LEADING ISSUES IN
ECONOMIC DEVELOPMENT

Leading Issues in Economic Development

THIRD EDITION

GERALD M. MEIER
STANFORD UNIVERSITY

NEW YORK
OXFORD UNIVERSITY PRESS
1976

For Daniel—

PREFACE TO THE THIRD EDITION

Development economists must operate in an imperfect second-best world, away from the simplified premises of neoclassical economics. Their subject matter is therefore not yet a coherent or self-contained discipline. Denied recourse to a set of general principles, perhaps the student's most sensible introduction to economic development is through a study of a number of "leading issues" that are at the time a major preoccupation of the development economist and development practitioner.

As reflected in this new edition, the "leading issues" now coalesce in a central theme: policies which are designed to eradicate poverty, reduce inequality, and deal with problems of employment. This does not mean that analysis of the overall process of development is any the less important, but it does require more attention to the connections between these particular objectives and the more aggregative analysis. This theme also calls for forward-looking analysis to determine the position of the developing countries under new international trade and monetary regimes. But in evaluating possible alternatives, the discussion must also give due attention to what has gone wrong in the past, and to theoretical analyses that might contribute to improved policy formulation.

This new edition, therefore, incorporates extensive changes. I have added new chapters. I have also extensively modified all the earlier chapters, replacing most of the earlier selections with new selections that better illuminate the central theme of this edition. New selections are also included to raise the level of theoretical analysis and provide more empirical relationships. I have also taken the opportunity to add more of my own Notes and to revise the Notes contained in previous editions.

My overriding objective remains the same as stated in the first edition—to present a new kind of course book for the study of economic development. The evolution of the subject confirms my belief that it can best be studied in a manner different from the usual approaches of either a textbook or a book of readings. I have therefore chosen to concentrate on relatively few issues that are now of central concern to development economists. On each of these strategic issues, I have then brought to bear a variety of materials that should be looked at simultaneously. And to provide additional direction and cohesion, I have written a substantive commentary through a series of connecting text Notes. These Notes integrate or supplement the other selections. In some instances, I have introduced a Note to treat a topic more expeditiously than could be done through separate readings; in other instances, a Note is designed to cover a topic that is not yet adequately treated in the literature, or to tie one issue with another.

Even more than in earlier editions, it should now be emphasized that greater importance is to be attached to the interrelatedness of the readings on each issue—*taken as a set*—than to any one particular reading. Each selection should acquire added significance through its contextual position, and the materials should be enhanced by their very combination. This is especially true for the interrelations among the various materials that deal with analysis, policy implications, and the results of development programs.

The interrelatedness among the chapters is also more pronounced now than in earlier editions. All the issues bear on the central theme of poverty, inequality, unemployment. The dominance of this theme gives more of a progressively interrelated argument to the subject and makes this edition more cohesive.

In restraining myself from proceeding in too many directions, I have had to exclude a considerable amount of subject matter that should eventually become part of the development economist's education. I have not ventured far into the formal methodology of development programming or planning techniques. Any excursion into the design of numerical, dynamic, multisector development planning models would rapidly become another course in its own right. Similarly, the range of country studies is now so extensive that the use of country examples can serve only to illustrate a more general problem or principle. Full-scale country studies have to be sought elsewhere. Nor is there as much crossing of the boundaries of economics into the noneconomic issues of development as the political scientist or sociologist would desire. I can only plead that an introductory book in development economics cannot offer everything for everyone. I hope that the introduction is sufficiently stimulating, and enough questions bordering on these other areas are raised, to encourage the student to proceed to further readings. (The select bibliographies at the end of each chapter may be a guide.)

I wish to express my appreciation to the authors and publishers who have granted permission to use excerpts from articles, books, and other publications in which American or foreign copyrights exist. Specific acknowledgment is given with each selection. Some parts of the original versions of the selected materials have been omitted out of consideration for relevancy and the avoidance of repetition; tables and diagrams have been renumbered; and some footnotes have been omitted, while others have been renumbered.

As in previous editions, many of the revisions in this edition have been inspired by my students at Stanford University and by lecture audiences in developing countries. Their challenging questions and incisive observations have meant much to me. As a master of data sources and a friend of all librarians, Mark Eaker has provided invaluable research assistance. Christiane Jose has accomplished a *tour de force* in cheerfully and efficiently guiding the manuscript from handwritten scrawls to the printer.

Finally, I want to acknowledge my substantial intellectual debt to members of the Institute of Development Studies (University of Sussex), the series of Cambridge Conferences on Development, and the Institute of Commonwealth Studies (Oxford). My visits there always turn into tutorials of reeducation—and eventually reappear in new editions of this book.

G.M.M.

August 1975
Stanford, California

CONTENTS

V. MOBILIZING DOMESTIC RESOURCES

VI. MOBILIZING FOREIGN RESOURCES

LEADING ISSUES IN
ECONOMIC DEVELOPMENT

CHAPTER I

International Poverty and Inequality

We are concerned in this book with nothing less than the future well-being of two-thirds of the world's population—the poverty-ridden peoples in the less developed countries of Asia, Africa, and Latin America. It is indeed sobering that, two centuries after the Industrial Revolution, most of the world remains poor, still suffering from inadequate standards of living.

The World Bank now emphasizes that the failure to achieve a minimum level of income above the "poverty line" has kept some 40 per cent of the peoples in the less developed countries in the condition of "absolute poverty"—a condition of life so degraded by disease, illiteracy, malnutrition, and squalor as to deny its victims basic human necessities. The persistence of absolute poverty, despite respectable achievements in rates of growth in GNP, is now of more concern than that of relative poverty, or of a "widening gap" between the rich and poor countries.

Our objective is to examine the central issues raised by the challenges of eradicating absolute poverty, reducing inequality, and creating employment opportunities. These challenges now require the international community to reassert the development priority and reshape development policies.

This reorientation has significant implications for the way development economists view the development process. It is more effective to adopt a positive approach to the promotion of development policies than to concentrate on "vicious circles of poverty" or the "causes" of poverty. Development is a process of cumulative change that results from positive forces that raise productivity.

A major theme of this book is the emphasis on discovering and promoting these positive forces that raise real income per head, create more employment opportunities, and achieve a wider distribution of the gains from development.

These forces of development are not, however, readily identifiable. After the disappointing record of development efforts, economists can no longer rely on simple causal relations that emphasize development planning, capital accumulation, and foreign aid. The forces of development are too complex, subtle, and insufficiently known to yield to any simple formula.

One way of recognizing that a wide range of development forces must be identified is to realize at the outset that the development process encompasses more than the economic theory of production. Empirical studies of the sources of growth in output in a number of countries have demonstrated that much of the increase in aggregate production over a long period cannot be explained by an increase in only the standard physical inputs of the factors of production. A large part of the increase in total output remains to be attributed to some "unexplained residual factor" in the economy's aggregate production. In studies of several advanced countries, the "residual factor"—the unisolated source of growth—is left to account for 50 per cent or more of the increase in total output.[1] The residual is what Abramovitz calls a "measure of our ignorance" of the determinants of a rise in productivity—the complex of little understood forces which cause output per unit of utilized resources to rise.[2] Is the residual to be attributed to some intangible "human factor," perhaps related to Marshall's observation that "Man is subject to increasing returns"? Is it a matter of "creativity" or "drive for dynamic efficiency," perhaps related to motivational changes? Is it disembodied labor-saving technological change, perhaps related to better management, organization, and work procedures which reduce the labor requirement per unit of output?[3] Is it dependent on the degree of competitive pressure and motivational efficiency, perhaps related to what Leibenstein simply calls "X-efficiency"?[4] Or is it a matter of "learning by doing," such that advances in knowledge accrue from the accumulation of experience in the production process (as measured, say, by cumulated past investments), and the production function accordingly exhibits increasing returns to scale?[5]

The fundamental question remains: What are the other sources of growth that can be identified in the catch-all of the "residual" and introduced as an "input," amenable to policy promotion? Another theme of this book, therefore, is the need to proceed beyond a narrow economic theory of production to a broader interpretation that requires

[1] R. Solow, "Technical Change and the Aggregate Production Function," *Review of Economics and Statistics,* August 1957, pp. 312–20; John W. Kendrick, *Productivity Trends in the United States,* Princeton, 1961; Edward F. Denison, *Why Growth Rates Differ,* Washington, D. C., 1967, especially Chaps. 1, 20, 21; Sherman Robinson, "Sources of Growth in Less Developed Countries: A Cross-Section Study," *Quarterly Journal of Economics,* August 1971, pp. 391–408.

[2] Moses Abramovitz, "Resource and Output Trends in the United States Since 1870," *American Economic Review, Papers and Proceedings,* May 1956, pp. 11–14. Also see, T. Balogh and P. P. Streeten, "The Coefficient of Ignorance," *Bulletin of the Oxford Institute of Economics and Statistics,* May 1963, pp. 99–107.

[3] Cf. Dale W. Jorgenson, "The Embodiment Hypothesis," *Journal of Political Economy,* February 1966, pp. 1–12.

[4] Harvey Leibenstein, "Allocative Efficiency vs. 'X-Efficiency,' " *American Economic Review,* June 1966, pp. 392–415.

[5] Kenneth J. Arrow, "The Economic Implications of Learning by Doing," *Review of Economic Studies,* Vol. 29, 1962, pp. 155–73.

attention to "efficiency" in the utilization of inputs, and a wider understanding of an economy's "learning process."

An additional theme is that national development must now occur within the international context of the coexistence of rich and poor countries. Capital, technology, knowledge, values, and institutions are more readily transferable from rich to poor countries than ever before. There may, however, be drawbacks as well as advantages in being a late-comer to development, and the late-developing country is increasingly aware of the need for "appropriate" transfers. There is now a more imaginative search for means by which to raise the benefit-cost ratio of these transfers to the developing countries.

At the same time, the greater interdependence between the developed countries (DCs) and less developed countries (LDCs) gives the LDCs new negotiating strategies for designing trade, investment, and international monetary arrangements. The LDCs have assumed an enhanced role in shaping the emergence of a new international economic order to replace the old Bretton Woods system. The contentions of the United Nations Conference on Trade and Development (UNCTAD), and the criticisms of the General Agreement on Tariffs and Trade (GATT) and the International Monetary Fund (IMF), must receive serious attention because the future of national development will be closely related to reforms in international trade and monetary arrangements.

The time has also come for a reassessment of development planning and policymaking. Many have become disenchanted with centralized detailed planning as it has been practiced in some LDCs. But even for a "lighter" type of framework planning, indicative planning, sectoral planning, the simpler monetary and fiscal policies, or only project evaluation—even for these less ambitious policies, the quality of policymaking must be raised. The analysis of what policies are needed, choice of policy instruments, and methods of implementation must all be improved. Intimately related to improvement in policymaking is the role to be assigned to the market price system and decentralized decision-making. The removal of price distortions and the use of the market as an instrument of policy are aspects of this theme of improving the quality of development policymaking.

To begin the pursuit of these several themes, this first chapter emphasizes new initiatives to reduce international poverty and inequality. Chapter II then provides some perspective from the viewpoints of theory, history, and political economy. Against this background, Chapters III and IV introduce the core problems of dualism and unemployment. Chapters V to VII proceed to relate the new initiatives to resource mobilization and allocation in developing countries that are characterized by dualism and unemployment. Chapters VIII to XI examine specifically the policy issues of human-resource development, agricultural strategy, industrialization strategy, and trade strategy. The final chapter offers a more general evaluation of development policymaking and planning.

We might reach a clearer understanding of the meaning of economic development by first considering some of the misconceptions of development (section I.A). The dimensions of the problems of absolute poverty and income inequality are outlined by the selections in section I.B. These selections give special emphasis to the problems involved in the measurement of poverty and inequality, both among nations and within a nation. Finally, the selections in section I.C indicate some bases for reorienting development strategy toward the objectives of employment, distribution, and growth.

Throughout this chapter, we should be aware that poverty, inequality, and unemployment are related phenomena. Given a population's average income level, a higher level of inequality will tend to be associated with a higher level of poverty. This poverty may be expressed in absolute terms—as a number of people below a "poverty line." When, however, the poverty line is established with reference to some socially accepted "minimal" standard of living, the average income level is likely to become a reference level, and measures of absolute poverty then also reflect an aspect of relative inequality as well. The president of the World Bank, for instance, spoke in 1975 of the "absolute poor" as those having a per capita income below $50, or less than one-third of the average per capita income of their country.

Poverty is also closely related to unemployment and underemployment. As emphasized in selections in this chapter, growth does not necessarily generate employment; nor does growth necessarily benefit those suffering absolute poverty. Despite the attainment of the Development Decades' target growth rates of 5 or 6 per cent in GNP, many LDCs have witnessed rapidly rising numbers of unemployed and a greater number in absolute poverty. The dominant question of this chapter is, therefore: Who benefits from development?

I.A. MISCONCEPTIONS OF DEVELOPMENT—NOTE

Dissatisfaction with the results during the first generation of development in the 1950s and 1960s has led to a refocusing of strategy to meet the second-generation problems of development. The growth of GNP is no longer regarded as the main objective or index of development—but no single criterion can be readily substituted. To the dismay of the purist—but not to the surprise of the development practitioner—it is difficult to give one precise meaning to "economic development." Perhaps it is easier to say what "economic development" is *not*.

At the outset it should be recognized that economic development is not equivalent to the total development of a society: it is only a part—or one dimension—of general development. We usually focus on the nation-state as the unit of development, but "national development" is a term which encompasses—at a minimum—social and political development, as well as economic development, in the building of national identity. Depending on the orientation of one's discipline, it is also possible to consider other types—for example, legal or administrative development. The interrelationships among these various types of development are extremely important. A major question implicit in our entire subject is how sociocultural and political development contribute to economic development, and are in turn determined by it. It will be apparent that much more interdisciplinary study is needed to determine how economic and noneconomic forces interact.

It is also necessary to caution against equating economic development with either "economic independence" or "industrialization." As a result of their colonial history and newly acquired political independence, many poor countries have expressed discontent with their "dependence" on export markets and foreign capital. Such "dependence" is often interpreted as synonymous with "foreign domination" or "exploitation"—to be avoided now by import-substitution policies and restrictions on the inflow of private foreign capital. The emphasis on national independence through "inward-looking" policies, and the advocacy of policies to avoid "foreign domination" become part of an ideology that might be called the "economics of discontent." But the "economics of discontent" should not be confused with the economics for development (see Chapter II). National independence and the process of national consolidation may be called as it is in India, "emotional integration";[1] but this is not to say that this noneconomic objective also contributes to economic development. "Inward-looking" policies are most likely to run counter to economic development, as is argued more fully in Chapter XI, below.

Another aspect of the economics of discontent is the poor country's protest against being a primary-producing country. Industrialization tends to be viewed as a superior way of life; rich countries are believed to be rich because they are industrialized; and poor countries are believed to be poor because they are primary-producing. Whether an industrial society enjoys a superior way of life is, however, a noneconomic question. The relevant economic question for a poor country is whether agricultural development or industrial development is now the appro-

[1] Gunnar Myrdal, *Asian Drama*, New York, 1968, pp. 53, 722–3.

5

priate strategy for accelerating the country's economic development.

Economic development is not to be equated simply with industrialization for several reasons. First, the concentration of a large percentage of production in the primary sector is in itself not a cause of poverty: the cause is the low productivity in agriculture. A poor country's high ratio of agricultural population to total population is also more appropriately viewed as a consequence, rather than a cause, of poverty. Whenever the agricultural population is poor, the nonagricultural population serving the agricultural population tends to be relatively small in size and also at a low level of living. When the rural sector is prosperous, the nonrural sector tends to be large and also prosperous.[2]

Second, progress in industrialization is highly dependent upon agricultural development. Without the necessary support of improvements in primary production, the policies of industrialization will be severely handicapped. In Chapter IX, below, we shall examine the essential ways in which the rate of industrialization depends upon surmounting the limitations of the agricultural bottleneck.

Third, economic development is much more than the simple acquisition of industries. It may be defined as nothing less than the "upward movement of the entire social system";[3] or it may be interpreted as the attainment of a number of "ideals of modernization," such as a rise in productivity, social and economic equalization, modern knowledge, improved institutions and attitudes, and a rationally coordinated system of policy measures that can remove the host of undesirable conditions in the social system that have perpetuated a state of underdevelopment.[4]

These views also imply that economic development involves something more than economic growth. Development is taken to mean growth plus change; there are essential qualitative dimensions in the development process that may be absent in the growth or expansion of an economy through a simple widening process.[5] This qualitative difference is especially likely to appear in the improved performance of the factors of production and improved techniques of production—in man's growing control over nature. It is also likely to appear in the development of institutions and a change in attitudes and values.

If we turn from what economic development is not, and attempt to consider its meaning more directly, we immediately encounter ambiguities because the ideal of economic development tends to be associated with different policy goals. The phenomena that one chooses to denote as "economic development" are very much a matter of what one values as the economy's policy goals. And any definition of development inevitably becomes a "persuasive definition," implying that development—as so defined—is a desirable objective.

Although requiring careful interpretation, perhaps the definition that would now gain widest approval is one that defines economic development as the *process* whereby the *real per capita income* of a country increases over a *long period* of time—subject to the *stipulations* that the number below an "absolute poverty line" does not increase, and that the distribution of income does not become more unequal. We emphasize *process* because this implies the operation of

[2] For an elaboration of primary production as only an associative–rather than causative–characteristic of poverty, see S. Kuznets, *Economic Change*, New York, 1953, pp. 222–5; J. Viner, *International Trade and Economic Development*, Oxford, 1953, p. 50; G. M. Meier and R. E. Baldwin, *Economic Development*, New York, 1957, pp. 315–16.
[3] Myrdal, *Asian Drama*, p. 1869.

[4] C. E. Black, *The Dynamics of Modernization*, New York, 1966, pp. 55–60.
[5] See, for example, the account of recent growth—but not development—in Liberia: R. W. Clower et al., *Growth Without Development*, Evanston, 1966.

certain forces in an interconnected and causal fashion. In the following chapters we want to examine the process of economic development as a form of progressive action—a working-out of certain principal forces that reveal the inner structure or "logic" of an economy's development. To interpret development in terms of a process involving causal relationships should prove more meaningful than merely to identify development with a set of conditions or catalog of characteristics. If our interest in the development of a poor country arises from our desire to remove mass poverty, then we should also emphasize as the primary goal a rise in *per capita* real income rather than simply an increase in the economy's real national income, uncorrected for population change. For, if the criterion were only an increase in real national income, then it would be possible for aggregate output to rise without a per capita improvement in living standards. Population growth may surpass the growth of national output, or run parallel with it; the result would be falling, or at best constant, per capita income, and we would not consider this as economic development.

We also stress a *long period* of time because what is significant from the standpoint of development is a sustained increase in real income—not simply a short-period rise such as occurs during the upswing of the business cycle. The underlying upward trend over decades—at least two or three decades—is the stronger indication of development. From this standpoint, a five-year development plan is only the start of the development process, and it remains to be seen whether there is the power to sustain the process so that per capita real income continues to rise over the longer period. There is a vital distinction between *initiating* development and the more difficult task of *sustaining* development over the longer run.

Although the increase in real income per head can be adopted as the primary goal, it has also become common to interpret economic development in terms of a number of subgoals or particular categories of the overall primary objective. Thus, a certain distribution of income is another policy objective. A diminution in economic inequality is a generally stated objective of development plans. Most students of development would also undoubtedly qualify the primary goal by requiring that the absolute number of people below a minimum level of real income should also diminish at the same time that real per capita income rises. Otherwise it is conceivable that if there is population growth, the numbers of those living below a poverty line may actually have grown while there has been a rise in the average income of the population as a whole. When a dual economy exists—with a division between the modern money economy and the traditional indigenous economy—it is also possible for all of the increase in total income to occur in the modern economy,[6] and income per head might still rise even though there had been no change in the indigenous economy. Judgment on the distribution of income is thus an integral part of the development problem.

A few of the many possible other subgoals may be the specification of a minimum level of consumption, a certain composition to the consumption stream, a maximum level of unemployment that will be tolerated, avoidance of marked disparities in the prosperity and growth of different regions within a country, diversification of the economy, and the attainment of the "ideals of modernization" listed above (p. 6).

Owing to this variety of policy objectives, the emphasis on various dimensions of economic development will vary at different times and in different countries. We should, therefore, beware of interpreting economic development as meaning economic progress or an increase in economic welfare. An increase in real per capita income is not by itself a sufficient condition. Per capita real income is only a partial index of economic welfare because a judgment regarding eco-

---

[6] The problem of dualistic development is discussed fully in Chapter III, below.

nomic welfare will also involve a value judgment on the desirability of a particular distribution of income. All observers would not, therefore, definitely say that economic welfare has increased even if per capita income has risen, unless the resultant distribution of income is also considered desirable.

Economic welfare poses not only the question of distributive justice. There are also the prior questions of what is the composition of the total output that is giving rise to an increase in per capita real income, and how this output is being valued. Whether a larger total output corresponds to individual preferences—let alone the more difficult test of collective choice—depends as much on what is produced and its quality as it does on the quantity produced. The valuation of the output may also be biased insofar as it is valued by market prices. These prices become the equivalent of weights, but they have been affected by the distribution of income: with a different distribution of income, prices would be different, and both the composition and value of the national output would also be different.[7] Market prices will also have limited value insofar as they do not reflect external diseconomies or social costs.

If such considerations of the composition of aggregate output, its valuation, and its distribution make it difficult to equate economic development with economic welfare, it is all the more unreasonable to claim that economic development means an increase in social welfare in general. Economic welfare is but a part of social welfare, and even if in the course of a country's development all the conditions necessary to promote economic welfare have been satisfied, this need not also mean that social welfare has been promoted. For the process of development has a profound impact on social institutions, habits, and beliefs, and it is likely to introduce a number of sources of tension and

discord. Some aspects of human welfare might suffer if relations that were once personal become impersonal, the structure and functions of the family change, the stability in one's way of life is disrupted, and the support and assurance of traditional values disappear. Tensions also arise when the inequalities in income distribution, both among individuals and among regions in the developing country, tend to increase; when development creates "open unemployment" as well as employment; and when the pressures of excessive urbanization occur.[8] In a fundamental sense, discords arise from the contrasts between the modern and the backward—from the superimposing of modern functions on traditional institutions.

In sum, even though it is conventional to begin with an increase in per capita real income as the best available overall index of economic development, we shall abstain from labeling this an increase in economic welfare, let alone social welfare, without additional considerations of various subgoals and explicit recognition of the value judgments regarding at least the composition, valuation, and distribution of the expanded output. The student of development must adopt such a cautious approach as a result of the strictures of welfare economics and the need for clarity on value premises in social research.

Even more, the policymaker must adopt such an approach because in many countries it has become only too painfully apparent that despite growth in aggregate output there can still be a larger number of people below the poverty line, rising unemployment, and greater income inequality. The quality of development is completely masked if the policymaker does not pierce

[7] See S. K. Nath, "Welfare Economics, Economic Growth, and the Choice of Techniques," *Journal of Development Studies*, January 1968, pp. 230–31.

[8] For these and other sources of tension that may accompany development, see E. H. Phelps Brown, *Economic Growth and Human Welfare*, Delhi, 1953, Chap. 2; W. Arthur Lewis, "Economic Problems of Development," in *Restless Nations: A Study of World Tensions and Development*, New York, 1962; Black, *Dynamics of Modernization*, pp. 26–34.

the aggregate measure of GNP and consider its composition and distribution.

Thus, an International Labour Organization report on Colombia says, "The root of the discontent with economic growth as a supreme objective has been the dawning realization that even when it is rapid, it has generally, as in Colombia itself, been accompanied by rising unemployment and widening gaps between the rich and the poor, and between town and country—very possibly by actual increases in the numbers living below some poverty line, wherever this is drawn. ...To try to solve the unemployment problem by just accelerating overall economic growth is therefore to take on, voluntarily, the task of Tantalus—the target recedes as one reaches it. What is needed is to change the nature of the process of economic growth."[9]

Development economists no longer worship at the altar of GNP, but concentrate more directly on the quality of the development process. In the words of a former chief economist for the government of Pakistan, "the problem of development must be defined as a selective attack on the worst forms of poverty. Development goals must be defined in terms of progressive reduction and eventual elimination of malnutrition, disease, illiteracy, squalor, unemployment and inequalities. We were taught to take care of our GNP as this will take care of poverty. Let us reverse this and take care of poverty as this will take care of the GNP. In other words, let us worry about the content of GNP even more than its rate of increase."[10]

Years before the start of the United Nations' first Development Decade, Professor Viner had offered a similar warning that should have received more attention. He stated that:

[9] International Labour Organization, *Towards Full Employment—A Program for Colombia*, Geneva, 1970.

[10] Mahbub ul Haq, "Employment and Income Distribution in the 1970's: A New Perspective," *Pakistan Economic and Social Review*, June-December 1971, p. 6.

While the supplementing of data as to economic aggregates by *per capita* averages provides additional and often essential information . . . even this does not suffice for some purposes. Let us suppose, for instance, that a country which has embarked on a programme of economic development engages in periodic stock-taking of its progress, and finds not only that aggregate wealth, aggregate income, total population, total production, are all increasing, but that *per capita* wealth, income, production, are also all increasing. All of these are favourable indices, but even in combination do they suffice to show that there has been "economic progress," an increase in economic "welfare," rather than retrogression?

Suppose that someone should argue that the one great economic evil is the prevalence of a great mass of crushing poverty, and that it is a paradox to claim that a country is achieving economic progress as long as the absolute extent of such poverty prevailing in that country has not lessened or has even increased? Such a country, nevertheless, might be able to meet all the tests of economic development which I have just enumerated. If its population has undergone substantial increase, the numbers of those living at the margin of subsistence or below, illiterate, diseased, undernourished, may have grown steadily consistently with a rise in the average income of the population as a whole. . . .

Were I to insist, however, that the reduction of mass poverty be made a crucial test of the realization of economic development, I would be separating myself from the whole body of literature in this field. In all the literature on economic development I have seen, I have not found a single instance where statistical data in terms of aggregates and of averages have not been treated as providing adequate tests of the degree of achievement of economic development.[11]

[11] Jacob Viner, *International Trade and Economic Development*, Oxford, 1953, pp. 99–100.

Long after Viner's warning, Hollis Chenery introduced the World Bank's influential study on *Redistribution with Growth* with this statement: "It is now clear that more than a decade of rapid growth in underdeveloped countries has been of little or no benefit to perhaps a third of their population. Although the average per capita income of the Third World has increased by 50 percent since 1960, this growth has been very unequally distributed among countries, regions within countries, and socio-economic groups. Paradoxically, while growth policies have succeeded beyond the expectations of the first Development Decade, the very idea of aggregate growth as a social objective has increasingly been called into question."[12]

This questioning has become common among development policymakers. In assessing foreign aid, a chairman of the Development Assistance Committee of the Organization for Economic Cooperation and Development has reviewed the "state of mind which existed widely ten years ago among donors and why it was wrong. Four specific examples will illustrate how illusory was our previous confidence that our knowledge and experience make the task relatively simple:"

i) Until recent years the view was widespread, even among people who should have known better, that our remarkable progress in science and technology had found answers to all the real problems faced by the developing countries at their low levels of civilisation. All that was needed to lift them up to our superior level of performance was a massive effort of technological transfer. It would work quite simply and fast. It sounded highly patronising and it was. And it was also quite wrong. Their climates and soils, their raw materials, their factor costs of labour and capital, the priority needs of their peoples, the threats of tropical insects, fungi, bacteria, viruses, etc., to their peoples, animals and plants, were all different from ours. On many points each country presents unique problems.

ii) We took for granted that GNP growth, largely concentrated in the industrial sector, would bring with it automatically full employment and the eradication of poverty as it had seemed to do for us. We failed to remember that during our period of early industrialisation, population growth was slow, technology quite labour-intensive, emigration was relatively easy if you could not find a job, and there was no competition from already highly industrialised societies or restrictions by them on access to their markets. We also overlooked how badly many people lived in the early industrialisation period.

iii) We assumed that the greatest service we could do their people was to give them the chance to enjoy schooling like ours. More schooling was the universal key to prosperity and the good life. It may be, if of the right kind, but our present set-up, what we gave and they welcomed, was far from what they needed.

iv) It occurred to few of us that the reductions in mortality we were bringing their peoples would cause a dramatic and harmful population explosion. Why? Because we had never had to deal with this phenomenon, our drastic fall in mortality rates occurring after we had reached a level of education, incomes and urbanisation that provided the motivation and ability to control family size by individual choice.[13]

Other misconceptions could be added to this list. Most important are some that arise through the limitations of economic theory, as will be discussed in the next chapter.

If there were misconceptions during the first generation of development, the second

---

[12] Hollis Chenery et al., *Redistribution with Growth*, London, 1974, p. xiii.

[13] OECD, Report of Director of Development Advisory Committee, *Development Cooperation 1973 Review*, Paris, 1973, p. 31.

generation of development calls for a basic reconsideration of the meaning of development and a fundamental redirection of development policy. Instead of any aggregate, or even per capita, index of "development," direct attention must be given to the achievement of better nourishment, better health, better education, better living conditions, and better conditions of employment for the low-end poverty groups in the poor countries of the world. Instead of seeking "development" as an end, it must be viewed as a means—as an instrumental process for overcoming persistent poverty, absorbing the unemployed, and diminishing inequality. To help illuminate this process is the intention of this book.

I. B. DIMENSIONS OF DEVELOPMENT

I.B.1. Indicators of International Poverty—Note

The extreme degree of inequality that now characterizes international living standards can be seen in various indices. Not only is the distribution of world income highly unequal; there are also inequalities in other relevant indicators of development such as technology, consumption of energy, education, and health.

Table 1 presents comparative data for developed and less developed areas in several important series. Especially significant are the contrasts in the series of population, gross national product, education, health, and such "real" indices as passenger motor vehicles, energy consumption per capita, and cement production per capita. These non-monetary indices have been found to have a high correlation with real private consumption per head. This table clearly emphasizes the gap in living standards between the developed and less developed countries.

It should, however, be noted that there are considerable differences among the LDCs. Latin America is not as poor as Africa or Asia. There are also marked disparities within each region: some countries in Latin America, for example, are poorer than the richer countries in Africa or Asia (see Table 2, below). It remains striking, however, that per capita income would have to grow at a rate of more than 3 per cent a year in most of the African and Asian countries even to reach by the end of this century the average income levels already attained in Latin America. Since the populations of Africa and Asia are likely to continue increasing on average by more than 2 per cent annually, the domestic product would have to grow at

an average rate of more than 5 per cent a year over the rest of this century even to reach current Latin American levels.

For a more detailed summary of GNP per capita in a large number of countries as of 1967 and 1973, one should give attention to Table 2. Again, the wide differences between rich and poor countries are evident in this table.

There are, however, a number of statistical difficulties involved in using low per capita income as an index of poverty. Prominent among these are the problems of aggregation, especially in a dual economy; the arbitrary valuation of nonmarket activities; the inadequacy of converting national income statistics at official exchange rates; and the welfare qualifications associated with the changing composition of output and the distribution of income.[1]

In order to avoid these difficulties, several studies have attempted to make international comparisons of standards of living by using "nonmonetary" indicators.[2] A

[1] For a more thorough consideration of these difficulties, see W. J. Barber, "A Critique of Aggregate Accounting Concepts in Underdeveloped Areas," *Bulletin of the Oxford University Institute of Economics and Statistics,* November 1963; R. S. Thorn, "Per Capita Income as a Measure of Economic Development," *Zeitschrift für Nationalökonomie* 28, 1968, pp. 206–16; Simon Kuznets, *Six Lectures on Economic Growth,* Glencoe, 1959, pp. 13–28; Gunnar Myrdal, *Asian Drama,* New York, 1968, Chaps 11, 12, Appendix 13; Dan Usher, "Income as a Measure of Productivity," *Economica,* November 1966.

[2] These are summarized in Wilfred Beckerman, *International Comparisons of Real Incomes,* Devel-

TABLE 1. Comparisons Between Developed and Less Developed Countries

| Item | Unit | Developed Countries[1] | | Less Developed Non-Communist Countries[2] | | | | | |
		Total	United States	Total	Latin America	East and South-East Asia	South Asia	Near East	Africa
Population:									
Total (mid-1972)	millions	664	209	1832	291	333	714	147	306
Annual growth (1963–1972)	per cent	.9	1.1	2.8	2.9	2.8	2.7	2.6	2.6
Persons per square km.	number	17	22	27	15	86	141	22	12
Education:									
Literacy	per cent	97	99	50	76	55	27	36	26
Students enrolled at third level (1970)	per cent	8.8	9.0	2.4	2.7	3.0	3.0	3.0	1.2
Life expectancy	years	71	71	48	57	53	44	58	41
Calorie supply per capita	% of established standards	116	118	98	95	96	97	99	101
Real indices:									
Energy consumption per capita (1972)	kilograms of coal equivalent	6393	11611	373	967	277	174	913	168
Passenger motor vehicles (1970)	per 100 population	25.3	42.5	.8	3.5	.5	.1	.9	.6
Cement production per capita (1972)	1000 metric vans	489	359	65.5	114	80	26	209	36

[1] Developed countries—United States, Canada, Japan, S. Africa, Australia, New Zealand, E. E. C., E. F. T. A., Iceland, Ireland, Finland.

[2] Underdeveloped countries—Latin America: 20 republics (excluding Cuba) plus Jamaica and Caribbean islands; South East Asia, Afghanistan, Ceylon, India, Nepal, Pakistan; East Asia: Countries of S. E. Asia plus China (Taiwan), Hong Kong, South Korea; Near East: Cyprus, Greece, Iran, Iraq, Israel, Jordan, Kuwait, Lebanon, Saudi Arabia, Syria, Turkey, U. A. R., Yemen; Africa: Does not include South Africa nor U. A. R. The "total" column for the less developed non-Communist areas is the sum of these 5 regions plus Spain, Oceania and Puerto Rico.

Sources: Population series: U.N. *Demographic Yearbook*, 1972; Real indices: U.N. *Statistical Yearbook*, 1973; Health series: U.N. *Statistical Yearbook*, 1973; World Bank, *Trends in Developing Countries*, 1973; Education series: UNESCO *Statistical Yearbook*, 1972; World Bank, *Trends in Developing Countries*, 1973.

major effort in this direction has been made by Beckerman, who sought to discover

opment Center of OECD, Paris, 1966, Chap. 4. A ranking of countries that takes into account not only per capita income but also other indications of social and political development is provided in I. Adelman and C. Taft Morris, *Society, Politics, and Economic Development. A Quantitative Approach*, Baltimore, 1967.

which nonmonetary indicators are highly correlated with some meaningful national accounts aggregates, and how, given estimates of the former and the nature of the statistical relationship, to "predict" real per capita consumption from the nonmonetary indicators. The main reason for experimenting with this method is the greater availability of data on nonmonetary indicators than on na-

TABLE 2.   Per Capita Gross National Product (U.S. Dollar Equivalent) (Constant 1972 Prices)

Country	GNP Per Capita		Country	GNP Per Capita	
	1967	1973		1967	1973
Switzerland	$4806	$5971	Malaysia	394	474
United States	4964	5815	Nicaragua	426	461
Sweden	4728	5563	Tunisia	305	436
Canada	3929	4961	Guatemala	327	406
Denmark	3713	4770	Zambia	382	376
Australia	3385	4084	Rhodesia	311	376*
Japan	2048	3456	Colombia	292	349
New Zealand	3019	3359*	So. Korea	199	336
United Kingdom	2459	2850	Ecuador	260	335
Israel	1516	2213	Paraguay	285	327
Spain	1148	1576	El Salvador	303	307
Greece	950	1513	Morocco	250	282
Venezuela	1069	1206	Honduras	251	273
Portugal	708	1103	Ghana	276	265
Argentina	936	1102	Philippines	183	216
Panama	674	867	Thailand	167	203
Mexico	649	787	Kenya	129	163
Chile	702	763	Bolivia	125	150
Costa Rica	528	653	Tanzania	100	115
Uruguay	576	616	India	95	102
Iran	365	600	Malawi	86	100
Taiwan	351	560	Pakistan	92	97
Peru	488	536	Indonesia	66	88
Brazil	357	536	Ethiopia	81	87
Turkey	367	476			

*1972
Source: AID, *Gross National Product, Growth Rates and Trend Data*, Report RC-W-138, May 1, 1974.

tional accounts aggregates and the apparent scope for finding fairly close correlations between certain of such indicators and independent estimates of real per capita consumption.[3] The nonmonetary indicators used as "explanatory" variables in the final computations were: steel consumption, cement production, number of letters sent, stock of radio receivers, stock of telephones, stock of road vehicles, and meat consumption—all on a per capita basis.[4] The final

predictions for 1960 are compared, in Table 3, below, with the results that would be obtained by using official exchange rates to convert national accounts estimates of private consumption. Some major differences between the proposed nonmonetary and national accounts series can be noted.

In a later study, Beckerman and Bacon measured the international inequality of the

[3] Beckerman, *International Comparisons*, p. 28.
[4] Ibid., p. 29. See also Jan W. Duggar, "International Comparisons of Income Levels: An Addi-

tional Measure," *Economic Journal*, March 1968, pp. 109–16; U. N., "Concept of Development and its Measurement," *International Social Development Review*, No. 2 (1970).

distribution of consumption based on more reliable and extensive data.

Table 4 presents estimates of the size distribution of the world's consumption in terms of the percentage of the world's consumption that is enjoyed by each successive 10 per cent of the world's population. According to the table, it can be seen that the poorest 10 per cent of the world's population accounts for only 1.6 per cent of world consumption, whereas the top 10 per cent enjoys 35.2 per cent of world consumption. In other words, the average per capita consumption of the top 10 per cent is twenty-

TABLE 3. Predicted Indices of "Real" Private Consumption Per Head in 1960 (USA in 1960 = 100) from Modified Non-Monetary Indicator Method

Rank	Country	Index based on proposed method	Index at official exchange rates	Rank	Country	Index based on proposed method	Index at official exchange rates
1	USA	100.0	100.0	30	Algeria	13.8	..
2	Sweden	77.4	54.5	31	Yugoslavia	13.5	6.1
3	Canada	77.0	73.9	32	Mexico	13.4	16.2
4	Australia	65.4	57.2	33	Greece	12.7	16.4
5	UK	61.7	49.9	34	Malaya	12.6	264·9
6	Denmark	59.2	46.6	35	Cuba	12.2	447·7
7	Switzerland	59.1	55.6	36	Brazil	12.1	6.4
8	New Zealand	58.6	56.0	37	Colombia	11.4	10.9
9	Norway	57.4	34.9	38	Federation of Rhodesia	11.2	5.4
10	Germany	56.1	41.2				
11	France	54.3	47.4	39	Turkey	9.8	27.2
12	Belgium	53.6	48.3	40	China (Mainland)	9.4	..
13	Netherlands	45.0	31.3	41	Iraq	9.0	..
14	Finland	41.3	32.5	42	Syria	8.6	..
15	Austria	40.8	29.2	43	Peru	8.1	..
16	Italy	30.8	22.3	44	Morocco	8.1	6.7
17	Japan	28.7	12.6	45	Tunisia	7.9	..
18	Israel	27.8	45.8	46	Taiwan	7.4	5.4
19	South Africa	26.0	35.8	47	Iran	7.3	..
20	Roumania	25.2	..	48	Egypt	6.4	..
21	Argentina	23.8	18.5	49	Ceylon	5.3	5.8
22	Lebanon	22.8	..	50	Ghana	4.8	7.9
23	Ireland	22.0	27.5	51	Saudi Arabia	4.0	..
24	Hong Kong	19.6	..	52	Thailand	3.7	4.0
25	Spain	19.5	13.6	53	Congo (Leopoldville)	3.2	..
26	Venezuela	18.9	31.8	54	India	3.1	..
27	Portugal	17.0	11.6	55	Nigeria	2.6	..
28	Chile	16.9	20.9	56	Indonesia	2.4	..
29	Uruguay	16.2	..	57	Pakistan	2.3	..

Source: Wilfred Beckerman, *International Comparisons of Real Incomes*, Development Center of OECD, Paris, 1966, pp. 36–7.

TABLE 4. Distribution of World Real Consumption by Decile of Population

Population Decile*	1954–55			1962–63		
	Per Capita Consumption†	Share in Total Consumption	Cumulative share	Per Capita Consumption	Share in Total Consumption	Cumulative share
0–10	50·2	·011	·011	83·6	·016	·016
10–20	64·0	·014	·025	83·6	·016	·032
20–30	68·5	·015	·040	94·0	·018	·050
30–40	82·2	·018	·058	104·5	·020	·070
40–50	173·6	·038	·096	177·6	·034	·104
50–60	264·9	·058	·154	282·0	·043	·158
60–70	447·7	·098	·252	522·3	·100	·258
70–80	666·9	·146	·328	825·2	·158	·416
80–90	1,091·8	·239	·637	1,211·7	·232	·648
90–100	1,658·2	·363	1·000	1,838·5	·352	1·000

*10% of population = 154 million in 1954–5 and 184·1 million in 1962–3.
†Total consumption = $703,514 million in 1954–5 and $961,095 million in 1962–3 at US (1960) prices.
Source: Wilfred Beckerman and Robert Bacon, "The International Distribution of Incomes," in Paul Streeten (ed.), *Unfashionable Economics: Essays in Honour of Lord Balogh*, London, 1970, p. 62.

two times as great as that of the bottom 10 per cent. Explaining these results, Beckerman and Bacon state that

In absolute amounts and in terms of the basic units used for the underlying equations, which are US dollars in 1960 prices, the average annual consumption per head of the top 10 per cent was about $1,840 in 1962–3, whereas it was about $84 in the bottom 10 per cent, or $1.60 per week. Since the conceptual basis for these estimates is such as to allow for international differences in price levels (since the correlations are with control data in terms of "real" consumption), it is clear that it would not be possible to live on $1.60 per head per week alone. The explanation is partly that many fail to live on this, but it is largely that these estimates correspond to the normal national accounting estimates of consumption, and, as such, are composed almost exclusively of consumption that has passed through the market economy. The lower the income level of a country, the lower, in general, is the relative importance of the market economy in total consumption. Nevertheless, even after making due allowance for this, it is clear what is meant, in absolute terms, by international differences in income levels.[5]

Although the foregoing tables reveal the extremes that exist among rich and poor countries in various indicators of living standards, it is a further cause of concern that the gap between rich and poor countries tends to be widening.

Table 5 reveals the considerable differences in the growth records of individual countries. It is a disturbing fact that the

[5] Wilfred Beckerman and Robert Bacon, "The International Distribution of Incomes," in Paul Streeten (ed.), *Unfashionable Economics: Essays in Honour of Lord Balogh*, London, 1970, pp. 61–2.

majority of countries with Gross Domestic Product per capita of less than $300 had growth rates of total output per annum of less than 5 per cent in the period 1960–70. Table 6 also shows that the rate of growth in per capita GNP has been considerably slower in less developed areas than in the developed areas during the period 1960–73.

The absolute gap in per capita income has accordingly widened. Even if the LDCs were to enjoy a much higher rate of growth in per capita income than in the rich countries, the

TABLE 5. Income Levels and Rates of Growth of Total Output of Selected Developing Countries, 1960–70

GDP Per Capita in 1970 / Growth Rate of Total Output per Annum; %	Under $100	$100 to under $200	$200 to under $300	$300 to under $500	$500 and more
7 and more		So. Korea Thailand		Taiwan Iran	Israel Spain Greece Mexico
5 to under 7	Pakistan	Philippines Kenya	Bolivia Honduras Ecuador	Nicaragua Malaysia El Salvador Turkey Guatemala Colombia	Costa Rica Venezuela
3 to under 5	Ethiopia India	Ceylon Uganda Tanzania	UAR Paraguay Rhodesia Morocco	Zambia Peru Tunisia	Chile Argentina
Under 3			Ghana		Uruguay

Source: OECD, *Development Assistance, 1971 Review*, Paris, December 1971, p. 117.

TABLE 6. Trend of Per Capita GNP, 1960–73 (Constant 1972 Prices)

Year	1960	1961	1962	1963	1964	1965	1966	1967	1968	1969	1970	1971	1972	1973
Developed	100.0	102.7	107.4	111.1	116.9	121.9	127.5	131.1	137.5	143.4	146.5	150.4	157.2	165.8
Less Developed	100.0	103.0	105.4	108.4	112.6	115.0	117.9	120.6	125.5	131.1	136.5	140.7	145.8	157.2

Source: AID, *Gross National Product, Growth Rates and Trend Data*, Report RC-W-138, May 1, 1974.

gap in absolute levels of per capita income would still tend to widen—unless the LDCs were to have an incredibly high rate of growth. In actuality, the annual growth of per capita income at the end of the 1960s was less than 2 per cent in Latin America, only about 2 per cent in East Asia, merely 1 per cent in Africa, and only about ½ per cent in South Asia. At these rates, a doubling of per capita income in East Asia would take nearly thirty-five years, in Latin America more than forty years, in Africa almost seventy years, and in South Asia nearly a century and a half.

We must also realize that a quick reversal of these trends in international development cannot be expected. Incomes in the rich countries have grown over a long period of time, and it is the power of compound interest over the long run that accounts for their presently high standards of living. The rich countries, however, now have a large base of income, so that even if poor countries were to grow at a much higher rate than the rich countries, the absolute gap in per capita income would nonetheless still widen between the rich and poor countries. (A 10 per cent rate of growth in a per capita income of $200 gives an increment of income of only $20, whereas a rate of growth of only 2 per cent of a per capita income of $2000 gives an increment of $40.)

Finally, we should recognize that the problem of international inequalities is further aggravated by the fact that the internal distribution of income within a poor country also tends to be highly unequal—more unequal within poorer countries than within richer countries. This is indicated by the selections that follow.

I.B.2. Relative and Absolute Poverty*

What is the extent of relative and absolute poverty in underdeveloped countries and does it vary systematically with the level of development? What evidence is there on the relationship between growth and inequality and how far can this relationship be affected by policy? What are the economic characteristics of the poor and what do they imply for distributional strategies? . . .

RELATIVE INEQUALITY

The conventional approach to income inequality is to define the problem in purely relative terms. A familiar technique for this purpose is to measure inequality by the extent to which the income share of groups of individuals or households differs from their

*From Montek S. Ahluwalia, "Income Inequality: Some Dimensions of the Problem," *Finance and Development*, September 1974, pp. 3–7. Reprinted by permission.

population share. In this section, we will examine the problem in terms of income shares of the lowest 40 per cent, the middle 40 per cent, and the top 20 per cent of households ordinally ranked by income. . . .

Tables 1, 2, and 3 present income share data for sixty-six countries cross-classified according to different levels of overall inequality and per capita income levels. The tables distinguish between three inequality levels defined as high, moderate, and low (according to specified ranges of the share of the lowest 40 per cent) and three income groupings defined as high, middle, and low (according to specified ranges of per capita GNP). The extent of inequality varies widely among countries but the following broad patterns can be identified.

The *socialist countries* have the highest degree of overall equality in the distribution of income. This is as we would expect, since income from the ownership of capital does not accrue as income to individuals. The

TABLE 1. Cross-classification of Countries by Income Level: High Inequality (Share of Lowest 40% less than 12%)[1]

	Country (Year)	Per Capita GNP US$	Lowest 40%	Middle 40%	Top 20%
Income up to $300	Kenya (1969)	136	10.0	22.0	68.0
	Sierra Leone (1968)	159	9.6	22.4	68.0
	Iraq (1956)	200	6.8	25.2	68.0
	Philippines (1971)	239	11.6	34.6	53.8
	Senegal (1960)	245	10.0	26.0	64.0
	Ivory Coast (1970)	247	10.8	32.1	57.1
	Rhodesia (1968)	252	8.2	22.8	69.0
	Tunisia (1970)	255	11.4	33.6	55.0
	Honduras (1968)	265	6.5	28.5	65.0
	Ecuador (1970)	277	6.5	20.0	73.5
	El Salvador (1969)	295	11.2	36.4	52.4
	Turkey (1968)	282	9.3	29.9	60.8
Income from $300 to $750	Malaysia (1970)	330	11.6	32.4	56.0
	Colombia (1970)	358	9.0	30.0	61.0
	Brazil (1970)	390	10.0	28.4	61.5
	Peru (1971)	480	6.5	33.5	60.0
	Gabon (1968)	497	8.8	23.7	67.5
	Jamaica (1958)	510	8.2	30.3	61.5
	Costa Rica (1971)	521	11.5	30.0	58.5
	Mexico (1969)	645	10.5	25.5	64.0
	South Africa (1965)	669	6.2	35.8	58.0
	Panama (1969)	692	9.4	31.2	59.4
Income above $750	Venezuela (1970)	1004	7.9	27.1	65.0
	Finland (1962)	1599	11.1	39.6	49.3
	France (1962)	1913	9.5	36.8	53.7

Note: The income shares of each percentile group were read off a free-hand Lorenz curve fitted to observed points in the cumulative distribution. The distributions are for pretax income. Per capita GNP figures are taken from the World Bank data files and refer to GNP at factor cost for the year indicated in constant 1971 U.S. dollars.

[1] The data used in the tables in this article are largely taken from Jain, S. and Tiemann, A. 1973, *Size Distribution of Income: A Compilation of Data*, Development Research Center Discussion Paper No. 4, World Bank, Washington, D.C.

TABLE 2.   Cross-classification of Countries by Income Level: Moderate Inequality (Share of Lowest 40% between 12% and 17%)

	Country (Year)	Per Capita GNP US$	Lowest 40%	Middle 40%	Top 20%
Income up to $300	Burma (1958)	82	16.5	38.7	44.8
	Dahomey (1959)	87	15.5	34.5	50.0
	Tanzania (1967)	89	13.0	26.0	61.0
	India (1964)	99	16.0	32.0	52.0
	Madagascar (1960)	120	13.5	25.5	61.0
	Zambia (1959)	230	14.5	28.5	57.0
Income from $300 to $750	Dominican Republic (1969)	323	12.2	30.3	57.5
	Iran (1968)	332	12.5	33.0	54.5
	Guyana (1956)	550	14.0	40.3	45.7
	Lebanon (1960)	508	13.0	26.0	61.0
	Uruguay (1968)	618	16.5	35.5	48.0
	Chile (1968)	744	13.0	30.2	56.8
Income above $750	Argentina (1970)	1079	16.5	36.1	47.4
	Puerto Rico (1968)	1100	13.7	35.7	50.6
	Netherlands (1967)	1990	13.6	37.9	48.5
	Norway (1968)	2010	16.6	42.9	40.5
	Germany, Fed. Rep. (1964)	2144	15.4	31.7	52.9
	Denmark (1968)	2563	13.6	38.8	47.6
	New Zealand (1969)	2859	15.5	42.5	42.0
	Sweden (1963)	2949	14.0	42.0	44.0

observed inequality in these countries is due mainly to inequality in wages between sectors and skill classes. Since the structural factors operating toward equality are the strongest in these countries, their average income share of the lowest 40 per cent— amounting to about 25 per cent of total income—may be taken as an upper limit for the target income share to which policymakers in underdeveloped countries can aspire.

The *developed countries* are evenly distributed between the categories of low and moderate inequality. The average income share of the bottom 40 per cent amounts to about 16 per cent, which is lower than the average for socialist countries but better than most of the underdeveloped countries .... Most of the *underdeveloped countries* show markedly greater relative inequality than the developed countries. About half of the underdeveloped countries fall in the high inequality range with another third displaying moderate inequality. ... Those of the underdeveloped countries classified in the low inequality category have income shares for the lowest 40 per cent averaging 18 per cent, as is the case with the most egalitarian of the developed countries. Against this, however, half the underdeveloped countries show income shares of the lowest 40 per cent, averaging only 9 per cent. . . .

ABSOLUTE POVERTY

The extent of relative inequality in underdeveloped countries is an important dimension of the problem of income distribution, but it tells us little about the extent of absolute poverty. Yet much of the current interest in income distribution is not simply due to a concern with relative inequality. It is more often a concern with absolute standards of living in terms of calorie intake and nutrition levels, clothing, sanitation, health, education, and so on. . . . The incidence of poverty in underdeveloped countries defined in absolute terms has powerful appeal for dramatizing the need for policy action in both domestic and international spheres. Estimates of this type have been attempted for some countries using arbitrary poverty lines for each country to measure population below these levels. Similar estimates can be derived for the underdeveloped countries in Table 1 by combining income share data

TABLE 3. Cross-classification of Countries by Income Level: Low Inequality (Share of Lowest 40%, 17% and above)

	Country (Year)	Per Capita GNP US$	Lowest 40%	Middle 40%	Top 20%
Income up to $300	Chad (1958)	78	18.0	39.0	43.0
	Sri Lanka (1969)	95	17.0	37.0	46.0
	Niger (1960)	97	18.0	40.0	42.0
	Pakistan (1964)	100	17.5	37.5	45.0
	Uganda (1970)	126	17.1	35.8	47.1
	Thailand (1970)	180	17.0	37.5	45.5
	Korea (1970)	235	18.0	37.0	45.0
	Taiwan (1964)	241	20.4	39.5	40.1
Income from $300 to $750	Surinam (1962)	394	21.7	35.7	42.6
	Greece (1957)	500	21.0	29.5	49.5
	Yugoslavia (1968)	529	18.5	40.0	41.5
	Bulgaria (1962)	530	26.8	40.0	33.2
	Spain (1965)	750	17.6	36.7	45.7
Income above $750	Poland (1964)	850	23.4	40.6	36.0
	Japan (1963)	950	20.7	39.3	40.0
	United Kingdom (1968)	2015	18.8	42.2	39.0
	Hungary (1969)	1140	24.0	42.5	33.5
	Czechoslovakia (1964)	1150	27.6	41.4	31.0
	Australia (1968)	2509	20.0	41.2	38.8
	Canada (1965)	2920	20.0	39.8	40.2
	United States (1970)	4850	19.7	41.5	38.8

with total income estimates obtained from the national accounts. For each country we have estimated (see Table 4) the population living below two arbitrary "poverty lines" of annual per capita incomes of US$50 and US$75 (in 1971 prices). . . .

The countries included in Table 4 account for about 60 per cent of the total population of the developing countries excluding China. About a third of this population falls below the poverty line defined by US$50 per capita and about half falls below

TABLE 4. Estimates of Population Below Poverty Line in 1969

Country	1969 GNP Per Capita	1969 Population (Millions)	Population Below US$50		Population Below US$75	
			Millions	% of Total Population	Millions	% of Total Population
LATIN AMERICA						
Ecuador	264	5.9	2.2	37.0	3.5	58.5
Honduras	265	2.5	.7	28.0	1.0	38.0
El Salvador	295	3.4	.5	13.5	.6	18.4
Dominican Republic	323	4.2	.5	11.0	.7	15.9
Colombia	347	20.6	3.2	15.4	5.6	27.0
Brazil	347	90.8	12.7	14.0	18.2	20.0
Jamaica	640	2.0	.2	10.0	.3	15.4
Guyana	390	.7	.1	9.0	.1	15.1
Peru	480	13.1	2.5	18.9	3.3	25.5
Costa Rica	512	1.7	–	2.3	.1	8.5
Mexico	645	48.9	3.8	7.8	8.7	17.8
Uruguay	649	2.9	.1	2.5	.2	5.5
Panama	692	1.4	.1	3.5	.2	11.0
Chile	751	9.6	–	–	–	–
Venezuela	974	10.0	–	–	–	–
Argentina	1054	24.0	–	–	–	–
Puerto Rico	1600	2.8	–	–	–	–
Average and Total	*545*	244.5	26.6	*10.8*	42.5	*17.4*
ASIA						
Burma	72	27.0	14.5	53.6	19.2	71.0
Sri Lanka	95	12.2	4.0	33.0	7.8	63.5
India	100	537.0	239.0	44.5	359.3	66.9
Pakistan (E&W)	100	111.8	36.3	32.5	64.7	57.9
Thailand	173	34.7	9.3	26.8	15.4	44.3
Korea	224	13.3	.7	5.5	2.3	17.0
Philippines	233	37.2	4.8	13.0	11.2	30.0

Country	1969 GNP Per Capita	1969 Population (Millions)	Population Below US$50		Population Below US$75	
			Millions	% of Total Population	Millions	% of Total Population
ASIA, continued						
Turkey	290	34.5	4.1	12.0	8.2	23.7
Iraq	316	9.4	2.3	24.0	3.1	33.3
Taiwan	317	13.8	1.5	10.7	2.0	14.3
Malaysia	323	10.6	1.2	11.0	1.6	15.5
Iran	350	27.9	2.3	8.5	4.2	15.0
Lebanon	570	2.6	–	1.0	.1	5.0
Average and Total	*132*	872.0	320.0	*36.7*	499.1	*57.2*
AFRICA						
Chad	75	3.5	1.5	43.1	2.7	77.5
Dahomey	90	2.6	1.1	41.6	2.3	90.1
Tanzania	92	12.8	7.4	57.9	9.3	72.9
Niger	94	3.9	1.3	33.0	2.3	59.9
Madagascar	119	6.7	3.6	53.8	4.7	69.6
Uganda	128	8.3	1.8	21.3	4.1	49.8
Sierra Leone	165	2.5	1.1	43.5	1.5	61.5
Senegal	229	3.8	.9	22.3	1.3	35.3
Ivory Coast	237	4.8	.3	7.0	1.4	28.5
Tunisia	241	4.9	1.1	22.5	1.6	32.1
Rhodesia	274	5.1	.9	17.4	1.9	37.4
Zambia	340	4.2	.3	6.3	.3	7.5
Gabon	547	.5	.1	15.7	.1	23.0
South Africa	729	20.2	2.4	12.0	3.1	15.5
Average and Total	*303*	83.8	23.8	*28.4*	36.6	*43.6*
Average and Grand Total	*228*	1200.3	370.4	*30.9*	578.2	*48.2*

Note: —negligible.

US$75 per capita. Much of this is clearly due to the low levels of per capita income of many countries rather than to highly skewed income distribution patterns. India, Pakistan, Bangladesh, and Sri Lanka with 55 per cent of the total population together account for about 75 per cent of the population living below US$50. These countries are all characterized by low to moderate inequality. More interestingly, the table shows that a high per capita income does not ensure that there is no "absolute poverty" problem. Differences in patterns of income distribution between countries mean that the poverty problem may be equally serious in countries with very different per capita income levels. Both Ecuador and Sri Lanka have about a third of the population below the US$50 poverty line even though Ecuador's per capita income is three times as high. . . . These estimates provide some indication of the scale of absolute poverty in underdeveloped countries and its relationship to per capita GNP and the distribution of income. Much of the poverty problem is a direct reflection of low levels of per capita income, but skewed distribution patterns are also important. Observed differences in the degree of inequality are such as to offset per capita incomes which are two or three times higher. It follows that development strategies which succeed in raising the level of per capita income may not have much impact on the poverty problem if they are accompanied by a deterioration in relative income shares.

GROWTH AND THE LOWEST 40 PER CENT

The above discussion of distributional patterns . . . has been limited to describing existing conditions. We have not considered whether these conditions are improving or deteriorating over time. Yet it is precisely these questions that are most often raised in evaluating performance and designing policy.

Measuring changes in distributional conditions can be done in terms of either relative income shares or absolute incomes. The limitations of a purely relative approach are self-evident: changes in relative equality tell us little about changes in income levels of the poor unless we also know what has happened to total income. An alternative approach which places greater emphasis on absolute income levels of the poor is to consider whether the levels of living of the poor have improved over time.

Systematic examination of such trends calls for time series data on both the distribution of income and the growth of income. Unfortunately time series data on the distribution of income are not available even for most developed countries. At most, we have a collection of countries for which distribution data are available for two points in time. These data can be combined with national accounts data to give us rough estimates of the income accruing to the lowest 40 per cent at two points in time. Figure I.1 plots the estimated annual growth rate of income of the lowest 40 per cent against the rate of growth of GNP for 18 countries . . . . Countries above the 45 degree line are countries in which the income share of the lowest 40 per cent increased over the period so that the estimated rate of growth of income for this group is higher than for the economy as a whole. Countries below the 45 degree line are countries in which the relative income shares of the lowest 40 per cent declined.

The scatter suggests considerable diversity of country experience in terms of changes in relative equality. . . . Both Peru and Sri Lanka, for example, experienced the same rate of GNP growth over the respective periods reported, but income of the lowest 40 per cent grew over 8 per cent per annum in Sri Lanka—compared to only 3 per cent in Peru—because of improvements in relative income shares. In other cases, a high rate of growth of GNP offsets a deterioration in relative income shares to produce substantial increases in income of the poor. Mexico and Brazil, for example, experienced an increase in inequality in terms of relative income shares but income of the lowest 40 per cent grew by about 6 per cent per annum in both cases.

Since individual observations are subject to substantial error, it is perhaps more important to look for patterns in the data. The evidence suggests that there is no strong pattern relating changes in the distribution of income to the rate of growth of GNP. In both high-growth and low-growth countries there are some which have experienced improvements and others that have experienced deteriorations in relative equality. The absence of any marked relationship between income growth and changes in income shares is important for policy purposes. It suggests there is little firm empirical basis for the view that higher rates of growth inevitably generate greater inequality. This may have

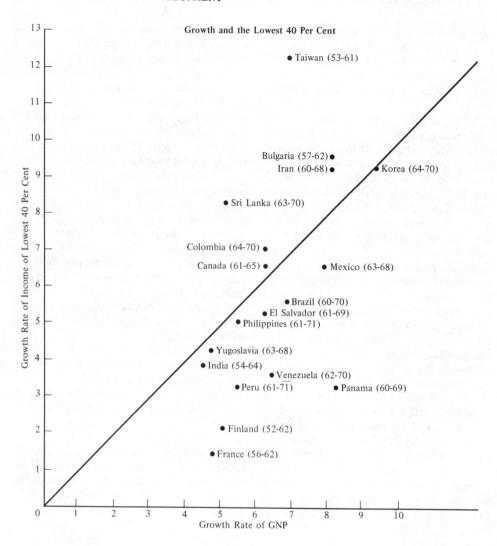

FIGURE I.1.

happened in particular cases but an explanation for this must be sought in the circumstances of each particular case and not in terms of a generalized relationship. . . .

DETERMINANTS OF INEQUALITY

Ideally the determination of relative income shares should be analyzed in the con-

text of a fully developed theory of the size distribution of income. Such a theory should take into account not only the economic factors affecting the distribution of income, but also the political and institutional context in which these factors operate. Needless to say, we are far from having such a comprehensive theory. There are, however, several partial hypotheses about particular factors affecting the distribution of income which provide some of the elements of a comprehensive theory. As a first step in the analysis we need to study the empirical validity of these hypotheses using available data.

In the absence of time series data, such tests must rely heavily on cross-country data of the type discussed above. Cross-country differences in income inequality can be explained in terms of various "explanatory variables" reflecting different influences on distribution patterns. Associative relationships of this type cannot, of course, be presented as proof of causality, but they help to indicate relationships which deserve further study. . . . In this section we present preliminary results (obtained by the World Bank's Development Research Center) using multiple regression to estimate equations "explaining" variations in the income share of the top 20 per cent, the middle 40 per cent, and the lowest 40 per cent.

The results of our cross-section analysis may be summarized as follows:

The explanatory variables used included both structural variables such as the level of per capita income and the share of agriculture in GDP and other variables which can be influenced by policy such as the rate of growth of the economy, the rates of enrollment in primary and secondary schooling, and the rate of growth of population. The variables explain about half of the observed variation in income shares across countries. The large proportion of variation unexplained is not surprising. We have not considered a number of potential explanatory variables which can be identified a priori. The most important of these is the concentration of wealth (including agricultural land) and mechanisms perpetuating this concentration pattern. Other economic factors that may be relevant are various institutional and market mechanisms that discriminate against low-income groups. The influence of these factors could not be explained due to lack of data and the difficulty in specifying an appropriate explanatory variable.

There is some confirmation of the hypothesis that income inequality first increases and then decreases with development. . . .

Education is positively related to equality in terms of income shares of the lowest and middle group. . . .

The growth of population is positively related to inequality as measured by the income share of the lowest 40 per cent. . . .

The cross-section evidence does not support the view that a high rate of economic growth has an adverse effect upon relative equality. Quite the contrary, the rate of growth of GDP in our sample was positively related to the share of the lowest 40 per cent, suggesting that the objectives of growth and equity may not be in conflict. . . .

I.B.3. Variables Affecting Income

Distribution*

In an extension of the methodology of our previous work[1] our study of growth and equity relates interactions among changes in economic and social structure to two dimensions of social equity, namely political participation and income distribution. The analysis relates to the period 1957–68 for 43 underdeveloped countries.[2]

With respect to the distribution of income, the statistical technique is based on an analysis of variance which seeks to 'explain' variations in the dependent variable. In fact, three dependent variables for the 43 countries are constructed from the basic income distribution data shown in Table 1. They are:

(a) The income share of the lowest 60 per cent of the population;

(b) The income share of the middle quintile of the population;

(c) The income share of the wealthiest 5 per cent of the population.

The statistical analysis attempts to assess the relative importance of 35 independent variables in explaining inter-country differences in patterns of income distribution. The six most important variables are found to be: the rate of improvement in human resources; direct government economic activity; socio-economic dualism; the potential

for economic development; *per capita* GNP; and the strength of the labour movement.[3]

It must be stressed that the generalizations that follow, in this section and elsewhere, depend crucially on a dynamic interpretation of the cross-section results. This assumes that in its growth path a typical underdeveloped country will embody the average characteristics of the group of countries which are associated with successive levels of development. These generalizations, though stated as fact, should thus properly be regarded as suggestive hypotheses, worthy of consideration by policymakers and still in need of further study.[4]

The relationship between levels of economic development and the equity of income distribution is shown to be asymmetrically U-shaped, with more egalitarian income distributions being characteristic of both extreme economic underdevelopment and high levels of economic development. Between these extremes, however, the relationship is, for the most part, inverse: up to a point, higher rates of industrialization, faster increases in agricultural productivity, and higher rates of growth all tend to shift the income distribution in favour of the higher-income groups and against the low-income groups.

The beneficiaries of economic development, as well as the processes by which the poor are penalized by economic develop-

*From Irma Adelman, "Growth, Income Distribution and Equity-Oriented Development Strategies," *World Development,* February-March 1975, pp. 67–73. Reprinted by permission.

[1] I. Adelman and C. Taft Morris, *Society, Politics and Economic Development: A Quantitative Approach* (Johns Hopkins Press, 1967).

[2] I. Adelman and C. Taft Morris, *Economic Growth and Social Equity in Developing Countries* (Stanford Press, 1973).

[3] For a discussion of the statistical technique and its results, see Adelman and Morris, *Economic Growth and Social Equity,* op. cit., chapter 4. The indicators for the independent variables are defined in chapters 1 and 2.

[4] Apart from this methodological issue, on the validity of the data, ibid., pp. 155–8.

TABLE 1. Income Distribution Estimates (Percentage Shares by Population Groups)

	Country	0–40	40–60	0–60	60–80	80–100	95–100
1.	Argentina	17.30%	13.10%	30.40%	17.60%	52.00%	29.40%
2.	Bolivia	12.90	13.70	26.60	14.30	59.10	35.70
3.	Brazil	12.50	10.20	22.70	15.80	61.50	38.40
4.	Burma	23.00	13.00	36.00	15.50	48.50	28.21
5.	Ceylon	13.66	13.81	27.47	20.22	52.31	18.38
6.	Chad	23.00	12.00	35.00	22.00	43.00	23.00
7.	Chile	15.00	12.00	27.00	20.70	52.30	22.60
8.	Colombia	7.30	9.70	17.00	16.06	68.06	40.36
9.	Costa Rica	13.30	12.10	25.40	14.60	60.00	35.00
10.	Dahomey	18.00	12.00	30.00	20.00	50.00	32.00
11.	Ecuador	16.90	13.50	30.40	15.60	54.00	33.70
12.	El Salvador	12.30	11.30	23.60	15.00	61.40	33.00
13.	Gabon	8.00	7.00	15.00	14.00	71.00	47.00
14.	Greece	21.30	12.30	34.10	16.40	49.50	23.00
15.	India	20.00	16.00	36.00	22.00	42.00	20.00
16.	Iraq	8.00	8.00	16.00	16.00	68.00	34.00
17.	Israel	16.00	17.00	33.00	23.90	43.10	16.80
18.	Ivory Coast	18.00	12.00	30.00	15.00	55.00	29.00
19.	Jamaica	8.20	10.80	19.00	19.50	61.50	31.20
20.	Japan	15.30	15.80	31.10	22.90	46.00	14.80
21.	Lebanon	7.20	15.80	23.00	16.00	61.00	34.00
22.	Libya	.50	1.28	1.78	8.72	89.50	46.20
23.	Malagasy	14.00	9.00	23.00	18.00	59.00	37.00
24.	Mexico	10.50	11.25	21.75	20.21	58.04	28.52
25.	Morocco	14.50	7.70	22.20	12.40	65.40	20.60
26.	Niger	23.00	12.00	35.00	23.00	42.00	23.00
27.	Nigeria	14.00	9.00	23.00	16.10	60.90	38.38
28.	Pakistan	17.50	15.50	33.00	22.00	45.00	20.00
29.	Panama	14.30	13.80	28.10	15.20	56.70	34.50
30.	Peru	8.80	8.30	17.10	15.30	67.60	48.30
31.	Philippines	12.70	12.00	24.70	19.50	55.80	27.50
32.	Rhodesia	12.00	8.00	20.00	15.00	65.00	40.00
33.	Senegal	10.00	10.00	20.00	16.00	64.00	36.00
34.	Sierra Leone	10.10	9.10	19.20	16.70	64.10	33.80
35.	South Africa	6.11	10.16	16.27	26.37	57.36	39.38
36.	Sudan	15.00	14.30	29.30	22.60	48.10	17.10
37.	Surinam	22.26	14.74	37.00	20.60	42.40	15.10
38.	Taiwan	14.20	14.80	29.00	19.00	52.00	24.10
39.	Tanzania	19.50	9.75	29.25	9.75	61.00	42.90
40.	Trinidad & Tobago	9.42	9.10	18.52	24.48	57.00	26.60
41.	Tunisia	10.62	9.95	20.57	14.43	65.00	22.44
42.	Venezuela	13.40	16.60	30.00	22.90	47.10	23.20
43.	Zambia	15.85	11.10	26.95	15.95	57.10	37.50

Source: I. Adelman and C. Taft Morris, *Economic Growth and Social Equity in Developing Countries* (Stanford Press, 1973), p. 152.

ment, vary with the level of development of the country. At the lowest level of development, as economic growth begins in a subsistence agrarian economy through the expansion of a narrow modern sector, inequality in the distribution of income typically increases greatly, the income share of the poorest 60 per cent declines significantly, as does that of the middle 20 per cent, and the income share of the top 5 per cent increases strikingly. In these countries the path toward sustained economic growth is eventually blocked unless either the country is sufficiently large or redistributive policies are sufficiently important to generate an internal market for growth.

Once countries move successfully beyond the stage of sharply dualistic growth, the middle-income receivers are the primary beneficiaries of the widening of the base for that economic growth which follows. The position of the poorest 40 per cent typically worsens both relatively and absolutely, even where a transition from sharply dualistic growth to more broadly based economic growth is accomplished. Even when relatively high levels of development have been attained and the capacity for more broadly based economic growth has been established, the poorest segments of the population typically benefit from economic growth only where widespread efforts are made to improve the human resource base.

Finally, it should be noted that, in order to reach the relatively small positively correlated portion of the equity-level-of-economic-development curve, a country must be among the upper half of those underdeveloped countries at the highest level of development. Indeed, in the absence of domestic policy action aimed specifically at redirecting the benefits of growth, a nation must attain a level of development corresponding to that which exists among the socio-economically most developed of the underdeveloped countries (Argentina, Chile, Taiwan, Israel) before the income distribution tends to become as even as it is in countries that have undergone virtually no

economic development (e.g., Dahomey, Chad, Niger).

With regard to political participation, perhaps the principal lesson suggested by our results is that increases in political participation are by no means automatic consequences of socio-economic development in underdeveloped countries.[5] The early stages of social mobilization and economic modernization generate pressures for political and administrative reform and a general transformation of the political élite. For these pressures to lead to viable forms of political participation requires both the institutionalization of socio-economic interest groups and the evolution of mechanisms for sharing political and economic power among them which are sufficiently equitable to be generally accepted. Success in accommodating these demands on the political system tends to reduce social tensions, but the process of inducing the necessary political changes is fraught with social conflict and often accompanied with violence. If the resultant instability exceeds the capacity of the system to integrate conflicting claims peacefully, authoritarianism and the suppression of incipient participant institutions may postpone indefinitely the development of modern forms of participation.

THE POLITICS OF EQUITABLE GROWTH

The major unresolved question posed by equity-oriented development economics is: 'Is equitable growth possible within existing socio-political structures?' A subsidiary question is: 'If not, what socio-political structures are most conducive to equitable economic growth?'

Neither question can be answered unequivocally at this time, and I shall not theorize on the answers. Instead I shall limit myself to a few remarks based on empirical evidence that may be suggestive in developing answers to these questions.

[5] ibid., chapter 3.

1. Greater political participation, that favourite remedy of Western democracy for making equitable economic growth politically possible, does not appear to redistribute income to the poor. To the extent that it is effective at all, it tends to redistribute income from the upper- towards the middle-income groups.[6]

2. Greater government ownership of productive enterprise, that favourite remedy of the socialist world for making equitable economic growth politically possible, also does not appear to redistribute income to the poor. It reduces the income share of the upper 5 per cent dramatically, but the benefit of the redistribution redounds to the next quintile in the income scale.[7] It also tends to reduce the growth rate relative to the free enterprise growth rate, thus providing less to redistribute.

3. There appears to be an uncomfortable trade-off between freedom of action in the economic arena and the equity of the distribution of income. Such a conflict is evident in Yugoslavia, for example, where, after the adoption of a more liberal and decentralized economic policy, inequalities in the distribution of income have started reasserting themselves disconcertingly quickly. . . .

The reason why the political climate is so important is that asset redistribution and the redistribution of opportunities for access to asset accumulation are a necessary first step for the initiation of equitable growth. (The latter has been an actual precondition in all successful equitable growth countries to date.) But in all successful countries that redistribution has been followed by a host of primarily growthmanship-oriented policies to maintain the value of the redistributed assets. Poor economic management or excessively slow growth rates have invariably negated the intent of redistributive efforts both by producing a drastic fall in the value of the redistributed assets (witness the host of abortive land reforms and enterprise nationalizations) and by providing unforeseen and undesirable windfall profits for the upper 20 per cent of the population.

EQUITY-ORIENTED DEVELOPMENT STRATEGIES

The results of the statistical analyses performed by Morris and myself suggest that equitable growth requires a major reorientation of development strategies. The most hopeful redirection to emerge from this work is towards human-resource-intensive development patterns.[8] It is significant that all five Western countries which have successfully combined accelerated growth with improvements in the share of income accruing to the poor have followed a strategy consistent with this result, in that each has stressed export-oriented growth based on labour-and-skill-intensive exports. That is, they have all adopted human-capital-intensive development strategies, in which broad-based massive investment in the improvement of the educational level of the population was phased into the subsequent creation of productive employment opportunities.

GROWTH AND INCOME DISTRIBUTION

Before discussing policy implications, it may be worth-while to examine the relationship between growth and income distribution. Both cross-sectional and time series evidence suggest the following rather complicated relationship between the rate of economic growth and the change in the share of income accruing to the poorest 40 per cent of the population (see Figure I.1 in I.B.2, p. 25).[9]

[8] It will be recalled that the rate of improvement in human resources is shown to be of great significance in the statistical analysis of variations in the dependent variables.

[9] These relationships are supported by a cross-section regression analysis in Adelman and

[6] ibid., p. 179.
[7] ibid., p. 179.

1. Real rates of *per capita* economic growth below 3.5 per cent tend to be associated with declines in the share of income of the poor. At current rates of population growth, this puts the minimum required growth rate of real GNP around 5.5 per cent.

2. Higher rates of growth are a necessary *but not a sufficient* condition for substantial improvements in the share of income of the poor.

3. High growth rates tend to lead to improvements in the income of the poorest 40 per cent of the population only if accompanied by a human-resource-intensive development strategy pursued within a not sharply dualistic growth pattern.[10]

The economic responses underlying these observations (admittedly somewhat oversimplified) are:

1. Where growth is slow, the adverse equity effects of development are due primarily to deterioration of the position of the small farms in the agricultural sector and to the population impact of modern health measures on low-income families. Capital-intensive industrialization does not tend to generate sufficient employment to absorb the labour force released by higher agricultural productivity. Subsistence farmers, tenants, and other small farms cannot take full advantage of modern methods, and cannot compete with plantations or large mechanized farms. The resultant fall in real income (due both to lower product prices and higher money costs) is especially hard on the subsistence and tenant groups. In the industrial sector, modern industry tends to displace cottage and handicraft workers, while the wage gains of the employed are largely eroded by the inflationary impact of tariff-supported import-substitution industrialization.

2. Under moderately rapid capital-inten-

sive growth, dualistic or otherwise, changes in product mix and technology within both agricultural and non-agricultural sectors, rapid expansion of the urban industrial sector, continued rapid population increases, migration to the cities, lack of social mobility, and inflation all operate to the detriment of the urban and rural poor.

As economic growth spreads, regional income inequality increases as the concentration of rapidly growing, technologically advanced enterprises in cities widens the gap between rural and urban *per capita* income. Within the urban sector, the spread of capital-intensive methods, which results from the ease with which owners of modern large-scale enterprises can obtain capital abroad, and from the preferences of entrepreneurs for advanced technologies, intensifies the accumulation of assets into the hands of a relatively small number of owners of modern enterprises. This labour-saving bias of technological advance, the rapidity of urban population growth, the migration to the cities of unemployed rural workers, and the lack of social mobility all tend to swell the numbers of the urban impoverished and decrease the income share of the poorest segments of the urban population.

In the rural sector, meanwhile, agricultural output expands, and the inelasticity of international and domestic demand for many agricultural products tends to reduce the real income of agricultural producers. Import substitution policies, which raise domestic consumers' goods prices above international levels, contribute further to decreasing real income among the poorest groups. Simultaneously, mechanization in industry continues to reduce greatly the earnings of large numbers of artisans and cottage workers; where cheap manufactures are permitted to flood domestic markets, the destruction of handicraft industries contributes further to reducing incomes and increasing unemployment among both the rural and urban poor. Finally, inflation depresses the real income of large groups of low-income workers.

Morris, *Economic Growth and Social Equity*, op. cit., appendix C.

[10] Panama, Mexico, and the Middle Eastern oil economies fail to meet either of these requirements.

An analogous process takes place at high rates of growth whenever the pattern is highly capital-intensive (and therefore dualistic).

3. When the rate of labour absorption in high productivity employment can exceed the rate of growth of the urban proletariat, wage rates and employment for both unskilled and semi-skilled workers will tend to rise faster than GNP. Wage differentials in industry will tend to narrow, as skilled and white-collar wage rates will not rise as fast. The consequent shift of the distribution of money income towards the lower 40 per cent will then tend to raise the demand for the outputs of agriculture. If, in addition, the industrialization process is export-oriented, domestic prices for light consumer goods need not rise above international prices and gains in money income need not be as thoroughly eroded. The differential between rural and urban incomes then narrows, both because of the continuing outward migration from agriculture and because the income elasticity of demand for agricultural products starts raising agricultural incomes more than price inelasticity will decrease them. In short, once the rates of increase of productive wage employment

exceed additions to the labour force, the spread effects of growth can start outweighing its backwash effects and the benefits of growth can start percolating downwards.

As indicated earlier, the minimum rate of growth at which this scenario can take place is estimated empirically at 5.5 per cent. An independent semi-empirical approach leads to a similar figure. Thus, at current average labour—output ratios, labour absorption in industry proceeds at about half the rate at which industrial output rises. Since, for an average developing country, the current rate of urban population growth (natural increase plus immigration) is about 4 per cent per year, an annual rate of growth of industrial output of at least 8 per cent is required merely to absorb new increments. A growth elasticity for industrial output with respect to GNP of approximately 1.3 per cent leads to a figure of about 5 per cent as the minimum turnaround rate of GNP growth. If the process of industrialization is more labour-intensive, or if the elasticity of industrial growth with respect to output is higher, or the rate of population growth lower, the turnaround will occur at lower GNP growth rates; if the rate of growth of GNP is more rapid, the turnaround will occur sooner.

I.C. NEW INITIATIVES IN
DEVELOPMENT

I.C.1. Successful Development
Strategies*

Because of the interdependence of the various aspects of structural change, we cannot hope to explain development very adequately as the sum of separate influences, which is the hypothesis underlying most econometric studies. I will therefore supplement these conclusions by examining the development strategies of rapidly growing countries to try to identify the kinds of policy that have led to successful growth.

From 75 countries with per capita incomes of less than $600 (in 1964 prices) for which the World Bank has compiled fairly complete statistics for most of 1950–69, I have chosen 29 that have sustained relatively high growth rates throughout, making some allowance for countries starting with a very large agricultural sector. The average growth rates of 26 of them were at least 5.5 per cent for the period covered; Pakistan, Malaysia, and Peru were added as borderline cases.[1]

My analysis of the sources of sustained growth concentrates on three aspects displayed in Table 1: (1) the volume and financing of investment as between domestic savings and external sources (columns 8–11); (2) the role of trade and natural resources (columns 13–16); and (3) the pace of transformation of the economy, as evidenced by the lead or lag of industrialization compared with the normal patterns (columns 17–20). The last two characteristics were measured by the deviation of a country's trade and production patterns from the normal for its income level and size.

To evaluate the role of external resources we need to know how far investment in these countries was financed by external capital, whether this external dependence was reduced over time, and how the productive structure was adapted to maintain sectoral balance. Table 1 gives several measures of structural change relevant to these processes.

A preliminary analysis of these data shows quite different patterns of resource use as between those countries (mainly small) with ample supplies of foreign exchange from aid or primary exports and those (mainly large) that lack such external sources. Hence the strategies of successful growth are grouped into four types:

A. High Capital Inflow: More than 30 per cent of investment financed by aid or other foreign sources for at least the first decade.

B. High Primary Exports: Primary exports at least 50 per cent and usually 100 per cent above normal levels. High primary exports seem more important in character-

*From Hollis B. Chenery, "Growth and Structural Change," *Finance and Development Quarterly,* Vol. 8, No. 3, 1971, pp. 21–5. Reprinted by permission.

[1] Other countries that appear to have had growth rates of this magnitude, but are omitted for lack of comparable data are Albania, North Korea, Libyan Arab Republic, Rumania, Saudi Arabia, and North Viet-Nam. Czechoslovakia, Eastern Germany, and Italy are also omitted since they were already relatively developed in 1950.

TABLE 1. A Classification of Development Strategies of High Growth Countries

	1950 GNP Per Capita US$ (1964)	Population 1960 (Millions)	GDP Growth 1950–60 (% a year)	GDP Growth 1960–69 (% a year)	Population Growth 1950–69 (% a year)	Increase in per capita GNP (Ratio 1969/1950)	Investment Ratio 1950–55	Investment Ratio 1960–69	External Finance: (Ratio F/I 1950–60)
A–Strategy: High Capital Inflow									
(1)	(2)	(3)	(4)	(5)	(6)	(7)	(8)	(9)	(10)
Israel	534	2.1	10.4	8.7	4.2	2.54	.31	.24	66.7
Taiwan	95	10.6	8.1	9.9	3.2	2.71	.14	.23	39.3
Jordan	88	1.7	9.0	8.3	2.7	2.52	n.a.	.17	181.8
Greece	268	8.3	5.8	7.3	0.9	2.66	.18	.27	43.3
Puerto Rico	478	2.4	6.0	8.3	1.1	2.00	.20	.27	81.3
Korea, Rep. of	78	24.7	6.0	9.3	2.7	2.31	.12	.20	65.4
Panama	307	1.1	4.8	8.1	3.1	1.80	.11	.19	55.0
B–Strategy: High Primary Exports									
Thailand	68	26.4	6.4	8.2	3.0	2.06	.13	.21	14.5
Trinidad and Tobago	335	0.8	7.9	6.9	2.5	2.25	.24	.25	25.1
Jamaica	231	1.6	7.5	3.8	1.8	1.79	.13	.24	47.9
Malaysia	185	8.1	4.1	6.7	3.0	1.67	.10	.16	−72.7
Iran	137	21.5	6.2	8.1	2.8	2.04	n.a.	.16	13.6
Nicaragua	197	1.4	5.5	6.9	3.2	1.74	n.a.	.18	n.a.
Venezuela	502	7.3	7.7	4.5	3.8	1.68	.25	.21	4.7
Ivory Coast*	139	3.7	n.a.	8.8	3.3	n.a.	.14	.17	−30.6
Iraq	106	6.9	9.9	6.5	3.1	2.45	.16	.15	−9.9
Zambia	113	3.2	5.7	6.8	2.9	1.82	.24	.27	−9.1
C–Strategy: Moderate Capital Inflow									
Mexico	277	36.0	5.8	7.1	3.3	1.72	.16	.20	11.1
Turkey	154	27.5	6.3	5.9	2.6	1.88	.13	.17	13.8
Peru	194	10.0	5.2	5.3	2.7	1.53	.20	.19	n.a.
Philippines	107	27.4	6.6	4.7	3.3	1.52	.12	.19	13.9
Pakistan*	70	100.2	2.6	6.0	2.5	1.30	n.a.	.16	n.a.
Costa Rica	264	1.3	6.6	6.5	3.6	1.60	.18	.06	22.7
Singapore	434	1.6	5.4	7.0	3.6	1.51	n.a.	.13	n.a.
D–Strategy: Low External Dependence									
Japan	251	93.2	8.3	11.1	1.1	4.85	.29	.36	−0.5
Yugoslavia	187	18.4	7.1	6.0	1.2	2.63	.38	.32	9.5
Spain	240	30.3	6.2	7.4	0.9	2.85	.21	.23	3.0
Bulgaria	157	7.9	10.9	7.5	0.8	4.35	.17	.30	n.a.
Brazil	142	69.7	6.8	5.5	3.1	1.63	.15	.18	7.3

Sources: IBRD and Chenery, Elkington, and Sims (1970).

§ Columns 17 and 19: 1950 except 1960.

† Columns 17 and 19: 1950 except 1955.

*Countries having more than 50 per cent of GNP from agriculture in 1950.

£Singapore, 1951–60. Goods only.

The basic data are those compiled and circulated in January 1971 by the Economic Program Department, Socio-Economic Data Division, IBRD, under the title World Tables. References are to that volume unless otherwise noted. The data came from the UN, IBRD Country Reports, and national sources. The sample includes all countries having adequate data and a 5.5 per cent or more GDP growth rate plus several borderline cases (see text).

Col. 2: 1950 GDP per capita (1960 for Ivory Coast) in 1964 U.S. dollars from Table IV, Col. 17.

Col. 3: 1960 (midyear) Population, except Jordan, Greece, and Yugoslavia 1961 (Table II, Col. 1).

Cols. 4 and 5: Annual Average Growth Rate of Total Gross Domestic Product: at constant market prices whenever possible, otherwise at constant factor cost (Table 1, Col. 2). Data available only to 1967 for Jordan and Nigeria, 1968 for Trinidad and Tobago, Iran, Pakistan, Sudan, and Bulgaria.

Col. 6: Annual Average Growth Rate of Population 1951–69 (Table I, Col. 1).

Col. 7: Increase in per capita GNP 1951–69 (Table IV, Col. 17).

Cols. 8 and 9: Investment Ratios, averages of 1950 and 1955 and of 1960, 1965, 1968, and 1969, respectively, from Table IV, Col. 1 (Gross Domestic Product) and Col. 2 (Gross Domestic Investment).

Cols. 10 and 11: Balance of Payments Current Deficit 1951–60 and 1961–68 or 1961–69 as available, from Table IV, Col. 8.

Col. 12: Ratios for each period were obtained by dividing the gross addition to capital stock by the

External Finance: (Ratio F/I 1960–69)	Capital Output Ratio	Primary Exports/GNP (Ratio 1960)	Trade Orientation Index	Export Growth 1950–60 (% a year)	Export Growth 1950–69 (% a year)	Industrial Production Ratio to Normal (1950)	Industrial Growth (% a year)	Primary Production Ratio to Normal (1950)	Primary Production Growth 1950–69 (% a year)	
(11)	(12)	(13)	(14)	(15)	(16)	(17)	(18)	(19)	(20)	(1)
A–Strategy: High Capital Inflow										
65.0	3.8	.061	M	21.8	15.4	1.28	11.9	.42	7.2	Israel
13.4	1.9	.103	M	6.8	23.6	1.22	16.1	.77	9.3	Taiwan
109.1	n.a.	.145	B	15.3	10.4	.91§	15.2	.40§	8.3	Jordan
32.8	3.4	.084	B	11.7	11.4	.90	8.0	.93	3.8	Greece
79.0	3.3	n.a.	M	10.3	10.8	.90	6.5	.80	−1.6	Puerto Rico
53.0	2.4	.044	M	9.1	29.1	.80†	16.9	1.03†	3.9	Korea, Rep. of
23.2	2.4	.340	P	4.3	13.2	1.02	14.2	.80	5.7	Panama
B–Strategy: High Primary Exports										
93	2.3	.171	P	3.8	10.4	1.08†	8.7	.91†	4.6	Thailand
26.6	n.a.	.630	n.a.	5.9	10.8	.96	10.0	1.32	5.1	Trinidad and Tobago
25.0	3.8	.330	P	14.0	6.3	1.19†	5.0	1.32†	2.6	Jamaica
−5.5	2.9	.316	P	0.4	6.8	.58§	6.4	1.23§	5.1	Malaysia
−0.5	2.0	.202	P	1.7	10.7	n.a.	11.2	n.a.	3.9	Iran
26.6	2.7	.261	P	7.6	10.4	n.a.	7.6	n.a.	3.6	Nicaragua
−7.3	4.0	.310	P	7.7	0.6	n.a.	10.5	n.a.	5.7	Venezuela
−11.9	2.1	.312	P	6.4	13.0	.60§	n.a.	1.41§	3.9	Ivory Coast*
−13.8	2.1	.334	P	14.8	6.3	.71†	6.8	1.49†	7.1	Iraq
−31.1	4.0	.454	P	10.1	13.1	.76†	13.8	1.53†	2.6	Zambia
C–Strategy: Moderate Capital Inflow										
9.5	3.0	.078	B	5.4	7.9	.93	7.4	.90	3.9	Mexico
13.5	2.7	0.22	B	4.5	7.6	.72	11.5	1.26	3.5	Turkey
12.3	4.1	.169	P	8.9	8.6	.95	7.5	1.02	2.5	Peru
16.0	2.8	.141	B	3.0	6.9	.71	8.5	.90	4.9	Philippines
24.3	2.5	.143	P	1.9	5.4	.58	15.0	1.13	2.7	Pakistan*
28.6	3.6	.215	P	4.5	9.0	1.1	9.8	1.20	3.5	Costa Rica
n.a.	2.0	.093	B	1.2¶	11.2	.41	14.8	.23	2.3	Singapore
D–Strategy: Low External Dependence										
−0.1	3.0	.010	B	16.5	16.1	.91†	16.3	.92†	3.6	Japan
5.4	n.a.	.014	M	14.1	13.3	n.a.	10.0	n.a.	3.2	Yugoslavia
9.6	4.5	.066	B	7.4	14.0	1.06†	10.0	n.a.	3.1	Spain
n.a.	n.a.	.045	M	18.0	14.2	n.a.	17.0	n.a.	6.9	Bulgaria
3.9	2.8	.084	B	0.4	6.6	1.02	7.8	.81	2.6	Brazil

increase in GDP and the two ratios averaged (Table III, Col. 16). For several countries only one figure for Gross Marginal Capital-Output Ratio was available.

Col. 13: Primary Exports/GNP. Per cent primary of total value of exports, derived from *UN Yearbook of International Trade Statistics*. Primary exports were defined as Food (0), Unmanufactured tobacco leaf (121), Inedible (2 up to 266 Synthetic Fibers), Crude or partly refined oil (33), Natural gas (341.1), Oils and fats (4), Wild animals (941). Per cent exports of GDP from IBRD, Table III, Col. 4. Figures for Iran, Iraq, Trinidad and Tobago, and Venezuela revised to include refined petroleum and petroleum products and Zambia to include copper products.

Col. 14: M = manufacturing orientation, B = balanced, P = primary orientation, according to the deviation from the normal production of manufactured goods and primary products in exports, as measured in Chenery and Taylor (1968).

Cols. 15 and 16: Annual Average Growth Rate of Exports of Goods and Services (Table I, Col. 8) defined to exclude factor and transfer payments to and from abroad.

Cols. 17 and 19: Ratio of actual industrial and primary productions to the normal level for a country of the same income a head and size (from Chenery, Elkington, and Sims, 1970).

Col. 18: Annual Average Growth Rate of Manufacturing Production 1951–69 from Table I, Col. 7. Generally computed from country indices of manufacturing production published by UN Statistical Office.

Col. 20: Annual Average Growth Rate of Primary Production 1950–69. Primary is defined as agriculture plus mining. Per cent shares of GDP were obtained from Table IV, Cols. 6 and 7, and applied against the IBRD total GNP (Table IV, Col. 16).

izing this pattern than a high capital inflow, although they sometimes go together.

C. *Moderate Capital Inflow:* Countries with 10–30 per cent of their investment externally financed during most of the period.

D. *Low External Dependence:* Countries having none of these sources.

High Capital Inflow

The seven countries that achieved high growth rates using substantial amounts of external capital received support for reasons that are largely political; all these countries, except Korea, are small. They typically started the period in political difficulties and with unfavorable natural resources. Capital, mainly public, of some 5 to 10 per cent of GNP has flowed in for substantial periods. In all, investment in the second decade has substantially increased and dependence on foreign capital diminished while shifting to private sources.

A high development assistance strategy essentially permits a country to expand its most readily growing sectors without worry about short-term balance of payments problems. Generally aid has substituted initially for agricultural production, but both industry and primary production have grown quite rapidly. The normal stage of specialization in primary exports is thus bypassed and manufactured exports (or tourism) develop instead.

Success in a high-aid strategy normally requires a substantial reduction in the dependence on capital inflows after a decade or so. All but Puerto Rico and Jordan have achieved this result by high growth rates of both saving and exports, and all seven countries have grown very rapidly in the second decade.

The high-aid strategy has not always been so successful, but considering the unsettled political and economic conditions in which it has typically been attempted it has turned out remarkably well. Other high-aid countries (and their decade growth rates) are

Cyprus (4.5, 4.7), Tunisia ("not available," 4.4), and Bolivia ("not available," 5.1). However, the total population of Group A countries is only 50 million, and no large country is now likely to receive such substantial resources from abroad.

High Primary Exports

Development led and financed by primary exports is the traditional colonial strategy and one followed by many non-colonial countries blessed with rich natural resources. Ten countries with a total population of 85 million followed it successfully over the past 20 years. Their natural resources attract private investment, but after several decades amortization and profit remittances typically make the net inflow zero or negative.

Although, like aid recipients, the primary exporters have relatively high imports, their productive structure is strikingly different. Industry is typically lower than normal and primary production significantly higher. Even in the successful countries the growth rate is closely linked to export growth and recently in a few favored cases to tourism.

Sound development by this route eventually requires a country to become less dependent on primary exports and shift toward a more balanced production and trade structure. Successful countries such as Thailand, Trinidad and Tobago, and Iran, have—like high-aid recipients—achieved this reduced dependence by rapid industrialization without lowering the growth rate. A smooth transition is fairly exceptional, however, since most countries delay the needed structural change until demand for their primary exports declines, as in prewar Argentina, Brazil, and Chile and postwar Colombia, Uruguay, and Ghana.

Moderate Capital Inflow

Seven countries have achieved substantial growth with only moderate primary exports and dependence on external capital. This strategy is typical of medium-sized and large countries with primary exports less than 15 per cent of GNP and trade affecting the productive structure less than in the smaller export-oriented countries. Since large countries' import needs are less, moderate aid may still finance a substantial proportion of them, thus preventing a balance of payments bottleneck from inhibiting their initial accelerated growth. Most countries in this group previously depended heavily on primary exports but have industrialized sufficiently to achieve an average productive structure for their level of income.

Success in moderate-aid countries has been similar to that in high-aid ones, but less spectacular. Both savings rates and exports have normally risen in the second decade to adequate levels for fairly rapid growth. However, the poorer countries in this category will probably still need external finance for more than a fifth of their imports to sustain 6 per cent growth rates.

Since few countries have the option of high-aid or high-primary-export strategies, most have attempted the development strategy outlined here. Medium and small economies depending on primary exports such as Ceylon, Chile, Colombia, Ghana, and Uruguay have found the subsequent transformation to a more balanced structure particularly difficult. Manufacturing offers limited scope for economical import substitution in small countries, so continued growth requires either a shift to manufactured exports or development of new primary exports. In the past few years, Colombia has been actively promoting nontraditional exports of both types.

Low External Dependence

Relatively few countries have been successful in economic development with low levels of both primary exports and external capital. This strategy requires the early development of manufactured exports to cover minimum import needs, a hard task for very poor countries. This more self-sufficient pattern typically requires relatively more than average capital per unit of output. Rapid growth therefore demands high investment rates.

The most successful countries employing this strategy, Japan and Yugoslavia, have achieved high growth rates through very high domestic savings and investment. Japan has long since ceased to be "underdeveloped" but Yugoslavia provides something like a model of the possibilities—and problems—of such development.

Exports in Group D countries have grown very rapidly except in Brazil. Argentina, Burma, and India also attempted self-sufficient development but with notable lack of success because of inadequate stress (until recently) on exports or agricultural development. Aid donors however share responsibility for India's failure to achieve more rapid growth: they provided considerably less capital per capita than they did to other countries with comparable performances.

These four developmental strategies are distinguished primarily by different priorities in shifting resources and so transforming the economy to meet the needs of sustained growth. In the accumulation of capital and skills, successful development patterns look more alike: virtually everywhere rapid growth and a rising savings rate go together, so that either capital inflow can be reduced or the growth rate further accelerated. The experience of slower-growing countries is very different, suggesting that the greater profitability of investment at higher growth rates significantly affects the supply of savings. Experience to date, therefore, shows increased self-reliance accompanying rapid growth; only for slow-growing countries does dependence on aid tend to be perpetuated.

In deciding where to give aid, an important consideration is the attractiveness of rapidly growing countries to private investors. Rapid export growth is the main support of a country's foreign debt service capacity. Private capital and hard loans therefore have increasingly replaced concessional lending to several countries (the Republic of China, Korea, Thailand) which a decade earlier interested few foreign investors.

OBJECTIVES OF DEVELOPMENT

While economic development can be measured in terms of inputs and outputs, its aim is a transformation of the economy and the society, and the only true measure of success is the degree to which this trans-formation is achieved. Rates of progress toward this goal largely depend on the starting point. It appears to be as difficult for the poorest countries to achieve 5 per cent growth in GNP as for the $300 country to achieve 7 per cent, and the 6 per cent target for all developing countries might be better conceived in these terms. It may indeed turn out that in more primitive societies growth rates in excess of 5–6 per cent produce social stresses (at present little understood) that are not conducive to sustained growth. If so we should seek not a maximum but an optimum rate of development at each stage.

I.C.2. Redefining Objectives: Growth and Distribution*

So long as economists were willing to assume the possibility of unrestricted transfers among income groups, they found no conflict in principle between the objectives of distribution and growth. Once it is recognized that large-scale transfers of income are politically unlikely in developing countries, however, it becomes necessary to evaluate the results of any development policy in terms of the benefits it produces for different socio-economic groups. While this idea has been accepted in the recent literature of project evaluation, it has found little reflection in the methodology of macroeconomic planning and policy formulation.

An index of economic performance reflecting these objectives can be developed as follows. Assume a division of society into N socio-economic groups, defined by their as-sets, income levels, and economic functions. For purposes of policy analysis, it is necessary to distinguish several poverty groups such as small farmers, landless laborers, urban underemployed, and others according to the similarity of their responses to policy measures. In order to illustrate the problem of evaluation, we will classify merely by income size into ordinally ranked percentile groups.

Assuming a division by income level into quintiles, the rate of growth of income of each group, g_i, can be taken to measure the increase of its social welfare over the specified period. The rate of increase in welfare of the society as a whole can therefore be defined as a weighted sum of the growth of income of all groups:

$$G = w_1 g_1 + w_2 g_2 + w_3 g_3 + w_4 g_4 + w_5 g_5 \quad [1]$$

where G is an index of the growth of total social welfare and w_i is the weight assigned to group i.[1]

*From Montek S. Ahluwalia and Hollis B. Chenery, "The Economic Framework," in *Redistribution with Growth,* joint study by World Bank's Development Research Center and Institute of Development Studies, University of Sussex, Oxford University Press, New York, 1974, pp. 38–43, 48–9. Reprinted by permission.

[1] This measure can be applied either to the income or the consumption of each group. When

A summary measure of this type enables us to set development targets and monitor development performance not simply in terms of growth of GNP but in terms of the distributional pattern of income growth. The weights for each income class reflect the social premium on generating growth at each income level; they may be set according to the degree of distributional emphasis desired. As the weight on a particular quintile is raised, our index of the increase in social welfare reflects to a greater extent the growth of income in that group. Thus if we were only concerned with the poorest quintile we would set $w_5 = 1$ and all other $w_i = 0$, so that growth in welfare would be measured only by g_5. This approach is closely related to the more formal approach to welfare choices using explicit social welfare functions to measure improvements in welfare.

In these terms the commonly used index of performance—the growth of GNP—is a special case in which the weights on the growth of income of each quintile are simply the income share of each quintile in total income. The shortcomings of such an index can be seen from the following income shares for the different quintiles, which are typical for underdeveloped countries:

Quintiles	1	2	3	4	5	Total
Share in Total Income	53%	22%	13%	7%	5%	100%

The combined share of the top 40 percent of the population amounts to about three-quarters of the total GNP. Thus the rate of growth of GNP measures essentially the income growth of the upper 40 percent and is not much affected by what happens to the income of the remaining 60 percent of the population.

An alternative welfare principle that has considerable appeal is to give equal social value to a one-percent increase in income for any member of society. On this principle, the weights in equation [1] should be proportional to the number of people in each group and would therefore be equal for each quintile. Thus a one-percent increase in income in the lowest quintile would have the same weight in the overall performance measure as a one-percent increase in income for any other quintile, even though the absolute increment involved is much smaller for the lowest quintile than for the others.

When we use the growth of GNP as an index of performance, we implicitly assume that a dollar of additional income creates the same additional social welfare regardless of the income level of the recipient.[2] Given the typical income shares of the different quintiles, it follows that a one-percent growth in income in the top quintile is given almost eleven times the weight of a one-percent growth in the lowest quintile (in the preceding example) because it requires an absolute increment which is eleven times as great. In contrast to the GNP measure, the equal weights index gives the same weight to a one-percent increase in income in the lowest quintile as it does to a one-percent increase in the highest quintile. In this case a dollar of additional income in the lowest quintile is valued at eleven times a dollar of additional income in the highest quintile.

Many individuals (and some countries) may wish to define social objectives almost exclusively in terms of income growth of the lowest groups, placing little value upon growth in the upper-income groups beyond its contribution to national savings and investment. The welfare implications of such a "poverty weighted" index are stronger than those underlying either the rate of growth of

---

applied to income, the weight assigned should take account of the contribution made by each group to the financing of investment and government expenditure. For long run simulations of policy an index based on consumption only is preferable.

[2] This statement has to be qualified to allow for the higher savings of the upper income recipients and their greater contribution to future growth. In a more complete analysis, the increase in social welfare can be measured by the weighted growth of consumption rather than income.

GNP or the "equal weights" index, since it would be a welfare function based primarily on the lower-income groups.

Weighted indexes of the sort discussed above provide a very different evaluation of performance in many countries than is obtained from conventional measures. This can be illustrated using data for the fourteen developing countries for which we have observations at two points in time. The numerical results presented here are subject to the limitations of the data and are essentially "illustrative" to show the potential usefulness of weighted growth indexes in evaluating performance. They are not presented as definitive assessments of country experience.

Table 1 shows the difference in estimates of welfare increments based on three different weighting systems: shares of each quintile in GNP (giving the rate of growth of GNP); equal weights for each quintile; and "poverty weights" of 0.6 for the lowest 40 percent, 0.3 for the next 40 percent, and 0.1 for the top 20 percent.[3] The following differences can be observed among the countries when comparing GNP growth with the other two indexes.

(i) In four countries (Panama, Brazil, Mexico, and Venezuela), performance is worse when measured by weighted indexes. In these countries the data show that relative income distribution worsened over the period considered, i.e., growth was disproportionately concentrated in the upper-income groups. The indexes giving greater weight to the growth of income in lower-income groups are therefore lower than the rate of growth of GNP.

(ii) In four countries (Colombia, El Salvador, Sri Lanka, and Taiwan), the weighted indexes are higher than GNP growth. In these countries the data show that distribution improved over the period, i. e., the growth of incomes in lower-income groups

[3] In terms of weights for unit increments, these weights imply that a dollar of income accruing to the bottom 40 percent is worth 33 times a dollar accruing to the top 20 percent, instead of 11 times as with equal weights.

was faster than that in higher-income groups.

(iii) In five countries (Korea, the Philippines, Yugoslavia, Peru, and India) the use of weighted indexes does not alter the GNP measurement of growth to any great extent. In these cases the data show that distribution remained largely unchanged and all income classes grew at about the same rate. In general the extent to which a weighted index of growth diverges from the growth rate of GNP and the direction of divergence are measures of the extent and direction in which growth is distributionally biased.

It is important to note that the proposed index is a measure of the *increase* in welfare rather than of total welfare. Increasing equality is indicated by a weighted growth rate in excess of GNP growth and increasing inequality by the opposite difference. The measure cannot be used to compare performance among countries without allowing for their initial distribution of income. For example, Table 1 shows inequality increasing in both Brazil and India, but in India the starting point was a relatively equal distribution in 1954 while in Brazil distribution was already quite unequal in 1960.

We recognize that the use of such indexes for evaluation of performance will be severely limited by the initial lack of accurate data. For the present they are perhaps more valuable as analytical devices to be used in redefining the objectives of development strategy. They help to clarify both the statement of distributional objectives and the limits of acceptable trade-offs between growth and income distribution. In particular, the use of welfare indexes emphasizes the importance of increasing the rates of growth of income in the poverty groups instead of focusing on the static picture of income inequality.

TOWARD A THEORY OF DISTRIBUTION AND GROWTH

The preceding section suggests that the objective of distributive justice is more usefully conceived of as accelerating the development of the poorer groups in society

TABLE 1. Income Distribution and Growth

| Country | Period | I. Income Growth | | | II. Annual Increase in Welfare | | | III. Initial Gini Coefficient |
		Upper 20%	Middle 40%	Lowest 40%	(A) GNP Weights	(B) Equal Weights	(C) Poverty Weights	
Korea	1964–70	10.6	7.8	9.3	9.3	9.0	9.0	.34
Panama	1960–69	8.8	9.2	3.2	8.2	6.7	5.6	.48
Brazil	1960–70	8.4	4.8	5.2	6.9	5.7	5.4	.56
Mexico	1963–69	8.0	7.0	6.6	7.6	7.0	6.9	.56
Taiwan	1953–61	4.5	9.1	12.1	6.8	9.4	10.4	.55
Venezuela	1962–70	7.9	4.1	3.7	6.4	4.7	4.2	.52
Colombia	1964–70	5.6	7.3	7.0	6.2	6.8	7.0	.57
El Salvador	1961–69	4.1	10.5	5.3	6.2	7.1	6.7	.53
Philippines	1961–71	4.9	6.4	5.0	5.4	5.5	5.4	.50
Peru	1961–71	4.7	7.5	3.2	5.4	5.2	4.6	.59
Sri Lanka	1963–70	3.1	6.2	8.3	5.0	6.4	7.2	.45
Yugoslavia	1963–68	4.9	5.0	4.3	4.8	4.7	4.6	.33
India	1954–64	5.1	3.9	3.9	4.5	4.1	4.0	.40

Note: The rates of growth of income in each income group were calculated as follows: income shares were applied to GNP (constant prices) to obtain the income of each group in each year. The growth rate is the annual compound growth rate estimated from the two endpoint income estimates for each income group. Sources of income share data for each country are identified in Chapter I. GNP series are from the World Bank data files. Equal weights imply a weight of 0.2, 0.4, and 0.4 for the three income groups while poverty weights are calculated by giving weights of 0.1, 0.3, and 0.6 respectively.

rather than in terms of relative shares of income. As a way of implementing this approach, we can visualize the role of the state as using available policy instruments (including the allocation of investment in physical and human capital) so as to maximize a welfare function of the type just described. State intervention of this sort requires both an analysis of the determinants of income in poverty groups and of the linkages between the incomes of different groups. The fact of income linkages is crucial for any analysis of distributional problems since they impose important constraints on policy. Thus tax-financed transfers from the rich to the poor may raise the income of the poor but, if they reduce savings and capital accumulation by the rich, they may in time lead to lower income in the poorer groups. An analysis of these interactions requires an integration of growth and distribution theory.

Distribution of Income and Capital

Existing theories of income distribution are of only limited value in establishing an analytical framework for comprehensive governmental action because they are somewhat narrowly focused on the functional distribution of income between labor and capital. Most theories conceive the central problem of income distribution as the determination of the levels of employment and remuneration of the factors of production, usually grouped into capital and labor. They differ mainly in their assumptions about market behavior and the way in which wages and product prices are determined. Neoclassical theory assumes competitive equilibrium in all markets and thus derives factor returns from pure production relationships and demand patterns, given factor supply conditions. At the other extreme, the classical and Marxist wage theory that forms the basis for most dual economy models assumes relatively fixed real wages with all surplus value appropriated by the owners of capital.

The inadequacy of existing theories for our purposes arises less from the lack of consensus as to the determinants of the functional division of income than from the omission of other aspects of the problem. The available evidence on the nature of poverty in underdeveloped countries shows that half of the poor are self-employed and do not enter the wage economy. Most wage-earners are already in the middle-income groups, so that policies affecting the split between wages and profits mainly concern the upper end of the distribution.

The principal element that is missing from existing theories is an explicit treatment of the distribution of the various forms of assets.[4] A more general statement would recognize that the income of any household is derived from a variety of assets: land, privately owned capital, access to public capital goods, and human capital embodying varying degrees of skills.

We distinguish four basic approaches to the problem of raising the welfare of the low-income groups: (i) *Maximizing GNP growth* through raising savings and allocating resources more efficiently, with benefits to all groups in society. (ii) *Redirecting investment* to poverty groups in the form of education, access to credit, public facilities, and so on. (iii) *Redistributing income* (or consumption) to poverty groups through the fiscal system or through direct allocation of consumer goods. (iv) *A transfer of existing assets* to poverty groups, as in land reform. In most countries some elements of each of these approaches will be applicable, depending on the initial economic and social structure.

[4] Recognition of the importance of asset distribution is common to neoclassical theorists as well as to Marxists, but it has not been incorporated in empirical models.

The advantages and limitations of each strategy will vary with the circumstances of each country, and an assessment of these considerations is necessarily a matter of detailed study. Nevertheless, it is useful to consider some broad characteristics of each strategy in a relatively pure form. The general conclusions from the analysis in this volume can be summarized as follows:

(i) Maximizing the growth of GNP involves some measures that benefit all groups, as well as others—such as favoring high-savings groups through lower income taxes or wage-restraint policies—in which there is a conflict with distributional objectives. Because of the relatively weak income linkages between the poverty groups and the rest of the economy, their growth tends to lag until the expansion of employment creates a shortage of unskilled labor and hence an upward pressure on wage rates. Although—as suggested by Table 1—the poor may be better off even in this case than with slower GNP growth, the welfare effects of a maximal growth strategy can almost always be improved by adding transfers.

(ii) As compared to maximal growth of GNP, increased investment in the physical and human assets of the poverty groups is likely to require some sacrifice of output in the short run because returns on investment in human capital take longer to develop. Even so, the welfare index will be higher because these investments lead to income growth in target groups which have higher welfare weights. While this strategy has a short-run cost to the upper-income groups, in the longer run they may even benefit from the "trickle up" effects of greater productivity and purchasing power of the poor.

(iii) General transfers of income in support of consumption can also raise the weighted welfare index in the short run, but they have too high a cost in terms of foregone investment to be viable on a large scale over an extended period. Nevertheless, some direct consumption supplements for specific target groups (child nutrition, maternal health services) are a necessary supplement to an investment-oriented strategy, since they are the only way to alleviate some types of absolute poverty.

(iv) Political resistance to policies of asset redistribution makes this approach unlikely to succeed on any large scale in most countries. However, in areas such as land ownership and security of tenure, some degree of asset redistribution is an essential part of any program to make the rural poor more productive. Beyond this essential minimum, a vigorous policy of investment reallocation in a rapidly growing economy may well be a more effective way of increasing the productive capacity of the poor than redistribution from the existing stock of assets, which is likely to have a high cost in social and political disruption.

(v) In the longer term, population policy can have an important influence on both the distribution of incomes and the level of consumption in the poverty groups. Our simulations show a tendency of income distribution to worsen with population growth above 2.5 percent per year, while with more optimistic assumptions it tends to improve. There is considerable demographic evidence that investments in the health, education, and economic growth of the poverty groups may also contribute to a reduction of fertility and hence indirectly to better income distribution.

Particular emphasis is given in this volume to directing public investment to raise the productive capacity and incomes of the poor. There is a strong analogy between this strategy and an international strategy of assisting investment in poor countries. In both cases transfers of resources which increase productive capacity and lead to greater self-support in the future are both more efficient and more attractive to donors than continuing subsidies for consumption. In both cases it should be possible to get greater political support for the more developmental approach.

I.C.3. Strategic Policy Issues—Note

From the preceding discussion of trends in international development and the disappointing record of the 1950s and 1960s, we are now left with three overriding questions: (1) What have been the constraints on the *attainable* rates of development in the LDCs? (2) Why have the *actual* rates of development been below the attainable rates in most of these countries? and (3) What policies in a strategy of development can now eradicate absolute poverty, reduce inequality, and provide more employment opportunities? These questions will dominate much of the analysis throughout this book.

Many of the readings in subsequent chapters will consider whether the development process is now encountering increasingly severe—or even intractable—difficulties. It will become apparent that there is a divergence of view on whether the limitations to development are to be located mainly within the economies of the LDCs or whether external obstacles to development are the villains of the piece. There are also differing conclusions as to whether the obstacles are best removed by promotion of the market mechanism or comprehensive central planning.

Behind the disappointing statistical record lie four major constraints that have limited the attainable rate of development in most of the less developed world. One major constraint stems from the low level of savings. The inability to mobilize sufficient domestic resources, or to supplement domestic resources with external resources, has continued to inhibit development. An increase in the ratio of savings to national income is still imperative in most, if not all, of the LDCs. If it had not been for foreign assistance, the ratio of net savings to domestic product would actually have fallen in many countries during the 1960s. Indeed, in some countries, no increase in per capita income would have been realized if there had not been a capital inflow. It is, however, disturbing that the rate of increase of gross capital formation has slowed down in many countries, and it is indeed questionable in many LDCs whether the domestic savings rate and capital inflow are now sufficiently high to sustain a satisfactory rate of development. Problems associated with the savings constraint will be examined in Chapters V and VI.

Another bottleneck relates to the agricultural sector. Agricultural production constitutes a large share of the gross domestic product of developing countries, and agricultural commodities account for a considerable part of the value of their total exports. For the majority of developing countries, a major restraint on their development rate during the 1960s was the slow growth of their agricultural output in general and of food crops in particular. Agricultural output has generally increased only a little faster than population in the LDCs. For all LDCs, the average annual rate of growth in agricultural production has declined from 3.5 per cent in 1950–55 to 3.2 per cent in 1955–60 and to 2.8 per cent in 1961–71.[1] There is bound to be a close association between the agricultural performance and the overall growth rate of developing countries: in the "high-growth" developing countries (as measured by rate of growth in GNP) the average rates of increase in agricultural production and food production were 4.5 per cent and 4.4 per cent, respectively, during the period 1960–66; in "medium-growth" countries, the rates were 2.6 and 3.2 per cent, respectively; in the "low-growth" countries, 0.9

and 0.8 per cent, respectively.[2] In Latin America, food production per head was practically at a standstill during the 1960s. In many LDCs, the demand for food has grown faster than food production, and an increasing number of LDCs have become net importers of food. Many developing countries spend a quarter to one-third of their foreign exchange on food imports. This weak performance of the agricultural sector has been pervasive, and the agricultural bottleneck remains one of the most difficult of developmental problems. In Chapter IX, we shall stress the importance of agricultural development as a necessary basis for industrial development, and we shall examine the interactions between industry and agriculture.

As distressing as is the lag in the agricultural sector, and not unrelated to it, is the lag in the export sector. The foreign exchange constraint—or deterioration in the capacity to import—is an acute limitation on the size of development plans. During the 1960s, the value of exports from developed countries rose considerably more rapidly than from LDCs. The ratio of value of exports from LDCs to total world exports declined from approximately 25 per cent in 1955 to 20 per cent in 1965 and to only 17 per cent in 1972. At the same time, development programs have stimulated the demand for imports. It is also contended that for structural reasons the demand for imports rises more rapidly than national product and also exceeds the rate of increase in exports. The import demand by LDCs has thus risen more than their capacity to import based on export earnings. Compounding the difficulties, the net inflow of foreign capital has slowed down, debt servicing of amortization and interest on public debt has risen markedly, and income payments of dividends and profits on private direct foreign investment

[1] FAO, *The State of Food and Agriculture 1973*, Rome, 1974, p. 22.

[2] Report of UNCTAD secretariat, *Review of Recent Trends in Trade and Development 1968*, TD/B/184, September 13, 1968, pp. 36–7.

have grown, so that the import surplus that can be supported by external financial resources has also diminished.[3] The official holdings of foreign exchange reserves have also been limited, and only a few LDCs have improved their international liquidity position; for most of the LDCs, official reserves are scarcely sufficient to cover more than a few months' import needs in the event of a decline in foreign exchange availabilities from export receipts or external financial sources. Except for some oil-exporting countries and a very few other exceptional developing countries, the foreign exchange constraint has persisted as a severe limitation on a country's development program by making it impossible to fulfill import requirements. The problems of mobilizing external resources are discussed in Chapter VI; the related notion of a "widening trade gap"—and its policy implications with respect to import substitution and export promotion—are considered in Chapter XI.

4, Finally, another major constraint is connected with the need for human-resource development. The policy problems relating to the need for social development are now among the most critical of all development problems. It has become increasingly apparent that an improvement in the quality of human life cannot be simply awaited as an ultimate objective of development but must instead be viewed as a necessary instrument of development. There is a need not only to increase the quantity of productive factors, but even more so to improve the quality of human beings as economic agents. If development is growth *plus* change, and change is social and cultural as well as economic, then the qualitative dimensions of development become extremely significant in terms of human-resource development. Without such change, the process of development will not become self-sustaining.

[3] See data in Chapter VI; also Report by the Secretary-General of UNCTAD, *New Directions in International Trade and Development Policies,* TD/B/530 (February 1975), Chap. 1.

This qualitative change requires increasing emphasis on investment in human capital and on measures to modify social and cultural values. Recognizing that the problem of controlling population growth has now reached serious dimensions throughout most of the underdeveloped world, many would also argue that population control policies are essential for a rise in the standard of living in many poor countries. Unless this is done, it will be all the more difficult to improve the quality of the population and the potential for development will not be realized. As with social development, however, the attainment of control over population growth is ultimately dependent upon noneconomic factors in the development process. If the Development Decades of the future are to offer a truly significant advance in well-being, the ultimate question to be answered is not how much economic change the poor country can absorb—but rather how much social change its people can absorb and how quickly.

Although we do not minimize the significance of noneconomic factors in the process of modernization, we shall emphasize in this book the strategic economic policy issues connected with a relaxation of the savings, agricultural, foreign exchange, and human-resource constraints.

These constraints—multiple in number and both internal and external to the developing country's economy—aggravate the problem of development. The problem is all the more complicated by the question of trade-offs between growth, employment, and equity. Is there a conflict between increasing output and increasing employment? Given that capital is a scarce resource, is the type of production that economizes on the use of capital per unit of output consistent with maximizing employment? Or does output have to be sacrificed in providing more employment? The conflict lies not so much between current output and current employment, but between current employment and the growth rate of employment and output in the future. We shall return to this issue in Chapter IV, where the possible trade-off between output and employment is examined more fully in selection IV.E.1.

Another troublesome trade-off is between output and equity. Does social justice have to be sacrificed for greater output? Or is it possible to achieve what might be termed "efficient equality"—that is, an increase in equality together with an increase in output? Does this also hold in intertemporal terms— that is, is it possible to have both greater equality and greater output in the present period and in future periods as well? Or is it more probable that a country can have greater equality and greater output in the future only if it endures greater inequality in the present?

These issues will be examined in the following chapters.

I. SELECT BIBLIOGRAPHY

The Bibliography following each chapter offers supplementary readings on special topics. The following abbreviations are used:

AER: American Economic Review
EDCC: Economic Development and Cultural Change
EJ: Economic Journal
IBRD: International Bank for Reconstruction and Development
IDR: International Development Review
ILO: International Labour Organization
ILR: International Labour Review
JDE: Journal of Development Economics
JDS: Journal of Development Studies
JEL: Journal of Economic Literature
JPE: Journal of Political Economy
OECD: Organization for Economic Cooperation and Development
OEP: Oxford Economic Papers
QJE: Quarterly Journal of Economics
RES: Review of Economics and Statistics
UNCTAD: United Nations Conference on Trade and Development
UNIDO: United Nations Industrial Development Organization
WD: World Development

1. Various interpretations of the meaning of "economic development" can be noted in the following: Dudley Seers, "What Are We Trying to Measure," *JDS*, April 1972; ____, "The Meaning of Development," *IDR*, December 1969; H. Myint, *Economic Theory and the Underdeveloped Countries*, New York, 1971, Chaps. 1–3; Nancy Baster (ed.), *Measuring Development*, London, 1972; Paul Streeten, "Alternatives in Development," *WD*, February 1974; Gunnar Myrdal, *Asian Drama*, New York, 1968, Chaps. 2–3, Appendix 1; Jacob Viner, *International Trade and Economic Development*, Oxford, 1953, Chap. 6; S. H. Frankel, *The Economic Impact on Underdeveloped Societies*, Oxford, 1953, Chap. 3; H. Leibenstein, *Economic Backwardness and Economic Growth*, New York, 1957, Chap. 2.

The relation between development and welfare is considered in W. A. Lewis, *The Theory of Economic Growth*, London, 1955, Appendix; ____, "Economic Problems of Development," in *Restless Nations: A Study of World Tensions and Development*, New York, 1962; S. K. Nath, *A Reappraisal of Welfare Economics*, London, 1969, Chap. 9; R. G. Ridker, "Discontent and Economic Growth," *EDCC*, October 1962; M. Abramovitz, "The Welfare Interpretation of Secular Trends in National Income and Product," in Abramovitz et al., *The Allocation of Economic Resources*, Stanford, 1959; James A. Mirrlees, "The Evaluation of National Income in an Imperfect Economy," *Pakistan Development Review*, Spring 1969.

2. A few outstanding quantitative analyses of the economic structure of LDCs are: H. B. Chenery and M. Syrquin, *Patterns of Development, 1950–1970*, London, 1975; S. J. Patel, "The Economic Distance Between Nations," *EJ*, March 1964; Dudley Seers, "A Model of Comparative Rates of Growth in the World Economy," *EJ*, March 1962; Wassily Leontiéf, "Structure of the World Economy," *AER*, December 1974; Simon Kuznets, *Six Lectures on Economic Growth*, Glencoe, 1959; ____, *Modern Economic Growth: Rate, Structure, and Spread*, New Haven, 1966; E. E. Hagen, "Some Facts About Income Levels and Economic Growth," *RES*, February 1960; Dan Usher, *The Price Mechanism and the Meaning of National Income Statistics*, Oxford, 1968; H. B. Chenery, "Patterns of Industrial Growth," *AER*, September 1960; H. B. Chenery and L. Taylor, "Development Patterns: Among Countries and Over Time," *RES*, November 1968.

3. The statistical record of the first two Development Decades can be documented from a large number of United Nations publications, particularly the Economic Surveys of the several regional commissions; annual U. N. yearbooks on national accounts, demography, trade; and the UNCTAD documents. Also useful is the OECD Development Center, *National Accounts and Development Planning in Low-Income Countries*, Paris, 1974. The statistical record should be interpreted in light of Simon Kuznets, "Problems in Comparing Recent Growth Rates for Developed and Less Developed Countries," *EDCC*, January 1972; Irving B. Kravis et al., *A System of International Comparisons of Gross Product and Purchasing Power*, Baltimore, 1975.

4. An excellent survey of the problems of income distribution is presented by W. R. Cline, "Income Distribution and Development," *JDE*, February 1975; this article reviews general distributional theories, recent theoretical and empirical work on relationships between development and income distribution, and policy instruments for redistribution.

Foremost analytical discussions are: A. K. Sen, *On Economic Inequality*, Oxford, 1973; A. B. Atkinson, "On the Measurement of Inequality," *Journal of Economic Theory*, September 1970; a critique by P. T. Bauer and A. R. Prest, "Income Differences and Inequalities," *Moorgate and Wall Street*, Autumn, 1973.

Empirical studies include: Felix Paukert, "Income Distribution at Different Levels of Development," *ILR*, August-September 1973; I. Adelman and C. T. Morris, "An Anatomy of Income Distribution in Developing Nations," *Development Digest*, October 1971; I. Kravis, "A World of Unequal Income," *Annals*, September 1973; J. Pen, *Income Distribution*, New York, 1971, Chaps. 4–5; D. J. Turnham, "Income Distribution: Measurement and Problems," in Society for International Development, *International Development 1971: Development Targets for the 70's: Jobs and Justice*, Baltimore, 1972; Shail Jain and A. E. Tiemann, "Size Distribution of Income: Compilation of Data," IBRD, Discussion Paper No. 4 (mimeo), August 1973; S. Kuznets, "Economic Growth and Income Inequality, *AER*, March 1955; W. R. Cline, *Potential Effects of Income Redistribution on Economic Growth*, New York, 1972; Albert Fishlow, "Brazilian Size Distribution of Income," *AER*, May 1972; Harry Oshima, "Income Inequality and Economic Growth: The Postwar Experience of Asian Countries," *Malayan Economic Review*, October 1970; Richard Webb, *Government Policy and the Distribution of Income in Peru, 1963–1973*, Princeton, 1974; K. Griffin, "An Assessment of Development in Taiwan," *WD*, June 1973; R. M. Sundrum, "The Distribution of Income in the ECAFE Region," *Economic Bulletin for Asia and the Far East*, December 1972; R. Weisskopf, "Income Distribution and Economic Growth in Puerto Rico, Argentina, and

Mexico," *Review of Income and Wealth,* December 1970; V. M. Dandekar and N. Rath, "Poverty in India," *Economic and Political Weekly,* January 2, 1971; Mahbub ul Haq, "Employment and Income Distribution in the 1970s," *Development Digest,* October 1971; A. O. Hirschman and M. Rothschild, "Changing Tolerance for Inequality in Development," *QJE,* November 1973.

CHAPTER II

Economics *for* Development

All the theories of development, whether classical, Marxian, Schumpeterian, or Neo-Keynesian, are ways of talking systematically about the development process—but in abstract terms and from the outside. They relate to the economics *about* development. This approach, however, is far different from the economics *for* development—the economics that the development practitioner must use in formulating and administering an actual development program in a specific environment. In the administration of a development program, the development practitioner cannot rely simply on the analyst's view of development "from the outside." He must be concerned with applying economic principles to specific problems embedded within the general development process. This he cannot do by merely being knowledgeable about the latest development model. And yet, it is unfortunate that a development theory has only too often been misread as if it provided a recipe for successful development, and access to the teachings of modern economics has been thought to bestow some new magical quality.

Since the disillusioning experience of postwar development efforts, however, a reaction has been setting in against such a naïve approach. In the LDCs, modern economics is losing its mystique and policymakers are seeking more relevant analyses. If we emphasize the constraints on development, we must ask just what is the relevance of economic theory and history in understanding how these constraints might be relaxed.

It might be thought that we must depart radically from "Western economics" and introduce a completely different system of economic thought in order to reach a fuller understanding of development problems. After all, economic analysis has matured in the more advanced industrial nations, and the problems that have preoccupied economists' attention in these countries might be considered to have little pertinence for less

51

developed economies. In this vein, one could argue for new approaches in economic theory to fit the problems and interests of poor countries. The selections in II.A pursue this question.

If we are to appreciate fully the variety, complexity, and pervasiveness of development problems, we must be aware of their historical dimension. Historical perspective is one of the best safeguards against taking a superficial view of these problems. Section B therefore considers the relevance of historical experience in contributing to our understanding of the sources of development. It does so, in part, by focusing upon Professor Rostow's provocative application of a stage approach to the course of development. As a grand historical thesis, Rostow's analysis of stages of growth has continued to command attention. Its appeal has been especially strong in the less developed countries. But it has received substantial criticism, and some of these critiques deserve equal attention for their concern with those historical factors neglected by Rostow.

Basic to Rostow's original analysis in his *Stages of Economic Growth* was his sketch of a dynamic theory of production which emphasizes the composition of investment and the growth of particular sectors in the economy. This theory of production allowed Rostow to identify certain "leading sectors," the growth of which is thought to be instrumental in propelling the economy forward. Rostow also indicated that a sequence of optimum patterns of investment can be postulated from a set of optimum sectoral paths determined by the level of income and population, by technology, by the quality of entrepreneurship, and by the empirical fact that deceleration is the normal optimum path of each sector. The actual course of investment, however, generally differs from these optima inasmuch as they are influenced not only by private choices, but also by the policies of governments and the impact of wars. Nonetheless, Rostow believes that, at any period of time, leading sectors can be identified, and the changing sequence of leading sectors plays an important role in Rostow's stages of growth. The sequence of stages suggests, in turn, that a succession of strategic choices is open to societies, and that political and social decisions about the allocation of resources are made in terms beyond the usual market processes. Of Rostow's five stages of growth, the most relevant for presently poor countries are the first three—the "traditional society," the emergence of the "preconditions for take-off," and the "take-off."

Other selections in section II.B criticize Rostow's stage theory and suggest different viewpoints for attempting to draw some conclusions regarding the correspondence and variation between past and present efforts at development. The Note on "Future Development in Historical Perspective" (II.B.4) places special emphasis upon some of the differences between past and present cases of development—differences which give rise to problems that will receive extensive consideration in subsequent chapters.

In the last section, we consider styles of development that are alternatives to neoclassical theory and Western historical examples. Among alternative ideologies, the Marxist and "dependencia" schools are most prominent. Among countries, particular attention should be given to the unusual development strategies of China, Cuba, and Tanzania. By illustrating the policy options for rural development, the last selection considers different styles in development—the technocratic, reformist, and radical.

II.A. RELEVANCE OF THEORY

II.A.1. The Limitations of the

Special Case*

This paper is the reaction of an economist who, after several years of work overseas on problems of economic development, has had an opportunity to reflect on the usefulness of his subject. If the tone is rather sharp in places, I must ask the reader to understand that close personal contact with the problems of backward countries instils, for many reasons, a sense of urgency and some impatience. Economics seems very slow in adapting itself to the requirements of the main task of the day—the elimination of acute poverty in Africa, Asia and Latin America—just as the previous generation of economists failed to cope realistically with economic fluctuations until after the depression had brought politically catastrophic results. . . .

If there was ever a time when one could see a major revolution in doctrine looming ahead, it is today. And the reasons are, as always, because the existing body of theory cannot explain what has to be explained, nor can it give the help that is politically essential. What has to be explained is why economies grow at different rates, and the help that governments need most desperately is advice on how to stimulate development.

It is clear where the force which will disrupt the subject is emerging. In the past five years, impatience with poverty has grown, but development has either slowed down in the poorer economies or been accompanied by increasingly severe tensions

*From Dudley Seers, "The Limitations of the Special Case," *Bulletin of the Oxford Institute of Economics and Statistics*, Vol. 25, No. 2, May 1963, pp. 77–9, 81–5, 96–8. Reprinted by permission.

(e.g., payments deficits and inflation). In some of these, for example Argentina and Chile, the political position is now critical, and yet conventional economics does not have a great deal to offer by way of useful advice. Development is still considered as merely one branch, more an appendage than an essential element, of the syllabus. One hears the term "development economists" as if they were a race apart.

The political dangers are now so obvious that this state of affairs cannot continue. There are many pressing questions on which professional help has so far been very meagre. When is it justifiable to use labour-intensive but out-of-date techniques? How can one decide what to spend on education as opposed to capital investment? And on secondary education as against primary? Can capital-output ratios be used as a guide to savings needs, and if so which, and with what qualifications? To what extent, and when, does economic size limit growth? How does export diversification help to stimulate development? What sort of central bank should an exporter of primary products have? And so on and so on.

Attempts to deal with problems such as these will end, if the history of economic thought is any guide, by changing the attitude to development in industrial economies, and therefore the whole body of economic theory.

One obstacle to the reconstruction of economics is that we have not really grasped, still less accepted, the point that the subject we have inherited was built in and for countries with which the profession was familiar, namely developed industrial economies. To paraphrase a dictum of E. H. Carr: Before you study economics, study the economist; before you study the economist, study his historical and social environment.

The whole business is made much more difficult by the widespread practice that authors and lecturers have, of not merely concentrating on the economics of some developed industrial country, but presenting it as universally valid. Textbooks or lecture courses with quite general titles, such as "Economic Principles," "Banking" or "Public Finance," turn out to be really treatises about economic principles, banking or public finance in the United States, the United Kingdom or a typical developed economy.

In this respect economists are somewhat less than rigorous. A book is not called "Principles of Astronomy" if it refers only to the earth or the solar system or even the local galaxy. We justifiably expect a lecture course on geology to deal with other continents besides the one on which the author happens to live, unless the title is duly qualified. Even sociologists generally avoid this error.

The common failure to specify the frame of reference, which is so liable to mislead students and to hinder the subject's development, is at first sight puzzling, because the developed industrial economy is by no means typical. Viewed from the point of view of either history or geography, it is an extremely rare case, and obviously so. There have been only a few such economies for a few decades; even now they cover only quite a small fraction of mankind. It may be argued that economics is international in its scope, and provides an adequate basis for work anywhere. In fact, this *is* argued, and *must* be argued, since every aging doctrine must defend itself as best it can. (*A priori,* one can predict the moves of the defence just as in a taut chess game.) But here we can apply an empirical test. Are economists in fact successful when working in nonindustrial countries? I would put in evidence (though you may have to take my word for it) a point on which there is widespread agreement, that economists are [of] very

little use working on the problems of underdeveloped countries, until they have done so for some years, and then only if they are unusually adaptable. Engineers are probably more useful than economists on economic problems in these parts of the world, at least until the latter have had two or three years' experience. There is so much for economics graduates to unlearn—and unfortunately the abler the student has been in absorbing the current doctrine, the more difficult the process of adaptation.

In any case it is inherently implausible that a "general theory," or even propositions of any generality, can be derived from the experience of a few countries with highly unusual, not to say peculiar, characteristics. Teaching which concentrates on this type of economy is somewhat distorted, and the distortion is dangerous if those teaching fail to stress continually that they are dealing with what is a highly special case.

The typical case is a largely unindustrialized economy, the foreign trade of which consists essentially in selling primary products for manufactures. There are about 100 identifiable economies of this sort, covering the great majority of the world's population. This is also fortunately the most interesting and important type of economy, for it is here that economic problems are really acute and the economist's help is most needed. . . .

CHARACTERISTIC FEATURES OF THE SPECIAL CASE

What are the features of the private-enterprise industrial economy that make it of limited professional relevance for work in other economies? I can only indicate these here in note form.

I. *Factors of Production*
a. *Labour.* Literate and mobile, mostly in employment; highly organized; racial, religious and linguistic differences not sufficiently important to break up the labour supply; substantial quantities of skilled and professional workers.

b. *Land.* Most available land cultivated, and by private owners (or farmers with secure leaseholds) in plots of economic size.

c. *Capital.* All sectors heavily capitalised, with spare capacity; integrated and comprehensive systems of transport and power.

d. *Enterprise.* A wide field from which enterpreneurs can be drawn, and a favourable climate for enterprise; firm legal basis for corporations.

II. *Sectors of the Economy*

a. *Agriculture.* Wholly commercial, and flexible in response to price changes or technical advances; foreign ownership rare; extensive marketing network for foods.

b. *Mining.* Of limited size and in the hands of local firms.

c. *Manufacturing.* Diversified, with a large metal-using industry producing (*inter alia*) machinery and vehicles; some areas of competition.

d. *Overall.* Manufacturing much larger than either agriculture or mining; natural resources adequately surveyed.

III. *Public Finance*

a. *Revenue.* Strong reliance on direct taxes relative to import or export duties; tax laws enforceable.

b. *Expenditure.* Includes big outlays on social security and agricultural subsidies, relatively little on public works.

IV. *Foreign Trade*

a. *Exports.* Consist of several products for which there is a large internal market, and for which price and income elasticities are fairly high; export prices determined by local costs and stable; exports sold to many countries.

b. *Imports.* Consist largely of primary products (some of which are also produced domestically) which come from many countries, and for which the income elasticity of demand is not high.

c. *Capital.* Long-term capital flows and profit remittances of secondary importance.

V. *Households*

a. *Income.* Distribution moderately equal (post-tax); very few living at subsistence level.

b. *Expenditure.* Food not overwhelmingly important; standardisation and mass production possible, because of equal distribution of income, national promotion and homogeneity of tastes; prestige of local manufactures high.

VI. *Savings and Investment*

a. *Savings.* Mobilized by a capital market, comprising a stock exchange, a bond market and an extensive nationally owned banking system, with a central bank and a managed currency; personal savings significant.

b. *Investment.* High (probably over 20 per cent of G.D.P.); but import content very low.

VII. *Dynamic Influences*

a. *Trade.* No chronic tendency to deficit because of income elasticities (see above).

b. *Population.* Growth of population slow (less than 2 per cent a year), and urbanisation relatively moderate.

c. *Aspirations.* Envy of foreign living standards not high or spreading as a cause of discontent.

In brief, what is assumed is an autonomous and flexible socio-economic structure, in which each human being responds individually to the material incentives offered, and which is subject to no formidable exogenous strains.

The extent to which various economic principles rely on the assumptions set out above is a matter of opinion. There are propositions of a very elementary sort which have some general validity (e.g., those showing the implication for prices if demand and supply curves have certain shapes and shift in one direction or another). But macro-economics is another matter. The burden is surely on those who claim that this is not highly specific to show how any macro-economic model fits various non-industrial economies, each with its own institutions and productive structure.[1]

It cannot even be taken for granted that the aggregative categories with which we now work (such as "labour," "full employment," "savings," etc.) are going to prove useful in non-industrial economies.

The major inadequacies of conventional economics for those dealing with the typical case are that analysis focuses on the wrong factors, and the models do not fit at all closely the way in which non-industrial economies operate.

One respect in which analytical emphasis is rather inappropriate is that although time can often be ignored when deriving propositions for developed economies, it certainly cannot in economies which are underdeveloped. In Asia, say, the need for social and economic development would be urgent even if there were neither population pressure nor rising aspirations. Consequently, purely static propositions are mostly irrelevant, if not actually misleading. Moreover, the fashionably uncommitted attitude to growth, intellectually cloaked in positivism, while perhaps justified by local circumstances in developed economics, has little place when one is dealing with economic problems in a more general sense.

The second error in emphasis is that insufficient attention is paid to the social structure, feudal land systems, conventional work practices, the existence of foreign firms, disparities between regions, racial barriers, etc. It is arguable how much such factors hamper progress in industrial countries, but there is little doubt that they are more serious overseas as obstacles to growth. Conventional economics contains little discussion of the economic implications of policy tools such as land reform, nationalization, or capital levies, still less raising the educational

level of the adult labour force. In brief, institutions are taken as given, whereas the question is precisely what institutions to change and how.

Thirdly, improvements in nutrition, housing, and health services are treated, if at all, as increases in consumption, rather than as influences on output. (This is still also partly true of education.) Here again, this is understandable in societies where economic progress is not conditional on raising the quality of labour.

It may be argued that false emphasis merely renders much of modern economics irrelevant. However, habituation, hour after hour, year after year, to static models, assuming given institutions and neglecting the determinants of human capacity, makes a student gradually unfitted to understand, let alone solve, the problems of non-industrial societies.

Similarly, years of study and work with models devised to explain industrial economies make it hard for economists to grasp the operation of a very different type of economy. One main difference is that (except for a few large economies such as India), activity and employment in the non-industrial economy depend very much, in both the short- and the long-term, on the export sector. Moreover, the nature of the response to changes in exports depends on the organization of this sector, especially whether taxes, profits of foreign companies, or peasant incomes absorb the highest share of increments in income. It also depends on the type of product (particularly whether there is any significant domestic market). The role of the export sector is rarely stressed in conventional economies, and this for a very good reason—in an industrial economy hardly any major sector sells the greater part of its output overseas.

This leads to another point. Non-industrial economies cannot be understood unless studied in the context of the world economy. The sales of their particular primary products, and thus their development, are determined by (i) the rate of growth of the

[1] An E.C.L.A. study, *Inflation and Growth in Latin America,* assembles available Latin American material to show the extent to which these various assumptions are valid in the 20 republics of that region.

industrial economies that buy from them, (ii) the income-elasticities of demand for the commodities they export (which reflect, *inter alia,* the substitution of artificial materials for natural ones), (iii) protective measures that limit imports into industrial economies, (iv) influences on the distribution of the remaining markets between various suppliers (company policy, preferential tariff arrangements, etc.). One could argue that industrial economies would also be easier to understand, if the same approach were adopted. But they do not absolutely require this treatment—it may be reasonable to treat them, which is often done implicitly or explicitly, as if they were closed economies.

Of course, the development of non-industrial economies may become also partly independent of export performance. This implies, however, import substitution, which necessarily involves for these economies (in contrast to those which are already developed), the founding of completely new manufacturing industries. This in turn requires investments in transport and energy, and (defining "investment" slightly differently) in education, etc., and involves a shift in the composition of imports. But the substitution process eventually reaches a limit, which is set (in the main) by natural resources and the size of the local market. However, this process and these limitations are hardly discussed at all in conventional economics, which is so "global" that it misses essential characteristics of development.

Finally a word should be said about some of the peculiarities of fiscal and monetary sectors which affect the operation of industrial economies.

For example, because of the heavy weight of direct taxes and the scale of unemployment benefits, the public sector automatically compensates, in some measure, for fluctuations in the private economy. In non-industrial economies, on the other hand, a slump in trade can rarely be overcome by throwing the budget into deficit, because the only means of covering it will probably be to run down reserves. (This is obviously true of one particular type of non-industrial economy, an "open" economy; there a payments deficit appears immediately, if internal activity is maintained in a slump.) So the government may in time be compelled to raise taxes or reduce outlays, aggravating the initial downward impulse. Another feature of the fiscal system in industrial economies, but not in others, is that it operates to spread income more widely over the country's various regions and thus ensures that none get left far behind in an economic advance.

While all industrial economies have virtually complete monetary autonomy, this is by no means universally true. Even the larger non-industrial economies, which manage their own currencies, lack many of the means of influencing the supply of money, such as open-market operations; moreover, foreign companies and foreign banks, which draw finance from, or supply it to, their head offices, may be quantitatively important and their operation may affect the money supply more than any steps taken by the local central bank.

Because of their financial systems, industrial economies have boundaries corresponding to their political frontiers. But, when we look at the other types, we may wonder whether the nation is the correct unit of analysis at all. If fiscal and monetary systems are very tenuous, geographical or racial or religious barriers may seal off parts of the nation into virtually self-contained sub-economies. For this reason, national averages (e.g., income levels, wage levels, price levels, etc.) may have little meaning, whether used for comparison with other countries, or for measuring progress over time. . . .

The Degree of Generalization Possible

Simple explanatory models can now be constructed for various individual economies, and these could be developed into models for the different types of economy. Steps in this direction, when they have been assimilated, will be particularly helpful to teachers working overseas who are anxious to try to relate material to their pupils' needs. At present they have to provide their own gloss on the available texts, such as Samuelson's, and this is of course a poor substitute for the texts that are needed. . . .

But it would be worthwhile to attempt something more general. There are so many common characteristics that it would now be possible to write a text covering what is, and will be for several decades, the typical case in economics, the unindustrialized economy, even though such a text would at present be very rudimentary. For all such economies, a dynamic approach is needed, with heavy emphasis on trade, and therefore on

the organization of the world economy and on the operation of commodity markets. There are certain similarities in their social and economic structures and in their problems, especially if they are grouped according to the stage of development. Their growth processes show common features, and require analysis at a low level of aggregation. Recognisable patterns can be seen in the way they respond to short-period fluctuations, and again more so if we group them this time, according to the organization of the leading export sector. . . .

A useful guide in the reconstruction of economics which is now starting could be the following modest but revolutionary slogan: Economics is the study of Economies.

II.A.2. Economic Theory and Agrarian Economics*

According to some recent studies, more than 1.3 billion people still live in a self-subsistence economy, that is, as peasants. Most of these also live on the verge of starvation. Asia and Africa, which together represent more than 60 per cent of the world's population, produce only a little more than 30 per cent of the world's agricultural output. Conservative estimates show that if basic nutritional needs for the entire population of the world are to be met, it is necessary that the food production be increased by at least 30 per cent.[1] Neither the overwhelming numerical importance of peasant economy nor the scarcity of food is a new economic development peculiar to our own time.

*From N. Georgescu-Roegen, "Economic Theory and Agrarian Economics," *Oxford Economic Papers*, Vol. 12, No. 1, February 1960, pp. 1–6. Reprinted by permission.

[1] The above data are found in W. S. and E. S. Woytinsky, *World Population and Production*, New York, 1953, pp. 307, 435 *passim*.

In spite of all this, agrarian economics—by which I mean the economics of an overpopulated agricultural economy and not merely agricultural economics—has had a very unfortunate history. Non-capitalist economies simply presented no interest for Classical economists. Marxists, on the other side, tackled the problem with their characteristic impetuosity, but proceeded from preconceived ideas about the laws of a peasant economy. A less known school of thought—Agrarianism—aimed at studying a peasant economy and only this. An overt scorn for quantitative theoretical analysis prevented the Agrarians from constructing a proper theory of their particular object of study, and consequently from making themselves understood outside their own circle. There remain the Standard economists (as a recent practice calls the members of the modern economic school for which neither Neo-Classical nor General Equilibrium suffices as a single label). Of late, as economic development has become tied up with precarious international politics, Standard economists have been almost compelled to come to grips with the problem of underdeveloped economies, and hence with non-capitalist economics. But in their approach they have generally committed the same type of error as Marxists.

Thus, the agrarian economy has to this day remained a reality without a theory. And the topical interest of a sound economic policy in countries with a peasant overpopulation calls for such a theory as at no other time in history. . . .

THEORY AND REALITY

Theory is in the first and last place a logical file of our factual knowledge pertaining to a certain phenomenological domain. Only mathematics is concerned with the properties of "any object whatever," for which reason since Aristotle's time it has been generally placed in a special category by itself. To each theory, therefore, there must correspond a specific domain of the reality. In any science, the problem of precisely circumscribing this domain faces well-known difficulties. Where physics ends and chemistry begins, and where economics ends and ethics begins, are certainly thorny questions, although not equally so. Here, however, I want to discuss a quite pedestrian query pertaining to the problem of the proper domain of a theory. And this query is: Can an economic theory which successfully describes the capitalistic system, for instance, be used to analyse successfully another economic system, say feudalism?

Let us observe that a similar question hardly ever comes up in the physical sciences, for no evidence exists to make physicists believe that matter behaves differently today than yesterday. In contrast, we find that human societies vary with both time and locality. To be sure, one school of thought still argues that these variations are only different instances of a unique archetype and that consequently all social phenomena can be encompassed by a single theory. This is not the place to show precisely where the weakness of the various attempts in this direction lies. Suffice it to mention here that when the theories constructed by these attempts do not fail in other respects, they are nothing but a collection of generalities of no operational value whatever. As Kautsky once judiciously remarked, "Marx designed to investigate in his 'Capital' the capitalistic mode of production [and not] the forms of production which are common to all people, as such an investigation could, for the most part, only result in commonplaces."[2] For an economic theory to be operational at all, i.e. to be capable of serving as a guide for policy, it must concern itself with a specific type of economy, not with several types at the same time.

What particular reality is described by a given theory can be ascertained only from the latter's axiomatic foundation. Thus, Standard theory describes the economic process of a society in which the individual behaves *strictly* hedonistically, where the entrepreneur seeks to maximize his cash-profit, and where any commodity can be exchanged on the market at uniform prices and none exchanged otherwise. On the other hand Marxist theory refers to an economy characterized by class monopoly of the means of production, money-making entrepreneurs, markets with uniform prices for all commodities, and complete independence of economic from demographic factors.[3] Taken as abstractions of varying degree, both these axiomatic bases undoubtedly represent the most characteristic traits of the capitalist system.[4] Moreover, far from being abso-

[2] Karl Kautsky, *The Economic Doctrines of Karl Marx*, New York, 1936, p. 1.

[3] I refer to the fact that the assumption of a permanent reserve army simply means that at the subsistence wage-rate the supply of labour is "unlimited" both in the short and in the long run, while Classical economics held that this was true only in the long run. *Infra*, p. 18 n.

[4] We have left out the surplus value proposition from the Marxist axioms because this proposi-

lutely contradictory, they are complementary, in the sense of Bohr's Principle of Complementarity.[5] This is precisely why one may speak of Marx as "the flower of Classical economics."[6]

A far more important observation is that the theoretical foundations of both Standard and Marxist theories consist of cultural or, if you wish, institutional traits. Actually, the same must be true of any economic theory. For what characterizes an economic system is its institutions, not the technology it uses. Were this not so, we would have no basis for distinguishing between Communism and Capitalism, while, on the other hand, we should regard Capitalism of today and Capitalism of, say, 50 years ago as essentially different systems.

As soon as we realize that for economic theory an economic system is characterized exclusively by institutional traits, it becomes obvious that neither Marxist nor Standard theory is valid as a whole for the analysis of a non-capitalistic economy, i.e. of the economy of a society in which part or all of the capitalist institutions are absent. A proposition of either theory may eventually be valid for a non-capitalistic economy, but its validity must be established de novo in each case, either by factual evidence or by logical derivation from the corresponding axiomatic foundation. Even the analytical concepts developed by these theories cannot be used indiscriminately in the description of other

economies. Among the few that are of general applicability there is the concept of a production function together with all its derived notions. But this is due to the purely physical nature of that concept. Most economic concepts, on the contrary, are hard to transplant. "Social class" seems the only exception, obviously because it is inseparable from "society" itself (save the society of Robinson Crusoe and probably that of the dawn of the human species). This is not to say that Marxist and Standard theories do not provide us with useful patterns for asking the right kind of questions and for seeking the relevant constituents of any economic reality. They are, after all, the only elaborate economic theories ever developed.

All this may seem exceedingly elementary. Yet this is not what Standard and (especially) Marxist theorists have generally done when confronted with the problem of formulating policies for the agrarian overpopulated countries. And, as the saying goes, "economics is what economists do."

A REALITY WITHOUT THEORY

As has often been remarked, economists of all epochs have been compelled by the social environment to be far more opportunistic than their colleagues in other scientific fields, with the result that their attention has been concentrated upon the economic problems of their own time.[7] And as the transition of economic science from the purely descriptive (i.e. taxonomic) to the theoretical stage coincided with the period during which in Western Europe feudalism was rapidly yielding to capitalism, it was only natural that the latter should become the ob-

---

tion—as we shall argue later—belongs to feudalism, not to capitalism.

[5] This principle by which Bohr overcame the impasse created by the modern discoveries in physics states that reality "cannot be comprehended in a single picture" and that "only the totality of the phenomena exhausts the possible information about objects." Niels Bohr, *Atomic Physics and Human Knowledge,* New York, 1958, pp. 40 *passim.*

[6] Terence McCarthy in the Preface to the English translation of K. Marx, *A History of Economic Theories,* New York, 1952, p. xi.

[7] The point finds an eloquent illustration in the vogue that the problem of economic development has recently acquired among Western economists: we have reached the point where the development of underdeveloped nations is as much an economic problem of the West as of these other nations.

jective of the first theoretical economists. That may explain only why most Western economists have been interested in developing the theory of the capitalist system, but not why none attempted a theory of a noncapitalist economy. The only explanation of this omission is the insuperable difficulty in getting at the cultural roots of a society other than that to which one actually belongs. And, as we have seen, an intuitive knowledge of the basic cultural traits of a community is indispensable for laying out the basis of its economic theory.

By its very nature, a peasant village is the milieu least fit for modern scientific activity. The modern scientist had therefore to make the town his headquarters. But, from there, he could not possibly observe the life of a peasant community. London, for instance, offers indeed "a favorable view . . . for the observation of bourgeois society"—a circumstance immensely appreciated by Marx[8] — but not even a pinhole through which to look at a peasant economy. Even if, unlike Marx, an economist was born in a village, he had to come to town for his education. He thus became a true townee himself, in the process losing most, if not all, *verstehen* of the peasant society. It was natural, therefore, that to Marx as well as to other Western economists (to those coming from a peasantless country, especially) the peasant should seem "a mysterious, strange, often even disquieting creature."[9] Yet none showed Marx's unlimited contempt for the peasantry. For him, the peasantry was just a bag of potatoes, not a social class. In the *Communist Manifesto* he denounced "the idiocy of rural life" to the four corners of the world. But these Marxist hyperboles apart, there is, as we shall presently see, a spotless rationale behind Marx's attitude towards the peasant.

The difference between the philosophy of the industrial town and of the agricultural countryside has often attracted the attention of sociologists and poets alike.[10] But few have realized that this difference is not like going to another church, and that it involves every concrete act concerning production and distribution as well as social justice. Undoubtedly the basis of this difference is the fact that the living Nature imposes a different type of restriction upon *homo agricola* than the inert matter upon *homo faber*.

To begin with, no parallelism exists between the law of the scale of production in agriculture and in industry. One may grow wheat in a pot or raise chickens in a tiny backyard, but no hobbyist can build an automobile with only the tools of his workshop. Why then should the optimum scale for agriculture be that of a giant open-air factory? In the second place, the role of the time-factor is entirely different in the two activities. By mechanical devices we can shorten the time for weaving an ell of cloth, but we have as yet been unable to shorten the gestation period in animal husbandry or (to any significant degree) the period for maturity in plants. Moreover, agricultural activity is bound to an unflinching rhythm, while in manufacture we can well do tomorrow what we have chosen not to do today. Finally, there is a difference between the two sectors which touches the root of the much discussed law of decreasing returns (in the evolutionary sense). For industrial uses man has been able to harness one source of energy after another, from the wind to the atom, but for the type of energy that is needed by life itself he is still wholly dependent on the most "primitive" source, the animals and plants around him. These brief observations are sufficient to pinpoint not

[8] K. Marx, *A Contribution to the Critique of Political Economy*, Chicago, 1904, Preface, p. 14.

[9] Karl Kautsky, *La Question agraire*, Paris, 1900, p. 3.

[10] In the Western literature, Oswald Spengler is probably the best known author for placing a great historical value upon this difference. See especially his *The Decline of the West*, New York, 1928, vol. ii, ch. iv.

only why the philosophy of the man engaged in agriculture differs from that of the townee but also why agriculture and industry still cannot be subsumed under the same law. Whether future scientific discoveries may bring life to the denominator of inert matter is, for the time being, a highly controversial—and no less speculative—topic.

Probably the greatest error of Marx was his failure to recognize the simple fact that agriculture and industry obey different laws; as a result he proclaimed that the law of

concentration applies equally well to industry and agriculture.[11] To repeat, Marx had no opportunity to observe a peasant economy. Nor is there anything in his vast literary activity to indicate that he ever studied a non-capitalist agriculture.[12]

[11] K. Marx, *Capital*, Chicago, 1906, i, ch. xiv, sec. 10.

[12] Kautsky, *La Question agraire*, p. xii. Also F. Engels in the Preface to the third volume of *Capital* (Chicago, 1909, p. 16).

II.A.3. Use and Abuse of Development Models*

The following criticism is not intended as a rejection of all models in the analysis of underdevelopment and in planning for development. All thought presupposes implicit or explicit model building and model using. Rigorous abstraction, simplification and quantification are necessary conditions of analysis and policy. But models must be realistic, relevant and useful. The trouble with many current models is that they are shapely and elegant, but lack the vital organs.

SYSTEMATIC BIASES

Model thinking shows four systematic biases, which are related to each other and overlap, and which can be called:

1. Adapted *ceteris paribus* or automatic *mutatis mutandis;*
2. One-factor analysis;
3. Misplaced aggregation;
4. Illegitimate isolation.

*From Paul Streeten, "The Use and Abuse of Models in Development Planning," in Kurt Martin and John Knapp (eds.), *The Teaching of Development Economics,* Frank Cass & Co., Ltd., 1966, pp. 57–63, 65–9. Reprinted by permission.

1. *Adapted Ceteris Paribus or Automatic Mutatis Mutandis.* It is interesting to note that the conclusions of orthodox liberal and of Marxian economics, though derived from very different premises, converge in this respect. The separation of parameters from variables in Western orthodox models is partly determined by what is appropriate for advanced industrial nations, partly by ideology and vested interests, and partly by convenience of analysis. Thus psychological attitudes and valuation and social institutions are normally assumed to be given and adapted. We assume that there is a legal framework, that contracts are enforced, that an efficient civil service carries out government orders and an honest judiciary adjudicates; that people are able and willing to work if opportunities arise; that they are literate, skilled and able to co-operate with discipline, appearing on time and carrying out orders; that money spent is efficiently spent and not diverted into the pockets of corrupt officials; that alternatives are considered largely on their pecuniary merits, etc. It follows that none of these matters is considered a suitable area for planning.

In the Marxian scheme (though not always in Marx's own writings), what are parameters become dependent variables. Cultural, political and social institutions are the superstructure, which is determined by the methods of production. It reflects these conditions and gives rise to tensions and contradictions in due course. These tensions between the degree of development of the forces of production and the prevailing relations of production (the institutions and attitudes) in turn give rise to revolution. After the revolution the attitudes and institutions reflect the new conditions of production. Hence social, cultural and political attitudes and institutions, the so-called "relations of production," though dependent variables, are, after a time-lag, adjusted to the extent required by the dynamic productive forces. Once again, though for fundamentally different reasons, planning the superstructure is not in question. It would be futile before the revolution and unnecessary after it. It was indeed for their attempts to speculate on how social attitudes and institutions could and should be reformed that Marx and Engels ridiculed the "Utopian" thinkers. Yet, in many ways the early Utopian socialists were more akin to modern planners, including the planners in Soviet Russia, than many of the cruder versions of Marxian thought.

Thus the conservative judgment that a reform of attitudes and institutions is undesirable, and the Marxian judgment that it is either impossible or inevitable, lead to the same conclusion, distracting attention from conscious policy directed at a radical reform of the so-called "non-economic" factors in economic development. It is, of course, true that textbooks, articles and plans pay lip service to the need to reform the social framework before economic planning can begin. But these declarations are usually forgotten later when the discussion turns to the conventional concepts of income, employment, savings, investment, etc. At that stage either the assumption of *ceteris paribus* is tacitly reintroduced, so that the conventional economic variables can be considered in isolation, or the assumption of automatic *mutatis mutandis* is made, implying that where other things cannot be assumed constant, they will without special policies be adapted to the required extent as a result of economic transformation.

The intellectual framework, which reflects this bias, is supported by value judgments and by vested interests. As we shall see, reforms of institutions and human attitudes violate entrenched interests and are therefore more painful to implement than financial expenditure programmes.

In a bias-free model, the distinction between parameters and variables would be determined, not by ideological preconceptions, but by the situation to which the model is intended to apply and by the questions asked about this situation. To be useful, models will have to be, at least initially, much more specific to individual cases and much less general and "theoretical." In particular, the distinction between parameters and variables should not run along the line drawn between "economic" and "non-economic" factors operating in a situation. Thus social and political reform should neither "precede" nor "follow" economic development: social reform must accompany development, reinforce it, create the conditions necessary for it, but is itself promoted and determined by development. The process is one of continual mutual causation.

2. *One-Factor Analysis.* Although economists ought to be particularly trained to discern interdependence and particularly immune to uni-causal explanations, it is a fact that frequently one factor is selected as the strategic factor in development, although the choice of this factor is subject to fashion and ideology. If the Physiocrats stressed *Land* as the source of all wealth and the classical economists *Labour, Capital* has recently played the strategic role. Keynes's emphasis on the income-creating aspect of capital was combined with Marx's emphasis on its output-creating aspect in the Harrod-Domar model which has strongly influenced planners. The relationship which equates the rate of growth of income to the savings ratio divided by the capital output ratio has been

one of the chief vehicles by which Western economic thought has been carried into the plans and discussions of the plans of under-developed countries. Capital is sometimes re-garded as a necessary and sufficient condi-tion of growth, sometimes as the strategic variable. It became soon obvious, however, that numerous other conditions both ac-count for past growth in advanced countries and are required for development in under-developed countries. But instead of embark-ing on a careful analysis of the necessary co-ordination of policies in particular cases, a new one-factor analysis has tended to re-place the old one. *Education* is now the craze and one cannot open a journal or read a speech concerned with development with-out being told of the high returns that "in-vestment in human beings" yields. There is often little thought as to education of whom, for what, how long, in conjunction with what other measures. It is interesting to speculate what other factors will be singled out as discussion progresses. "Research and Development" are already popular, and per-haps we shall soon study the returns from appropriate child-training, which produces experimental innovating personalities, or from expenditure on child prevention.

3. *Misplaced Aggregation.* Almost all con-cepts formed by aggregation suitable for analysing Western economies must be care-fully reconsidered before they can be ap-plied to underdeveloped economies. "Capi-tal," "income," "employment," "unemploy-ment," "price level," "savings," "invest-ment," presuppose conditions which are absent in many underdeveloped countries. "Employment" presupposes a fairly homo-geneous, mobile labour force, willing and able to work and responsive to incentives. In a society of isolated communities, some of them apathetic or with religious prejudices against certain kinds of work, illiterate and unused to co-operation, the notion "Labour Force" does not make sense. Similarly "un-deremployment" or "disguised unemploy-ment" presupposes that if only demand and machines were available, men and women would be able and willing to work. In fact,

much more would be required: a break-down of caste prejudices, of apathy, of lack of interest in money rewards, of resistance to co-operation, discipline and punctuality, etc. Any attempt to calculate "disguised un-employment" also presupposes a value judg-ment as to the length of the appropriate working day and working week.

If economies are divided into sectors be-tween which there is little or no substitu-tion, either in consumption in response to changes in relative prices, or in production in response to changes in relative factor re-wards, aggregation of incomes or prices is inappropriate. Even though the indigenous sector may sell its surplus in the market, and even though some of its members may occa-sionally participate in the transactions of the money sector, if the indigenous sector neither depends upon nor interacts with the capitalist sector, aggregation can be meaning-less. The income of an industrial enclave may grow, while real income per head of the indigenous population stagnates or declines. In what sense is "average income" rising? The problem is not merely how to get at the facts in the indigenous sector and how to appraise them properly. More fundamental is the problem what weights to attach to a small decline of essentials and to a large increase of non-essentials. Paasche and Las-peyres indices may give contradictory re-sults. Habits of thought induce us to use concepts which are applicable to one set of conditions, because substitution is possible, responses exist, and value judgments are ap-propriate, in an entirely different context, where these presuppositions of legitimate ag-gregation are absent. The statistical manifes-tation of this would be contradictory results according to which of several equally plausi-ble sets of weights were applied to the same change. Using base period weights, we should register a rise in income per head, and therefore conclude that development is pro-ceeding, while we have begged the political question "development for whom?"

The distinction between consumption and investment can have various justifica-tions. In the context of development, it is based upon the assumption that investment enables us to produce more later than we would otherwise have done, while consumption is current enjoyment. But if more food and better health now reduce apathy and raise ability to work, they share in the characteristics of investment: consumption, too, is productive of more output. If different investment projects require different sums to bribe corrupt officials, what guide is their cost to the resources used up? To abstract from the differences in such cases is to pour out the baby with the bath water.

It is correct to say that a man is male, a woman female, but it does not make sense to ask: "Is your family male or female?" One can discuss the differences between the British and the French Constitutions, and also the connections between the Cabinet, Parliament and the Church of England, but it does not make sense to ask "What transactions go on between the House of Commons and the British Constitution?"[1] Similarly, it is what philosophers call a "category mistake" to ask what is the capital, income, employment, price level, etc., of a society sharply divided into non-communicating sectors. Just as words can be spelt, but letters of the alphabet cannot be spelt, not because it is very difficult but because it is an improper request,[2] so asking questions about certain aggregates commonly used in advanced industrial countries in the context of underdeveloped countries, is improper. The solution of a jigsaw puzzle consists in putting each piece where it belongs, not in lumping them together arbitrarily.

Two separate problems arise here. First, category mistakes are made where a category is applied to a field of experience to which it is inappropriate. It is quite possible for this category to be appropriate for advanced countries, but not for underdeveloped ones, just as it is legitimate to ask in some cities "Where is the University?" but not in Oxford.

[1] Gilbert Ryle, *The Concept of Mind*, pp. 17 and 168.
[2] *Op. cit.*, p. 206.

Secondly, there are instances in which the category *might* be appropriate if we knew what it meant when applied to a situation of underdevelopment. Thus the distinction between consumption and investment can be misplaced aggregation in either sense, depending upon the definition. If investment is defined as "abstaining for the sake of higher consumption later" the first problem may arise. But if investment is defined as any input which yields higher output later, irrespective of whether it involves "abstaining" or not, the second problem arises and the error is not a conceptual one but simply of failing to group certain activities under "investment" which, in advanced countries, are classified as "consumption."

4. *Illegitimate Isolation.* The converse of misplaced aggregation, but related to one-factor analysis, which is a particular manifestation of it, is the bias of illegitimate isolation. It consists in assigning the role of sufficient condition to what may or may not be one of several necessary conditions of development. If a component is illegitimately isolated from its necessary complements, and then aggregated with others similarly isolated, we get a combination of misplaced aggregation and illegitimate isolation. The case can be illustrated by successive missions going to a country. The first says entrepreneurial *incentives* are inadequate, and if we nurse these by *low taxes,* resources will soon become available. The next goes and says *resources* are the bottleneck and decisions will soon come forth if we set free resources by *high taxation* to generate a high budget surplus. But the correct policy would be high taxation of certain incomes and property, perhaps land, combined with generous investment allowances and incentives where these yield results. The division should not be resources *versus* incentives, but certain incentives combined with certain resources.

Education, which is now often advocated as a panacea, may simply result in a group of educated unemployed and unemployables, as in India. Equipment may lie unused and unmaintained. Irrigation water flows unused

and reservoirs are silting, because "investment" has not been co-ordinated with the
right kind of education, land reform and
civil service reform. The price we pay for
misplaced aggregation and illegitimate isolation is wasted resources and possibly hard-
ened resistance to and growing cynicism
about the process of development.

II.A.4. Economics as a Form of Technical Assistance*

Has the economist a place in a programme of
technical assistance? Is a knowledge of modern economic theory and analysis a useful or
necessary input in a programme designed to
foster economic growth in a foreign economy? These questions provide the theme for
the following tentative observations. . . .

Some years ago Lord Robbins, in an address on "The Economist in the Twentieth
Century,"[1] discussed the contribution of
economists in government service. He suggested that it was the command of the somewhat elementary and trite platitudes of economics which was particularly useful in this
context. More recently, Professor Simon
Rottenberg, an economist with extensive experience of development problems, expressed substantially the same view in the
field of development economics.[2]

I agree with these assessments. We should
note, however, what is meant by these platitudes or simple fundamentals. I take it that
they include such matters as the treatment
of supply and demand as being functionally
related to price, and of cost as opportunity
cost; the theory of relative prices; the implications of comparative advantage and costs,
and the functional relationships between the
flow of money incomes, the volume of employment and the balance of payments.

Such fundamentals are clearly relevant to
economic policy-making, notably to the
assessment of alternative policies and the
efficiency of different specific measures.
They apply to public finance, especially to
the assessment of the incidence and other
effects of different taxes and items of government expenditure. But their scope extends far beyond these important spheres.
For instance, recognition of the effects of
prices on supply, or of the presence and
relevance of costs, is necessary to assess the
implications of such diverse measures as licensing of transport or processing enterprises; prescription of minimum physical
standards for export products; the payment
of uniform prices to producers, irrespective
of their location; imposition of minimum
wages; prescription of rents or leasing of
government-owned land at uniform rates, regardless of its fertility and location; and
many other measures which affect incomes,
opportunities and the efficient use of resources.

The neglect of the importance of cost
largely explains the confusion between technical and economic efficiency implicit in
such measures as the prescription of minimum physical standards for export products,
and other similar measures adopted in many
underdeveloped countries, including those
whose governments have economic advisers
or even lavishly-staffed planning units.[3] Yet

*From P. T. Bauer, "Economics as a Form of
Technical Assistance," *Manchester School of Eco-
nomics and Social Studies,* May 1967, pp. 111–16.
Reprinted by permission; revisions by author.

[1] *Economica,* May, 1949.
[2] "Economic Instruction for Economic
Growth," *Economic Development and Cultural
Change,* October 1964.

[3] An analogous instance of the identification or
rather confusion of technical and economic effi-

these are measures which can be assessed largely on the basis of economic reasoning since they do not raise wide political and social issues. They are often costly in the sense that a given volume of output could be produced with an appreciably smaller volume of scarce resources; they serve also to retard the expansion of production for the market and the spread of the exchange economy in many poor countries; and the retardation of the spread of the exchange economy has far-reaching adverse effects on development.

The establishment by statute or by organised labour of minimum wages is now widespread in the underdeveloped world. The effects and implications of this measure cannot properly be assessed without reference to elementary economic theory. Even without econometric or statistical investigations it is possible to form some idea of such relevant factors as the presence or absence of monopoly, or the factors affecting the elasticity of demand for the product, or the elasticity of supply of complementary resources, or the elasticity of substitution between resources. Without some grasp of elementary economics these factors will be overlooked, as indeed they very generally are. This defect in turn makes it impossible to select the industries for the imposition of minimum wages to secure the most effective achievement of any specific policy objective.

The relevance of elementary economic considerations is also clear in more specialised aspects of technical assistance. For in-

ciency is the ban on the use or importation of second-hand machinery. For instance, in the 1950's the import of second-hand machinery into Egypt was banned for some years. This type of equipment is often available more cheaply to underdeveloped countries because it has lost its usefulness in advanced countries where wages are higher, while it is still valuable in countries where they are lower. In these circumstances a ban on the import of second-hand machinery deprives the country of a comparatively cheap addition to its productive equipment.

stance, prices, costs and returns are clearly relevant when choices are being made between alternative agricultural or industrial technique. Costs depend on factor prices and resource availabilities, and these often differ for different types of producer even within the same economy or country. Thus, for instance, the most suitable planting density in rubber growing differs between estates operating with large capital and expensive hired labour forces on the one hand, and small-holdings with little capital and without hired labour, on the other; and the optimum planting density varies also with differences in expected prices and costs. Thus the optimum planting density can be determined only after taking into account both economic and technical factors.

Various forms of restrictionism, particularly but not only those directed against foreign or minority personnel or capital, are widespread in underdeveloped countries. These measures substantially damage the development prospects of these countries; they inflict hardship on many people in the country concerned; and they often exacerbate social and political tensions. A reasonable grasp of the nature and sources of income, of the theory of relative prices, and of the implications of competitive or complementary relationships between resources, helps both to understand the forces behind these tendencies, and also to analyse some of their effects and implications.

With few and normally irrelevant exceptions, incomes represent payments to owners of productive resources for services supplied, and not money extracted from others without return. The contrary view that incomes, especially those of certain groups, are somehow extracted from others or payments imposed on others, is politically influential, popular and appealing. . . .

The simple propositions of economics are also necessary for the effective use of its more advanced techniques. Thus the adoption of ostensibly sophisticated planning techniques or techniques of project appraisal is irrelevant if alternative uses of resources are disregarded in the process of applying them to specific projects or sectors. It is not that recent advances in economic analysis may not be relevant for and applicable to the problems of underdeveloped countries. But their use is misconceived or even mischievous when it is accompanied by gross neglect or apparent ignorance of elementary but basic economic considerations, and by a disregard of the implications of the institutional backgrounds.

As an effortless but firm grasp of the obvious is a hall-mark of expert knowledge, so the neglect of simple fundamentals and of patent empirical evidence reflects its absence. It seems paradoxical that in spite of important technical advances in so many branches of economics, and in spite of enormous interest (or at least output) in development economics, there is now a substantial lack of fundamental expertise in this branch of the subject. The eagerness with which the latest refinements in economic theory and analysis are, or appear to be, embraced by the practitioners of development economics is misplaced if at the same time they disregard elementary economic and institutional considerations.

II.A.5. Economic Theory and

Development Policy*

There are many distinguished economists who would be impatient with my proposal to start from the existing theoretical framework and to try to improve its applicability to the underdeveloped countries in the light of accumulating experience and factual knowledge. They would say that the existing "Western" economic theory is so intimately bound up with the special conditions, problems and preconceptions of the industrially advanced countries that large portions of it have to be abandoned before we can come to grips with the problems of the underdeveloped countries.

These economists have advanced three main types of criticism against the existing economic theory.

First, they question the "realism" of trying to apply the standard models of theoretical analysis meant for the advanced countries to the different economic and institutional setting of the underdeveloped

*From Hla Myint, "Economic Theory and Development Policy," *Economica*, Vol. 34, No. 134, May 1967, pp. 119–21, 123–7. Reprinted by permission.

countries. I have no quarrel with this line of criticism. In fact I shall be giving illustrations of other types of lack of realism in applying economic theory to the underdeveloped countries which are not mentioned by the critics. But it seems to me that this is not an argument for abandoning existing economic theory but merely an argument for trying to improve its applicability.

Secondly, the critics question the "relevance" of the static neo-classical economics concerned with the problem of allocating given resources within an existing economic framework to the problem of promoting economic development in the underdeveloped countries, which are concerned with increasing the amount of available resources, improving techniques, and generally with the introduction of a dynamic self-sustaining process of economic change, disrupting the existing framework. Here again I agree that we do not possess a satisfactory dynamic theory for studying development problems. In fact, I would go further to say that the recent developments in dynamic economic theory in terms of growth models are not very relevant and are not meant to be relevant for the underdeveloped countries.[1] But I do not accept the conclusion which the critics have drawn: that the static theory of efficient allocation of given resources is irrelevant for the underdeveloped countries. I shall come back to this point in a moment.

Thirdly, the critics maintain that orthodox economic theory is inextricably bound up with preconceptions and biases in favour of orthodox economic policies of *laissez-faire*, free trade and conservative fiscal and monetary policies. They believe that these orthodox economic policies are generally inimical to rapid economic growth, which can be promoted only by large-scale government economic planning, widespread protection and import controls, and deficit financing of development programmes, if sufficient external aid is not available. Thus they propose that large chunks of existing economic theory, particularly the orthodox neo-classical theory, should be abandoned to pave the way for the adoption of these new development policies.

There are two questions here. The first is the general question whether the new policies are always more effective than the orthodox policies in promoting economic development in the underdeveloped countries. The second is the more specific question whether there is an unbreakable ideological link between orthodox economic theory and orthodox economic policies, so that if we wish to adopt the new development policies we must necessarily abandon large chunks of existing theory.

The underdeveloped countries vary widely among themselves and I, therefore, find it difficult to accept the general presumption that the new policies will be always better for their economic development, whatever their particular individual situation. . . . Whether we like it or not, it is no longer an open question whether the underdeveloped countries should choose the orthodox or the new type of development

[1] Cf. Sir John Hicks, *Capital and Growth,* Oxford University Press, 1965, p. 1.

policies. One after another they have already made their choice in favour of the new policies, which have now become a part of conventional economic wisdom. Accepting this as one of the facts of life, the more immediately relevant question seems to be the second question, whether large chunks of the orthodox economic theory have now become obsolete because the underdeveloped countries wish to plan for rapid economic development.

I shall argue that this is not so; that on the contrary, the orthodox economic theory assumes a greater significance in the context of the new "progressive" development policies. I shall show that even if development planning is to be regarded as new and radical policy, the *theory* underlying development planning is, technically speaking, quite orthodox and conventional. Similarly, I shall show that the orthodox theory of international trade can be made to support more liberal and generous trade and aid policies towards the underdeveloped countries, if we choose to use it in this way. What I am saying is not new. It is merely a restatement of the familiar doctrine that economic theory is "ethically neutral" and can be made use of in the more efficient pursuit of the economic objectives to be chosen by the "value judgments" of the policy maker.

However, let us start by a closer look at the question of "realism" in applying existing economic theory to the underdeveloped countries. Some critics speak of "existing theory" as though it were contained in a modern textbook like Samuelson. Properly speaking, it should include the whole corpus of Western economic theory, offering a wide choice of theoretical models, ranging from those of the older economists writing at earlier stages of economic development to the highly complex and abstract models of contemporary economic theory. To my mind a very important cause of lack of realism arises from the wrong choice of theoretical models to be applied to the underdeveloped countries. Much in the same way as the governments of the underdeveloped countries succumb to the lure of the "steel mills" embodying the most advanced and capital-intensive type of Western technology, many development economists have succumbed to the lure of the intellectual "steel mills" represented by the latest and most sophisticated theoretical models. This is where, I believe, the greatest mischief has been done. This is why I have always maintained that a good development economist should also be something of an applied historian of economic thought.

If it is unrealistic to apply highly sophisticated theoretical models meant for the complex economic structures of advanced countries to the simpler economic structures of underdeveloped countries, has this been corrected by the new theories of development and underdevelopment which are specially meant for the underdeveloped countries? Looking at these new theories, which became popular during the 1950's, such as the "vicious circle," the "take-off" or the "big push," it does not seem to me that these have stood up to the test of realism any better. The weakness of these new theories is that they try to apply a composite model of the underdeveloped country, incorporating certain special features of some type of underdeveloped country, to all the underdeveloped countries. The "vicious circle" theory assumes poverty and stagnation caused by severe population pressure on resources; the "take-off" theory assumes the pre-existence of a fairly high level of development in the political, social and institutional framework; the "big push" theory assumes both and also an internal market large enough to support a domestic capital goods sector. By the time we have incorporated all these special features into a composite model, the number of the underdeveloped countries to which this model might apply becomes limited to one or two countries, such as India and possibly Pakistan.

The limitations of these new theories of development, particularly the "vicious circle" theory, can be illustrated by looking at the broad dimensions of the economic performance of underdeveloped countries during the decade 1950–60. During that decade, compared with the 4 per cent average annual growth rates for the advanced Western countries, the G.D.P. of underdeveloped countries as a group grew at the average annual rate of 4.4 per cent, giving them a growth in *per capita* incomes of a little over 2 per cent per annum.[2] This may or may not be very much, but the really interesting thing is that the G.D.P. of some underdeveloped countries was growing at a faster rate than the average, say between 5 per cent and 6 per cent, while that of other countries barely kept up with their population increase. Thus instead of the earlier *simpliste* view according to which all underdeveloped countries are caught up in a vicious circle of stagnation and population pressure, we are led to the question why some underdeveloped countries grow faster or slower than others.

When we try to answer this question, we become very aware of the differences between the underdeveloped countries, in size, in the degree of population pressure over natural resources, in the conditions of world demand for their exports and in their general level of economic development and political stability. These differences will by themselves explain quite a lot of the differences in the growth rate between different underdeveloped countries. If, in addition, we want to say something about development policy, we shall have to choose a fairly uniform group of countries where the basic social and economic differences are small enough for us to isolate the effect of economic policy....

Let me now conclude my remarks on the "realism" of applying economic theory to the underdeveloped countries by drawing attention to the dangers of trying to be too different from the standard models of economic analysis. These arise from selecting the "queer cases" in the standard Western models of analysis, and in taking it for granted that these exceptions to the stan-

[2] United Nations, *World Economic Survey 1963*, Part I, p. 29.

dard case must automatically apply to the underdeveloped countries because they are so different from the advanced countries in social values and attitudes and institutional setting. Such for instance is the famous case of the "backward sloping supply curve of labour" attributed to the underdeveloped countries by many writers, who also speak of the "demonstration effect" and "the revolution of rising expectations." Such too is the belief that the people of the underdeveloped countries, being more communally minded, will take more easily to co-operative forms of economic organisation (while writers on the co-operative movement in the underdeveloped countries frequently complain about the lack of co-operative spirit and the excessive individualism of the people). Yet another example is the generalisation that the people of the underdeveloped countries naturally lack entrepreneurial ability, irrespective of the economic policies followed by their governments. If one were to tell the politicians of the underdeveloped countries that their people are lazy, stupid, lacking in initiative and adaptability, one would be branded as an enemy; but if one were to rephrase these prejudices in another way and say that the people lack entrepreneurial capacity, one would be welcomed for giving "scientific" support for economic planning. To take just one more example, there is the hoary belief that peasants in the underdeveloped countries do not respond to economic incentives, while agricultural economists have been accumulating abundant evidence to show that peasants do respond to price changes by switching from one crop to another or by bringing more land under cultivation. The real problem is how to introduce new methods of cultivation which will raise productivity: this is a difficult practical problem, but in principle it is not all that different from, say, the problem of introducing new methods to raise productivity in British industry.

This is where I think that a closer co-operation between economics and other branches of social studies is likely to prove most useful, both in getting rid of questionable sociological generalisations and also in tackling the more intractable problems of analysing social and economic change. . . .

Let me now turn from the "realism" to the "relevance" of the existing economic theory to the underdeveloped countries. The problem of promoting rapid economic development in these countries may ultimately lie in the realm of social and economic dynamics of the sort we do not at present possess; and there is nothing in my argument to prevent anyone from launching into new dynamic theoretical approaches to the underdeveloped countries. But in the meantime, it is dangerously easy to underestimate the significance of the orthodox static theory of the allocation of given resources to the underdeveloped countries. The affluent Western economies with their steady rates of increase in productivity may be able to take a tolerant attitude towards misallocation of resources. But the underdeveloped countries are simply too poor to put up with preventable wasteful use of their given meagre economic resources. In particular, they can ill afford the well-recognised distortions of their price systems, such as the excessively high levels of wages and low levels of interest in their manufacturing and public sectors compared with those in the agricultural sector, and the overvaluation of their currencies at the official rates of exchange. Having to bear the brunt of low earnings and high interest rates discourages the expansion of agricultural output both for export and for domestic consumption and this in turn slows down the over-all rate of growth of the economy. Higher wages attract a large number of people from the countryside to the towns, but only a small proportion of this influx can be absorbed because of the highly capital-intensive methods adopted in the modern import-substituting industries. This aggravates the problem of urban unemployment and the problem of shanty towns, which increases the requirements for investment for housing and social welfare. The scarce supply of capital tends to be wastefully used, both in government prestige projects and in private industry, because of the artificially low rates of interest. This is aggravated by the over-valuation of currencies and import controls in favour of capital goods, which positively encourage the businessmen who are fortunate enough to obtain import licences to buy the most expensive and capital-intensive type of machinery from abroad.

These then are some of the glaring sources of wastefulness which can be reduced by a better allocation of resources. Now I should point out that just because the orthodox neo-classical theory is concerned with the efficient allocation of *given* resources, it does not mean that it becomes unimportant in the context of aid policies to increase the volume of resources available to the underdeveloped countries. On the contrary, a country which cannot use its already available resources efficiently is not likely to be able to "absorb" additional resources from aid programmes and use them efficiently. That is to say, a country's absorptive capacity for aid must to a large extent depend on its ability to avoid serious misallocation of resources. A similar conclusion can be drawn about an underdeveloped country's ability to make effective use of its opportunities for international trade. If we find that a country is not making effective use of its already available trading opportunities, because of domestic policies discouraging its export production or raising the costs in the export sector, then we should not expect it to benefit in a dramatic way from the new trading opportunities to be obtained through international negotiations.

This is a part of the reason why I have suggested that orthodox economic theory, instead of becoming obsolete, has assumed a greater significance in the context of the new "progressive" policies for promoting economic development in the underdeveloped countries. Let me illustrate this argument further by examples from development planning theory and from recent discussions

about the appropriate trade and aid policies.

I think that a great deal of confusion would have been avoided by clearly distinguishing the *policy* of development planning and the economic *theory* which underlies development planning, which is, as we shall see, only an application of the traditional theory of the optimum allocation of the *given* resources. This confusion was introduced during the 1950's when it was the fashion to try to make out the case for development planning mainly by attacking the orthodox equilibrium and optimum theory. At the macro-economic level, there were theories of deficit financing trying to show how economic development might be accelerated by forced saving and inflation, or by making use of "disguised unemployment" for capital formation. More generally, the theories of the "vicious circle," the "big push" or the "unbalanced growth" tried to show, in their different ways, the desirability of breaking out of the static equilibrium framework by deliberately introducing unbalances and disequilibria which would start the chain-reaction of cumulative movement towards self-sustained economic growth. Ironically enough, when the underdeveloped countries came to accept the need for development planning and to ask how this might be done efficiently, it turned out that the economic theory required for this purpose is basically nothing but the traditional equilibrium and optimum theory.

Thus according to the present-day textbooks on development planning,[3] the first task of the planner is to test the feasibility of the plan at the macro-economic level by making sure that the aggregate amount of resources required to carry out the plan does not exceed the aggregate amount of resources available. That is to say, deficit

[3] See particularly, *Development Planning,* by W. Arthur Lewis, Allen and Unwin, 1966; also, *Development Planning: Lessons of Experience,* by Albert Waterston, Oxford University Press, 1966 and W. B. Reddaway, *The Development of the Indian Economy,* Allen and Unwin, 1962.

financing and inflation are to be avoided and this is to be checked at the sectoral level by ensuring that the projected rate of expansion of the services sector does not exceed the possible rate of expansion in the output of commodities by a certain critical margin. The next task of the planner is to test the consistency of the plan at the sectoral and micro-economic level to make sure that the demand and supply for particular commodities and services are equated to each other, and that there is an equilibrium relationship between the different parts of the economy, not only within any given year, but also between one year and another during the whole of the plan period. Finally, if the plan is found to be both feasible and consistent, the task of the planner is to find out whether the plan adopted is an optimum plan in the sense that there is no alternative way of reallocating the given resources more efficiently to satisfy the given objectives of the plan.

If this standard formulation of development planning is accepted, then there is no fundamental theoretical difference between those who aim to achieve the efficient allocation of the available resources through the market mechanism and those who aim to achieve it through the state mechanism. Both accept the optimum allocation of resources as their theoretical norm and their disagreements are about the *practical* means of fulfilling this norm. In any given situation, they will disagree how far planning should be "indicative" or "imperative," that is to say, how far the task of allocating resources should be left to the decentralised decision-making of the market or to the centralised decision-making of the state. But technically speaking they are using the same type of economic theory—the extension of the orthodox neo-classical theory in the pursuit of their different practical policies.

From a theoretical point of view, the great divide is between those who believe that economic development of the underdeveloped countries can be promoted in *an orderly manner* by a more efficient allocation of the available resources, which are assumed to be steadily expanding between one period and another through good management of domestic savings and external aid, and those who believe that only sudden disruptive and *disorderly* changes such as social revolutions and technical innovations can bring about economic development. Now this second revolutionary approach to economic development may well be the correct approach for some underdeveloped countries. But it is difficult to see how this can be incorporated into the planning approach. Development planning is by definition an orderly approach: on the other hand, genuinely far-reaching and disruptive social changes cannot be turned on and turned off in a predictable way and incorporated into the planning framework. Those who advocate the necessity of breaking out of the static equilibrium framework by deliberately introducing unbalances and tensions, are in effect advocating at the same time the need to break out of the planning framework. Thus one may advocate social revolution now and planning later but not advocate social revolution and planning at the same time without getting into serious contradictions. Further, it should be pointed out that the revolutionary approach to economic development is by no means the monopoly of the critics of the private enterprise system. The case for *laissez-faire* can be made, not on grounds of static allocative efficiency, but on the ground that it imparts a "dynamism" to the economy by stimulating enterprise, innovation and savings. Schumpeter's picture of the disruption of the existing productive framework through a process of "creative destruction" by innovating private entrepreneurs, is a well-known illustration of this type of revolutionary approach to economic development.

II.A.6. Limits of Economic Theory—Note

It has long been said that "The Theory of Economics does not furnish a body of settled conclusions immediately applicable to policy."[1] But in few, if any, areas of economic policy does the distance between theory and policy tend to be as great as it is for development problems. Some reasons for this have been offered in the foregoing selections, especially in terms of the limited relevance of the special case of "Western" economic theory and the abuse of models.

As a summary of the strictures expressed above, we may again emphasize the economics *for* development. To improve our understanding of development problems, the literary economist is now being asked to provide more operational concepts and empirical constructs instead of "empty stages of growth" (II.B.2) or ambiguous phrases such as "big push" (X.A.1) or "balanced growth" (X.A.3). The mathematical economist is being asked to be more aware of the limits of mathematical programming in a less developed country. The econometrician is being cautioned to recognize the simplifying assumptions to which he resorts in order to keep his models within manageable dimensions.[2]

In reconsidering policies to eradicate poverty and reduce inequality, the development economist must rethink some basic premises of both price theory and income theory. Price theory has to be extended to consider problems of intertemporal allocation of resources and the implications of prices for the mobilization of resources. A "correct set of prices" is needed not only for allocational objectives during a given period of time, but even more importantly as proper signals and sufficient incentives for the fuller utilization and mobilization of resources over time. The development economist needs to understand more precisely just what is meant by "getting prices right" in this dynamic context.

The conventional Keynesian type of income theory also leaves the development economist perplexed about the causes of unemployment and what might be effective policies for fuller employment. The investment multiplier of Keynesian economics was first identified as an employment multiplier, and more employment was expected to parallel greater output. But notwithstanding the rise in their investment ratios and growth in GNP, many developing countries have at the same time experienced rising unemployment. The unemployment problem may be related to the inappropriate set of prices and to structural phenomena which have been ignored by income theory. As indicated frequently in this book, the unemployment problem in LDCs is not of the Keynesian variety, and the policy implications of income theory have to be modified for LDCs.

Local economists in the developing countries are also beginning to realize that in many cases they have neglected solutions to immediate and crucial needs by overreaching for sophisticated techniques of analysis and highly formalized long-range planning models. The vogue for long-term plans to the neglect of a more concentrated effort to improve current policymaking has been decried by Sir Alec Cairncross in these words:

For young mandarins who have recently returned from the universities of the West, initiated into the abracadabra of input-out-

---

[1] J. M. Keynes, General Editorial Introduction to Cambridge Economic Handbooks Series.

[2] See, for example, Alfred H. Conrad, "Econometric Models in Development Planning—Pakistan, Argentina, Liberia," in Gustav F. Papanek (ed.), *Development Policy—Theory and Practice*, Cambridge, 1968, Chap. 2.

put analysis, linear programming and other mysteries, the preparation of long-term plans is a very beguiling operation, and one full of intellectual challenge even when the practical outcome may be highly obscure. On the other hand, the short-term management of an economy that is subject to rapid changes in circumstances offers harsher and more restricted choices with little scope for subtlety.[3]

Whether it be due to the operation of an international "demonstration effect" in governmental policymaking or the dominant influence of intellectuals on planning commissions, there has been in many developing countries an overly keen receptivity for the most refined model, the newest technique, the latest element of expertise. It has, however, become increasingly apparent that the use of the latest technique is likely to be premature, and that the attraction to the highest style analysis may be without practical effect.

To overcome this artificiality and remoteness, the economics for development must have more direct relevance to the problems of the less developed countries. This necessitates both modification and extension of traditional Western economic theory. As already emphasized by Seers (II.A.1), we are prone to generalize from the special case of Anglo-Saxon economics. Instead, we must be aware of the different institutional relationships and different behavioral relationships in the LDCs. This does not mean that traditional theory has no value, but simply that it is necessary to modify conventional economic theory to take account of particular circumstances that alter the institutional framework and cause some behavioral relationships to differ in the poorer countries from what they are in more advanced economies.

[3] A. K. Cairncross, *The Short Term and the Long in Economic Planning,* Tenth Anniversary Lecture, Economic Development Institute, Washington, D. C., January 6, 1966, p. 7.

Although it cannot be gainsaid that problems of underdevelopment are different in degree—and, to some extent, even in kind—from those encountered in developed countries, nevertheless it would be overreacting to conclude that entirely different economic tools and principles are needed to analyze these problems. The progress that has been made in development economics has actually been mainly within the framework of traditional economic analysis. Many tools of traditional economics and many principles of accepted economic theory have proved directly applicable to the problems of poor countries, and some conceptions and techniques can become more useful with some ready-made modification or extension.

What has become clear, however, is that we must frequently be prepared to depart from traditional assumptions when analyzing problems of development. We must recognize that the premises of accepted economic theory may have to be altered to make the theory more immediately relevant to countries that have a different social system and economic structure from those to which Western economists are accustomed. The development economist's task is made difficult not because he must start afresh with a completely new set of tools or because he confronts wholly different problems, but because he must acquire a sense of the different assumptions that are appropriate to analyzing a problem within the context of a poor country.[4] In particular, this calls for special care in identifying different institutional relations,[5] in assessing the different

[4] Cf. W. B. Reddaway, "The Economics of Under-Developed Countries," *Economic Journal,* March 1963, pp. 1–2.

[5] At first sight, it might be thought that behavioral relations are also of a different kind. On closer examination, however, the usual postulates of rationality and the principles of maximization or minimization appear to have quite general applicability. For illustrative evidence, see P. T. Bauer and B. S. Yamey, *The Economics of Under-Developed Countries,* London, 1957, pp. 91–101; W. J. Barber, "Economic Rationality and Behavior Pat-

quantitative importance of some variables, and in allowing some elements that are usually taken as "given" to become endogenous variables in development analysis.

When examining the materials of the following chapters, we should therefore be alert to the efforts being made to adapt our conventional way of thinking about economic problems to the particular context of development problems. For some issues, the adaptation is made explicit: the key factors distinguishing the situation in a poor country from that in an advanced economy are recognized, and a new set of assumptions is explicitly adopted—for example, the existence of a subsistence sector, or disguised unemployment, or an unorganized money market may require modification of the usual assumptions of macroanalysis. In other instances, some concepts are introduced out of consideration for the special conditions in poor countries—for instance, "social dualism," the structuralist view of inflation, or noneconomic criteria for investment. Whether they are introduced explicitly or are only implicit, we should be aware that these considerations of the relevance of conventional economic analysis constitute a major theme of this book. This problem of adapting our accepted tools and principles is, in a fundamental sense, an overriding general issue in development economics.

If there has been a tendency to generalize too much from the special case of Anglo-Saxon economics, there has also been a tendency for development economists to overemphasize the case of India. India is a special case of underdevelopment, distinguished from other developing countries: there is acute population pressure on natural resources; there is a low ratio of foreign trade to national income; manufactured goods are exported; there is a real potential for a capital-goods sector oriented toward the domestic market; and the quality of India's administrative and planning machinery is exceptionally high in comparison to that of most of the other LDCs.[6] In fact, no country—certainly not India—can be considered a representative poor country. Although all share the common problem of poverty, the poor countries are heterogeneous in their structural characteristics. Their individual characteristics must be taken into account when strategies of development are proposed. It will certainly not do to generalize from the case of India.

A way to avoid improper generalization would be the comparative analysis of development in the context of some typology of development. For analytical purposes, different countries might be "typed" and compared according to structural conditions or behavioral patterns over time. Countries might be typed, for instance, according to the "stage" they have reached in the sequence of growth. Rostow does this by identifying all societies, in their economic dimensions, as lying within one of five categories: the traditional society, the preconditions for take-off, the take-off, the drive to maturity, and the age of high mass-consumption (II.B.1, II.B.2). Alternatively, countries could be typed by the character of their development process. Thus, Hoselitz suggests a typology encompassing "expansionist versus intrinsic," "dominant versus non-dominant," and "autonomous versus induced" characteristics of the growth process.[7] Or,

[6] Hla Myint, "Economic Theory and the Underdeveloped Countries," *Journal of Political Economy,* October 1965, pp. 488–91.

terns in an Underdeveloped Area: A Case Study of African Economic Behavior in the Rhodesias," *Economic Development and Cultural Change,* April 1960, pp. 237–51; W. O. Jones, "Economic Man in Africa," *Food Research Institute Studies,* May 1960, pp. 107–34.

[7] Bert F. Hoselitz, "Patterns of Economic Growth," *Canadian Journal of Economics and Political Science,* November 1955, pp. 416–31. "Expansionist versus intrinsic" refers to whether the process of growth is capital-widening and involves methods of production that provide extensive employment of labor; "dominant versus non-domi-

following Seers's suggestion,[8] a typology by structure of production is possible: for example, foodstuff-producing (and subdivided into plantation or peasant production units), raw-materials producing (also subdivided into plantation or peasant units), or mineral-producing. Although comparative studies according to some typology may eventually prove instructive, such studies are only now beginning in any full-scale fashion and we cannot include them as a dominant theme in this book. Instead we may find it presently more instructive to emphasize the developmental constraints that are now generally relevant for most of the LDCs.

Even though we shall not use any comprehensive typology, we shall have occasions to be concerned with some different types of developing countries—such as the labor surplus type of economy (Chapter III), the capital-poor type (Chapters V and VI), the human-resource-poor type (Chapter VIII), and the export-oriented type (Chapter XI).

If we choose to concentrate on analyzing the constraints on development, then we must not only modify traditional Western economics but also extend it in the sense of asking some new questions. The major concern of neoclassical economics has been with the short-period analysis of resource alloca-

tion. In this analysis, it is assumed that population, "state of the arts," institutions, and supply of entrepreneurship are all given. But the very essence of the development process is that these parameters become variables. What is normally taken as "given" in static analysis must actually be explained when the problem is one of secular change. Economics must be broadened—indeed, must at times become interrelated with other disciplines—in order to explain the determinants of population growth, technological progress, institutional change, and increase in the supply of entrepreneurship.

If this broader approach is not undertaken, we shall remain ignorant of a large part of the development process. "Investment in man," "human capital," the "economics of manpower"—these new interests are becoming an essential part of the economics for development. Chapter VIII examines the problems of human-resource development. The international transmission of knowledge is also influential in determining the pace and pattern of the recipient country's development. The appropriateness of this transfer will be questioned at various points in our discussion. This chapter has already queried the appropriateness of some of the economics knowledge that is being transmitted internationally. The international transfer of technology will be considered in Chapter VI, and the international transfer of social technology will be examined in Chapter VIII.

At the same time that more consideration is being given to the role of human resources, the economics for development must become broader in scope to include a larger array of factors in the development process. Modern economics has acquired its high degree of rigor at the expense of narrowing the questions it asks. But economic development is necessarily concerned with larger questions, and it must be viewed as a social study that cannot be reduced to a matter of pure technics. Development economists must consider an unusually wide

---

nant (or satellitic)" refers to the degree of dependence upon one or more foreign countries in the course of development ("dominant" means autarky in trade and no capital borrowings); "autonomous versus induced" relates to the role of active government participation in the development process.

A penetrating discussion of the usability of "contrary pairs" as types of industrial development is presented by Alexander Gerschenkron, "Typology of Industrial Development as a Tool of Analysis," in *Continuity in History and Other Essays*, Cambridge, 1968, pp. 77–97.

[8] Dudley Seers, "An Approach to the Short-Period Analysis of Primary-Producing Economies," *Oxford Economic Papers*, February 1959, pp. 1–36.

range of factors, even if some of the relevant factors do not lend themselves to quantification or to the precise analysis that characterizes other branches of economics.

Some of the most critical factors might be recognized from a study of economic history. A discussion of the relevance of historical experience follows.

II.B. PERSPECTIVE OF HISTORY

II.B.1. Rostow and Marx—Note

It has always been tempting to search for regularities in history, and many writers have adopted a uni-directional view of development in terms of some pattern of stages. As summarized by Professor Kuznets, "a stage theory of long-term economic change implies: (1) distinct time segments, characterized by different sources and patterns of economic change; (2) a specific succession of these segments, so that *b* cannot occur before *a*, or *c* before *b*; and (3) a common matrix, in that the successive segments are stages in one broad process—usually one of development and growth rather than of devolution and shrinkage. Stage theory is most closely associated with a uni-directional rather than cyclic view of history. In the cyclic view the stages are recurrent; in a uni-directional view, a stage materializes, runs its course, and never recurs. Even in the process of devolution and decline, the return to a level experienced previously is not viewed as a recurrence of the earlier stage."[1]

The central question raised by Kuznets is: How can such a simple design be a summary description or analytic classification of a vast and diverse field of historical change sufficiently plausible to warrant the formulation and persistence of many variants?

At one extreme, Adam Smith referred to the sequence of hunting, pastoral, agricultural, commercial, and manufacturing stages. At the other, Karl Marx related Hegel's thesis, antithesis, and synthesis to the Marxian stages of feudalism, capitalism, and socialism. Most recently, Professor Walt Ros-

tow attempted to generalize "the sweep of modern economic history" in a set of stages of growth, designated as follows: the traditional society; the preconditions for take-off; the take-off; the drive to maturity; the age of high mass-consumption.[2]

The "take-off" is meant to be the central notion in Rostow's schema, and it has received the most critical attention. The take-off is interpreted as "a decisive transition in a society's history"—a period "when the scale of productive economic activity reaches a critical level and produces changes which lead to a massive and progressive structural transformation in economies and the societies of which they are a part, better viewed as changes in kind than merely in degree." The take-off is defined "as requiring all three of the following related conditions":

(1) a rise in the rate of productive investment from, say, 5% or less to over 10% of national income (or net national product);

(2) the development of one or more substantial manufacturing sectors, with a high rate of growth;

(3) the existence or quick emergence of a political, social and institutional framework which exploits the impulses to expansion in the modern sector and the potential external economy effects of the take-off and gives to growth an on-going character.[3]

[1] Simon Kuznets, "Notes on Stage of Economic Growth as a System Determinant," in Alexander Eckstein (ed.), *Comparison of Economic Systems,* Berkeley, 1971, p. 243.

[2] W. W. Rostow, "The Stages of Economic Growth," *Economic History Review,* August 1959; *The Stages of Economic Growth,* Cambridge, 1960; *The Economics of Take-Off Into Sustained Growth,* London, 1963.

[3] Rostow, *The Stages of Economic Growth,* pp. 36–40.

Of the earlier proponents of stages, only Marx commands Rostow's explicit attention. Indeed, Rostow presents his analysis as an alternative to Marx's theory of modern history. Describing his system as "A Non-Communist Manifesto," Rostow poses his five stages of growth against Marx's stages of feudalism, bourgeois capitalism, socialism, and communism.

We can recognize some broad similarities between Rostow's analysis and Marx's sequence. Both are audacious attempts to interpret the evolution of whole societies, primarily from an economic perspective; both are "explorations of the problems and consequences for whole societies of building compound interest into their habits and institutions";[4] and both recognize that economic change has social, political, and cultural consequences.

From other viewpoints, however, there are fundamental differences. The basic Marxian problems of class conflicts, exploitation, and inherent stresses within the capitalist process find no place in Rostow's analysis. Nor does Rostow reduce the complexities of man to a single economic dimension. Rostow recognizes that, in terms of human motivation, many of the most profound economic changes must be viewed as the consequence of noneconomic human motives and aspirations. Instead of limiting human behavior to simply an act of maximization, Rostow interprets net human behavior "as an act of balancing alternative and often conflicting human objectives in the face of the range of choices men perceive to be open to them."[5] Rostow allows for the different facets of human beings, and interprets the total performance of societies as an act of balance in the patterns of choice made by individuals within the framework permitted by the changing setting of society. Rostow insists that although his "stages-of-growth are an economic way of looking at whole societies, they in no sense imply that the

worlds of politics, social organization, and of culture are a mere superstructure built upon and derived uniquely from the economy."[6] On the contrary, what most concerns Rostow is how societies go about making their choices and balances: "the central phenomenon of the world of post-traditional societies is not the economy—and whether it is capitalist or not—it is the total procedure by which choices are made."[7] Marx's assumption that a society's decisions are merely a function of who owns property is therefore rejected as inaccurate; instead it is maintained that "one must look directly at the full mechanism of choice among alternative policies, including the political process—and indeed, the social and religious processes—as independent arenas for making decisions and choices."[8]

The implications of this broader view of human motivation become especially significant when Rostow's interpretation of post-traditional societies is contrasted with Marx's account of the post-feudal phase. Thus, Rostow concludes that his account of the break-up of traditional societies is

based on the convergence of motives of private profit in the modern sectors with a new sense of affronted nationhood. And other forces play their part as well, for example the simple perception that children need not die so young or live their lives in illiteracy: a sense of enlarged human horizons, independent of both profit and national dignity. And when independence or modern nationhood are at last attained, there is no simple, automatic switch to a dominance of the profit motive and economic and social progress. On the contrary there is a searching choice and problem of balance among the three directions policy might go: external assertion; the further concentration of power in the centre as opposed to the regions; and economic growth.[9]

[4] Ibid., p. 148.
[5] Ibid., p. 149.

[6] Ibid., p. 2.
[7] Ibid., p. 150.
[8] Ibid.
[9] Ibid., p. 152.

This approach may have more immediate relevance for the problems now confronting many underdeveloped countries than Marx's narrower view that political behavior is dependent on economic advantage, and that the decisions of capitalist societies are made simply in terms of the free-market mechanism and private advantage.

Moreover, as Rostow observes, the Marxian sequence suffers by basing its categories on only one historical case: the case of the British take-off and drive to maturity. Rostow reminds us that Marx had presented his whole system before any other society except Britain had experienced the take-off, and instead of revising his categories so as to be more applicable to other cases, Marx merely generalized and projected his interpretation of the British case. A concentration on the British case, however, misses the variety of experience in the evolution of different societies, and makes the Marxian analysis of the "march of history" unduly rigid and artificial. If for no other reason than that it draws upon a far wider range of historical knowledge, and is thereby more comprehensive and less doctrinaire, Rostow's analysis can claim to be a superior alternative to the Marxian sequence.

Nonetheless, if Rostow's thesis is to assert with a high degree of generality that it is able to trace a structure of history in the form of a sequence of stages, then it must also answer a number of criticisms that have commonly been levied against stage-theorists. ("Stage-making" approaches are misleading when they succumb to a linear conception of history and imply that all economies tend to pass through the same series of stages. Although a particular sequence may correspond broadly to the historical experience of some economies, no single sequence fits the history of all countries. To maintain that every economy always follows the same course of development with a common past and the same future is to overschematize the complex forces of development, and to give the sequence of stages a generality that is unwar-ranted. A country may attain a later stage of development without first having passed through an earlier stage, as stages may be skipped, and different types of economies do not have to succeed or evolve from one another. The sequence is also blurred inasmuch as frequently the stages are not mutually exclusive, and characteristics of earlier stages often become mixed with characteristics of later stages. Anyone who attempts to impose upon economic history a one-way course of economic evolution is bound to be challenged, since it is difficult to accept one unique schema as the only real framework in which the facts truly lie; the same facts can be arranged in many patterns and seen from many perspectives.[10] What matters, therefore, is how suggestive and useful Rostow's pattern is in providing answers to our questions as we attempt to make sense out of the past and make the future more predictable. This comes down to the question of the adequacy of Rostow's pattern in helping us isolate the strategic factors which make for change, especially those factors that constitute the necessary and sufficient conditions for determining the transition of an economy from a preceding stage to a succeeding stage.

In this respect, Rostow's efforts are more substantial than those by other proponents of stages. Recognizing how important the search for strategic factors is, Rostow adopts an approach that is more analytical and related to a wider range of issues than any of the approaches of his predecessors. His argument abounds with terms such as "forces," "process," "net result," "inner logic"—all indicative of his desire to present an analytical, not merely a descriptive, set of stages. According to Rostow, the "analytic backbone" of his argument is "rooted in a dynamic theory of production," and he believes that his set of stages reveals a "succes-

[10] Although Rostow gives little attention to the problem, his analysis raises many questions related to basic social theory. In this connection, it is illuminating to consult Isaiah Berlin, *Historical Inevitability*, London, 1954, especially sections 2, 8.

sion of strategic choices" that confront a country as it moves forward through the development process. On this basis, perhaps the most illumination can be gained from Rostow's analysis by interpreting each stage as posing a particular type of problem, so that the sequence of stages is equivalent to a series of problems that confront a country in the course of its development. Rostow's ulti-

mate objective, however, has been to present through his set of stages a theory about economic growth and a means of uncovering both the uniformities and the uniqueness of each nation's experience. To be in a better position to judge how successful Rostow has actually been in fulfilling these claims, we should now consider the following appraisal of his analysis.

II.B.2. Empty Economic Stages?*

Professor Rostow's bold generalisations ordering the process of economic growth are no less controversial now than they were in 1960 and of no less interest. Scholars and planners continue to wrestle with the same basic problem of economic development, but in a context considerably influenced by Rostow's writings. The appearance of this volume affords us all a valuable opportunity to re-examine and rethink the issues that have evolved in the debate of almost a decade upon the concept of take-off.[1]

THE TWO THEORIES OF TAKE-OFF

Despite frequent clarifications and restatements by Rostow of the concept of take-off in the course of his two essays and liberal participation in the discussion, its underlying duality is not resolved. The implicit recognition that there are indeed two theories of take-off is perhaps one of the

most fruitful contributions made by the Conference. At one level the take-off is a sectoral, non-linear, threshold notion. This is the realm of the leading sector, with its forward, backward and spreading effects breathing regular innovation into the heretofore slumbering *corpus economicum*. It is the domain of certain crucial industries, such as those of coal, iron and engineering. Economic growth is viewed as a constant struggle among a succession of activities first accelerating and decelerating.

The other level is highly aggregative. Here the setting is that of the familiar Harrod-Domar model in which the rate of growth of income is the product of an average propensity to save and the inverse of a reasonably stable capital-output ratio. Take-off then consists of a recognisable discontinuity in the observed growth of income *per capita*, which under these conditions means a sharp increase in the savings rate:

*From Albert Fishlow, "Empty Economic Stages?" *Economic Journal*, Vol. 75, No. 297, March 1965, pp. 112–16, 120–25. Reprinted by permission.
[1] A review of W. W. Rostow, ed., *The Economics of Take-off into Sustained Growth*, Proceedings of a Conference held by the International Economic Association (London: Macmillan & Co. Ltd., 1963).

It is . . . useful to regard as a necessary but not sufficient condition for the take-off the fact that the proportion of net investment to national income (or net national product) rises from, say, 5% to over 10%, definitely outstripping the likely population pressure (since under the assumed take-off circumstances the capital output ratio is low) and yielding a *distinct* rise in real output per capita.[2]

The theories, of course, are not mutually exclusive. But neither are they ever integrated into a single framework. The discussion of interindustrial relationships takes for granted the availability of resources and emphasises instead the power of the demand nexus in stimulating growth among complementary activities. Its purpose is the exposition of a mechanism for transmitting autonomous impulses affecting one sector to the economy as a whole. Not only output but also technology is involved. The final objective is a description of how the industrial matrix—its quantities *and* coefficients—undergoes a decisive and discontinuous transformation. The aggregate model takes as its starting-point, on the other hand, the constraint of savings, and hence investment, without which growth cannot attain regularity at high rates. Within an environment where the inducement to invest is the limiting factor, rather than savings, the sectoral approach seems much the more fruitful. The propensity to save is dependent not so much upon consumer decisions as those by entrepreneurs, and the elasticity of resources and automaticity of technological advance is high. Some underdeveloped countries may indeed fit such a mould; Professor Hirschman's writings stress this theme, and in this volume Professor Leibenstein also argues that such a shift in emphasis to investment rather than concentration upon savings is desirable.

Yet Rostow fails to elaborate the conditions under which one approach rather than the other yields a more cogent explanation of how growth took root, or how the two are related. This explains why Professor Solow is troubled by the absence of any coherent theory and why Rostow's reply to him is unsatisfactory. By shifting between

[2] W. W. Rostow, *The Stages of Economic Growth* (Cambridge, 1960), p. 37.

them in almost random fashion Rostow does the concept of take-off little service. And by not introducing resource constraints and a more adequate discussion of technological diffusion into his sectoral theory he deprives it of a clarity and consistency that the aggregate model does enjoy. Furthermore, the data required to establish the acceleration in income *per capita* and savings proportions are easier to come by than the detailed analyses of individual countries, and Rostow confines himself with infrequent exception to such evidence. Thus, while he frequently protests the neglect of his sectoral approach, the blame resides not only on his critics.

THE USEFULNESS OF THE AGGREGATE APPROACH

The result, then, is that it is the aggregate notion of take-off that has become most bruited about. How well does it perform? Not very, I believe. Despite its elegant simplicity, the conception of growth as a resultant of the savings rate and the aggregate capital-output is singularly inappropriate for a society in transformation. Even if formally correct, it obscures and misleads concerning the fundamental forces at work. The national capital-output ratio lacks behavioural content. Its constancy subsumes complementary changes in other inputs, such as labour and entrepreneurial skills, not to mention technological progress. It excludes the important category of human capital. Its stability is consistent with wide-ranging shifts in industrial composition and investments in which we precisely are interested. And as pointed out above, the savings propensity itself can hardly be regarded as subject to autonomous change. Were the question merely one of history, the observed regularity of the ratio might suffice and causality be regarded more lightly. In a world where take-off has become a goal, and policies are at issue, there can be no such facile resolution, particularly when some of the careful qualifications stated by Rostow are lost in the midst of a widening audience. Professor Cairncross' essay speaks cogently and quite usefully to these matters in more detail, and it is unnecessary to elaborate further here.

Thus, at best the regularity hypothesised by Rostow—the sharp increase in the savings rate and accelerated growth of *per capita* income within the span of a generation—provides us with entrée to the problems of transition rather than its solution. Unfortunately, however, the hard facts of developmental experience cast considerable doubt upon such a convenient and universal order. Drawing upon data for Japan, Sweden, Germany, Britain, Canada and the United States, Professor Kuznets forcefully denies that such discontinuity is common to all. Rather he sketches a picture of economies initially blessed with respectable savings proportions and growth rates, and experiencing gradual increases in both well beyond what have been denoted as the take-off decades. Sometimes, in his zeal, his conclusions overreach his own evidence. For Germany and Japan the available series begin during the supposed take-off; hence the relevant comparison with the earlier magnitudes is excluded. Similarly, for Britain the discontinuity in the annual rate of change of aggregate product understates the break in the *per capita* series after 1785. Moreover, even such a rise in the growth rate of total output as from 0.9% prior to 1770 and 1.5% from 1770 to 1880 should not be dismissed too lightly. Finally, more recently compiled data for countries such as Italy and Denmark appear to fit the original Rostow specification very well indeed.[3]

These amendments to Kuznets' findings are not to argue for the validity of the Rostow conjecture. Still other countries, like Norway, do not conform at all, and recently compiled United States evidence stands in even greater contradiction than that available to Kuznets in 1960. The increase in the share of output devoted to domestic capital formation from the 1830s on appears to be substantially more modest than that observed in other economies: the gross rate starts at 15% in 1834–43, changes little during the *ante bellum* period and increases (in part due to relative price changes) to about 25% in the postwar decades.[4] There is obviously a variety of national experiences to be reckoned with. Some economies may have executed the requisite *saltus* in aggregate terms, while others pursued a more gradual course. (Appropriately enough, Kenneth Berrill finds the same diversity in the dependence upon foreign capital in the course of development.) Since both groups attained the same conversion to economic growth rooted in a modern technology, the Rostow hypothesis must be adjudged of limited merit.

Note also the additional and unfortunate rigidity imposed by enmeshing the take-off within a full-blown stage theory of economic evolution. Like most nineteenth-century conceptions of progress, the path is orderly and monotonic: societies move through each of the stages in succession. But unfortunately excluded by such a hierarchy are many of the most interesting cases—economies that entered well into the transition phase but did not succeed. Some of the nations of Latin America seem to have been so beset. At the end of the nineteenth and beginning of the twentieth century, the pace of development quickened in that part of the world as it did in Russia and Italy, among others. In Mexico, between 1895 and 1910, one set of *per capita* income estimates places growth at 1.6% annually, or faster than Britain and possibly even Russia during their take-offs. Nor was it simply exploita-

[3] Reported in Simon Kuznets, "Long Term Trends in Capital Formation Proportions," *Economic Development and Cultural Change*, Vol. IX, No. 4, Part II (1961).

[4] These are the estimates of Robert E. Gallman and will appear in his "Gross National Product in the United States, 1834–1909," to appear in Vol. 29 of *Studies in Income and Wealth*.

tion of mineral resources: manufacturing expanded at the salutary rate of 5% per year as well. Again, in Argentina the net national capital formation proportion averaged some 20% in the years 1900–15, with annual growth of product of almost 3%. Much social overhead capital had been accumulated, and in Argentina, at least, much human capital as well.[5] Many of these same features are common to Chile. Yet retrospectively, the anticipated prize of sustained growth did not materialise. Must we then agree that take-off did not occur since "the subsequent periods of stagnation or relapse . . . are clear" (p. 27)? Why not take-off, followed by structural difficulties that left such economies modernised only in certain, but not all, respects?

The unnecessarily narrow Rostow view is imposed by the logic of a stage theory without an endogenous propulsive force. Take-off accordingly must be defined not in terms of the extent and nature of the inner transformation, but the later accomplishment of continuing flight. For only then, precisely by reference to the self-sustained character of subsequent growth, can we be certain take-off has occurred. In turn, the pre-conditions have been satisfied, since they are specified only as those permitting take-off to occur. The minimum social overhead capital, the rise of a large enough entrepreneurial class, the prior sufficient growth in agricultural productivity, are all ratified. The other, and necessary, way of articulating the three central stages of the global theory is to specify the conditions for moving from one to the other independently of later events; this in turn means a complete theory of social change, including non-economic factors. Rostow, despite even more than customary obeisance to the latter, never successfully integrates them into his analysis, precisely for the reason that the linkage he

[5] For Mexico, see *México, Cincuenta Años de Revolución* (México City, 1960), Vol. I, p. 585; for the Argentine data, see Kuznets, "Long Term Trends in Capital Formation Proportions."

imposes runs in the opposite temporal direction.

The consequence is a non-operational concept. To talk knowingly of countries in the world to-day as in the pre-conditions phase or the midst of take-off is sheer guesswork, unrelated to the theory itself. This is why it is possible (so far) to be right with the assessment of Mexico but wrong with Argentina. In neither instances are objective criteria invoked. The consequence of this counter-temporal linkage is to rob the take-off phase at the same time of its attractiveness as a decisive period—possibly one of many—in the growth of a society and to reduce it to a mechanical construct whose identification within a specific set of years is more to be worried about than an elaboration of its content. . . .

THE SECTORAL VARIANT OF TAKE-OFF

The aggregate approach to take-off has not fared well. It is unable to deliver the universal, endogenous theory of development it promises. But such deserved criticism should not obscure the many insights take-off has to offer at the sectoral level. There its great strength is an explicitly partial orientation emphasising process, and so subject to empirical test. Rostow's various views may be summarized by the following interrelated propositions:

1. Successful industrialisation is unbalanced in the sense that a single, or limited number of industries, is the source from which an initial acceleration ramifies through the economy. There is a consequent discontinuity in production of manufactures.

2. Such leading sectors have three paths of influence upon the economy: forward, lateral and backward linkages, of which the latter route has historically predominated.

3. Certain industries have played the rôle of leading sector in a number of different countries, notably the railroad.

4. The development of certain subsidiary activities—coal, iron and machinery—is a good index of the extent of industrialisation and the probability of its continuation.

5. Industrial, rather than agricultural, growth affords the initial basis for sustained development.

Now, to be sure, these propositions are by no means proven. Indeed, one can set out many concrete instances in which the Rostow examples purporting to establish one or more of the points is grossly in error. Not the least of these deal with the supposed importance of the railroad in triggering take-off. In the United States, for example, the role played by the railroad before 1860 in developing for the first time a machinery industry is clearly mis-stated. The reason locomotives and other equipment were produced domestically so soon after the introduction of the railway was that machinery firms were already in existence to serve the textile and steamboat interest. Virtually all the locomotive firms grew out of such origins. Nor did their specialised production dominate the industry anything like the mistaken horse-power estimates Rostow cites. Where the unique significance of the railway resides with respect to engineering inputs is in its substantial maintenance requirements. Widely dispersed repair shops training pools of local talent undoubtedly were a significant factor in technological diffusion.

What is more, the entire emphasis upon the industrial consequences following from the backward linkage of railroadisation as being crucial in the United States misses the point. At the time when pig-iron output first underwent apparent rapid increase in the 1840s iron rail demand was an insignificant proportion of the whole. Coal, too, was a minor need for railroad operations in an era of wood-burning engines. Rather what made the rapid projection of the railroad in the 1850s so consequential was the impetus it gave to agricultural expansion. In this and other instances Rostow tends to understate the role of the market, actual and antici-

pated, in favour of derived demand nexuses. While the latter may to-day be more potent, we should not re-write history in its image. Modernisation may proceed impelled by relative prices as well as by government, and by way of forward linkages as well as backward.

It also follows that yet another proposition closer study may amend and qualify is the extent to which commercial agriculture may serve as a leading sector. Professor Bulhões treats the case of the state of São Paulo in Brazil, where he outlines a sequence leading from expanding coffee production to social overhead investment to industrial diversification. The evolutionary process in this instance contradicts both the Rostow and Gerschenkron emphasis. For new countries, drawing extensively upon immigration and capital imports, and with large land resources, this may be the natural pattern. One may cite the United States, Canada, Australia and New Zealand. Where such a process is arrested, as in Brazil and Argentina, it may cause sustained growth to be much more difficult to achieve than might otherwise be the case. Ungrasped opportunities may exact a continuing toll as a disadvantage of forwardness.

On the other hand, Professor Boserup's comprehensive essay defends what has almost come to be the conventional view that industrialisation proceeds despite agriculture rather than as a consequence of a progressive primary sector. "In the normal course of events, new things do not originate in the agricultural milieu" (p. 205). At best, rising agricultural productivity serves as a precondition for take-off, and some type of institutional reform is required to raise supply elasticities. Within the European and South Asian context of sedentary agriculture, one can find little fault with these conclusions; the principal caveat is the applicability of the results to more recently settled lands.

These limitations are of no matter. Much more detailed research is required before the central tenets of the hypothesis can be fairly evaluated and suitably qualified. That the sectoral variant of take-off both permits and structures such research is testimony to its usefulness. Indeed, Rostow himself in this volume has restated the mechanism in such a way as to further its application. By making more explicit the type of linkages by which leading sectors transmit their impulses he considerably improves upon the earlier version, which tended to stress the observed rate of growth of the leading sector as a measure of significance. The legitimate criticisms of Kuznets, that leadership represents a combination of internal growth, weight within the industrial matrix and the magnitude of other effects, thus are fully met. . . .

With the forward, backward and lateral linkages spelled out in this fashion, Rostow's leading sectors now become virtually the historical analogue of Hirschman's strategy for contemporary unbalanced growth. Certain activities have capacity for greater influence than others because they have more dispersed, or larger, demands upon manufactures as a whole, or some critical subset; other sectors pass along their output not to consumers directly but to other industries for further processing, and so present a potential force from the side of supply; finally, some industries, by virtue of location, or training of a skilled labour force, or demonstration effects, operate beyond inter-industrial relationships. Leading sectors presumably possess some critical combination of all three, the first two of which, at least, are subject to well-defined empirical investigation.

There is much to be done to extract the potential gains of this approach. Forward linkages, which are more behavioural in their inducements than the technically determined backward linkages, are yet to be suitably defined. Various proposed measures within the input-output framework, such as the proportion of sales to industrial purchasers versus final demand or more detailed summaries of the inverse matrix of tech-

nological coefficients to rank the absorptive consequences of an initial expansion in output, do not fully render the market dimensions of this supply influence.[6] The extent to which backward linkages have been emphasised may reflect the better analytical basis for measuring derived demands as much as their differential importance.

Nor can we ignore the very real data limitations. Complete, disaggregated industrial matrices are not now available, and perhaps never can be, far distant into the past. None the less, in most actual instances relatively few, but significant, interactions are involved. However crude the first historical applications of the leading sector concept inevitably turn out to be, they promise to add a considerable sophistication to our studies of past industrialisations, successes and failures. The input-output apparatus so mobilised distinguishes clearly between the magnitude of direct and indirect effects, and settles the recurrent question raised at this Conference and elsewhere of whether rates of growth or absolute increments are the relevant criteria of the importance of a single industry by placing its contribution in an appropriate multi-sector context.

This comparative-statical framework, however enlightening, does not exhaust the content of initial industrialisation. But neither does it fully render the concept of take-off. Rostow's category of lateral linkages is an attempt to introduce further elements of change into the picture. That such a grouping is too broad and nebulous to serve the needs of empirical research is not to deny his recognition of the problem. In preference to that procedure, it would seem better to retain the input-output context and to interpret the entire array of technical

[6] Albert Hirschman, *The Strategy of Economic Development* (New Haven, 1958), pp. 106–7, uses the sales ratio measure. P. N. Rasmussen, *Studies in Inter-Sectoral Relations* (Copenhagen, 1956), develops an index of sensitivity of dispersion that "expresses the extent to which the system of industries draws upon industry no. i" (p. 135).

coefficients not as constants but as variables themselves subject to change as a function of changes in output of certain industries or specific coefficients.[7] Not only do we thereby faithfully translate the Rostow emphasis upon productivity change as one of the fundamental influences upon modern growth but we retain the applicability of many of the initial Rostow propositions. Take-off becomes a sectoral joint theory of output change *and* technological diffusion.

So interpreted, the leading sector becomes not only the agent of triggering quantity response in other industries but also of disseminating modern techniques. It therefore is likely to be a new industry itself using advanced technology, a description consistent with the broad contours of historical industrialisations. Corresponding to the discontinuity in industrial production is a threshold level of acceptance of novel methods. Here is where the thrust of non-economic influences should be directed: which social circumstances are barriers and aids to technological change. Once the level of resistance has been overcome, diffusion is assumed to be regular and continual. Industrial growth typically, then, will continue at high levels for backward economies as they absorb better production techniques.

Such a prominent place for technology in the schema reinforces the logical basis for many of the earlier Rostow conjectures concerning the pattern of industrialisation. The physical presence of an industry like machinery—in contrast to dependence upon imports—is indeed a good guide to successful industrialisation. It creates a national vested interest committed to technological progress and obsolescence while at the same time reducing uncertainty by assuring close con-tact between supplier and user of the new techniques. Where maintenance needs are apt to be crucial, proximity is no small comfort. Needless to say, the portrait of an industrial matrix expanding by initial augmentation of sectors utilising modern technology gives greater weight to the preference for manufactures over agriculture as a vehicle of growth.

Whether these statements suffice or other propositions relating to technological diffusion are substituted, the important point is that productivity increase is afforded an explicit and central position in the hypothesis. This is a great advance beyond the simple capital-accumulation models still current—and underlying the aggregate version of take-off itself. Much must be done to implement the approach, both analytically and empirically. Historical initial conditions must be allowed to influence the propositions, thereby softening the claims of universality.[8]

The take-off phase itself must be integrated into later, sustained growth. Are long savings a miniature replay of the initial discontinuity postulated, as Rostow sometimes seems to suggest? How are the initial resource constraints imposed by inadequate capital formation resolved over time in response to industrialisation? How do increases in agricultural productivity become regular, not as a pre-requisite of the industrial surge, but as a resultant? Without a respectable rate of growth of agricultural product, rapid national income advance is almost impossible. Finally, much systematic historical research lies ahead. We do not even know at the present what the rôle of productivity change was, or is, in the contemporary world in the first stages of industrialisation!

---

[7] It is useful in this context to note the identity between a geometric index of productivity change and that obtained from the changing matrix of technical input-output coefficients. See Evsey D. Domar, "On the Measurement of Technological Change," *Economic Journal*, Vol. LXXI (1961), pp. 709–29.

[8] Recent Latin American experience where rapid increase in the manufacturing sector has not led to continuing growth is an obvious case in point. For Chile, see Marto A. Ballesteros and Tom E. Davis, "The Growth of Output and Employment in Basic Sectors of the Chilean Economy, 1908–1957," *Economic Development and Cultural Change*, Vol. XI, no. 2 (1962), 153.

The sectoral variant of take-off thus can serve as the basis for important and relevant research into many still unresolved problems of economic growth.[9] While economic theorists wrestle with the implications of embodied and disembodied technical progress, and empirical workers extend the frontiers of measurement of productivity, it is only appropriate that historians bring to bear accumulated experience upon technological diffusion and its contribution to successful industrialisation.

CONCLUDING COMMENT

The appearance of *The Economics of Take-off* marks a turning-point in a debate that has now been carried on for almost a decade. Here for the first time is a systematic confrontation of the take-off hypothesis with a considerable segment of historical experience. The aggregate version of the concept emerges qualified at best: Rostow's readiness to accept any number of amendments is testimony less to the flexibility of the notion than to its failure to fit well the actual diverse paths of development. The test of the hypothesis afforded by

[9] For one related attempt see Hollis B. Chenery, Shuntaro Shishido, and Tsunehiko Watanabe, "The Pattern of Japanese Growth, 1914–1954," *Econometrica*, Vol. XXX, no. 1 (1962), 114–118 especially. Although they fail to carry the analysis of technological change very far, their results illustrate the potential returns from sectoral analysis.

the recent quantitative research upon historical patterns of growth constitutes the principal contribution of the volume. The papers and discussion based less factually have a correspondingly lesser impact, in no small measure because their relationship to the take-off is more tenuous. Yet despite this progress the Conference achieved in its examination of the discontinuity of modern economic growth, important questions remain. It is for this reason that I have tried to suggest a new focal point for the discussion by differentiating between the aggregate and sectoral approaches to take-off, and to the role technological change plays in the last. Where there is little reason to accept the complete explanation of national income growth Rostow offers, there is good cause to pursue his many suggestions concerning the process by which industrialisation becomes rooted. Rostow, paradoxically, is at his best read as a prospectus rather than as a treatise.

The loss of grandeur in the descent from manifesto to partial hypothesis must not be exaggerated. It is a rare occasion when operational, albeit partial, theories pregnant with potential are put forward. The conception of take-off is just such an event. Professor Clapham, some forty years ago, chided his theoretical colleagues for providing him with empty boxes. Better that historians to-day recognise the important possibilities of take-off in structuring inquiry than to continue to expound (or to reject out of hand) a grand set of stages that lamentably are sometimes vacant.

II.B.3. Economic Backwardness in

Historical Perspective*

The map of Europe in the nineteenth century showed a motley picture of countries varying with regard to the degree of their economic backwardness. At the same time, processes of rapid industrialization started in several of those countries from very different levels of economic backwardness. Those differences in points—or planes—of departure were of crucial significance for the nature of the subsequent development. Depending on a given country's degree of economic backwardness on the eve of its industrialization, the course and character of the latter tended to vary in a number of important respects. Those variations can be readily compressed into the shorthand of six propositions.

1. The more backward a country's economy, the more likely was its industrialization to start discontinuously as a sudden great spurt proceeding at a relatively high rate of growth of manufacturing output.[1]

2. The more backward a country's economy, the more pronounced was the stress in its industrialization on bigness of both plant and enterprise.

3. The more backward a country's economy, the greater was the stress upon producers' goods as against consumers' goods.

4. The more backward a country's economy, the heavier was the pressure upon the levels of consumption of the population.

5. The more backward a country's economy, the greater was the part played by special institutional factors designed to increase supply of capital to the nascent industries and, in addition, to provide them with less decentralized and better informed entrepreneurial guidance; the more backward the country, the more pronounced was the coerciveness and comprehensiveness of those factors.

6. The more backward a country, the less likely was its agriculture to play any active role by offering to the growing industries the advantages of an expanding industrial market based in turn on the rising productivity of agricultural labor.

...the differences in the level of economic advance among the individual European countries or groups of countries in the last century were sufficiently large to make it possible to array those countries, or group of countries, along a scale of increasing degrees of backwardness and thus to render the latter an operationally usable concept. Cutting two notches into that scale yields three groups of countries which may be roughly described as advanced, moderately backward, and very backward. To the extent that certain of the variations in our six propositions can also be conceived as discrete rather than continuous, the pattern assumes the form of a series of stage constructs. Understandably enough, this result obtains most

---

*From Alexander Gerschenkron, *Economic Backwardness in Historical Perspective*, Cambridge, Mass.: Harvard University Press, copyright, 1962, by The President and Fellows of Harvard College, pp. 353–9. Reprinted by permission.

[1] The "great spurt" is closely related to W. W. Rostow's "take-off" (*The Stages of Economic Growth*, Cambridge University Press, 1960, Chap. 4). Both concepts stress the element of specific discontinuity in economic development; great spurts, however, are confined to the area of manufacturing and mining, whereas take-offs refer to national output. Unfortunately, in the present state of our statistical information on long-term growth of national income, there is hardly any way of establishing, let alone testing, the take-off hypotheses.

naturally with regard to factors referred to in proposition 5, where quantitative differences are associated with qualitative, that is, institutional, variations. . . .

Such an attempt to view the course of industrialization as a schematic stagelike process differs essentially from the various efforts in "stage making," the common feature of which was the assumption that all economies were supposed regularly to pass through the same individual stages as they moved along the road of economic progress. The regularity may have been frankly presented as an inescapable "law" of economic development.[2] Alternatively, the element of necessity may have been somewhat disguised by well-meant, even though fairly meaningless, remarks about the choices that were open to society.[3] But all those schemes were dominated by the idea of uniformity. Thus, Rostow was at pains to assert that the process of industrialization repeated itself from country to country lumbering through his pentametric rhythm. . . .

The point, however, is not simply that these were important occurrences which have just claims on the historian's attention. What matters in the present connection is that observing the individual methods of financing industrial growth helps us to understand the crucial problem of prerequisites for industrial development.

The common opinion on the subject has been well stated by Rostow. There is said to be a number of certain general preconditions or prerequisites for industrial growth, without which it could not begin. Abolition of an archaic framework in agricultural organization or an increase in the productivity of agriculture; creation of an influential modern elite which is materially or ideally interested in economic change; provision of

what is called social-overhead capital in physical form—all these are viewed as "necessary preconditions," except that some reference to the multifarious forms in which the prerequisites are fulfilled in the individual areas are designed to take care of the "unique" factors in development. Similarly, the existence of a value system favoring economic progress and the availability of effective entrepreneurial groups basking in the sun of social approval have been regarded as essential preconditions of industrial growth.

These positions are part and parcel of an undifferentiated approach to industrial history. But their conceptual and empirical deficiencies are very considerable, even though it is by no means easy to bid farewell to this highly simplified way of viewing the processes of industrialization. It took the present writer several years before he succeeded in reformulating the concept of prerequisites so that it could be fit into the general approach premised upon the notion of relative backwardness. . . .

There should be a fine on the use of words such as "necessary" or "necessity" in historical writings. As one takes a closer look at the concept of necessity as it is appended to prerequisites of industrial development, it becomes clear that, whenever the concept is not entirely destitute of meaning, it is likely to be purely definitional: industrialization is defined in terms of certain conditions which then, by an imperceptible shift of the writer's wrist, are metamorphosed into historical preconditions.[4]

The recourse of tautologies and dexterous manipulations has been produced by, or at any rate served to disguise, very real empirical difficulties. After having satisfied oneself that in England certain factors could be reasonably regarded as having preconditioned the industrialization of the country, the tendency was, and still is, to elevate them to the

---

[2] See, for example, Bruno Hildebrand, *Die Nationalökonomie, der Gegenwart und Zukunft und andere gesammelte Schriften*, 1, Jena, 1922, p. 357.

[3] See Rostow, *The Stages of Economic Growth*, pp. 118f.

[4] It is not surprising, therefore, to see Rostow at one point (p. 49) mix conditions and preconditions of industrial development very freely.

rank of ubiquitous prerequisites of all European industrializations. Unfortunately, the attempt was inconsistent with two empirical observations: (1) some of the factors that had served as prerequisites in England either were not present in less advanced countries or at best were present to a very small extent; (2) the big spurt of industrial development occurred in those countries despite the lack of such prerequisites.

If these observations are not ignored or shrugged away, as is usually done, they quite naturally direct research toward a new question: in what way and through the use of what devices did backward countries *substitute* for the missing prerequisites? . . . It appears, on the one hand, that some of the alleged prerequisites were not needed in industrializations proceeding under different conditions. On the other hand, once the question has been asked, whole series of various substitutions become visible which could be readily organized in a meaningful pattern according to the degree of economic backwardness. . . . [I] t is easy to conceive of the capital supplied to the early factories in an advanced country as stemming from previously accumulated wealth or from gradually plowed-back profits; at the same time, actions by banks and governments in less advanced countries are regarded as successful attempts to create *in the course* of industrialization conditions which had not been created in the "preindustrial" periods precisely because of the economic backwardness of the areas concerned. . . .

. . . the area of capital supply is only one instance of substitutions for missing prerequisites. As one looks at the various patterns of substitution in the individual countries, taking proper account of the effects of gradually diminishing backwardness, one is tempted to formulate still another general proposition. The more backward was a country on the eve of its great spurt of industrial development, the more likely were the processes of its industrialization to present a rich and complex picture—thus providing a curious contrast with its own preindustrial history that most often was found to have been relatively barren. In an advanced country, on the other hand, the very richness of its economic history in the preindustrial periods rendered possible a relatively simple and straightforward course in its modern industrial history.

Thus, the concept of prerequisites must be regarded as an integral part of this writer's general approach to the industrial history of Europe. At the same time, it is important to keep in mind the heuristic nature of the concept. There is no intention to suggest that backward countries necessarily engaged in deliberate acts of "substitution" for something that had been in evidence in more advanced countries. Men in a less developed country may have simply groped for and found solutions that were consonant with the existing conditions of backwardness. In fact, one could conceivably start the study of European industrializations in the east rather than in the west of the Continent and view some elements in English industrial history as substitutions for the German or the Russian way of doing things. This would not be a very good way to proceed. It would make mockery of chronology and would be glaringly artificial. True, some artificiality also inheres in the opposite approach. It is arbitrary to select England as the seat of prerequisites. Yet this is the arbitrariness of the process of cognition and should be judged by its fruits.

The main advantage of viewing European history as patterns of substitutions governed by the prevailing—and changing—degree of backwardness lies, perhaps paradoxically, in its offering a set of predictabilities while at the same time placing limitations upon our ability to predict. To predict is not to prophesy. Prediction in historical research means addressing intelligent, that is, sufficiently specific, questions as new materials are approached.

II.B.4. Future Development in

Historical Perspective—Note

"The historian is a prophet looking backwards"—this dictum is apt for the economic historian concerned with development. Rostow's analysis, for instance, presumes that the choices now confronting the poor countries may be revealed in the light of the stages of preconditions and take-off that the currently rich countries experienced in earlier centuries, and that historical perspective may contribute to the formulation of development policy. From this viewpoint, Rostow's analysis may be most instructive for many countries that have not yet passed successfully through the take-off stage: it may point up the similarities and differences between past and present take-offs, and suggest what policy implications flow from the differences.

With respect to the role of particular sectors of the economy, Rostow observes many problems and patterns familiar from the past. He submits that present take-offs depend, as in the past, on the allocation of resources

to building up and modernizing the three non-industrial sectors required as the matrix for industrial growth: social overhead capital; agriculture; and foreign-exchange-earning sectors, rooted in the improved exploitation of natural resources. In addition, they must begin to find areas of modern processing or manufacture where the application of modern technique (combined with high income- or price-elasticities of demand) are likely to permit rapid growth-rates, with a high rate of plow-back of profits.[1]

It will be instructive to reconsider these conclusions after reading Chapters VII–XI below, where questions not recognized by Rostow are raised regarding the allocation of investment resources and the role of industrialization.

Further, Rostow believes that for the presently underdeveloped nations, the inner mechanics of the take-off involve problems of capital formation, just as in the past. If their take-offs are to succeed, the underdeveloped countries "must seek ways to tap off into the modern sector income above consumption levels hitherto sterilized by the arrangements controlling traditional agriculture. They must seek to shift men of enterprise from trade and money-lending to industry. And to these ends patterns of fiscal, monetary, and other policies (including education policies) must be applied, similar to those developed and applied in the past."[2]

Again, this interpretation of the take-off should be critically reexamined after reading Chapter V, below, where a case is made against assigning as much importance to the role of capital accumulation as Rostow does. Rostow also notes some political and sociocultural similarities between past and present take-offs. As in the past, political interest groups range from defenders of the *status quo* to those prepared to force the pace of modernization at whatever cost; there exists the balance between external expression of nationalism in almost every case; above all, "there is continuity in the role of reactive nationalism, as an engine of modernization, linked effectively to or at cross-purposes

---

[1] W. W. Rostow, *The Stages of Economic Growth,* Cambridge, 1960, p. 139.

[2] Ibid.

with other motives for remaking tradition-alist society."[3]

Historical cases of successful take-offs also indicate a contemporary catalogue of necessary social change:

how to persuade the peasant to change his methods and shift to producing for wider markets; how to build up a corps of tech-nicians, capable of manipulating the new techniques; how to create a corps of entre-preneurs, oriented not towards large profit margins at existing levels of output and technique, but to expand output, under a regime of regular technological change and obsolescence; how to create a modern pro-fessional civil and military service, reason-ably content with their salaries, oriented to the welfare of the nation and to standards of efficient performance, rather than to graft and to ties of family, clan, or region.[4]

On the basis of the foregoing similarities, Rostow regards the process of development now going forward in Asia, the Middle East, Africa, and Latin America as analogues to the stages of preconditions and take-off of other societies in earlier centuries. But there are also differences—by way of different kinds of problems now confronting poor countries, and in the manner in which some problems, although similar in kind to those of the past, are now expressed in different degrees of intensity and complexity. Espe-cially significant is the fact that the poor countries now stand in a different relation-ship to rich countries than was true when the presently rich countries were poor. These differences are extremely important, and they deserve more attention than Rostow gives them. For insofar as most of these differences aggravate the problems of the take-off, they warn against letting the success-stories of past take-offs lull us into too easy an interpretation of the develop-ment task. Nor should we equate the LDCs

to the early stages of the presently devel-oped countries. The persistence of under-development in the world economy poses some refractory problems that were absent in earlier cases of successful development. If we recognize these differences, we may hesitate to join Rostow in concluding that in the end the lesson of history is that "the tricks of growth are not all that difficult."[5]

In the first place, poor countries are attempting to accelerate their development from a lower economic level than was true for the presently rich countries at the time of their rapid rates of development. As Kuznets observes,

Output per capita is much lower in the underdeveloped countries today than it was in the presently developed countries at the date of entry—a period rather than a point of time—into modern economic growth, i.e., when growth of per-capita product (with an already high rate of population growth) began to accelerate, the shift toward non-agricultural sectors occurred, modern tech-nology (modern by the times) was adopted, and so forth. However difficult the compari-son of per-capita gross product at such distances of time and space, the weight of the evidence clearly suggests that, with the single and significant exception of Japan (the records for which are still to be fully tested), the pre-industrialization per-capita product in the presently developed coun-tries, at least $200 in 1958 prices (and significantly more, in the offshoots over-seas), was appreciably higher than per-capita product in underdeveloped countries in the late 1950s—certainly in most of Asia and Africa, and in a good part of Latin America.

Yet this statistical difference in aggregate output per capita is less important than what it represents. It implies that even today these underdeveloped countries still have such a low product per capita that they are not at the same stage as the presently developed countries were at their initial stage of

[3] Ibid., p. 140.
[4] Ibid.

[5] Ibid., p. 166.

modern economic growth. This seems to be the case despite access to modern technology and despite the existence of a modern sector within these countries (no matter how small). These underdeveloped countries are either at some earlier stage within the long-term trend of the presently developed countries—in terms of the Western European sequence perhaps at the period of city formation in the early Middle Ages; or, what is far more defensible, they are at some stage in a sequence of long-term growth separate and distinct from that of the Western European cradle of the modern economic epoch and are following a time and phase sequence that may be quite different.[6]

Not only do poor countries now confront the strategic policy issues of development from an absolutely lower level of per capita income than did the presently developed countries, but their relative positions are also inferior compared with other countries—unlike the position of the early comers to development that entered the industrialization process from a position of superior per capita income relative to other countries. The implications of attempting to develop rapidly from a lower level of per capita income, and from a relative position that entails more pressures of backwardness, should receive a fuller treatment than Rostow's analysis provides.

Gerschenkron's suggestive analysis, outlined above, can provide a more profound understanding of these implications. We should examine, as does Gerschenkron, the processes of industrial development in relation to the degree of backwardness of the areas concerned on the eve of their great spurts of industrialization. Gerschenkron's approach has distinct advantages over Rostow's in maintaining that it is only by comparing industrialization processes in several countries at various levels of backwardness that we can hope to separate what is accidental in a given industrial evolution from what can be attributed to the historical lags in a country's development, and that it is only because a developing country is part of a larger area which comprises more advanced countries that the historical lags are likely to be overcome in a specifically intelligible fashion.[7]

Another fundamental difference is that many of the poor countries have not yet experienced any significant degree of agricultural improvement as a basis for industrialization. The failure to have yet undergone an agricultural revolution makes the present problem of accelerating development far more difficult than it was for the now developed countries when they entered upon their industrial revolutions. It is fairly conclusive that productivity is lower in the agricultural sector of underdeveloped countries than it was in the pre-industrialization phase of the presently developed countries. Although direct evidence of this is unavailable, it is indirectly confirmed by data suggesting that the supply of agricultural land per capita is much lower in most underdeveloped countries today than it was in presently developed countries during their take-off, and that there is a wider difference between per worker income in agricultural and nonagricultural sectors in the underdeveloped countries today than there was in the preindustrial phase of presently developed countries.

The more severe population pressures in the underdeveloped areas constitute another essential difference. Rates of population increase in these areas are higher than those that generally obtained during the Western cases of development in the past. Even

[6] Simon Kuznets, "Notes on Stage of Economic Growth as a System Determinant," in Alexander Eckstein (ed.), *Comparison of Economic Systems,* Berkeley, 1971, pp. 254–5.

[7] Alexander Gerschenkron, *Economic Backwardness in Historical Perspective,* Cambridge, 1962, p. 42. For the application of this general conception of a system of gradations of backwardness to particular countries, see Chaps. 1, 4, 7, 8.

though not all the poor countries are now densely populated, the rate of population growth is, or gives indications of soon becoming, a serious problem for most of them. And, unlike the earlier cases in which population growth was induced by, or at least paralleled, a higher rate of development, the present growth in population is simply due to the introduction of public-health measures that lower death rates. This acts as an autonomous factor, quite unrelated to the rate of internal development. Moreover, unlike the European industrial countries that began lowering their birth rates before their sharpest declines in mortality, the poor countries now will not do so until long after their mortality has reached a modern low level. Given the fact that many poor countries are already experiencing population pressures more severe than those that confronted the currently rich nations when they were in their early phases of development, and that other poor countries may face a population problem in a relatively short time, the need to attain increases in production sufficient to outstrip potential increases in population is now more acute than it ever was in Western countries at the beginning of their industrialization.

Sociocultural and political differences also account for some obstacles to development that are now more formidable than in the past. Unlike the social heritage with which Western countries entered the take-off stage, the social structure and value pattern in many poor countries are still inimical to development. The structure of social relations tends to be hierarchical, social cleavages remain pronounced, and mobility among groups is limited. Instead of allowing an individual to achieve status by his own efforts and performance, his status may be simply ascribed to him, according to his position in a system of social classification— by age, lineage, clan, or caste. A value system that remains "tradition-oriented" also tends to minimize the importance of economic incentives, material rewards, inde-

pendence, and rational calculation. When the emphasis is on an established pattern of economic life, family obligations, and traditional religious beliefs, the individual may simply adopt the attitude of accepting what happens to exist, rather than attempting to alter it—an attitude of resignation rather than innovation. Within an extended family system or a village community, the individual may resign himself to accepting group loyalties and personal relationships which remain in a stable and tradition-dominated pattern, assigning little importance to material accomplishments and change. Even though they may have latent abilities, individuals may lack the motivations and stimulations to introduce change; there may not be sufficiently large groups in the society who are "achievement-oriented," concerned with the future, and believers in the rational mastery of nature. The positive value which the traditional way of life still holds for many of the people in a poor country inhibits the necessary orientation toward the future, and change is either resisted or, if accepted, is restricted to fringe areas.

In short, the cultural context in many poor countries may not yet be as favorable to economic achievement as it was in Western countries. This is not, of course, to assume simply that, because the West is developed, Western values and institutions are therefore necessary for development, and that Western cultural patterns must be imported into the poor countries. Many Western values and institutions may be only accidentally associated with Western development, and many values and institutions in poor countries are not obstacles to development. But though the West need not be imitated, some institutional changes and modifications in the value structure are necessary if the inhibiting institutions and values are to be removed. To allow poor countries to enter into the development process with as favorable a cultural framework as did the currently developed nations, there must be changes in their cultures so that new wants, new beliefs, new motivations, and new institutions may be created. Until these cultural changes are forthcoming, an acceleration of development will be more difficult to achieve than it was in the past.

If the degree of sociocultural development has been less than what occurred in the past, so too has there been a difference in political development. In many poor countries, the political foundations for developmental efforts are not yet as firm as they were in Western development. Whereas the currently developed countries had already enjoyed a long period of political independence and a stable political framework before their periods of rapid economic development, most of the currently poor countries have only recently acquired a real measure of political independence. Political instability, undifferentiated and diffuse political structures, and inefficient governments are still only too prevalent. In some countries, government leadership has yet to be exercised by groups that do not have vested interests in preserving the *status quo*; in others, there is still a wide gap between the traditional mass and a modern elite which controls the central structures of government and is the main locus of political activity.[8]

All the foregoing differences might be subsumed under a more general observation that it matters a great deal for the course of an individual country's development where that country stands relative to other countries. This has already been alluded to by Gerschenkron for European cases of development. With more direct reference to the problems of the presently poor countries, Professor Streeten has argued persuasively that the fact that advanced industrial societies already exist when countries embark on development, makes a number of important differences to the development prospects of the less developed societies.[9]

On the one side, the coexistence of rich and poor countries now has a number of drawbacks for the less developed countries. A suggestive list follows.[10]

1. The most important difference is that the advanced state of medical knowledge that can be borrowed from rich countries makes it now possible to reduce deaths cheaply and rapidly, without contributing to an equivalent reduction in births—thereby presenting the LDCs with more difficult population problems than the now advanced countries faced in their pre-industrial phase.

2. Modern technology in rich countries evolved under conditions of labor scarcity and has therefore been designed to save labor in relation to capital. But the transfer of labor-saving technology to LDCs, which is encouraged by attitudes toward modernization and by the prestige of Western technology, tends to aggravate the underutilization of labor in the LDCs.

3. The knowledge of organizations and institutions that prevail in the advanced countries may be ill-adapted to the needs of LDCs. The adoption of the trade union structure, for example, may be inappropriate for conditions of labor surplus. Or public expenditure on social welfare services developed in advanced industrial welfare states may be premature for LDCs. Or large-scale business enterprises may be undesirable in lesser-developed economies. The transfer of inappropriate institutions to the LDCs may impede their development.

4. Technical progress in advanced economies has harmed the trade prospects of the less developed countries that depend on the export of primary products by facilitating

---

[8] For a discussion of the difference between Western and non-Western political systems, see G. A. Almond and J. S. Coleman (eds.), *The Politics of the Developing Areas*, Princeton, 1960.

[9] Paul P. Streeten, "The Frontiers of Development Studies; Some Issues of Development Policy," *Journal of Development Studies*, October 1967, pp. 2–24.

[10] Streeten fully elaborates this list and some other differences, ibid., pp. 3–7.

the substitution of synthetics for natural products, by reducing the input of raw materials per unit of industrial output, and by shifting demand away from products with a high primary import content.

5. The land-rich or capital-rich countries which at one time served as an outlet for labor surplus countries are no longer receptive to immigration; with accelerated population growth and the intensified underutilization of labor, the development pressures are thus all the greater. At the same time, the scarce resources of capital and skilled individuals are drained off to the rich centers and away from the poor peripheral countries.

Streeten has rightly emphasized that it is this coexistence of rich and poor countries, rather than the intentional or unintentional exploitation of colonialism or neocolonialism, which can have detrimental effects on development efforts. And he properly concludes that it is this coexistence which sets limits to the ready transfer of the lessons of one historical setting to the entirely different present setting of poor countries vis-à-vis much more advanced countries.

Beyond the coexistence of rich and poor countries, we should also recognize that the attempts of many poor countries to develop simultaneously may also intensify the task for any one of the LDCs. The policies adopted by each country in its effort to develop may hinder the development of another country. Thus the poor countries compete among themselves in attempting to increase their exports, in attempting to attract private capital and skilled services, in attempting to foster industrialization via import-substitution policies, and by way of other restrictive nationalistic policies which have beggar-my-neighbor (usually a poor neighbor) effects.

Although these several differences now aggravate the problem of development, there are some dissimilarities which, on the other side, make the problems less difficult. Some advantages may accrue to presently poor countries from their position of being late-comers to development. Most helpful now may be the ability of the poor countries to draw upon the accumulated stock of knowledge in countries that have already developed. Not only may improved productive techniques and equipment be derived from these countries; more generally, they may benefit from the transference of ideas in the realm of social techniques and social innovation as well as technological. As we have already seen, however, the value of this imitative ability is debatable, since it is still necessary to modify and adapt—not simply imitate—the technological and social innovations within the context of the borrowing country's environment. This problem receives fuller treatment in Chapter VI, below. And aside from the requirements of readaptation, there also remains the ultimate difficulty of having change accepted and integrated into the recipient society. We should not, therefore, accept too readily the view that by drawing upon the lessons and experiences of countries that have developed earlier, the latecomers are in a position to telescope the early stages of development.

The existence of many advanced countries that have already reached a high level of development, which was not the case when these same countries were in their preindustrial phase, may now, however, help to ease the development of poor countries by providing a flow of resources from the rich to the poor countries. Never in the past has there been so much international concern with the desirability of increasing trade, technical assistance, private foreign investment, and the flow of public funds as objectives of development policy. But how effective foreign economic assistance may actually prove to be is, of course, another matter. Some judgment on this may be had from Chapter VI, below.

Finally, there is now a strong conscious desire for development on the part of national leaders in many countries. The national interest in deliberate and rapid development, the willingness of national authorities to assume responsibility for directing the country's economic development, and the knowledge of a variety of policies that a government can utilize to accelerate development—all these give new dimensions to the role that the State may play in the development of emerging nations. Through governmental action, to a degree unknown in Western development, a more favorable environment for a take-off might be created. Nonetheless, as will be appreciated time and again in subsequent chapters, the mere act of development planning cannot be expected to remove the difficult choices and decisions that must be made to accelerate development.

Depending on how much importance we attach to each of the various differences between past and present conditions, we may reach contrasting conclusions as to whether present conditions are more or less favorable than in the past for the acceleration of development. But in the final analysis, what will decide whether a poor country will succeed is whether its government can implement effectively the possible policies that might make the country's development potential realizable, and whether its people are prepared to bear the costs that accelerated development will necessarily entail. Regardless of whether we interpret conditions in the currently poor countries as being on balance more or less favorable, we must not expect these countries to follow simply the historical patterns of presently developed countries. We must still give due weight to the severity of the particular problems confronting these countries. And we must determine what policies might now be most effective in removing the barriers to development. With the benefit of historical perspective, however, we should be better able to appraise the significance of these present-day development problems and their various policy implications.

II.C. ALTERNATIVES IN

POLITICAL ECONOMY

II.C.1. An Economic Reappraisal

of China*

... In spite of the economic setbacks of 1960–61 caused by the Great Leap Forward and the Soviet withdrawal of technicians, and in spite of the disruptions resulting from the Cultural Revolution in 1967–69, China has managed an overall rate of economic growth that has kept well ahead of the increase in population. Most of the rise in per capita product has resulted from growth in the producer-goods sector, but if 1963 is used as a base year rather than 1957, there has also been some increase in the per capita availability of consumer goods.

INVESTMENT AND PLANNING IN INDUSTRY

Let us turn our attention now to the factors responsible for this quite respectable economic performance. One factor of major importance has apparently been the maintenance of a high rate of investment. While there are no official figures on the investment rate, it is possible to arrive at some general conclusions on the basis of what we know about the producer-goods sector. Thus, it is clear from the reasoning in the preceding sections that the share of producer goods in China's GNP has doubled between 1957 and 1972, and we know that these goods are generally used for one of three purposes—*i.e.,* for investment, as inputs into other producer and consumer goods, and for

*From Dwight H. Perkins, "Looking Inside China," *Problems of Communism,* November 1973, pp. 5–12. Reprinted by permission.

the production of military equipment. Given the much higher rate of growth in the output of producer goods as compared to that of consumer goods, the proportion of total producer-goods output used as inputs into the production of consumer items has undoubtedly declined. As for the military share of producer goods output, even though China's expenditures on military equipment and installations have risen sharply, particularly since 1960 when Soviet military supplies were cut off, it is unlikely that they could have absorbed all of the very marked increase indicated above in the overall share of producer goods in GNP. Hence, the most plausible conclusion is that there was a rise in the proportion of such goods allocated to investment.

A second major factor in China's economic performance over the past decade has been the regime's arrival in the early 1960's—after years of experimentation and changing policies—at settled ways of organizing the economy that have evidently proven effective. Because the organization of the industrial sector is quite different in form, if not in spirit, from that of agriculture, the two will be dealt with separately. Let us look at the industrial sector first.

In the early 1950's, China introduced the highly centralized Soviet system of planning and control, complete with a powerful planning commission in Peking which, in principle, was expected to exercise direct control over all industrial firms above the handicraft level. However, because China had tens of thousands of industrial firms with widely different technologies and, in many cases, with primitive accounting procedures, it was found to be totally impossible for the central authorities to keep track of performance at the plant level in each of these enterprises. To remedy this situation, it was decided in late 1957 and early 1958 to decentralize authority over production and even over investment choices, but this decision was carried out in such a way during 1958 and 1959 that there was in fact no authority responsible for coordinating inputs and outputs. The result was chaos, with firms churning out items that were often of low quality and of little use to anyone.

Beginning in the early 1960's, order was restored—not by recentralizing economic authority in Peking, but by placing it in the hands of provincial and county (*hsien*) planning and control organs. Individual firms still had to meet essentially physical output targets and stay below targeted levels of input use, but principal responsibility for drawing up these targets was in the provincial and county seats, not in Peking. Only a few enterprises were controlled at the national level, and the number of firms in this category appears to have declined throughout the 1960's. As long as most of a firm's inputs were purchased within a given region and its output sold within that same region, there was no need for coordination on a national scale.[1]

With regard to the impact of the Cultural Revolution on the economic structure, the available evidence suggests that it was largely limited to the manner in which the planning and control apparatus conducted itself, and that it entailed few major changes in the *formal* planning system. How the Revolution affected the behavior of the economic apparatus can be inferred from criticisms that began to appear in the Chinese press in the

[1] The planning and organization of Chinese industry are discussed at greater length in D. H. Perkins, "Plans and Their Implementation in the People's Republic of China," *Papers and Proceedings of the American Economic Association*, May 1973.

early 1970's with respect to the conduct of cadres during the 1967–69 period. The criticisms implied that many cadres had failed to distinguish "rational rules and regulations from revisionist practices of controlling, restricting and repressing the working masses" and had taken the mistaken position that "all rules and regulations which obstruct anarchism are no good." Such complaints strongly suggest that the Cultural Revolution witnessed a recurrence of at least some of the excesses that had marked the 1958–59 Great Leap Forward. As indicated earlier, however, the excesses of the Cultural Revolution period slowed growth only temporarily, mainly because they were not allowed to get out of hand as in 1958–59. Thus, the early 1970's were dominated by calls in the press to end anarchy, to strengthen management and accounting, to make more careful inventories of warehouses, to pay more attention to veteran workers, and to emphasize product quality. At the same time, a number of individuals who had been severely criticized during the Cultural Revolution as architects of the economic policies of the early 1960's, most notably Ch'en Yun, were rehabilitated—another possible sign of a return to the main lines of pre-Cultural Revolution policy for the economy.

Other key features of the industrial policies of the 1960's that have continued unchanged into the early 1970's include special emphasis on the development of military equipment industries, on rapid expansion of agricultural support industries (most notably the chemical fertilizer industry), and on a major increase in the number of rural-based small-scale firms of many types.

The effort to expand small-scale rural industry merits closer attention. Rural China has always had small-scale handicraft industries for the processing of food and similar activities, but what is different today is that the concept has been extended to a number of industries that hitherto were not typically either small in scale or rural-based. This effort, too, began during the Great Leap Forward, when there was a drive to develop small enterprises such as the much-publicized "backyard" iron and steel furnaces. As in the case of so many other activities connected with the Leap, implementation of the program, though energetic, was poorly thought out and resulted in waste of raw materials and poor quality of output. Most of the backyard furnaces were closed down in the early 1960's, as were many other small plants, but in others an attempt was made to rationalize production procedures rather than to close the plants down altogether. Apparently the effort was deemed successful, for the number of small plants was once again on the rise by the mid-1960's. By 1970, thousands of such enterprises dotted the countryside, and hundreds—perhaps even thousands—more were built in 1971 and 1972.

Although there are many kinds of small-scale firms, they are centered mainly in five industries: iron and steel, cement, chemical fertilizer, energy (coal and electricity), and machinery (chiefly farm-machinery repair shops, but also production of simple tools). The development of rural-based cement and chemical fertilizer plants is, perhaps, the most unusual aspect of the program in comparison to what is found in other less-developed countries today. In 1971, some 60 percent, or 10 million gross tons, of China's total chemical fertilizer output was produced in such small rural plants, while 40 percent of China's cement output was produced by 1,800 small enterprises (the addition of 600 more small cement plants during 1972 brought the percentage of total cement production up to 48).

Unfortunately, we do not yet have enough information to judge whether the development of these small-scale rural plants makes possible more efficient use of China's endowment of productive resources, characterized by surplus labor and short capital. What we do know is that such enterprises have helped to familiarize millions of Chinese farmers with modern industrial tech-

nology. This effort seems bound to produce both economic and social benefits, the latter by breaking down the sharp distinction that exists in so many less-developed societies between the sophisticated, modernized cities and a primitive countryside.

AGRICULTURAL ORGANIZATION AND POLICY

It is agriculture, however, that lies at the heart of China's economic problems, for the agricultural sector must not only provide the ever-increasing amounts of food required by the country's mounting population but also generate surpluses needed to help finance the development of industry. As pointed out earlier, while the rate of growth in industry has far exceeded that of agriculture, the latter has shown marked improvement since the early 1960's, so that output is now expanding at a pace more than adequate to take care of population growth. Let us now look at the changes in agricultural organization and policies that have brought about this significant improvement.

During the period extending from the start of agricultural collectivization in China in the winter of 1955–56 up to 1962, the Chinese Communist regime experimented with a wide variety of organizational forms. In 1958 and 1959, under the banner of the Great Leap Forward, virtually all remaining non-collectivized farming activities (the peasants' private plots and the small free markets) were abolished, and the farmers were organized into communes of 4,000–5,000 families each, with control over their activities centralized in the hands of the commune leadership. These innovations, however, contributed to a sharp recession in agriculture which forced a reversal of policy. In the depths of the rural depression in 1961, many areas experimented with something called the "agricultural responsibility system," which was tantamount to a virtual abandonment of collectivized agriculture.

This period of instability in agricultural policy ended in 1962, when China finally settled on a basic organizational structure for agriculture which has not undergone any major changes since. The larger existing communes were split up into several smaller ones, and at the same time authority over the planning and management of labor and crops was decentralized to a considerable degree from the commune to a small subunit of the commune, the production team. The production team was also made the accounting unit, a change which meant in effect that whatever profits (or losses) the individual team made (after taxes) were no longer pooled and shared with the entire commune but accrued to the team itself. Whereas several thousand families had shared the fruits of their collective labor in the initial communes, now only several dozen families did so. Even before this, moreover, small private plots and rural free markets had been reinstituted in order to revive declining food production, and these institutions were continued after 1962.

There have, of course, been minor adjustments in this basic organizational pattern since 1962. Over the next few years, for example, the amount of land in private plots (which were supposed to be kept to about 5 percent of total cultivated acreage) appears to have increased slightly. During the Cultural Revolution, there was some talk of restricting or abolishing private plots, as well as of recentralizing more authority in the hands of the production brigade (a unit above the team but below the commune), but little if anything was actually done along these lines. The rural areas were generally kept out of the mainstream of the Cultural Revolution, and they appear to have suffered little disruption of any kind in that period—certainly not enough to affect crop output.

As of 1971 and 1972, there continued to be little indication of any major change in rural organization or general agricultural policy. If anything, it is possible that the independence of the individual production teams may have increased, inasmuch as "self-reliance" has been the leitmotif of the "Learn from Tachai" Campaign, which has played such a big role in the Chinese countryside in recent years. The basic idea of "self-reliance" is that all units should try to produce as much of their own needs as possible and thus minimize their dependence on others; however, this sort of self-sufficiency necessarily implies a reduction in the influence of outsiders on decision-making at the production-team level. The higher authorities must instead resort to more indirect methods of exercising control.

INCOMES POLICY AND GROWTH

One further matter that merits attention here is the rather unusual fact that China has endeavored to couple its pursuit of rapid economic growth with a policy of eliminating inequalities in income distribution. This sets the PRC clearly apart from the rest of the less-developed countries of the world. Although a good many of the latter have espoused some form of "socialism" during the past few decades, it has in most instances been socialism for the rich, and particularly for the bureaucracy. Great effort has been made in these countries to find jobs in state enterprises and government offices for the newly-emerging elite, but relatively little has been done to keep the incomes of this elite from rising too far above those prevailing among the great majority of the people.

The PRC has deliberately followed a different path. One of the central purposes of the Cultural Revolution, for example, was to prevent or reverse the rise of a new elite class based on the party-government bureaucracy. As a result of this effort, all but a handful of cadres in the various government and party offices are now required to go to the countryside and work at unskilled jobs for considerable periods, and youth, instead of moving steadily up the educational ladder, are expected to spend several years at manual labor before they can even be considered for admission to university. Numerous other measures have been adopted with a similar purpose.

Apart from such measures to prevent the reemergence of elitist attitudes, the Communist regime set out from the beginning to reduce the range of income differentiation between different types of labor as well as between different levels of skill and responsibility. While substantial disparities in income still remain, these disparities have certainly been sharply reduced in comparison to those that existed in China before 1949 or presently exist in other less-developed nations. However, most of the steps in this direction were taken in the 1950's, and there has since been a slackening of efforts to push ahead with income equalization as this policy has come into conflict with the requirements of growth and the policy of self-reliance.

In sum, China still seems to remain committed to the principle of equalizing incomes, though the pace of such efforts has naturally slowed down by comparison with the rapid and drastic changes of the 1950's. The fact is that the PRC is still a relatively poor country and cannot afford to push the redistribution of income too vigorously at the price of markedly slowing down the rate of economic growth. During the Cultural Revolution the pursuit of social goals closely related to issues of income distribution did slow down or stop growth for a time, and it consequently was an effort that could not be sustained indefinitely. China has not abandoned these social goals in the early 1970's, but it does appear to have given them a lower priority in a generally successful effort to accelerate growth.

II.C.2. Maoist Development Strategy*

What possible relevance has China's attempts at rural development to other underdeveloped countries? To begin to answer this, it is first necessary to specify exactly what the Maoist strategy for economic development is, within which rural development is contained. Since this strategy is an evolving one and has already taken several twists and turns, one cannot be certain of getting it right. But as of now the overall development strategy appears to consist of the following steps.

1. Destroy the feudal-landlord-bureaucrat class structure, and redistribute land, other assets, income, and power to the peasants and workers.

2. Establish socialist relations of production as soon as possible, and use the Party to

*From John G. Gurley, "Rural Development in China," in Edgar O. Edwards (ed.), *Employment in Developing Nations,* Report on a Ford Foundation Study, Columbia University Press, New York, 1974, pp. 399–403. Reprinted by permission.

educate peasants and workers in socialist values and ideals. That is, nationalize industry as soon as feasible and bring about cooperativization in the countryside without waiting for agricultural mechanization; begin transforming the superstructure into a socialist one.[1]

3. Establish a full planning mechanism to take the place of market-price-determined allocation of resources and distribution of incomes, and go all out for industrialization, but emphasize those industries having direct links to agriculture.

[1] This is because, if mechanization is introduced in an essentially individualistic, private-enterprise framework, the fruits of the new technology will be captured by only a few, leaving the majority of peasants resentful and ready to "break the machines." Also, capitalist development creates capitalist people. Under certain circumstances, according to Mao, it is necessary to change the superstructure in order to release the productive forces of society. See point 5.

4. Achieve high rates of capital forma-tion by encouraging savings at all levels and the use of the savings at each level for self-financed investment. Encourage rural areas, in particular, to produce whatever can be produced by small-scale, indigenous methods, to finance these investments from their own savings, and to manage these industries themselves. Capital goods that can be produced only by large-scale, modern methods should be financed and managed at higher political levels.

5. Develop and release human energy and creativity by promoting socialist values ("serve the people," selflessness, collective incentives) over bourgeois values (individ-ualism, selfishness, materialism), by provid-ing health-care facilities everywhere, educating as many people as possible, providing worthy goals that inspire people to work hard, and encouraging basic decision-making at the lowest possible level.

6. Carry out a continuing revolution at all levels of society, and maintain the dicta-torship of the proletariat.

It seems to me that the Maoist strategy, *considered as a whole,* probably has very little relevance to governments of most underdeveloped countries today, for it involves breaking the power of ruling classes and their foreign supporters, opting for socialism and eventually communism over capitalism, for full-scale industrialization over trade, commerce, and agrarianism, for continuing revolutionary activity over orderly procedures. Since most "third-world" countries today play more or less subordinate and dependent roles in the international capitalist system, serving the wealthier countries of that system with raw materials, oil, cheap labor, or additional markets, for them to follow China's path would mean first breaking out of this global system and then taking their chances on an all-out development effort with their own resources plus whatever aid can be obtained

from socialist countries.[2] This may be a program favored by some classes in these poor countries, but it is hardly a prescription that would be appealing to their govern-ments and propertied classes. Furthermore, such thoughts are anathema to the United States, as the leader of global capitalism, the duty of which is to try to prevent such breakaways through some combination of economic aid, military aid, counterinsur-gency, cultivation of domestic elites, or force. The alliance between the U.S., on the one hand, and the propertied classes and elites in the poor countries, on the other, is a powerful one.

That is the overall picture. It stresses that one thing *does* depend on another in Maoist strategy, and indeed this is so in any development strategy. To make any substan-tial headway, the problem of underdevelop-ment often has to be tackled as a whole, not piecemeal. For example, in the Chinese experience, rural industrialization depended on the general acceptance of goals other than profits and efficiency. This general acceptance in turn was based on the prior inculcation of socialist values throughout the society, which were reinforced daily by the prior establishment of socialist institutions, including a full planning mechanism. These socialist relations of production could be developed only by the prior breakup of the old class structures of society. And so on.

I have emphasized the holistic view, the Maoist way. I now wish to ask whether other underdeveloped countries can benefit, to some extent at least, from separate parts of China's total experience. Some socialist poli-cies should be adaptable to capitalist devel-opmental programs.

[2] This is also true for the ruling classes of the major oil-producing countries, who may gain some advantages over the industrial capitalist countries but who are so greatly dependent on international monopoly capital that they (or most of them) would not dream of breaking out of this global system.

It is well to recognize at the beginning that many Chinese policies for development are universally known and in fact have been acquired by China from the theoretical and practical work of bourgeois economists and other development experts, as well as from the experience of the Soviet Union. To this extent, China has learned from others, and there are, of course, no reasons why other countries cannot take advantage of the same information. I refer to policies of raising capital formation relative to consumption to attain higher growth rates, of encouraging saving for this purpose through taxation, financial institutions, and in other ways, of using relative factor supplies to good advantage, of aiming for developmental government budgets and moderate growth rates of the money supply, of utilizing aid and trade efficiently, and so on. Much of China's overall performance can be explained "simply" in terms of the very high investment and saving ratios that were attained by 1953–54 and were more or less maintained thereafter. (Recall, however, that to attain *these* the old class structures were overthrown by revolution. That is what lies behind "simply.") And larger shares of this total capital formation were applied to agriculture in the 1960s, which goes a long way in explaining China's recent gains in rural development. Thus, much of the story is standard fare, known to everyone.

But, while China has learned much from others, she may also be able to teach a few things. First, China has demonstrated the importance of industrialization to economic development; that the large resources initially devoted to iron and steel, machine-building, non-ferrous metals, oil, electric power, and chemicals were indispensable in establishing a base for later advances in agriculture, transportation, consumer goods, and military weapons, and in freeing the economy from its dependency on foreign direction and influence. The initial stress on heavy industry, rather than on infrastructure and consumer goods, was made possible only by socialist aid and trade. Despite the growing bitterness between the U.S.S.R. and China, no other country has ever received so much help toward full-scale industrialization as China did during the 1950s. This is something of a lesson in itself.

Second, China has shown, especially during the 1960s, *how* to industrialize without generating social problems that threaten eventually to blow the society sky high. China has involved increasing numbers of people, especially in the rural areas, in industrial activities in order to break down the potentially antagonistic relations between city and country and between workers and peasants; to spread knowledge of industrial processes as widely as possible so as to promote talent, ingenuity, confidence, and the scientific attitude among masses of workers and peasants; and to transform rural areas into self-reliant agrarian-industrial-cultural local economies, which are attractive places to live and which can, at least partly, break their dependent relationships with higher political units, including the state. This is relevant for other poor countries because it demonstrates a pattern of industrialization that does not generate severe imbalances between urban and rural areas, between rich and poor, between employed and unemployed, or between one region and another. The lesson that many developing countries are learning from their own experience is that high output growth rates are often the "good face" on an increasingly diseased body. Thus, the last annual report of the World Bank, after noting the respectable growth rates of many underdeveloped countries, went on to say: "Statistics conceal the gravity of the underlying economic and social problems, which are typified by severely skewed income distribution, excessive levels of unemployment, high rates of infant mortality, low rates of literacy, serious malnutrition, and widespread ill-health." The statistics also conceal the growing urban problems, foreign debt difficulties, social unrest, and much else in many of these countries. Perhaps the most important message that China can send to other poor people is that not one item in the above list applies to her.

The third lesson is the importance of raising work motivation and how to do it. Capitalist economists have concentrated far too much on how to reallocate economic resources to attain higher levels of national output and far too little on how to get people really interested in their work and so willing to exert great efforts to achieve their goals. I think that China has shown that the latter is much more important than the former; that people who really want to work completely eclipse the effects of nice adjustments toward more competitive markets and fine calculations regarding factor inputs.

The Maoists believe that they have inspired and enabled people to work hard by altering their work environments, changing their incentives, and providing them with education, good health, and technical training. The first point is that, in capitalist development, to raise growth rates of national output, it is necessary to do it in such a way as to reinforce the existing class structures of society and the values which support such structures. The pursuit of higher growth rates, therefore, has generally reduced many human beings to unthinking, specialized, manipulated inputs in the production process, in which hierarchical structures of capitalists and workers, bosses and "hands," mental experts and manual workers, face each other in more or less antagonistic relationships. Such alienated work environments lower the general intelligence, initiative, and willingness to work hard of broad masses of workers, which are the obvious costs of pursuing growth in the context of such sharp class alignment. The Maoists feel that the development of people as full human beings, working in a warm, egalitarian, and cooperative atmosphere, leads to the rapid development of material output; that the former is possible only in

the absence of capitalist or feudal class structures; and that the latter is desirable only within the context of the former.

Thus, the Chinese lesson, in this regard, is that it is possible to increase greatly the overall productivity of peasants and workers by establishing less alienated work environments. In the absence of full-scale revolution, underdeveloped countries might benefit from China's experience by questioning their own organizations of work both in the countryside and in the cities, and by experimenting with other forms. Are existing organizations efficient from a factor productivity point of view, or are they mainly efficient in channeling part of the economic surplus to a landed aristocracy or to a capitalist class? Do work organizations exist to maintain discipline and order or do they promote energy and initiative? And, if the former, why? Are they designed to set off one group of workers against another to the benefit of the dominant class and to the detriment of factor productivity? China may have much to teach us in this regard.

Work motivation in China has also risen, according to the Maoists, because of an increase in socialist consciousness among the masses of workers and peasants, which means that collective incentives—the willingness to work hard for increasingly larger groups of people without expectation of personal gain—have gained over individual ones. Maoists believe that people are inspired and can see real meaning in their lives only if they are working for goals worthy of human beings and not merely for their own selfish, material welfare. Indeed, people throughout China *do* seem inspired in this way, for whatever reason, and seem not only completely involved in their present accomplishments but in achieving the plans for the future: "In two years, we'll have this and have a good start on that, and then . . . " Just about everyone talks this way.

Further, with regard to work motivation, it is necessary to repeat that increasing numbers of people are able to work hard and more effectively by being more literate, having better health and improved nutrition, and having more technical training.

Finally, the Chinese Communist Party has developed high motivation among its own cadres to "serve the people" in honest and incorruptible ways. The work motivation and collective incentives engendered within this large group have been of vital importance in getting policies translated into proper actions at all levels, in ways that do not dissipate the intentions of the policymakers. The CPC has for several decades now demonstrated the importance of having such cadres for the actual realization, as

contrasted to the verbalization, of national goals.

China offers other lessons, too, which there is space only to mention: how to adapt education to the needs of an industrializing society; that it is not necessary for economic development to invite foreign capital into the country; the desirability of maintaining rather stable prices of important commodities over long periods of time; and so on.

The principal lesson, however, is the necessity of breaking out of all dependency relationships with advanced industrial countries and pursuing the course of self-reliance, both at the national and the local levels.

II.C.3. Cuba's Development*

In Cuba, the development strategy has put heavy emphasis on the elimination of poverty, through a sharp reduction in inequality. The degree of equality in Cuba is now probably unique. It is a case, therefore, highly pertinent to the issues of this report: if one could set up an experiment in the social sciences, it might well look like Cuba.

Economic data on Cuba are scarce and it is impossible here to deal at all fully with the results of the revolution. But it seems broadly that, although there was a spurt forward in many productive sectors immediately after the revolution, the national income rose only about in line with population from 1961 to 1968,[1] and then declined

in the following three years.[2] The main issue therefore appears to be whether redistribution has inhibited growth.

But this is misleading. Before trying to explain what has occurred, I would like to point out that to discuss the "trade-off" in these terms is theoretically mistaken when elimination of poverty is the central objective. Then the important question to pose about a country's performance is not, how much did the nation's income grow? But rather, whose income grew? And what sort of production increased? Increases in the income of the top 20 percent have no direct impact on absolute poverty—they aggravate relative poverty (i.e., inequality). Besides, if the object is to change the existing distribution of income, this implies the inappro-

*From Dudley Seers, "Cuba," in Hollis B. Chenery et al., *Redistribution with Growth*, Oxford University Press, New York, 1974, pp. 262–8. Reprinted by permission.

[1] See Dorticos (1972). It is not clear whether adjustment had been made for price changes, but the most favorable assumption is that he was using a fixed-price comparison. Since wages and prices were frozen for much of this period, it would not matter greatly. However, since the Marxist defini-

tion of income was presumably used, the actual rise was somewhat higher; this definition excludes the social services, the most dynamic sector.

[2] For figures from which the following can be inferred, see the unsigned "La Perspectivas Desarrollo de la Economia Cubana, 1971–75," *Economia y Desarrollo* no. 13 (September-October 1972), p. 194.

priateness of prices produced by this distribution and used in estimates of growth.[3]

It is often argued that, however narrowly the benefits of growth are concentrated, poverty can be cured one day in the future by redistributing the national product after it has increased. The political assumptions of this argument are questionable because growth makes those who benefit from it more powerful. But in any case, the conclusion does not necessarily follow even in purely economic terms. Because of the specificity of assets, it depends on what types of production increased—one cannot cure poverty by redistributing cosmetics or casino tickets.

In the case of Cuba, there is indeed a question about the consistency of objectives, but it cannot be posed in such naïve terms. The movement of an aggregate has particularly little meaning when far-reaching changes take place in the structure of production and income, including the emigration of a large fraction of those who were formerly rich. The question which *is* raised is the slowness in improving the lot of the poor. In the first few years after the revolution, dire poverty and unemployment were virtually eliminated.[4] But further progress in the production of necessities, especially food, or of goods which could be exported, was slow. Sugar output in the 1970s (except for the special effort which produced 8.5 million tons in 1969/70) has not exceeded typical prerevolutionary levels. From 1962 to 1968/69 nonsugar agricultural output fell by 18 percent[5] and supplies of consumer goods, including necessities such as food, grew tighter. Progress in rehousing those in slum or overcrowded dwellings was slow. It

is true that teaching and medical services, which are essential to the elimination of poverty, expanded rapidly. But the infant mortality rate obstinately remained around 40 per 1,000.[6]

The key question is not whether the redistribution and the associated use of moral rather than material incentives caused the per capita incomes to rise little if at all between 1958 and 1971, but whether they contributed to the failure to make further substantial inroads into poverty after 1961.

THE PRE-REVOLUTIONARY SITUATION

This issue should be looked at in historical perspective. In the 1950s, Cuba was beset by serious social problems. Open unemployment was some 16 percent in 1956/57,[7] poverty was widespread, with a large fraction of the population illiterate and undernourished (especially those in large rural families).[8] This was not, however, due to inadequate national income, which at about $500 a head[9] was quite high enough to make acute poverty unnecessary.

The distribution of this income was however highly concentrated, and so was access to medical and educational facilities. Although no coefficient of concentration can be estimated, Cuba must have been among those countries in which it was "relatively high" (i.e., > 0.5). At its roots

[6] In fact this rate had been 35 in 1953. It is possible to ascribe the rise to 38 in 1966 to improvements in statistical collection. JUCEPLAN (1967) estimates that the correct figure should have been 39 in both years. But the further increase to 41 in 1968 suggests that poverty was proving an intractable problem. However, the rate fell back to 36 (a provisional figure) in 1971, according to United Nations (1973).

[7] Consejo Nacional de Economia (1958).

[8] The sample surveys of rural workers carried out by the Catholic University Group (ACU) demonstrate this. For example, less than 10 percent of homes had running water.

[9] Oshima (1961). His reference is to the position in 1957.

[3] There are additional problems of measuring, or even defining, the national income in countries with large rural populations.

[4] A comparison of nutritional surveys in 1967 with those made a decade earlier showed "a definite improvement" in the state of nutrition. See Navarro (1972).

[5] Acosta (1972).

lay a highly concentrated distribution of property, especially of land, 9 percent of the landowners holding 73 percent of the land.[10] Many factories and much land belonged to foreign companies. Contrasts between incomes, housing, health, and educational levels in Havana and the rural areas were particularly marked.

There seemed little prospect of the chronic poverty being alleviated. Up to the 1920s, the Cuban economy had advanced rapidly—with sugar output reaching 5 million tons in the mid-1920s—but it developed severe inequalities in the process. In the following three decades, progress was slow. Increased sugar output was restrained by quotas and industrialization was hindered by the Reciprocal Trade Agreement (1934) with United States. Apart from tourism (the benefits of which largely accrued either to foreigners or to groups and areas already rich) there was little dynamic in the economy, which had considerable surplus capacity in capital as well as labor. A succession of dictatorships notorious for their inefficiency and corruption repressed the political forces that favored the redistribution of income.

STEPS AFTER THE REVOLUTION TO
REDISTRIBUTE INCOME

Most of the implements of redistribution ... were used after the revolution. (a) *Assets were redistributed.* Tenants of small-holdings and houses became their owners.[11] In addition, nationalization, starting with foreign-owned companies and landholdings, spread to all productive assets. There was no compensation for U.S. asset-holders and, though most local property-owners were paid annuities, these involved a degree of expropriation. Much property (especially housing) was abandoned by emigrants. (b) *Public investment and consumption were concentrated on the poor,* especially health and educational services. Particular attention was paid to the reduction of illiteracy, and there was a very big increase in adult education at all levels, including technical training. The expansion of public expenditure made big inroads into unemployment, and by being concentrated in rural areas it helped reduce the urban-rural imbalance. (c) *Income was redistributed* in three ways. (i) Wages were increased, especially at lower levels, the effective minimum becoming nearly 100 pesos a month by 1971 for both agriculture and industry.[12] Pensions were made universal and raised to levels near or at the corresponding wage levels. At the other end of the scale, salary rates for managerial jobs were reduced, few being left above 300 pesos, so that a span of about 3-to-1 covered the great majority of wage and salary rates.[13] (ii) Piece rates and other incentive payments were abolished, and claims for overtime discouraged.[14] Stress was laid, especially in education, on moral incentives, made concrete in medals, titles, and the like to take the place of financial acquisitiveness. (iii) Charges for medical attention, schooling, and some other services (e.g., water, school meals, entrance to sporting events, local telephone calls) were eliminated, as were loan obligations of smallholders. Basic foodstuffs were put on ration and their prices were kept low, and so were the prices of other basic goods and services such as bus journeys. Consequently the range of real

---

[10] Estimates of INRA before the land reform.
[11] After the second stage of the agrarian reform in 1963, 24 percent of the land remained in private hands; much of this was incorporated in the state sector after the Third Reform of 1968/69. See Acosta (1972).

[12] At the time of the revolution, 1 peso officially equalled US$1; they were perhaps also roughly equal in purchasing power. Since then, the price structure has changed so much in Cuba that comparisons are now difficult, if not meaningless.
[13] An official currently in a senior post was allowed a personal supplement to maintain his income level.
[14] However, workers in establishments with good records of attendance and voluntary work were allowed higher pensions when they retired.

incomes became even less than that of money incomes.

A feature of this report is attention to the political conditions for a poverty-oriented strategy. In Cuba the government was strong enough after the revolution to put the redistributive measures into effect. The political power both of the poor rural areas (where the revolution originated) and also of many urban dwellers had been mobilized. The military and police forces, which had been an integral part of the former régime, and might have attempted to overthrow the new one, were disbanded and replaced, and many of the rich started to emigrate.

CAUSES OF PRODUCTION PROBLEMS

These measures had an impact on poverty.[15] Why was the improvement not sustained? Of course, at this stage, fifteen years after the revolution, a thoroughgoing evaluation would be premature. Evaluations of the social progress of the Soviet or Chinese revolutions after only fifteen years would have proved misleading. Nevertheless it is possible to indicate some elements in the explanation.

In other contexts, it might have been expected that the reduced concentration of income would lead to a fall in investment. However, this has not happened in Cuba. Investment has been almost completely under public control, and has been supported by heavy aid, especially from the Soviet Union. It has been more than 20 percent of the national income (though the

[15] A "poverty-weighted" national income would show a sharp rise in the first few years after the revolution, though perhaps an index giving all the weight to the bottom 40 percent would be more meaningful—at least in Cuba. Such an index would not allow, of course, for the rise in the welfare of the poor due to public services (especially education and health) and to changes in the price structure (especially reduction of prices for necessities).

percentage might have been lower if growth had been faster).

Part of the explanation of production difficulties lay in the international context. The loss of professional and skilled manpower through emigration to the United States aggravated production problems. So did the switch to Soviet and East European sources of supply for intermediate products and equipment—especially spare parts, as a result of a trade embargo—and to the same sources of technical expertise. (Cuba was neglected by many aid agencies, even multilateral ones.) Moreover, part of the country's resources were tied up in military preparations to deal with possible invasions, especially after the Bay of Pigs.[16]

Yet by the early 1970s these problems had been eased. In many sectors, the loss of qualified personnel had been offset by the results of the big increase in education and training programs; the conversion to COMECON sources of inputs had been very largely completed; and the threat of invasion had dwindled. Indeed the trade embargo and military intervention were in some respects economic assets. They provided an excuse for shortages; by stimulating nationalism, they also encouraged voluntary labor, which was extensively used to break production bottlenecks. The cutting of trade and other links with countries in the Western Hemisphere reduced the "demonstration effect" of standards of consumption which could not be afforded by the population as a whole as well as the influence of technical assistance which would doubtless have been inappropriate for Cuba's development strategy.

A main cause of production problems has to be sought in economic management. The economy has lacked the central rationale of

[16] It is interesting to speculate what the production experience of Cuba would have been—and whether less egalitarian policies would have been followed—if instead of embargo, blockade, and invasion, Cuba had received external support from capitalist countries in the early years of the revolution.

either a price system or an overall development plan,[17] which was a contributory
factor in policy mistakes[18] (e.g., reversals of
sugar policy). Moreover, financial accounting
was abandoned for both individual enterprises and the economy as a whole.

Managers of factories and farms ceased to
keep accounts, or even to know their costs
of production (the economy being in effect
treated as one big enterprise without inter-
departmental invoices). This not only caused
inefficiency (including hoarding of labor);
project evaluation also became practically
impossible.

No attempt was made to match rises in
wages, pensions, public services, or investment (or reductions in prices) by measures
to absorb the consequent increases of purchasing power, and the government has
persistently rejected a currency reform
(apart from a confiscation of large notes
soon after the revolution). So cash in the
hands of the public rose to very high
levels:[19] retail inventories virtually disap-
peared (except for reading matter and phar-
maceuticals); and long queues had become a
familiar sight. There appears also to have
been a considerable black market.[20]

---

[17] There *have* been, however, medium-term
physical plans for particular sectors, and annual
plans for foreign exchange, labor use, and key
products.

[18] For example, several reversals of sugar
policy, most notably the early decision to uproot
15 percent of the acreage given to sugar on the
grounds that planned "industrialization and diversification" would make it necessary. Replanning
took place in the mid-1960s. For a highly critical
account of Cuban agricultural policies see Dumont
(1970), especially Chapter V; also, "El Sector
Agropecuario en la década 1959–69," Instituto de
Economía, Universidad de la Habana. Mimeographed. Havana, 1971.

[19] About 3.3 billion pesos at the end of 1970,
or more than the total annual wage bill. See
Dorticós (1972).

[20] According to the Prime Minister's May 1,
1971, speech, the highly specific nature of the
rationing system encouraged ration-swapping
(which is the starting point of a black market).

The market imbalance had results somewhat inconsistent with social objectives. A
family's consumption level came to depend
partly on whether its members had between
them the time and stamina needed for
queuing, which penalized the elderly and
those with children under school age, and
partly on access to official transport, can-
teens, and so forth.

The market imbalance also meant a
vicious circle: queuing led to absenteeism
and production difficulties, which in turn
aggravated the shortages. Moreover, since
many families could not spend the wages of
their employed males, the government made
little progress in its attempt to mobilize the
female labor reserve of 1.5 million. In
addition, the prevalance of absenteeism and
black market operations impaired the appeal
to moral incentives.

Cuban experience in the 1960s, therefore,
turns out not to have been a proper test of
an egalitarian policy, which does not necessarily entail the abandonment of financial
controls or complete abolition of material
incentives. It is possible, however, that all
these policies had their roots in the years of
guerrilla warfare, when there was, of course,
no need for accountancy or an appeal to
material incentives.[21]

THE RECENT CHANGE IN STRATEGY

In 1970 this complex of problems grew
worse, partly because of the diversion of
labor to the attempted sugar crop of 10
million tons. A sweeping change of policy
took place, designed to increase material
incentives as well as to restore financial
balance, both overall and for production
units.[22] Prices of "nonessential" goods were

---

[21] Another contributing factor may have been
the euphoria which followed the successful repul-
sion of the Bay of Pigs invasion.

[22] A recent policy statement by Fidel Castro
[November 25, 1973, before the 13th Congress of
the CTC] admitted implicitly that the distribution
of income had not been closely enough geared to

raised sharply, those of restaurant meals being at least doubled and of rum trebled. New production norms were introduced. An "antiloafing" law was passed. Television sets, refrigerators, and even apartments started to be offered as prizes for good records of attendance and production. It was decided to make cars available to technicians and union officials. Wage increases were linked to productivity. Some pension rates were lowered (for those yet to retire). Accounting was reintroduced and a standard system adopted in 1973. Government statements stressed the importance of saving materials and electricity.

A development plan for the period 1971–75 was also prepared. Although this plan focuses conventionally on a high growth rate (11 percent),[23] it could be argued that aggregates have more significance now that income is distributed more equitably, poverty has been reduced, and production is concentrated on necessities.

It is far too early to see the impact of the new policies on equality, production, or poverty. However, cash in the public's hands has fallen;[24] queues have shortened; absenteeism has declined; and the national income is reported to have risen by 9 percent in 1972, despite a poor sugar crop, and 13 percent (very provisionally) in 1973.[25] The quality of underutilized capital and human resources in 1971 certainly permitted a surge forward in output, including foodstuffs.

However, the new policies may well cause some of what was previously disguised unemployment (because of the hoarding of labor) to emerge into the open. Additionally, the distribution of consumption is becoming rather less equal. The growth in production, therefore, may not mean a comparable rise in consumption at the lowest levels.

While interpretation of Cuban experience is complicated by the temporary abolition of financial controls, it suggests that very drastic redistribution, especially if it takes the form of abolishing incentives, may interfere with the reduction of poverty (at least in a society which has been conditioned to expect personal rewards). Now that financial controls are being introduced, it will be easier to assess whether what is still a highly egalitarian society has the dynamic potential to complete the task of eliminating poverty.

---

productive contribution. Before reaching communism, which implied distribution according to need, it was necessary first to apply "the inexorable law" of socialism, that each should be paid according to his labor.

[23] See "La Perspectivas Desarrollo de la Economia Cubana, 1971–75," p. 194, loc. cit. The growth rate of agriculture, apart from sugar, is put at the very high rate of 16.4 percent.

[24] Castro, loc. cit. The reduction had been 1.23 billion pesos in two and a half years.

[25] Ibid.

References

Acosta, J. 1972. Land Reform Laws in Cuba and the Peasants Private Sector. *Economia y Desarrollo*, No. 12 (July-August): 84–115.

Consejo Nacional de Economia. 1958. *Simposia de Recursos Naturales.* Havana.

Dorticos, O. 1972. Development of Cuban Economy: Analysis and Perspectives. *Economia y Desarrollo* No. 12 (July-August): 28–62.

Navarro, V. 1972. Health, Health Service and Health Planning in Cuba. *International Journal of Health Services* 2 (August): 406.

Oshima, H. 1961. The National Income and Production of Cuba in 1953. *Food Research Institute Studies* 2 (November): 213–227.

United Nations. 1973. *Multi-National Corporations in World Development.* New York.

II.C.4. Tanzania's Development*

Since Independence, Tanzania has attained a moderate but fairly steady growth rate. Between 1964 and 1972 the country has averaged about 5 percent a year in real terms, compared to 3 percent over the 1961–64 period and somewhat less over the previous decade. The relevant policy-change dates were Independence in 1961, the first comprehensive planning exercise in 1964, and serious priority to asset and income redistribution in 1967. Independence was followed by planning and growth, but no correlation between egalitarianism and growth in the short run is evident. External factors—weather, rundown of diamond production, export prices—have been moderately worse since 1967 (albeit aid levels have been higher), giving credit to the tentative conclusion that concentration on egalitarian and socialist measures has been at least neutral in its impact on growth.

The shift to a more radical policy initially arose from a realization that the 1961–67 period had seen the first steps toward the emergence of elites in a form likely to "nationalize" the colonial structure rather than lead to egalitarian socialism. These elites included Tanzanian large farmers, small businessmen, intellectuals, managers of the parastatals and the private sector, senior civil servants, and political leaders. As these were at most weak proto-elites in 1967, the 1967–73 strategy has been largely prophylactic, freezing the citizen tap, squeezing the small private sector modestly, nationalizing the large private sector, and seeking to build up the economic and political power of the poor through asset creation, expenditure redirection, and participation.

*From Reginald H. Green, "Tanzania," in Hollis B. Chenery et al., *Redistribution with Growth,* Oxford University Press, New York, 1974, pp. 268–73. Reprinted by permission.

In 1972, average output was about $100. The poorest 40 percent of the population had per capita incomes below $50 and about one-sixth of total income while the richest 20 percent had per capita incomes over $190 and slightly over half of total income. This probably represents a shift of about 8 percent away from the top quintiles since 1967, a gain of about 2.5 percent to the bottom two quintiles and a gain of 5.5 percent to the middle two quintiles. Public consumption was about 10 percent of GDP; investment was of the order of 24 percent. The impact of direct and indirect taxes and use of public services would probably raise the bottom two quintiles' share to about one-fifth of total income and reduce the top quintile's to somewhat under half. The very top end of the income distribution is dominated by some 5,000 expatriates who provide high-level skills. The lowest two quintiles are predominantly rural. The urban unemployed and informal sectors are relatively small absolutely and in comparison with other African countries. Nonagricultural recorded wage employment has grown over 6 percent a year for half a decade, tending to match the rate of urbanization.

The public sector citizen wage/salary range runs from Sh 3,600 to Sh 58,000 per year. As three-quarters of large- and medium-scale economic activity is in this sector, and the share is rising, this set of scales is increasingly dominant. Medium-size citizen private business and professional incomes are—in perhaps 3,000 to 5,000 cases—near or above the top of this range, but unlikely to grow absolutely in levels or numbers. With all land state-owned, and the rural emphasis on *ujàmaa* (cooperative) villages, there now is virtually no chance that the 10,000 or so citizen-farm families with incomes (cash and kind) above Sh 10,000 will expand individually or as a class to dominate the agricultural sector.

From 1967 to 1973, urban wage/salary inequality sharply fell, large-scale landlord holdings experienced a total takeover (with very limited compensation), the retailer profit margin growth reversed, and a broadening of the rural/urban gap halted. While the actual distribution of income was only marginally better in 1973 than in 1967, the trend appears to be positive and built on programs which should sustain it and allow the growth needed to finance it.

INSTRUMENTS OF REDISTRIBUTION

Asset redistribution has centered on nationalization and directly productive public investment, rural infrastructure creation, and *ujàmaa* village promotion and support.

By 1972, three-quarters of large- and medium-scale economic activity were in the public sector, compared with perhaps one-fifth in 1966. The contribution of national parastatals and cooperatives to monetary GDP was estimated to be about 23 percent, and to monetary fixed investment, 57 percent, while their net cash flow (before tax and depreciation) was almost 40 percent of domestic savings. Although under one-third of parastatal assets were nationalized—as opposed to created by public investment—the 1967–71 nationalizations shifted the actual balance and planning outlook radically.

Decentralization and institutional reform have raised the share of recurrent and public investment expenditure directed to rural areas and altered the balance significantly toward poorer farmers. Probably half of public capital and recurrent annual expenditure from 1967 to 1972 has been shifted to the bottom two quintiles. This includes expenditure on selective input subsidies, rural adult and rural skill education, initial materials and food-*cum*-feeder roads, seeds, cattle for

ujàmaa villages, water and health expenditure directed toward *ujàmaa* villages, and additional expenditure on rural roads and services. Given that this capital formation, enhancing human skills and creating public assets, amounted to about 3 percent of GDP, it formed a major redistribution effort in favor of the rural poor.

Ujàmaa (cooperative or communal) villages now number about 7,000, with about 3 million participants or over a quarter of rural Tanzanians. There is a clear geographic and income group correlation between poverty and *ujàmaa* village membership. Priority for rural capital and recurrent services plus provision of training for internal technical and farm management strengthening is designed to provide both immediate increases in living standards and medium-term increases in productive capacity. The rapid growth of the villages and the relatively low rate of members leaving suggest that the former goal is being attained; results in increasing productivity are unclear or mixed (as would be expected in a program only in its fourth year, with most villages under two years old). Some major achievements, e.g., regionally with maize at Dodoma, have been recorded.

Price changes have included an income policy which has narrowed the pretax range between the highest to the lowest paid public sector (including parastatal) worker from over 70-to-1 at Independence to about 18-to-1 today. Taking account of direct and indirect taxation, and the greater increases in prices affecting the higher-income groups, the effective differential in terms of consumption standards has fallen from about 60-to-1 to perhaps 13-to-1, including fringe benefits and access to public services. This policy has included absolute cuts followed by a six-year freeze at the top and a threefold increase at the bottom. Price controls have been used to raise rural prices—though not necessarily above import parity given recent world price increases—and to squeeze distributive sector margins. The latter had more than doubled (in percentage terms) over the 1970–73 period so that the measures seem to have aided income distribution with fairly minimal effects on production or investible surplus. Individual cases of serious allocative inefficiency have arisen, e.g., in rice and meat where urban land interests and rural producer or public investible surplus interests clashed. Viable compromise solutions mediating among the goals have usually been reached, though sometimes with severe delays.

Similarly, credit planning has been used to force both more effective purchasing use of commercial credit and more effective bill collection. Domestic credit formation growth has been cut from over 20 percent in between 1969 and 1971 to under 10 percent in 1971/72 and 1972/73, with little evident loss in output growth.

In the productive sector, nonagricultural employment has grown on average by 6.5 percent per year. This suggests that the incomes policy has led to improved use of labor (organizational rather than capital-intensive in nature) and that demand increases in the mass market have more than offset any tendency for modern sector expansion to lag.

Government expenditure, while still urban biased, has risen rapidly and is less urban biased than personal income; it has been steadily pushed toward such areas as rural water, rural health centers, primary and mass adult education, agricultural services, and feeder roads. The taxation system is fairly progressive, with incidence ranging from perhaps 3 percent to 5 percent on the bottom two quintiles, to 17.5 percent on urban minimum wages, and 30 percent to 40 percent at $3,000.

An important regulation is the rule forbidding leaders of the party, middle and senior civil servants, and middle and senior public productive sector employees from having second jobs, earning rental or share incomes, or running any business except a small farm without permanent (as opposed to seasonal) paid labor. Spouses of these individuals face similar restrictions. This code is enforced with relative strictness even at the rural level, although its impact there is less.

GOVERNMENT OBJECTIVES

In the case of Tanzania, the direction of change clearly flows from the government's commitments to egalitarian, participatory, self-reliant socialism and to the increasingly clear articulation of these commitments since the Arusha declaration of 1967.

Rural priority has led directly to support of *ujámaa* villages, rural credit and services, reconstruction and expansion, tax revision, and decentralization. Seventy percent to 75 percent of the population is dependent on small individual or communal agricultural holdings (*not* 95 percent, as sometimes stated) and the implications of this fact for egalitarianism are clearly grasped.

The alleviation of poverty is usually formulated in terms of creating conditions allowing every able-bodied Tanzanian to earn enough to meet a minimally acceptable standard of personal consumption and have free access to education (including adult literacy and vocational training), health, pure water, and information. Minimum wages, rural services and investment programs, and abolition of all school fees and all direct taxes on increases below the minimum wage flow from this objective.

The reduction of inequality has been viewed as calling for the concentration of all gains on households at or below income levels of Sh 12,000 per year in the urban areas and Sh 6,000 per year in the rural areas. Greatest emphasis has been on households at or below Sh 3,000 per year. This concentration has led to public sector salary cuts in 1961 and 1966 and freezes since; reconstruction of parastatal scales to parallel civil service ones; increased taxation (direct and indirect) on the top two quintiles;

steady reduction of the role of private business especially new, large, domestic private business; and the extinction of the large-scale private landlord class.

The active participation of Tanzanians in decisions directly affecting themselves has been regarded as a positive end in itself. This has led to decentralization of regional and district government, broad controls of budget and other activities being allotted to regional and district development councils. Greater participation of workers is being introduced in parastatal management as well as in *ujamaa* village organization. There has also been a tendency toward more regional, district, and cooperative activity on the small business level where it is not well handled (or not handleable) by the national parastatals.

Socialism is seen as necessary for participation, national self-determination, and egalitarianism. Tanzanian objectives emphasize these as well as the extension of the public sector in production. With 75 percent of large-scale economic activity and about 80 percent of monetary fixed capital formation in the public sector, the results of this objective in terms of the mode of production are clear at the macro level. The decentralization thrust into small-scale activity is less clear.

Self-reliance, or national self-determination, is seen as requiring the dominance of Tanzanian ownership, management, investment, savings, and decision-making in the economic as well as social and political spheres. This national posture has led to a stress on raising domestic surplus generation and broadening Tanzanian participation in decisions as well as to a more mass-oriented demand and capacity-oriented approach to production and service development.

The generation of an investible surplus has been seen as critical to achieving all other objectives, even if on occasion conflicting in detail with some of them. From the surplus has flowed a high ratio of tax to monetary GDP (about 40 percent) and the large cash flow (pretax profit plus depreciation) surpluses of Tanzanian parastatals, Tanzanian share of multinational parastatals, cooperatives, and *ujamaa* villages.

PROBLEMS

Three very evident problems are: containing inflation (largely imported) without damaging egalitarianism or the generation of investible surplus, maintaining incentives and morale at both the bottom and the top, and sustaining the growth in management capacity necessary to operate coordinated, decentralized planning involving multiple instruments.

In the context of an open economy with limited and late data, rapid changes in world prices greatly hamper effective planning. Because there is no desire to erode the purchasing power of the minimum wage, the effective rural consumption power, or public sector investible surplus, price management poses technical and political conflicts. At best these result in pressures for greater efficiency or in trade margins going to upper income (proprietor or employee) consumption; at worst to serious delays and some internal inconsistencies.

Morale and incentives pose problems at the top and bottom. With the slower pace of citizen promotion, increasing numbers of senior citizen managers and civil servants face falling real incomes. Managerial and civil service salary scales in the three neighboring countries and in the joint East African services may be 50 percent to 200 percent higher, and Tanzanians are acutely aware of this fact. As well, Tanzanians face the special strains of a more participatory and decentralized system. However, morale is in fact probably better than five years ago and at least as good as in Kenya or Zambia. At bottom the problems are low absolute gains and the time lag in attaining them, particularly for the very poor now farming, or having in the past three years farmed, *ujámaa* villages. In some cases rural asset creation (largely government but significantly self-help) has provided tangible gains, and in others initial output expansion has been significant, but real problems exist for many villages in maintaining momentum.

Management efficiency is needed because the margins for waste are low, especially with large-scale economic activity dominated by the public sector and public expenditure significant and rising. Efficiency is hard to achieve because decentralization and use of multiple institutions and instruments in the context of poor communications, patchy and often unreliable data, and scarce manpower pose very taxing demands. Equally radical change is harder to manage effectively than incremental growth within a fixed structure.

II.C.5. Styles of Development*

In discussing policy one must beware of the fallacy of eclecticism, that is, in the words of Marshall Wolfe, 'the assumption that countries can borrow freely bits and pieces of policies that are alleged to have been successful in other settings.' Although governments seldom are consistent in everything they do, their objectives, programmes and policies tend to have a certain coherence or internal logic which makes it difficult for them to benefit from the experience of other nations where objectives and policies may be radically different. This does not imply that the government of no country can borrow from any other, but it does imply that borrowing is likely to be most successful when it is from a similar country.

Intuition tells us that, say, Pakistan could and would borrow development policies more readily from India than from China, despite her political hostility towards India and her friendship toward China. Similarly, North Vietnam would be more likely to emulate Chinese policies than those of the Philippines. In a sense, the Chinese 'style' of development is incompatible with that of Pakistan, and the Cuban style is incompatible with that of, say, Guatemala. Of course, countries differ primarily in degree, not in kind; policies, objectives and ideologies are scattered along a spectrum in multidimensional space. Nonetheless, three distinct strategies or approaches to development in general and rural problems in particular can be detected: we shall label these the technocratic strategy, the reformist strategy and the radical strategy.

These three strategies define three points on a spectrum—viz. the extremes and the middle—and thus do not constitute a taxonomy. It is for this reason that few countries can be placed firmly under one category or another; most occupy neither an extreme position nor the mid-point, but are distributed (probably skewed right) along a continuum. It is important to recognise that the classification we propose rests on social and political considerations, namely the intended beneficiaries of agrarian policy.

Our three strategies differ in their objectives (or the priorities they attach to various objectives), in the ideology which is used to mobilise support and action, in the dominant form of land tenure institution (and in the pattern of property rights), as well as in the way the benefits of the economic system and growth process are distributed. These differences in objectives, ideologies, institutions and distribution constitute differences

*From Keith Griffin, "Policy Options for Rural Development," *Oxford Bulletin of Economics and Statistics,* November 1973, pp. 239–43. Reprinted by permission.

in style. Differences in style, in turn, are related to the classes or 'core combination'[1] on which the government depends for support.

Most underdeveloped countries have pursued a strategy for rural development which is located toward the technocratic end of the spectrum. The prime economic objective has been to increase agricultural output, either by incorporating more conventional inputs such as land, as in Brazil, or by encouraging farmers to adopt an improved technology, as in the Philippines. The economic system has been justified essentially in terms of a liberal capitalist ideology: emphasis is placed on competition, free markets and widely dispersed private property as sufficient conditions for achieving the objective. In practice, property ownership is highly concentrated and this is reflected in the dominant form of land tenure institutions, viz., latifundia, plantations, large corporate farms and various types of tenancy arrangements. The benefits of technical change and higher output accrue, at least in the first instance, to the landowning elite and other men of property. Inequality of income, far from being deplored, is welcomed, since it is assumed that the rich will save a large proportion of their extra income and thereby contribute to faster accumulation and growth. In other words, the concentration of income and wealth is one of the ways whereby the output objective is expected to be achieved.

The reformist strategy, on the other hand, is basically a compromise between the two extreme positions, and governments which adopt this style of development run the risk of committing the fallacy of eclecticism. Reformist governments tend to vacillate in their choice of policies and one frequently encounters inconsistencies between what a government proclaims and what it actually does. Nonetheless, this style of rural development places priority on redistributing income to some sections of the community (particularly the middle peasantry) and accordingly attributes lower priority than the technocratic strategy to increasing agricultural output. Attempts are made to reconcile greater equity with faster growth by changing agrarian institutions. Quite often, however, the reforms are partial, fragmented and incomplete, and concentrated in certain regions to the exclusion of others, with the consequence that this style creates a dualistic or bi-modal agricultural sector. This is very clear in Mexico, where a policy of redistributing land in favour of the peasantry was followed in the populous areas in the south while a policy of encouraging capital intensive farming on large holdings was pursued in the irrigated areas of the north. Similarly, in Egypt, the original thrust of the reform movement was to encourage labour intensive farming on cooperatives and small holdings, but more recently there has been a shift in favour of more capital intensive techniques on larger 'new farms'.

The ideology associated with this style of rural development usually is nationalist and occasionally is populist. The dominant land tenure institutions tend to be family farms, but if the dualism is pronounced one may find small cooperatives and minifundia confronting large capitalist farms or neo-latifundia. In practice the beneficiaries of the strategy often are the middle peasants on the family farms and large 'progressive' farmers on substantial holdings. Several of the 'progressive' farmers who benefit from a reformist strategy may be of urban origin, e.g., retired army officers, civil servants or politicians. The redistribution of income that occurs, thus, is largely from the upper income groups to the middle; those in the lowest deciles of the income distribution may receive higher earnings, e.g. because of greater employment opportunities, but they are unlikely to improve their relative share—or to increase their political influence.

Finally, the objective of the radical strategy is first and foremost to achieve rapid

[1] See Warren F. Ilchman and Norman Uphoff, *The Political Economy of Change*.

social change and a redistribution of political power. Next in priority comes a redistribution of wealth and income (in that order) and, lastly, higher production. In short, the objectives are greater mass participation, economic equality and faster growth. No conflict is seen between the first two objectives; indeed they are merely different aspects of the same thing, and these, in turn, need not conflict with the third. If there is a conflict, however, the growth objective would give way to the quest for social, political and economic equality.

The radical strategy is supported by the ideology of socialism. Agrarian socialism, particularly its Asian variant, is based on the assumption that it is possible to mobilise an untapped resource potential, namely, human labour. This involves extending the number of days worked, increasing the intensity of effort and raising the efficiency and inventiveness of labour. This can be done, however, only if social and economic inequalities are reduced, since equal sacrifices are incompatible with a system of unequal rewards. Rough equality is achieved by abolishing private property in land and establishing collectives, communes or state farms. These institutions, evidently, tend to favour small peasants and landless labourers.

Implicit in this strategy is a profound scepticism of the desirability of relying on unregulated market forces for development. Considerable emphasis is placed on the immobility and specificity of resources and great importance is attached to exploiting unique local opportunities. In contrast to the first two styles of development, the radical strategy, especially as applied in China, places relatively little emphasis on national agricultural planning, the manipulation of macro-economic aggregates or price signals. Instead more attention is concentrated on the locality; solutions to problems are sought at the local level rather than in general, national policies. Motives and atti-

TABLE 1. Styles of Rural Development

Development strategy	Objectives	Major beneficiaries	Dominant form of tenure	Ideology	Representative countries
Technocratic	increase output	landowning elite	large private and corporate farms, plantations, latifundia, various tenancy systems	capitalist	Philippines, Brazil, Ivory Coast
Reformist	redistribute income (and wealth); increase output	middle peasants, 'progressive' farmers	family farms, cooperatives	nationalist	Mexico, Egypt
Radical	social change; redistribute political power, wealth and output	small peasants and landless labourers	collectives, communes, state farms	socialist	China, Algeria, Cuba

tudes, even morality, are believed to be capable of being changed (witness the search for a 'new socialist man'); moreover, institutional arrangements are treated as variables and considerable experimentation with alternative means of organising production and consumption is permitted; and if a particular locality encounters a difficulty, local initiative rather than outside assistance is expected to be relied upon.

The three styles of rural development represent, therefore, three distinct approaches to the agricultural sector and to the people who live and work within it. The major characteristics of these three styles are summarized in Table 1. A study of countries which have adopted different styles of development should be highly instructive, e.g., in determining the social and economic consequences of a particular technical change, but it is doubtful if governments following one style can or would wish to borrow policies used by countries following either of the other two styles.

II. SELECT BIBLIOGRAPHY

1. Some of the earlier theories of economic development—in particular, those of the classical economists, Marx, neoclassicists, and Schumpeter—are reviewed in G. M. Meier and R. E. Baldwin, *Economic Development: Theory, History, Policy*, New York, 1957, Part 1. An outstanding interpretation of analyses of economic development in the history of thought is provided by Lord Robbins, *The Theory of Economic Development in the History of Economic Thought*, New York, 1968.

2. Incisive appraisals of the state of development economics are presented by Paul Streeten, "Social Science Research on Development," *JEL*, December 1974; _____, *The Limits of Development Studies*, Leeds, 1975.

Major criticisms of the "relevance and realism" of traditional economic theory for developmental problems are presented by Gunnar Myrdal, *Economic Theory and Underdeveloped Regions*, London, 1957; _____, *Asian Drama*, New York, 1968, Part 1, Appendix 6. In connection with these criticisms, it is also instructive to read Dudley Seers, "Why Visiting Economists Fail," *JPE*, August 1962; Martin Bronfenbrenner, "Balm for the Visiting Economist," *JPE*, June 1963; Douglas Rimmer, "The Abstraction from Politics: A Critique of Economic Theory and Design with Reference to West Africa," *JDS*, April 1969.

For some well-balanced critiques of modern theories of development, the following may be noted: W. B. Reddaway, "The Economics of Under-Developed Countries," *EJ*, March 1963; Polly Hill, "A Plea for Indigenous Economics: The West African Example," *EDCC*, October 1966; Wolfgang Stolper, "Contribution of Economic Research to Economic Development," in E. A. G. Robinson (ed.), *Economic Development of Africa South of Sahara*, New York, 1964; H. Leibenstein, "What Can We Expect from a Theory of Development?" *Kyklos*, Vol. 19, No. 1, 1966; Lloyd Reynolds, "The Content of Development Economics," *AER*, *Papers and Proceedings*, May 1969; Ursula Hicks, "Learning About Economic Development," *OEP*, February 1957; Kurt Martin and John Knapp (eds.), *The Teaching of Development Economics*, London, 1966; P. T. Bauer, *Dissent on Development*, Cambridge, 1972, Chaps. 8–9, 20–22.

3. For a more detailed exposition of Rostow's general thesis, and criticisms levied against it, see the papers presented at the International Economic Association's conference, published in W. W. Rostow et al., *Economics of Take-Off into Sustained Growth*, London, 1963.

Several other critiques deserve special mention: K. Berrill, "Historical Experience: The Problem of Economic 'Take-Off,'" in K. Berrill (ed.), *Economic Development with Special Reference to East Asia*, London, 1964, Chap. 7; Henry Rosovsky, "The Take-Off into Sustained Controversy," *Journal of Economic History*, June 1965; P. Baran and E. Hobsbawm, "The Stages of Economic Growth," *Kyklos*, Volume 14, No. 2, 1961; P. T. Bauer and Charles Wilson, "The Stages of Growth," *Economica*, May 1962; S. G. Checkland, "Theories of Economic and Social Evolution: the Rostow Challenge," *Scottish Journal of Political Economy*, November 1960; E. E. Hagen, *On the Theory of Social Change*, Homewood, 1962, Appendix 2; D. C. North, "A Note on Professor

Rostow's 'Take-Off' into Self-sustained Economic Growth," *The Manchester School,* January 1958; Goran Ohlin, "Reflections on the Rostow Doctrine," *EDCC,* July 1961; G. L. S. Shackle, "The Stages of Economic Growth," *Political Studies,* February 1962. But see Rostow's second edition of *The Stages of Economic Growth,* Cambridge, 1971, and *Politics and the Stages of Growth,* Cambridge, 1971.

4. No attempt can be made to do justice to the innumerable historical studies of development. Only a few survey studies can be singled out: R. M. Hartwell, "The Causes of Industrial Revolution: An Essay in Methodology," *Economic History Review,* Vol. 18, No. 1, 1965; Richard A. Easterlin, "Is There a Need for Historical Research on Underdevelopment?" *AER,* May 1965; Barry E. Supple, "Economic History and Economic Underdevelopment," *Canadian Journal of Economics and Political Science,* November 1961; John C. H. Fei and Gustav Ranis, "Economic Development in Historical Perspective," *AER,* May 1969; J. Hughes, *Industrialization and Economic History,* New York, 1970, Part II; J. R. Hicks, *A Theory of Economic History,* London, 1969.

An interesting collection of "successful and promising beginnings" of development is contained in Malcolm E. Falkus (ed.), *Readings in the History of Economic Growth,* New York, 1968; also, Barry E. Supple (ed.), *The Experience of Economic Growth,* New York, 1963.

5. For alternative approaches and some ideological, sociocultural, and political critiques of the "orthodox" doctrine of development, see the various readings in H. Bernstein (ed.), *Underdevelopment and Development,* London, 1974; N. E. Uphoff and W. F. Ilchman, *The Political Economy of Development,* Berkeley, 1972; C. K. Wilber (ed.), *The Political Economy of Development and Underdevelopment,* New York, 1973.

Latin American theories of dependency are presented in *Dependence and Under-development in the New World and the Old,* special issue of *Social and Economic Studies,* March 1973; Fernando Henrique Cardoso, "Dependency and Development in Latin America," *New Left Review,* July-August 1972; O. Sunkel, "National Development Policy and External Dependence in Latin America," *JDS,* October 1969; ——, "The Pattern of Latin American Dependence," in V. L. Urquidi and R. Thorp (eds.), *Latin America in the International Economy,* New York, 1973; Ronald Chilcote, "Dependency: A Critical Synthesis of the Literature," *Latin American Perspectives,* Spring 1974; David Ray, "The Dependency Model of Latin American Underdevelopment: Three Basic Fallacies," *Journal of Inter-American and World Affairs,* February 1973; Clive Y. Thomas, *Dependence and Transformation,* New York, 1974; George Cumper, "Dependence, Development and the Sociology of Economic Thought," *Social and Economic Studies,* September 1974; P. J. O'Brien, "A Critique of Latin American Theories of Dependency," in I. Oxaal et al. (eds.), *Beyond the Sociology of Development,* London, 1975.

Other readings on alternatives in political economy are André Gunder Frank, *Latin America: Underdevelopment or Revolution,* New York, 1970; ——, *Capitalism and Underdevelopment in Latin America,* New York, 1967; ——, "Development of Underdevelopment," *Monthly Review,* September 1966; Alec Nove, "On Reading André Gunder Frank," *JDS,* April-July 1974; Celso Furtado, *Development and Underdevelopment,* Berkeley, 1967; Tamás Szentes, *Interpretations of Economic Underdevelopment,* Budapest, 1969; ——, *The Political Economy of Underdevelopment,* Budapest, 1971; René Dumont and Marcel Mazoyer, *Socialism and Development,* New York, 1973; Aghiri

Emmanuel, "Myths of Development versus Myths of Underdevelopment," *New Left Review*, May-June 1974; T. Weisskopf, "Capitalism, Underdevelopment and the Future of Poor Countries," *Review of Radical Political Economics*, Spring 1972.

The literature on international dependency also overlaps with that on multinational enterprises as listed in the Bibliography to Chapter VI, below, and that on imperialism in Chapter XI.

6. Some readings on the economy of mainland China are: A. Eckstein et al., *Economic Trends in Communist China*, Chicago, 1968; ——, "Economic Growth and Change in China," *The China Quarterly*, April/June 1973; ——, *China's Economic Development*, Ann Arbor, 1975; D. H. Perkins, *Market Control and Planning in Communist China*, Cambridge, 1966; ——, "Plans and their Implementation in the People's Republic of China," *AER*, May 1973; —— (ed.), *China's Modern Economy in Historical Perspective*, Stanford, 1975; L. Huberman and P. Sweezy, "The Cultural Revolution in China," *Monthly Review*, January 1967; B. M. Richman, *Industrial Society in Communist China*, New York, 1969; L. G. Reynolds, "China as a Less Developed Economy," *AER*, June 1975; D. Keesing, "Economic Lessons from China," *JDE*, March 1975; Nicole Ganière, *The Process of Industrialization in China*, an analytical bibliography prepared by OECD Development Center, May 1974; special issue on "China's Road to Development," *WD*, July 1975 (with bibliography).

CHAPTER III

Dualistic
Development

Having considered in the preceding two chapters the general context of developmental problems and some approaches to their analysis, we are now ready to turn directly to a more detailed examination of the development process. We begin by focusing on an outstanding characteristic of LDCs—that of "dualism." In many LDCs, a modern commercialized industrial sector has developed alongside a traditional subsistence agricultural sector, resulting in what is termed a dual economy. Although only relatively few LDCs have yet entered into a Rostovian process of self-sustained growth, most of them do exhibit some elements of modernization in one sector or in parts of their economies. The contrast in economic and social organization between the advanced exchange economy and the backward indigenous economy is one of the most striking—and puzzling—characteristics of a poor country. Professor Kuznets relates the dualism of the domestic economy to the fact that the LDCs are late-developing countries.

It is a crucial characteristic of the presently underdeveloped countries that they *are* underdeveloped while others are much more developed—and this situation has lasted a long enough time to affect markedly the structure of the underdeveloped countries; and also to cover several phases in the changing impact of the developed upon the underdeveloped parts of the world.

This impact, in the broadest terms, is the introduction of a modern component into the structure of the otherwise traditional underdeveloped countries. The magnitude of this component, its specific economic content, and the way in which it was introduced, confined, or encouraged, could and did vary widely. In a territory with colonial status a substantial modern sector often emerged but was organized by Western entrepreneurs of the metropolitan country. In a politically independent underdeveloped country with an export sector oriented toward the developed countries' markets the economic organization was and is quite different from that in a country with domestically oriented agriculture or industry. And in some others, a few members of the native elite educated in some Western lore are participating in administration and attempting to introduce Western elements into what may still be a purely traditional economic society.

Obviously, in the countries that are still underdeveloped, this modern component, even if in existence for a long period, has not expanded sufficiently to shift the country to developed status, and in most cases has not even raised its per-capita product to an intermediate level. Given the long coexistence of developed and underdeveloped economies, it is no exaggeration to argue that a major result of such coexistence in the underdeveloped economies is their dual structure. There are two distinct components, the modern and the traditional; and in marked contrast with the past record of the presently developed countries, the two components continue to perform without the modern one, despite its greater productivity, rapidly outpacing the other. It is the *persistence* of the dual structure and the confinement or limitation of the modern sector that are crucial, for the two have operated simultaneously but for a shorter period in the developed countries also.[1]

If we are to identify the structural relationships involved in the development process, we must understand the dual structure of the modern and traditional, and we must consider how the acceleration of development will entail a higher rate of structural transformation in a developing country. We should therefore explore several questions about dualism: What conditions have given rise to a dual economy? In what sense is a dual economy also a labor surplus economy? How can the absorption of the indigenous economy into an expanding modern economy be accomplished?

To begin to answer these questions, this chapter must first clarify the meaning of "dualism." The term came into prominence in association with the colonial status of many underdeveloped countries. A history of nineteenth-century Jamaica, for example, is entitled *Two Jamaicas*.[2] Two cultures—two ways of life—were represented by the "African Jamaica" and the "European Jamaica":

Jamaica, as a society, was not only molded by the plantation economy, it was created by it. . . . Although Jamaican society of the early nineteenth century was unified with peculiar single-mindedness in the business of producing sugar and coffee, the unity hardly penetrated beyond the common economy endeavor. Jamaicans were divided legally into the three castes of free whites, colored people with limited privileges, and Negro slaves. Of the three divisions, the white and colored people had something in common as the heirs of European culture as it existed in Jamaica. The Negroes stood apart as a separate group, not only because they were slaves, but because their cultural heritage was still largely African.[3]

More recently, a Jamaican economist has brought the story up to date—but still in terms of the legacy of a plantation economy with characteristics of dualism that impede development.

[1] Simon Kuznets, "Notes on Stage of Economic Growth as a System Determinant," in Alexander Eckstein (ed.), *Comparison of Economic Systems*, Berkeley, 1971, pp. 256–7.

[2] Philip D. Curtin, *Two Jamaicas: The Role of Ideas in a Tropical Economy 1830–1865*, Westport, 1955.

[3] Ibid., pp. 22, 23.

Initially plantations have an important development impact for several reasons: they create an infrastructure of social capital, they bring previously unused land into production thereby increasing output and income, they provide former subsistence farmers with the wherewithal to produce for markets and so to bring about a transformation of "primitive" subsistence economy to money and exchange economy, and, in many countries, they have been responsible for the introduction of scientific farming. These developments have been hindered somewhat by the frequent foreign ownership of plantations, the high import content of plantation investment, and the relatively high import propensity of consumption in plantation society. Nevertheless, the net development impact is large enough to bring about a transformation from a condition of undevelopment to one of underdevelopment. Plantation economy never gets beyond the stage of underdevelopment. For within the system itself there are structural factors which impede further economic progress for plantation society as a whole. In both economic and socio-political terms, the system influences the human element in ways that seriously retard development and transformation and the institutional arrangements that exist contribute to perpetuation of a continued state of underdevelopment. The factors operating in this direction are numerous and have considerable weights which when aggregated explain why plantation economy has been left behind in the backwash created by metropolitan economic and social advances.[4]

The prominence of dualism in African economies has also been stressed in a United Nations study:

The most significant economic development in Africa since the beginning of this century has been the enlargement of the money economy involving the shift of resources from subsistence production to production for sale. Initially the traditional economies of the continent were basically organized for the needs and with the resources of self-contained rural communities. Such subsistence economies may be characterized by three related features: i. Lack of specialization on a significant scale. . . . ii. Lack of regular production of a surplus with a view to sale. . . . iii. Stationary technology . . .

The combination of these three features composes a pattern of static economy which almost all African economies at the turn of the preceding century exemplified with relatively inconsequential differences among them. The vicious circle of stagnancy in which the traditional economies were caught has been broken by the rise of exchange activity, the main impetus to which has come from outside through foreign business enterprise and government administrations which have provided the means and incentives to bring certain of the products of Africa within reach of world markets. . . .

The evidence of this and other studies suggests that most African economies may be represented by some form of model, the basic feature of which is a distinction between a traditional economic system and a modern exchange system. The effect of economic development which springs from the exchange economy is to encroach upon the traditional economy, drawing part of its productive resources into the orbit of the exchange economy.[5]

---

[4] George L. Beckford, *Persistent Poverty, Underdevelopment in Plantation Economies of the Third World*, New York, 1972, pp. 210–11.

[5] United States, Department of Economic Affairs, *Structure and Growth of Selected African Economies*, New York, 1958, pp. 1–5.

Postwar experience in Southeast Asia has also been interpreted in terms of open dualistic economies in which the transition process from a colonial epoch to that of modern economic growth involves a gradual modification of the land-based export economy of the colonial heritage through an industrialization process toward a modern growth epoch.

More specifically, the colonial heritage left the economy: (1) compartmentalized into two insulated parts: a modern export-oriented enclave and a large, backward, traditional agricultural sector; (2) dominated by the export of land-based resources . . . while the development of other domestic primary resources (i.e., entrepreneurship, skilled labor and capital) was discouraged; (3) a small and weak industrial sector. [Therefore] transition growth requires the integration of the agriculture and industrial sectors, the growth and development of indigenous factors of production, industralization, and the modernization of traditional agriculture. The focal point of transition growth analysis is to investigate the process through which these interrelated changes occur as modern growth is gradually initiated.[6]

The preceding quotations suggest that it is necessary for students of economic development to become aware of how dualism has arisen, its manifestation in the postcolonial period, and its implications for the future structural transformation of developing economies. One explanation of dualism, propounded principally by J. H. Boeke and other Dutch economists in their studies of Indonesian development, emphasizes the differing social organizations and cultural contrasts that result in "social dualism." The selections in section III.A critically examine this interpretation.

The attention to dualism now centers less upon its sociocultural aspects, and more upon its purely economic features, especially in terms of the effects of a dual economy on the pattern of development. Underemployment is commonly believed to be a dominant feature of densely populated underdeveloped countries, and the labor force is continually increasing with population growth. It is therefore important to consider how dualism is related to the problem of providing adequate employment opportunities for the currently underemployed workers and for the increase in the labor force.

In this connection, one version of dualism looks to resource endowments and differences in the production functions in the two sectors as the basis of a "technological dualism" which, in turn, has resulted in an inadequate number of openings for productive employment. The Note on "Technological Dualism" sets forth this argument (III.B).

There has been much confusion over the phenomena of unemployment, underemployment, and disguised unemployment in the traditional sector of a poor country. The materials in Section III.C are therefore designed to clarify the effects of a dualistic structure on employment by examining the concept of the "labor surplus economy."

Several models of development have focused on the structural formation of a dual economy. Prominent among these is the Fei-Ranis model of a labor surplus economy which is characterized by the coexistence of a relatively large and overwhelmingly stagnant subsistence agricultural sector in which institutional forces determine the wage rate, and a relatively small but growing commercialized industrial sector in which competitive conditions shape the labor market. In such a labor-surplus dualistic economy, labor is a nonscarce factor while capital is extremely scarce. Development therefore

---

[6] Douglas S. Paauw and John C. H. Fei, *The Transition in Open Dualistic Economies: Theory and Southeast Asian Experience*, New Haven, 1973, p. 225.

requires that "the center of gravity must continuously shift towards industry through the continuous reallocation of labor from the agricultural to the industrial sector: the related criterion of 'success' in the development effort is thus a rate of industrial labor absorption sufficiently rapid to permit the economy to escape from the ever-threatening Malthusian trap.[7]

Perhaps most celebrated of the labor surplus models is Sir Arthur Lewis's analysis of "Development with Unlimited Supplies of Labor." The Note on "Inter-Sectoral Relationships in a Dual Economy" (III.D) summarizes this model, emphasizing the interaction between an advanced "capitalist" sector and an indigenous "noncapitalist" sector in a developing economy, and indicating how resources can be drawn into the modern exchange system through capital accumulation in the expanding capitalist sector. The Lewis model is helpful in explaining the mechanism by which the proportion of domestic savings in the national income increases during the course of development of a dual economy whose growth is due to the expansion of capitalist forms of production. As the model explains, capitalist sector growth turns on the higher than average propensity to save from profit income, and on the rise of the share of profits in the national income in the early stages of development. The noncapitalist sector, in turn, serves as a reservoir from which the expanding capitalist sector draws labor. The model therefore has significant policy implications for labor absorption and for the employment problem—a problem to which we shall return frequently in subsequent chapters.

[7] John C. H. Fei and Gustav Ranis, *Development of the Labor Surplus Economy*, Homewood, 1964, p. 3.

III.A. SOCIAL DUALISM

III.A.1. Dualistic Economics*

It is possible to characterize a society, in the economic sense, by the social spirit, the organizational forms and the technique dominating it. These three aspects are inter-dependent and in this connection typify a society, in this way that a prevailing social spirit and the prevailing forms of organization and of technique give the society its style, its appearance, so that in their inter-relation they may be called the social system, the social style or the social atmo-sphere of that society.

It is not necessary that a society be exclusively dominated by one social system. Where this is the case or where, at least, one social style prevails, the society in question may be called homogeneous; where, on the contrary, simultaneously two or more social systems appear, clearly distinct the one from the other, and each dominates a part of the society, there we have to do with a dual or plural society. It is, however, advisable to qualify the term dual society by reserving it for societies showing a distinct cleavage of two synchronic and full grown social styles which in the normal, historical evolution of homogeneous societies are separated from each other by transitional forms, as, for instance, precapitalism and high capitalism by early capitalism, and which there do not coincide as contemporary dominating fea-tures. Without this qualification it would be impossible to distinguish between homo-geneous and dual societies, because every society, in its progression, will show, beside the prevailing social system, the remains of the preceding and the beginnings of its future social style. But, exactly when and

where this is a process of endogenic social progression, of evolution, ultimately homo-geneity will appear because one system, be it a mixture, penetrates through all the strata of society. By this qualification it becomes self-evident that a society maintains its homogeneous character when its late-capitalistic social system is gradually super-seded by a socialistic system that has grown up internally, even when this process of supersession momentarily stirs up the most violent disturbance, war or revolution, in short gives clear proofs of a *temporary* social dualism. In a dual society, on the other hand, one of the two prevailing social systems, as a matter of fact always the most advanced, will have been *imported from abroad* and have gained its existence in the new environment without being able to oust or to assimilate the divergent social system that has grown up there, with the result that neither of them becomes general and characteristic for that society as a whole. Without doubt the most frequent form of social dualism is to be found there where an imported western capitalism has penetrated into a precapitalistic agrarian community and where the original social system—be it not undamaged—has been able to hold its own or, expressed in opposite terms, has not been able to adopt the capitalistic principles and put them into full practice. When stated in these general terms the case of social dualism is widespread. Therefore, although in this treatise most of the data are drawn from Indonesia, this should not be inter-preted to mean that social dualism is an Indonesian specialty. Far from it: rather it may be found to exist in the largest part of the world, and if most of the arguments relate to Indonesia, the explanation is that originally this book treated of Indonesia

*From J. H. Boeke, *Economics and Economic Policy of Dual Societies*, New York, 1953, pp. 3–5. Reprinted by permission.

only, that the author is most familiar with that country, and that no other country illustrates more clearly the characteristics of a dual society.

On the basis of the foregoing argument we now come to the following definition: Social dualism is the clashing of an imported social system with an indigenous social system of another style. Most frequently the imported social system is high capitalism. But it may be socialism or communism just as well, or a blending of them. Nevertheless even in that case it remains advisable to keep the term social dualism because this emphasizes the fact that the essence of social dualism is the clash between an imported and an indigenous social system of divergent character.

Every social system has its own economic theory. A social economic theory is always the theory of a special social system. Even if it announces itself as a general theory still it is historically determined. Therefore the economic theory of a dualistic, heterogeneous, society is itself dualistic. It has to describe and to explain the economic interactions of two clashing social systems. Indeed it will be realistic and not pure theory in so far as it has to be based on historical facts, generalizing them in an "ideal-typical" (Max Weber) way. In so far it even will have to be three economic theories combined into one: the economic theory of a precapitalistic society, usually called primitive economics, the economic theory of a developed capitalistic or socialistic society, usually termed general economic theory or summarily social economic theory, and the economic theory of the interactions of two distinct social systems within the borders of one society, which might be called dualistic economics, if this term had not better been reserved for the combined economic theory of a dual society as a whole.

III.A.2. A Critique of Boeke's "Dualistic Theory"*

The economist who is trying to provide a systematic analysis of the development of underdeveloped areas has two choices before him. He may integrate orthodox economic and social theory, as it exists in advanced western countries, and choose assumptions appropriate to the institutional framework of underdeveloped areas; or he may endeavor to develop a distinctive theory which is applicable only in underdeveloped areas. Perhaps the leading exponent of the latter approach is Dr. J. H. Boeke, who has recently restated and elaborated his special

theory of underdeveloped areas.[1] Dr. Boeke's "dualistic theory" is of special interest and importance because of his years of reflection as Professor of Eastern Economics at Leiden University. While his

[1] J. H. Boeke, *Economics and Economic Policy of Dual Societies*, New York, 1953 (hereinafter referred to as Boeke, *Economics . . .*); "Three Forms of Disintegration in Dual Societies," lecture given in the course on Cooperative Education of the International Labour Office, Asian Cooperative Field Mission, October 1953, and published in *Indonesië*, Vol. 7, No. 4, April 1954, hereinafter referred to as Boeke, "Three Forms . . ."; and "Western Influence on the Growth of Eastern Population," *Economia Internazionale*, Vol. 7, No. 2, May 1954, hereinafter referred to as Boeke, "Western Influence. . ."

*From Benjamin Higgins, "The Dualistic Theory of Underdeveloped Areas," *Economic Development and Cultural Change*, January 1956, pp. 99–108, 111–12. Reprinted by permission.

theory is based largely on Indonesian experience, Boeke feels that it has general applications. An analysis based largely on Indonesian experience may prove to have less general application than Boeke believes; meanwhile, as one of the few attempts at a general theory of economic and social development of underdeveloped areas, Boeke's theory enjoys considerable vogue. Also, to the degree that Boeke reflects attitudes of the former Netherlands East Indies Government, his ideas are of considerable historical interest.[2]

Dr. Boeke gives the following formal definition of a dual society:

Social dualism is the clashing of an imported social system with an indigenous social system of another style. Most frequently the imported social system is high capitalism. But it may be socialism or communism just as well, or a blending of them.[3]

This dualism, he says, is a "form of disintegration, [which] came into existence with the appearance of capitalism in pre-capitalistic countries."[4] The invading force is capitalism, but it is not colonialism. Colonialism is a "dust-bin term"; both it and "the antithesis native-foreign" are "objectionable," and

. . . it is to be hoped that with the obtaining of national sovereignty the true character of economic dualism will be acknowledged sincerely and logically, for its negation is decidedly not to the interest of the small man.[5]

On the other hand, dualism is for Boeke virtually synonymous with "Eastern."

Dualism arises from a clash between "East" and "West" in the sense in which these terms are used in Rudyard Kipling's famous phrase, "East is East and West is West and never the twain shall meet." While cautioning that "the only true and really cogent antithesis is represented by the words *capitalistic* and *non-* or *pre-capitalistic*," Dr. Boeke contends that "we may use the term 'eastern economics' instead of 'dualistic economics' because both terms cover the same situation, to wit, the situation that is typical for the countries in South and East Asia."[6]

The pre-capitalistic or eastern sector of a dualistic economy has several characteristic features. One of these is "limited needs," in sharp contrast with the "unlimited needs" of a western society. Accordingly,

. . . anyone expecting western reactions will meet with frequent surprises. When the price of coconut is high, the chances are that less of the commodities will be offered for sale; when wages are raised the manager of the estate risks that less work will be done; if three acres are enough to supply the needs of the household a cultivator will not till six; when rubber prices fall the owner of a grove may decide to tap more intensively, whereas high prices may mean that he leaves a larger or smaller portion of tapable trees untapped.[7]

In short, in the familiar terminology of western economics, the pre-capitalistic sector of the eastern economy, in contrast to the "homogeneous" western economy, is characterized by backward-sloping supply curves of effort and risk-taking.

Such needs as there are in eastern societies are social rather than economic. It is what the community thinks of commodities that gives them their value.

If the Madurese values his bull ten times as much as his cow, this is not because the

[2] For evidence that the whole structure of government in the Netherlands Indies rested on a theory of "dualism," see Rupert Emerson, *Malaysia*, New York, 1937, esp. pp. 420–25.

[3] Boeke, *Economics . . . , op. cit.*, p. 4.

[4] Boeke, "Three Forms . . . ," *op. cit.*, p. 282.

[5] Boeke, *Economics . . . , op. cit.*, p. 20.

[6] *Ibid.*, p. 12.

[7] *Ibid.*, p. 40.

former is ten times as useful to him in his business as the latter, but because the bull increases his prestige at the bull races.[8]

A closely related feature, in Boeke's view, is the almost complete absence of profit-seeking in an eastern society. Speculative profits are attractive to the Oriental, but "these profits lack every element of that regularity and continuity which characterizes the idea of income."[9] Similarly, there is no professional trading in the eastern village community. Eastern industry is characterized by "aversion to capital" in the sense of "conscious dislike of investing capital and of the risks attending this," only slight interest in finish and accuracy, lack of business qualities, failure to come up to even the minimum requirements of standard and sample, lack of elasticity of supply, lack of organization and of discipline, and corrective local specialization. All this is said to be in sharp contrast to the industry of the westernized, capitalistic sector of underdeveloped areas. The Oriental is, unfortunately, totally lacking in organizing power where modern western enterprises are concerned. Where western industry is dominated by common sense reason, eastern society is molded by "fatalism and resignation."[10]

Because of these great differences between eastern and western economies, western economic theory is totally inapplicable to underdeveloped areas. "We shall do well," Dr. Boeke sternly admonishes, "not to try to transplant the tender, delicate hot-house plants of western theory to tropical soil, where an early death awaits them."[11] Western economic theory, he says, is based on unlimited wants, a money economy, and many-sided corporative organizations, none of which exists in the rural sector of eastern societies. Western theory is designed to explain capitalistic society, whereas the eastern village is pre-capitalistic. He is particularly critical of any effort to explain the allocation of resources or the distribution of income in terms of marginal productivity theory, mainly because of the great immobility of resources in an eastern society.

This picture of the nature of underdeveloped areas leads Professor Boeke to pessimistic views on the chances for success of recent efforts to develop them, economically and socially, along western lines. At best, these efforts are likely to be abortive; at worst, they may hasten retrogression and decay. Perhaps Boeke's strongest statement of this conclusion is his most recent. We cannot reverse the process of social disintegration in dual societies, he says, "because it is not possible to transform the operating forces into the opposite of what they are. The contrast is too all-inclusive, it goes too deep. We shall have to accept dualism as an irretrievable fact."[12] The acceptance of social and economic dualism leads to two policy conclusions: "First, that as a rule one policy for the whole country is not possible, and second that what is beneficial for one section of society may be harmful for the other."[13]

Even in agriculture, efforts to bring about improvement in methods may cause retrogression instead, especially if "mental attitudes" of farmers are not changed in the process. For "capitalism can only be realized by capitalist minded individuals," and if the foreign experts "try to attain their objectives merely by technical, outside means . . . only one result can be expected: an accelerated increase in population which . . . makes the problem more insoluble than ever." Worse, if the innovation is a technical or economic failure, "the result will be increased indebtedness." Meanwhile, the culture of the village community is "perfectly adapted to the environment"; and the methods of eastern agriculture "could hardly be improved

---

[8] *Ibid.*, pp. 37–8.
[9] Boeke, *Economics . . .* , p. 41.
[10] *Ibid.*, pp. 101–2 and 106.
[11] *Ibid.*, p. 143.

[12] Boeke, "Three Forms . . . ," *op. cit.,* p. 289.
[13] *Ibid.*, p. 289.

upon."[14] The existing agricultural system is a result of adaptation, and is not at a low stage of development.

Dr. Boeke doubts whether the Javanese cultivator can turn to new crops. Nor does he think that Indonesians could

X   assume part of the work of the western enterprises, the agricultural part, so as to allow entrepreneurs to devote their energies exclusively to the industrial aspect of the business. This would mean that what is now one united concern, one business, what is being nursed and developed in serried areas, uniformly raised, scientifically guarded and improved, qualified on the basis of the knowledge of market requirements, promoted by means of cheap and plentiful capital, brought into immediate contact with industrial processing, would begin to disintegrate and retrogress at all these points. The present organization of these enterprises is the product of a long history, and handing over cultivation of these products to the petty native peasant would mean a return to an arrangement in the main abandoned as inefficient.[15]

As for industry, "Eastern business will always present a very different appearance from western, even in cases where the two are concerned in the production of the same commodity." Technological progress along western lines is impossible. "There is no question of the eastern producer adapting himself to the western example technologically, economically or socially." Indeed, if eastern enterprises endeavor to imitate western methods, they will merely lose their competitive qualities.[16] Efforts to industrialize Indonesia, along western mechanized lines, have left Indonesia "further from self-sufficiency than it was a century ago," while its national small industry "has for the most part been ruined in the course of modern development."[17]

Similarly, Dr. Boeke does not believe that there is anything government can do about unemployment in underdeveloped areas. He distinguishes five kinds of unemployment: seasonal, casual, unemployment of regular laborers, unemployment of urban white collar workers, and unemployment among Eurasians (he does not specifically mention disguised unemployment). All five kinds of unemployment, Dr. Boeke says, "are beyond the reach of government help," because dealing with them "would entail a financial burden far beyond the government's means."[18]

5) Economic development of any kind is hampered by limited, wants and still more limited purchasing power. Either an increase in supply of foodstuffs, or industrialization, will lead to a glutting of markets, a fall in prices, and havoc. Even the transmigration programme, on which the Indonesian government has placed so much hope for economic development, is of little use, according to Boeke. It only transplants Java's population problem to the Outer Islands, while Java itself is worse off than before.[19]

Any effort on the part of the West to improve these harassing conditions by educating Indonesian leaders in the western tradition can only hasten decay.

[14] Boeke, Economies . . . , op. cit., p. 31; and "Three Forms . . . ," op. cit., p. 292. These remarks apply to Indonesia. "Eastern agriculture in some other countries provides plenty of room for improvement, and even in Java agricultural experts can suggest ways of raising productivity significantly."

[15] Boeke, Economics . . . , op. cit., pp. 193–4.

[16] Ibid., p. 103. See also p. 217, where Boeke argues that "native industry," because it has "practically no organization," is "without capital, ignorant of the market," and "technically helpless," cannot compete with western enterprise, and will suffer trying to do so.

[17] Ibid., p. 227.

[18] Ibid., pp. 318–19.

[19] Boeke, Economics . . . , op. cit., pp. 187, 182–3.

In my opinion, here the western influence tends to divert the attention of the leading classes from their own society to the new and promising western power. The masses, however, unable to follow their leaders on their western way, thus lose the dynamic, developing element in their culture. Eastern culture in this way comes to a standstill, and stagnation means decline.[20]

Again, "the penetration of the West . . . has deprived the villages . . . of their leaders in a social and cultural respect."[21]

In the field of international relations as well, the outlook for the underdeveloped area is dismal. For

after the Second World War disintegrating forces have asserted themselves and binding forces have grown weaker in the international field as well. I am alluding to the formation of new sovereign nations and to the decline of the uniting influence of colonial and imperial powers on all the dual countries.[22]

Dr. Boeke has little to suggest by way of positive policy, as a substitute for the "technical- and capital-assistance" approach which he deplores. However, his idea seems to be that any industrialization or agricultural improvement must be "a slow process," small-scale, and adapted to a "dualistic" framework. "The conclusion to which these arguments about industrialization as well as about agricultural reforms lead us can be no other than the one already expressed, to wit, that social-economic dualism, far from being considered as a passing phase the termination of which may be hastened considerably by a western policy of integration, must be accepted as a permanent characteristic of a large number of important countries, permanent at least within a measurable distance of time." We must have a "dichotomy of social-economic policy, which is fundamentally different according to the social groups at which it is aimed."[23]

What this policy means in concrete terms is not spelled out. "I will expose no plans," says Dr. Boeke, except to stress the need for "village restoration." This restoration will not take place through a revival of the rural gentry, but must "follow more democratic ways." New leaders must spring from "the small folk themselves," and must be accompanied by "a strong feeling of local social responsibility in the people themselves." Just how all this is to be accomplished Professor Boeke does not say; but the sphere of action must be small, the time slow, and the goal won by "faith, charity, and patience, angelic patience."[24]

In examining this discouraging analysis of the prospects for underdeveloped areas, I wish first to record certain differences between Dr. Boeke's impressions of eastern society and my own. Let us return to Dr. Boeke's emphasis on "limited wants," or backward-sloping supply curves of effort and risk-taking. There is an all-important difference between saying that the people of underdeveloped countries really cannot envisage a standard of living higher than their own, or that they could think of no satisfactory way of spending increases in income, and saying that they see no simple way of raising their standard of living by their own efforts or enterprise. The last of these statements is to some extent true, and the reasons for it receive attention below. The first two are definitely not true, especially in Indonesia. There, both the marginal propensity to consume and the marginal propensity to import are high. Wants of the villagers, far from being limited, are so many

---

[20] *Ibid.*, p. 39.
[21] Boeke, "Western Influence . . . ," *op. cit.*, p. 367.
[22] Boeke, "Three Forms . . . ," *op. cit.*, p. 294.

[23] *Ibid.*, p. 293.
[24] Boeke, "Western Influence . . . ," *op. cit.*, pp. 366–9.

and varied that any "windfall," occurring initially through increased exports, is quickly spent on imported semi-luxuries unless rigorous import and exchange controls are applied to prevent it. Far up the great rivers of Kalimantan (Borneo), hundreds of miles into the jungle, good rubber prices result in a spate of orders for bicycles, mattresses, watches, fountain pens, and the like. Sampans in the remotest canals are loaded with Australian tinned milk and American tinned soup. The same is true of the other islands as well. Indeed, the limitless wants of the Indonesian people confront the authorities concerned with import and foreign exchange controls with their major problem. To turn these wants into a wellspring of economic growth, the people must be shown the connection between satisfaction of their wants and their own willingness to work, save, and take risks—a difficult but not impossible task.[25]

Dr. Boeke himself recognizes the high income elasticity of demand for semi-luxuries, largely imported.[26] Why, then, does he attach such importance to "limited needs," contending that in "diametric opposition" to western economies with their "limitless needs," the economic motive does not work continuously in eastern society, calling for a distinct "theory of values?"[27]

Having seen enterprises efficiently organized and operated by Orientals, along western lines, I do not share Dr. Boeke's pessimism regarding possibilities of technological progress in eastern industry. Dr. Boeke's characterization of the Oriental casual worker as "unorganized, passive, silent, casual"—a kind of behavior which, he says, "is characteristic of the Easterner"—seems inconsistent with the growing strength of organized labor in Indonesia, India, and

elsewhere.[28] Similarly, it is hard to reconcile Dr. Boeke's isolation of "repugnance to alienation from the village community" with the continued growth of the large cities in Indonesia. This movement can no longer be explained in terms of rural insecurity; nor are employment opportunities better in the cities. It would seem that the life of the larger cities, with their cinemas, cafes, shops, libraries, and sports events, has proved attractive to villagers who get a taste of it; the result is congestion, inadequate community facilities, and unemployment in the larger cities. It is also hard to reconcile Dr. Boeke's argument that native agriculture cannot compete with western, with the postwar growth of small-holders' rubber exports, which has recently constituted the larger share of rubber exports of Indonesia, despite an increase in total exports.

Some degree of "dualism" certainly exists in underdeveloped areas. In most of them, it is possible to discern two major sectors; one which is largely native, in which levels of technique, and levels of economic and social welfare are relatively low; and another, usually under western leadership and influence, in which techniques are advanced, and average levels of economic and social welfare are relatively high.

There is then no denying the existence of this "dualism," although it is perhaps less sharp than Dr. Boeke suggests, seems to be becoming still less sharp and does not prove by its mere existence that it is immutable. But is this dualism a special feature of "eastern" countries? Merely to raise the question is to answer it. Dr. Boeke himself

---

[25] This point is made, in different terms, by Professor D. H. Burger, "Boeke's Dualisme," *Indonesië*, Vol. VII, No. 3, January 1954.

[26] Boeke, *Economics . . . , op. cit.*, p. 249.

[27] *Ibid.*, p. 39.

[28] *Ibid.*, p. 145. At one point (p. 144), Dr. Boeke seems even to deny the possibility of growth of labor organizations. Because of the nature of agricultural enterprises, which are scattered and more likely to support each other in their common interests than to compete, every effort at organization could be nullified, Dr. Boeke argues. The fact is, however, that it is precisely in plantation agriculture that the Indonesian trade union movement is strongest.

suggests at one point that dualism exists in other underdeveloped areas, including those of Latin America and Africa, as well as those of the Orient. But there is perhaps no country in which "dualism" is more striking than in Italy, with its industrialized and progressive North, and its agricultural and stagnant South. Indeed, one could go further, and argue that some degree of dualism exists in virtually every economy. Even the most advanced countries, such as Canada and the United States, have areas in which techniques lag behind those of the most advanced sectors, and in which standards of economic and social welfare are correspondingly low. . . . Most economies can be divided into distinct regions, with different degrees of technological advance.

Dr. Boeke does say that the term "dual society" should be reserved for "societies showing a distinct cleavage between two cynchronic and full grown social styles."[29] But does this qualification help? What is "full grown"? Where does one find a "full grown" capitalism side-by-side with a "full grown" pre-capitalistic society, with nothing in between? And, if such countries could be found, would it be helpful to classify all other countries as "homogeneous"? It seems more realistic to rank countries on a more or less continuous scale of homogeneity, perhaps with Dr. Boeke's native Holland at the upper end, as a country exhibiting an extraordinary degree of homogeneity.

In sum, it seems to the present writer that Dr. Boeke exaggerates the degree of "dualism" in such countries as Indonesia; the contrast between the advanced and underdeveloped sectors appears to me to be less sharp than Boeke contends, and to be diminishing. Nor can I see that such dualism is specifically eastern. Contrasts between the levels of technique and of economic and social welfare, and even contrasts in economic and social behavior, can be found among different sectors of many western

economies. To my mind, it is Dr. Boeke's "homogeneous" societies that are rare. . . .

Professor Boeke stresses the need for a distinctive economic and social theory for underdeveloped countries, but he does not really provide one. His "theory" consists in description of eastern society, and demonstration that it lacks those features of western society which have resulted in the economic and social development of the West. Since eastern society is so different, it follows, in Professor Boeke's mind, that such economic and social development on western lines is impossible for the East. My own belief is that an explanation of the relative stagnation of the underdeveloped areas can be found, by applying familiar tools of economic and social analysis, within a model defined by appropriate institutional assumptions. It is my further belief that given such an explanation of underdevelopment the solution to the problem will suggest itself.

I do not deny that some existing social and cultural institutions of underdeveloped countries differ from those of the West in a manner constituting a barrier to economic development. Institutions, however, can be changed, as they were changed in Europe and in the New World during the periods of rapid economic and social advance in those areas. The time has not yet arrived for a definitive analysis of the sociological factors in economic development of underdeveloped areas, and certainly this is not the place for such an analysis. Elsewhere,[30] however, I have indicated four kinds of sociological barriers to economic development. First is the dilution of incentives to save, invest, work, and restrict family size in an undivided family system. In contrast to a society in which the single family is the basic unit, a society organized around the undivided family—which can become almost coter-

---

[29] Boeke, Economics . . . , op. cit., p. 3.

[30] Benjamin Higgins, "Economic Development of Underdeveloped Areas: Past and Present," Ekonomi dan Keuangan Indonesia, December 1954.

minous with the village—does not guarantee to a man's immediate family all the benefits, if he works harder, saves more, accepts greater investment risk, or practices birth control. Any gains resulting from such decisions are divided among a group so large that the relation of a particular family's standard of living to its own decisions is a very loose one. Second is the limited scope of entrepreneurial spirit in underdeveloped areas. In many of these countries a feudal attitude towards commerce and industry still prevails, among educated people. There, as in Europe generations ago, "the gentleman does not sully his hands in trade." Innovation in the economic sense is accorded little reward or respect. Yet development of the capitalist type cannot take place without capitalists. Third is what has been referred to above as the "backward-sloping supply curve" of effort and risk-taking. To have an incentive to work harder or better, or to take additional risk with one's capital, one must have a clear picture of the more ample life which additional income will bring. A strong spirit of emulation, or a high "demonstration effect," occurs only where some people are currently demonstrating the effects of additional effort or risk-taking. If life in the villages has been much the same for generations, and no one in the village has before him the picture of people moving to ever higher standards of living through their own efforts or their willingness to risk capital, the expenditure of additional effort, or the acceptance of additional risk, will seem rather absurd. In many Oriental villages, there are virtually only two classes: rich and poor. Nothing approaching the more or less continuous gradation of modes of life found in the West exists in such villages. There is no lower-middle, middle-middle, and upper-middle class through which to move, and a single jump from lower to upper class occurs very rarely, and is hard to imagine, apart from political upheavals. The fourth sociological problem might be termed the "population multiplier." Boeke points out that industrial investment in Indonesia led to no decline in the proportion of the labor force engaged in agriculture, and implies that the occupational structure is essentially immutable in underdeveloped countries—"traffic in these densely populated regions has to remain within limited bounds, otherwise it creates havoc." I believe that the explanation of stable occupational structure is quite different. In the absence of any control of population growth, industrialization, by producing an initial rise in *per capita* income, permits a more rapid increase in the native population. If the bulk of industrial investment goes into export industries (such as plantations, mining, and petroleum), or into production for the limited western market (automobiles, tires), as it did in Indonesia, rather than production for the home market combined with measures to generate domestic demand for manufactured goods, most of the increase in population *must* find employment in agriculture, or remain unemployed.

Such institutional factors are indeed obstacles to economic development. They must be taken into account in any complete analysis, and still more in any recommendations for policy. But they are not immutable; the recent experience of Japan, and some recent anthropological studies of primitive cultures subjected to the "shock" of occupation by American armed forces and similar cases, suggest that cultures can change with astonishing rapidity, and apparently with little pain, if the right formula is found.

III.B. TECHNOLOGICAL DUALISM—NOTE

One of the most important effects of dualistic development is its influence on the pattern of employment. Several writers have suggested that the labor employment problems of a poor country are due to the existence of "technological dualism"—that is, to the use of different production functions in the advanced sector and the traditional sector.[1] In this interpretation, dualism is associated with "structural unemployment" or "technological unemployment"—a situation in which productive employment opportunities are limited, not because of lack of effective demand, but because of resource and technological restraints in the two sectors.

The traditional rural sector is said to have the following characteristics: it is engaged in peasant agriculture and handicrafts or very small industries; the products can be produced with a wide range of techniques and alternative combinations of labor and capital (improved land)—that is, the sector has variable technical coefficients of production; and the factor endowment is such that labor is the relatively abundant factor, so that techniques of production are labor-intensive (in the sense that relatively large amounts of labor and relatively small amounts of capital are used).

In contrast, the modern sector is composed of plantations, mines, oil fields, or large-scale industry; there is either in fact, or entrepreneurs believe there is, only a very limited degree of technical substitutability of factors, so that production is characterized by fixed technical coefficients; and the production processes in this sector are relatively capital-intensive. This situation can be represented by a production function as in Figure III.1, where the points a, b, c, etc., denote the fixed combinations of factors—capital (K) and labor (L)—that would be used to produce the outputs q_1, q_2, q_3, etc., irrespective of what the relative factor prices might be.[2] The line OE joining the points a, b, c, etc., represents the expansion path of this sector, and its slope is equal to a constant, relatively capital-intensive factor ratio.

Only when capital and labor are actually available in proportions equal to the fixed capital-labor ratio is it possible that both factors can be fully utilized simultaneously. If the actual factor endowment is to the

---

[1] As an alternative to Boeke's sociological theory of dualism, the theory of technological dualism has been emphasized by Benjamin Higgins, *Economic Development*, New York, 1968, (revised edition), pp. 17–20, 296–305. The theory of technological dualism incorporates the "factor proportions problem," as discussed by R. S. Eckaus, "The Factor Proportions Problem in Underdeveloped Areas," *American Economic Review*, September 1955. Earlier references include Joan Robinson, *The Rate of Interest and Other Essays*, London, 1952, pp. 110–11; M. Fukuoka, "Full Employment and Constant Coefficients of Production," *Quarterly Journal of Economics*, February 1955.

[2] Units of capital (K) are measured on the vertical axis, and units of labor (L) on the horizontal axis. The curve q_1 is an isoquant representing a certain level of output; as drawn, the output q_1 can be produced only with the unique combination of factors at point a (OK$_1$ of capital and OL$_1$ of labor). The curves q_2, q_3, etc., represent different levels of output, with output increasing along the expansion line OE. Output can be increased, however, only by increasing the use of K and L in the constant proportions given by the slope of OE.

MRS =

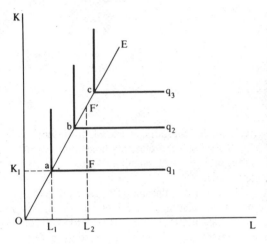

FIGURE III.1.

right of line OE—say, at point F—there must then be some unemployment of labor in this sector. To produce an output of q_1 the sector will use OK_1 units of capital and OL_1 units of labor; even though OL_2 units of labor are available, the excess supply of labor will have no effect on production techniques and L_1L_2 units of labor will remain in excess supply, regardless of the relative factor prices of capital and labor. Only if the capital stock were to increase in the amount indicated by the length of the dashed line FF' could the redundant labor be absorbed in this sector. Failing a sufficient accumulation of capital, the excess labor supply will simply remain unemployed, or must seek employment in the traditional sector.[3]

[3] It is interesting to note that Marx had a similar view of the problem of unemployment: according to Marx, the amount of employment offered by capitalists depends upon the amount of capital in existence, and there is unemployment because there is insufficient capital to employ all the potentially available labor. If A represents the total labor available, and N the amount of employment required to work the existing stock of capital at its normal capacity, then (A—N) is Marx's "reserve army of unemployed labor." Cf. Robinson, *Rate of Interest*, pp. 110–11, n.2.

Having in mind the different production functions in the two sectors, we may now summarize the argument that technological dualism has intensified the problem of employment in dual economies. In many countries, the advanced sector was initially developed by an inflow of foreign capital. As foreign enterprises operated under efficient management with modern production techniques, output in this sector expanded. At the same time, however, population was growing—in some cases at a rate considerably in excess of the rate at which capital was accumulating in the advanced sector. And since production processes in this sector were capital-intensive, and fixed technical coefficients were used, this sector did not have the capacity to create employment opportunities at a rate sufficient to absorb the greater labor force. While investment and output expanded in the advanced sector, capital accumulation was nonetheless slow relative to population growth, and labor became a redundant factor in this sector. Entry into the traditional rural sector was then the only alternative open to surplus labor.

As the labor supply increased in the traditional sector, it may have been possible initially to bring more land under cultivation, but eventually land became relatively scarce. Labor increasingly became the relatively abundant factor, and since technical coefficients were variable in this sector, the production process became ever more labor-intensive in the traditional sector. Finally, all available land became cultivated by highly labor-intensive techniques, and the marginal productivity of labor fell to zero or even below: "disguised unemployment" began to appear.[4] Thus, with continuing population growth, the limited availability of capital caused a surplus of labor to arise in the traditional rural sector. Given the labor surplus, there was no incentive in the traditional sector to move along the production function toward higher capital-labor ratios

[4] Higgins, *Economic Development*, p. 330.

and thereby achieve an increase in output per man.

Further, it is contended that, over the longer run, technological progress did not ease this situation. For in the modern sector technological progress favored more capital-intensive techniques, so that it was all the more difficult to increase employment opportunities in this sector as investment and output expanded. At the same time, there was no incentive in the rural sector to introduce labor-saving innovations (even if it were assumed that the technical possibilities were known and the necessary capital was available).

It has also been suggested that the locus of technological progress is such that a capital-intensive invention affects the choice of technique in only those cases in which the cost of labor to capital is high, but not when it is low as in the traditional sector. As Professor Leibenstein argues,[5] this is because the gradual type of technological progress, which, through redesign and general improvement, increases the effectiveness of given types of machines and tools, is more likely to cause a shift of points on the production function in this region of high rather than low capital-labor ratios, such as in the shift from q to q' in Figure III.2. In the traditional sector, where the capital-labor ratio is low, there is less likelihood of recognizing opportunities for gradual inventions and improvements, the scale of operations may not be sufficient to support any new equipment, and there may be a lack of the complementary inputs needed to adopt some type of new capital good. Accordingly, it is maintained that there is little tendency for the isoquants to shift at points with low capital-labor ratios. If the expenditures line EE' in Figure III.2 represents the existing ratio of labor cost to capital cost (in this case: relatively low wage rates, as reflected in the slope of EE'), then the shift in the

[5] Harvey Leibenstein, "Technical Progress, the Production Function and Dualism," *Banca Nazionale del Lavoro Quarterly Review*, December 1960, pp. 13–15.

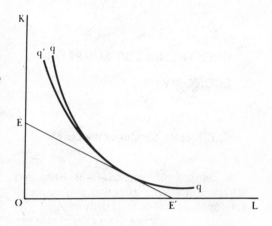

FIGURE III.2.

capital-intensive portion of the isoquant has no effect on the choice of technique in the traditional labor-intensive sector.

Although the theory of technological dualism indicates why factor endowment and the differences in production functions have resulted historically in the rise of underemployment of labor in the traditional sector, its empirical relevancy can certainly be questioned. Has production in the advanced sector actually been carried on with fixed coefficients? Even if an advanced, capital-intensive process was initially imported, was there subsequently no adaptation to the abundant labor supply? Was technical progress actually labor-saving in the advanced sector? These questions call for empirical studies beyond the highly impressionistic statements contained in the foregoing summary of the theory of technological dualism.

Finally, greater clarity is needed on the nature of the unemployment or underemployment in the traditional sector. Ambiguity surrounds the concept of excess labor supply. And the actual extent of "disguised unemployment" may be considerably less than might be inferred from the foregoing analysis. This issue will be examined in the next section.

III.C. THE LABOR SURPLUS ECONOMY

III.C.1. Labor Surplus on the Land*

The concept of surplus farm labor has attracted increasing attention in the underdeveloped countries, especially in Asia. The simplest definition of it implies that some labor could be withdrawn from subsistence farming without reducing the volume of farm output. In technical terms, the marginal productivity of labor is believed to be zero. If this is true, it has some far-reaching implications. But is it true? Is it even conceivable? Some economists have had serious doubts on this score. It must be admitted that the idea of "disguised unemployment," as it is usually called, has sometimes been carelessly formulated and inadequately substantiated.

The subject must be viewed in relation to the general population problem. The crucial fact is that world population has doubled in the last hundred years. About two-thirds of the increase has taken place in the underdeveloped areas, chiefly in Asia, largely through a fall in death-rates. This has been part of the uneven impact of Western civilization on the rest of the world. Now in the poorer countries as a rule the majority of the population works in agriculture to start with, for basic and obvious reasons. Just as food is the major item of consumption in low-income communities, so the struggle for food takes up most of their time and resources. In such countries rapid population growth naturally leads, and in some has already led, to excess population on the land.

Consider for a moment the effects of population growth in a community of peasant cultivators. Numbers are increasing while land, capital and techniques remain unchanged. Alternative employment opportunities may be lacking because of the rigid social structure, and may actually be decreasing because of the decline of traditional handicraft industries due to the competition of imported manufactures.

With the growing pressure of people on the land, farms become smaller and smaller. What is more, farms are divided and subdivided into tiny strips and plots. Accordingly it seems to me that agricultural unemployment in densely populated peasant communities may be said to take at least two basic forms: (1) underemployment of peasant cultivators due to the small size of farms; (2) unemployment disguised through fragmentation of the individual holding. . . .

To the extent that the labor surplus is absorbed—and concealed—through fragmentation, it cannot be withdrawn without bad effects on output unless the fragmentation is reversed and the holdings are consolidated. Over a limited range the marginal productivity of labor might be zero without any such reorganization. It could be zero over a much wider range if the remaining factors of production were appropriately reorganized, which would require for one thing a consolidation of plots. Appropriate reorganization of the other factors of production is clearly a necessary and a reasonable pre-requisite for purposes of policy as well as analysis.

There are a number of empirical studies that tend to confirm this general picture.

*From Ragnar Nurkse, "Excess Population and Capital Construction," *Malayan Economic Review*, October 1957, pp. 1, 3–5. Reprinted by permission.

142

The evidence can never be entirely satisfactory in a matter such as this where some things, including the weather, would have to be held constant and others subjected to a reorganization which may necessitate a revolutionary change in rural life, bringing inevitably other changes with it. Nevertheless the connection between over-population and fragmentation goes a long way to make the existence of surplus farm labor plausible.

On a theoretical view of the matter it is clear that excess population can be so great in relation to land and capital that the marginal productivity of labor is reduced to zero. There are, however, two reasons why some economists have found this idea difficult to accept. First, anyone trained in Western economics would have to ask: Who would employ these people if their product is zero? Or else one might ask: How can these marginal people live, what do they eat, if they really produce nothing?

The answer to the first question is that in many countries the wage-labor system, which Western economists are apt to take for granted, hardly exists. The prevailing condition in subsistence farming is one of peasant family labor.

The answer to the second question—how can they live?—is that they live by sharing more or less equally in the total product of the farm, which includes the product of intra-marginal labor and of any land and capital goods the peasants may own. The product from these factors goes into the same pot and the members of the household eat out of that same pot. These institutional arrangements are foreign to the economies of business enterprise, and so the conditions which they make possible may seem paradoxical.

If this sharing of food is considered a little further the ultimate limit to the multiplication of people on the farms becomes starkly plain.[1] If the average total product per person falls below the physical level of subsistence, the outcome is the Malthusian state of starvation cutting down numbers or at least checking their further increase. At the point where this average product equals the physical subsistence level, the marginal product of labor may well be zero or even negative.[2] Still, it need not be as low as zero. Conversely, if and when labor's marginal product is zero, the average product need not be as low as the physical subsistence level; it may be a little above that level.

In any case, excess population necessarily implies that the marginal product is less than the average. In this state of affairs further population growth brings down the average level of consumption. Why? Because the additional labor contributes less than the average worker previously, and so it pulls down the average product per head. If the average product is as low as we know it to be, it does not seem far-fetched to suppose that in some cases the marginal product of labor may be zero. The upshot of the argument does not, of course, depend on its being exactly zero, although this is a convenient case on which to concentrate the analysis. The essential point is that the marginal workers live, in effect, on a subsidy if their own contribution to output is less than their intake of food and other necessities.

The relationship between total product and total population is illustrated in the accompanying diagram (III.3). Average product per head is reflected in the slope of the vector from the origin to any point on the curve. The marginal product is reflected in the slope of the curve itself at any given point. The average product per head reaches a maximum at A (where the angle AOL is

---

[1] The analysis concentrates on the subsistence farm sector. The reader should bear in mind that even the most backward economy usually contains other sectors also, including export production, commerce, government and even some industrial activity.

[2] Professor J. E. Meade has shown this very clearly in his book, *The Theory of International Economic Policy;* Vol. II, *Trade and Welfare,* issued under the auspices of the Royal Institute of International Affairs, London: Oxford University Press, 1955, Chapter 6 and Appendix 1.

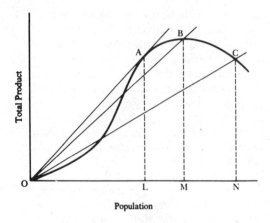

FIGURE III.3.

largest) and declines thereafter as population increases further. The marginal product becomes zero at B (where the average product measured by the angle BOM may still be substantial). If population increases beyond M, the marginal product becomes negative and the average product continues to fall. If we suppose that the average product at N represents the absolute physical minimum of subsistence, then population cannot increase beyond N. This supposition is of course purely arbitrary and illustrative. Actually the physical subsistence level of average product per head may lie, not in the range of negative marginal productivity, but conceivably at B or somewhere between A and B where marginal product is still positive. The diagram merely illustrates the possibilities and does not, of course, tell us what actually happens.

It must be conceded that this view of the matter is essentially that of "optimum population" theory (in the diagram the optimum size of population is OL). Now this theory has sometimes been criticized as being an unrealistic exercise in comparative statics. It assumes that nothing changes except the number of people—and, in response thereto, the volume of total product. It abstracts from, and ignores, any connections that may exist between population size on the one hand and, say, the state of techniques or the volume of capital on the other hand. It holds all other things constant. Is this not bound to lead to a distorted view of reality?

The criticism may be perfectly valid with regard to population trends in the Western world. But if we consider Asia over the last hundred years, I am not sure that the objection has much force. I began by saying that the population explosion in Asia, due largely to the fall in death-rates, reflects the *uneven* impact of Western civilization. The point is precisely that while population has doubled, other things such as techniques, capital supplies and cultivable land have remained *too much the same.* Therein lies the whole problem. Of course, there has been some advance in these other things too, but not nearly at the same rate as in population. In Asia there has been nothing like the advance that accompanied population growth in the West. In this state of affairs it seems to me that the "optimum population" approach, questionable though it may be in the West, has a good deal of validity in the East. The economic problem of the East has been largely a consequence of dynamic population growth in an otherwise relatively static environment.

"Optimum population" theory directs attention chiefly to the variation of *average* product as the size of population varies. We have found it at least equally important to consider the *marginal* product. The question might be asked: Why this obsession with the margin? Why not stress the obvious fact of a low general level of productivity? The answer is that the marginal approach is useful here because of the need to take away some labor from current production for work on capital construction.

III.C.2. Unemployment in Underdeveloped Countries*

In the literature before the Great Depression unemployment was usually regarded as a temporary maladjustment of demand and supply of labor. It was explained in terms of cyclical or other shifts in demand, low mobility of labor and sluggish price and wage adjustment.

The Great Depression and the Great Keynesian Simplification (of economics) born of the depression experience has made the world employment conscious. Under-employment equilibrium (with or without competition) is regarded as the rule and full employment the rare exception. According to the predominant simpler versions of the new doctrine there is practically always some slack in the economy and this slack is always due to insufficiency of effective demand. The unemployment is either open or disguised. The phrase "disguised unemployment" was coined by Mrs. Robinson and used to designate workers, who having lost well-paid positions in industry to which their skill and training entitles them, are doing odd jobs, raking leaves or selling apples to eke out a miserable living.

Keynesian unemployment, open or disguised, was thought to exist only in rich industrial countries. Poor and underdeveloped countries are spared this particular scourge, because they still have plenty of investment opportunities and their poverty keeps the rate of saving low.

According to ultra modern i.e. Post-Keynesian theory, disguised unemployment exists also in underdeveloped countries, typically and chronically (but by no means exclusively) in agriculture. Disguised unem-

*From Gottfried Haberler, "Critical Observations on Some Current Notions in the Theory of Economic Development," *L'Industria*, No. 2, 1957, pp. 3–5. Reprinted by permission.

ployment is said to be present if a part of the labor force, say 5%, can be removed from the farms without reducing aggregate output; in fact aggregate output may even increase when the input of labor is reduced. It is, in other words, a case of zero (or negative) marginal productivity of labor.

The term "disguised unemployment" is surely not a good one, because most of the writers who believe that such conditions are widespread in the underdeveloped world (e.g. Arthur Lewis, Ragnar Nurkse, P. N. Rosenstein-Rodan) do not wish to suggest that disguised unemployment in underdeveloped countries is curable by the same easy methods as disguised and open cyclical or secular unemployment in industrial countries. A mere strengthening of effective demand by means of easy money policy and deficit spending is not only insufficient but positively harmful.

The modern theory of disguised unemployment can be regarded as an extreme version of the well known theory of protection associated with the name Mihail Manoilesco and the theory is, in fact, being utilized for the justification of import restrictions.[1] While Manoilesco only claimed

[1] For example, in numerous publications of ECLA. See esp. *International Co-operation in a Latin American Development Policy*, United Nations, 1954. It is interesting to note that the originators of the idea (Nurkse and Rosenstein-Rodan) are careful to point out that conditions in the sparsely populated countries of Latin America are not the ones where one would expect disguised chronic unemployment. They refer specifically to old thickly populated countries such as Egypt, India and South East Europe. This has not prevented ECLA from embracing the idea wholeheartedly and to make it a cornerstone of its highly protectionist and interventionist policy recommendations.

that the marginal productivity of labor in agriculture was low compared with other branches of the economy, the modern theory of disguised unemployment goes the whole hog and maintains that it is zero or possibly negative.

To my mind, the claims of the proponents of the theory of widespread disguised unemployment are tremendously exaggerated. I can perhaps better explain what I think is wrong with the theory of disguised unemployment by stating positively what in my opinion is actually true in varying degrees in various countries, not only in underdeveloped but in developed countries as well: If it were possible to improve methods of production in agriculture; if the skill of farm laborers is increased; if social habits could be changed, a new spirit implanted and the resistance to moving to and living in cities and to working in factories could be overcome; if technology in industry could be changed so as to employ unskilled rural workers; if capital and other cooperating factors (entrepreneurs, managers, skilled foremen, etc.) could be provided in larger quantities and better quality; if and to the extent that all these things happen or are done, agriculture can release a lot of labor without loss of output and industrial output be stepped up at the same time.

Now there is no doubt that all these things gradually do happen and did happen all the time in developed as well as underdeveloped countries. In fact, economic development largely consists of these changes. Furthermore, few would deny that many of these changes and improvements can be speeded up by appropriate policies (although, if the measures taken are inappropriate or the dosage incorrect, the result will be a slow-down rather than a speed-up) and that for some of these changes to happen Government action is indispensable. But it is very misleading to speak of disguised unemployment. In that sense there always was disguised unemployment in developed as well as underdeveloped countries and practically everybody is a disguised unemployed, even in the most highly developed countries, because each of us will produce more ten years hence when technology has made further progress, skill and training have been further improved, the capital stock increased, etc.

The cases where after removal of a part of the labor force output remains unchanged (or even rises) without capital having been increased, technology improved, social habits changed, etc., or where such changes can be expected to be the automatic and immediate consequence of a prior reduction in labor input, must be comparatively rare and inconsequential compared with the increase in output due to the gradual introduction of all those changes and improvements.

The theory of disguised unemployment is often associated with the proposition that the capital-labor proportion is fixed—forgetting conveniently other productive agents. In other words production functions (isoquants) are said to have rectangular (or at least angular) shape. In some modern highly mechanized industries one may sometimes find situations faintly approaching this case. But the assumption that this should be the case in more primitive economies (agriculture) and should be a chronic situation seems to me preposterous.

III.C.3. The Concept of "Disguised Unemployment"*

The term "disguised unemployment" is commonly used to designate a situation in which the removal from a working combination of factors of some units of labor, nothing else of consequence or worth mentioning being changed, will leave the aggregate product of the working combination undiminished, and may even increase it. To say that there is "disguised unemployment" is therefore equivalent to saying that in that working combination the marginal productivity of labor is zero or almost zero and may even be a negative quantity. The "unemployment" may be only metaphorical, since there may be hard work even at the margin, when "unemployed" must mean "unproductively employed." But sometimes it is intended to be realistically descriptive, as when it is used to include seasonal unemployment; in such cases, I do not know what the adjective "disguised" is supposed to mean. I will in this note treat "seasonal unemployment" as a distinct phenomenon not obviously presenting a serious problem and not obviously having any peculiar relationship to agriculture in underdeveloped countries. As I look at the agricultural world with my inexpert eye, it seems to me that agricultural employment is most seasonal, is least continuous, in the temperate zones where agriculture is most "developed" and yields the highest levels of average and marginal product per labor-year.

As an intermittent phenomenon, resulting from the vagaries of weather and human error, zero marginal productivity of labor in agriculture is a commonplace concept. But

*From Jacob Viner, "Some Reflections on the Concept of 'Disguised Unemployment,'" in Contribuicoes à Análise do Desenvolvimento Econômico, Livraria Agir Editôra, Rio de Janeiro, 1957. Reprinted by permission.

how can a priori the possibility of zero marginal productivity of employed labor, as a chronic phenomenon, be plausibly established? One way that has been suggested is on the assumption that the (average and marginal) technical coefficients of production are constant, so that the addition to a working combination of more units of labor will add nothing to the aggregate product unless additions are made also to the quantities used of all (or of some) of the other factors of production—Pareto's "fixed coefficients," or Frisch's "limitational factors."

I am not aware that anyone has ever given a convincing illustration of a technical coefficient which is "fixed" in a valid economic sense. The plausibility of the idea has resulted, I believe, from the confusion of chemical ingredients of a product, or actual engineering elements in a productive process, with potential economic input-items in a productive process. If iron ore, or coal, were as expensive per ton as gold I am sure that the steel industry would find ways of appreciably reducing the amounts of iron ore, or of coal, it uses to produce a ton of steel of given specific character, even though the chemical constituency of the steel were invariant, and, moreover, it would readily find ways of changing the chemical constituency of a ton of "steel" without reducing its suitability for its ordinary uses, and this not only in the long run but in the very short run. As far as agriculture is concerned, I find it impossible to conceive of a farm of any kind on which, other factors of production being held constant in quantity, and even in form as well, it would not be possible, by known methods, to obtain some addition to the crop by using additional labor in more careful selection and planting of the seed, more intensive weeding, cultivation, thinning, and mulching, more painstaking harvesting, gleaning, and cleaning of the crop. Even supposing that there were such a farm, on which every product had technically and economically fixed ingredients, labor would still have positive marginal productivity unless there were not only fixed technical coefficients of production for all the economically relevant potential products of the farm, but the proportions between the technical coefficients were uniform for all of these products. For if these proportions are different as between different products, then it will always be possible by appropriate change in the product-mix, in the direction of more production of those products whose labor technical coefficients are relatively high, to absorb productively any increment of labor.

Unless one assumes non-economic motivation on the part of employers, there is difficulty also in conceiving why they should hire at any wage-rate additional units of labor beyond the point at which they know the labor will add less in value to the product than the wage-cost, to say nothing of the case where the labor will add nothing to and may even subtract from the product. The employer may, of course, be ignorant as to the facts, but I know of no experience to persuade me that the speculative economist is on such matters better informed than the experienced farmer in immediate touch with reality. This is probably what W. A. Lewis has in mind, although I cannot find that he anywhere explicitly says so, when he concedes that in agriculture "disguised unemployment" occurs only for peasant or self-employed labor, and not for plantation labor.[1] Since there is a good deal of plantation agriculture in underdeveloped countries, this is an important limitation of the applica-

bility of the concept of "disguised unemployment." But it raises its own difficulties. In Brazil, for instance, I take it that agriculture is even in the same localities a mixture of hired labor on plantations, of self-employed labor on owned (or rented?) small farms, and of squatter labor. Should there not be a tendency for equalization of the marginal productivity of labor in all agrarian uses where labor can fairly readily move from one type of use to another? Where there is labor-mobility, marginal productivity of labor must rise substantially above zero in peasant or squatter agriculture or sink to zero or near-zero on the plantations. This would especially be the case, for a reason to be explained later, if a member of a peasant or squatter family would not lose access to the family supply of food by taking employment on a nearby plantation. When I was in Brazil, I heard of complaints by plantation owners in districts in which there was also peasant and squatter agriculture of "shortage of hands" (*falta de mao*). I don't see how this can be reconciled with the prevalence of zero marginal productivity of labor, whether on the plantations or for self-employed agricultural labor. . . .

W. A. Lewis has suggested, as an explanation of "disguised unemployment" in agriculture that, when "there are too many persons on too little land" the farmer cannot afford to keep cattle, so that the land gets no manure and land is put under the plough which ought to be left in forest or in fallow; arid land is over-cropped, so that fertility is destroyed.[2] . . . Given the situation as Lewis describes it, the *long run* marginal productivity of labor could be zero or negative, but it would be in the long run interest of the owner of the crowded farm not to over-work it. Genuine unemployment on the farm, or employment of the "surplus" labor only on such tasks as would not impair fertility, would in the long run be more profitable than full employment, but the shortsighted-

[1] *The Theory of Economic Growth*, Homewood, 1955, pp. 326–7. In "Economic Development with Unlimited Supplies of Labour," *The Manchester School*, May 1954, pp. 141–2, the presence of "disguised unemployment" is claimed for hired agricultural labor also, although in lesser degree than for self-employed labor.

[2] *The Theory of Economic Growth, op. cit.*, pp. 327–8.

ness of the owner, or the hunger of his family, might nevertheless trap him into exploiting the short-run marginal productivity of labor, which I would expect to be always positive in a situation such as here described. Lewis concedes that this phenomenon of impairment of soil-fertility through over-crowding would be present only in "over-populated areas," and lists China, India, Japan, Java, Egypt, some countries in the Middle East, Kenya, and some small islands as the only countries in this category. Latin America and Eastern Europe, which many writers have regarded as subject to "disguised unemployment," are thus excluded by Lewis, and, as we have seen, he would exclude also the plantation agriculture of any country.

Ragnar Nurkse has suggested that where "disguised unemployment" prevails in agriculture, it would be desirable to transfer the surplus labor off the farms to produce capital goods, while keeping the consumption of food by the population as a whole constant through taxation or direct controls.[3] This would be relevant for Lewis's type of zero or negative marginal productivity of agricultural labor resulting from loss of fertility of soil through over-crowding and over-cropping. But as I have pointed out, it would not be a solution in the short run, for in the short run transferring labor out of agriculture would, or might, reduce the total output. N. Koestner has objected against Nurkse's argument that it fails to take account of the fact that the urban workingman needs more calories than the idle rural inhabitant.[4] But for Lewis the "disguised

[3] *Problems of Capital Formation in Underdeveloped Countries*, Oxford, 1953, pp. 36 ff.

[4] "Some Comments on Prof. Nurkse's Capital Accumulation in Underdeveloped Countries," *L'Egypte contemporaine*, XLIV, April 1953, p. 9. Nurkse, however, as far as I can see, has made a more than adequate concession on this point. See his original discussion in *Some Aspects of Capital Accumulation in Underdeveloped Countries*, Cairo, 1952, p. 25, (repeated in substance in his *Problems of Capital Formation*, p. 39): "A food deficit may

unemployed" of agriculture may be working as hard as anyone else, and may in fact need more calories for farm-work than they would need for factory-work. They are "idle" in the sense only that their work is unproductive. On the other hand, Nurkse, does not mention the inevitable and possibly appreciable loss of food involved in deterioration, spoilage, and spillage when the food is consumed in the city instead of on or near the farm where it is produced.

Still another kind—or source—of zero or less marginal productivity of agricultural—or urban—labor can be conceived of, and may even be important in practice, although I have not encountered it in the literature, and it would not be a simple matter, even if it existed, to demonstrate the fact. Suppose that given the "quality" of the labor force and the supplies of other productive resources, the marginal productivity function of labor could be represented, in the familiar manner, by a slowly-descending curve which within the range of observation remains substantially above the zero-productivity level. Suppose, however, that the quantity of food available for the farm family depends wholly on the output of the farm, that the food is shared by all members of the family, and that when it falls below a certain quantity per capita the energy and productive will and capacity of the worker-members of the family decline. It then becomes conceivable that if some of the members of the family, including working-members, were removed from the farm (or if the whole family were removed from the farm, and the farm joined to a similar adjoining farm) and if those removed could no longer draw on the food-resources of the farm, the labor remaining on the farm would acquire a sufficiently higher marginal productivity curve, so that the farm would produce more than it did before when the

arise also from the investment workers, the previous unemployed in disguise, having to eat a little more than before because they are now, perhaps, more actively at work."

number of workers was greater. In such a case, much of what has been said about "disguised unemployment" and about appropriate remedies for it would be relevant. Not so, however, Nurkse's proposal of removal of some of the workers off the farms without termination of their dependence, direct or indirect, on the farm for their food. Unless the per capita food consumption on the farm was increased, there would in this case be a reduction in the total food output of the farm if any of its workers were removed.

Let me now, as my last illustration, suggest the possibility of a special kind of unemployment which is not "disguised" or "hidden," but is open and voluntary. This is the kind of unemployment which would result from a rise in productivity, or in income per time-unit of labor, when the supply curve of labor was of the kind to which many years ago I gave the label of a "rising-backward supply curve." When income per time-unit of labor and aggregate income per laborer both rise, the laborer's relative valuation of marginal units of leisure and of wages per unit of labor may so change as to make a shorter working-day, week, or year attractive even at the cost of a smaller increase in the size of the pay envelope. (For labor paid on a piece-rate basis and for self-employed labor a similar adjustment may occur through reduction in the intensity rather than in the duration of the labor.) The English mercantilists of the eighteenth century thought that this was the usual pattern of behavior of labor, and therefore believed in the inexpediency of high wages. There is no reason why such behavior should be peculiar to agricultural labor, but it may be that it is more likely to be prevalent for habit-ridden rural populations, as an initial response to the availability of choice between higher income or less—or less intensive—labor.

Lewis claims that "disguised unemployment" is not confined to agriculture, but is in underdeveloped countries common also in cities in the form of over-staffed retinues of domestic servants and of over-crowded service occupations where self-employment is the rule.[5] To make plausible the argument that maintenance of a large retinue of domestic servants is a symptom of "disguised unemployment" any more in the city of an underdeveloped country than it would be in London or Paris, one must assume, as Lewis does, that provision of employment for persons who otherwise would be openly unemployed is a major motive of the employers in the underdeveloped countries. Nurkse has claimed that the attractiveness of the consumers' goods of advanced countries to the population of underdeveloped countries operates as a serious barrier both to the development of their own industries and to capital formation.[6] Since industrialization in underdeveloped countries, when not directed otherwise by government, tends to concentrate on consumers' goods of advanced-country types, a shift of taste away from Lewis's type of domestic service to tangible consumers' goods should promote instead of retarding industrialization, although I do not venture to guess whether it would promote or work against "economic welfare."

I refrain from discussing here the appropriateness of the application of the term "underemployment" to agriculture, even to American agriculture, merely to signify either allegedly low-productivity employment or considerable seasonal unemployment, in the absence of convincing evidence that the employment is not reasonably "productive" when everything relevant to "real income" and to available alternatives is taken into account or that we know how to grow spring wheat or cabbages in an American winter.[7] If we must do without the

[5] *The Manchester School*, May 1954, pp. 141–2.

[6] *Problems of Capital Formation, op. cit.*, Chap. 3.

[7] Cf. Arthur Moore, "Underemployment in American Agriculture," National Planning Associa-

spring wheat or the cabbages if we are to escape the seasonal unemployment, perhaps it is sensible to reconcile ourselves to its persistence. I find it unhappy semantic usage also to label as "underemployment" and as "disguised unemployment" labor which

tion, Planning Pamphlets No. 7, Jan. 1952; *Underemployment of Rural Families*, Materials Prepared for the Joint Commission on the Economic Report, February 1951.

would be "unnecessary" to maintain product undiminished if "intensity of work per hour" were raised,[8] since this would lead to the conclusion that there was "underemployment" and "disguised unemployment" in the most prosperous American urban industries even when overtime work was common.

[8] Chiang Hsieh, "Underemployment in Asia," *International Labour Review*, LXVI, June 1952, p. 709.

III.C.4. Dualism and Wage Differentials*

We have noted that the level of wages is generally higher in the modern sector than in the traditional sector of the underdeveloped country. How far does this imply the existence of a dualism in the labour market, discouraging the expansion of the modern sector and distorting the allocation of resources in the opposite direction from that caused by financial dualism? Without entering into a detailed enumeration of the possible causes of the wage differentials between the two sectors, we may consider them under three heads.

First, there are the wage differences which reflect genuine economic differences in skills, in costs of living, etc. which clearly do not distort the allocation of labour between the two sectors.

Next, there is the less well-recognized fact that in the underdeveloped countries the wage rate in the modern sector reflects the payment to the head of the family to induce him to move with his dependents on a permanent basis to the place of his work, whereas the wage rate in the traditional

*From H. Myint, *Economic Theory and The Underdeveloped Countries*, Oxford University Press, New York, 1971, pp. 331–40. Reprinted by permission.

sector reflects the payment to a single worker on a casual or temporary basis. Now even in the absence of government regulations and trade union pressure, the larger-scale concerns in the modern sector may prefer to pay higher wages to obtain a regular labour force, for at least two reasons. First, the gains in productivity from a stable labour force and a low rate of turnover may more than pay for the higher wage bill. Second, if the concerns are run by foreign entrepreneurs or managers, they do not have the necessary local knowledge and skills in labour relations to cope with the casual type of labour. Indeed, from their point of view the cost of re-adapting their whole system of production and organization to make use of the cheaper casual labour would be much too high and they would be prepared to pay considerably higher wages to obtain a labour force approximately similar to the type of regular labour force they are used to in their own countries. Historically, this can be illustrated by the contrasting labour policies adopted in the development of the textile industry by foreign entrepreneurs in India and by indigenous entrepreneurs in Japan. The former recruited their labour force from adult males, paying them a wage rate sufficient to maintain their dependents; the latter took advantage of the cheaper, but equally efficient, labour of young farm girls available for a few years before they got married.[1] The present-day expansion of the modern manufacturing sector in the underdeveloped countries relies heavily on foreign managers and technical experts, not to speak of the branch factories of international corporations set up to jump the tariff and import controls. Thus we have a pattern of wage policy and labour organization based on a high differential between the ruling wage rate in the regular labour market and that in the unorganized market for casual labour. How are we to interpret this type of wage differential between the modern and the traditional sector? In so far as the large-scale modern concerns are willing to pay a higher wage rate, voluntarily and without any external pressure, there can be no distortion of resource allocation originating from the labour market. Yet the wage differential is associated with a distinct dualism in industrial organization and may be a sign of managerial rigidity on the part of the modern sector failing to make a more effective use of the abundant supply of casual labour. In so far as this creates a distortion, it is not due to a high wage rate discouraging the expansion of the larger-scale economic units in the modern sector, but due to an insufficient development of the small-scale indigenous economic units which are more likely to be able to take advantage of the abundant supply of casual labour.

Lastly, we have the factors which arbitrarily widen the wage differential between the modern and the traditional sectors and

[1] For a comparative analysis of the labour policies adopted in the development of the textile industry in India and Japan see S. J. Koh, *Stages of Industrial Development in Asia*, University of Pennsylvania Press, 1966, Chs. II and III; see also W. W. Lockwood, *The Economic Development of Japan*, Princeton, 1954, pp. 213–14; for a theoretical analysis of this point, see D. Mazumdar, "Underemployment in Agriculture and the Industrial Wage Rate," *Economica*, November 1959.

clearly distort the allocation of labour between the two. However, these need to be disentangled from the concept of "disguised unemployment." A familiar argument for the protection of domestic manufacturing industry based on this concept may be summarised as follows. Because of heavy population pressure on existing land, the marginal product of labour in agriculture is reduced to zero. But the income level in the traditional sector is equal not to the marginal product but to the average product of labour on land because of the prevalence of the extended family system sharing the total output among its members. In recruiting labour from the traditional sector the modern sector must pay a wage rate equal to the income level in the traditional sector plus an incentive margin. Thus the modern sector is being penalised by having to pay a wage rate high above the social opportunity cost of labour as measured by its marginal product in agriculture, and in order to correct this distortion the modern manufacturing industry should be given tariff protection.

In order to argue that a person in the traditional sector can enjoy an income equal to the average product of labour even when his marginal product is zero we need, first of all, to assume that his family owns the land and that he is being supported in a state of "disguised unemployment" out of what is, properly speaking, rent from the land. Once we introduce the landlords into the picture, then the income left to the family after paying economic rent must be wage income: i.e. the marginal product of family labour on land must be positive. Even if the family owns the land, the marginal product of labour on the farm will not be zero if there are alternative opportunities of using some part of the family labour elsewhere. Once we introduce some form of market for agricultural labour, the marginal product of labour on the family farm will approximately reflect the wage rate in the neighbourhood. Finally, even in the absence of landlords and a labour market, the marginal product of labour on the family farm will not be zero unless we are prepared to make the highly unrealistic assumption that the marginal disutility of work on the farm is zero. But the notion of the zero marginal product is not needed for the purpose of showing the existence of a distortion in the labour market. All that we need for the purpose is to show that there are certain factors arbitrarily or artificially widening the wage differential between the modern and the traditional sector beyond the extent required to reflect the genuine economic differences in the two sectors.

It is possible to find three such factors. The first consists of the various government regulations on labour and minimum wage rates. These exert a differential effect in that while they can be strictly enforced in the bigger economic units in the modern sectors they are unenforceable for the small economic units in the traditional sector. The second arises from the greater ease with which the urban labour force in the manufacturing sector can organize itself into strong trade unions restricting free entry of labour. The third factor is important in countries which have a prosperous foreign-owned export industry such as petroleum or copper. Here the high wage rates which the trade unions are usually able to extract out of the export sector tend to spread, by a series of sympathetic wage rises, into the rest of the modern sector, imposing a heavy burden both on the domestic manufacturing industry and on the public sector. While all these three factors can cause a serious distortion in the allocation of resources, none of them constitutes an argument for special protection of domestic industry. The distortions have to be cured by reforms within the labour market. In particular the third source of distortion is similar to the point we have discussed in connection with "disguised unemployment" in agriculture. Here also the distortion arises from the fact that the rent income which the government should have extracted from the foreign companies in the extractive industries and

kept for its own use has been unjustifiably permitted to inflate the wage level in the modern sector above the marginal productivity of labour.

Finally, we may turn to the main argument for domestic industrialization which underlies much of the current writings on economic dualism in the underdeveloped countries. This argument combines the concept of "disguised unemployment" with that of technological dualism and attempts to make out the case for the expansion of domestic manufacturing industry, not in terms of deviations from the static optimum but in terms of "dynamic" considerations. Thus it is argued that, given the heavy pressure of population on land, it is no longer possible for the underdeveloped countries to absorb any more labour in agriculture: the only way of absorbing the surplus labour is through the expansion of the manufacturing sector. But the underdeveloped countries are obliged to import modern technology in a ready-made form from the advanced countries: this means that the expansion of the manufacturing sector has to be based on methods of production which are not only capital-intensive but also require capital and labour in fixed proportions.[2] In terms of the static optimum theory, this pattern of economic development goes against the grain of the factor endowments in the underdeveloped countries, but it is argued that it can be justified on two grounds. First, given the factor disproportionalities and technological rigidities which characterise the dualistic economic structure of the underdeveloped countries, there is really very little scope for smooth and flexible substitutions and adjustments assumed in a neo-classical model of the economic system. Second, the "dynamic" gains from the expansion of the modern manufacturing industry will tend to outweigh the static losses from the distortion in the allocation of resources.

[2] Cf. R. S. Eckaus, "The Factor-Proportions Problem in Underdeveloped Areas," *American Economic Review*, September 1955.

We shall now show that these arguments do not stand up to a critical scrutiny and that they seriously underestimate the scope for the introduction of labour-intensive methods of production both in agriculture and in the manufacturing sector by appropriate domestic economic policies. Even the exponents of the population pressure argument recognise that the underdeveloped countries in Africa and Latin America are not so thickly populated as some of the Asian countries. Thus they tend to use countries such as India or Pakistan as prime examples of agricultural overpopulation. But a broad survey of the Asian agricultural scene is sufficient to cast doubts on the assumption that the agricultural sector in these countries is so saturated with labour that there is no further scope for the introduction of labour-intensive methods along any known lines. As a matter of fact, the highest population densities on land and the smallest-size peasant holdings are to be found in countries such as Japan, Taiwan and Korea. On the other hand, these countries are also outstanding illustrations of how agricultural output can be rapidly increased by intensive methods of farming based on small peasant holdings provided that appropriate economic policies are followed. These include (a) the adequate provision by the government of agricultural inputs, notably the irrigation facilities which enable multiple cropping on the same piece of land, reduce seasonal unemployment and encourage the use of fertilisers and improved seeds; and (b) improvements in agricultural credit and marketing. Compared with the genuinely intensive agriculture of Northeast Asia, the agriculture in the so-called overpopulated countries of India and Pakistan may not unfairly be described as an inefficient *extensive* type of farming offering great potentialities for the introduction of labour-intensive methods.[3] In terms of our analysis, the agri-

cultural backwardness of these countries may be attributed to two types of dualism: (a) unequal provision of government economic services to the modern manufacturing sector and to the agricultural sector with some degree of dualism within the agricultural sector itself, created by unequal access to public economic facilities between the larger and the small farmers; and (b) financial dualism, which is a serious obstacle to the adoption of improved methods by small farmers. Thus it is no accident that

in Japan, where the rural and small-scale industrial sectors are more integrated in the organized credit market (more than half of all agricultural credit is provided by financial institutions), interest differentials are much smaller: on the average, interest rates are lower in the traditional sectors, but considerably higher in the fully organized sector, than in India and Pakistan.

Let us now turn to the argument that the scope for substitution of labour for capital is severely limited by the need to adopt modern technology in the manufacturing sector and that, given this technical rigidity, the only method of absorbing surplus labour is to expand the size of the manufacturing sector on a capital-intensive basis. This implicity identifies the manufacturing sector with the larger-scale modern style factories. But in many underdeveloped countries small-scale industries of various types employ by far the largest proportion of the labour and contribute a substantial proportion of the output of the manufacturing sector.[4] If we define the manufacturing

---

[3] For two very important recent contributions to this subject, see Shigeru Ishikawa, *Economic Development in Asian Perspective*, Kinokuniya,

Tokyo, 1967, Ch. 2 and also charts 2–4; and G. Myrdal, *Asian Drama*, 1968, Vol. I, Ch. 10 and Vol. II, Part V.

[4] For quantitative evidence for the importance of small-scale industries in the underdeveloped countries, see S. Kuznets, *Modern Economic Growth: Rate, Structure and Spread*, 1966, table 8.1 and pp. 417–20; also E. Staley and R. Morse, *Modern Small Industries for Developing Countries*, 1965, Ch. 1.

sector to include both its modern segment of the larger-scale economic units and its traditional segment of the small-scale economic units, then one thing becomes clear: even if all the large-scale modern factories operated rigidly on the basis of fixed technical coefficients, there would still be considerable scope for increasing the proportion of labour to capital in the manufacturing sector as a whole by substituting the output of the small-scale economic units for that of the larger-scale units. As we have seen, the possibilities in this direction are greater than generally allowed, for two reasons: first, the modern factories set up for the purpose of import substitution in many underdeveloped countries are predominantly in the field of light consumers' goods which are also produced by the traditional sector; and second, the lower quality of the products of the small-scale industries is compensated for by their cheaper prices. But, as we have shown, this overlap in the range of goods produced by the larger and the smaller manufacturing units is associated with and attributable to the glaringly unequal terms on which capital funds, foreign exchange and economic services provided by the government are made available to the two types of manufacturing industry by the prevailing policy of domestic industrialization. These policies may be said to protect the larger-scale modern factories not only from foreign competition but also from the domestic competition of the small-scale economic units. Thus it would seem reasonable to expect that a reduction in the unequal access to scarce economic inputs between the larger-scale and small economic units would make the latter more competitive and increase their share of the manufacturing output, thereby raising the proportion of labour to capital employed in the manufacturing sector as a whole. A reduction of economic dualism in this sense would have the effect of encouraging a greater degree of economic specialization between the larger and smaller economic units and thus introduce a new pattern of complementary economic relationships between the two types of manufacturing industry.

Complementary relationships based on vertical linkages between different industries are a familiar theme in development economics. But so far the analysis has been handicapped by confining the concept of complementarity only to the modern segment of the manufacturing sector. Further, given the popularity of the input-output models, complementarity tends to be interpreted in purely technical terms: in terms of fixed technical co-efficients linking up insufficiently disaggregated sectors. When, however, we broaden the concept of complementarity to the possible economic linkages between the larger and smaller industries and apply the older Adam Smithian notions of division of labour and specialization[5] to the situation, we begin to have a richer understanding of the possible complementary relationships within the manufacturing sector which would have the effect of introducing a greater degree of economic flexibility into the domestic economic organization of the underdeveloped countries. With a reduction in dualism, the small economic units may be typically expected to take over a larger share of the output in the light consumers' goods industries while the larger economic units shift into the production of inputs for the small industries. As a matter of fact, the small industries in the underdeveloped countries have shown considerable enterprise in changing over from their traditional materials to new imported materials in such inputs as dyes, yarns, plastics, etc. and this is the reason why they are so handicapped by foreign exchange controls which restrict their access to imports. But the division of labour between the larger-scale and the small economic units may take various other patterns: the larger economic units may subcontract any part of their productive

[5] See G. J. Stigler, "The Division of Labour is Limited by the Extent of the Market," *Journal of Political Economy*, June 1951.

processes to the small economic units; the small economic units may set up repair shops and other servicing activities for the bigger economic units; and so on. In general, given easier access to capital and foreign exchange, the small economic units may be expected to increase their share of economic activities in the manufacturing sector whenever their lower overhead costs and their access to cheap family and casual labour give them a comparative advantage over the larger economic units. These various possibilities are well illustrated by the history of the economic development of Japan, where the small industries have played a very important role. Significantly, the growth of the small industries was greatly facilitated by access to cheap electric power—a reduction of the dualism in the supply of public economic services. W. W. Lockwood describes the development of complementary economic relations between the larger-scale economic units and the small economic units as "a skillful utilization of Japan's limited capital resources and technical experience to employ a large and expanding population in productive pursuits."[6]

[6] W. W. Lockwood, *The Economic Development of Japan*, 1954, p. 211. See also the rest of his Ch. 4.

III.D. INTERSECTORAL RELATIONSHIPS IN A DUAL ECONOMY—NOTE

When a dual economy exists, the ultimate question for the country's future development is how the modern exchange sector is to expand while the indigenous sector contracts. This requires an analysis of the interrelationships between the two sectors. Sir W. Arthur Lewis has offered a perceptive analysis of this problem.[1] This note summarizes Lewis's model and assesses its relevance for contemporary problems of development.

Lewis analyzes the process of economic expansion in a dual economy composed of a "capitalist" sector and a "noncapitalist" sector. The capitalist sector is defined as that part of the economy which uses reproducible capital, pays capitalists for the use thereof, and employs wage-labor for profit-making purposes. Capitalist production need not be restricted to manufacturing; it may also be in plantations or mines that hire labor and resell its output for a profit. The capitalist sector may also be either private or public: again, the distinguishing feature of the capitalist sector is the hiring of labor and sale of its output for a profit, which can be undertaken by public enterprise as well as private. The subsistence sector is that part of the economy which does not use reproducible capital and does not hire labor for profit—the indigenous traditional sector or the "self-employment sector."[2] In this sector, output per head is much lower than that in the capitalist sector; given the available techniques, the marginal productivity of a laborer in agricultural production may be zero as a limiting case. As a result of institutional arrangements, such as the family farm or communal holdings of land, members of the farm labor force consume essentially the average product of the farm's output even though the marginal product of some farm

[1] W. Arthur Lewis, "Economic Development with Unlimited Supplies of Labour," *The Manchester School*, May 1954, pp. 139–91; "Unlimited Labour: Further Notes," ibid., January 1958, pp. 1–32. "Reflections on Unlimited Labor," in Luis Eugenio Di Marco (ed.), *International Economics and Development, Essays in Honor of Raùl Prebisch*, New York, 1972, pp. 75–96. The analysis has been extended in some respects by Professors Gustav Ranis and J. C. H. Fei, "A Theory of Economic Development," *American Economic Review*, September 1961, pp. 533–65; "Innovation, Capital Accumulation, and Economic Development," ibid., June 1963, pp. 283–313; *Development of the Labor Surplus Economy: Theory and Policy*, Homewood, 1964; "Agrarianism, Dualism, and Economic Development," in I. Adelman and E. Thorbecke (eds.), *The Theory and Design of Economic Development*, Baltimore, 1966.

[2] The characterization of this traditional agricultural sector as the "self-employed" sector is suggested by Kazushi Ohkawa, "Balanced Growth and the Problem of Agriculture—with Special Reference to Asian Peasant Economy," *Hitotsubashi Journal of Economics*, September 1961, pp. 13–25.

Professor Reynolds has also proposed that a four-sector model would be more relevant—with the "traditional sector" divided into the rural sector and the urban trade-service sector, and with both an industry subsector and a government subsector in the "modern sector." The urban trade-service sector employs people with little skill and little initial capital, and there is relative freedom of entry. For a discussion of the different production functions in these four sectors, see Lloyd G. Reynolds, "Economic Development with Surplus Labor: Some Complications," *Oxford Economic Papers*, March 1969, pp. 89–103. Reynolds's urban trade-service sector bears some resemblance to the "informal sector" discussed in Chapter IV, below.

laborers may be well below the average product.

A fundamental relationship between the two sectors is that when the capitalist sector expands, it draws labor from the reservoir in the noncapitalist sector. For countries that have experienced high rates of population growth and are densely populated, it is assumed that the supply of unskilled labor to the capitalist sector is unlimited. Labor is "unlimited" in the sense that when the capitalist sector offers additional employment opportunities at the existing wage rate, the numbers willing to work at the existing wage rate will be greater than the demand: the supply curve of labor is infinitely elastic at the ruling wage. According to Lewis, one condition for this is that the ruling wage of the capitalist sector exceeds the earnings in the noncapitalist sector of those who are willing to transfer themselves. The other condition is that any tendency which the transfer may set in motion for earnings per head to rise in the noncapitalist sector must initially be offset by the effect of increases in the labor force (natural increase, immigration, or greater female participation).[3] A large component of the unlimited supply of labor from the noncapitalist reservoir of labor is composed of those who are in disguised unemployment in agriculture and in other overmanned occupations such as domestic service, casual odd jobs, or petty retail trading. Another source of labor is women who transfer from the household to commercial employment, and the labor force has also grown as a result of the population increase. The large pool of unskilled labor enables new industries to be created or old industries to expand in the capitalist sector without encountering any shortage of unskilled labor.

The wage which the growing capitalist sector has to pay is determined in Lewis's model by what labor earns in the subsistence sector. Peasant farmers will not leave the

family farm for wage employment unless the real wage is at least equal to the average product on the land.[4] Capitalist wages, as a rule, will have to be somewhat higher than subsistence earnings in order to compensate labor for the cost of transferring and to induce labor to leave the traditional life of the subsistence sector (Lewis observes that there is usually a gap of 30 per cent or more between capitalist wages and subsistence earnings). At the existing capitalist wages, however, the supply of labor is considered to be perfectly elastic.

This situation is illustrated in Figure III.4, where OA represents subsistence earnings, OW the real wage rate in the capitalistic sector, and WS the perfectly elastic supply of labor. Given a fixed amount of capital at the outset, the demand for labor is initially represented by the marginal productivity schedule of labor, $N_1 D_1$ in Figure III.4. If we assume profit maximization, capital will then be applied up to the point where the current wage equals the marginal productivity of labor. If OW is the current wage, the amount of labor employed in the capitalistic sector is OL; beyond L, workers earn whatever they can in the subsistence sector. The total product $N_1 PLO$ in the capitalist sector will then be divided between wages in the amount OWPL and the capitalists' surplus or profits in the amount WPN_1.

In tracing the process of economic expansion, Lewis emphasizes that the key to the process is the use of the capitalist surplus. The driving force in the system is generated by the reinvestment of the capitalist surplus in creating new capital. As the capitalist sector expands, labor withdraws from the subsistence sector into wage employment, the surplus then becomes even larger, there is still more reinvestment of profits, and the process continues on progressively absorbing surplus labor from the subsistence sector.

---

[3] Lewis, "Reflections on Unlimited Labor," p. 77.

[4] As noted in III.C.1, above, even though the marginal product of labor is zero in disguised unemployment, a member of the extended family shares in the total product and receives approximately the average product.

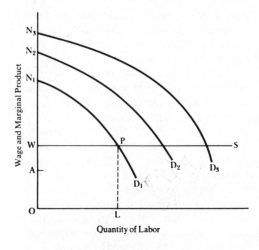

FIGURE III.4.

Figure III.4 illustrates this process by the outward shift of the demand for labor, from $N_1 D_1$ to $N_3 D_3$ over time. When some of the initial surplus WPN_1 is reinvested, the amount of fixed capital increases, and the schedule of the marginal productivity of labor is then raised to the level of say, $N_2 D_2$. Both the capitalist surplus and capitalist employment are now larger. Further investment then raises the marginal productivity of labor to, say, $N_3 D_3$. And so the process continues.

The growth in capitalist profits is crucial in this process, and the share of profits in the national income is of strategic importance. This will be determined by the share of the capitalist sector in the national output and by the share of profits in the capitalist sector. As the capitalist sector expands, and the wage-price ratio remains constant, the share of profits in national income increases. And since the major source of savings is profits, savings and capital formation also increase as a proportion of the national income.

Barring a hitch in the process, the capitalist sector can expand until the absorption of surplus labor is complete, and the supply function of labor becomes less than perfectly elastic. Capital accumulation has then

caught up with the excess supply of labor; beyond this point real wages no longer remain constant but instead rise as capital formation occurs, so that the share of profits in the national income will not necessarily continue to increase, and investment will no longer necessarily grow relative to the national income.

In their two-sector model, Professors Ranis and Fei consider disguised unemployment to exist in the agricultural sector when the marginal physical product of labor is less than its average product which is the institutional wage under the extended family system in agriculture. When labor has a marginal product of zero, it is termed "redundant labor." In the Ranis-Fei model the horizontal supply curve to the capitalist sector is then considered to end when the redundant labor force in the agricultural sector is taken up and a relative shortage of agricultural goods appears, so that the terms of trade turn against the capitalist sector that is trading with the agricultural sector. This upward trend in the labor supply curve is later accentuated by a rise in the agricultural real wage traceable to the removal of disguised unemployment and the commercialization of agriculture so that real wages become determined by competitive market forces, not by the non-market institutional average product.[5] When the marginal product is equal in the capitalist and noncapitalist sectors, the analysis then becomes the same as in the usual neoclassical one-sector economy.

In Lewis's model, the expansion process might be cut short, however, by a rise in real wages and a reduction in profits that halts capital accumulation before the excess labor supply is completely absorbed. This may be due to a rise in average product in the subsistence sector because the absolute number of people in this sector is being reduced without a fall in total output, or labor productivity happens to increase in the subsistence sector, or the terms of trade turn against the capitalist sector.

[5] Ranis and Fei, "A Theory of Economic Development," pp. 539–40.

If, for instance, the capitalist sector produces no food, and the demand for food rises as the capitalist sector expands, then the price of food will rise in terms of capitalist products—that is, the terms of trade turn against the capitalist sector. In order to keep the real income of workers constant, capitalists then have to pay out to labor a larger part of their product as wages, thereby reducing their profits.

The possibility that industrialization can be inhibited by a deterioration in the terms of trade for the industrial sector points up the extreme importance of providing an agricultural surplus for consumption in the expanding industrial sector. This is one of several reasons why agricultural output must expand along with industrial development. This problem, together with other relationships between industry and agriculture, will be discussed more fully in Chapter IX, below.

It should, of course, be recognized that if the country earns sufficient foreign exchange, the capitalist sector could overcome the agricultural constraint on its further expansion by importing the necessary food and raw materials from overseas instead of being limited by domestic agricultural output. But if export earnings are insufficient, then the failure of exports to keep pace with needed imports will constrain the rate of growth of output.

Although the Lewis model highlights some basic relationships in dualistic development, its applicability has been questioned on several counts. Some critics believe that the model rests on the existence of disguised unemployment in the noncapitalist sector, and they contend this is unrealistic. The strict interpretation of disguised unemployment is that the marginal productivity of labor, over a wide range, is zero—that is, labor is redundant or in surplus and can be withdrawn without any loss of output even if no change in production techniques or use of other productive resources occurs. But the existence of disguised unemployment is not necessary for the expansionary process

that Lewis describes; all that the model needs is the fact that supply exceeds demand at the current wage. It is therefore not necessary to say anything about the productivity of marginal units of labor in the reservoir, beyond noting that it must be less than the wage offered by capitalists. Moreover, although Lewis refers to the zero marginal productivity of labor as a limiting case, he means by this the marginal product of a *man*, not the marginal product of a *manhour*. "For example, in many countries the market stalls (or the handicraft industries) are crowded with people who are not as fully occupied as they would wish to be. If ten percent of these people were removed, the amount traded would be the same, since those who remained would do more trade. This is the sense in which the marginal product of men in that industry is zero. It is a significant sense, and its significance is not diminished by pointing out that the fact that others have to do more work to keep the total product constant proves that the marginal product of manhours is positive."[6]

This interpretation of zero marginal productivity of labor is similar to that offered by A. K. Sen, who distinguishes between the amount of labor and number of laborers. In considering the question why labor would be applied beyond the point where the marginal productivity of labor becomes zero, Sen suggests that the correct answer is "not that too much labour is being spent in the production process, but that too many laborers are spending it."[7] It is *laborers* who are abundant; *labor-time* is employed only up to the point where its marginal product is zero. In this situation, disguised unemployment takes the form of a smaller than "normal" number of working hours per head per year: although the marginal productivity of labor is just equal to zero at the margin, the marginal productivity

[6] Lewis, "Reflections on Unlimited Labor," p. 79.

[7] A. K. Sen, *Choice of Techniques*, Cambridge, 1968, pp. 3–5.

of the laborer is zero over a wide range. If each laborer is working a number of hours that is less than the "normal" hours of work per laborer, then the same total product could be produced by fewer laborers working normal hours. There are surplus laborers so that output over some range is independent of the number of workers. Although each laborer must work more hours if fewer laborers are to produce the same output as did the larger number, this does not mean a reorganization of production through a change in production techniques or an increased supply of another factor; it does, of course, involve some sacrifice of leisure.

It is difficult to estimate empirically the amount of surplus labor. Lewis simply states:

Nobody denies that in the overpopulated countries handicraft workers, petty traders, dock workers, domestic servants, and casual workers have a lot of spare time on their hands, and that most of them (except the domestic servants) would be glad to exchange extra work for extra income at the current rate. Neither does anybody deny that there is much seasonal unemployment in agriculture. The dispute is confined to the situation on small family farms at the peak of the agricultural season, in some parts of Asia and the Middle East.

I do not believe that the productivity of a manhour is zero in agriculture, domestic service, petty retailing, handicrafts, or any other part of the noncapitalist reservoir. Nevertheless, I have seen nothing in the now vast literature of underemployment to alter my belief that in India or Egypt one could mobilize a group equal to, say, ten per cent of the unskilled noncapitalist labor force without significantly reducing the output of the noncapitalist sectors from which they were withdrawn.[8]

Another type of underemployment that characterizes some LDCs may, however, create more difficulties for the Lewis analysis. A type of "traditional" underemployment arises when sociocultural determinants of the division of labor between men and women in the traditional sector leave the men underemployed. In some African economies, for instance, it is common practice for the men to clear and prepare the land for cultivation while the women do the routine work of sowing and cultivating. The men are left in surplus supply in agriculture, but they then frequently become migrant laborers in the exchange sector. As temporary immigrants from the traditional sector, they might work in industry or mining on a seasonal basis, or even for a year or two, and then return to their peasant farms.[9] The migration of labor for short periods might have only a negligible effect on agricultural output, but several studies have shown that adult manpower cannot be spared from the traditional system of agriculture for more than two or three years without reducing output.[10] This special situation of temporary labor migration does not conform to a precise interpretation of disguised unemployment. It is more enlightening to analyze the labor supply as a case of joint supply whereby workers are being supplied jointly to the advanced sector and the traditional sector over a period of time. An important part of this problem is to determine whether and for how long an individual will offer his labor for wage employment in the wage sector.[11]

[8] Lewis, "Reflections on Unlimited Labor," pp. 81–2.

[9] Informative discussions of migrant labor are presented by Guy Hunter, *The New Societies of Tropical Africa*, Oxford, 1962, pp. 93–101, 191–203; W. J. Barber, *The Economy of British Central Africa*, Stanford, 1961, pp. 71–3; W. Elkan, "Migrant Labor in Africa: An Economist's Approach," *American Economic Review, Papers and Proceedings*, May 1959, pp. 188–97; W. Watson, *Tribal Cohesion in a Money Economy*, Manchester, 1959.

[10] Barber, *Economy of British Central Africa*, pp. 72–3, and other references listed in note 9.

[11] See E. J. Berg, "Backward-Sloping Supply Functions in Dual Economies—The African Case,"

The case of a migrant labor force, however, poses special problems that cannot be adequately analyzed in Lewis's model. To make it more relevant for this type of situation, the Lewis model has been modified by Professor Barber in his analysis of the interaction between the indigenous economy and the expanding money economy in British Central Africa.[12]

Another difference is that even if an unlimited supply of unskilled labor is assumed to exist, it is nonetheless generally true that in poor countries skilled labor is in very short supply. Lewis recognizes this problem, but discounts its importance by considering it to be only a temporary bottleneck which can be removed by providing the facilities for training more skilled labor. This will, however, at best involve a time lag, and recent experience in developing countries indicates that the problems of skill formation are not quickly overcome for uneducated and untrained manpower.

A more serious limitation of the Lewis model is that it simply takes for granted the demand side of the investment process. Can we assume, as Lewis does, that a capitalist class already exists? A major obstacle to development in many countries still may be the absence of a capitalist class with the necessary ability and motivation to undertake long-term productive investment. We must confront the problem of how a class of private capitalists is to emerge, or else we must rely at the outset on the presence of foreign capitalists or a class of state capitalists. The analysis of the behavior in the capitalist sector may have to be modified, according to which type of capitalist class exists.

Further, it is assumed that whatever the capitalist sector produces, it can sell; no allowance is made for a problem of aggregate demand. But why should this be true if the output is to be sold within the capitalist sector itself, or if the product is an export good? The remaining alternative—that the capitalist sector sells to the noncapitalist sector—presents a special difficulty. For then productivity must rise in the noncapitalist sector in order to ensure an adequate market for the output of the capitalist sector. But if real wages rise in the noncapitalist sector, the supply-price of labor to the capitalist sector will then be higher, profits will be reduced, and the expansionary process may stop before all the surplus labor is absorbed.

Despite these restrictions on its direct applicability, the Lewis model retains high analytical value for its insights into the role of capital accumulation in the development process. What is clearly of prime significance is the way investment becomes a rising proportion of national income.

Lewis wanted his model to explain rising savings and profit ratios, and he states that "the chief historical example on which the model was based was that of Great Britain where ... net savings seems to have risen from about 5 per cent before 1780 to 7 per cent in the early 1800s, to 12 per cent around 1870, at which level it stabilized. A similar rise is shown for the United States [between the 1840s and 1890s] .... Similar changes can be found since the second world war for many less-developed countries such as India or Jamaica."[13]

Along with the expansion of the capitalist sector and the rise in investment, the model also indicates that—short of the model's turning points—labor will be continually absorbed from the reservoir of the noncapitalist sector, and that disguised unemployment or underemployment or surplus labor will continually diminish. Despite two Development Decades, however, and rising investment ratios and expansion of the capitalist sectors in most of the LDCs, the persistence of surplus labor remains as acute

---

Quarterly Journal of Economics, August 1961, pp. 468–92.

[12] Barber, *Economy of British Central Africa*, pp. 180–88.

[13] Lewis, "Reflections on Unlimited Labor," p. 75.

in these countries as it was when Lewis first presented his model in 1954. A generation later, as we review the Lewis model, we find that the creation of employment is still a major challenge for poor countries. We now turn to that problem—and to some of its manifestations that the Lewis model did not adequately anticipate.

III. SELECT BIBLIOGRAPHY

1. The major study of social dualism is J. H. Boeke's *Economics and Economic Policy of Dual Societies,* New York, 1953. This is a revised version of two earlier books: *The Structure of the Netherlands Indian Economy,* New York, 1942, and *The Evolution of the Netherlands Indies Economy,* New York, 1946. An excellent discussion of special aspects of Boeke's thesis is provided by Royal Tropical Institute, *Indonesian Economics,* The Hague, 1961. The collection of essays in this volume examines the fundamentals of dualism and the applicability of the concept.

Also instructive are Boeke, "Capitalist Development in Indonesia and in Uganda: A Contrast," in UNESCO, *Social Change and Economic Development,* Paris, 1963; J. S. Furnivall, *Netherlands India. A Study of Plural Economy,* Cambridge, 1939; John Rex, "The Plural Society in Sociological Theory," *British Journal of Sociology,* June 1959; Y. Itagaki, "A Review of the Concept of the 'Dual Economy,' " *The Developing Economies,* June 1968; Manning Nash, "Southeast Asian Society: Dual or Multiple," *Journal of Asian Studies,* May 1964.

2. Excellent survey articles of various interpretations of disguised unemployment are those by Howard S. Ellis, "A Note on Unemployment in Underdeveloped Countries," *Zeitschrift Für Nationalökonomie,* Vol. 26, 1966; Charles H. C. Kao et al., "Disguised Unemployment in Agriculture: A Survey," in Carl Eicher and Lawrence Witt (eds.), *Agriculture in Economic Development,* New York, 1964; Nurul Islam, "Concepts and Measurement of Unemployment and Underemployment in Developing Countries," *ILR,* March 1974. An extensive bibliography of the phenomenon of disguised unemployment is available in *Development Digest,* July 1966.

Special attention should be called to some empirical studies of disguised unemployment: P. N. Rosenstein-Rodan, "Disguised Unemployment and Underemployment in Agriculture," *Monthly Bulletin of Agricultural Economics and Statistics,* July/August 1957; Harry Oshima, "Underemployment in Backward Economies—an Empirical Comment," *JPE,* June 1958; N. K. Sarkar, "A Method of Estimating Surplus Labour in Peasant Agriculture in Over-Populated Under-Developed Countries," *Journal of Royal Statsitical Society,* Vol. 120, Pt. 2, 1957; John W. Mellor and Robert D. Stevens, "The Average and Marginal Product of Farm Labor in Underdeveloped Economies," *Journal of Farm Economics,* August 1956; Folke Dovring, "Underemployment in Traditional Agriculture," *EDCC,* January 1967; T. W. Schultz, "The Doctrine of Agricultural Labor of Zero Value," in *Transforming Traditional Agriculture,* New Haven, 1964; Morton Paglin, " 'Surplus' Agricultural Labor and Development: Facts and Theories," *AER,* September 1965; Bent Hansen, "Employment and Wages in Egypt," *AER,* June 1969. A thorough review of the difficulties in applying the Western concept of unemployment to labor in Asia is presented in Gunnar Myrdal, *Asian Drama,* New York, 1968, Appendix 6.

3. A number of two-sector models have been formulated to emphasize the developmental relationships between the agricultural and industrial sectors. Besides the Lewis and Ranis-Fei models, special consideration should be given to Dale W. Jorgenson, "The

Development of a Dual Economy," *Economic Journal*, June 1961; ——, "Testing Alternative Theories of the Development of a Dual Economy," in I. Adelman and E. Thorbecke (eds.), *The Theory and Design of Economic Development*, Baltimore, 1966; ——, "Surplus Agricultural Labour and the Development of a Dual Economy," *OEP*, November 1967. The Jorgenson model is examined by Alvin L. Marty, "Professor Jorgenson's Model of a Dual Economy," *Indian Economic Journal*, Vol. 36, 1965; R. Ramanathan, "Jorgenson's Model of a Dual Economy—an Extension," *EJ*, June 1967.

Also significant are S. Wellisz, "Dual Economies, Disguised Unemployment and the Unlimited Supply of Labour," *Economica*, February 1968; G. E. Cumper, "Lewis's Two-Sector Model of Development and the Theory of Wages," *Social and Economic Studies*, March 1963; J. M. Hornby, "Investment and Trade Policy in the Dual Economy," *EJ*, March 1968; Kazushi Ohkawa, "Balanced Growth and the Problem of Agriculture—with Special Reference to Asian Peasant Economy," *Hitotsubashi Journal of Economics*, September 1961; A. K. Sen, "Peasants and Dualism with or without Surplus Labor," *JPE*, October 1966; A. K. Dixit, "Optimal Development in the Labour Surplus Economy," *Review of Economic Studies*, January 1968; R. A. Berry and R. Soligo, "Rural-Urban Migration, Agricultural Output, and the Supply Price of Labour in a Labour-Surplus Economy," *OEP*, July 1968; Harry T. Oshima, "The Ranis-Fei Model of Economic Development: Comment," *AER*, June 1963; R. Mabro, "Industrial Growth, Agricultural Underemployment and the Lewis Model—The Egyptian Case, 1937–65," *JDS*, July 1967; ——, "Employment and Wages in Dual Agriculture," *OEP*, November 1971; Lloyd Reynolds, "Economic Development with Surplus Labor: Some Complications," *OEP*, March 1969; William Barber, "Dualism Revisited," in Paul Streeten (ed.), *Unfashionable Economics*, London, 1970; H. G. Johnson, "An Informal Classical Model of the Current Development Problem," in W. Sellekaerts (ed.), *Economic Development and Planning*, White Plains, 1974.

4. Although they focus on the optimal investment allocation between consumer goods and capital goods, the models of optimal growth paths have some affinity with the two-sector models. For readings on optimal growth paths, see the Bibliography in Chapter VII.

CHAPTER IV

The Employment Problem

What policies can improve the utilization of labor in the poor countries? We can begin to provide some answers to this question if we consider what has gone wrong with the Lewis model of labor transfer—why urban unemployment has increased and why the labor reservoir in the noncapitalist sector still remains so large after more than two decades of developmental effort since Lewis propounded his model. The Note at the start of this chapter examines how some important conditions of the Lewis model have failed to be fulfilled in reality. Other selections, however, indicate ways by which the explanatory power of the model could be improved. Specifically, it is suggested that the analysis give more attention to the interrelations between the rural and urban sectors, the existence of an informal (nonmodern, noncapitalist) sector alongside the organized (modern, capitalist) sector in urban areas, and to the need for improving the quality of employment in the informal sector as well as the quantity of employment throughout the economy. Capitalist and noncapitalist subsectors are within both the rural and urban sectors, giving the economy the characteristic of "double dualism." Unemployment and underemployment are not confined to the rural areas, but comparable problems of open unemployment, inadequate incomes, and low productivity have also arisen in urban areas.

Estimates of the magnitude of the employment problem are necessarily imprecise because of the ambiguities in the conceptual meaning of "unemployment" and "underemployment," lack of data, and statistical pitfalls in measurement. To begin with, however, we should consider the determinants of the labor supply as related to population growth and labor force participation. Although slow increases in labor demand aggravate the imbalance between labor supply and labor demand, many development economists emphasize the high rate of population growth as the main cause of this imbalance. Rates of growth of the labor force in LDCs are, in total, more than twice as great as in the developed countries. Studies by the United Nations imply an overall increase of some 25 per cent per decade, or almost 40 per cent in the LDCs' labor force during the period 1965–80.[1] It is indeed striking that the International Labour Organization estimates that labor force participation in the LDCs will increase by 850 million between 1970 and 2000. This is equivalent to the total developed countries' population of 1950, and amounts to approximately two times the developed countries' labor force of 1950.

While in this chapter we shall recognize only how population growth underlies the increase in labor supply, we shall consider in Chapter VIII the requirements for human-resource development. The interrelations between population growth, labor force participation, and investment in human capital are of utmost importance for the employment problem.

The selections in section IV.B outline various dimensions of the employment problem. Following the analysis of the ILO mission to Colombia, this section serves to emphasize that the employment problem is not one problem but three: (1) the shortage of work opportunities, (2) inadequate incomes from work, and (3) underutilized labor resources. Within each of these categories, different types of unemployment and underemployment can be identified, both visible and "disguised."

Rural-urban migration, as examined in section IV.C, is central to the problem of growing urban unemployment. The model by Todaro emphasizes a migration function which hypothesizes that the relevant urban income is the present value of expected earnings (that is, a rational calculation by an individual migrant that allows for the probability of the migrant obtaining urban employment). In a distorted labor market, growing urban unemployment is consistent with equilibrium in this model, and rural-urban migration is assumed to occur until there is equality between the actual rural wage and the expected urban wage. Although the specific character of the probability function for urban employment can be questioned, the migration function is analytically useful in explaining why policies which are devoted only to raising urban labor demand cannot be relied upon to reduce urban unemployment.

The high rate of population growth has also been the main cause of the high density of land occupation in the rural areas; this, in turn, has been in many countries an underlying factor in the high rate of migration from rural to urban areas. The accelerated rural-urban labor migration has produced extremely high rates of growth of the active population in urban areas that have far exceeded the growth of urban employment opportunities, culminating in rising levels of urban unemployment. Given the limited employment opportunities in the modern sector of urban areas, an increasing share of the urban labor force has become unemployed, or has drifted into the tertiary sector, or what has come to be called the "informal sector." As unemployment and underemployment have been transferred from the rural sector, the absorption of labor in the informal sector has become in many respects an extension into the urban areas of the traditional rural subsistence economy.

As discussed in section IV.D, another ILO mission to Kenya has given considerable emphasis to the role of the "informal sector." In almost every area of Kenyan activity, there appears to be a sharp and analytically significant dualism between the protected, organized, large-scale, foreign-influenced, formal sector and the unprotected, unorganized, small-scale, family-based and essentially self-reliant, informal sector. The mission argued that to infer the growth of total employment, let alone the volume of unemployment, from the growth of formal sector employment can be very misleading. It has become a general phenomenon in the urban areas of the LDCs that during the past two

---

[1] United Nations, *The World Population Situation,* New York, 1969.

decades the number in the informal sector has increased absolutely and as a proportion of the labor force. The size of urban areas has commonly doubled within a decade, and with such high urban growth-rates, unemployment and underemployment have also risen.

An entire set of policies is now needed that will concentrate on employment in the urban informal sector and the rural sector, as well as on demand in the organized urban sector. The underutilized labor reservoir in the traditional sector and open unemployment in the urban area are problems in their own right. Employment problems, however, pervade the economy, and pervasive policies are therefore needed, as emphasized in section IV.E. Several of this chapter's selections can be read as a plea for a set of interrelated policy measures rather than partial measures. While some specific policies are discussed in section IV.E, subsequent chapters will also relate to the employment problem, especially in connection with the transfer of technology, income distribution, education, and trade expansion. Section IV.E analyzes the central question of whether there is a conflict between output and employment. Is maximum production compatible with maximum employment? From a comprehensive analysis of the employment problem, we should become aware that the objectives of greater utilization of labor, diminution of poverty, and improved income distribution are complementary, not competitive objectives.

IV.A. GROWTH WITHOUT
EMPLOYMENT—NOTE

Although Lewis's two-sector model did not so intend it, the capitalist sector in his model has, in practice, been identified with industry or the urban sector, while the noncapitalist sector has been identified with agriculture or the rural sector. Many development plans have been premised on the objectives of transferring resources out of agriculture to the industrial-urban sector and achieving a marked decline in the relative size of the agricultural labor force. It was another of the earlier beliefs of development planning that the process of industrialization could provide a substantial growth of employment opportunities in the modern urban sector. And yet, one of the most perplexing—and serious—problems now confronting many LDCs is their growing level of urban unemployment in the modern industrial sector. Perplexing—because the level of unemployment has risen in spite of a rise in the rate of investment and an expansion in output. Serious—because unemployment intensifies social resentment and political unrest. As elaborated in Chapter I, the increase in the absolute number of unemployed questions the very fact of whether development is occurring.

Although we may wish for more refined statistics,[1] a number of studies have emphasized the broad dimensions of the problem: industrial employment has lagged behind growth in industrial output, behind growth of the urban population, and even behind the general growth rate of population. Only a portion of the annual increase in the urban labor force has been absorbed in the urban industrial sector.

In Latin America, the differential was especially great: urban population during the decade of the 1950s grew at an annual average rate of 5.6 per cent, while industrial employment grew at a rate of only approximately 2.0 per cent. During the decade of the 1960s the growth rate of output was almost twice as fast as that of employment—some 4.9 per cent in aggregate output as against only 2.8 per cent in aggregate employment. In manufacturing, the annual growth rate of output was 5.9 per cent, but only 2.3 per cent in employment in the manufacturing sector. In contrast, between 1960 and 1969, the annual growth of output in the service sector was 7.3 per cent, but the annual growth rate of employment in this sector was more than 8 per cent. As other sectors failed to provide sufficient employment to absorb increases in the labor force, the service sector acted as an employer of last resort with increasing numbers in small-scale, self-employed types of trade and commerce, domestic service, and government employment.[2]

For Asian countries, the annual growth in real national income was approximately 4.5

---

[1] For some problems of statistical coverage and a discussion of statistical methods, see Edgar O. Edwards (ed.), *Employment in Developing Nations,* New York, 1974, *passim*; David Turnham, *The Employment Problem in Less Developed Countries,* Paris, 1971; Erik Thorbecke, "The Employment Problem: A Critical Evaluation of Four ILO Comprehensive Country Reports," *International Labour Review,* May 1973.

[2] United Nations, *Economic Survey of Latin America 1969,* New York, 1970, Tables I-22 and I-23.

Other factors contributing to the expansion of the service sector are analyzed by M. A. Katouzian, "The Development of the Service Sector: A New Approach," *Oxford Economic Papers,* November 1970, pp. 373–82.

per cent for 1950–64, but in the same period the full-time equivalent employment rose at a rate of only 1.5 per cent per year.[3]

The problems in Africa are comparable. The annual rates of growth in total non-agricultural employment during the period 1955–64 were actually negative in a number of African countries: –0.5 per cent in Kenya; –0.7 per cent Malawi; –0.4 per cent Tanzania; –0.1 per cent Uganda; and –0.9 per cent Zambia.[4] At the same time, the growth in nonagricultural output was sizeable: between 1954 and 1964, annual rates of increase of nonagricultural output were approximately 6.5 per cent in Kenya, 7.7 per cent in Uganda, 7.5 per cent in Tanzania.[5] Only some 15 to 20 per cent of the nonagricultural employment in these countries was in manufacturing and public utilities; the largest component, ranging from 45 to 60 per cent, was in trade, commerce, and services.

In numerous developing countries, despite creditable rates in aggregate growth, it is not uncommon for the rate of *open* unemployment (not disguised unemployment or underemployment) in major urban areas to be as high as 15 to 20 per cent. Even worse, the rates of urban unemployment in the age group 15–24 are generally about double the rates of unemployment among the urban labor forces as a whole.[6] All this suggests that the Keynesian unemployment model does not fit these countries. But even more, it indicates that the actual course of industrialization has deviated considerably from Lewis's model of development with unlimited supplies of labor. As we saw in

III.D, the essence of the Lewis model is that wages in the modern sector are based on the average product of labor in the traditional rural sector, but are somewhat higher—for unskilled labor, normally about 50 per cent above the income of subsistence farmers—in order to attract labor into the modern sector and compensate for the higher cost of urban living and any nonpecuniary disadvantages. At this higher wage rate, the modern sector is able to draw as much labor as it wants without at the same time attracting "much more than it can handle."[7] Further, the model postulates that wage rates should not rise with increasing productivity, but rather that capital formation and technical progress in the capitalist sector should raise the share of profits in the national income. To the extent that the profit ratio rises, there should then be capital-widening investment in the industrial sector—so that the demand for labor continues to rise and more industrial workers are employed at a constant real wage. Finally, after the surplus labor is absorbed, wages begin to rise.

In actuality, however, the real income gap between the modern and rural sectors has been much greater than allowed for in the Lewis model. The wage rate in the modern sector has been higher than that needed to cover the cost of transfer and the higher urban costs of living. And the differential above rural income has widened. The wage level in the industrial sector has risen in spite of open unemployment and before the surplus labor of the rural sector has been absorbed. It has also continued to rise in many of the LDCs, although the average product in agriculture may have been even stagnant in some economies. Instead of Lewis's suggested 50 per cent differential, the average real wage for workers outside of agriculture has commonly been two to three

[3] Harry T. Oshima, "Labor-Force 'Explosion' and The Labor-Intensive Sector in Asian Countries," *Economic Development and Cultural Change*, January 1971, p. 162.

[4] C. R. Frank, Jr., "Urban Unemployment and Economic Growth in Africa," *Oxford Economic Papers*, July 1968, Table 2, p. 254.

[5] Ibid., p. 253.

[6] See Edwards, *Employment in Developing Nations*, p. 13.

[7] W. A. Lewis, *Development Planning*, London, 1966, pp. 77–8, 92. Also, Lewis, "Unemployment in Developing Areas," in A. H. Whiteford (ed.), *A Reappraisal of Economic Development*, Chicago, 1967, p. 5.

times greater than the average family income in the traditional sector.[8]

Most importantly, the inflow of labor to the modern sector has actually been "more than it can handle": contrary to what is to be expected from the Lewis model, an exceedingly high rate of unemployment has materialized in the modern sector. Those formerly in disguised unemployment in the rural sector have, in effect, transferred into visible unemployment in the modern sector.

The reasons for this can be found in some of the actual deviations from the conditions of the Lewis model and in some structural distortions that have been perpetuated by inappropriate policy measures.

The rate of urbanization has indeed been high. The amenities and public services of the urban area are attractive in themselves to labor from the rural sector. But the strongest inducement has been the widening income difference between urban wages and rural income at the same time as rural employment opportunities have not expanded. Fundamentally, it can be submitted that the growing rate of open unemployment in the urban area has been due to a premature increase in the industrial wage level combined with a premature reduction in agricultural employment.[9] To a lesser extent, but still significantly in some countries, labor has been released from the very labor-intensive indigenous handicraft industries which cannot compete with the growth in new manufacturing activities. "Rationalization" of labor practices in the tertiary sector has also tended to increase the supply of labor to the urban-industrial sector.

As already noted, the urban wage level has not been controlled by real earnings in agriculture. Urban wages have instead risen independently through the wages policies of the government and trade unions.[10] Trade union pressures have increased in many countries, and labor-supported governments have shown some sympathy to such pressures. Moreover, the monopolistic structure of many product markets has facilitated the passing on of higher wages in the form of higher prices. In several countries, union pressure in crucial sectors of the economy— for instance, oil, copper, bauxite—has been instrumental in setting a pattern of wage increases in other sectors.

More significantly, governmental policies have been the direct instruments for raising urban wages. The public sector is frequently the largest sector of wage employment and also the only sector that is highly organized. Wages in the public sector have risen rapidly and have commonly acted as the base for a wider pattern of wage increases. In Kenya, for example, wage rates in public services rose at an average annual rate of almost 11 per cent during 1954–64, and by almost 10 per cent per annum in all employment.

---

[8] H. A. Turner, *Wage Trends, Wage Policies, and Collective Bargaining: The Problems for Underdeveloped Countries*, Cambridge, 1965, p. 13. Urban wages have been estimated to be two to four times higher than agricultural wages in Africa; Carl Eicher, *Employment Generation in African Agriculture*, July 1970, p. 10. See also H. A. Turner and D. A. S. Jackson, "On the Determination of the General Wage Level–A World Analysis; or 'Unlimited Labor Forever,'" *Economic Journal*, December 1970, p. 848.

[9] In Africa, the unemployment among school leavers is one indication of this. Not only are there school leavers within the city, but also those who attend schools in villages reject the traditional occupations on the land and migrate to the cities in search of wage-paid jobs. See A. Callaway, "Education Expansion and the Rise of Youth Unemployment," in P. C. Lloyd et al. (eds.), *The City of Ibadan*, Cambridge, 1968, pp. 197–209.

[10] Lewis did recognize the effects of minimum wages and union action as being among the various possibilities that could cause the process of absorbing surplus labor from agriculture to come to a premature halt: Lewis, "Economic Development with Unlimited Supplies of Labor," *The Manchester School of Economic and Social Studies*, May 1954, pp. 172–3. But the model as explained in Chapter III, above, is allowed to run its course without this restraint coming into effect.

In his *Development Planning*, however, Lewis does concentrate more on the resultant unemployment; pp. 76–87.

During the same period, however, total employment did not grow at all, while population and the labor force grew by 3 per cent per annum.[11]

In newly independent countries, the salary scales are still basically those that were paid to expatriates during the earlier colonial period; but this scale does not now conform to the utilization of the domestic supply of labor, and it puts undue pressure on the wage structure.[12] Nor can the heightened expectations from the extension of education be fulfilled. Further, minimum wage regulation has been influential in raising urban wages and in having a great impact on the total wage structure in a developing country. The minimum wage in a dominant industry is frequently negotiated with the government on a basis of "an ability to pay" criterion; but this wage tends to spread through other industries. The increase in the minimum wage will have considerable effect in raising the whole wage scale since the wages being received by most of the unskilled workers are at or near the current minimum wage.[13] The generalization of a minimum wage may then become highly unrealistic as it is oblivious to conditions of supply and demand in the labor market, living standards in the traditional sector, and the effects on the wage structure as a whole. Workers who were only marginally useful— but nonetheless employed at the lower wage—become redundant when the minimum wage rises.

Minimum wage policies for unskilled labor have the effect of making the skilled-unskilled wage differential too narrow, as has happened in many African and Asian countries. Market forces of supply and demand are left to determine wages for skilled labor, but demand rises only slowly so that the market-determined wage for skilled labor also tends to rise slowly. If governments then insist that unskilled wages should increase independently of demand and supply conditions in the unskilled labor market, there is a likelihood that unskilled wages will increase faster than skilled wages, and that relatively low-wage labor will become overvalued.[14]

In default of adequate profit taxation or other tax policy, governments have also found it convenient in effect to "tax" companies—especially foreign companies— through wage increases. The government's policy of encouraging higher wages may initially be directed only at foreign companies in order to prevent "excess" profit repatriation and to raise the share of income for domestic factors. But the demonstration effect of higher wages in the foreign enterprises also causes a spread of higher wages to other enterprises.

In a distorted labor market (i.e., workers of the same skill level receive different wages in different industries), migration occurs largely in response to wage differentials and in spite of higher unemployment levels in high wage areas.[15]

[11] *Kenya Development Plan,* Nairobi, 1966, pp. 27–8.

[12] For a more extensive discussion of this problem in connection with manpower planning, wages, and incentives, see the references listed in the Bibliography at the end of this chapter.

[13] For African examples, see Frank, "Urban Unemployment and Economic Growth," p. 263; also, B. I. Cohen and N. H. Leff, "Employment and Industrialization: Comment," *Quarterly Journal of Economics,* February 1967, pp. 162–4; Elliot Berg, "Major Issues of Wage Policy in Africa," in A. M. Ross (ed.), *Industrial Relations and Economic Development,* London, 1966, pp. 186–8, 200–203.

[14] Koji Taira, "Wage Differentials in Developing Countries: A Survey of Findings," *International Labour Review,* March 1966, pp. 286–7.

[15] For an instructive application of "the wage-gap model," see Gene M. Tidrick, "Wage Spillover and Unemployment in a Wage-Gap Economy: The Jamaican Case," *Economic Development and Cultural Change,* January 1975, pp. 306–24. Tidrick supplies other empirical references in support of the wage-gap hypothesis that whereas the rate of modern-sector employment growth is largely a function of wage trends, the level of unemployment is a function of the wage structure (pp. 306–7, 322).

Although government policies have supported urban wage increases, no particular attention has been given to the level of agricultural wages. The result has been a widening gap between the urban and agricultural wage levels.

Such a large differential has served to attract the disguised unemployed from the rural sector to the urban sector, but at the same time it has kept industrial labor overpriced. Moreover, the differential between urban and rural wages has proceeded to widen in face of the substantial and growing urban unemployment.[16] With the rising expectational wage, it has become increasingly difficult to absorb the excess supply of labor.

Although the Lewis model envisages sufficient capital-widening investment in the industrial sector to absorb the labor inflow, the actual result has been a substitution of capital for labor in the modern sector. Contrary to the model, wage rates in many of the LDCs have actually risen more rapidly than productivity. Real wages have risen at rates comparable to those in the advanced industrial countries. But whereas in the industrial countries real wages have increased roughly in line with average national productivities, the rise of wages in the developing countries often implies an increase considerably faster than that in real national product per capita.[17] In many African and Latin American countries, average real wages in the urban sector have been rising some 4 to 5 per cent per annum, compared with an increase in real product per capita of only some 1 to 1½ per cent per annum.[18]

The consequence of this has been the use of more capital-intensive production methods, either through the introduction of labor-saving machinery in response to rising wages or through improvement in personnel and production management practices which have trimmed the labor requirements per unit of output.

Capital-intensive methods of production have also been subsidized by other price distortions—especially through too low a rate of interest and too low a price for foreign exchange. When interest rates in the urban sector do not reflect the true scarcity of capital, a bias is imparted to capital-intensive production methods. This is often intensified by inflation which lowers the real rate of interest below the nominal rate, possibly even to a negative real rate. So too is there a bias toward more advanced production techniques when the LDC's currency is overvalued in terms of foreign currency, and the true cost of importing machinery is hence undervalued. Governments have also lowered the relative price of producers' equipment by such measures as allowing duty-free importation of equipment, a preferential exchange rate, and making available foreign exchange for servicing loans from overseas machinery suppliers. When domestic enterprises are protected by tariffs and import quotas, the pressure to economize on capital is also less than it would be in more competitive markets.

A close observer of African unemployment has summarized succinctly how factor-price distortions have aggravated the unemployment:

With the benefit of hindsight, it is now becoming painfully apparent how the conventional wisdom of economic development theory which placed top priority on the rapid accumulation of capital as the key to successful economic progress in the 1950s

---

[16] Turner, *Wage Trends*, p. 17.

[17] Ibid., p. 12.

[18] Ibid., pp. 13–14. It is, of course, a complex problem to measure industrial output and industrial labor productivity in the LDCs, especially in view of import restrictions which raise the domestic price of expanding industries and hence require some deflation of the money value added domestically.

The changing structure of output, retardation in growth of output, and increases in productivity per worker have undoubtedly exacerbated the slow growth of employment.

and early 1960s has led to the serious employment predicament of the 1970s. Typically, a spectrum of policy devices ranging from overvalued exchange rates to accelerated capital depreciation allowances, tax rebates, licensing agreements, and negative effective rates of protection for imported capital goods was instituted, which effectively pushed the price of capital well below its real opportunity cost. On the other hand, in their natural and understandable desire to raise the standard of living of their working populations, African governments acquiesced to pressure both from trade unions and from civil servants in setting urban wage rates at levels considerably in excess of rural average incomes and the over-all opportunity cost of urban labour.

This combination of underpriced capital and overpriced labour has no doubt been a factor in retarding the expansion of urban employment opportunities by encouraging capital-labour substitution in the production process. Moreover, this implicit bias towards relatively capital-intensive methods of production has been aided and abetted by the policies of national aid agencies which continue to insist on tying considerable proportions of their aid to the importation of their own nation's capital equipment. The impact of this distorted factor-price structure is felt not only in urban areas where sophisticated modern equipment is being installed in almost all newly established industries, but also in rural agricultural areas where premature tractor mechanisation is being encouraged by similar policies relating to the importation of farm machinery.

The widespread existence of undervalued capital prices and wages in excess of labour's opportunity cost has also contributed to the influx of rural migrants in spite of the relatively slow growth of urban job openings. By mechanising their production efforts, employers in the modern sector are able to offer relatively high wages for their limited number of employees and unions are able to justify these high wages on the basis of rising levels of labour productivity even though

this higher productivity is due not so much to the skills of the workers as to the equipment they are using.[19]

It is most significant that the strategy of industrialization via import substitution has dominated the expansion of the industrial-urban sector. In Chapter XI, we shall examine in some detail the policies used to promote the home replacement of imported final goods. At this point, we need only recognize that the attempt to industrialize via import substitution has generally been accompanied by inflation and an overvalued exchange rate. These policies have resulted in a distorted price structure in many LDCs: too low a rate of interest in the urban sector, too low a rate for foreign exchange, and too high a level of urban wages.

The capital-intensive bias is also supported by a number of other measures. Employers tend to seek means of reducing their labor requirements when the government uses wage policies as a substitute for social legislation by requiring family allowances, pensions, licensing and health measures, or other fringe benefits bordering on social insurance. Officially required fringe benefits and wage supplements may commonly amount to as much as 30 to 40 per cent of the basic wage. When the employers are foreign enterprises, they are also likely to be simply imitating the advanced techniques of production known in the advanced country—techniques which are appropriate for the factor supply of the advanced country but not for the labor surplus of the less developed country.

Contrary to the Lewis model, the expansion of the modern sector has also tended to slow down in many LDCs. Being based on import substitution, the industrial sector might be expected to have initially a substantial rate of growth as imports are

---

[19] Michael P. Todaro, "Income Expectations, Rural-Urban Migration and Employment in Africa," *International Labour Review,* November 1971, pp. 396–7.

replaced. But this may be a once-for-all expansion with little subsequent reinvestment—unless the home market continues to grow, or the process of import substitution can proceed on from the final stages of production down through the production process to the replacement of intermediate goods, or the import-replacement industry is able to gain a competitive advantage in export markets. As we shall see, however, such opportunities for the continual expansion of the modern sector have not materialized, and the capital-widening investment of the Lewis model with an ever-expanding demand for the surplus labor has not been sustained.[20]

[20] See XI.C. It is also illuminating to note Professor McKinnon's demonstration that, with tariff differentials, a rise in money wages relative to intermediate input prices in the protected industry can cause the use of labor to fall per unit of output of the protected import-substitute commodity as the use of imported intermediate inputs expands.

At the same time as domestic policies have had the effect of subsidizing capital-intensive import-substitution industries, they have implicitly imposed a levy on domestic agriculture. This has gone against an expansion in labor-intensive agricultural output and a rise in rural employment.

For these various reasons the employment problem has become a central problem of development. Unemployed or under-employed rural labor have not been able to be fully absorbed in an expanding industrial sector, as the earlier labor surplus models suggested would happen. Unemployment, underemployment, low productivity employment, and the "working poor" are all aspects of the employment problem. The problem is not confined to one sector, but pervades the entire economy.

R. F. McKinnon, "Intermediate Products and Differential Tariffs: A Generalization of Lerner's Symmetry Theorem," *Quarterly Journal of Economics*, November 1966, pp. 613–14.

IV.B. DIMENSIONS OF THE EMPLOYMENT PROBLEM

IV.B.1. Population and Labor Force*

A number of main population prospects confronting LDCs merit special emphasis. Although many are well known in broad terms, the often novel orders of magnitude involved and their often novel causal concomitants mark so remarkable a break between recent LDC demographic history and earlier DC [developed country] history that fresh comparative perspectives are required. For this purpose, it is useful to focus on comparative DC magnitudes about 1920, when practically all DC areas had achieved far longer or sustained development than is true of practically all LDC areas today.

To begin with, the population in LDCs today is over 2.5 billion, a figure which exceeds (a) total world population as recently as 1950, (b) the current DC total of about 1 billion, and (c) the 1920 DC total by a factor of 3 to 4. As just noted, the last comparison has interest because of its relation to economies which had already experienced a considerable history of development; conversely, nearly all but a small part of the 1970 LDC population has not yet done so. In simple numerical terms, well over 3 times as many persons today live in societies which have failed to achieve long-term development transitions as had completed such transition, or were well under way to completing it, by the 1920s.

Adding prospective growth in numbers from 1970 to 2000—between two and just

*From George J. Stolnitz, "Population and Labor Force in Less Developed Regions: Some Main Facts, Theory and Research Needs," in Edgar O. Edwards (ed.), *Employment in Developing Nations,* Report on a Ford Foundation Study, New York, 1974, pp. 235–9. Reprinted by permission.

over three billion according to the range of UN projections, but with growth of well over two billion seemingly almost certain barring major catastrophes—the LDC populations which have either just begun a first major development transition, or are yet to embark on it, will total at least 4.5 to 5.5 billion by the end of the century. Relative to the 1920 DC population, these end-century orders of magnitude represent multiples of six to eight, say seven in conservative, rounded terms. Even relative to the DC population in 1970, the corresponding multiple is easily likely to be five or higher.

Since the age interval 15–65 accounts for about three-fifths of total population size and change, the UN year-2000 projection ("medium" variant) implies a rise of about 1.5 billion for this span of the main labor force ages. The rise alone is over twice the 1970 DC number in this age span and the end-century size more than five times that level. Both multiples are considerably larger, of course, relative to the corresponding DC number in 1920.

Labor force projections to the year 2000, made by ILO as of the mid-1960s, suggest an end-century LDC total of about 1.9 billion. Merely the 1970–2000 rise, about 850 million, would match the total DC population as recently as 1950, be more than double the DC labor force of that year and be about one-third higher than the entire year-2000 DC labor force.

Again using 1920–30 as a DC historical benchmark, we find that any reasonably foreseeable size of end-century LDC labor force will surely be far more than twice the entire DC population of a half-century ago and easily five times its labor force.

Subsequent ILO projections, though oriented to a "perspectives plan" or 15-year period rather than the futurist 30-year period of the above projections, and though using more recent bases for its assumptions, show essentially the same results for over-lapping years. Interestingly, merely the 1970–85 rise in LDC labor force, projected at about 400 million, turns out to be far higher than total DC labor force in 1920–30.

A further main set of interactions between population and labor force in LDC areas revolves about their urban-rural composition. Such interactions cast light, in particular, on mobility prospects or needs, given the fact that urban and rural employment often differ so radically in nature and policy issues.

Once again the same kinds of broad comparative perspectives stand out clearly, using UN urban-rural projections as a data base. Although the specific techniques underlying the UN projections are much less refined than in the case of labor force or population, with even the distinction between urban and rural open to serious question, the main indications are unambiguous. Using 20,000 as a minimum population size for defining "urban" localities leads to a projected series (consistent with the UN "medium" total population projection) which more than doubles during 1960–80 and again doubles during 1980–2000. Such "urban" size, despite its functionally conservative definition, can by 1980 be expected to exceed the entire DC population (urban plus rural) as of 1920 and would by the year 2000 be well over twice this total.

Much the same comparisons would hold if "urban" were identified according to national definitions, a second approach used by the UN in making its urban-rural projections.

If the 1960 LDC "rural" population is defined as persons living in areas other than 20,000-plus localities, its 1.7 billion size is about 2.5 times the 1920 DC total population size and 3.5 times the DC rural population of that year. The projected 1960–2000 rise in the LDC rural population (same definition) approximately doubles these multipliers, while similar orders of magnitude are found to hold when "rural" is identified, alternatively, according to national definitions.

In the main, these LDC-DC comparisons reflect differential national rates of growth, not numbers of countries. There are, of course, many more LDC than DC entities, but this is not the main underlying factor. Rather, it is that national LDC population and labor force growth rates, the corresponding rural rates, and many or most urban rates will over the next 30 to 40 years almost surely exceed by far the DC national growth parameters of the past and, even more surely, prove to be far beyond the DC rates in prospect. The population growth rates typically anticipated in the UN regional and national projections for LDC areas tend to exceed by 50 to 100 percent margins even the maximum rates found historically over decadal or generational-length periods in Europe, the only long-settled DC region as of the nineteenth century and thereby the closest historical analogue we have today to future long-run changes under early industrialization.

In addition to dealing with LDC employment issues in comparative static terms, therefore, or even in terms of possible long-run dynamic equilibrium, we need to consider the size and variability of growth itself as possibly important explanatory elements. As yet we appear to know little about long-term processes of labor absorption under very high growth of labor supply in long-settled areas. Although size of labor force may be primary—in one sense must be so, since size and growth can always be regarded as numerical transformations of each other—growth as such may not be an unimportant additional causal factor for purposes of analyzing LDC employment and unemployment propensities.

POPULATION-LABOR FORCE LINKAGES

Among the numerous processes which can be analyzed formally in relating population trends to labor force, seven in particular are singled out for discussion below. That discussion, brief as it must be, focuses on internal distribution and ignores external migration. The seven relationships are:

1. Effects of changes in vital (birth and death) rates of labor force size and growth.
2. Comparative influence of population trends and those in labor force participation (activity) rates on future size and changes in labor force.
3. Effects of age structure on aggregate activity and absorption rates.
4. Mortality or morbidity factors in relation to participation rates.
5. Fertility and female participation rates.
6. Urban-rural distribution and participation rates.
7. Sex composition effects on participation rates.

Basic Underlying Propositions

Before discussing these relationships as they may apply in LDC settings, three points of underlying interest should be made. These, in formal terms, apply to all populations, whether DC or LDC.

First, whatever the size of the population growth rate, its mortality and fertility components have separate significance. A 20 per 1,000 or two percent growth rate when crude birth and death rates are 40 and 20 per 1,000 has different implications from one arising out of a 30-10 mix and the same would be true of any other mix and size of components. The reason is age structure. Mortality declines tend to have only limited effect on age composition, partly because such declines tend to be spread, albeit unevenly, over many ages rather than a few, and partly for other technical reasons. A fertility change, in contrast, has immediate impact on the young ages only and a continuation of such change over the long run has analogous impact, raising the proportion of young in the event of an upward fertility movement and lowering it when the

movement is downward. The main reason for the substantially higher dependency ratios found in LDC regions, involving much larger proportions of population under age 15 along with much smaller proportions over 65, is their higher fertility, not their higher mortality. Most of the differences would remain if LDC death rates were to shift, whether suddenly or more gradually (the specific time path doesn't matter greatly), to DC levels.

Other things equal, future declines in LDC mortality can be expected to affect total numbers in essentially one-to-one ratio to deaths averted annually, while leaving age structure and dependency ratios essentially unchanged (the latter would be somewhat raised, if anything, by the rising fraction under 15). Fertility declines would also affect numbers in one-to-one fashion, but would in addition significantly alter age composition and dependency ratios. Hence, an equal decline in birth and death rates, while leaving the growth rate unchanged, would begin to diminish dependency immediately because of fertility effects; labor force would rise because of reduced mortality, but this would be in terms of numbers, not of relative size.

Second, neither the extent of unemployment and underemployment, nor their spatial distribution, is likely to have significant effect on mortality. Limited effects may well exist, particularly where labor underutilization is severe, but if so their visibility seems very low. Barring extreme breakdown, such as under famine or civil war conditions—and often to a surprising extent even when such conditions exist—it is government policy and action with respect to death and disease control measures which are likely to be the crucial or strategic determinants of trend. The unprecedented mortality declines found in many LDC regions over the past two or three decades have been associated with enormous ranges of variation in rates of economic growth and development, levels of living, degrees of underemployment and patterns of urban-rural distribution or redistribution. Briefly,

LDC mortality levels or trends appear to be very largely exogenous to employment processes, at least over very broad ranges of development and perhaps uniquely so today compared to earlier periods.

Third, the impact of fertility declines on labor force numbers involves very long lags, even when the declines are large. The point is familiar but its quantification is well worth illustrating. Using the ILO projections as example, a sudden halving of LDC fertility in 1975 (below those already posited) would only reduce male labor force by one-eighth as of the year 2000 (from about 1.28 to 1.11 billion). This would not be a trivial effect, of course, but the extreme nature of the assumption suggests that a reduction of one-twentieth or five percent would be closer to the most we can expect over the next quarter-century.

It is true that the full array of consequences might be broader than those on age structure alone, since fertility declines also might give rise to changing female activity rates, changing wage differentials by age, associated shifts in patterns of labor force entry or retirement, and changing factor proportions. However, even if some or all of these might be relevant for a fuller model of effects, it seems unlikely that the total impact from all sources would be substantially different from the above age-related effects alone.

IV.B.2. Measurement of the "Unemployment Equivalent"—Note

If there is not one employment problem but many, there must be various approaches to the measurement of unemployment, and the relevant approach must depend on the particular problem or policy question at hand. It has already been emphasized, however, that the employment problem in LDCs cannot be interpreted as simply a Keynesian type of involuntary unemployment. A pervasive problem is that of the "working poor"—those who actually work long hours but earn only a low income below a poverty line. The disguised unemployed constitute another major dimension of the employment problem. Beyond measures of "open involuntary unemployment," it is just as important—if not more so—to have measures of the "underemployed" and "disguised unemployed."

We might usefully think of a range of unemployment, beginning at one extreme with open unemployment in the urban area, defined as "zero hours work and zero income." Beyond this extreme, we can apply four major criteria for determining whether a person may be called unemployed or underemployed: (1) the time criterion, (2) the income criterion, (3) the willingness criterion, and (4) the productivity criterion.[1] Thus, we may call a person unemployed or underemployed if either: (1) by the time criterion, he is gainfully occupied during the year for a number of hours (or days) less than some number of normal or optimal hours (or days) defined as full employment hours or days; or (2) by the income criterion, he earns an income per year less than some desirable minimum; or (3) by the willingness criterion, he is willing to do more work than he is doing at present—he may either be actively searching for more work or be available for more work if it is offered on terms to which he is accustomed; or (4) by the productivity cri-

---

[1] These criteria are presented by Raj Krishna, "Unemployment in India," *Economic and Political Weekly,* March 3, 1973, p. 475.

terion, he is removable from his present employment in the sense that his contribution to output is less than some normal productivity, and therefore his removal would not reduce output if the productivity of the remaining workers is normalized with minor changes in technique or organization.

Another study also emphasizes that there are several dimensions of underutilization of labor:

In addition to the numbers of people unemployed, many of whom may receive minimal incomes through the extended family system and therefore not rightly classified with the very poor, it is also necessary to consider the dimensions of (1) time (many of those employed would like to work more hours per day, per week or per year), (2) intensity of work (which brings into consideration matters of health and nutrition), and (3) productivity (lack of which can often be attributed to inadequate, complementary resources with which to work). Even these are only the most obvious dimensions of effective work, and factors such as motivation, attitudes, and cultural inhibitions (as against women, for example) must · also be considered. Our discussions have thrown up the following forms of underutilization of labor, which may indicate the diversity of the phenomenon but which further study will probably show to be incomplete:

1. *Open unemployment*—both voluntary (people who exclude from consideration some jobs for which they could qualify, implying that they have some means of support other than employment) and involuntary.
2. *Underemployment*—those working less (daily, weekly, or seasonally) than they would like to work.
3. *The visibly active but underutilized*—those who would not normally be classified as either unemployed or underemployed by the above definitions, but who in fact have found

alternative means of "marking time," including

(a) *Disguised underemployment.* Many people seem occupied on farms or employed in government on a full-time basis even though the services they render may actually require much less than full time. Social pressures on private industry also may result in substantial amounts of disguised underemployment. If available work is openly shared among those employed, the disguise disappears and underemployment becomes explicit.

(b) *Hidden unemployment.* Those who are engaged in "second choice" nonemployment activities, perhaps notably education and household chores, primarily because job opportunities are not (i) available at the levels of education already attained, or (ii) open to women, given social mores. Thus, educational institutions and households become "employers of last resort." Moreover, many of those enrolled for further education may be among the less able, as indicated by their inability to compete successfully for jobs before pursuing further education.

(c) *The prematurely retired.* This phenomenon is especially apparent, and apparently growing, in the civil service. In many countries, retirement ages are falling at the same time that longevity is increasing, primarily as one means of creating promotion opportunities for some of the large numbers pressing up from below.[2]

Different estimates of "unemployment" will be possible according to which criterion or various combinations of the different

[2] Edgar O. Edwards (ed.), *Employment in Developing Nations*, New York, 1974, pp. 10–11.

criteria are applied. A gross measure of the employment problem might be termed the "unemployment equivalent"—that is, the sum of those in open unemployment plus a measure of the "equivalent" of the underemployed. Conventional measures underestimate both the size of the labor force and the amount of unemployment. In addition to the "involuntary unemployed" (those "seeking work at the existing wage-rate"), there are many others who are not seeking work because they estimate that the probability of finding employment is too low, or they lack skill qualifications, or suffer from malnutrition or ill health. Even more, there is a part of the labor force that may be actually employed but only for a limited time in part employment or seasonal employment. There is also a portion of the labor force that constitutes the "working poor." Finally, there are those who, while working, are unproductive: they are "underemployed," and they constitute part of the "labor reserve" that could through effective policy measures be allowed to work more hours or more productively. Just what these policy measures might be is the concern of a large part of the remainder of this book. The essential point here is that a labor reserve does exist, and that because of the underutilization of labor this reserve exceeds the conventional measures of "unemploy-

ment"—but the amount of labor surplus or labor reserve cannot be precisely measured in terms of any static comparison. It is necessary to recognize that the size of the labor reserve will be a function of policy changes that affect the behavior of labor. Myrdal's cautionary approach to the problem of labor utilization in South Asia should be generalized to other LDCs:

Every attempt to look upon the underutilized labor in South Asian countries as a labor reserve implies a policy assumption. The size of the labor reserve is a function of the policy measures to be applied. It cannot be defined—and therefore ascertained empirically and measured—in an "objective" way as merely related to facts and independent of policy assumptions. . . .

It [the labor reserve] has to be studied realistically as a functional relationship between policy measures, on the one hand, and the input and efficiency of labor, on the other hand, during a period of time and in a particular situation.

As an ultimate goal, the planner and policy-maker must aim to absorb the total labor reserve by utilizing the labor force fully at higher levels of labor efficiency and still higher levels of labor productivity.[3]

[3] Gunnar Myrdal, *Asian Drama,* abridged edition, New York, 1971, pp. 226–7, 229–30.

IV.B.3. Review of the Evidence*

We begin with the approach which has been applied more widely than any other in empirical work and from which almost all the information we have about trends in

*From David Turnham, *The Employment Problem in Less Developed Countries,* OECD Development Center Studies, Paris, 1971, pp. 41–3, 47–50, 52–9, 64–6, 68–71. Reprinted by permission.

unemployment is derived. The definitional framework here is set up to enumerate those members of the population who are seeking work or additional work at going wage rates and who are not in fact employed; properly carried out therefore the procedure identifies the group who are involuntarily unemployed. Involuntary unemployment covers anyone unemployed who is or would be as efficient at a job as someone actually doing it and who would accept the same wage.

In application to less developed countries there are a number of reasons why it is difficult to identify this group of people.

The Participation Rate Problem

Clearly, if a substantial group who would, in certain circumstances, accept work are by definition excluded from the labour force, then a significant aspect of the unemployment problem tends to get overlooked. However, it is not entirely clear that the bias in sample survey or census definitions of labour would necessarily lead to this result. Recent studies in the United States which are focused on the effects of income level and prospects for employment on participation are of interest in this context. These studies take account of two rather different reactions to a low income/poor job prospect situation. The first type of reaction is embodied in the "discouraged worker" hypothesis: potential workers drop out of the labour market when prospects for finding work are poor but would accept suitable work if it were available. On the other hand, it is argued that there may also be groups who supplement family income by taking up paid work which would not be accepted if family income were higher. Thus, the "additional worker" hypothesis, postulates that as job prospects/family income situations improve, participation rates would fall.

So far as we know these hypotheses have not been tested for any less developed country although such tests might be possible for the few cases where sample surveys providing data on participation rates have been undertaken for several years. There seems little doubt that measured participation in developing countries could be considerably affected, in principle in either direction, by such phenomena. A study of female participation rate differences by family income level, for example, would be of interest in this context.

A priori reasoning perhaps suggests that in terms of the measurement procedures commonly adopted in less developed countries, the "bias" is likely to be toward understatement of unemployment. "Discouraged workers" tend to get left out and "additional workers" tend to be included when they are working. In rural areas particularly, statistics of the employed tend to get inflated by the inclusion of many part time or seasonal workers—married women, young and old dependents etc. and this helps create an illusion that rates of unemployment are very low.

However, it seems likely that the "discouraged worker" effect would be most important among young age groups, partly because more in these groups are dependents and partly because, as we shall see shortly, measured unemployment among these groups tends, despite discouragement, to be extremely high. Measured participation rates are indeed often very low and there are usually large groups who describe themselves as "students" or "homeworkers" and are therefore not counted among unemployed workers.

The Effect of the Structure of Activity

Characteristically, across all age groups, measured rates of open unemployment are usually much higher in urban than in rural areas and this is partly explained by differences in the structure of activity, in particular, differences in the importance of household and non-household enterprise between urban and rural areas. Clearly among family workers and self-employed workers unemployment is difficult to identify and measure. The self-employed worker is unlikely to look for other work during a period when he has little to do in his own enterprise and is unlikely to treat his working dependents any differently; adjustments to conditions of trade are more likely to occur through lengthening and shortening of working hours.

Statistical and Technical Problems

As a practical matter, there are virtually no useable unemployment statistics to be got as a by-product of some other public activity. Employment exchange records for example are almost useless as there seems to be no important less developed country for which an effective policing system either ensures that the unemployed register or that those finding employment take their names off the register (an automatic elimination of those not re-registering is sometimes used). Most schemes of this kind are voluntary and many mix registrations of those unemployed with those employed and seeking better employment. In practice therefore almost all we know about rates of unemployment is derived from sample survey and census data.

There are considerable problems in sample enquiries of this nature especially when dealing with illiterate and non-numerate rural populations to whom straightforward questions about duration and intensity of work may make little sense, whose activities are hedged about by custom and tradition and to whom the notion of finding work by actively seeking it might seem absurd. The expertise demanded in framing the sample questions and in obtaining meaningful answers is therefore rather high (that such people are scarce is one reason why there are so few useable statistics).

EMPIRICAL EVIDENCE OF OPEN
UNEMPLOYMENT IN DEVELOPING
COUNTRIES

Data relating to the full-time unemployed for less developed countries which keep or have kept a regular survey are shown in Table 1. It is to be emphasised that in regard to the trend in unemployment in less devel-oped countries, this table includes very nearly all the information we have, and even here changes in sample design and date of enquiry affect the results.

It is worth emphasising that many of these rates are high *despite* all the problems of measurement discussed above, and that with labour force growing at 2 or 3 per cent, even a constant percentage rate of unemployment implies considerable growth in the number of unemployed.

Much more information is available on a cross section basis, as many countries have undertaken one or more special surveys, especially in urban areas. Some information is available from population census statistics as well, particularly those of the post 1960 period when more questions about unemployment were introduced. However, differences in concept and definition from one enquiry to another argues against close comparisons of levels of unemployment in different countries and most of our attention will be focused on the structural characteristics of unemployment.

There seems little doubt that surveys directed to conditions in urban areas have most chance of providing useful information and much of the discussion which follows is based on results from about twenty such enquiries. From them a surprising degree of similarity in certain characteristics of the unemployed group seems to emerge.

In most cases the rate of unemployment among young workers is double or more than double that applying to the labour force as a whole. It is worth pointing out that the difference between rates found for the 15–24 groups and groups over 24 is a good deal bigger than this. In Malayan towns for example, the overall rate of 9.8 per cent is made up from rates of 21.0 per cent for 15–24 age group and only 4.6 per cent for workers over 24, so that the rate for the former group is four and a half times greater than the rate for the latter group. Our cut off point-age 15, admittedly arbitrary, is intended to remove the effect of the inclusion of very young workers who are often

TABLE 1. Unemployment as a Percentage of the Labour Force: Sample Survey Statistics

	1957	1958	1959	1960	1961	1962	1963	1964	1965	1966	1967	1968
Africa:												
UAR	5.1	3.4	4.9	4.8	3.2	1.8	..	*1.5*	..	..	..	*3.2*
Asia:												
Korea[1]			3.8	4.8	2.3	8.4	8.1	7.7	7.4	7.1	6.2	5.1
Philippines	7.9	8.2	6.8	6.3	7.5	8.0	6.3	*6.4*	7.1	7.1	8.0	7.8
Taiwan							*5.3*	4.4	3.4	3.1	2.3	1.7
America:												
Argentine (Gran Buenos Aires)									5.3	5.6	6.4	5.0
Chile (Gran Santiago)	6.4	9.5	7.4	*7.4*	6.7	5.3	5.1	5.3	5.4	5.4	6.1	*6.0*
Colombia (Bogota)[2]							8.7	7.2	8.8	11.5	12.7	11.6
Panama							*5.8*	*7.4*	7.6	5.1	6.2	9.1
Puerto Rico[3]	13.0	13.9	13.8	12.1	12.6	12.6	11.8	11.1	12.0	12.3	12.2	*11.6*
Trinidad and Tobago									14.0	14.0	15.0	14.0

[1] New series from 1962.
[2] 14 plus until 1965, thereafter 10 plus.
[3] Revised series after 1960.
Source: *International Yearbook of Labour Statistics, 1968, 1969.*
Note: Figures in italics are at monthly dates different from those used elsewhere in the series.

anyway excluded by definition and which in some enquiries only seem to get included if they are employed. In some countries, however, unemployment rates (whether meaningful or not) are extremely heavy among this group—in Taiwan, for example, the unemployment rate for 12 to 14 year olds can be calculated as 16 per cent in 1966 when the rate applicable to the 15 plus labour force was only 2.6 per cent.

A number of other striking characteristics of unemployment tend to follow directly from the relative young average age of the group who are subject to it.

The proportion of "inexperienced" workers tends to be considerable. Lack of experience is variously defined from e.g. having never worked before, to having never held a particular job more than two or three weeks. Depending partly on definition, the proportion of inexperienced unemployed to total unemployed seems to vary from about 20 per cent to over 60 per cent. Inexperienced

workers are very heavily concentrated at the young end of the age distribution (though slightly more so for men than for women).

Relative to the whole working population, the unemployed as a group tend to be better educated, especially where young and inexperienced unemployed are numerous.

One other generalisation suggested by these illustrations (and we have not seen this contradicted by other evidence) is that rates of unemployment are relatively low among highly educated people. It seems that it is among the middle group—primary and secondary school leavers—where unemployment rates are highest. It would of course be much more directly relevant for policy purposes were it possible to make these comparisons at an age-specific level but such data are rarely available. In the case of Malaya, where the data are available, one is struck not only by the extraordinary high rates among some of the groups distinguished but also by the high rate for the illiterate group. However, illiterates are still, on an age-specific basis, much less likely to be unemployed than others.

Persons of dependent status or not heads of households tend to be relatively heavily represented among the urban unemployed. Again, the statement can only be supported by fragmentary evidence, but is not contradicted by any evidence that we know about.

Interpretations of the Evidence about Open (Urban) Unemployment

How do we interpret these findings and what is their significance in relation to the general employment problem? Why is open unemployment so concentrated in these particular socio-economic groupings? These are not questions to which much attention seems to have been given either at the theoretical or empirical level although different explanations yield rather different implications for an assessment of the "size" of the unemployment problem and the remedial policies needed. Two interpretations seem possible. One could simply argue that 15 per cent open unemployment does indicate the magnitude of an over-all gap between supply and demand for labour and that young and inexperienced people are particularly affected because these are the most vulnerable groups in the labour surplus economy; older people cling to their jobs and previous work experience commands a premium which in a more balanced market would be translated into a wage differential, but in the surplus economy enables jobs to be got and held. Standard explanations for high unemployment then follow, e.g. that rates of increase in the demand for labour are insufficient in relation to increases in the supply because capital requirements per unit of output are inelastic and because capital accumulation does not proceed fast enough. "Solutions" then involve some combination of faster capital accumulation and growth, and reducing the rigidity of the capital-output ratio.

A different interpretation of the unemployment problem begins from the proposition or assumption that some work is always available in the traditional sector and that additional numbers can be accommodated there partly through work sharing and partly through accepting lower income for a given effort. The question to focus on therefore, according to this argument, is the reason why some groups tolerate open unemployment in preference to traditional sector low productivity work. One possible answer is as follows:

Having regard either to past trends in wage increases in "modern" sector employments or to current wage differentials between these employments and those available in the traditional sector, the decision of a school leaver to spend time looking or waiting for the "right" job is in many countries a perfectly sensible one. It may, similarly, be perfectly rational for parents or others to maintain the school leaver during the process in the hope of later "pay-off". As family responsibilities grow or when family support is no longer forthcoming, the unsuccessful job hunter is absorbed into the traditional sector where some income generating occupation can be got, albeit less satisfying and less financially rewarding.

This argument is more closely related to the special characteristics of the structure of open unemployment—the importance of young and relatively well educated people, and of persons of dependent status. It also receives some support from the findings of a few surveys which have directly investigated job aspirations. These tend to show a marked preference among school leavers for non-manual work often considerably at variance with the existing structure of occupations. It may be objected that these questionnaires throw little light on what work would in fact be accepted if it were offered and may reflect no more than an expression of wishful thinking of little relevance to economic behaviour; but the notion that there exists a massive gap between the aspirations of increasingly modern-minded young job seekers and the opportunities which can be provided is fairly widespread.

Finally, this explanation for open unemployment enables us to interpret the otherwise puzzling finding of a few surveys showing rates of unemployment separately for natives and migrants into urban areas. These surveys tend to show *lower* rates of unemployment, especially at young age groups, for migrants than for native born workers.

A conclusion to this line of argument would be that the existence of a high wage, high status, modern sector in the towns together with a level of family income high enough to support the young adult job seeker are sufficient to explain why urban unemployment is so high. It would follow from this argument that a tendency for urban unemployment to grow would be closely linked, on the one hand, to educational developments and, on the other, to the existence of relatively high wages in favoured job categories and growing real income among urban family groups.

Rural Unemployment

It is much more difficult to describe the unemployment situation in rural areas partly because, as we argued earlier, the conventional approach through sample survey enquiry is much less satisfactory but partly also because there is a pronounced lack of well conducted enquiry at the macroeconomic level. What scattered studies there are tend to suggest quite considerable differences in employment situations from one country or region to another. Where the standard sample enquiries have been extended to the rural area the results, not surprisingly, indicate considerably lower levels of open unemployment than is found for urban areas.

Table 2 gives some comparisons for urban and rural rates of unemployment for survey enquiries and for censuses where the latter

used definitions and were implemented in such a way as to provide *some* basis for a belief that unemployment was properly identified. But quite large differences between the census and the survey data reported for Venezuela and Panama suggest that the estimates (especially census estimates) should be treated with considerable reserve. Even where investigation is thorough, however, rural unemployment rates might in general be expected to turn out very low.

UNDEREMPLOYMENT STUDIES

If open unemployment is largely confined to groups in special economic circumstances, an obvious area to research for evidence of a wider involuntary unemployment problem is the work activity of the employed labour force. In particular, it is often argued that underemployment in rural areas is an important explanation for persistent net migration to towns where rates of open unemployment are much higher. A number of countries have instituted or maintained enquiries into "visible" underemployment: those seeking more work at going wages and unable to find it.

These enquiries, perhaps surprisingly, have not so far produced results which indicate any vast quantity of visible underemployment. Practical objections to the procedure are rather serious; short period surveys do not provide very reliable indicators of activity in agriculture because of seasonal variation, memory demands on self-employed respondents in particular are heavy and calculations of additional hours of work wanted rely on subjective assessment of a particularly doubtful kind. But where attempts have been made to convert extra work demanded into an equivalent percentage of full time unemployed, the addition is usually rather meagre—2 or 3 per cent—although the proportion of the employed labour force wanting *some* additional work may be quite high. Uncritical use of this ratio—"30 per cent of the labour force is

TABLE 2. A Comparison of Urban and Rural Rates of Unemployment

		Urban Rate	Rural Rate	Notes
Africa:				
Cameroons	1964			
	Males	4.6	3.4	Survey
Morocco	1960	20.5	5.4	Census
Tanzania	1965	7.0	3.9	Survey
Asia:				
Ceylon	1959/60	14.3	10.0	Survey
	1968	14.8	10.4	Survey
China (Taiwan)	1968	3.5	1.4	Survey
Korea	1965	12.7	3.1	Survey
India[1]	1961/62	3.2	3.9	Survey
Syria	1967	7.3	4.6	Survey
Iran	1956	4.5	1.8	Census
	1966	5.5	11.3	Census
Philippines	1967	13.1	6.9	Survey
West Malaysia	1967	11.6	7.4	Survey
America:				
Chile	1968	6.1	2.0	Survey
Honduras	1961	13.9	3.4	Census
Jamaica	1960	19.0[2]	12.4[3]	Census
Panama	1960	15.5	3.6	Census
	1967	9.3	2.8	Survey
Uruguay	1963	10.9	2.3	Census
Venezuela	1961	17.5	4.3	Census
	1968	6.5	3.1	Survey

[1] The unemployed "available" but "not seeking" work are included in rural areas but not in urban areas. Deducting this group might reduce the rural percentage rate by about one third. The urban figure relates to the age group 15–60.

[2] Kingston.

[3] All Jamaica less Kingston.

Sources: See Appendix [not reprinted].

underemployed" etc.–is clearly very misleading without reference to the amount of extra work which is wanted and to the circumstances in which it is wanted. Usually found in these surveys is a wide range in actual hours worked, an average for hours worked which is often surprisingly high considering the presence of genuine short time working, and a relationship between time worked and extra time wanted which does not fall sharply at any particular level of actual hours worked. In particular, people wanting additional work are often quite numerous among those already working long hours. It may be inferred from all this that the concept of a normal work week does not fit too easily into the circumstances of less developed countries.

We consider first data relating to the urban sector. Table 3 illustrates the situation in regard to actual working hours.

The proportion working less than 40 hours per week seems to vary from under 10 per cent in the case of Taiwan up to perhaps

30 per cent in the case of Venezuela. The equivalent average hours worked is more rarely reported but rough calculations and some estimates suggest that it is unlikely to be less than 40 hours per week for any of the studies reported above and for most of them considerably more.

It is perhaps worth adding as a rider to the table that the variability of wage work is usually a good deal less than for self-employed and family workers, though not necessarily higher on average (family workers are usually less intensively employed than other groups however). Young and very old workers can account for a considerable part of the group working short hours. Thus, in the Philippines some 39 per cent of male workers aged 10–14 worked less than 20

TABLE 3. Variations in Weekly Hours Worked in Urban Areas

| | Percentages of Employed at Work | | | | |
	Hours Worked				
Ceylon, January 1968	*1–20*	*21–49*	*50+*		
Males	5.0	65.3	29.7		
Females	5.6	69.0	25.4		
Chile, December 1968	*1–14*	*15–34*	*35–40*	*41–48*	*49+*
Males	0.8	5.7	17.8	41.7	34.0
Females	2.1	11.8	15.4	31.9	38.8
China (Taiwan), 1966[1]					
Non-agricultural industries	*1–17*	*18–41*	*42–48*	*49+*	
Males	2.2	4.6	35.6	57.6	
Females	5.0	10.2	31.9	52.9	
Korea, 1963–67 average					
Non-farm households	*1–18*	*19–29*	*30–39*	*40–49*	*50+*
Both sexes	3.5	5.3	8.2	22.2	60.8
India, 1961/62	*1–14*	*15–28*	*29–42*	*43–56*	*57+*
Both sexes	2.9	6.5	14.9	56.5	19.2
Philippines, 1962					
Non-agricultural industries	*1–19*	*20–34*	*35–40*	*41–48*	*49+*
Males	3.4	7.8	21.3	32.5	35.0
Females	11.8	17.7	21.3	18.0	31.2
Singapore, 1966	*1–19*	*20–34*	*35–44*	*45–54*	*55+*
Both sexes	1.3	7.4	30.1	31.1	30.1
Tanzania, 1965	*1–14*	*15–29*	*30–39*	*40–48*	*49+*
Both sexes	2	4	10	42	42
Thailand, August–November 1968					
Bangkok-Thonburi	*1–19*	*20–29*	*30–39*	*40–49*	*50+*
Males	2.6	1.1	18.1	35.6	42.6
Females	2.1	2.8	19.8	27.6	47.7
Venezuela, March 1969	*1–14*	*15–30*	*31–40*	*41–48*	*49+*
Both sexes	0.4	10.0	30.0	39.1	20.5

[1] The definition of employed workers excludes those working less than 18 hours wanting more work: we have added to the estimates of those working 1–17 hours all experienced unemployed whose last job was outside agriculture.

Sources: See Appendix [not reprinted].

hours and 12 per cent of those aged between 15 and 19, while for groups aged between 20 and 64 years the corresponding average was under 2 per cent; for those over 65, some 7 per cent worked less than 20 hours.

Table 4, which provides some indication of the differences in hours worked between urban and rural areas for a few countries, shows the somewhat greater importance of low working hours in the rural sector.

The differences are usually considerably bigger for women than for men and greater in Asia than in Latin America. Few surveys however permit proper identification of the

Underemployment in Rural Areas

TABLE 4. Hours Worked in Rural and Urban Areas—Survey Data

	Percentages of Employed Persons Working Less than X Hours		
	Rural	Urban	Notes
Ceylon, 1968			
Less than 20 hours:			
Male	10.7	5.0	
Female	17.5	5.6	
Chile, 1968			
Less than 41 hours:			
Male	18.2	24.3	
Female	31.5	29.3	
China (Taiwan), 1966			Non-agricultural and
Less than 42 hours:			agricultural workers
Male	4.8	5.2	
Female	19.1	12.1	
Korea, 1963/67 average			Farm and non-farm
Average less than 40 hours:			households
Both sexes	46.0	17.0	
India			
Less than 43 hours:			
1958/1959 Both sexes	41.2		
1961/1962 Both sexes		24.3	
Philippines, 1962			Agricultural and non-
Less than 40 hours:			agricultural industries
Male	30.4	14.8	
Female	71.2	36.7	
Tanzania, 1965			
Less than 40 hours:			
Both sexes	40	18	
Venezuela, 1969			
Less than 41 hours:			
Both sexes	39.3	40.4	

Sources: See Appendix [not reprinted].

seasonal influence, though clearly if surveys are repeated sufficiently often there is no reason why seasonality in work input should not be distinguished. One case where surveys are sufficiently frequent is that of Korea.

Clearly when account is taken both of variation in hours worked and of variation in employment the seasonal factor is of considerable importance, especially in a situation where one crop (rice in this case) is predominant.

But despite the shorter and more variable work week in agriculture, the evidence is not too strong that a great volume of involuntary unemployment exists, though again there is little evidence to the contrary.

SURPLUS LABOUR APPROACHES

Partly because survey procedures are considered unsatisfactory and partly also because not much survey information has been available, a good deal of work has gone into the measurement of what is variously called surplus labour or disguised or hidden unemployment, especially in agriculture.

Much measurement work has been concerned to assess the quantum of involuntary unemployment which may be either missed by survey enquiry or which is unknown because surveys have not been undertaken. These measures relate to what is sometimes called "static" surplus. They are based on a consideration of how labour time is actually used in comparison with what, in local circumstances, might be the amount of labour which could "reasonably" be provided.

In our judgment this approach offers no advantage over well conducted survey estimation and indeed the problems which arise in constructing such estimates include precisely those which render survey results dubious. Chief among such problems are (a) what participation rate or set of rates to choose in defining the surplus and (b) what current activities are to be counted as work activities.

The second problem we have already touched upon in dealing with survey estimates of rural employment and static surplus calculations offer little new guidance. The emphasis on on-farm or field work typical in such studies can be useful however, in recalling the importance of this problem; by the nature of the method, surveys can rarely get beyond recording what the respondent says his total work activity has been. On the other hand, surplus labour calculations can be extremely misleading where off-farm activities are neglected entirely and these there is a tendency to ignore.

The participation rate problem is the more difficult issue. It seems clear that the amount of work time likely to be available in total will be some function of the wage offered; even if adult males are rather rigid in work norms, women, old and young household-members are likely to be more flexible. The amount of work forthcoming is also likely to depend on the type of extra work available and under what conditions it is offered—for example, whether it is "light" work suitable for women or whether it is work which can be done on or off the farm, etc. For these reasons it does not seem possible to arrive at any estimate of surplus without reference to specific assumptions in regard to its utilisation but such assumptions are in fact rarely explicitly made.

Calculations of "dynamic" labour surplus do have a considerable advantage over survey techniques or static surplus calculations in that they attempt specifically to allow for disguised unemployment i.e. where part of the time spent at work, or some part of the employed labour force, is effectively non-productive.

We have already argued that time worked in low income situations is only one dimension of labour input. In particular, when the opportunity cost of work time is low, it is likely that more time will be spent at work than otherwise; if work intensity were increased the same output could be got with fewer work hours. Similarly, where holdings are fragmented, much time can be spent between cultivated areas which would be saved if holdings could be consolidated. Much evidence suggests that larger farms are cultivated much more extensively than small farms so that while labour is more intensively used on small farms and yields are higher, output per man hour is lower. Land reform could promote a better distribution of available labour over land, and raise output per unit of labour. If a lot of work time is in fact wasted because of these sorts of inefficiencies then the results of static calculations or surveys are seriously misleading. The difficulty with dynamic surplus concepts, however, is to know where to stop. Clearly, once begun with structural and institutional changes which raise labour productivity it is a short step to considering other changes—for example in cultivation practises—which might yield also large increases in productivity and hence generate large labour surpluses. In practice these sorts of change, for example, the introduction of new seeds and fertiliser or simple tools, may in fact be a good deal easier to implement than organisational changes. Thus once the Pandora's box of possible assumptions in regard to productivity change is opened convincing estimates are hard to establish. As well, the reader is often left in some doubt as to whether great or small changes are needed in, for example, incentives, institutions, or in health and nutrition, to realise the surplus. Thus, as with static surplus, dynamic surpluses can only be useful if a particular change in circumstances is envisaged and details of how it is to be brought about are specified.

A possibility which has attracted a good deal of attention in the literature is that the marginal product of labour in traditional agriculture is actually zero. Zero marginal product can be interpreted in two ways: (i) that the value of extra work for a day or an hour is actually zero or (ii) that some people are marginal in the sense that simply removing them would stimulate those

remaining to compensate by working harder.

The second is perhaps the more plausible formulation. In this case, following the withdrawal of marginal workers (who we will assume to have, on average, the same economic characteristics as those who remain), output will be unchanged if the total number of hours worked is unchanged.

It is probably true to say that continuing interest in these possibilities owes more to theoretical convenience than to any strong support from empirical investigations. A number of models embody as a leading feature the assumption that there is surplus labour in traditional sectors which becomes available to the modern sector at a constant real wage. But where labour force in total grows at 2 or 3 per cent per annum the supply of workers to the modern sector may anyway be assured and whether the supply is perfectly elastic ("unlimited") or only very nearly so, may not make a great difference either, although some convenient simplifications in the arithmetic of the models may disappear.

The Income Approach to Underemployment

Whether or not we agree that a particular situation exhibits labour surplus (according to one or more of the several of the available concepts), we can at least agree that the basic sine qua non for the condition is low productivity working. Indeed we would argue that a more comprehensive focus on the central problems in situations of this kind is encouraged by direct statements in terms of productivity rather than in terms of surplus labour. Certainly, the earlier concern with a freely available supply of labour to the modern sector which encouraged the surplus labour perspective is now inappropriate.

An alternative approach which, we believe, offers more hope of substantial improvement in existing knowledge about the employment situation, would reinstate the survey technique but make work income and the circumstances in which it is derived the central subject for investigation rather than employment and unemployment as such.

An operational procedure would be (*i*) to calculate average income among fully employed workers; (*ii*) to take one half or one third of the average so defined and to identify the group of full-time (and potential full-time) workers whose income falls below this level and (*iii*) examine the circumstances of this group—activities (and the lack of them); status-employees/self-employed, etc; sociological and demographic features—race, family size, sex, age and so on. A practical yardstick of employment situation is then the percentage of the low paid workers in the total and a worsening or improvement in the situation would be judged by reference to increases or falls in the proportion over time. Alternatively, some fixed level of real income could be taken as the dividing line and development over time judged by reference to changes in the workers who receive less than this income. The unemployed would of course be included under this approach.

IV.B.4. The Employment Problem in

Colombia*

There are three distinct but related dimensions to the employment problem:

(a) Many people are frustrated by lack of employment opportunities; they include both those without work and those who have jobs but want to work longer hours or more intensively.

(b) A large fraction of the labour force, both urban and rural, lack a source of income both reliable and adequate for the basic needs of themselves and their dependants.

(c) A considerable volume of unutilised or under-utilised labour forms a potential productive resource, which ought to be brought into use.

Although the term "unemployment" is most commonly applied to the first of these categories, we cannot ignore the second way in which the employment provided by the economy is inadequate. For in the last resort, the real tragedy of those without jobs is the poverty into which they slip, and which they share with all those with very

*From ILO (Seers Mission), *Towards Full Employment: A Programme for Colombia*, Geneva, 1970, pp. 15–26. Reprinted by permission.

low incomes. After all, the ultimate object of policy is not just to provide more jobs, but to provide work which is socially productive *and yields enough income for a reasonable standard of living.*

Access to reasonable levels of income has received emphasis as part of the employment problem in recent years, particularly in studies of Latin America and other developing areas, but the justification for this approach should perhaps be spelled out. Raising the incomes of the poor involves many of the same issues as providing work opportunities, when they are regarded as objectives of policy, and to some extent to achieve one is to achieve the other. So it is reasonable to treat them together. But they may also be incompatible at times: for example, the higher wages are, the more difficult it may be to increase the number of jobs. To emphasise the two dimensions of the employment problem does not tell one how to handle such dilemmas, but it does help to prevent a misleading preoccupation with just one facet of it.

The third dimension is also important, but from a different viewpoint. Removal of this sort of wastage is not an objective of policy *per se,* but should rather be considered a means of raising output and thus providing the resources for eliminating poverty.

The extent of the employment problem in Colombia must therefore be judged by all these three yardsticks, not just by one alone. As far as possible, moreover, each needs to be applied separately in urban and rural contexts, because it has both different causes and different effects in the two cases. Actually, we were able, because of shortage of data, to analyse only the three aspects of the employment problems for urban areas, though we have added a short section on the same aspects of the problem as they appear in rural areas.

URBAN EMPLOYMENT

The Shortage of Urban Work Opportunities

Two groups of people suffer from shortage of work opportunities: those without work and those in work but working short hours. In both cases, the numbers involved are almost certainly a good deal larger than the observed numbers actively seeking work or longer hours, because of the "disguised element"–the unemployed (or underemployed) who are not openly seeking work (or more work) but would do so if open unemployment were to decrease. Table 1 gives estimates of the order of magnitude of both open and disguised rates in urban areas for persons lacking work opportunities in Colombia in 1967. (The year 1967 was one of rather low economic activity, but the general scale of the problem is too big for the figures to be greatly affected by year-to-year economic fluctuations.)

While the table suggests that open unemployment of the total labour force is probably the largest element, it accounts–at least among men–for less than half the total lack of work opportunities. (Among women, the rate of open unemployment in 1967 was extremely high, having apparently increased sharply over the previous three years.)

By its very nature, disguised unemployment is, of course, difficult to quantify. To make estimates which are at all adequate one needs detailed sample surveys covering work motivation and intentions. In the absence of these, rather sweeping assumptions have to be made.

However, the rates of labour participation in Colombia–i.e. the proportion of the population of working age which is in the labour force–provide a clue to its extent. These are low in comparison with many other Latin American countries (let alone with countries enjoying higher income levels) or even compared with what they used to be in Colombia, and the declines in these rates since 1951 strongly suggest that disguised unemployment has grown in recent years. These suspicions are strengthened by more careful studies showing that the higher the level of unemployment the lower the tendency for people to seek work. The estimates in table 1 therefore, though inevitably very rough, derived from changes in labour participation rates, give perhaps a reasonable order of magnitude.

On underemployment, data can be found in the periodic sample surveys carried out by a number of universities. This is not as large as one might expect; the full-time equivalent of short hours is in total only about 5 per cent of total employment, as items 3 and 4 in table 1 indicate. Fewer than half of those working short hours are openly seeking more work, though no doubt more would do so if they had any prospects of finding it, i.e. there must be some further (disguised) underemployment among those working part time.

In any case the figures are misleadingly low. Part of the explanation for the small extent of underemployment shown reflects the definition used–the data are of hours worked per week, and not the time usefully employed in earning money. If statistics based on the latter approach were available, we would undoubtedly find larger numbers

TABLE 1. The Extent of Urban Work Opportunities, 1967 (Percentage of Active Urban Labour Force)

	Total	Males	Females
1. *Open unemployment* (persons without work and seeking it)	14	12	19
2. *Disguised unemployment* (persons without work and who would probably seek it if unemployment were much lower)	(7)[1]	10	_[2]
3. *Open underemployment*[3] (persons working less than 32 hours per week and seeking to work longer)	2	2	1
4. *Disguised underemployment*[3] (persons working less than 32 hours per week, who would probably seek longer hours if the opportunity were available)	3	2	4
Total[4]	(25)[1]	25	(25)[1]

[1] Incomplete total.

[2] No estimate possible but probably substantial.

[3] The proportion of the labour force working less than 32 hours a week is larger than this figure which is obtained by expressing the number of hours of underemployment in units of 48 hours (i.e. in its full-time equivalent) before the percentage is worked out.

[4] Totals may differ from the sums of items because of rounding.

Source: Surveys of eight of the largest cities.

for this item, since in many occupations (e.g. shining shoes) people have to wait long intervals between opportunities of earning incomes.

However, there are reasons to believe that the working of "short time" in most jobs is rather limited. Employers are encouraged by labour legislation (often with the support of their employees and the unions) to employ their existing labour force for longer hours rather than to take on more people. It is also no doubt true that many of those who are self-employed (such as shopkeepers) work very long hours to obtain an income at all adequate. The result is not only that under-employment is small, but also that this very situation makes unemployment somewhat larger.

The total effect of all four elements of work shortage is considerable—a lack of opportunities equivalent to some 25 per cent of the urban labour force in 1967, even on the incomplete figures available.

Unemployment is subject to cyclical fluctuations and, at least so far as open unemployment in Bogotá was concerned, 1967 was a particularly bad year. But for reasons given later in the report, there is no doubt that the long-run trend in unemployment is upward. This is confirmed by data for Bogotá (the only city for which there is a regular series), though these probably have a downward bias. They show open unemployment at 7 per cent of the labour force for 1964 and 10 per cent for 1969, despite relatively prosperous conditions in the latter year. But figures for other cities at various dates also suggest a rising trend.

Inadequate Urban Incomes

The second approach to the problem of employment is to measure the active labour force with very low incomes. This aspect of the problem is of particular importance in a country where the majority of families in the urban areas have no other source of income than what they can earn. The Government has but a limited capacity to redistribute income by direct transfer payments and the provision of free or subsidised services—and this would be true even if taxation were increased as we suggest later. So relieving the poverty of the poorest sections of the population—which is acute—depends heavily on the provision of jobs, with reasonable wages.

Purely in order to indicate the magnitude of urban poverty, we show in table 2 estimates for 1967 of the proportion of the labour force with incomes of less than 200 pesos monthly, a daily equivalent of less than 8 pesos (or about 50 US cents), assuming employment of twenty-six days a month. (Taking this particular level does not by any means imply that 200 pesos is considered to have been, even in 1967, an adequate income for a single person, let alone for a family—data in the source are tabulated by 100-peso intervals and 200 happens to be the highest figure shown below the lowest minimum wage.)

The figures show that a third of the urban labour force received less than 200 pesos a month (indeed more than half received less than 400 pesos). The "hard core" was the open unemployed, with no earnings at all.

Ideally, one would like to relate figures on income distribution to data on size of family and to some measure of family needs for basic expenditure on food, clothing and shelter. Unfortunately, no such statistics exist at present, although there is evidence that the diet of a big fraction of the urban population is inadequate (in terms of basic nutritional needs) and their housing well below minimum standards of public health.

One can, however, relate the levels of earnings to minimum wages. In 1967 the lowest levels of non-agricultural minimum wages were 9.80 pesos daily in the "low cost" areas and 11.20 pesos in the "high cost" cities, such as Bogotá or Medellín. (The highest levels of minimum wages applied to the larger manufacturing firms and were 11.20 pesos in the "low cost" areas and 14 pesos in the "high".) Thus, in 1967, a third of the urban labour force received at the very most about three-quarters of the lowest of the minimum wage rates.

A major conclusion can therefore be deduced, in spite of the margins of uncertainty in the figures. A very large proportion

TABLE 2.   The Extent of Extreme Urban Poverty, 1967 (Percentage of the Active Urban Labour Force)

	Total	Males	Females
Unemployed—open	14	12	19
—disguised	(7)[1]	10	—[2]
Occupied but with incomes below 200 pesos monthly[3]	12	6	24
Total—all with incomes below 200 pesos monthly	(33)[1]	28	(44)[1]

[1] Incomplete total.

[2] No estimate possible but probably substantial.

[3] Including those under 15 years of age. These account, however, for only about 2 per cent of the total urban labour force; to exclude them from the data on earnings would thus make very little difference to the over-all picture.

Source: Numbers unemployed: see table 1. Those with low incomes: see CEDE: *Encuestas urbanas de empleo y desempleo*, 1969 (averages for eight cities).

of the active labour force has an inadequate income, by any standards, and this proportion is considerably more than that of the unemployed or underemployed. Poverty therefore emerges as the most compelling aspect of the whole employment problem in Colombia.

Unutilised or Under-utilised Reserves of Urban Labour

This is the third dimension of the employment problem. Here, the point of concern is not with the human consequences of lack of work or low income but with the economic potential of labour not used to the full. From this point of view, unemployment need not necessarily be considered a burden for policy makers. It can be looked on as a potential asset. To treat it as a liability is one indication of how one's values become distorted during a period of large-scale unemployment. There is this reserve of human resources available, if only the will and the way could be found to mobilise them for national development; certainly the long-term outlook for reaching high living standards would be in some ways more bleak if there were neither spare labour nor spare land to be brought into production. (Still, it is also understandable that in present circumstances large-scale unemployment should be considered a problem rather than an opportunity.)

Table 1 has already indicated part of Colombia's surplus labour reserves in 1967. This showed the proportions lacking the opportunities to work as much as they were willing and able to do. Taking all groups together, the total proportion in 1967 was the full-time equivalent of a quarter of the active labour force. The other component consists in another form of disguised underemployment, namely persons employed full time but in work where their contribution to output is low or even zero, even though they statistically appear as occupied in the sector. Where there is chronic unemployment, some

workers, usually in family businesses, substitute their own production for part of someone else's. This is particularly common in the service sector, but it can be found in other sectors, too.

By its very nature, it is almost impossible to obtain adequate evidence on this phenomenon. There is first the difficulty of distinguishing low productivity due to this cause from low productivity due to shortage of complementary capital or land or to lack of motivation or to ill health. Even if one can make this distinction, a measure of the *extent* of this form of disguised underemployment would require making an estimate of the amount by which labour productivity could be raised *before* it reached a ceiling set by the supply of the other factors of production.[1] The whole question raises a series of difficult conceptual and empirical issues, which could be quantified only if we had data from inquiries in depth.

But the difficulties of measurement should not lead one to ignore the problem, particularly as various clues suggest it is both large and of growing importance. It has been estimated that in 1964 the equivalent of 13.5 per cent of the non-agricultural labour force was underemployed in this sense[2] and the percentage could well be larger in other countries.[3] One should admit, however, that almost any figure is possible, depending on the breadth of one's definition and the boldness of one's guesswork. To the extent that one can rely on the national income data for commerce and finance, productivity in these sectors fell by 8 per cent from 1951

[1] More strictly, before the marginal productivity of labour in all sectors became the same.
[2] Dieter K. Zschock: *Manpower Perspective of Colombia* (Princeton University, 1967).
[3] Studies in Chile and Peru, for instance, have suggested that in those countries almost 30 per cent of the non-agricultural labour force was underemployed. See Esteban Lederman: *Los recursos humanos en el desarrollo de América latina,* Cuadernos del Instituto Latinoamericano de Planificación Económica y Social, No. 9 (Santiago de Chile, 1969), p. 13.

to 1964 and by a further 4 per cent in the whole service sector over the following three years. This alone would suggest considerable and growing surpluses of labour in the service sector, quite apart from under-utilised labour elsewhere.

Thus, the third approach to the problem of employment suggests that in 1967 there was a pool of unemployed, underemployed or unproductively employed labour, equivalent to at least a third of the whole urban labour force. This total pool of surplus labour has tended to grow over the years; it is clear that the part we can measure (very roughly), open unemployment, has risen since 1964, and it seems very likely that the remainder has too.

RURAL EMPLOYMENT

Even fewer and weaker statistics are available on the employment problem in the rural areas than for the towns. This is a serious hindrance to policy making; special surveys and the regular collection of basic data should be instituted as a matter of urgency.

In the absence of hard statistics, one can only surmise on the facts. But one can begin with three broad generalisations. The first is that the rural situation varies sharply from area to area. Differences in rates of unemployment between towns have already been noted: patterns of land ownership, crops, marketing and communications are so dissimilar between different parts of the country that it is absurd to talk of the rural situation as if it were everywhere the same.

The second point is that rural employment varies considerably over the year. While agriculture's natural cycle from planting to harvesting creates peaks of labour demand, at which periods almost any additional labour (longer hours or more people) can add to the yield, much less labour is needed during the slack seasons. To some extent, the peaks and troughs occur at different times for different crops, so the total demand for agricultural labour shows less seasonal variation. But this is truer for the country as a whole than for separate regions. There is a marked pattern of local specialisation, leading to temporary migration from one area to another which mitigates the extremes of imbalance between the supply and demand for rural labour over the year. Small-scale handicrafts and local industry also provide work for some people during the slack periods in agriculture, particularly in the rural areas and in the small towns, although such possibilities are insufficient to remove seasonal fluctuations in the rural employment pattern. Thirdly, the nature of rural life often makes nonsense of over-precise urban concepts like "active labour force" or even "unemployment." Using our three approaches to the employment problem avoids some of the worst confusions, but great difficulties of definition still remain.

The Shortage of Work Opportunities

Census results tell us nothing, really, about how much surplus labour there is in rural areas, because of the great difficulty of interpreting them. At any one date, the surplus will differ from one district to another, anyway, according to local crop patterns and the movement of migrant labour. It is likely, however, that in most areas there are some periods in the year, at least, when labour is scarce; investigations in other countries have shown that this is normally the case. Professor Berry, who has made the most detailed recent study of the question, told us that he believed that there is little unemployment at peak periods. Supporting evidence is the fact that labour does migrate in some volume to help with certain crops.

Thus the real problem of shortage of work opportunities occurs during seasonally slack periods—though we do not know how long they last or how severe they are. It then often takes the form of part-time work, especially on the family farm, rather than unemployment in the sense of seeking work.

(In many rural areas, there would really be no point in "seeking work"—everyone will know whether or not the local large-scale farmers are offering jobs.)

Inadequate Incomes

Migration, whether temporary or permanent, is also evidence of the low income of many of those living in the country areas. Here we do have some rough data—in table 3 (though for *agricultural* rather than *rural* incomes). It shows that many people have a very low income indeed, even in relation to the minimum wage in rural areas, which amounted to about 1,100 pesos in 1960, in annual terms. Perhaps one in six of the agriculturally occupied (wage earners plus self-employed) received less than this, which was equivalent to less than US$200.

A major reason for these low incomes is that 40 per cent of families are estimated to have less than two hectares each, and 6 per cent to have none at all. Although many of them work part of the year as labourers on other people's farms, this still does not provide an adequate income.

What makes this poverty much more serious is the limited availability in the rural areas of any of the basic government services. In terms of health, education, basic sanitation or clean water, many of these rural communities have only the barest minimum, if that.

We just do not know how this situation has changed over the last decade, important though it would be to have such information, but there are reasons for suspecting that at any rate it has not improved much. Government measures to provide additional land and aid to production have benefited only a small proportion of poor farmers. Moreover, though physical output (excluding coffee) has risen by nearly 3.5 per cent per year between 1960 and 1967, much of the increase seems to have come from the large producers. Professor Berry has estimated (in unpublished material) that real wages in the countryside have changed little since 1935—a fall in the following 15 to 20 years being made up by a rise which, however, apparently ended in 1963. It is worth noting that rapid migration to the towns has continued, in spite of growing urban unemployment.

Unutilised or Under-utilised Labour

We start here, as for urban labour, with the volume of open unemployment and

TABLE 3.   Income Distribution of the Occupied Labour Force in Agriculture, 1960 (Percentages)

Annual Income[1] (Thousand Pesos)	Percentage of Those Occupied in Agriculture	Cumulative Percentage of Those Occupied in Agriculture	Cumulative Percentage of Incomes
0–1	9	9	2
1–1.5	33	42	13
1.5–2	22	64	23
2–3	12	76	30
3–5	10	86	41
5–10	9	95	57
Over 10	5	100	100

[1] "Income" refers only to incomes from agriculture (though subsequent research shows that it makes little difference when other rural incomes are covered). Income in kind is included.
Source: Unpublished estimates by Professor Berry.

underemployment—though we have no data for these categories. Because of the fluctuation in activity, there is a labour reserve at certain times of the year which could be temporarily employed. Some labour indeed is, through migration, working on nearby farms or taking jobs in other industries, but the unused capacity is still considerable—because of the facts that peak demands on various farms in areas specialising in coffee or other crops coincide, that rural industry scarely exists, and that rural public works are not on a large scale.

In addition, there is "disguised" underemployment, even harder to define, let alone measure, in the rural context. In principle there are certainly people, very large numbers in fact, who are working with low productivity because family holdings are too small, or the land is too poor. In some areas, at least, they could be moved to adjacent land which is being underused and could be cultivated without big needs of capital; where this could be done without causing crops in the neighbourhood, which they would otherwise have picked, to go to waste (which raises the problem of the seasonal peak again), we could call this another facet of disguised unemployment. One would imagine that the small proprietor would often be able both to produce more, if he had the land, and yet also at certain times of the year help with the harvest of others. The relatively very low yields per man currently obtained on minifundia are a clue that the net effect could be a rise in output.

There clearly is therefore a labour reserve in agriculture bigger than just the open unemployment, though its dimensions are unknown. Judging from the slow rise of productivity in agriculture (about 2 per cent a year), disguised unemployment, at least, is almost certainly growing—indeed one could expect little else since there are greater and greater numbers of people per hectare on the smallholdings as the population rises. Because of its seasonality and other special characteristics of the rural sector, there are particular problems about mobilising the labour surplus at all fully.

IV.C. RURAL-URBAN MIGRATION

IV.C.1. A Model of Rural-Urban Migration*

In this section I would like to set forth briefly a theoretical framework which yields some important insights into the causes and mechanisms of rural-urban migration in tropical Africa. No attempt will be made to describe this model in any great detail since that has been done elsewhere.[1] I believe that the model can usefully serve two purposes: first, to demonstrate why the continued existence of rural-urban migration in the face of rising levels of urban unemployment often represents a rational economic decision from the point of view of the private individual; and second, to demonstrate how such a theoretical framework can be used in an analysis and evaluation of alternative public policies to alleviate the growing urban unemployment problem.

THE INDIVIDUAL DECISION TO MIGRATE: SOME BEHAVIOURAL ASSUMPTIONS

The basic behavioural assumption of the model is that each potential migrant decides whether or not to move to the city on the basis of an implicit, "expected" income maximisation objective. There are two principal economic factors involved in this decision to migrate. The first relates to the existing urban-rural real wage differential that prevails for different skill and educational categories of workers. The existence of large disparities between wages paid to urban workers and those paid to comparably skilled rural labourers has long been recognised as a crucial factor in the decision to migrate.[2] The increasing divergence between

*From Michael P. Todaro, "Income Expectations, Rural-Urban Migration and Employment in Africa," *International Labour Review*, November 1971, pp. 391–5, 411–13. Reprinted by permission.

[1] A more detailed description and development of the over-all features of the model can be found in Michael P. Todaro: "The urban employment problem in less developed countries: an analysis of demand and supply", in *Yale Economic Essays*, Vol. VIII, Fall 1968, pp. 331–402; idem: "A model of labor migration and urban unemploy-

ment in less developed countries", in *American Economic Review*, Mar. 1969, pp. 138–148; and John R. Harris and Michael P. Todaro: "Migration, unemployment and development: a two-sector analysis", ibid., Mar. 1970, pp. 126–142.

[2] Some of the more recent studies identifying economic forces as principal factors affecting the decision to migrate include Ralph E. Beals, Mildred B. Levy and Leon N. Moses: "Rationality and migration in Ghana", in *Review of Economic and Statistics*, Nov. 1967, pp. 480–6; John C. Caldwell: *African rural-urban migration. The movement to Ghana's towns* (New York, 1969); Lowell E. Gallaway: "Industry variations in geographic labor mobility patterns", in *Journal of Human Resources*, Fall 1967, pp. 461–74; J. Gugler: "On the theory of rural-urban migration: the case of sub-Saharan Africa", in J. A. Jackson (ed.): *Sociological studies Two: migration* (Cambridge, University Press, 1969), pp. 134–155; John R. Harris and Michael P. Todaro: "Urban unemployment in East Africa: an economic analysis of policy alternatives", in *East African Economic Review*, Dec. 1968, pp. 17–36.

urban and rural incomes has arisen both as a result of the relative stagnation of agricultural earnings (partly as a direct outgrowth of post-war bias toward industrialisation at the expense of agricultural expansion) and the concomitant phenomenon of rapidly rising urban wage rates for unskilled workers. For example, in Nigeria Arthur Lewis noted that "urban wages" are typically at levels twice as high as average farm incomes. Between 1950 and 1963 prices received by farmers through marketing boards in southern Nigeria fell by 25 per cent while at the same time the minimum wage scales of the Federal Government increased by 200 per cent.[3]

In Kenya average earnings of African employees in the non-agricultural sector rose from £97 in 1960 to £180 in 1966, a growth rate of nearly 11 per cent per annum. During the same period the small farm sector of Kenya experienced a growth of estimated family income of only 5 per cent per annum, rising from £57 in 1960 to £77 in 1966. Consequently, urban wages rose more than twice as fast as agricultural incomes in Kenya so that in 1966 average wages in the urban sector were approximately two-and-a-half times as high as average farm family incomes.[4] Moreover, the urban-rural income differential in Kenya in 1968 varied considerably by level of educational attainment. For example, whereas farm income was approximately K£85 in 1968, individuals with zero to four years of primary education in urban areas earned on the average K£102, those with five to eight years of primary education earned K£156, while migrants who had completed from one to six years of secondary education earned on the average K£290 per annum in 1968.[5]

A final example of the growing disparity between urban and rural incomes can be gleaned from Uganda data. During the period 1954 to 1964 agricultural incomes remained essentially unchanged while minimum wages in government employment in Kampala rose by almost 200 per cent from £31 to £90 per annum.[6] It should be noted that in Uganda as in most other African nations the minimum wage often acts as the effective rate which determines the level at which more than 50 per cent of urban unskilled workers are paid. It is also the key weight in the over-all wage structure since when the minimum wage changes, the entire wage structure tends to move with it.[7]

The second crucial element, which for the most part has not been formally included in other models of rural-urban migration, relates to the degree of probability that a migrant will be successful in securing an urban job. Without introducing the probability variable it would be extremely difficult to explain the continued and often accelerated rate of migration in the face of sizeable and growing pools of urban unemployed. Arguments about the irrationality of rural peasants who unwittingly migrate to urban areas permeated by widespread unemployment are as ill-conceived and culture-bound as earlier assertions that peasant subsistence farmers were unresponsive to price incentives. The

[3] W. Arthur Lewis: *Reflections on Nigeria's economic growth* (Paris, OECD Development Centre, 1967), p. 42.

[4] Dharam P. Ghai: "Incomes policy in Kenya: need, criteria and machinery", in *East African Economic Review*, June 1968, p. 20.

[5] For an analysis of the relationship between education and migration in Africa, see Michael P. Todaro: "Education and rural-urban migration: theoretical constructs and empirical evidence from Kenya", paper prepared for the Conference on Urban Unemployment in Africa, Institute for Development Studies, University of Sussex, Sep. 1971, especially pp. 16–30.

[6] J. B. Knight: "The determination of wages and salaries in Uganda", in *Bulletin of the Oxford University Institute of Economics and Statistics*, Aug. 1967, pp. 233–264.

[7] For a useful discussion of the relationship between wages and employment in Africa, see Elliot J. Berg: "Wage policy and employment in less developed countries", paper prepared for the Overseas Study Committee Conference "Prospects for Employment Opportunities in the Nineteen-Seventies", University of Cambridge, 1970.

key, in my opinion, to an understanding of the seemingly paradoxical phenomenon of continued migration to centres of high unemployment lies in viewing the migration process from an "expected" or permanent income approach where expected income relates not only to the actual wage paid to an urban worker, but also to the probability that he will be successful in securing wage employment in any given period of time. It is the combination and interaction of these two variables—the urban-rural real income differential and the probability of securing an urban job—which I believe determine the rate and magnitude of rural-urban migration in tropical Africa.

Consider the following illustration. Suppose the average unskilled or semi-skilled rural worker has a choice between being a farm labourer (or working his own land) for an annual average real income of, say, 50 units, or migrating to the city where a worker with his skill or educational background can obtain wage employment yielding an annual real income of 100 units. The more commonly used economic models of migration, which place exclusive emphasis on the income differential factor as the determinant of the decision to migrate, would indicate a clear choice in this situation. The worker should seek the higher-paying urban job. It is important to recognise, however, that these migration models were developed largely in the context of advanced industrial economies and, as such, implicitly assume the existence of full employment or near-full employment. In a full employment environment the decision to migrate can in fact be predicated solely on securing the highest-paying job wherever it becomes available. Simple economic theory would then indicate that such migration should lead to a reduction in wage differentials through the interaction of the forces of supply and demand, both in areas of out-migration and in points of in-migration.

Unfortunately, such an analysis is not very realistic in the context of the institutional and economic framework of most of the nations of tropical Africa. First of all, these countries are beset by a chronic and serious unemployment problem with the result that a typical migrant cannot expect to secure a high-paying urban job immediately. In fact, it is much more likely that upon entering the urban labour market the migrant will either become totally unemployed or will seek casual and part-time employment in the urban traditional sector. Consequently, in his decision to migrate the individual in effect must balance the probabilities and risks of being unemployed or underemployed for a considerable period of time against the positive urban-rural real income differential. The fact that a typical migrant can expect to earn twice the annual real income in an urban area that he can in a rural environment may be of little consequence if his actual probability of securing the higher-paying job within, say, a one-year period is one chance in five. In such a situation we could say that his actual probability of being successful in securing the higher-paying urban job is 20 per cent, so that his "expected" urban income for the one-year period is in fact 20 units and not the 100 units that the fully employed urban worker receives. Thus, with a one-period time horizon and a probability of success of 20 per cent it would be irrational for this migrant to seek an urban job even though the differential between urban and rural earnings capacity is 100 per cent. On the other hand, if the probability of success were, say, 60 per cent, so that the expected urban income is 60 units, then it would be entirely rational for our migrant with his one-period time horizon to try his luck in the urban area even though urban unemployment may be extremely high.

If we now approach the situation more realistically by assuming a considerably longer time horizon, especially in view of the fact that the vast majority of migrants are between the ages of 15 and 23 years, then the decision to migrate should be represented on the basis of a longer-term, more permanent income calculation. If the migrant anticipates a relatively low probability of finding regular wage employment in the initial period but expects this probability to increase over time as he is able to broaden his urban contacts, then it would still be rational for him to migrate even though expected urban income during the initial period or periods might be lower than expected rural income. As long as the present value of the net stream of expected urban income over the migrant's planning horizon exceeds that of the expected rural income, the decision to migrate is justified.

The mathematical details of our model of rural-urban migration are set forth in the Appendix to this article. For our present purposes, suffice it to say that the model attempts to demonstrate the conditions under which the urban-rural "expected" income differential can act to exacerbate the urban *unemployment* situation even though urban *employment* might expand as a direct result of government policy. It all depends on the relationship between migration flows and the expected income differential as expressed in an "elasticity of migration response" term developed in the Appendix.

Since the elasticity of response will itself be directly related to the probability of finding a job and the size of the urban-rural real income differential, the model illustrates the paradox of a completely urban solution to the urban unemployment problem. Policies which operate solely on urban labour demand are not likely to be of much assistance in reducing urban unemployment since, in accordance with our expected income hypothesis, the growth of urban employment *ceteris paribus* also increases the rate of rural-urban migration. If the increase in the growth of the urban labour force caused by migration exceeds the increase in the growth of employment, the level of unemployment in absolute numbers will increase and the unemployment rate itself might also increase. This result will be accentuated if, for any increase in job creation, the urban real wage is permitted to expand at a greater rate than rural real income. A reduction or at least a slow growth in urban wages, therefore, has a dual beneficial effect in that it tends to reduce the rate of rural-urban migration and increase the demand for labour.

A second implication of the above model is that traditional methods of estimating the "shadow" price of rural labour to the urban sector will tend to have a downward bias if the migration response parameter is not taken into account. Typically, this shadow price has been expressed in terms of the marginal product of the rural worker who migrates to the city to secure the additional urban job. However, if for every additional urban job that is created more than one rural worker is induced to migrate, then the opportunity cost will reflect the combined loss of agricultural production of all those induced to migrate, not just the one who is fortunate enough to secure the urban position. It also follows that whenever there are sizeable pools of urban unemployed, traditional estimates of the shadow price of urban labour will reflect an upward bias.

APPENDIX

A Mathematical Model of Rural-Urban Migration

Consider the following formulation of the theory of rural-urban migration used in this article. I begin by assuming that individuals base their decision to migrate on considerations of income maximisation and that their calculations are founded on what they perceive to be their expected income streams in urban and rural areas. It is further assumed that the individual who chooses to migrate is attempting to achieve the prevailing average income for his level of education or skill attainment in the urban centre of his choice. Nevertheless, he is assumed to be aware of his limited chances of immediately securing wage employment and the likelihood that he will be unemployed or underemployed for a certain period of time. It follows that the migrant's expected income stream is determined both by the prevailing income in the modern sector and the probability of being employed there, rather than being underemployed in the traditional sector or totally unemployed.

If we let $V(0)$ be the discounted present value of the expected "net" urban-rural income stream over the migrant's time horizon; $Y_{u, r}(t)$ the average real incomes of individuals employed in the urban and the rural economy; n the number of time periods in the migrant's planning horizon; and r the discount rate reflecting the migrant's degree of time preference, then the decision to migrate or not will depend on whether

$$V(0) = \int_{t=0}^{n} [p(t)Y_u(t) - Y_r(t)] \; e^{-rt}dt - C(0)$$

is positive or negative, where

C (0) represents the cost of migration, and

p (t) is the probability that a migrant will have secured an urban job at the average income level in period t.

In any one time period, the probability of being employed in the modern sector, $p(t)$, will be directly related to the probability π of having been selected in that or any previous period from a given stock of unemployed or underemployed job seekers. If we assume that for most migrants the selection procedure is random, then the probability of having a job in the modern sector within x periods after migration, $p(x)$, is:

$p(1) = \pi(1)$
and

$p(2) = \pi(1) + [1-\pi(1)] \pi(2)$
so that

$p(x) = p(x-1) + [1-p(x-1)] \pi(x)$
or

$$p(x) = \pi(1) + \sum_{t=2}^{x} \pi(t) \prod_{s=1}^{t-1} [1-\pi(s)]$$

where

$\pi (t)$ equals the ratio of new job openings relative to the number of accumulated job aspirants in period t.

It follows from this probability formulation that for any given level of $Y_u(t)$ and $Y_r(t)$, the longer the migrant has been in the city the higher his probability p of having a job and the higher, therefore, is his expected income in that period.

Formulating the probability variable in this way has two advantages: (1) it avoids the "all or nothing" problem of having to assume that the migrant either earns the average income or earns nothing in the periods immediately following migration: consequently, it reflects the fact that many underemployed migrants will be able to generate some income in the urban traditional sector while searching for a regular job; and (2) it modifies somewhat the assumption of random selection since the probability of a migrant having been selected varies directly with the time he has been in the city. This permits adjustments for the fact that longer-term migrants usually have more contacts and better information systems so that their expected incomes should be higher than those of newly arrived migrants with similar skills.

Suppose we now incorporate this behaviouristic theory of migration into a simple aggregate dynamic equilibrium model of urban labour demand and supply in the following manner. We once again define the probability π of obtaining a job in the urban sector in any one time period as being directly related to the rate of new employment creation and inversely related to the ratio of unemployed job seekers to the number of existing job opportunities, that is—

$$(1) \; \pi = \frac{\gamma N}{S-N}$$

where γ is the net rate of urban new job creation, N is the level of urban employment, and S is the total urban labour force.

If w is the urban real wage rate and r represents average rural real income, then the "expected" urban-rural real income differential d is—

$$(2)\ d = w \cdot \pi - r$$

or, substituting (1) into (2)—

$$(3)\ d = w \cdot \frac{\gamma N}{S-N} - r$$

The basic assumption of our model once again is that the supply of labour to the urban sector is a function of the urban-rural *expected* real income differential, i.e.—

$$(4)\ S = f_s(d)$$

If the rate of urban job creation is a function of the urban wage w and a policy parameter a, e.g. a concentrated governmental effort to increase employment through a comprehensive programme of industrial import substitution or, as in the case of Kenya, the 1964 and 1970 Tripartite Agreements to raise employment levels, both of which operate on labour demand, we have—

$$(5)\ \gamma = f_d(w;a)$$

where it is assumed that $\dfrac{\partial \gamma}{\partial a} > 0$. If the growth in the urban labour demand is increased as a result of the governmental policy shift, the increase in the urban labour supply is—

$$(6)\ \frac{\partial S}{\partial a} = \frac{\partial S}{\partial d}\frac{\partial d}{\partial \gamma}\frac{\partial \gamma}{ga}$$

Differentiating (3) and substituting into (6), we obtain—

$$(7)\ \frac{\partial S}{\partial a} = \frac{\partial S}{\partial d} w \frac{N}{S-N} \cdot \frac{\partial \gamma}{\partial a}$$

The absolute number of urban unemployed will increase if the increase in labour supply exceeds the increase in the number of new jobs created, i.e. if—

$$(8)\ \frac{\partial S}{\partial a} > \frac{\partial (\gamma N)}{\partial a} = \frac{N \partial \gamma}{\partial a}$$

Combining (7) and (8), we get—

$$(9)\ \frac{\partial S}{\partial d} w \frac{N}{S-N} \cdot \frac{\partial \gamma}{\partial a} > \frac{N \partial \gamma}{\partial a}$$

or—

$$(10)\ \frac{\partial S/S}{\partial d/d} > \frac{d}{w} \cdot \frac{(S-N)}{S}$$

or, finally, substituting for d—

$$(11)\ \frac{\partial S/S}{\partial d/d} > \frac{w \cdot \pi - r}{w} \cdot \frac{(S-N)}{S}$$

Expression (11) reveals that the absolute level of unemployment will rise if the elasticity of urban labour supply with respect to the expected urban-rural income differential, $\dfrac{\partial S/S}{\partial d/d}$, (what I have called elsewhere the "migration response function") exceeds the urban-rural differential as a proportion of the urban wage times the unemployment rate, $\dfrac{S-N}{S}$. Alternatively, equation (11) shows that the higher the unemployment rate, the higher must be the elasticity to increase the level of unemployment for any expected real income differential. But note that in most developing nations the inequality (11) will be satisfied by a very low elasticity of supply when realistic figures are used. For example, if the urban real wage is 60, average rural real income is 20, the probability of getting a job is ·50 and the unemployment rate is 20 per cent, then the level of unemployment will increase if the elasticity of urban labour supply is greater than ·033, i.e. substituting into (11) we get—

$$\frac{\partial S/S}{\partial d/d} = \frac{\cdot 50 \times 60 - 20}{60} \times \cdot 20 = \cdot 033$$

Clearly, much more needs to be known about the empirical value of this elasticity coefficient in different African nations before one can realistically predict what the impact of a policy to generate more urban *employment* will be on the over-all level of urban *unemployment*.

IV.C.2. Urban Unemployment*

Migration from rural areas accounts for half of urban population expansion. The many studies on the causes of this migration have shown so many "push-pull" aspects and such variety in its composition, not only between countries but also between regions of the same country and over time, as to make generalizations hazardous. Differences in social norms, including the degree of "emancipation" which the towns offer, in existing links with urban families, in prevailing conditions in the towns and the countryside, particularly the dynamism of urban economic growth and the availability of additional agricultural land, all influence the flow.

That greater opportunities are seen in the towns primarily in terms of income seems clear enough. There is considerable evidence that the migrants, or at least those who stay, are generally successful in this respect, even though there may be a period of waiting during which support is received from friends and relatives. Unemployment among migrants of a few years' residence is generally noticeably lower than urban averages.

The attraction of amenities as such seems of less immediate significance. Use of amenities generally requires payments and is therefore conditional on earning a sufficient income. Conversely, attempts to restrain migration by deliberate policies of restricting the growth of urban services appear to have been unsuccessful. Migrants generally seem to regard living conditions even in squatter settlements as no worse than those they have left. And certainly the life-style is generally considered more attractive. Surprising to the town dweller the neon lights and billboards may also appear more beautiful to the migrants than the countryside.

As a very tentative generalization, the migratory movement has slowed significantly

*From World Bank, *Urbanization,* Sector Working Paper, Washington, D.C., 1972, pp. 10–12, 14–17, 21–3, 80–82. Reprinted by permission.

only when the absorptive capacity of the towns in terms of economic growth remains stagnant and urban unemployment is persistently high. There are, however, isolated cases such as Taiwan where prolonged and successful rural development of a labor-intensive nature has been accompanied by significantly lower than average migration.

The marginal nature of rural to town migration deserves emphasis. Important as the migration is in relation to existing urban population, it is nevertheless equivalent to only a fraction even of the *increase* in rural population. If the population of the rural areas is six times the population of the urban areas (as in the most populous of the developing countries), and the rate of natural increase the same as in the towns, then migration equivalent to only one-sixth of the additions to rural population will double the urban population growth rate.

These considerations throw some light on the variations in urban growth rates between countries and regions of the developing world. Urban population growth is most rapid where total population growth is particularly high as in South America, or where, as in Africa, a somewhat more modest population growth is accompanied by a particularly high proportion of rural to total population. The unexpectedly slow rate of urbanization in India in the 1960s appears to be associated with very slow economic growth and very heavy unemployment in some of the major towns, such as Calcutta.

Projections of future urbanization levels depend on the assumptions made as to changes in population and urbanization trends as the process of development continues, and as to the speed of the rise in income levels. The estimates given below are from United Nations sources. Comparisons with other estimates do not indicate important divergencies over the next two decades due to the strong influence of the existing age structure and the limited potential for changes in birth rates over this period. Even for the year 2000, the differences can be considered marginal in relation to the size of the problem—similar levels of urban population would be reached a few years earlier or later. Thereafter divergencies become much more marked.

The projected increase in the urban population of the developing countries in the 40 years from 1960 to 2000 is over one billion, more than four times the increase in the previous 40 years and about three times the total urban population of the developed world in 1960. If this appears scarcely plausible, the projected increase in rural population appears equally so. The one and a half billion increase foreseen is three times that of the previous 40 years and almost as large as the total rural population in 1960. An increase of at least 50% in the ratio of rural population to agricultural land may be implied for many countries. Yet there is no indication that total population will increase less than assumed so as to be able to reduce either rural or urban estimate without increasing the other.[1]

Perhaps the most striking feature of the urbanization process in the developing countries has been the rapidity of growth of large cities. Many are more than doubling in population and perhaps tripling in area within a decade. This phenomenon is not confined to any region. Abidjan grew from 69,000 in 1950 to well over 500,000 today; Lagos from under 250,000 to 1,500,000; Bangkok from less than 1,000,000 to 3,000,000; and Bogota from 650,000 to over 2,500,000.

URBAN EMPLOYMENT, INCOME
DISTRIBUTION AND LIVING CONDITIONS

The malaise of urban centers in the developing countries is only too evident in the

[1] Such evidence as exists suggests that both total and urban population in 1970 were somewhat higher than the projections. For the developing

squalor of the rapidly growing slums and unauthorized settlements, the deterioration in many public services, the extreme shortage of housing, and the congestion in the streets. Less immediately evident, but certainly no less important, are the growth of unemployment and the worsening of income distribution.

Data on urban employment are sadly inadequate partly because the wage-paid element of the labor force is generally very low and the conceptual difficulties in defining "unemployment" and measuring "income" for the remainder are considerable. Scattered evidence suggests that unemployment in urban areas, as variously defined, is much more often above 10% than below, and is over 20% in some countries and, more frequently, for the 15 to 24 age group. There are again, however, a few significant exceptions both among countries with a strong record of rural development, such as Taiwan, and among those with particularly high urban and industrial growth, for example, Korea. For large cities, the position appears worse than for the smaller urban centers. In some major African cities estimated unemployment exceeds 30%.

The urban unemployment situation appears generally to have worsened over the last two decades, though it is by no means clear whether unemployment plus underemployment is worse than in the countryside. The limitations of modern industry as a means of absorbing the available manpower have become increasingly evident. The growth rate in industrial employment tends to be only about half that in industrial output. Nor does this take into account the repercussions that expansion of modern in-

world as a whole, the *increase* in urban population between 1960 and 1980 may equal the *total* urban population of the developed world in 1960. It may be noted that the projected rural population of the developing countries would still approximate about 70% at the end of the century and the 30% urban population would correlate with a national income per capita average of only a little over $200.

TABLE 1.   Urban/Rural Population of Developing Countries

	1920	1940	1960	1980	2000
Urban (above 20,000) Population (Millions)	69 (6%)	128 (9%)	310 (15%)	693 (22%)	1,436 (31%)
Rural and Small Town Population (Millions)	1,118 (94%)	1,346 (91%)	1,705 (85%)	2,431 (78%)	3,235 (69%)
Annual rate of increase					
—in urban population		3.1%	4.5%	4.1%	3.7%
—in rural population		0.9%	1.2%	1.8%	1.4%

Source: Table 32 in "Growth of the World's Urban and Rural Population, 1920–2000." UN 1969. Estimates are an average of four alternative series based on existing trends and weighted for each region according to the assumptions judged most relevant.

TABLE 2.   Estimates of Migrants as a Percentage of Recent Population Increases

City	Period	Total Population Increase (Thousands)	Migrants as a Percentage of Total Population Increase
Abidjan	1955–63	129	76
Bogota	1956–66	930	33
Bombay	1951–61	1,207	52
Caracas	1950–60	587	54
	1960–66	501	50
Djakarta	1961–68	1,528	59
Istanbul	1950–60	672	68
	1960–65	428	65
Lagos	1952–62	393	75
Nairobi	1961–69	162	50
Sao Paulo	1950–60	2,163	72
	1960–67	2,543	68
Seoul	1955–65	1,697	63
Taipei	1950–60	396	40
	1960–67	326	43

Source: World Bank, *Urbanization*, Washington, D.C., 1972, p. 80.

dustrial output may have in reducing employment in small-scale handicrafts—though this may in some cases be more than offset by employment directly created in associated service industries.

Estimates by the International Labour Office (ILO) indicate that even after allowing for a decline in participation rates, the total labor force of developing countries will expand by at least 25% between 1970 and 1980.[2] Such a rate is unprecedented even in countries which had large-scale immigration, such as the United States. This surge in the labor force derives from the lagged effect of the earlier surge in life expectancy at birth. With few exceptions a continuance of this trend in labor force at least until the middle 1980s is implied by the pattern of birth and mortality rates over the last two decades.

Growth in urban labor force is likely to be particularly rapid. The natural increase will be high as a result of past immigration which has tended to raise the average age in the countryside and lower it in the towns.[3] Moreover, in many developing countries, and in large regions within others, the availability of suitable land for agriculture is already very restricted and the median size of farms small. In such cases, any acceleration in the growth of rural labor force can be expected sharply to increase pressures to migrate, further intensifying urban employment problems.[4]

The wide divergence between urban employment patterns in developing countries and those in developed countries deserves

[2] As workers in urban centers enter the labor force later and retire earlier than in agriculture, the urbanization trend of itself tends to reduce participation in the labor force.

[3] Where migration has been predominantly of unaccompanied male workers, the impact on future labor force may not occur.

[4] Where, as in many African countries, additional cultivable land is relatively abundant and a large part of rural migration is to colonize new areas, the increased rural labor force may have less urban impact.

emphasis. "Dualism" in the countryside between modern and traditional agriculture is paralleled in the cities by a dualism between the small modern wage-paid sector and the much larger traditional or "bazaar" sector. A large part of this latter group is covered in conventional terminology under the "service sector"; yet its functions are much wider than the nomenclature indicates. A multitude of small enterprises generally exists in shantytowns as in older areas of the cities. Casual labor and petty trading are highly important not only as a source of employment but also for the economic functioning of the cities and the economizing of scarce resources, in re-use of products as well as in reduced needs for equipment and buildings. Though productivity is low compared to the modern sector, it is far superior to unemployment and in all probability exceeds productivity in marginal employment in agriculture.

Unfortunately, concentration of attention on industry has resulted in little analysis of the much larger "service" sector of urban employment. Little is known of its composition and functioning or its linkages with the modern sector. Yet there is no evidence that it will decline in importance in the near to medium future. Even looking further into the future, employment in manufacturing seems most unlikely ever to attain the levels of 40% or more of the total reached in the developed countries. The reason is simply that advances in technology are progressively reducing the proportion of labor in the manufacturing process. Machines are more efficient than they were and power is more readily available.

The functions of the city and composition of employment are thus likely to remain very different from the present or earlier situation in developed countries. There is no inevitable technical connection between industrialization and urbanization. Solutions based on historic Western typology are most unlikely to be appropriate for the urban employment problems of the developing countries. In the developing countries, the service industry predominates over manufacturing industry in the majority of urban centers and is likely to continue to do so.

Closely associated with the employment problem is that of income distribution. It is widely recognized that a large gap exists between incomes in the towns and those in the countryside. Average Gross Domestic Product (GDP) in the major urban centers of the developing countries may be three to five times that of rural areas, with a somewhat lower differential for the smaller towns. Even allowing for higher prices in the towns, the gap is wide and, on somewhat scant evidence, appears to be widening. A similar situation of polarization of incomes has developed within the urban centers with a small and increasingly wealthy group separated socially and often physically from the poorer mass of the population.

In large part, this situation reflects the impact of the technological revolution, an impact much sharper than it was in today's developed countries. The differences between productivity in the modern and the traditional sector are much greater than they used to be—for production of non-agricultural goods, for agriculture, and for services. Not until modern technologies have spread much more widely in both town and countryside will the underlying causes abate. While the choice of technology alternatives will play a large part in the speed of diffusion of impact, the time required must be measured in decades for most developing countries.

Present trends and the pressures of population and labor force thus indicate a further worsening of income distribution over the near future at least. Sharp gains in the small modern sectors of both urban and rural areas will be paralleled by more rapidly rising numbers in the more traditional sectors. Not only are considerations of equity and social unrest involved. A more even income distribution would also create the basis for mass markets for manufactured goods of lower

import content and provide a stimulus to growth and urban employment.

With a few notable exceptions, the high natural growth of urban population, the inflow of poor rural migrants, and the increasing unemployment and imbalance in income distribution, have been reflected in a deterioration in urban living conditions. The shortcomings of present living conditions are, it is true, generally less for the migrants than those they have left in rural areas. Parallels can, moreover, readily be found in many industrial cities of the nineteenth century, in the inadequacy of sewerage for instance. What is most disturbing is rather the scale of the problem and the prospect of urban populations increasingly outdistancing the urban services and housing available.

Many big cities are experiencing shantytown population growth in excess of 20% a year and a doubling of slum and shantytown population within the next four to six years is now in prospect. The shantytown population already accounts for a third or more of the total population in many cities. Such settlements are therefore very quickly becoming, if they have not already become, the major part of the city in terms of living conditions and urban pattern. Though varying widely in type, social structure and the degree of poverty, they are in large part characterized by absence of even minimal standards of housing, water supply, sewerage, streets, and social facilities.

Housing conditions are generally poor in the extreme. The case of Calcutta where more than two-thirds of families are reported as living in one room is only slightly more drastic than for many other cities of Asia, Africa and Latin America. Housing construction is typically running at a quarter or less of estimated minimum requirements.[5] The World Health Organization (WHO) estimates that only a quarter of the urban populations currently receive public water supply in house or courtyard and only

[5] UN Document A/8037—21 August 1970.

a further quarter is supplied from public standpipes.[6] The situation for sewerage is certainly worse with the backlog of requirements rapidly growing. . . .

It is clear that urbanization problems have reached a magnitude and importance necessitating explicit consideration in overall national development policies. It is no less clear that considerations of social policy, equity and regional balance—in large part involving value judgments—as well as more narrowly defined economic considerations, must play a considerable role in determination of national urbanization policies.

One school of thought holds that much greater emphasis should be placed on creating jobs and improving amenities in the countryside. Urban pressures would thereby be lessened through a reduction in migration. Income disparities between town and country and between different regions would also be narrowed, and help provided to the rural poor, who have as yet received little or no benefit from economic development. And if, unfortunately, it has to be accepted that large-scale unemployment is inevitable for at least several years to come, "Planners should ask themselves: Where is it more convenient for the unemployed to be, in the country or in the city? In the country, of course."[7] Both infrastructure and welfare requirements will be less in rural areas than in the cities not only because costs may be lower, but also because lower standards are accepted. The foreign exchange element of the infrastructure and of the spending from rural incomes will also be lower.

Those who hold this view contend that the existing urbanization trend, particularly to big cities, is biased by a number of influences. Costs of relocation of migrants are not sufficiently taken into account in considering urban employment, nor in assessing the benefits of labor-saving investments in

agriculture. Failure to charge industrialists with the full social costs of their operations, including pollution and congestion, biases location and investment towards the big city. Above all, the concentration of political power produces a very favored position for big cities in the allocation of investment resources. Such influences operate through the allocation of development funds and favored treatment for various types of permits. Perhaps more importantly, policies such as those toward exchange and interest rates swing the terms of trade between town and country in favor of the former.

On this view, in short, attention and investment have been unduly concentrated on urban areas and on accompanying capital intensive projects which, while they may provide the greatest returns on outlay, do not maximize the use of the nation's total resources. Or more extremely, the urban population is increasingly a parasitic growth, its privileged position based on exploitation of the rural surplus. What is generally implied is that a given total of local resources and foreign exchange can, with appropriate policies, achieve more in the countryside than in the cities in creating employment, raising living standards, and also possibly in output. By reducing migration, cities will be relieved of a corresponding burden of expenditure.

The opposing view sees the solution of rural poverty in accelerated migration to the towns. Urbanization is expected to continue to offer the most important opportunities for increasing employment, output and savings, and thus also the possibilities for increased future investment in both town and country on any but a short view. Concentration of activities in towns provides the basis for specialization, and for increased productivity in manufacturing and supporting services. Large, flexible labor markets with diversified skills are needed to match changing patterns of production. Cities provide concentrated markets for the output and are the link with the outside world through which technological know-how flows. The

[6] WHO Document A23/P&B/5, 10 April 1970.
[7] Professor Edmundo Flores, "Economic Growth and Urbanization," Rehovot Conference paper, 1971.

concentration of population also permits standards of education and health not possible in the countryside if only on account of distances. The informal spread of knowledge of modern methods can be as important as the more formal training possibilities.

Urbanization is considered a necessary condition for increasing productivity in rural areas by providing markets for agricultural products and, most importantly, stimulating specialization of agriculture between regions. Urban activities provide agricultural inputs and incentive goods, and indirectly promote use of modern techniques. Only by rapid migration can the population of rural areas be brought into balance with rural resources and productivity, incomes raised, and the poverty of the lowest income rural groups, the landless and marginal farmers, reduced. The dualism between "modern" and "traditional" sectors existing in the countryside will inevitably increase as commercialized agriculture and new techniques spread until the countryside as a whole enters the modern sector. This situation is a long way away and will be retarded by anti-migration policies.

That migration of rural labor to higher incomes in the towns may increase disparities between regional average income levels is not denied. But the relevance of such statistical measures of income balance is questioned if the persons who move are better off while those left in the rural areas are at least marginally better off. Reduced densities as a result of migration should, in most circumstances, result in higher average productivity per man in the rural areas since there will be less fragmentation and fewer inhabitants in the less productive areas. The national, as opposed to regional, income distribution should be improved. Higher incomes of the remaining rural population will, moreover, provide additional markets for urban products.

On this view, in brief, the real problem is rural overpopulation not urban overpopulation. The question which should be posed is accordingly not how many should be in towns, but how few are needed in agriculture. As for the basic problem of harmful population growth, the greater the urbanization, the sooner a declining rate can be expected.

IV.D. THE URBAN INFORMAL SECTOR

IV.D.1. The Informal Sector in Kenya*

The problem with employment is that the statistics are incomplete, covering a major part of wage-earning employment and some self-employment in the larger and more organised firms but omitting a range of wage earners and self-employed persons, male as well as female, in what we term "the informal sector".

The popular view of informal-sector activities is that they are primarily those of petty traders, street hawkers, shoeshine boys and other groups "underemployed" on the streets of the big towns. The evidence suggests that the bulk of employment in the informal sector, far from being only marginally productive, is economically efficient and profit-making, though small in scale and limited by simple technologies, little capital and lack of links with the other ("formal") sector. Within the latter part of the informal sector are employed a variety of carpenters, masons, tailors and other tradesmen, as well as cooks and taxi-drivers, offering virtually the full range of basic skills needed to provide goods and services for a large though often poor section of the population.

Often people fail to realise the extent of economically efficient production in the informal sector because of the low incomes received by most workers in the sector. A common interpretation of the cause of these low incomes (in comparison to average wage levels in the formal sector) has been to presume that the problem lies within the informal sector; that it is stagnant, non-dynamic,

*From ILO Mission, *Employment, Incomes, and Equality: A Strategy for Increasing Productive Employment in Kenya*, Geneva, 1972, pp. 5–8, 503–8. Reprinted by permission.

and a net for the unemployed and for the thinly veiled idleness into which those who cannot find formal wage jobs must fall. It is hardly surprising that this view should be widespread, for academic analysts have often encouraged and fostered such an interpretation. Further, from the vantage point of central Nairobi, with its gleaming sky-scrapers, the dwellings and commercial structures of the informal sector look indeed like hovels. For observers surrounded by imported steel, glass and concrete, it requires a leap of the imagination and considerable openness of mind to perceive the informal sector as a sector of thriving economic activity and a source of Kenya's future wealth. But throughout the report we shall argue that such an imaginative leap and openness of mind is not only necessary to solve Kenya's employment problem, but is entirely called for by the evidence about the informal sector. There exists, for instance, considerable evidence of technical change in the urban informal sector, as well as of regular employment at incomes above the average level attainable in smallholder agriculture. The informal sector, particularly in Nairobi but to varying degrees in all areas, has been operating under extremely debilitating restrictions as a consequence of a pejorative view of its nature. Thus there exists an imminent danger that this view could become a self-fulfilling prophecy.

Later we explain how employment in the informal sector has grown in spite of obstacles and lack of outside support: the evidence suggests that employment has probably increased a good deal faster in the informal than in the formal sector. It is therefore impossible to judge how the employment problem has changed merely from the data on employment in the formal sector.

Our analysis lays great stress on the pervasive importance of the link between formal and informal activities. We should therefore emphasise that informal activities are not confined to employment on the periphery of the main towns, to particular occupations or even to economic activities. Rather, informal activities are the way of doing things, characterised by—

(a) ease of entry;
(b) reliance on indigenous resources;
(c) family ownership of enterprises;
(d) small scale of operation;
(e) labour-intensive and adapted technology;
(f) skills acquired outside the formal school system; and
(g) unregulated and competitive markets.

Informal-sector activities are largely ignored, rarely supported, often regulated and sometimes actively discouraged by the Government.

The characteristics of formal-sector activities are the obverse of these, namely—

(a) difficult entry;
(b) frequent reliance on overseas resources;
(c) corporate ownership;
(d) large scale of operation;
(e) capital-intensive and often imported technology;
(f) formally acquired skills, often expatriate; and
(g) protected markets (through tariffs, quotas and trade licenses).

Our strategy of a redistribution from growth aims at establishing links that are at present lacking between the formal and the informal sectors. A transfer of incomes from the top income groups to the working poor would result in new types of labour-intensive investments in both urban and rural areas.

This should not only generate demand for the products of the informal sector but also encourage innovations in labour-intensive techniques in this sector. The various policies which we recommend in other parts of the report are intended to reduce risk and uncertainty on the part of those employed in the informal sector and to ensure a dynamic growth of this large segment of the Kenyan economy.

Unemployment is often analysed as simply the result of the first type of basic imbalance, between a rapidly growing labour force and a more slowly growing number of job opportunities. If population, it is said, grows at 3.3 per cent as in Kenya, and enumerated wage-earning employment grows—as in Kenya since 1964—at 1.9 per cent, increasing unemployment results.[1] And as long as the divergent growth rates continue, the prospect of growing unemployment in the future seems inevitable. Economic growth even at Kenya's recent rates of 6 to 7 per cent is no protection, it is argued, since inappropriate technologies and rising wages increase productivity so rapidly that growth is robbed of its power to increase the number of jobs faster than the labour force. Although this explanation has sometimes been used in Kenya, it should by now be clear why we have found it seriously deficient, and in some respects seriously misleading, as the main explanation of the Kenyan situation. It ignores the fact that the bulk of the population works on the land, not in wage-earning jobs. It depends crucially on the statistics of the growth of enumerated employment in the formal sector, whereas— as we stated earlier—enumerated employment ignores a large and apparently growing amount of employment in the "informal sector". Thirdly it focuses too exclusively on jobs, instead of on opportunities for earning a reasonable income.

[1] The imbalance is even greater if one compares growth rates of the urban population or of the number of school leavers with the growth of enumerated employment.

But apart from these weaknesses, the explanation just discussed analyses the situation exclusively in terms of over-all imbalances, giving no weight to imbalance between the structure of skills and aspirations of the labour force and the structure of incentives and incomes from work. It pays no attention to the variations in the incidence of employment problems seasonally, regionally, by age or by sex.

There are also marked contrasts between the relative security and income levels of those with wage-earning jobs in the bigger firms and those self-employed in the informal sector. These sharp inequalities inevitably create strong ambitions to migrate to the towns, to strive for higher education, to search for a job. As long as extreme imbalances persist, so will unemployment, since large differentials will always attract a margin of job seekers to hover in the towns, near the chances of the good jobs, in the hopes of snapping one up. This explains why the analysis of inequality is fundamental to the explanation of employment problems in Kenya.

But unemployment is not only the result of imbalance in differentials and opportunities. Even with perfect equality, unemployment could arise. Fast rates of population growth, of urbanisation and school expansion inevitably make it more difficult to absorb the growing labour force and reduce the time that might otherwise be available for structural adjustments. Here a second set of imbalances arise—dynamic imbalances relating to the structure of economic growth in the economy and to the constraints upon it. Rapid growth is needed, but rapid growth can itself generate imbalances which will frustrate its continuation—most notably a shortage of foreign exchange, of domestic savings, of skills and entrepreneurship, of demand or of the political support needed to keep the system workable. For this reason our report is not merely concerned with alleviating unemployment, poverty and gross inequality, but with economic growth on a pattern which can be sustained in the future,

and which generates wider and more productive employment opportunities in the process. . . .

THE RELATION BETWEEN THE FORMAL AND INFORMAL SECTORS

The process of economic transformation and growth in Kenya has been marked by growing inequalities in the distribution of wealth and income among Africans. The usual explanation is the traditional-modern division of the economy, in which the westernised modern sector is the source of dynamism and change and the traditional sector slowly withers away. This view does not correspond to the reality of Kenya; we reject it for that reason, and because it ignores the dynamism and progressive elements indigenous to the Kenyan economy. We have considerable evidence to refute a view that attributes the sources of economic and social change almost exclusively to outside forces.

Furthermore, the traditional-modern analysis focuses only on the positive effects of the westernisation of the Kenyan economy and ignores the negative effects. In particular, it ignores inter-sectoral dynamics, which are the key to the employment problem. The accumulation of wealth in a small part of the modern sector is the consequence of the concentration of political power in that sector, and has given rise to the development of an impoverished and economically deprived modern sub-sector. The slums of Nairobi, Mombasa and to a lesser extent other urban areas are completely modern and due to the differences of wealth and income between different sectors of the economy. These differences draw migrants towards the concentrations, and bring about the modernisation of almost the entire economy, but not the spread of wealth. Because of the slow growth of high-wage employment, migration to urban areas by income seekers has led to the growth of a low-income periphery. This low-income sector is peripheral both literally and figuratively. In Nairobi it sprang up, and continues to grow, just outside the borders of the wealthy urban zone, to supply goods and services to the fortunate few inside that zone and to its own population. Figuratively, it is peripheral in that it has only fortuitous and restricted access to the sources of wealth.

Characteristics and Dynamics of the Informal Sector

We describe these two urban sectors as being the "formal" and the "informal" sector. This designation is not intended to contribute to an academic proliferation of labels; we merely seek an analytical terminology to describe a duality that avoids the bias against the low-incomes sector inherent in the traditional-modern dichotomy. Both sectors are modern; both are the consequence of the urbanisation that has taken place in Kenya over the last 50 years. We might have used the terms "large-scale" and "small-scale", but those terms are purely descriptive and tell us nothing about why one sector is large-scale and the other is small-scale. An explanation of this is central to explaining and solving the employment problem in Kenya. One important characteristic of the formal sector is its relationship to the Government. Economic activities formally and officially recognised and fostered by the Government enjoy considerable advantages. First, they obtain the direct benefits of access to credit, foreign exchange concessions, work permits for foreign technicians, and a formidable list of benefits that reduce the cost of capital in relation to that of labour. Indirectly, establishments in the formal sector benefit immeasurably from the restriction of competition through tariffs, quotas, trade licensing and product and construction standards drawn from the rich countries or based on their criteria. Partly because of its privileged access to resources, the formal sector is characterised by large enterprise, sophisticated technology, high wage rates, high average profits and foreign ownership.

The informal sector, on the other hand, is often ignored and in some respects helped and in some harassed by the authorities. Enterprises and individuals within it operate largely outside the system of government benefits and regulation, and thus have no access to the formal credit institutions and the main sources of transfer of foreign technology. Many of the economic agents in this sector operate illegally, though often pursuing similar economic activities to those in the formal sector—marketing foodstuffs and other consumer goods, carrying out the repair and maintenance of machinery and consumer durables and running transport, for example. Illegality here is generally due not to the nature of the economic activity but to an official limitation of access to legitimate activity. Sometimes the limitations are flouted with virtual abandon, as in the case of unlicensed *matatu* taxis; sometimes the regulations are quite effective. The consequence is always twofold: the risk and uncertainty of earning a livelihood in this low-income sector are magnified, and the regulations ensure a high quality of services and commodities for the wealthy few at the expense of the impoverished many.

The formal-informal analysis applies equally well to the agricultural sector. The parallels are obvious and striking. The division between favoured operators with licences and those without in urban areas is reproduced in agriculture between those who grow tea and coffee with official sanction and those who do so illegally. Similarly, with other agricultural products such as beef, there are those whose wealth enables them to conform to and benefit from standards officially laid down, while others can make a livelihood only by contravening the regulations. In the agricultural sector extension services take the place of the industrial estates and of loans from the Industrial and Commercial Development Corporation in the urban areas: farmers whose wealth and income allow them to conform to bureaucratic criteria benefit. Perhaps the most striking rural-urban parallel is with illegal rural squatters, who move unofficially on to land scheduled for resettlement and face a continual danger of eviction. Their similarity to urban squatters is obvious—both are irresistibly drawn to real or perceived sources of wealth, despite legal restrictions of access.

In the Introduction to this report we considered the characteristics, other than relation to the Government, that distinguish the informal sector from the formal. These characteristics of the informal sector, both agricultural and non-agricultural, result in low incomes for those who work in it. A natural consequence of these low incomes is that monetary exchanges within the informal sector are different in quality from those in the formal sector. A most important consequence of a low income is the primacy of risk and uncertainty. The loss a small farmer or a small entrepreneur can bear is disproportionately smaller than that which can be borne by a wealthy operator, particularly when the former has no access to institutionalised sources of credit. As a consequence, the entrepreneur in the informal sector must act continually to protect himself against risk. Accordingly he establishes semi-permanent relations with suppliers and buyers, frequently at the expense of his profits. For the same reason he may be hesitant to innovate, particularly in agriculture, for he cannot take the chance of failure. These characteristic behavioural responses are not inherent in the informal sector; they are adaptive responses to low income.

As pointed out in our report, a rate of increase of employment in the formal sector high enough to reduce the relative size of the informal sector seems to us to be beyond the bounds of possibility for the foreseeable future. An absolute reduction is much less likely still. On the basis of any reasonable calculation, the urban informal sector in 1985 will include a larger proportion of the urban labour force than it does today. We do not view this inevitable development with dismay, for we see in the informal sector not

only growth and vitality, but also the source of a new strategy of development for Kenya. The workshops of the informal sector can provide a major and essential input for the development of an indigenous capital goods industry, which is a key element in solving the employment problem. The informal sector is not a problem, but a source of Kenya's future growth. In addition, it is in its workshops that practical skills and entrepreneurial talents are being developed at low cost. Many of its enterprises are inefficient technically and economically, and will disappear in the process of growth; but this applies equally to the formal sector, where tariff and quota protection, access to capital goods below world market prices and other restrictions on competition perpetuate gross operating inefficiencies that go hand in hand with sophisticated technology.

Despite the vitality and dynamism we see in the informal sector, we do not delude ourselves that it will develop successfully under present conditions. Although it has the potential for dynamic, evolutionary growth, under the existing nexus of restrictions and disincentives, the seeds of involutionary growth have been sown. Unlike the determinants of growth of the formal sector, the determinants of the informal sector are largely external to it. The relevant question is not whether the informal sector is inherently evolutionary or involutionary, but what policies should be followed to cause evolutionary growth. Irrespective of policy changes, the informal sector will grow in the next 15 years. If policy continues as at present, the growth will be involutionary and the gap between the formal and informal sectors will widen. The employment problem will then be worse.

A Model of Inter-sectoral Flows

The purpose of this section is to identify the major factors determining employment in the informal sector. The model used is a simple identity rather than a behavioural model. The points may seem self-evident, but we feel it is useful to make them, because linkages between the small-scale, informal sector and other sectors of the economy have generally been ignored.

From the writings of economists on urban areas in poor countries it appears that the criterion authors use for dividing the urban economy is not the modernity of activities but their enumeration in government labour force surveys.[2] The relation between the two urban sectors implicit in this analysis can be called the "residual" model. The residual model is based on the presumption that the informal sector is a reservoir of unemployment and marginally productive activity into which those who cannot obtain paid jobs in the formal sector sink, barely making ends meet by begging, hawking or embarking on petty crime. In short, the activities in this sector are seen as providing no economic service or commodity. The demand for labour in the sector is presumed to be static. Popular though this view is, we do not feel that it is particularly useful. It asserts *a priori* a characteristic of the informal sector (unemployment) that can be determined only empirically. The mechanism of the residual model can be summarised briefly. The informal or "tradi-

tional" urban sector has a static demand for labour, or a demand for labour that is quite income-inelastic.[3] Therefore, an increase in the number of persons seeking a living in the informal sector (for example, after a reduction of employment in the formal sector) merely drives down average earnings in that sector; and if average earnings are at subsistence level, the influx presumably results in unemployment. A further prediction of this type of model when it incorporates a rural sector is that if average earnings in the urban informal sector are not below those in rural areas, migration will result. Facts mentioned in the first part of the report cast doubt on this last prediction for Kenya.

This view of the informal sector ignores linkage effects and product substitution, which we feel are at present quite significant in Kenya, and should be strengthened in the future. To identify these linkages we use a four-sector model of the economy, which distinguishes between smallholder agriculture, the informal (non-agricultural) sector, the private formal sector and the government sector. The outputs of these sectors are X_1, X_2, X_3 and X_4 respectively. The output of the informal (non-agricultural) sector is by definition given by the following input-output row:

$$(1) \quad X_2 = a_{21}X_1 + a_{22}X_2 + a_{23}X_3 + a_{24}X_4 + X_{2F}$$

The symbol a indicates input-use coefficients, and X_{2F} is the final demand for informal-sector output. From our observations and reading in Kenya we can make up a list of the most important goods and services supplied by the informal sector to itself and the other three sectors.

---

[2] "A more meaningful distinction than that of employed-underemployed-unemployed is between those employed in establishments employing five or ten workers which are usually covered in annual labour surveys . . . and the rest of the labour force. The larger establishments . . . can generally be characterised as modern-sector establishments, as opposed to the smaller-scale establishments which are better characterised as traditional. Employees in traditional establishments are generally underemployed under most definitions of the term, while modern sector employees can be thought of as fully employed. . . ." Charles R. Frank, Jr., "The problem of urban unemployment in Africa," in R. G. Ridker and H. Lubell (eds.), *Employment and unemployment problems of the Near East and South Asia* (Delhi, Vikas, 1971), pp. 785–786.

[3] This, of course, is also an empirical question, and the assumption of a low income elasticity of demand is rather arbitrary. The over-all income elasticity of demand for the output of the informal sector, for example, is sensitive to the distribution of income.

Using sector	Goods and services supplied
1. Agriculture	Grain-grinding, building materials, transport, marketing, repair and maintenance.
2. Informal	Furniture for commercial use, tools, transport, repair and maintenance.
3. Private formal	Marketing and distribution, transport, furniture, repair and maintenance.
4. Government	Construction, furniture, transport.
5. Final demand	Clothing, prepared food, furniture, repair and maintenance.

In our report we have discussed in detail the ways of increasing the final demand for informal-sector products and strengthening linkages between the informal and other sectors. Here we restrict ourselves to a discussion of the most important parameters of identity (1) above. The strategy we have suggested for Kenya would have the effect in time of strengthening the linkages of the informal sector and fostering a dynamic growth of its final demand; this implies a shift in the composition of output from relatively capital-using to relatively labour-using production processes. In short, we foresee the production of certain types of commodities and services with more labour for a given level of output. This will not occur, of course (indeed, the reverse will occur), unless the present development strategy is radically altered.

Identity (1) can be solved for informal-sector output as follows:

$$(2) \quad X_2 = \frac{1}{1-a_{22}}(a_{21}X_1 + a_{23}X_3 + a_{24}X_4 + X_{2F}).$$

If we assume the capital stock of the informal sector to be constant, then a change in X_2 production is—

$$\Delta L_2 \frac{\Delta X_2}{\Delta L_2}, \quad \text{where} \quad \frac{\Delta X_2}{\Delta L_2} \text{ is, at the limit, the}$$

marginal product of labour in the informal sector. This allows us to write (2) in terms of employment:

$$(3) \quad \Delta L_2 = \frac{1}{1-a_{22}} \frac{\Delta L_2}{\Delta X_2} [\Delta (a_{21}X_1 + a_{23}X_3 + a_{24}X_2 + X_{2F})].$$

While extremely simple, (3) is useful in analysing the growth of employment in the informal sector.

It is obvious that an increase in any X will increase employment in the informal sector if none of the input coefficients is zero. For a given increase in total output, the effect on employment in the informal sector is determined by the values of the coefficients and the composition of the increase in output in terms of $X_1, X_2, \ldots X_{2F}$. The effect of the recommendations in the main report is—

(a) to increase the size of the coefficients; and
(b) to shift the composition of future increases in output towards the sectors where the coefficients are highest.

Even if steps are taken to induce the private formal sector and the Government to shift purchases of inputs towards sector 2, there are significant technological and consumer taste influences militating against success. The extent of potential linkages between sector 2 and sectors 3 and 4 (parameters a_{23} and a_{24}) is strongly related to the nature and pace of technical change occurring outside Kenya. This, in turn, is related to the choice of products, particularly in sector 3. Sector 3 products, which require sophisticated technology for quality reasons (and constantly undergo labour-saving technical change), are unlikely to provide much scope for subcontracting or for intermediate inputs supplied by small producers. Thus the choice of products must be determined either through the redistribution of income or through direct restrictions. In addition, active measures must be taken to increase the technical capacity of the informal sector to supply inputs.

The model used here needs to be elaborated along behavioural lines, and an attempt must be made to estimate the parameters. Data are lacking, though we have made very rough calculations, based on arbitrary but moderate assumptions, that indicate that the present situation in sectors 1, 2 and 3 and shifts in government purchases within the present structure of public demand imply an intermediate demand for sector 2 output of almost £70 million. This very rough calculation indicates that there is considerable scope for employment in the informal sector in Kenya. Further, we feel that this model, with an attempt to estimate its parameters, represents a more fruitful approach to an understanding of the informal sector than the analysis underlying the residual model.

IV.D.2. Unemployment in Kenya*

Another way of understanding the flaw at the centre of the mission's thinking is to examine more closely its concept of the 'informal sector', which it clearly regards as a major conceptual advance. The 'informal sector' consists of things 'done in a certain way'—a way characterized by ease of entry into the activity concerned, reliance on indigenous resources, family ownership, smallness of scale, labour intensiveness and 'adapted technology', skills acquired outside the formal school system and unregulated and competitive markets. The question is, the mission says, why this way of doing things provides such low incomes for those who do them. The answer, it believes, is three-fold. First, the low income of those it caters for; second, official discouragement, owing to a 'pejorative' official view of the value of such activities; and, third, lack of demand from the 'formal sector', public and private. Therefore, it proposes that besides increasing the incomes of the poor the government should turn from harassing to fostering the 'informal sector', and should also start placing official orders with it, and inducing firms in the 'private' ('formal') sec-

*From Colin Leys, "Interpreting African Underdevelopment: Reflections on the ILO Report on Employment, Incomes and Equality in Kenya," *African Affairs*, October 1973, pp. 425–8. Reprinted by permission.

tor to do likewise. From being the Cinderella of underdevelopment, the 'informal sector' could thus become a major source of future growth.

In one sense this argument is almost true by definition. *If* the incomes of the poor were doubled and *if* foreign owned firms were induced to place orders for their inputs with small-scale local family businesses instead of abroad, and *if* the government placed its orders with such businesses and *if* no legal obstacles were placed in the way of such businesses multiplying, then it is fairly clear that such businesses would multiply. What is much more doubtful is whether the 'informal sector' would continue to exhibit the characteristics which the mission now admires; and even more interesting, perhaps, is the question of what would be gained if it did.

For what, after all, is the 'informal sector'? In illustrating the concept the mission generally refers to self-employed craftsmen and the like in the towns: 'a variety of carpenters, masons, tailors and other tradesmen, as well as cooks and taxi-drivers, offering virtually the full range of basic skills needed to provide goods and services for a large though often poor section of the population'; 'the carpenter at work behind his dwellings, the tailor inside an unmarked mud and plaster hut, or the *matatu* (illegal taxi) driver who is out earning fares'. Elsewhere, it recognizes that squatters on unused private or state land also fit the definition of the 'informal sector'. But, in spite of the fact that its interest in the 'informal sector' is primarily in its labour-intensive character, it refers much less often to the fact that it consists also, and predominantly, of wage-workers; and this omission also enables the mission to write as though the *wholly* unemployed were somehow 'outside' the sector altogether. Yet, what stands out about the so-called 'informal sector' is that it denotes primarily a system of very intense exploitation of labour, with very low wages and often very long hours, underpinned by the constant pressure for work from the 'reserve army' of job seekers. The mission noted evidence that in 1970 the lowest paid workers in Nairobi worked the longest hours; almost 30 per cent of those earning less than 200 shillings per month were working over 60 hours per week. On smallholdings in the rural areas in 1968 wages were in some places as low as 50 cents a day, and the rate most often given was between 1/50 and 2/– a day.[1] The "informal sector" is in fact a euphemism for cheap-labour employment, based on landlessness and unemployment, and, as the mission notes, the bulk of it is 'economically efficient and profit-making.'[2]

A second fundamental feature of the 'informal sector' is that the economic activities (and inactivities) it comprises are linked intimately to the so-called 'formal sector'. What they do is to provide goods and services at a very low price, which makes possible the very high profits and wages of the 'formal sector' (i.e. the monopolistic sector). Smallholders provide cheap food crops, pastoralists provide cheap beef, petty traders provide cheap distribution, 'subsistence' transporters provide cheap communications,

the makers of shoes out of old tyres and the bicycle repairers and the charcoal burners and sellers provide cheap goods and services designed for the poverty life-style of those whose work makes the 'formal sector' profitable, and which enable them to live on their wages. From this point of view the sort of urban activities mainly considered by the mission are only a small part of the far larger system of exploitation on which the 'formal sector' rests, including, of course, the so-called 'formal' agricultural sector, for which specially low legal minimum wages are set—not to mention such features as the even lower wages actually paid in the African-owned large farm sector, and the revival of squatter labour. The 'informal sector' of the mission's report is, then, only a—somewhat romanticized—part of the whole range of low-return activities which generate surplus for appropriation by the owners of foreign capital and by the compradors. The mission's prime concern in its celebration of the 'informal sector' is to 'rehabilitate' it; to deny that it consists mainly of 'the street hawker, the bootblack, and the youths idling on street corners'—those in occupations deemed to be 'unproductive' and 'parasitic'—and to insist that the 'bulk' of it is 'productive'. But perhaps the conventional image of the 'informal sector' as consisting of people like prostitutes, hawkers and bootblacks symbolizes a truth which is lost sight of in the mission's report; i.e. that the carpenter, the squatter and the woman labourer working on a smallholding for 1/50 shillings per day have in common with the prostitute and the bootblack the fact that they too are forced to sell something very cheaply, without which the wealth of the rich would be impossible.

At any rate, it is rather ironic that the mission sees one of the main keys to an employment-oriented development strategy as consisting in effecting links between the 'informal sector' and the 'formal sector'. What this really means is that the sort of links which the monopolistic, mainly for-

[1] Mimeographed draft of J. Heyer, D. Ireri and J. Moris, "Rural Development in Kenya" (Institute for Development Studies, Nairobi, 1969), p. 167.

[2] ILO Report, p. 5.

eign, sector has *not* previously found it profitable to have with small-scale African firms, and which the government itself has hitherto had mainly with foreign firms, should now be added to the vital if less direct links which already exist between foreign capital and the government on the one hand, and the rest of the economy on the other. Provided the new goods and services which foreign capital would procure from the 'informal sector' were cheap enough to compensate it for what it would lose in not buying from its own sources of supply abroad, no doubt it would be happy to collaborate. But this could only happen if, in addition to 'informal' wage rates remaining extremely low, a good deal of regulation and protection was introduced to govern these transactions. The mission, for instance, envisages special training schemes for 'informal' producers entering into arrangements to supply goods to 'formal sector' enterprises, state loans for plant, long-term purchasing contracts and the like; what would still be 'informal'—i.e. competitive—about the activities involved in this process would evidently be only the wages paid.[3] Significantly enough, when it discusses trade unions, the mission does not say whether or not it envisages union organization developing among the workers in the greatly expanded 'informal sector' which it wishes to create, and in general its discussion of 'industrial relations' scarcely seems to envisage the possibility of a conflict of interests between employers and workers, as the remarkable last sentence of the following passage indicates:

'It is hoped [the report does not say by whom] that increased trade union activities in the rural sector may help to bring about

an improvement in the working and living conditions of rural workers. . . . They could exert effective pressure when necessary, to protect the interests of small farmers, casual workers and landless labour. . .'[4]

In a word: by talking of two 'sectors', the mission saw a duality (the word is theirs) where there was a unity—between the mass of very low incomes in general and the high profit levels of most firms; and it ignored a vital divergence of interest—between the employers and the workers within the so-called 'informal sector'. The most probable effect of the mission's proposals—even in the unlikely event of its recommendations on income redistribution and the circumscription of foreign capital being implemented— would be primarily to direct business to low-wage African-owned enterprises, and to enable a new stratum of the African petty-bourgeoisie to transcend the limitations of the competitive market and achieve a measure of protection among the ranks of the auxiliary bourgeoisie.[5]

It is true that, because African small firms tend to be more labour-intensive than large foreign ones, the problem of *un*employment would probably be relieved;[6] but it is not

[3] For instance, the mission recommended with regard to government building that 'the de facto policy of awarding construction contracts to enterprises paying less than official minimum wages could be made official . . .'"

[4] ILO Report, p. 259.

[5] One problem not adequately discussed in the report is the extent to which consumer tastes have already been moulded by advertising and conspicuous consumption by the rich so that any substantial increase in the incomes of the working poor would expand demand for 'formal sector' products (such as bread, leather shoes, bicycles, etc.) rather than for 'craft-produced' cheap goods.

[6] This is on the assumption that the steps recommended against the excesses of foreign firms with regard to surplus transfer, etc., and other measures would not reduce the overall growth rate of a minimum of 6 per cent per annum assumed by the mission. The mission's judgment that its recommendations would not, on balance, do this seems well founded, but with an important proviso: this would depend on the balance of its proposals being faithfully reflected in the balance of the measures adopted. If they were implemented selectively, and

clear how the mission's proposals in this area would relieve the problem of the 'working poor'. On the contrary, one might almost say that the real meaning of the mission's proposals about the 'informal sector' is that exploitation should be spread more evenly.

Nor—finally—is it clear how, after the recommended redistribution of income has been initially brought about, the problem of inequality and unemployment is not to reappear. The mission's treatment of this point is brief, and can be quoted in full:

'It cannot be emphasised too much that our strategy is based not on permanent transfers of income to the lowest income group through redistribution from the top, but on investment to provide the unemployed and

especially if the redistribution of income were much less than it recommended, balance of payments constraints and other problems might well reduce the overall rate of growth so that the level of *un*employment was not materially reduced.

the working poor with the basis for earning reasonable minimum incomes the levels of which can be raised over time. Initially, the target would be to double the present average income of the lowest income group by giving an income to the unemployed and raising the incomes of the working poor. Our hope and expectation is that once this has been achieved the economic system which will have been created as a result of the new strategy will continue afterwards to make for more equal income distribution and an economic growth which is the healthier and faster for being more widely shared and more equitably distributed.'

The mission's faith in the possibility of a reformed capitalism, free from contradictions, is made even more clear when it goes on to say that 'an employment strategy can be sustained only on the basis of a national consensus, when all concerned feel that they benefit fairly.'[7]

[7] ILO Report, p. 114.

IV.E. EMPLOYMENT
STRATEGIES

IV.E.1. Conflicts between Output and Employment Objectives*

Neither of the objectives, maximum output and maximum employment, are unambiguous. The output objective is ambiguous because output at any time consists of a heterogeneous collection of goods. Types of employment, in duration—daily, weekly and seasonally—in effort and by regions, etc. also differ. In addition, both output and employment occur over time. Current levels of output and employment may influence future levels. Weighting therefore both intra- and inter-temporally is crucial to the *definition* of the objectives. However, we shall begin by ignoring these ambiguities and assume that our sole concern is with current levels of output and employment, and that maximizing current levels automatically leads to achievement of future objectives, or put more formally, that maximizing current levels of output and employment is equivalent to maximizing the present value of the entire streams of output and employment over time. We shall also begin by assuming that there is a single index for output and employment.

CONFLICTS RESULTING FROM SCARCE COMPLEMENTARY FACTORS OF PRODUCTION

We can then rephrase the question and ask: is maximum current production compatible with maximum employment? On the face of it, the answer seems to be an obvious 'yes'. More men must surely be able to produce more. It is hard to picture conditions in which it is impossible to find anything useful to do for extra hands.

At a given time, with a given stock of capital equipment (inherited from the past), the employment of more men on that equipment is likely to increase output, though it could be that, as a result of the reorganization of the work, of less efficient production methods used, of people standing in one another's way or of a fall in efficiency for some other reason, the extra workers do not add to, or even subtract from, production. However, the choice facing a country is not simply a question of employing additional men with the existing capital stock but of the type of new equipment to install, and in this decision about the nature of new investment there can be a conflict between output and employment. Given that the total funds available for new investment are limited, using the funds for equipment to employ people in one way will inevitably mean *not* using the same funds for some other equipment which may involve *less* employment but might also produce more output. Maximizing output involves using scarce resources as efficiently as possible. If capital is the scarce resource, it involves minimizing the capital-output ratio. The type of production this requires may be, but need not be, consistent with maximizing employment.

Suppose in the textile industry the minimum capital-output ratio is associated with fairly modern style industry. If £100,000 is available for investment in textiles, if the

*From F. Stewart and P. P. Streeten, "Conflicts between Output and Employment Objectives," in R. Robinson and P. Johnston (eds.), *Prospects for Employment Opportunities in the 1970s*, HMSO, 1972, pp. 367–73, 375–8, 381–4. Reprinted by permission.

capital-output ratio is 2·5, and if the capital cost per work place for this type of factory is £1000 (assuming a firm degree of utilization of capacity), then investing all funds in this modern factory will involve extra employment of 100 and extra output of £40,000. An alternative way of investing the funds might be to introduce hand-spinning. Suppose for this the capital-output ratio was 5·0 and the cost per work place £100; then the extra output resulting from using the funds for hand-spinning would be £20,000 and the extra employment generated 1000. In this case there is a fairly dramatic conflict between employment and output maximization. It should be noted that this conflict (which is a fairly realistic one if one examines actual figures for costs, etc. in the textile industry)[1] arises because the more labour-intensive method in the sense of the method which uses a lower capital-labour ratio or shows lower cost per work place, actually involves *more capital per unit of output* than the capital-intensive method. Some theoretical models assume this can never happen. It would be true that it could not, if all techniques of production were invented and developed simultaneously, since the labour-intensive methods which use more capital would never be developed. But in fact methods of production are developed over an historical period with the more labour-intensive methods generally originating from an earlier period. One reason why this sort of situation develops is the existence of economies of scale; as machinery

[1] Bhalla (1964), suggests that the capital-output ratio (including working capital as well as fixed capital) using factory methods in cotton spinning is about three quarters of that using the hand Ambar Charkha methods. Bhalla's analysis of rice-pounding (1965), suggests a similar conflict here; the technique which maximizes employment (or has the lowest cost per work place), the pestle and mortar, requires nearly twice the capital per unit of value added compared with the large sheller machine. The latter requires investment per work place of about 100 times as great as the former.

has been adapted for larger-scale production the capital costs in relation to output have tended to fall, so that for large-scale production the later and more capital-intensive methods tend to economize on capital in relation to output. For small-scale production the older machinery may remain efficient.[2] Implicit in this example is the assumption that there is a specific level of employment associated with each technique, and thus that it is sensible to talk of a 'cost per work place'. In fact, the number of people employed with any given machine may vary. . . .

So long as output is responding positively to additional workers the level of employment associated with a given machine will depend partly on the level of wages. Even where output is invariant with respect to employment the actual employment associated with given machinery may depend partly on real wages since managerial effort may be substituted for employment as real wages rise. Thus the employment level associated with any given machine may not be independent of the wage rate. In the examples above some wage level is implicitly assumed in associating each machine with a unique output and employment level. A range to represent output and employment at different wage levels would have been a more realistic representation. If one assumes that continuous variations in output are associated with continuous variations in employment for each machine, but that there is diminishing marginal product as employment is increased, one is back in a neo-classical world where there are variable factor proportions and any amount of capital (or any machine) may be associated with any level of employment. In this neo-classical world the limit to employment is set by the real wages workers demand. There

[2] The importance of scale in determining the efficient range of production possibilities is emphasized by many empirical studies, including Boon (1964); Strassmann (1968).

can be no conflict between output and employment because every type of machine can be associated with any amount of employment. Thus if the modern factory methods were employed in spinning, the extra 900 workers could be employed in the factory and would each add to output. At least as much employment and more output could result from choice of the factory alternative. We do not believe that this is a realistic assumption. Though some variation in employment is possible with any given machine, there comes a point at which the machine is operating at its maximum pace, when additional workers do not increase output. There is thus a limited range of employment possibilities associated with each machine, which means that there can be a conflict between output and employment. Put in another way, for any positive real wage there comes a point at which it is no longer worth while employing extra workers with a particular machine. This point may be reached at a lower employment level and a higher output level for one machine than for another. In this case there is a conflict between output and employment, which is independent of any institutional or other lower limit on the level of real wages.

Just as some economists assume that such a conflict between output and employment cannot arise, others assume not only that it has arisen in the past, but also that it necessarily must arise. The capital-intensive methods of production, it is claimed, will always involve lower capital costs per unit of output (and higher costs per work place) than the labour-intensive methods.[3]

This position is as extreme as the other. There is considerable evidence that in many industries, and in many processes, the more labour-intensive methods also save capital per unit of output.[4] In these cases maximizing employment and output are consistent. Probably of more significance is the possibility of devoting research and development (R and D) efforts to the labour-intensive methods (in the sense of low capital cost per work place) so that they become efficient as compared with capital-intensive methods. Present possibilities reflect the fact that almost all R and D is concentrated on producing methods suitable for the developed world, in which labour is scarce; the labour-intensive methods currently available are generally the products of earlier and less sophisticated science and technology. [. . .]

REASONS FOR PREFERRING EMPLOYMENT TO OUTPUT

If a conflict between maximizing current output and employment were inevitable, why should we wish to sacrifice output to employment? Four possible answers occur to us, though others might think of additional reasons. First, employment creation and the consequential wage payments may be the only mechanism by which income can be redistributed to those who would otherwise remain unemployed. With an efficient fiscal system, taxation combined with unemployment relief, free social services and other forms of assistance to the unemployed could be used as an engine of redistribution. In an underdeveloped society, loyalty to the extended family may induce the employed wage earner to share his wages with his often

---

[3] See, for example, Kaldor (1965, pp. 28–9): 'There is no question *from every point of view* of the superiority of the latest and more capitalistic technologies' (our italics). Similar emphasis on the overall superiority of capital-intensive techniques is found in Amin (1969, pp. 269–92).

[4] A. K. Sen suggests that in cotton weaving the capital-output ratio is the lowest for the most labour-intensive technique, the fly shuttle hand loom, and highest, nearly 2½ times as big, for the automatic power loom (again including working capital). Evidence for the existence of a range of efficient techniques in a number of industries below a certain critical scale of output is also contained in Boon (1964).

large extended family. But if neither fiscal system nor family provide a systematic channel of redistribution, job creation may have to be used for this purpose. Production will then be sacrificed for better distribution and, as a means to this, greater employment.

2, Second, unemployment is demoralizing. To feel unwanted, not to be able to make any contribution, lowers a man's morale and makes him lose his self-respect. The preservation of self-respect is worth sacrificing some production. As Barbara Ward has said, 'of all the evils, worklessness is the worst'— clearly not only and even not mainly because, and if, it lowers national product. It is worth sacrificing production to reduce this evil.

3, Third, it might be thought that work is intrinsically good, whatever its impact on morale, self-respect and other subjective feelings. The Puritan ethic may commend job creation as valuable irrespective of its contribution to production. Puritanism played a valuable part in making desirable the necessary but unpleasant sacrifices which promoted the industrial revolution in Britain. Whether this ethic, where it has been adopted in the developing world (and it is notable that most Puritan-like statements tend to come from expatriates) should be encouraged and where it has not been adopted should be promoted, if it leads to a situation which impedes rather than speeds up development by requiring the adoption of inefficient techniques to compensate for the masochistic value placed on work, is another question. Other aspects of Puritanism are certainly conducive to development; to the extent that Puritanism is a package deal, this aspect may have to be accepted along with the rest.

4, Fourth, there are obvious political disadvantages and dangers in widespread unemployment and non-employment. This is an important reason for valuing employment since, in so far as anyone does, it is the politicians who lay down 'the objective function' of society. Political instability may, in

any case, eventually endanger output levels and growth. [...]

The desire for employment which is so apparent in many countries cannot be entirely divorced from the desire for higher incomes. Many of those seeking urban employment are looking for work *at the going wages* in the organized industrial sector, where wages are generally considerably higher than incomes obtainable elsewhere. Discussion of the need for rural employment opportunities to reduce the underutilization of labour normally takes place in the context of the need to create opportunities for increasing incomes through fuller labour utilization. Again the need is for incomes as much as for work. It is unlikely that the unemployed, or those scratching a living in the rural areas, would be prepared to suffer some loss in *their* incomes for the sake of more work. What is wanted is increased opportunities to work *and* earn higher incomes. Because both work and higher incomes are required it is difficult to disentangle the two. Clearly, the desire for redistribution of income is of prime importance. To achieve this redistribution, employment opportunities may be needed but the sacrifice, or trade-off involved may be of the income of the better-off for the sake of that of the worse-off, rather than of output for the sake of employment. However, it can be argued that it is not just a question of income redistribution but of providing a chance to *earn*, not simply receive, the higher incomes.

These are the only reasons we can think of as to why the employment objective might conflict with the output objective, and sacrifice of output to employment, *properly defined*, is justified. But what are the proper definitions? As argued in the first paragraph, objectives are ambiguous. Two types of ambiguity are relevant. First, national product consists of a heterogeneous collection of goods, 'of shoes, and ships and sealing wax, of cabbages' (and possibly of the services of kings) and it accrues to different people, in different regions, with varying needs. In putting all these together we must use a system of weighting the different items and different sets of weights may lead to contradictions. One set may give the impression that we are sacrificing product for employment, another may not.)

(2) Another ambiguity arises because both production and employment occur in time and stretch into the future. An infinite number of time profiles within any horizon that we care to consider can be drawn up. Any profile for either of our two objectives that lies all the way below another profile of the same objective can be dismissed as inefficient. But in order to choose between those that intersect at some moment of time, we must make additional choices in the light of our policy objectives. What if 5 per cent less employment now gives us 15 per cent more employment in two years' time? What if a rise of 10 per cent in employment now prevents us from employing an additional 5 per cent of a vastly larger labour force in 10 years and after? We must turn to the problems of *weighting* and *timing*.)

WEIGHTING: TIME

Another serious ambiguity arises from the fact that sacrifices now may yield gains in the future. We must consider two opposite sets of circumstances: first, where less production and more employment now lead to more production later)than would otherwise have been possible; second, where less employment and more production now lead to more employment later)than would otherwise have been possible.

In order to illustrate the first case, let us return to the situation where men were demoralized by unemployment. We then regarded self-respect and high morale as ends in themselves. But we may also regard them as necessary for the continued employability of men. If men remain unemployed for long, their skills as well as their attitudes deteriorate and they are incapable of producing as

much later. This situation cannot be remedied by unemployment assistance, for it is only on the job that ability to work and motivation are maintained. Just as machines sometimes have to be kept going in order to prevent attrition or rust, so workers and teams of workers have to be kept busy to prevent them from becoming rusty or apathetic. Current employment, even where there is nothing to show for it, can be regarded as a form of investment—human maintenance—which prevents future deterioration of productivity. In addition men's productive capacity, their ability to work, their initiative and organizational ability and their concentration may not merely be maintained but may actually be increased by working. This form of learning by working means that the greater current employment opportunities, the greater is future productive capacity.

The second case works in the opposite direction and is possibly the most important way in which an apparent conflict between employment and output arises. Here we maximize production in the short run, even though it means tolerating now more nonemployed, because the extra production enables us to generate more jobs later than would otherwise have been possible. If there is a current conflict between output and employment, it must be remembered that output is useful not only for itself, but can be used to generate more employment.

The inter-temporal 'trade-off' between employment now and employment tomorrow arises because, by tolerating more unemployment now for the sake of producing more, we can provide the men (and their children) with more jobs later. This is only partly a matter of investment, i.e. producing now the machines, or resources with which to buy the machines, that will give jobs tomorrow. A greater volume of food which provides better nutrition for the workers and their children, of health measures and of certain forms of education can also contribute to greater employment (and fuller labour utilization) in the future. The point leads once again to income distribution, but this time not valued independently as desirable, but as instrumental to faster growth. The choice between maximum employment and maximum output reduces to one between jobs now or later, because more output can promote more, and more effective, employment in the future. To raise employment means sacrificing not only output now (and, on our assumption, the rate of growth of output) but also the rate of growth of employment. This means that at some future date the level of employment will be lower than it would otherwise have been. To go back to the example discussed earlier, suppose in each case, modern factory and hand spinning wheel, 20 per cent of income generated is saved. The factory solution will involve £8000 investment available in the next year, while the hand wheel alternative will involve £4000. The divergence will get greater in subsequent years. The factory alternative will lead to an annual growth in income (and assuming the same £1000 a work place technology is adopted, in employment) of 8 per cent per annum while the hand spinning wheel alternative will lead to 4 per cent annual growth in output and employment. (This ignores the impact of extra consumption on growth.) The diagram [Figure IV.1] illustrates the possibilities [. . .] .

As to the right choices, a good deal will depend upon our time horizon and on certain future developments. As far as employment is concerned, the life span of one generation and perhaps its children will be relevant, but few societies would be prepared to tolerate widespread unemployment over two generations to improve the job prospects of their great-grandchildren. This is not only because we show less concern for our great-grandchildren, but also because we may rightly hope that their prospects will improve for other reasons, such as the development of more appropriate technologies, improvements in motivation, administration, education, etc. Given the time horizon, we might say that, on the other hand, the richer society of tomorrow can look better after its unemployed and to be unemployed then will be a smaller hardship. On the other hand, with present trends of growth of the labour force in less developed countries and likely opportunities for jobs, the total number of unemployed is increasing rapidly. While the lot of a given number of unemployed will therefore be better in the future and the burden of maintaining them lighter, the number to be looked after will be larger. In the more distant future, however, we may assume that population control will have become effective or new scope for migration will have opened up. In view of all this, it seems right to discount future jobs and to give more weight to more jobs now and in the near future.

On balance it seems that the discount rate that we should apply to employment may be less than the one we apply to output. The main argument for applying a discount rate to output is that the marginal utility of income is less for a richer society. This does not apply in the same way to employment— i.e. the value of extra employment generated does not decline as the level increases— though increasing *incomes* per head may make employment in the future less important as a means of income redistribution. On the other hand, the contrasts between those employed and those not employed and the

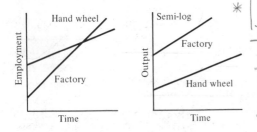

FIGURE IV.1.

accompanying resentment may work the other way. Poverty in the midst of affluence is worse than plain poverty widely shared. This, and the question of numbers, suggests that it may be correct to give greater relative weight to future as against current employment than to future as against current output. *i.e. wt to future emplt > future ot*

Planners must know not only their preferences between the present and the future, for both output and employment, but also what opportunities there are for trade-offs. Conflicts between current levels of growth rates of output and employment may arise either because growth rates are determined by savings rates (or, more generally, developmental expenditure rates), savings rates by income distribution and income distribution by employment levels, or because growth rates are determined by the allocation of a given savings ratio between sectors and this allocation has different effects on employment.

It is common to assume in this context that a capital-intensive technique leads to a higher savings ratio for the same income level than a labour-intensive technique. On this assumption, lower employment now can give faster growth of both output and employment. Those who make this assumption (Sen, 1968; Little and Mirrlees, 1968) assume:

1. That a higher proportion of profits is saved than of wages (at its most extreme this assumption is that all profits are saved, all wages consumed); and that consumption makes no contribution to future growth;
2. That wage rates do not depend on techniques;
3. That the government is incapable of securing the savings ratio it desires by taxing wage earners and generating adequate public savings or using inflation to reduce real wages.

Since the growth rate is the product of the savings ratio and the output/capital ratio, the effect on the growth rate of raising the savings ratio by increasing the capital-intensity of technique adopted will depend on the consequences for the output/capital ratio.

TECHNICAL PROGRESS

Until now we have ignored technical progress and assumed that output and employment grow at the same rate if a single technique is chosen and adhered to over time. In practice technical possibilities available increase over time. Generally technical progress take a form which involves increasing labour productivity, so that the rate of growth of employment is less than the rate of growth of output. This phenomenon—output increasing faster than employment—has been observed in many developing countries. The precise form that technical progress takes will affect the terms of any conflict between output and employment.

If technical progress is disembodied, affecting existing capital equipment as much as new and therefore unrelated to the rate of investment, and if it increases the labour productivity associated with techniques of varying capital intensity to the same extent, then the technique which maximizes the rate of growth of output will be the same as the technique which maximizes the rate of growth of employment, though the latter will be lower than the former. If technical progress is embodied, affecting only new investment, the greater the rate of investment, the greater the increase in labour productivity. Hence for any increase in growth rate, resulting from an increase in the investment ratio, there will be a less than proportionate increase in the rate of growth of employment. Similarly, if labour productivity is positively related to the scale of production, measures which speed up the growth of output (whether they be investment or other means) will increase the growth of employment less than proportionately. Relationships of this type have been observed for developing countries, though the relationship appears less strong than for developed countries (Oherlihy, 1970). Since the growth in output remains bigger than the associated growth in labour productivity, the technique which increases the growth rate of output will also increase the growth of employment, but the gains in terms of growth of *employment*, will be less than the gains in terms of growth of *output*.

Technical developments are likely to affect some techniques more than others. In particular, research, development and use of techniques in the developed countries is virtually confined to techniques of high, and increasing, capital-intensity. Thus for these techniques labour productivity and often capital productivity as well, may rise over time, while the more labour-intensive techniques may be unaffected by technical progress. The labour-intensive techniques may therefore become inferior over time and their use may involve a sacrifice of output as compared with the later techniques.

However, for labour-intensive techniques various improvements are likely to result from their widespread use, including a fall in their cost simply as a result of economies of scale in their production. Labour-intensive techniques are also often easier to produce in the developing countries, because they are often of simpler design and more (in number) are required in a particular country so that some of the economies of scale may be exploited. Current relative costs and efficiency of different techniques may therefore fail to reflect potential relative costs after technical progress through use has been realized. They may also fail to take into account the differing possibilities for local production and repair of the different techniques. This means that current possibilities may understate the likely implications for output of labour-intensive techniques; the conflict between employment and output may therefore be less in reality than at first appears.

THE PRODUCT-MIX

So far we have assumed the composition of consumption goods to be determined and have varied only the techniques of producing them and the allocation of investment between sectors. If different consumption goods require different proportions of labour and capital, we can raise the level of employment without varying the techniques of producing any product by enlarging the share of labour-intensive products at the expense of capital-intensive products. If there are opportunities for international trade on favourable terms, this is an obvious solution. If, however, a changing composition involves changing the products consumed at home, the question is whether, with a proper system of weighting, losses in consumers' welfare would arise. If the labour-intensive products are also those largely demanded by the poor, we have already seen that a fall in output may be an optical illusion and that the weights derived from a more equal income distribution might show a rise. There may also be external diseconomies of consumption or buying as a result of created wants or of habits. If a product is wanted (a) because others buy it or (b) because it was bought in the past or (c) wants are created through advertising, and if these features are peculiar to the capital-intensive products, its elimination may lead to smaller welfare losses (in cases (b) and (c) after a time) than the expenditure values would indicate or it may lead to welfare gains.

The scope for changing the consumers' product-mix in a labour-intensive direction is generally considered somewhat limited, apart from possibilities of international trade, by the need for a reasonable balance in the composition of demand. We cannot expect people to consume all food and no clothes for example, or to have more haircuts at the expense of bicycles. But the conclusions drawn from this, in terms of the narrow scope for product substitution, arise partly from a mistaken definition of product. Any given need may be fulfilled by a number of different products: nylon or cotton shirts fulfil the need for clothing, wooden houses, mud huts, reinforced concrete multi-storey buildings fulfil the need for shelter. While maintaining a reasonable balance in terms of needs (clothing, housing, shelter, etc.), there is considerable scope for substitution towards more labour-intensive products for the fulfilment of each need. The possibilities of concentrating more on labour-intensive products to fulfil each need may therefore extend the scope for using the product-mix to increase employment opportunities.

References

Amin, S. (1969), "Levels of remuneration, factor proportions, and income differentials with special reference to developing countries," in A. Smith (ed.), *Wage Policy Issues in Economic Development,* Macmillan.

Bhalla, A. S. (1964), "Investment allocation and technological choice—a case of cotton spinning techniques," *Economic Journal,* Vol. 4, pp. 611–22.

——, (1965), "Choosing techniques: hand pounding vs. machine-milling of rice: an Indian case, *Oxford Economic Papers,* Vol. 17, pp. 147–57.

Boon, G. K. (1964), *Economic Choice of Human and Physical Factors in Production,* North Holland.

Kaldor, N. (1965), in R. Robinson (ed.), *Industrialization in Developing Countries,* Cambridge University Press.

Little, I. M. D., and Mirrlees, J. (1968), in *Manual of Industrial Project Analysis in Developing Countries,* Vol. 2, p. 42.

Oherlihy, C. St. J. (1970), "Wages and employment," Meeting of Directors of Development Training and Research Institute, ILO (mimeo).

Sen, A. K. (1968), *Choice of Techniques,* Blackwell.

Strassmann, W. P. (1968), *Technological Change and Economic Development,* Cornell University Press.

IV.E.2. Four Steps to Full Employment*

It is no secret that our [West Indian] economic situation is rather patchy. Mining is our only really prosperous industry, but while mining contributes significantly to incomes in Trinidad, Jamaica and Guyana, especially through the public revenue, it provides very little employment indeed. All our other industries expect to be subsidised in one way or another; tourism and manufacturing by exemptions from taxation and by government loans or guarantees; and agriculture by low interest rates and heavy expenditures on agricultural research and

*From Sir Arthur Lewis, "Four Steps to Full Employment," Presidential Address to the Board of Governors of the Caribbean Development Bank, April 1972, reprinted in *International Development Review,* Vol. 14, No. 2, 1972, pp. 2–9. Reprinted by permission.

education. In the territories with minerals the revenues provided by the mines keep everything else afloat. In the territories without mines, the economy is kept going by various forms of taxing industries with one hand and subsidising them with the other.

Apart from minerals, our basic industries are in poor shape. Agriculture is a dying industry. Cocoa, cotton and arrowroot have been disappearing from our list of exports. The banana output is falling. Imports of food grow by leaps and bounds every year. Sugar, after some years of decline, has received a new shot in the arm from the recent increase in prices, but still does not expect to be able to fill its quotas. Manufacturing grows, but rather slowly by comparison with other less developed countries, where growth rates of 10 to 15 per cent per annum are common. In consequence we are much less advanced in import substitution than the countries of Asia or Latin America, and are only just beginning to be aware of the rapidly growing world trade in a wide variety of diversified light manufactures other than garments.

The sad consequence of this relative stagnation, as we all know too well, is rising urban unemployment. Our young people are deserting the countryside and flocking into the towns. Some find work in the tourist industry; others in our rapidly expanding public services—as teachers, nurses, policemen, soldiers or clerks; or in the industries where we "take in each others' washing"—shopkeeping, hairdressing, television and similar commercial services. But the growth rate of our basic industries is not adequate to support our continually rising populations, and we have record unemployment rates, especially among the young. This situation is very much in the public eye because of its dangerous political potential. But it is also an agonising human problem, in its own right, that so many of our youngsters, on leaving school, may tramp the streets for a whole year or two before finding their first job. No one of us deserves happiness while this condition lasts.

WHY IS THERE NOT FULL EMPLOYMENT?

If we are to change this situation, we must first understand it. Why is our economy not able to provide full employment? The simple answer is, because our money costs of production are too high in relation to world prices. Potential investors are continually making feasibility studies with a view to starting new manufacturing industries, or extending agricultural output, or building new hotels. Some of these come out on the positive side, especially in tourism and manufacturing, and so some new employment is created. But not enough come out right to absorb our labor force. Our costs are too high; if they were lower,

more new industries would be started, and existing industries would expand faster.

Our governments recognize that this is the problem. This is why they are forced to offer the wide range of tax exemptions and other privileges which, of course, reduce the benefit from such new enterprises as are actually started. But though our governments recognise the situation, our people do not. The man in the street has, instead, been taught, in the usual manner, to put all the blame on foreign devils. Unemployment is due, we are told, to the fact that foreigners control our economy. It is true that foreigners control much of our economy, and that this is both undesirable and unnecessary (I will return to this in a moment), but it is not true that this is why our costs are so high, or why we have so much unemployment. On the contrary, in our current situation, where we save so little and train so few of our own people, if there were fewer foreigners we would have even more unemployment. This is the reason why our governments are constantly on the look-out for potential foreign investors; this, rather than any lack of patriotism on their part.

Our costs have become too high because our money incomes are determined for all economic activity by what the richest industries can afford to pay, namely the mines and the tourist industry, without regard to the productivity levels of other industries. In fact the expansion of mines threatens to destroy all other economic activity, while itself providing an almost negligible amount of employment. Of course incomes in other industries have not reached the level of incomes in the mines, but they are always striving to get there. In the process, costs in other industries are raised beyond what productivity can support and the result is massive unemployment.

When one says of an economy that its money costs of production are too high in relation to world prices for it to be able to provide full employment, this is the classic definition of an overvalued currency. Nearly all West Indian currencies are heavily overvalued, in relation to our foreign trade policies and our current levels of money income and productivity; this is the basic reason for our high and steadily mounting unemployment. It used to be considered immoral to make such a remark in these islands, since the preservation of our parity with sterling was regarded as the first priority of economic policy. But now that the British pound devalues regularly, and even the mighty US dollar has insisted on being allowed to fall, we are able to look at our own situation more objectively.

If maintaining parity with sterling no longer has first priority in economic policy, what should? In general, economists dislike the very notion of priority; normally everything is important; we make marginal adjustments to equate our satisfactions all along the line. The notion of priority belongs to abnormal situations, to states of emergency; so if one is looking for priorities one has to seek them where the emergency lies. To my mind there is no doubt that the great emergency in our country is high and rising unemployment, especially among our young. To eliminate this should be the prior goal of all our economic policies, and whenever we hear or read any policy prescription, we should test it against its likely effect on the overall record of employment.

In many third world countries unemployment is an insoluble problem because there is a vast reservoir of rural labour pouring into the towns faster than it can be absorbed. We are more fortunately placed, because our agricultural labour force is already much reduced—down to 20 per cent in Trinidad and Barbados and to 30 per cent in Jamaica. Neither is our problem the Keynesian deficiency of monetary demand which engrosses the attention of the large, nearly self-contained industrial economies; ours is a small population, with access to vast markets. Given top priority, we could achieve full employment in about a decade. . . .

Since the situation is that our exchange rates, trade policies, money incomes and productivity levels are mutually inconsistent, the problem can be solved, conceptually, by operating on any one of these four variables. In practice, no one of these, taken by itself, is capable of solving the problem within the feasible rates of change. We need to operate on all four, in mutual support.

EXCHANGE RATES

Take first the foreign exchange rate. Gross overvaluation, such as most of us suffer from, cannot in practice be cured without some measure of devaluation. However, devaluation raises the cost of living, and so generates increases in money incomes which raise domestic costs. If the increase in domestic costs is proportionately as great as the fall in the rate of exchange, the devaluation achieves absolutely nothing.

Some rise in money incomes is inevitable, but the rise does not have to be as great as the devaluation. Whether it is or not will depend on the level of community discipline. There are countries which can devalue effectively, as shown by a considerable change in their balance of payments. There are also other countries which cannot devalue effectively because they lack the necessary discipline to keep money costs under control in the face of increased prices of imports.

Where the cost of living is closely related to the foreign exchange rate, as it is in our area, some countries try half-devaluation, i.e., a system of multiple exchange rates. Importers, for example, may continue to pay $4.80 for a pound, but exporters may be given say $6.00 for every pound they bring in—thereby stimulating employment in the export industries without raising the price of imports. Some multiple systems are very complicated, having a separate exchange rate for each of several types of imports and exports, tourism and other services. Administration then becomes complicated, and evasion and corruption spread. Moreover, the cost of living cannot be insulated; any system which effectively increases import substitution is going to raise the cost of living; and any system which makes exporting more remunerative is going to raise domestic prices by increasing domestic demand. So multiple exchange rates afford only temporary relief; as domestic prices rise and evasion spreads, devaluation is ultimately inevitable.

Much of the recent abortive discussion in the West Indies springs from the conviction that these territories do not have the necessary social discipline to devalue the currency effectively, with the result that devaluation would raise money incomes in the same proportion, and so have no effect on the level of employment. Actually no country can escape devaluation forever if its other economic policies are driving it in that direction. If it persists in clinging to a rate which gets more and more out of line, the change, when it comes, is mammoth, as recently in Ghana. And if then its social discipline is inadequate, devaluation becomes an annual (or now in some cases monthly) event, instead of a small adjustment to be made once or twice in a decade.

I do not know how much social discipline is possible in the West Indies, but other elements have also been in the back of our minds, three of which are erroneous. One is the belief that devaluation would move the terms of trade against us, which is true of tourism, but not of our visible imports and exports. Another is the pre-Keynesian idea that the foreign exchange rate must be correct if the foreign exchange reserves are not diminishing. The balance of payments can balance at any exchange rate, at the expense of employment. One has therefore to determine where one's priority lies. A third thought, which we have retained from the nineteenth century, is the orthodox longing to duplicate the phenomena of the gold standard, by hook or crook. Actually, the orthodoxy among international bankers is coming steadily to be the reverse of this; namely that the appropriate relationship between the world's major currencies in our day is one of continuous floating. I am not arguing that currencies should float, or that we must do what other people do. But I do believe that we should try to cleanse our minds of the brainwashing of nineteenth century economic orthodoxies.

FOREIGN TRADE POLICY

As I have said, devaluation is not the only remedy. But if one is convinced that it will not work, one must then put even more effort into the other three possible solutions. The principal objective of devaluation is to cut imports and increase exports. This can also be approached in other ways.

There is great scope for reducing imports. We import too much fish, meat, animal feedingstuffs, maize, cotton, vegetable oils, footwear, textiles, and light metal manufactures, to take just the leading items of which we could produce substantially more at home. CARIFTA enables us to export more to each other, and is an essential part of our effort to reduce imports from the outside world. We cannot solve our problem simply by reducing imports, partly because our natural resource base is inadequate, and partly because a growing population with a rising level of living is bound to put continuous pressure on imports. We cannot reduce imports absolutely, but we can over a transition period prevent imports from rising as fast as national income.

Since imports are bound to grow absolutely, our exports must also grow. The future for our agricultural exports is most uncertain. These have depended on special preferences and quotas in the UK, Canada and the USA where continuance is increasingly in doubt; this will continue to be a major area of diplomatic activity. Our tourist industry still has great possibilities, especially if we can tap the mass tourist market, but growing hostility towards this trade on the part of our intellectuals casts a shadow of doubt over its future. The only sphere which offers us unlimited possibilities is world trade in manufactures. We continue to exaggerate the difficulties, and to over-emphasise the garment industry. As for the difficulties, one should note that Hong Kong ships half its manufactured exports to the United States, and gets beyond tariffs and quotas, although its wage level and transport costs are substantially higher than ours. The opportunities outside textiles are immense. Hong Kong got its first electronics factory in 1961, with 54 workers; now employs more than 40,000 in this trade; has also huge numbers in plastics, toys and many other light industries. Why did this happen there and not here? World trade in manufactures is enormous, and has doubled every ten years; there is plenty of room for us if we try.

When an overvalued currency is keeping imports high and exports low, one can take counteracting measures to stimulate domestic production. The most important of these are the application of tariffs and quotas to imports, and the granting of subsidies to import substituting or to exporting industries. We have done some of this. We have a tariff system, but it was not designed to keep out imports, and our rates are low when compared with the rest of the third world. We also have a few quotas. Direct monetary subsidies to industry are rare, but we have various substitutes, including exemptions from taxation and the free provision of government services. Looked at from the point of view of a policy to stimulate domestic production, our trade armoury is rather amateurish, and clearly also not very effective.

Measures of this kind do little for exports; these depend on having an appropriate rate of exchange, since GATT frowns on direct money subsidies to exports. Quotas and tariffs can make an immense difference to production for the home market. However, like devaluation, they raise the cost of living, so this argument against the one is no less effective against the others, except that

tariffs and quotas resemble multiple exchange rates rather than straightforward devaluation. Given that one wishes to increase exports as well as to restrain imports, the current consensus of international opinion that foreign exchange policy should play a larger role in regulating foreign trade than tariffs or quotas or subsidies is probably correct. What cannot be right is to use neither instrument effectively.

PRODUCTIVITY

A country which simultaneously maintains an overvalued currency and neglects to use tariffs, quotas or subsidies in adequate measure could achieve equilibrium with full employment only by reducing money costs; i.e., either by lowering money income per head, or by increasing productivity.

There is certainly immense scope for increasing productivity in the West Indies. Our sugar costs much more to produce than Australia's, although our wages are a small fraction of hers. We get 4 tons of bananas per acre instead of 12 tons; 300 pounds of cocoa instead of 1,000 lbs.; 800 lbs. of maize instead of 4,000 lbs., and so on all along the line in agriculture. Equally in manufacturing industry we would sell all we could produce if our productivity equalled that of Hong Kong or Singapore.

Our deficiencies are partly of training, partly of organisation and partly of capital.

In terms of numbers, our biggest training gap is in agriculture, where we have hundreds of thousands of people working who have had no agricultural training beyond what they pick up from overseers. Our small farmers ought all to have gone to agricultural institutes. Of course they would then not be content to farm two acres; they would need from 25 to 100 acres, according to their abilities and crops; and this is what they should have, since no community can hope to build a decent standard of living on 2-acre farms, unless the land is wet enough to yield three crops of cereals or vegetables in a year. This brings us into organisation. Land reform, coupled with a great increase in the number of farm schools, is an essential ingredient in agricultural productivity.

We are equally badly served in manufacturing industry. To begin with, in the industrial countries, the child begins to play with mechanical toys at home from a very early age. By the time he is ten he is thoroughly at home with nuts and bolts and springs and the elementary principles of traction. We ought to use our primary schools to give our children what they do not get at home, by putting into the schools mechanical toys, simple tools, wood to work with and clay, and inserting periods of play into the curriculum during which our young may, through their own playful curiosity and manipulative experience, become familiar with concepts that are fundamental to later factory practice. We also need, as is obvious to everybody, much more occupational training in the ages running from 15 to 18, both in our ordinary schools and also in special post-secondary institutes for mechanics, secretaries, para-medical personnel, and a wide range of technicians. Our shortages of personnel trained at this level are a major cause of low productivity.

It is also clear that much of our finest brain power runs to waste. We have a substantial university population but it is recruited almost entirely from our middle class. Since our middle class is still tiny, most of our first class brain power is still locked away in the social class whose children do not get beyond primary school. We worry about the brain drain into foreign countries, but there is a much greater waste of brains right here at home. We ought to improve our methods for finding the youngsters of poor families who have first class ability; we should enrich this ability with special attention, and make sure that it goes all the way through to the top of the educational ladder. We are failing to mobilise and train enough of our first class talent; this is a basic cause of our low productivity.

In addition to more skill, we must raise productivity by employing more capital per head. This is true not only of manufacturing industry but also of agriculture, which will not hold its labour force unless its productivity permits earnings comparable with those of urban occupations. We need an immense investment of capital, both to bring productivity per head in line with money incomes and also to create new opportunities for employment.

It is tempting to argue the contrary; that our industries are not under-capitalised but over-capitalised. One can always make work by reducing productivity; somebody said recently that if the automatic telephone system were scrapped and the United States returned to manual operation, it would take all the adult women in the country to handle the current volume of calls. I fully agree that we ought temporarily to go in for a lot of make-work projects to get our young people off the streets. Some, such as housing, would also be very valuable in themselves. But make-work is not a permanent solution to our problems. Having limited natural resources we have to live by foreign trade, and we can compete in foreign markets only if our productivity matches our wage levels; since wages are almost certain to go on rising, productivity must keep rising too. Also, even in sheltered industries, our objective is to keep raising our standard of living, which means more output per head. While temporarily making work, we must keep our eyes all the time on the conditions required for attaining full employment with the highest productivity which our resources permit.

One of these conditions is a high level of domestic capital formation. Over and above what may be invested in mining, which employs so few, we need to invest about 20 per cent of gross domestic product every year if we are to approach and hold full employment.

Where is this to come from? We are already excessively dependent on foreign investment, and unless we save more, we can solve our employment problem only by depending even more on foreign capital. This is a subject much overgrown with confusion. We are being fed with many slogans—"black power," "ending neo-colonialism," "controlling our own destiny," "vesting our resources in the community" and so on. But if we are to provide employment for our young people we must either save out of our own incomes, or else depend on foreign capital. The precondition for realising all these comforting slogans is a much higher level of domestic saving—unless one is willing to sacrifice the employment of the poor to the chauvinist sentiments of well-paid intellectuals.

What has gone wrong? At our level of national income per head, that is to say excluding the earnings of foreign firms, we ought to be able to save nearly 20 per cent of national income, but we are nowhere near this figure. The strategy of inviting foreign investment which we have followed over the past two decades presupposed that we would use the occasion of the increase in national income, which would result, to increase quite sharply the ratio of domestic savings. We would thereby first become self-sufficient in capital, and thereafter be able to buy the foreigners out. We have indeed had very substantial increases in income per head during these twenty years, such that by now we should no longer need foreign capital, except for major developments in mining. Jamaica seems to have seized the opportunity to raise its domestic savings ratio, but most of our other territories have let the opportunity pass by, and are proportionately as dependent on foreign saving now as they were when real income was only half as high.

Why have we wasted our substance in this way? In the first place, in so far as personal consumption goes, we are still a thriftless people. We are all trying to keep up with the Jones's and living to the limit of our borrowing capacity. In this we differ from say the average Japanese, who saves 20 per cent of his personal disposable income; but we are not very different from other third world

people. Personal saving is low in the developing world, and will expand only as new standards of values and new institutions stimulate habits of thrift.

For this reason it is widely recognised that the secret of capital formation in poor countries, whether socialist or capitalist, is to have a high level of public saving, that is to say a wide gap between the public revenue and public expenditure on current account; in other words a substantial budget surplus, as well as substantial profits by public enterprises. This is effectively the only way to rid ourselves of dependence on foreign capital in the near future.

You will recognise of course how far we are from this. Many of our governments have no budget surplus at all, and in most the public enterprises are run at a loss, so that they are a drain on savings in other sectors, rather than a source of saving. The enormous expansion of the public revenues which has occurred over the past twenty years has been matched by an equal expansion of public expenditure on current account. Our population grows so fast that the budgets for schools, hospitals, prisons, housing subsidies and other government services are simply insatiable. On top of this, independence on a retail basis has brought a superstructure of overseas representation and continual attendance at international meetings which eats up a lot of money. Our governments are just as spendthrift as our people. So public saving fails us just as badly as private saving.

In the circumstances I see no immediate reduction in our dependence on foreign capital; on the contrary, I see a substantial increase if any substantial inroad is to be made into current unemployment. But I would hope that we are capable of learning, and could now set ourselves goals of saving, private and public, which will enable us to get ourselves out of this frightful situation within the next two decades. I call the situation frightful, partly because foreign capital is expensive; partly because the dependence is to some extent self-perpetuating, since a substantial proportion of saving comes from profits; and partly because it is politically explosive, since the slogan-makers emphasise the remuneration of the foreign capital which gives us employment, rather than our own failure to save out of the personal incomes and public revenues which the investment generates. We could have got ourselves out of this situation during the last two decades if we had tried. We shall have no excuse for failing to try during the next two decades.

MONEY INCOME

Finally we come to our fourth variable, money income per head. Money costs are a function of money income and productivity, and could be kept constant if productivity rose as fast as money income per head. Unfortunately this is almost impossible to achieve without control of money incomes. Annual increases in productivity are normally in the range of 2 to 4 per cent, whereas annual increases in money income per head tend to range much higher. Overvaluation cannot be rectified merely by increasing productivity; it calls also for restraint of money income.

This problem is universal in Western type democracies. It does not exist in the Communist countries, because there the unions have no bargaining power; the governments fix both wages and prices. A large number of third world countries, especially in Africa and Asia, have also got around the problem by clipping the powers of trade unions. Western democracies are almost without exception launched on the same road, under different names—"incomes policy," "guidelines," "wage freeze," "Phase II" and so on. It is highly improbable that the West Indies will escape having to adopt the sorts of laws and institutions which so many other kinds of countries seem to have found inevitable.

Experience teaches certain lessons. One is that a government cannot get away with simply freezing the existing distribution of income. Even in comparing one wage with another, some wages are too low, whether in relation to the cost of living, or because more recruits are needed in some expanding industries or occupations. A wages board must have a philosophy of relative wages, and flexibility to put it into effect. If it is to have moral authority, it must show that it recognises wrongs and is in the forefront of trying to rectify them; and not just waiting until strikes are threatened. Besides wage differentials, the ratio of wage income as a whole to national income is also of general concern. Every year when government, employers and unions meet to bargain about wages, the government is expected to say what it is going to do by way of taxation or provision of schools or other social services as the unions' price for acceptance of wage restraint. Attempts at wage control which do not embody an active policy to improve the distribution of income are bound to fail within the democratic context.

It follows, secondly, since changes in income distribution are required, that control of money incomes is more politically feasible if output per head is rising than if it is falling. Then it is possible for everybody to be better off, some more so than others. Attempts to make some much better off at the expense of worsening the position of others always lead to a breakdown of society and to bloodshed. Redistribution of income and vigorous economic growth must go together.

Incomes policy faces greater difficulties in the West Indies than it does in Europe or North America. One difficulty is that imports enter to a greater extent into the cost of living here than there. A rise in the price of imports, whether due to market forces or due to devaluation, raises the cost of living, and has to be accommodated by higher money incomes. The cost of living need not rise by as much as the price of imports, but to prevent this requires smart footwork on the part of the authorities; a quick raising of wages in response to rising prices, combined with maintaining a differential between foreign and domestic prices. For a wages board, lagging behind or giving too much are equally disruptive policies.

A second difficulty is that some foreign-owned industries can afford to pay much more than other industries. As we have seen, this is one cause of our troubles, since in doing so they destroy more employment in the other industries than they create in their own. If they are not allowed to pay higher wages there must be some other way of ensuring that an appropriate part of the wealth they create accrues to nationals of the country. The appropriate way is to charge what the economist calls a "rent," which may take the form of a royalty, or of special taxation on extractive industries. As oil-producing and copper-producing countries have shown, there are many devices by which a government can get an adequate share of profits without having to pay excessive wages to the workers of one industry at the expense of employment in other industries.

Our third special difficulty is that it is not as easy here, as it is in Europe and North America, to squeeze those at the top and in the middle on behalf of those at the bottom. This is because of their greater mobility. We can squeeze those who live on rents, whether of land or ores, because they cannot take these natural resources away. But we cannot both attract foreign capital and exploit it; we can exploit what has been already invested, but will then inevitably discourage new investment. We can also not so easily exploit our professional classes—nurses, doctors, engineers and so on—as we used to, because, with the relative lifting of colour barriers all over the world, these can now get better jobs in other countries; better not just in money, but since our social and political climates are hostile to professional people, better also in working conditions and in job satisfaction.

Taking all this together, an incomes policy is just as necessary in this part of the world as it is elsewhere, but needs even greater sophistication if it is to work without curtailment of democratic liberties. If we fail to make it work, we may easily become one of those countries where the currency has to be devalued every month.

CONCLUSION

My theme is easily summarised. It is that our economic policies lack a crucial element: namely measures to bring our money costs into line with international prices. All of us who are concerned with making new investments and creating new employment—and this is what the Caribbean Development Bank is all about—are operating with our hands tied behind our backs because, in this crucial aspect, economic policies inhibit investment, and are inadequate to cope with this basic cause of unemployment.

Unemployment is our most important problem. We have mesmerised ourselves into thinking that it cannot be solved, and is therefore something that we have to live with, but this cruel resignation is unnecessary. We have not one solution, but four, corresponding to the four variables in the situation: the rate of exchange, foreign trade policy, productivity and incomes policy. We need more positive action on all four, since the feasibility of success through any one depends on what is happening simultaneously to the other three.

IV.E.3. Policy Implications—Note

While this chapter has outlined some dimensions of the employment problem and has suggested broad strategies of employment creation, we are left with numerous specific policy questions that need to be clarified. All the remaining chapters will bear on the formulation of a set of employment policies by relating to the mobilization and allocation of investment resources, agricultural development, industrialization programs, and trade strategy. At this point, however, it may be useful to offer some general principles underlying possible policy options for slowing down the rise in unemployment. Their validity will then be explored in greater detail in subsequent chapters.

a. If urban unemployment is to be reduced, policy measures must reduce the rural-urban drift. To this end, a reduction of urban-rural real income differentials would be most helpful; but this is probably the most difficult objective to achieve. According to the Todaro model of labor migration (IV.C.1), the larger the gap between urban and rural nominal wages, the higher must be the urban unemployment rate before migration in excess of job opportunities ceases. As long as urban wages rise more rapidly than average rural incomes, rural-urban migration will continue in spite of rising levels of urban unemployment. All policies that would redress the imbalance between urban and rural income levels would therefore be desirable—urban wage restraint, adjustment of minimum wage rates, revision of the tax structure, a comprehensive national income and wages policy.

A number of institutional and political considerations, however, militate against the efficacy of these policies, and it is not realistic to expect any strong downward pressure on urban wages. An effective "wages policy" has proved difficult in the developed—let alone newly developing—countries.

b. If it is difficult to institute a "wages policy" that would increase urban employment, it is all the more important to emphasize the "supply side" of the problem. When the urban sector cannot absorb the inflow of labor from the rural sector, special consideration must be given to policies that will remove the causes of the rural "supply push" and help contain the labor force in rural areas. Urban problems are in a fundamental sense rural problems: urban "pull" must be offset by lessening the "push" through rural development.

The modern sector must avoid producing what can be produced in the rural sector—e.g., village handicraft employment should not be displaced if this entails the wasteful use of capital in the modern sector to produce an output which could be produced equally well by surplus labor. It is to be recalled that in Japan's case of successful development, both agriculture and village industry became more labor-intensive. There may also be a considerably greater scope for rural-based industry involving simple technology and the processing of agricultural materials.

Beyond this, however, a full-scale program of rural development is needed to absorb and retain large amounts of manpower. If the rural to urban migration is to be reduced, it is necessary to modify policies that have turned the terms of trade against the agricultural sector. Ceiling prices on foodstuffs, export taxes or restrictions on primary products, and tariff protection on industrial inputs and consumer goods have acted as disincentives to agricultural producers while they have artificially increased the urban-rural differential.

Efforts should also be made to disperse to the rural sector some of the amenities and public services now concentrated in urban areas. Readier access to such services as public utilities, health, education, and entertainment in the rural areas may amount to an increase in the rural social wage, and diminish the attractions of the city.

Of greatest consequence will be the type of strategy pursued for developing the agricultural sector. As elaborated in Chapter IX, the most important factor influencing a developing country's ability to absorb a growing labor force into productive employment is whether a labor-using, capital-saving type of approach to agricultural development is followed (as in Japan and Taiwan). For most developing countries, the employment potential in rural modernization can be greater than that of the modern urban sector—provided that the countries avoid implicit taxation of agriculture and "unduly labor displacing" measures in agriculture.

c. If the previous strategy of industrialization via import substitution has resulted in "urban bias"—that is, distortions that favor the urban, import-substituting, modern sector at the expense of the rural sector,[1] then in the future the promotion of nontraditional exports may allow a strategy of industrialization via export substitution that creates more employment, among other advantages. Chapter XI discusses various policies—notably those connected with trade policy and foreign investment—that are needed to make export substitution effective.

The distortions in the price structure also create divergences between domestic and international prices that inhibit the country's exports. To the extent that the comparative advantage of the country lies in labor-intensive commodities, the employment-intensity of trade can be raised by "getting prices right" and by establishing an efficient commodity composition of exports.

d. More effort is also needed to devise a range of technological choices that are superior to the country's indigenous traditional technology but are not as advanced and labor-saving as are the modern machines and equipment that have been imported from advanced industrial countries. As discussed in Chapter VI, the transfer of "appropriate" technology has important consequences for employment in both the urban industrial sector and the rural agricultural sector.

The choice of a more labor-intensive production technique may, of course, conflict with other investment criteria—in particular, the maximum absorption of labor may yield only a low return per unit of capital and not maximize the future rate of growth in output. This conflict has been noted in selection IV.E.1, above. The crucial consideration is the emphasis on devising new technology that is "capital-stretching" in an efficient way—that is, the labor-intensive equipment should raise the labor/capital ratio without also raising the capital/output ratio. A more appropriate technology would in effect retain the essential quality of the tool element in physical equipment without the superfluous labor-saving appendages of the advanced technology of industrial countries.

To lessen the bias toward relatively capital-intensive techniques, it is again necessary to stress the removal of factor price distortions. Given that there is a positive elasticity of substitution of labor against capital,[2] it would become less profitable to use capital-intensive technologies if interest rates were increased, foreign exchange became more expensive in terms of home currency, and the increases in urban wages were restrained.

e. As long as labor is induced to migrate from the rural sector and the manufacturing

---

[1] Michael Lipton, "Urban Bias and Rural Planning," in Paul Streeten and Michael Lipton (eds.), *The Crisis of Indian Planning,* London, 1968, pp. 89–95.

[2] For a careful empirical study that suggests that considerable substitution possibilities exist in a number of manufacturing industries, see Howard Pack, "The Employment-Output Trade-Off in LDCs—A Microeconomic Approach," *Oxford Economic Papers,* November 1974.

sector cannot absorb labor in sufficient quantities, it will be necessary for labor to seek employment in the tertiary sector. Labor has done so in many of the LDCs, and employment in services and commerce has actually risen more rapidly than in other sectors. In Latin America, for instance, employment in the tertiary sector rose by more than 4 per cent per annum over the period 1950–65, while employment in industry increased only by approximately 2.8 per cent per annum, and the percentage of the labor force in the services sector (excluding construction and utilities) rose from 24 per cent to 30 per cent.[3]

From the standpoint of providing an employment outlet, it is therefore advisable not to promote too rapid an increase in efficiency in employment practices in the service sector. As remarked by Professor Galenson,[4] the pushcarts should not be too readily replaced by the supermarket; the bicycles by the trucks; a casual but large labor force by a permanent and stable but smaller labor force. The inefficient use of labor in the tertiary sector will not, of course, have the undesirable cost effects that would occur if this were done in the import-replacement or export sectors. In the production of nontradable commodities it may therefore be important to be unimportant about seeking the least cost combination of factors when this would displace labor.

Emphasizing that "Asian countries will be forced to develop the labor-intensive sectors

---

Pack concludes that "correct relative factor prices, if acted upon, should induce both a correct industry choice as well as optimum choice of technique, thus maximizing national income as well as the use of labor" (p. 403).

[3] United Nations, ECLA, "Structural Changes in Employment within the Context of Latin America's Development," *Economic Bulletin for Latin America*, October 1965, pp. 163–87.

[4] W. Galenson, "Economic Development and the Sectoral Expansion of Employment," *International Labour Review*, January-June 1963, pp. 505–19.

if jobs are to be created for the increasing waves of youngsters coming into the labor market," Oshima has stated that

the nonagricultural labor-intensive sector is very large, perhaps engaging two-thirds to three-fourths of the nonagricultural labor force. It is a sector that provides employment using the least amount of capital, in terms of capital efficiency uses the less scarce type of capital and saving, requires material inputs which are domestically produced, utilizes labor not appropriate for modern industries, and produces goods of the traditional type, consumed by lower-income families located in various parts of the country instead of being concentrated in the cities. It is an excellent complement to modern industrialization for underdeveloped countries where modern types of inputs and factors are scarce—whether these be capital and savings, skills, infrastructure, inputs, etc.[5]

A recent OECD study calculated that on average in the developing countries the manufacturing sector employs 20 per cent of the labor force, and the unemployment rate and underemployment rate together average 25 per cent. The increase in labor productivity is assumed to be 2.5 per cent a year, the rate achieved between 1955 and 1968. In order to absorb an increase in the labor force growing at 3 per cent a year (a conservatively low estimate), industrial production would have to increase at the exceptional rate of 18 per cent a year—a rate beyond the achievement of any LDC. To eradicate within a decade the existing rural and urban unemployment and underemployment it would have to increase by 30–35 per cent a year. Not surprisingly, the report concludes: "Thus eradication of general underemploy-

[5] Harry T. Oshima, "Labor-Force 'Explosion' and The Labor-Intensive Sector in Asian Growth," *Economic Development and Cultural Change*, January 1971, p. 178.

ment through the development of industrial employment is a practical impossibility in the medium term."[6]

f. If open unemployment persists and its unfavorable social and political repercussions are to be avoided, the government will itself have to provide employment opportunities. On public work projects, or elsewhere in the public sector, labor may then be receiving a wage greater than its marginal product. Thus, there comes about in the public sector a situation similar to the disguised unemployment that exists in agriculture (in the sense of the real wage being greater than the marginal product of labor). But if it is decided that labor should not remain unnecessarily idle, then in a labor surplus economy the labor will have to be used even to the point where its social marginal product becomes zero.

g. Finally, more attention must be given to the "supply side" of the problem in terms of population control policy and the "outputs" of the country's educational system. Growth in the labor force is a derivative of the population growth rate and the labor participation rate. But since there is about a 15-year lag between a decline in the birthrate and a decline in the labor force entry rate, any deceleration of population growth can only have long-run effects and is not a relevant instrument for short-term policy. Investment in human capital may, however, influence employment more readily. In this connection, some relevant points will be noted in the chapter on human-resource development, below.

From even this summary listing of policy implications, it should be apparent that employment policies only make sense within the context of an overall development strategy. An integrated set of employment policies has to provide for the mobilization

and allocation of domestic and foreign resources so as to achieve more labor-intensive output growth, investment in human capital, a more labor-intensive industrialization program, an agricultural program that is itself labor-absorbing and also contributory to industrialization, access to more appropriate technology, and the slowing down of population growth.

The range of policies extends from measures that can be instituted immediately to other measures that can take effect only in the long run. With respect to employment in Africa, for example, Todaro has proposed the following short-run policies: (1) the elimination of present factor-price distortions, (2) the establishment of a "dual" wage structure through the use of wage subsidies in some combination with a policy of wage restraint, (3) the immediate creation of new types of employment opportunities through various voluntary agreements, and (4) the restriction of excess emigration through the use of moral exhortation to return to the land, the adoption of forced controls on the movement of people, or the establishment of urban labor exchanges to regulate and control the process of job placement.[7] The most important medium term strategies include (1) the establishment of a comprehensive incomes policy, (2) the acceleration of rates of industrial and urban output growth, and (3) the intensification of efforts to stimulate agricultural and rural development.[8] Long-run policies would include the establishment and maintenance of an effective program to limit rapid population growth, and efforts to plan for the eventual development of domestic labor-intensive capital goods industries.[9]

[6] Quoted in Jonathan Power, "Why Going Back To The Land Is The Only Hope For The Third World," *The London Times,* October 18, 1974, p. 18.

[7] Michael P. Todaro, "Income Expectations, Rural-Urban Migration and Employment in Africa," *International Labour Review,* November 1971, p. 396.

[8] Ibid., p. 402.

[9] Ibid., p. 407.

Logical as the foregoing policies may be, they will not be implemented unless political conditions are supportive. The authors of three important ILO employment reports state that the partial implementation of their reports

raises questions such as what weight a government actually gives to employment objectives, what freedom of manoeuvre it possesses given its relationships to key interest groups, both domestic and foreign, what costs would be involved in adopting an employment-oriented strategy, and how those who would benefit from such a policy could be made more vocal and more powerful . . .

We now see more clearly that the heart of employment strategy lies not in making economic projections, or finding ways of removing biases towards capital intensity, but in the balance of political forces, and the capacity of political leadership in government and outside to mobilize support in ways which will make changes successful.[10]

[10] Richard Jolly, Dudley Seers, and Hans Singer, "The Pilot Missions under the World Employment Programme," in *Strategies for Employment Promotion,* ILO, Employment Research Papers, 1973.

The need for "political will" and "the establishment of a social consensus as to the need for such a change in the nature of the development path" are also emphasized by the employment mission to the Philippines as the most important task facing the country; Gustav Ranis, "Employment, Equity, and Growth: Lessons from the Philippine Employment Mission," *International Labour Review,* July 1974, pp. 25–6.

IV. SELECT BIBLIOGRAPHY

1. The most comprehensive surveys of employment problems are: David Morawetz, "Employment Implications of Industrialization in Developing Countries," *EJ*, September 1974; Edgar O. Edwards (ed.), *Employment in Developing Nations*, New York, 1974; Henry Bruton, "Economic Development and Labor Use: A Review," *WD*, December 1973.

2. The ILO's World Employment Programme has produced several Mission reports that merit attention: *Towards Full Employment: A Programme for Colombia*, Geneva, 1970; *Matching Employment Opportunities and Expectations. A Programme of Action for Ceylon* (Sri Lanka), Geneva, 1971; *Employment, Incomes and Equality. A Strategy for Increasing Productive Employment in Kenya*, Geneva, 1972; *Employment and Income Policies for Iran*, Geneva, 1973.

An evaluation of these reports is presented by E. Thorbecke, "The Employment Problem: A Critical Evaluation for Four ILO Comprehensive Country Reports," *ILR*, May 1973.

3. Features of rural-urban migration are examined in more detail in the following: J. R. Harris and M. Todaro, "Migration, Unemployment and Development: A Two-Sector Model," *AER*, March 1970; ——, "Urban Unemployment in East Africa," *Eastern Africa Economic Review*, December 1968; ——, "Wages, Industrial Employment and Labour Productivity: The Kenyan Experience," *Eastern Africa Economic Review*, June 1969; J. B. Knight, "Wages and Employment in Developed and Underdeveloped Economies," *OEP*, March 1971; C. R. Frank, Jr., "Urban Unemployment and Economic Growth in Africa," *OEP*, July 1968; H. Oshima, "Labor-Force 'Explosion' and the Labor-Intensive Sector in Asian Growth," *EDCC*, January 1971; J. C. Caldwell, *African Rural-Urban Migration*, Canberra, 1969; G. E. Johnson, "The Structure of Rural-Urban Migration Models," *Eastern Africa Economic Review*, 1971; J. E. Stiglitz, "Rural-Urban Migration, Surplus Labour, and the Relationship between Urban and Rural Wages," *Eastern Africa Economic Review*, 1969; D. Warriner, "Problems of Rural-Urban Migration," *ILR*, May 1970.

Studies on urban employment problems are rapidly increasing in number. See, for example, Kingsley Davis, *World Urbanization, 1950–1970*, Berkeley, 1969; T. G. McGee, *The Urbanization Process in the Third World*, London, 1971; Harold Lubell, *Urban Development and Employment: The Prospect for Calcutta*, Geneva, 1974; H. Joshi and V. Joshi, *Surplus Labour and the City; Theory, Evidence, and Policy*, Bombay, 1975; J. Weeks, "Policies for Expanding Employment in the Informal Urban Sector of Developing Economies," *ILR*, January 1975.

4. An excellent introduction to problems of manpower and educational planning is F. Harbison and C. A. Myers, *Education, Manpower and Economic Growth*, New York, 1966. Also of special interest are J. R. Sheffield (ed.), *Education, Employment, and Rural Development*, Nairobi, 1967; UNESCO, *Manpower Aspects of Educational Plan-*

ning, Paris, 1968; R. G. Hollister, "Economics of Manpower Forecasting," *ILR,* April 1964; Lloyd G. Reynolds, "Relative Earnings and Manpower Allocation in Developing Countries," *Pakistan Development Review,* Spring 1969.

Other special problems of manpower and education are considered in A. Callaway, "Unemployment Among African School Leavers," *Journal of Modern African Studies,* Vol. 1, No. 3 (1963); W. Galenson, *Labor in Developing Economies,* Berkeley, 1962; S. C. Sufrin, *Unions in Emerging Societies,* Syracuse, 1964; A. M. Ross (ed.), *Industrial Relations and Economic Development,* London, 1966; Peter Kilby, "Industrial Relations and Wage Determinants: Failure of the Anglo-Saxon Model," *Journal of Developing Areas,* July 1967; B. C. Roberts, *Collective Bargaining in African Countries,* London, 1967; Walter Adams (ed.), *The Brain Drain,* New York, 1968.

Problems of the wage structure are considered in A. D. Smith (ed.), *Wage Policy Issues in Economic Development,* London, 1969; Elliot Berg, *Wages and Employment in Less Developed Countries,* Ann Arbor, 1970; H. A. Turner and D. A. S. Jackson, "On the Determination of the General Wage Level—A World Analysis; or Unlimited Labor Forever," *EJ,* December 1970; H. A. Turner, "Wage Planning, Growth and Employment in Less Developed Countries," *ILR,* May 1970; J. R. Weeks, "Wage Policy and Colonial Legacy—A Comparative Study," *Journal of Modern African Studies,* October 1971.

5. Specific policies directed to the employment problem will be considered in subsequent chapters, but some general employment strategies can be noted in the following: W. Galenson (ed.), *Essays on Employment,* Geneva, 1971; Alan Peacock and G. K. Shaw, *Fiscal Policy and the Employment Problem,* Paris, 1971; G. Ranis, "Industrial Labor Absorption," *EDCC,* April 1973; ——, "Output and Employment in the '70's: Conflict or Complements," in R. G. Ridker and H. Lubell (eds.), *Employment and Unemployment Problems in Southeast and South Asia,* Delhi, 1971; H. Pack, "The Employment-Output Trade-off in LDCs—A Microeconomic Approach," *OEP,* November 1974; M. S. Ahluwalia, "Taxes, Subsidies and Employment," *QJE,* August 1973; Hans Singer and Richard Jolly, "Unemployment in an African Setting," *ILR,* February 1973; Mark Blaug, "Employment and Unemployment in Ethiopia," *ILR,* August 1974; Mark W. Leiserson, "Employment Perspectives and Policy Approaches in Indonesia," *ILR,* April 1974; W. Robinson, "Types of Disguised Rural Unemployment and Some Policy Implications," *OEP,* November 1969; special issue of *ILR,* May 1970, on "Economic Research for the World Employment Programme"; Louis Emmerij, "A New Look at Some Strategies for Increasing Productive Employment in Africa," *ILR,* September 1974.

CHAPTER V

Mobilizing Domestic Resources

Even though labor may be abundant, the output of an LDC remains limited by a shortage of capital. It is widely recognized that the LDCs must make additional efforts to mobilize and achieve effective use of their internal resources. The mobilization of domestic resources—along with the mobilization of external resources (to be discussed in the next chapter)—requires policies to facilitate the process of capital accumulation. Many economists emphasize capital accumulation as the major factor governing the rate of development. Professor Rostow, for example, specifies a rise in the rate of productive investment to over 10 per cent of national income as a necessary requirement for a country's take-off (II.B.2). Similarly, in presenting his model of a dual economy (III.D), Sir Arthur Lewis contends that

The central problem in the theory of economic development is to understand the process by which a community which was previously saving and investing 4 or 5 per cent of its national income or less, converts itself into an economy where voluntary saving is running at about 12 to 15 per cent of national income or more. This is the central problem because the central fact of economic development is rapid capital accumulation (including knowledge and skills with capital).[1]

[1] W. Arthur Lewis, "Economic Development with Unlimited Supplies of Labour," *The Manchester School,* May 1954.

The discussion of technological dualism (III.B) also implied that development requires primarily large amounts of capital investment, especially in the underdeveloped sector.

Certainly there has been no tendency among development economists to under-estimate the importance of capital. On the contrary, it has been stressed so much that a reaction has set in, and there is a strong counterview that the role of capital has received excessive attention to the neglect of other essential components of the development process. The materials in section V.A present opposing views on the legitimacy of emphasizing capital as the key variable determining the rate of development. Since capital-output ratios have figured prominently in the discussion of capital accumulation, the Note on capital output ratios clarifies various interpretations of the capital-output ratio, and at the same time levies a number of criticisms that restrict the use of a capital-output ratio in practice (V.A.3).

To the extent that an increase in the rate of investment is necessary or desired, a developing country must mobilize the required savings. The Note in section V.B focuses on this issue by outlining the various sources of capital formation. In examining these sources, we should assess each source of capital formation from the wider standpoint of how its contribution to the flow of resources for developmental purposes can be intensified.

Section V.C turns to the importance of the government's role in raising the volume of public savings. The discussion emphasizes that the financing of the government's share in economic development should be analyzed from two basic points of view. First, an adequate amount of taxation is needed to provide the government with a noninflationary means for purchasing investment goods out of revenue. Second, in attempting to intro-duce an effective tax system and reorient tax policy to the tasks of development, it is necessary to recognize the peculiar characteristics of the LDCs and to give particular attention to the probable effects of different kinds of taxes on private incentives to work, save, and invest. Special consideration must now also be given to the impact of public finance on the distribution of income.

Of increasing interest are the problems of financial development—the manner in which financial institutions and financial policies may help overcome the shortage of capital and influence a country's pattern of development. Economic theory has been generally conducted in "real" terms, such as national product in physical units, production functions, capital-output ratios. And yet, for an understanding of the process of develop-ment we must consider how the financial superstructure and the real infrastructure interact, and what are the effects of such interaction on development.

The selections in section V.D ask some basic questions about the contribution of financial development to economic development. What are the alternative techniques available to each country for mobilizing its economic surplus and channeling capital flows? What are the relationships between finance and the rate and pattern of develop-ment? These general questions should help to place in perspective the empirical studies of particular financial institutions or the financial development of individual countries.

It is especially important to consider the need for more efficient capital markets to improve the quantity and quality of capital formation. "Financial repression" is charac-teristic of inefficient capital markets and the consequence is the substitution of direct, microeconomic measures that distort prices and the allocation and mobilization of resources.

Although much of the discussion in this chapter is designed to indicate various ways of mobilizing resources for developmental expenditures without causing inflation, many countries have in practice desired a higher rate of investment than could be maintained by noninflationary sources of finance. Recourse to the substitute method of monetary expansion and credit creation has become common. Increased spending of an inflationary sort is therefore an important issue of development policy. On this issue, however, there are marked differences of opinion regarding the causes and consequences of inflation.

We try in section V.E to sort out these differences and reach some assessment of the effects of inflation in LDCs. To do this, we shall examine in analytical terms the main forces and consequences of inflation. Why are the LDCs so prone to inflation? How might inflation be stopped? Would it do more harm than good to stop inflation in a developing country?

Against the background of this general analysis, we shall also give specific attention to the problem of inflation in Latin America. These materials center on the issues between the traditional "monetarist" view of inflation and the contrasting "structuralist" view. Different interpretations of the causes of inflation lead naturally to divergent conclusions on policies for curbing inflation. While the orthodox prescription has been to restrain demand by the exercise of monetary and fiscal discipline, this policy is criticized by "structuralists" as being concerned with only the "propagating" factors of inflation or the "symptoms" instead of the underlying real structural causes. In contrast, the structural position looks to the supply side of the problem and stresses the need for social and economic reforms to correct basic structural imbalances.

There is no denying that underdeveloped countries are especially prone to inflationary pressures, and that the policies available to an underdeveloped country for effectively controlling inflation are more limited than those in an advanced country. What remains controversial, however, is whether these inflationary pressures encourage or inhibit development. This issue is discussed in section V.E, with arguments presented both in favor of and against the method of development through inflation.

Besides the usual points advanced in favor of inflation, consideration is given to the following special contentions: inflation permits the employment of underemployed workers; monetary or credit expansion is necessary to allow the "development authorities" to bid resources away from consumption; in the early stages of inflation, the "money illusion" may induce factors of production to work more intensively; the period of inflation may be short, since it will increase investment which, in turn, will expand total output, and a large portion of the increment in output may then be saved and taxed to offset the rise in investment; and none of the alternative methods of financing a rise in investment is any less free of hardships.

As for the case against inflation, the following arguments are especially persuasive: inflation has harmful effects on the efficient allocation of resources, being particularly detrimental in creating distortions in investment patterns; balance of payments pressures result from the adverse impact on exports, the spillover into imports, and the discouragement of foreign investment; the volume of resources available for domestic investment may actually fall as voluntary savings decline and incentives are diminished; and the government lacks the power to constrain the inflation and prevent the pressures from becoming progressively severe.

V.A. THE ROLE OF CAPITAL

V.A.1. Capital Accumulation and

Development*

The general rate of development is always limited by shortage of productive factors. If any one scarce factor associated with under-development should be singled out, it would be capital. The final goal of development programming is, therefore, to find the best way of breaking the vicious circle between capital shortage and under-development and to design the most efficient and optimum rate of capital accumulation.

It would be an over-simplification, of course, to regard economic development as a matter of capital accumulation alone. Other things are needed in addition, such as entre-preneurship and training of workers and public administrators. Yet these are seldom possible without some increase in the stock of capital. Therefore capital accumulation may very well be regarded as the core process by which all other aspects of growth are made possible.

Capital increases by investment, and more investment necessitates more savings or foreign assistance. Foreign assistance, if not in the form of grants, means some burden in the future. The extent to which foreign loans can be serviced and repaid will ulti-mately depend on what can be saved at home in the future. Domestic savings are, therefore, the more reliable source of invest-ment to break the vicious circle of poverty and under-development. But domestic savings can be increased only by a sacrifice in consumption which has to be compared with the future increases in consumption it promises. Investment, moreover, yields dif-ferent results, depending on the industries in which it is made. In order, therefore, for the government of an under-developed country to design an appropriate plan for develop-ment, it must be informed of the quanti-tative aspects of savings and investment, and their effects on production and consump-tion.

These quantitative aspects are of crucial importance in determining the most de-sirable rate of development. It is impor-tant, for one thing, particularly when population is growing rapidly, to estimate the rate of development that would be needed to bring about an improvement in *per capita* income or a high rate of employ-ment for the growing work force. Another element which may play a role in estimating a minimum rate of development is the neces-sity to give a certain minimum size to some projects in order that they are at all econom-ically sound. In some industries where so-called "indivisibilities" play a role, there are such minimum sizes of projects. For the country as a whole, this may mean that only a "big push," as it has been called, can really help to start the process of development. Although this may produce results which appear ambitious in the light of current efforts, it provides a fair indication of the tasks involved in the planning effort.

Whatever the initial approach, there are some useful concepts which should be borne in mind in planning the rate of development. These concepts may conveniently be described in terms of investment. There is, first, the concept of a *minimum rate of investment*, which measures the rate needed to prevent *per capita* income from falling in the face of population growth. A rate of investment somewhat above this minimum is

*From United Nations, ECAFE, *Programming Techniques for Economic Development,* Report of the First Group of Experts on Programming Tech-niques, Bangkok, 1960, pp. 8–13.

the lowest target at which any plan should aim, even though this may involve a heavy effort when population is growing rapidly. For some countries this may be a rate that can be easily attained on the basis of an effort which does not require any fundamental policy decisions, any changes in attitudes or behaviour patterns, or any improvements in techniques, skills and methods of business or public administration. For these countries, the minimum rate of investment is clearly too low, and is useful only for reference.

A second concept of use in this context is that of a *practical maximum rate of investment.* In theory a maximum rate of investment may refer to a level of capital accumulation which involves saving and investing at least all income above, say, a subsistence level. Clearly, such a maximum is of no practical significance. A practicable maximum may, therefore, be determined differently in the light of the extent to which the population would be willing to accept austerity now, so as to enjoy a higher standard of living in the future. The planner must form his best judgment as to what this practical maximum would be. The rate just defined above is the one to be determined by an evaluation of people's potential propensity to save.

A third concept is that of the highest rate of investment consistent with *absorptive capacity.* Absorptive capacity depends on natural resources, taxes, the labour supply, the level of labour, technical and managerial skills, entrepreneurial capacity, the efficiency of public administration, the extent of "technology-mindedness" of the population, and so on. Such capacity sets a limit to the amount of efficient investment physically possible, and although it can itself be increased through further investment, it does effectively limit the rate of development possible, particularly in the short run. Maximum absorptive capacity may, of course, permit of a higher rate of investment than that allowed by the ability of the population to save. In this case, it would be the role of

an ideal international policy to fill the gap and to raise investment to the highest level consistent with absorptive capacity. On the other hand, where absorptive capacity is below the practicable rate of savings, both national and international policies should be directed towards raising such capacity. These policies would then constitute the initial phase of a long-term plan.

Thus, one of the logical ways to start planning the general rate of economic development is first to estimate the amount of domestic savings and capital imports that could be expected with no change in economic policies; then to calculate the rate of growth that this level of savings and investment would provide; and finally to compare it with the desired rate of growth. Usually, the ratio of saving to income is fairly stable over long periods of time, and these saving-income ratios are lower in under-developed countries (under 10 per cent) than in higher advanced countries (about 15 per cent). Any empirical estimation of this ratio must start with the observation of the rates of savings experienced by the country in the recent past. The estimates may be based on data for incomes and the savings of households, business and government, or domestic investment *minus* capital imports. It may also be possible to base the estimates on the experiences of comparable countries, keeping in mind the differences in income levels.

After estimating the current rate of savings, the crucial question will be what amount of net national output may be expected from the investment to be made on the basis of the estimated savings. A number of studies have been made on the amount of capital required to increase output by one unit per annum in each sector of the economy and for a national economy as a whole. This amount is called the "capital-output ratio," or "capital coefficient."

Available data clearly show that for a number of countries, e.g., the Federal Republic of Germany, Japan, Norway, the United Kingdom and the United States, the capital-output ratio for a national economy as a whole remains stable over somewhat longer periods at a level of 3 to 4. This fact may well be explained by complementarities of industrial activities, or it may be that the increases in the capital-output ratios in some manufacturing industries are compensated by decreases elsewhere, possibly by external economies due to better transport or organization of the economy. Even though there are variations, it is perhaps one of the most useful parameters with a fair degree of stability. For post-war years the coefficient was found to be 2.6 for Ceylon, 2.3 for India, 4.7 for Japan, 2.3 for Malaya, etc. A better use of already existing idle capacity may have been responsible for the low values found for Ceylon, India and Malaya. These values can be expected somewhat to rise in the future. Since, moreover, the capital coefficients differ so much from one industry to another, and, in some cases, from one technique to another, it is conceivable that capital-output ratios will change in the future, depending upon the industrial structure of the economy and on the techniques to be chosen. Nevertheless, fairly reliable estimates of capital-output ratios can be made for most countries.[1] If exact estimates are difficult, the maximum and minimum values of possible estimates may be taken, and some alternative rates of development calculated.

This capital-output ratio may be considered, at this stage of our programming, as a tentative figure, and may be adjusted later as improved information, based on detailed sectoral studies, becomes available.

Although the capital-output ratio is usually calculated as the "average" capital-output ratio, what really matters is the "marginal" or "incremental" capital-output ratio: we need information on the capital required to *increase* the national output. If we want to increase output by 20 and estimate the capital-output ratio as 4, then the required addition to the capital stock, to be provided by new investment, is 80. Evidently the figure 4 in this example stands for the "incremental capital-output ratio."

Given estimates of the current rate of savings and the capital-output ratio, the rate of economic growth, in terms of national output, could be projected in the following way. If the current level of national output is 1,000, and the saving ratio is 0.06, domestic savings would be 60, which may be invested to generate the increased national output. With a capital-output ratio of 4, this amount of savings and investment could generate an increase in national output of 15, not more. An increase in national output of, say, 20 will not be possible, because the amount of investment required for this purpose is 80, which exceeds the current savings of 60. Hence, the increase in output warranted by the savings of 60 is $60 \div 4 = 15$, which gives the growth rate of 1.5 per cent in national output. The rate of growth in national output can thus be calculated by dividing the saving ratio by the capital-output ratio.

This method of projecting the future level of national output can be checked by other ways of forecasting, e.g. extrapolation of past figures. If the projected national income shows a lower growth rate than actual income did in the past, it may be that the saving ratio has been underestimated or the capital-output ratio overestimated. If the ratios are right, a slowing down of economic growth must be expected. Another check would be to divide the projected national output by the numbers in the active labour

---

[1] One may wonder if it is safe to assume that national output is proportional to (or a linear function of) capital only. In general, national output would be technically related to the employment of labour and capital, and this relation would change through time. To base the projection of national output mainly on the capital-output ratio implies a certain type of technical change in the relevant future. There are some other econometric models, such as the Douglas function, which may be usefully applied to some countries. Details of this type of possible formulation are omitted from the text here.

TABLE 1.   Rate of Economic Growth in Terms of National Output

National Output (1)	Saving Ratio (2)	Saving (3)	Investment (4)	Capital-Output Ratio (5)	Increase in National Output (6)
1,000	0.06	60	60	4	15

$$\text{Growth rate (G)} = \frac{(6)}{(1)} = \frac{15}{1,000} = \frac{(2)}{(5)} = \frac{0.06}{4} = 0.015$$

force, to obtain an index of the average productivity of labour in the future. If this index does not rise as much as the past trend, the estimates of parameters should again be reconsidered. If they are correct, inefficiency or unemployment must be expected in the future, unless measures are taken to prevent them.

The rate of growth of an economy will be somewhat less than shown by the preceding calculations, if the gestation period of the investment envisaged is large. The calculation above tacitly assumes that capital created by the investment in one period can be used productively in the following period. If, however, the gestation period of some investment project is longer than one year, say three years, then capital available for productive use will not increase before three years. At that time, the level of national income will be higher, and hence the rise in production, as a percentage of total national income, is somewhat less. This means that the extension of the gestation period has the same effect as the decline in the saving ratio, or the increase in the value of the capital-output ratio. If this is the case, then the rate

of economic growth computed in the preceding way must be adjusted downward. Needless to say, a lengthening of this time lag has further adverse effects, owing to the additional postponement of the fruits of investment.

If such projections of current trends show no significant rise in the people's standard of living, there is a definite need to increase the growth rate of national output. Suppose that the expected population increase is 1.5 per cent a year, the saving ratio 6 per cent, and the capital-output ratio 4. This will leave the standard of living unchanged, and represents the minimum rate of investment as defined [above]. If the *per capita* national income must increase by, say, 2 per cent a year, the national income must increase by 1.5 + 2.0 = 3.5 per cent every year. This means that, with the same capital-output ratio, the saving ratio must be increased from 0.06 to 0.14, requiring a considerable adjustment in policy measures. If such a sudden rise in the saving ratio is difficult to achieve, the targets for improvements in living standard must be lowered to what was called . . . the practical maximum rate of investment.

V.A.2. The Cost of Capital

Accumulation*

If the ambition is to grow as rapidly as the countries of Europe and North America have grown during the past century, the desired growth rate is about 2 per cent per head per annum. Allowing for population growth, this in most of the poorer countries means that national output should grow by about 4 per cent per annum. Higher rates than this are stated as objectives in some development plans, but 4 per cent is so difficult to attain that it is really quite an ambitious target.

Economic growth at about 4 per cent per annum requires that a country withhold from personal consumption about a quarter of the national output. One half of this or about 12 per cent of national output, is needed to provide an adequate framework of public services, the other half is required for capital formation. The need for capital formation, or investment, is familiar; a word should be said about the framework of public services.

The governments of these countries ought to spend every year about 3 per cent of national income on education, 2 per cent on public health, 3 per cent on economic services such as communications, agriculture, and geology; and about 4 per cent on general administration and welfare. This cost, aggregating 12 per cent of national income, is somewhat higher than in the more developed countries, who can provide the same range of public services more intensively for 10 per cent of national income. This is mainly because the average public servant is paid more in relation to average national income in a poor than in a rich country—a fact

*From W. Arthur Lewis, "Some Reflections on Economic Development," *Economic Digest*, Pakistan Institute of Development Economics, Karachi, Vol. 3, No. 4, Winter 1960, pp. 3–5. Reprinted by permission.

which mainly reflects the shortage of educated persons. Expenditure on the public services is just as necessary to growth as capital investment. Law and order, education, agricultural extension, geological survey, public health and such services are foundations of economic growth.

As for capital investment, no catalogue is necessary. The most urgent need of most developing countries is for better transport, especially roads and harbours. The next priority is water—its conservation for agricultural, industrial and domestic purposes. Then there is the tremendous need for capital for housing in all our rapidly expanding cities. Many people think of capital primarily in terms of manufacturing industry and electric power, but even in the most advanced countries less than one-third of capital investment is in factories. Public services, utilities and housing are the great eaters up of capital investment, without which other productive activities could not take place. . . .

Nowadays in most underdeveloped countries people know what economic growth requires; the difficulty is to make available the quarter of the national income which it costs. Personal consumption, which should only be 75 per cent of the national income, is nearer 85 per cent, leaving for the public services and for capital formation together only about 15 per cent instead of the 25 per cent they need. How is this transition to be effected?

The problem is not new. The countries which are now developed have all had to make this transition during their "industrial revolutions" or "take-off periods." In the Soviet Union the transition has been achieved in effect by taxation which is a form of compulsory saving. Elsewhere it came automatically, over a fairly long period, as a by-product of the rise of a capitalist class to dominance in the economic system.

Capitalists are distinguished from other dominant classes by their passion for saving and for productive investment. Earlier dominant classes had different ambitions. Priestly classes saved, but they invested their wealth more usually in monuments and churches than in factories and farms. Landowners saved, but in their heyday they used their savings to buy more land, rather than to invest in improving land, and the persons from whom they bought were usually selling in distress to finance consumption. Nowadays landowners in developed countries have learned to behave like capitalists, but elsewhere landowners are still not prone to productive investment. The capitalist was the first dominant type to make saving and productive investment into a religion of life.

As capitalism develops within a backward economy, the proportion of the national income accruing as capitalist profits increases all the time, and so the share of the national income saved and invested grows automatically all the time, until the economy is fully converted to capitalism, when the share of profits in the national income is stabilised. All the countries now developed have gone through this process, except the U.S.S.R.; and the countries now in line for development can tread the same path if they so desire.

For the most part they do not so desire. This is not primarily because of anti-capitalist ideology. Most of the leaders of new states proclaim some sort of socialist leaning, but within a year or two of taking office their desire for development proves stronger than their antipathy to capitalism; and they adopt programmes for stimulating private capital investment; for stimulating even indeed the foreign private capital investment which they have hitherto denounced. Their main objection to relying solely on the growth of private capitalism is that it is so slow. By this method it may take any-

thing up to a century to raise the rate of domestic saving from 5 to 10 per cent. Most political leaders want quicker results than this.

Taxation provides a more rapid alternative. If 20 per cent of national income is raised in taxes, of which 12 per cent is spent on government services, the other 8 per cent, added to 5 per cent of private saving, makes a respectable level of capital formation. Countries which have followed this path in recent years include Ghana, Burma, Ceylon and China.

This relatively high level of saving out of taxes, 8 per cent of national income, accords very well with the modern pattern of demand for capital. For nowadays half of investment is done by public agencies anyway, in electric power, communications, water supplies, schools and other public services; so there is no longer need to rely on private savings for financing investment of this kind. In addition, many private investors look to public agencies for finance, whether for private housing, for agricultural credit, or for manufacturing industry. So it is quite appropriate for the major part of saving to be done on public account.

Neither can it be said that 20 per cent is too much of the national income to take in taxes. Developed countries take 30 per cent or more. In Asia and Latin America the distribution of income is even more uneven than it is in Europe and North America. The top 10 per cent of the population gets 40 per cent of the national income; landlords think nothing of taking half the peasants' produce as rent. There is a large surplus over and above what the masses of the people receive for their consumption, and it is not too much to ask that some of this surplus be mobilised for economic development. Admittedly it cannot be done all at once. But there is no technical obstacle in the way of raising the share of taxes in the national income from 10 to 20 per cent over a period of ten years.

This can be done even in egalitarian countries, such as we find in West Africa, where land is plentiful, and where there are very few rich persons. Output is growing in these countries anyway; so it is possible to raise the proportionate share of taxes in national income over a period of time without actually reducing the absolute level of consumption per head.

What is lacking in most of these countries is not the means but the will.

V.A.3. Criticisms of the Capital-Output Ratio—Note *Reddaway*.

A capital-output ratio is frequently employed to estimate the amount of investment needed to achieve a certain rate of growth in income. This was done explicitly in ECAFE's calculations of capital requirements (V.A.1) and implicitly by Professor Lewis (V.A.2). A definite causal relationship between the growth of capital and of output, however, cannot be as readily assumed as the foregoing selections would imply. And it is misleading to suppose that the whole of any increase in output is due simply to capital accumulation.

Many conceptual difficulties and statistical pitfalls surround the derivation and use of capital-output ratios. Even after it is decided which of the several possible definitions of "capital" and "output" are best to use, and some solution to the problem of valuation is accepted, there still remain ambiguities. It is first necessary to distinguish between the average and the marginal capital-output ratio. The average ratio is the value of the total stock of capital divided by total annual income; the marginal—or incremental—ratio for the entire economy is the value of the addition to capital (net investment) divided by the addition to income (net national income). The marginal ratio need not, of course, equal the average ratio, and even though any change in the average ratio may be expected to be slow, the marginal ratio can vary a great deal more.

In framing a development plan, it is common practice to calculate the amount of additional capital required to produce a one unit increase in annual output at the margin. For this purpose, a marginal capital-output ratio is used. Net investment is estimated over the plan-period; the increase in net output (or income) is estimated between the year before the plan-period and the last year of the plan. All measurements are made at the same price level. The use of a marginal capital-output ratio in this fashion has been inspired to a large extent by the Harrod-Domar theory of growth, which relates a country's rate of growth of income to its savings-income ratio and marginal capital-output ratio.[1] The Harrod-Domar analysis, however, relates to an advanced economy, and it seeks an answer to the question of how much national income would have to grow to induce sufficient investment to maintain this rate of growth in income. For a poor country, the relevant problem is not that of sustaining a certain rate of growth, but rather the prior task of initiating or generating a higher growth rate in the first place.

[1] Evsey Domar, "Expansion and Employment," *American Economic Review,* March 1947, pp. 34–5; "The Problem of Capital Formation," *American Economic Review,* December 1948, pp. 777–94; "Economic Growth: An Econometric Approach," *American Economic Review, Papers and Proceedings,* May 1952, pp. 479–95; R. F. Harrod, "An Essay in Dynamic Theory," *Economic Journal,* March 1939, pp. 14–33; *Towards a Dynamic Economics,* London, 1948; W. J. Baumol, *Economic Dynamics,* New York, 1951, Chap. 4.

3. (Moreover, it is important to be clear whether all other productive factors that must cooperate with capital are also assumed to increase when capital increases. In an advanced economy an adequate supply of cooperant factors is likely to exist. The institutional, political, and social prerequisites for development also already exist. When using the marginal capital-output ratio under these conditions, it is reasonable to make a *mutatis mutandis* assumption that the supply of other necessary factors is forthcoming. But in a poor country where the cooperant factors tend to be in short supply, and the other prerequisites for development may not yet exist, it is not legitimate to consider an increase in capital as a sufficient condition for an expansion in output. Even though investment may be a necessary condition, an increase in output may still not be produced unless other conditions are also fulfilled along with the increase in capital supply. Since an expansion in output depends on many factors of which capital formation is only one, greater output may require changes in other factors along with an increase in capital. Or output may even increase independently of investment. Even if we accept the assumption that there is a fixed relationship between capital and output as determined by technical factors, it does not follow that we can infer from this relationship that only capital is needed to increase output. We must also consider explicitly the effect of other variables on output—for example, the supply of trained manpower, entrepreneurship, institutional arrangements, attitudes, etc. To ignore these other variables or simply to assume that accommodating changes occur, and then to attribute all of the output-increment to investment, is to take a too mechanical—and too easy—view of the changes that are necessary for an increase in output.)

4. (On the other hand, exclusive attention to a capital-output ratio may exaggerate the need for investment, insofar as output may be increased by changes in other factors

without requiring a sizeable amount of investment, or even any additional capital. If, for instance, unutilized capacity exists, it is possible to raise output with the fuller utilization of the existing capital stock or without requiring much more capital. Or there may be considerable opportunity to raise output by applying better methods of production to existing plant. To avoid taking either an overoptimistic view of what can be accomplished by capital accumulation alone, or an overpessimistic view of how much investment is needed, we should guard against a too simple use of capital-output ratios.)

5. (For the purpose of clearly recognizing the changing circumstances that may occur when additions to the capital stock are made, it is helpful to distinguish between the "net marginal capital-output ratio" and the "adjusted marginal capital-output ratio."[2] The net ratio interprets the marginal capital-output ratio as net of any changes in other factors; it considers the capital-output ratio with a *ceteris paribus* assumption—the supplies of all other factors are held constant. The adjusted ratio, however, refers to what the capital-output ratio would be if it were adjusted to a given specific increase in the supply of other factors; it assumes that investment is accompanied by changes in other output-yielding variables. For a given increment in output, the net marginal capital-output ratio is higher than the adjusted marginal capital-output ratio. Capital requirements will therefore be underestimated if they are initially based on an adjusted marginal capital-output ratio, but the other output-yielding factors do not actually accommodate themselves to the growth of capital as expected.)

6. (In calculating capital requirements, a development plan usually concentrates on an overall or global capital-output ratio for the

[2] Such a distinction is suggested by Harvey Leibenstein, *Economic Backwardness and Economic Growth*, New York, 1957, p. 178.

entire economy. But this ratio depends on capital-output ratios in the various sectors of the economy, with the overall ratio being an average of the sectoral ratios, weighted by the increases in sectoral outputs. Since the overall ratio will be affected by the changing composition of output and investment among the several sectors, it is essential to analyze the capital-output relationships at the sectoral level.)

Recognizing the problems raised above, W. B. Reddaway has offered a summary of what needs clarification when considering a marginal capital-output ratio for a sector. He states that it would be desirable to divide the increase in output for a sector between two dates into these components:[3]

Output. (i) Increase due to better methods applied to old plant, involving little or no net capital expenditure (called P for progress). (ii) Changes due to fuller (or lower) utilization of old plant, as a reflection of changes in demand (called D). (iii) Changes due to introduction of double-shifts, etc. (S). (iv) Changes due to better weather (W). (v) Changes of the kind for which a certain relationship between capital and output may reasonably be assumed as "given" by technical factors—at least if we assume a fixed number of shifts, fairly full utilization, and no shortage of labor; the bringing into use of new steel mills is a good example. If the capital cost of these is x and the capital-output ratio in a new mill is r, then the increase in annual output = x/r.

Investment. Investment in the period will consist of x, plus any capital expenditure designed to save labor without increasing output (M for "modernization") and plus (or minus) an adjustment for the difference between expenditure on construction in the period and completion (L for "lag").

Observed Capital-Output Ratio. If we work from historical statistics (or from figures for future years included in a plan)

the traditional marginal capital-output ratio for a sector is then equal to

$$\frac{x + M + L}{\frac{x}{r} + P + D + S + W}$$

If we consider only the first term in the numerator and the first term in the denominator—ignoring changes in M, L, P, D, S, and W—we are then using the capital-output ratio in an oversimplified way. Only if these other changes are small relative to x and x/r can the marginal capital-output ratio be considered approximately equal to r. But this is to treat the ratio as if it were simply a technical relationship applicable to a new plant; in practice, the actual ratio is likely to differ from r, depending on the values of the other terms in the above ratio.[4] Although M, D, S, and W may be relatively small, P will not be insignificant if there are large opportunities for increasing output by methods which involve negligible amounts of investment, and L will not be small if much of the period's investment goes into projects that are not completed during the period. When P is significant, the observed marginal capital-output ratio will be lower than if simply r is estimated; and when L is significant, because new investment projects take a long time to complete and considerable construction is started in the period, then the observed ratio will be higher than simply r. These considerations caution us against assuming that the marginal capital-output ratio is constant, even at the sectoral level.

At the aggregate level, the difficulties are compounded. Even in the simplest (but most special) of cases—namely, production coefficients fixed in all sectors and relatively small values for all the other variables that might affect output—the overall marginal capital-output ratio will still not be fixed, since sectoral output may vary with changes in demand. More generally, the overall ratio

---

[3] W. B. Reddaway, *The Development of the Indian Economy,* Homewood, 1962, pp. 207–8.

[4] Ibid., pp. 208–9.

will vary according to a number of conditions, some of which may allow only a small additional income to be generated when more capital is accumulated, while others may contribute to a large increment in output. Thus, the following conditions will tend to make the capital-output ratio high: the sectoral pattern of investment is biased toward heavy users of capital, such as public utilities, public works, housing, industry rather than agriculture, and heavy industry rather than light industry; there is excess capacity in the utilization of capital; other resources are limited, and capital is substituted for these limitational factors; capital is long-lived; the rate of technological and organizational progress is low; and investment is for completely new units of production rather than simply for extensions of existing plant.

In contrast, the marginal capital-output ratio will be lower when the composition of output is biased toward labor-intensive commodities, the average life of capital is shorter, the rate of technological and organizational progress is high, and when some capital expenditure allows fuller use of previously unutilized capacity, increases the productivity of labor, allows capital-saving innovations, opens up new natural resources, or permits the realization of economies of scale.

From such considerations, we must conclude that the marginal capital-output ratio is unlikely to be constant over time. A projected ratio must be estimated over the period for which investment requirements are being calculated, and it may then turn out that there is a wide discrepancy between the actual ratio and the projected ratio.

V.A.4. The Place of Capital in Economic Progress*   Cairncross

Capital occupies a position so dominant in the economic theory of production and distribution that it is natural to assume that it should occupy an equally important place in the theory of economic growth. In most of the recent writings of economists, whether they approach the subject historically (e.g. in an attempt to explain how the industrial revolution started) or analytically (e.g. in models of an expanding economy) or from the side of policy (e.g. in the hope of accel-

*From A. K. Cairncross, "The Place of Capital in Economic Progress," in L. H. Dupriez (ed.), *Economic Progress,* Papers and Proceedings of a Round Table held by the International Economic Association, Louvain, 1955, pp. 235, 236–7, 245–8; Cairncross, *Factors in Economic Development,* George Allen and Unwin, London, 1962, pp. 111–14. Reprinted by permission.

erating the development of backward countries), it is the process of capital accumulation that occupies the front of the stage. There is an unstated assumption that growth hinges on capital accumulation, and that additional capital would either provoke or facilitate a more rapid rate of economic development even in circumstances which no one would describe as involving a shortage of capital.

Yet there seems no reason to suppose that capital accumulation does by itself exercise so predominant an influence on economic development. In most industrialized communities the rate of capital accumulation out of savings is equal to about 10 per cent of income. If one were to assume that innovation came to a standstill and that additional investment could nevertheless yield an average return of 5 per cent, the consequential rate of increase in the national income would normally be no more than ½ per cent per annum. We are told that the national income has in fact been rising in such communities at a rate of 2–3 per cent per annum. On this showing, capital accumulation could account for, at most, one-quarter of the recorded rate of economic "progress." Nor were things very different in the nineteenth century. . . .

Even this way of putting things exaggerates the rôle of capital in economic development. For the yield on additional capital would rarely be as high as 5 per cent if there were not a discrepancy between the existing stock of capital and the stock appropriate to the existing state of technique. If innovation in the broadest sense of the term were at a standstill, accumulation would continue until the rate of interest fell to a point at which saving ceased. The sole object of accumulation in those circumstances would be to take advantage of the progressive cheapening of capital in order to introduce more roundabout methods of production, not to keep pace with current developments in technique. Ordinary observation suggests, however, that the scope for investment *in industry* to take advantage merely of lower rates of interest, once the long-term rate is below 5 per cent, is extremely limited, although there may be a good deal more scope in other directions where capital charges form an unusually high proportion of the final cost (e.g. in the erection of dwelling-houses, public buildings and the like).

The contribution of capital to economic progress is not, however, confined to the usufruct of additional capital assets, similar to those already in existence. It embraces three distinct processes. (First, a greater abundance of capital permits the introduction of more roundabout methods of production or, to be more precise, of a more roundabout pattern of consumption. This covers the freer use of capital instruments in the production of a given product, the use of

more durable instruments, and a change in the pattern of consumption in favour of goods and services with relatively high capital charges per unit cost.) (Secondly, the accumulation of capital is a normal feature of economic expansion, however originating. This is the process normally referred to as widening, as opposed to deepening, the structure of production. It may accompany industrialization, or any change in the balance between industries that makes additional demands on capital; or it may accompany an extension of the market associated with population growth, more favourable terms of trade, or the discovery of additional natural resources. Thirdly, additional capital may be required to allow technical progress to take place. It may either finance the discovery of what was not known before or more commonly, the adaptation of existing knowledge so as to allow of its commercial exploitation through some innovation in product, process or material.)

Now of these three, the first is generally of subordinate importance; it is unusual for capital accumulation, unassisted by other factors, to bring about a rapid increase in income. The second, which also abstracts from any change in technology, accounts for nearly all the capital accumulation that has taken place in the past; forces making for rapid increase in income may be largely nullified unless they are reinforced by a parallel increase in capital. It is to the third, however, that one must usually look—at least in an advanced industrial country—for the main influences governing the rate of growth of real income per head. Whatever may have been true in the past, it is now technical innovation—the introduction of new and cheaper ways of doing things—that dominates economic progress. Whether technical innovation, in the sectors of the economy in which it occurs, makes large demands on capital is, however, very doubtful. Many innovations can be given effect to in the course of capital replacement out of depreciation allowances, which, in an expanding economy, may be fully as large as net savings. Others may actually reduce the stock of capital required. Existing buildings and existing machines can often be modified so as to allow most of the advantages of the new techniques to be gained. It is economic expansion, far more than technological change, that is costly in capital. . . .

Given that the national income is increasing, whether under the influence of technical progress, population growth, or some other factor, there is good reason to expect that additional capital will be required in some important sectors on a comparable scale. Habits of thrift—a phrase that must now be stretched to include not only the practices of corporations in adding to reserves but the propensities of Finance Ministers—appear to admit of capital accumulation at a rate of about 2½ per cent per annum, and this has in recent years been close to the rate of growth of income. Provided, therefore, that the capital requirements of industry—the main sector left out of account—are also increasing at this rate, the capital-income ratio will remain constant and the whole of the country's thrift will be effectively mobilized. There can be no guarantee, however, that industry's requirements will in fact mount at this rate, even in the long run. In the short run, for reasons that are familiar, the whole process of capital accumulation may be thrown out of gear.

Now the significant feature of this argument is that it hinges far more on the indirect than on the direct demand for capital. It assumes that technical progress operates largely in independence of capital accumulation and that capital is needed, not in order to allow innovations to be made but in order to consolidate the improvements in income that innovation brings about. Moreover, it implies that if, at any time, the process of innovation creates a bulge in the demand for capital, it should be possible to adapt the pattern of investment so as to accommodate the high-yielding requirements of industry by displacing part of the larger, but less remunerative, requirements of house-building, stock-building, and so forth.

It is hardly necessary to show that this implication may be mistaken. Public policy may maintain the demand for capital in the sectors capable of compression or the capital market may be so organized that industry is unable to draw capital from the sources that finance other forms of accumulation. But unless the bulge is a very large and consistent one it is doubtful whether innovation need suffer greatly.

The effect of technical progress is generally to widen the divergence between the actual stock of capital and the stock consistent with the full exploitation of current worker opportunities. Some part of the additional capital will be needed to finance the innovations in the sectors of the economy in which they arise; some will be linked with the innovations directly, either because associated industries are offered a wider market or because social capital has to be provided in an area where it has become insufficient; some will be linked indirectly, in the way already outlined, because the increased expenditure of consumers will give rise to a derived demand for capital. Now it is common to find that, particularly with a major advance in technique, the influence which it exerts on the scope for eventual capital accumulation is far more profound than its immediate impact on the current flow of capital formation. There is generally a chain reaction, strung out through time, one physical asset being wanted only after another has been created. Although the full consequences may be entirely foreseeable, development does not work up to its full momentum until a whole series of changes have occurred: an extension of capacity here, an application of the new technique there; a shift of location in one industry, a building up of new attitudes in another. The introduction of the steam engine, for example, brought into existence a large reservoir of projects that trickled out into capital formation all through the nineteenth century: the stock of capital appropriate to existing technique was far above the existing stock both because the steam engine was capable of wide application and because many industries that themselves made no use of it (such as bridge-building) were transformed in scale or (like agriculture and many pursuits ancillary to it) in location.

Moreover, because the chain reaction takes time and the innovation is, *ex hypothesi,* a profitable one, the process is to a large extent self-financing. If there is a spate of such innovations, interest and profits are likely to show some response and a corresponding shift in the ratio of savings to income will ease the heavier burden of finance. It may happen, however, that the situation is not regulated in this way: interest rates may be sticky upwards as well as downwards. The probable outcome will then be a series of spurts in investment, followed by periods of indigestion. . . .

A variant of this situation is one in which there has been a considerable lag behind the known opportunities for the fruitful use of capital at existing rates of interest. A country may fail to make use of technical knowledge available elsewhere and suddenly become alive to the possibilities of applying that knowledge. At that stage its capital requirements will increase discontinuously and the additional capital which it requires before bumping up against the limits of technical advance may be very large. It appears to be this situation that is in the minds of those who assume that the injection of additional capital into a country's economy will almost automatically speed up its economic progress. Sometimes the argument is framed more specifically in terms of a shift of employment from agriculture to industry, with a large net gain in productivity from the shift, and the large capital investment needed to accomplish it operating as a brake.

This is a complex situation and it may exist in some underdeveloped countries. But it is by no means obvious that additional capital, whether borrowed from abroad or accumulated through the exertions of surplus labour in the countryside, would by itself suffice to start off a cycle of industrial-

ization. The problem is often one of organization quite as much as of capital creation: of training managements and men; of creating new attitudes towards industrial employment; of taking advantage of innovations that need little capital and using the resulting gains to finance investment elsewhere.

On the whole, there is a greater danger that the importance of capital in relation to economic progress will be exaggerated than that it will be underrated. How many successful firms, looking back over their history, would single out difficulty of access to new capital as the major obstacle, not to their growth, but to the adoption of the most up-to-date technique? How many countries in the van of technical progress have found themselves obliged to borrow abroad? It is where there has been a lag, where technical progress has been too slow, that capital is called upon to put matters right. No doubt where capital is plentiful, more risks can be taken and development is speeded up, so that rapid development and rapid capital accumulation go together. But the most powerful influence governing development, even now, is not the rate of interest or the abundance of capital; and the most powerful influence governing capital accumulation, even now, is not technical progress. . . .

There is general agreement that, in all countries, the process of economic growth and capital accumulation are closely interconnected. It was in terms of this interconnection that the earliest theories of economic development were formulated; and in the work of modern economists, output is still assumed to be limited by capital, whether there is abundant labour or not. A high rate of capital formation usually accompanies a rapid growth in productivity and income; but the causal relationship between the two is complex and does not permit of any facile assumption that more capital formation will of itself bring about a corresponding acceleration in the growth of production.

In industrial countries this is only too obvious. Capital formation may assume forms, such as house-building or an addition to liquid stocks, that are unlikely to add very perceptibly to productivity although they may yield a sufficient return to make them worth while. If all capital formation were of this character, or represented an enlargement of the capital stock with assets broadly similar to those already in existence, it would be hard to account for the rates of growth actually recorded. A moment's reflection will show that even an average return of 10 per cent to capital in a country saving 10 per cent of its income annually would raise income by no more than 1 per cent per annum.[1] Similarly, efforts to impute the recorded expansion in industrial production to the additional labour and capital contributing to it invariably leave a large unexplained residual.[2] It is necessary, therefore, to take account of other influences, such as technical progress and improvements in social and economic organization, which may operate through investment, or independently of it, so as to raise the level of production. These influences, if they take effect uniformly throughout the economy in competitive conditions, will tend to swell the national income without raising the average return to capital, the extra output slipping through to the consumer, the wage-earner or the government.

How far it is correct to attribute an expansion in output to high investment, when high investment is only one of the factors at work is necessarily debatable. It

[1] This point is developed in my "Reflections on the Growth of Capital and Income" (*Scottish Journal of Political Economy,* June 1959). See also the comments by E. Lundberg, "The Profitability of Investment" (*Economic Journal,* December 1959).

[2] See, for example, W. B. Reddaway and A. D. Smith, "Progress in British Manufacturing Industries in the Period 1948–54" (*Economic Journal,* March 1960) and O. Aukrust, "Investment and Economic Growth," *Productivity Measurement Review,* February 1959.

would certainly be legitimate if capital formation was lagging behind, and finance could be identified as a bottleneck in the process of expansion. It might also happen that the rate of technical advance was itself controlled by the scale of investment, not merely because capital formation was the means by which new techniques were adopted but also because high investment created an atmosphere favourable to experimentation and innovation. There is undoubtedly some tendency for all the symptoms of rapid growth to show themselves simultaneously. But there is no invariable dependence of growth on a high rate of capital formation and it is easy to imagine circumstances in which efforts to increase capital formation may actually slow down the progress of the economy.[3]

Moreover there is some justification for turning the causal relationship the other way round. If income is growing fast, investment opportunities are likely to be expanding correspondingly fast, so that the growth in income draws capital accumulation along behind it. The biggest single influence on capital formation is market opportunity, and many types of capital accumulation are likely to be embarked upon only when income is booming. If capital formation does not respond, its failure to do so will certainly act as a drag on the expansion in output. But there is no reason why it should bring it to a halt, and, given a re-arrangement of the investment pattern, income might grow a long way before the shortage of capital became acute. In the meantime the rapid growth in income, particularly if it were accompanied by high profits, would be likely to generate additional savings and so mitigate any symptoms of capital shortage that manifested themselves.

All this presupposes that a spurt in income could precede an acceleration of investment, and that capital formation is subordinate to other elements in the process

[3] The ground-nuts scheme in Tanganyika is an extreme example.

of growth. These suppositions are not altogether extravagant. Technical progress does not always involve high net investment: indeed it may permit of a *reduction* in the stock of capital or an expansion in output without any comparable investment. A change in the pattern of investment could also, by enforcing the continued use or overloading of old types of plant, make possible a far more rapid construction of those newer types which bear the fruits of technical progress in greatest abundance.

Attempts are sometimes made to settle the issue by citing the apparent constancy of the capital-income ratio and deducing from this the "neutrality" of technical progress. But the capital-income ratio is affected by many things other than technical progress: the distribution of consumers' expenditure between capital-intensive and labour-intensive products; indivisibilities in past investment—for example, in the transport and communication network; changes in the pattern of trade; investment in social assets such as roads, schools, and hospitals to

which no income is imputed; and so on. Even if these influences, too, are neutral and if the capital-income ratio does remain constant—and neither of these assumptions seems well-founded—the fact that capital and income grow at the same rate tells us nothing about the causes of growth in either. There is no reason at all why one should rule out the suggestion that the same circumstances that favour rapid growth of income are also favourable to a rapid growth of investment.

This may seem a rather arid and irrelevant issue: arid, because if capital requirements must keep pace with the growth of income that is all we need to know for practical purposes; irrelevant, because the issue relates to experiences in industrial rather than pre-industrial countries. But when it is so commonly urged that countries will be able to take-off if only they are provided with sufficient capital from outside, the issue seems neither arid nor irrelevant. For this thesis assumes the very causal relationship that is in dispute.

V.B. SOURCES OF CAPITAL FORMATION—NOTE

Whether it be financed from internal sources or external, by noninflationary or inflationary means—the accumulation of capital in any developing economy requires the mobilization of an economic surplus. If investment is to increase, there must be a growing surplus above current consumption that can be tapped and directed into productive investment channels. The different ways of financing capital formation will entail different institutional arrangements (for example, the plowing back of industrial profits into investment would imply a different institutional framework from that of financing through taxation by the state). It should be recognized, however, that the process of capital formation involves three essential steps: (1) an increase in the volume of real savings, so that resources can be released for investment purposes; (2) the channeling of savings through a finance and credit mechanism, so that investible funds can be collected from a wide range of different sources and claimed by investors; and (3) the act of investment itself, by which resources are used for increasing the capital stock.

The first requirement—an increase in the volume of real savings—is of fundamental importance if a higher rate of investment is to be achieved without generating inflation. This crucial step of mobilizing savings should not be confused, however, with the monetary financing of investment. The significance of financial institutions lies in their making available the means to utilize savings. As one study of the role of financial institutions concludes:

However poor an economy may be there will be a need for institutions which allow such savings as are currently forthcoming to be invested conveniently and safely, and which ensure that they are channelled into the most useful purposes. The poorer a country is, in fact, the greater is the need for agencies to collect and invest the savings of the broad mass of persons and institutions within its borders. Such agencies will not only permit small amounts of savings to be handled and invested conveniently but will allow the owners of savings to retain liquidity individually but finance long-term investment collectively.[1]

Although the existence of a more developed capital market and financial intermediaries will aid in the collection and distribution of investible funds, they in no way lessen the need for real saving. The rate of investment which it is physically possible to carry out is limited by saving, and a "shortage of capital"—in the sense of a shortage of real resources available for investment purposes—cannot be solved merely by increasing the supply of finance. Indeed, it is comparatively easy to introduce institutional arrangements to increase the supply of finance, and a lack of finance need not persist as a serious bottleneck. Once a sizeable class of savers and borrowers come into being, financial intermediaries are likely to appear, and lending institutions are readily created. But the creation of new financial institutions is no substitute for the necessary performance of real saving.

It is therefore important to be clear on the various sources from which the necessary savings can be mobilized to provide the wherewithal for capital expenditure. From internal sources, an increase of savings may be generated voluntarily through a reduction

---

[1] Edward Nevin, *Capital Funds in Underdeveloped Countries,* London, 1961, p. 75.

in consumption; involuntarily through additional taxation, compulsory lending to the government, or inflation; or, finally, by the absorption of underemployed labor into productive work. From external sources, the financing of development may be met by the investment of foreign capital, restriction of consumption imports, or an improvement in the country's terms of trade.

An increase in voluntary saving through a self-imposed cut in current consumption is unlikely when the average income is so low. At best, it can be hoped that when income rises, the marginal rate of saving may be greater than the average rate. Instead of relying on voluntary saving, the government will normally have to resort to "forced" saving through taxation, compulsory lending, or credit expansion. The efficacy of credit expansion and its resultant inflationary consequences are discussed in V.E. As for taxation, the country's "taxation potential" depends upon a variety of conditions—the level of per capita real income, the degree of inequality in the distribution of income, the structure of the economy, the political leadership and administrative powers of the government. It is generally true in underdeveloped countries that the actual ratio of tax revenue to national income is at present less than the tax potential. The potential can be more fully exploited, especially if the increase in taxation is undertaken gradually over a number of years. The saving that is forced by additional taxation, however, is likely to be less than the additional tax revenue, since there may be a reduction in private voluntary saving instead of a fall in consumption by the full amount of the tax. Nonetheless, an increase in taxation remains the most expeditious way of meeting a rise in capital expenditure. There is only narrow scope in a poor country for the practice of compulsory saving through the practice of compulsory purchase of nonnegotiable government bonds. Of greater practical significance may be the operation of state marketing boards which have a statutory monopoly over export crops. These boards may compel native producers to save by purchasing the native's produce at prices below world prices.

Finally, another internal source of saving is represented by the "investible surplus" of underemployed labor. If this "investible surplus" is utilized in productive activity, the national output would be increased, and the required savings might be generated from the additional output. It should also be noted that the direct formation of capital through the use of underemployed labor can be obtained by what is termed the "unit multiplier" method.[2] If labor does have zero productivity in agriculture, it can be withdrawn and put to work on investment projects (construction, irrigation works, road building, etc.) without a drop in agricultural output. Most of the payment of the additional wages will be directed towards foodstuffs, and agricultural income will rise. The higher income may then be taxed, and the tax revenue can finance the investment project. If taxes are levied in an amount equivalent to the additional wage-bill, there will be no change in consumption but income will have risen by the amount of the investment. When the investment projects are completed there will be an increase in output, and some of this increase in income may also be captured through taxation. How much scope there is for this method of direct investment in kind depends upon the ease with which labor can be attracted to investment projects, the degree to which labor can form capital directly without requiring additional investment expenditure, the absence of an adverse effect on agricultural output, and the capacity to offset the investment with taxation. We shall consider more thoroughly the general problem of taxation in section C of this chapter.

When we look to external sources of financing development, the capital assistance provided by foreign economic aid and the

[2] James S. Duesenberry, "Some Aspects of the Theory of Economic Development," *Explorations in Entrepreneurial History*, Vol. 3, No. 2, pp. 65–7.

private investment of foreign capital are of most importance. The next chapter examines the contribution of foreign aid and private foreign investment. Some contribution may also come from a restriction of consumption imports. Provided that there is not simply a switch in expenditure from imports to domestic consumption, the level of savings will then rise. Imports of capital goods can then be increased, and this will represent a genuine addition to the rate of capital formation: the increase in the flow of investment goods imported is, in this case, matched by an increase in the flow of domestic income saved. If, however, consumers increase their domestic spending when they can not import, then resources will be diverted from domestic capital production in favor of the increased domestic consumer spending, and the increase in imports of investment goods will be offset by reduced domestic investment. An increase in saving is therefore necessary if the restriction of consumption imports is to result in an increase in total net capital formation.[3]

A similar analysis applies to changes in the terms of trade. When export prices rise, the improvement in the country's commodity terms of trade makes it possible for the country to import larger quantities of capital goods. But again, this source of capital formation will not be fully exploited unless the increment in domestic money income due to the increase in export proceeds is saved. If the extra income merely increases consumer spending on home produced or imported goods, the opportunity for new saving is lost. The extra resources made available by the improvement in the terms of trade must be withheld from consumption and directed into investment.[4] Either a corresponding increase in voluntary saving or in taxation is necessary to give the

country a command over additional imports of investment goods.

A special word should be added about consumption and capital formation. We have implied above that present consumption is at the expense of future output; as usually stated, it is believed that restraints on consumption are needed to divert resources from the production of more consumer goods to capital accumulation. But is this always true? Can a case be made that—in the context of a developing country—an increase in current consumption may actually lead to an expansion in future production?

When the level of living is as low as it is in an LDC, the distinction between consumption and investment becomes overdrawn insofar as private consumption may well have a positive marginal productivity. The reason is not that consumption will augment resources, but that a rise in consumption may improve labor quality and efficiency and hence allow better use to be made of the existing labor resources. The consumption of health-improving goods should improve the ability to work and increase the intensity of work. The greater consumption of foodstuffs that aid nutrition is especially significant. For it has now been established by medical scientists that improper food, especially a diet low in protein, can in itself impair the physical and mental development of children from birth.[5]

In an empirical study of the impact of components of "labor quality" on the growth of output, Professors Galenson and Pyatt have demonstrated that an increase in consumption may improve labor quality. The components of labor quality examined are calories per head, investment in dwellings, higher education, health indicators, and social security benefits. Of these various components, better diet is shown to have the

---

[3] Cf. Ragnar Nurkse, *Problems of Capital Formation in Underdeveloped Countries,* Oxford, 1953, pp. 111–16.

[4] Ibid., pp. 97–103.

[5] *Pre-School Malnutrition: Primary Deterrent to Human Progress,* National Academy of Sciences, National Research Council, Washington, D.C., 1966; N. S. Scrimshaw, "Infant Malnutrition and Learning," *Saturday Review,* March 16, 1968, pp. 64–8. See further, VIII.B, below.

greatest impact on labor productivity and growth of output.[6]

Certain policy implications follow from the view that private consumption may be productive. In its efforts to raise the community's marginal rate of saving, the government should put more emphasis on taxation and on business saving through profits rather than on individual saving through a curtailment of consumption. But there should at the same time be an improvement in the pattern of consumption so that it might contribute as directly as possible to increasing efficiency. What is needed is a selective increase in consumption. Luxury consumption, for instance, should be taxed, and the import-replacement of consumer goods should be limited insofar as this policy has become suboptimal (see XI.C). There should, however, be an increase in consumption that favors the rural population if this will help overcome the agricultural bottleneck. In this connection, we should note Professor Myint's observation that "incentive consumer goods" can be a useful means of encouraging peasants to enter the money economy: a rise in the aspiration to consume these goods may lead to the sale of a food surplus and may encourage better methods of production that will increase the food surplus in the future.[7]

In its most general terms, the principle that consumption can be productive raises the complex problem of specifying criteria for intertemporal efficiency in consumption, and then shaping policy instruments to meet these criteria. If we take the largest view, this brings us to the very frontier of multisectoral intertemporal models where we should attempt to interrelate an optimal consumption policy with an optimal capital policy. The problem of the total amount of investment that can be made in the future then becomes a function of investment allocation and the pattern of consumption in the present period. We need not be overwhelmed at this point by the complexities of such a model, but we shall return in Chapter VII to the problem of optimal investment allocation.

[6] W. Galenson and G. Pyatt, *The Quality of Labour and Economic Development in Certain Countries,* ILO, Geneva, 1964, pp. 15–19, 87–8.

Another study has shown that, in the rural areas of Asia, an insufficiency of calories may take the form of inadequate work effort after the peak season. See Harry T. Oshima, "Food Consumption, Nutrition, and Economic Development in Asian Countries," *Economic Development and Cultural Change,* July 1967, pp. 390–91. Cf. also, F. A. O., *Nutrition and Working Efficiency,* Rome, 1962; Gunnar Myrdal, *Asian Drama,* New York, 1968, pp. 1912–19. But see Elliott J. Berg, "Major Issues of Wage Policy in Africa," in A. M. Ross (ed.), *Industrial Relations and Economic Development,* London, 1966, pp. 190–96. Professor Berg argues that under conditions of migrant labor and a joint family system, higher income does not necessarily lead to better nutrition. He also contends that better nutrition is not sufficient to improve individual efficiency unless there are also present the necessary motivation and essential cooperant factors with labor.

[7] Hla Myint, *The Economics of the Developing Countries,* London, 1964, pp. 88.

V.C. THE GOVERNMENT AS SAVER

V.C.1. The Taxation Potential*

Problems of taxation, in connexion with economic development, are generally discussed from two different points of view, which involve quite distinct, and often conflicting, considerations: the point of view of *incentives* and the point of view of *resources*. Those who believe that it is the lack of adequate incentives which is mainly responsible for insufficient growth and investment are concerned with improving the tax system through the granting of additional concessions of various kinds, with less regard to the unfavourable effects on the public revenue. Those who believe that insufficient growth and investment is mainly a consequence of a lack of resources are chiefly concerned with increasing the resources available for investment through additional taxation, even at the cost of worsening its disincentive effects.

In my opinion a great deal of the prevailing concern with incentives is misplaced, except in particular cases, such as tax concessions granted to foreigners which *may* increase the inflow of capital from abroad. It is shortage of resources, and not inadequate incentives, which limits the pace of economic development. Indeed the importance of public revenue from the point of view of accelerated economic development could hardly be exaggerated. Irrespective of the prevailing ideology or the political colour of particular governments, the economic and cultural development of a country requires the efficient and steadily expanding provision of a whole host of non-revenue-yielding services—education, health, communications

*From Nicholas Kaldor, "Taxation for Economic Development," *Journal of Modern African Studies*, Vol. 1, No. 1, 1963, pp. 7–11, 13. Reprinted by permission.

systems, and so on, commonly known as "infrastructure"—which require to be financed out of government revenue. Besides meeting these needs, taxes or other compulsory levies provide the most appropriate instrument for increasing savings for capital formation out of domestic sources. By reducing the volume of spending by consumers, they make it possible for the resources of the country to be devoted to building up capital assets.

Of course, it is possible to allow unchecked consumer spending to bid up prices until only relatively few can afford to buy. Inflation can thus succeed in setting free resources for capital development—at some cost. But it is a clumsy and ineffective instrument, since a large part of the enforced reduction in the consumption of the mass of the population, brought about by the rise in prices in relation to incomes, is wasted in the increased luxury consumption of the profit-earning classes. Also, it is difficult to conceive of inflation as more than a temporary instrument for mobilising resources; once wages rise in consequence of the rise in prices, the rate of price-inflation is accelerated, without securing any further savings.

Ruling out inflation as a deliberate instrument, it may be asked: What are the most appropriate taxes that can be relied on for maximum revenue? This question does not admit of any general answer in the widely varying conditions of "under-developed" countries. The only feature that is common to them is that they all suffer from a shortage of revenue. This is partly because they have a low "taxation potential"—which may be defined as the maximum proportion of the national income that can be diverted for public purposes by means of taxation. But more important, in my view, is the fact that the taxation potential in such countries is rarely fully exploited.

There is a glaring discrepancy, in most under-developed countries, between the amount of incomes of various types as computed by the method of national output statistics, and the incomes declared in tax returns or computed on the basis of tax receipts. In the "developed" countries the national income estimates based on the "income" and the "output" method of computation are more easily reconciled, and do not reveal such glaring differences. It is probably not exaggerated to say that the typical under-developed country collects in direct taxation no more than one-fifth or possibly only one-tenth of what is due. The difficulties are many. Bad tax laws or bad tax administration—or both—are not only to be explained by lack of knowledge, of understanding, or of administrative competence; they are also the result of resistance from powerful pressure groups who block the way to effective tax reform. Accelerated development in all such cases is predominantly a political issue; expert advice can point the way, but overcoming resistance to more effective policies for mobilising resources must depend on the collective will, operating through political institutions. Many under-developed countries suffer, not only from lack of revenue, but also from an irrational scale of priorities in the allocation of public funds. Too much may be spent on the (real or fancied) needs of defence, or for ostentatious purposes of various kinds—such as public buildings and ornaments, lavish diplomatic missions, etc. There is nothing much for the economist to say about all this, beyond noting the facts.

What determines the taxation potential of a country? It is obviously greatly dependent on (i) real income per head; (ii) the degree of inequality in the distribution of income; (iii) the relative importance of different kinds of economic activity (such as the production of cash crops, subsistence agricul-

ture, and so on) and their social and institutional setting; and (iv) the administrative competence of the tax-gathering organs of the government.

It is a commonplace to say that taxes can only be paid out of the "economic surplus"—the excess of production over the minimum subsistence needs of the population. Moreover, in so far as such surplus is not consumed by the people to whom it accrues, but is saved and invested, it can only be made available for the purposes of public expenditure at the cost of reducing the rate of capital accumulation of the community. This in turn is bound to react adversely on the country's economic development, unless the capital investment which is reduced thereby itself served the purposes of inessential or "conspicuous" consumption (such as luxury housing). It would be more correct to say, therefore, that the taxation potential of a country depends on the *excess of its actual consumption over the minimum essential consumption of the population.*

In practice, however, the minimum essential consumption of a community cannot be defined or measured; it is not just a matter of the strict biological requirements of subsistence (which themselves vary greatly with climate and location) but of social conventions and habits, and the actual standards of living to which the bulk of the population of any particular community has become accustomed. Since governments ultimately depend on the consent of the people whom they govern, it is impossible as a matter of policy to reduce, by means of taxation, the actual standard of living of the mass of the population very far below the currently accepted standards. If this were not so, the taxation potential would vary enormously with the actual level of real income per head. Supposing this potential were 10 per cent in a country with an income per head of £20 a year, it would be no less than 82 per cent in a country whose income per head is £100 a year. Yet even the richest countries with the highest incomes per head find it very difficult to raise more than 30–35 per cent of their gross national product in taxation.[1]

It is the highest income groups that offer the highest potential yield to the tax collector; in other words, the taxation potential of any country is strongly dependent on the prevailing inequality in the distribution of the national income. This in turn is closely linked to the relative importance of incomes derived from property, as against incomes derived from work, and to the degree of concentration in the ownership of property. As between two countries with the same real income per head, the accustomed standard of living of the bulk of the population will evidently be the lower in the country in which a larger share of total incomes accrues to a minority of wealthy individuals; and it will be this country that has the higher taxation potential.[2]

From this point of view the underdeveloped countries of different regions of the globe (or even individual countries within the same region) show the widest differences. At one end of the scale a country such as India, with a very low income per head of population, has a high ratio of property income in total income (a ratio that is comparable to that of the country with the highest income per head, the United States) and in consequence has a relatively high taxation potential in relation to real income per head. In many of the countries of Latin America the share of the national income accruing to property owners is even higher than in any European or North American country, and the proportion of the national income that is taken up by their consumption may be three to four times the corresponding proportion in highly developed countries such as the United States or the United Kingdom. At the other end of the scale there are some underdeveloped countries, particularly in Africa, in which incomes derived from property ownership are relatively insignificant and in which a wealthy property-owning class can hardly be said to exist. From the point of view of taxation potential the African countries thus appear to be less favourably placed, in relation to the distribution of real income per head, than the countries of Asia or Latin America.

It is possible on the other hand that there is scope for additional taxation at the other end of the income scale. For example, the amount of food produced in a country may be limited, not by the availability or fertility of land, nor by knowledge or ability, but by the immediate needs of the agricultural population, who prefer to have maximum leisure and a minimum of material income, and therefore work just hard enough to cover their essential needs. In such circumstances additional taxes levied on them would tend to make them work harder and produce more—i.e., reduce their leisure, rather than their standards of material consumption. Taxation would then act as an incentive to produce more, rather than force

[1] Over a period of time it may be possible of course to increase quite substantially the proportion of the national income collected in taxation without any actual reduction in the standard of living, insofar as real incomes per head are rising. This is particularly important in those cases where incomes are rising fast on account of increasing yields or higher export prices for the main crops.

[2] This is not to suggest that either the inequality of incomes or the inequality in standards of consumption could be eliminated by taxation. It is not possible or expedient to prevent the owner of the successful business from enjoying the fruits of his success during his lifetime—any more than it is possible to prevent scarce talent from earning its high reward in a socialist state. But clearly not all forms of economic privilege fulfil any positive social function—absentee landlords for example—and the experience of western Europe and North America has shown that the consumption of the entrepreneurial class can be reduced within wide limits, by means of progressive taxation, without interfering either with incentives or the means of continued growth and accumulation. It is consumption, rather than saving out of profits, which shows wide differences between countries, according to the nature of their tax systems.

the people to consume less, and this may not encounter the same kind of resistance, particularly if the increase in taxation is a gradual one. From this point of view, the countries of Africa—where, in general, shortage of land is not a critical factor in agricultural production—are more favourably placed than those of Asia.

There are some under-developed countries which, while they lack a domestic property-owning class, have important foreign enterprises in their territory for the exploitation of valuable minerals or the produce of plantations, so that a considerable share of their gross *domestic* product accrues to non-residents. Since the right of a country to tax all income arising within its jurisdiction is now firmly established, this provides a source of taxation that is essentially similar to that of a wealthy domestic property-owning class. . . .

Under-developed countries differ also as regards the relative magnitude of the non-monetised or subsistence sector, and the monetised or market-exchange sector, as well as the nature of the prevailing type of enterprise in each. The most appropriate forms of taxation will be different in an economy where commercial and manufacturing activities are carried on by small traders than in one where they are concentrated in the hands of large-scale business enterprises. Similarly, the prevailing forms of land tenure, the nature of social and family relationships, or the extent of economic inequality call for differing methods of taxa-

tion of the subsistence sector. The general tendency in most under-developed countries is to throw a disproportionate share of the burden of taxation on the market sector, and an insufficient amount on subsistence agriculture. The reasons for this are partly administrative and partly political: taxes levied on the agricultural community are far more difficult to assess and collect, and are socially and politically unpopular because they appear unjust; the people in the subsistence sector are, individually, always so much poorer than the people in the market sector. Yet . . . it is the taxation of the agricultural sector that has a vital role to play in accelerating economic development; the disproportionate taxation of the market sector tends to retard economic progress by reducing both the resources and the incentives for accumulation.

Our general conclusion so far is that the question: "Which taxes are the most appropriate for securing maximum revenue in an under-developed country?" can only be answered in concrete terms in the light of the particular circumstances of each individual country. The main considerations that are relevant in this connexion are: (i) the forms of land tenure, and the distribution of land ownership; (ii) the nature of enterprises in the so-called "secondary" and "tertiary" sectors of the economy; (iii) the role of foreign enterprise; (iv) the nature of exports and of imports; and (v) the competence of the administrative organs of the government.

V.C.2. Trends in Taxation*

Developing nations continue to increase their levels of taxation as measured by the ratio of their total taxes (excluding social security contributions) to gross national product (GNP). This is shown in a recent updating in March 1975 *Staff Papers,* "Tax Ratios and Tax Effort in Developing Countries, 1969–71," by Raja J. Chelliah, Hessel J. Baas, and Margaret R. Kelly.

The earlier report first outlined the major changes in the levels and composition of taxes between two three-year periods, 1953–55 and 1966–68, for a sample of 30 countries and then examined in detail the structure of taxation in the countries surveyed during the latter period. More importantly, the study attempted to measure relative tax effort in the sample countries during 1966–68, and the updating applies its methodology to data for 47 of the 50 countries covered in the original study. All these countries, except Argentina, had a per capita income below $1,000; the group thus encompassed most low-income countries.

OVERALL TAX RATIOS

The earlier study noted that tax ratios—the ratio of total taxes, excluding social security contributions, to GNP—had increased in the developing countries included during the interval between 1953–55 and 1966–68. This trend continued after 1968; the average tax ratio for 1969–71 was 15.1 per cent, compared with 13.6 per cent for 1966–68.

In spite of the general increase in tax ratios in developing countries, the average level of taxation in these countries is still considerably less than in developed coun-

*From Raja J. Chelliah, "Trends in Taxation in Developing Countries," *IMF Staff Papers,* July 1971, as summarized in *IMF Survey,* June 3, 1974, pp. 162–4. Reprinted by permission.

tries. The average tax ratio in 16 of the developed countries of Europe and North America was 26.2 per cent in 1969–71. Moreover, most of these countries raise an amount equal to more than 20 per cent of their GNP in taxes, exclusive of social security contributions. The difference between the two groups of countries is greater if social security contributions are included, in which case the average tax ratio for the developed countries of 34 per cent is more than double the developing countries' average ratio of 16 per cent.

COMPOSITION OF TAX REVENUES

Taxes on international trade constitute the largest share of total taxes collected in developing countries, followed closely by taxes on domestic production and internal transactions, and by income taxes (including royalties on minerals). The composition of taxes in the 1969–71 period was not markedly different from that in 1966–68. However, there was a further shift—continuing the trend noticed between 1953–55 and 1966–68—from property and poll taxes to income taxes. The latter increased from an average of 23.5 per cent of the total in 1966–68 to 27.3 per cent in 1969–71. The increase in income taxes was also partly at the expense of indirect taxes, which declined from 65.8 per cent in 1966–68 to 63.9 per cent in 1969–71. Within the category of indirect taxes, there was a decline both in taxes on international trade and on production and internal transactions. This shift to direct taxes took place in more than half the countries.

An examination of the pattern of taxation in relation to GNP shows that property taxes are of little importance—less than 1 per cent of GNP—in most of the countries. In about two thirds of the countries studied, income taxes were equivalent to more than 2 per cent of GNP, and over a quarter of the countries raised more than 5 per cent of GNP in income taxes, including royalties on minerals. The average ratio of income taxes to GNP in the 23 countries with the highest per capita income was 6.7 per cent, against 2.8 per cent in the 24 countries at the lower end of the per capita income scale. The average ratio of international trade taxes to GNP was 4.1 per cent in the first group and 5.4 per cent in the second. The average ratio of production taxes in the two groups was 5.0 and 4.7 per cent, respectively, compared with the groups' overall average tax ratios of 16.8 and 13.5 per cent.

TABLE 1.   Tax Ratios[1] and Indices of Tax Effort of Selected Developing Countries

Taxes as Per Cent of GNP			Index of Tax Effort		
	1969–71[2]	1966–68		1969–71[3]	1966–68
Zambia	31.34	28.6	Brazil	1.806	1.779
Zaïre	29.36	23.4	Tunisia	1.639	1.297
Guyana	23.42	20.6	Egypt	1.487	1.343
Brazil	22.86	20.8	Ivory Coast	1.471	1.429
Tunisia	21.71	20.7	Sudan	1.440	1.098
Iran	21.58	18.0	Sri Lanka	1.374	1.270
Venezuela	20.43	20.7	Senegal	1.342	1.382
Ivory Coast	19.80	19.7	Republic of China	1.304	1.116
Chile	19.60	19.2	Zaïre	1.276	1.435
Jamaica	19.36	16.7	Morocco	1.224	1.163
Malaysia	19.30	17.1	Turkey	1.197	1.164
Egypt	19.19	17.5	Malaysia	1.193	1.016
Sudan	18.22	13.0	Korea	1.181	0.972
Senegal	18.11	16.8	Chile	1.159	1.176
Morocco	17.81	16.5	Ghana	1.154	1.015
Republic of China	17.76	13.1	Zambia	1.111	1.175
Sri Lanka	17.67	16.3	India	1.093	1.052
Trinidad and			Kenya	1.090	1.155
Tobago	17.66	15.2	Guyana	1.059	1.027
Ghana	15.78	13.4	Mali	1.055	1.365
Turkey	15.58	14.1			
			Tanzania	1.034	1.063
Korea	15.40	12.6	Ecuador	1.002	0.978
Kenya	14.43	12.2	Jamaica	0.993	1.031
Peru	14.18	13.7	Argentina	0.973	1.098
Tanzania	13.86	11.1	Costa Rica	0.970	0.813
Ecuador	13.42	12.9			
			Venezuela	0.958	0.971

Taxes as Per Cent of GNP			Index of Tax Effort		
	1969–71[2]	1966–68		1969–71[3]	1966–68
India	13.39	12.2	Burundi	0.946	0.863
Argentina	13.38	13.3	Thailand	0.925	0.996
Singapore	13.21	11.8	Iran	0.913	0.972
Mali	13.16	13.4	Colombia	0.901	0.803
Costa Rica	13.11	12.4			
			Peru	0.874	0.923
Colombia	12.47	10.6	Paraguay	0.867	0.801
Thailand	12.42	12.4	Trinidad and		
Burundi	11.45	10.4	Tobago	0.834	0.701
Honduras	11.31	10.5	Upper Volta	0.817	1.183
Togo	11.28	9.5	Honduras	0.800	0.752
Lebanon	11.24	10.9	Singapore	0.796	0.752
Paraguay	10.89	9.7	Lebanon	0.782	0.858
Upper Volta	10.33	11.4	Togo	0.739	0.706
Indonesia	10.05	6.9	Pakistan[4]	0.728	0.752
Philippines	9.12	9.1	Ethiopia	0.705	0.783
Pakistan	8.76	8.3[5]	Philippines	0.683	0.771
Ethiopia	8.61	8.6	Indonesia	0.658	0.618
Bolivia	8.24	8.7	Guatemala	0.618	0.647
Guatemala	7.93	7.9	Rwanda	0.602	0.704
Rwanda	7.89	8.3	Mexico	0.490	0.771
Mexico	7.11	6.8	Bolivia	0.459	0.538
Nepal	4.45	3.2	Nepal	0.374	0.300

[1] As is well known, international comparisons of tax ratios are subject to limitations. Here it should be mentioned, in particular, that (a) in several cases local government tax revenues are not included, or could not be included in full and (b) in a few cases GDP figures have had to be used in the denominator. Where local tax revenues have not been covered, they are generally understood to be less than 10 per cent of the total.

[2] Ranked according to tax ratios.

[3] Ranked according to index of tax effort.

[4] On the basis of the tax ratio of 12 per cent in 1972–73, the present Pakistan's tax effort index works out to 1.028.

[5] Pakistan before partition.

Data: IMF Fiscal Affairs Department.

Regional variations in average tax ratios range from 17.9 per cent for Middle Eastern and North African countries to 12.7 per cent for those of Asia and the Far East. The Middle Eastern and North African countries also have higher than average income taxes and taxes on production, whereas tropical Africa is the most dependent on international trade taxes. The Asian and Far Eastern countries have the lowest average total tax ratio and also the lowest ratio of income taxes and of total direct taxes to GNP. The

TABLE 2. Sources of Tax Revenue in Selected Developing Countries (Data are for 1969–71; Figures are Per Cent of Total)

	Taxes on Income[1] (1)	Taxes on Property (2)	Poll and Personal Taxes (3)	Total Direct Taxes (Cols. 1 + 2 + 3)	Taxes on International Trade (4)	Import Taxes (4a)	Export Taxes and Other (4b)	Taxes on Production and Internal Transactions (5)	Total Indirect Taxes (Cols. 4 + 5)	Other Taxes (6)
Average	27.30	4.85	1.43	33.58	32.09	24.43	7.66	31.86	63.95	2.47
Bolivia	17.31	3.93	–	21.24	52.96	39.60	13.36	25.78	78.74	–
Brazil	13.21	0.41	–	13.61	7.42	3.44	3.98	67.13	74.55	11.83
Burundi	19.49	2.99	12.69	35.17	42.34	26.38	15.96	22.46	64.80	–
Chile	32.71	4.89	–	37.60	11.00	11.00	–	50.67	61.67	0.71
Republic of China	9.54	14.53	–	24.07	26.17	22.45	3.72	48.64	74.81	1.12
Colombia	34.60	9.04	–	43.64	19.93	15.42	4.51	26.51	46.44	9.92
Costa Rica	20.80	1.72	–	22.52	32.72	27.86	4.86	42.10	74.82	2.64
Ecuador	13.02	8.95	–	21.97	50.62	40.18	10.43	26.90	77.52	0.49
Egypt	23.12	3.24	–	26.36	31.32	31.32	–	34.87	66.19	7.45
Ethiopia	23.52	5.18	–	28.70	38.78	27.04	11.74	32.52	71.30	–
Ghana	21.39	1.77	–	23.16	46.68	15.07	31.61	30.16	76.84	–
Guatemala	12.80	5.37	–	18.17	30.61	25.60	5.01	51.22	81.83	–
Guyana	36.56	7.87	–	44.43	36.93	34.55	2.38	15.26	52.19	3.36
Honduras	27.08	3.11	–	30.19	32.05	23.83	8.22	37.76	69.81	–
India	18.65	7.81	–	26.46	11.34	8.91	2.43	62.20	73.54	–
Indonesia	40.63	–	–	40.63	32.51	25.42	7.09	26.86	59.37	–
Iran	73.61	–	–	73.61	18.32	17.77	0.55	7.16	25.48	0.90
Ivory Coast	15.37	3.68	–	19.05	56.83	37.84	18.99	20.24	77.07	3.88
Jamaica	45.63	6.10	–	51.73	22.43	22.43	–	25.81	48.24	–
Kenya	39.02	0.45	2.83	42.30	32.47	31.82	0.65	20.12	52.59	5.11
Korea	33.72[2]	3.81	–	37.53	12.27	12.27	–	49.77	62.04	0.43
Lebanon	12.78	12.50	–	25.36	44.46	36.47	7.99	30.16	74.62	–
Malaysia	28.55	0.48	–	29.03	36.27	24.83	11.44	19.53	55.80	15.17
Mali	9.90	1.02	16.18	27.10	26.87	19.76	7.11	32.91	59.78	13.12
Mexico	54.14	...	–	54.14	11.17	9.61	1.56	33.21	44.38	1.48
Morocco	22.62	4.55	–	27.17	18.01	16.10	1.91	52.51	70.52	2.29
Nepal	4.95	23.81	–	28.76	45.37	38.63	6.74	24.98	70.35	0.89
Pakistan	15.20	3.83	–	19.03	25.71	...	...	55.24	80.95	–
Paraguay	10.22	5.76	–	15.98	37.55	34.87	2.68	45.82	83.37	0.63
Peru	30.23	3.78	–	34.01	25.26	25.26	–	37.41	62.67	3.32
Philippines	28.65	4.39	...	33.04	24.36	19.52	4.84	41.28	65.64	1.31

	Taxes on Income[1] (1)	Taxes on Property (2)	Poll and Personal Taxes (3)	Total Direct Taxes (Cols. 1 + 2 + 3)	Taxes on International Trade (4)	Import Taxes (4a)	Export Taxes and Other (4b)	Taxes on Production and Internal Transactions (5)	Total Indirect Taxes (Cols. 4 + 5)	Other Taxes (6)
Rwanda	18.09	4.95	11.44	34.48	48.22	29.61	18.61	16.24	64.46	1.03
Senegal	21.73	5.04	3.59	30.36	47.29	41.87	5.42	21.87	69.16	0.48
Singapore	34.57	27.15	–	61.72	19.45	19.45	–	16.44	35.89	2.39
Sri Lanka	18.74	4.27	–	23.01	46.79	15.99	30,80	30.20	76.99	–
Sudan	9.73	1.07	–	10.80	54.34	39.76	14.58	34.85	89.19	–
Tanzania	28.12	0.08	5.05	33.25	33.60	29.46	4.14	29.09	62.69	4.05
Thailand	15.01	3.01	–	18.11	37.36	29.72	7.64	44.41	81.77	0.12
Togo	16.23	1.11	–	17.34	43.57	29.99	13.58	31.20	74.77	7.89
Trinidad and Tobago	56.30	6.78	–	63.08	19.78	19.78	–	17.13	36.91	–
Tunisia	29.91	3.63	1.66	35.20	9.59	6.13	3.46	52.42	62.01	2.76
Turkey	35.53	10.04	–	45.57	22.77	22.77	–	31.66	54.43	–
Upper Volta	13.92	2.36	12.45	28.73	53.96	49.82	4.14	17.03	70.99	0.28
Venezuela	83.37	0.48	–	83.85	7.16	6.28	0.87	8.98	16.14	–
Zaïre	25.20	1.22	–	26.42	66.04	24.28	41.26	7.25	73.29	0.29
Zambia	60.13	0.97	–	61.10	26.25	9.46	16.79	9.59	35.84	3.06

[1] Including royalties on minerals.
[2] Includes land tax.
Data: IMF Fiscal Affairs Department.

percentage variation between regions is least in the case of import taxes.

TAX EFFORT

The evaluation of tax effort or performance on the basis of a simple comparison of tax ratios fails to take account of the fact that some countries have a greater potential for raising taxes than others and can thus be said to have a greater taxable capacity. As a measure of tax performance the study calculated for each country an index of tax effort by dividing each country's actual tax ratio by a calculated or "predicted" ratio obtained by measuring, through regression analysis, the relative influence of major economic factors affecting the capacity to levy and pay taxes. The rationale behind this procedure is the assumption that the predicted tax ratio represents that ratio which the given country would achieve if it had used its capacity to the average extent. It was hypothesized that the average level of income, the degree of "openness" of the economy, and the composition of gross domestic product (GDP) would each have a significant impact on the taxable capacity of a country. It was found that the share of mining in GDP was the most significant factor affecting tax ratios in developing countries and it seemed appropriate to use it to represent the composition of income. The ratio of exports to GNP basically determined their relative capacity to import taxable goods and hence the size of the foreign trade

TABLE 3. Regional Variations in Levels of Taxation (Per Cent of GNP, for Selected Developing Countries in 1969–71)

	Taxes on Income[1]	Taxes on Property	Poll and Personal Taxes	Total Direct Taxes	Taxes on International Trade	Taxes on Production and Internal Transactions	Total Indirect Taxes	Total Taxes
Middle East and North Africa	5.63	0.77	0.05	6.45	4.80	6.23	11.03	17.90
Tropical Africa	4.34	0.34	0.57	5.25	6.92	3.18	10.10	15.79
South America	4.96	0.62	–	5.59	3.36	5.86	9.22	15.05
Central America and the Caribbean	5.43	0.74	–	6.17	3.95	3.98	7.93	14.27
Asia and the Far East	2.99	0.98	–	3.94	3.65	4.89	8.54	12.87
Average for the sample	4.49	0.68	0.17	5.32	4.68	4.56	9.23	15.10

[1] Including royalties on minerals.
[2] Excluding social security contributions.
Data: IMF Fiscal Affairs Department.

sector; so it was chosen as a proxy for the degree of "openness" of the economy. The tax effort equation was formulated to include as explanatory factors the per capita nonexport income, the share of mining in GDP, and the ratio of nonmineral exports to GNP.

It should be noted that for conceptual reasons (explained in the original study) and because of limitations inherent in the data used, due caution must be exercised in interpreting the tax effort indices. Furthermore, it is not intended here to convey the idea that there is economic merit in a high level of taxation as such, regardless of other circumstances and factors.

It was found that, generally, countries with above average tax ratios (above 15.01 per cent) have tax effort indices that are above unity, and vice versa. Of the 12 countries with tax ratios above 19 per cent, six– Brazil, Egypt, Ivory Coast, Malaysia, Tunisia, and Zaïre–are among those with the highest indices of tax effort. The high tax ratios exhibited by these countries may be attributed partly to above-average tax effort. But there are several exceptions to the rule: Iran, Jamaica, and Venezuela all have high tax ratios but have tax effort indices of less than one. Futhermore, some countries with tax effort indices above unity are able to achieve only modest tax ratios. Of the countries with tax ratios below 10 per cent, all have tax effort indices below 0.710.

V.C.3. Taxation of Agriculture—Note

Some reference has already been made to the taxation of agriculture, but since it can play so critical a role in accelerating development it merits special attention. Although a large proportion of the population is still engaged in subsistence agriculture, and a high proportion of the national output comes from this sector, the tax system in most of the newly developing countries has tended to place the main burden of taxation on the monetized or market sector. Taxes that are levied on the subsistence sector are undoubtedly more difficult to administer, and they are bound to be politically unpopular. When, however, a disproportionate share of taxation falls on the market sector, it may adversely affect the country's rate of development by reducing both the sources and incentives to saving. And unless the agricultural sector is taxed in order to expand the "agricultural surplus," the growth of the nonagricultural sector may be retarded. As development proceeds, the proportion of the working population engaged in nonfood production increases; to make this possible, the marketable surplus from agriculture must also rise—that is, the proportion of food produced in the agricultural sector which is not consumed by the food producers must increase and be transferred to the nonagricultural sector. To accomplish this requires either taxes in money which impel greater deliveries to market, taxes in kind or compulsory sales to the government, or a deterioration in the terms of trade of the agricultural sector vis-á-vis the nonagricultural sector. This is the same problem that we discussed previously in connection with the Lewis model (III.D): the growth of the demand for labor in the nonagricultural sector is dependent upon an increase in the supply of food which goes to the market.

Taxation of the agricultural sector may also serve as an important policy instrument in underdeveloped countries: the incentive and distributional use of taxation may be utilized to redirect agricultural production, encourage the more efficient use of the land, accomplish changes in land tenure, promote new productive investment in agriculture, and stimulate movement of redundant labor from agriculture to nonagriculture employment.

Although taxes may be used for such nonfiscal purposes as bringing idle lands into production and breaking up large landed estates, some tax specialists have argued that

the best approach to land taxation for most poor countries is to focus directly on the objective of revenue, not on various refinements intended to improve the allocation of resources within the agricultural sector or the private distribution of incomes in rural areas. These other objectives are valid but less important than achieving an effective land tax in the circumstances of most, though not all, developing countries. Attempts to achieve them are likely to confuse the main issue [of establishing a solidly based simple property tax with meaningful rates] and to make its attainment more difficult.... The most essential requirement for any effective land tax system is a land registry, preferably centralized; in addition, all land taxes except the simplest land area tax also require a clearly established and effective valuation procedure.[1]

Various types of taxes on land, agricultural produce or agricultural incomes are possible. One of the oldest forms of taxation is an annual tax on land. Such a tax, expressed for instance as a percentage of the

[1] Richard M. Bird, "Agricultural Taxation in Developing Countries," *Finance and Development,* September 1974, pp. 42–3.

value of the produce per acre, may be objected to as being regressive in its incidence, but the tax could be made progressive on the owners of larger size holdings. If it were based on the potential productivity of the land, a land tax might also be used to promote improved methods of cultivation. Professor Stephen R. Lewis, Jr., has emphasized that

with increased concern about questions of income distribution and employment, the land tax takes on some added significance. A tax on the value of agricultural land would raise the cost of not using land most productively relative to labor and capital, and would encourage more intensive land use. This would especially affect larger landowners who may be underutilizing land and who would have added reason (with an effective land tax) either to cultivate more intensively themselves or to increase the tenant population on their lands.

There are considerable problems in introducing progressivity into systems of land taxation, as is well known. However, some form of land tax progressivity would be most desirable from the point of view of its employment effects, its complementarity to land reform policy and its effects on equity. Recent papers on Pakistan and Colombia, as well as numerous earlier studies, point to the desirability of increasing the rate of tax as size of holdings increases, but there are always problems in combining a tax on land with a tax on persons. Some variant on the type of "agricultural income tax" which is used in parts of the South Asian subcontinent may be appropriate. This tax is in effect a progressive surtax on land tax paid. The rate of "agricultural income tax" (which is of course misnamed) rises as the total amount of land tax paid by any single reporting unit increases. To ensure effective enforcement, it would be necessary to combine a progressive land tax surcharge system with that of the income tax, thus making some crosschecks available with another system of collection and helping to ensure that ownership was translated into taxable spending or income units.

Despite a fairly widespread agreement on the desirable features of some kind of tax on agricultural land related not to actual but to potential value of output there has certainly been no comparable widespread move to introduce or to improve land tax systems. The fundamental problems are political, though there are also some major administrative problems in countries that do not have established land records and surveys. However, the administrative problems are worth trying to overcome if one thinks of a reasonable time horizon for tax reforms and for establishment of an enduring system of taxation. With the alarming increase of population pressure on land, the virtues of a land tax, especially one in which progressivity can be included, are worth the initial administrative outlays.[2]

If the marketing system is controlled by the government, another possibility is to levy produce taxes. When the government buys an agricultural crop and sells it through official markets at fixed prices, it can pay the seller the price net of tax, and collect the actual tax later from the buyer (a wholesaler or other intermediary). This type of tax, however, is difficult to administer when prices are not controlled; nor can it readily make allowances for differences in family status or for costs of production, or be levied at other than proportional rates.

In general, the taxation of agriculture is easier when plantation agriculture prevails or native farmers are producing cash crops for export. Where a large proportion of total produce is exported, the government can tax agriculturists through export levies, or can

[2] Stephen R. Lewis, Jr., "Agricultural Taxation and Inter-Sectoral Resource Transfers," *Food Research Institute Studies in Agricultural Economics, Trade, and Development,* Vol. 12, No. 2, 1973, pp. 108–9.

force savings through the operation of a state agricultural marketing board that pays the producers less than the international prices received by the board. A serious drawback of export taxation is the possible disincentive effect on export production, and the taxation may cause a shift of productive effort from exports to production for the home market.

In the absence of a land tax or income tax, the rural sector can be taxed indirectly through consumption taxes on commodities from the nonagricultural sector. By turning the terms of trade against farmers, these taxes may tend to increase the marketed surplus of agricultural products. Again, however, the scope for this type of taxation is still limited in most developing countries.

Considering the obstacles connected with a land tax or produce taxes, some economists have suggested that the most practicable way to tax income arising in agriculture is to develop a form of personal tax or "simple" income tax.[3] This may prove useful for taxing people with incomes below the exemption level of a proper income tax and for reaching subsistence agriculture and the production of output for the domestic market.

Such a tax was effectively utilized in Uganda. Known as the graduated tax, the Uganda tax was administered as follows. Local tax authorities first drew up a list of the main sources of income and wealth in the area (crops, cattle, trading, transport, wages, salaries, etc.). Calculations were then made of the taxable capacity of different types of income or income-yielding assets. In the case of a crop such as coffee, for instance, each tree was assumed to yield a certain income for the year. This yield was placed somewhat below the level that could be achieved by an average farmer on average

land, so as to encourage output. Corresponding values were placed on the other sources of income or potential income, so that the income of individual taxpayers could be aggregated. Rates of tax were then imposed, and these were graduated for broad income categories.

This sort of tax has several distinctive features: it provides direct taxation on individuals who are too poor and illiterate to be taxed through a proper income tax; it can be based on a measure of the individual's taxable capacity rather than on only his money income; it can take account of factors that influence taxable capacity such as the possession of assets and the consumption of unmarketed produce; its revenue is more stable than would be a tax that is assessed wholly on agricultural produce; it can provide incentives to make farming improvements (through the setting of standard unit rates of return above which all production is tax free); and its assessment does not require the taxpayer to make out a complicated tax declaration but can be levied simply and inexpensively by local assessment committees.

None of the foregoing taxes is free of administrative and political problems. At present a variety of fiscal instruments is used to tax agriculture directly: taxes on land area, on land value, on net income; marketing taxes, export taxes, land transfer taxes, and special assessments; taxation through marketing boards, and exchange rates that implicitly "tax" the exporter through maintenance of an overvalued domestic currency. Notwithstanding the variety of tax techniques, two features dominate agricultural taxation: the level of agricultural taxation in most LDCs is still low, and export taxes remain the most important source of government revenue from agriculture. This can be noted in Table 1 (below).

It is clear that if the government is to succeed in raising the level of agricultural taxation, more consideration must be given to

[3] Cf. David Walker, "Taxation and Taxable Capacity in Underdeveloped Countries," in E. F. Jackson (ed.), *Economic Development in Africa*, Oxford, 1965, pp. 142–6.

TABLE 1. The Pattern of Agricultural Taxation

Share of Total Tax Receipts Produced by Agricultural Taxes	Number of Countries Having a Given Type of Tax				Total Direct Agricultural Taxes
	Personal	Export	Land	Other	
Less than 4 per cent	9	27	26	3	15
5 to 9 per cent	4	13	18	0	20
10 to 20 per cent	4	16	4	0	23
Over 20 per cent	2	2	0	0	11
Number of countries in sample	19	58	48	3	69

Source: Richard M. Bird, *Taxing Agricultural Land in Developing Countries* (Cambridge, Mass.: Harvard University Press, 1974), p. 32.

reform of agricultural taxation—with less reliance on export taxes because of their disincentive effects and the instability of the revenues which they produce, and with more reliance on heavier taxes on agricultural land.

V.C.4. Public Finance and Inequality*

Traditionally, the fiscal system has been considered, as a recent Colombian plan put it, "the most effective and least disruptive instrument of the State for bringing about better distribution" (*Guidelines for a New Strategy,* National Planning Department, 1972). For decades it has been a common, if often merely implicit, assumption of economists that any unwelcome effects on distribution resulting from other government policies or from the general course of economic growth could be readily corrected by means of the fiscal system. Not only has the fiscal system been thought of as the supreme equalizer of public policy, but it is also commonly considered to be used extensively for this purpose, at least in the industrial countries. This fiscal redistribution is assumed to take place both through progressive income taxes (which take relatively larger shares from the rich than from the poor) and through expenditure programs which transfer income to the poor and provide them with proportionately larger benefits from free government services.

Recently, however, increasing doubt has been expressed about the efficacy of the fiscal system as an instrument of redistribution. For example, Mahbub ul Haq of the World Bank referred in a recent speech ("Employment in the 1970's: A New Perspective," *International Development Review,* December 1971) to the prevalence of "misguided faith in the fiscal systems of the developing countries and a fairly naive understanding of the interplay of economic and political institutions." Until recently this misguided faith was taken to justify the preoccupation of development economists with growth policies to the neglect of income distribution policies. "We know now," Mr. Haq went on, "that the coverage of

*From Richard M. Bird, "Public Finance and Inequality," *Finance and Development,* March 1974, pp. 2–4. Reprinted by permission.

these fiscal systems is generally narrow and difficult to extend." It is thus coming to be the new conventional wisdom that the fiscal systems of developing countries have not done much to alter the distribution of incomes generated by the economic system—and, indeed, that they cannot do much.

Two reasons have been offered in support of this distributional pessimism. The first is that only a relatively small part of the national income in most developing countries is channeled through the fiscal system so that its potential as a redistributor is inherently limited. The second is that, because extensive direct income transfers are impractical in poor countries, the major task of redistribution falls on the tax system, but the tax systems in most poor countries are not, in fact, progressive. On the contrary, they are either *regressive* (that is, fall relatively more heavily on the poor) or exhibit, at best, a sort of wandering proportionality from income class to income class. Furthermore, it is generally argued, this failure to tax the rich more heavily than the poor is not offset on the side of public expenditures by policies which tend to spend more on those things which benefit the poor rather than the rich. In fact, some studies indicate that, at least in some countries, most of the benefits from public expenditure accrue to the better-off section of society, thus accentuating the general ineffectiveness, or even perversity, of the fiscal system as a means of correcting the distribution of income and wealth.

This picture is indeed a somber one. Fortunately, however, this pessimism is only partly supported by the facts. In the first place, quite a few developing countries, such as Brazil and Tunisia, collect 20 per cent or more of the national income in taxes. These countries would thus appear to have substantial scope for redistributing income through the fiscal system if they chose to do so. On the other hand, it is true that many other countries, ranging from India to Guatemala, collect a considerably smaller proportion of the national income in taxes, and thus, on

the face of matters, would find it more difficult to alter substantially the general pattern of income distribution through fiscal means. Even in these cases, however, it would, in theory, be possible to reduce inequality significantly by taxing the rich—although this would in itself do very little to help improve the lot of the poor since taxes can only make the rich poorer, not the poor richer. This brings us back to the second reason for distributional pessimism noted above: the observed regressivity of the fiscal systems in developing countries.

Here again, the facts do not appear quite as gloomy as some seem to believe. A recent intensive review in the Fund of the large number of studies on the distributional impact of fiscal systems in developing countries suggests that the great variation within the developing world makes it very difficult to generalize about the progressivity or regressivity of taxes. About half of the tax incidence studies examined (in total there were 67 studies covering 23 countries) indicated that the tax system was at least mildly progressive, with the remainder exhibiting proportionality or even regressivity over some ranges of the income distribution. Although the incidence of expenditure systems has been less studied (13 studies for 9 countries) the results were again mixed, with half of the studies suggesting a regressive (which means pro-poor in this case) pattern and the remainder more or less proportionality. It should be remembered, however, that even a high degree of *relative* favoritism for the poor in expenditures may still mean that far less is spent on them than on the rich in *absolute* per capita terms. It is the latter which is important so far as redressing unequal income distribution is concerned, and one might in fact argue that *more* in absolute terms must be spent on the poor than on the rich if public expenditure policy is to be truly equalizing in its effects. No country examined came even close to meeting this standard.

Although the conceptual and statistical bases of these studies of tax and expenditure incidence leave a great deal to be desired, it can at least be concluded that the available evidence provides no reason for believing that the fiscal system in developing countries is inevitably regressive and ineffective as a means of distributing income. On the contrary, at least in the more advanced of the developing countries—in which the size of the government budget also tends to be relatively greater—there appears to be considerable scope for affecting distribution through the fiscal system if the countries want to do so.

TAXATION AND RESOURCE ALLOCATION

Rather than throwing up one's hands in despair, then, it seems worthwhile to look a little more closely at how tax and expenditure policy can be used to affect the distribution of income and wealth in a developing country. The first point to note in this respect is that the implicit taxes and subsidies which are introduced into the economy of many countries by fiscal (and other) policies which distort relative prices may well be more important than the explicit taxes and expenditures which appear in the budget. In countries with considerable unemployment, for example, payroll taxes which raise the private cost of employing workers above the social cost may lead to fewer workers being employed in the modern sector than would otherwise be the case. Similarly, exemptions from customs duties for imported capital equipment, especially in countries with overvalued exchange rates, tend to maintain the cost of capital at artificially low levels and to encourage the relative expansion of capital-intensive lines of production, particularly by the larger firms which have easier access to import licenses and foreign suppliers' credits and which tend anyway to use less labor per unit of capital. Furthermore, tax and other incentive policies which induce more investment through lower capital prices will tend, simultaneously, to reduce the desired level of utilization of existing capital equipment

(which depends in part on the relative prices of capital and labor), and hence will further reduce employment.

The misallocation of resources resulting from such capital-favoring policies has recently received much attention in countries concerned, as are most developing countries, with an excessive and growing amount of open urban unemployment. The substantial distributional implications have not been so commonly noted although it is clear that policies which tend to lower the price of capital and raise the price paid to labor will tend, perhaps paradoxically, to increase the inequality of the distribution of income earned through work through their effects on employment and the choice of technology. A reversal of such policies will thus tend to reduce inequality. In short, in countries where fiscal policies have artificially fostered economic growth by lowering the relative price of capital below that which should prevail in the light of the scarcity of capital and the abundance of unskilled labor, a reversal of these policies should have substantial and beneficial allocative and distributive effects. Indeed, this appears to be one of the few instances in development economics in which one can, so it seems, have one's cake and eat it too.

One way in which tax and expenditure policy may affect the distribution of income and wealth is thus through policies which affect employment and the relative rewards received by labor and capital and which thus alter the pattern of economic activity and the distribution of income and wealth generated by that activity: this may be called *primary redistribution.* The effect of taxes on the structure of industry and the demand for unskilled labor may well be the single most important distributional aspect of tax policy in developing countries.

TAXING WEALTH

A second way in which tax policy can alter this initially-generated distribution is through the taxation of wealth. It is true that taking away wealth from the few, however wealthy, and giving it to the many, however poor, would not in most developing countries have much visible impact on the well-being of most people, given the relative numbers in the two groups. However, this is, in a sense, irrelevant since the primary aim of taxing wealth—in addition to encouraging the more efficient utilization of capital—is not to make the poor richer but to make the rich less powerful. One relevant point of particular interest in many developing countries is that an effective land tax will in itself tend to have an initial primary redistributive impact through reducing land prices. A more important point is that heavier taxes on wealth (or on income from capital) *must* be imposed to offset the effects on incomes of the higher returns to owners of capital—the rich—which would result from those policies designed to raise the relative price of capital to its true scarcity value in poor countries. If this is not done, the presumably undesirable distributional impact of making wealthy capitalists wealthier will have to be counted as a partial counter-balance to the poverty-relieving effect of increasing employment through more rational factor pricing.

There are, of course, well-known limitations in most countries on the political and administrative feasibility of land taxes, net wealth taxes, and death taxes. There is also some possibility of adversely affecting savings, though the importance of this effect is generally greatly exaggerated: there are few other taxes which can tap the same segments of the population with less adverse impact than wealth taxes. Although the impact of wealth taxation will no doubt usually be minor, on the whole it seems clear that those who wish to use the fiscal system for redistributive purposes should pay much closer attention to the role of wealth taxation, both as a means of redistribution in itself and as a support for such more direct approaches to the problem as land reform and more rational factor prices.

TAXING INCOME

The other approach to fiscal redistribution, and a more traditional focus for fiscal discussion, is to redistribute income after it has been initially distributed by the workings of the economic system: this may be called *secondary redistribution.* Conventionally, it is argued that the major instrument which should be used for this purpose is a global progressive personal income tax. Unfortunately, in many developing countries this tax is neither global in coverage (since many forms of income escape effective taxation), nor (for that reason) particularly progressive nor, indeed, really on personal income. In fact, the income tax in practice all too often amounts to a tax on certain forms of earned income, with only scattered coverage (largely through presumptive assessments) of many of the other forms of income—rents, dividends, interest, profits—which accrue particularly to the better-off groups in society.

In the political and administrative circumstances of many developing countries, an attempt to levy a truly effective personal income tax may in fact end up by imposing a still heavier burden on income from labor while continuing to fail to reach income from property effectively. The same degree of failure in attempts to tax wealth—if one may speak in this very relative fashion—is likely to lead to much better results, both distributionally and allocatively. While the potential of the income tax to produce significant revenues over the long run should not be neglected, it would thus be a mistake to rely solely upon it to correct all distributional ills. In many countries, progressive taxes on consumption combined with wealth taxes may prove as good or better for this purpose.

THE ATTACK ON POVERTY

More generally, as noted above, taxes cannot make the poor richer, which is, after all, the main concern of distributional policy. Even the complete removal of all taxes on the poorest members of society would not make them much better off, simply because of the low *absolute* amounts of income and tax involved. Furthermore, many of the poorest people, particularly those in rural areas, take part only marginally in the economic life of the country and are thus little affected by taxes. While the regressivity of the tax system, where it exists, ought to be reduced as much as possible in order not to make things worse, it is clear that, if our main concern is with poverty as such, with the waste and misuse of human resources and the stunted opportunities in life afforded those with incomes below some minimum level, any fiscal corrective must be exercised primarily through the expenditure side of the budget.

Two major points may be mentioned on the effects of public spending on distribution in developing countries. First, expenditures on health, education, and similar government activities related directly to the well-being of individuals can clearly be so directed as to benefit most the poorer members of society. The fact that in some countries it appears that education expenditures have in reality helped most those who need it least—for example, by subsidizing university education for the children of the well-to-do—does not affect this conclusion. What it does do is reinforce the importance of being *selective* and of paying careful and close attention to the precise nature of expenditures if one is concerned with the distributional impact. It is obvious, for example, that money spent on primary education in the rural areas will do more to benefit the poor than the same amount spent on university education in the capital city. The poor, like the rich, are by no means a homogeneous group, and policies designed to help particular subgroups of the poor will need, as a rule, to be selective and often localized in their incidence.

V.D. FINANCIAL DEVELOPMENT

V.D.1. Financial Structure and Economic Development*

During economic development, as their incomes per capita increase, countries usually experience more rapid growth in financial assets than in national wealth or national product.[1] During the past century and a half, this has been true for the United States. Financial assets there were only about one-half the level of national wealth in the early 1880's, but they have been considerably larger than real wealth in recent years. Financial assets have grown much faster than gross national product in the United States: the ratio increased from about unity at the beginning of the last century to 4.5 now.

Japan has had a similar experience. There the ratio of financial assets to real wealth rose from perhaps 10 percent in 1885 to over 150 percent in recent years. In the Soviet Union, this ratio moved up from 10 percent in 1928 to 35 percent a few years ago. Financial growth in excess of real growth is apparently a common phenomenon around the world.

In somewhat rougher outline, this same picture is revealed by comparison among

*From John G. Gurley and Edward S. Shaw, "Financial Development and Economic Development," *Economic Development and Cultural Change,* Vol. 15, No. 3, April 1967, pp. 257–65, 267–8. Reprinted by permission.

[1] The measurements we use for relative growth in financial assets, tangible assets, and income are based consistently on nominal values except when deflated values are mentioned explicitly. Financial assets include all intangible assets—claims against both nonfinancial spending units (primary securities) and financial institutions (indirect securities). . . .

countries at any moment of time. Countries that are poor in income per capita generally have very low ratios of financial to real wealth. The present ratio in Afghanistan and Ethiopia, for instance, is probably little higher than 10 or 15 percent, comparable to the Japanese ratio in 1885 but lower than the ratio in the United States 150 years ago. The ratio is somewhat higher, from 30 to 60 percent, in more prosperous countries such as Argentina, Brazil, Guatemala, Mexico, the Republic of Korea, Venezuela, and Yugoslavia. India, though less developed than most of these countries, has a financial ratio of around 35 percent. In still more highly developed countries, the proportion of financial to real wealth often lies in the range of 80 to 100 percent. France, Israel, West Germany, and several other countries are in this range. However, the Soviet Union has a low financial ratio for its income per capita, about 35 percent, while Japan (150 percent), Switzerland (over 200 percent), and the United Kingdom (215 percent) have exceptionally high ones.

At the present time, national stocks of financial assets vary from 10 to more than 200 percent of national real wealth. As the foregoing examples suggest, differences in income per capita go a long way toward explaining this variety of financial experience. The United States does have a higher financial ratio than France, France than Mexico, and Mexico than Afghanistan. Over time, for any one country as its income per capita increases, financial assets rise relative to national real wealth.

REASONS FOR SECULARLY RISING
FINANCIAL RATIOS

The relationship between growth in financial assets and growth in real wealth and income per capita may be analyzed in various ways. For example, financial development depends on division of labor that is feasible only in the context of real development. Again, financial development depends on conditions of demand for and supply of financial assets that are sensitive to real development. We consider each of these approaches in this section.

Finance and self-sufficiency are antonyms: Robinson Crusoes do not accumulate debt and financial assets. Finance is associated with division of labor in three senses: (1) division of labor in production that involves exchange of factor services and outputs implies lending and borrowing. In primitive market economies, these financial transactions are in kind. Subsequently, the diseconomies of finance-in-kind induce monetization. It seems to be the general rule that the pace of monetization exceeds the pace of real growth in diminishing degree. There is everywhere a limit, in terms of real wealth and income per capita, beyond which the stock of means of payment grows in step with wealth and income or even less rapidly. When money payments are ubiquitous, the ratio of money to income or of money to wealth hovers near to its secular peak.

In the United States, the ratio of the money supply to gross national product was only 7 percent in 1805. It doubled by 1850 and doubled again by 1900. Thereafter, the money-income ratio has shown no strong trend up or down: it is still around 30 percent. A similar pattern appears in cross-section comparisons. On the basis of data for 70 countries since World War II, one observes that the money-income ratio varies from approximately 10 percent or less in the poorest countries to 20 percent in countries with gross national product per capita of about $300. Then the rise in the ratio is retarded, though it continues to 30 percent and a little more.

(2) Finance is associated with division of labor between saving and investment. Where it is one sector in the community that releases factors of production from consumer goods industries and another sector that absorbs such factors into accumulation of real capital, financial assets and debt accumulate in both monetary and nonmonetary form. The rate of accumulation depends on the mix of techniques for transferring savings to investment.

This division of labor leads to issues of primary securities by ultimate borrowers (investors) and to acquisitions of financial assets by ultimate lenders (savers). In between lie the markets on which primary securities are bought and sold. During the growth process, the division of labor between saving and investing becomes more intricate, and this institutional evolution implies more rapid accumulation of primary debt and financial assets than of real wealth. Financial accumulation falls into step with real accumulation when the institutional evolution approaches its limit. Similarly, factor inputs of the financial sector increase more rapidly for a time than inputs of other sectors, but balanced growth of inputs comes eventually.

Primary security issues approximate 1 or 2 percent of gross national product in the poorer countries. The ratio generally lies within the range of 10 to 15 percent in wealthier countries. A similar contrast emerges from data for the United States: the issues-income ratio was apparently small during the early years of the nineteenth century, but it rose to more than 10 percent by the close of the century, and there it remains. During the nineteenth century in the United States, the stock of primary securities more than doubled relative to national wealth and income, and then changed little after 1900.

(3) There is division of labor in a third sense that promotes growth in both quantity and variety of financial assets. Specialization

develops between saving and ownership of primary securities. Financial intermediaries solicit savings, paying a deposit rate for them, and assume responsibility for savings allocation, charging a primary rate of interest to ultimate borrowers. The spread between the primary rate and the deposit rate compensates for factor costs and risks in intermediation. This spread shrinks during financial development. In combination with shifts in savers' tastes among financial assets, the relative rise in the deposit rate induces layering of indirect debt upon primary debt and growth in total financial assets of savers relative to national income and wealth.

There are countries which develop a comparative advantage in intermediation. They import primary securities and export indirect debt, earning the spread between the primary rate of interest and the deposit rate. Countries with a comparative disadvantage in intermediation prefer smaller factor inputs for the domestic financial sector. Exporters of intermediation have relatively high and rising ratios of total financial assets to income and wealth, but their portfolios of indirect financial assets follow a rising trend.

Stocks of nonmonetary indirect financial assets, including both domestic and foreign claims, rise almost without let-up during the development process. They were a negligible fraction of gross national product in the United States at the beginning of the nineteenth century. They rose almost continuously from that time, reaching 35 percent of gross national product by 1900 and 60 percent in the last few years. Cross-section data have very much the same story to tell: time and savings deposits, which comprise the bulk of nonmonetary indirect assets, are only 1 or 2 percent of gross national product in the poorest countries, 10 percent in countries with national products per capita of about $300 to $400, and 40 or 50 percent in the richer nations.

We have seen that financial assets accumulate as income and wealth grow. Our suggestion is that such accumulation reflects division of labor in production, saving and investment, and intermediation. Specialization in the use of productive factors generates a rising stream of income and a rising stock of both real and financial wealth.

The coincidence and interaction of real and financial growth can be explained also in terms of supply and demand conditions on real and financial markets. The income elasticity of savings is greater than unity at low levels of income, and the savings elasticity of demand for financial assets *en masse* seems to remain above unity as income rises. Though the secular decline in the real rate of interest that accompanies development tends to depress saving, trends in both explicit and implicit returns on financial assets and particularly on indirect financial assets stimulate portfolio demands. These trends can be attributed to technological change, to economies of scale, and sometimes to regulatory controls on markets for financial assets. Briefly, both income and price phenomena associated with real development stimulate finance.

The retroactive impact of finance upon the real world need not be explored carefully here. Anything that the financial sector does to accelerate savings, improve their allocation to investment, and economize costs in transmitting savings to investment implies an increase both in its own flows and stocks of financial assets and in flows and stocks of real output.

There are degrees and kinds of differences in national financial systems that cannot be explained by differences in income and wealth. . . .

ALTERNATIVE TECHNIQUES FOR MOBILIZING THE ECONOMIC SURPLUS

The principal reason for dissimilar financial structure at given national levels of income and wealth is that there are alternative techniques for mobilizing the economic surplus—for eliciting savings and allocating them to investment. The financial technique, or the debt-asset system, is only one method. Each of the other techniques is a substitute for it.

In its full detail, the list of alternative processes for putting saving to the service of selected investment is very long. However, the list may be compressed into two major classes: processes of internal finance and processes of external finance. In the former, the investor draws on his own savings. In the latter, the investor draws on the savings of others.

Internal finance itself comprises two principal techniques: self-finance and taxation. In self-finance, savings are put at the investors' disposal by adjustments in relative prices on commodity and factor markets and on markets for foreign exchange. The taxation technique employs taxes and other non-market alternatives to channel savings to the state for either governmental or private investment. Within external finance, the debt-asset system is the technique for mobilizing domestic savings. In addition, savings from abroad may be supplied by gift or loan, on the initiative of either private or governmental sources.

We condense the long list of alternative processes to four: self-finance and taxation, as internal finance processes; the debt-asset system and foreign aid, as external finance processes. This section has to do mainly with internal finance, but there are first a few comments on external finance to bring out the contrast between processes.

External Finance

The debt-asset system for mobilizing domestic savings depends upon and encourages division of labor between savers and investors, as well as between savers and intermediaries. It belongs in the context of decentralized decision-making, of market organization, of dependence upon relative prices to guide economic behavior. Market rates of interest, as one class of relative prices, bear a heavy responsibility for the rate and direction of investment.

The issue and accumulation of government debt is a component of the debt-asset system. It draws private savings through security markets and intermediaries to both private and governmental uses. The stock of government debt has a role to play in portfolio diversification that affects deeply the performance of the debt-asset system.

Internal Finance

The processes of internal finance—self-finance and taxation—are substitutes for the debt-asset system. Each of them involves more centralization of decision-making, less specialization between savers and investors. Each of them leads to a less elaborate financial structure.

Self-finance. The processes of self-finance involve adjustment in terms of trade on commodity, factor and foreign-exchange markets—"opening the scissors," as Paul Baran would have said, of relative prices to the advantage of an investing sector, forcing involuntary savings upon other sectors. These adjustments in relative prices may be imposed by government, socialist or capitalist, at a stable price level. They may be induced by government through inflation of the price level. They may be imposed by private investors with monopoly power on some commodity or factor market. The processes of self-finance can operate through socialist central planning, monopoly or state-directed capitalism, or inflation. . . .

Socialist extraction of savings depends upon prices paid and received by state enterprise, to a lesser extent upon taxation, and in minor degree upon accumulation by private savers of financial claims, including money, against the state. Private solicitation of savings for investment in private capital, including consumer durables, is unimportant, though expansion of consumer credit is to be anticipated. Allocation of savings according to plan can be achieved by simple transfers to state enterprise on the records of the state bank.

Socialist centralism foregoes most of the division of labor that we have stressed as one basis for relatively high finance-income ratios. Saving and investment are generated principally within the state sector, so that market transfers of savings at explicit rates of interest are as unnecessary as they are distasteful in socialist doctrine. Demand for financial assets in other sectors is depressed by constraints on personal income and wealth. It is depressed, too, because the state undertakes to supply various services for which people save in capitalist societies, because private bequests are minimized, and because reduced private risks imply reduced precautionary portfolios. Under these circumstances of demand and supply, there is little occasion for markets in either primary or indirect securities. Moreover, because of pressure for internal development, there has not been significant accumulation by socialist societies of financial claims abroad, and there has been no industry of financial intermediaries to export its services.

The process of socialist centralism reduces the dependence of economic units on a financial structure; contact is made less through financial markets and financial institutions and more through planning bureaus and other central coordinating devices; the order of the day is internal finance and balanced budgets, not external finance and the issue of new securities. The theory and design of socialist society are incompatible with relatively high ratios of financial assets to income and wealth.

Manipulation of the terms of trade between agriculture and industry, whether under socialism or capitalism, is a case of self-finance. It has been the socialist view that a preindustrial society could not mobilize its surplus effectively without collectivization of peasant farming. Only then could prices of agriculture be reduced relatively for the benefit of industrial investment. Or, as one knows from American experience, the scis-

sors can be opened in the farmer's behalf to increase his savings for his investment in agricultural capital.

Factor prices are an obvious target for techniques of self-finance. Peasant migration to the city depresses real wage rates and raises real profit rates, with the consequence that industry has access to flows of new finance for its own capital. Controls on rates charged by public utilities under foreign ownership can extract involuntary savings from abroad.

Overvaluation of domestic currency on the foreign exchanges may transfer real income from an exporting sector, with taste for imports of consumption goods or of foreign financial assets, to an importing sector that is accumulating plant and equipment. Depending upon relevant elasticities of demand and supply, overvaluation can also appropriate foreign savings for domestic use.

Inflation is a technique of self-finance. Because of its impact on relative prices, relative incomes, and relative wealth positions, inflation appeals to "structuralists" as a temporarily necessary alternative in some retarded societies where relative prices tend to move perversely for purposes of growth and where other techniques of mobilizing and allocating savings are underdeveloped. In the theory of structuralism, stagnation is the alternative if inflation is not used to generate savings among spending units with investment opportunities. The "cost-push" variant of structuralist doctrine accepts inflation as a corrective for relative-price distortions that tend to reduce the flow of savings into the retained earnings of business and its self-financed capital formation. Inflation is a second-best "income policy" to prevent dissipation of savings through consumption or underemployment. It is inferior, the argument goes, to productivity ceilings on factor prices, but it is preferable to stagnation.

Inflation in prospect affects anticipated relative yields on various types of wealth, financial and real, reducing real rates of return on assets with the more inflexible nominal rates and raising real prospective returns on assets with more flexible nominal rates. The inevitable result is to change rates of saving, allocation of savings, and channels by which savings flow. Self-finance gains at the expense of debt-asset finance. Foreign aid through intergovernmental loans and gifts may gain if inflation reduces domestic saving of the recipient country below a target level of investment. The channels that lose are debt-asset finance and also taxation, unless tax rates happen to be progressive to inflation.

Inflation transfers net worth as well as income. It taxes such forms of financial wealth as money balances, assessing creditors for the benefit of debtors, public or private. If the result is to depress the wealth position of savers and the debt position of investors below preferred levels, a temporary acceleration of saving, investment, and debt-asset finance can ensue. Needless to say, this result does not follow for gross inflation that is expected to continue.

Self-finance is centralist. It has been common in precapitalism, before the decentralizing evolution of commodity, factor, and financial markets. It is inherent in anti-capitalism, or socialism. Even in the general context of capitalism, there occur changes in the socioeconomic structure that involve reversion to self-finance. Degeneration in processes of debt-asset finance reduces saving and investment, but it can also divert funds into the channels of self-finance. Self-finance may increase if business firms combine to avoid encounters, as Baran puts it, with "the restraining hand of financial institutions." Cooperative credit among, say, consumers or farmers has been at times a way of detaching relatively small, homogeneous groups from reliance on broader security markets. The *mujin* and *kye* of the Far East, "traditional" credit institutions, are illustrations of cooperative saving-investment processes that border on both self-finance and the debt-asset system.

Taxation. The tax technique is a variant of internal finance, a way of mobilizing the economic surplus that implies centralized decision-making. While it is true that there are taxes which work to the benefit of debt-asset finance, there can be a structure of taxation which depresses demand for financial assets, displaces issues of securities by investors and intermediaries, and makes securities markets superfluous. The receipted tax bill is a substitute for the financial asset in spending units' portfolios.

CRITERIA FOR CHOICE AMONG ALTERNATIVE SAVING-INVESTMENT TECHNIQUES

We have defined four technologies or processes of eliciting and allocating savings: self-finance, taxation, debt-asset, and foreign aid. We have suggested that differences in the ratio of financial assets to income and wealth, between countries and between times for any one country, may reflect differences and changes in choice between the debt-asset technology and the others. In the present section, we consider some criteria for choice among the four technologies.

The objective of public policy regarding the saving-investment process, we assume, is to maximize the capital value of anticipated real consumption. Given a social discount rate, the technology or combination of technologies for eliciting and allocating saving is best which implies highest consumer welfare, counting government among consumers. The optimal consumption stream has the qualities of equity and stability that conform to a social welfare function.

The contribution of each saving-investment technology to consumer welfare has a positive (gross yield) component and a negative (factor cost) component, and the difference is the net yield of the technology. Additional real resources applied to a saving-investment technology may raise rates of saving and investment, the nation's capital stock, and hence the future flow of consumption. The gross yield of these real resources is the capital value of the economy's anticipated gross additions to its consumption stream. Factor cost is the capital value of the stream of final goods that could have been produced by the real resources if they had not been diverted to a saving-investment technology. The net yield is the difference between these two capital values.

We suggest that there is an optimal combination of saving-investment technologies for each economy in each phase of its development. This optimal combination has been attained when no gain in net yield can result from shifting factor inputs between technologies. Then no transfers of resources between technologies can advance the possibility frontier of anticipated consumption. If the optimal combination varies with the aggregate of factor inputs into all saving-investment technologies, one may wish to define the best combination more narrowly, as that which prevails when net yield is zero at the margin for all technologies. . . .

Bias and Evolution in Choice Between Technologies

Economic development is marked by iterative probing for the optimal combination of saving-investment technologies. The search is guided in part by principle and prejudice, in part by foreign example, by trial and error, and even by rational analysis. The combinations and permutations of technology are so numerous that no two countries are likely to follow the same probing sequence or, specifically, to reach the same ratio of financial assets to tangible wealth at any given level of real wealth or income per capita.

The probing sequence is most deeply affected by the economy's choice between self-finance with central planning and technologies that are compatible with decentralized decision regarding saving and investment. This is a choice between Left and Right. Advocates of either can design imposing proof that it is cheaper in resource imputs, more effective in eliciting and allocating savings, less vulnerable to instability in the consumption stream, and more compatible with the ethics of equity.

As the socialist sees decentralized finance, it is exorbitantly expensive in marble columns, bank presidents, and energy consumed in managing portfolios. It elicits too little in savings, because monopoly finance does not pay savers enough, because decentralized decisions pay too little attention to the consumer welfare of succeeding generations, or because savers do not measure accurately the rewards to saving. It allocates savings badly—on ostentation, on consumer durables, on military capital. Its allocation is biased by indifference to externalities of private investment, by hostility to public goods, by undervaluation of human capital. It is inherently unstable in the short run: variance in the future consumption stream is high. It reeks of inequity. Needless to say, the capitalist's view of socialist central planning is no less emphatic, using the same criteria of capitalized yield and cost.

As development proceeds, these blacks and whites of choice between technologies appear to shade off to greys of varying intensity. The probing process everywhere seems to lead toward a mixture of self-finance under central planning and decentralized processes. At the margin, neither black nor white has a long life expectancy. If we dared to suggest a Law of Financial Development, it would be this: each economy begins its development by intensive exploitation of a saving-investment technology that is chosen for historical, political, social, or perhaps economic reasons, and then, as this technology produces a diminishing net yield, experiments with alternative technologies that are marginally superior in terms of their capitalized returns and costs. Whatever the first choice may be, it is tilled intensively until there is obvious advantage in trying the extensive margin that involves a mix of processes for eliciting and allocating savings. Along the extensive margin, a socialist society may tolerate market as well as shadow rates of interest, and a capitalist society may put up with some centralized self-finance.

V.D.2. Demand-Following or Supply-Leading Finance*

Typical statements indicate that the financial system somehow accommodates—or, to the extent that it malfunctions, it restricts—growth of real per capita output. For example,

It seems to be the case that where enterprise leads finance follows. The same impulses within an economy which set enterprise on foot make owners of wealth venturesome, and when a strong impulse to invest is fettered by lack of finance, devices are invented to release it . . . and habits and institutions are developed.[1]

Such an approach places emphasis on the demand side for financial services; as the economy grows it generates additional and new demands for these services, which bring about a supply response in the growth of the financial system. In this view, the lack of financial institutions in underdeveloped countries is simply an indication of the lack of demand for their services.

We may term as "demand-following" the phenomenon in which the creation of modern financial institutions, their financial assets and liabilities, and related financial services is in response to the demand for these services by investors and savers in the real economy. In this case, the evolutionary development of the financial system is a continuing consequence of the pervasive, sweeping process of economic development. The emerging financial system is shaped both by changes in objective opportunities—the economic environment, the institutional framework—and by changes in subjective responses—individual motivations, attitudes, tastes, preferences.

The nature of the demand for financial services depends upon the growth of real output and upon the commercialization and monetization of agriculture and other traditional subsistence sectors. The more rapid growth rate of real national income, the greater will be the demand by enterprises for external funds (the saving of others) and therefore financial intermediation, since under most circumstances firms will be less able to finance expansion from internally generated depreciation allowances and retained profits. (The proportion of external funds in the total source of enterprise funds will rise.) For the same reason, with a given aggregate growth rate, the greater the variance in the growth rates among different sectors or industries, the greater will be the need for financial intermediation to transfer saving to fast-growing industries from slow-growing industries and from individuals. The financial system can thus support and sustain the leading sectors in the process of growth.

The demand-following supply response of the growing financial system is presumed to come about more or less automatically. It is assumed that the supply of entrepreneurship in the financial sector is highly elastic relative to the growing opportunities for profit from provision of financial services, so that the number and diversity of types of financial institutions expands sufficiently; and a favorable legal, institutional, and economic environment exists. The government's attitudes, economic goals, and economic pol-

*From Hugh T. Patrick, "Financial Development and Economic Growth in Underdeveloped Countries," *Economic Development and Cultural Change,* Vol. 14, No. 2, January 1966, pp. 174–7. Reprinted by permission.
[1] Joan Robinson, "The Generalization of the General Theory," in *The Rate of Interest and Other Essays,* London, 1952, pp. 86–87.

icies, as well as the size and rate of increase of the government debt, are of course important influences in any economy on the nature of the economic environment. As a consequence of real economic growth, financial markets develop, widen, and become more perfect, thus increasing the opportunities for acquiring liquidity and for reducing risk, which in turn feeds back as a stimulant to real growth.[2]

The demand-following approach implies that finance is essentially passive and permissive in the growth process. Late eighteenth and early nineteenth century England may be cited as a historical example. In fact, the increased supply of financial services in response to demand may not be at all automatic, flexible, or inexpensive in underdeveloped countries. Examples include the restrictive banking legislation in early nineteenth century France, religious barriers against loans and interest charges, and Gerschenkron's analysis of the abortive upswing of Italian industrial development in the 1880's "mainly, it is believed, because the modern investment bank had not yet been established in Italy."[3] In underdeveloped countries today, similar obstacles, together with imperfections in the operation of the market mechanism, may dictate an inadequate demand-following response by the financial system. The lack of financial services, thus, in one way or another restricts or inhibits effective growth patterns and processes.

Less emphasis has been given in academic discussions (if not in policy actions) to what may be termed the "supply-leading" phenomenon: the creation of financial institutions and the supply of their financial assets, liabilities, and related financial services in advance of demand for them, especially the demand of entrepreneurs in the modern, growth-inducing sectors. "Supply-leading"

has two functions: to transfer resources from traditional (non-growth) sectors to modern sectors, and to promote and stimulate an entrepreneurial response in these modern sectors. Financial intermediation which transfers resources from traditional sectors, whether by collecting wealth and saving from those sectors in exchange for its deposits and other financial liabilities, or by credit creation and forced saving, is akin to the Schumpeterian concept of innovation financing.

New access to such supply-leading funds may in itself have substantial, favorable expectational and psychological effects on entrepreneurs. It opens new horizons as to possible alternatives, enabling the entrepreneur to "think big." This may be the most significant effect of all, particularly in countries where entrepreneurship is a major constraint on development. Moreover, as has been emphasized by Rondo Cameron,[4] the top management of financial institutions may also serve as entrepreneurs in industrial enterprises. They assist in the establishment of firms in new industries or in the merger of firms (the advantages of economies of scale may be more than offset by the establishment of restrictive cartels or monopolies, however), not only by underwriting a substantial portion of the capital, but more importantly by assuming the entrepreneurial initiative.

By its very nature, a supply-leading financial system initially may not be able to operate profitably by lending to the nascent modern sectors.[5] There are, however, several ways in which new financial institutions can be made viable. First, they may be government institutions, using government capital and perhaps receiving direct government subsidies. This is exemplified not only by Russian experience in the latter half of the nine-

[2] Cf. W. Arthur Lewis, *The Theory of Economic Growth,* London, 1955, pp. 267–286.

[3] Alexander Gerschenkron, *Economic Backwardness in Historical Perspective—A Book of Essays,* Cambridge, 1962, p. 363. See also Chapter 4.

[4] Rondo Cameron, "The Bank as Entrepreneur," *Explorations in Entrepreneurial History,* Series 2, I, No. 1 (Fall 1963), pp. 50–55.

[5] Except in the extreme case where inherent profit opportunities are very high, and supply-leading stimulates a major entrepreneurial effort.

teenth century, but by many underdeveloped countries today. Second, private financial institutions may receive direct or indirect government subsidies, usually the latter. Indirect subsidies can be provided in numerous ways. Commercial banks may have the right to issue banknotes under favorable collateral conditions; this technique was more important in the eighteenth and nineteenth centuries (national banking in Japan in the 1870's; wildcat banking in the United States) than it is likely to be in present underdeveloped countries, where this right is reserved for the central bank or treasury. Nonetheless, modern equivalents exist. They include allowing private financial institutions to create deposit money with low (theoretically, even negative) reserve requirements and central bank rediscount of commercial bank loans at interest rates effectively below those on the loans. Third, new, modern financial institutions may initially lend a large proportion of their funds to traditional (agricultural and commercial) sectors profitably, gradually shifting their loan portfolio to modern industries as these begin to emerge. This more closely resembles the demand-following phenomenon; whether such a financial institution is supply-leading depends mainly on its attitude in searching out and encouraging new ventures of a modern nature.

It cannot be said that supply-leading finance is a necessary condition or precondition for inaugurating self-sustained economic development. Rather, it presents an opportunity to induce real growth by financial means. It thus is likely to play a more significant role at the beginning of the growth process than later. Gerschenkron implies that the more backward the economy relative to others in the same time period (and the greater the forced-draft nature of the economic development effort), the greater the emphasis which is placed on what I here term supply-leading finance.[6] At the same time, it should be recognized that the

[6] Op. cit.

supply-leading approach to development of a country's financial system also has its dangers, and they should not be underestimated. The use of resources, especially entrepreneurial talents and managerial skills, and the costs of explicit or implicit subsidies in supply-leading development must produce sufficient benefits in the form of stimulating real economic development for this approach to be justified.

In actual practice, there is likely to be an interaction of supply-leading and demand-following phenomena. Nevertheless, the following sequence may be postulated. Before sustained modern industrial growth gets underway, supply-leading may be able to induce real innovation-type investment. As the process of real growth occurs, the supply-leading impetus gradually becomes less important, and the demand-following financial response becomes dominant. This sequential process is also likely to occur within and among specific industries or sectors. One industry may initially be encouraged financially on a supply-leading basis and as it develops have its financing shift to demand-following, while another industry remains in the supply-leading phase. This would be related to the timing of the sequential development of industries, particularly in cases where the timing is determined more by governmental policy than by private demand forces.

Japan between the 1870's and the beginning of World War I presents an excellent example of the sequence of supply-leading and demand-following finance. A modern banking system was created in the 1870's, subsidized by the right to issue banknotes and by government deposits. These banks, in the absence of large-scale industrial demand for funds, initially concentrated their funds on financing agriculture, domestic commerce, and the newly important foreign trade. However, they also became the locus for much of the early promotional and entrepreneurial talent which initiated the industrial spurt beginning in the mid-1880's, especially in railroads and in cotton textiles (at first import-competing, and later export-oriented). The banks also became an early important source of industrial funds, albeit *via* an indirect route. The modern financial system thus was not only created in advance of Japan's modern industrialization, but, by providing both funds and entrepreneurial talent on a supply-leading basis, contributed significantly to the initial spurt. By the mid-1890's, the emphasis apparently moved from supply-leading to demand-following in the financing of the textile and other consumer goods industries. On the other hand, the financing of most heavy manufacturing industries continued on a supply-leading basis perhaps until World War I, with a considerable portion of external funds provided through the long-term loans of special banks established at government initiative and utilizing government funds. . . .

V.D.3. Organized and Unorganized

Money Markets*

The size of an organized money market in any country may be indicated by either or both of the following ratios, although neither measurement is perfect: the ratio of deposit money to money supply and the ratio of the banking system's claims (mostly loans, advances, and bills discounted) on the private sector to national income. . . .

The ratio of deposit money to money supply actually measures banking development of the money market. However, to the extent that the development of commercial banking is synonymous with the development of the money market, this ratio may be used as an indicator of the growth of a money market. In most underdeveloped countries, there are hardly any lending agencies of importance other than commercial banks. There are no discount houses or acceptance houses, and savings institutions (including life insurance companies) are in the early stages of development. . . .

*From U Tun Wai, "Interest Rates in the Organized Money Markets of Underdeveloped Countries," *International Monetary Fund Staff Papers,* Vol. 5, No. 2, August 1956, pp. 249–50, 252–3, 255, 258, 276–8; "Interest Rates Outside the Organized Money Markets of Underdeveloped Countries," ibid., Vol. 6, No. 1, November 1957, pp. 80–83, 107–9, 119–25.

Both ratios might be expected to be low in an underdeveloped country and high in a developed one. The ratio of deposit money to money supply should be higher in a more developed country because, with economic development, there is also development of the banking system. . . .

The structure of interest rates in the organized money markets of underdeveloped countries is usually more or less the same as in the developed ones. The short-term rate of interest is generally much below the long-term rate, as indicated by the spread between the government treasury bill rate and the government bond yield; the rate at which bills of exchange are discounted is also lower than the rate at which loans and advances are granted.

The lowest market rates are usually the call loan rates between commerical banks. The next lowest are those paid by commercial banks on short-term deposits, followed by the government treasury bill rate. Then come the rates at which commercial banks discount commercial paper, varying according to the type of security and the date of maturity. In most countries, especially in Asia, the government bond yield comes next, followed by the lending rates of commercial banks. . . .

In general, the level of interest rates in underdeveloped countries, even in organized money markets, is higher than in the more developed countries. The more notable difference between the two groups of countries, however, is that the range of interest rates is generally much wider in underdeveloped countries. The volume of loans granted at relatively low rates in an underdeveloped country is not very important, as only limited amounts of financial assets are available to serve as collateral for lending at low rates. It is usually the foreign business firms with longer experience and larger capital which are able to borrow at the lower rates. Most of the indigenous firms have to pay the higher rates; this is especially true where foreign banks occupy an important position in the banking system. . . .

Central banks have been established in most underdeveloped countries; in Latin America for the most part they were established in the twenties and thirties, whereas in Asia, except in India, Japan, and Thailand, they are of postwar origin. The statutes of a number of central banks in Asia (for example, Burma and Ceylon) have granted them wide power including that of control over the rates at which commercial banks may grant loans, but these powers have not so far been exercised. Where central bank lending to commercial banks is substantial, one would naturally expect changes in the bank rate to be reflected immediately in market rates. Where such lending is nominal, the influence would be felt directly only if marginal lending should influence the market rate. . . .

In spite of the small direct dependence of commercial banks on the central banks for funds, the latter are able to influence market rates by changes in the bank rate because of their economic, and at times their legal, position in the domestic money market, with wide powers for selective credit control, open market operations, and moral pressures.

The general expectation is that the long-term trend of interest rates in underdeveloped countries, at least in the organized markets, should be downward. Generally speaking, in these countries the banking systems and with them the money markets are likely to develop at a faster rate than the other sectors of the economy. The long-term supply of loanable funds therefore tends to increase more rapidly than the long-term demand. Where, for one reason or another, the growth of banking has been restricted or the banking system subjected by law to many restrictions, including controls on interest rates and of the purposes for which loans may be granted (as in a number of countries in Latin America), the long-term trend of interest rates may, however, not be downward. . . .

In [the above] examination . . . of the interest rate structure and the lending practices of organized money markets in underdeveloped countries, . . . it was shown that these differed much less than might have been expected from those prevailing in most developed countries. In underdeveloped countries, however, unorganized money markets also play a very important role, and any study of credit conditions in these countries that is to be adequate must be extended to cover the unorganized as well as the organized markets. Efforts have often been made to repair the deficiencies of the unorganized markets by government action designed to stimulate the development of cooperative credit or to provide credit through agricultural banks, etc.; it is convenient to include these government-sponsored institutions in a study of unorganized money markets in general.

Interest rates in the unorganized money markets of underdeveloped countries are generally very high in relation both to those in the organized money markets and to what is needed for rapid economic development. These high interest rates are caused by a disproportionately large demand for loanable funds coupled with a generally inelastic and limited supply of funds. The large demand stems from the special social and economic factors prevalent in the rural areas of underdeveloped countries. The low level of income leaves little surplus for saving and for the accumulation of capital for self-financing of agricultural and handicraft production. The uncertainty of the weather, which affects crop yields and incomes, causes an additional need for outside funds in bad years. A significant portion of the demand for loanable funds in rural areas is for financing consumption at levels much higher than are warranted by the low income of the peasant. . . .

The supply of loanable funds in the unorganized money markets is very limited and inelastic because the major source is the moneylender, and only very small quantities are supplied by indigenous bankers and organized institutions, such as cooperative credit societies and land mortgage banks. The moneylender in most cases is also a merchant or a landlord and therefore is willing to lend only at rates comparable with what he could earn by employing his capital in alternative uses which are often highly profitable. The lenders in the unorganized money markets do not have the facilities for mobilizing liquid funds available to commercial banks in organized markets and therefore the supply of funds is rather inflexible. Since the unorganized money markets are generally not closely connected with the organized money markets, there is little possibility of increasing the supply of loanable funds beyond the savings of the lending sector of the unorganized money markets. The limited supply of loanable funds indeed reflects the general shortage of capital in underdeveloped countries.

The disadvantages of the high rates of interest in the unorganized money markets are well known and include such important effects as "dead-weight" agricultural indebtedness, alienation of land from agriculturalists to moneylenders and the agrarian unrest that is thus engendered, and a general slowing down of economic development. . . .

The organized money markets in underdeveloped countries are less fully integrated than the money markets in developed countries. The unorganized money markets in underdeveloped countries are even more imperfect, and indeed it is questionable whether the existing arrangements should be referred to as "markets." They are much less homogeneous than the organized markets and are generally scattered over the rural sector. There is very little contact between the lenders and borrowers in different localities. The usual textbook conditions for a perfect market are completely nonexistent: lenders and borrowers do not know the rates at which loans are being transacted in other parts of the country; the relationship between borrower and lender is not only that of a debtor and creditor but is also an integral part of a much wider socioeconomic pattern of village life and rural conditions.

In unorganized money markets, moreover, loans are often contracted and paid for not in money but in commodities; and the size of the average loan is very much smaller than in the organized money markets. Both borrowers and lenders in the two markets are often of quite different types. In the organized money markets, the borrowers are mainly traders (wholesale and retail) operating in the large cities and, to a less extent, manufacturers. Agriculturalists rarely account for a significant portion of demand except in those underdeveloped countries where export agriculture has been developed through plantations or estates. In the unorganized money markets, the borrowers are small agriculturalists, cottage industry workers, and some retail shopkeepers. The lenders in the organized money markets consist almost exclusively of commercial banks. In the unorganized markets, the suppliers of credit consist of a few financial institutions, such as cooperatives, private and government-sponsored agricultural banks, indigenous bankers, professional moneylenders, large traders, landlords, shopkeepers, relatives, and friends. Proper records of loans granted or repaid are usually not kept, and uniform accounting procedures are not adopted by the different lenders. Loans are granted more on a personal basis than in the organized money markets, and most of the loans granted by the moneylenders and by other noninstitutional sources are unsecured beyond the verbal promise of the borrower to repay.

The unorganized money market may be divided into three major parts: (1) a part in which the supply is dominated by indigenous bankers, cooperatives, and other institutions, and the demand by rural traders and medium-sized landlords; (2) a part in which the demand originates mainly from small agriculturalists with good credit ratings, who are able to obtain a large portion of their funds from respectable moneylenders, traders, and landlords at high but reasonable rates of interest, i.e., rates that are high in relation to those prevailing in the organized money market but not exorbitant by the standards of the unorganized money market; (3) a part in which the demand originates from borrowers who are not good credit risks, who do not have suitable collateral, and who in consequence are driven to shady marginal lenders who charge exorbitant rates of interest. . . .

Many explanations have been offered for the high interest rates that generally prevail in unorganized money markets. One theory is that interest rates are high there because they are determined by custom and have always been high. This might be called the theory of the customary rate of interest. . . .

The theory of customary rates is not satisfactory, however, because it does not explain how or why the custom of high rates developed. The true explanation has to be found in the economic and social conditions of underdeveloped countries, which cause the demand for loanable funds to be large in relation to the available supply. Some writers tend to explain the high rates of interest in terms of demand factors while others emphasize supply.

The demand for funds, in relation to the supply, is large because the average borrower in the unorganized money market has a very low income and therefore has no surplus funds to finance his business operations. The majority of the cultivating tenants—one of the most important groups of potential borrowers—have to borrow money not only for investment in land, cattle, etc., and for working capital to make purchases of seeds and fertilizers, but also for their minimum basic necessities of food, shelter, and clothing.

On the supply side, there is a general shortage of capital in underdeveloped countries and an inadequate level of domestic savings. Also, the small amount of domestic savings is not channeled effectively into the unorganized money market because of the absence of proper financial and credit institutions which not only would integrate the organized and unorganized money markets but also would facilitate the mobilization of savings in the rural areas. . . .

The difference in the levels of interest rates between the organized and unorganized money markets stems partly from the basic differences between the sources of supply of funds in the two markets. In an organized money market, facilities for the expansion of credit are open to the commercial banks, which have the use of funds belonging to depositors. These banks are therefore able to charge relatively low rates of interest and yet make satisfactory profits for the shareholders. On the other hand, moneylenders in an unorganized money market have little influence on the supply of funds at their disposal and, furthermore, their supply price tends to be influenced by the alternative uses to which their funds can be put.

A number of institutional factors are also responsible for high rates of interest in unorganized money markets. The size of the loan is usually small and thus the fixed handling charges are relatively high. Defaults also tend to be larger in unorganized money markets. These higher defaults are due not so much to a lower standard of morality and willingness to repay debts as to the fluctuations in prices and incomes derived from agricultural products, which reduce the ability of the agriculturalists to repay debts at inopportune times. . . .

Another general factor causing high rates of interest is experience in regard to inflation. While this is probably of importance in many Latin American countries, it hardly seems relevant for prewar colonial territories which, by their rigid currency exchange standards, had maintained fairly stable conditions but still had high interest rates in the unorganized money markets. The large development programs in most underdeveloped countries, however, constitute possible inflationary pressures and may be considered as a factor in maintaining high rates of interest.

The list of causes of high interest rates could be extended to include other social and economic factors in underdeveloped countries—even to fairly remote factors, such as the system of land tenure which prevents land from being used as collateral. A general statement, however, is that interest rates in the unorganized money markets of underdeveloped countries are high because the economy is underdeveloped and the money market unorganized. . . .

Any program to bring down interest rates in unorganized money markets must be comprehensive and should be guided by the principle that interest rates can be lowered only by reducing the demand for loanable funds as well as by increasing the supply. The demand for loanable funds for financing consumer expenditures can be reduced by changing social habits and concepts of acceptable standards of well-being. India has passed a law limiting the amount of expenditures which may be incurred for religious and social occasions. Such laws will not prevent people who are bent on spending money for such purposes from doing so; but it is believed that the masses, who are forced by custom to maintain levels of expenditures much above their income, will welcome this law and use it as an excuse to cut unnecessary consumption expenditure.

A reduction in borrowing for productive purposes may not be desirable, especially as the amount of self-financing which can take its place is negligible. Such borrowing can be reduced in the long run only through an increase in savings from higher agricultural output and income. It is not sufficient that the ability of the farmer to save be increased. The willingness to save must also be created. The problem of cheap agricultural credit is inseparable from the whole problem of agricultural development, including such measures as increasing the use of fertilizers and proper seeds; making available adequate marketing facilities, including proper grading, transportation, and storage of crops; and providing an efficient agricultural extension service.

There is no question that merely increasing the supply of loanable funds without reducing or limiting the demand will not solve the problem of high rates of interest. Experience in many underdeveloped countries, especially in Southeast Asia, indicates that an increase in supply merely stimulates demand (mainly for financing consumption) and does not lower the general level of interest rates.

Even if it is true that the cure for high rates of interest is to be found more on the demand side than on the supply side, the supply of credit should also be increased. Supply should be increased in such a way that legitimate credit needs are met at cheaper rates without encouraging borrowing for consumption. This can be achieved by increasing the supply of institutional credit while at the same time taking steps to discourage borrowing from noninstitutional lenders. In this connection, it could be argued that legislation regarding moneylenders which has had the effect of drying up noninstitutional credit may be a blessing in disguise—although in a manner different from that intended by legislators.

Increasing the supply of institutional credit is a difficult problem, but the efforts of governments have had a fair degree of success. One problem is that of getting the commercial banks to lend more to agriculture. This problem cannot be solved merely by opening more branches, because even at present agriculturalists who are fairly close to the big cities are as isolated from the organized money market as others living some distance away from the cities. The opening of more bank branches is desirable, but the branches' business will as likely as not be confined to financing local retail and wholesale trade.

One way of inducing the organized financial institutions to lend more to agriculture is by making agriculturalists more credit-worthy and generally reducing the risks of lending by lessening the impact of some of the natural calamities (floods, plant and animal diseases); improving the human factor, i.e., reducing carelessness and increasing honesty; reducing the uncertainties of the market through crop insurance, stabilized agricultural prices, etc. The lenders might also take certain steps, such as spreading loans between different types of borrower and region and supervising the use of loans for productive purposes.

SUMMARY

The unorganized money market is generally larger than the organized money market. Its nature and working are quite different from that of the organized money market. Noninstitutional sources of supply, such as moneylenders, landlords, shopkeepers, relatives, and friends, are more important than credit institutions and thus business is carried on in a personal way and not subjected to standardized procedures.

The direct connection between the two money markets is rather poor and is less close than the connection between the organized money markets in underdeveloped countries and world money markets. The organized and unorganized money markets are, however, loosely connected through large exporters, wholesalers, and landlords who borrow in the organized market and carry out some relending in the unorganized market.

Interest rates in the unorganized money market range from fairly low rates charged by the cooperative credit societies to the very high and exorbitant rates charged by loan sharks to borrowers with poor credit ratings or to those in urgent need of funds. The major portion of the loans, however, are granted at rates in between these two extremes. It is estimated that in the majority of countries the weighted average rate of interest in the unorganized money market must lie between 24 per cent and 36 per cent per annum.

The high rates of interest prevailing in the unorganized money market have been a heavy burden to the agriculturalists. Annual interest payments have been fairly large in relation to the net income of the farmer, thus reducing his ability to make improvements on the land.

The high rates of interest are due to both demand and supply factors and stem from the economic and social conditions prevailing in underdeveloped countries. The need for funds by agriculturalists is more urgent than the need of borrowers in the organized money market, because the low level of agricultural income makes it practically impossible for the farmer to set aside funds for self-financing. The supply is small because of the low savings, even of those in the upper income brackets, and the lack of institutional arrangements to mobilize and channel the available savings into the unorganized money market. It seems, however, that the exorbitant rates of interest charged by loan sharks and unscrupulous moneylenders are due mainly to the semimonopolistic position occupied by them.

Generally speaking, there are no seasonal and cyclical fluctuations in interest rates, such as occur in the organized money market. The rates charged by moneylenders and by credit institutions do not vary with the cycle. The quantities lent, however, have varied, with the supply from credit institutions expanding more rapidly in the boom and contracting much faster in the slump. Since the rate charged by credit institutions is much lower than the rate charged by moneylenders, the weighted average rate of interest in the unorganized money market has fallen in the boom and risen in the slump; this is the opposite of the movements in the organized money market.

Governments have attempted to influence the cost and availability of credit in the unorganized money market through direct lending to the agriculturalists and by controlling the rate of interest and the conditions of moneylending. Although some success has been achieved, these measures, generally speaking, have not as yet lowered rates of interest, partly because of inflationary pressures created by deficit financing for such lending and other expenditures and partly because controls have been evaded.

In view of the fact that the unorganized money market is larger than the organized money market, and since the two markets have not been closely connected, the use of orthodox monetary policy as an instrument of economic policy has very limited possibilities in underdeveloped countries. The cost and availability of credit in the unorganized money market can be influenced by the central bank either by improving the link between the two money markets or by having a large amount of credit supplied by it directly or indirectly through credit institutions and even through moneylenders. There are inflationary dangers in the latter approach, but the art of central banking in underdeveloped countries is to be able to steer the monetary system into a position of dependence on the central bank without inflation, so that when inflationary pressures arise, the authorities can cut credit not only in the organized money market but also in the unorganized money market.

V.D.4. Financial Repression and

Liberalization*

Numerous decentralized economies with low levels of per capita income and wealth have been attracted at times to a development strategy that results in "shallow" finance. By distortions of financial prices including interest rates and foreign-exchange rates and by other means, it has reduced the real rate of growth and the real size of the financial system relative to nonfinancial magnitudes. In all cases this strategy has stopped or gravely retarded the development process. A new strategy that has the effect, among others, of "deepening" finance—a strategy of financial liberalization—has invariably renewed development. Liberalization matters in economic development. It is *not* our theme that only financial liberalization matters. On the contrary, financial liberalization is appropriately linked with complementary measures that reach beyond the financial sector.

*From Edward S. Shaw, *Financial Deepening in Economic Development,* Oxford University Press, New York, 1973, pp. 3–14. Reprinted by permission.

NOMINAL FINANCE AND REAL FINANCE

The first step in clarifying the developmental role of finance is to distinguish real values and real rates of return for financial assets from their nominal counterparts—to cleanse the analysis of money illusion. Where the strategy of financial repression is in effect, nominal aggregates of money, for example, or government securities and social trust funds commonly rise at some buoyant rate. At the same time, these aggregates deflated by any broadly inclusive index of prices for domestic goods and services are rising less rapidly or falling. Nominal finance is taking the high growth path, real finance the low one. Then finance in the real sense is shallow, partly because it is being taxed by inflation.

The experience of four countries during 1963–68 illustrates divergence between nominal and real financial growth.

Uruguay realized nominal growth of 710 per cent in money, time, and savings deposits whereas real values declined by 55 per cent. In the race between growth in nominal

TABLE 1. Patterns of Growth in Money *Plus* Time and Savings Deposits

Indexes of Nominal Values				
	Ghana	Thailand	Iran	Uruguay
1963	1.00	1.00	1.00	1.00
1968	1.63	1.96	2.16	8.10
Indexes of Real Values				
1963	1.00	1.00	1.00	1.00
1968	1.01	1.74	2.00	0.45

Source: International Monetary Fund, *International Financial Statistics.*

pesos and inflation, the latter was an easy winner. Ghanaian policy expanded the nominal stock of cedi liquid claims whereas the real stock remained constant. Iran and Thailand achieved financial deepening, real financial growth absorbing the increment in nominal claims. The Uruguayan economy collapsed during 1963–68, and the Ghanaian economy retrogressed whereas both Iran and Thailand realized growth in real income and consumption. Analysis of the bearing of finance on these differences in growth experience starts with the observation that nominal values and real values in terms of the new cedi, rial, baht, and peso took dissimilar relative paths.

Where finance is shallow, in relation to national income or non-financial wealth, one finds that it bears low, often negative real rates of return. Holders of financial assets including money are not rewarded for real growth in their portfolios: they are penalized. During 1965–69 the proportion of money balances to gross national product in Ghana declined from 14.4 per cent to 10.7 per cent. The nominal explicit rate of interest on money balances was zero, but the average real rate of return was negative 8 per cent, the realized average rate of inflation.

Trade unions and employers appreciate the difference between nominal and real wage rates and wage incomes. Financial authorities are rarely as sophisticated about nominal and real financial rates of return,

flows, and stocks. They seem to miss the point, for example, that money has four prices. One price is simply unity (column 1, Table 2), a decreed price for the money unit—one new cedi, one baht, one rial, one peso. Another price is $1/P$ (column 2, Table 2), an index for the purchasing power of money over some assortment of goods and services. The money stock valued at the first unit of account or accounting price is the nominal stock M, whereas the money stock valued at its relative worth in goods and services is the real stock M/P.

If the second price of money and the real money stock are to be positive, the marginal unit of money must yield valuable services. These services may be in kind, including benefits to consumer welfare or to productivity, but they may also take the form of a third explicit price. It is a real deposit rate of interest d, the sum of any nominal rate of interest d on money balances and the rate of change $\dot{P}$ in money's second price: $d = \underline{d} - \dot{P}$. For the new cedi in 1969, nominal deposit rate was nil, $\dot{P}$ was negative 10.8 per cent, and so d or the real yield of Ghanaian money balances was also negative 10.8 per cent. The fourth price of money is a foreign-exchange rate, the ratio of exchange between one money, perhaps a new cedi, and another money, perhaps a dollar. Financial analysis would be simpler if there were just one exchange rate between two moneys rather than a real or purchasing-power-parity rate as well as a nominal rate and forward or future rates as well as present or spot rates.

TABLE 2. Two Prices and a Rate of Interest for Money: The Case of New Cedis

	Nominal Price	Relative Price	Real Yield (%)
1965	1.00	1.00	—
1966	1.00	.79	−21.0
1967	1.00	.80	1.3
1968	1.00	.83	3.7
1969	1.00	.74	−10.8

Source: Central Bureau of Statistics, *Economic Survey, 1969*, Accra, Ghana, 1970.

Multiple pricing characterizes all financial assets, non-monetary assets as well as money. The same distinctions arise between nominal and real amounts of finance, between nominal and real rates of return. A distinction exists too, between instruments of financial policy, with some bearing on nominal amounts of finance and some bearing on real amounts. . . . Financial deepening results from appropriate real-finance policy. The principal instruments of this policy bear on real rates of return to real stocks of finance. Shallow finance is partly the consequence of distortions in prices of finance.

MEASURES AND INDICATORS OF FINANCIAL DEEPENING

Numerous indicators or measures register financial deepening. Here it is sufficient to mention only a few. One class pertains to financial stocks. When financial policy has been liberalized and distortions in financial prices have been removed or reduced, reserves of liquidity increase. For example, the central bank typically builds up its international liquidity and takes less recourse to detailed intervention, through rations or licenses, on the foreign-exchange markets. Farmers substitute balances of financial assets for working capital in the form of rice or wheat or other commodity inventories that are costly to maintain. Buyers and sellers in all markets accumulate average balances of liquid assets that make it unnecessary to waste resources on inconveniences of barter. Stocks of financial assets aggregatively grow relative to income or in proportion to tangible wealth, and their range of qualities widens. There is a lengthening of maturities, and a wider variety of debtors gains access to the financial markets. The menu of financial assets is diversified so that borrowers may adjust their debt structures and lenders their portfolios by relatively small degrees at the margin.

Financial flows can be read easily for evidence that finance is deepening. Where it is shallow, for example, an economy depends relatively heavily on its government fiscal budget and on its international capital accounts for the flows of savings that finance capital growth. Deepening eases the strain on taxation and moderates demand for foreign savings. Flight of savings abroad by one device of smuggling or another and demand for construction of dubious social productivity are common evidence of an aversion to finance. Deepening stops and reverses capital flight and diverts savings from those skeletons of partially complete office and apartment buildings. The velocity of money diminishes.

In the context of shallow finance, organized finance is dominated by the banking system and other finance flows through the foreign exchanges or through the curb market of moneylenders and cooperative societies. The banking system behaves as a high-cost, high-profit oligopoly. Finance through the foreign exchanges is dominated by external grants of aid, high-cost suppliers' credits, and direct investment from abroad. The curb is limited to short-term transactions at some high risk from borrower default and governmental repression. The deepening of finance increases the real size of the monetary system, and it generates opportunities for the profitable operation of other institutions as well, from bill dealers to industrial banks and insurance companies. Deepening involves specialization in financial functions and institutions, and organized domestic institutions and markets gain in relation to foreign markets and the curb.

Financial prices are perhaps the least ambiguous evidence. Where finance is shallow, demand for financial assets is repressed by low real rates of interest and supply of primary securities on these terms is repressed by credit rationing. Even the curb market is subject to usury laws and regulations. The financial markets are required to trade at interest rates that overvalue the future in terms of the present. Deepening implies that interest rates must report more accurately the opportunities that exist for substitution of investment for current consumption and the disinclination of consumers to wait. Real rates of interest are high where finance is deepening. Differentials between rates tend to diminish—for example, between loan and deposit rates and between rates on the organized markets and rates on the curb.

Shallow finance is commonly associated with overvaluation of domestic money on the official markets for spot foreign exchange. Regulatory policy demands a premium on domestic balances in terms of foreign balances as well as a premium in present balances on future balances. It discourages exporting and saving but encourages importing and consumption. Deepening ensues when these biases in relative prices are removed. The evidence one looks for is a decline of the discount on domestic money in the black markets and the forward markets for foreign exchange.

OBJECTIVES OF FINANCIAL DEEPENING

Financial liberalization tends to raise ratios of private domestic savings to income. Some of the gain may be illusory: savings may be drawn to uses that are counted in national income accounts and away from capital flight in various forms that defy measurement. Some of the gain must result from higher rewards to saving—higher real rates of interest and opportunities for diversifying savers' portfolios of domestic assets. Again, real growth of financial institutions provides more investors with access to borrowing and gives them incentive to save and to accumulate the equity that makes borrowing cheaper. Finally, there seems to be a shift of savers' planning horizons to the more distant future and improvement in income expectations that reduces relatively the attraction of consumption now.

Savings tend to rise in the government sector. When finance is shallow, in decentralized economies, government savings are characteristically low. Government depends on the inflation tax for command over resources, and the typical inelasticity of tax revenues and profits of government enterprise to inflation reduces government savings in the conventional sense. Savings from the foreign sector also respond to liberalization. Capital flight of domestic funds is reversed, and there is easier access to foreign capital markets when distortions of such relative prices as interest rates and foreign-exchange rates are corrected. In some circumstances the inflow of foreign funds reaches proportions that are not easy to absorb at a stable domestic price level.

Liberalization permits the financial process of mobilizing and allocating savings to displace in some degree the fiscal process, inflation, and foreign aid. Fiscal technique is backward in lagging economies. Its capacity to draw revenues is strained by demands for government consumption and, in the usual case, for some minimal social security. Additional demands upon it for the purpose of financing investment tend to have effects upon economic efficiency and social equity that offset benefits of capital accumulation. Foreign aid has been, in some important degree, a substitute for domestic savings: the aid gap is partly an expression of excess demand for savings in economies that employ relative price to repress savings of their own. Technocratic planning models may define ranges of per capita income in which developing economies generate shortages of savings and foreign exchange, but correction of distorted relative prices has a remarkable way of making the models irrelevant.

Liberalization opens the way to superior allocations of savings by widening and diversifying the financial markets on which investment opportunities compete for the savings flow. In the repressed economy savings flow mainly to the saver's own investments: self-finance prevails. In the liberalized economy savers are offered a wider menu of portfolio choice. The market for their savings is extended; a broader range of selection in terms of scale, maturity, and risk becomes available; and information for comparison of alternatives can be obtained more cheaply. Local capital markets can be integrated into a common market, and new opportunities for pooling savings and specializing in investment are created.

The extended capital markets, where prices in the form of interest rates can be used to discriminate between investment alternatives, seem to be a congenial context for appearance of new investing firms and innovative investment projects. They generate competing proposals for the disposition of savings. In this respect, the contrast with financially repressed regimes can be striking. There savings flow through narrow channels which are not subject to the discipline of relative price, into the repetitive projects of established firms, especially government enterprise and traditional trading firms. Too often the search for investment uses of savings is casual and opportunistic, with little reference to comparative rates of return. Financial depth seems to be an important prerequisite for competitive and innovative disposition of savings flows. It is no accident that marginal ratios of investment to output are high where finance is shallow.

Unemployment in lagging economies is partly the result of financial repression. Scarce savings supply labor inadequately with the tools of its trades. To make matters worse, the low interest rates that inhibit savings combine with relatively high minimum-wage rates to guarantee that labor is supplied with the wrong tools. Investment flows to capital-intensive production even though capital is scarce and labor plentiful. The status of labor is not improved by the overvalued exchange rates that conceal the comparative advantage of labor-intensive agriculture and indigenous manufacturing.

Financial liberalization and allied policies tend to equalize the distribution of income. It appears that elasticities of substitution of labor against capital may be high in some lagging economies and that a rise in interest rates and foreign-exchange rates relative to

wage rates may both raise employment and increase the wage share of income. Again, liberalization reduces the monopoly rents that flow from import and other licenses to the few importers, bank borrowers, or, for example, consumers of electric power. Furthermore, the twists in terms of trade against farmers, for example, or against workers that are applied in a regime of repression to extract profits and savings for investors can be replaced by measures of finance and taxation that achieve as much growth of capital with less abuse of equity and less hazard for political and social stability.

Liberalization and deepening of finance contribute to the stability of growth in output and employment. There can be less stop-go. One reason for this is that some of the more ample savings flow may be used to finance larger international reserves. More flexible foreign-exchange rates can also absorb some of the shocks of international trading. If both the current balance on international account and the domestic savings flow respond to treatment, the economy becomes less vulnerable to the ebb and flow of supplier credits and foreign aid. From the standpoint of stability, it is perhaps most important that liberalization can reduce dependence on bursts of inflation and the inflation tax to balance fiscal budgets and can bring monetary variables under discipline.

The name of the policy game in repressed economies is interventionism. Because monetary variables are out of hand, there seems to be need for price control in detail. Because the exchange rate is overvalued, complex tariff schedules, import licenses, and differentiated export bonuses are put into force. Because savings are scarce, credit is rationed loan by loan. An economy that immobilizes critical relative prices must fall back upon contrivances of interventionism to clear markets. A burden is put upon the civil service that it cannot carry, and the costs in both inefficiency and corruption are high. It is a principal purpose of liberalization to substitute markets for bureaus.

THE ORIGINS AND CONTEXT OF FINANCIAL REPRESSION

Financial repression has its typical complements in development strategy. It is part of a package. As we have suggested, overvaluation of the domestic currency in terms of foreign monies is another part. Whereas financial policy including inflation reduces real rates of interest and makes savings appear cheap, so cheap that they must be rigorously rationed, exchange-rate policy holds down the domestic price of foreign exchange. There is excess demand for both savings and foreign exchange. In the rationing of foreign exchange, preference commonly goes to capital equipment or, once the equipment has been installed, to its spare parts and replacements and to materials that it processes.

Another part of the strategy reduces relative prices for domestically produced primary products. Industrial raw materials are made cheap for the urban industrial establishment that benefits, too, from low rates of interest and from cheap imports. Foods are made cheap for the urban working class in order to temper its wage demands. Primary products are diverted from export markets, and imports of substitutes have a claim of high priority for scarce foreign exchange when domestic supplies run short.

The strategy produces a dual labor market. A relatively small fraction of the labor force is recruited for capital-intensive industry that benefits from low rates of interest, low rates of foreign exchange, and cheap prices for domestic inputs. Industrial labor unionizes and is granted minimum-wage rates that, despite erosion in real terms during inflation, draw rural labor into urban unemployment. Basic amenities for the urban population impose a growing burden on the government budget and reduce government's contribution to the flow of savings.

Fiscal policy in this context is easy to predict. By one device or another, including marketing boards, substantial revenues are collected from traditional exports. Excises on some items of luxury consumption and duties on imports of goods that compete with products of capital-intensive industry are other ranking revenue sources. Real property is taxed lightly, if at all; various tax concessions are arranged for the industrial enclave; and public enterprise supplies cheaply, or at a loss, various utilities that, like savings and foreign exchange, are rationed in some degree of compliance with a plan of industrialization. Total revenues tend to be inelastic to both inflation and growth in real national output.

Excess demand for savings spills into the capital account of the balance of international payments. In the worst of circumstances, it draws on high-cost, short-term credits until some solution is found for funding. It may be satisfied by direct private investment from abroad and by grants of official aid, some of them with local-currency counterparts that provide a measure of relief for the fiscal budget.

This is a strategy of transformation and structural change. It manipulates a congeries of relative prices—for savings, foreign exchange, basic materials, labor, government services—and it resolves by rationing the excess demands that emerge at these prices. The general purpose, of course, is to break away from relatively low levels of income and consumption by changing the national matrix of products and their inputs. It is an inferior strategy under the best of circumstances and a self-defeating strategy in the usual case: the excess demands or "gaps" that it generates on some markets and the excess supplies that occur especially in markets for labor and for products of capital-intensive industry prove impossible to close at desired or acceptable growth rates of income and consumption. They repress development.

V.E. INFLATION AND ITS
EFFECTS

V.E.1. Inflation and Development

Policy*

The first question to be discussed is whether the mobilization of an economy's resources by development policy inevitably involves inflation. It is contended here that some degree of inflation—but a moderate degree only—is the logical concomitant of efficient economic mobilization. The argument rests on two propositions. One is that so long as inflation proceeds at a rate low enough not to disturb seriously the general confidence in the stability of the value of money its effects are primarily to redistribute incomes, and to do so to an extent that does not involve serious social consequences, rather than to produce significant misallocations of resources, such as those which occur when people come to expect inflation and seek to protect themselves from it by holding goods instead of money and by using political means to safeguard their real incomes. The other proposition is that, owing to the various rigidities and immobilities characteristic of any economy, but particularly of underdeveloped economies, upward movements of wages and prices can help to reallocate labour and resources and to draw labour out of traditional or subsistence sectors into the developing sectors of the economy. It is important to note that this proposition, like the first, presumes a general expectation of stability in the value of money, as a precon-

*From Harry G. Johnson, "Is Inflation the Inevitable Price of Rapid Development or a Retarding Factor in Economic Growth?" *Malayan Economic Review*, Vol. 11, No. 1, April 1966, pp. 22–8. Reprinted by permission.

dition for the offer of higher wages and prices to serve as an inducement to mobility.

The second proposition implies that some inflationary pressure in the economy will assist the task of mobilizing resources for development; the first implies that such inflationary pressure will not introduce offsetting distortions causing significant real losses to the economy as a whole, but will instead mainly involve transfers of income within the economy, the social consequences of which will be small enough to be acceptable. Efficient policy-making will therefore involve arriving at a trade-off between the mobilizing and redistributive effects of inflation that will involve some positive rate of inflation. The indicated optimum rate of inflation is likely to be significantly higher for an underdeveloped than for an advanced economy for two reasons: first, the sophisticated financial system of an advanced economy provides many more facilities for economizing on the use of money in face of expected inflation; and second, the superior mobility of resources of an advanced economy implies that the increase in total output achievable by inflationary means is relatively much smaller. Thus one might expect that whereas "tolerable" price stability in an advanced economy is frequently defined as a rate of inflation of no more than one to two per cent a year, the tolerable degree of stability for an underdeveloped economy might be in the range of a four to six per cent annual rate of price increase. (Harberger has suggested that a 10 per cent annual rate of inflation represents the outside limit of inflation justifiable by this line of argument.)[1] This analysis, of course, relates to purely domestic considerations and ignores the balance-of-payments or exchange-rate implications of internal price trends.

The foregoing remarks relate to the question of inflation as a consequence or aspect of economic development policy, and to the argument that some degree of inflation is the necessary price of rapid development. It has been argued that a modest rate of inflation is a logical part of an efficient development policy, in the sense that the "price" may purchase gains in efficiency of resource allocation and utilization that outweigh the costs. The argument now turns to the second problem raised by the question, the effectiveness or otherwise of inflationary financing of development programmes.

The deliberate use of inflationary policies to promote economic development has been recommended on theoretical grounds by certain economists, and the fact that many underdeveloped countries have for one reason or another resorted to such policies has led a number of other economists to condone or find merit in inflation as a means to economic development. This article will not attempt to survey all the theoretical arguments—in particular, it will not go into the structuralist *versus* monetarist debate over inflation in Latin America—but will instead outline the major theoretical and practical arguments for inflation as a means to development, and discuss the major defects of inflationary development policy in practice.

The main theoretical arguments for inflationary development policies derive from two systems of economic thought, the Keynesian theory of income and the quantity theory of money. The Keynesian approach to the question (which derives from the Keynes of the *Tract* and the *Treatise* as much as from the Keynes of the *General*

Theory) argues that inflation will promote growth in two ways: by redistributing income from workers and peasants, who are assumed to have a low marginal propensity to save, to capitalist entrepreneurs, who are assumed to have a high marginal propensity to save and invest; and by raising the nominal rate of return on investment relative to the rate of interest, thus promoting investment. Neither of these arguments, however, is either theoretically plausible or consistent with the facts, at least so far as sustained inflationary processes are concerned. Both rest on the arbitrary and empirically unsupported assumption that entrepreneurs realize that inflation is occurring, whereas the other members of the economy do not, or at least do not realize it fully. As to the first, the theoretical prediction is that all sectors of the economy the prices of whose services are upwards-flexible will come to anticipate inflation, so that no significant redistributions of income will take place; this prediction accords with the mass of the available evidence. As to the second, the theoretical expectation is that free-market interest rates will rise sufficiently to compensate holders of interest-yielding assets for the expected rate of inflation; this expectation also accords with the mass of the available evidence. This argument for inflation, therefore, is valid only under two possible sets of circumstances: first, in the early stages of an inflationary development programme, while the mass of the population (especially the workers and the savers) still has confidence in the stability of the value of money; and second, when inflationary financing is accompanied by governmental policies of holding down the wage and interest costs of business enterprise. Such policies would generate distortions in the allocation of resources, which might offset any benefits to growth from the inflationary policy; in particular, the contrary view has been argued that inflation will discourage the supply of saving for investment.

The quantity theory approach, on the other hand, adopts the more realistic as-

[1] Arnold C. Harberger, "Some Notes on Inflation," in Werner Baer and Isaac Kerstenetzky (eds.), *Inflation and Growth in Latin America,* Homewood, Ill.: Irwin, 1964.

sumption that in a sustained inflationary process the behavior of all sectors of the economy will become adjusted to the expectation of inflation, and that consequently the effect of inflation will be, not to redistribute income from workers or savers to capitalist entrepreneurs, but to redistribute it from the holders of money balances—who are the only losers from an inflation that is anticipated—to the monetary authorities who issue money the real value of which steadily depreciates. Inflation imposes an "inflationary tax" on holdings of money, which consists in the real resources that the holders of money have to forego each period in order to restore the real value of their money holdings. The presence of this tax, in turn, encourages the public to attempt to evade the tax by reducing their holdings of money, shortening payments periods, holding inventories of goods instead of cash, and so forth; these efforts involve a waste of real resources and a reduction of real income, representing the "collection cost" of the inflationary tax. On the other hand, the real resources collected by the inflationary tax are available for use in the development programme; and if they are used for investment, the inflationary policy may accelerate economic growth. It should be noted, however, that in the transitional stages of an inflationary development policy, or in the process of acceleration of such a policy, whatever contribution to growth there is may be outweighed by the increased waste of resources produced by the increase in the inflationary tax.

In practical experience, resort to the inflationary tax as a method of financing economic development is generally prompted by the inability of the developing country to raise enough revenue by taxation and by borrowing from the public to finance its development plans, either as a result of the low income and taxable capacity of the economy, or more commonly as a result of inability to command the necessary political consensus in support of the necessary sacrifices of current income. Unfortunately, the same characteristics of underdevelopment that limit the capacity to finance development by orthodox fiscal methods also place rather narrow limits on the possibility of financing development by inflation. In particular, underdevelopment implies a relatively smaller use of money than is common in advanced countries, and therefore a relatively smaller base on which the inflationary tax can be levied.

Before discussing this point in detail, it is appropriate to refer to a related question that figured large in the development literature of about a decade ago, the question of the extent to which development can be financed by monetary expansion without producing inflationary consequences. The answer, clearly, is that such financing can be safely pursued up to the limit set by the growth of demand for money consequent on the expected growth of the economy at stable prices, plus the growth of demand for money associated with the monetization of the subsistence sector (where relevant), minus the portion of the growth in the money supply that must be created against private debt. The magnitude of the resources that can be made available for financing development by this means, however, depends on the magnitude of the absolute increase in the money supply permitted by these factors or, to put it another way, on the rate of growth of the demand for money, the ratio of money to income, and the portion of the additional money that can be used to finance public spending. Thus, for example, with a rate of growth of demand for money of 6 per cent, half of which can be used to finance public spending, the budget deficit financed by monetary expansion would be 3 per cent of the initial money supply. If the ratio of money supply to national income were in the neighborhood of two-fifths, as is common in advanced countries, this would make 1.2 per cent of national income available for development investment; if, on the other hand, the ratio of money supply to national income were in the lower neighborhood of one-fifth, as is common in underdeveloped countries, only one half of one per cent of national income would be available for development investment.[2] The difference in the order of magnitude of the money-to-income ratio explains both why budget deficits in underdeveloped countries are more frequently associated with inflation, and why in such countries inflationary financing of development is more frequently resorted to, than in advanced countries.

In the same way as it limits the scope for non-inflationary deficit financing of development, the restricted use of money in underdeveloped countries limits the extent to which inflation can make resources available for economic development through the inflationary tax. Ignoring the possibilities of non-inflationary financing by monetary expansion due to the growth and monetization of the economy, the yield of the inflationary tax as a proportion of national income will be the product of the money-to-income ratio, the rate of inflation, and the proportion of the increase in the money supply captured for financing development. Thus, with the assumed money-to-income ratio of one-fifth and an assumed capture rate of one-half, a 10 per cent rate of inflation would secure 1 per cent of national income for the development programme, and so on. The money-to-income ratio, however, is not insensitive to the rate of inflation, but is on the contrary likely to decrease appreciably as the rate of inflation rises, thereby setting limits to the possibilities of development finance by these means. Further, it should be noted that insofar as development financing depends on a growth of demand for money resulting from monetization of the economy, inflation is likely to reduce that growth by inhibiting monetization, so further reducing the net amount of resources

gathered for development finance through inflation. . . .

The circumstances in which inflation is resorted to in underdeveloped countries, however, are far from the most favorable conceivable, and their inflations are extremely likely to proceed in such a way, and to be accompanied by such other economic policies, as to exercise a serious retarding influence on economic growth. Specifically, inflationary financing may impede growth in three major ways, each contrary to the assumptions of the inflationary tax model.

In the first place, contrary to the assumption that prices throughout the economy adjust freely to inflation, the government of a developing country employing inflationary development policies is likely to be under strong political pressure to protect important sectors of the community from the effects of inflation, through control of food prices, rents, urban transport fares, and so on. Such controls inevitably distort the allocation of resources within the economy, and particularly their allocation to private investment in growth. Fixing of low prices for food inhibits the development of agricultural production and the improvement of agricultural technique; control of rents, on the other hand, may unduly foster the construction of new housing to accommodate those who cannot find rent-controlled housing or to enable landlords to evade rent controls. All these policies tend to promote urbanization, which involves expenditure on social overhead and may increase the numbers of the urban unemployed. Moreover, control of prices of food, and particularly of fares on state-owned transport facilities, may involve the state in explicit subsidies on the one hand and budget deficits on the other, so that the proceeds of the inflationary tax are wasted in supporting the consumption of certain sections of the population rather than invested in development. Such phenomena are widely observable in the underdeveloped countries of the world. (They are also observable in advanced countries, but

[2] The illustrative numbers used are derived from J. J. Polak, "Monetary Analysis of Income Formation and Payments Problems," *International Monetary Fund Staff Papers,* November 1957, Table on p. 25.

the latter can easily afford the wastes of resources involved).

Second, contrary to the assumptions of the inflationary tax model, inflation typically does not proceed at a steady and well-anticipated rate, but proceeds erratically with large politically-determined variations in the rate of price increase. These variations in the rate of inflation divert a great deal of the effort of private business into forecasting and speculating on the rate of inflation, or hedging against the uncertainties involved. They also destroy the possibility of rational calculation of small margins of profit and undermine the incentives to strive constantly to reduce costs and improve performance, which striving is the key to the steady increase of productivity in the industrially advanced nations.

Finally, the inflationary tax model assumes either a closed economy or a country on a floating exchange rate system. In reality, countries—especially underdeveloped countries—are exposed to competition in and from the world economy, yet they display a strong propensity to maintain fixed exchange rates and to defend them to the limit of their exchange reserves, borrowing powers, and ability to use exchange controls. In this kind of setting inflation introduces a progressive tendency toward exchange rate overvaluation, balance-of-payments difficulties, and resort to increasing protectionism, which in turn results in the diversion of resources away from export industries and toward high-cost import-substituting industries, and a consequent loss of economic efficiency. While the appearance of growth may be generated by the establishment of import-substitute industries, the reality may be lost in misallocation of resources produced by protectionism and the inefficiency of exchange control procedures. Moreover, eventually the increasing overvaluation of the currency is likely to force a devaluation, coupled with a monetary reform involving drastic domestic deflation. This experience, in addition to the immediate disturbing effects of deflation in interrupting the growth of the economy, has the long-run effect of damaging the stability and confidence of expectations on which the process of investing in the growth of the economy depends.

To summarize, this article has argued the following propositions. First, an efficient development policy should plan on some modest degree of inflation as a means of more fully mobilizing the economy's resources; in this limited sense, inflation is an inevitable price of rapid development. Second, while a policy of financing development by deliberate inflation has strong attractions theoretically and politically, the possibilities of stimulating economic development by these means are quite limited. Third, inflationary development policies in practice are unlikely to achieve this stimulating effect, but on the contrary likely to retard economic growth, by distorting the allocation of resources and wasting the inflation-gathered development resources on consumption, by increasing uncertainty and reducing incentives for innovation and improvement, and through their balance-of-payments effects by fostering the inefficiencies of protectionism and exchange control.

V.E.2. Monetarism and Structuralism in

Latin America*

The controversy between "monetarists" and "structuralists" in Latin America has been exaggerated beyond all bounds. While rather virulent in theoretical disquisitions, it narrows down substantially when practical policy recommendations have to be formulated.

One cruel fact that the structuralists must face, when entrusted with policy responsibilities outside the academic wards, is that structural adjustments inevitably take a long time, while the combat to inflation, if it is to succeed, needs fairly quick, visible results; and those can be obtained much more expeditiously (though often at the cost of painful side effects) through the demand side—via monetary and fiscal policies—than through the supply side (unless foreign aid is available in unlimited amounts). I do not, of course, deny that the purely monetary or fiscal solution may not be durable or consistent with stable growth unless adjustments are also made on the supply side. The truth is, that in the short run, all structuralists when entrusted with policy-making responsibilities become monetarists, while all monetarists are, in the long run, structuralists. Thus, we might jocosely define a monetarist as a structuralist in a hurry and a structuralist as a monetarist without policy-making responsibility.

Let us try to determine at this stage what the controversy is not. It is not a quarrel between those economists and policy-makers who recognize the existence of structural rigidities and those who do not. All recog-

*From Roberto de Oliveira Campos, "Economic Development and Inflation with Special Reference to Latin America," in OECD, *Development Plans and Programmes,* OECD Development Center, Paris, 1964, pp. 129–37. Reprinted by permission.

nize that structural problems do exist. It is not a controversy between those who favor economic growth and development and those who do not. It is not a debate between those who advocate an economic policy which permits the economy to grow and those who advocate a restrictive monetary policy in an attempt to hold down the money supply and keep prices absolutely constant.

The basic controversy lies in the tendency of economists of the structuralist persuasion to view monetary expansion and inflation as an unavoidable feature of structural change and economic growth in Latin America; and correlatedly to claim that the attempt to avoid monetary expansion and inflation will only hamper structural changes and economic growth. If other descriptions are needed, one might say that the structuralists would hold that the permissiveness of the monetary and fiscal policy of the monetary authorities is simply a reflection of exogenous factors, particularly the decline in import capacity, while the monetarists would hold that this fatalistic result is not inevitable, and that inflation cannot be blamed exclusively or even predominantly on "exogenous" factors, but rather on the "policies of inaction" pursued by most of the Latin American Governments.

Another "spurious" presentation of the controversy is to take the view that monetarists in Latin America are slavishly following monetary tenets of classical liberalism, by adhering strictly to the quantity theory in money and banking, to free trade views in matters of international trade, to non-intervention doctrines insofar as Government activities are concerned, and generally by ascribing lower priority to development than to stabilization and by neglecting the special problems of structural under-employment or unemployment in underdeveloped countries. . . .

THE MONETARIST VIEW ON INFLATION AND GROWTH

Apart from a small current of thought that approaches the question of inflation and development from the viewpoint of value judgments, and that, by questioning the social advantage of inflation-financed development, tends to ascribe high social priority to stabilization, the bulk of the monetarists in Latin America appear to recognize the social priority of development, while insisting that continued and stable growth can best be attained in an environment of monetary stability. Their position can be thus summarized:

1. The only possible contributions of inflation to growth derive:

a. From the forced saving mechanism, through which the decline in real wages due to rising prices and the wage lag would increase investible profits. Thus inflation would act as a disguised taxation on consumers and savers to the benefit of investors;

b. From the assumption that the pressure of inflationary demand would permit a fuller utilization of manpower and resources, while conversely the attempt to combat inflation by wiping out excess demand might bring employment and resource-utilization down to the level permitted by bottleneck factors;

c. From the assumption that inflation would stimulate bold entrepreneurship and reward investors at the expense of conservative savers or rentiers. Against these supposed advantages, the monetarists raise a formidable number of qualifications: (i) the forced savings device can act only temporarily for discontinuous inflation, but has its efficacy lowered or destroyed when inflation is chronic and becomes a part of the expectation of wage earners, who devise defense mechanisms to prevent a decline in real wages. It is true that in dual societies, in which because of institutional factors real wages in some urban industries are set above the limit of marginal productivity, it is possible, because of the continuous migration of under-employed rural labor to the city, and given the relative rigidity of factoral proportions of labor and capital in modern technology, to depress the real urban wage for protracted periods; this, however, only prolongs a little bit the usefulness of the forced savings mechanism but does not guarantee its continuity; (ii) such transfer of resources as may take place from consumers to the Government or to investors may be offset by luxury consumption of the entrepreneurial group, by the lower efficiency of government investments or by bottlenecks in the import capacity; (iii) while inflation encourages the adventurous entrepreneur, it tends to discourage risk-taking in basic enterprises of a long maturation period.

2. Inflation discourages the inflow of foreign capital and renders more difficult the absorption of financing from foreign governments and institutional organizations.

3. Inflation tends to impair the qualitative composition of investments. It discourages investments in basic industries and infrastructural services which are either price-controlled or require long gestation periods, or both. It weakens or prevents the creation of credit and capital markets and stimulates speculative investments in inventories.[1]

4. The structural thesis exaggerates the two basic alleged rigidities: the inelasticity of the food supply and the inelasticity of exports. The reasoning of the structuralists starts from the premise of a total sectoral incompressibility of prices, so that any upward price pressure would result in a rise in the

[1] These results need not necessarily occur. For a different view, see Werner Baer, "Inflation and Economic Efficiency in Brazil," paper presented at the Rio de Janeiro Conference on Inflation and Development, January, 1963. . . .

general price level. Thus the pressure of population growth and rising urban incomes would tend to raise, through a chain-reaction mechanism, first the price of agriculture goods, secondly the general price level and thirdly wages, thus creating an inflationary spiral of a structural nature. Similarly, the inelasticity of world demand for primary export would tend to lower the export capacity below import requirements for growth, rendering necessary an accelerated process of import substitution. But, at least initially, import substitution tends to be inflationary because of the relative inefficiency of the new industries during the learning period, this cost pressure being aggravated by the need for exchange devaluations in an attempt to restore external balance. The monetarists would argue that the alleged structural inelasticity of food supplies is often not structural at all. It stems frequently from the fact that the administrative control of food prices, designed to protect the urban consumer, cuts off the agricultural producer from price and market stimuli, so that the inelasticity of food supply, rather than being an inherent structural characteristic, may be a distortion induced by administrative controls. While in some cases the structure of land tenure would prevent in any event the diffusion of market incentives, thus rendering structural reform a precondition for increasing food production, this situation occurs only rarely. As to industrial import substitution, while it is not denied that it carries a built-in inflationary pressure, at least if the industrial expansion takes place at constant cost, the cost-push arising therefrom has been grossly exaggerated. Thus, assuming that imports for a typical underdeveloped country represent 10 per cent of national product, that real income is rising at 6 per cent per annum, that exports are stationary and that the income-elasticity of demand for imported products equals 2, and finally, that the needed customs protection for the national substitutes is 100 per cent—all of those factors would not entail a price increase above 1.2 per cent per annum,

a margin vastly surpassed in the inflated economies of Latin America.

CRITICISM OF THE MONETARIST APPROACH

The monetarist approach has curiously enough been attacked from two conflicting vantage points. It is argued, on the one hand, that it is too strong because controls will restrain investment, generating unemployment and losses in real output, thus not only aggravating the supply problem but also arousing political instability. Some argue, on the other hand, that it is too weak, because without the leverage of fiscal policies it does not really control excess demand nor go to the heart of structural and institutional problems.

Four points may be readily granted. The *first* is that the only meaningful interpretation of the monetarist approach is that it encompasses not only the use of traditional monetary weapons—the efficacy of which is by definition very limited in the rather primitive financial markets characteristic of the less developed countries—but also of fiscal policies. The *second* is that the effectiveness of monetary weapons, *stricto sensu*, is considerably greater in the case of *demand inflation* than of *cost inflation.* This is particularly true if the problem is that of a wage spiral, where the reduction of the quantity of money may stop the rise in prices but *only* at the expense of employment. The *third* point is that monetary tools, as distinct from fiscal policies, are inappropriate when the problem is to curb consumption (which can only be achieved via fiscal policies), the effectiveness of monetary restraints being greater if the objective is to restrain investment.

The *fourth* point is the asymmetrical effect of monetary policies; through a combination of quantitative and qualitative credit controls it is possible to orient a selective expansion of certain economic sectors but much harder to enforce a selective restriction of undesirable sectors.

The net upshot of these observations is that monetary weapons, though an indispensable ingredient in anti-inflationary programmes, have to be used in a prudent combination with fiscal policies. The shortcomings to their application arise not only from asymmetrical effects—they affect investment more than consumption, their efficiency is greater in reducing demand than costs—but from the limited organization and responsiveness of money and credit markets in the less developed countries. Fiscal policies, particularly when designed to curb luxury consumption by taxation of wealthier groups so as to raise the marginal tax rate above the average rate, have undoubtedly a fundamental role to play in anti-inflation programmes.

The applicability of monetary policies depends, of course, on the speed desired in checking inflation and on the degree of flexibility of the wage pattern and labor organisation. The latter factor is a major determinant of the possibility of utilization of credit controls without untoward unemployment effects.

THE "STRUCTURALIST" VIEW

The "structuralist" school stresses the "structural vulnerability" of Latin American economies to inflation because of two alleged basic rigidities.

The first one is the slow and unstable rate of export growth, which is held to be chronically inadequate to support the needed rate of development; the sluggish growth rate makes necessary a continuous and sharp effort of import substitution, creating a cost-push because of the substitution effort itself; the instability of the growth rate in turn creates occasional contraction of government tax revenues arising from exports, precisely when government expenditures need to be increased to offset the depressant effect of the stagnation or recession of the export sector; finally, the secular trend towards deterioration of the trade of primary products creates an additional complication, further limiting the potentialities of growth of the export income, and reinforcing the trend toward periodical exchange rate devaluation.

The second one is the inelasticity of agricultural production, due largely to defective patterns of land tenure which decrease the responsiveness of food production to price stimuli.

The cost-push in Latin American economies would thus come from a fourfold direction: cost of import substitution, rise in agricultural prices, deterioration of the terms of trade and exchange rate devaluation.

Fortified with those tenets, the structuralists proceed to inveigh against what they call the "orthodox" monetary policies advised by the International Monetary Fund, which in their view do not go to the heart of the problem—structural change—and have depressant effects, manifested in a decrease in the level of investment, in the contraction of the private sector due to the incompressibility of the public sector and in the deflationary effects of unemployment and the wage lag. Thus stability is achieved only at the expense of growth.

CRITICISM OF THE STRUCTURALIST APPROACH

While the structuralists are very articulate in their diagnosis of Latin American inflation and in their strictures on monetarism, they are far less explicit on practical policy recommendations. These do not go usually beyond the expression of pious hopes for structural changes, which because of their long-run nature are not serviceable recipes for the short-run cure of inflation.

The structuralist tends therefore to advocate gradualism in anti-inflationary programmes and to postulate an increase in foreign aid and international financing as major factors in helping to buy time for the needed structural changes.

One of the most cogent and articulate criticisms of the structuralist interpretation of Latin American inflation has been put forward recently by Arthur Lewis in his

"Closing remarks at the Conference on Inflation and Development in Latin America," convened in January, 1963 in Rio de Janeiro.

Lewis' initial and important contribution is to stress the difference between *self-liquidating* and *spiral inflation*, the first being relevant and the second irrelevant for economic development. Through *self-liquidating* inflation limited policy objectives can be attained, such as altering permanently the distribution of income in favor of investment. The *spiral* inflation, in turn, does not serve any growth objective but is rather a political phenomenon, arising from tensions in the society.

The *first* stricture of Lewis is to question the alleged inevitable sluggishness of the export sector of primary producing countries. He mentions that between 1950 and 1960, the quantum of trade in primary products grew by 6 per cent, only slightly under the rate of growth of manufactured exports, which was 7 per cent. While Lewis is right in excoriating the excessive importance attributed by the structuralist school to the "structural" sluggishness of the export sector in Latin America, he dismisses altogether too glibly the trade problem, which is real. In particular, he overlooks the fact that:

a. Part of the statistical expansion of exports of primary products in the last decade did not come from the underdeveloped countries but from the industrialized countries. The latter expanded their export of primary products by 57 per cent while the former by only 14 per cent. Thus not only world trade in manufactures expanded at a faster rate, but the lion's share of primary exports was taken by the industrialized countries themselves. Latin American exports were also greatly affected by a price decline since 1953. While world trade grew in volume by 50 per cent between 1953 and 1960, raw material prices declined by 7 per cent. Brazil expanded its volume of exports by 20 per cent in the above period, while unit prices fell by 37 per cent.

b. The trade experience with which Professor Lewis is most familiar is that of the sheltered trade area of the British Commonwealth countries. But Latin America was for all practical purposes, until the recent creation of LAFTA, an unsheltered trade area, and the GATT report on "Trends in International Trade" presents conclusive evidence that trade within sheltered areas has been expanding at a substantially faster rate than the trade of unsheltered areas.

Just as Professor Lewis appears to minimize unduly the importance of the decline in the import capacity of Latin America, the "structuralists" of ECLA overestimate its explanatory and causal role in the process of inflation. As Professor Grunwald has pointed out, despite a decline in the export quantum over the last decade, the Latin American countries managed to maintain or even to increase their import quantum by depletion of exchange reserves and/or increase in international indebtedness.[2]

It is true that this does not quite solve the problem, particularly in those countries where the decline in export activity requires compensatory government policies for domestic expansion, or where fiscal revenues are greatly dependent on export taxation. But the brunt of the argument is taken. The two main weaknesses of the structuralist view on trade are then:

a. that some of the sluggishness in the export growth is not really structural but results plainly from the failure to exploit, because of overvalued exchange rates, export opportunities that may still exist;

b. the import quantum has been maintained, on the average, for Latin America, despite the decline in export revenues, so that there has been no inflationary decrease in the availability of import goods.

[2] Grunwald, "Invisible Hands in Inflation and Growth," p. 11, paper submitted to the Rio de Janeiro Conference on Inflation and Development, January, 1963. [W. Baer and I. Kerstenetzky (eds.), *Inflation and Growth in Latin America*, Homewood, 1964.]

The *second* stricture of Professor Lewis concerns the wage push. He tends to deny any special characteristic to the Latin American wage scene, as compared to other underdeveloped regions more successful in controlling inflation; he also writes off the wage spiral in Latin America as simply a political problem, resulting from the low degree of sympathy of trade unions for their governments. It is impossible to deny, however, that there are vast differences between Latin America and other underdeveloped regions of Africa or Asia in a number of respects. There is less surplus labor in Latin America, the degree of labor organisation is greater, there is more responsiveness to Western consumption habits and less passivity in claiming social benefits. Even within Latin America, there are substantial regional differences, the difficulty of preventing a wage spiral being directly related to the degree of labor union organisation, which seems greater in the Argentine and Chile, much lower in Mexico, Peru and Colombia, while Brazil holds an intermediate position.

The *third* stricture of Professor Lewis concerns the alleged rigidity of agricultural production. He is right in pointing out that pressure on food supplies is not peculiar to the underdeveloped countries of Latin America and that structuralists underestimate the possibility of corrective adjustments by increasing the propensity to export or by reducing the propensity to import.

What might be said by way of conclusion is that the basic flaws in the structuralist argument seem thus to lie in that:

a. no separation is made between autonomous structural rigidities and induced rigidities resulting from price or exchange controls or mismanaged government intervention;

b. the quantitative importance of the cost-push generated by import substitution, or by losses in import capacity through the decline in terms of trade, is greatly exaggerated; while those factors might account for a moderate inflationary pressure, they are of little use to explain the massive and chronic inflation in Latin America.

V.E.3. Inflation and Growth*

It is abundantly clear from the available evidence that there is no close relation between the rate of inflation and the rate of economic growth. There have been countries with low rates of inflation which have had the full gamut of experience with respect to economic growth. The same is true with respect to high rates of inflation. It seems to me that we cannot accept a position at either extreme, either one which holds that having a substantial inflation would rule out

*From Arnold C. Harberger, "Some Notes on Inflation," in Werner Baer and Isaac Kerstenetzky (eds.), *Inflation and Growth in Latin America,* Richard D. Irwin, Inc., Homewood, 1964, pp. 320–28. Reprinted by permission.

the possibility of a substantial rate of progress in real income or one which holds that some inflation is necessary in order to achieve a high rate of economic growth. Whatever connections we may establish between the rate of inflation and the rate of economic progress are likely to be rather weak, tenuous links rather than strong and fundamental relationships.

In this paragraph I set out what I believe to be the principal argument against inflation as the promoter of economic growth. This argument is not really an argument against inflation itself, but rather an argument against the way inflations appear to have worked in practice. It is possible to imagine an inflation which went on steadily at, say, 30 percent per year, and which was completely and accurately anticipated by everybody, and in which the separate prices of all the different commodities and services in the economy rose steadily at the same pace. This "ideal" type of inflation is not what we have observed in the real world. The inflations of the real world are, by and large not at all accurately anticipated, and in them there occurs substantial disparity in the rates of rise of the prices of different types of goods and services. The failure to anticipate accurately and, in particular, the disparity in the pace of adjustment of particular prices blur, so to speak, the vision of the people who are responsible for economic organization. In a country which has a stable general price level it is possible for entrepreneurs to make a judgment that a new process will save, say, two cents in the dollar of production costs, and it is likely that within a stable environment such a new process would in fact be adopted with alacrity. If, however, the economy is undergoing an inflation of, say, 20–30 percent per annum it will be difficult for entrepreneurs to act on this kind of improvement. They will not know whether the saving of two cents in the dollar of costs will be erased by a rise in wages or in prices of materials in the very near future. During any big inflation all absolute prices are constantly adjusted. They adjust at different rates, and in a pattern which is not at all precisely predictable. I would venture to guess that where in a stable environment entrepreneurs would be happy to make alterations in their method of production on the basis of information which appeared to suggest a saving of two cents in the dollar of costs, in an inflationary environment entrepreneurs might require information suggesting that they might save ten cents in the dollar of costs before they would be willing to undertake a substantial overhaul of their methods of production. This obviously means that fewer growth-producing innovations will take place in an inflationary setting than in a more stable environment.

The above should not be taken as presenting a total picture. Inflation sometimes can help to keep the economy operating at its full potential. Economists like to pretend that it is possible to maintain full employment while keeping the general price level constant. The evidence, however, does not appear to corroborate the economists' view. Moreover, a little reflection will indicate that the economic policy of a country probably should have a certain inflationary bias. Consider the economic costs to a country of having, on the one hand, a situation in which there are present inflationary pressures whose ultimate effect would be to raise the price level by 5 percent; consider, on the other hand, a situation in which there are present deflationary pressures whose ultimate effect would be to lower the price level by 5 percent. In both of these cases there would exist inequities due to the differential impact of inflation or deflation on different groups in the economy. By and large, those who would gain from inflation would lose from deflation, and I do not see any reason to consider that, on equity grounds, inflation is either better or worse than deflation. However, allowing deflationary forces to work themselves out would entail, in virtually any present-day economy, substantial unemployment of labor, and perhaps also of capital resources. This effect is present when the pressures are deflationary and absent when the pressures are inflationary. It seems to me self-evident that the social costs of allowing deflationary pressures at the rate of, say, 5 percent per annum are very much greater than the social costs of allowing inflationary pressures at the rate of 5 percent per annum to work themselves out in the economy. So long as there is this asymmetry between the social costs of a deflation of x percent per annum and the social costs of inflation of x percent per annum, it is clear that public policy should not operate on the assumption that one is as bad as the other. Some bias toward inflation should result from any rational calculation of the costs and benefits involved. The way in which this bias toward inflation might reasonably work itself out would be through a monetary and fiscal policy which was tight in periods of boom, and sufficiently loose in periods of slack to produce some rise in the general price level, as a consequence of the effort to eliminate or reduce the slackness in the economy. Just to put an order of magnitude on the kind of inflation that might result from this sort of policy, I can easily imagine that it could produce inflation at an average rate of 1, or 2, or 3 percent per annum. So as not to err in my judgment, let me set the limit at something like 10 percent per annum. It seems to me that it would be extremely difficult to defend a policy which produced inflation at more than 10 percent per annum on the ground that this rate of inflation was necessary to eliminate slackness in the economy.

It is my impression that the basic force which has created the inflationary pressure in Latin-American countries has been a chronic budget deficit. But I think it is important to realize that budget deficits do not invariably produce inflation, and that there is a reasonable amount of room in which budget policy can move without having inflationary consequences.

Economic growth is the principal reason that budgetary deficits can be maintained continuously without necessarily producing inflation. In a growing economy some provision must be made for a secular increase in the money supply if stable prices are to be maintained. If economic growth is taking place at 3 percent per year in real terms, it is likely that the increase in the money supply required for price stability will be somewhat greater than 3 percent per year, for the evidence from a number of countries suggests that the income elasticity of demand for real cash balances is typically somewhat in excess of unity. Moreover, if, as may be the case in some developing economies, there is a secular tendency for the real rate of interest to fall, there will arise from this source also a tendency for secular increase in the demand for real cash balances. It is thus possible that

a country with a 3 percent rate of growth of real income might be able to sustain a 4 or 5 percent rate of growth of the money supply without inducing inflation.

One can conceive of many ways of providing the increase in money supply necessary for maintaining price stability. At the base of the money supply we have what has come to be called high-powered money— currency plus the deposit liabilities of the central bank. (It is called high-powered money because it can serve as reserves on the basis of which a secondary expansion in the money supply can take place, via deposit creation in the commercial banks.)

The money supply in the hands of the public and the government may be conceived as representing the liabilities of the banking system as a whole, at least in those cases where currency consists overwhelmingly of central bank notes. Any increase in the money supply will, accordingly, have as its counterpart some increase in the assets of the banking system as a whole, and an increase in bank assets can represent either private sector obligations or public sector obligations, or both. If a 5 percent per annum increase in the money supply is desired, it could, in principle, have as its counterpart exclusively increased holdings of government obligations by the banking system. It is unlikely, however, that such an extreme position would represent wise policy for the long run, for this would mean that there would be no expansion of bank loans and investments in the private sector, in spite of the fact that the economy as a whole was growing. A situation which appears to me more reasonably to approximate a sensible norm for the long run is that the banking system's holdings of both private obligations and government obligations would expand at roughly similar rates. (I do not mean to imply by this that there is any profound reason for maintaining a fixity in the proportions of the two classes of assets held by the banking system; I only suggest that maintaining a fixed ratio seems to be a more plausible norm than concentrating all increases in bank assets in one sector or the other.) Let us suppose a situation in which the assets of the banking system consisted initially of half public and half private sector obligations, and in which these proportions are to be maintained throughout the process of money supply expansion. Then, assuming that the money supply is to be expanded at the rate of 5 per cent per year, half of this expansion would be accounted for by increases in bank holdings of government obligations. On this account alone, one could justify a government deficit which each year was equal to 2½ percent of the country's money supply.

Unfortunately, the amount of deficit that can be justified in these terms is substantially less for underdeveloped countries than for advanced countries. In advanced countries the money supply often amounts to a third or a half of a year's national income, so that a government deficit equal to 2½ percent of the money supply would amount to between, say, ⅞ of 1 percent and 1¼ percent of the annual national income. In underdeveloped countries, on the other hand, the money supply typically amounts to something between one fifth and one tenth of a year's national income. Here, a deficit equal to 2½ percent of the money supply would amount to between ¼ of 1 percent and ½ of 1 percent of a year's national income.

I do not mean to imply by the above that somewhat larger deficits would not in some cases be possible. Certainly, where there exists a tradition of government bonds being sold to and held by the general public, there would presumably be some possibility of having a secular expansion in this class of government obligations, and it is also possible that some governments would be able to obtain a secularly increasing volume of credit from abroad. But, having mentioned these possibilities, I shall now put them aside.

The fact that the money supply amounts to such a small fraction of annual national income in most underdeveloped countries operates to produce a particular proclivity to inflation. Suppose, on the one hand, an advanced country in which the money supply amounts to one half of a year's national income. Let this country experience a deficit amounting to 2 percent of a year's national income, and let this deficit be financed by the sale of bonds to the banking system. The resulting increase in the money supply might range between 4 percent and, say, 8 percent. (The 4 percent figure assumes that the government divided its sales of bonds between the central bank and the commercial banks in such a way that the government absorbed the full increase in the money supply. The 8 percent figure assumes that the government sold the bulk of its bonds to the central bank, and that there was a secondary expansion of money supply on the basis of the reserves thus created, the secondary expansion being equal in magnitude to the amount of primary increase in the money supply.)

Suppose, now, an underdeveloped country in which the money supply amounts to only one tenth of a year's national income, and suppose, once again, a government deficit equal to 2 percent of a year's national income. In this case, on the same assumptions used above, the resulting increase in the money supply would range between 20 percent and 40 percent rather than between 4 percent and 8 percent. The same deficit (expressed in terms of national income) goes a great deal farther in generating price inflation in the underdeveloped country of the above example than in the advanced country. This is an unfortunate fact, particularly so since it is likely that underdeveloped countries in general have less refined means of controlling their budgetary situation than are available to more advanced countries. I do believe, however, that this simple reason goes far to explain why inflation has been so much more serious a problem in underdeveloped countries than in advanced countries.

It is highly unlikely that any country can avoid a substantial rate of inflation if its government has a perennial and large deficit of which a significant proportion is financed by the sale of bonds to the central bank.

This has been the case in many Latin-American countries, and the record clearly bears out the above proposition. It is possible, for a time, to offset the inflationary pressures generated by the sale of government bonds to the central bank, through contractions in the amount of credit granted by the banking system to the private sector. But there are limits to the use of this offsetting device (if private sector credit is contracted by a certain amount each year, it will some day be cut to zero). Moreover, long before the ultimate limit is reached, the squeeze on private sector credit is likely to have other undesirable effects. It seems to me that the efforts made in many Latin-American countries to stem the tide of inflation have very often been of this type. I would conclude that programs designed to stem the rate of inflation should be assigned very low probability of success unless they include a serious attack on the problem of chronic and substantial budget deficits. Purely monetary measures will not be sufficient so long as chronic deficits of substantial size persist.

It is more difficult to obtain general agreement about the role of wages in the inflationary process than about the points already discussed. But it is possible that agreement can be achieved as to what wages *can* do, as distinct from the way in which they do in fact operate. In this and the next five paragraphs I shall accordingly focus on the possible ways in which wages might work in the inflationary process. First, an autonomous rise in wages *can* cause a rise in the general price level even if the money supply is held constant. If the money supply is held constant in the face of rising wages it is likely that the level of output will be reduced and the rate of unemployment increased. If the monetary authorities are sufficiently stonyhearted, and refuse to increase the money supply even in the face of substantial unemployment, it is likely that ultimately the rate of unemployment would be reduced again, either through wages being forced down or through rises in produc-

tivity, which gradually produce a situation in which the economy can attain full employment at the given wage level. But either of these processes of adjustment is likely to be slow and painful, entailing substantial amounts of unnecessary unemployment if the autonomously-set wage is significantly above the equilibrium wage. The lesser evil is surely for the monetary authorities to add sufficiently to the money supply to permit the economy to produce at or near full employment in the face of the new, higher level of wages.

An autonomous rise in wages, above and beyond that justified by recent productivity increases in the economy, is fairly easy to identify in an environment in which prices have been stable for a period preceding the wage rise. We have indicated above that such a wage rise would probably cause a rise in the price level, regardless of whether it was "financed" by the monetary authorities or not. But where the process goes from here is a matter about which we can be less sure. If workers are willing to see the apparent gain in real wage implicit in the initial wage rise partly or wholly eroded by subsequent increases in prices, then there is no reason to expect a continuing inflation. The price level will adjust to the autonomous wage rise, but it will be a once-and-for-all adjustment, so to speak. On the other hand, if workers bargain for, and get, a second rise in wages to compensate them for the loss in purchasing power coming from the price rise caused by the first rise in wages, then a second round of price rises will be initiated. This process can continue indefinitely, at least in the case where the monetary authorities "finance" each successive wage rise. In short, if in the first instance an unrealistic level of real wages is set (unrealistic in the sense of precluding full employment), and if workers successfully bargain for the re-establishment of this unrealistic real wage after every successive round of price increases, then a continuing inflation can be generated, especially if the monetary authorities "finance" the successive wage rises in the effort to generate full employment. This is a real case of wage inflation.

In order for an autonomous wage rise to function in the way indicated in the preceding paragraph, it must be fairly general. If the autonomous rise occurs only in a limited sector of the economy, it is likely that the unemployment generated by the wage rise will be small, and it is possible that the people who become unemployed as a result of the wage rise will find employment elsewhere in the economy (through wages in the rest of the economy rising less rapidly than they otherwise would have done). Moreover, the workers in the affected areas would have to have substantial bargaining power in order to be able to enforce successive readjustment of real wages to an unrealistic level, or the government would have to intervene to strengthen the position of the workers. My own judgment is that these conditions may have been met in Argentina, where the real wages of urban workers were raised to unrealistic levels during the Peron era, and where a tradition of strong unionism remained after Peron fell. It is possible, though less probable, that these conditions were met in Chile. The possibility emerges because of the responsiveness of private sector wages to the readjustments periodically made by the government in the *sueldo vital*. It is less probable because, by and large, unions are not particularly strong in Chile, and because in the course of Chile's great inflation of the last two decades the share of wages in the national income actually fell quite perceptibly. This last piece of evidence makes it hard (though not impossible) to argue that real wages were being maintained at unrealistically high levels.

It should be recognized that the mere existence of periodic and substantial readjustments of wages does not in itself imply that wage rises are an autonomous force in the inflationary process. Perhaps the simplest way to demonstrate this is to talk in terms of the Chilean tradition of annual readjustments. Suppose that these adjustments take place every year in January, and envision a process in which prices rise fairly steadily through the year while wages rise in discrete and substantial steps each January. Real wages will then be highest in January of each year, and will be progressively eroded by the steady rise of prices during the year, only to take a big jump upward when a new readjustment is declared the next January. Now we can conceive of a "right" order of magnitude for the real wage—that real wage which would have to rule if the economy were to maintain reasonably full employment in an environment of reasonably stable prices. It is to be presumed that somewhere during the downward drift of real wages which takes place each year this "right" real wage will prevail. The question is, will this point be in January, at the beginning of the process, or in December, when real wages are lowest, or somewhere in between? If real wages are "right" in January, they are never "too high"; in this case it would be utterly wrong to attribute to wages an autonomous, causal, inflationary impact. The fuel for inflation would be coming from somewhere else, most likely from monetary expansion. If so, then the increase in money supply necessary to finance this January's wage rise will already have been issued last year. This January's wage rise, bringing wages up to their "right" level, will not require any additional expansion of the money supply in order to maintain full employment.[1] If, on the other hand, real wages are "right" in December of each year, then they are above the "right" level during all the rest of the year. Here wages should certainly be assigned an autonomous role in the inflationary process; indeed, this is precisely the case referred to above.

Between the extremes discussed in the preceding paragraph, there exists a whole

[1] Certain assumptions about the dynamic processes involved in inflation would require qualification of this statement. I do not want here to get into an involved analysis of the problem. The basic point is that if real wages are never higher than the "right" level, wages cannot be assigned an autonomous, causal role in the inflationary process.

continuum of possibilities—real wages can be "right" at any time from February through November. If the truth is anywhere within this continuum, wages will play what I have called a transmitting role in the inflationary process. On the one hand, the wage rise of this year will be influenced by the price-level rise of last year; on the other hand, some additional expansion of the money supply will likely be necessary this year, in order to prevent the development of serious unemployment in the face of this year's wage rise, and this in turn will add fuel to this year's price inflation. It is probably idle to quibble about the point in the February-November range at which we would begin to consider that wages become an autonomous force in the inflation, for their transmitting role must be recognized to exist at any point in this range. But I think it should be accepted that in an inflation in which wages definitely did not play an autonomous role, but which was expected to continue, it would be perfectly reasonable for the January readjustment to incorporate some anticipation of the inflation expected for the coming year. That is, it would be reasonable to expect real wages to rise above the "right" level in January. In a rough way, I would argue that the dividing line should be based on the average real wage

for the year. If, on the average, real wages were above the "right" level, I would argue that wages were exerting an autonomous force in the inflation. If, on the other hand, real wages averaged out to be lower than the "right" level, I would find it difficult to argue that they were playing an autonomous role. Nonetheless, even when real wages averaged less than the "right" level, they could be playing a very significant transmitting role in the inflationary process.

Implicit in the above analysis is the idea that wages need not be playing the same role throughout a protracted inflation. The Chilean government, in particular, has followed quite different policies in deciding on the wage readjustments to be granted at different points in time. There have been times when the wage readjustments exceeded the rate of price rise since the preceding adjustment by a substantial amount, and other times in which the readjustments fell far short of the rate of price inflation experienced in the preceding year. Efforts to establish empirically that wages always play the same role, and in the same way, are thus likely to be frustrated, and theories in which a particular role of wages is critical are unlikely to fit the facts. . . .

V. SELECT BIBLIOGRAPHY

1. The following references are recommended to those who wish to pursue further the issue of the importance of capital in the development process: M. Bronfenbrenner, "The Appeal of Confiscation in Economic Development," *EDCC*, April 1955; A. K. Cairncross, "Reflections on the Growth of Capital and Income," *Scottish Journal of Political Economy*, June 1959; ____, "The Contribution of Foreign and Indigenous Capital to Economic Development," *International Journal of Agrarian Affairs*, April 1961; W. A. Lewis, *The Theory of Economic Growth*, Homewood, 1955, Chap. 5; S. H. Frankel, "Capital and Capital Supply in Relation to the Development of Africa," in E. A. G. Robinson (ed.), *Economic Development for Africa South of the Sahara*, New York, 1964; A. Sturmthal, "Economic Development, Income Distribution and Capital Formation in Mexico," *JPE*, June 1955; S. P. Schatz, "The Role of Capital Accumulation in Economic Development," *JDS*, October 1968.

Reviews of the theoretical and empirical literature on savings rates in LDCs are provided by R. Mikesell and J. Zuiser, "The Nature of the Savings Function in Developing Countries," *JEL*, March 1973; H. S. Houthakker, "On Some Determinants of Saving in Developed and Underdeveloped Countries," in E. A. G. Robinson (ed.), *Problems In Economic Development*, New York, 1965.

The topic of capital coefficients receives more specialized treatment in the following: V. V. Bhatt, "Capital-Output Ratios of Certain Industries: A Comparative Study of Certain Countries," *RES*, August 1954; K. Martin, "Capital-Output Ratios in Economic Development," *EDCC*, October 1957; W. B. Reddaway, "Some Observations on the Capital-Output Ratio," *Indian Economic Review*, February 1960; H. Leibenstein, "Incremental Capital-Output Ratios and Growth Rates in the Short Run," *RES*, February 1966; Gunnar Myrdal, *Asian Drama*, New York, 1968, pp. 1968–93; A. H. Studenmund, "Towards a Better Understanding of the Incremental Capital-Output Ratio," *QJE*, August 1968.

2. Problems of taxation and the relative merits of alternative fiscal policies in developing countries can be examined in the following: R. M. Bird and O. Oldman (eds.), *Readings on Taxation in Developing Countries*, 3rd ed., Baltimore, 1975; R. M. Bird, *Taxation of Agricultural Land in Developing Countries*, Cambridge, 1974; John F. Due, *Taxation and Economic Development in Tropical Africa*, Cambridge, 1963; ____, *Indirect Taxation in Developing Countries*, Baltimore, 1970; A. R. Prest, *Public Finance in Underdeveloped Countries*, London, 1962; U. K. Hicks, *Development Finance*, Oxford, 1965; R. J. Chelliah, *Fiscal Policy in Underdeveloped Countries*, London, 1970; R. A. Musgrave, *Fiscal Systems*, New Haven, 1969; Nicholas Kaldor, *Indian Tax Reform*, New Delhi, 1956; ____, "Will Underdeveloped Countries Learn to Tax?" *Foreign Affairs*, January 1963; A. M. Martin and W. A. Lewis, "Patterns of Public Revenue and Expenditure," *The Manchester School of Economic and Social Studies*, September 1956; U Tun Wai, "Taxation Problems and Policies of Underdeveloped Countries," *IMF Staff Papers*, November 1962; H. P. Wald, *Taxation of Agricultural Land in Underdeveloped Economies*, Cambridge, 1959; R. Goode et al., "Role of Export Taxes in Developing Countries," *IMF Staff Papers*, November 1966; A. Andic and A. Peacock, "Fiscal Surveys and Economic Development," *Kyklos*, Vol. 19, No. 4, 1966; R. S. Thorn, "Evolution of Public Finances during Economic Development," *The Manchester School of Economic*

and Social Studies, January 1967; A. Peacock and S. Hauser (eds.), *Government Finance and Economic Development,* Paris, 1965.

3. Major analytical treatises on the financial system and resource mobilization are: E.S. Shaw, *Financial Deepening in Economic Development,* New York, 1973; R. I. McKinnon, *Money and Capital in Economic Development,* Washington, 1973.

Outstanding studies of the determinants of the size and character of a country's financial superstructure are those by Raymond W. Goldsmith, *The Determinants of Financial Structure,* Paris, 1966; _____, *The Financial Development of Mexico,* Paris, 1966.

The development of banking and financial institutions can be considered in the following: A. I. Bloomfield, "Central Banking in Underdeveloped Countries," *Journal of Finance,* May 1957; S. Boskey, *Problems and Practices of Development Banks,* Baltimore, 1959; L. V. Chandler, *Central Banking and Economic Development,* Bombay, 1962; W. Diamond, *Development Banks,* Baltimore, 1957; _____, *Development Finance Companies,* Baltimore, 1968; J. Marquez, "Financial Institutions and Economic Development," in H. S. Ellis (ed.), *Economic Development for Latin America,* New York, 1961; Edward Nevin, *Capital Funds in Underdeveloped Countries,* London, 1961; R. S. Sayers, "Central Banking in Under-Developed Countries," in *Central Banking After Bagehot,* Oxford, 1957; S. N. Sen, *Central Banking in Under-Developed Money Markets,* 3rd ed., Calcutta, 1961; David Krivine (ed.), *Fiscal and Monetary Problems in Developing States* (Proceedings of the Third Rehovoth Conference), New York, 1957; Anand G. Chandavarkar, "How Relevant is Finance for Development?" *Finance and Development,* September 1973.

4. General aspects of the problem of inflation in less developed countries are examined in the following: A. P. Thirwall, *Inflation, Saving and Growth in Developing Economies,* London, 1974; E. M. Bernstein and I. G. Patel, "Inflation in Relation to Economic Development," *IMF Staff Papers,* November 1952; M. Bronfenbrenner, "The High Cost of Economic Development," *Land Economics,* August 1953; Henry J. Bruton, *Inflation in a Growing Economy,* Bombay, 1961; Bent Hansen, *Inflation Problems in Small Countries,* Cairo, 1960; Nicholas Kaldor, "Economic Growth and the Problem of Inflation," *Economica,* August 1959; F. Pazos, "Economic Development and Financial Stability," *IMF Staff Papers,* October 1953; V. K. R. V. Rao, "Deficit Financing, Capital Formation and Price Behavior in an Underdeveloped Economy," *Indian Economic Review,* February 1953; J. H. Adler, "Deficit Spending and Supply Elasticities," *Indian Journal of Economics,* Vol. 36; _____, "Note on 'Spurt' Inflation and Economic Development," *Social and Economic Studies,* March 1961; H. W. Singer, "Deficit Financing of Public Capital Formation," *Social and Economic Studies,* September 1958; A. C. Harberger, "Using the Resources at Hand More Effectively," *AER,* May 1959; Dudley Seers, "Normal Growth and Distortions: Some Techniques of Structural Analysis," *OEP,* March 1964; M. J. Mamalakis, "Forced Saving in Underdeveloped Countries: A Rediscovery or a Misapplication of a Concept?" *Economia Internazionale,* May 1964; G. S. Dorrance, "Rapid Inflation and International Payments," *Finance and Development,* June 1965.

5. An excellent guide to the literature on the "structuralist school" is contained in Dudley Seers, "A Theory of Inflation and Growth in Under-developed Countries Based on the Experience of Latin America," *OEP,* June 1963. For additional readings on inflation in Latin America, the following may be consulted: Werner Baer, "Inflation and Economic Growth: An Interpretation of the Brazilian Case," *EDCC,* October 1962; _____, "The Inflation Controversy in Latin America: A Survey," *Latin American Research*

Review, Winter 1967; ____ and I. Kerstenetzky (eds.), *Inflation and Growth in Latin America,* Homewood, 1964; David Felix, "Structural Imbalances, Social Conflict, and Inflation," *EDCC,* January 1960; ____, "An Alternative View of the 'Monetarist'– 'Structuralist' Controversy," in A. O. Hirschman (ed.), *Latin American Issues,* New York, 1961; G. Maynard, "Inflation and Growth: Some Lessons to be Drawn from Latin-American Experience," *OEP,* June 1961; Celso Furtado, "Industrialization and Inflation," *International Economic Papers,* Vol. 12, 1967.

A comprehensive bibliography is provided in K. Griffin, *Financing Development in Latin America,* New York, 1971.

CHAPTER VI

Mobilizing Foreign Resources

The overriding concern of this chapter is how to improve the process of transferring resources from rich to poor countries—whether this transfer be in the form of public financial aid, or private foreign investment, or a nonmonetary transfer of managerial and technical knowledge. This is not merely a matter of a greater amount of resources; there is now even more discussion about the "appropriateness" of the transfers from the developed to the less developed countries. In view of the redefining of development objectives, it is now important that the transfers to the poor countries contribute to more employment and greater equality. It cannot simply be assumed that the stock of resources and the stock of knowledge that now exist in the developed countries are in this sense "appropriate" for the late developing countries.

Section VI.A focuses on issues that are of most analytical and policy interest in the transfer of foreign aid. Public financial aid—i.e., concessional finance, or the "grant equivalent" in the capital inflow—has a twofold function. It supplements the LDC's low domestic savings and hence helps fill the resources gap or "saving gap," and also provides additional foreign exchange and thereby helps fill the "foreign exchange gap." The "two-gap analysis" of the role of external aid is also significant in indicating that one gap may be greater than another *ex ante*: if, for example, the foreign exchange gap is greater than the saving gap, foreign aid becomes the means of permitting the required imports so that the full saving potential can be realized and resources will not be left underutilized because of an import bottleneck. The necessary identity of the savings-investment and export-import gap *ex post* is brought about by a process of adjustment.

In terms of policies, we should recognize what are the costs of aid to the donor countries and what are the benefits received through aid by the recipient countries. The related problem of debt servicing now calls for more policy attention in view of a more than threefold expansion in external public indebtedness of the developing countries during the 1960s, and the presently large percentage of export receipts that must be devoted to debt servicing. There is also considerable controversy over the contribution that aid makes to development; some economists dissent from the conventional view by arguing that as an instrument of development, aid is generally of limited value—let alone an indispensable instrument—because it cannot substantially affect the basic factors which are needed to promote the material progress of the people in the aid-receiving countries. Others, however, emphasize the need to improve the quality of the aid relationship—not only from the standpoint of the more conventional "performance criteria," but now also in the context of meeting the needs of target poverty groups, redistribution, and employment. The more socially oriented measure of "performance" associated with the redefinition of development objectives raises some difficult questions for a redirection of aid policy.

If the real amount of resource flows through financial aid has diminished, it is important to discover alternative means of providing aid. One alternative is related to the current demands for international monetary reform. Differences of opinion now exist as to whether proposals for an increase in international liquidity should also provide a link to development finance. The Note on "The International Monetary System and Development Finance" (VI.B) discusses this issue. Other measures of providing aid through trade policy will be noted in Chapter XI.

The discussion in section VI.C is concerned with policy measures that a developing country might take to obtain a more substantial contribution from private foreign capital to its development program. To assess the potential contribution of private foreign investment, the Note (VI.C.1) first outlines the benefits and costs of various forms of private foreign investment viewed in terms of the recipient country's development program. As an agent of private foreign investment, the multinational enterprise merits special consideration. Against this conceptual background, we might better appraise the nature of the bargaining process between host countries and foreign investors.

In the final section, we explore further the possibility of securing a more effective transfer of managerial and technical knowledge to the LDCs. The technology that has been imported from developed countries may have an excessive capital-bias, be inappropriate for the recipient country's factor endowment, and aggravate the problems of unemployment and inequality. While the recipient country may want a technology that raises the labor-capital ratio, it wants to avoid at the same time an increase in the capital-output ratio: efficient capital-stretching innovations are needed. This is not only a matter of new R & D efforts devoted to the requirements of a new technology. The problem of technology transfer is much wider—ranging from questions about the composition of an "appropriate" product mix to policies of bargaining over the terms and conditions of technology importation.

VI.A. PUBLIC FINANCIAL AID

VI.A.1. Calculation of Capital Requirements*

The word "requirements" is used in this context as indicating a need for a transfer of goods and services in order to achieve certain targets; these may be target rates of growth for the economies as a whole, or they may be target rates of investment, although, where this is so, investment is normally thought of as being the means by which rates of growth of income are increased. The basic idea, however, is that such estimates of capital inflow or capital requirements shall be related to a generally recognizable and agreed aim, and that this aim should include the transformation of the recipient economy in such a way as to increase permanently its ability to contribute to economic welfare. They are not normally regarded as subsidies to current consumption, although such capital flows may include such subsidies within a suitable framework of foreign aid.

TWO APPROACHES

There are two possible approaches to making such estimates and both are based on the idea that increased income and wealth depend fundamentally upon the application of more capital, either to increase output directly when used in combination with local resources, or indirectly when the use of such capital will lead to a more effective use of other resources.

The first approach is to make an overall estimate of the uses that are made of the

*From E. K. Hawkins, "Measuring Capital Requirements," *The Fund and Bank Review: Finance and Development,* Vol. 5, No. 2, 1968, pp. 2–5. Reprinted by permission.

output of goods and services, with particular reference to the share that is allocated to consumption and the share that is allocated to investment. It is then argued that the future growth of the economy depends on a suitable increase in the share of goods and services allocated to investment. An attempt is made to estimate the effect upon the future growth of income of any additional investment so as to be able to assess how much capital is needed to achieve a given rate of growth. This is then compared with the estimated ability of the economy to make available such a share of resources. (In other words, how much saving can an economy at a particular stage of development carry out?) The difference between these two estimates will then give some indication of the required size of the capital inflow from abroad.

Such estimates are made without any consideration of the specific form that the investments are likely to take. By contrast, the second approach builds up such an overall estimate from below by a detailed study, on a project-by-project or a sector-by-sector basis, of the need for capital. An examination is then made of the possible sources of such capital locally, and a discrepancy will thus emerge between the needs for the development of all the projects under consideration and the resources which can be made available. This difference is the required capital inflow from overseas, the counterpart of which can be the estimate reached by the first approach mentioned.

These two approaches are different not only in their nature, but in their provenance. The first approach corresponds to the various calculations of capital requirements which have been made in the last 20 years by the United Nations and by the U.S. Government. The second approach is, generally speaking, the one followed by the World Bank in producing the estimates which have been developed in recent years by its own thinking on the subject.

There is a further important difference, however, in the manner in which this subject has been treated by other international organizations and the way in which it has been viewed by the World Bank Group. Estimates made outside the Bank have all been concerned with the requirements aspect of capital inflows. They begin by specifying a target rate of growth which is to be the aim of the developing country and then proceed to estimate the amount of capital which would be needed to reach that target. In the estimates made by the World Bank Group no explicit target is used; instead, the estimates emerge from a multidimensional examination of the economy in question and represent the amount of capital which the Bank feels might be used in an effective way in the future, provided that certain levels of economic performance are achieved and suitable policies are followed by the country concerned....

THE "TWO-GAP" APPROACH

Attention is also focused, however, on what is thought to be a more important limitation on development: a possible shortage of foreign exchange, as a result of which countries may be unable to acquire from abroad the goods and services necessary for promoting domestic development. This approach has become known as the "two-gap" approach because it operates in two dimensions; while continuing to argue that development is a function of investment it also holds that such investment, which requires domestic savings, is not sufficient to ensure that development takes place. It must also be possible to obtain from abroad the goods and services that are complementary to

those available at home. In most developing countries the structure of the economy is so simple that it can produce only a limited range of products when relying solely on domestic sources. In these circumstances an act of saving, by itself, even though it releases resources for investment purposes, may not make available the correct kind of resources. In physical terms a country may be unable to produce the cement, steel, or machinery which go into the various projects required to raise income in the future, although it may be able to make the necessary savings by cutting down on consumption. Unless these savings can be used to purchase the necessary goods and services from overseas no progress can be made.

Estimates made as a result of this approach start from certain basic relationships which are generally accepted as holding true for all countries. The usages of modern national accounting are designed to express the fact that the amount that can be invested in any country is identical with the amount that is saved; that is to say, only those goods and services which are not consumed can be deployed to increase future income through investment. At the same time, if these resources are to be supplemented from abroad, such a flow of resources will appear in this accounting framework as an excess of imports over exports. It will, in fact, always appear twice, first as the difference between investment and the amount that can be saved within the economy and second as an equal excess of imports and services over exports of goods and services.

THE FOUR IMPORTANT MAGNITUDES

Calculations of capital requirements proceed on the basis of projections of the four important magnitudes: savings, investments, exports, and imports. A target rate of growth is specified, and then the amount of additional capital that will be required in order to reach that target rate of growth is estimated. This gives a figure for capital requirements which can be compared with the likely availability of domestic savings. At the same time it is possible to make projections of the likely behavior of exports and imports. The former will depend on the supply of goods and services available, or likely to be available, for export from the domestic economy, the state of the world markets, and the economic health of the developed countries which are the markets for such exports. A similar estimate can be made for import requirements. All these projections (which are of course capable of much subdivision) can be made independently of one another, and it follows that there is very little likelihood that such independent projections will all arrive at an answer which satisfies the basic accounting relationship already referred to above. Projected investments may well exceed projected savings; projected imports, on the other hand, may exceed the projected exports by a different amount. However, national income accountancy demonstrates that the excess of investment over savings must necessarily be equal to the excess of imports over exports and this must hold true at all points of time. It follows that there is something inconsistent about the projections that have been made independently. The two-gap method, therefore, is essentially a way of ensuring that inconsistencies, which may be *implicit* in other ways of making projections, are brought out into the open.

Estimates of capital requirements made by this method, therefore, yield not one, but two figures for consideration. . . . The use of this approach requires either that the projections include the necessary changes in the structure and the behavior of the economy which will make the two estimates consistent with each other, or that a decision has to be made that the larger of the two gaps will be the more significant and will be taken as the required capital inflow from abroad.

A "THREE-PHASE" APPROACH

A variant on the approach has also been followed by . . . Hollis B. Chenery and Alan M. Strout, who, in a study[1] prepared for the U. S. Agency for International Development (AID), employed a three-phase approach, where an attempt was made to specify in quantitative terms the constraint on development arising from the limit of absorptive capacity.[2] This work has had a considerable influence on discussions of the subject. In their study, various constraints—a savings constraint, the foreign exchange constraint, and the limitation of absorptive capacity—come into operation for a particular developing economy at various stages of its growth. They focus special attention on two aspects: first, the savings behavior of the economy concerned, or its ability to refrain from consumption and allocate additional resources to investment; and second, the question of absorptive capacity, viewed, in this instance, as a performance factor. In other words, if absorptive capacity is increasing over the years, it can be regarded as a measure of the improved economic performance of the country concerned, and of its ability to make better use of capital from abroad. In their work they spelled out the operation of these three constraints in terms of three different stages of development. An interesting feature of this study is its extensive coverage on a country basis, since the model was applied to 50 developing countries and totals obtained for a spectrum of different assumptions.

This three-phase approach can be useful for expository purposes, but it can only be an approximation to the real life problems

[1] Hollis B. Chenery and Alan M. Strout, "Foreign Assistance and Economic Development," *American Economic Review,* September 1966.

[2] Absorptive capacity covers all the ways in which the ability to plan and execute development projects, to change the structure of the economy, and to reallocate resources is circumscribed by the lack of crucial factors, by institutional problems, or by unsuitable organization. Not only the structure of the economy but also the utilization of its existing capacity will have an important bearing on a country's absorptive capacity. Cf. J. H. Adler, *Absorptive Capacity: The Concept and Its Determinants,* Brookings Institution, Washington, 1965.

of many developing countries where the three constraints often coexist and interact with one another. It has been found, for example, that the limitations of absorptive capacity may apply only to particular sectors of the economy, while other parts of the economy are able to absorb more capital than can be obtained from local sources of savings. This coexistence of the various constraints on development is in many ways a central characteristic of an underdeveloped country.

One limitation of all the approaches detailed above is precisely that they operate at a highly aggregate level. Any aggregative approach of this kind treats all units of investment as if each were adding to a volume of

capital which is homogeneous. In practice this is only true of the monetary units in which capital and investment are measured. It is convenient to measure investment and capital in monetary terms, but the money values often only hide the significance of the specific nature of the investment item. Cement once incorporated into a highway cannot be used for other purposes; steel once built into a building must yield additional wealth in that form, otherwise the investment will have been wasted. It is the underlying importance of this aspect of development which emphasizes the project and sector approach to the measurement of capital requirements.

Do you agree with the view that a constant flow of fin. res. and techⁿ is a sufficient condⁿ for the ecoⁿ devpt. of an UDC? Give reasons for your answer.

VI.A.2. Two-Gap Analysis*

Many recent writings on development economics have suggested that "saving" and "foreign exchange" constitute two separate and independent constraints on the attainable rate of economic growth [4] [5] [8] [9] [10] [12]. The well-known empirical work of Professor Hollis Chenery is based explicitly on this distinction [4] [5]. Estimates of the "trade gap" which must be covered if the LDCs are to achieve a given growth rate make use of the same idea [1] [13] [14]. The existence of a "foreign exchange constraint" has also been held to require a complete revision of trade theory [8]. The purpose of what follows is to bring out clearly the assumptions behind the analytical distinction between saving and foreign exchange constraints and to criticise models which use this distinction in deriving conclusions about trade and aid policy.

*From Vijay Joshi, "Saving and Foreign Exchange Constraints," in Paul P. Streeten (ed.), *Unfashionable Economics*, London, 1970, pp. 111–15, 117–21, 127–8. Reprinted by permission.

A SIMPLE MODEL

The distinction between saving and foreign exchange constraints has generally been made in the following way. The rate of investment in an economy is ordinarily determined by its willingness and ability to mobilise savings. This is a "saving constraint". But in LDCs generally (or at any rate in some LDCs) the willingness to save, *though it exists*, is frustrated by the inability to acquire through trade the imports which are required to produce investment goods. This situation is described as a "foreign exchange constraint".

In order to understand the logic of this distinction, it is helpful to employ the standard two-good static model which is used in international trade theory. The relation of the concepts under consideration to orthodox trade theory is interesting in itself; more importantly, the simple two-good model brings out the assumptions involved more transparently than the models generally used in this context. Consider in Figure VI.1 an

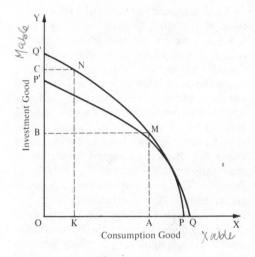

FIGURE VI.1.

economy producing two goods: a consumption good X and an investment good Y. It is an open economy and given the structure of demand and of international relative costs, X is the exportable and Y is the importable. With given stocks of factors of production at a point in time, PP' is the domestic transformation curve. If the economy were closed, this curve would also represent the maximum quantities of X and Y available to the economy. The absorption possibilities of the open economy are traced out by the curve QQ'. This is the "availabilities envelope".[1] It tells us the maximum quantities of X and Y which the economy can obtain by making efficient use of both production and trade. If the economy were to receive foreign aid this would shift the availabilities enve-

lope outward. We assume that foreign aid is zero in the initial situation.[2]

The next step in orthodox welfare analysis would be to introduce an objective function in the form of a system of community indifference curves between consumption and investment. The welfare economic problem is the maximisation of this objective function subject to the constraint represented by the availabilities envelope. If this is the complete specification of the problem, then the analysis of saving and foreign exchange constraints cannot get off the ground. In this problem, the only constraint is the availabilities envelope which separates those points which are *technically* feasible from those which are not. So long as the "efficiency conditions" are satisfied and the economy operates efficiently on the frontier of the envelope QQ', the optimum point can be reached. This optimum point, which could be represented geometrically by the tangency between the availabilities envelope and the highest possible indifference curve, explicitly balances the community's desire to save with its desire to invest; so the notion of a saving *constraint* seems completely out of place. Furthermore, even if we postulate that some efficiency conditions cannot be satisfied, this simply means a different maximisation problem and a different optimum point. There cannot be any constraint to maximisation as such, other than *all* the constraints of the particular maximum problem.

In order to bring out the meaning of the popular distinction between saving and foreign exchange constraints, we must get away from this approach. The most convenient way to set up the problem is to suppose that

---

[1] The "availabilities envelope" (sometimes known as the "Baldwin envelope") is constructed by combining the domestic transformation curve and the foreign offer curve. For derivation, see [2]. It is assumed, for convenience, that PP' and QQ' are concave to the origin. It would be possible, though tedious, to drop this assumption.

[2] The analysis would be unaffected if we assumed a given positive amount of aid in the initial situation. Note that aid availability is assumed to be a parameter outside the control of the economy. It is also assumed in this simple model that aid received affects only the availabilities envelope and nothing else. In particular, it does not affect the domestic willingness to save.

the utility function to be maximised is specified *by the Planning Commission,* and to suppose further that this function does not have consumption as an argument.[3] Social welfare is increased by increasing investment and consumption has no value in itself. This does not, however, mean that consumption is irrrelevant. In order to increase investment the Planning Commission must persuade or force people to consume less but there may well be a limit to the reduction in consumption that people will tolerate. Thus, consumption enters the problem as a *constraint* on the saving which the planners can extract from the community.[4] Now return to Figure VI.1. Suppose the economy happens to be at *M* with consumption *OA* and investment *OB*. Assume that *OK* is the minimum level to which consumption can be forced down. The Planning Commission reduces consumption and increases investment starting from *M*, but it is prevented from going further than *N*, with consumption *OK* and investment *OC*. At *N* there is a pure "saving constraint". The idea of a constraint must be carefully interpreted. There is still an optimum point, given the constraint. One can always maximise in the sense of doing the best that is possible under the circumstances and given the problem, *N is* the best point. But there is a pure saving constraint in the sense that *given* the availabilities envelope, the *sole* reason for the inability of Planning Commission to increase investment (and therefore welfare) *beyond N* is its imperfect control over domestic consumption.[5]

[3] The analysis will later be extended to cover the case where both consumption and investment enter into the planners' utility function.

[4] What the minimum consumption limit actually is will presumably be influenced, though not entirely determined, by the *private* utility function which is different from the *planners'* utility function.

[5] Professor C. Kennedy, in a recent article [7] argues that there can be no such thing as a "saving constraint" because saving is not a "resource". The above should make clear that no such suggestion is involved. A saving constraint is simply a shorthand

All this is perfectly straightforward. What then is a pure "foreign exchange constraint"? One can get a bit confused here. It is tempting to reason in the following way: Consider any volume of investment which is inside the availabilities envelope. If this cannot be achieved by the planners, then this failure must be the result of a pure "saving constraint". A pure foreign exchange constraint must therefore refer to any situation where the planners are aiming for an investment target which is outside the availabilities envelope. This argument, however, does not go far enough. The distinction between saving and foreign exchange constraints is *not* designed simply to make the obvious point that there are some targets which are technically feasible and some which are not. This applies to every country whether "less developed" or otherwise. If this were the basis of the distinction, then any country could claim to face a foreign exchange constraint by raising its target high enough. We shall soon see that a foreign exchange constraint does indeed imply that planners want more investment than is technically feasible but it implies something more as well.

To understand the concept of a pure foreign exchange constraint, begin again with a *given* availabilities envelope and recall that pure saving and foreign exchange constraints are supposed to be mutually exclusive. In a pure foreign exchange constraint situation, saving is, *ex hypothesi, not* a constraint. In other words, we have to envisage a situation in which an increase in investment is impossible *although* more saving can be enforced. Consider Figure VI.2. QQ' is again the availabilities envelope but it has a different *shape* from QQ' in Figure VI.1. There is now a completely flat portion RQ' signifying that beyond R transformation of X into Y is impossible. Note that this requires two conditions: (a) that the underlying rate of transformation in domestic production is zero

expression for the constraint on increasing investment imposed by the minimum level to which consumption can be squeezed.

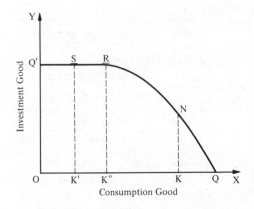

FIGURE VI.2.

over the relevant range and (b) that the rate of transformation through trade is zero signifying that the elasticity of reciprocal demand is unity or less. Now consider different minimum consumption limits. Suppose minimum possible consumption is OK. Then at N there is a pure saving constraint precisely as in Figure VI.1. Next suppose that minimum possible consumption is OK'. In this case, beyond R no increase in investment (and therefore welfare) is possible even though the planners can extract more saving because transformation possibilities are completely exhausted. In the region RS we have a pure "foreign exchange constraint".[6] Note that in the limiting case when the minimum consumption limit is OK'' we do not have a *pure* foreign exchange constraint. In this case there is *both* a saving and a foreign exchange constraint at R; each constraint is separately sufficient to prevent further investment.[7]

[6] Thus the term "foreign exchange constraint" is really rather a misnomer. Superficially it might seem to refer simply to lack of foreign trade possibilities, but a flat stretch of the availabilities envelope is in fact made up of two *separate* rates of transformation—the domestic and the foreign—being simultaneously equal to zero.

[7] Observe that if the availabilities envelope QQ' were continuously downward sloping (as in Fig.

To summarise: the distinction between saving and foreign exchange constraints assumes a given availabilities envelope, efficient policies in production and trade and a social utility function dictated by the planners which is different from the private utility function. Attention is directed towards those situations in which an increase in investment would increase welfare. The distinction then turns on what constitutes *at the margin* the effective constraint on increasing investment. An increase in investment is constrained solely by "saving" if, at the margin, transformation possibilities (domestically and/or through foreign trade) still exist but cannot be utilised because domestic consumption has reached its minimum tolerable level. An increase in investment is constrained solely by "foreign exchange" if, at the margin, more saving can be extracted, but the possibilities of transforming consumption into investment domestically *and* through trade have fallen to zero.[8]

Our simple model can be used to illustrate some familiar themes in recent literature. The first is the idea that aid can be seen as performing two independent functions. It increases the amount of resources devoted to capital formation over and above what the economy can provide. In this role it supplements domestic saving. On the other hand, it

VI.1) there can never be a *pure* foreign exchange constraint. Transformation of consumption into investment is now possible right up to the point Q' where consumption falls to zero. In the theoretically conceivable case where zero consumption is possible, there would be a foreign exchange constraint at Q' but there would, of necessity, be a saving constraint as well. A pure foreign exchange constraint requires that transformation possibilities should fall to zero at positive levels of consumption.

[8] Since we have assumed that the availabilities envelope is concave to the origin, a zero marginal rate of transformation implies that there is also a *total* constraint on transformation. If the assumption of concavity were dropped, the presence of a total constraint would have to be separately specified.

(2) also increases the economy's ability to import the goods it wants. In this role it provides foreign exchange and helps the balance of payments. Though, seen as an accounting fact, aid performs both these functions simultaneously, which particular function is tion, aid clearly acts as a substitute for domestic saving which has reached its maximum limit. If saving could be increased, aid could be reduced. Here the saving function of aid is the main one. However, in a foreign exchange constraint situation, it is not a substitute for domestic saving. Aid is irrevocably necessary to increase investment and remains necessary even if consumption could be reduced to zero. Here it is the foreign exchange providing function of aid which is crucial.

Our model can also throw some light on the "aid *versus* trade" issue. So far we have considered the *direct* provision of aid as the only way of reaching a target in the presence of a constraint. In fact anything which results in an *exogenous* improvement in the foreign offer curve (and therefore an outward shift in the availabilities envelope) might do equally well. In this case, however, it becomes difficult to separate the "increased trade" from the disguised aid. It is fairly clear that "increasing access to markets" (by e.g. reduction of tariff barriers) which increases opportunity to trade at prevailing prices should be classified as "increased trade"; and that actually *raising* selling prices of exports involves an element of aid. The whole issue of distinguishing between "aid" and "trade" in actual policy measures is very complex.[9] But we can make a few straightforward points comparing "increased trade" in the sense of increasing trade opportunities at prevailing prices with the provision of aid in the form of a direct grant:

(a) An improvement in trade opportunities shifts the availabilities envelope

outwards and must clearly enable the planners to increase investment and welfare.

(b) However, though increased trade *could* improve the situation this is not automatic. Trade opportunities have to be seized and this involves more saving. Aid involves no sacrifice for the recipient and enables the economy to obtain investment goods without any cost. But the provision of an equivalent amount of investment goods through trade may require a more than acceptable increase in saving.

(c) If we consider the situation in terms of the model . . . in which both consumption and investment enter into the planners' utility function, then it is furthermore clear that there is a *welfare* cost attached to obtaining more goods through trade (except possibly in a pure foreign exchange constraint situation). This is of course justified so long as the benefit from the goods obtained exceeds the cost. But again, aid is a pure benefit. The direct provision of goods through aid is necessarily more "efficient" than their indirect acquisition through trade.[10]

IDENTIFYING CONSTRAINTS

While a valid conceptual distinction can thus be drawn between a saving and a foreign exchange constraint it is clearly not easy to identify them in practice. Before the

[9] There is a good discussion of some of the issues involved in [6].

[10] This analysis is highly simplified and I have only drawn those conclusions which are implicit in the simple model. In fact, aid and trade have very complex effects. The discussion later in the paper goes part of the way towards introducing realism. Note also the assumption above, that aid is entirely used for investment. Clearly, if it was consumption goods which were desired and aid was used for that purpose, the conclusions about aid and trade would still hold.

analysis can be applied we have to be sure that the target is not being held up (wholly or partly) by misallocation of resources or by some institutional factors which are capable of being changed.

The simple model above assumes that the economy behaves efficiently so that it is always on the frontier of the availabilities envelope, not inside it. It also assumes that the planners cannot by their own actions shift this frontier. In practice neither of these assumptions may hold; there may be a number of respects in which changes in policy if carried through would increase investment (or growth). Of course there will also be in many cases "structural" obstacles to such changes in policy.[11] The identification of constraints then becomes a matter of judgment. Depending on the time-horizon we have in mind, we may place explicit restrictions on changes in the pattern of consumption, the distribution of income, the level and growth of employment, the freedom of government policy with regard to the exchange rate and so on.[12] Obviously the more restrictions we admit, the easier it becomes to find "constraints". In judging the conclusions of any model which purports to tell us whether a country faces a saving or a foreign exchange constraint we must judge the reasonableness of the explicit and implicit institutional and policy restrictions it takes as given; we must also judge whether even given these restrictions the best possible use is being made of the country's resources. If the inefficiencies are very significant or if the institutional and policy assumptions are unreasonable then the whole distinction between saving and foreign exchange constraints begins to lose its point.

Note that the reasonableness or otherwise of objectives or restrictions is partly a matter of value judgment, partly a matter of judgment about the feasibility of doing certain things.[13]

CHENERY-TYPE MODELS

Let us now consider the models which have been proposed by Professors Chenery, McKinnon and others. I shall not discuss the working of these models in any detail because they have become widely known but simply indicate the similarities and differences between these and the simple model I have used.

Note first the similarities. Though these models allow trade in intermediate and capital goods as well as in final goods and though they allow output to increase over time, these features do not in themselves make any difference to our analysis. Given a time-horizon we still have a locus of maximum availabilities over time. The connection with my model is now obvious. If the actual rate of growth can be raised by increasing the rate of saving there is clearly a pure saving constraint on growth. If the actual rate of growth has reached its maximum limit before the saving rate has reached its upper limit there is a pure foreign exchange constraint on growth. Such a situation would again imply that the marginal rate of return to saving domestically and through trade is zero *in spite of* efficiency in production and trade; if the planners are optimising it must also mean (with the usual reservations about

[11] Economic theory cannot deal satisfactorily with structural obstacles. They are either put into the *ceteris paribus* clause in which case they are considered "given"; or they are not in which case they represent an "inefficiency" which can be corrected by the price system. The truth is more complex. On this see Lord Balogh [3] and Appendix 2, Vol. III of [11].

[12] This is done in Chenery-type models. See in particular [4].

[13] It might be thought that one way to dilute the concept of a foreign exchange constraint would be to say that it occurs when the economy finds itself in a situation where the terms on which consumption can be transformed into investment become "very unfavourable" though not actually zero. On logical grounds, this is a saving constraint; further, a clear political judgment is involved in deciding what "very unfavourable" terms are.

kinks) that they regard consumption as valueless at the margin.

Indeed, in some ways the Chenery-type models are even more restrictive than my simple model. Not only do they, on the whole, ignore welfare questions but they also make severe assumptions about production and trade possibilities. The flexibility of possible import-substitution is eliminated by postulating technologically fixed import coefficients. The flexibility of possible export expansion is eliminated by assuming an exogenously given maximum export revenue which is not amenable to influence by the planners. The possibility of varying investment requirements is eliminated by assuming a constant capital-output ratio. In other words, the model becomes essentially a very simple linear model. This model has been extensively used in estimating aid requirements. The typical argument goes as follows: Assume that the target is to increase GNP by a prescribed compound growth rate over a prescribed time-horizon T. Assuming a given incremental capital-output ratio, investment requirements in the terminal period (I_T) are determined. Initial savings are known. On the basis of this and a linear Keynesian saving function we can calculate total potential savings (S_T) in the terminal year. Then the difference between investment and saving ($I_T - S_T$) is the "saving gap" which must be covered by foreign assistance. However, there are also certain import requirements which the system has to fulfil. Required imports in the terminal year (M_T) are determined on the basis of initially observed imports and a fixed marginal propensity to import. Maximum potential exports (X_T) are given exogenously. Then ($M_T - X_T$) is the "foreign exchange gap" or "trade gap". Given that successful achievement of the target requires that *both* investment and import requirements be satisfied, required foreign aid inflow is determined by the *larger* of the two gaps. Of course, *ex post*, the two gaps must be equal. The adjustment is brought about either by savings or exports falling

below the projected level.[14] Note that a saving gap larger than the foreign exchange gap implies that the economy is or will in the course of growth run into a pure "saving constraint". On the other hand, a foreign exchange gap larger than the saving gap implies that the economy is or will run into a pure 'foreign exchange constraint'.

It is important to remember that the gap analysis depends crucially on the assumed constancy of the parameters. If the relevant parameters were not fixed and unalterable, a planning authority could by efficient planning reduce both gaps and, in particular, bring the larger of the two gaps towards equality with the smaller, thus reducing foreign aid requirements. Of course, it is still possible for the two *ex ante* gaps to differ in spite of perfect planning. But this would occur only when all possibilities of reducing investment requirements and of operating on exports and imports, which are consistent with maintaining the growth target, have been exhausted. It is important to ask in connection with these models whether their technological and trade assumptions and the institutional and other restrictions which underlie these are reasonable.

FOREIGN AID AND THE GAP ANALYSIS

To summarise the foregoing analysis:
1. The pseudo-mathematical certainty of the two-gap models conceals important judgments about domestic objectives and the technological and institutional restrictions on their attainment. This must be borne in mind when faced with the seemingly objective division of countries into those that face saving constraints and those that face foreign exchange constraints.[15] There is a recommendation that is implied in this division

---

[14] Thus, as in our simple model, Keynesian adjustment problems are assumed away.

[15] Chenery and Strout [5] divide countries into those where the saving gap is greater than the foreign exchange gap and *vice versa*.

given the related idea that aid shows higher "productivity" in a foreign exchange constraint situation and the related moral view that aid should be given to those who "help themselves". The dependence of the conclusions of such models on the political and other assumptions is important for recipients as well. Assuming that recipients want to make do with as little aid as possible[16] they must take maximum advantage of technological flexibilities and try to break institutional obstacles. A model of the two-gap type is therefore at best only a first approximation in calculating aid requirements. What is required is an analysis of the costs in terms of domestic objectives of reducing the gaps.
2. While both gaps are based on a mechanistic model, a foreign exchange gap which is larger than the saving gap is more suspect than the other way round. Such a situation can arise only when all possibilities of import substitution and export promotion have been exhausted. It is unlikely to be realised in practice and on examination will generally be found to be the result of some other domestic objective; indeed quite often simply of an unwillingness to save.
3. The gap analysis conducted on an aggregate plane diverts attention away from the specific needs (e.g. specific types of technical assistance) that foreign aid can most usefully fulfil.

CONCLUSION

It would seem that the distinction between a saving and a foreign exchange constraint is of very limited usefulness. Theoretically, it is based on very extreme assumptions which reduce its value as a classification of reality. It might have some limited use in a rough, short-run calculation of aid requirements though the institutional assumptions need to be looked at very carefully. Over the longer run it is not of much

[16] Even if aid is in the form of outright grants, there might be political strings attached.

use. Indeed it may be positively harmful. For it lends academic respectability to the view that LDCs are hampered in their development solely by *external* factors. In fact *internal* measures by the LDCs are of great importance; failure to realise this can be very damaging, especially at the moment when foreign aid prospects look so gloomy.

References

[1] Balassa, B., *Trade Prospects for Developing Countries*, Richard D. Irwin, Homewood, Illinois 1964.

[2] Baldwin, R. E., "Equilibrium in International Trade: A Diagrammatic Analysis", *Quarterly Journal of Economics*, 1948.

[3] Balogh, T., "Economic Policy and the Price System", *UNECLA Economic Bulletin for Latin America*, 1961. Reprinted in *The Economics of Poverty* by T. Balogh, Weidenfeld & Nicolson, London 1966.

[4] Chenery, H. B., and Bruno, M., "Development Alternatives in an Open Economy," *Economic Journal*, 1962.

[5] Chenery, H. B., and Strout, A. M., "Foreign Assistance and Economic Development", *American Economic Review*, 1966.

[6] Johnson, H. G., *Economic Policies Towards Less Developed Countries*, Allen & Unwin, London 1967.

[7] Kennedy, C., "Restraints and the Allocation of Resources", *Oxford Economic Papers*, 1968.

[8] Linder, S. B., *Trade and Trade Policy for Development*, Praeger, New York 1967.

[9] Little, I. M. D., and Clifford, J., *International Aid*, Allen & Unwin, London 1965.

[10] McKinnon, R. I., "Foreign Exchange Constraints in Economic Development", *Economic Journal*, 1964.

[11] Myrdal, G., *Asian Drama,* Allen Lane, the Penguin Press, London 1968.
[12] Patel, I. G., "Trade and Payments Policy for a Developing Economy" in R. F. Harrod and D. C. Hague (eds), *International Trade Theory in a Developing World,* Macmillan, London 1964.

[13] UN, *Towards a New Trade Policy for Development,* report by the Secretary-General of the UNCTAD, New York 1964.
[14] UN, *World Economic Survey 1963,* part I, chapter 3.

"Foreign Aid often affects adversely the major factors behind material progress." Discuss.

VI.A.3. Benefits and Costs of Aid*

It is possible to evaluate the quantity of all forms of resource transfer from developed countries to developing countries by a common measure—the so-called grant equivalent, or real resource cost. By this method, grants, loans of whatever term or condition, contributions in kind, technical assistance, and foreign private investment can be valued at their net resource cost to donors, or their net benefit to recipients.

The method is based on reducing all loans to their grant equivalent, by estimating the present value of future repayment streams to donors and to recipients. These values will ordinarily differ as between donors and recipients for the same loan, because donors could have invested the sum they loaned at a rate of return that is different from the rate which the recipient could earn from investing the same sum domestically. If these alternative rates of return are known, the grant equivalent of the loan can be calculated by methods described below.

A second element in determining real costs and benefits is to make allowance for excess costs of aid-tying, when they exist. These costs will also normally be different for donor and recipient, even when the same goods are being valued.

*From John Pincus, *Costs and Benefits of Aid: An Empirical Analysis,* Report for UNCTAD, TR/7/Supp. 10, October 26, 1967, pp. iv–v, 2–4, 11, 13–15, 19–20, 24–8, 31–3, 35, 38–41. Reprinted by permission.

In view of the perspectives on aid flows which the grant equivalent method offers and of the link which it provides between "qualitative" and "quantitative" factors in the flow of resources from developed to developing countries, further application and refinement of the method would be desirable.

The chief policy objectives of this study are:

a. to strengthen the recipients' case for easing the terms of aid;
b. to make explicit the costs to recipients of tied aid, thereby strengthening the case for untied borrowing;
c. to draw attention to the conflict of immediate self-interest by clarifying the distinction between real costs to donors and real benefits to recipients;
d. to facilitate donors' burden-sharing analyses by providing greater comparability between different forms of aid;
e. to demonstrate the inadequacy of any single measure as a comprehensive guide to donors' aid efforts. . . .

ALTERNATIVE MEASURES OF RESOURCE FLOWS

How large is the financial contribution that rich countries make to poor ones? The question seems simple, but there is no single answer or, more exactly, the answer depends on the definition adopted.

In theory, the flow of financial resources can be defined in the following different ways:

a. gross, without subtracting return flows of interest, amortization, dividends, capital repayment and capital exports;
b. net, to subtract some or all of these items and reinvested earnings of enterprises;
c. to include or exclude private investment;
d. in so-called "real cost" terms, designed to measure the sacrifices made by donors;
e. in "real benefit" terms, designed to measure the benefit to the recipient;
f. in balance-of-payments terms, designed to show the direct and indirect effects of flows of financial resources on the foreign exchange position of both exporters and importers of capital.

This analysis is concerned with items (d) and (e) in the foregoing list—real cost and real benefit. What is the meaning of "real costs" or "real benefits" in this connexion? The real cost of capital flows for a capital exporter is the income he foregoes as a result of the outflow of capital in the light of alternative possible uses of the same funds. For a capital importer the real benefit is measured by the net increment in income made possible by investing the capital inflow received, as compared with making the same investment with capital from other sources. Both real costs and real benefits can be measured approximately using existing data sources, although precise estimates would require a more comprehensive research effort than has yet been undertaken.

In order to examine the method, it is necessary to introduce the concept of a grant equivalent as a method of measuring capital flows. It is clear that for many purposes it would be a mistake to give equal weight to each dollar of capital outflow. A grant of one dollar costs the donor more than a ten-year interest-free loan of the same amount. That loan, in turn, costs him more

than a credit, payable in one year, bearing 6 per cent interest. Therefore, the problem is how to find a method that will give each form of capital outflow its appropriate weight.

The answer is found by referring to a table of annuity values. Banks, insurance companies and other financial institutions are often faced with the need to put a present valuation on future cash flows. For example, a customer might ask an insurance company how much he would have to pay today in order to be assured of an annuity income of $1,000 annually starting at age 60, twenty years from now, the income to continue for his normal life expectancy of twelve years thereafter. If the insurance company assumes that it can invest the customer's payment now at an interest rate of 5 per cent (over and above administrative costs, profits, etc.), then it can answer his question by referring to a table that shows the amount of money that one must invest today at 5 per cent return in order to produce the required sum of money from twenty to thirty-two years hence. Thus, to produce $1,000 twenty years from now it is necessary to invest $358.94 today at 5 per cent. Adding up this series of terms for the twelve-year period starting twenty years from now produces a sum amounting to $3,507.49. This is the sum of money that the customer would have to invest today at 5 per cent (excluding charges for the insurance company's costs and profits) in order to receive $1,000 per year for twelve years, starting twenty years from now and ending twelve years thereafter.

We can look at the same numbers a little differently and say that the present value of an annual income of $1,000 from 1987 to 1998 is $3,507.49, when discounted at an interest rate of 5 per cent. In other words, that future flow of income is worth $3,507.49 today.

The same analysis can be applied to the international flow of resources. Country A lends $1 million to country B at 3 per cent interest, to be repaid over twenty years in equal annual instalments, after an initial five-year grace period on amortization. This means annual interest payments of $30,000 for the five-year grace period and annual payments of $67,215.71 for twenty years thereafter. What is the present value to the lender of this future flow of repayments? The answer depends on the rate at which the lender could invest the funds if they were not lent to country B. If the funds are raised by taxation, then the alternative is the long-term rate of safe return that private investors could earn, which is approximated in most capital-exporting countries by the going rate for real estate mortgages. If the rate were 3 per cent, the same rate as the actual loan, then the present value of the repayment flow would be $1 million. If the rate were higher, say, 6 per cent, then the present value of the repayment flow to the lender would be less than $1 million, because he could have invested the money at a 6 per cent return instead of a 3 per cent return. In the example cited here, the present value would be $702,487. In other words, with long-term domestic investments yielding 6 per cent, country A incurs a cost of $297,513 (equal to $1 million minus the present value of $702,487), when lending $1 million to country B at an interest rate of 3 per cent, repayable over twenty years with a five-year grace period.

This cost of $297,513 (amounting to nearly 30 per cent of the face value of the loan in this example) is called the "grant equivalent" of that particular loan, because it represents the present value of the foregone return on capital. It arises from the difference between market rates of return on investment (assuming that market rates reflect the social return to capital) and the lower return forthcoming from the actual loan made to country B. The grant equivalent will be a higher proportion of the face value of the loan, (a) as the market rate of interest diverges more from the interest rate of the loan; and (b) the longer the grace period and the amortization period.

If the market rate of interest is equal to the loan rate, then the present value equals the amount of the loan and the grant equivalent is zero. If the market rate of interest is lower than the loan rate, then the "subsidy" to the borrower is negative, from the lender's viewpoint. . . .

DONOR'S COST APPROACH

From this analysis we can develop a set of rules for determining real costs of capital flows to donors, as well as the real benefits to recipients. Let us begin with donors' official capital flows.

In principle a grant is 100 per cent grant equivalent. The grant equivalent of each official loan can be calculated, as described above, by computing the present value of the repayment streams of interest and amortization, discounted at each donor's market long-term interest rate. The difference between the amount of the loan and the present value is the grant equivalent.[1]

These two steps do not complete the task of estimating the real cost of donor's aid. Donor aid is often in the form of contributions in kind, such as surplus agricultural commodities. This aid should be valued depending on the case either at domestic prices or world market prices; or, if the quantity is large relative to world trade, at the additional revenue it would bring if sold on the world market. (mkt clearing ps)

Most official aid is tied to procurement in the donor country. To the extent that the costs of tied aid exceed the costs of procurement on a competitive world market, should aid be valued at world market prices for real cost comparison purposes?

With a few exceptions, world prices are not the appropriate guide to donors' real

---

[1] If we assume that the alternative use of the loan funds is non-subsidized international official lending, rather than domestic investment, then the appropriate discount rate is the International Bank's borrowing rate, as discussed below.

costs. Donors may often be high-cost producers of goods exported under foreign-aid financing, because of the effects of protective tariffs on the structure of domestic production and costs. Thus, if a donor country exports as aid the products of its protected machine tool industry at prices 25 per cent above world market levels, this is not necessarily an indication that its prices are 25 per cent above its real cost. It may simply be a high-cost producer of machine tools.

On the other hand, if the donor's tied aid price (normally equivalent to its domestic market price) is higher than the donor's normal commercial export price, there is a margin between prices and real costs because the donor is charging the recipient a higher price than it costs him to produce the goods for export. This element of monopoly pricing is, in effect, a subsidy from the donor Government to the producer (or, if the aid is in the form of loans, a subsidy from recipient to producer). . . .

It is therefore possible to compute the real cost of official aid to donors in a full-employment economy as the sum of the following elements:

a. Grants, including technical assistance, at nominal value;

b. Loans, of any terms and conditions, valued at the difference between their nominal value and the present value of repayments with present value discounted at a rate reflecting the market rate of return on long-term capital investment;

c. Contributions in kind valued at world market prices (or when large quantities are involved, at market clearing prices);[2]

d. Sales or loans, repayable in recipients' inconvertible currency, valued as grants, after making allowance for funds actually spent by the lender in the borrowing country.

---

[2] These are valued at world prices rather than domestic prices because this item in practice consists almost entirely of United States farm surpluses for which foreign, rather than domestic, sales represent the only genuine alternative.

Before going on to discuss the matter from the viewpoint of recipients, a few points concerning the assumptions and methods of donors' cost analysis are in order. First, this analysis is based on the assumption that resources in donor countries are relatively fully employed. If they are not, the only loss involved in resource transfers, including grants, is that stemming from the difference between capital depreciation arising from producing goods exported under the aid programme and capital depreciated when machinery and equipment are left idle. Naturally, in an underemployed donor economy there is always the alternative of devoting the resources to domestic projects rather than to foreign aid and in that sense there is a "cost" to aid. But it is not a real resource cost, unless the proposed domestic projects are actually adopted and also succeed in restoring full employment. If the domestic projects are not adopted, then they cannot be counted as cost in a period when there are no available opportunities for profitable use of capital and labour.

A second assumption implicit in the real cost analysis is that prices of goods and services reflect the operation of competitive markets for merchandise, labour and capital. To the extent that monopoly elements affect prices, then the real cost of goods exported is less than the market price. Although monopoly elements are undoubtedly widespread in capital-exporting countries, the excess cost so produced is considered to be only a small fraction of national product. Therefore, the use of market prices as an indicator of real costs introduces only negligible overstatement and one that is probably roughly equal as among donor countries. This overstatement is probably considerably smaller than that introduced by the discrepancy between tied aid prices and commercial export prices for the same products, as discussed above.

It should also be noted that the grant equivalent of each year's commitment or flow of resources is measured without sub-

grant equiv means donor's cost

tracting the current year return flow elements that stem from debt servicing of prior loans. This follows because the grant-equivalent approach is in effect a netting out of future return flows. It is the difference between nominal values and grant-equivalent values that gives rise to debt service payments. To subtract those payments out would therefore be a form of double counting.

RECIPIENTS' BENEFIT APPROACH

The same real-cost analysis for capital flows can be applied from the viewpoint of recipients' benefit. The values will normally diverge from those shown . . . under the donors' cost definition, for several reasons.

1. Firstly, the interest rate for discounting will usually be different in donor and recipient countries. The higher the long-term real rate of interest in the recipient country, the larger the grant equivalent of a loan. Thus, for the $1 million loan cited above, offered at an interest rate of 3 per cent for twenty years, with a five-year grace period and a donor's discount rate of 6 per cent, the donor's grant equivalent was $297,513. For a recipient who would have to pay 8 per cent in order to raise capital domestically, the grant equivalent of the same loan would be $437,780. Naturally, if the recipient's discount rate is lower than the donor's, the grant equivalent to recipients will be less than that to donors.

2. Secondly, in cases where foreign-exchange controls are practised, one appropriate rate for discounting is that which the recipient would have to pay on the international securities market, as measured for example by bond rates (including flotation costs) for countries that are able to float international market loans (for example, Mexico, Jamaica, Israel); or by the effective rates of suppliers' credit in other cases.[3]

[3] In pure theory the appropriate rate of discount for recipients could be viewed as the mar-

3. Thirdly, from the viewpoint of aid recipients, tied aid may reduce the grant equivalent of aid if the prices charged for goods by the supplier exceed the world price. Thus the calculation of effective rates of interest charged for suppliers' credits, as discussed in the preceding paragraph, should include an adjustment of effective interest rates to allow for the difference, if any, between suppliers' prices and world prices. The appropriate adjustment for over-pricing of tied aid is very difficult to calculate because of the differences in the quality and specifications of goods supplied by different exporters. Relatively accurate estimates of the costs of tied aid are possible only for standardized commodities such as agricultural products, raw materials, and semi-finished bulk goods. For many consumer goods, machinery and other forms of capital equipment, problems of non-comparability arise to impede the price comparisons.

4. A fourth difference between the donors' cost and recipients' benefit estimates concerns the "grant equivalent" of private investment. From the viewpoint of the national economy, the grant equivalent is the difference between the discounted value of foreign investors' future return on investment (where the percentage return on investment is used as the rate of discount) and the host country's own discount rate for capital. If the investor's rate of return is higher than the host country's borrowing rate for foreign capital of the same maturity, then the "grant equivalent" is negative. . . .

In practice, the only way to measure foreign investors' discount rates of return on equity investment is to make three simplifying assumptions: (i) new investment will earn the same average rate of return as existing investment; (ii) future rates of return will be the same as current rates; (iii) foreign

ginal social rate of return for capital at equilibrium exchange rates. Thus, in countries with over-valued currencies, the recipients' discount rate would have to be increased to take account of over-valuation.

investors will reinvest depreciation allowances, so the income stream arising from the investment stream can be assumed to continue indefinitely.

This type of calculation necessarily abstracts from certain technical assistance and technology transfer elements inherent in much private investment, unless these accrue to the investor in the form of higher rates of return. Both of these effects (training and "know-how") add to the recipient's benefit and thus, in effect, raise his rate of discount and hence also the grant-equivalent ratio of each unit of private capital inflow. However, the practical difficulties of measurement are so great that it is best treated as a qualitative consideration.

All these considerations—the difficulty of establishing appropriate discount rates or appropriate values for tied aid, and the simplifying assumptions required for calculating recipients' benefits from private investment—have the effect of reducing the accuracy of estimated grant equivalents for recipients' benefits, as compared to those based on a donor's cost definition.

POLICY IMPLICATIONS

The analysis outlined in this study leads to certain implications for aid policy. Firstly, it demonstrates clearly that, even within current budgeted levels for official aid, the benefit to recipients could be substantially increased.

Within the loan category, a shift to longer-term loans and lower rates of interest would have a similar effect. . . . The real cost and benefit analysis leads to the same conclusion as recent analysis of debt-service problems. The conclusions of the two types of analysis are in accord because (debt service obligations) per unit value of aid received increased commensurately with the decline in grant equivalent per unit value of aid offered. Thus, real cost and benefit considerations and debt-service considerations

combine to provide a single argument for easing aid terms and conditions.

Naturally, a shift to softer aid terms increases the real cost to the donor. Whether this increase is greater or smaller than the increase in benefit to the recipient depends in pure theory on the rate of return to capital in the two countries. If it is higher in the donor country his cost increase from softer lending is greater per dollar of aid than the increase in the recipient's benefit. If the return to capital is higher in the recipient country than in the donor country, then the donor's cost increase per dollar of aid is less than the recipient's benefit increase.[4]

However, this theoretical approach to real cost and debt service problems neglects a major element. The basic test of appropriate grant equivalent ratios or—what amounts over time to the same thing—appropriate debt service levels, is not the relative return to capital in donor and recipient countries, but the general economic situation of donor and recipient. As Ohlin has said "It might well be argued that a country that qualifies for foreign assistance has no debt servicing capacity at all. Debt service competes with essential imports for foreign exchange earnings which are regarded as insufficient, and the investment needs for inadequate [domestic] savings. When debt is serviced in such a situation, it is in recognition of the fact that fulfilment of obligations is a prerequisite for further assistance, but no one expects a country in this position to liquidate its external debts."[5] Looked at in this way, the case for raising the donors' grant equivalent per dollar of capital transfer becomes overwhelming. This point has been brought home recently by the evident inability of some under-developed countries to repay conveniently their accumulated debts.

[4] Cf. Wilson Schmidt, "The Economics of Charity: Loans versus Grants," *Journal of Political Economy*, August 1964, pp. 387–395.

[5] Goran Ohlin, *Foreign Aid Policy Reconsidered*, Development Center, OECD, Paris, 1966, p. 88.

As Ohlin has pointed out, when net lending continues at the rate of several billion dollars annually, international aid is sure to produce a debt of colossal magnitude, which may in itself discourage further lending.

2.
Aid tying

A second set of policy implications arising from the analysis of this report is the significance of aid-tying for donors and recipients. For donors, as we have seen, the principal issues are balance-of-payments effect and the creation of long-term markets for output. The real cost savings to donors stemming from aid-tying under full employment conditions are probably small.

For recipients, on the other hand, the real value of aid, particularly in the form of loans, may be substantially reduced by requirements for tying. This is the more likely to be true as the recipient finds it difficult to shift its foreign spending to compensate for the tying requirement. Naturally, if the alternative to tied aids is no aid, the recipient may still be better off if he accepts the high effective interest rates implicit in tied loans. However, it may often be the case that recipients are unaware of the increased burden of repayment effectively imposed on them by tied lending. . . .

It is clear . . . that the effective rate of interest on tied lending is significantly higher than the apparent rate. The differences between the two rates are in some instances perhaps so large that, if made explicit, borrowers might prefer to switch their capital sources to untied lending, even at high nominal rates of interest.

3. A third set of policy implications relates to burden-sharing questions. The foregoing analysis leads to the conclusion that some form of grant element approach is more appropriate than the unweighted summing of grants and loans, as a method for comparing the aid efforts of donor nations. This type of analysis also clarified the role of private investment in burden-sharing computations. As a general rule, private investment, except to the extent that it includes a subsidy from the donor Government, should not be included as a real cost to donors. Therefore, it cannot be weighed in the same scales as official aid for burden-sharing purposes.

4. Fourthly, there are clearly a number of policy aspects, both for burden-sharing considerations and for considerations of total capital flows, that cannot be effectively measured by the methods used in this report. The grant equivalent of resource flows is of little value for considering balance-of-payments problems which often affect donors' and recipients' policies towards both official and private capital flows. Nor, does it enable policy-makers to distinguish among the genuinely qualitative effects of aid, including such complex economic problems as the relative productivity of various forms of aid and of aid from various donors, as well as the relative ability of recipients to make use of the various forms of resource flows.

VI.A.4. Determinants of Debt-Servicing Capacity*

In discussing the ability of countries to service external debt, it is essential to distinguish among different categories of debt. A particular debt will or will not be serviced on schedule depending on the terms of other loans contracted to finance the country's total resource gap. It is, therefore, best to look at the total blend of capital entering a country and consider the blend most suitable to the country's present and prospective position. For this purpose, one may distinguish the following categories of official capital provided to developing countries:

(a) Concessionary financing, almost exclusively public, including loans with interest of 3 per cent or less and grants.

(b) "Conventional" loans, with interest above 3 per cent but more typically between 5 and 8 per cent or higher and maturities over 10 years, including privately placed bonds, IBRD and regional development bank loans.

(c) Export or commercial credits, provided to finance export trade of industrial countries, with a variety of terms centering around 5–8 per cent interest (depending on the extent of subsidy provided) and maturities depending on the value of the contract and the characteristics of the project for which the goods are used, but usually 10 years or less.

(d) Eastern European credits (characterized by low interest, about 2½ per cent, and relatively short maturities, 10 years or less).

The "strongest" countries will be able to finance their capital needs with predominantly hard loans—i.e. mostly with "conven-

*From Barend A. De Vries, "The Debt Bearing Capacity of Developing Countries—A Comparative Analysis," *Banca Nazionale del Lavoro Quarterly Review,* March 1971, pp. 12–18. Reprinted by permission.

tional" loans or export credits. The weaker a country's ability to service loans, the softer must be the blend, i.e. the greater its concessionary component.

The factual analysis in the present paper is based on data about grants and loans, with maturities over one year, provided by "donor" governments or guaranteed by recipient governments. Assessment of countries' debt bearing capacity must, however, also cover short-term credits and, more generally, the flow of finance from private creditors (industrial firms or banks) to private debtors without government guarantee and including short-term (mostly commercial) loans. They may at times bulk large in the capital flow to individual countries. Commercial credits when excessive (or in arrears) have, at times, been consolidated into longer-term public debt. In addition, the assessment must consider the role played by private investment. The "servicing" of private investment does not proceed according to the same kind of schedules as used for loan capital, but nevertheless imposes a long-term claim on the economy which must be taken into account in analysing the country's balance of payments prospects.

PRINCIPAL DEVELOPMENT STAGES

The successive stages of development can be characterized by countries' dependence on foreign capital, the level of debt contracted and the level of income achieved. In the early stage of development countries tend to have a relatively small dependence on external capital. They may even have a resource surplus, being mostly exporters of primary products, while the rest of the economy and society is left undeveloped. Since the amounts to be financed are small, external debt is also small. As development gathers momentum, the external resource need—the "gap"—increases and, after perhaps many years, reaches a peak. The gap will start to decline after the country has made certain critical achievements, which will depend on its development strategy, its resource base, geographical location, etc. Examples of these achievements are the production of a sufficient range of import substitutes, overcoming stagnation in traditional export markets and development of new export products and markets, and mobilization of sufficient domestic resources to finance its own investments. As the gap starts to decline, the debt contracted to finance it will continue to rise as long as new debts are needed to cover the resource gap. In fact, the debt continues to rise even after the gap turns into a surplus and as long as the surplus is less than the interest needed to pay debts outstanding. Once the surplus is large enough to cover interest on outstanding debt the country will be able to start reducing its debts.

In the sequence of growth-and-debt stages described, a basic assumption is that income rises in subsequent phases, i.e. the capital mobilized domestically and borrowed abroad is effectively used to increase output. The more effective the use of capital the quicker the country will be able to reduce its gap. Accordingly, it will be possible to distinguish subsequent phases in which first the gap, next the debt and finally the income level increases. In the later phases the gap declines first and next the debt, while the income level continues to rise. This sequence of events results in the following phases.

Phase	Gap	Debt	Income
I A	Low	Low	Low
II A	High	Low	Low
III A	High	High	Low
III B	High	High	Middle
IV A	Low	High	Middle
V	Low	Low	High

In the sequence of phases countries are depicted as evolving, over a period of years, a stronger basic balance of payments position as measured by the relative extent of its dependence on external capital. It should not be denied, of course, that payments positions may be subject to considerable short-term fluctuation or that, regardless of income level, countries may follow policies which greatly affect their dependence on outside capital. The basic question is whether the country's policies promote growth and reduce its longer term dependence on external assistance. The gap may be kept small by direct controls which may be harmful to growth. Empirical evidence does not conclusively suggest that long-term development proceeds according to the sequence presented. Various factors may, in fact, help countries to accelerate their move from one stage to another or may explain why countries do not neatly fit into any of the phases presented:

(a) The debt burden may remain "low" because the country has received loans on predominantly soft terms [e.g. Chad and Congo (B)]. On the other hand, an unfavorable debt structure may increase the debt burden even while the resource gap and the income level are still low.

(b) A successful export orientation makes it possible to reach middle level income without developing a large resource gap [e.g. China (Taiwan) and Peru].

(c) Private investment finances a substantial portion of the resource gap and enables the country to keep down the debt burden (e.g. Malaysia). A number of countries manage to finance a substantial portion of a relatively large resource gap with private capital and thus have at present a low public external debt burden (e.g. Greece, Jamaica, Portugal and Spain) . . . .

Against the background of the growth-and-debt sequence one can derive two basic criteria for determining a country's ability to service debt:

(a) The more "developed" the country, the greater its debt bearing capacity: as the country approaches the end of the sequence, its need for external capital is reduced relative to its own resources and its ability to service debt improves.

(b) The more effective its policies are in moving toward the next "phase" of the sequence, the greater its ability to service loans.

Clearly, debt servicing capacity will tend to be greatest in the last phase. In this phase countries may be able to finance their external capital needs on hard terms even though their growth policies may not in all cases be very effective. Next in line would be countries which have reached the higher income level while their debt is still relatively high.

For remaining phases the second consideration is critical. In the earlier development phases a slow growth rate may require a very low average interest rate if countries' debt repayment capacity is not continuously and progressively to fall short of their debt obligations.[1]

[1] In long-term debt-and-growth analysis a critical question is whether the debtor country can reach a point at which its "savings surplus" increases faster than the interest on its debt. If, over the longer term, interest increases faster than the savings available to repay debt, the country's debt will increase continuously. The interest rate at which this explosive debt situation occurs, the so-called critical interest rate, can be derived from the country's growth parameters (growth of product, the marginal savings rate and the capital output ratio). The slower the growth rate, the lower the marginal savings rate, and the less productive its capital investment the lower is the critical interest rate.

VI.A.5. Adverse Repercussions of Aid*

Aid is an inflow of subsidised or *gratis* resources, and in this sense enriches the recipients. But unlike manna from heaven, it does not descend indiscriminately on everybody. It sets up a whole variety of damaging repercussions, and these have to be taken into account.

1. Official aid reinforces the disastrous tendency to politicise life in poor countries, the trend towards *politique d'abord*. This tendency operates even without aid, but is buttressed and intensified by it. The hand-outs increase the power, resources, and patronage of governments compared to the rest of society; and this is exacerbated by the more favourable treatment of governments which try to establish state-controlled economies. Many Third World governments, especially in Africa, could not operate their close economic controls without expatriate staffs,

*From P. T. Bauer, "Foreign Aid, Forever?" *Encounter,* March 1974, pp. 18–20, 22–3, 25. Reprinted by permission.

employed under various aid programmes. Politicisation of life provokes political tension because it becomes supremely important, often a matter of life and death, who has the power—witness Indonesia, Nigeria, Pakistan, Tanzania, Uganda, and Zaire (the Congo). This politicisation diverts the attention, energies, and activities of able and enterprising people from economic activity to politics and administration, sometimes from choice (because this diversion is profitable), but quite often from necessity (because economic or even physical survival comes to depend on political developments and administrative decisions.

2. Besides politicising life and thereby contributing to social and political tension, official aid similarly reinforces the pursuit of policies damaging to material progress (and often also inhuman). Many recipient governments restrict the activities of highly productive and economically successful minorities—Chinese in Indonesia, Asians in Africa, Indians in Burma, Europeans everywhere.

And many have also maltreated and persecuted politically ineffective groups, especially ethnic minorities. Such policies reduce current and prospective incomes in these countries, and widen income differences between them and the West. Even where it does not promote economic advance, aid represents current resources accruing to the governments, resources which are available for the purchase of imports or for the distribution of largesse, so that it helps governments temporarily to conceal from their own people some of the economic consequences of their actions.

3. Aid often supports extremely wasteful projects which make large losses year after year, and which can absorb more local resources than the value of their output. For political reasons such hopeless projects often have to be continued for years after it has become plain that they are thoroughly wasteful.[1]

4. Aid is often linked to balance-of-payments deficits of the recipients, especially when these deficits are considered as the results of laudable official efforts to speed up progress. Balance-of-payments crises in the course of development planning are especially useful in supporting appeals for aid: governments of poor countries are understandably encouraged to embark on ambitious plans involving large expenditures financed by inflationary monetary and fiscal policies, and also to run down their foreign-exchange reserves. Inflationary policies, pay-

ments difficulties, and the detailed economic controls which they promote, all engender a widespread feeling of insecurity or even a crisis atmosphere, a sequence which inhibits domestic saving and investment and even promotes a flight of capital. These sequences, in turn, serve as arguments for further external assistance.

5. The insistence on the need for external assistance obscures the necessity for the people of poor countries themselves to develop the facilities, attitudes, and institutions which are required if these societies are to achieve sustained substantial material progress. Indeed, this insistence on external aid helps to perpetuate the ideas and attitudes widespread in these countries, which are damaging to economic progress: that opportunities and resources for advance of oneself and one's family must come from someone else—the state, the rulers, one's superiors, richer people or foreigners. In this sense aid pauperises those it purports to assist.

6. Aid frequently influences policies into inappropriate directions by promoting unsuitable external models, such as Western-type universities whose graduates cannot get jobs, Western-style trade unions which are only vehicles for the self-advancement of politicians, and a Western pattern of industry even where quite inappropriate (e.g. national airlines and steelworks).[2]

7. Aid is money which could be used more productively in the donor countries (or, at any rate, by their citizens), so that it reduces the combined national incomes of donors and recipients. It also retards the material advance of the donors by affecting adversely their own balance-of-payments; and payments difficulties in donor countries have often brought about restrictive domestic economic policies—with adverse effects on the Third World's export markets.

---

[1] This consideration applies not only to industrial ventures and other familiar prestige projects, but often also to agricultural schemes. For instance, some years ago Tanzania received substantial amounts of bush clearing equipment under a Yugoslav aid scheme. The equipment was designed for use in temperate climates. The attempt to keep it going rather ineffectively in Tanzania absorbed large amounts of labour and scarce water for cooling. Protracted pressure by external advisers was required before the government agreed to abandon the equipment. (The episode bears some resemblance to the celebrated "groundnut scheme" of the late 1940s in the same area.)

[2] See Harry Johnson's critical account of the general Western intellectual misconceptions which helped to form the "Afro-Asian" ideology: "A Word to the Third World", *Encounter,* October 1971.

8. As a result of the operation of various sectional interests, the most important donor countries erect substantial barriers against the exports from the less developed countries to whom they are giving aid. Foreign aid unfortunately diminishes the political resistance in the recipient countries to the erection of these barriers, both within the donor countries and by spokesmen of recipient countries.

All these adverse repercussions (and the list could easily be extended), even when taken together, do not mean that foreign aid cannot promote development. But it is certainly unwarranted to assume that it must do so simply because it represents an inflow of subsidised resources. Aid may well improve current economic conditions in the recipient countries.

But the contribution of aid to long-term development is at best marginal. It means that some investible funds are available more cheaply than would be the case otherwise. These funds are likely to be less productive than capital supplied commercially since their use cannot be adjusted so readily to market conditions including supplies of complementary factors. And when capital is productive, it will usually be generated locally or be readily available from abroad on commercial terms.

Moreover, the crucial personal and social determinants of development are apt to be affected adversely by the repercussions of the inflow of aid. These adverse repercussions are likely to offset, or more than offset, the benefits from the inflow of subsidised investible funds in otherwise propitious circumstances. There is, therefore, not even a general presumption that aid is more likely to promote development rather than retard it. As it has operated in the past and as it is likely to operate in the foreseeable future, any general presumption would tend to be in the very opposite direction . . . .

Three further variants of the general argument for aid deserve to be noted: the popu-

lation explosion; large-scale starvation; and the widening gap.

1. The rapid growth of population in the Third World (the so-called population explosion) does not rescue the conventional arguments for aid. For it reflects a fall in mortality, a longer life-expectation of both infants and adults, i.e. some improvement in basic conditions. This improvement is omitted in conventional statistics of per capita incomes, as they do not recognise health, life-expectation and the possession of children as components of living standards.

2. It is often asserted that without foreign aid there would be widespread starvation in the Third World. These countries are supposed to be living at below-subsistence levels and under persistent threat of starvation, while at the same time alarm is expressed at the growth of their populations—a paradox which is seldom noticed. If there is not enough food for the existing population, there could be no large-scale increase in numbers. Much aid directly or indirectly finances uneconomic enterprises or activities which produce neither food nor exports to purchase it.

The widening gap is another plausible but insubstantial argument for aid. To begin with, the argument again prejudges the effects of aid by implying that aid promotes the long-term improvement in living standards in poor countries. Aid certainly removes resources from the donors; but this does not mean that it improves incomes or living standards of the recipients. To make the rich poorer does not make the poor richer. The impact of aid on differences in income and living standards cannot be judged without examining the factors behind these differences and also the likely effects of aid in specific instances.

3. The concept of the so-called gap is vague to a degree. There is continuous gradation and no clear gap or discontinuity in the international range of per capita incomes. The distinction between what are called rich and poor countries on the basis of per capita incomes depends simply on where the line

between the two categories is drawn; and in the absence of clear discontinuity this is quite arbitrary. Consequently the difference in per capita incomes between the two categories is similarly arbitrary. Moreover, many Afro-Asian lands in recent years have developed much faster than most rich countries— South Korea, Thailand, Hong Kong, Malaysia, Kenya, the Ivory Coast, Nigeria, as well as some Latin American countries. The oil states of the Middle East (usually included in the less developed world) have per capita incomes among the highest in the world. Thus the difference in conventionally measured per capita incomes between some of these countries and many developed countries has narrowed and not widened in recent years or decades. The arbitrary and crude aggregation of the developed and less developed world conceals far-reaching differences within these aggregates, including differences in material prosperity and rates of progress.

When referring to international income differences and to the widening gap, aid advocates often suggest that the higher income of the West has been somehow secured at the expense of the Third World. This has been a familiar theme of Marxist and Leninist pamphlets, and of the arguments of so-called Third World politicians. In recent years it has increasingly found its way into the advocacy of aid.

These allegations are quite without substance. The poorest societies in the less developed world are those with the fewest (or no) external economic contacts, so that their poverty cannot be the result of deprivation by external powers. Conversely, those involved in extensive foreign trade are the most prosperous. Obvious examples are Malaysia and Ghana, not to speak of the oil-producing countries. The material prosperity of Western societies and of Japan is the achievement of their own people, whose activities have also promoted such economic advance as has taken place in the Third

World. But the advocacy of aid is presumably made easier by suggesting the contrary. . . .

⨯ The belief that foreign aid is the discharge of a moral obligation to help the poor is perhaps the most influential argument—or rather, emotion—behind the advocacy of aid in popular discussion. I thought it appropriate to postpone discussion of this argument until after consideration of the more technical or systematic arguments for aid and of its major results and implications, since a worthwhile assessment of the morality of aid must be affected by its results.

4. The suggestion that aid represents the discharge of moral duty is usually based on the poverty of the Third World as compared to the West. However, this argument prejudges a) the effects of aid by taking it for granted that aid is bound to raise living standards in the recipient countries. I have shown that this belief is quite unwarranted. I have noted also that the standard international income comparisons bandied about in this context are worthless, and further that much of aid benefits the relatively well-off in the recipient countries and leaves the poorest untouched or even affects them adversely. Nor is this all. Foreign aid often facilitates the pursuit of measures which provoke or exacerbate political tension, increase the flow of refugees, and thus promote much suffering and human misery.

b) The conduct of many aid-recipient governments in the Third World clearly offends the most elementary moral principles. The expulsion of tens of thousands of Asians from Uganda is only the most widely publicised and, therefore, the most familiar instance. Large-scale maltreatment of minorities, including expropriation and expulsion, has taken place since World War II in many aid-receiving countries, including Burma, Burundi, Sri Lanka, Egypt, Indonesia, Iraq, Nigeria, Pakistan, the Sudan, Tanzania and Zaire. In some of these countries there have been large-scale massacres.

Many of the aid lobbyists seem to be sublimely uninterested in the social results of aid, or in the policies it buttresses. Morality appears to be satisfied as long as the donors are made to feel guilty and are divested of a goodly portion of their resources.

The argument that aid is the discharge of moral duty to help the poor is open to a further objection; and to some it may even be more fundamental. The implicit analogy between foreign aid and the morality of voluntary charity fails. Foreign aid is taxpayers' money—the donors have to pay whether they like it or not. By and large they do not even know that they do in fact contribute to aid. Aid lobbyists do not give away their own money. They propose taxes on others.

The moral obligation to help one's fellow man rests on persons who are prepared to make sacrifices. It cannot be discharged by entities such as governments.

Foreign aid also differs from voluntary charity in various other ways. For instance, unlike voluntary action it cannot easily be directed to the specific needs of groups or persons, since it is distributed to governments and not to voluntary organisations or to individuals.

The few people in poor countries who know about aid sense that it differs radically from voluntary charity. This is one reason why they suspect statements about its alleged humanitarian quality.

VI.A.6. Improving the Quality of

Aid—Note

Neither the volume of foreign economic aid in real terms, nor the volume of aid in relation to the national incomes of contributing countries, has been very impressive. UNCTAD II proposed that developed countries should allocate at least one per cent of their GNP to assistance purposes (official and private). The Pearson Report on aid, at the end of the 1960s, complained that "in the last years of this decade, the volume of foreign official aid has been stagnant. At no time during this period has it kept pace with the growth of national product in the wealthy nations."[1]

Contrary to the Pearson Report's call for action, however, the real volume of official development assistance actually declined by seven per cent during the period 1969–75. Throughout this period, the U.S. share of total official development assistance fell steadily from 58 per cent in 1967 to 32 per cent in 1973; in real resource value, U.S. concessional assistance declined from $3.5 billion in 1967 to $2.0 billion in 1973; and as a per cent of its GNP, U.S. concessional assistance fell from 0.43 per cent in 1967 to 0.23 per cent in 1973. For the 17 donor countries of the OECD, the share of GNP devoted to concessional aid declined from 0.42 per cent in 1967 to 0.30 per cent in 1973.[2] In view of the small amount of concessional capital that is forthcoming, and the fact that the net transfer of resources has declined, it is all the more essential to improve the quality of foreign aid.

The donor nations as well as the recipients must now bear a responsibility for improving the aid relationship. Specifically,

[1] Report of the Commission on International Development (Lester B. Pearson, chairman), *Partners in Development*, 1969, p. 4.

[2] OECD, *Development Cooperation*, 1974 Review, November 1974, p. 14.

there are three major ways the donors might improve the quality of foreign assistance: by untying their aid, by giving more scope to program aid, and by operating more within a multilateral context.

Aid may be tied by both source and end-use: the recipient country may not have the freedom to apply the aid to imports from sources other than the donor country, and the use of aid may be restricted *via* specification of commodities or projects. Aid-tying has a cost to the recipient countries; if it is tied by project as well as by source, the switching possibilities in the use of the aid are severely limited, and the costs of tying can be quite significant to the recipient country. Aid-tying is essentially a protectionist device, reducing the real value. The direct costs of tying aid can be estimated as the difference between the cost of importing from the tied source and the cost of importing the same commodities from the cheapest source. According to a recent study by Professor Bhagwati,[3] the limited general evidence available indicates that the direct costs alone of aid-tying are equivalent to a significant proportion of the value of the tied aid and almost certainly account on the average for as much as one-fifth of the value of tied aid. In specific cases, price differentials amounting to 100 per cent or more are not uncommon.

In addition to the direct costs incurred, tying of aid may have significant indirect costs for the recipient country by causing a distortion of development priorities. The distortion in the allocation of investment resources can be especially deleterious by biasing the recipient's development program toward those projects that have a high component of the special import content allowed for under the conditions of the tied aid and avoiding those projects with a large amount of "local costs" that cannot be covered by aid. "Double-tying"—by donor pro-

[3] Jagdish N. Bhagwati, *The Tying of Aid*, Study prepared for UNCTAD secretariat, TD/7/Supp. 4, November 1, 1967, pp. 1–3. See also VI.A.3.

curement and project restriction—can only too readily artificially alter the relative priority of different projects and bias investment toward import-intensive projects.

Donor countries have argued for aid-tying by source on the basis that it prevents a deterioration in the donor's balance of payments. A strong competitive element is, however, present in aid-tying: when a donor country that has a balance-of-payments deficit ties its aid, another country that may actually be a surplus country responds by also tightening restrictions on its aid. Because of this competitive element in aid-tying, a realistic process of aid-untying would now have to be gradual and simultaneous for all donor countries, and would have to allow countries with balance-of-payments deficits to untie a smaller percentage of their aid at each stage than surplus countries.

It is also proposed that the costs of tying be reduced by (a) treating the excess costs of tied aid to the recipient countries as a subsidy on exports from the donor country rather than as aid; (b) granting waivers for imports by the recipient country from other developing countries; (c) avoiding the tying of aid by both source and project, as this form of tying can lead to serious monopolistic exploitation; (d) encouraging to the greatest possible extent competitive international tendering on aid-financed projects; and (e) acceptance of debt-service payments in the products or currencies of debtor countries.[4]

Although project-type loans have had most appeal to the donor countries, it can be argued that more development assistance should be on a general program basis. It is first of all illusory to believe that aid for a certain project is financing that particular project: it is impossible to limit the effects of aid only to the project to which aid is ostensibly tied. Aid is fungible, and the aid is actually financing the marginal project that would not have been undertaken but for the

[4] Ibid., pp. 3, 51–3.

receipt of aid. Moreover, the efficacy of any one project is a function of the entire investment program; what ultimately matters is how the recipient country allocates its total investment expenditures. When aid is limited to specific projects, it becomes difficult to provide more aid for education, agriculture, small-scale industry, and administrative services which are not visible as large projects but which are extremely important for development. Most significantly, it should be noted that the subsequent uses of the income generated from a project are of more importance than the initial benefits from the project. To determine the effectiveness of aid, it is necessary to consider not only the initial increment of income resulting from the receipt of aid, but also whether the increment in income is subsequently used to relax one of the constraints on development, or is instead dissipated in higher consumption or used to support a larger population at the same low per capita level of income. Insofar as the most effective use of aid depends upon the operation of the whole set of development policies in the recipient country, program aid rather than project aid may be considered the more appropriate context from the start.[5]

The argument that the quality of development assistance can be improved by untying aid and shifting to nonproject aid is also an argument for extending the scale and range of aid efforts on a multilateral basis. In contrast to bilateral aid, multilateral aid has several distinct advantages: it is less influenced by the donor's interests; the undesirable effects of tying are more easily avoided; it can more readily harmonize and improve the financial terms of aid (unlike bilateral aid, which allows one country to insist on hard terms while another offers aid on soft terms); it facilitates coordination of aid programs among the various aid sources and with the development priorities of the

[5] See Hans W. Singer, "External Aid: For Plans or Projects?" *Economic Journal*, September 1965, pp. 539–45.

recipient countries; and it provides the opportunity for more aid consortia and consultative group arrangements to bring together the aid donors assisting a group of developing countries. If regional integration can contribute to development, then attention should also be given to the means of distributing aid through regional development institutions. Aid programs can then avoid being piecemeal and fragmentary, and there can be more opportunity for the active participation of recipient countries in the aid process.

What matters for securing the effective use of aid is not only its specific form or the terms on which it is rendered by the donor, but also the extent to which aid is successfully integrated by the recipient country into its development plan. Clarity on the objectives of foreign assistance is the necessary first step in determining how much aid is needed by a recipient country. The essence of capital assistance is the provision of additional resources, but external assistance should add to—not substitute for—the developing country's own efforts. If financial assistance from abroad is to result in a higher rate of domestic investment, it must be prevented from simply replacing domestic sources of financing investment or from supporting higher personal consumption or an increase in nondevelopmental current expenditures by the government.

It has become increasingly evident that not every poor country is immediately able to employ considerable amounts of capital productively, in the sense of having the investment cover its costs and also yield a reasonable increase in income. At least in the short run, the country may not have the capacity to absorb a large amount of real productive capital because complementary factors are in short supply, knowledge and skills are limited, and well-conceived projects are not readily forthcoming. The deficiencies in managerial, technical, supervisory, and skilled manpower seriously restrain absorptive capacity. For this reason, the productive use of capital assistance may depend heavily upon the effectiveness of technical assistance, since the contribution of technical aid is essentially to raise absorptive capacity. Once the pace of development gains momentum, the absorptive capacity will be higher, and foreign capital can then be utilized more effectively.

When foreign aid is available on a general purpose basis, the allocation of the foreign capital is decisive in determining whether it contributes as much as possible to raising the growth-potential of the recipient country. The efficient allocation of investment resources then depends upon the application of investment criteria in terms of the country's entire development program, and domestic policy measures must be adopted to supplement the use of foreign assistance. Regardless of the amount of aid received, the formation of capital depends, in the last resort, on domestic action.

It is appropriate therefore to emphasize the necessity of self-help measures: unless recipient governments adopt policies to mobilize fully their own resources and to implement their plans, the maximum potential benefits from aid will not be realized. As the record of foreign assistance in several countries shows, external aid may be incapable of yielding significant results unless it is accompanied by complementary domestic measures such as basic reforms in land tenure systems, additional taxation, investment in human capital, and more efficient government administration.

In this vein, a former administrator of AID has made the following observations:

The United States has increasingly come to realize that the power of aid as a catalyst is at least as important, probably more important, than aid as a method of transferring resources. This means that we have become less exclusively concerned with putting more wine into old bottles, e.g. providing project aid to the public sector, and more with fashioning new bottles, i.e. providing support for commodity import programs benefiting millions of farmers and small and medium-scale industrial entrepreneurs. We have, in short,

come to realize that as an essential part of any aid package, we must have agreement with the recipient on the appropriate policy package which will move the system away from enclaved development and towards a more broadly based participation of its people in productive and innovative activity.[6]

Several countries may now be cited as having embarked on more effective development programs, supported and even conditioned by foreign aid.

The Taiwan success story is well known. After 1960 a substantial volume of additional aid was dove-tailed with major policy changes, including a land reform, import liberalization, devaluation and fiscal and monetary reform. This combination resulted by 1963 in domestic saving rates in excess of 20%, in growth rates of 6–8%, an increasing inflow of private foreign capital and, by 1965, in the cessation of further concessional AID assistance. Taiwan thus, in fact, "graduated" twice, first from a security/stability situation to a (basically) development situation, and second from an aid to a self-sustaining growth situation.

Korea is a second case in point. The so-called reconstruction period characterized by a government attempting to patch up by direct action the wounds of partition and war ended around 1960. By 1963 the back of the inflationary spiral, which had diverted energies into the search for quick financial returns and away from those relatively fine allocative decisions which yield better developmental performance, had been broken. In 1964, Korea devalued, unified its exchange rate and gradually liberalized its imports until, by 1967, about 90% of all non United States financed imports were admitted on an automatic replenishment basis. Moreover, in the complementary domestic credit sector interest rates moved toward higher and more nearly unitary levels providing, for the first

[6] Gustav Ranis, "Why Foreign Aid?" *Ventures*, Fall 1968, p. 25.

time, incentives for domestic saving and investment. The change in overall performance of the Korean economy has been little short of spectacular. From negative saving rates in the 1958–62 period, and at 5.8% as late as 1962–64, Korea is now experiencing saving rates in excess of 13 and 14%. Manufacturing output rose by 24% in the 12 months after devaluation, as compared to an 8% increase over the preceding 12 months. Exports also responded extremely well to the devaluation/liberalization package, growing at a 29% annual rate during 1962–66, compared to 15% in 1958–62.[7]

Although these success stories are still few in number, they do point up the case for "performance" as the criterion for allocating aid. The "performance criterion" would have a country qualify for aid according to its performance in accomplishing such objectives as raising its marginal rate of saving, lowering its incremental capital-output ratio, and reducing its balance-of-payments deficit.[8] The purpose of this criterion is to allow aid to exert positive leverage in having the recipient countries meet specified standards in their development policies and to ensure that the limited amount of aid is allocated to those countries where it will be most productive.

Several objections may be raised, however, against the "performance criterion" for aid allocation. It does not allow a country to qualify for aid simply on the basis of "need"; and yet, this may be an essential part of any foreign assistance program. The "performance criterion" is actually designed as a measure of the recipient country's progress toward a termination of external aid, but it may be argued that the transfer of resources from rich to poor countries should become a permanent feature of the international economy. Indeed, the performance criterion sidesteps questions of equity: a country may reach a state of self-sustaining growth and thus not qualify for additional aid, but still have a per capita real income lower than another country which has not yet reached self-sustaining growth and is still receiving aid even though it has a higher per capita income. Finally, the performance criterion might be interpreted as simply indicating that a country can absorb more capital, rather than that it needs aid: the fact that a country receives low marks on performance may be the very indication that it needs a larger component of aid in its capital inflow. It has been contended, for example, that many of the African countries cannot absorb much more capital, but they still require more aid proper.[9]

Because the emphasis is now on the problems of absolute poverty, unemployment, and inequality, the performance criterion is less controlling of aid allocations than simpler evidence of need. Special consideration must now be given to the lowest income countries that are extremely vulnerable to foreign exchange needs; the World Bank advocates a substantial increase in aid to countries with per capita incomes below $200, and is focusing concessional IDA lending entirely on the poorest countries. "The inference follows that the international community needs not only to mobilize more development assistance, but to direct such assistance increasingly to the poorest among and within developing countries. . . . The vast majority of the poorest in developing countries live in the rural areas. In recent years, therefore, the Bank has sought increasingly to support rural development projects designed to improve productivity, particularly among small farmers and the landless."[10]

The use of income distribution criteria and employment criteria may also improve the efficacy of foreign assistance. An expan-

---

[7] Ibid., p. 27.
[8] H. B. Chenery and A. M. Strout, "Foreign Assistance and Economic Development," *American Economic Review*, September 1966, pp. 728–9.

[9] I. M. D. Little and J. M. Clifford, *International Aid*, London, 1965, pp. 235–6.
[10] World Bank, *Annual Report 1974*, p. 14.

sion of lending activities in agriculture, education, and population sectors may support employment and income distribution objectives. More generally, the emphasis on these objectives now requires a shift in the orientation of aid away from capital-intensive projects, investments in urban rather than rural areas, projects in the modern rather than the traditional and informal sectors, and away from large rather than small projects.[11]

Instead of imposing a rigid and quantitative interpretation of the performance criterion, it is more appropriate to interpret it as simply reemphasizing the necessity of self-help measures and the requirement that foreign aid should avoid supporting domestic policies that turn out to be counterproductive to the recipient country's development. From this viewpoint, the granting of program aid, the insistence on self-help measures, and the concern over "performance," are all interdependent elements in the aid relationship—a relationship that is necessarily reciprocal with respect to donor and recipient behavior.

Just as the absence of complementary domestic policies may limit the effectiveness of aid, so too may its impact be neutralized by changes in the other components of the total flow of resources from rich to poor countries. The total flow is affected by private foreign investment, export earnings, and the terms of trade, as well as by foreign aid. It is therefore essential to recognize the relationships between capital assistance, private foreign investment, and international trade. The contribution of international assistance will be greater if public loans and grants are not competitive with, but instead stimulate, private foreign investment. Public aid for economic overhead facilities can create opportunities for private investment, and the private investment can, in turn, ensure fuller use of these facilities and raise their financial and economic return. Similarly, policies should be pursued that will bolster export earnings so that the inflow of development

capital will be able to do more than simply offset a weak trend of export earnings or a deterioration in the recipient country's terms of trade. Of particular concern now is the need for policies that stabilize the poor countries' foreign exchange earnings; this problem is examined in XI.B, below.

Finally, attention should be given to ways of minimizing the burden of debt-service payments. When the return flow of interest and amortization payments exceeds the inflow of new capital assistance, the country confronts a transfer problem and must generate an export surplus. If the country is to accomplish this without having to endure the costs of internal and external controls, or currency depreciation, its development program must give due consideration to the country's debt-servicing capacity.

This becomes part of the problem of selecting appropriate investment criteria. To provide for adequate servicing of the foreign debt, the inflow of capital should increase productivity sufficiently to yield an increase in real income greater than the interest and amortization charges. If this is done, the economy will have the capacity to raise the necessary funds—either through a direct commercial return or greater taxable capacity. Moreover, to provide a sufficient surplus of foreign exchange to avoid a transfer problem, the capital should be utilized in such a way as to generate a surplus in the other items of the balance of payments equal to the transfer payments abroad. This does not mean that a project financed by foreign aid must itself make a direct contribution to the balance of payments, for the ability to create a sufficiently large export surplus depends on the operation of all industries together, not only on the use made of foreign investment. The basic test for the allocation of capital aid is not simply a narrow balance of payments criterion, but rather the more general criterion that capital should be invested in the form that yields the highest social marginal product. As long as capital is distributed according to its most productive use and the excess spending associated with inflation is avoided, the necessary export

[11] ILO, *Time for Transition*, Geneva, 1975, p. 62.

surplus can be created indirectly. The allocation of foreign aid according to the criterion of productivity will also be the most favorable for debt servicing, since it maximizes the increase in income from a given amount of capital, thereby contributing to the growth of foreign exchange availabilities.

The problem of the growing burden of debt-servicing will also be eased for the aid-receiving country when capital assistance is offered at lower interest, for longer terms and with more continuity, and when the creditor country follows a more expansionary domestic policy and a more liberal commercial policy. As noted earlier (VI.A.4), these considerations are becoming critical for many countries that have already reached a point at which an increasing share of their current earnings of foreign exchange is being required for amortization and interest payments. For some of the LDCs, debt-service accounts for 20 per cent or more of total commodity export earnings.[12]

[12] It is estimated that by 1980 as many as 17 developing countries, accounting for 52 per cent of

It is now clear that a substantial increase in the gross flow of resources will be required in the immediate future simply to maintain the net transfer of resources to developing countries at its present relatively low level, let alone to increase it. Any given annual gross flow of loans, at given maturities and interest rates, will build up a progressively rising flow of interest and amortization payments which will ultimately exceed the gross flow itself. If the rate of gross aid cannot be increased, then to maintain the net transfer of resources and ease the problem of balance-of-payments adjustment, it would be most helpful if a larger proportion of "aid" took the form of grants or loans at very long term and at very low interest. In this way loans would have a larger grant equivalent, and the flow of capital would correspond more closely to pure aid.

total debt-service payments, might surpass the 20 per cent mark; UNCTAD, *Debt Problems of Developing Countries*, TD/B/C.3/109, April 1973, p. 12.

VI.B. THE INTERNATIONAL MONETARY SYSTEM AND DEVELOPMENT FINANCE—NOTE

What emerges from the preceding selections is that foreign aid has been declining just at a time when there is a greater capacity to use aid more effectively and when the need in many countries has become even more urgent. It is understandable that the LDCs have therefore sought new measures for the extension of foreign aid. If aid is not forthcoming in sufficient amounts in the traditional form of open aid explicitly granted by donor to recipient, then the transfer of resources from rich to poor countries must come via other policy instruments. Most prominent in UNCTAD discussions are the attempts to have aid increased in a "disguised" form through trade policy (i.e., through international commodity agreements and preferences on manufactures) and through reform of the international monetary system. In Chapter XI we shall examine the scope for aid through trade policy. Here we consider the merits of introducing a stronger component of development finance into the international monetary system.

New international monetary arrangements have been evolving since August 15, 1971 when the United States suspended convertibility of the dollar into gold, and a regime of floating exchange-rates for most major currencies emerged. There has been official intervention in exchange markets, however, so that the floats have been "managed" within limits. Although rates were not fully flexible, the old par system of the IMF was dismantled, and a debate emerged over establishment of a new exchange-rate system to improve the balance-of-payments adjustment process. This debate was also closely related to the question of how payments imbalance might be settled more readily with greater international liquidity. And this, in turn, raised the issue of supplementing development aid by linking the creation of additional international reserves with assistance to developing countries. The general position of LDCs, as represented by the Lima Action Program and statements of UNCTAD,[1] has been in favor of very limited flexibility or a return to a fixed exchange-rate system and the creation of additional international liquidity in the form of a fiduciary instrument like Special Drawing Rights (SDR).

In the debate over flexible exchange-rates, some special arguments relate to LDCs with respect to whether (i) rates are fixed or flexible between developed countries (DCs) and LDCs, and (ii) rates are fixed or flexible among the DCs.

The LDCs may favor fixed rates among the DCs, but some management of a "crawling peg" between the LDC currency and DC currencies. Several LDCs have used some form of "crawling peg" to offset their differential rates of inflation and to leave their real effective exchange-rate fairly constant. These include Brazil (a "trotting peg"), Colombia, the Philippines, Korea, Malaysia, Morocco, Yugoslavia, and Indonesia.

In favor of greater flexibility, it is claimed that flexible rates depoliticize the problem of devaluation. LDCs tend to maintain overvalued disequilibrium rates, protected by trade and exchange restrictions, and are reluctant to devalue for political reasons; but

[1] G. M. Meier, *Problems of A World Monetary Order*, New York, 1974, pp. 224–35.

this tendency to postpone adjustment would be overcome if depreciation of the deficit country's currency came about automatically under freely fluctuating rates. Although devaluations have not met with political favor, a study of some two dozen currency devaluations in LDCs shows that the action has generally been successful in improving the balance of trade.[2]

Most of the LDCs, however, favor fixed rates between their currencies and those of other countries with which they have most of their trade and financial relations. Being generally a small open economy, the LDC believes it is advantageous to maintain convertibility at a fixed price into the currency of some major country with which the small LDC trades extensively or on which it depends for capital for investment.

Perhaps even more persuasive than the positive case for pegging to a major currency, is the negative case against flexible rates for LDCs. It is argued that flexible rates have several special disadvantages for LDCs. The problems of overcoming uncertainty and risk aversion may be especially severe for an LDC which does not have well-established forward exchange markets and which would have to diversify its reserve and debt portfolios to reduce exchange-rate risks. The facilities for a forward market between foreign currency and domestic currency are usually extremely thin in the LDC, and it is too facile to believe that forward cover can be provided the LDC's exporters by utilizing forward markets in the developed countries. Flexible rates intensify the complexity of portfolio management of reserves for LDCs, and reserves held in a depreciating currency would lose purchasing power. The creation of uncertainty for the foreign investor who wants to reconvert funds into the creditor's currency can also become a significant deterrent to capital inflow. The real value of the repayment bur-

den of servicing external debt could also be severe if the debt is denominated in an appreciating currency.

Further, freely fluctuating rates tend to inhibit regional integration among LDCs unless the countries can agree to a joint float. Finally, exchange-rate depreciation for an LDC would be ineffective as an adjustment mechanism to the extent that domestic inflation persists, the LDC's demand for imports is a function of its output and is unresponsive to price changes, the LDC's marginal propensity to save is a constant that cannot be readily altered by relative price changes, and the LDC's exports have a low price elasticity of demand (i.e., conditions of a "structural disequilibrium"). Thus, on grounds of both inefficacy and undue burden, the LDCs tend to reject fluctuating exchange-rates.

The strength of these arguments can only be assessed in comparison with what are the feasible alternatives to flexible rates. If rates are to change only infrequently, but the changes are very large, then the uncertainty and risk aversion may be even greater than under more frequent, but smaller, rate changes. If the alternative to adjustment through rate flexibility is the imposition of trade restrictions, or is a policy of national income contraction, then the alternative costs may be greater than any burden imposed by rate flexibility. It is therefore not sufficient simply to point out that there are costs involved in rate flexibility: in the absence of access to unlimited international liquidity, there will be some costs to any remedial policy for correcting a balance-of-payments deficit. The objective is to discover the least-costly remedial policy.

Even if it is granted that the LDC wants to peg its currency to a DC currency, the question still remains whether fixed or flexible rates among the DCs themselves would be of most advantage to the LDCs. Again, this depends on the feasible alternatives for the DCs. The dominant concern of the LDC should be expansion of its exports to the DCs. Trade with the DCs is by far the largest

[2] Richard N. Cooper, *Currency Devaluation in Developing Countries*, Princeton Essays in International Finance, No. 86, June 1971.

source of foreign exchange for the LDCs. (In 1973, the LDCs received $145 billion in foreign exchange, of which $125 billion came from exports, $11 billion from net private capital inflow, and $9 billion in official development assistance.) It is therefore of utmost importance that the DCs refrain from imposing trade barriers on imports from the LDCs, and that the DCs promote a high rate of domestic expansion so that imports from LDCs will be maintained. If flexible rates among the DCs will provide an effective adjustment mechanism, so that trade controls or deflation can be avoided, then flexibility among DC-rates will be best from the viewpoint of the LDCs.[3]

With flexibility among DC-currencies, the LDC can then peg either to a key currency (dollar, franc, mark, yen), to a bundle of currencies, or to the SDR. Which is most desirable for the LDC will depend on the diversification of its trade and financial transactions with "the rest of the world." Technically, to reduce its loss of control over its effective exchange-rate, the small LDC should peg to a weighted average of key currencies. If the objective is to keep its domestic prices in line with the "world" price level, the weights will have to correspond to those of each major country contributing to such a price level. If the goal is to maintain balance-of-payments equilibrium by adjusting the effective exchange-rate, more complicated calculations of multiple-currency pegging will be necessary, involving price elasticities by countries and forecasts of future trade patterns. Because of the complicated calculations required to maintain some target trade-weighted exchange-rate

(and how should financial flows be weighted, as compared with trade flows?), the LDCs are more likely to opt for pegging to the SDR. Since June 1974 the SDR has been defined in terms of a basket of 16 major currencies, and it is undoubtedly operationally simplest to peg to a "standard basket" SDR.

To the extent that the mechanism of adjustment is more effective through flexible rates and disabsorption policies, there is less need for the creation of additional reserve assets. But to the extent that countries are unwilling to bear the costs of adjustment, or countries welcome continual surpluses while corresponding deficits are much less readily tolerated, there will have to be an autonomous inflow of new reserve assets into the system. In the past, the inflow of reserves that were available unconditionally to settle imbalances in international transactions came from new gold production or from the increase in dollar holdings of central banks acquired as the United States ran a balance-of-payments deficit.

In the course of discussions on international monetary reform it was increasingly argued that the SDR should become the principal asset of settlement between central banks, and, in time, the principal reserve asset of the system, rather than being just a supplement to gold and dollars. It is a common judgment that if countries must suffer deflation or impose restrictive measures on trade and capital movements in order to protect their international reserves, then there is a shortage of international liquidity. Even though one cannot specify the "right" amount of international liquidity,[4] one can certainly maintain that countries are revealing a shortage of international liquidity

[3] For a comprehensive discussion, see William R. Cline, *Interests of The Developing Countries in International Monetary Reform*, Brookings Staff Paper, 1975. Cline concludes that the empirical evidence of currency changes in the early 1970s indicates that the LDCs' fears of flexible rates have generally been unwarranted, and that the LDCs' gains from an improved monetary system should greatly exceed any external costs to them from flexibility in DC-rates.

[4] It is illusory and misplaced precision to specify an "optimum amount" of international liquidity by relating the "need" to such variables as imports, variations in foreign trade, imports and capital flows, past deficits, domestic money supply, or current liabilities. See Fritz Machlup, "The Need for Monetary Reserves," *Banca Nazionale del Lavoro*, September 1966, pp. 175–222.

when the rate of international economic growth is retarded and there is a retreat from liberalization of trade in order to husband reserves. This trend became progressively stronger during the postwar period as the supply of traditional reserve assets failed to expand sufficiently, and the reserve-currency countries were under continual pressure. But how much liquidity should be created? Who is to control the creation of the additional liquidity? How is the increase to be distributed? And what are to be the benefits to the LDCs?

Even if the LDCs were not to share in the control of the creation of additional liquidity, or were not to receive directly any of the initial increase in liquidity, they would still benefit indirectly from any plan that expanded world reserves. For to the extent that such an expansion forestalls the developed countries from adopting beggar-my-neighbor policies, or allows a relaxation of such restrictive measures, the developing countries will benefit. If as a result of access to new reserves, a developed country can have a higher rate of domestic growth without encountering a balance-of-payments constraint, then the demand for imports from LDCs can rise. If a developed country is enabled to remove restrictions on the outflow of private foreign investment, then again the LDCs may benefit. Or if monetary policy—previously kept "tight" out of consideration for the balance of payments—is eased, the LDCs and international institutions specializing in development assistance may have greater access to the capital markets of developed countries. And most importantly, if developed nations no longer have to plead that pressures on their balance of payments prevent an increase in foreign aid or the untying of aid, then the recipient LDCs will benefit. The needed increase in foreign aid, the generalized untying of aid, and the softening of the terms of aid, advocated in VI.A.6, are dependent upon the creation of additional international liquidity.

Although these indirect benefits are of value, the LDCs have argued for more than this indirect assistance: they have wanted development finance to be linked with liquidity creation.[5] A scheme of international monetary reform would then be of direct benefit to the LDCs in that it would directly provide additional aid in the process of creating additional international liquidity.

The standard argument against linking liquidity creation and development finance is, of course, that the need for reserves and the need for development finance are two distinct issues and that therefore the LDCs are mixing up two separate questions. It is argued that the need for reserves is to cover a temporary imbalance, while the need for long-term development finance is to cover a chronic balance-of-payments gap. If the amount of liquidity to be created is determined by development finance, then, it is argued, there will be too much liquidity. Moreover, it is contended that the developing countries would not conserve an addition to their reserves but would instead spend it, contrary to the notion that the creation of liquidity should meet the demand for liquid assets to hold as precautionary balances, not to spend as transaction balances.

Against this scepticism, proponents of a direct link between monetary reform and the provision of development finance offer several counter-arguments. In brief:

i. The need for more reserves by LDCs is especially acute. It is contended that there is a widening trade gap, primary product export earnings fluctuate widely, and the mechanism of adjustment to a balance-of-payments deficit operates more slowly in an LDC than in an advanced economy.[6] There is therefore a justification in initially distrib-

[5] See Y. S. Park, *The Link Between Special Drawing Rights and Development Finance*, Princeton Essays in International Finance, No. 100, September 1973.

[6] But cf. A. Kafka, "International Liquidity: Its Present Relevance to the Less Developed Countries," *American Economic Review, Papers and Proceedings*, May 1968, pp. 596–607.

uting an increase in international liquidity to LDCs.

ii. As for the contention that an increase in reserves would allow the developing countries to escape from balance-of-payments discipline, it is replied that for an LDC the so-called "discipline of the balance of payments" does not in reality lead to deflationary (or disinflationary) monetary and fiscal policies but instead merely to import restrictions. An increase in reserves would therefore not actually have the undesirable effect of removing balance-of-payments discipline but rather the favorable effects of supporting the liberalization of trade.

iii. The argument that developing countries are incapable of conserving an increase in additional reserves is also denied. Contrary to the usual impression, the statistical evidence does not support the view that the typical or average LDC behavior is to increase overseas expenditure by an amount corresponding to any increase in reserves.[7]

iv. Finally, even if the developing country did choose to spend an increase in its reserves on additional imports, some would argue that this is quite legitimate. For if the additional liquidity has not been acquired subject to specific conditions on its use, then—as the owner of unconditional liquidity—the developing country should be able either to spend it or hold it.[8] From this standpoint, there is no reason why more severe provisions should be imposed on an LDC than on any other country that receives additional liquidity.

When the Special Drawing Account was established in the IMF in 1969, the emphasis was only on liquidity-creation, and a link to development finance was not incorporated in the facility for Special Drawing Rights.

The establishment of this facility provided, through deliberate international decisions (an 85 per cent majority vote of IMF members was required to create SDRs), a major new supplement to existing reserve assets, on a permanent basis, backed by the obligation of Fund members to accept the SDRs and pay a convertible currency in return. The first allocation of SDRs amounted to $9.5 billion over the period 1970–72. SDRs were allocated to each participating member country according to its quota in the IMF; such an allocation did not favor the LDCs and was criticized by those who advocate a direct or "organic" link between liquidity-creation and liquidity-distribution in favor of the LDCs. Since the SDR was redefined in 1974 in terms of a "standard basket" of 16 major currencies, it has been increasingly used as a numéraire in international transactions. Whether the SDR is to become the principal reserve asset will depend on the future volume of new SDRs that are created and their substitution for other reserve assets. SDRs are transferred by debiting the SDR account of the user and crediting the SDR account of the receiver, with the user country acquiring convertible currency from the receiving member—provided that the member drawing upon other members shall not make use of its SDRs in excess of 70 per cent of its average cumulative allocation over a five-year average period, and a member's obligation to provide currency will not extend beyond the point at which its holding of SDRs exceeds twice its cumulative allocations.

In the initial creation of SDRs, there was no direct connection with foreign aid, but the LDC members of the IMF share along with other Fund members through additions to their reserves in proportion to their quotas, and they benefit indirectly to the extent that the SDRs allow an increase in aid expenditure and trade liberalization on the part of developed countries.

The LDCs still advocate, however, either an organic link through an increase in SDR allocations to the LDCs, or allocation of

[7] Report of the Group of Experts, *International Monetary Issues and the Developing Countries*, UNCTAD, 1965 (66.II.D.2) paragraphs 35–6; Paul P. Streeten, "International Monetary Reform and the LDCs," *Banca Nazionale del Lavoro*, June 1967, pp. 8–9.

[8] Streeten, "International Monetary Reform," p. 9.

SDRs to development agencies that could use these funds for long-term loans to the developing countries, or a contribution by developed countries of a certain proportion of their SDR allocation to multilateral development agencies, or the transfer to development agencies of reserve currencies received by the IMF in exchange for a special issue of SDRs.[9] If the problem of liquidity-creation at first dominated the establishment of the SDR facility (the original Rio Agreements of 1969), the ensuing years of discussion about international monetary reform have raised more critical questions regarding the distribution of SDRs.

Although the SDR-aid link issue poses important questions for both the technical operation of the international monetary system and moral judgments of international distributional equity, the quantitative impact of any flexible SDR-aid link scheme will only be marginal relative to the foreign exchange that LDCs derive from trade and capital movements.

The LDCs must support policies that provide more aid and more trade and more capital inflow—not policies that entail any trade-offs among the sources of foreign exchange.

[9] Details of proposals for an organic link are presented in Park, *Special Drawing Rights and Development Finance*, pp. 9–11.

While the SDR-aid link may have only marginal significance for the receipt of foreign exchange by the LDCs, as compared with expansion by the developed countries and greater market access in the developed countries, nonetheless the idea of linking reserve creation to development assistance has symbolic value in terms of distributional equity. If international poverty is a manifestation of international inequality, the channeling to LDCs of a part of the share of SDRs formerly going to industrial countries would be at least a welcome symbol of a deliberate effort to transfer resources from rich to poor countries.

It may also be argued that if "objective indicators" are introduced imposing international rules that limit a country's freedom regarding reserve composition, these rules should be more lenient for LDCs. A wider range for "objective indicators" might be permitted for LDCs than DCs, in view of the greater fluctuation in export earnings of LDCs than DCs, and in deference to the need of the LDCs to acquire liquidity at less cost than on private capital markets.

Finally, if international monetary reform should involve the demonetization of gold by gradual sales to private markets of the gold holdings of the IMF and central banks, the profits from such transactions might be directed as aid to the LDCs.

VI.C. PRIVATE FOREIGN INVESTMENT

VI.C.1. Benefits and Costs of Private Investment—Note

Although public foreign capital has been the dominant source of international financing of development, increasing attention is now being focused on the contribution that might come from foreign private sources. Despite the past dominance of public capital, there is still a widespread belief that capital from official sources is only a transitional arrangement and that foreign economic aid should be gradually replaced by private foreign investment. Although this cannot realistically be expected to occur in the near future, nonetheless the potential role for private foreign investment appears to be broadening. Several new features offer more scope for private overseas investment. Unlike the earlier days of comprehensive central planning, a lighter type of planning is now being practiced in many of the LDCs and more attention is being given to the private sector (see XII.A). The rise of the multinational enterprise also provides a new potential (see VI.C.3). Import-substitution policies also induce an inflow of foreign capital, especially for the creation of "tariff factories." And if the LDCs are granted tariff preferences on exports of manufactured goods, this concession can be among the most significant of inducements to private foreign capital.[1]

Finally, foreign aid has been complementary to private foreign investment by acting as bond credit, which allows the creation of the social overhead capital and infrastructure necessary to attract a subsequent flow of private capital from overseas. Indeed, it has been stated that far from competing with private foreign investment, foreign aid is really a precondition for its success: thus, Professor Rosenstein-Rodan estimates that every $100 million of long-term (today necessarily public) lending creates good investment opportunities for private investment of between $30 and $40 million.[2]

Considerable interest is now being shown in measures that might promote private foreign investment and allow it to make a greater contribution to the development of the recipient countries. In an attempt to promote a larger flow of private capital to developing nations, several capital-exporting countries have adopted a range of measures that include tax incentives, investment guarantees, and financial assistance to private investors. International institutions are also encouraging the international flow of private capital; the International Finance Corporation, for instance, cooperates directly with private investors in financing new or expanded ventures.

Of far greater influence, however, than the measures adopted by capital-exporting nations or international organizations are the policies of the capital-recipient countries themselves. Controls exercised by the host country over the conditions of entry of foreign capital, and restrictions on the remit-

[1] See H. G. Johnson, "LDC Investment: The Road is Paved with Preferences," *Columbia Journal of World Business*, January–February 1968, pp. 17–21.

[2] Inter-American Development Bank, *Multinational Investment in the Economic Development and Integration of Latin America*, Bogotá, April 1968, p. 62.

eign capital, regulations of the operation of foreign capital, and restrictions on the remittance of profits and the repatriation of capital are far more decisive in determining the flow of foreign capital than any policy undertaken by the capital-exporting country.

Policies of the host country are now being adopted in the context of development planning, and their rationale and effects have taken on new dimensions in this light. No longer is it simply a matter of private investors dismissing investment prospects with the complaint that a "favorable climate" does not exist; nor need host countries contend that an inflow of private capital entails nothing but "foreign domination." The meaning of a "favorable climate" calls for reinterpretation in terms of development planning, and the effects of foreign investment in countries that are newly independent should not be analyzed as if the undesirable features in the history of colonialism need be repeated. The central problem now is for the recipient country to devise policies that will succeed in both encouraging a greater inflow of private foreign capital and ensuring that it makes the maximum contribution feasible toward the achievement of the country's development objectives.

The practice of development planning need not in itself be inimical to the promotion of a larger inflow of private capital. If a development plan reserves some areas of investment for the public sector, there is at least, on the other side, a clear statement of policy regarding areas in which private investment is desired. For a development plan may expressly define the particular role assigned to the private sector, indicate more clearly the existence of investment opportunities, facilitate advance calculation, and reduce the foreign investor's uncertainties regarding his position vis-à-vis the domestic private and public industrial sectors.

Although the prevalence of national development plans does not necessarily limit the scope for private activity and may actually promote more attractive business opportunities, it does not mean that private inves-

tors must share with the government a common interest in accelerating development. The tasks of development require both more effective governmental activity and more investment on the part of international private enterprise. But the private investor must be aware of the developmental objectives and priorities of the host country and understand how his investment fits into the country's development strategy. The contribution of private foreign capital has to be interpreted in terms beyond private profit. At the same time the government must recognize that if risks are too high or the return on investment is too low, international private investment will be inhibited from making any contribution at all. Development planning now requires the government to influence the performance of private foreign investment, but in doing this, the government should appreciate fully the potential contribution of this investment, and it should devise policies that will meet the mutual interests of private investor and host country. This calls for more intensive analysis of the consequences of private foreign investment and for more thought and ingenuity in devising new approaches that favor the mobilization of private foreign capital while ensuring its most effective "planned performance" in terms of the country's development program.

At present, the policies taken by the developing countries reveal a mixed picture of restrictions and incentives. On the one hand, the foreign investor's freedom of action may be restricted by a variety of governmental regulations that exclude private foreign investment from certain "key" sectors of the economy, impose limitations on the extent of foreign participation in ownership or management, specify conditions for the employment of domestic and foreign labor, limit the amount of profits, and impose exchange controls on the remission of profits and the repatriation of capital.

On the other hand, a progressive liberalization of policy towards private foreign capital has occurred during recent years. Many countries now recognize that an inflow of private capital may offer some special advantages over public capital, and a number of investment incentive measures have been recently adopted or are under consideration. These incentive devices include assistance in securing information on investment opportunities, the provision of supplementary finance, establishment of economic overhead facilities such as in industrial estates, protective tariffs on commodities that compete with those produced by foreign investors, exemptions from import duties on necessary equipment and materials, the granting of exchange guarantees or privileges, tax concession schemes for the encouragement of desired new investments, and special legislation for the protection of foreign investments.

To remove the ambivalence that characterizes these policies, it is desirable to reexamine the role of private foreign capital more systematically by appraising the prospective benefits and costs of private foreign investment. Such an appraisal may then provide a more rational basis for determining what type of policy is most appropriate for securing the maximum contribution from private foreign investment.

From the standpoint of national economic benefit, the essence of the case for encouraging an inflow of capital is that the increase in real income resulting from the act of investment is greater than the resultant increase in the income of the investor.[3] If the value added to output by the foreign capital is greater than the amount appropriated by the investor, social returns exceed private returns. As long as foreign investment raises productivity, and this increase is not wholly appropriated by the investor, the greater product must be shared with others, and there must be some direct benefits to

other income groups. These benefits can accrue to (a) domestic labor in the form of higher real wages, (b) consumers by way of lower prices, and (c) the government through higher tax revenue. Beyond this, and most importantly in many cases, there are likely to be (d) indirect gains through the realization of external economies.

An increase in total real wages may be one of the major direct benefits from an inflow of foreign capital. This can be recognized in Figure VI.3 where the line EG illustrates the marginal productivity of capital in the capital-recipient country, given the amount of labor. If initially the domestically owned capital stock is AB, total output is ABCE. We shall assume that profits per unit of capital equal the marginal product of capital, and that total profits on domestic capital are ABCD, and total real wages are CDE. Let there now be an inflow of foreign capital in the amount BF. Total output then increases by the amount BFGC, and the profits on foreign capital are BFGH of this amount. Since the profit rate on total capital has fallen, profits on domestic capital are reduced to ABHI. But the total real wages of

[3] Much of the following analysis is based on Sir Donald MacDougall, "The Benefits and Costs of Private Investment from Abroad: A Theoretical Approach," *Economic Record*, March 1960, pp. 13–35; Paul Streeten, *Economic Integration*, second edition, Leyden, 1964, Chap. 5.

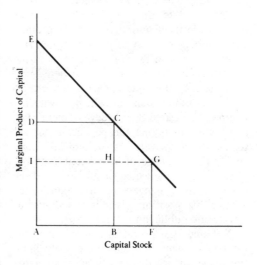

FIGURE VI.3.

labor are now GIE, with the increase in real wages amounting to DCGI. Although in this case, with a given marginal productivity of capital schedule, most of labor's gain—the amount DCHI—is merely a redistribution from domestic capitalists, there is still a net increase in the real incomes of domestic factors, represented by the rise in real wages in the amount CGH.

For a developing country, the inflow of foreign capital may not only be significant in raising the productivity of a given amount of labor but may also allow a larger labor force to be employed. If, as was contended in the discussion of dualistic development in Chapter III, a shortage of capital in heavily populated poor countries limits the employment of labor from the rural sector in the advanced sector where wages are higher, an inflow of foreign capital may then make it possible to employ more labor in the advanced sector. The international flow of capital can thus be interpreted as an alternative to labor migration from the poor country: when outlets for the emigration of labor are restricted, the substitution of domestic migration of labor into the advanced sector becomes the most feasible solution. The social benefit from the foreign investment in the advanced sector is then greater than the profits on this investment, for the wages received by the newly employed exceed their former real wage in the rural sector, and this excess should be added as a national gain.

Domestic consumers may also benefit from direct foreign investment. When the investment is cost-reducing in a particular industry, consumers of the product may gain through lower product prices. If the investment is product-improving or product-innovating, consumers benefit from better quality products or new products.

In order that labor and consumers might enjoy part of their benefit from the higher productivity in enterprises established by foreign investors, the overseas withdrawal by the investors must be less than the increase in output. But even if the entire increase in productivity accrues as foreign profits, this requirement may still be fulfilled when the government taxes foreign profits. For many countries, taxes on foreign profits or royalties from concession agreements constitute a large proportion of total government revenue. The fiscal benefit derived from foreign investment is evident from the fact that the share of government revenue in the national product of countries that have received substantial foreign investment (Iraq, Venezuela, Peru, Ceylon, Costa Rica, Guatemala) is considerably higher than in most of the other low-income countries.

The most significant contribution of foreign investment is likely to come from external economies. Direct foreign investment brings to the recipient country not only capital and foreign exchange but also managerial ability, technical personnel, technological knowledge, administrative organization, and innovations in products and production techniques—all of which are in short supply. This ensures in the first instance that a project involving private foreign investment will be adequately formulated and implemented, unlike the situation that has frequently confronted public economic aid when the recipient country has not had the talent or inclination to undertake adequate feasibility studies and formulate projects that might qualify for public capital. The preinvestment survey, act of investment, and operation of the investment project are all ensured in private foreign investment. One of the greatest benefits to the recipient country is the access to foreign knowledge that private foreign investment may provide—knowledge that helps overcome the managerial gap and technological gap. The provision of this knowledge can be interpreted as "private technical assistance." The private technical assistance and the demonstration effects that are integral features of private foreign investment may spread and have beneficial results in other sectors of the economy. The rate of technological advance in a poor country is highly dependent on the rate of capital inflow. New techniques accompany the inflow of private capital, and by the example they set, foreign firms promote the diffusion of technological advance in the economy. In addition, foreign investment may lead to the training of labor in new skills, and the knowledge gained by these workers can be transmitted to other members of the labor force, or these workers might be employed later by local firms.

Private foreign investment may also serve as a stimulus to additional domestic investment in the recipient country. This is especially likely through the creation of external pecuniary economies.[4] If the foreign capital is used to develop the country's infrastructure, it may directly facilitate more investment. Even if the foreign investment is in one industry, it may still encourage domestic investment by reducing costs or creating demand in other industries. Profits may then rise and lead to expansion in these other industries.

Since there are so many specific scarcities in a poor country, it is common for investment to be of a cost-reducing character by breaking bottlenecks in production. This stimulates expansion by raising profits on all underutilized productive capacity and by now allowing the exploitation of economies of scale that had previously been restricted. When the foreign investment in an industry makes its product cheaper, another industry that uses this product benefits from the lower price. This creates profits and stimulates an expansion in the second industry.

There is also considerable scope for the initial foreign investment to produce external investment incentives through demand creation in other industries. The foreign investment in the first industry can give rise to profits in industries that supply inputs to the first industry, in industries that produce complementary products, and in industries

[4] The various meanings of "external economies" are clarified by T. Scitovsky, "Two Concepts of External Economies," *Journal of Political Economy*, April 1954; H. W. Arndt, "External Economies in Economic Growth," *Economic Record*, November 1955.

that produce goods bought by the factor-owners who now have higher real incomes. Similar effects may also follow from investment that is product-improving or product-innovating. A whole series of domestic investments may thus be linked to the foreign investment.

Against these benefits must be set the costs of foreign investment to the host country. These costs may arise from special concessions offered by the host country, adverse effects on domestic saving, deterioration in the terms of trade, and problems of balance-of-payments adjustment.

To encourage foreign enterprise, the government of the host country may have to provide special facilities, undertake additional public services, extend financial assistance, or subsidize inputs. These have a cost in absorbing governmental resources that could be used elsewhere. Tax concessions may also have to be offered, and these may have to be extended to domestic investment since the government may not be able to discriminate, for administrative and political reasons, in favor of only the foreign investor. Moreover, when several countries compete among themselves in offering inducements to foreign capital, each may offer more by way of inducement than is necessary: the investment may be of a type that would go to one country or another, regardless of inducements, but the foreign enterprise may "shop around" and secure extra concessions. Without some form of collective agreement among capital-receiving countries regarding the maximum concessions that will be made, the cost of "overencouraging" certain types of foreign investment may be considerable.

Once foreign investment has been attracted, it should be expected to have an income effect that will lead to a higher level of domestic savings. This effect may be offset, however, by a redistribution of income away from capital if the foreign investment reduces profits in domestic industries. The consequent reduction in home savings would then be another indirect cost of foreign investment. But it is unlikely to be of much consequence in practice, for it would require that foreign investment be highly competitive with home investment. In a poor country, it is more probable that foreign capital will complement domestic investment and will give rise to higher incomes and profits in other industries, as already noted.

Foreign investment might also affect the recipient country's commodity terms of trade through structural changes associated with the pattern of development that results from the capital inflow. If the inflow of capital leads to an increase in the country's rate of development without any change in the terms of trade, the country's growth of real income will then be the same as its growth of output. If, however, the terms of trade deteriorate, the rise in real income will be less than that in output, and the worsening terms of trade may be considered another indirect cost of the foreign investment. Whether the terms of trade will turn against the capital-receiving country is problematical depending on various possible changes at home and abroad in the supply and demand for exports, import-substitutes, and domestic commodities. It is unlikely, however, that private foreign investment would cause any substantial deterioration in the terms of trade. For if an unfavorable shift resulted from a rising demand for imports on the side of consumption, it would probably be controlled through import restriction. And if it resulted, on the side of production, from a rising supply of exports due to private direct investment in the export sector, the inflow of foreign capital would diminish as export prices fell, thereby limiting the deterioration in the terms of trade. Moreover, if the deterioration comes through an export bias in production, it is still possible that the factoral and the income terms of trade might improve even though the commodity terms of trade worsen, since the capital inflow may result in a sufficiently large increase in productivity in the export sector.

Of greater seriousness than the foregoing costs are those associated with balance-of-payments adjustments. Pressure on the balance of payments may become acute when the foreign debt has to be serviced. If the amount of foreign exchange required to service the debt becomes larger than the amount of foreign exchange being supplied by new foreign investments, the transfer mechanism will then have to create a surplus on current account equal to the debit items on account of the payment of interest, dividends, profits, and amortization on the foreign borrowings.[5] When a net outflow of capital occurs, a reallocation of resources becomes necessary in order to expand exports or replace imports. To accomplish this, the country may have to endure internal and external controls or experience currency depreciation. The adverse effects of these measures of balance of payments adjustment must then be considered as indirect costs of foreign investment, to be added to the direct costs of the foreign payments.

The direct costs in themselves need not be a matter of great concern. For even though part of the increased production from the use of foreign capital has to be paid abroad in profits or interest—and this is a deduction that would not be necessary if the savings were provided at home—this is merely to say that the country must not expect to get an income from savings if it does not make the savings.[6] What is fundamental is that the country does have additional investment, and the benefits from this may exceed the direct costs of the foreign savings that made possible the capital formation.

The indirect costs, however, are rightly a cause of concern, insofar as the capital-receiving country may be unable or unwilling

[5] The length of time which elapses before this occurs will depend on the growth in new foreign investment, rate of interest and dividend earnings, and the amortization rate. Cf. E. D. Domar, "The Effect of Foreign Investment on the Balance of Payments," *American Economic Review*, December 1950, pp. 805–26.

[6] Cf. J. R. Hicks, *Essays in World Economics*, Oxford, 1959, p. 191.

to endure a loss of international reserves and does not want to impose measures of balance-of-payments adjustment in order to find sufficient foreign exchange for the remittance of the external service payments. External measures such as import quotas, tariffs, and exchange restrictions may suppress the demand for imports, but they do so at the expense of productivity and efficiency. Internal measures of higher taxation and credit tightness involve the costs of reduced consumption and investment. And the alternative of currency devaluation may cause the country to incur the costs of a possible deterioration in its terms of trade, changes in income distribution, and necessary shifts of resources. To avoid, or at least minimize, these indirect costs, the role of private foreign investment must be related to the debt-servicing capacity of the host country. And this depends on the country's development program as a whole, since the ability to create a sufficiently large export surplus rests on the operation of all industries together, not simply on the use made of foreign investment alone.

In the past there has been a general tendency for poor countries to overestimate the costs of foreign investment and to discount the benefits, especially the indirect benefits. Now, however, there is wider appreciation that within the context of a development program and with a careful appraisal of the prospective benefits and costs of foreign investment, policies may be devised to secure a greater contribution from the inflow of private capital. Instead of discouraging investment from abroad simply because it involves some costs, the newly developing countries are increasingly recognizing that they should attempt to devise policies that will encourage the maximum feasible contribution. Although the formulation of specific policies must depend on particular conditions in each country, we may at least suggest some of the principal considerations that might shape these policies.

In general, the attraction of private foreign investment now depends less on fiscal action, upon which most countries have concentrated, and more on other conditions and measures that guarantee protection of the investment and provide wider opportunities for the foreign investor. If private foreign investment is to be encouraged, it is necessary to allay the investor's concern over the possibilities of discriminatory legislation, exchange controls, and the threat of expropriation. Investment guarantees may be utilized more effectively to lessen the investor's apprehension of nonbusiness risks. Either unilaterally or through bilateral treaties, governments can offer some assurances designed to reduce the likelihood of expropriation or of impairments of investors' rights and to assure investors of an adequate recourse if such impairments should occur.[7] It has always been difficult to secure agreement by both investing and recipient countries on a uniform set of substantive rules, as in a multilateral investment charter.[8] The World Bank has, however, succeeded in establishing an International Center for Settlement of Investment Disputes, which provides facilities for the settlement, by voluntary recourse to conciliation or arbitration, of investment disputes arising between the foreign investor and the host government.

Finally, along with assurances against the occurrence of risk and measures for the adjustment of investment disputes, considerable attention is being given to the possibilities of providing guarantees under which the investor will be compensated for any loss he may suffer from other than normal business

[7] For a detailed review of the various measures that might be adopted, see United Nations, Economic and Social Council, *The Promotion of the International Flow of Private Capital: Further Report by the Secretary-General*, Document E/3492, Geneva, 1961, Chap. 3.

[8] For a survey of various proposals, see Earl Snyder, "Foreign Investment Protection: A Reasoned Approach," *Michigan Law Review*, April 1963, pp. 1087–1124; *The Encouragement and Protection of Investment in Developing Countries*, International and Comparative Law Quarterly, Supplementary Publication No. 3, 1962.

causes. Although such a guarantee is something of a measure of last resort, it does help to minimize the investor's risk and gives some advance assurance of a reliable "safety margin." Some capital-supplying nations have provided insurance coverage, but the insurance of investments in developing countries might be made more effective through the establishment of a multilateral investment insurance program as opposed to participation in a number of bilateral programs.

While investment guarantees may help in removing "disincentives" to foreign investment, the attraction of private capital depends even more on positive inducements in the form of greater opportunities for profit-making. The private investor's first concern is whether his costs will be covered and a profit earned. Many developing countries now offer special tax concessions that provide a tax holiday or reduce the rate of tax on profits, but these measures are not effective unless the investment yields a profit. The foreign investor is likely to be less interested in receiving an exemption after a profit is made than he is in being sure of a profit in the first instance. It is therefore most important to raise his profit expectations. To do this, it may be necessary to undertake additional public expenditures, especially in developing the country's infrastructure and in ensuring a supply of trained labor. Yet rarely is a government willing to undertake expenditures expressly for the purpose of attracting foreign investment; instead of incurring the present cost of additional expenditures, most governments prefer to assist foreign investors through a future sacrifice in revenue. Though more politically feasible, tax concessions are not likely to be the most powerful inducements that the host country can offer to encourage a flow of investment.

At the same time, their use can be overdone. They involve a cost to the government not only in terms of a revenue foregone, but also in terms of equity and administrative costs. More importantly, the LDCs may offer excessive concessions in their efforts to attract foreign investment. If an investment

is going to occur in one LDC or another (for example, in order to secure a raw material supply), but each LDC competes against the other in offering concessions, then the LDCs are likely to overconcede.[9] When tax concessions are granted to existing investments, in order not to discriminate, there is simply a windfall. Moreover, the concessions are likely to attract the quick speculative type of foreign investment which is in the country only to take advantage of the concessions and leaves as soon as these are withdrawn. Finally, if the benefits of foreign investment are realized for the host country during the early years of the investment, there is no case for prolonging the concessions beyond this relatively short period.

Newly developing nations are now mainly interested in having foreign enterprises contribute to their industrialization, rather than following the historical pattern of being directed to agriculture or mining. In most cases, however, the size of the domestic market has remained too small to offer much attraction. As a development program proceeds, domestic markets may widen, and this limitation will be reduced. Much can also be done to widen markets and establish a more substantial base for industry by promoting regional markets through arrangements for a common market or a free trade association. The general problem of regional integration is examined in Chapter XI, but it should be noted here that the establishment of a customs union or free trade area may have considerable potential for attracting invest-

[9] Cf. Dudley Seers, "Big Companies and Small Countries," *Kyklos*, 1963, pp. 601–3; R. H. Green and Ann Seidman, *Unity or Poverty?*, Baltimore, 1968, pp. 99–131.

Several studies indicate that tax incentive programs have not been effective. See, for example, Jack Heller and Kenneth M. Kauffman, *Tax Incentives for Industry in Less Developed Countries*, Cambridge, 1963, pp. 60–66; M. C. Taylor, *Industrial Tax Exemption in Puerto Rico*, Madison, 1957, pp. 143–9; Peter Kilby, *Industrialization in an Open Economy: Nigeria, 1945–66*, Cambridge, 1969, pp. 132–4.

ment to the development of manufacturing industry.

Even more significant than regional preferential arrangements would be a general preferential system by which developed countries granted preferences to all LDCs on their exports of manufactures and semi-manufactures. Such a system may offer considerable attraction to private foreign investment, especially by inducing the transfer of production facilities required from the developed preference-granting countries to the less developed preference-receiving countries in order to turn labor and raw materials into saleable products and obtain the dual advantages of tariff-free or preferential market access and lower labor costs.[10]

In considering measures to encourage foreign investment, a developing country does not want, of course, to seek foreign capital indiscriminately. The objective is to ensure that the investment supports activities from which the recipient nation may derive maximum national economic gain, as assessed through benefits and costs. To achieve the most effective utilization of foreign investment in terms of its entire development program, the country may have to adopt policies, such as preferential tax treatment or other incentives, that will attract private capital into activities where it will have the maximum catalytic effect of mobilizing additional effort. From this standpoint, it is especially important that policies affecting the allocation of foreign capital be based on an awareness of the external economies that can be realized from different patterns of investment. Beyond a consideration of the direct increase in income resulting from the investment and other short-term criteria, it is important to look to the more indirect and longer-run possibilities—from the widening of investment opportunities to even the instigating of social and cultural transformations.

Finally, the recipient country may be well advised to emphasize a partnership ar-

rangement between foreign and domestic enterprise. A joint international business venture that involves collaboration between private foreign capital and local private or public capital is a promising device for protecting international investment, integrating foreign investment within a development program and safe-guarding against an enclave type of investment, stimulating domestic management and investment, and reducing the transfer burden and balance-of-payments difficulties.

The alternatives of a 100 per cent foreign-owned enterprise and a joint venture are, however, only two of a number of possible arrangements for securing a mix of foreign capital, management, and technology. The major question is whether there are other means of transferring scarce managerial and technical knowledge without having to be in joint supply with capital as in a foreign direct investment. As already noted, the cost for foreign equity capital is high, even post-tax. The host country may well consider this cost excessive for the foreign managerial and technical knowledge which it desires but which cannot be acquired through a direct foreign investment without the high payment for equity capital with which it is in joint supply. The new approach to foreign investment has therefore been to focus on alternative arrangements for securing capital, management, technology, and marketing capabilities without the foreign ownership and control that has commonly been associated with foreign direct investment. It may be possible to "unwrap" the bundle of inputs that come in the package of direct foreign investment and secure inputs that are more appropriate for the needs of the recipient country, or that cost less when they are not tied to equity capital.

The problem for the host country is to evaluate the benefits and costs of alternative arrangements for importing the investing firm's capabilities, and then to secure by inducements and regulations the best feasible alternative. The alternative arrangements span an entire spectrum. At one end of the

[10] Johnson, "LDC Investment," p. 19.

spectrum is the traditional form of direct investment involving 100 per cent foreign equity ownership and no time-limit on the existence of the foreign-owned enterprise in the recipient country. This arrangement is appropriate for only those sectors where the joint mix of capital, technology, and management cannot be supplied in any other way and the investment continues to provide a properly discounted benefit-cost ratio greater than that of unity for an unlimited time period. Moving on from this arrangement, the host country may initially allow 100 per cent ownership but then insist that any expansion of the enterprise occur through national participation. It may further limit the time of foreign control by requiring a national majority equity holding to emerge within a certain period. There may be a "fadeout" provision such as Decision 24 of the Andean Common Market, which requires multinational corporations to fade down from 100 per cent to 49 per cent ownership over a period of 15 or 20 years. [11] There may be other requirements and means for disinvestment over time.[12] Moving still further to a dilution of the foreign equity, the host country may insist at the very outset on a joint venture and may also establish a limited time for any foreign equity participation. At the other end of the spectrum, the host country may exclude foreign equity altogether and seek the managerial and technological knowledge through other contractual arrangements that might allow the transfer of technical and managerial skills without being tied to equity capital. Licensing agreements, technical services agreements, engineering and construction contracts, management contracts, and coproduction agreements can prove to be of considerable benefit to a developing country—

supplying the needed foreign knowledge at a lower cost than must be paid when the knowledge comes with equity capital.[13]

Some doubts may, however, be expressed that the LDCs can indeed realistically expect to receive foreign technological and managerial knowledge without equity capital. This may prove difficult or impossible for the latest technology or research-and-development type of enterprise because the discoverer and owner of such technology normally wishes to retain control. But this does not apply to the older, more standardized types of technology. Assuming that the demand for such technical services should increase, then it can be expected that a supply of such services will be induced.

Similarly, it can be contended that a management contract is not an effective instrument for the discovery of investment opportunities as distinguished from simply the operation of an investment. This may be true, but in the LDCs the discovery of new investment opportunities is not as relevant as in more advanced countries, and the crucial need is still much more for simply the adaptation, imitation, widening, and deepening of existing methods of investment.[14]

Finally, it may be doubted whether there will be sufficient motivation when there is no equity interest. But managerial fees can be graduated according to profits, and even other objectives such as foreign exchange savings realized. Other incentive devices—short of ownership—can also be utilized.

In general, these contractual arrangements are extremely flexible devices for securing the transfer of the nonmonetary resources of management and technology; they may be adapted to widely diverse circumstances; and their utility in meeting a variety of objectives is becoming increasingly

[11] Andean Foreign Investment Code, Commission of the Carthegena Agreement, International Legal Materials, Vol. 2, 1972.

[12] Albert O. Hirschman, *How to Divest in Latin America, and Why*, Princeton Essays in International Finance, November 1969.

[13] A coproduction agreement allows a national firm in the LDC to acquire imported equipment and technology in return for payment "in kind" by exporting its products for a number of years to the guaranteed market overseas.

[14] See Inter-American Development Bank, *Multinational Investment*, p. 61.

appreciated. Together with the fact of development planning, these new approaches to international investment are causing both the foreign investor and the recipient country to consider the benefits and costs of foreign investment in a newer light. This approach can be particularly efficacious when activities are reserved under a development program for public ownership or for majority ownership by local nationals, but there is still a need for seeking technical information or managerial services from abroad.

If the technical and managerial components of direct foreign investment can be secured through contractual nondirect investment devices without having to grant its supplier a controlling equity interest, and if financial aid is provided from foreign public sources of capital (either directly or indirectly through a development bank or development corporation), then the recipient LDC may benefit from an optimal mix of public financial aid and private technical assistance.

The potentialities for combining local public or private ownership with technical assistance from private foreign enterprise and capital assistance from public sources deserve considerable emphasis.

VI.C.2. The Terms of Investment*

There is a general presumption that migratory flows of capital searching for higher rates of return than can be earned at home result in a more productive use of resources and thus in a net benefit that is shared mutually between investing and host countries. There are echoes of comparative advantage here, with factor movements seen as a substitute for product flows. But while the early proponents of comparative advantage theory could easily demonstrate the general result that trade confers mutual benefits, their insistence that this was so in practically all cases has not survived subsequent scrutiny. Could the same not also be true of international investment? We might usefully develop here a concept analogous to the commodity terms of trade, to refer to the distribution of gains from foreign investment between the investor and the host economy, calling it the *"terms of investment"*. This might be defined as the ratio between the

*From Tony Killick, "The Benefits of Foreign Direct Investment and its Alternatives: An Empirical Exploration," *Journal of Development Studies*, January 1973, pp. 301–9, 310–11, 312–14. Reprinted by permission.

net social benefits accruing to the host economy and the private returns accruing (abroad) to the investor. In the general case we would expect the ratio to be positive but there might be cases in which direct investment does actual net harm to the host economy, in which case the ratio would be negative.

Possibly the most influential and least vulnerable argument in favour of foreign direct investment is that it is better than none at all. Implicit here is the assumption that this form of investment at least produces some positive benefits for the host economy and that there is no alternative to it. In fact, there is always at least the alternative of waiting until such time as it is possible to mobilize domestic resources, or until foreign participation can be secured on more favourable terms of investment. The decision whether or not to wait, and for how long, becomes a problem in discounting. But the alternatives need not be so stark as between permitting a foreign capitalist to do now what otherwise will have to be postponed. There may be a choice between the importation of the technically efficient productive methods of industrial nations, typically demanding large inputs of capital and managerial skills, and 'backward' indigenous techniques requiring little of either. This is a possibility that may exist, for example, when plantation investment is proposed, and in the manufacture of some simple consumer goods. It is a possibility that exists when economic minerals are found on or just under the surface of the land, as in the case of the Sierra Leone diamond industry examined below. In these circumstances there is no clear distinction between the choice of foreign or domestic exploitation and the choice of production techniques.[1]

To assess the benefits to the Sierra Leone economy of the different types of mining activity the paragraphs that follow examine the extent to which the alternative modes of operation (a) contribute directly to national value added from a given volume of output,[2] (b) generate linkage effects of the type recorded in an input:output matrix and (c) generate external economies. The choice of the mining sector is a significant one, for in choosing between alternative modes of production the decision is especially critical in the case of mineral extraction. In the nature of things, this is a once-and-for-all process and the problem therefore arises of how to derive the maximum benefit for the national economy from the exploitation of this scarce resource.

Sierra Leone possesses characteristics similar to those of a number of low-income countries, especially in Africa. It is small when measured by the size of its population

(2·5 million in 1968), tiny when measured by the size of its GDP (£145 million in 1968–69) and minuscule when measured by the size of its market for manufactures (perhaps £50 million) [U.N., 1969, pp. 606–14]. It is dominated by primary production, with agriculture and mining contributing over half the GDP. There is little manufacturing; the output of this sector (including handicrafts) is about 6 per cent of estimated GDP. It is heavily dependent on foreign trade; imports and exports of goods and services in 1966–67 to 1968–69 were equivalent to about 55 per cent of GDP. It is sparsely populated and estimates of the rate of growth of population range from 1 per cent p.a. upwards.

The bulk of private foreign capital in the country is invested in mining and trading, especially the former. Mineral production contributed about 15 per cent of the GDP in 1966–67 to 1968–69 and in 1967 earned almost 90 per cent of total export receipts. Minerals produced are wholly for export and, with one small exception, are shipped abroad in an unprocessed state. The production of diamonds is the most important mining activity but iron ore, bauxite and rutile are also exported in significant amounts. During the nineteen-sixties the mining of these latter three minerals was solely undertaken by wholly-owned subsidiaries of companies registered in Britain and the United States. The structure of the diamond industry was more interesting. About two-fifths of diamond production was recovered by a wholly-owned subsidiary of a British firm, the Sierra Leone Selection Trust. The remainder of output was won by Africans working in small teams and using only the simplest equipment—buckets, spades, bowls, sieves and, in some cases, mechanical pumps. This part of the industry will be described in more detail later; for the present attention will be confined to the activations of the foreign mining companies.

We commence with an examination of the direct contribution of the foreign mining companies to various national accounting

---

[1] Since the period to which this study relates a different kind of choice has been made, for during 1969 the Government of Sierra Leone announced its intention of taking a controlling share in the foreign mining concerns operating in the country, on the Chilean model.

[2] The emphasis here is on the contribution to the *national* economy as distinguished in national accounting from the domestic economy. There may be a major difference between these because of the return flow of profits and other foreign factor rewards.

concepts, given by the statistics in Table 1. The value obtained for gross domestic value-added is £9·63 million (item 3). This is gross because it includes depreciation and domestic because it includes the factor rewards of non-nationals. This sum was equivalent to 8·7 per cent of the mean value of the GDP

TABLE 1. Output, Inputs and Value-Added of Mining Companies

	£ million[a]
1. Gross output.[b]	13·23
2. *less* Material inputs	
(i) Imported	2·36
(ii) Locally produced	1·24
3. Gross domestic value-added	9·63
of which:	
4. Wage and salary payments[c]	
(i) To expatriates	0·90
(ii) To Sierra Leoneans	1·55
5. Direct tax payments[d]	2·65
6. Depreciation[e]	1·18
7. Profits[f]	3·26
8. Errors and omissions[g]	0·09
9. Gross national value-added (3 minus 7)[h]	6·37
10. Net national value-added (9 minus 6)	5·19
11. Item (10) as % of item (1)	39%
12. Item (10) as % of item (3)	54%
13. Production costs (2 + 4 + 6)	7·23
14. Production costs as % of gross output	55%

[a]To minimize distortions created by temporary abnormalities the values recorded are the means of the years 1963–65.
[b]Taken as equivalent to export values.
[c]Including payments in kind.
[d]Including diamond marketing rules service fees.
[e]As recorded in company returns.
[f]Including undistributed profits but after tax and depreciation.
[g]This is the difference between item 3 (assumed to be correct) and the sum of items 4 to 7. The error is most likely to have resulted from poor wage and salary statistics.

[h]Besides deducting profits from gross domestic value added there would be a case for doing the same with wage and salary payments to expatriates (see item 4 (i) of Table 1). This has not been done in the table because these workers are residents of Sierra Leone on the usual national accounting definition [*U.N., 1960, p. 7*]. Very few of them, on the other hand, will stay for more than a few years and meanwhile they will remit substantial proportions of their current incomes to their home countries. It was estimated that some 32% of expatriates' current incomes are repatriated and another 22% spent on imported goods and services [*Killick and During, 1969, p. 292*]. Thus, it could be plausibly argued that of the average payment of £0·9 million to expatriates only about £0·4 million truly contributed to national value-added. This figure, moreover, makes no allowance for the often substantial lump-sum repatriation of accumulated savings at the end of an expatriate's sojourn in Sierra Leone and this is another factor which worsens the terms of investment.
Source: T. Killick and R. W. During, "A Structural Approach to the Balance of Payments of a Low-Income Country," *Journal of Development Studies*, Vol. 5, No. 4, 1969, and previously unpublished data.

at factor cost in 1963–64 to 1965–66. If gross domestic value added is the relevant indicator, it is evident that the mining companies made a significant contribution to income, output and expenditure in Sierra Leone during this period. But a much better indication is given by figures which have been adjusted for the outflow of profits, for these accrued entirely to the incomes and asset values of foreigners and are excluded from estimates of the national product. We call the adjusted figure gross national value added, which is shown in item 9 of Table 1 as £6·37 million.

This shows that one-third of domestic value-added was made up of a profit element accruing to non-residents and it will be seen from the table that the profit was about 25 per cent of gross revenue. This suggests that investment by these companies is not a cheap way for Sierra Leone to obtain capital. However, profits are more appropriately set against the capital investment that produces them. If we measure profits against the mean value of fixed assets employed this calculation results in a rate of return to fixed capital of 24 per cent p.a., net of Sierra Leone tax, although it should be added that aggregation of the profits of the companies in question conceals large differences in their individual records over these years. Moreover, the profit figures in Table 1 include undistributed profits; of the £3·26 million total profits after Sierra Leone tax some £1·28 were reinvested and did not, therefore, truly represent a 'leakage' from the Sierra Leone economy. With this said, however, the very substantial profits revealed here do suggest that the ratio of private profits to social returns was on the high side and the terms of investment somewhat to the disadvantage of the host country. Given that we are dealing with the once-for-all exploitation of mineral resources, the possibility remains a real one that greater benefit could be secured for the national economy by an alternative arrangement for the utilization of these resources.

All in all, the results summarised below point to the conclusion that the companies' capacity to contribute to national income is limited by high profits and the high import-content of depreciation expenditures. To put the matter another way, expansion by the mining companies which increased GDP by 1 per cent in a given period would, on the

National Accounting Magnitude	Mean Contribution to Total of Mining Companies, 1962–65
G.D.P.	8·7%
G.N.P.	5·9%
N.N.P.	5·2%

record of 1963–65, increase the NNP by only 0·6 per cent. The achievement would be yet less favourable were we also to deduct the transfers and imports of expatriate company employees.

We turn now from the directly measurable impact on the national income to the more elusive linkage and external economy effects of the mining companies.

INDUSTRIAL LINKAGES

There are good reasons for expecting weak linkages in this case: the national economy is a very small one at an early stage of development, the companies are undertaking primary production and will thus have small requirements for inputs from other sectors of the economy, and since all output is sold abroad there are no forward linkages. The small size of any backward linkages is demonstrated by the estimate that inputs of local materials and non-factor services averaged £1·24 million per annum, or 9·4 per cent of gross output. Information on this aspect was admittedly poor but even if the estimate is subject to a margin or error as large as ±50 per cent the nature of the conclusion would be unchanged. If the strength of industrial linkages is considered as a factor bearing upon the terms of investment, the near absence of these in the operations of mining companies in Sierra Leone must be taken as worsening the terms of investment to the host country.

EXTERNAL ECONOMIES

There are those who argue that the external economy effects of foreign direct investment are likely to be particularly important and although no very systematic analysis is possible here of all the potential external economies which might raise social benefits relative to private returns, there is something to be reported, and various points are dealt with in the following sub-paragraphs.

(a) *Employment*: Since there is a high incidence of unemployment in Sierra Leone whose reduction is regarded as an economic objective in its own right, the creation of employment may be regarded as a type of external economy, to the extent that the social opportunity cost of labour is less than the going market wage. Productive techniques employed by the mining companies are rather capital intensive, with fixed assets of £3,560 for every person employed. Total numbers employed by the companies averaged 7,790 over 1963–65. This was equivalent to 0·83 per cent of the total labour force in the census year 1963, even though their contribution to the GDP was 8·7 per cent. The relatively small number of jobs created by the companies must have limited their ability to make a favourable impact on the creation of a permanent wage-labour force and on the rates of urbanization and social change. This question of employment creation is discussed more fully in following paragraphs.

(b) *Creation of skills:* It would not be correct to say that the companies use local labour only in jobs requiring no skills. The two larger companies have their own training schemes for mechanics and other artisan skills and they send some of their more promising workers for further training overseas. While some of the skills imparted may be fairly specific to mining there is no doubt that a 'wastage' of trained workers into other sectors has occurred and this may be reckoned an external economy in the strict Marshallian sense. It is still true, however, that for higher-level technical personnel the companies remained heavily reliant upon expatriates in this period. It is, moreover, doubtful whether there has been much spill-over of managerial skills from the companies into other sectors. Until recently they relied very largely upon expatriates to fill most supervisory and managerial posts and only in rare cases would these employees go on to secure employment elsewhere in the local economy. As can be seen from Table 1 item 4,

payments to expatriates are estimated to have taken up £900,000 out of an annual total wage bill of £2,450,000, even though they comprised under 3 per cent of the numbers employed. It should in fairness be added that there was some change during the nineteen-sixties and, even prior to nationalization, Africanization could have been expected increasingly to penetrate into supervisory, higher-technical and managerial positions. The small external economies created in the past may in this context be a rather poor guide to the future position.

(c) *Infrastructure:* The creation by the companies of infrastructural facilities whose utilization is not exclusive to the mining sector is another form of external economy. In this connection, the diamond company maintains some 60 miles of road and this is undoubtedly used for purposes additional to the company's. The company extracting iron ore operates a 50-mile railway to its own port at Pepel but the use of this is largely confined to the haulage of ore. Both the main companies have built housing and hospitals for its employees and the latter are also used by local communities. In short, it seems probable that the infrastructure created by the mining companies generates real but not massive external economies. This, however, is a matter that would warrant considerably more investigation.

(d) *Taxability:* Tax receipts from foreign investors can be treated as a species of external economy in cases where a shortage of government revenue operates as a development constraint and where taxation of foreign concerns yields revenue in excess of what would be possible under an alternative industrial structure. In Sierra Leone during the years in question a strong case could be made out that both these conditions were fulfilled. During these years the government ran into increasing financial difficulties, stemming partly from an inelastic tax structure, and as a result of these had recourse to IMF stand-by support and deflationary fiscal policies. We shall see later that the rate of taxation of the mining companies, on the average and at the margin, was much higher than on the largely indigenous Alluvial Diamond Scheme. It can be calculated from Table 1, items 5 and 7 that tax payments were 45 per cent of pre-tax profits. Tax agreements were subsequently revised and substantially larger revenues could be expected thereafter.

(e) *Foreign exchange*: The treatment of the foreign exchange earnings of the companies is somewhat similar, for in this period the non-mining sector of the economy was running large and increasing balance of payments deficits which contributed to a crisis in 1966 and the need to obtain IMF support. In other words, the official rate of exchange did not at this time reflect the true value to the economy of foreign exchange and the social benefit derived from the net foreign exchange earnings of the companies was in excess of their 'market' value. This case is strengthened by the recurring nature of the country's balance of payments difficulties and her decision to follow Britain's devaluation of 14·3 per cent in November, 1967. The study of the direct effects of the mining companies on the balance of payments showed that, overall, the companies were making foreign exchange available at the rate of £9·0 million p.a., and if we multiply this by the 'shadow price' of 1·143 (using the new exchange rate established at end-1967) it increases to

£10·3 million p.a. [*Killick and During, 1969, p. 280*]. However, the net benefit to the current account was much smaller than the value of exports and the ability of the companies to provide so much foreign exchange depended upon an importation of capital funds which may or may not have continued in the future. Moreover, when we took certain indirect factors into account, such as the imports and transfers of company employees, the overall contribution of foreign exchange fell to £5·7 million p.a. (at the then existing exchange rate), or only 43 per cent of the value of export earnings.

The discussion of this section can be summarized as demonstrating that a number of factors limited the value of investments by foreign mining companies to Sierra Leone's economy. Among these were low ratios of net national value-added to gross output and gross domestic value-added, slight industrial linkages, high capital intensity and heavy dependence on expatriate skilled manpower. Some external economies were generated to set against the unfavourable factors, notably a diffusion of lower-level technical skills, fairly large tax payments and substantial net earnings of foreign exchange. In general, however, the balance of the argument is consistent with the views of those who stress the factors making for unfavourable terms of foreign investment. The next stage of this study is to make a comparison with the economic benefits derived from an alternative method of exploitation, as it exists in the diamond industry.

An interesting aspect of the Sierra Leonean case is that the diamond industry in this period exhibited a markedly dualistic character. On the one hand a British company, Sierra Leone Selection Trust (SLST), won diamonds using techniques requiring large inputs of capital and managerial expertise. This company usually accounted for about two-fifths of diamond output. The rest, on the other hand, was won by African diggers using tiny amounts of capital and economising on managerial skills. This sub-industry has a four-tier structure. There are, firstly, the labourers who do the digging, who are called tributors: the estimated number of these has fluctuated around 30,000 in recent years. These are organized into gangs, at the second level, by people misleadingly called diggers. Thirdly, there are dealers who buy diamonds from the diggers and dispose of them legally to the Government Diamond Office or illegally by smuggling them to Liberia or elsewhere. The Government Diamond Office, which is a marketing organisation managed for the government by a subsidiary of the de Beers Group, forms the final tier. The whole is known locally as the Alluvial Diamond Scheme and for convenience it will in what follows be referred to as the ADS.

All the tributors and diggers are African, mostly Sierra Leonean but with an admixture of people from other West African states. Although there is a substantial minority of Sierra Leoneans among the dealers, in value terms an overwhelmingly large part of dealing is undertaken by Lebanese residents. It would therefore be rather misleading to describe this as an indigenous industry for, in common with the rest of the mining sector, the ADS has come to depend upon foreign enterprise.

Comparisons between the ADS and the mining companies are made much more difficult by the fact that there is practically no solid information about the distribution of the earnings of the former. For the purpose of the balance of payments study this problem was tackled by making two alternative sets of assumptions, designed to illustrate the extreme possibilities. The main bone of contention relates to the repatriated profits of the Lebanese dealers, with apparently knowledgeable opinion differing greatly on this point. Our alternative assumptions assume in the 'high-benefit' case repatriated profits 2½ per cent of gross domestic value added and 25 per cent in the 'low-benefit' case, these proportions being chosen to illus-

trate the extreme possibilities. In the judgment of the author *the true proportion is likely to be considerably nearer to 2½ per cent than 25 per cent.* Details of the full range of assumptions made are set out in Killick and During [*1969, Table A*].

Estimates comparable with those in Table 1 are set out below, showing both high and low-benefit cases. The output figures include a provision for smuggled diamonds. There is no depreciation figure in Table 2 and hence no distinction between gross and net value added. This is because only tiny amounts of fixed capital are employed in the ADS and the figures on imported materials [*item 2 (i)*] are in this case calculated to include replacement buckets, spades, and other simple pieces of equipment.

The figures tabulated permit a number of direct comparisons between the ADS and the companies. It can rightly be protested that the relevant comparison is with the diamond mining concern (SLST) only, not with all the companies taken together. Unfortunately, such a comparison would not be possible without disclosing confidential information but the nature of results based upon a direct comparison is indicated in the text.

The first comparison is of the proportions of net national value added to (a) gross output and (b) gross domestic value-added:

| | *Net National Value Added as Percentage of:* | |
	Gross Output	*Gross Domestic Value Added*
Companies	39%	54%
ADS (high-benefit)	97%	98%
ADS (low-benefit)	74%	75%

From the point of view of the host country, the objective is to maximize the contribution to national income from the exploitation of a given deposit of diamonds. What is demonstrated here is that *even on the most pessimistic assumptions* the extraction of a given value of diamonds by the techniques embodied in the ADS makes a clearly superior contribution to national income than extraction of minerals by the technically superior methods of the companies. This important conclusion holds also for a direct comparison with the diamond company, for SLST's figures are only slightly higher than those for all the companies. The relative disadvantage of the companies is derived partly from their proportionately greater use of material inputs, and partly from the greater 'leakages' from the national income in the form of depreciation and profit repatriations.

Another interesting aspect of these statistics is revealed by a comparison of the bottom lines of Tables 1 and 2, which compares costs of production relative to gross output. It can be seen that the production costs of the companies are smaller relative to output than in either ADS case. The same is true of a direct comparison between SLST and the

ADS. In that sense the companies are clearly the more efficient procedures, and yet they make a smaller contribution to the national income. The lesson to be drawn from this apparently paradoxical result is that when the greater part of profits is repatriated a country should not necessarily opt for 'efficient' low-cost, high profit methods of production. . . .

Turning now to a comparison of *industrial linkages*, it is obvious from a glance at the estimates of material inputs [*Table 2, item 2 (ii)*] that the ADS possesses virtually no backward linkages with other productive sectors and, since all production is directly exported, there are no forward linkages either. It may be protested that the figures for inputs are merely the numerical results of more-or-less arbitrary assumptions. This is conceded but everyone connected with the

TABLE 2. Output, Inputs and Value-Added of Alluvial Diamond Scheme, on Alternative Assumptions

	(£ million)[a]	
	High-benefit case (1)	Low-benefit case (2)
1. Gross output[b]	12·30	12·30
2. *less* Material inputs		
(i) Imported	0·10	0·10
(ii) Locally produced	0·02	0·02
3. Gross domestic value added	12·18	12·18
of which:		
4. Payments to tributors	4·26	3·04
5. Payments to diggers and other Sierra Leoneans	5·78	4·87
6. Tax payments	0·91	0·61
7. Current consumption and local savings of dealers	0·91	0·61
8. Repatriated profits of dealers	0·30	3·04
9. Gross national value added		
(= net national value added) (item 3 minus 8)	11·88	9·14
10. Item (9) as % of item (1)	97%	74%
11. Item (9) as % of item (3)	98%	75%
12. Production costs (2 + 4 + 5)	10·16	8·03
13. Production costs as % of gross output	83%	65%

[a]Values are the means of the years 1963–65.
[b]Taken as equivalent to officially recorded exports plus an allowance for smuggling.
Source: As for Table 1.

industry agrees that material inputs are very small indeed, so that our conclusion is firm even though the figures are only illustrative. This test is thus to the advantage of the companies. Small as their linkages were seen to be they are, in the backward direction, certainly more powerful than those of the ADS. And what is true of the companies collectively holds also for SLST alone.

The last subject of comparison is *external economies*. The following sub-paragraphs correspond to those on the externalities of the companies.

(a) *Employment*: The number of tributors employed in the ADS, about 30,000 in recent years, is about four times greater than employment in all the companies, because of the labour-intensive techniques used, and, since full employment is itself a policy objective, the greater capacity of the ADS to create jobs is one of its advantages. Thus, to obtain an annual gross output of £1 million the companies employed about 590 workers in this period whereas the ADS employed about 2,400. However, the work involved is not of the kind usually described as wage labour and does not do much either to create a permanent modern labour force or urbanisation in its beneficial aspects.

(b) *Creation of skills*: There is no diffusion of skills comparable with the case of the companies. This is because fewer skills are called for and many of the skills that are needed, e.g. in sifting alluvial deposits or in valuing diamonds, are highly specific. It is even less likely that the ADS has generated a diffusion of managerial skills than that the companies have. This is similarly due to the small usage and specificity of managerial expertise in the ADS.

(c) *Infrastructure*: The ADS has produced little social overhead capital, partly because of its lightweight end-product—diamond marketing does not need major roads or railways. Power and piped water are not used; housing is so primitive as to have caused official concern in the past.

(d) *Taxability*: The ability of the government to tax the ADS is markedly weaker in comparison with the companies. Tax evasion is easy because of the small risks involved in smuggling such an easily concealed commodity over long and inaccessible frontiers. In fact, an attempt in 1967 to raise the export duty payable on ADS diamonds had to be abandoned because it was resulting in disproportionately more smuggling and correspondingly smaller sales through official channels. In 1963–65 tax revenues attributable to the ADS were a little over 5 per cent of mean annual exports, as compared with 20 per cent for the mining companies and a higher figure yet for SLST by itself.

(e) *Foreign exchange*: During the period reviewed the ADS was a large net earner of foreign exchange. Measuring its direct impact on the balance of payments, net earnings were estimated at between £27 million and £36 million over the three years, which figures fell to £18 million and £12 million, after taking certain indirect factors into account. A comparison with SLST revealed that in its direct effect on the balance of payments even the ADS low-benefit case yielded higher net foreign exchange earnings, relative to its exports, than the companies (or SLST taken separately). Taking indirect factors into account raised the relative overall contribution of SLST slightly above the ADS low-benefit figure. Since the true contribution of ADS is likely to lie nearer to the high-benefit limiting case, we may be fairly confident that for every pound's worth of exports the technically primitive part of the diamond industry brings greater net relief to the balance of payments than the modern mining company. If it is the case, however, that the company achieves a higher extraction rate than the ADS, it is an open question which would achieve the greater net foreign exchange earning from a given alluvial deposit. . . .

Comparison of the ADS and the foreign company has shown that each has its strong points and weaknesses. The company has larger, even though small, backward connections with other productive sectors; it contributes more to the diffusion of modern skills; it has created more valuable contributions to the country's infrastructure; it is much more amenable to taxation. The Alluvial Diamond Scheme, on the other hand, produces a substantially larger contribution to national income from a given gross domestic value-added, and almost certainly from diamond deposits of a given value; it creates more employment; it produces a larger net relief to the balance of payments from a given value of production, although not necessarily from a given deposit.

Considerably more information would be needed and for a longer period of time before any final judgment could be formed. Crucial data on the distribution of the gross income of the ADS and on extraction rates achieved from the two methods are lacking and we cannot confidently generalize from a study of only three years. Nevertheless, the balance of advantage does appear to lie fairly firmly with the ADS. The one really solid advantage of the company is its superior taxability, but against this must be set the greater overall impact of the ADS on the Sierra Leone economy.

The question arises, to what extent can these results be attributed to the nationality of ownership of the alternatives and to what extent is it derived from the radically different techniques of production employed? To

some extent it is unreal to attempt a sharp distinction between these two factors. Given the stage of development of Sierra Leone's economy, the importation of foreign capital and management was at the material time practically the only feasible means of creating technologically advanced mines. However, the question does have some point, not least because of the recent nationalization agreement. The answer is that both techniques and nationality of ownership matter. Technical contrasts result in big differences in depreciation costs, in somewhat different patterns of inputs, and thus in contrasting employment-creating effects. These factors help to explain the differences in the ratios of net national value added to gross output, in the linkage effects, and in externalities. The nationality of ownership, on the other hand, affects the outflow of profits and the extent to which expatriates are employed in technical and managerial posts. Nationality therefore also influences the ratios, linkage effects and externalities.

What conclusions may be drawn from this study which have a more general validity? In a number of respects the foreign mining companies in Sierra Leone are archetypal of the foreign enclaves about which so much has been written. They were in the period covered wholly foreign-owned, they engaged in primary production for export and thus had only slight connections with other productive sectors, they made substantial post-tax profits. Even so, it has been possible to demonstrate that they did make positive and significant contributions to the Sierra Leonean economy. Thus, while the terms of investment may well be described as having been unfavourable to Sierra Leone, our conclusions do not support those who argue that receipt of foreign capital in these forms may do positive harm. We have also shown the possibility, on the other hand, that exploitation of the country's alluvial diamond deposits by technically simple, high cost and labour-intensive methods might have brought a larger social benefit than was obtained from the expatriate diamond mining concern. This emphasizes the importance of considering all the available alternatives when determining in which activities foreign investment should be encouraged or discouraged, although the range of choice available in other industries and in other countries may often be more limited than in the case discussed here. If an important new diamond field were discovered in Sierra Leone (an unlikely but not impossible event) the government would be mistaken to decide that this should be mined by modern methods, with or without foreign participation, except after very careful consideration of the rival claims of the ADS.

Implied in this view is a familiar warning against confusing technical with economic efficiency. There is a fairly generally held view in Sierra Leone that the creation of the ADS was economically harmful to the country and was justified only on political grounds. Our results do not support that view. There is a sense in which SLST belongs technically to a different age from the Afri-

can diggers, working with bucket and spade, and we have seen that it is SLST which is the lower-cost producer. But it is the ADS, by utilizing in a greater degree locally available resources, which imparts a greater dynamic to the economy.

Various factors have been isolated here which have a direct bearing upon the distribution of gains from foreign direct investment, which may be influenced by state action. We are reminded, for example, of the importance of taxation paid by foreign companies for the GDVA:NNVA ratio and for externalities; governments can influence the distribution of gains by varying their tax provisions. Efforts directed towards changing the employment and training policies of foreign concerns and the extent to which they utilize domestic as against imported materials can also influence the benefits accruing to the national economy. Low-income countries perhaps possess a greater power of control over their terms of investment than over their terms of trade.

VI.C.3. Multinational Enterprises in

Developing Countries—Note

The multinational enterprise (MNE)—with facilities in many countries and responsive to a common management strategy—has gained increasing prominence as an instrument for private foreign investment in developing countries. While the capital, technology, managerial competence, and marketing capabilities of an MNE can be utilized for a country's development, there is also a fear that the MNE may dominate the host country or impose excessive costs.

Criticism of the MNE is but the latest attempt to dispel complacency over the relevance of the neoclassical theory of international trade for development problems. As we shall see in Chapter XI, critics of the

neoclassical trade theory first attempted to discredit the theory's power to explain historical development by arguing that international trade had actually operated historically as a mechanism of inequality. After the establishment of the postwar international economic institutions, the argument shifted to a criticism of the alleged biases and deficiencies of the international institutions comprising the Bretton Woods system. And now the MNE has become the object of criticism, with pessimistic warnings about future detriment to the developing countries if the MNE is not sufficiently regulated.

Does the evaluation of the operation of the MNE, however, call for more than a social benefit-cost type of analysis, such as outlined in the previous selection (VI.C.1)? Why should the MNE be analyzed differently from a "simple" type of foreign direct investment from one home country to a single host country? The essential question is what difference does the attribute of "multinationality" make to the analysis?

True, an MNE is likely to have the power of an oligopoly; but so too may some "simple" foreign enterprises or domestic independent companies. True, an MNE may be a vertically integrated enterprise that uses transfer prices for intrafirm trade; but so too may "simple" foreign investment. True, an MNE may be involved in the costly process of import substitution; but so too may a simple foreign enterprise or a national firm. True, an MNE may be depleting too rapidly a wasting asset; but so too may other forms of investment that are not multinational in character. In assessing the contribution of a foreign investment by an MNE, we have to be clear on whether what is being assessed is the *investment project* per se, the *foreignness* of the investment, the *multinationality* of the investment, or some *alternative* institutional arrangement for acquiring the ingredients of the direct investment package.

The distinguishing feature of an MNE is that the range of its major decisions (finance, investment, production, research and development, and reaction to governmental policies) is based on the opportunities and problems that the MNE confronts in all the countries in which it operates. In utilizing its "global scanning capacity" to determine its investment plan, worldwide sourcing strategies, and marketing based upon expectations of returns and risk factors, the MNE concentrates on the total net worth of the investor's interests, not that of an individual subsidiary alone.

Although these features of foreign investment associated with "multinationality" do not call for a different type of analysis from the general benefit-cost analysis already discussed, the multinational firm is characterized by some behavioral differences that broaden the reach and increase the intensity of both the benefits and costs of foreign investment. As Caves has indicated,[1] a national branch of a multinational firm might behave differently from an equal-sized independent company for three reasons:

(1) *Motivation.* The multinational firm maximizes profits from its activities as a whole, rather than telling each subsidiary to maximize indpendently and ignoring the profit interdependences among them. The multinational firm also spreads its risks, and could therefore behave quite differently in an uncertain situation from an independent having the same risk-return preference function.

(2) *Cognition and information.* Its corporate family relations give the multinational unit access to more information about markets located in other countries—or to information to which it can attach a higher degree of certainty.

(3) *Opportunity set.* The set of assets held by a multinational unit can differ from a national firm's in various ways—perhaps most notably in its skill in differentiating its product and its financial capacities.

Although Caves's analysis is concerned with the differences in market behavior between a national branch of a multinational firm and an equal-sized independent company, these behavioral differences are also relevant as between a multinational firm and a "simple" type of foreign enterprise in the developing country.

These behavioral differences can be especially significant in: first, promoting foreign investment; second, allowing the MNE to act as a unit of real economic integration; and

[1] Richard E. Caves, *International Trade, International Investment, and Imperfect Markets*, Princeton University Special Papers in International Economics, No. 10, November 1974, pp. 21–2.

third, endowing the MNE with greater bargaining power.

The growth of MNEs tends to promote more foreign investment because the MNE is less of a risk-averter when it operates in a number of countries, produces a number of products, practices process specialization, and enjoys greater maneuverability with respect to marketing opportunities and conditions of production than does a firm with a narrower range of activities.

Emphasizing the interrelations between output and input flows in international trade, Baldwin has stated:

When the international firm becomes economically viable in a particular industry, not only is it possible to transfer knowledge, capital, and technical and managerial labor across borders more efficiently, but these transfers tend to be economically feasible with smaller product markets than is the case when the optimum size of productive units is small. Moreover, because of the pecuniary and technological externalities that exist among intermediate sectors in a vertical product line, it may not be economically profitable from a private viewpoint to add a new product to a country's production list unless the international firm mechanism is utilized.[2]

The MNE is also a unit of integration in the world economy. The transmission of factors (capital, skills, technological knowledge, management) via the MNE, together with the MNE's economies of scale in R&D and marketing, make it a unit of real international integration. By its multinational operations and intrafirm transactions, the MNE transcends the national barriers to commodity trade and impediments to international factor movements. As a planning unit that makes resource allocation decisions, the MNE becomes the mechanism for making effective the LDC's potential comparative

advantage. The MNE provides the complementary resources of capital, technology, management, and market outlets that may be necessary to bestow an "effective" comparative advantage to the labor-surplus factor endowment in the host country.

This can also be evaluated as efficient international production. The MNE views production as a set of activities or processes, and the global strategy of the MNE amounts in essence to the solution of activity models of production, with production processes in many countries. A competitive equilibrium solution to the programming problem is imposed within the MNE when it operates efficiently as a planning unit, and each process is in the solution basis. Regulatory interference with the MNE will alter the equilibrium basis, and some processes formerly in operation may become inefficient to use. The likelihood for a labor-surplus economy is that labor becomes unemployed for lack of cooperating factors previously supplied by the MNE. Or if workers were formerly employed in a lower productivity occupation, there is a loss in real wages.

This interpretation of the MNE as an efficient technical and allocational unit of integration means that while intrafirm trade conforms to *corporate* advantage, it is also identical with the realization of *comparative* advantage. If the nation-state fragments the world economy through restrictions on commodity and factor movements and thwarts international economic integration, the MNE may serve a complementary—rather than competitive—function to the nation-state: the MNE may be the vehicle for evoking in practice the principle of comparative advantage in world trade, for trade in both outputs and inputs. The internal resource allocation in the MNE is a substitute mechanism for the market, but when it realizes comparative advantage in processes and activities, the resource allocation decisions of the MNE will be more efficient than those in unintegrated markets that are characterized by imperfections and uncertainty. For global technical efficiency, the world economy is the territorial unit of international production

[2] R. E. Baldwin, "International Trade in Inputs and Outputs," *American Economic Review, Papers and Proceedings*, May 1972, p. 433.

(not the nation-state, which is a unit of international politics).

What, however, is the distribution of gains between the MNE and host country? More pointedly, how might the net benefit for the host country be raised? This is the crucial question posed by the attribute of "multinationality." For multinationality instills foreign investment by an MNE with greater bargaining power because of its tendency to be of larger size, its capability to exercise wider options, and its capacity to avoid some forms of regulation that cannot reach beyond national jurisdiction.

These powers are especially suspect when they coalesce in the practice of transfer pricing. The host country may believe that transfer pricing allows the MNE to minimize taxes, escape from tariff charges, or be the means of remitting profits from a subsidiary to the parent company that would otherwise not be allowed by exchange restrictions.[3]

If the MNE is concerned with overall profit, not profit at any particular stage, then the dominant motivation behind the pricing structure in a vertically integrated operation is to gain maximum advantage vis-à-vis the different governmental rates of taxation and regulation of international capital flows. Transfer prices or cost allocation techniques then acquire an artificial quality in the absence of "arm's-length" transactions.

The developing country's desire to regulate transfer pricing is only a special instance of the general problem of how the bargaining process between the host government and MNE distributes the fruits of the foreign investment—more technically, the extent to which the developing country can capture from the MNE a greater share of the MNE's quasi-rents on its supply of technological knowledge, management, and capital. In the

most formal terms, the problem is for the host government to devise an optimal welfare tax on foreign capital which improves the terms of foreign borrowing.[4]

The more general problems of bargaining between host government and MNE have been summarized as follows:[5]

For the transfer of a certain "package" of know-how, capital, management and inputs there is a range of values which would be acceptable to both sides but which both sides have an interest in concealing. The ability to conceal the relevant values is however much greater for the MNE than for the host country.

In settling the bargain and in drawing up the contract, a large number of items may be for negotiation, in addition to income and sales tax concessions and tariff and non-tariff protection of the product. Among these are:

(a) specific allowances against tax liabilities, such as initial or investment allowances, depletion allowances, tax reporting techniques, loss offset provisions, etc.;

(b) royalty payments, management fees and other fees;

(c) duty drawbacks on imported inputs for exports;

(d) content of local inputs;

(e) profit and capital repatriation;

(f) structure of ownership and degree and timing of local participation;

(g) local participation in management at board level;

(h) obligations to train local labour;

(i) transfer pricing;

(j) rules and requirements relating to exporting;

(k) degree of competition and forms of competition; price control and price fixing;

(l) credit policies (e.g., subsidized interest rates);

[3] For an analysis of the adverse effects of the transfer pricing mechanism, see Constantine Vaitsos, *Intercountry Income Distribution and Transnational Enterprises*, Oxford, 1974, Chapter 6; S. Lall, "Determinants and Implications of Transfer Pricing by International Firms," *Bulletin of the Oxford Institute of Economics and Statistics*, August 1973.

[4] W. M. Corden, *Trade Policy and Economic Welfare*, Oxford, 1974, pp. 339–40, 345–7, 355–64.

[5] Paul Streeten, "The Multinational Enterprise and The Theory of Development Policy," *World Development*, October 1973, pp. 8–9.

(*m*) extent of capitalization of intangibles;

(*n*) revalorization of assets due to currency devaluation;

(*o*) subsidies, e.g., to energy, rent, transport; or export expenses such as insurance, freight, promotion;

(*p*) place and party of jurisdiction and arbitration;

(*q*) time and right of termination or renegotiation.

A contract between the MNE and the host government will contain provisions under some of these headings. Such possible contracts can be ranked in an order of preference by the MNE and by the government. If both the MNE and the government prefer a certain contract to another, the latter can be eliminated. The only complication here is that either party has an interest in concealing the fact that its interest coincides with that of the other party. For by appearing to make a concession, when in fact no concession is made, it may be spared having to make a concession on another front where interests conflict.

But leaving this complication aside, amongst the contracts that remain when those dominated by others have been eliminated, the order of preference for the MNE will be the reverse of that for the government. If the least attractive contract from the point of view of the MNE is outside the range of contracts acceptable to the government, no contract will be concluded. But if there is some overlap, there is scope for bargaining. The precise contract on which the two partners will settle will be determined by relative bargaining strength.

Ranking of Contracts in Order of Preference

MNE	Government	
	F	
A	C	↑
B	(E)	
C	(D)	Range of bargaining
(D)	B	
(E)	A	
F		↓

E and D are ruled out because both the MNE and the government prefer C; F is ruled out because it is unacceptable to the MNE.

At the same time, in determining the relative value of the different contracts, the host government will find cost—benefit analysis useful. By comparing the present value of the stream of benefits with that of the costs the disparate components in the bargain can, at least in principle, be made commensurable. Cost—benefit analysis and bargaining-power analysis are not alternative methods of approach but are complementary. Cost—benefit analysis will not tell a government whether a particular project is acceptable or not, i.e., whether it falls within the acceptable bargaining range, but it will help it to rank those that are acceptable.

VI.D. TRANSFER OF
TECHNOLOGY

VI.D.1. Science and Technology for Poor
Countries*

Until a few years ago nobody would have doubted that the tremendous development of the world's technological power, both of science (know-why) and of technology (know-how), presented great advantages for the late comers in the process of development of the poorer countries of today. Surely the more accumulated knowledge to draw from, the easier development must become?

So to a point, reality seemed to support this view unquestionably held by practically all economists. Germany and the US developed more rapidly than the UK, the pioneer country of the industrial revolution. But then Russia in turn, and even Argentina and Southern Brazil, looked like catching up rapidly, and so did a little later, Australia and Canada. Even the growth of the poorer countries of today, on an overall view, is quite fast by historical standards, with growth rates of GNP of 5 to 6 per cent. If this does not result in corresponding rises in per capita income, this is due to faster rates of population growth than the rich countries of today had to contend with at any time in their history, when they also had emigration outlets not open to the developing countries of today. Rapid population increase is a different problem, though for our present subject it may be relevant to reflect that the reduction in mortality rates is itself part of the impact of the rich countries' technology—in this case, health technology.

*From Hans W. Singer, *The Strategy of International Development*, Macmillan, London, 1975, pp. 189–95, 203–6. Reprinted by permission.

But there is now a spreading recognition that even growth rates of 5 per cent, 6 per cent or more of GNP do not represent real development—quite apart from the fact that so much of the growth is slowed up by population increase. It is now clear that rapid growth of output can, and does, go hand in hand with increased impoverishment of large sections of the population, a rapid rise in the number of people living below any acceptable poverty line, rise in underemployment, and a general failure in the development process to involve larger numbers of the population. Hence, I think we are bound to say that in the overall picture we do not see a satisfactory development of the poorer countries, and this in spite of the unprecedented accumulation of know-why and know-how. Why is this?

My thesis is that it is precisely *because* of the accumulation of science and technology, or rather because of the specific nature of this accumulation, that we witness such widespread failures of real development among the late comers, belying the unthinking optimism of earlier days.

This thesis can be best illustrated by pointing to two striking disproportions. The first disproportion can be seen in the fact that with a rate of population increase at least three times higher than in the rich countries, the developing countries of today—per million population—have to create three times as many new jobs; yet they have to do this with resources which are only perhaps one-twentieth or less than those of the rich countries. This means that resources per job required are only one-sixtieth or less. This in turn means that if the developing countries of today tried to create jobs of the same kind and with the same technology as the rich countries of today, only one-sixtieth of their new job-seekers, i.e. less than 2 per cent, would in fact be employed at "modern" standards. The rest, over 98 per cent, would remain unemployed. In reality, of course, the situation is not quite as crass as that. Many more of the jobs will be in rural sectors and other occupations requiring less capital per job, and in many ways, the technology used even in similar jobs, will be less capital-intensive and hence require fewer resources. But all the same, our numerical exercise is sufficiently close to the way in which things are moving in the developing countries of today to be meaningful.

The other disproportion can be seen in the present distribution of the creation of new knowledge and technology as between rich and poor countries. Here we face the difficulty that the 'creation of new science and technology' is not directly measurable. However, as often in economics, e.g. in national income statistics, where we cannot measure the total output of something, we may be able to measure the total input or cost which goes into the production of the output. For example, in national income statistics we cannot really measure the output of civil servants or university professors, so we substitute the salaries paid to them. In this way we use input figures as a proxy for output figures. We do so without too much worry even though we know perfectly well that a good civil servant or university teacher may be worth to his country many more times more than his salary, while a bad civil servant or teacher may make a strong negative contribution.

In the creation of science and technology, we can also in principle and increasingly also in actuality, measure the inputs of countries of such a creation. These are the so-called R & D expenditures—research and development expenditures—which include basic and applied research, as well as pilot and prototype development, before investment takes over. To these expenditures should be added expenditures for the necessary infrastructure of scientific and technological services—laboratories with their equipment, research institutes, patent offices, scientific and technological laboratories, training institutions, etc. The rich countries of today, with less than one-third of the world's total population, account for pretty close to 99 per cent of total R & D expenditures. The same applies to the scientific and technological infrastructure expenditures. The poor countries, with more than twice the population, account for only 1 per cent. Expressed on a *per capita* basis, we have here a disproportion of over 200:1, an even more striking disproportion than the one of 60:1 applying to resources available per population required.

The point of the thesis here presented is that these two disparities are very closely connected; in fact, they are two sides of the same coin. Taken together, they share the falsity of the optimistic claim that there is a simple accumulation of science and technology which favours the newcomer in development. Ninety-nine per cent of the total creation of new science and technology being in the rich countries, this naturally represents a system of solving the problems of rich countries by methods which are suited to the circumstances and requirements of the rich countries. The vast preponderance of the new science and technology in the rich countries also ensures that the little that is done in the developing countries fails to reach the minimum scale at which it is effective, and that the scientists and technologists, as members of the scientific community, will accept the definitions of priority problems and suitable methods of those 99 per cent of their colleagues who live in the rich countries. They themselves will, in any case, have been trained in this image. The result is an international technology which, as shown by the first disparity, leads to a situation where growth is concentrated upon a small modern sector, while the resources of the poorer countries are insufficient to spread participation in growth over more than a minority of the population and thus convert growth into real development.

There is still another way of presenting this: the picture of a simple accumulation of knowledge, an increasing store on which the late comers can draw, is false. What we see is much more comparable to a flow than to simple accumulation. New science and new technology is created at one end, but displaces science and technology previously existing. Being located in the rich countries with their dynamic search for new knowledge and their vastly and increasingly different requirements, priorities and factor endowments, it is not surprising that the knowledge displaced or submerged at one end, may be more useful to the developing countries than the new knowledge added at the other end. Therefore it is by no means clear that from the point of view of the poorer countries of the world, there is in fact an accumulation of knowledge in the relevant science.

The brain drain is perhaps the clearest and most visible expression of the big social effect which the vast concentration on science and technology in the rich countries has on the poor countries. The tendency for scientists and technologists to migrate from the poorer countries is not only due to the attraction of higher salaries, but also to the intercultural advantages to a scientist or technologist to have contact with a much wider scientific community and to be properly supported by an ample infrastructure of equipment, laboratory and publication facilities, assistance, etc. The brain drain from rich to poor countries is clearly contrary to the global priorities which require more, rather than less, emphasis on the problems of the majority of mankind living in the poorer countries, and of more, rather than less, balanced distribution of R & D work between the two groups of countries. It is also directly harmful to the *developing* countries, in so far as they are losing their scarce intellectual élite and all the costs of training and education embodied in them.

However, we must make a qualification to this last statement. Although the brain drain—I would prefer to call it the *external* brain drain—is so visible and measurable because it involves movement of people across national boundaries, yet in practice, the more important brain drain may be, what I would call, the *internal* brain drain. By this I mean the tendency already noted above that the scientists and technologists of the poorer countries will in fact behave as members of the scientific community with its centre of gravity in the rich countries rather than as citizens of their own countries. If you want a Nobel Prize or recognition from your peers, or even your articles published in the leading journals, you must work on the 'frontiers of science'. But it is the rich countries which decide where the 'frontiers of science' are. Parenthetically we may add that in addition to the external and internal brain drain, there is what I call the fundamental brain drain. This is the failure of human brains to develop to their full potential as a result of malnutrition of young children in the crucial period of nine months after birth until three years after birth (when most of the human brain should be developed). Brain development being development of protein synthesis, it depends crucially upon nutrition, and the vast majority of children in the poor countries—and they in turn are the vast majority of all children born in the world today—do not receive sufficient calorie-protein in the right combination to guarantee full brain development. This combination of brain drains—external, internal, and fundamental—represents a tremendous development obstacle, much more so than the limits of the neo-classical models: saving, investment, foreign exchange, etc.[1] Certainly, they must make us extremely doubtful about the alleged advantages to the late comer.

Apart from the brain drain, another unfavourable social effect upon the developing

[1] One is reminded here of the point so brilliantly emphasized by Leibenstein that the allocative efficiency so much worried about by the prevailing schools of thought among economists, is much less important than what he calls "X-efficiency."

countries which we can fairly clearly identify is the considerable scientific and technological effort devoted to the development of synthetic substitutes replacing natural materials on which the developed countries depend for their export proceeds. It is not so much that such research and development takes place, but that it is not balanced by corresponding efforts towards the improvement of natural products or of other local products of developing countries. By and large, it is true that our technological power has increased to a degree where we can best consider the R & D machinery as an established industry in which outputs depend more or less predictably on inputs. Just as we know that in the case of a shoe factory, if you feed in leather and tanning materials, equipment and labour, etc., at one end, shoes will pass out at the other end; so in the case of the R & D industry we can assume that if you feed in certain problems at one end, the solution of these problems will pass out at the other end. If it seems to those now in a position to make these decisions right and profitable to feed into the R & D machinery the problem of synthetic coffee, synthetic cocoa, or synthetic tea, which is indistinguishable from the natural product or even superior to it, we need have no doubt that such synthetic substitutes will pass out in due course. But we need hardly underline what this will do to the economies of countries such as Kenya which relies on coffee, or Ghana which relies on cocoa, or Ceylon which relies on tea. The point is that the decisions of what problems are being fed into the R & D machinery are being made in the rich countries in the light of their priorities and requirements.

GAP BETWEEN POTENTIALS AND REALIZATION

What are the main elements which have been responsible for the limited impact of science and technology in the developing countries? They are:

(a) The weakness of scientific institutions in the less developed countries;

(b) The 'weight' and orientation of advanced country science and technology and its impact on the developing countries;

(c) The problems of access by the developing countries to world science and technology;

(d) The obstacles to the application of new technologies arising from underdevelopment itself.

There is, however, an additional factor which must be kept in mind. This is the very lop-sided nature of the present international division of labour in science and technology. . . .

REMEDIES

What then is the nature of the action required? One of the goals must clearly be to increase the national power to create science and technology by the developing countries themselves, and direct it to their own problems and resources. As already explained at present only 1 per cent of the world's R & D expenditures are within the developing countries and the great bulk of these are wasted from our point of view. With three or four exceptions—India, Brazil, Mexico, Israel—the national capacity of developing countries is negligible or non-existent. At present, developing countries as a whole spend perhaps as little as 0·1 per cent of their GNPs on this vital factor in development as compared with 2½–3 per cent in the rich countries. The United Nations has set a target of 0·5 per cent of GNP to be spent by developing countries on R & D alone, and a similar proportion on the scientific and technological infrastructure. This is probably the maximum rate of expansion possible in view of the built-in limits of training and supply of skilled personnel and the building up of institutions. Perhaps even more important is to make certain that these resources are more effectively used to solve the developing countries' own problems than is the case at present. This will often require regional collaboration by the neighbouring countries; it is not realistic for small and poor countries to develop a reasonably full range of activities.

While such an expansion would still leave developing countries by 1980 with only a very small share of global R & D work, it could at least be sufficient to carry the creation of science and technology in developing countries beyond the threshold below which ineffectiveness and brain drain are almost inevitable results. More specifically, it should give developing countries the minimum bargaining strength to enable them to select more purposefully and effectively the technology which they have to import from abroad, and to negotiate on more equal terms with those who carry the new technology: exporters of capital goods, foreign investors, aid donors, patent and licence holders, etc.

This last point is crucial. It is sometimes said that poor countries should not waste their resources in developing national capacities since they can import from abroad all the technology which they need. In the first place, this is not true because the technology which they specifically need may often simply not exist. But more importantly, the statement is inconsistent: a country which has no national capacity cannot know what technology is available to be imported, what the most suitable technology for itself is, where the best sources for such technology are, and what the best forms are in which such technology should be embodied—let alone bargain effectively about the terms on which such imports take place. It is often said that Japan is an example of a country which relied on imported technology, but research shows that Japan had an infinitely higher capacity to substitute, select and adapt, even copy and negotiate, than most of the developing countries of today. Thus, logically, the strengthening of the national capacity of developing countries must have priority.

In this endeavour however they will need the aid of the rich countries of today for a long time to come. Much of the aid presently being given results in the transfer of capital-intensive technology inappropriate to the circumstances of the aided countries and incapable of exercising the broad catalytic effect which would involve widening circles in the development process. This is particularly the case where the aid is given in the form of imported capital equipment for agreed projects, and is tied to the capital goods industries of the donor country. It would be far better if more aid were given directly for the development of national scientific and technological capacity inside developing countries to develop the use of local materials and local labour for types of product representing their genuine development priorities. Such aid could consist of equipment for laboratories, in sending technological assistance experts, in providing libraries and continuing contacts with visiting scientists and technologists, links with research institutes of the rich countries, etc.

The United Nations has suggested a target which in effect would amount to one-seventh of the total aid now flowing to be given in this form. This would not seem to be an excessive proportion.

But all this would still leave a big gap compared with the minimum that is required. To fill the gap it would be necessary for the rich countries deliberately to use at least a small part of their tremendous technological power inside their own countries for purposes of specific benefit to developing countries. To be sure, a little is already being done in this direction. There are institutes of tropical medicine, of tropical agriculture, tropical health, etc.; here and there, a little scattered work is being done on labour-intensive or small scale technologies inspired by the needs of poorer countries. But all this amounts to less than 1 per cent of the total R & D expenditures of the rich countries. The United Nations has suggested that this percentage be raised to 5 per cent. Such a target would of course be meaningless unless we specify for what purposes this should be earmarked. It is not enough to say: 'Spend 5 per cent of your R & D expenditure on things which benefit developing countries,' for this is too vague and rich countries would claim that practically everything they spend is potentially useful for developing countries. For this reason, the priority areas to which such earmarked R & D resources should be directed would have to be specified; the empty boxes will have to be filled. This was perhaps the most important indirect benefit from thinking about higher targets—the need to be specific. As a result the United Nations has specified thirty-one priority areas ranging from such things as spreading the Green Revolution of high-yielding varieties to such crops as mil-let, sorghum and cassava, to new fishing methods to fill the protein gap for young children, to new hydrographic surveys, control of live-stock diseases and development of cheap construction materials and roofing materials suitable for tropical housing. Just as the increased effort by the developing countries requires collaboration among them, so will an increased allocation of rich countries' R & D resources be the more effective if they do this through concerted action and international collaboration. . . .

VI.D.2. Inappropriate Products and

Inappropriate Technology*

Among the most important, and least emphasized, ways in which imported technology may be inappropriate lies in the nature of the products.

The basic human needs—for food, drink, shelter, warmth, entertainment and companionship—are broadly common to all mankind. But the ways in which these needs are fulfilled (and the extent to which these and others are fulfilled) is dependent in large part on the amount, characteristics and distribution of goods in a society. Products can be regarded as bundles of characteristics fulfilling various needs (and wants) more or less efficiently. The characteristics of a product are its attributes: its colour, weight, size, function. A list of the characteristics of a product indicates the various needs it may fulfill. Thus a shirt may provide protection against cold or heat, may demonstrate by its cleanliness and smartness, a certain status in

*From Frances Stewart, "Technology and Employment in LDCs," World Development, March 1974, pp. 21–3; also in Edgar O. Edwards (ed.), Employment in Developing Nations, Columbia University Press, New York, 1974, pp. 90–94. Reprinted by permission.

society, may impress potential employers, may by its colour and decoration give pleasure to onlookers, and may, if drip dry, avoid the need for ironing. It may fulfill these needs more or less well and may be acquired for any or all of these reasons.

Products are indivisible. If one acquires a particular product for one of its characteristics one unavoidably has to acquire the other characteristics too. The only way to avoid unwanted characteristics is to find some product without them (e.g. a non drip dry shirt). A particular product may be described as having excessive characteristics or embodying excessive standards, in relation to a particular consumer, or set of consumers, when it has characteristics which the consumer does not want, or standards in excess of those needed to fulfill the purpose for which the product is required. An example of excess standards is of a brick strong enough to support a four storey building, used for a single storey house.

Just as any one product fulfills a number of needs, so any one need can normally be fulfilled by a variety of products. The need for accommodation may be fulfilled (more or less well) by the pavements of Calcutta, caves, mud huts, multistorey apartments, or a palace; the need for transport, by a basket, a wheelbarrow, an airplane or a space ship. The number and nature of the products fulfilling a particular need depend on the specific nature of the need: the more narrowly it is specified the fewer products which fulfill it. An airplane is no good for transporting bricks from one end of a village to the other; a wheelbarrow may be of some use for collecting rocks on the moon, but not for bringing them back to earth.

As people (and societies) get richer they do not simply consume the same as before but more of it—10 maunds of rice a year instead of 2; the nature of the products they consume changes. The same broad needs are fulfilled by a different set of products, embodying a different (on the whole more satisfying, more sophisticated) set of characteristics, with higher standards. Rice tends to be replaced by wheat and by meat; Jatra by movies and by radio; radio is replaced by television, first black and white and then in colour. Cars take over from horse or human powered vehicles, and the cars become more sophisticated, faster, quieter, even safer. Changes in the nature of products consumed is an essential aspect of getting richer; long before modern science and technology made possible the sort of product replacement described above, richer societies and people were distinguished from their poorer contemporaries by the nature of the goods they consumed, as well as by their quantity—by their silks and their palaces. Modern science and technology made possible various products on a systematic basis. These new products are both cause and consequence of higher incomes; higher incomes provide the purchasing power and hence the markets which make it worth developing new products; and the technological developments make possible the mass production of sophisticated goods, embodying new materials, which are the basis of the increases in incomes.

Figure VI.4 illustrates the nature of technological developments in developed countries. Three interconnecting cycles have been distinguished. First, on the left, that of increases in per capita incomes providing an incentive for technological developments which lead to higher labour productivity, thus making possible further increases in incomes. Secondly, on the right, higher incomes providing an incentive for technological developments involving new and improved products, while these new products are in turn an essential aspect of further increases in incomes. Thirdly, in the centre, higher incomes leading (with constant propensity to save) to higher savings per man

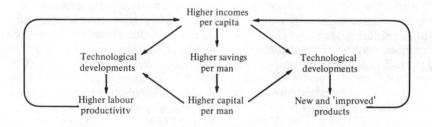

FIGURE VI.4. *Technological development in a (dynamic) closed system*
Note: The arrows indicate the direction of causality.

and consequently greater capital accumulation per man, thus influencing and making possible technological developments of both types, techniques and products. In practice it is not easy to distinguish between these types of technological developments, since many changes in techniques also involve new products—new machines or other inputs, or changed characteristics of old products. The evidence suggests that the bulk of technical developments involve new products (and *ipso facto* changed methods of production). Most products change, at least in terms of detailed physical characteristics, in a dynamic economy over time. Product developments like technique developments reflect the society in which they are developed. They do so in two ways. On the side of production they require capital intensive techniques related to the resource availability of the economies at the time when they are first produced. On the demand side they are products designed for levels of income typical in the societies in which they are developed. With technological developments in products, as well as in techniques, almost entirely confined to the rich countries, the products developed are inappropriate to poorer countries, being designed for much higher income levels, and embodying therefore many characteristics which are excessive in relation to what average consumers in poorer countries can afford. For example, detergents possess various advantages over soap—they are labour saving and produce a 'whiter' wash. But they also involve a far more capital-intensive technology than some methods of producing soap, and their additional qualities may not be a sensible way for a poor society to spend its income. Such a society might well be better off with a poor quality soap that everyone could afford than sophisticated detergents whose consumption must be confined to a rich minority.

Developing countries are thus just as much in need of appropriate products, as of appropriate techniques. Inappropriate products are products with excessive characteristics and standards in relation to needs and income levels of the country in question. Some characteristics may be excessive in the sense that they are neither useful nor wanted, they have to be acquired. In this they resemble the appendix in the human body—more expensive to remove than to ignore. Much more common are products whose characteristics are excessive in relation to the poverty of society but which are nonetheless desired by those who consume them. Cars, washing machines—almost any of the products of modern developed country consumer durable industries provide examples. They are not confined to consumer durables: the standard of durability and strength of textiles may be excessive; similarly of building materials and also other qualities such as heat and sound insulation.

Consumption of rich country products *requires* an unequal income distribution in a much poorer country. Take the example of housing. Most people can afford to spend about one fifth of their income on housing. In the U.K. with average earnings per man of around £1,500 this is consistent with a typical house with a capital value of around £5,000. But if similar housing standards were adopted in India, with average incomes about one twentieth of those in the U.K. each person would need to spend £300 a year, which is more than the average income, on housing. Obviously this is impossible. There are two alternatives: modifying housing standards so that the cost of an average house is consistent with expenditure of one fifth of average income—i.e. providing houses in India whose purchase price was around £200. Or, providing £5,000 houses identical to those produced in the U.K. and allowing (or generating) sufficient inequality of income distribution to enable some of the population to enjoy incomes at least as high as the average in the U.K. and so be able to afford the £5,000 houses.

Houses are not, in general, transferred lock, stock and barrel to developing countries, though many building standards are. But other products are transferred complete with all characteristics. The consumption of such products raises the same issues. Either standards have to be modified so that less costly products can be consumed by all, or the products are transferred intact and their consumption by a few deprives the rest of the population of the possibility of consumption. Private cars are an example. In most developed countries a family with average income can afford a car. In developing countries a market for cars for private consumption is only possible with a highly unequal income distribution—the cheapest car available costs about ten times the average income per head in India.

Medicine provides an example. Most research has been devoted to high income medicine in the developed countries. Medicine of similar standards and nature has been adopted in many developing countries, with the result that medical facilities tend to be concentrated in the towns and on the relative rich. Drug production is capital intensive, while its administration and other medical attention is highly skill intensive. Unequal access to medical facilities is the inevitable result of providing developed-country-type facilities for some. China, in contrast, with a far more equal income distribution, has made a determined attempt to develop a more appropriate pattern of medicine, making selective use of modern and traditional techniques, and introducing 'barefoot doctors.'

The example illustrates the close connection between income distribution and the nature of products. Once an unequal income distribution is established, emanating from the system of production, it is extremely difficult to make a radical change towards more appropriate products which are consistent with a quite different and more egalitarian income distribution. Traditional products, and those recently developed in and for the poorer sections of the community, are much more appropriate in characteristics and in methods of production. They are so by necessity. The labour intensity of traditional forms of entertainment, of housebuilding and of road construction, of carpentry and of spinning, arose from the fact that the people who used and developed them could afford only very limited amounts of capital. Similarly, traditional products are designed for poor consumers and do not contain excessive standards. There have also been some product developments in the poor sectors, also of an appropriate nature. In Kenya used tyres are used to manufacture sandals, and also the base of beds. But lacking all resources—of capital and science—they are inevitably outshadowed by developments in the modern sector of the economy.

The transfer of developed countries' products reinforces the dualistic nature of development, and the unequal income distribution between the two sectors, described earlier.

VI.D.3. Progressive Technologies*

This paper will discuss the choice of technologies for developing countries. The word choice is used advisedly. The theme will be that technology is an important variable in

*From Keith Marsden, "Progressive Technologies for Developing Countries," *International Labour Review*, May 1970, pp. 475–80, 494–502. Reprinted by permission.

development strategy, not an immutable force requiring adjustments in other factors to make way for it. Indeed, technology may have greater inherent flexibility in the short and medium terms than the human factors (skills, attitudes, behaviour, propensities and motivations) which co-operate with it in production. It will be suggested that government has a vital role to play in influencing investment decisions, directly and indirectly, so that they result in the optimum utilisation of available resources. . . .

SOME REASONS WHY THE DIRECT TRANSFER OF TECHNOLOGIES FROM INDUSTRIALISED TO DEVELOPING COUNTRIES MAY BE INAPPROPRIATE

Capital is Dearer and Labour Cheaper in the Developing Countries

In the advanced economies labour is scarce and dear, and capital relatively plentiful and cheap. The opposite is true of most developing countries. It follows that a machine that is economic with wage rates of $2 an hour and interest charges of 4 per cent per annum may be uneconomic when interest charges are 15 per cent (or should be) and wages $0.10 an hour.

Large-scale Production may be Inefficient in the Conditions Prevailing in Some Developing Countries

Much modern technology has been designed for use in large-scale plants. Certain prerequisites of large-scale operations have therefore to be fulfilled before it can be employed economically. These are not always present. Large-scale capital-intensive production is not efficient if markets are small, scattered, highly seasonal or fragmented; if distribution channels are not well organised; if workers are not used to factory discipline; if management does not know the necessary managerial techniques or, though aware of them, cannot implement them because they conflict too strongly with accepted customs, beliefs, systems of authority, etc., of the employees; of if there are no service engineers who can get the complicated machinery going again when it breaks down. Scarce capital is wasted if it is invested under such circumstances. And these

are factors that cannot be changed overnight by a simple planning decision. . . .

Advanced Technologies may Reduce Both Employment and Real Incomes in Certain Circumstances

Even when run below capacity, advanced machinery can often make products cheaper than is possible by traditional methods. As a result a large number of indigenous craftsmen may be put out of business even when the innovation is a product not previously produced within the country. In the mass market there are very few new items which do not have their equivalents among traditional products and, where incomes are static, the traditional product will often be replaced by the new one.

The redundant workers may not be absorbed into the new factories because machinery is being employed instead of labour and the difference in productivity is so great. Some consumers may receive some benefit through lower prices, but this may be offset by a decline in average real income in the community at large. This will occur if—

(a) the new substitute product has a higher proportion of imported materials and components than the old; and

(b) resources cannot be easily transferred to satisfy higher monetary demand for other products, because the surplus capital is tied up in specialised equipment and the unemployed labour lacks the educational background or the social mobility needed in the new occupations.

The fact that many countries are experiencing growing unemployment, a rising import bill and domestic inflation all at the same time would tend to confirm this explanation. In this case the persons who gain most from the technical change are the inhabitants of the already rich countries exporting the machinery, the materials and components required by the new technologies. In other words, the main benefits "leak" abroad. So in these cases there is little opportunity to compensate the unemployed by transfer payments from those with higher real incomes elsewhere, or to wait until a long-term growth in employment opportunities absorbs them.

This is the crucial difference between the industrialised nations, which have initiated technological change themselves, and the developing countries, which acquire new methods only from abroad. In the first group, technology "producers" and technology "users" have established close interrelationships which facilitate the flow of knowledge between them. The sources of innovation are widely diffused throughout the economy. Each change is relatively small in relation to what has gone before. Innovations represent not just advances in scientific knowledge in the abstract but economic solutions to specific problems. The demand for new products springs out of larger incomes. Even when substitution occurs, the decline in the sector employing an obsolete technology is more than offset by the expansion in those using and making the new. Resources are progressively transferred from one to the other, although the geographical concentration of declining industries still presents difficulties (depressed areas).

In the developing countries, however, the innovation may take the form of an alien "transplant" that kills off competing activities in the traditional sectors but has to be fed through external linkages established with suppliers abroad to be kept alive itself. This is because the indigenous industry lacks the specific skills, materials and equipment to satisfy its immediate requirements, and time and money are too short for it to make the necessary adjustments. Decades or even centuries of development cannot be compressed into the couple of years it takes to build a plant and get it running. Thus the innovation may make little contribution to the spread of employment or to raising the skills upon which self-sustained growth depends. The backwash effects can exceed the spread effects, and the technological and income gap becomes wider.

SOURCES OF PROGRESSIVE TECHNOLOGY AND WAYS OF INCREASING ITS AVAILABILITY

The optimum choice can only be made if a full range of alternatives is available. Unsuitable techniques are often applied because there is nothing else on the market except machinery which has been designed to meet other needs. The full spectrum of scientific and technical knowledge must be brought to bear. The brand new, the present day and the past are all potential sources which should be tapped. Let us examine the sources in more detail and put forward some ideas of how their yield can be increased by international action.

Specially Designed Technologies

The most effective means of overcoming economic backwardness would be to apply accumulated scientific knowledge to the solution of the particular problems of the developing countries. There is undoubtedly a great need for new technologies which will incorporate recent inventions but at the same time take account of the scarcity of capital and of certain managerial and operative skills in the developing world. Innovation is required too so that local raw material can be substituted in certain processes for the different types which are imported at present. Varying climatic conditions may demand new solutions to familiar problems. . . .

Technological research institutes are now being set up in some countries under United Nations Special Fund auspices. But only the surface of the problem is being scratched. If just a small proportion of the ingenuity and creativity which goes into satisfying the exotic demands of an affluent society could be diverted to this end, a very real contribution to overcoming world-wide poverty could be made. Perhaps each of the advanced countries could earmark a certain percentage of its aid funds to sponsor research of this kind, preferably within the developing countries themselves so that it is based upon first-hand knowledge of the local situation.

Modern Technologies

As emphasized previously, modern up-to-date technology from the most industralised countries can play a part. To deprive oneself completely of these techniques would be just as wasteful as their indiscriminate application in the past. What types are likely to pass through the screen that has been proposed? One can distinguish four main groups.

The first consists of technical know-how with little or no capital element. Improved ways of making or growing things as a result of a deeper understanding of the chemical, physical and biological properties of products and materials fall into this category. The quicker this knowledge is incorporated into current practice the better, and extension services and demonstration units have vital roles in this dissemination. There would appear to be no major economic obstacles, though social resistance may be encountered.

The second group consists of technologies where the tool element can be easily separated from the labour-saving element. One particular process in a series of operations may have to be performed by a particular machine if consistent quality and precision in the final product are to be maintained. The ancillary operations, particularly materials handling, can be carried out by hand methods if labour is abundant and cheap.

The third category covers machines which replace non-existent human skills, or skills which would be more expensive to train in terms of educational facilities.

The fourth embraces all those modern technologies that may be the only effective means of exploiting a country's physical resources, which would otherwise lie idle, and which could form the basis of other indigenous industries.

Long-established Designs

Classic designs which have proved themselves at a similar stage of development in the now advanced economies could still be relevant to the developing countries. They may not be included in the current machinery catalogues because they have been superseded in the advanced countries by more expensive, labour-saving devices. They have to be dug out of the archives of patent offices and long-established machinery manufacturers. Trade associations could carry out such sifting and collating, sponsored by multilateral or bilateral aid funds. They, in turn, would send the designs to the research institutes in the developing countries, which would disseminate technical specifications, blueprints, drawings, etc., to the engineering workshops and manufacturing firms.

The major international companies which set up subsidiaries in the developing countries could contribute considerably in this. The Philips electrical concern has given a lead by establishing a pilot radio assembly plant in Holland where simple, commonly available tools are tried out in conditions which simulate those encountered in its overseas operations.

The Intermediate Technology Development Group in the United Kingdom has published, in collaboration with the Confederation of British Industry, a buyers' guide which advertises the simple kinds of tools and equipment that might fill the gap between traditional hand methods and sophisticated technologies. Second-hand machinery is another cheap, readily available source which could be utilised more often...

POLICY MEASURES TO FACILITATE THE IMPLEMENTATION OF PROGRESSIVE TECHNOLOGY

The need for discrimination has been demonstrated, various yardsticks proposed and possible sources of supply of progressive technologies indicated. International action to increase the availability has been outlined. What remains to be examined is the most crucial aspect of all–how to ensure that these ideas are turned into cold metal and bricks and mortar with the desired character-istics in the countless investment decisions being made throughout the developing world.

This is no easy task. A general awareness of the issues involved is insufficient. When the investment is in the public sector, the officials responsible may take a broad na-tional view. But they may lack a first-hand acquaintance with the down-to-earth, practi-cal operating details which have a bearing on the decision. Private industrialists will na-turally tend to seek private advantage, which may not be identical with social welfare, as we have seen. All in all, it sounds like a counsel of perfection to expect the individ-ual investor to be, on the one hand, omni-scient, i.e. familiar with all the alternatives available and able to make a quantitative judgment on each and, on the other hand, dedicated to the common good. i.e. to reject the pursuit of private gain whenever it con-flicts with the interests of the whole commu-nity (even if he could perceive or acknowl-edge it).

In other words, it is unrealistic to think in terms of providing each potential investor with a check-list of do's and don'ts, together with a full inventory of alternative tech-niques, and just to wait until common sense and social justice prevail. This would be ad-ministratively unworkable and psychologi-cally unsound. The only practical approach is for governments to create a legislative framework and a general economic climate in which individual investment decisions, public and private, tend to coincide rather than conflict with the national interest. What is advantageous for the enterprise must also be advantageous from the point of view of the national economy. Only if there is such a coincidence of these interests can decision-making be decentralised and dif-fused and the price mechanism left to deter-mine the distribution of resources between competing ends. This would not prevent spe-cial cases from being examined individually by the direct application of the investment criteria I have indicated.

What specific measures could be taken by governments to create the economic and le-gal environment most conducive to optimum choice and, once selected and installed, to ensure that progressive technology is utilised efficiently? Some possible steps are listed below.

(1) The formation of customs unions with other States at a similar stage of devel-opment and with complementary resources. These would encourage a new international division of labour and a competitive stimulus for efficiency, while avoiding head-on, heavily one-sided encounters between rich and poor nations in the international trade and technology fields.

(2) Higher official interest rates to raise the price of capital vis-à-vis labour costs. This would tend to bring more labour into productive employment as well as increase the propensity to save. It should be made clear that this is not to suggest that govern-ments should pay a higher interest rate on what they borrow from advanced countries or international agencies.

(3) Providing indigenous industries with ample scope to expand, develop and diver-sify over time without bumping their heads against competing industries which are tech-nically more advanced because greater re-sources (uneconomically priced) have been placed at their disposal. Giving a clear run ahead to indigenous entrepreneurs is likely

to be more conducive to growth and development than imposing protective subsidies and quotas in an attempt to have the best of both worlds.

(4) Tax concessions and political guarantees to attract foreign capital and know-how, accompanied by legislation requiring all companies to buy a certain proportion of raw materials, components and replacement machinery locally within a fixed time period (as in Mexico).

(5) The setting up of documentation and information centres to keep track of past and current technological developments throughout the world. These would establish close liaison with international and other national advisory services for the selection of equipment.

(6) The provision of widespread primary and technical education facilities at the appropriate level, combined with night-school tuition and upgrading courses for practising operatives, supervisors and managers. Vocational, instructor and management training institutes sponsored by the ILO already function in many countries, while UNESCO programmes cover school, college and university education.

(7) Training courses for managers and planners in feasibility study and cost/benefit analysis techniques to increase the "rationality" of investment decisions and in the use of other management tools (e.g. work study) which will increase the efficiency of existing manufacturing methods. The ILO and UNIDO are operating here.

(8) The encouragement, by state subsidies, grants, etc., of trade and research associations for each industry, sponsored and run by the members themselves. Special budgets could be allocated for importing standard machines to be stripped down, adapted and eventually reproduced locally.

(9) The institution of incentive rewards schemes for inventions, as well as patent protection for local adaptations of foreign designs.

(10) The formation of common facility co-operatives and joint production work-shops to raise the productivity of artisan and handicraft industries.

(11) The provision of extension services for small-scale entrepreneurs, providing advice on product and process development, technical skill formation and the selection and use of appropriate technologies. Again, the ILO is active in this work through small-industry institutes and experts on individual assignment.

(12) Long-term planning of manpower and skill requirements in the various sectors of the economy, closely related to the foreseen rate and character of technical change.

(13) The adoption of factory legislative and safety regulations which provide adequate working conditions and safeguards for all groups of workers but do not create dual standards (i.e. for those within and those outside the practical jurisdiction of the laws) and act as barriers to expansion for the smaller enterprises.

(14) The creation of central quality-control and inspection schemes to ensure that products destined for export meet external quality standards, but without imposing unrealistically high standards on total production within the country.

(15) Priority in the allocation of import licences for machinery and materials to organisations that have already demonstrated the aptitudes, skills and motivations required for success in the export markets.

(16) Systematic market research surveys abroad to identify precise consumer needs (and appropriate distribution channels) which might be satisfied by the use of relatively labour-intensive techniques. UNCTAD and GATT have already sponsored and carried out such investigations on behalf of member governments.

(17) The establishment of special small-business development banks to reduce the differentials in capital accessibility between the traditional and the modern sectors. The World Bank is giving technical and financial assistance in this area.

(18) The planned distribution of industry to backward areas to provide more em-

ployment opportunities outside the major cities and to reduce income inequalities between regions. Processing of agricultural and other land-based products are obvious choices (the FAO has substantial interests in this field).

(19) Financial incentives (e.g. tax rebates on training costs) to international companies to set up apprentice training schools, management development programmes and planned succession to management positions for indigenous staff. This would reduce the foreign exchange costs of expatriate staff, while ensuring that their essential expertise in operating, servicing and managing more advanced technology is passed on to local personnel.

(20) Devaluation of currencies to ensure that the importer has to pay the real cost of foreign machinery and materials, and that a proper evaluation is made in initial feasibility studies.

(21) State-financed hire-purchase and rental schemes with lower interest rates for imported second-hand machinery and locally made equipment.

(22) Subsidised factory premises in provincial towns and villages to slow down the population drift to the cities. The subsidies could be equivalent to the cost of housing and other facilities which would otherwise have to be provided in the cities.

(23) "Tax holidays" for foreign machinery and component manufacturers who set up local design and production plants to develop indigenous techniques.

(24) Public information campaigns to increase the prestige and consumer acceptance of indigenous technologies and products.

Where such policies and programmes have been introduced, the results are promising. They appear to open up new avenues for a dynamic attack on poverty in the developing countries in which the progressive and widespread introduction of new methods (new, that is to say, compared with *their* traditional ones) could lead to a better use of their current resources and achieve a rapid and sustained growth shared by the whole people.

VI.D.4. Capital-Stretching Innovations*

First and foremost, it should be remembered that, unlike in an advanced country where technological change is viewed as rather automatic and routinized or as capable of being generated through R & D expenditures according to some rules of cost/benefit analysis, in the contemporary developing societies technological change cannot either be taken for granted or afforded through basic R & D allocations. In this situation, we cannot avoid the question of what, given the

*From Gustav Ranis, "Industrial Sector Labor Absorption," *Economic Development and Cultural Change*, April 1973, pp. 392–7. Reprinted by permission.

existence of a shelf of technology from abroad, is the pattern by which the typical less developed economy, in fact, manages to innovate. This question in turn forces us to look at least at the following dimensions more carefully: (1) the precise nature of that technology shelf, (2) the availability within the LDCs of required initial managerial and entrepreneurial capacity, and (3) the changing nature of that required managerial and entrepreneurial capacity in the course of transition to modern growth.

The technology shelf developed in the mature industrial economies abroad may be described by a set of unit activities following a smooth envelope curve as in figure VI.5. A

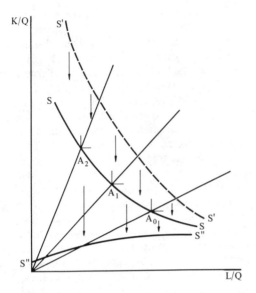

FIGURE VI.5.

particular technology can be described by an L-shaped contour producing one unit of output with a given pair of capital and labor coefficients. The technology shelf is composed of the complete set of such activities or technologies which have been demonstrated to be feasible somewhere in the advanced countries at some historical point in time, including the present. Since there exists a number of technology-exporting countries—for example, the United States, Germany, the United Kingdom, and Japan—with continuous technological transfers among themselves as well as with the LDCs, it is not unreasonable to postulate the existence of a single technological shelf for the lending world as a whole. For example, unit technology A_0 may have been generated in Germany in 1920, A_1 in the United States in 1920, and A_2 in the United States in 1950. In other words, as we move to the left along the shelf we run into more "modern " technology, that is, technology of more recent vintage and of higher capital intensity. As

capital per head increases this means that the typical worker has learned to cooperate with more units of capital of increasing technical complexity. This capital-deepening process, in other words, is more complicated than the textbook version of "homogeneous" labor being equipped with more units of "homogeneous" capital.

At any point in time the typical LDC is, then, theoretically free to borrow a particular unit activity from anywhere along this shelf. What technology is chosen and what happens as an immediate and ultimate consequence of that choice, that is, what secondary processes and reactions are set off, is, of course, all part and parcel of the innovation process taken as a whole. The quality of that process, each step of the way, in turn depends on both the economic environment, that is, the nature of the relative price signals, and on the entrepreneurial, managerial, and skilled labor capacity of the borrower.

The role of innovation must therefore be seen as intimately related to the stage in which the developing economy finds itself. In other words, the role of technological change in output and employment generation must be viewed as sensitive to the same discernible phases of growth as the economy moves in transition from open agrarianism to Kuznets' modern economic growth. In the first postindependence or import-substitution phase previously mentioned, an effort is made to increase the supply of domestic entrepreneurship and the economy's learning capacity, partly through the importation of people via aid but mainly through the system of protection established by government policies. In fact, the most reasonable explanation for the import-substitution syndrome is that it is a response to a real (or imagined) shortage of entrepreneurship and that it permits time, through informal learning by doing or more formal educational processes, for this entrepreneurial capacity to develop.

In terms of figure VI.5, this means that, although the technological shelf may look as indicated by curve *SS*, the *actual* choices available to the developing country during the import-substitution phase are more aptly described by $S'S'$. In other words, due to the inadequate state of entrepreneurial capacity during the early postindependence period of physical controls, the efficiency of generating output per unit of capital in the borrowing country is likely to be substantially below that in the lending country. This is likely to be more true the more capital intensive the import, that is, the further removed from the cultural inheritance and experience of the borrower. Such technological imports are often accompanied by imported engineers, even managers and supervisors—adding up to what is called a "turn-key project." The most advanced and sophisticated technology can, of course, be made to "work," in the physical sense, even in the most backward developing economy. But a shiny new plant imbedded in a society many decades distant is bound to be substantially less efficient. This is true for a thousand direct reasons, such as the absence of even minimal skilled labor supplies, domestic subcontracting, and repair and maintenance possibilities, as well as for many more subtle sociological reasons which enter into the total milieu in which the plant is required to operate. The more sophisticated and removed from the rest of the economy the technological transplant, in other words, the greater the relative inefficiency, as indicated by the shape of the $S'S'$ curve.

If and when the economy then moves away from the import-substitution phase and enters into the second phase of liberalization and export substitution, a second important, if unintentional, type of innovation is likely to appear, namely, a reduction in the extent of the inefficiency of the original transplanted technology. Call it X efficiency if you like, but the cost of the pure transplantation is likely to be reduced, quite unintentionally, that is, largely as a result of factors external to the profit-maximizing behavior of the productive unit itself. This increase in productive efficiency over time will increase in quantitative significance as the import-substitution hothouse tempera-

ture is gradually turned down and a more competitive efficiency may be represented by the arrows tending, over time, to move $S'S'$ back toward the original SS position.

Another more conscious and quantitatively more important type of innovation begins to gather importance during this same second phase of transition. This phenomenon may be called innovational assimilation—innovating "on top of" imported technology in the direction of using relatively more of the abundant unskilled labor supply. As the economy shifts from a natural-resource-based growth pattern in the import-substitution phase to a human-resource-based system in the export-substitution phase, there is an increasing sensitivity to the continuously changing factor endowment, first in terms of the efficient utilization of the domestic unskilled-labor force, and later in terms of the incorporation of growing domestic skills and ingenuity. In other words, the appropriate type of technology finally in place must be one in which not only the initial choice from the shelf but also the adaptations and adjustments consciously made thereafter, in response to changing domestic resource and capability constraints, play an important role.

The more liberalized the economy, in terms of the government's performing a catalytic role through the market by indirect means rather than trying to impose resource allocation by direct controls, the better the chances that the millions of dispersed decision makers can be induced, by the sheer force of profit maximization, to make the "right" decision. As the gap between shadow and market prices narrows—coupled with the expectation of continued labor surpluses for years to come—we would expect transplantation choices to become more flexible, that is, labor intensive. However, since shelf choices are likely to continue to be severely constrained—partly by a lack of illumination of substantial portions of it, partly by such institutional inhibitions as prestige, aid tying, and so forth—we can realistically expect relatively less benefits from liberalization to accrue in the transplantation process. On the other hand, we can expect much more from the assimilation type of innovational behavior which now tends, for the same reasons, to be more slanted in a labor-using direction. In the typical labor surplus type of economy—or one likely to become one over the next decade (as is probably the case in much of Africa)—all this means a much greater possibility for the efficient accommodation of pure labor services.[1] Whether this will lead to a sectoral output shift in favor of labor-intensive export commodities or a mix change predominantly addressed to the domestic market, of course, depends on, *ceteris paribus*, income elasticities of demand, the government's fiscal prowess, and the type (e.g., size) of the economy. Moreover, no strong generalization as to the relative importance of shifts in output mix versus changes in technology for given mixes is likely to be valid. It should be clear, however, that the important issue is that the search for innovation can now be considered a conscious activity of the individual entrepreneur and—given the combination of more realistic relative price signals after liberalization plus greater entrepreneurial capacity— that it is likely to be mainly directed toward various forms of indigenous capital stretching on top of the imported technology. Such capital stretching can be represented by a reduction in the capital coefficient per unit of output. The effective postassimilation set of unit technologies, that is, *after* domestic assimilation, may thus be represented by curve $S''S''$ in figure VI.5, with the strength

[1] It is important to emphasize the word "efficient" since I am not concerned here with the, possibly also legitimate, objective of employment creation as a separate social goal, to be weighed against output growth.

of the indigenous labor-using innovative effort indicated by the amount of the "downward" shift in the capital coefficient.

It should be noted here that a negatively sloped technology shelf, for example, SS, representing pure technological transplantation, permits, as we move to the left, higher labor productivity levels, but only at increasing capital cost. In a country characterized by capital scarcity this may mean increased technical unemployment (à la Eckaus) and hence a lower value of per capita income for the economy—in spite of the higher level of labor productivity achieved. Domestic capital stretching, however, can materially affect that situation by enabling more workers to be employed per unit of the capital stock. If the postassimilation unit technology set, $S''S''$, for example, is upward sloping from left to right, higher labor productivity levels become consistent with lower capital/output ratios.

In summary, once the overall policy setting has turned more favorable and permitted the economy to enter the second phase of transition, it is this indigenous capital-stretching capacity which I consider to be of the greatest importance—especially for the contemporary developing economy facing the formidable labor force explosion predicted for the seventies and eighties. It is in this specific area also where the skepticism of planners, engineers, and aid officials generally is most pronounced—especially with respect to the full range of technological choice really available when all the dust has settled. Historical examples from the Japanese case, as well as contemporary evidence from Korea and Taiwan, permit us to demonstrate the existence and potential importance of such capital-stretching innovations for the labor surplus developing country.

VI.D.5. Bargaining and Technology

Importation*

Technology, being a form of information, is 'non-exhaustible'. Its use contrasts with the usage (or consumption) of an item which is 'individually owned', in which case the availability to others (or to the same person in the future) is at least partially reduced through wear and tear. Technology, then, is by nature 'jointly' and not 'individually' owned. The usage of information by a person or firm does not in itself reduce its present or future availability. Information is 'non-exhaustible'; the price mechanism that could satisfy the efficient transfer of 'individually' owned goods is inappropriate in this case.

The marginal cost of using or selling an already developed technology is zero for the owner of that technology. Where cases of adaptation arise, the owner incurs certain costs which can be estimated and usually do not exceed a figure in the tens of thousands of dollars. In several industries the sellers of technology to developing countries have themselves copied such technology from the originators who incurred the R and D expenses. On the other hand, from the point of view of the purchaser, the marginal cost of developing an alternative technology with his own technical capacity might amount to millions of dollars. Or he might be unable to develop it, or at least think so, in which case his relative marginal cost is infinite. Given market availabilities, the price between zero or tens of thousands of dollars, and millions of dollars or infinite is, in turn, determined solely on the basis of a crude relative bargaining power. There is no price which *a*

*From Constantine V. Vaitsos, "Bargaining and the Distribution of Returns in the Purchase of Technology by Developing Countries," *Bulletin of the Institute of Development Studies*, October 1970, pp. 16–23. Reprinted by permission.

priori can be claimed to be more or less appropriate within the two limits specified.

A further consideration arises as to whether information, technology or ideas are 'owned', to start with, in accordance with the traditional definition of property. Ideas can certainly be captive either legally, i.e. patent privileges, or technically, i.e. in a case where they are kept secret, or when a potential user does not have the knowledge to absorb and use certain information. But can they be 'owned'? Furthermore, how can 'ownership' be claimed in inventions or ideas when any advancement in thought is a result of dependence on and further elaborations of previous inventions or ideas? The distinction between 'ownership' and 'captivity' leads us to the following consideration. In part of the market of technology commercialization an external mechanism is interposed so as to create, artificially, a scarcity which in turn results in a price system. Such interposition is achieved through patents.

The second assumption made about the price system as an efficient means of allocating resources implies that 'the parties participating in an exchange are able to assess the values of the economic units transacted'. Here again the existing market of technology commercialization not only differs from that of the price system, but also places the purchaser in a structural position of basic weakness. In the formulation of the demand for technology, or for information in general, the prospective buyer needs information about the properties, potential results, alternative offers, etc., of the item he intends to purchase. In this respect the technology market is no different from all other markets. Yet quite often, the item itself that one needs to purchase, i.e. technology, is at the same time the information that is needed in order to make a rational decision to buy it. What is needed is knowledge about knowledge, which could effectively be one and the same thing. As a result the assumed roles of an efficient market mechanism break down, at least on the part of the buyer. In evaluating contracts of technology purchase by developing countries, one is immediately struck by the total vagueness by which technical assistance is being acquired contractually. The licensor is quite generally left with complete freedom to transfer whatever he decides while the purchaser has explicit and fixed conditions with respect to payments, terms of obligations, etc. The buyer, quite often, does not know what to ask.

The properties of the market of technology transfer are therefore such that the mechanism that best describes its functioning is the process of bargaining (and not the traditionally defined market-price system). The buyer is, moreover, placed in a position of structural weakness in the formulation of his demand for information. We now have to consider why developing countries confront, in addition, other problems which further diminish their relative bargaining power and hence increase the cost of technology acquisition. . . .

The process of industrialization through final product import substitution of the 'late late-comers' has been such that developing countries basically confine themselves to the transformation (and not properly the production) of products that have been imported from abroad. Within this context technology purchase involves, to a great extent, know-how embodied in intermediate products and capital goods. As a result purchases of the latter are tied-in with the purchase of technology. Tie-in arrangements resulting from contractual terms and/or technical requirements and/or ownership ties, have properties which make the market price system a poor mechanism to distribute benefits while protecting the interests of developing countries.

Markets where prices are settled through bargaining, like the labor market, have generally developed explicit institutional methods and rules upon which negotiations are settled. Such methods enable the participating parties to protect their interests by the proper definition of the negotiable elements, maximum and minimum positions of bargaining, identification of areas where the other party is most or least likely to 'give in', etc. Industrialized countries, both because of the sophistication and size of their companies, and because of the existence of specialized government agencies (see MITI and JETRO in Japan) have enabled their technology buyers to negotiate with considerable knowledge and intelligence. Developing countries, however, in spite of being highly dependent upon foreign technology, have not yet shown an awareness of the critical problems involved.

To start with, a large part of foreign know-how is introduced through the establishment of foreign-owned companies. Such subsidiaries lack even a minimum negotiating position since their interests are, presumably, identified with those of their parent corporation and not with the host country. For example, it is not uncommon to encounter cases where a foreign wholly-owned subsidiary has capitalized in its books technology that originated from the parent corporation. As a result it could be (a) paying royalties, (b) reducing its tax payments through depreciation 'charges' of intangible assets, (c) having lower tax coefficients in countries where taxable profits are related to 'invested' capital, and (d) claiming higher capital repatriations in countries with exchange controls, all for the same know-how. Clearly a foreign-owned subsidiary does not need to capitalize technology since 100 per cent of its capital is already owned by its parent.

Institutional mechanisms and procedures to handle adequate bargaining of foreign-technology purchases are lacking not only in cases of parent–subsidiary situations, or with respect to the proper definition of implicit costs that result from intermediate product overpricing—an item which is usually left out of the negotiating process. Procedures are also inadequate for the evaluation of even the explicit, negotiable elements in technology purchase such as royalty payments. They are usually negotiated on the basis of sales, and not with respect to the income-generating effects of technology, such as profits for firms and domestic value-added for countries. As a result of this misspecification of the 'economic effects' of a particular know-how purchase one encounters cases where royalty payments, which appear quite 'reasonable' with respect to sales, amount to a multiple of profits or value-added.

The inadequacy of the present bargaining system stems partly from the lack of any adequate specifications of what is meant by technology importation. When evaluating contracts in developing countries one generally encounters the tautological definition that technological purchase implies the importation of know-how. The issue arises as to what, at least operationally, is the technology that a country is importing for a given industry, or process or product. Is it technical assistance which is transmitted through personnel, or a manual with production specifications, or a license of a patent (which clearly is not technology but the legal permission to use technology), or know-how already embodied in intermediate products and machinery, or factory layouts, or what? Each of these different types of technology importation has different potential alternative sources of supply and hence different alternative prices; each expresses different types and degrees of dependence between technology supplier and receiver;

each has attached to it different types of obligations and rights for the contracting parties, etc. The type of technology needed by developing countries in their present industrial stage is amply available around the world. Therefore, the breakdown of what is collectively referred to as technology importation and the exact specification of each of its parts would make it possible to transform a market which is at present almost totally monopolistic into a competitive one. The degree of this competitiveness will depend on the amount of information a potential buyer has in the pursuit of information purchase.

CONCLUDING REMARKS

Countries do not make resource allocations on education, defense, space programs, public health, etc. on the basis of the market-price system. The particular characteristics of the 'markets' in these areas are quite distinct from the properties and image we inherited from the 'economic liberalism' of the previous century. Nations have, thus, attempted to introduce other means in order to allocate resources and distribute benefits. (Some of them, like the voting process, do not even fall within the strict definition of economic market system.) Technology importation has structural properties that make the market-price mechanism totally inadequate in the process of defending the interests of the receiving countries. Once this has been understood, a new system, long overdue, can be developed which enables developing countries to take advantage of technology.

VI. SELECT BIBLIOGRAPHY

1. Some fundamental theoretical formulations of the foreign exchange constraint, two-gap analysis, and foreign capital requirements are presented in the following studies: R. McKinnon, "Foreign Exchange Constraints in Economic Development," *EJ*, June 1964; H. Chenery and I. Adelman, "Foreign Aid and Economic Development: The Case of Greece," *RES*, February 1966; ____, and A. MacEwan, "Optimal Pattern of Growth and Aid: The Case of Pakistan," *Pakistan Development Review*, Summer 1966; ____, and A. Strout, "Foreign Assistance and Economic Development," *AER*, September 1966; J. Vanek, *Estimating Foreign Resource Needs for Economic Development*, New York, 1967; John Adler (ed.), *Capital Movements and Economic Development*, London 1967; A. Sengupta, "Foreign Capital Requirements for Economic Development," *OEP*, March 1968; H. J. Bruton, "The Two Gap Approach to Aid and Development: Comment," *AER*, June 1969; D. Lal, "The Foreign Exchange Bottleneck Revisited," *EDCC*, July 1972.

2. The following consider the objectives and means of foreign economic aid: E. Hawkins, *The Principles of Development Aid*, London, 1972; I. M. D. Little and J. M. Clifford, *International Aid*, Chicago, 1966; John White, *Pledged to Development*, London, 1967; ____, *The Politics of Foreign Aid*, London, 1974; A. O. Hirschman and R. M. Bird, *Foreign Aid: A Critique and a Proposal*, Princeton, 1969; Pearson Commission Report, *Partners in Development*, New York, 1969; R. E. Asher, *Development Assistance in the Seventies*, Washington, D.C., 1970; ____, and E. S. Mason, *The World Bank Since Bretton Woods*, Washington, D.C., 1973; T. Byres (ed.), *Foreign Resources and Economic Development*, London, 1972; Paul G. Clark, *American Aid for Development*, New York, 1972; W. L. Thorp, "Foreign Aid: A Report on the Reports," *Foreign Affairs*, April 1970; P. Rosenstein-Rodan, "International Aid for Underdeveloped Countries," *RES*, May 1961; W. E. Schmidt, "The Economics of Charity: Loans versus Grants," *JPE*, August 1974; A. Carlin, "Project Versus Program Aid," *EJ*, March 1967; I. Adelman and C. T. Morris, "Performance Criteria for Evaluating Economic Development," *QJE*, May 1968; Joan M. Nelson, *Aid, Influence and Foreign Policy*, New York, 1968; C. R. Frank, Jr., "Optimal Terms of Foreign Assistance," *JPE*, September-October 1970; ____, *Debt and Terms of Aid*, Washington, D.C., 1970; K. B. Griffin and J. L. Enos, "Foreign Assistance: Objectives and Consequences," *EDCC*, April 1970; G. Papanek, "The Effect of Aid and Other Resource Transfers on Savings and Growth in Less Developed Countries," *EJ*, September 1972; T. Weisskopf, "The Impact of Foreign Capital Inflow on Domestic Savings in Underdeveloped Countries," *Journal of International Economics*, February 1972.

Critical views of foreign aid are presented by P. T. Bauer and J. B. Wood, "Foreign Aid: The Soft Option," *Banca Nazionale del Lavoro Quarterly Review*, December 1961; ____, and Barbara Ward, *Two Views on Aid to Developing Countries*, London, 1966; Milton Friedman, "Foreign Economic Aid: Means and Objectives," *Yale Review*, Summer 1958.

3. For an evaluation of the role of multinational enterprises in LDCs, the following may be consulted: D. Lal, *Appraising Foreign Investment in Developing Countries*, London, 1975; C. Vaitsos, *Intercountry Income Distribution and Transnational Enterprises*, Ox-

ford, 1974; B. I. Cohen, *Multinational Firms and Asian Exports*, New Haven, 1975; Paul Streeten, "The Multinational Enterprise and the Theory of Development Policy," *WD*, October 1973; ____, "Costs and Benefits of Multinational Enterprises in Less Developed Countries," in J. H. Dunning (ed.), *The Multinational Enterprise*, London, 1971; Stephen Hymer, "The Multinational Corporation and the Law of Uneven Development," in J. Bhagwati (ed.), *International Economics and World Order to the Year 2000*, New York, 1972; ____, "The Efficiency (Contradictions) of Multinational Corporations," *AER*, May 1970; O. Sunkel, "Big Business and 'Dependencia,' " *Foreign Affairs*, April 1972; R. E. Caves, "International Corporations: The Industrial Economics of Foreign Investment," *Economica*, February 1971; R. H. Mason, "Some Observations on the Choice of Technology by Multinational Firms in Developing Countries," *RES*, August 1973; Edith T. Penrose, "Some Problems of Policy Toward Direct Private Foreign Investment in Developing Countries," *Middle East Economic Papers*, 1962; J. N. Behrman, "Promoting Development Through Private Direct Investment," *AER*, May 1960; C. P. Kindleberger, *American Business Abroad*, New York, 1969, Chap. 5; H. G. Johnson, "The Efficiency and Welfare Implications of the International Corporation," in C. P. Kindleberger (ed.), *The International Corporation*, Cambridge, 1970; A. O. Hirschman, *How to Divest in Latin American and Why*, Princeton, 1969; G. K. Helleiner, "Manufactured Exports from Less Developed Countries and Multinational Firms," *EJ*, March 1973; R. Vernon, *Sovereignty at Bay*, New York, 1971; ____, "Foreign Operations," in J. W. McKie (ed.), *Social Responsibility and the Business Predicament*, Washington, D.C., 1974; ____, *The Operations of Multinational United States Enterprises in Developing Countries*, New York, 1972; Hans Singer, "The Distribution of Gains Between Investing and Borrowing Countries," *AER*, May 1950; T. G. Parry, "The International Firms and National Economic Policy," *EJ*, December 1973; G. L. Reuber et al., *Private Foreign Investment in Development*, Oxford, 1973.

A large volume of literature on the multinationals has been published by the United Nations; see in particular, United Nations Secretariat, *Multinational Corporations: A Selected Bibliography*, ST/LIB/30, August 1973 (mimeo); *United Nations, Multinational Corporations in World Development*, New York, 1973; see also an annotated bibliography by S. Lall, *Foreign Private Manufacturing Investment and Multinational Corporations*, New York, 1975.

4. The following consider both the analytical and organizational aspects of the international transmission of technical and managerial knowledge to the LDCs: Jack Baranson, "New Technologies for Emerging Economies," *Harvard Business Review*, July-August 1961; ____, "Transfer of Technical Knowledge by International Corporations to Developing Countries," *AER*, May 1966; K. E. Lachmann, "The Role of International Business in the Transfer of Technology to Developing Countries," *American Society of International Law Proceedings*, 1966; Peter Gabriel, *International Transfer of Corporate Skills*, Boston, 1967; D. L. Spencer and A. Woroniak, *The Transfer of Technology to Developing Countries*, New York, 1967; A. K. Cairncross, *Factors in Economic Development*, London, 1962, Chap. 11; Kenneth J. Arrow, "Classificatory Notes on the Production and Transmission of Technical Knowledge," *AER*, May 1969. A comprehensive bibliography has been compiled by Jack Baranson, *Technology for Underdeveloped Areas: An Annotated Bibliography*, New York, 1967.

On the problem of "appropriate" technology, the following are noteworthy: the special issue on "Technology," *WD*, March 1974; special issue on "Science and Technology in Development," *JDS*, October 1972; G. K. Helleiner, "The Role of Multinational

Corporations in the Less Developed Countries' Trade in Technology," *WD*, April 1975; A. S. Bhalla (ed.), *Technology and Employment in Industry*, Geneva, 1975; Amartya Sen, *Employment, Technology and Development*, Oxford, 1975; Jack Baranson, *Industrial Technologies for Developing Countries*, New York, 1969; David Felix, "Technological Dualism in Late Industrializers," *Journal of Economic History*, March 1974; W. P. Strassman, *Technological Choice and Economic Development*, Ithaca, 1968; Charles Cooper (ed.), *Science, Technology and Development*, London, 1973; Louis T. Wells, Jr., "Economic Man and Engineering Man," *Public Policy*, Summer 1973; C. Vaitsos, "Patents Revisited: Their Function in Developing Countries," *JDS*, October 1972; Edith Penrose, "International Patenting and the Less Developed Countries," *EJ*, September 1973; G. Ranis, "Industrial Sector Labor Absorption, " *EDCC*, April 1973; Frances Stewart, "Trade and Technology in Developing Countries," in Paul Streeten (ed.), *Trade and Developing Countries*, London, 1973; Paul Streeten, "Technology Gaps Between Rich and Poor Countries," *Scottish Journal of Political Economy*, November 1972; United Nations, *The Acquisition of Technology from Multinational Corporations by Developing Countries*, New York, 1974; OECD Development Center, "Low-Cost Technology," Paris, 1975 (mimeo); ____, *Choice and Adaptation of Technology in Developing Countries*, Paris, 1974.

A series of reports by the United Nations Institute for Training and Research (UNITAR) are highly instructive; so too are the Industrial Planning and Programming Series of UNIDO, and reports of UNCTAD.

CHAPTER VII

Allocating Investment Resources

Having considered the overall contribution of capital to development, and the various ways of financing a higher rate of investment, we now turn to the remaining problem of how to determine the allocation of investment resources. When investment resources are as scarce as they are in a poor country, the rational allocation of capital is of the greatest importance. If public investment absorbs a large percentage of the total resources available, or the state attempts to influence the direction of private investment, it becomes necessary to establish "investment criteria" for determining the optimal investment allocation.

The rationale of investment allocation is discussed in the Note in section VII.A. It will become readily apparent that the establishment of investment criteria raises problems regarding not only the precise formulation of these criteria, but also possible conflicts among the criteria. For example, on the basis of the existing relative scarcities of factors, it may appear sensible to minimize the capital-output ratio and adopt less capital-intensive techniques of production; however, to maximize the available investible surplus and attain the maximum growth rate, the optimal technique may have to be highly capital-intensive. Although the materials in this chapter set forth the different investment criteria that have been formulated, we should not examine them with the expectation of resolving their differences and determining from them a single definitive criterion. For, as is stressed in VII.A, the relevance of each criterion depends on judgments about social objectives, designation of the time period involved, and specification of various constraints. Since a number of alternative variables may be maximized, and the maximization may occur over different periods of time and various constraints may be introduced, it should be apparent that different criteria are warranted for different sets of conditions. The disagreement over alternative investment criteria thus stems from the variety of conditions assumed.

In section VII.B, we examine these different investment criteria more closely. We shall concentrate on the problems of determining the best utilization of investment resources among different sectors in the economy and the choice of the optimum technique of production. Although several investment criteria have been propounded, we shall give primary attention to the following: minimum capital intensity (minimum capital-output ratio), maximum social marginal productivity of capital, maximum surplus over wages available for investment ("marginal reinvestment quotient"), and maximum employment absorption.

Some principles of project evaluation are discussed in section VII.C. These are normative principles that a government should be mindful of in its public expenditure policy, particularly in investment planning. Whether the project is to be undertaken by a public authority, or public decision-making is involved in screening private projects, there should be some guidelines by which the government authority can compare and evaluate alternative projects. In recent years the methodology of project appraisal has been formulated more rigorously by two studies in particular: *Guidelines for Project Evaluation* (UNIDO, 1972), and I.M.D. Little and J.S. Mirrlees, *Project Appraisal and Planning for Developing Countries* (1974).

These studies are notable for their application of welfare economics to investment planning. Although no summary can do them justice, section VII.C offers some indication of the issues raised in these studies. We must be especially aware of the conditions that give rise to the particular need for social cost-benefit analysis in LDCs, and we must understand how "shadow prices" can be utilized as a means of correcting market prices for the divergences between market prices and social benefits and social costs. The distortions that prevail in a developing economy are commonly in foreign trade prices, factor markets, the nonoptimal income distribution, and in the use of nonoptimal taxes and subsidies. In correcting for these distortions, the practice of project appraisal is an exercise in the theory of the second-best.

VII.A. THE RATIONALE OF
CAPITAL ALLOCATION—NOTE

In development planning, the problem of allocating investment resources involves several choices—the choice of how much investment is to be made) within the various sectors in the economy, the (choice among various projects within a sector,) and the (choice of techniques for a particular project.)

In a developing country, these choices become especially complex for two basic reasons: first, (there is uncertainty regarding the determinants of development, so that no "correct" criterion can be offered with respect to investment policies designed to maximize the rate of development;) and second (market imperfections, externalities, and disequilibrium prices make market criteria unreliable or irrelevant, so that decisions about capital allocation must be made outside the market mechanism.)

The selection of sectors, projects, and techniques is complicated by the existence of any number of development objectives. There are no simple technical criteria for the ranking of investment priorities: instead, capital allocation is very much a matter of judgment, since the optimal allocation depends upon what objective is being maximized and over what period of time. The objective may be maximum real national income, maximum real per capita income, maximum per capita consumption, or maximum employment. Each of these objectives may also be subject to a number of stated constraints; for example, the objective may be to maximize real per capita income, subject to the constraints that the income distribution is not worsened in the process or that the balance of payments does not deteriorate.

The problem is complicated further by the treatment of time: Over what time period is the objective to be maximized? Some discounting procedure will be necessary in order to maximize the present value of the target variables through which one judges the objective. It is therefore not surprising that different investment criteria are applicable, depending upon different objectives to be achieved over different periods of time.[1]

The problem of allocating capital among sectors is a recurrent theme in this book—especially as a problem in capital allocation between agriculture and industry, and between import substitutes and exports. The problems of choice of projects and choice of techniques are discussed in this chapter. Rather than anticipate these discussions, we might more profitably concentrate here on some fundamental distinctions that underlie the analysis of investment criteria: the distinctions between the static and dynamic aspects of the problem, between micro- and macroefficiency, and between economic and noneconomic criteria of capital allocation.

One way of interpreting investment criteria is as a subproblem of the more general problem of choice among alternative time paths obtainable by an economy from some given initial and anticipated future conditions. The choice is made by maximizing some social welfare function, as will become apparent in the following selections. We must, therefore, keep the different social welfare functions and the different time ho-

[1] See Harvey Leibenstein, "Why Do We Disagree On Investment Policies for Development?" *Indian Economic Journal*, April 1958, pp. 369–86.

rizons of the various authors in mind when we compare their proposals. This problem has been neatly summarized by T. N. Srinivasan, and it merits a rather complete statement. Srinivasan considers

(a) the Social Marginal Productivity (SMP) criterion of A. E. Kahn and Hollis Chenery, (b) the Marginal Per Capita Reinvestment Quotient (MRQ) criterion of Walter Galenson and Harvey Leibenstein, (c) the Marginal Growth Contribution (MGC) criterion of Otto Eckstein, and (d) the Reinvestible Surplus criterion of Maurice Dobb and A. K. Sen.[2]

The social welfare function implicit in Kahn's work and made explicit by Chenery is a function of several variables, of which Chenery considers national income and balance of payment to be the most important. The problem they solve is the allocation of a *given* rate of investment of *one* period between alternative projects in such a way as to maximize the average annual increment in social welfare. This annual average is to be computed through a discounting process; the way in which the discount factor is to be chosen is not explained. Chenery's procedure is to rank projects according to their SMP and choose projects in decreasing order of SMP until the given rate of investment is exhausted. The SMP of a project is defined

[2] The relevant articles and books are: A. E. Kahn, "Investment Criteria in Development Programs," *Quarterly Journal of Economics,* February 1951, pp. 38–61; Hollis B. Chenery, "Application of Investment Criteria," *Quarterly Journal of Economics,* February 1953, pp. 76–96; Walter Galenson and Harvey Leibenstein, "Investment Criteria, Productivity, and Economic Development," *Quarterly Journal of Economics,* August 1955, pp. 343–70; Otto Eckstein, "Investment Criteria for Economic Development and the Theory of Intertemporal Welfare," *Quarterly Journal of Economics,* February 1957, pp. 56–85; Maurice Dobb, *Economic Growth and Planning,* 1st. ed., New York, 1960, pp. 29–75; A. K. Sen, *Choice of Techniques, An Aspect of the Theory of Planned Economic Development,* 1st ed., Oxford, 1960, pp. 21–51.

by Chenery as the average annual increment in national income (plus balance of payments effect) resulting from the marginal unit of investment in that project. The increment in national income is to be computed after applying some corrections to market prices which take into account the divergence between social and private benefits that occur when external economies, unused resources, tariffs, and subsidies are present.

In summary, the Kahn-Chenery approach is static since the choice variables belong to a single period. In computing the increment to the flow of national income resulting from the given investment, planners need to know the future product and factor prices. But future relative scarcities of various factors and products will themselves depend on the current rate and composition of investment. The same remark applies to the corrections with which Chenery wants to alter the market prices. By taking a static view Kahn and Chenery are implying either (a) that the projected investment is too "small" to affect the future course of prices, or (b) that the future course of prices is independent of current choices. Either assumption is untenable in the context of economic development.

Galenson and Leibenstein also criticize Chenery for using tools of economic statics in analyzing the problem of economic growth. The social welfare index they propose instead is an increasing function of the per capita output potential at some future point in time. The per capita output potential at any point in time depends, in their view, on a number of factors, of which capital per worker and the quality of the labor force are important. Capital per worker at any future point in time T depends on the accumulation of capital from now until T and the size of the labor force at T. Galenson and Leibenstein conclude that the "best allocation of investment resources is achieved by equating the MRQ of capital in its various alternative uses."[3] The MRQ of a

[3] Galenson and Leibenstein, "Investment Criteria," p. 351.

project is determined by the annual surplus it generates over and above wage and depreciation costs, taking into account the contribution of the project toward improving the quality of the labor force and bringing about a decline in its rate of growth. Galenson and Leibenstein come to an empirical judgment that the MRQ is likely to be higher in capital intensive than in labor intensive projects.

Galenson and Leibenstein have been criticized by John Moes,[4] Francis M. Bator[5] and others for the extreme nature of the assumptions needed to validate their theoretical and empirical conclusions. Even if one grants their assumption that only profit earners save, it is by no means necessary that profit maximization should always imply maximization of the capital labor ratio. Their prescription that governments in underdeveloped countries should maintain artificially high wages to induce producers to choose high capital labor ratios is questionable. If one is interested in retarding the rate of growth of the labor force, investing in capital intensive projects in a labor surplus economy is surely an indirect and perhaps an inefficient method. Lastly, the objective of maximizing the per capita output potential (d) at some future point in time implies that a one commodity economy is being considered. This criterion is not very meaningful in an economy with more than one commodity. . . .

(c)   Eckstein tries to synthesize the Kahn-Chenery approach and the Galenson-Leibenstein approach. His social welfare function is the sum of the discounted value of the stream of consumption resulting from a given current investment $\bar{K}$ and the future reinvestments occasioned by it. Current investment is to be divided among alternative projects which differ in their output stream

and reinvestment potential. All reinvestments (at future points in time) are to be directed to a single project. Maximizing his social welfare function, Eckstein arrives at his MGC criterion. The optimal allocation of $\bar{K}$ results when the amounts invested in each project are such that the MGC's of the different projects are equal. The MGC of a project is the sum of two terms, (a) the present value of the project's direct contribution to the consumption stream and (b) the present value of the consumption stream resulting from reinvestments associated with the project. Eckstein also tries to determine the rate of investment itself by determining the interest rate through a marginal utility approach.

Eckstein's approach is subject to a number of criticisms. First, if one wants to consider an infinite time horizon as Eckstein does, one cannot proceed as if capital were the only scarce factor at all points in time. Second, there is no reason to direct all reinvestments to one project. One can, at the very least, postulate that the same projects are available at all future periods of time as at the beginning.[6]   The approaches of Dobb and Sen are very similar and we shall discuss only that outlined by Sen. Sen considers an economy consisting of two sectors, an advanced sector and a backward sector. The backward sector produces a single consumer good, corn, presumably using only labor. The advanced sector about to be initiated consists of two departments, one which produces corn, using labor and machines, and one which produces machines, using only labor.[7] The corn productivity of labor in department 1 depends on the capital intensity of the process

[4] John Moes, "Investment Criteria, Productivity and Economic Development: Comment," *Quarterly Journal of Economics,* February 1957, pp. 161–4.

[5] Francis M. Bator, "On Capital Productivity, Input Allocation and Growth," *Quarterly Journal of Economics,* February 1957, pp. 86–106.

[6] Eckstein is aware of this problem but he does not offer a complete solution. (Eckstein, "Investment Criteria for Economic Development," p. 72.)

[7] In Chapter 3 of his book, Sen relaxes the assumption that capital goods can be produced only with labor. But he does not go beyond stating that a solution to the problem of choice of capital intensity in the two departments is not impossible. (Sen, *Choice of Techniques,* Chap. 3.)

used. The capital intensity of a process is measured by the number of man years required in department 2 to produce enough capital (machines) to equip one laborer in department 1. The wage rate to be paid to laborers in the advanced sector is assumed given. The total wage bill in the advanced sector is to be met from corn production within the sector except in the first period, when the advanced sector is being initiated. The wage bill of the first period is to be met by an amount of corn surplus extracted from the backward sector.

Sen considers three possible objectives for his economy: (1) maximizing the corn output of the second period in the advanced sector, (2) maximizing the rate of growth of corn output, and (3) maximizing the undiscounted sum of the stream of output of corn over T periods of time. Naturally the optimal capital intensities for attaining the three objectives are different.

One can agree with Sen in dismissing the first objective as clearly not the one to be pursued if one is interested in the problem of growth, for maximization of total corn output need not necessarily result in maximum surplus (over wages) for reinvestment unless the wage rate is zero.[8] One can even construct examples in which maximization of corn output of the second period yields a negative surplus. But the second objective, maximizing the rate of growth of corn output by maximizing the rate of surplus in each period, is based on the assumption that

(surplus b.)

any rate of growth can be sustained indefinitely by withdrawing labor from the backward sector without reducing its output. Once we introduce a limit to the withdrawal of labor from the backward sector, the optimal capital intensity under the second objective may be different. The third objective completely ignores the time path of consumption by considering only the aggregate consumption over an interval of time. Furthermore, such an approach precludes consideration of an infinite time horizon because undiscounted aggregate consumption over an infinite time horizon may well be infinite.

Thus our brief review of the more important articles in the literature reveals that most of these authors analyze the problem of growth in a static framework. Even the analysis of Galenson and Leibenstein, considered by them to be dynamic, is static in our view because they limit themselves to the objective of maximizing per capita output potential at some chosen point of time in the future. They therefore have a finite time horizon and hence static tools could be used to analyze their problems. Sen and Dobb do introduce dynamic elements explicitly in their model, but they fail to consider restraints, such as the availability of labor, that may become operative at future points in time.[9]

The value of Srinivasan's review is in calling attention to the distinction between the static and dynamic aspects of the problem of capital allocation. In his own model, Srinivasan demonstrates that there exists a maximum sustainable rate of consumption per worker for an economy with two sectors: a machine-producing sector and a sector that produces a homogeneous consumer good. This maximum but sustainable rate of consumption is achieved along a "terminal

---

[8] Let $\bar{s}$ be the surplus corn extracted from the backward sector in the first period. Assume with Sen a lag of one year in the production of machines and no lag in the production of corn. Let a be the capital intensity chosen and w the wage rate. Then the total output of corn in the advanced sector in the second period is $\dfrac{\bar{s}}{wa} f(a)$ where f(a) is the corn productivity of labor when capital intensity a is used. But surplus over wages is $\dfrac{\bar{s}}{wa} [f(a) - w]$. The maximization of one is not equivalent to that of the other.

[9] T. N. Srinivasan, "Investment Criteria and Choice of Techniques of Production," *Yale Economic Essays*, Vol. 2, No. 1, 1962, pp. 59–63.

path." Srinivasan also examines time paths that result from maximizing two specific welfare functions: (a) consumption per worker at some chosen time T in the future, and (b) the discounted sum of the future stream of consumption per worker. A number of other analyses that attempt to determine optimal growth paths are listed in the Bibliography at the end of this chapter.

Another problem of capital allocation is to reconcile what might be called microefficiency with macroefficiency. At the micro-level it may be perfectly rational for an individual firm to utilize a capital-intensive method of production. This may result in technical efficiency in the sense of minimizing production costs. And yet, this choice of technique may not correspond to economic efficiency in the sense of an efficient allocation of resources from the standpoint of the entire economy. If the economy is a labor-surplus economy and has a low real wage rate, it need not be true that a capital-intensive technique of production which achieves technical efficiency for the firm is also the technique of production which will achieve economic efficiency for the entire economy. The conflict between micro- and macroefficiency is likely to occur in a developing economy because of the highly distorted price structure that perpetuates excess supplies or excess demands. As noted time and again, capital goods tend to be priced too low in the industrial sector of many LDCs, whereas labor is priced too high. The result is a capital-intensive urban sector surrounded by an economy that remains short of savings and with a surplus of labor.

This problem has been stated in somewhat different terms, but quite strikingly, by Lauchlin Currie as follows.

One of the most glaring contrasts, especially in an underdeveloped country, is afforded by the firm where economic motivation has full play, and the economic system, whose calibrations have been distorted in an irrational manner. Let me give one of a thousand possible illustrations.

In a tropical city in Colombia is a relatively small but modern synthetic fiber plant, highly capital-intensive, with air-conditioning, humidifiers, supplementary electric power that switches on in six seconds upon the failure of municipal power, and so on—apparently a very efficient operation. The labor requirements are so small that a taxi suffices to bring and deliver the requisite night shift of women employees.

In the same city, in the main street, twenty-one shoeshine able-bodied men, not boys, were counted in one block. (L surplus)

A well-trained economist would have no difficulty in explaining this contrast in terms of the inequality of incomes and the consequent existence of sufficient demand for man-made fibers, in terms of the capital-employment ratio in that industry as determined by modern techniques, in terms of inadequate saving and capital formation to give better employment with modern technical practices and so on. And yet, rationally considered, the explanation makes little sense.

With a changed calibration of the system or the economic machine—less demand for synthetic fibers, more demand for mass consumer goods, more price flexibility, competition and factor mobility or substitutes to take adequately their place—the same capital (both domestic and imported) could have yielded as high or higher returns and could have been consistent with much greater employment and yielded much greater and widespread well-being. The efficiency of the firm is a splendid thing. But infinitely more important in dealing with the economics of developing countries is the efficiency of the economic system in making the best use of available resources—human, natural, and man-made. The profit motive continues to work to the end that in each plant fewer people can produce more goods. What is not working is the mechanism for picking up the released people (and millions more) and putting them to equally useful, remunerative work.[10]

The conflict between micro-and macro-efficiency is not confined to industry, but may equally well occur in agriculture. It has, for instance, been pointed out that the seed-fertilizer revolution is likely to give an impetus to premature tractor mechanization. The rapid initial increase in cash income increases the ability and the incentive to invest in such equipment; but in economies in which the absolute size of the farm labor force is increasing rapidly, investment in tractor mechanization is likely to be uneconomic from the macro viewpoint even though it is profitable for the large-farm operators. The saving in labor costs as determined by market wage rates is likely to be considerably higher than the marginal productivity of the labor that is displaced, but the social costs of exacerbating problems of underemployment and unemployment do not enter into the private assessment of costs and returns. In this case again, price distortions tend to accentuate the difference between private marginal productivity of investment in labor displacing mechanization and the social marginal productivity, so as to encourage the premature mechanization.[11]

Finally, from the viewpoint of noneconomic analysis, the criteria of capital allocation may be quite different from that based on only economic analysis. If one asks what is required socially and culturally for economic development, he may prescribe a different investment pattern from that based solely on economic efficiency. This is because the investment pattern may change key values and institutions in the developing society, and these in turn will affect the rate of economic development. It has, for example, been suggested that widespread use of motors and machines will affect values in such a way as to make behavior more conducive to development.[12] This is then an argument in favor of capital-intensive techniques of production even though it may be contrary to the relative factor supply.

For illustrative purposes, some other noneconomic criteria of investment might be as follows: invest in industries that require prolonged and high-level training for labor so as to justify sending children at an early age to training schools, where they can get not only skills but also new values; invest in projects that transform village life by drawing people to centers of employment away from the village because, by preventing impersonal relations, village life is a major source of opposition to change; invest in projects that will mean employment of women outside the home, for women tend to be the most conservative members of a culture and if they are to transmit new values and new norms to their children they must be influenced by outside sources. Such noneconomic considerations may contradict economic criteria, but they must still be an essential part of the total assessment of investment criteria. The difficult task, therefore, is not to establish various investment criteria—but to resolve a conflict among the criteria. This will be apparent in the following selections.

In the last analysis, the application of criteria for the use of investment resources cannot be separated from national objectives or the country's development plan. As stated in the UNIDO *Guidelines,*

The main reason for doing social benefit-cost analysis in project choice is to subject project choice to a consistent set of general objectives of national policy. The choice of one project rather than another must be

[10] Lauchlin Currie, *Accelerating Development,* New York, 1966, p. 56.

[11] Bruce F. Johnston and John Cownie, "The Seed-Fertilizer Revolution and the Labor Force Absorption Problem," *American Economic Review,* September 1969, pp. 573–4.

[12] David C. McClelland, *The Achieving Society,* New York, 1961, pp. 399–403.

viewed in the context of their total national impact, and this total impact has to be evaluated in terms of a consistent and appropriate set of objectives.

The avoidance of a complete dichotomy between project choice and national planning is one of the main reasons for doing social benefit-cost analysis. When one project is chosen rather than another, the choice has consequences for employment, output, consumption, savings, foreign exchange earning, income distribution and other things of relevance to national objectives. The purpose of social benefit-cost analysis is to see whether these consequences taken together are desirable in the light of the objectives of national planning.[13]

Any method of ranking projects involves adjustments or corrections of market prices in order to reflect more closely social benefit of outputs and social cost of inputs. Project evaluation involves first an assessment of conditions that cause a divergence between market price and marginal social value and marginal social cost. The most significant distortions for which corrections usually have to be made in a developing economy are those in foreign trade, in factor markets, and those caused by nonoptimal taxes and subsidies. Selection VII.C.3 will present in more detail the conditions which make cost-benefit analysis desirable in developing countries.

"Shadow prices" or "accounting prices" must be calculated to adjust market prices for these distortions. Assumptions must then be made about future changes in the distortions over the lifetime of the project. A relevant discount rate must be applied to arrive at some present value of net benefit. And the valuation must be expressed in terms of a unit of account, or numéraire. In the UNIDO approach, the choice of

numéraire is "aggregate current consumption measured at domestic market prices"; in the Little-Mirrlees approach, the numéraire is current savings measured at world market prices expressible in convertible foreign currency.[14]

Although different methods of project evaluation may be applied, the method used cannot—from a formal point of view—make any difference to project selection if a number of projects are to be ranked. The project ranking will be the same under each method, provided the same economic assumptions and judgments about the correction of market prices are made. The variation in project appraisal by two different project evaluators cannot arise from formal differences in their methods of analysis, but only from differences in their judgments of divergences between market price and marginal social value and marginal social cost, and from differences in their correction of these distortions.

Stated in somewhat different words, differences in project evaluation can be interpreted in terms of differences in the project evaluators' judgments about what function is to be maximized and the kinds of constraints that are worth bothering about.[15] Project evaluation is an exercise in planning which is, in turn, an exercise in constrained maximization. The choice of the objective function to be maximized and the selection of the constraints that are judged relevant will therefore determine the shadow prices that are used to correct market prices.[16]

[13] UNIDO, (P. Dasgupta, A. Sen, and S. Marglin), *Guidelines for Project Evaluation*, New York, 1972, p. 11.

[14] As explained in VII.C.3, below, the UNIDO numéraire puts a premium on savings, and the Little-Mirrlees procedure penalizes consumption.

[15] Partha Dasgupta, "A Comparative Analysis of the UNIDO Guidelines and the OECD Manual," *Bulletin of the Oxford University Institute of Economics and Statistics*, February 1972, pp. 48–9.

[16] As Dasgupta expresses it, "The shadow price of a given resource is the increase in the maximum value of the objective when ceteris paribus the economy is endowed with a unit more of the resource. As such it is the 'marginal product' of the resource, the 'product' being reflected in the value

In accord with the underlying theme of this book, we would emphasize the net contribution of a project towards the national objective of improving the time profile of aggregate consumption, the objective of improving the distribution of income, and the objective of increasing employment.[17] But even if project evaluators agree on what the objective function's ingredients should be, they may differ in their interpretation of what the constraints happen to be, and on what measures can be taken to remove nonoptimal government policies. As Sen emphasizes, "one of the most complex aspects of the exercise of project appraisal is the precise identification of the project evaluator's areas of control. This will affect the nature of the exercise that he has to solve and the shadow prices that will be relevant for his evaluation."[18] To the extent that constraints persist and distortions cannot be removed, they must be taken into account by the project evaluator. The precise method of project evaluation will therefore differ according to the particular conditions in a particular country at a particular time. In any particular evaluation, however, some of the issues raised and some of the suggestions made in the following selections may prove useful.

---

of the objective function. It is immediately clear then that the shadow price of a resource depends both on the objective function and the nature of the constraints that the system faces." (Ibid., p. 49).

[17] These national objectives are also emphasized in the UNIDO *Guidelines,* Chaps. 4–8.

[18] A.K. Sen, "Control Areas and Accounting Prices: An Approach to Economic Evaluation," *Economic Journal,* March 1972, p. 499.

VII.B. PUBLIC INVESTMENT CRITERIA

VII.B.1. Survey of Criteria for Allocating Investment Resources*

Economists have put forward a number of criteria and techniques for allocating investment resources to different sectors or projects in planning the development of underdeveloped economies. Although many of these criteria and techniques differ in their approach to the problem, some are closely connected. The differences in approach usually reflect different evaluations as regards the objectives of economic development, and this suggests a basis for determining the order in which the criteria may conveniently be studied.

The most general objective of economic development is to maximize the national income or the rate of economic growth. Accordingly, the criteria which are most appropriate for allocating the available investment resources in the pursuit of this objective will be considered together in this note, as a first group. Included are the capital-output ratio or rate of capital turnover, . . . social product analysis, and the rate of savings and reinvestment. . . .

The incremental capital-output ratio (or capital coefficient) seeks to represent the amount of additional investment required to produce an additional unit of output. The ratio is usually based on an analysis of past experience where possible, but may allow for anticipated changes in the future period. The over-all capital-output ratio can be used

as a tool for estimating capital requirements for the whole economy, while capital-output ratios for individual sectors, industries or processes may be used to estimate capital requirements sector by sector or project by project.

This concept assumes a stable relationship between capital and output, which is more likely to be the case in the over-all economy. However, the sectoral capital-output ratios may vary widely with the stage of economic development, the pattern of investment, the relative importance of non-capital inputs, and the amount of investment in complementary sectors.

The capital-output ratio when applied as a priority criterion is synonymous with the capital-turnover criterion suggested by J. J. Polak.[1] It is maintained that, to maximize income, choice should be made of investment projects with a low capital-output ratio, i.e. a high rate of capital turnover. However, this criterion has some serious limitations. Firstly, the time element plays a key role, since quick maturing projects with a lower capital-output ratio in the short run do not necessarily have a lower ratio in the long run. Secondly, the supplementary benefits of an investment project to other economic activities are neglected. In view of project complementarity, in fact, a project

*From United Nations, ECAFE, "Criteria for Allocating Investment Resources among Various Fields of Development in Underdeveloped Countries," *Economic Bulletin for Asia and the Far East,* June 1961, pp. 30–33.

[1] J. J. Polak, "Balance of Payments Problems of Countries Reconstructing with the Help of Foreign Loans," *Quarterly Journal of Economics,* February 1943, pp. 208–40. Reprinted in American Economic Association, *Readings in the Theory of International Trade,* pp. 459–93.

with a higher capital-output ratio should not necessarily be accorded a lower priority.[2] Thirdly, when applying this concept to agriculture in under-developed countries, it should be noted that the magnitude of fixed capital investment may be quite small in proportion to total inputs, e.g. of working capital such as fertilizer, so that the fixed capital-output ratio may vary rather widely due to factors other than capital investment.[3] . . .

Two main proposals for applying [the social product] criterion have been advanced. One is the *national produce (or consumption)* test suggested by J. Tinbergen.[4] This is based on an assessment of the project's direct, indirect and secondary consequences, all values of which are reckoned at "accounting prices" as referred to later. "Indirect consequences are those to be expected in the absence of further changes in total national income," while "secondary consequences consist of the changes in production which are the consequence of the change in national income, both in the short and the longer run, connected with the new production."

The other proposal is the *social marginal productivity* (SMP) criterion which was first advanced by A. E. Kahn.[5] H. B. Chenery[6]

[2] United Nations, Economic Commission for Asia and the Far East, "Problems and Techniques of Economic Development Planning and Programming with Special Reference to ECAFE Countries," *Economic Bulletin for Asia and the Far East,* November 1955, pp. 25–62.

[3] United Nations, Economic Commission for Asia and the Far East, *Report of the FAO/ECAFE Expert Group on Selected Aspects of Agricultural Planning,* Bangkok, 1961 (mimeographed).

[4] J. Tinbergen, *The Design of Development,* Baltimore, 1958.

[5] A. E. Kahn, "Investment Criteria in Development Programmes," *Quarterly Journal of Economics,* February 1951, pp. 38–61.

[6] H. B. Chenery, "The Application of Investment Criteria," *Quarterly Journal of Economics,* February 1953, pp. 76–96.

attempts to quantify the SMP principle by applying it to a number of empirical situations in several countries. In allocating investment resources, one should take into account "the total net contribution of the marginal unit to national product, and not merely that portion of the contribution (or of its costs) which may accrue to the private investor." The efficient allocation is the one which maximizes the value of national product, and the rule for achieving this is to allocate resources in such a way that the social marginal productivity of capital is approximately equal in the different uses.

As a rule, the SMP is not correlated with the rate of capital turnover referred to earlier. The results obtained from the two criteria will diverge, especially widely in the case of projects which create greater external economies. As a practical rule of thumb, nevertheless, Kahn admits that the capital-turnover criterion is useful where capital is relatively scarce and labour extremely plentiful, except that some investments which clearly relate to a bottleneck in development may be capital-intensive. In case the social opportunity cost of labour is very close to zero, the SMP criterion will in fact approximate the capital-turnover criterion. Chenery also considers that the rate of capital turnover is "particularly useful in choosing among projects within a given sector."

The SMP criterion is expressed in terms of a once-for-all effect on the national income, and does not include the specific multiplier effect of investment on future income levels. In other words, it does not take account of what happens to the final products—this determines in part the investment rate in future which in turn determines the level of future incomes. Nor does it take account of changes in the nature and quality of the factors of production such as population and labour force that may, in part, be an indirect consequence of the current investment allocation.

From the criticisms mentioned above of the SMP criterion comes the argument by W.

Galenson and H. Leibenstein[7] that the appropriate goal of development should be the maximization of *per capita* output, or average income, at some future point in time, rather than the maximization of national income now. Hence, the correct criterion for investment must be to maximize the rate of savings and thus of reinvestment, and to "choose for each unit of investment that alternative that will give each worker greater productive power than any other alternative." It is assumed that profits are largely saved for reinvestment and that wages are largely spent. The best allocation of investment resources is to be achieved, it is claimed, by distributing the available capital among the various alternative uses in such a way that "the marginal *per capita* reinvestment quotient" of capital is approximately equal in the various uses. Apart from human factors such as the quality of the labour force, it is the capital-labour ratio (or capital intensity) that determines output *per capita.* As a corollary, the reinvestment criterion favours capital-intensive projects even where capital is scarce. . . .

However O. Eckstein[8] considers that it might be desirable to employ fiscal means to attain an income distribution which will yield sufficient savings, rather than to depend on planned investment based on the reinvestment criterion. Furthermore, "endless growth for its own sake does not make too much sense," or there may be circumstances in which the current consumption may be a more immediate concern. Consequently, at a later stage of development or even in the present in some instances, the reinvestment criterion may have to be tem-

pered by the consideration of the value of current consumption to the community.

It is often argued that, since underdeveloped economies are generally characterized by massive underemployment along with scarcity of capital, one should select those investment projects that substitute abundant labour for scarce capital, or, in other words, mobilize the maximum amount of labour per unit of investment. The maximization of employment may also be a social and political objective. The employment absorption criterion has a family relationship with the case for low capital intensity, i.e. low capital-labour ratio.

The maximum labour absorption, however, does not necessarily lead to the maximization of the addition to total output. Adherence to capital-saving and labour-intensive investments may result in perpetuation of low labour productivity. Moreover, a course of maximizing the rate of investment may do more within the not so distant future to provide work for the underemployed than the capital-saving and labour-intensive use of the existing investment potential can do in the immediate future. . . .

A variant of the employment absorption argument is found in a doctrine advanced by R. Nurkse.[9] He draws attention to the potential savings concealed in rural underemployment and proposes to mobilize the underemployed for capital formation. This proposal implies that the output of the formerly excess labour when productively employed less minimum maintenance costs of that labour, can be used entirely for the production of capital goods. This involves essentially a plan for forced savings out of the labour of the previously disguised unemployed. Although admitting that there may be circumstances under which it would be best to put into effect Nurkse's proposal, Leibenstein suspects that "there is no evi-

[7] W. Galenson and H. Leibenstein, "Investment Criteria, Productivity and Economic Development," *Quarterly Journal of Economics,* August 1955, pp. 343–70.

[8] O. Eckstein, "Investment Criteria for Economic Development and the Theory of Intertemporal Welfare Economics," *Quarterly Journal of Economics,* February 1957, pp. 56–85.

[9] R. Nurkse, *Problems of Capital Formation in Underdeveloped Countries,* Oxford, 1953, pp. 36–47.

dence to lead us to believe that the particular technique suggested by Nurkse is the best way of obtaining the forced savings, or that the amount so obtained is the optimum amount."[10]

Since foreign exchange, a factor which is vital to the development of an underdeveloped economy, is usually scarce in underdeveloped countries, the balance of payments effect assumes importance as a criterion for the allocation of investment resources and the determination of priorities. It is often advocated that priority should be given to those projects which minimize balance of payments deficits or, in other words, increase the supply of foreign exchange or economize the use of it.

The balance of payments effect has two different aspects, namely the effects during the investment phase which are always negative, and the operating effects. J. J. Polak[11] classifies investments into three types according to whether the operating effect is positive, neutral, or negative. Type I includes exports and substitutes for imports, Type II replacements for goods at present consumed, and Type III goods sold in the home market in excess of the demand resulting from increase in real incomes. He maintains that the amount of investments in Type I sectors must be sufficiently large for the resulting positive balance of payments effects to offset the negative effects of investments of Type III and of the investment phase of all types of projects. However, this is not a very operational approach, because the output of many commodities may fall into several categories. Moreover, it does not tell what changes should be made in the programme in case the criterion is not satisfied.

In quantifying the SMP principle, H. B.

Chenery[12] incorporates the balance of payments effect. He suggests that a premium should be attached to foreign exchange earning or saving. This premium mathematically "represents the amount oi increase in national income which would be equivalent to an improvement of one unit in the balance of payments under specified conditions." It generally "measures the average overvaluation of the national currency at existing rates of exchange, taking into account the expected effect on imports and exports of the whole investment programme and also the balance-of-payments position at the beginning of the period."

The difficult foreign exchange situation currently prevailing might result in overemphasis on balance of payments effects in investment allocations. This criterion, therefore, needs to be balanced by the consideration of comparative advantages in the long run.

Whatever the criteria for resource allocation, difficulties arise in the measurement of present and future benefits from a given project and of the costs that are incurred in obtaining such benefits. Market prices, particularly those of the factors of production, form a very imperfect guide to resource allocation in under-developed economies, because there exist fundamental disequilibria which are reflected in the existence of massive underemployment at present levels of wages, the deficiency of funds at prevailing interest rates and the shortage of foreign exchange at current rates of exchange. The equilibrium level of wage rates will be considerably lower than market wages, while equilibrium interest rates will probably be much higher than market rates.

If a criterion is to be based on the concept of social product, it will be essential to remedy this defect. To do this, the use of "accounting prices" or "shadow prices" which truly

[10] H. Leibenstein, *Economic Backwardness and Economic Growth,* New York, 1957, p. 261.

[11] J. J. Polak, "Balance of Payments Problems of Countries Reconstructing with the Help of Foreign Loans," *Quarterly Journal of Economics,* February 1943, pp. 208–40.

[12] H. B. Chenery, "The Application of Investment Criteria," *Quarterly Journal of Economics,* February 1953, pp. 76–96.

reflect intrinsic values of factors of production is suggested by J. Tinbergen[13] and by H. B. Chenery and K. S. Kretschmer.[14]

In the application of this theory, however, a certain arbitrariness may enter into the assessment of these intrinsic values. Shifts in accounting prices which may arise from the realization of investment programmes are difficult to predict. Moreover, the application of accounting prices might result in favouring, more than long-term considerations would warrant, those projects which are labour-intensive, which create or save foreign exchange and which promise a quick yield on the capital employed.

The concept of accounting prices has to be made precise before it can be applied in

[13] J. Tinbergen, *The Design of Development,* Baltimore, 1958.

[14] H. B. Chenery and K. S. Kretschmer, "Resources Allocation for Economic Development," *Econometrica,* October 1956, pp. 365–99.

the actual preparation of economic plans. A recent attempt at greater precision defines accounting prices as "the values of the marginal productivity of factors when a selection of techniques has been made which produces the maximum possible volume of output, given the availability of resources, the pattern of final demand and the technological possibilities of production,"[15] It would then be for the government to calculate marginal productivity of factors and manipulate the system of subsidy and taxation in such a way that the supply prices of factors to the producers became equal to the value of their marginal productivity. However, even apart from the difficulties in calculating the marginal productivity of the factors, the problem of producers' response to changes in taxes and subsidies would also have to be studied.

[15] A. Quayyum, *Theory and Policy of Accounting Prices,* Amsterdam, 1959.

VII.B.2. Choice of Technology as a

Problem of "Second Best"*

Before one can enter the debate on the complex question of the choice of technology in the context of development planning, certain preliminary issues have to be cleared up. These include the concept of technical efficiency, which is one of the dominant concepts in the field of policy-oriented economics.

Suppose we are considering some technical choice *i* which permits the production of an output combination *x* using an input

*From A.K. Sen, "Choice of Technology: A Critical Survey of a Class of Debates," in UNIDO, *Planning for Advanced Skills and Technologies,* Industrial and Planning Programming Series No. 3, New York, 1969, pp. 45–9. Reprinted by permission.

combination *y*. If it is possible to produce the same bundle of commodities *x* with less of at least one, and no more of any, of the inputs, then the technical choice *i* is not efficient. This is simply because efficiency implies producing a given quantity of output with as few inputs as possible. Similarly, if with that collection of inputs *y*, an output combination can be produced which exceeds *x* in at least one, and is no less in terms of any, of the outputs, then again the technical choice *i* must be regarded as inefficient. This is because efficiency also implies that for any given collection of inputs we should try to get the maximum of outputs.

In fact, we can combine the two criteria together by treating inputs as negative outputs.[1] Thus defined, what efficiency requires is that no more of any one output can be obtained given the amount of the others.

This takes us a certain distance, but not very far. If a certain technical choice leads to a greater output of a given commodity and a lower output of some other commodity than a different technical choice would do, the criterion of technical efficiency does not help us at all. Both these technical choices may satisfy the test of efficiency and yet we may be left with a problem still to be solved.

The concept of technical efficiency is often applied at a given point of time, but there is no difficulty in extending it over time. All we need to do is treat a certain commodity today as different from the same commodity tomorrow. In other respects the definitions, concepts and criteria need not be altered. The same problem of incompleteness persists, naturally, even in this extended view of technical efficiency, embracing more than one point in time. In fact, in comparing two alternative technological possibilities, we might face a possibility of having more of a certain commodity at point of time t and less of some commodity at a point of time (t + 1). Once again the criterion of technical efficiency cannot solve this problem.

The main usefulness of the criterion of efficiency is that it permits a preliminary sorting out. A number of technological possibilities may be eliminated on grounds of inefficiency, and then we shall be left with a set of efficient technological possibilities, the choice between which must be made on the basis of some other criterion. Efficiency is like a test applied in the "qualifying round", and it needs to be supplemented by some other criterion to determine which is the winner amongst those alternatives that have qualified.

This is where the notion of optimality comes in. This is one of the basic concepts used in economics: an optimum choice represents the "best" among the feasible alternatives. Naturally, if we are to choose the optimum combination we must have some criteria for discrimination between the various alternatives.

A preliminary point of logic may be cleared up at this stage. We can distinguish between two conditions for rational choice: the existence of either a "complete ordering" or a "choice set". The former requires that any two alternatives should be consistently comparable with each other in terms of some ordering relation, such as "being at least as good as . . .". This property is sometimes called "connectedness". Another required condition is "transitivity", which demands that if x is regarded as being at least as good as y, and y is regarded as being at least as good as z, then x should be regarded as at least as good as z.[2] When these conditions are satisfied, a complete ordering exists over the relevant conditions.

The existence of a choice set is somewhat different. This requires the existence of some alternative which is regarded as at least as good as every alternative in the available set. This simply means that a "best" alternative exists. The existence of a choice set may be regarded as sufficient for the purposes of choosing an optimal policy.

It is important to note that the existence of a complete ordering is neither a sufficient, nor a necessary condition for the existence of a choice set. It is not sufficient because, although we may be able to order alternatives in a certain fashion, if there is an in-

---

[1] See Debreu, p. 56. A good introduction to the problems of efficiency can be found also in Koopmans.

[2] On the logic of ordering, see Arrow and Debreu. It may be noted that the way we have defined any two alternatives being comparable not only guarantees "connectedness" but also yields "reflexivity" which requires that every alternative be regarded as "at least as good as" itself. When the alternatives considered are the same, what was defined as "connectedness" is in fact a condition of "reflexivity". By and large in optimal policy decisions, reflexivity is not a major source of worry; in fact, a minimal degree of sanity seems to be sufficient. The real problem arises with connectedness and transitivity. On this, see in particular Arrow.

finite number of them, it is possible that no best alternative may exist. For example, alternative 2 may be preferred to 1, alternative 3 to 2, alternative 4 to 3, and so on, *ad infinitum*. It is not a necessary condition because, although we may be able to compare some alternative with all the others and find it to be at least as good as them all, there may, nevertheless, be intransitivities, or a lack of connectedness. For example *x* may be regarded as better than *y* and also better than *z*; but we may not be able to compare *y* and *z* by the criterion we are using. Even so, we may feel safe in choosing *x*, since it is the best alternative, although we cannot compare its two inferiors *y* and *z*.

In spite of this difference between the conditions for the existence of a choice set and those for the existence of a complete ordering it is clear that there is an intimate relationship between these two aspects of rational choice. In fact, most of the discussions on optimality have been concerned with obtaining a criterion for a complete ordering, and it has been supposed that this in itself will guarantee the identification of a best alternative. This presupposition makes eminently good sense when the number of alternatives is finite, when a consequence of the existence of a complete ordering is the existence of a choice set. When, however, the number of alternatives is infinite, this consequence may or may not follow. Furthermore, even when a complete ordering does not exist we may still be able to find what is the best thing to do. Although we shall not be concerned very much in this paper with this contrast it is important for us to bear in mind the difference between these two requirements of rational selection. Indeed, in some problems the distinction can be extremely important.

Whether we prefer a choice set or a complete ordering, we need some method of ordering, a criterion to tell whether a certain alternative *x* is better or worse than, or indifferent to, another alternative *y*. The concept of technical efficiency can be used partly for this purpose, and we may find that *x* is more

efficient than *y* and simply eliminate *y*. However, as we noted before, this does not help when *x* and *y* are both efficient. Much of the debate on the choice of techniques is concerned with supplementing the criterion of technical efficiency by some other criterion that will permit us to choose between the efficient alternatives. In the discussion that follows we shall be concerned with a choice among a set of efficient alternatives, and shall assume that the inefficient ones have already been pruned away.

We shall thus have no further use for the concept of efficiency as such, which (it will be assumed) has done its job, and the discussion will concentrate on some supplementary criteria to take us beyond efficiency. The lively debate on technological choice which has taken place over the last two decades has been concerned with methods of supplementing the relatively uncontroversial criterion of technical efficiency. To this range of problems we now turn.

SUBOPTIMALITY OF SAVINGS RATE AND CHOICE OF TECHNOLOGY AS A PROBLEM OF "SECOND BEST"

Investment decisions can be classified into various types, according to whether they depend on the optimum size of investment, the optimum capital-intensity, or the optimum sectoral allocation. While it is important that we recognize these investment decisions to be different, we cannot regard them as independent. Indeed, much of the controversy on the choice of technology concerns the dependence of the amount of savings on the factor proportions selected.

A simple illustration may bring out the difference between some of the schools of thought. It may be argued that wage earners tend to have a higher propensity to consume than profit earners. This is likely to be spectacularly true in a socialist economy, where the profits are earned by the state, but it may hold good even in the case of a privately-owned enterprise. Given this assump-

$$MPC_w > MPC_\pi$$

tion, it appears that the proportion of additional income that is saved will depend on the distribution of that additional income between the wage earners and the profit earners. And this distribution, in its turn, depends on the choice of technology, since a more labour-intensive technique will (other things being equal) tend to lead to a higher share of wages.

A special case of this has been much discussed: the assumption that the wage earners have a propensity to consume of 1 and profit earners have a propensity to consume of 0. This is, however, a rather limited case, and the problem with which we are concerned relates to much more general conditions, viz, the propensity to save of profit earners is systematically higher than that of wage earners. Given this assumption a direct link would be established between the degree of labour intensity chosen and the proportion of the additional income that will be saved.

Situations often occur in which one technique will lead to a higher amount of total output and another technique will generate a higher amount of total savings. If we wish to attach additional weight to the savings generated, over and above the weight that is attached to all output (be it saved or consumed), then clearly this will affect our decisions regarding which techniques to choose.

For the purpose of this discussion total output and total savings may be regarded as two separate commodities, even when they are assumed to be physically homogeneous, as in some simple models. The question of economic efficiency discussed in the last section may be applied to such a case. Any technique which generates less of either total savings or total output and no more of the other may be simply rejected as inefficient. But after this preliminary pruning operation had been carried out, we would be left with a set of techniques that could not be compared purely on efficiency grounds. We should then have cases in which a higher amount of total savings results in a lower amount of total output. What our choice is in

such a situation will depend crucially on the additional weights to be attached to savings as against output.

At this stage we might ask: Why must we attach any additional weight to savings as such? After all, savings involve a certain sacrifice of present in favour of future consumption, and what reason is there for us to believe that it is always better to sacrifice present consumption for a corresponding future amount? Indeed there is no such compelling reason in general. What the debate on choice of technology did was to assume (often implicitly) a suboptimal rate of savings, some outside constraint preventing the savings rate from rising to the optimal level. As a consequence there was always reason to look kindly on any policy which led to a higher proportion of savings.

Why this suboptimality should arise is itself a complex question. In the case of private-enterprise economy it can certainly be argued that the rate of savings may be considerably below optimal.[3] In particular, it has been argued that people might be willing to sign a contract forcing everyone to save a certain amount for the future, even when they may not do it individually under the market mechanism: a situation of this kind has been christened the "isolation paradox".[4]

There seems to be considerable agreement at a practical level regarding the need for raising the rate of saving in many underdeveloped countries. Indeed one has only to look through the planning documents of a variety of countries to see that one of the persistent themes is the need for a higher rate of saving and a higher rate of growth.[5] These doecuments are clearly based on certain assumptions, usually implicit, about the

[3] See Pigou, Ramsey, Baumol, Dobb, Sen (1961, Feb. 1967), Marglin (Feb. 1963, May 1963), Feldstein, and others.

[4] Sen (1961). See also Baumol, Marglin (Feb. 1963), Harberger, Lind, Phelps, and Sen (Feb. 1967).

[5] See R. F. Kahn for a review of some of the planning documents in this context.

objectives to be achieved by the economy, in terms of which the existing rates of saving appear to be below optimal. Sometimes the arguments are fairly sophisticated,[6] sometimes not.

Whatever the reasons for the suboptimality of the savings rate, it seems to be clear that this is a persistent diagnosis for most under-developed economies. In the presence of such suboptimality it is not difficult to see why additional weight has to be attached to the part of the additional income that is saved and invested as against the part that is consumed. It is in this context that much of the controversy on the problem of choice of technology in recent years become fully clear.

Essentially the problem is that of choice of technology in a world of suboptimal savings. It can also be viewed as a problem in the theory of "second best".[7] Since misallocation at the margin of choice between savings and consumption is due to some specific constraint, this will be reflected in the choice of the degree of labour intensity implicit in the technological selection. The problem would have been totally different if the case had been one of allocating an optimal of savings among techniques with varying degrees of labour intensity.

A distinction should be made in this context between

(a) a general equilibrium formulation where the amounts of savings, the degrees of labour intensity, and the pattern of investment are to be simultaneously selected; and

(b) a partial equilibrium formulation where the technical choice is confined to finding an optimal labour intensity for a marginal project.

In the former case the inoptimality of the savings rate should not be assumed although it may result from the allocational exercise. In the latter case an over-all suboptimality of savings may be taken as given, since the project in question is too small to affect the over-all inoptimality of savings.

Some kind of an objective function may be given which depends on technical choice and the proportion of savings. In the absence of any constraint on savings, our choices should lead to an optimal situation with the usual marginal equalities, if the exercise is of the former kind: in the absence of a specific constraint on the rate of savings, the rate of transformation between consumption at time t and the consumption at time $(t + 1)$ will equal the rate at which we are ready to substitute the one for the other.[8] There will then be no need for a marginal preference in favour of future consumption, implying additional weight on the savings generated. Even in the general-equilibrium framework, if some outside constraint is imposed which prevents the rate of saving from rising above a certain level, a suboptimality of savings can result. It will then be appropriate to attach additional weight to savings as against the part of the income immediately consumed.

Such constraints can arise for a variety of reasons, including political difficulties in taxation. The planners may want a higher rate of saving in terms of the objectives assumed by them, but fail to achieve this for fear of political reactions.[9] Given this political constraint the suboptimality of the savings rate that may be generated will tend to influence the optimal technical choice in the direction of relatively more capital-intensive tech-

[6] Optimum savings models have generally tended to yield extremely high rates of savings, very much in excess of the usual rates observed anywhere in the world. See, among others, Tinbergen (1957, 1962), Goodwin, Chakravarty, and Sen (1967).

[7] See Lancaster and Lipsey.

[8] This is on the assumption of smooth differentiability. When there is only a limited number of basic alternatives, with resultant "kinks" in the transformation surfaces, the corresponding rule will take the form of a set of inequalities. See Dorfman, Samuelson, and Solow.

[9] Whether this range of problems can arise in a fully socialist economy is a matter for discussion. For some indications that they do, see Pajestka and Marglin (Jan. 1966).

niques, as implying a relatively higher rate of savings.

This is precisely where a different school of thought may make itself heard, arguing that such political constraints do not in fact occur, that the total amount of income to be saved can be determined by the planner in any way he likes, and that he can then see that this decision is executed through the machinery at his disposal, such as wages and incomes policy, taxation policy and monetary policies. If this is true then the link snaps between the choice of techniques and the proportion of income saved. Then technical choice may be made with the main purpose of maximizing the amount of output,[10] and the proportion of the output to be invested can be decided at a separate stage.

In the context of such an assumption it will be right to argue that the amount of income generated in a surplus-labour economy ought to be maximized even at the expense of savings. This argument could spring from the assumption either that there is no suboptimality of savings or that the proportion of income that can be saved, even if constrained, is not dependent on the distribution of income. Various elaborations of these arguments can be found in economic literature.

Having commented on what appear to be some of the major issues that divide the different schools of thought in the debate on technical choice, we may now proceed to discuss the controversy itself in some greater detail. We develop a general framework in the next section and then express the various criteria in terms of comparison and contrast. This general framework uses a very simple model with one homogeneous commodity, which nevertheless illustrates almost the entire controversy that has taken place in recent years on choice of techniques for an

under-developed economy. At a later stage, in the context of a model on concave programming, we shall discard this assumption, and discuss the problem in a multi-commodity context.

A GENERAL FRAMEWORK

Let there be a production function relating output (Q) to labour (L) and capital (K).

$$Q = Q(L, K) \qquad (1)$$

We assume this to be homogeneous of the first degree, i.e. with constant returns to scale. Let the wage rate be given by w, the propensity to consume of wage earners by c_1 and the propensity to consume of profit earners by c_2. The amount of the income that is saved is represented as S, which is expressed by the following relationship:

$$S = L w (1 - c_1) + (Q - L w)(1 - c_2). \quad (2)$$

We assume that the supply of labour is unlimited.[11] The object of the exercise is to maximize a certain weighted sum of output and savings.[12] It is to be remembered that savings S is a part of output Q, so that the weight attached to S is in the nature of a premium, i.e. it is an additional weight, over and above the weight that S receives as a part of Q. Let this premium on savings be given by λ, which we have taken to be positive, since we have assumed the savings rate

[11] For a contrast of views on the empirical acceptability of this assumption, see Nurkse, Lewis (1954, 1955, 1958), Eckaus, Mellor and Stevens, Rosenstein-Rodan, Leibenstein, Viner, Haberler, Oshima, Fei and Ranis Schultz, Jorgenson (1966), Marglin (1966), Sen (Oct. 1966, Feb. 1967), and Mehra.

[12] In a general equilibrium framework the weights should vary with the choice of techniques, and the objective function should be "non-linear". However, in the case of a small project, the total savings and the consumption for the economy as a whole may not be much affected by the marginal choice. There the weights can be taken as given, much as the perfectly competitive firm takes prices as given.

[10] The implicit framework here is that of a one-commodity model, but the corresponding conditions for a multi-commodity model are easy to obtain.

to be suboptimal.[13] The object therefore, is to maximize the following welfare function

$$V = Q + \lambda S. \qquad (3)$$

Given the amount of capital the problem of the choice of techniques is simply to find the right amount L, which will determine the appropriate degree of capital intensity (K/L). Due to the assumption of constant returns to scale, it does not matter how we choose K, for the discussion is all in terms of ratios per unit of capital. It is clear that the first order condition of maximization of the objective function is given by the following when K is given:

$$\frac{\partial V}{\partial L} = 0. \qquad (4)$$

Given the equations (1), (2) and (3) it can be seen that the conditions of maximization given by equation (4) requires the following:

$$\frac{\partial Q}{\partial L} [1 + \lambda (1 - c_2)] = \lambda w (c_1 - c_2). \qquad (5)$$

As a condition on the marginal productivity of labour we can re-write relationship (5) as follows, defining that magnitude to which the marginal product of labor is to be equated as "the real cost of labour" (w^*):

$$w^* = \frac{\partial Q}{\partial L} = \left[\frac{(c_1 - c_2)\lambda}{1 + (1 - c_2)\lambda} \right] w. \qquad (6)$$

Much of the controversy on the choice of technology for an under-developed economy with surplus labour can be seen to be variations on the theme represented by equation (6). With this general framework we can sort out the different contributions in this controversial field.

One clarifying remark should be made before we proceed further. The evaluation of alternative techniques depends crucially on the value of λ, i.e. on the additional weight to be attached to investment as against consumption. The value of λ in its turn depends on the relative weights to be attached to consumption today as against that in the future. What we are really attempting, therefore, is to provide a one-period model which tries to catch the essence of comparison of the relevant sets of time series of consumption representing alternative technological possibilities.

That the problem of choice of techniques cannot be solved except in terms of making explicit value judgements about alternative sets of time series has been discussed by Sen[14] who also argued that the different criteria proposed really boil down to doing this very thing in a highly implicit manner.[15] . . .

References

K. J. Arrow, *Social Choice and Individual Values*, New York, 1951.

W. J. Baumol, *Welfare Economics and the Theory of the State*, London, 1952.

S. Chakravarty, "Optimum Savings with Finite Planning Horizon", *International Economic Review*, Sept. 1962.

G. Debreu, *The Theory of Value*, London, 1959.

R. Dorfman, P. A. Samuelson, and R. M. Solow, *Linear Programming and Economic Analysis*, New York, 1958.

M. H. Dobb, *An Essay on Economic Growth and Planning*, London, 1960.

R. S. Eckaus, "Factor Proportions in Under-developed Countries", *American Economic Review*, Vol. 45, Sept. 1955.

C. H. Fei and G. Ranis, *Development of Labor Surplus Economy: Theory and Policy*, Homewood, 1964.

---

[13] The choice discussed here is for a marginal project. A wider exercise should take λ as a variable. The optimality conditions, however, will remain the same for appropriate values of λ.

[14] Sen (1957).

[15] Explicit attempts at making these comparisons can be found in Sen (1957, 1968). This problem has been penetratingly studied by Marglin (Jan. 1966).

M. S. Feldstein, "The Social Time Preference Discount Rate in Cost-Benefit Analysis", *Economic Journal,* June 1964.

R. M. Goodwin, "The Optimum Path for an Underdeveloped Economy", *Economic Journal,* Dec. 1961.

G. Haberler, "Critical Observations on Some Current Notions on the Theory of Economic Development", *L'Industria,* Vol. 2, 1957.

A. C. Harberger, "Techniques of Project Appraisal", National Bureau of Economic Research, Conference on Economic Planning, 1964.

D. W. Jorgenson, "Testing Alternative Theories of the Development of a Dual Economy", in I. Adelman and E. Thorbecke (eds.), *The Theory and Design of Economic Development,* Baltimore, 1966.

____, "Subsistence Agriculture and Economic Growth", *Oxford Economic Papers,* 1967.

R. F. Kahn, "The Pace of Development", in Hebrew University, *The Challenge of Development,* Jerusalem, 1958.

T. C. Koopmans, *Three Essays on the State of Economic Science,* New York, 1957.

K. Lancaster and R. G. Lipsey, "The General Theory of Second Best", *Review of Economic Studies,* Vol. 24, 1956.

H. Leibenstein, "The Theory of Underemployment in Backward Economies", *Journal of Political Economy,* Vol. 65, Apr. 1957.

W. A. Lewis, "Economic Development with Unlimited Supplies of Labour", *Manchester School,* May 1954.

____, *The Theory of Economic Growth,* London, 1955.

____, "Unlimited Labour: Further Notes", *Manchester School,* Jan. 1958.

R. C. Lind, "The Social Rate of Discount and the Optimal Rate of Investment: Further Comment", *Quarterly Journal of Economics,* May 1964.

S. A. Marglin, "The Social Rate of Discount and the Optimal Rate of Investment", *Quarterly Journal of Economics,* Feb. 1963.

____, "The Opportunity Costs of Public Investment", *Quarterly Journal of Economics,* May 1963.

____, *Industrial Development in the Labour-Surplus Economy,* mimeographed, Jan. 1966.

____, "Mr. Jorgenson Against the Classics", in I. Adelman and E. Thorbecke (eds.), *The Theory and Design of Economic Development,* Baltimore, 1966.

S. Mehra, "Surplus Labour in Indian Agriculture", *Indian Economic Review,* Apr. 1966.

J. W. Mellor and R. D. Stevens, "The Average and Marginal Product of Farm Labor in Underdeveloped Economies", *Journal of Farm Economics,* Vol. 38, Aug. 1956.

R. Nurkse, *Problems of Capital Formation in Underdeveloped Countries,* Oxford, 1953.

H. T. Oshima, "Underemployment in Backward Economies: An Empirical Comment", *Journal of Political Economy,* Vol. 66, June 1958.

J. Pajestka, "Some Problems of Economic Development Planning", in Oscar Lange (ed.), *Problems of Political Economy of Socialism,* New Delhi, 1962.

E. S. Phelps, *Fiscal Neutrality toward Economic Growth,* New York, 1965.

A. C. Pigou, *Economics of Welfare,* 4th ed., London, 1932.

F. P. Ramsey, "A Mathematical Theory of Saving", *Economic Journal,* Dec. 1928.

P. N. Rosenstein-Rodan, "Disguised Unemployment and Underemployment in Agriculture", *Monthly Bulletin of Agricultural Economics and Statistics,* Vol. 6, July-Aug. 1957.

T. W. Schultz, *Transforming Traditional Agriculture,* New Haven, 1964.

____, "Significance of India's 1918-1919

Losses of Agricultural Labour—A Reply", *Economic Journal*, Vol. 77, Mar. 1967.

A. K. Sen, "Some Notes on the Choice of Capital-Intensity in Development Planning", *Quarterly Journal of Economics*, Nov. 1957.

_____, "On Optimizing the Rate of Saving", *Economic Journal*, Vol. 71, Sept. 1961.

_____, "Peasants and Dualism with or without Surplus Labour", *Journal of Political Economy*, Oct. 1966.

_____, "Terminal Capital and Optimal Savings", in C. H. Feinstein *et al.* (ed.), *Capitalism, Socialism and Economic*

Growth, Essays in Honour of Maurice Dobb, Cambridge, 1967.

_____, "Isolation, Assurance and the Social Rate of Discount", *Quarterly Journal of Economics*, Feb. 1967.

_____, *Choice of Techniques*, Oxford, 1960; 2nd ed., 1962; 3rd ed., 1968.

J. Tinbergen, "The Optimum Rate of Saving", *Economic Journal*, Dec. 1957.

_____, "Optimum Savings and Utility Maximization over Time", *Econometrica*, Apr. 1962.

J. Viner, "Some Reflections on the Concept of 'Disguised Unemployment' ", *Contribucoes a Analise do Desenvolvimento Economico*, 1957.

VII.B.3. Choice of Techniques in a Labor Surplus Economy*

Let us assume that the Government intends to make a certain amount of investment and is considering a number of alternative blueprints involving different techniques of production.[1] Of the alternatives some could possibly be rejected outright. If, for example, technique A leads to a smaller flow of

*From A. K. Sen, "Choice of Techniques of Production: With Special Reference to East Asia," In Kenneth Berrill (ed.), *Economic Development with Special Reference to East Asia*, Macmillan & Co. Ltd., London: St. Martin's Press, New York, 1964, pp. 386–7, 389–96. Reprinted by permission.

[1] We shall assume throughout this paper that the technique chosen does not affect the total amount of investment that can be made. In many cases, this is not a good assumption. See, in this connexion, "Some Notes on the Choice of Capital-Intensity in Development Planning," by the writer, the *Quarterly Journal of Economics*, November 1957, pp. 566, 568, 577–82; see also C. P. Kindleberger, *Economic Development*, New York, 1958, pp. 174–5.

output per year than does technique B, and if both sets of plants have the same gestation lag, the same length of life, and the same requirement of labour and other current inputs per year, the technique A is definitely "inferior." Similarly, if technique A leads to an equal flow of output per year over an equal life after an equal lag, as does technique B, and if it requires more labour, or other current inputs, per year, then again, A is distinctly "inferior."[2] In the same way, if

[2] The larger employment flow resulting from technique A cannot be considered to be a good thing in itself, for, if we like to have additional employment with the same volume of output, we can employ, in the case of choosing technique B, some people to dig holes, thus making the employment and the output figures equal to those with technique A. The point is, however, that we can, if we like economic growth, employ them in the capital goods sector. Given the level of real wages, the flow of employment possibility depends entirely on the output of consumer goods, so that the technique that maximizes the latter also maximizes

technique A leads to an equal flow of output per year and has the same current input requirement per year, but has a shorter life of plants with the same gestation lag, then it is, again, of not much use. We do not need much economics to reject these alternatives. Problems of real choice arise when one good thing clashes with another.

The classic case of technological choice is the one where the ratio of the initial investment to the consequent output flow is reduced by raising the ratio of employment flow to investment. At first sight it looks as if the techniques chosen in economies with surplus labour should be such that the ratio of output flow to capital investment is maximized (given the life of the plants, the gestation lag, and the requirements of raw materials), even if this involves a larger labour requirement than some other alternatives. Labour is available, and must be fed anyway, so that employment of more labour does not seem to cost anything to the society. This is, however, not quite the whole picture. Additional employment tends to produce additional consumption via the creation of additional wages bills. Total consumption may go up in two ways, viz., through an increase in the amount of consumption of the people who are newly employed and through that of the people who were previously supporting these unemployed people and have now more elbow room. It is, thus, possible that while the choice of a more labour-intensive technique will add to output, it will add more to consumption, reducing the volume of investible surplus. If the policy objective is the maximization of the growth rate, we may choose more capital-intensive techniques than when it is the maximization of immediate output per unit of investment. If our objctive is something intermediate between the maximization of immediate out-

put and the maximization of the growth rate, we might choose techniques that are in between these. Various intermediate criteria can be put forward. We shall not, here, go further into this question. Our object is only to refer to this rather elementary conflict of values as a background to what we are going to discuss.

CONDITIONS OF LABOUR SUPPLY

The main question that we would like to discuss in this note concerns the much discussed desirability of choosing a lower degree of mechanization in the underdeveloped economies than that in the advanced countries. We shall try to see the assumptions on which this proposition is based, and try to examine whether this could be considered to be a useful guide to policy. While discussing this, a number of other policy propositions might, incidentally, come to light. We shall assume in the first part of this study that a lower degree of mechanization, defined as the value of the amount of machines employed with one man at a time, always implies a lower degree of capital intensity (i.e. a lower ratio of capital investment to the consequent flow of employment per year). Towards the latter part of this note, this assumption itself will be examined.

The argument for a lower degree of capital intensity seems to be based mainly on two aspects of the relevant labour statistics: first, that there is, in most of these economies, a considerable surplus of unemployed labour, and second, that the real wage rate per unit of labour is also lower.[3] If the objective is the maximization of immediate output given the level of investment, the implications of the first are obvious. Since labour has no opportunity cost, we should

---

the former. Given the total amount of investment in the consumer goods sector, the technique with the least capital-output ratio also maximizes the employment possibility in the short run.

[3] Two other arguments refer to (a) the lower foreign exchange requirement and (b) the shorter gestation lag of less mechanized production processes.

not hesitate to choose a technique that uses a lot of labour per unit of investment provided that it gives a larger flow of output (given the lags and the life of the plants). In economies where additional employment in any field can be provided only by reducing employment in other fields, the alternative productivity of labour must be deducted from the addition in the field under review to obtain the *net* contribution of additional employment, given the amount of investment. Thus, with this policy objective, it would appear that the degree of capital intensity chosen should be lower in the under-developed economies than in the advanced ones.

This argument is, to a certain extent, valid, but questions can be raised about the availability of a surplus labour force in a number of under-developed countries. It can be said, broadly speaking, that a great many doubts can be raised about the validity of this empirical assumption for a considerable part of Africa (excluding the extreme north, e.g. Egypt), though the assumption is possibly right for the bulk of Asia. It is of some interest to study the historical reasons for such a division between the "under-developed" economies, and one wonders whether the differences in the relative timing of the growth of settled agriculture explain this dichotomy. This is a question we shall not try to answer here, but we must recognize that all under-developed economies do not necessarily have surplus labour. It can be maintained, however, that even in the areas which have no surplus labour, the opportunity cost of labour (i.e. alternative productivity) will tend to be much lower than in the advanced economies. Thus, the proposition that the techniques maximizing output would tend to be relatively less capital-intensive in the under-developed economies compared with those in the advanced countries, remains (given other assumptions) valid. In most of East Asia, where considerable volumes of surplus labour are known to exist, this result is, of course, especially relevant.

Immediate output maximization is not, however, a universally accepted policy objective, for it might be achieved, beyond a point, at the cost of economic growth. But even from the point of view of maximizing the rate of growth, the result is likely to hold good. Since the levels of real wages are lower in the under-developed countries, the consumption-creating effects of additional employment are weaker. In so far as the additional demand for labour in the economy will tend to raise the level of real wages, and therefore of real consumption, there will be an increase in the cost of labour from the point of view of growth. In an under-employed, backward economy, however, the only cost from the point of view of growth is the additional consumption, since there is no output sacrificed. The fact that the level of real wages in the under-developed economies will tend to be lower than the alternative productivity in the advanced economies will lead to the discussed results, even if there were no increase in the real wage rate in the fully employed advanced economies due to the additional demand for labour. It seems, therefore, that there is a *ceteris paribus* case for a lower capital intensity in the under-developed economies.

SOME DOUBTS

We must now examine closely a number of implicit assumptions on which the above conclusion is based. First, we have assumed that while the real wage rate is lower in the under-developed economies, the productivity, given the technique of production, is the same. Due to the inexperience of the labour force, in the under-developed countries, with industrial techniques, and due to things like undernourishment, the productivity of labour in these economies might be lower, for the same technique of production. This means that while an additional unit of employment might add rather little to consumption, it might also add relatively less to the product given the technique of production. This tends to weaken the argument for using relatively labour-intensive techniques on the ground of the low level of real wages or of low opportunity cost.[4] What it means, in terms of common sense, is that labour in efficiency units is not necessarily very cheap. One should, however, add that in so far as this phenomenon of lower productivity is due to lack of experience, the force of this consideration will weaken in the long run. A second point, which is perhaps more important, is that the productivity of labour in the under-developed economies might not be uniformly lower for all techniques. For certain traditional crafts, the skill of the artisans in many of the under-developed countries is well known. In so far as the productivity is lower mainly in mechanical production, this argument might, in fact, weaken, rather than strengthen, the case for mechanization. There is no doubt, however, that the force of the argument will be in the opposite direction in the choice between two varieties of mechanical production equally unfamiliar to the new workers.

Another implicit assumption that could be challenged is the actual existence of a large number of alternative techniques from which we can choose. In some industries, techniques cannot be varied to any considerable extent, and in others such variations may lead to such enormous differences in the quality of the product that the variability may not be of much use. While the Chinese have shown that even steel can be made by cottage industrial techniques, the quality of such steel has restricted its use to a few goods. In other fields, e.g. in splitting atoms, it may not be very fruitful to look for labour-intensive techniques to suit the under-developed nations. This lack of choice would reduce the empirical content of the

[4] See, on this question, "Second Thoughts on Capital Intensity of Investment," by Maurice Dobb, *Review of Economic Studies*, Vol. XXIV, No. 1, pp. 37–8.

proposition that we are discussing.[5] It should, however, be added here that while variations in the main lines of production might be very limited, that in the complementary fields (e.g. in building operations, in transporting things from one part of the factory to another) would be considerable.

THE COMPOSITION OF COMMODITIES

The fact that there are quite a lot of differences in the possible degrees of capital intensity in the production of different products has led many economists to assume a greater degree of variability than is perhaps legitimate. The choice between commodities cannot be discussed in the same terms as the choice between techniques to produce the same commodity, for different commodities may not be good substitutes for each other. Thus, the argument for labour-intensive production techniques cannot be based, beyond a point, on this type of choice. The transport provided by the railways, or by the buses, is undoubtedly a relatively capital-intensive product, while the shoes made by cobblers are undoubtedly not so; still, we cannot recommend replacing railways and buses by labour-intensive shoes. Certain degrees of substitutability are, of course, present between various commodities, and these can certainly be exploited for the purposes of choosing relatively labour-intensive techniques.[6] It should also be mentioned that

[5] Adam did not have to worry about the alternative ways of investing a rib, for the very same reason.

[6] It is sometimes difficult to tell whether we are discussing the choice between two commodities or between the same commodity made by different techniques, since the quality varies, in some cases, with the techniques of production. While thermal electricity is as good as hydro-electricity and additional food grains produced by irrigation might not differ appreciably from those made with more fertilizers, cloth made in the mills is not the same as hand-spun and hand-woven cloth, and hand-made

the poverty of many under-developed countries tends to make a number of "basic" consumer goods, which have nothing much in common in their use, act as substitutes of each other. It has been observed, for example, that in some parts of rural India kerosene is, to a certain extent, a substitute for sugar. The substitutability between commodities at different stages of production is, however, on the whole very limited, so that the not infrequent advice given to the under-developed nations to go in for "light" industries like cotton-textile or bicycle-making, rather than "heavy" industries like steel-manufacture, has rather limited validity. The degree of substitutability is, of course, increased by international trade, but its use is restricted by transport costs, the response of terms of trade to an expansion of exports or imports, the uncertainty (economic and political) associated with international trade, and the untradeability of some commodities, notably services.[7] Thus, the solution of choosing labour-intensive techniques indirectly, via the choice of the "right" types of industries, might not take us very far.

The problem of the interdependence between the commodities may affect the case

for labour-intensive methods of production even *within* one industry. The relatively labour-intensive techniques, to be at all considered, must involve a higher output-capital ratio, which normally means that they would also involve a higher ratio of raw material flow to the investment of capital, since the raw material content of the output is often rather constant. As the production of many raw materials (mineral and agricultural) might be subject to diminishing returns, due to the fixity of natural resources, an expansion of the raw material requirement is likely to raise its price compared with other prices. Thus, in choosing between alternative techniques of production in the secondary sector, we may have to use a relatively higher price for the raw materials if we choose less capital-intensive techniques. This will act, *ceteris paribus*, against the choice of such techniques. I need hardly add that the importance of this consideration will vary from case to case, and need not always be very important.

TECHNICAL PROGRESS

We have discussed the problem so far in terms of given production functions, but there is also technological progress. This technological progress, it might be added, would not be independent of the techniques chosen now. The use of mechanized techniques today might improve the possibilities offered by such methods through innovation. This could not be said, it might be argued, to the same extent about traditional non-mechanized methods of production, for they have been in use for a very long time and have absorbed whatever improvements are possible. This argument is not entirely correct, since the application of some elements of modern production methods, e.g. the use of power, can often bring about revolutionary improvements in the production possibilities offered by small-scale

---

shoes are not the same as machine-made ones. It is, of course, a tautology to say that the degree of substitutability will be greater between the same commodity made by different techniques than between two different commodities, since that is how we decide whether two different products should be called varieties of the same commodity or two different commodities altogether.

[7] The problem of inter-industrial allocation of investment is easy to solve in terms of either of two extreme assumptions, viz. (*a*) that the commodities are perfectly complementary to each other without any element of substitutability, which is what is implied in the input-output analysis with unique input-coefficients, and (*b*) that they are completely substitutable, which is what is implied (normally implicitly) in using constant relative prices to determine the "best" fields for investment. The intermediate cases are, however, much more complex.

labour-intensive methods. . . . Japan provides abundant examples of this. Thus, the fact that the range of technological knowledge will itself be affected by the techniques chosen today need not destroy the case for choosing relatively labour-intensive techniques. It is possible, however, that in some economies it is anticipated that, given the growth prospects, the excess labour force would soon be absorbed, so that a movement towards a greater degree of mechanization would soon be, so to say, inevitable. In these cases there would be a number of reasons for considering the mechanized techniques more favourably, even for the choice faced now. In the first instance, an expansion of technical knowledge about mechanized production processes would be of considerable importance. While the underdeveloped nations might make use of the techniques used in the West, the changes necessary to suit the conditions of the availability of specific raw materials and other factors in the particular economies would have to be studied. Secondly, experience of modern industrial work would be of use for the labour force in the future. Finally, in the case of durable plants, there would be less cost of obsolescence. Thus, these long-run considerations might, to some extent, change our preference for labour-intensive techniques.

MECHANIZATION AND CAPITAL INTENSITY

In spite of all the questions we have raised above, there is little doubt that the case for choosing relatively labour-intensive techniques in the under-developed economies is not bad in many sectors of production. Provided we recognize that the case for this is not as simple as it looks at the first sight and that we have to investigate a number of things before we can say anything definitely, the proposition we have been examining can be accepted. We should not assume, however, that the case for a lower

degree of capital intensity is, necessarily, a case for a lower degree of mechanization. This is a question that we had postponed for a later discussion. What we mean by "mechanization" and by "capital-intensity" is, of course, a matter of definition, but since the terms have certain meanings in economic discussions, we have here an empirical question disguised in definitional form. By the degree of mechanization we normally mean the amount of machinery (valued in terms of costs of production) employed per person at a time. This is a ratio of two *stock* figures, viz., machines to labourers. The degree of capital intensity, however, is the ratio of the stock of investment (in fixed capital *and* in working capital) to the *flow* of labour (per day, or month, or year) working with it. The two can, and in fact, in many cases, do, move in opposite directions. There are two important reasons for this dichotomy. First the degree of mechanization will depend mainly on the technical possibilities at any point of time, whereas the degree of capital intensity, being a ratio of a flow figure to a stock figure, will depend also on the proportion of the time for which the plants are worked. For example, given the extent of mechanization, multiple-shift working will reduce the capital intensity of investment. Secondly, capital consists not merely of machines but also of working capital, and this is something that the degree of mechanization naturally leaves out. The inclusion of working capital into the picture would tend to weaken the case for less mechanized techniques, for, given the average lag between current inputs and outputs and the requirement of current inputs other than labour, a less mechanized technique will have a higher ratio of working capital to fixed capital. This consideration is often extremely important since handicraft production normally involves very little fixed capital.[8] A technique

[8] For an actual example of this in terms of the Indian cotton textile industry, see "Working Capital and the Rate of Surplus," by the writer, *Economic Weekly*, Annual Number, 1958.

may require no machines and still be extremely capital intensive.

The effect of the other reason for the divergence between capital intensity and mechanization, viz. the proportion of the time for which the plants are worked, will also tend to go against the less mechanized techniques. Because of the problems of industrial organization, many of the less mechanized techniques can be usefully employed only in small-scale industrial production and not in factory production. Precisely the reverse is true for many of the mechanized techniques. Now, most small-scale industries work only one shift a day for obvious social reasons, whereas many factories work round the clock, and those that do not, can do so if necessary with less trouble than the small-scale industrial units. This means that the degrees of capital intensity tend to be less different from one another than the degrees of mechanization, and, indeed, sometimes a lower degree of mechanization might involve a higher degree of capital intensity. It must be pointed out, therefore, that the case for relatively less capital-intensive techniques of production discussed above does not necessarily imply a case for less mechanized production.

VII.C. PROJECT APPRAISAL

VII.C.1. Plans and Projects*

A sound development plan requires a great deal of knowledge about existing and potential projects. This is obvious enough for a short-term operational plan (3–5 years) which should, among other things, contain firm and realizable plans for Government expenditure in different sectors. But it is just as true for a perspective plan, which covers a period of, say, 10–15 years.

Such a perspective plan will lay down target rates for gross national production, consumption, and also for investment and its financing by both domestic and foreign savings. For this to be done, it is clear that a relationship has to be assumed between the level of investment during the plan period (and also for several years prior to the plan period) and the rate of growth of domestic product which depends more or less closely on that level of investment.

This connection between investment and the rate of growth cannot be properly estimated without a great deal of knowledge about actual and potential investment projects. . . .

In principle, there are an infinite number of feasible plans, only one of which is the best of all. One can never hope to arrive at this optimum plan. But unless one strives continually to direct one's investment to those sectors where it would yield the most benefits to the economy, and within sectors to projects which yield most, one will certainly end up with a plan which is very far short of what could be achieved. Thus, if the division of investment between different sec-

*From Ian M. D. Little, "Project Analysis in Relation to Planning in a Mixed Economy," in OECD Development Center. *Development Problems*, Summary of Papers at the Colombo Seminar, Paris, 1967, pp. 47, 49–52, 54–65. Reprinted by permission.

tors of the economy is to be rational, it is essential that the costs and benefits of many different projects in each sector should be assessed on a comparable basis. Here, one must admit that there are limits to what economic analysis can achieve. No matter the sector of activity, costs are relatively easy to estimate on a comparable basis. But this is not always true of benefits. For instance, although there is by now a considerable body of work concerned with estimating the benefits of education and medical expenditure, one cannot be proud of, or place much confidence in, the results as yet. But no such strong reservations need be made in the important spheres of economic infrastructure, industry proper, and agriculture. In these spheres, although it is of course true that formal estimates of cost and benefit always go wrong, nevertheless it would be highly obscurantist to suggest that one should not try to peer into the future at all. And, if one is going to peer into the future, it is important to make sure that the manner in which it is done does not lead to biases as between different sectors and different projects. . . .

I have laboured the point that realistic plans cannot be formulated in the absence of a great deal of project planning, and without proper economic appraisal of projects. But it is also true that a good economic appraisal of projects often cannot be made without a plan.

Project appraisal obviously requires an estimate of the demand for the product. But how can one estimate the domestic demand for any product unless one has some idea of how the economy will develop? And how the economy develops in turn depends at least partly on the long-range plans and policies of the Government. . . .

In presenting the twin propositions that

448

"plans require projects" and "projects require plans," it may seem that an insoluble chicken and egg dilemma has been posed. If good plans cannot be formulated without a proper economic appraisal of projects, and if the real value of projects cannot be properly ascertained, except within the framework of a plan, where does one start? But the chicken and egg analogy is false, as one is never totally devoid of knowledge. Inadequate plans are first formulated using inadequate methods of project appraisal. These in turn should permit improvements in project analysis and appraisals, and so on. Macro-economic planning can be gradually improved in the light of improvements in micro-economic planning, and vice versa. By such iteration and reiteration, one gradually tries to come near to optimum planning.

PROFITABILITY ANALYSIS

In principle, one can approach an optimum investment plan only if all new projects are compared with each other with a view to seeing that none are rejected which are superior to any of those selected. In principle, of course, this implies that public sector projects are compared with those in the private sector, both being evaluated in the same manner. But in this section, I shall neglect the special problems which arise from trying to compare public and private projects, and I shall speak *as if* all projects were in the public sector. The proper integration of the public and private sectors will be briefly considered later.

In this section also, I shall concern myself only with the analysis of gross profits, that is, profits before depreciation is subtracted. Or to use another terminology, with pre-tax cash flows. Of course, decisions in the public sector should not necessarily be based on profitability, since there are many reasons for thinking that profits are not always a good measure of the net benefit to society. Nevertheless, profitability analysis and social cost-benefit analysis have much in common, and it is therefore convenient, first, to set

out the proper principles for the former, and then to modify it in such a way as to turn it into a social cost-benefit analysis. This helps to bring out the differences between the two, differences which are important in that the private sector will make its own decisions on the basis of profits alone (albeit net of tax).

A. The Basic Predictions. The basic figures required for economic appraisal, whether or not the appraisal limits itself to considering only actual cash flows, consists of a prediction of

a. all receipts from the sale of outputs of the project for each year of the life of the project, these including the sale of any buildings and equipment remaining at the end of the life of the project, and

b. all expenditures on goods and services according to the year in which they are made, from the date of the first expenditures until the end of the life of the project. These expenditures include capital expenditures, whether for initial equipment or for replacement, as well as all current costs.

Current expenditures may be subtracted from current receipts. One then has two streams, the first consisting of net current receipts (gross profits), and the second consisting of capital expenditures, whether for initial equipment or replacement. . . .

So far, it has been assumed that a single well-defined project is up for consideration. But, in principle, no such finalized version of the project should come forward without much consideration having been given to alternative ways of doing more or less the same thing. First, there is always the question of whether it would not have been better to design the project on a larger or a smaller scale. Secondly, given the scale, there are usually numerous alternative techniques which might have been employed. Each of these many alternatives arising out of possible differences of scale and techniques is in principle another project, which has been rejected. Each of these will have had techni-

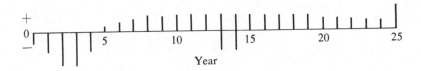

FIGURE VII.1. [1]

cal, managerial, and economic aspects. Were these alternatives properly assessed from these different angles before rejection? Naturally, one cannot fully evaluate a myriad of different possibilities before one of them is put forward for final consideration. Perhaps the most one can say is that those responsible for putting forward the final project, should be as aware as those who exercise the final choice of the need for proper appraisal and of the methodology which the final choosers operate. But, also, where important and feasible variants present themselves, and the economic choice is not obvious, the initiating departments should be encouraged to consult with the central project evaluators.

  B. *The Profitability Criterion.* I can now turn to describing the kind of analysis which the evaluators should conduct upon the basic figures already described. A diagram may be helpful here—see Figure VII.1 above:

—Above the line is measured the current cash flow (gross profits before depreciation). The exception is the last year, where the positive amount includes the disposal value of the terminal equipment.

—Below the line we have investment expenditures including replacement.

—The sum of the positive and negative items is the cash flow.

—Twenty-five years are included in the diagram. This is arbitrary, but unless the discount rate (see below) is extremely low, what happens after 25 years is very unlikely to make a significant difference.

Now suppose that the project can borrow any sums of money required at a fixed rate of interest. Using this market rate of interest, the next step is to discount all the net current receipts, and the investment expenditures back to the present, and add up.[1] This result is known as the *Present Value.* In symbols,

$$\sum_{t=1}^{t=25} \frac{X_t}{(1 + r)^t}$$

where X_t is the cash flow in year t, and r is the rate of interest.

  Ignoring risk (about which I shall say a few words later) it is logical to make any investment which results in a positive present value.

  A closely allied, but nevertheless different, procedure is to experiment until one has found that rate of discount which makes the present value equal to zero.

  In symbols one solves the equation

$$\sum_{t=1}^{t=25} \frac{X_t}{(1 + y)^t} = 0$$

for y. The solution (y) is called the *"Internal Rate of Return."* In a riskless situation, it

---

[1] Discounting simply means working compound interest backwards. For instance, £100 cumulated for two years at 10% interest becomes £121. £121 discounted at 10% for two years is £100.

pays to invest if the internal rate of return exceeds the rate of interest (if $y > r$).

The present value method is technically superior, since the internal rate of return can give an incorrect result in special circumstances. I shall not go into this. The only, but not unimportant, advantage of the internal rate of return (given that it does give the correct result) is that it is more familiar to administrators and businessmen. It is in fact the proper way to calculate what is familiarly and loosely known as the "yield."

Either of these methods is known as *"discount of cash flow analysis."* The point of using cash flow, rather than profits, is that replacement expenditures are explicitly accounted for, and the usual rather arbitrary methods of allowing for depreciation of capital are thereby avoided. The annual figures are gross of depreciation, but the final result is a *net* present value or *net* yield. The logic of the method is impeccable. It is now used by the most sophisticated firms in making their investment decisions, although the great majority still use much more rudimentary methods.

I have so far dealt with riskless cases only. There is no one correct method of allowing for risks. Two methods of approaching the problem are discussed briefly below.

First, one can use a higher rate of interest than the market rate for discounting purposes, or require that the internal rate of return substantially exceeds the market rate before embarking on an investment. The advantage of this is that the reduction of expected net receipts is greater the further in the future they are (and risks presumably increase with time). But it is rather mechanical, and leaves open the choice of how great the risk discount should be, and also the question of whether and how this risk discount should be varied between different classes of projects. While uniformity has advantages in preventing unconscious and irrational preferences from biasing the result,

there is the corresponding disadvantage that risks do differ between projects, and that they can to some extent be broken down for separate consideration instead of being lumped together in an overall risk allowance.

The second method is to try to make a high and a low estimate for each expenditure and receipt, and so produce a high and a low estimate of the present value, or the internal rate of return. The final step consists of some subjective evaluation of the result—and choice!

What I have said about risk is, of course, quite inadequate. But the subject had to be mentioned, if only because private entrepreneurs certainly make some allowance, however informal, while the subject is often not even mentioned where public sector projects are concerned.

SOCIAL COST-BENEFIT ANALYSIS

Three modifications may be made to the gross profitability analysis discussed above in order to turn it into a social cost-benefit analysis. They are as follows:

1. Other prices than those actually reigning may be used to value the inputs and outputs of the project. This is discussed below under the heading of *Shadow Prices.*

2. An allowance may be made for benefits or costs which arise elsewhere in the economy as a result of the operation or construction of the project. This will be discussed under the heading of *External Effects.*

3. The annual benefits and costs may be differently treated in a social cost-benefit analysis, as compared to a profitability analysis, in order to arrive at an investment criterion. Thus neither "present value" nor "the internal rate of return" may be appropriate. It is in fact necessary to introduce a new concept, the *"benefit-cost ratio."*

VII.C.2. Social Cost–Benefit Analysis*

In offering guidelines for the use of cost–benefit analysis in developing countries we pay special attention to industry and agriculture, as well as to infrastructural projects where the output has a market price. Education, health, and defence are neglected. This is not meant to imply that useful work is not going on in these fields: Certainly, cost-effectiveness analysis can be applied. But it is still very controversial whether full cost–benefit analysis in such sectors, where benefits are particularly difficult to measure, is as yet sufficiently soundly based to be a good guide for policy makers.

Thus we are concerned with the application of cost–benefit analysis precisely in fields in which it is considered unnecessary in developed economies. The justification for this can only be that it is felt that within such sectors of more advanced economies the price mechanism works in such a way that profits are a reasonable measure of net benefit, but that this is not true of most developing countries.

Why should one start with the presupposition that actual prices are very much worse reflectors of social cost and benefit than is the case in advanced economies? The main reasons are briefly adumbrated below.

Inflation

Very rapid inflation is more common in developing countries, particularly in South America. This is no accident. The very urgency of the desire to develop rapidly results in a constant tendency for demand to outrun supply: furthermore, lagging supply in the sectors which are most resistant to change, particularly agriculture, results in sectoral price rises which tend to transmit themselves across the board, and may virtually force the monetary authority to increase total money demand if a recession of activity is to be avoided.

If inflation proceeded uniformly so that relative prices were unaffected, it would not be a reason for prices to be a poor measure of real costs and benefits. But this, for institutional and political reasons, is seldom the case. For example, governments in such circumstances will often use price controls in selected fields where they can in practice be operated. This makes activity in these fields relatively or absolutely unprofitable, without regard to the net benefit of such activities.

A particular case of such control concerns the price of foreign exchange, which brings us to the next reason.

Currency Overvaluation

In almost all countries, the government "manages" the price of foreign exchange. With inflation, if the exchange rate is unaltered, domestic prices get out of line with world prices. This implies that on average, the rupee[1] prices of imports and exports are too low relative to those of goods which are not traded. So long as the currency is not devalued to rectify the situation, the demand for foreign exchange for imports and

*From I. M. D. Little and J. A. Mirrlees, *Project Appraisal and Planning for Developing Countries*, Heinemann, London, 1974, pp. 29–37. Reprinted by permission.

[1] We use 'rupees' to stand for the domestic currency unit, and 'dollars' to stand for a unit of foreign exchange. This is solely because it is awkward not to have a short familiar expression for these units: forced to choose, we selected rupees and dollars as being the units of the largest non-communist developing and developed countries respectively.

other purposes will exceed the supply, and the government will be forced to restrict imports, often in ways which open up gaps beween the market prices of goods and the real cost of procuring them. But some governments faced with a price inflation do not resort to import controls in order to maintain the domestic currency overvaluation, but devalue more or less frequently. If inflation is rapid and the government devalues periodically but not very frequently, then it is inevitable that the currency will be alternatively undervalued and overvalued. If the inflation is slow, the government usually tries to avoid devaluation, and long periods of overvaluation are likely.

Wage Rates, and Underemployment

It has been seen that the theory of competition requires that the marginal product of labour (the extra output resulting from the employment of a small extra amount of labour) be equal to the wage paid.

Because of monopoly power, and immobility, there are undoubtedly serious imperfections in the labour markets of many industrialized countries. But these imperfections are not usually thought to cause major intersectoral distortions of the pattern of production (regional distortions may be an exception, and here wage subsidies have been used). On the other hand, it is often argued that this is the case in many developing countries.

In "modern" sectors of the economy—including modern industry and commerce, government, and plantations—it is common to find that unskilled workers earn three or four times as much as casual rural labour, a difference far greater than can be accounted for by the difference in the cost of living; and therefore that the cost of employing people in these sectors is apparently much greater than the loss of rural production, assuming that such rural earnings are a fair measure of labour's marginal contribution to production. It has been argued that the earnings of casual labour overstate the marginal product of labour. This is because, in most developing countries, the greater part of rural labour is family labour. Since a dependent member of the family cannot be sacked, he may "earn" (i.e. consume) as much as a hired man but yet have a lower marginal product. As against this, in some places it is probable that the marginal product of a hired man is greater than his earnings because the employing farmers exercise some monopsonistic power.

That men by working are unable to contribute as much to production as they consume is what is meant by underemployment. The extended family system permits underemployment in the towns as well as the countryside. If relief were given institutionally, via unemployment benefits, the very low productivity urban activities—petty trading, car-watching, etc.,—would largely disappear and more people would become openly and wholly unemployed, a circumstance which would, of course, imply that wages did not reflect the social cost of employment.

The real cost of employing a man in the modern sector is still a subject of controversy, mainly because insufficient is known about the effects on the traditional sectors including agriculture, and because these effects will vary widely from country to country, and perhaps from region to region, or even town to town. However, there is rather wide agreement that modern sector wages almost everywhere overstate, perhaps greatly overstate, the social cost of employment.

Imperfect Capital Markets

Where risks are equal, interest rates on loans should be equal, if profits are to measure net social benefits. Interest rates have such an enormous range in many developing countries, that it is implausible to suggest that this is just a measure of differential risks. Other factors operate, such as government intervention, ignorance, and monopoly elements in the supply of capital, to widen the range from low to almost astronomical rates.

Large Projects

It is more common in developing countries—especially in small countries with, as yet, little development—that a project will be so large as to have important repercussions on profits elsewhere in the economy. In these circumstances, as we have seen, the profitability of the project itself cannot be regarded as a good measure of net social benefit.

Inelasticity of Demand for Exports

In a number of developing countries, a large part of export receipts is accounted for by one, two, or three export commodities. Where a country also accounts for a considerable part of total world production, then it can influence, within limits, the price it obtains by restricting sales—which is, of course, an abrogation of the conditions of perfect competition. The free market price cannot then correctly measure the benefit, because, like any monopolist, the country would gain if it exported less at a higher price.

This, in turn, implies that the country would gain by devoting rather less resources to producing these primary commodities, and rather more to others, or to industrialization. This situation can be best rectified by suitable export taxes on the commodities, together with other policies (including use of the revenue thus raised) which encourage the transfer of resources. Some countries recognize this situation and do in fact use export taxes. But the situation has also been used as an argument for encouraging industry by protection—which brings us to our next section.

Protection—Import Quotas, Tariffs, Export Disincentives

The protection of domestic industry may be a deliberate interference with the price mechanism designed to make it operate in a manner more conducive to society's benefit than would a laissez-faire commercial policy. A well-designed interference, in the shape of special encouragement of industrialization, may well make industrial profits a better guide to social advantage than they otherwise would be, either for the reasons given above, or for other reasons.

The main way in which industry is specially encouraged is by tarrifs and import quotas. Thereby, the domestic price of the output is kept above the import price. But the outputs of one industry are often the inputs of another. Consequently, when an industry contemplates exporting, it finds that the very system which protects it in its home market puts it at a positive disadvantage in export markets; whereas reason suggests that if industrial production is worth special encouragement, then it is worth special encouragement, and not actual discouragement, in producing for export. Thus tariff protection, like currency overvaluation, implies that the rupee price obtainable for an export underestimates the social value of that export. Some developing countries have taken measures to offset this effect, but such measures are often insufficient, and not very scientifically devised in such a way as to make the rupee price measure the benefit to the country.

Apart from the fact that protection discourages exports of both industrial and agricultural products, it is also the case that different industries receive enormously different degrees of protection, usually for no apparently rational economic reason. This situation has arisen partly because countries have selected industries or plants (or have agreed to protect private initiatives) without the kind of economic appraisal being advocated here. Protection has followed the establishment of industries, rather than itself being used as a screening device.

Another reason why the relative gap between domestic and world prices is highly divergent as between industries is the extensive use of import quotas. A country runs into balance of payments problems. The situation is brought under control by restricting imports and, naturally, the least essential goods are most restricted. The result may be a growth of domestic industry, behind protective quotas, which bears little relation to the long-run comparative advantage of the country. If a wrong industry gets established it handicaps any other industry which uses its output. For instance, steel-using industries will be handicapped by a high-cost local steel plant, unless the latter is subsidized so that it can supply at prices no higher than the import price. It is our belief that bad management of foreign trade or foreign exchange is one of the principal reasons why internal prices get highly distorted, and hence lead to industrial investments which are of little or no benefit to the country concerned.

We have now outlined seven important and fairly non-controversial reasons why the price mechanism and the profit motive may not work as closely for the social advantages as in developed countries. Other more general reasons could be adduced, such as ignorance of opportunities and techniques, inertia, short-sightedness, lack of a market economy, and greater fragmentation of markets leading to local monopoly power; but these have relatively little direct bearing on project evaluation especially in the public sector. We turn now to a further three reasons, which may be more controversial.

Deficiency of Savings, and Government Income

Two projects may have the same net profit, but a different effect on the relative amount of extra consumption, savings, and taxation.

As we saw, economic theory often treats savings and investment as of equal value. This is really a facet of the principle of consumers' sovereignty. It is assumed that it can make no difference to benefit whether some extra income is consumed, or saved and hence made available for investment. This is reasonable for an individual who freely chooses whether to spend or not. For him, an extra dollar of savings is worth the same as an extra dollar of consumption. But is it true for society?

To cut a long story short, if the government believes that rather more savings and rather less current consumption would be good for society, there may be a conflict. The point is that savings can be transformed into investment, and investment can produce extra future consumption for a sacrifice of present consumption: and the government may put a relatively higher value on the consumption of people in the future than do private persons. Furthermore, private persons may be inhibited from saving by income and other taxes which have the effect of double-taxing savings. We have already referred to these problems above, where it was argued that the rate at which society ought to discount the future may differ from the rate at which a firm can borrow. Thus, if the government chooses a discount rate for projects which is lower than the market rate of interest,[2] this is in effect to say that it considers future consumption to be more valuable than is indicated by the aggregate choices of private individuals. If the public saved more, interest rates would be lower, and the government pleased. In other words, the government considers present savings to be more valuable than present consumption.

Governments can reduce aggregate private consumption, and thus increase savings, by

[2] 'The market rate of interest' may be quite a wide band in developing countries, even if we restrict the meaning of 'the market' to that for medium and large scale industrial borrowing.

taxation. On the other hand, taxation has administrative and political costs. So perhaps it is money in the hands of the government which should be considered to be more valuable than private consumption: this view is strengthened by the fact that a rational government should see to it that the value of its expenditure at the margin is equal in all lines, whether it be defence, agricultural extension, education, or investing in industry. Many people will be rather unwilling to accept that money in the hands of the government is more useful than many kinds of private expenditure, especially when governments are seen to waste money and promote silly investments. But the project evaluator may in any case have to take a government view. This is a difficult and controversial matter, which will be taken up again.

Finally, it should be noted that although discussion of this problem has arisen mainly in the context of developing countries, it seems to us that it arises also in the case of rich countries.

The Distribution of Wealth

The preceding section was largely concerned with the distribution of benefits, as between the present and future. But there is also a problem of the distribution of benefits today—the problem of inequality, to which we have already referred. There is a dilemma here, for inequality tends to promote savings, and help future generations. This is especially true of corporations: company profits belong mainly to the rich, but are one of the main sources of saving. The dilemma can be made less acute insofar as public savings can, by increased taxation, take the place of savings of the rich; but there is a limit to this, and some element of dilemma remains.

The extent to which project selection should concern itself with different kinds of inequality will come up again. There is the additional important question of how far a practicable criterion for project selection can take proper account of inequalities.

External Effects

Some economists believe that external economies are of special importance in developing countries: that some industries have important beneficial effects on others in ways which cannot be, or anyway are not, reflected in the price obtainable for the output of the industry, or in the price it pays for its inputs. There has been much speculation and debate on this subject. But there is very little positive evidence. Certainly there has been much naive wishful thinking—for instance, that the provision of electricity, steel, or transport, would somehow create its own demand.

It was already shown that many of the more obvious external effects can be allowed for by a suitable definition of the project to be considered. But others will remain.

SOCIAL OBJECTIVES AND THE NOTION OF ACCOUNTING PRICES

A rather strong case has now been presented for saying that a project's anticipated receipts and expenditures cannot be relied upon to measure social benefits and costs in most developing countries. It is believed that this is true also of more developed economies, but to a lesser extent. There is therefore a strong *prima facie* case for the use of cost–benefit analysis.

We have seen that the basic idea of such an analysis is to use hypothetical rather than predicted actual prices when evaluating a project. The rate of discount may also not correspond to any actual interest rate. These 'shadow' prices, as they are often called, are chosen so as to reflect better the real costs of inputs to society, and the real benefits of the outputs, than do actual prices.

The name 'shadow price' is perhaps unfortunate. It suggests to many, even to some economists, that an analysis based on them is remote from reality, and therefore academic and highbrow, and so is to be distrusted. Of course, shadow prices may be unreal in that they are not the current prices of goods in a market. But then no price in a project analysis can ever be an actual price—for every price assumed in such an analysis necessarily lies in the future. The whole point of a shadow price is indeed that it shall correspond more closely to the realities of economic scarcity and the strength of economic needs than will guesses as to what future prices will actually be. From now on we shall use the term "accounting prices".

It is worth emphasis that if any input or output is valued at a different price from that actually expected to be paid or received by the project, then, in our terminology, a social accounting price is being used. In this sense, most project appraisals have made use of accounting prices. For instance, it is widely accepted in project analysis that indirect taxes on inputs should not be counted as costs. Or again, for some years now, direct imports and exports of projects have often been valued at c.i.f. or f.o.b. prices (border prices, as we shall term them) by, among others, consultants working for the IBRD. Some evaluators may think that they are not using shadow prices when they make such adjustments. That is a matter of terminology. What we want to make clear is that, in our terminology, they are using accounting prices.

While accounting prices have been in use for some time, they have seldom been used in a comprehensive and systematic way, but rather haphazardly. This is dangerous. Once some important prices become badly distorted—e.g. the price of labour or foreign exchange—the repercussions are widespread. Every price is then liable to need adjustment. What we are primarily concerned with in this book is to show how a whole set of accounting prices can be systematically and logically estimated and applied, yielding a practical method of analysis which can be expected to measure net social benefit better than ordinary profitability analysis. Being practical precludes perfectionism. We make no claim that accounting prices can be exact reflections of social costs and benefits—merely much better reflections than actual prices for many projects in many countries. Nor, of course, is it claimed that the use of accounting prices is a very satisfactory method of dealing with distortions. Many of the distortions can be fully dealt with only by removing them—that is, by adopting policies which lead to proper correspondence of prices, and costs and benefits. There may be yet others which, because of the difficulty of measuring them in a reasonably objective way, cannot be satisfactorily allowed for in a usable and politically acceptable criterion. These have to be left to the judgment of the politician and his advisers.

VII.C.3. Distortions in Factor Markets*

It is appropriate to begin by stating the obvious: cost-benefit analysis is undoubtedly the most used, and arguably the most useful, form of *applied welfare economics*. Its theoretical basis as well as its limitations are therefore necessarily those of its parent, *theoretical welfare economics*. This paper is not

*From Deepak Lal, *Methods of Project Analysis: A Review*, World Bank Staff Occasional Papers No. 16, Johns Hopkins University Press, Baltimore, 1974, pp. xiii–xvii, 24–38. Reprinted by permission.

for those who deny any practical use for theory, but for those who whilst recognizing the limitations of theoretical welfare economics nevertheless feel that in our present state of knowledge it provides the only basis for making an economic assessment of investment plans and proposals.

The purpose of any project selection procedure must be to provide a decision rule for accepting or rejecting a project. The net present value (NPV) or the internal rate of return (IRR) of the project are the indices usually used. Our chief concern in this paper will be with first, what should be included in the time stream of benefits and costs; secondly, what are the relevant values of the various cost-benefit components; and thirdly, how the discount rate (or rates) needed for determining the *NPV,* or the cut-off *IRR* at which projects are accepted, should be chosen. Most of the differences in the alternative procedures relate to apparently differing prescriptions in these three respects.

It will be repeatedly emphasized in this paper that any substantive differences among the alternative procedures are in large part dependent upon differing assumptions about the relevant aspects of the economic environment in which the investment decisions are being made. One of the basic purposes of this paper will be to demonstrate that, *in principle,* most of the suggested procedures are equivalent, if the same assumptions are made about the economic environment, though naturally there are differences in *emphasis* as to which set of assumptions is more relevant for LDC's in general, and more importantly in the *practical* problems of estimating the relevant values to be included in the *NPV/IRR* index, with accuracy and ease.

The reason why *in principle* most of the methods are equivalent, given the same basic assumptions about the economic environment, is their common lineage—theoretical welfare economics. One of its basic results is that in a perfectly competitive economy (with no uncertainty about future tastes and technology), allocation of resources on the basis of market prices of goods and factors (for which markets exist) would result in Pareto optimality for a given income distribution.[1] Market prices of goods and factors

would equate and equal the marginal social cost (*MSC*) of producing and the marginal social value (*MSV*) of using the relevant goods/factors. For a truly marginal investment project (in the sense that it does not alter the *MSV* and *MSC*'s of the output it produces and inputs it uses as a result of its operation), the values of the output and inputs at market prices would provide the correct values to be used in determining the net present value of the project.[2] Market prices would be the "shadow" prices to be used in project selection.

If the investment project being considered is not marginal (or if there are externalities), and does affect the *MSV* and *MSC*'s of its output and inputs, then the relevant measures of the social benefits and costs of the project will be the change in the consumers' and producers' surpluses caused by the project. This, in principle, will be the procedure recommended by *all* the project selection procedures we shall consider. In the case of the perfectly competitive model, valuation of the changes in producers' and consumers' surpluses, at market prices, will provide the correct indication of the net social benefits of the project.

---

[1] Pareto optimality necessitates that for a given distribution of income:

(i) the marginal rates of transformation in production of different commodities are equal to their marginal rates of substitution in consumption,

(ii) the marginal rates of substitution between any pair of factors are the same in all the industries in which they are used,

(iii) the marginal rates of substitution of any pair of commodities is the same for all individuals consuming both goods.

Given that the above conditions hold, a Pareto optimum will exist, such that for the given income distribution it will not be possible to make one person better off without making someone else worse off. Treating the same physical commodity at different dates as many different commodities, equivalent intertemporal marginal equivalences for an efficient intertemporal program can be derived. See Dorfman, Samuelson and Solow [2].

[2] The net benefits being discounted at the optimal discount rate which equates the marginal rate of transformation (*mrt*) in production of present into future consumption, to its marginal rate of indifferent substitution (*mrs*) in consumption, determined in a perfect market for intertemporal consumption.

To the extent, however, that the perfectly competitive paradigm does not hold— for example due to the existence of monopolies, taxes and subsidies, externalities, and/or increasing returns—market prices will no longer indicate the *social* costs and benefits of using and producing different commodities. The social cost to be included in the *NPV/IRR* index of social profitability, properly defined, will still be the marginal social cost of the various inputs used, and the social benefit will be the marginal social value of the output produced. However, the breakdown of the perfectly competitive assumptions results in market prices no longer equating and equaling the *MSC* and *MSV* of the relevant commodities. The market price will not equal either the *MSV* or *MSC*—and in some cases of rationing may not equal either. The problem then is to adjust the market price to obtain the relevant "shadow" prices, which are therefore generally needed in investment appraisal because of the divergence between the *MSC* and *MSV* of the relevant commodities.

If neutral fiscal devices (lump-sum taxes and subsidies) are feasible, then a full Pareto optimum could still be achieved if the government eliminates the divergence between *MSC* and *MSV* by suitably corrective tax-subsidy measures, thereby restoring the equivalence of *MSC* and *MSV* with the market price of the commodity. However, for obvious reasons it will not be possible, in most cases, to cure the divergence in this manner. In that case, the divergence between the *MSC* and *MSV* of the commodity may have to be taken as a datum (or a constraint) and the "shadow" prices corresponding to this constrained (or "second-best") welfare optimum will need to be computed. A large number, if not most, of the shadow prices which we shall consider are of this "second-best" kind.

Second, even if the government can eliminate the divergence between *MSC*'s and *MSV*'s by suitable tax-subsidy policy, it may take time for the divergence to disappear. Then current market prices will not equate

the *MSC* and *MSV* of the relevant commodities, but it is expected that future market prices will. As investment takes time and its effects are extended into the future, it is clearly the *MSC*'s and *MSV*'s of the relevant inputs/outputs appropriately dated which will be relevant in working out the project's social profitability. If it appears likely that in the future an existing divergence between *MSC* and *MSV* will be corrected, the appropriately dated price which reflects the social cost/benefit of the project will not be the current market price, nor the current *MSC* and *MSV* of the commodity, but rather the "equilibrium" price which is expected to prevail in the future. In this sense, even when an economy is moving towards an optimal set of market prices, from a distorted current set, it may be necessary to use "shadow" prices corresponding to the *future* optimal market prices, rather than the *current* market or shadow prices for pricing inputs and outputs which form the time stream of benefits and costs of the investment project.

Third, even for a perfectly competitive economy, there will be different Pareto optima associated with different income-distributions. Judging between these different Pareto optima will necessarily involve normative judgments about the desirability of particular income distributions.[3] Even if agreement can be reached on the desired income-distribution, there will still be the problem of legislating this "optimal" distribution. Again if neutral fiscal devices in the form of lump-sum taxes and subsidies are feasible, the government would be able to achieve a Pareto optimum with the optimal distribution of income. If however, as is more likely, neutral fiscal instruments are

[3] It being noted that investment projects affect both the intratemporal as well as the intertemporal distribution of income; the former by the distribution of their net benefits amongst contemporaries at a point in time, and the latter by the distribution of net benefits as between generations, over a period of time.

not available, then the distributional effects of investment projects will also have to be computed, and judged against and along with their purely "production" or "efficiency" effects. These problems open up other areas where there may possibly be conflicting judgments, and hence prescriptions for project selection procedures.

Practical Problems

These theoretical problems are compounded by practical ones. First, even though there may be agreement about the nature of the correct prices to be used in project selection, there may, nevertheless be disagreement as to whether or not the existing divergences between MSV's and MSC's which affect these prices will continue into the future or whether they will change. Depending on what assumption is made about the future course of the economy, the "second-best" or "first-best" shadow price will be the relevant one to choose.[4] In a sense, this is an empirical question; but to the extent that future government policies are normally unknown, the element of judgment involved in deciding which of these alternative assumptions is relevant, when considering existing distortions in commodity and factor markets, will be of paramount importance in deciding which is the correct "shadow" price to use. Hence it is important to remember that differing prescriptions on alternative evaluation procedures will most often be due to differing implicit assumptions about the current and, more importantly, the future economic environment.

Second, though we have been discussing the evaluation of a particular project and the social valuation of its inputs and outputs in what may appear to be a partial equilibrium framework, in principle, any proper investment criteria must take account of the total

[4] The second-best shadow price is that associated with continuing divergences, the first-best, that with no divergence, between MSV and MSC.

(direct and indirect) or what are termed the general equilibrium effects of the investment project. Thus for instance if an industrial project employs some seemingly underemployed labor in the urban sector, the ultimate effects via the impact on rural-urban migration could be a significant change in total output of the economy. The shadow wage rate will then in this case have to incorporate both the direct and indirect (via migration) effects of increasing industrial employment. The MSC's and MSV's which are taken as the "shadow" prices in determining the social profitability of the investment project, must therefore be the general equilibrium "shadow prices." This might appear to be an impossible task, but the relative merits of alternative investment appraisal procedures will depend upon their success in taking account of the general equilibrium effects of projects, which will in turn, if the procedures are to be *practical*, necessitate making certain simplifying assumptions about the economic environment. Once again, these assumptions, though empirical in nature, require judgment, and hence there can be disputes as to whether or not the simplifying assumptions are "realistic" or relevant or both.

For all the above reasons, even though all the procedures we will consider start from the same theoretical foundations, and hence are identical if equivalent assumptions are made, they may nevertheless differ to the extent that, in practice, they emphasize one set of assumptions about the economic environment rather than another. Hence, the continuing charges and countercharges that a particular procedure has ignored or assumed away an important aspect of reality, and is hence invalid; as well as the impression conveyed to neutral observers of shadow boxing on the part of different protagonists, and bafflement at the conflicting claims and counterclaims that are made for different procedures. This, however, does not imply that in practice certain procedures are not more general and easier to apply than others.

However, it may be more important to begin by realizing that the similarities amongst the procedures are far greater than the differences. . . .

DISTORTIONS IN FACTOR MARKETS

In this part we relax the assumption made that factor markets are perfectly competitive. We now introduce factor market distortions but, for simplicity and clarity, assume away all other distortions. Thus the domestic market prices of the two primary factors will no longer be taken to equal their *social* opportunity costs, as we had hitherto assumed. Distortions in both the markets for labor and capital have been discussed in the project evaluation literature. The two fully fledged evaluation procedures, the UNIDO and Little-Mirrlees procedures, identify the same distortions and, except for some differences in assumptions about the likely future changes in some of the divergences, provide identical rules in principle, except for a difference in numeraire. The UNIDO procedures take current consumption as their numeraire, the Little-Mirrlees current savings.[5] Note that current savings generate the time stream of future consumption. As consumption, following the practice in theoretical welfare economics, is identified as the source of economic welfare, this means that the net benefits will be dated consumption, and there will be the problem of making commensurable present consumption and future consumption. As long as the same relative price between present and future consumption is used to "add up" the intertemporal net benefits of the project, it does not matter which of the two relevant "commodities" (present consumption or future con-

sumption [savings]), we take as our numeraire.[6]

We turn first to examine the adjustments necessary to take account of the distortions in the market for capital.

Capital

Savings and investment are the means for changing the time shape of the intertemporal consumption stream which is feasible given resource and technological transformation constraints. The capital market intermediates between those making savings and investment decisions. In a perfect capital market, the social return from one unit of current savings (the net present value of the consumption stream made possible by one unit of current savings) at the margin, is equal to the social value of one unit of current consumption. The former will depend upon the opportunities open to society in production, to convert one unit of present consumption into future consumption—that is, the social productivity of investment—the latter on the weight society places on one unit of future consumption in terms of present consumption—the social rates of time preference. In a perfect capital market, the rate of interest R will equal and equate the marginal rate of transformation (mrt) of present into future consumption, and the marginal rate of indifferent substitution (mrs) of present and future consumption. That is $R = mrt = mrs$, of the two "commodities" present and future consumption. Distortions in the capital market will drive a wedge between the components of the above marginal equivalence, so that $mrt \neq mrs$. Moreover, the rate of interest may not equal either the mrt or mrs. Furthermore, if the

---

[5] More precisely the *LM* numeraire is "uncommitted social income measured at border prices." It need not be saved, but could be spent on uses (like administration, health, law and order, et cetera) which are considered as useful as savings by the government.

[6] The only difference will be the "cosmetic" one that the appropriate discount rate to be used with savings as the numeraire will generally be *higher* than that to be used with consumption as the numeraire.

capital market is segmented, there may be a multiplicity of rates of interest.

Two basic sources of distortion have been identified as causing the divergence between the mrt and mrs of present and future consumption. One is due to the presence of externalities, the other to the presence of monopolistic or fiscal distortions or both in the capital market. We will consider the causes and adjustments for the former type of distortion, the causes of the latter type being self-evident, and the remedies being similar to those suggested for the former type.

The source of the externality in the capital market is due to the interdependence and the mortality of private savers. Being mortal, they cannot be expected to extend their altruism to the infinite generations which are properly the concern of a society, which at least in principle, is immortal. As a result, the savings (future consumption) generated, *ceteris paribus*, as a result of the decisions of private savers is likely to be less than socially optimal. Furthermore, *if* private savers knew that everyone else was going to save at the socially optimal rate, then they too would agree to save at this rate. Hence, the externality. The result is that the private rate of time preference is higher than the social. Under laissez faire, a perfect capital market would insure that enough savings would be invested until the social return to investment (savings) fell to the private rate of time preference. That is the private marginal rate of substitution (mrs_p) in consumption would be equated to the private and *ex hypothesi, social*, marginal rate of transformation (*mrt*) in production, of present into future consumption. However, as the externality causes the marginal *private* rate of substitution to be higher than the marginal *social* rate of substitution (*mrs*), we have $mrs_p = mrt > mrs$.

Once again the first best solution would be to cure the above divergence, by appropriate tax-subsidy policy; in this case by using fiscal policy to raise the savings rate in the economy till mrs_p and *mrt* had become equal to *mrs*. Note that as the savings level is raised toward the optimal level, *mrs* will rise and mrs_p and *mrt* will fall.

However, the government may have imperfect control over savings in the economy, and may not be able to legislate the optimal savings rate by direct fiscal means. In that case, it will be necessary to take account of the divergence in the *mrt* and *mrs* in the capital market. As long as the divergence exists, current savings are socially more valuable than current consumption. Hence, if the government can indirectly, through its choice of projects, influence the savings rate, this "savings constraint" may be overcome over time till savings and consumption are considered to be equally socially valuable. The way in which the government could influence the savings-consumption balance of the economy through project choice is by influencing the choice of techniques and by choosing projects whose benefits tend to be saved and reinvested rather than consumed.

The way in which both the UNIDO and *LM* [Little-Mirrlees] procedures take account of the divergence is by differentially weighting the project's net benefits which are consumed and those which are saved. *The only difference between the procedures in principle is the difference in numeraires.* Whereas (a) the UNIDO procedures use *present consumption* as the numeraire, and put a *premium on savings*, (b) the *LM* procedures use *current savings* as the numeraire, and *penalize consumption*. To see this, consider the following simple algebraic example.

Algebraic Example: First, consider the procedure adopted in the UNIDO *Guidelines*, which takes *consumption as its numeraire*. Assume that the net benefits from a project in any year (t) are Bt, and that of these 0 percent in any year are saved and reinvested and $(1 - 0)$ percent are consumed. The social rate of time preference today is d_0, and the social return to investment today is r_0 ($r_0 > d_0$). Moreover, over time, the divergence between r and d is likely to diminish, till T years from today the divergence will disappear (the level of savings will be optimal). Finally, the project incurs capital costs of K in the base year, yielding the stream of net benefits for N years.

To obtain the social profitability of the project we first note that the opportunity cost of the capital costs K is the present value of the future consumption which would have resulted if Rs K of present investment were made at the current social rate of return to investment, r_0. Thus, if Rs 1 of current investment, which is assumed to remain intact forever, leads to net output of Rs 1.1 in the next period, $r_0 = 1.1/1 = .1$. Part of this return (θ) will be saved and invested. Hence, the increase in investment next year $(t = 1)$ will be $[1 (1 + r_0) - 1] \theta = r_0 \theta$. Total investment next year will therefore be $(1 + r_0 \theta)$. The year after next $(t = 2)$ investment will increase by $[(1 + r_0 \theta)(1 + r_1) - (1 + r_0 \theta)] \theta = (1 + r_0 \theta) r_1 \theta$. Total investment in year $t = 2$ will therefore be $[(1 + r_0 \theta) r_1 y \theta + (1 + r_0 \theta)] = (1 + r_0 \theta)(1 + r_1 \theta)$. Hence, by year T, when the savings constraint ceases to operate, total investment would have accumulated to: $(1 + r_0 \theta)(1 + r_1 \theta) \ldots (1 + r_{T-1} \theta)$. To get the present value of this accumulated investment which, *ex hypothesi*, is as valuable as an equal amount of consumption at T, we have to discount its value back to the present $(t = 0)$ at the changing social rates of time preference $(d_0, d_1, d_2 \ldots d_T)$, period by period. This present value is:

$$(1 + r_0 \theta)(1 + r_1 \theta) \ldots (1 + r_{T-1} \theta)/ (1 + d_1)(1 + d_2) \ldots (1 + d_T) \qquad (1)$$

In addition to this accumulated investment, the initial Rs 1 of investment will have resulted in consumption of $(1 - \theta)(1 + r_0 \theta)$ in $t = 1$; of $(1 - \theta)(1 + r_0 \theta)(1 + r_1 \theta)$ in $t = 2$; and hence in year t of $(1 - \theta)(1 + r_0 \theta)(1 + r_1 \theta) \ldots (1 + r_{t-1} \theta)$. The present value of this stream of consumption is:

$$\sum_{t=0}^{T} \frac{(1 - \theta)(1 + r_0 \theta) \ldots (1 + r_{t-2} \theta)(1 + r_{t-1} \theta)}{(1 + d_1) \ldots (1 + d_{t-1})(1 + d_t)} \qquad (2)$$

Confining our time horizon to T, the present value of the stream of consumption made possible by Rs 1 of investment today (s_0) is then:

$$s_0 = (1) + (2) \qquad (3)$$

The social opportunity costs of capital expenditure of K today are therefore $s_0 K$.

The benefits are B_t in year (t), of which θB_t will be saved and invested. The value of this savings in terms of consumption at date t will be given by the social opportunity cost of investment in year t, which on an analogous argument to that for deriving s_0, will be s_t. The rest of the benefits $(1 - \theta) B_t$ will be consumed in year t. Hence, the present value of the stream of net benefits will be given by:

$$\sum_{t=0}^{N} \frac{(1 - \theta) B_t + s_t \theta B_t}{(1 + d_1)(1 + d_2) \ldots (1 + d_t)} \qquad (4)$$

and the *NPV* of the project will be given by:

$$NPV = (4) - s_0 K \qquad (5)$$

Thus on the "generalized" UNIDO procedures[7] it is necessary to know both the changing social return to investment (the r_t's) as well as the changing social rates of discount (the d_t's). Moreover, the discount rate used to obtain the *NPV* of the project will be the social discount rates d_t's.

The alternative *LM procedure* takes *savings as its numeraire*, and uses the own rate of return on investment (called the accounting rate of interest, *ARI*) as the discount rate. However, as we will show, it is identical to the "generalized" UNIDO procedures, except for the change in numeraire. Following the same argument as before, and making

[7] "Generalized" because, as the next section explains, the way in which s is calculated on the UNIDO *Guidelines* assumes that its value remains constant over time. This, in practice, is likely to be an implausible assumption. But as the above account suggests, the UNIDO approach can be generalized, so that it is identical to the *LM* one, except for the change in numeraire.

the same assumptions, we found that Rs 1 of investment yielded a present value of total future consumption generated by the investment of s_0. That is, Rs 1 of current savings (investment) is worth s_0 of present consumption. Consumption therefore has $(1/s_0)$ the value if the same resources had been invested. In year 1, therefore, the value of $(1 - \theta)(1 + r_0\theta)$ consumption generated is $(1 - \theta)(1 + r_0\theta)/s_1$. In year t, the value of the consumption generated from the net benefits of the project will be $B_t(1 - \theta)/s_t$.

In each year there will also be yB_t savings generated, and these will be valuable at par, as savings is our numeraire. The total value, in terms of savings of the net benefits in any year, will then be:

$$B_t(1 - \theta)/s_t + \theta B_t$$

These total savings benefits in each year have then to be discounted back to the present at the accounting rate of interest, (ARI) (p_t)[8] in each period to get the present savings value of the project. Hence, the NPV of the project on the LM procedures will be given by:

$$NPV = \sum_{t=0}^{N}$$

$$\frac{B_t(1 - \theta)/s_t + \theta B_t}{(1 - p_1)\dots(1 + p_{t-1})(1 + p_t)} - K \quad (6)$$

Note that as savings is our numeraire, the capital costs K, incurred in year 0 are valued at par.

[8] Thus, if say Rs 1 of investment today leads to a net return of Rs 0.1 tomorrow, of which half (.05) is saved and invested, and if consumption has no social value in terms of the numeraire savings, then the ARI is $.05/1 = .05$. If on the other hand, consumption and savings are considered socially equally valuable, then the ARI would be $.1/1 = 0.1$. In general if the value of one unit of consumption in terms of savings is $1/s$, the ARI in this example will be $(.05 + .05/s)$.

Moreover, the *LM Manual* derives a relationship between p_t, s_t, and d_t. It is:

$$s_t/s_{t+1} = (1 + p_t)/(1 + d_t) \quad (7)$$

Now *consider a two period case*, that is from $t = 0$ to $t - 1$. For the project to be acceptable *on the LM criterion*, the NPV given by (6) should be positive, that is:

$$\frac{B_1[(1 - \theta)(1/s_1) + \theta]}{(1 + p_1)} \geqslant K \quad (8)$$

Multiplying both sides of (8) by s_1, and then dividing both sides by $s\sqrt{s_0}$, we get:

$$\frac{B_1[(1 - \theta) + \theta s_1]}{s_1/s_0 \cdot (1 + p_1)} \geqslant s_0 K \quad (9)$$

From (7) the denominator of the *LHS* of (9) is equal to $(1 + d_1)$, hence, we get (9) equal to:

$$\frac{B_1[(1 - \theta) + \theta s_1]}{(1 + d_1)} \geqslant s_0 K \quad (10)$$

as the criterion for accepting a project on the *LM* procedure.

But now consider the same two period case *on the UNIDO procedures*; the acceptance criterion is that the NPV given by (5) be positive; and it can be seen from (4) and (5) that this gives the identical result (10) as the criterion of acceptability. *Hence, the two procedures LM and UNIDO are identical* in terms of the information needed to take account of suboptimal savings. The differences in the discount rates on the two procedures (the ARI on the LM, the social rate of discount on the UNIDO) *merely reflect a change in numeraire.*

LM and UNIDO in Practice: To show the equivalence *in principle* of the two procedures, in the above algebraic example, we had assumed that the value of s is calculated on the UNIDO procedures *on the LM assumption* that savings and consumption will be equally valuable T years from today. *In practice*, however, the formula given by UNIDO to calculate the value of s assumes that the divergence in the relative social value of aggregate consumption and savings, and hence the value of s *remains constant* till infinity. Thus the UNIDO formula for calculating s is:

$$s = (1 - \theta)r/(d - \theta r),$$

where y = marginal propensity to save,
r = rate of return on investment, and
d = social rate of discount of consumption.

(See UNIDO [32], p. 175 onwards.) This equation will only provide meaningful values if $d > \theta r$, otherwise the social value of investment (s) will be infinite (see UNIDO [32], p. 189). There is no plausible economic reason why d must necessarily be greater than θr.[9] Moreover, the actual value of s given by the formula will be very sensitive to the values chosen for d, θ and r, and small differences in the values of these variables could lead to large differences in the value of s.

The assumption of a constant divergence in the relative social values of aggregate consumption and savings, and hence a constant s must therefore be rejected in favor of the more plausible *LM* assumption that this divergence disappears after T years and hence s will typically fall over time to a value of unity at T.[10]

Finally, it should be emphasized that both procedures require information on the social rate of discount and the social rate of return to investment in the economy. We

therefore next examine how these parameters can be estimated.

Estimating the Intertemporal Parameters:[11] The *LM Manual* gives a formula [12] relating the ARI_0 (p_0), and the social discount rate (d_0) to s_0 and T. This is:

$$s_0 = [1 + \tfrac{1}{2}(p_0 - d_0)]^T \qquad (11)$$

Given the definition of the ARI:

$$p_0 = r_0 [\theta + (1 - \theta)/s_0] \qquad (12)$$

Hence, substituting (12) into (11) we have:

$$s_0 = \left\{ 1 + \tfrac{1}{2} [r_0 (\theta + (1 - \theta)/s_0) - d_0] \right\}^T (13)$$

This formula succinctly expresses the various intertemporal parameters we need to estimate. These are r_0, d_0, T and θ; and given these s_0 will be determined.

The social return to investment is r_0 and θ is the percentage of this return saved; r_0 will thus be the return at accounting prices from marginal current investments. On certain plausible assumptions,[13] this return can be derived as a weighted average of social rates of profits on existing investments in the economy. θ, can be estimated from data on savings propensities and tax rates.

This leaves d_0, the social discount rate, and T the date when savings and consumption are expected to be equally valuable, to be estimated.

The social discount rates (d_t) reflect the distributional weighting given to income

---

[9] Thus Maurice Scott points out that "one could argue that d should be zero in Mauritius (with per capita consumption roughly constant) while y and r are both positive."

[10] Another consequence of assuming a constant s ($s_t = s_{t+1}$) is that from (7) above the discount rate ($p_t = d_t$) is the same on both *LM* and UNIDO procedures.

[11] A fuller discussion is contained in Lal [11].

[12] See Little and Mirrlees [14], p. 179, and Lal [10], Appendix II.

[13] See Lal [11] for the derivation of such a rate from a heterogenous capital dual economy model which avoids the capital theoretic problems arising for derivations based on aggregate production functions. This method is also similar to that advocated by Harberger; see his *Project Evaluation: Collected Papers*. Chicago; 1972. For an application of the method, see Lal [10], Appendix II.

(consumption) transfers between generations. In determining these weights it is plausible to assume that as a result of the normal processes of growth, future generations will in any case be richer than present ones. Just how much richer will depend upon the expected rate of growth per capita consumption over the future. Suppose the latter rate is g. Further assume that the elasticity of social marginal utility (defined as the percentage change in social utility resulting from a percentage change in consumption) with respect to per capita changes in consumption is e. Then it can be shown[14] that

$$d_t = (1 + g_t)^e - 1 \qquad (14)$$

This leaves T, which is rather harder to determine. However, from projections of expected growth rates of national income and savings, it may be possible to arrive at some estimate of the likely date by which savings are likely to be sufficient to give an adequate long term growth rate. This date can then be taken to be T.

Labor[15]

One of the most common forms of distortion identified in the project evaluation literature is in the labor markets of surplus labor economies, such that the wage rate does not equal the social opportunity cost of labor in the economy.

Two components have been traditionally identified in the social opportunity cost of labor in surplus labor economies. The *first* is the output foregone elsewhere in the economy, as a result of employing labor on the project. The *second* are the costs in terms of increased aggregate consumption that may

[14] Assuming a constant elasticity social utility function (U) which has per capita consumption (C) as one of its arguments, then $U = C^e$, and $d_t = (U_t^l/U_{t+1}^l)C$, and $g = (C_{t+1} - C_t)/C_t$. Hence $d_t = (1 + g)^e - 1$.

[15] This section is based on Lal [9], where a fuller treatment of the subject may be found.

result as more labor (which consumes most of its income) is employed on the project. If, due to the nonoptimality of savings (discussed above) present consumption is socially less valuable than current savings, then any increase in aggregate consumption, caused by increasing employment as a result of the project, will not be as valuable as the equivalent amount of savings. This factor will have to be reflected in the measure of the social opportunity cost of labor.

To concretize this, consider a particular formulation of the social opportunity cost of labor, that is the shadow wage rate (SWR) due to LM. Except for a change in numeraire, which LM take to be "savings" rather than consumption, their analysis is similar to other well-known ones due to Sen and Marglin, and which have been incorporated in the UNIDO procedures.

Assume first that the wage paid to a laborer in his new job, c, is above the value of the output foregone elsewhere by moving him from his previous employment, m. Second, given the nonoptimality of savings, and taking savings as the numeraire, one unit of current consumption is socially worth $(1/s)$ units of current savings. *The s factor is the same as in the discussion of capital* in the previous section. Then, the costs of employing one more person in the economy (in terms of savings) are given by:

$$SWR = m + (c - m) - (c - m)/s \qquad (15)$$

The first term on the *RHS* is the output foregone elsewhere in the economy, which has been traditionally identified with the marginal product of labor in agriculture. In addition, assuming that workers in both industry and agriculture consume all their incomes, the economy will be committed to providing them with extra consumption of $(c - m)$ as $c > m$. This increase in aggregate consumption must be at the expense of aggregate savings given the well-known Keynesian national income identities. But given the non-optimality of savings, this increase in aggregate consumption (decrease in savings) must represent a social cost. As, *ex hypothesi*, society values s units of consumption as equal in social value to one unit of savings, the net social cost of the increase in consumption (in terms of the numeraire, savings) will be

$$(c - m) - (c - m)s$$

which are the second and third terms of (15). The above expression reduces to:

$$SWR = c - (c - m)/s \qquad (16)$$

We now turn to the determination of the output foregone (m), and various other complications in determining the *SWR*, in the following sections.

Output Foregone: In most conventional analyses the output foregone m, in the above *SWR* formulation, has been identified with the marginal product of the relevant labor in its previous employment. While this would, given certain other assumptions to be discussed, be correct for labor which was previously in wage employment, it may not in general be correct for labor which was previously self-employed. This is an important consideration, in view of the fact that in most developing countries a substantial portion of the labor force is self-employed.

Moreover, in most conventional analyses it was also assumed that the marginal product of the laborer withdrawn from the traditional sector, agriculture, would be zero and hence $m = 0$. In a definitive analysis of dualism and surplus labor within a model of family farms on which there is equal work and income sharing, and which explicitly incorporated leisure as an argument in the individual peasant's utility function, Sen [28] demonstrated that zero marginal productivity was not a necessary condition for the existence of surplus labor. The necessary and sufficient conditions are given by a constant disutility of effort, which implies a constant marginal rate of substitution between income and leisure over the relevant range of hours worked per man, in the tradi-

tional sector. Given this, output in the traditional sector would not fall with the withdrawal of workers, and hence for them $m = 0$, even though the marginal productivity of labor was positive in the traditional sector. Thus, in general, for a family farm worker withdrawn from a farm without any hired labor, the change in output will not equal his marginal product.

Divergence Between Average and Marginal Costs: Certain writers have noted that the conventional analysis may *understate* the extra consumption cost of industrial labor. This is due to the assumption made in these analyses that "agricultural" workers can be hired by the "industrial" sector at a constant real wage (W_i), which is either given by a constant institutional wage, or else by a constant supply price of labor to the industrial sector. Dixit [1] suggests that this assumption may be unrealistic, especially if there are terms of trade effects following a withdrawal of labor from agriculture. Then, if the industrial labor market is competitive, the supply price of labor to industry and hence the industrial wage will rise with increased industrial employment.[16] This will create a divergence between the *average (c)* and *marginal (c + Δc)* cost of hiring industrial labor. The extra consumption the economy will be committed to will then be given by the difference between the *marginal* cost

---

[16] In the simple closed economy two-sector model analyzed by Dixit [1], the supply price of industrial labor is equal to the income foregone by agricultural family workers moving to industrial jobs. In short run equilibrium their income foregone is determined by the average physical product of labor in agriculture (assuming equal income sharing among family farm workers) and the relative price of agriculture output. With the withdrawal of an agricultural worker, the average product of labor in agriculture rises, while total agricultural output (assuming no surplus labor) falls. This last factor leads to a rise in the relative price of agricultural output. The net effect is to raise the average value product of labor in agriculture and hence the supply price of labor to the industrial sector.

of hiring $(c + \Delta c)$ and output foregone, m. Hence:

$$SWR = (c + \Delta c) - (c + \Delta c - m)/s \quad (17)$$

and if the premium placed on savings is very high $(s \to \infty)$, the SWR will be higher than the market wage (c). Note, however, that if there is a constant institutional wage in the industrial sector, then $c = 0$, and the SWR will be given as before by (16).

Rural-Urban Migration: As certain models of the labor market in developing countries have emphasized, the impact on net output in the economy cannot be deduced from the impact effects on output in the sector from which the new worker may be withdrawn. Hence, to obtain the value of m, it will be necessary to trace through all the indirect effects, in terms of the rural-urban migration that may ensue, as the result of creating one new job in, say, the industrial sector. Thus, if for instance we have say a laborer A moving to the project and his wage in his previous employment was w, and on his moving to the project his previous job is filled by someone else, B, who in turn moves from a job which paid him Y $(w > Y)$, then the change in output (assuming that the two wage rates are determined in competitive markets for hired labor) by employing A on the project is not w but Y, as now the first round effect of A's migration—a fall of output of w in his previous employment—is offset by a rise in output in his previous activity by an equivalent amount when the other worker B replaced him, but which now results in the loss of output as a result of B's movement from his initial job to A's previous job of Y.

Furthermore, as a result of creating one more job in the "industrial" sector, more than one migrant may move from rural areas. If N people migrate, and the change in agricultural output as a result of one person's migration is Y, then the

$$SWR = c - (c - NY)/s \quad (18)$$

Harberger [12] has used one particular model of rural-urban migration due to Harris-Todaro [14], to derive the SWR as always equal to the market wage c. This is obtained as follows. Harris-Todaro assume that there is *no* surplus labor in agriculture. The migrants come to the cities because the expected income in the urban sector is just equal to the income they forego in agriculture. The expected urban income is determined by the probability (P) of finding urban employment at the industrial wage c, which, in the Harris-Todaro model, is determined by the equilibrium ratio of employed to the total labor force in the cities, say P.[17] Furthermore, it is assumed that agricultural workers receive their marginal product (say a). At the margin, therefore, migrant workers will equate their marginal product (incomes) in agriculture, a, to the expected wage in towns, Pc (That is, $a = Pc$.) When one more man is hired by the industrial sector the expected wage Pc rises as P rises. This induces rural-urban migration of $1/P$ workers, which restores the probability of finding a job in the urban sector to P, and the expected income to the equilibrium level Pc—when rural-urban migration ceases. Hence in expression (18) $N = 1/P$. Moreover, the "equilibrium" value of P is a/c (given the migration function $a = Pc$), and as the out-

[17] See Harris and Todaro [7], p. 128. This is also the assumption made by Harberger [5], p. 570. This formulation of P is unrealistic. A more likely determinant of the chances of a single migrant is given by the number of vacancies occurring per unit of time divided by the number of candidates for those vacancies, that is the urban unemployed. The latter in fact was the determinant of P in the earlier Todaro formulation (see [18], p. 142). But note that while these differing determinants of P will affect the "equilibrium urban unemployment" rate (which is the chief concern of other writers on rural-urban migration), the *"equilibrium" value* of P will be invariant to these alternative formulations of its determinants, as it will be determined by the rural-urban income differential. (In our formulation above, the equilibrium $P = a/c$.) For a fuller discussion see Lal [9].

put foregone per migrant on Harris-Todaro assumptions is the marginal product a, we have:

$$m = NY = (1/P)a = c$$

Substitution in expressions (16) or (18) yields $SWR = c$, the industrial wage. However, as has been pointed out above, in general it cannot be assumed that the change in output in the agricultural sector will equal the marginal product of labor. In that case, the change in output m within the Harris-Todaro migration model will be given by Y/P, where Y is the change in output in agriculture when one worker is withdrawn. As before we have $a = Pc$ (where a is the income the worker received in agriculture, which on a family farm would be equal to the average product of the farm if we assume equal income and work sharing on family farms). Hence $m = Y/P = Y$. Then c/a and the SWR given a Harris-Todaro-type migration function will be:

$$SWR = c - c\ (1 - Y/a)/s$$

From this it is obvious that, on the special Harris-Todaro assumption that $Y = a$, the SWR will equal c, the industrial wage. This is the Harberger derivation of the SWR, in his "Panama" example (see [6], p. 568 and following). More important, however, the Harris-Todaro-Harberger migration model is also restrictive in many other respects, some of which are more serious than others. First, it implicitly assumes that industrial wage-earners have tenure, as the rate of labor turnover in industry does not figure in their determination of P. Empirically, this assumption may not be too inaccurate, as the rate of labor turnover does not seem to be very high in the industrial sector in most developing countries. Second, they consider the migration decision as a one-period decision, whereas strictly it should be a multi-period decision in which the present value of the costs of migration should at the margin

be equal to the present value of the benefits from migration.[18] If, however, as seems likely, most migrants have a fairly high subjective rate of time preference (fairly short time horizon), then the use of a single period migration decision function may not be invalid. Third, Harris-Todaro do not incorporate any of the costs of migration (real and/or "psychic")[19] nor the relatively higher costs of urban living which the migrant would have to incur in their migration function. Finally, and most important, their migration model fails to take account of the existence of a fairly competitive "unorganized" (services and small industry) sector urban labor market with high labor turnover and easy entry for new workers, which is typical of many developing countries, and which provides some income to the migrants while they are searching for an "organized" (industrial) sector job at the high institutional wage c.

Thus it is essentially the last two features which need to be incorporated into a more general migration function. To derive the SWR for this more general migration model, we continue to assume that industrial wage earners can be taken to have tenure, and that a one-period decision model is a fair approximation to reality. However, we now assume that in addition to the agricultural income foregone, a, the migrant has to incur migration costs of d, which include both the real and "psychic" costs of migrating. Furthermore, if the migrant does not succeed in obtaining an industrial sector job at the high institutional wage of c, he can nevertheless find some employment in the "unorganized" urban labor market and derive an income w. Finally, we assume that by living in the town the migrant has to incur a relatively higher cost of living than in rural areas of u to maintain the same standard of living as he enjoyed in the countryside. If the chances of

[18] Todaro [18], p. 143, fn. 10, notes this.
[19] Though Harris-Todaro note the existence of these costs, see their [7], p. 129, fn. 8.

getting an "organized" (industrial) sector job are as before P, then at the margin the migrant will equate the costs of migration, which are given by $(a + d + u)$ with the expected benefits, $[Pc + (1 - P)w]$, that is in equilibrium:

$$a + d + u = Pc + (1 - P)w.$$

This yields the "equilibrium" value of $P = (a + d + u - w)/(c - w)$.

As before, with the creation of an extra industrial sector job $N = 1/P$ migrants will move from agriculture, and as the output foregone per migrant in agriculture is Y, we have the total output foregone, $m = Y \cdot (c - w)/(a + d + u - w)$, and the

$$SWR = c - [c - Y \cdot (c - w)/ \\ (a + d + u - w)]/s \quad (19)$$

and in this more general and more realistic migration model, the conclusion drawn by Harberger that the institutionally given industrial wage c, is the shadow wage, will not be valid.

Disutility of Effort: Finally, in addition to changes in output, there will also be changes in the aggregate disutility of effort (E) with increased employment. To evaluate these, assume initially that there are no imperfections in the labor market. Then, at the margin, utility maximizing workers will equate the disutility of increased effort with the utility from the increased incomes (which we assume are all consumed) this extra work makes possible. That is, the extra disutility of effort (E) must equal the change in workers' consumption (including those left behind on the farm) which is given by $(c - m)$—the difference between the industrial wage (assuming the new job is in industry, and the worker moves to it from agriculture) and the total output foregone by employing one more man in the industrial sector. The value in terms of savings of this change in disutility of effort (which so far is in terms of consumption equivalents) is $(c - m)/s$. If the value society places on the disutility of

effort is λ, then the SWR incorporating the costs of the disutility of effort will be:

$$SWR = c - (c - m)/s + \lambda (c - m)/s \\ = c - (c - m)(1 - \lambda)/s \quad (20)$$

Next relax the assumption that all labor markets are competitive, and assume that there is an institutional wage, c, in the sector to which the labor is moving which is above the supply price of labor L. The latter term includes all the private disutilities that may attach to the new job. Our earlier expression for the consumption equivalent of the net change in disutility $(c - m)$ will now be overstating the true change in disutility by $(c - L)$, which is the difference between the institutional wage c, and the supply price of labor L. The net change in disutilities in this more general case will therefore be given by $(c - m) - (c - L) = (L - m)$, and as before the value in terms of savings will be $(L - m)/s$, and the

$$SWR = c - (c - m)/s + \lambda (L - m)/s \quad (21)$$

If $\lambda = 0$, that is society places no value on the change in the private disutilities of effort, we get the traditional SWR as in (16) above. If, however, it is assumed that society should value disutilities of effort at their private costs, then $\lambda = 1$, and the

$$SWR = L + (c - L)(1 - 1/s) \quad (22)$$

The first term is the supply price of labor, the second is the value in terms of savings, of the extra consumption generated by the excess of the institutional wage over the supply price of labor. Thus, when $\lambda = 1$, we get the standard neoclassical result, that the SWR will be the supply price of labor, if there is no divergence between the social value of present consumption and savings, that is $s = 1$; and furthermore, that if $c = L$, that is, if labor markets are competitive, the SWR will equal the market wage c, no matter what the value of s, and irrespective of any divergence between m (the output foregone elsewhere in the economy), and the industrial wage c.

Alternative Formulations of the SWR: We can now, very succinctly, compare the various alternative *SWR's* that have been suggested in the literature.[20]

First, there is the view due to Galenson-Leibenstein [4] and Dobb [3] that the *SWR is the market wage*, that is $SWR = c$. For this to be the case, *either* $c = m = L$, or $m = 0$, $s \rightarrow \infty$, $\lambda = 0$, or $E = 0$.

Second, there is the view associated with Kahn [8] and Lewis [12] that the $SWR = 0$. For this to be the case: $m = 0$, $s = 1$, $\lambda = 0$, or $E = 0$.

Third, for Sen [17], Marglin [15] and to some extent UNIDO [19], the $SWR = c - c/s$. For this to be valid: $m = 0$, $\lambda = 0$, or $E = 0$.

Fourth, the *LM* [14] *SWR* is given by (16) above, $SWR = c - (c - m)/s$. For this to be valid: $\lambda = 0$. As they assume a positive marginal product in agriculture, E cannot be zero.

Finally, for Harberger [6], the *SWR is the supply price of labor L*, that is $SWR = L$. For this to be valid: either $\lambda = 1$, $c = L$, or $s = 1$.

Part of the differences relate to empirical matters, that is the value of m and E. But, in part, the differences relate to two value parameters, s and λ. The reasons why it may be necessary to take $s > 1$ have been given in the section on capital above. A number of reasons have been advanced by the present author, why it may also be desirable to assume that $\lambda = 0$, for developing countries.[21] However, the values assigned to these parameters must be in the nature of value judgments, and hence the possibility of conflicting advice on the different procedures. However, as this section has tried to show, if the same assumptions and value judgments are made, the alternative procedures will give identical answers, based upon the general expression for the *SWR* provided by (21) above.

---

[20] As most writers have not included rural-urban migration in their models for determining the *SWR*, this aspect is neglected in this section. The previous section has already dealt with the *SWR's* derived or derivable from the Harris-Todaro-Harberger-type models and a model developed in Lal [9].

[21] See Lal [9].

References

[1] A. K. Dixit, "Short-Run Equilibrium and Shadow Prices in the Dual Economy," *Oxford Economic Papers* 23 (1971): 384–400.

[2] R. Dorfman, P. A. Samuelson, and R. M. Solow, *Linear Programming and Economic Analysis*. New York: McGraw Hill (Rand Series), 1958.

[3] M. H. Dobb, *An Essay on Economic Growth and Planning*. London: Routledge & Paul, 1960.

[4] W. Galenson and H. Leibenstein, "Investment Criteria, Productivity and Economic Development." *Quarterly Journal of Economics* LXIX (1955): 343–70.

[5] A. C. Harberger, "Survey of Literature on Cost-Benefit Analysis for Industrial Project Evaluation" in *Evaluation of Industrial Projects*. New York: United Nations (UNIDO), 1968.

[6] A. C. Harberger, "The Social Opportunity Cost of Labour." *International Labour Review* 103 (1971): 559–79.

[7] J. R. Harris and M. P. Todaro, "Migration, Unemployment and Development: A Two-Sector Analysis." *American Economic Review* LX (1970): 126–42.

[8] A. K. Kahn, "Investment Criteria in Development Programs." *Quarterly Journal of Economics* LXV (1951): 38–61.

[9] D. Lal, "Disutility of Effort, Migration and the Shadow Wage Rate." *Oxford Economic Papers* 25 (1973): 112–26.

[10] D. Lal, *Wells and Welfare*. Paris: Organization for Economic Cooperation and Development, 1972.

[11] D. Lal, "On Estimating Certain Intertemporal Parameters for Project Analysis." IBRD mimeograph. Washington, D.C., 1973.

[12] W. A. Lewis, "Economic Development with Unlimited Supplies of Labour." *Manchester School of Economics and Social Sciences* 22 (1954): 139–91.

[13] I. M. D. Little and J. A. Mirrlees, *Manual of Industrial Project Analysis In Developing Countries, Volume II: Social Cost-Benefit Analysis.* Paris: Organization for Economic Cooperation and Development, 1968.

[14] I. M. D. Little and J. A. Mirrlees, "A Reply to Some Criticisms of the OECD Manual." *Bulletin of Oxford University Institute of Economics and Statistics* 34 (1972): 153–68.

[15] S. A. Marglin, *Public Investment Criteria.* Cambridge, Mass.: MIT Press, 1967.

[16] A. K. Sen, "Peasants and Dualism With and Without Surplus Labor." *Journal of Political Economy* LXXIV (1966): 425–50.

[17] A. K. Sen, *Choice of Techniques, An Aspect of the Theory of Planned Economic Development.* 3rd ed. Oxford: B. Blackwell, 1968.

[18] M. P. Todaro, "A Model of Labor Migration and Urban Development in Less Developed Countries." *American Economic Review* LIX (1969): 138–48.

[19] United Nations Industrial Development Organization [P. Dasgupta, A. Sen, and S. Marglin], *Guidelines for Project Evaluation.* New York: United Nations, 1972.

VII.C.4. Social Importance of

Employment Creation*

It was noted earlier that one reason why employment is valued is because of its impact on income distribution. An unemployed person does not have a source of income; although it is possible to give him some income through a dole, this practice may be difficult to follow. In most developing countries a dole for the unemployed is not provided. Undoubtedly part of the reason is that with a large volume of surplus labour a poor country can ill-afford a dole system, and productive employment even with low output is preferable. Partly also, with disguised unemployment it is not very easy to identify those to whom a dole should be paid. Under these circumstances, an expansion of employment in spreading

*From UNIDO, *Guidelines for Project Evaluation*, Project Formulation and Evaluation Series No. 2, New York, 1972, pp. 91–7. Reprinted by permission.

the real income very widely may contribute efficiently to the redistribution objective. As was noted earlier, many of the desirable aspects of employment creation, its impact on nourishment, on education etc. really relate to the fact that employment creates a source of livelihood for the family.

This being the case, it is worth considering whether employment should be valued separately in project selection in the light of its impact on income distribution, or whether income distribution should be given a specific value and employment treated as a means to it. Fundamentally, this is not a crucial question, since which way we do the calculation makes little difference so long as the link between employment and redistribution is clearly recognized and realistically calculated. However, from the point of view of the convenience of calculation this is a question of some importance.

If, on the one hand, we treat the income level of the poorer classes as the relevant item to which value is attached, that value will simply reflect the planners' idea of the relative importance of channelling consumption to the poor. The planners' evaluation need not be concerned with the precise calculation of the impact of employment on the consumption of the poor classes; this would be left to the project evaluator. If, on the other hand, the central policy makers attach precise value to employment, in estimating this value the policy makers will have to take into account the impact of employment on the consumption of the poor classes, and the value will have to be determined by considering this in conjunction with the innate importance of giving consumption opportunities to the poor. The second procedure is less direct than the first, and there are obvious advantages in following the first procedure. The project evaluator himself is in a better position to judge the precise impact of employment and other factors on income distribution, and it seems best to do this calculation directly and to leave the central policy makers in fixing social weights unencumbered by this complex detail. By valuing redistribution the division of labour between the project evaluator and the over-all policy maker will be more appropriate, and this is the procedure we follow in these Guidelines.

A more fundamental issue is why employment should be regarded as a vehicle of income distribution and why income cannot be redistributed more directly through taxation and fiscal policy. In principle there is no difficulty in paying a person a certain amount of money even without employing him in a project. Employment may be quite extraneous to the act of payment. The objection that paying someone without employing him will be unethical need not detain us; since we are considering the role of employment in income distribution, our real concern is with getting income to the poor person, whether or not he is employed. In fact, to the extent that work is regarded as unpleasant and leisure is regarded as valuable, paying people without making them work may well be considered a superior means of income redistribution than employment.

The picture is, however, not so simple. Payment without work may have important political and social repercussions. If the Government decides to give a number of people some income without work, the question would naturally be raised why these people rather than others are selected for such support. This question of selection arises even for employment when unemployment is widespread, and charges of favouritism in job giving are not uncommon. However, in the case of employment creation, there are at any rate some possible criteria for suitability for jobs and also some definite procedure for giving employment. Also, getting paid for one's job is considered a compensation for one's effort, even though the institutional wage rate may be regarded as very much in excess of the unpleasantness of work in a country with unemployment. However that may be, politically the question of arbitrariness in job distribution, while important, is not likely to be such an explosive issue as the giving out of income without work.

In some situations income may be redistributed better through a direct payment than through giving employment. In dealing with people with some crying need, e.g. medical facilities, it may be simpler to give income than to give jobs. It is not being suggested that employment giving is always the best means of redistributing income. It need not be so at all. But often employment will be an important vehicle of income redistribution and the fact that its political feasibility is somewhat greater than pure distribution of money, except in very special situations, cannot be overlooked.

It might be mentioned in this context that the possibility of corruption is perhaps also less when income is redistributed through employment rather than through subsidies. It has been found, for example, that in giving famine relief in countries like India, the system of paying wages to labour in specially devised work programmes is less open to misuse than the system of a direct dole. There are clearer records of employment and also less possibility of distributing money to nonexistent persons, which is not uncommon in the context of a pure dole in a country with a defective administrative system. This is another reason why employment may be an important means of redistribution.

Be that as it may, in considering project selection we should have to see the redistributional impact of employment creation as a possible part of the objectives of some projects. There is nothing strange about this. Basically, this is another reflection of a phenomenon we have outlined in several places in these Guidelines: the best economic possibilities are not the same as political feasibilities. The redistribution of income through employment may be feasible when pure redistribution without employment may not be, even when the latter may be economically perfectly possible.

What we are mainly concerned with is an understanding of how employment may affect income distribution. This will vary from project to project. One has to see to what extent additional employment will provide income to particularly depressed groups. We have already discussed earlier how the redistribution objective can be formulated in a variety of ways. One of the ways is to attach an additional weight to the consumption of depressed groups or classes. Sometimes when a whole region is known to be economically depressed, income generating in that region may be given a special weight. Quite clearly this will include the impact of employment because in estimating the income generated in that region, note must be taken of employment and wages paid out. If we are concerned with such broad considerations, no special efforts need be made to see that the effects of employment are reflected in the income-distribution objective; the procedure already suggested will do it very well.

However, sometimes we may wish to attach a special importance to income accruing to depressed groups within a specific region, and we may then wish to attach a special weight to the wages paid to that group. Regions very often are internally unhomogeneous, and it may be important to distinguish between the depressed and the not-so-depressed classes in a certain region.

While such a distinction requires a fairly detailed calculation, it does not really affect the principles. On the one hand, the work should consist of making precise estimates of the income generated that will be enjoyed by these specific depressed groups. On the other hand, the policy makers must indicate the additional value to be attached to the income thus generated. For most of these really depressed groups, income and consumption are practically identical, so that we shall not be far wrong if we treat the accrued income of these groups as equivalent to their present consumption. In determining the value to be attached to the present consumption of these poorer groups, the policy makers must note that consumption to these groups will, on redistributional grounds, be regarded as more important than the consumption of the average citizen of the country. As part of aggregate consumption, consumption of these depressed groups will receive a weight in any case in the system of evaluating benefits of the projects. The additional weight to be attached to the consumption of these groups may be reflected through putting a positive value on the consumption of this group over and above the value of aggregate consumption.

For assessing the impact on employment and sectional income, the precise pattern of disbursement between different categories of expenditures would have to be examined. Very often project data are provided in such an aggregate manner that the expenditures on wages are not separated, nor is it specified where the additional people to be employed would be found. In the context of the objective of redistribution in relation to employment it would be important to obtain this breakdown, and to check what part of the disbursement reflects the additional wage bill and also to whom these wages are to be paid, i.e. whether the workers come from particularly depressed classes on whose income we would like to place an additional weight.

Compromises in project evaluation would, of course, have to be struck between the demands of perfection and the constraints of practicability. In principle it would be best to determine the precise income level of each employed person and attach a variable weight to his respective consumption; the weight will go up as the average income level goes down. This will not, however, be possible to do in any detail. The calculation would have to be done in terms of broad categories.

SOCIAL COST OF LABOUR

So far we have concentrated on the benefit side of employment, making only passing references to costs. In a country with full employment the cost of employment of labour is fairly easy to calculate. A person can be employed in a certain project only if he is withdrawn from employment somewhere else. From the point of view of this project, therefore, the cost of employing him may be thought to be equal to what he would have produced had he been employed elsewhere. This measure of what he would have alternatively produced is sometimes called "the social opportunity cost" of labour, a term that is often used in project-evaluation literature. By employing the person here the society is foregoing the opportunity of employing him elsewhere, and thus the social opportunity cost measures the value of the alternative opportunity that the society is losing by putting him to work in the project under discussion.

Defined this way, the opportunity cost of labour will be positive when there is full employment, but if there is unemployed labour it should be possible to employ labour in this project without having to withdraw it from elsewhere. Thus, the opportunity cost of labour as defined above may well be zero in the context of an economy with unemployment. Does this mean that employment of labour is costless for an economy with unemployment? The answer is "not at all", since along with employment come other changes in the economy that may or may not involve specific costs from the social point of view.

A few of the simpler considerations may be mentioned first, followed by a more complex problem. Although labour may be unemployed, it does not follow that there is no unpleasantness of work, especially since working conditions in developing countries often tend to be extraordinarily bad. The unpleasantness of work for those who would have otherwise been idle cannot be dismissed. This point assumes particular importance when there is a transfer of labour from the rural areas to the harsh living conditions of the growing towns and cities in the poor countries. The conditions of living, including the sanitary facilities and other social amenities in some of the urban areas of the developing countries, are often miserable, and it must be assumed that there is some loss in making people work under such conditions. It is possible to feel that this is an unimportant consideration, since the worker in question prefers to take the job rather than be unemployed. However, this is not a convincing argument. The worker prefers this job because he is paid a certain wage, and while this wage may overcompensate him for the inconvenience of bad working and living conditions, this does not mean that the working and living conditions do not involve some suffering. Therefore, just as we must calculate the benefits from employment in terms of output creation as well as of income redistribution and other objectives, we must also take into account the social costs, if any, of additional employment, especially when it involves migration.

From the social point of view, a further consideration may arise because the Government may have to construct housing and other facilities in an area to which the workers may be moving, and these costs may not be borne, at any rate not fully, by the workers themselves. Because a large proportion of the capital expenditure of a project lies in the cost of townships, this could be an important cost related to employment. If the benefits from new houses and good working conditions are provided, they may be included among the benefits of the project, but the cost of townships and housing must be counted as part of the cost of employment creation of the project.

A more complex consideration relates to the impact of employment on the distribution of the current income between consumption and investment. When an additional person is employed, drawn from the pool of the unemployed, and he is paid wages, some additional purchasing power is generated, and this will reflect itself in an increase in consumption. Of course, increased consumption is desirable, and indeed, aggregate consumption is the first objective that we examined in the context of cost-benefit calculation. However, an increase in immediate consumption may be achieved, under most circumstances, only through a reduction in investment. If the policy makers feel that, on balance at the margin, consumption and investment are equally attractive from the point of view of the society, it makes no difference whether investment is cut a little to increase immediate consumption correspondingly or whether immediate consumption is somewhat reduced for the sake of expansion of a corresponding amount of investment. If, however, we are dealing with an economy where the policy makers feel that the over-all rate of investment is deficient, a reduction in investment for the sake of an expansion of immediate consumption may be regarded as a loss. One way of viewing this problem is to regard the price of investment in terms of immediate consumption to be greater than one. . . . The shadow price of investment, $P^{inv}(t)$, is a crucial factor in assessing the social cost of

employment, since the expansion of employment means a shift from investment to consumption, and the loss involved in this per unit is equivalent to the value of $[P^{inv}(t) - 1]$. If investment and consumption are already optimally distributed, i.e. there is neither underinvestment nor overinvestment, then the value of $P^{inv}(t)$ should be equal to 1 and the loss involved would be precisely 0. However, as is common in most developing countries, if the planners believe that the level of investment is too low, there will be a loss, since $P^{inv}(t)$ exceeds 1. The social cost of labour depends not merely on the social opportunity cost of labour but also on the shadow price of investment.

We may seem to be contradicting ourselves in some ways by regarding additional consumption generated through additional employment (a) to be a good thing because it leads to a better distribution of income, and (b) to be a bad thing because it leads to a shift from investment to consumption. This is, however, not a contradiction, and both facts are correct and relevant, though they work in opposite directions. A unit of income that accrues to a worker in a project rather than accruing to the project authorities can be viewed in one of two ways. To the extent that it reflects workers' consumption as opposed to average consumption of the community, it can be regarded as more valuable; to the extent that it reflects consumption rather than investment it must be regarded as less valuable if the country is suffering from a shortage of investment vis-à-vis consumption. The latter is the comparison of consumption with investment and the former is the comparison of consumption by a poorer group vis-à-vis that by a richer group. In making a detailed calculation of benefits and costs of a project both these considerations are relevant, but they will come into our estimation under different objectives and will work in different directions.

Under the broad hat of aggregate consumption would come the question of the relative weight of investment vis-à-vis average consumption today, since the impact of investment on future consumption is fully reflected in our estimation of the aggregate-consumption benefit. On the other hand, the special weight to be attached to the consumption of the poorer groups vis-à-vis average consumption today must come under the heading of the redistribution objective.

Employment creation will, therefore, come in both the benefit and the cost side under these two sets of objectives; additional employment will involve a cost through the "aggregate-consumption objective" and a benefit through the "redistribution objective".

VII. SELECT BIBLIOGRAPHY

1. The two outstanding volumes on theory of investment planning and project evaluation are UNIDO, *Guidelines for Project Evaluation*, New York, 1972; I. M. D. Little and James Mirrlees, *Project Appraisal and Planning for Developing Countries*, New York, 1974. Of special relevance to these studies are the Symposium on the Little-Mirrlees manual, special issue of *Bulletin Oxford Institute of Economics and Statistics*, February 1972; P. Dasgupta, "An Analysis of Two Approaches to Project Evaluation in Developing Countries," in UNIDO, *Industrialization and Productivity Bulletin*, No. 15, 1970; Deepak Lal, *Methods of Project Analysis: A Review*, Baltimore, 1974.

2. Useful approaches to rational choice systems and benefit-cost analysis are provided in the following: R. Layard (ed.), *Cost-Benefit Analysis*, London, 1972; E. J. Mishan, *Cost-Benefit Analysis*, New York, 1971; A. C. Harberger, *Project Evaluation*, Chicago, 1973; ____, "Three Basic Postulates for Applied Welfare Economics," *JEL*, September 1971; A. K. Dasgupta and D. W. Pearce, *Cost-Benefit Analysis, Theory, and Practice*, New York, 1972; A. R. Prest and R. Turvey, "Cost-Benefit Analysis: A Survey," *EJ*, December 1965; R. A. Musgrave, "Cost-Benefit Analysis and the Theory of Public Finance," *JEL*, September 1969; P. Dasgupta and J. E. Stiglitz, "Benefit-Cost Analysis and Trade Policies," *JPE*, January–February 1972; R. W. Broadway, "The Welfare Foundations of Cost-Benefit Analysis," *EJ*, December 1974; C. F. Azzi and J. C. Cox, "Equity and Efficiency in Program Evaluation," *QJE*, August 1973.

3. The following analyze the use of shadow prices in investment planning and project evaluation: A. K. Sen, "Control Areas and Accounting Prices," *EJ*, March 1972; E. Bacha and Lance Taylor, "Foreign Exchange Shadow Prices," *QJE*, May 1971; M. FG. Scott, "How to Use and Estimate Shadow Exchange Rates," *OEP*, July 1975; J. S. Flemming and M. S. Feldstein, "Shadow Prices in Industrial Project Evaluation," in UNIDO, Project Formulation and Evaluation Series, Vol. 1, *Evaluation of Industrial Projects*, New York, 1968, pp. 163–74; A. C. Harberger, "Survey of Literature on Cost-Benefit Analysis for Industrial Project Evaluation," ibid., pp. 229–246; ____, "On Measuring the Social Opportunity Cost of Labour," *ILR*, 1971; M. S. Feldstein, "The Social Time Preference Discount Rate in Cost-Benefit Analysis," *EJ*, 1964; S. Marglin, "The Opportunity Cost of Public Investment," *QJE*, May 1963; Agnar Sandmo and Jacques Dreze, "Discount Rates for Public Investment in Closed and Open Economies," *Economica*, November 1971; S. Lal, "Disutility of Effort, Migration and the Shadow Wage Rate," *OEP*, March 1973.

4. More general discussions of investment criteria are contained in the following: A. K. Bagchi, "The Choice of the Optimum Technique," *EJ*, September 1962; M. D. Bryce, *Industrial Development*, New York, 1960; S. Chakravarty, *The Logic of Investment Planning*, Amsterdam, 1960; H. B. Chenery, "The Application of Investment Criteria," *QJE*, February 1953; ____, and K. S. Krestschmer, "Resources Allocation for Economic Development," *Econometrica*, October 1956; Otto Eckstein, "Investment Criteria for Economic Development and the Theory of Intertemporal Welfare Economics," *QJE*, February 1957; W. Galenson and H. Leibenstein, "Investment Criteria, Productivity and Economic Development," ibid., August 1955; Koji Taira, "A Note on the Analytical Properties of Galenson-Leibenstein Investment Criterion," *Bulletin of Oxford Institute of Economics and Statistics*, Vol. 27, No. 2, 1965; W. Galenson and G. Pyatt, "The Choice of Technique Once Again: A Reply to Dr. Taira," ibid., August 1966; H. Leibenstein,

478

"Investment Criteria and Empirical Evidence—a Reply to Mr. Ranis," *QJE*, February 1963; J. A. King, *Economic Development Projects and their Appraisal*, Baltimore, 1967; A. K. Sen, *Choice of Techniques*, 3rd ed., Oxford, 1968; Stephen Marglin, *Approaches to Dynamic Investment Planning*, Amsterdam, 1963; Timothy King, "Development Strategy and Investment Criteria: Complementary or Competitive?" *QJE*, February 1966; A. O. Hirschman, *Development Projects Observed*, Washington, D.C., 1967.

5. Although the theory of optimal growth paths has been devised for advanced economies, some aspects of the theory relate to efficient capital accumulation and may be suggestive for the optimal allocation of investment between consumption and capital goods in a developing economy. An excellent survey article is F. H. Hahn and R. C. O. Mathews, "The Theory of Economic Growth: A Survey," *EJ*, December 1964. Among the many growth models, the following may be of special interest: M. Dobb, *An Essay on Economic Growth and Planning*, London, 1960; R. Findlay, "Optimal Investment Allocation Between Consumer Goods and Capital Goods," *EJ*, March 1966; L. Johansen, "Some Theoretical Properties of a Two-Sector Model of Optimal Growth," *Review of Economic Studies*, January 1967; L. G. Stoleru, "An Optimal Policy for Economic Growth," *Econometrica*, April 1965; S. Bose, "Optimal Growth and Investment Allocation," *Review of Economic Studies*, October 1968; A. K. Dixit, "Optimal Development in the Labour-Surplus Economy," ibid., January 1968; H. Uzawa, "Market Allocation and Optimum Growth," *Australian Economic Papers*, June 1968; Jaroslav Vanek, *Maximal Economic Growth*, Ithaca, 1968; R. R. Nelson and S. G. Winter, "Neoclassical versus Evolutionary Theories of Economic Growth: Critique and Prospectus," *EJ*, December 1974.

The Bibliography in Chapter XII also relates to this topic.

CHAPTER VIII

Human-Resource Development

Another strategic policy issue is the development of human resources. If the earlier faith in development through the accumulation of material capital has waned, it has in recent years been replaced by a new creed of investment in human capital. It is now widely believed that improvement in the quality of people as productive agents must be a central objective of development policies. But how are the abilities and skills of people to be improved, and their motivations and values modified so as to be more suitable for developmental efforts? This is clearly one of the most difficult questions we have encountered, and yet, on its answer is likely to depend a country's success in achieving self-sustaining development.

Part of the difficulty in formulating policy to improve the "human infrastructure" within a less developed country is that economists have only recently begun to analyze this question systematically; among the limitations of the special case (II.A.1) have been the assumptions that an educated and slowly growing population, skilled and mobile labor force, and wide supply of entrepreneurship are already existent. Perhaps the greater part of the difficulty, however, is that an answer to the question entails not only economic analysis but also sociological, psychological, and political considerations. The inherently multidisciplinary character of the answer has caused each discipline to acknowledge the question but to fall short of a satisfactory answer. This chapter, in concentrating on the economics of the problem, will not be immune to this same criticism, but it will at least attempt to fashion the economic analysis so that it might suggest some links with other disciplines.

Before considering policy measures related to the quality of the population we should first gain some perspective on the quantitative problem of population pressure. Section VIII.A examines the nature of the population explosion and its importance from the standpoint of its effects on the quality of population. Population is growing much faster in the LDCs than in the more developed countries, and the urban population is growing especially rapidly. The exacerbation of the employment problem is direct: the U.N. estimates that for every 100 workers in Africa in 1970, there will be 142 in 1985; for every 100 in Asia, 134; for every 100 in Latin America, 148. The effects of population growth on the quality of health facilities, nutrition, educational programs, and public services make it necessary to acquire a better understanding of demographic problems. It is now especially apposite to investigate whether population growth worsens absolute poverty and the maldistribution of income. And do absolute poverty and the maldistribution of income contribute, in turn, to high rates of fertility? Further, what are the socioeconomic correlates of declining fertility, and how might policies affect the correlates to reduce the rate of population growth? If public policies can reduce mortality rates, can they also reduce fertility rates?

Section VIII.B outlines some policies to improve health and nutrition conditions among the world's poor. Among the first to suffer from shortages or inadequacies of food are the children—a country's investment in the future. And children, along with their mothers, are numerically dominant in developing countries. In these areas one-fifth of the population is under the age of 5 years, two-fifths are below the age of 15 years, while mothers and children together account for over two-thirds of the total population. The children are the most vulnerable group. Of the 800 million children growing up at present in the developing countries, more than two-thirds will encounter sickness or disabling diseases either brought on or aggravated by protein-calorie malnutrition.[1] Malnutrition adversely affects mental progress, physical growth, productivity, and the working life span. In cost-effectiveness terms—let alone fundamental human rights—there can be high returns from programs to reduce the incidence of protein-calorie malnutrition.

Poverty is the major cause of disease in developing countries, and more than medical facilities is needed to improve health conditions. Health policies must be related much more to the environment and to changes in the ecological, cultural, and nutritional situation which permits disease to thrive in poverty areas. As with technology, so too is there a need for an "appropriate" transfer of medical knowledge and medical technology: health programs have been only too often biased toward a small section of the urban population, and to oversophisticated "curative" treatment rather than more basic, widespread "preventive" treatment.

As analyzed in section VIII.C, formal and informal education and training in both the modern and traditional sectors are clearly necessary for the development of human resources. Any cost-benefit analysis of the "returns" to education must incorporate the interactions between education and the economy, giving particular attention to education as an investment, the importance of rural education in a developing economy, and the interdependence between education, manpower requirements, and development. Although each individual commonly views his own education as a consumption good, it is more appropriately viewed from the standpoint of the economy's development as an investment good: to the economist, human beings can be conceptualized as human capital or embodied savings. It is then an economic problem to determine how much the economy should invest in human capital, and of equal importance, what the composition of that investment should be. The selections in section VIII.C therefore consider both the quantitative growth of education and the character of education needed in a developing economy.

[1] FAO, *Lives in Peril,* Rome, 1970, p. 7.

The final section on entrepreneurship indicates why entrepreneurship is a significant variable in the development process and considers some economic, psychological, and social factors determining the supply of entrepreneurship. Professor McClelland's analysis of achievement motivation provides an important explanation of the psychological determinants of entrepreneurship. It may be suggested, however, that successful entrepreneurship depends not only on an individual's motivation, but also on his abilities and a permissive environment which provides incentives and opportunities for entrepreneurs. Economists have tended to emphasize a favorable economic environment, but according to McClelland, whenever economic growth begins, some tiny community within the larger society which has played the major entrepreneurial role can nearly always be identified. "If economic opportunities are such important 'motivators,' why is it that they affect markedly such a small fraction of the total population? Some human factor would seem to be necessary to explain the responsiveness of the few and the indifference of the many."[2] The theory of achievement motivation predicts that those in the population who will take greater advantage of increased opportunities are precisely those relatively few individuals who have a high need to achieve. The policy implication, therefore, is that efforts must be undertaken to instill a higher need to achieve in a larger segment of the population. This conforms to the more general view expressed throughout this chapter that the key to development is man, and that his abilities, values, and attitudes must be changed in order to accelerate the process of development.

[2] David C. McClelland and David G. Winter, *Motivating Economic Achievement*, New York, 1969, p. 6.

VIII.A. POPULATION

VIII.A.1. Population and Poverty—Note

Few developmental problems evoke as much pessisism as does the rapid increase in population in poor countries. If economists value a higher rate of development, they still fear, as John Stuart Mill did, a growth in population that "treads close on the heels of agricultural improvement, and effaces its effects as fast as they are produced." It is not difficult to find a basis for this fear—in that a large part of the gain in aggregate income has been used simply to support a larger population at the same low per capita level of income.

This pessimistic outlook on population growth is as old as academic economics itself.[1] Long ago economics was designated the "dismal science." Originally this was because of the view of classical economists who, when considering the long-run development of an economy, could see only the eventual advent of a dismal "stationary state" in which the springs of economic progress would have evaporated, growth in output would no longer outstrip population growth, and wages would be at subsistence levels. So far, however, this pessimism has proved unfounded for industrial nations: the economic histories of these nations represent the success stories of economic progress—of the achievement of a high rate of increase in real income, so that population and per capita real income have both been able to increase. Indeed, when some economists thought that the Great Depression of the 1930s might indicate a state of secular stagnation in mature industrial nations, they were concerned lest population growth in

these countries actually be too slow. But although capital accumulation, technical progress, and the phenomenon of increasing returns to scale may have dispelled the shadow of Malthus from the few rich industrial countries, that shadow still hovers over the many poor agrarian countries. For these countries there may still be only too much truth in the classical doctrines of the Malthusian principle of population with its correlative theory of subsistence wages. In these countries, per capita income has remained pitifully low, and the alarming prospects of population growth have revived neo-Malthusian fears. Once again there is widespread concern that economic betterment will be thwarted by excessive population pressure and that, unless acceptable means are found for checking population growth, the "revolution of rising expectations" must remain unfulfilled. It has become common to hear the development problem summarized as one of "increasing the fertility of the soil and reducing the fertility of human beings."

It is extremely important, however, to realize that the population problem is much more than a food problem: it has wider ramifications that make it a general development problem. A high rate of population growth not only has an adverse effect on improvement in food supplies, but also intensifies the constraints on development of savings, foreign exchange, and human resources. Rapid population growth, which stems from high birth rates, tends to depress savings per capita and retards growth of physical capital per worker. The need for social infrastructure is also broadened, and public expenditures must be absorbed in providing these facilities for a larger population rather than in providing directly pro-

[1] The history of thought on population growth and development is traced by Lord Robbins, *The Theory of Economic Development in the History of Economic Thought*, New York, 1968, Lecture II.

ductive assets. Population pressure is also likely to intensify the foreign exchange constraint by placing more pressure on the balance of payments. In some cases, the need to import foodstuffs will require the development of new industries for export expansion and/or import substitution. Possibly the most serious disadvantage to a high rate of population growth in a poor country is that it makes the human resources constraint more difficult to remove. Larger numbers militate against an improvement in the quality of the population as productive agents. The rapid increase in school-age population and the expanding number of labor force entrants put ever-greater pressure on educational and training facilities and retard improvement in the quality of education. Similarly, too dense a population or a rapid rate of increase of population aggravates the problem of improving the health of the population. With the concern over unemployment and inequality, students of population are now also asking whether population growth intensifies the extent of absolute poverty and the maldistribution of income.

That these disadvantages have become very real for many LDCs can be recognized if we contrast the demographic patterns of rich and poor countries. One striking difference is that a much higher percentage of the total population in poor countries is in younger age groups, and life expectancy is much lower than in rich countries. In most of the LDCs, 40 to 50 per cent of the population is below fifteen years of age, whereas in developed countries the corresponding percentage is about 25 per cent. If the economically productive age bracket is taken as fifteen to sixty-five years, the percentage of population in this category is considerably less in poor countries than in rich. This "bottom heavy" age structure of population results in a high ratio of dependents to adult workers, which means the differentiation and productive power of the labor force are limited. Even worse, it means greater consumption and constitutes a major obstacle to an increase in savings in many

LDCs.[2] This high dependency ratio requires the economy to divert a considerable part of its resources, that might otherwise go into capital formation, to the maintenance of a high percentage of dependents who may never become producers or, if so, only for a relatively short working life.

Not only do most of the people in the world live in the less developed areas, but the concentration is increasing. In many LDCs, the populations are of the high-growth potential type. In these countries the simple application of modern public health measures has allowed the death rate to fall spectacularly to the low levels of the rich country, while birth rates have remained very high and resistant to change (except recently in a few countries, as noted in the next selection). If, as is true for many LDCs, the birth rate remains at a high level of about 40 per thousand while the death rate is reduced to about 10 per thousand, then the population will double within a generation. With the declining death rates, the rates of natural increase have risen in the LDCs to 2, 3, or even 4 per cent a year in regions of persistently high fertility. While the population in the rich countries, constituting 30 per cent of the world's population, is growing at an average of only 1 per cent or less, the population in the poor countries, amounting to 70 per cent of the world's population, is growing at an average rate of 2.5 per cent. Almost all the doubling times for populations in poor countries are more rapid than the world average: Ethiopia is 33 years; India, 28 years; North Korea, 25 years; Mexico, 21 years. During the next 25 years, about 85 per cent of the children born will be in the poor countries. Although population projections are necessarily tentative, and present trends are unlikely to continue for a long period, nonetheless Table 1 gives

[2] For empirical evidence that the dependency ratio is significant for a country's savings-income ratio, see UNCTAD, "Objectives for the Mobilization of Domestic Resources by the Developing Countries," TD/B/C.3/58, December 9, 1968, pp. 26–7.

TABLE 1. Population of the World and Eight Major Regions, 1920 to 1960, and Projected, 1960 to 2000, on Assumptions of Continuing Recent Trends.

Regions	Enumerated or Estimated			Projected	
	1920	1940	1960	1980	2000
Population (millions)					
World	1,862	2,295	2,990	4,467	6,504
More developed regions	606	730	854	1,052	1,266
Europe	327	380	425	497	568
Soviet Union	155	195	214	270	330
Northern America	116	144	199	261	333
Oceania	8.5	11.1	15.7	24	35
Less developed regions	1,256	1,565	2,136	3,415	5,248
East Asia	553	634	793	1,095	1,424
South Asia	470	610	858	1,486	2,354
Africa	143	191	273	457	818
Latin America	90	130	212	377	652
Increase, 20-year periods (per cent)					
World	—	23.2	30.3	49.4	45.6
More developed regions	—	20.5	17.0	23.2	20.3
Europe	—	16.2	11.8	16.9	14.3
Soviet Union	—	25.8	9.7	26.2	22.2
Northern America	—	24.1	38.2	31.2	27.6
Oceania	—	30.6	41.4	52.9	45.8
Less developed regions	—	24.6	36.5	59.9	53.7
East Asia	—	14.6	25.1	38.1	30.0
South Asia	—	29.8	40.6	73.2	58.4
Africa	—	33.6	42.9	67.4	79.0
Latin America	—	44.4	63.1	77.8	72.9

Source: United Nations, *World Population Prospects, as Assessed in 1968*, Table A.1.

some indication of the increase in world population and its distribution by the end of the century.

The population explosion that has been experienced during the last two decades in most of the LDCs is in marked contrast with the history of the presently rich industrial nations when they were in earlier phases of their development. In their nineteenth-century preindustrial phase, the countries of western Europe had a population growth that was generally less than half the rate now existing in the poor countries. Moreover, in the past the decline of the death rate in industrialized countries was mainly due to the development process itself—through such factors as improved diet, better housing, sanitation. The death rates declined as part of the general evolution of Western society—induced by improvements in economic conditions and accompanied by changes in social attitudes that allowed birth rates to begin falling before death rates reached their low levels. Now, however, mortality rates are falling in poor countries not because of development, but because modern medical knowledge and scientific techniques of death control can be readily transferred from the rich countries and applied in nonindustrial areas. Modern medical and public health advances have stimulated declines in mortality independently of economic development and social change.

A crucial question now is whether population control policies can also stimulate declines in fertility,[3] without having to wait for higher levels of economic and social development to bring about a "normal" decline in fertility. Can family planning programs be effective in the face of traditional beliefs and social institutions that have sustained fertility at a high level? Or can an adjustment of birth rates to the fall in death rates be induced only by long-run forces of development and the resultant changes in the traditional culture? Is the future of population growth essentially a question of the future of development?

This Note has reversed the last question and emphasized that the very future of development is itself dependent upon a reduction in heavy population pressures, lest it be increasingly difficult to remove the shortages of capital, foodstuffs, foreign exchange, and skills that now limit the rate of development. But the total discussion of this book can be interpreted as claiming that the potential for economic development is greater than the potential for population growth. To realize this potential as rapidly as possible, we must therefore recognize the beneficial effects that can come from declining fertili-

[3] A general fertility rate is number of births per 1000 women in reproductive ages 15–49.

ty, and consider the inclusion of policies of family planning as a complement to other policies of development planning. We must also give due weight to the belief that rapid population growth is a consequence as well as a cause of poverty. Declining fertility is highly correlated with a reduction in unemployment, improved status of women, better health care, more education, and greater income.

Many demographers believe the time is dropping rapidly for the demographic transition from high to low birth and death rates. One major study of recent trends in natality in the LDCs concludes:

The data support the following conclusion about recent changes in natality in less developed regions:

1. A growing number of countries have been entering the demographic transition on the natality side since World War II and after a lapse of some 25 years in which no major country entered this transition.

2. Once a sustained reduction of the birth rate has begun, it proceeds at a much more rapid pace than it did historically in Europe and among Europeans overseas.

3. The "new" countries may reduce birth rates quite rapidly despite initially higher levels than existed historically in western Europe.

4. Where available, the more refined measures of fertility, standardizing for differences in age structure, yield results similar to those for crude birth rates.

5. There is no direct evidence yet that current fertility reductions will terminate at levels significantly higher than those achieved in European countries and Japan.

The above observations are based primarily on the experience of a relatively few countries with good data. Similar reductions in natality are very likely occurring in a number of other countries lacking reliable annual vital statistics. But there is no evidence yet as to whether reductions in the birth rate have recently occurred, or not occurred, in large countries, such as China,

India, Pakistan, and Indonesia. What is happening in these countries will be crucial.

Efforts to identify "thresholds" for the initiation of fertility reduction are at a preliminary stage and their predictive capacity, although promising in some regions, remains to be fully tested. The relation between socioeconomic variables and fertility is clearly different within the different major cultural regions of the less developed world; quite different levels and kinds of development are associated with fertility reductions, for example, in east Asia and in Latin America. This confirms common sense and explains why efforts to relate socioeconomic measures and fertility "across the board" for all less developed countries have led to confusing results.

Finally, is there indeed a new or renewed demographic transition? The evidence suggests that there is. A rapidly growing number of countries of diverse cultural background have entered the natality transition since World War II and after a 25-year lapse in such entries. In these countries the transition is moving much faster than it did in Europe. This is probably related to the fact that progress in general is moving much faster in such matters as urbanization, education, health, communication, and often per capita income. If progress in modernization continues, notably in the larger countries, the demographic transition in the less developed world will probably be completed much more rapidly than it was in Europe.

It would be foolhardy, however, not to end on a word of caution. On any assumptions concerning the reduction of fertility that may occur with socioeconomic progress, it still follows that one may anticipate and must accommodate an enormous increase in the world population and that these increases will be greatest precisely in those countries economically least well-equipped to absorb the increase in numbers.[4]

[4] Dudley Kirk, "A New Demographic Transition?" in Study Committee, National Academy of Sciences, *Rapid Population Growth*, Baltimore, 1971, pp. 145–6.

VIII.A.2. Demographic Change and

Socio-Economic Change*

In 1970, the population of the world stood at about 3.6 billion. As a result of a birth rate of about 34 per 1,000 of the population and a death rate of 14, it was increasing at 2 per cent a year, perceptibly faster than in the previous decade. Even a subdivision by broad regions reveals contrasts that suggest a close relationship between demographic development and economic development. The regions with birth rates above the global average, for example, comprise the developing countries of Asia, Africa and Latin

*From United Nations, Department of Economic and Social Affairs, *World Economic Survey 1973: Part One, Population and Development*, New York, 1974, pp. 7–8, 13–18.

America, accounting in the aggregate for half the world population (see table 1).

Several of these developing regions, however, have relatively low death rates. The Latin American averages, for example, are much the same as that of Europe, ranging from 10 per thousand of the population in the tropical area of South America to 11 in the Caribbean. To some extent this similarity in crude rates stems from the difference in age composition: the Latin American population is a much younger one and its life expectancy at birth is still substantially less (around 60 years) than that of the European population (around 70 years). Nevertheless, the contrast between the patterns of birth rates and the patterns of death rates suggests

TABLE 1. World Population and Vital Rates, by Region, 1950–1970

Region	Population 1970 (Millions)	1965–1970 Average Annual Rate per 1,000 Population		Average Annual Rate of Growth (Percentage)	
		Birth	Death	1950–1960	1960–1970
Europe	462	18.0	10.2	0.80	0.85
Japan	104	18.0	7.0	1.17	1.05
USSR	243	17.9	7.7	1.74	1.24
North America	228	19.3	9.4	1.79	1.36
East Asian mainland	779	33.1	15.1	1.81	1.80
Temperate South America	39	26.3	9.1	2.07	1.83
Oceania	15	20.2	8.7	2.25	1.92
Caribbean	26	35.0	10.9	2.02	2.27
Africa	345	46.8	21.3	2.15	2.45
Polynesia and Melanesia	4	41.2	14.9	2.21	2.61
Southern Asia	1,126	44.3	16.8	2.14	2.63
Eastern Asia	47	35.0	10.7	1.59	2.64
Tropical South America	151	39.8	10.0	2.92	2.98
Central America	67	43.7	10.1	3.10	3.35
World total	3,635	33.8	14.0	1.82	1.98

Source: Centre for Development Planning, Projections and Policies of the United Nations Secretariat, based on "Demographic trends in the world and its major regions, 1950–1970" (E/CONF.60/CBP/14, April 1974).

that the course of demographic development is not shaped by a uniform set of influences. The range of mortality rates is appreciably wider than that of natality and the two may change quite independently.

The co-existence of high birth rates characteristic of one type of society with the low death rates typical of a quite different society implies a potential for explosive growth. It is important, therefore, for individual countries not only to be able to take their existing and emerging demographic circumstances fully into account in their socio-economic planning but also to be aware of how the key demographic variables may be affected by technological and economic development. This may be illuminated both by cross-country analysis and also—with due reservations about relevance to present-day problems—by an examination of demographic development in countries with appropriate records to draw on.

An analysis of the history of the countries that are now characterized as economically advanced suggests that there has always been a close relationship between demographic change and socio-economic change. The precise relationship has differed from country to country and, because it has been affected by a number of other factors—notably the population/resource balance, the prevailing technologies and the nature of the cultural and institutional heritage—it has also varied from time to time. Nevertheless, certain broad features of that relationship have remained sufficiently constant to suggest a pattern of tendencies and sequences that may help to throw light on the contemporary global scene with all its complicated diversity.

The basic pattern is a movement over time from a situation of high death rates and high birth rates to one marked by low death rates and low birth rates. In this transition the decline in death rates precedes the decline in birth rates. The lag between these two downward trends is the crucial demographic dimension, for on its length depends the magnitude of the population explosion implicit in the transition.

The factors inducing the decline in mortality and fertility are not only complex—and combined in different proportions at different times—but also subject to a feedback reaction from the vital changes themselves. Thus the process of economic and social development and the demographic transition are linked in a mutually causative fashion, death rates being reduced by improvements in the standards of living made possible by an economic diversification process which, in its turn, causes—and is, in varying degree, contingent upon—a reduction in fertility. The links are by no means uniform or automatic: they are shaped by the physical environment, by contemporary production techniques, by the mores of the society concerned and by the way in which the fruits of its economic progress are distributed. Nor, indeed, are changes in vital rates solely the result of the forces transmitted through these links: they can be directly affected by the application of new technologies. Evidence of this has been particularly persuasive in the post-war period which has seen a decline in death rates of unprecedented proportions brought about by advances in sanitary and medical procedures quite unrelated to the level of living of the population concerned. Whether similar changes can be effected in birth rates is still an open question: the decisions influencing fertility are more private and culture-bound and their responsiveness either to specific technological developments or to official exhortation is likely to be much less definite or rapid. . . .

THE GROWTH OF POPULATION

In most countries the difference between the vital rates determines the rate at which the population grows; in very few cases do the gains or losses from migration play a major role. Since the demographic transition that seems to occur in the course of socio-economic development begins with a decline in the death rate, to be followed—but only after a significant delay—by a decline in the birth rate, the early stages are marked by an appreciable rise in the rate of natural increase. As indicated in table 1 above, the peak rate of population growth is reached in the third phase of the transition: by this time death rates have dropped to a low level but changes in fertility have made very little progress. Even in the fourth phase, when birth rates are clearly moving downwards, their difference from the low rates that mortality has already attained may be great enough to yield a rate of natural increase higher than that typical of a high death rate-high birth rate pre-transition community. It is only in the final phase that the rate of natural increase falls sharply to the levels that characterize economically advanced countries.

Population Growth and Income

Some aspects of this transformation over time can be captured in a snapshot cross-country picture. This shows that in 1970 the lowest-income group of countries tended to have rates of population increase between 2 and 3 per cent a year: over 80 per cent of the countries with a *per capita* income of less than $200 were in this population growth rate category. Countries in the intermediate-income range—$200–$700 a year *per capita*—were divided more or less equally between the 2–3 per cent population growth category (reflecting the early stages of the decline in death rates) and the highest population growth category (in which low mortality and high fertility yielded an increase of over 3 per cent a year). Of the countries with higher *per capita* incomes (over $700 a year) three fourths had rates of population growth of less than 2 per cent a year and two thirds had rates of less than 1.5 per cent.

As for the remaining countries, special factors accounted for their being outside their income-population growth category. Many of the countries that had lower rates of population growth than might have been expected from their income status were among those registering emigration losses—Barbados, Cuba, Lesotho, Portugal and Yugoslavia, for example. At the other end of the spectrum some owed their high incomes to a particularly active export sector less than fully integrated with the domestic economy (as in the case of the Libyan Arab Republic, Panama, Surinam, Trinidad and Tobago and Venezuela, for example) or to exceptional immigration gains (as in the case of Australia, Hong Kong, Israel, Kuwait and Singapore).

Population Growth and Economic Growth

While there is thus a discernible pattern in the relationship between income levels and vital characteristics, demographic factors pale into insignificance among the determinants of economic growth. On the other hand, differences in the rate of increase in production and income do tend to induce movements of population, though these occur chiefly within countries rather than between countries. And with a few notable exceptions—in which differences in income levels play a more important role than differences in growth rates—international population movements are small in relation to natural increase. Though the rate of increase in population influences savings, especially in low-income countries, this effect tends to have a much smaller impact on the growth of output than do changes in technology or discoveries of natural resources. And even where population growth does seriously affect national savings, the impact on production may be more than offset by international movements of capital. It is not surprising, therefore, that a matrix of population and production growth rates for the 1960s reveals no systematic relationship pattern.

Changes in *per capita* income were much more sensitive to differences in population growth rates in the 1960s. There was a systematic increase in the proportion of countries with an average annual gain of less than 2 per cent in output per person—from zero among the countries in which population was expanding at less than 1 per cent a year and a sixth of those in the 1–2 per cent growth group to 37 per cent among those with a population growth rate of over 3 per cent a year. The proportion achieving an increase of over 3 per cent a year in *per capita* output fell away correspondingly—from 94 per cent in the countries with the lowest population growth rate to 26 per cent in those with the highest. The countries registering large gains in *per capita* income notwithstanding rapid population growth were chiefly major mineral exporters—Iran, the Libyan Arab Republic, Saudi Arabia and Surinam.

Population Growth and Savings

Relatively few of the countries with low rates of population growth have low savings ratios: in the period 1968–1970, for example, about half the countries in which population had been increasing at less than 1.5 per cent a year saved more than a fourth of their gross product while the proportion saving less than 15 per cent was not much more than an eighth. Correspondingly, the low savers were largely those with high population growth: less than an eighth of the countries in which population was increasing at over 2 per cent a year had savings ratios of more than 25 per cent.

The countries not conforming to this negative relationship between population growth and savings were in many cases subject to special influences. Among the low savers, for example, population was held down by net emigration from such countries as Barbados, Lesotho and Portugal. And among the high population growth countries, savings were boosted by the activities of mineral-exporting companies in the case of Kuwait, the Libyan Arab Republic, Saudi Arabia, Surinam, Venezuela and Zambia.

Population Growth and Urbanization

There is an inverse relationship between the rate of increase in population and the degree of urbanization. Among the low-growth countries (with population rising by less than 1.5 per cent a year) hardly any had an urban component of less than 30 per cent in 1970 and only a fifth had as much as 40 per cent of their population living in urban areas. Conversely, only a sixth of the countries in which population was increasing at between 2 and 3 per cent a year had an urbanization ratio of over 40 per cent.

This pattern did not carry over into the group of countries with the highest—more than 3 per cent a year—rate of population increase, however. Half this high-growth group had more than 40 per cent of its population living in urban areas. Though, in general, fertility tends to be lower in urban communities than in rural, this group combines the highest rate of population increase with the highest degree of urbanization. As the countries concerned were either Arab (Algeria, Iraq, Jordan, Kuwait, the Syrian Arab Republic and Tunisia) or Latin American (Colombia, El Salvador, Mexico, Panama, Peru and Venezuela), it is clear that the exception was more a reflection of cultural factors than of the process of economic development.

Population Growth and Education

Not unrelated to the extent of urbanization is the school enrolment ratio. In only an eighth of the countries in which population was growing at less than 1.5 per cent a year in the late 1960s was less than 60 per cent of the 5–19 age group enrolled in formal education. Conversely, among the countries with rapid population growth—over 2.5 per cent a year—only an eighth had an enrolment ratio of more than 60 per cent.

The highest concentration of low enrolment ratios, however, was in the intermediate-growth group in which population was increasing at 2.2–3.0 per cent a year: in almost half the countries in this group enrolment was less than a third of the relevant age bracket. In the Arab-Latin American group of high population growth countries, on the other hand, between 30 and 60 per cent of all 5–19 year old children were enrolled in school.

Cultural patterns again emerge in the sex composition of this school enrolment. In the high-growth group there was a sharp contrast between the representation of girls in the Latin American countries, on the one hand (over .85 per cent of the number of enrolled boys in most cases), and in the Arab countries, on the other (with less than 70 per cent of the number of boys). In none of the countries in which population was increasing at less than 1.5 per cent a year was female enrolment less than half of male enrolment. Among the higher-growth countries, however, low enrolment of girls was quite common: in over a fourth it was below 50 per cent of the male level and in almost half below 70 per cent. Even lower ratios were recorded in respect of secondary education: among the countries in which population was increasing at between 2.5 and 3 per cent a year, about a half had three boys in secondary school for every girl.

Population Growth and Nutrition

Just as the difficulty of providing adequate education facilities is magnified by a high rate of natural increase, so is the problem of feeding the population. Thus in the late 1960s, among the slow-growth countries only a handful had a daily average calorie intake of less than 2,600 per person and two thirds of them had an average of over 2,900 calories, available. Conversely, among the countries in which population was increasing more rapidly (at over 2 per cent a year), very few (about 9 per cent) had more than 2,600 calories available *per capita*. In this group, indeed, almost two thirds of the countries had an average daily intake of less than 2,300 per person.

Protein availability presents a very similar picture: around 80 per cent of the slow-growing countries had an average daily intake in excess of 80 grammes per person while in the case of the faster-growing countries (with population increasing at more than 2 per cent a year) about 80 per cent had a daily intake averaging less than 70 grammes per person.

For many countries the growth of population adds significantly to the food import bill. At the end of the 1960s, half the countries were spending more then $15 a year per person on basic food imports, and a fourth were spending more than $40. Most of these countries were in the high-income category but they also included a number of the smaller islands among the developing countries, as well as such countries as Chile and, among those with very high population growth, Costa Rica, Jordan, Lebanon and Panama.

Population Growth and Indicators of Economic Development

Though the pictures drawn in this section have all been static, they suggest that the demographic transition that was associated with the economic development of the countries that are now classified as more advanced is in various stages of fulfilment among the developing countries. Perhaps the most important aspect of the transition—arising from the fact that the decline in mortality precedes the decline in fertility by an indeterminate, but not inconsiderable, period—is the implicit increase in the rate of population growth as economic and demographic development proceeds. Thus the general inverse relationship between the rate of

population increase and the various criteria of the state of development is not smooth and continuous: it is deflected by the widening disparity between birth rate and death rate and the socio-economic difficulties caused by the resultant rise in the rate of natural increase which complicate the process of graduation to demographic maturity.

If countries are divided into five groups according to their current ratio of population growth, it is the middle groups—with a population of nearly 1.5 billion, increasing at between 2 and 3 per cent a year—that manifest most of the signs of underdevelopment (see table 2). These groups have the lowest degree of urbanization (24 per cent), the highest proportion of the labour force in agriculture (around two thirds), the highest density of occupation of land (over 300 rural persons per square kilometre of agricultural land) and the lowest *per capita* consumption of foodstuffs. The group with a population growth rate of 2.0–2.5 per cent a year had the lowest savings ratio (9.4 per cent of gross ·domestic product in 1968–1970), and the 2.5–3.0 per cent group had the lowest rate of increase in *per capita* income (2.1 per cent a year in the 1960s).

All these indicators show the group with the highest rate of population growth (over 3 per cent a year) to have an improved development status. Its higher rate of increase in population is itself the result of one of these improvements, namely, a considerable reduction in the average death rate—to only 12.5 per thousand.

Further along in the demographic transition is the small group whose average birth rate has dropped below 25 per 1,000 persons per annum, giving it a rate of population growth of 1.5 per cent plus, in this case, a small net gain from immigration. In these countries almost three fourths of the population live in urban areas; their average income is substantially higher and, on a *per capita* basis, rising more rapidly than in the groups with a faster population growth.

The group with the lowest vital rates and an average increase of population of only 0.9

TABLE 2. Socio-economic Characteristics of Countries Grouped According to Rate of Increase in Population

Indicator	Countries in which the Annual Average Percentage Rate of Increase in Population in 1960–1970 was				
	Less than 1.5	1.5–1.9	2.00–2.49	2.50–2.99	3.00 and over
Number of countries	34	8	36	34	28
Population, 1970 (millions):					
Total	1,011	59	293	1,175	285
Average	29.7	7.4	8.1	34.6	10.2
Crude birth rate, 1965–1970 average per thousand	18.3	23.3	42.1	43.9	44.6
Crude death rate, 1965–1970 average per thousand	9.2	8.5	19.4	17.1	12.5
Natural increase, 1965–1970 average per thousand	9.1	14.8	22.7	26.8	32.1
Age distribution, 1970 (percentage):					
0–14	26.5	30.5	41.5	43.1	45.7
15–64	62.7	62.3	55.0	53.7	51.2
65 and over	10.8	7.2	3.5	3.3	3.1
Percentage of population in urban areas, 1970	63	72	24	24	40
Percentage of labour force in agriculture, 1970	20	17	68	65	56
Average per capita income, 1970 (dollars)	2,213	1,873	313	166	409
Ratio of national savings to GDP, 1968–1970 (percentage)	26.1	21.4	9.4	13.4	18.7
Average annual increase in GDP, 1961–1970 (percentage)	6.2	4.2	4.7	4.8	5.8
Average annual increase in per capita GDP, 1961–1970 (percentage)	5.1	2.5	2.5	2.1	2.5
Average per capita calorie consumption, 1964–1966	3,090	3,066	2,183	2,168	2,287
Average per capita protein consumption, 1964–1966 (grammes)	90	94	57	54	60
Average density: persons per square kilometre, 1970	103	16	124	138	44
Average density: rural population per square kilometre of arable land	170	37[a]	365	300	190[b]

[a] Excluding Iceland.
[b] Excluding Kuwait.
Source: See table 1.

per cent a year comprises most of the industrialized countries. It has the oldest population: almost 11 per cent over 65 (about three times the average of the high-growth groups), almost 63 per cent in the working age bracket and only 27 per cent below 15 years old. Not much more than a third of this population lives in rural areas and only a fifth of the labour force works in agriculture.

VIII.B. HEALTH AND

NUTRITION

VIII.B.1. A Health Policy for

Developing Countries*

Before it is possible to formulate a sensible health policy for the developing countries, perhaps the most fundamental question to be answered is: "What really determines the overall health level of a population?" One obvious possible answer is health services, and the number of physicians or hospital beds: yet there is clear evidence that at best this is only a very partial answer. In the "west"–North-western Europe and the United States–life expectancy at birth rose from about 35–40 years in the eighteenth century, to 50–55 by 1900. Yet very little indeed of this progress can be attributed to medical science. By 1900 major discoveries in medicine and surgery had already been made, but only smallpox vaccination would have been in sufficiently general use to have had a significant effect on mortality in the population as a whole. One must therefore look to other factors—better nutrition, a slow improvement in hygiene habits, and from about 1870 the effects of a series of public health measures.

Equally, factors other than conventional health services are still of importance today. It is difficult to measure health coverage accurately because of problems of definition: however, one indication that "modern" personal health services may be of very limited importance in many developing countries is the high proportion of babies

*From M. J. Sharpston, "A Health Policy For Developing Countries," World Bank draft paper, July 1975. Reprinted by permission.

The views expressed in the article represent those of the author and not necessarily those of the World Bank.

delivered by native midwives or indeed by relatives; probably as many as three-quarters or more of all births in such countries as Colombia, Tanzania, Thailand, Peru, Tunisia, Sudan, or Venezuela. Yet despite this low coverage of the population by "modern" health services in many developing countries, health has improved substantially since World War II. Evidence of this is the population "explosion", most of which can certainly be attributed to decreased mortality rather than increased fertility. Average life expectancy at birth in the developing world has probably increased from about 32 years before World War II, to 49 years at the end of the 1960s. Though this is still far short of the 70 years or more now typical of a developed country, it represents a very dramatic fall in mortality, over a rather short period. Some of the fall is attributable to major health campaigns (a notable example is malaria eradication in the Indian sub-continent), but a large residual is left which can only be explained by broader factors. To understand fully how such broader factors operate, one must examine rather carefully what the real health problems of a typical developing country are, and what causes them.

THE ECOLOGY OF POVERTY AND
DISEASE

Man, the organisms which give him diseases, and the vectors (such as flies) which help transmit disease, are all part of an ecological system. It is the interaction of man and his environment which determines the

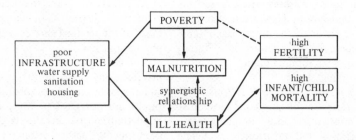

incidence of disease, i.e., how often disease is contracted. Curative health care services only very infrequently affect the incidence of disease, though they may mitigate its effects.[1] Rather, the disease pattern of a society intimately reflects its standard of living, and indeed its whole way of life. The diagram above shows some of the key factors which affect health in a typical developing country:[2]

In many societies, poverty is associated with high fertility. This has an obvious effect on the age-structure of the population. In any country, it is the old and the very young who are most susceptible to disease. Developing countries have proportionately very few old people, and many young children. As a result, diseases such as cancer and cardio-vascular conditions are a far smaller part of the disease pattern than in developed countries. On the other hand, up to a half of all deaths may be of those under five. In addition, the high level of fertility common in the developing world, and the short interval between births, also have a direct impact on health, largely because less nutrition and care is available for each child. Morbidity

and mortality in a large family are higher, and later children in the family are at a particular disadvantage. Furthermore, the health of the mother also tends to be worse in large families.

One of the most significant effects of the existence of large families living in poverty is malnutrition, which is of considerable importance as a direct cause of death. Still more importantly, malnutrition acts "synergistically" with disease agents to increase the incidence of clinical disease and aggravate its severity, essentially because it hampers the body's resistance mechanisms. Equally, disease can bring on malnutrition by increasing food requirements at a time when effective food absorption is often diminished.

At the same time, poverty makes itself manifest in poor physical infrastructure, including water supply, sanitation, and housing. In their turn, poor water supply and sanitation relate directly to a prevalence of diseases connected with human wastes, while poor housing is associated with the prevalence of air-borne diseases.[3] Among the diseases connected with human wastes are typhoid, dysentery, cholera, polio, and hepatitis. Diarrhoeal disease, also in this group, is probably the biggest single cause of death among children under five, and of illness in adults. Many worm diseases also belong to this group, including tapeworms, hook-

[1] For an account of the very limited effect on the incidence of disease of very high-level, very intensive and expensive health care, see Walsh McDermott, Kurt W. Deuschle and Clifford R. Barnett, "Health Care Experiment at Many Farms" in *Science*, January 7, 1972.

[2] I am indebted to Ms. S. E. Harvey for help with this diagram.

[3] In fact, poor housing also seems to affect the prevalence of other diseases, such as diarrhoeal diseases.

worms, and bilharzia (also called schistosomiasis). Air-borne diseases are the second
most important group. They are transmitted
by the breathing-in of the disease agent, and
include tuberculosis, pneumonia, diptheria, bronchitis, whooping cough, meningitis,
influenza, and measles.

In a major study of 22 locations in 8
Latin American/Caribbean countries, diseases from contamination by human wastes,
air-borne diseases, and nutritional deficiency
were responsible in all except two cases
(both in Jamaica) for over 70 per cent of
deaths under five—figures as high as 91 per
cent are found.[4] In other words, although
exotic tropical diseases can be of great importance in certain areas, in general they do
not constitute the key health problems of
the developing world. Rather, it is the generally mundane diseases of the core disease
pattern already described which really take
the biggest toll. However, official health statistics, collected usually from a few major
urban hospitals, will not necessarily show
that this is so—even in a developed country,
a health service "discovers" the illnesses for
which it is looking and to which it caters.

THE ALLOCATION OF RESOURCES DEVOTED TO HEALTH

In nearly all developing countries, the
bulk of government health expenditure is
allocated to curative services. A large part of
government funds are spent on hospitals,
particularly on in-patient services. In turn,
hospitals are concentrated in the urban
areas, and most of the patients also come
from the same urban area: organized referral

[4] Deaths due to congenital abnormalities or
perinatal causes excluded. Calculated from Ruth R.
Puffer, Carlos V. Serrano, *Inter-American Investigation of Mortality in Childhood, Provisional Report*, Pan-American Health Organization, September 1971. For a fuller account of the system of
disease classification used above, see M. J. Sharpston, *Factors Determining the Health Situation in
Developing Countries*, World Bank Staff Working
Paper, 1975.

is usually of insignificant importance. Some
rural inhabitants refer themselves—i.e., take
themselves into an urban centre—but even so
most of the medical care goes to a few urban
populations.[5]

The reasons why doctors, government or
private, congregate in the principal towns,
and the government doctors in the large hospitals, are not hard to find. The economic
opportunities are in the large towns—and
government doctors often do private practice, whether or not it is officially permitted.
Again, even if a doctor comes from the rural
areas originally (and, in fact, most come
from better-off households in the cities), by
the time he has completed his training he
usually has adopted the outlook of an urban
professional man: his friends will live in the
cities, and that is where the bright lights are.
Furthermore, he is likely to associate high
professional status with the sophisticated
treatment of "interesting" cases: this will
usually only be possible at a few major hospitals. Politically, private sector doctors will
usually be able to determine where they
practice, and so also will public sector doctors—doctors are a tight elite, with an arcane
expertise that touches the frightening mysteries of life and death: few laymen will
tackle them on their own terrain. In any
case, the lay elite—politicians, civil servants,
even trade union leaders—are also nearly all
urban, and will want "proper" (i.e., western)
levels of treatment for themselves and their
families. The result is that in most countries
the doctors stay almost exclusively in the
main towns, perhaps after a token year or so
of exile in the hinterland, soon after becoming qualified. Extra output of doctors by the
medical schools only leads to unemployment
or under-employment of doctors in the capital cities, probably coupled with emigration:
this, for example, is the case in the Philip-

[5] See M. J. Sharpston, "Uneven Geographical
Distribution of Medical Care: A Ghanaian Case
Study," in *Journal of Development Studies*, Vol. 8,
No. 2, January 1972. Similar statistics could be
produced for a very wide range of developing countries.

pines. The rural areas remain without doctors. On the other hand, the mere fact that doctors remain unemployed will not necessarily prevent the creation of new medical schools: the output of doctors is frequently determined by the political power and social aspirations of middle-class parents.

There is thus an impressive array of factors tending to concentrate the resources of the health services in a few urban areas. This situation can now be related to three main reasons why health coverage in developing countries tends to be low. The first reason is geographical: it is known that the great bulk of patients at a health facility come from the immediate vicinity, say, within five miles. Yet much of the population of most developing countries is dispersed and outside the immediate vicinity of a health facility. The second reason is administrative: it is very difficult to get referral systems to work. The transport from outlying areas to urban hospitals is not available, and few developing countries have an administrative control system strong and ruthless enough to prevent those in the immediate vicinity of a hospital from pre-empting the available beds. The third reason is cultural: particularly in Latin America, a peasant may feel that a doctor looks down on him, and prefer to go to a curandero. In Asia, people may have more faith in traditional healers, or go to western doctors only for certain conditions.[6] Thus even in the cities many people do not make use of official health services.

POLICIES FOR HEALTH DEVELOPMENT

It has been shown that poor health, poverty, and high fertility are intimately inter-

[6] A study in an Indian village showed that village women preferred the Family Health Worker for diarrhoea or fever, the private doctor for tetanus, and the faith healer for smallpox, chickenpox, or measles. See Rural Health Research Centre, Narangwal, Punjab, India, *Rural Health Services and Family Planning Utilization*, Annual Report of Population Research, 1972–73.

related. Any policy that raises income levels or equalizes income distribution is likely to improve nutrition, particularly among the poor: this will almost certainly improve health. Equally, any policy which lowers fertility will also tend to improve health.

More generally, health considerations need to be taken into account early on in all development planning, rather than having health regarded as a matter of giving more money to the Ministry of Health for a new hospital, or adding a clinic to a development project. For example, in agricultural development one should try to ensure that the crops grown in a region will yield a reasonably balanced diet, and avoid excessive emphasis on commerical cash crops. Large-scale water resource projects, particularly in previously arid areas, can create important health risks, of river blindness, schistosomiasis, and malaria. (A full list of countermeasures is not appropriate here: but, for example, sluice gates should be designed to minimize the breeding possibilities for simulium black fly, which is the vector of river blindness.)

HEALTH PROMOTION SERVICES

Whatever policy has been in theory, in fact—as evinced in the allocation of financial and manpower resources—there has often been an effective emphasis on sophisticated and expensive clinical practice by highly trained, highly paid physicians in large urban hospitals. At the same time, environmental health, water supply and sanitation have generally received little emphasis, except to a limited extent in a few major cities. While this may have corresponded to the realities of powerful social and political forces—the vested interests of an urban elite and of the medical profession—such activities have scarcely touched the health problems of the bulk of the population, who often live in rural areas out of reach of official personal health services, and whose health situation is hardly affected by episodic curative health care.

Essentially, a way has to be found of promoting health in a whole community, rather than concentrating on the treatment of illness in individuals on an intermittent basis. What is needed is to change the ecological and cultural situation which permits disease to thrive. At the same time, curative health care is a felt need of all peoples in all situations, and attempts at health education or environmental health are often likely to meet with little acceptance, if they are divorced from curative care. The problem is to ensure that curative care does not swamp environmental health, other preventive measures, and health education, but is in balance with them.

THE COMMUNITY-BASED HEALTH WORKER SYSTEM

To achieve this goal, it may be useful to consider an approach based on the promotion of health from within the community. (Since the population of most developing countries is predominantly rural, the concept of community-based health workers is discussed here in a rural context; but the basic idea is equally applicable to poor groups in an urban environment.) Essentially, a village would choose one or perhaps more of its members for health training;[7] in this way the health worker selected would be assured of the village's support. The health worker chosen could be male or female, an old traditional healer or birth attendant, or a young primary school graduate: the choice should reflect village cultural attitudes and literacy, though useful, would not be imposed as a qualification. The worker would then be given brief training—with frequent later refresher courses—in how to treat some of the commonest disease conditions

on a symptomatic basis, i.e., if there is this symptom, give this treatment. (A programme of this kind, to teach illiterate villagers, already exists in Niger.)

The teaching of clinical skills would of necessity be very limited; and indeed this would be desirable, in order to ensure adequate time for environmental and preventive health work, including family planning. Among other duties such workers could monitor the growth of young children for possible nutritional problems, provide nutrition education and organize self-help efforts in the fields of environmental health, water supply and sanitation, with such governmental help as could be made available and was absolutely necessary. (Pit latrines are a cheap and effective self-help technology for rural sanitation. The construction of good water systems may require more technical assistance—but just to put a rim around the village well and a cover over the top may be better than nothing.) Since the health worker would be diagnosing and prescribing drugs in his own right, to make health care provided in this way as effective as possible, it would be necessary to permit such a worker to use certain drugs which have perhaps more conventionally been limited to prescription by a physician. The appropriate question is not, "Could some people die from incorrect treatment or from side-effects?" but "Will more die if the village worker is, or is not, allowed to use this drug?"[8]

In all likelihood, and whether or not the community-based health workers chosen by their communities are traditional healers, the traditional health care system will continue to be important for a long while. It is therefore most important that community-based health workers who are not themselves part of the traditional health care system should co-operate with it.

[7] Arguably the government authorites should have some say in the selection process, especially if there are inegalitarian power structures at the village level. The practical operation of the system proposed here will depend very much upon how it fits into the local socio-political environment.

[8] This has been called "statistical morality." See Walsh McDermott, "Modern Medicine and the Demographic Disease Pattern of Overly Traditional Societies: A Technologic Misfit" in *Journal of Medical Education*, September 1966.

Community-based health workers would typically work on health matters part time. For example, it may be possible to include agricultural extension among the functions of a multi-purpose worker; this has proved a very successful combination in the Cali region in Colombia. Costs in connexion with a community-based health worker system would tend to be very low compared to a more conventional health service. In Niger, the continuous training of village aides costs only about $15 a year.

ADMINISTRATION AND SUPERVISION OF COMMUNITY-BASED HEALTH PROMOTION SERVICES

Immediately above the community-based health workers would come supervisory auxiliaries, who would be full-time community health promotion workers, and would have perhaps 18 months to 2 years of health training. Above this level, various models exist for the administration and supervision of community-based health services. One view is that they can be run from within the Ministry of Health, by a "primary care managerial physician." Compared to a typical "western" clinical physician, such a physician would have less clinical training. On the other hand, he or she would also learn much more about epidemiology, the science of the causation of diseases in their social setting. More generally, he or she would be trained in community health promotion on a continuing basis, rather than principally in episodic curative health care on an individual basis. Such a physician should be able to participate in a general effort at rural development, discussing health-related improvements with community leaders and motivating communities. Training as a referral physician, and in supervising auxiliaries and community-based health workers who would act as initial points of patient contact, would also be required. A knowledge of the costs of different types of health measures would also be needed. Lastly, there would be train-

ing in management and administration skills. Above all, such a physician should be prepared to serve in the rural areas for long periods, and not be likely to emigrate to developed countries. Clearly, such a "primary care managerial physician" is a very long way from a physician as produced in the great majority of medical schools in developing countries today: in his training certainly, but even more clearly in attitudes and motivation. One may also note that a conventional teaching hospital is probably one of the worst places to train managerial physicians: a physician with urban professional-class background, trained at a teaching hospital and then thrust our into some rural health facility is indeed "an elegantly trained person in inelegant surroundings."[9]

The remaining issue is whether or not the new form of health promotion service should come under the Ministry of Health. On grounds of organizational logic, there is an obvious case for this. On the other hand, it can also be argued that the only way to achieve early health coverage of the bulk of the population in the face of the somewhat conventional or gradualistic views of many Ministries of Health is to develop rural health promotion services through another agency, for example, a Ministry of Rural Development. In Tanzania the promotion of rural health services outside the Ministry of Health is in fact taking place.

OTHER METHODS OF HEALTH PROMOTION

The community-based health worker system should not be seen as the exclusive means of health promotion. Some diseases can be handled by generalized environmental control techniques, such as large-scale use of insecticides. Another possibility is organized co-operation with traditional healers, who, for example, are often very good at dealing with mental illness. Again, in addition to

[9] N. R. E. Fendall, *Auxiliaries in Medical Care*, New York, 1972.

new community-based health workers, it may be useful to give some simple training to others who could be concerned with health—from traditional birth attendants to owners of general stores to agricultural extension staff to party workers. Commercial trade channels can also be used for health purposes. Radio and posters can be used for health education purposes, and so can any form of entertainment or large gathering of people. Certain very carefully chosen forms of food fortification may also be logistically and financially feasible, and genuinely effective in raising health levels: for example, if salt is purchased from some central supply source, iodization of the salt may avoid thyroid deficiency and cretinism.

MAIN FEATURES OF A REFORMED HEALTH SYSTEM

It may be useful to summarize some of the main features of the health promotion system which has just been described:

a. Emphasis on active promotion of health in a whole community, rather than intermittent disease care for individuals.
b. The key worker is someone who belongs to the community, and is given some health training.
c. There is delegation of authority to diagnose and to treat illness, to auxiliaries and to community-based health workers.
d. The "western" clinical physician is seen as a poor technologic fit for the health problems of developing countries. The health system outlined here could be managed by non-physicians.
e. There is little emphasis on referral of difficult cases. Referral is not easy to

organize logistically or administratively, and it is more urgent to extend health coverage. This policy may result in some difficult cases dying: but a policy of stress on "adequate" referral facilities will result in many more *easy* cases dying, simply because health coverage is so low.

What has been given here is only the rough outline of an appropriate health policy for a developing country. Clearly the exact policy which is appropriate will depend upon local social, political and administrative conditions. It will also depend upon the existing structure of the medical profession and the Ministry of Health. Last but not least, it will depend upon the availability of financial and manpower resources, and logistical problems of communications in a particular country—a small, rich country like Singapore will be able to maintain a very different system to what would be workable in Chad. Nevertheless, it is probably generally true in most developing countries that in the past there has been far too much emphasis on referral facilities, rather than health promotion work at a community level. Talk about "health service pyramids" has often in practice been an excuse for concentrating resources at the apex of a pyramid rather than the base. The priority need in most developing countries is for better health coverage, and more emphasis on health promotion rather than health care. Accordingly, in nearly all developing countries every effort should be made to avoid construction of new hospitals, which are extremely expensive to build, but also very expensive to operate; which absorb vast amounts of high-level manpower; and which give a sophisticated clinical bias to the whole health system, and the prestige of ordering of its personnel.

VIII.B.2. Nutrition Objectives*

The mathematically precise economic growth models that have been in vogue since the 1940s seldom take explicit account of the notion of investment in human beings. Increases in tomorrow's income are assumed to result primarily from today's additions to material capital, and since consumption displaces capital investment, it becomes an enemy of growth, not a handmaiden. Consumption in the form of educational services, clothing, and eating of course have an instrumental impact on productivity, but since the effects of such consumption are difficult to identify, all growth in income is imputed to those more easily measurable factors included in the model. Expenditures on health and nutrition are also classified as consumption and thus fail to show up as factors affecting national growth.

Recently, however, the concept of capital has been extended to human beings. Development of the new theory was prompted by the discovery that "increases in national output have been large compared with the increases of land, man-hours, and physical reproducible capital. Investment in human capital is probably the major explanation for this difference." A significant part of economic growth in the United States and Western Europe, for example, has been attributed to education, and any residual growth to "knowledge."

In similar attempts to begin to measure economic returns to health investment, the cost of preventing a death is compared with the worker's future income, had he lived. Or the investment in human capital—the health, food, clothing, housing, education, and other expenditures necessary to enable a person to develop his particular skills—is measured against his loss through death any time prior to retirement. Those costs can also be measured against debility, where death is not a factor. Whether an illness results in temporary loss of work days or some temporary or permanent reduction in work capacity, the estimated loss in output added to the cost of medical care can be compared with proposed expenditures for preventing the occurrence of the illness in the first place.

Similar comparisons can be made of the benefits to be gained from expenditures on nutrition. Improved nutrition that returns an absent worker to the active labor force, or helps lengthen his working life span, or overcomes a debility that is reducing his productive capacity, or that enables a child to return to school or to improve his understanding or retention of things taught, or that enables an adult to absorb more effectively in-service training or the advice of an agricultural extension agent clearly raises the flow of earnings above what it would have been in absence of the improvement in well-being.

Once a person's well-being is stabilized, nutrition costs become a maintenance expenditure. Increments of nutrition no longer lead to increases in productivity. An improvement in nutrition thus can help to improve or maintain the productivity level of an active member of the labor force, or it can take the form of an investment—for example, helping to push up the expected lifetime earnings of a two-year-old child.

Savings on Medical Costs

One measure of the benefits of a nutrition program is in the medical costs saved through reduced demand for medical services. In Caribbean hospitals, 20–45 percent of the pediatric beds are filled by nutrition cases; in India, 15 percent; in Guatemala, 80

*From Alan Berg, *The Nutrition Factor*, Brookings Institution, Washington, D.C., 1973, pp. 16–29.

percent. Nearly half a million hospital in-patients from thirty-seven developing countries were officially registered for malnutrition in 1968 (actual numbers may be higher due to classification of nutritional ailments under other diseases). At an average cost of $7.50 a day for ninety days for each case,[1] costs for treating malnutrition are on the order of $340 million a year to the thirty-seven countries. If treatment were provided to the approximately 10 million preschool-aged children who need it[2]—without it, severe (third degree) protein-calorie malnutrition is generally fatal—annual costs would be on the order of $6.8 billion.

Clearly it is cheaper to prevent malnutrition than to cure it. However, as long as the elimination of, say, a case of kwashiorkor frees a bed and other medical resources for treatment of some other sick person who was otherwise unable to gain entry into the system, total hospital costs will not go down. Since unsatisfied demand for curative services is typical in low-income countries, reduction of malnutrition is not likely to bring about either a net reduction in medical expenditures or a slowing of the rate of growth in medical system investment. Adequate nutrition, however, would enable the medical system to increase the welfare and restore the productivity of all those persons in the queue who would be able to replace malnutrition patients in the system.

Reducing Productivity Losses

Another potentially large nutrition benefit for developing countries is the reduction in productivity losses caused by the debility

of a substantial portion of the labor force. Unfortunately, medical data of the kind needed for calculating debility seldom are available for poor countries, and even if clinical data are accessible, they do not include many of the sick who never enter the statistics because of the excess demand on the medical system. In any case, the synergistic interaction of malnutrition with much prevailing illness makes it difficult to pin down the exact contribution of each factor. Often malnutrition itself does not put sufferers into the queues.

An alternative approach to measuring productivity losses is through use of aggregative data on food supply and the occupational distribution of the labor force. From estimates of daily caloric need in different occupations, shortfalls in work capacity can be calculated for different levels of shortfall in caloric intake. Comparison of a country's average caloric need to average national caloric consumption then yields national working capacity shortfalls. For low-income countries these shortfalls are almost always very substantial, often as high as 50 percent. While this means of linking individual productivity to national productive capacity is conceptually useful, it relies on such aggregative data that its utility in estimating the cost of malnutrition is limited.[3]

Extending Working Years

Another cost of malnutrition is the reduced number of working years resulting from early death. For the majority of the

[1] Cost of hospitalization in Guatemala is $7.31 a day; in Uganda, $7.84 a day. This compares to national per capita health budgets in many countries of between $1 and $2 a year.

[2] An estimated 3 percent of the 325 million preschool-aged group in developing countries need such treatment; that is twenty times the number of medical facility cots available for children for all diseases.

[3] The example given here is based on the work of Hector Correa, who recognizes that because of data limitations many of his assumptions are heroic. A more refined model would offer finer breakdowns of the labor force, adjustment of work factors for local conditions and of caloric requirements by occupation and local conditions, and estimates of daily intake by income level and by season. It would still fail to take account of such important factors as employment opportunities, intra-family food distribution, the impact of cook-

developing countries, increases in the life expectancy of adults would add years to the working lives (rather than retirement years) of most adults. In countries where life expectancy at ten or twenty is particularly short, the added working years would be those when healthy adults would be at the peak of their powers and earning capacity.

Other things being equal, a lengthening of working life reduces the country's dependency ratio—the proportion of those in the population (largely the young) who produce no income to those who work. In 1960 for every 100 persons of working age in the typical developing country population, there were an estimated 76 dependents compared to only about 59 in the typical industrialized country. Lower dependency ratios, of course, increase per capita income and, potentially, per capita savings as family incomes are required to support fewer numbers.

The age structure and life expectancy rates of developing countries indicate that reductions in adult mortality would not only add years to income-generating lives and reduce dependency ratios, but increase the "yield" on education and other investments society makes in workers during their formative years. The advances are only potential, however, because they depend on productive employment being available.

The Problem of Surplus Labor

Restoring a worker to good health adds nothing to national production if no job exists for him. The apparent slow growth of employment opportunities compared with the growth of the labor force in poor countries is a common source of development economists' skepticism that better health and nutrition will bring economic benefits.

---

ing habits on nutrient content, the problems of efficiency of absorption, and the productivity impact of early malnutrition on mental and physical capacity.

Many countries have a substantial labor surplus in the form of seasonal idleness in agriculture, open urban unemployment, and part-time or work-sharing employment which has been called disguised unemployment. Hence the case for seeking productivity benefits from better nutrition, especially for the masses of the unskilled, would seem weak.

Yet, in rural areas of low-income countries, labor is more commonly in short supply than in surplus during harvest and other periods of intense activity. Do farm workers try to feed themselves seasonally to higher capacity, like draft animals? In fact, can they do so during the weeks preceding harvest, when cash income is at the lowest annual point and grain prices are at their peak? What happens to the productivity of workers who undergo alternating periods of well-being and malnourishment?

Open unemployment does not necessarily mean that production problems can be solved merely by hiring additional workers. Many functions impaired by a worker's malnourishment cannot be satisfactorily corrected by added hands. Most machine-paced operations have precisely defined needs for which the human work input cannot be divided among more workers to compensate for inefficiency. If a job is strictly machine paced, the worker would have narrow scope for reducing his performance below the machine's automatic demand. Malnutrition might then be reflected in shoddy output, particularly if the work is dependent on the worker's manual precision or strength. Malnutrition also is reflected in accident rates and poor work attendance. (In numerous instances, factories that have introduced feeding programs have experienced lower accident and absenteeism rates.)

In many urban centers the army of the unemployed is not the commonly perceived homogeneous collection of surplus (and impoverished) human energy. Considerable numbers of unskilled laborers are in the pool, but the rate of urban unemployment is sometimes greater among skilled and educated young people. In Malaya in 1965 the urban unemployment rate among males fifteen to twenty-four with secondary education was 30.9 percent; among those with primary education 19.5 percent; and among illiterates 10.4 percent. In urban areas of Venezuela in 1969 the unemployment rate among laborers with secondary education was 10.2 percent; among those with primary education 7 percent; and among illiterate laborers 4.3 percent. The young, who are conspicuous, often volatile, and therefore a problem, often choose to wait for the job in the field for which they are trained and in which they will earn the largest future stream of income. Since the educated unemployed do not normally compete with the unskilled, this type of unemployment is not relevant to the question of whether and how investment in the nourishment of the poor will pay off.

It is worth recalling that in many areas of the developing world, man-to-land ratios are relatively low and there appears to be no substantial "disguised unemployment" problem. Much of southeast Asia was historically what Adam Smith called a "vent for surplus" economy—that is, an economy in which only an increase in export demand was needed to motivate farmers to extend their area of cultivation, trading leisure for additional work to take advantage of a vent or opportunity for exporting the potential surplus. Though an increasing population makes this description less apt for southeast Asia today, it would fit many subsistence agricultural parts of Africa and South America.

The quality of labor. Productivity is of course more than a function of human energy, of numbers of workers. Energy loss is a limited basis for calculating the effect of malnutrition on national production. As development proceeds, human energy is replaced by machine energy; human quality becomes more important than sheer physical capacity. Demands on human physical energy output decrease as the proportion of the work force in agriculture declines. (Although this may sound like a long-term description of the development process, it is already

happening in some developing countries.) In agriculture, timely initiative, physical dexterity, and comprehension of increasingly sophisticated techniques all become critical to the successful exploitation of new technologies. In cultivating the new high-yielding grain varieties, farmers fall short of maximum returns because they fail, in varying degree, to apply the recommended practices. Some constraints, like inaccessibility or high cost of credit, are beyond the farmers' control. But errors of planting depth and timing, pesticide application, and fertilizer application rates and timing are not economic; they may reflect such factors as education, mental performance level, dexterity, and attention.

The small farmer exemplifies the problem. His decision making on the use of his own resources is not divisible. If malnutrition during his childhood limited his learning opportunity and undernourishment as an adult is compounding his disadvantages, his potential efficiency in making decisions is not increased by the presence of unemployed labor in the neighborhood.

Given the gross unemployment picture—and clearly this is one of the major challenges facing many countries—an economic, as distinct from welfare, case cannot be made for special expenditures merely to upgrade the potential productivity of those masses of unskilled, landless, adult workers who have dim prospects of gainful employment. There are, of course, other limiting factors in the picture besides malnutrition—poorly functioning extension and credit services, inadequate transport systems, inadequate equipment (perhaps exacerbated by policies encouraging capital rather than labor intensive technologies), illiteracy, and so on. Any presumption that improvements in nutritional status are a sufficient condition for realizable improvements in productivity would therefore be simplistic.

Yet, it would be equally simplistic to dismiss the productivity value of nutrition because of the existence of idle adults. To do so is to assume that underemployed labor is available (or can be made available) in the vicinity of an activity at the right time, that it possesses required skills, that it can be hired in fact, and that the work is technically capable of being divided among more workers than are currently employed. Often this is not the case. Much of the unemployed and underemployed today turns out to be a diverse and complex group that needs to be sorted out before conclusions are reached about the value of nutritional improvements. Moreover, recognizing the increasing importance of skilled manpower and general labor quality for future national growth, investment in large numbers of malnourished children today can improve the quality of a significant fraction of the future labor force. This is probably the area in which nutrition will prove critical to development in the long run. . . .

Other Economic Benefits

Nutrition programs promise a number of economic benefits in addition to the direct productivity benefits:

As the incidence of communicable diseases among the adequately nourished is lowered, the exposure of others to these diseases will be reduced.

The increased income of well-nourished workers (or well-nourished children when they enter the labor force) should improve the living standards of their dependents, thereby raising both their current consumption and their future productivity.

Housewives, whose activities are not measured in a market economy, should when better nourished improve performance on a number of economically important functions, not least of which is the quality of care for the young.

Returns may be raised on other investments closely related to human well-being, particularly education. (Low-income countries now spend nearly 4 percent of their gross national products on education, almost a third more than in 1960. The efficiency of

the education systems they support may be reduced as much as 50 percent by the dropout and repeater rates to which malnutrition contributes heavily.)

BENEFITS COMPARED WITH COSTS

Even where opportunities for returns to better nutrition appear to be significant, the costs must be weighed. Will the nutrition expenditure be less than the value of the expected increase in production? How will it compare with returns to alternative investments? The answers will depend on whose malnourishment is to be corrected, what increments in their productivity can be expected, how much the program will cost, whether its effects will be immediate or delayed, and what discount rate is applied to determine present value if benefits are delayed.

Productivity payoffs from nutrition investment can be anticipated for workers employed in machine-paced occupations in modern manufacturing sectors, students for whom malnutrition limits the potential joint returns from education and health expenditures, and small farmers facing the more exacting demands of new agricultural technologies. The widest and most lasting impact, however, probably would come from providing adequate nutrition to mothers in the last trimester of pregnancy—the critical period for fetal growth—and to children six months through two or three years of age (most of the needs before six months can be met through breast feeding). The greatest physiological need and greatest growth occur in the early years: 80 percent of eventual brain weight, for example, is reached by age two. During this time children require, relative to body weight, two and one-half times as much protein as adults; without adequate nourishment, they are susceptible to severe consequences of childhood infections such as measles and whooping cough and to diarrheal diseases. Even if a child's diet is fully adequate only in utero and during the critical early years of life, he probably will be brought closer to his growth potential. If, during adulthood, his energy intake level falls short of some desirable norm, his productivity will already have been ratcheted to a higher level—more relevant to a modern economy—than a lifetime at his current nutrition level could achieve.

Payoff on Child Nutrition Investments

An institutional feeding program designed to meet all nutritional deficiencies of a child from six months through his third year can cost roughly $8 a year or a total of $20.[4] (This *annual* cost to prevent malnutrition is approximately the same as the *daily* cost to treat it in a number of countries.) Suppose that the program averts a disability in a child's later performance. Assume also that if the disability were not avoided, the child would be able to produce (or earn) an annual income of $200 over a thirty-five-year period starting at the age of fifteen. How much of an increase above $200 would be required to make the nutrition investment break even?

Of course, returns beginning twelve years after an investment is made are remote, and they should be adjusted to account for the long waiting period. If a discount rate of 10 percent is used to convert future benefits to present value, an improvement of only 4 percent ($8) in annual earning capacity is needed to break even—the annual productivity increase is about the same as the annual cost of the feeding. Both the time stream and the discount rate are on the conservative side, however. In developing societies a child

---

[4] The $8 would meet deficiencies of a diet that currently satisfies three-fourths of a child's protein need and two-thirds of his caloric need. The estimate is based on the production and distribution costs of Bal Ahar, used in India's child feeding programs (the child feeding program is being used here only for illustrative purposes, and is not being suggested as the lowest cost means of achieving the nutrition goal).

often turns worker at eight or ten. Though a discount rate of 10 percent is commonly used for developing countries, it is probably too high for important irreversibilities—for assets or opportunities that once forgone can never be restored. The irreversibility of the human condition or opportunity resulting from malnutrition would place nutrition investments at the lower end of any discount range, increasing their competitive strength as investments.

Nonetheless, an increase in future productivity of 4 percent is a modest reflection of higher levels of performance. The actual rate of return will depend on a number of factors. The higher the initial income of the worker, the smaller proportionately need be the break-even increase in productivity. The larger his shortfall in working capacity due to malnutrition, the greater will be the increase in his performance from better nutrition. If his improvement in performance can move him upward in occupational groups, the gains may be more significant. Increased productivity ought also to include side benefits and enhanced returns to other investments. In a study that compared nutrition levels and IQ differences of Chilean children with IQ and productivity (or wages) of Chilean workers, the potential increase in earnings from child feeding that would offset protein-calorie deficiencies during the critical periods of early growth was estimated to range from 19 percent to 25 percent. Those rates are quite competitive with returns to education; in India, for example, education returns have been estimated in the range of 9 percent to 16 percent.

It would be hard to find a more favorable investment opportunity than avoidance of vitamin A blindness. Poverty-stricken societies where such blindness is considerable have few facilities for training the blind for productive occupations. The upkeep of the blind, minimal as it is, represents a total burden to their families or the society. Assuming that the average blind person could be sustained at a subsistence cost as low as $25 a year, the cost is 1,250 times the annual ingredient cost of the vitamin A needed for prevention. If vitamin delivery techniques should raise the cost several times, the arithmetic would still be highly favorable. The average blind person need only be in position, if sight loss were avoided, to produce a modest fraction of this annual consumption for the investment in his sight to yield an enormous return. For India the consumption burden (at $25 a year per person) of one million people blind from vitamin A deficiency will cumulate to $1 billion over their lifetimes. Similar returns can be made from investments to prevent what are in some places common cases of irreversible cretinism and deaf-mutism linked to endemic goiter. In parts of Bolivia, for example, 40–50 percent of the population is goiterous and 5–10 percent of these suffer from cretinism and deaf-mutism. Cost of the iodate to prevent goiter (and the equipment necessary to add the nutrient to salt) is one-sixth of a cent a year per person covered.

Many of the links between diet, performance potential, and economic returns are poorly understood and may remain so, given the complexities of human development and behavior. Little is known, for example, about the relative damage caused by different degrees of malnutrition at different ages and of varying durations. The major benchmark provided by medical science is the concept of "minimum daily requirements" of specified nutrients. Any sustained diet below the minimum daily requirement implies damage, especially in environments where widespread diarrhea and other ailments lead to heavy nutrient losses. Although it is known that the extent of damage increases as the level of nutritional deprivation falls—as a child moves from first to third degree malnutrition—the shape of the curve relating deprivation to loss of physical, motor, and mental development, and to the severity of nutrition-related diseases, is unknown. The threshold beyond which the extent of loss becomes serious cannot be defined, nor can the degree of mental or physical shortfall or other resulting damage that separates the

serious from the inconsequential be calculated.

Although it may never be possible to separate the mass of the world's malnourished children into neat groups whose potential performance can be forecast from specific investments in varying nutritional supplements, a clear line can be drawn between those who will live and the significant number of those who will die of malnutrition or related causes. Before children born today in developing countries reach their fifth birthdays, approximately 75 million youngsters will die of malnourishment and associated illnesses. The known numbers of those whose lives will be marked by illnesses that seriously strike the malnourished are so great, and the effects of malnutrition on educational and productive capacity so apparent, that investment in nutrition programs can almost be undertaken as an act of faith. . . .

Beyond Standard Economic Benefits

In economic terms the life of agricultural laborers and their families often would be categorized as "very poor" or "destitute." Yet, for all their economic privation, these rural families have the potential for enjoying a wide range of noneconomic goods—nature, love, friends, good talk at the coffee or tea stall, the joy of children. These enjoyments, independent of economic status, include some of the major sources of satisfaction in life, satisfactions which by their nature are not marketable services and are not quantifiable in the national accounts when the economist totes up the per capita availability of goods and services for personal "consumption." But those who are apathetic and physically drained by nutritional anemia or debilitated by the seemingly constant bouts with nutritionally related diarrheas cannot really savor these satisfactions. It is well-being, not income, that determines whether a man, rich or poor, has the capacity to enjoy these most fundamental sources of human satisfaction. Well-being is the primary requisite, the sine qua non, that determines the utility men derive from all other forms of consumption, whether measurable or not. The developing economies are not likely in the near future to provide a very much wider range of material goods to those in lower income levels. But it may be within the power of public policy to improve the level of nutrition, which in turn can increase the capability for a substantial portion of the population to enjoy whatever sources of consumption are available.

For societies whose prevailing philosophy places a premium on egalitarianism, the intellectual loss that is caused by malnutrition may be a strong obstacle to attaining this social goal. Nutrition is not, of course, a cure-all; educational barriers, for example, are immense. However, a malnourished child's chances for social mobility are greatly restricted no matter what is offered in education or other avenues designed by policy makers to facilitate upward movement within a society. Adequate mental development, hence adequate nutrition, would seem to be a prerequisite to other programs for mobility that are being developed as a matter of social policy. If a child lacks curiosity and mental energy—to say nothing of the possibility of mental capacity—the other opportunities are not significant.

Even more difficult to quantify than the costs of widespread malnutrition among the working masses—but no less real—is the loss to society of potentially outstanding individuals. Since the origin of so many superior people in the middle and upper class is a result of opportunity rather than genetic potential, it seems appropriate to ask how many potentially superior minds are lost because of malnutrition. If nutritional risk is as high as studies now indicate—affecting as much as half of some populations—a substantial number of potentially superior people will never come forward. They are not only the Tagores and the Gandhis but also the one-in-a-thousand or ten-thousand who can organize large resources, who is innovative, an entrepreneur, a mover of men. Considering how very thin in most countries is the leadership elite on whom rests the burden of the nation's success or failure, such losses would seem to inhibit the chances for eonomic development.

The purpose of national development—of forgoing consumption today in favor of more investment—is to generate a higher level of human well-being tomorrow for more people. To most people in low-income countries, that mostly means a better diet. Food is a major, perhaps the major, problem of their lives. It is central to both their consumption and their production activities. For a person living at the income level that characterizes the malnourished, typically 65–80 percent of income goes for food. As his income rises, the proportion devoted to buying more food declines, but generally the proportion remains high. The inadequacy and uncertain availability of food from year to year represents the condition of underdevelopment at its most immediate and palpable and dangerous level.

VIII.B.3. Food and Nutrition Planning*

The nutrition problem is commonly regarded as being, above all, a problem of protein deficiency. Seen in this light the solution lies in feeding more protein to those who are suffering from protein deficiency. Paradoxically enough, most of those suffering from protein deficiency eat more than enough protein to meet their protein requirements. However, because they do not eat, in total, enough calories, the protein that they eat is not utilised as protein for growth or maintenance of body tissue but as calories to supply their energy needs. People whose calorie intakes are adequate are not generally to be found suffering from protein deficiencies. (Gopalan 1968, Miller and Payne 1969, Sukhatme 1970a, b, Sukhatme 1972.)...

To advocate that protein deficiency should be made good with protein rich foods—especially with foods of animal origin—is to advocate expensive ways of feeding poor people or expensive ways for poor people to feed themselves. If such people were to eat fish, or milk, or meat, they would only improve their protein status if they ate enough to satisfy their calorie requirements—an expensive way of buying calories. Neither poor people nor poor country governments can afford to meet protein-calorie requirements in such ways and the attempt to do so could mean a gross misallocation of resources (Joy 1971a) ...

To see the nutrition problem as a 'protein crisis' is to place a mistaken emphasis on protein. Even more mistaken is to see the nutrition problem as primarily a *supply* problem to be solved by promoting farm production—of animal produce especially—

and by augmenting this with non-conventional foods—especially with such protein foods as single-cell protein, leaf protein, plankton and fish meal.

The basic fact about the nutrition problem is that it is primarily a *poverty* problem: a problem of ineffective demand rather than of ineffective supply; for food not just for protein....

Identification of Relevant Measures

Generally poor nutrition is associated with poverty *and also with change*, for poor nutrition is not necessarily a characteristic of rural subsistence communities. Population pressures, technological and structural changes and the social changes that accompany them lead to reduced holdings, landlessness and low output or earnings for many families. Some of the rural poor will migrate to the towns; commonly, more will choose to migrate than can be absorbed. Such a process is to be expected in most countries unless something is done to stop it. The countryside may not readily and automatically absorb a growing population; yet only after a fairly advanced stage of development can industrial and urban growth absorb the additional population from the 2–3 per cent per annum national population growth rates so common to poor countries (Dovring 1959). In some countries, development strategies encourage or allow a pattern of structural change which results in rejecting people from the rural economy in the sense that the number able to continue to subsist within it is reduced. Iran, for example, embarked on a strategy of modernising a section of its rural economy to the comparative neglect of the rest which was expected to be absorbed into the growing urban industrial sector. This has meant displacement from both the 'modernised' and

*From Leonard Joy, "Food and Nutrition Planning," *Journal of Agricultural Economics*, January 1973, pp. 1, 3, 5, 9–14, 19–20. Reprinted by permission.

the 'neglected' rural areas in a situation where, as it is now clear, the rural sector must continue to absorb a growth in population for at least thirty years. In this case, only a major revision of rural development strategy can prevent the emergence of malnutrition–and, if malnutrition is to be eliminated, the choice is between the revision of development strategy to prevent malnutrition and the treatment of malnutrition as it inevitably arises. The choice indeed, is between a strategy which aims to raise output and generate income among those who are poor and one which aims to raise the G.N.P., regardless of the emergence of poverty, in the expectation that poverty can then be treated by income transfers through subsidies, or applied nutrition programmes. No doubt mixed strategies are possible and they are likely to be optimal.

This seems to be the general situation in developing countries and the nature of this choice of prevention or treatment–or neglect–is beginning to be explored by many of them. It is certainly evident that reliance on growth of G.N.P. to eliminate poverty and malnutrition is to accept the existence of the problem in some cases for many decades (Berg 1970, Dandekar and Rath 1970, Sundrum 1972). Policies to 'increase rural incomes' may not solve the problem either where the accompanying structural change rejects rather than absorbs a growing labour force. The income increase may not be very well spread. Agricultural development strategies which seek to 'raise farm incomes' and 'promote supplies of protective foods' may still be such as to aggravate rather than reduce the nutrition problem. Thus, a scheme for promoting dairy production which assists wealthier farmers to start herds of exotic dairy cattle could (i) displace hired labour from crop cultivation when less labour-intensive dairy production was adopted; (ii) produce milk for supply to distant towns to people who could afford it and who are already adequately fed; (iii) accelerate the buying out of neighbouring small holdings for the expansion of highly profitable dairy

businesses. Such a policy might be successful in terms of 'raising farm incomes' and 'supplying protective foods' but its success would need to be qualified by the fact that it also depressed some rural family incomes and aggravated their nutritional problems. The point here is to attack not dairy farming schemes but the assumptions that (i) average income is an adequate index of success in removing poverty and (ii) supplies are more important than, or a sufficient pre-condition of, demand. In general, strategies of agricultural development which emphasise production as the major objective are likely to channel productive inputs to large farmers rather than small farmers, rich farmers rather than poor farmers, irrigated rather than dryland farmers and landlords rather than tenants. The nutrition problem is likely to be worst among small, poor, dryland, tenant farmers and the landless. (Though not all tenants are worse off than all landlords.)

The assumption that policies to maximise production do not necessarily allow for the optimisation (or maximisation) of *consumption* seems only gradually becoming evident. It is time to ask whether the most effective way of ensuring that everybody is fed is not to arrange to *generate* income for those unable to subsist rather than to *transfer* income to them. Transferring incomes turns out to be a difficult and expensive business and there is a limit to the extent of transfer that is feasible. Because of this, for many countries, an effective attack on poor nutrition must be a fine balance between a strategic attack on the removal of poverty and the adoption of programmes to ameliorate its effects. It is by no means clear that we should assume that strategies to attack poverty will retard growth.

So far as the planning process is concerned it is most important that the relative potential impact of strategies and programmes should be assessed. The nutrition problem needs to be defined and quantified not simply as it is but as it will be given present development strategies and forces for change. We need predictions of the quantitative and qualitative evolution of the problems and an identification of the pressures at work and the key policy variables which control these. We need to be able to identify alternative strategies and to attempt to predict their impact—on nutrition and on other goals.

On the programme side we need to assess the scope for treating particular aspects of the problem with particular programmes and policies (Call and Levison 1971, Joy 1971b). We need to know what scope there is for raising protein-calorie intakes by subsidising grain, or bread, to specific poorly-fed groups and at what cost; what scope there is for raising infant intakes (and health and growth rates) by the provision of special infant foods and so on. We also need to know, on the one hand, the effects of a successful nutrition policy upon prices and, on the other, the effects of an overall price policy for foods, or for specific food items, upon the intakes of the poorly fed and also, of course, upon such matters as total consumption, supplies, wages, and the general pattern and level of economic activity. . . .

Prediction—Appraisal—Design—Choice

Given an outline plan, its implications have then to be considered in further detail in relation to such questions as:

(i) What will be the overall impact on the nature and extent of malnourishment in the short run and in the long run?

(ii) What will be the consequences in terms of improved health and performance?

(iii) Have the appropriate priorities been asserted in determining who shall benefit and who not benefit?

(iv) What will be the consequences in terms of general equilibrium effects, especially for food and agriculture?

(v) What will be the consequences in terms of growth and other planning objectives?

(vi) Are the implied resources available? Do the benefits of their mobilisation for these programmes meet their opportunity costs?

The following discussion is a commentary on some issues raised in posing these questions.

No programme should be undertaken unless it is expected to lead to an improvement in the nutrition of the poorly nourished. Yet it is rare for a nutrition project to be presented with a statement of its expected impact on nutrient intakes. It is rarer still that a prediction is made of the impact upon health and performance. Quantitative assumptions of the nutritional impact of, for example, the substitution of existing maize varieties by high-lysine varieties, or of the subsidised manufacture of an infant food, or of a daily protein-rich biscuit to school children, or of a 10 per cent reduction in wheat price are surely essential before decisions can be made about their desirability. Without such detailed estimates with regard to each of the components of a nutrition plan no estimate of its overall nutrition impact is possible. Quantitative predictions of the further impact on height/weight gain, reduced morbidity and mortality, increased activity, output or rate of learning should also be attempted and one might reasonably doubt the value of projects where such predictions are not thought feasible—unless their purpose is precisely to test such impact.

Inevitably, in most countries, hard choices will need to be made in the allocation of scarce resources for nutrition programmes. Whatever strategies are pursued there will still be need for specific programmes to assist particular groups or to attack particular problems. Conventionally, the economist will seek to apply cost-benefit analysis to determine whether or not nutrition programmes compete with other alternative resource allocation proposals. While cost-benefit analysis may usefully contribute to decision-making its limitations are very sharply revealed in this context. A project to distribute vitamin A in India so as to prevent people going blind will, at the margin, simply make 40,000 of those joining the ranks of the unemployed each year sighted rather than blind. The increment to the *production* stream may be negligible and the net benefit: cost ratio less than 1. Even so, such a project may well be regarded as desirable. This brings home sharply the fact that economists too readily use marketed production as a proxy for consumption. We need constantly to be reminded that *we intend* planning decisions to be concerned with the pattern *of consumption* between people and over time, with welfare and the quality of life. We need to be reminded, too, that it is because the price system does not readily optimise for us in these respects that we may need to act against it as it operates with existing patterns of distribution not only of wealth and income, but also of social care and of political and bureaucratic access.

Nutrition planning which relies primarily on conventional cost-benefit analysis to identify 'economically' justifiable projects could lead to the rejection of almost all nutrition programme proposals. In effect it is this logic, though not the application of cost-benefit analysis, which has 'justified' neglect of nutrition planning in the past: the rate of return to nutrition improvement was thought to be low and consumption was postponed in favour of immediate investment (Berg 1971, Berg and Muscat 1971, Wilson 1971). Modification of cost-benefit analysis to meet criticisms of its income distribution assumptions might be attempted by valuing explicitly the increments of *consumption* resulting from a project at current prices weighted according to the initial level of income of the persons to whom the additional consumption benefits accrued.[1] Nonmarketed benefits would still need to be

[1] The Little-Mirrlees Manual proposes that, for industrial project evaluation, some system of weighting might be used in comparing rates of return to projects in rich and poor regions (Little and Mirrlees, 1969, pp. 39–45). This is offered as a practical alternative to weighting benefits accruing to different income groups; but it has only limited relevance to agriculture.

subjectively valued and the value of some benefits, for example the value of sight, might be assumed to be unaffected by the level of initial income. It does not, of course, follow that, even with these considerations accounted for, nutrition programmes could always be shown to be something that a country would choose to afford.

Not all nutrition benefits are as dramatic as the prevention of blindness where a modest intake of a cheap nutrient can have so striking an effect on personal welfare. In India, inadequate nutrition is the lot of a large section of the population. Protein-calorie malnutrition afflicts in the order of one-third of the population. Malnourished mothers produce underweight babies who fail to grow—first through shortage of breast milk then because of enteric and bronchitic diseases which, among their other effects, reduce intakes and absorption. Underweight infants become underweight children where these conditions are sustained and where, particularly, low-bulk high-energy foods and vitamin rich protective foods are insufficiently available because of their relatively high cost. Underweight children become underweight adults who survive the more readily for being underweight since the overhead costs of body maintenance are correspondingly lower. The obvious place to break this cycle seems to be with the pregnant mother. But how much is it worth doing anything for mothers unless health can be sustained through infancy and childhood? And what growth rates and adult body weights should be aimed for? (Sadre and Donoso 1969). Perhaps it is better to be small if poor? Should nutrition programmes be applied for the benefit of those who can more or less afford to subsist? Or should they be directed to those who are furthest below subsistence? These are the sorts of questions to be asked in ordering priorities of limited resources for nutrition programmes.

The direct cost of the food required for least-cost supplementation of inadequate diets may be relatively low. In Iran, with maybe 25–35 per cent of the population protein-calorie deficient, and in the order of 50–60 per cent deficient in vitamins, the direct food cost of making good intake requirements is estimated to be in the order of 1–2 per cent of the national income.[2] This may be a useful figure for estimating the size of the problem in a situation in which intakes could be raised by a direct subsidy to the affected people for precisely the extra intake they require. But, in practice, policy instruments tend to be less than precisely discriminating and the more one moves away from 'target group' approaches to 'blanket' approaches so the more does the cost of serving the target group rise.

Target group approaches may also be costly if one has to operate outside existing channels of distribution, as one might, for example, in trying to get special infant foods to poor rural families.

Where the aim is to raise total incomes to levels at which families will subsist, then the cost of clothing, shelter, medical and other expenses has to be covered and the costs are correspondingly higher. Even so, typically, 60–70 per cent or more of income may be spent on food, and incremental expenditures are likely to be in much the same ratio so that more than 60 per cent of extra incomes would be spent on extra food.

Dandekar and Rath (1970) calculated that the increase in total expenditure that would be required if all but the poorest 10 per cent of the Indian population were to be raised to minimum expenditure standard would be 5·62 per cent (i.e., an average 5·62 per cent above their existing expenditure level). Their increased expenditure on food grains would be 5·42 per cent, on pulses 8·06 per cent, on milk and milk products 8·06 per cent, on oil and oil seeds 6·50 per cent and on meat and fish 5·44 per cent. The order of increase in total demand for food grains would be around 1 per cent or so. (*N.B.* The data refer to the position in the early 1960's but it seems unlikely that the argument would be affected by updating

[2] Personal estimate.

the calculations.) This is an amount considerably less than the year to year fluctuation in supply and we might, with reasonable optimism, suppose it to be a readily achievable increase in the trend supply pattern. Even so, additional measures further to accelerate supply responses might be justified. But these are notional figures which would apply if efficient schemes for creating the required increment of effective demand could be devised. While planning and administration may be improved, past experience does not give grounds for optimism.

If it is difficult to transfer incomes, an even bigger nutrition planning problem is how to *generate* increased incomes for the poor. Possibilities considered for India include land redistribution, labour-intensive technologies, small farmer credit and extension programmes, and rural works programmes. The first of these might offer some scope for critical income redistribution if redistributed land were to augment holdings which are less than adequate; the second seems on the whole to be already about as fully exploited as would be beneficial and the third and fourth generally to have posed, so far, major problems of administration. While rural works employment programmes are being further explored and supported, past experience has revealed severe limits to their value as instruments of employment and income distribution policies. However, these limitations may not be inherent and we may still be hopeful that the radical review of these programmes currently being undertaken in India will reveal new scope for them as effective policy instruments. But we should also require that resources directed to such programmes will increase output, not simply transfer incomes, and to an extent which sufficiently approaches their rate of return elsewhere, if only to maintain the capacity to continue to transfer incomes.

Perhaps even more important than positive strategies is the avoidance of harmful strategies. The approach to rural development planning needs to be on an area basis in a way which asks directly what resource redistributing policies are relevant for reducing poverty—or, less ambitious, specifically for improving nutrition. Such a conscious concern for welfare objectives in the approach to planning, combined with a concern to identify target groups, and the causes as well as the symptoms of their condition, should lead to the identification of measures to improve conditions and to an understanding of the policies and programmes which are aggravating poverty and malnutrition. Thus, while from a national viewpoint the short-run adverse effect of, for example, land registration or consolidation programmes on rural poverty, or the longer-run effects of farm mechanisation, might be overlooked, they should be very clearly evident at the local level. It does not follow, of course, that problems that arise locally should be treated locally and the planning process must allow the possibility of more efficient non-local solutions. But problems which are not perceived locally may be overlooked nationally until they cumulate to the proportions of a national calamity and opportunities for anticipating problems or for finding specific local solutions may then have been missed.

This paper has purposely emphasised the priority that must be given to a concern for demand rather than supply. However, an effective food and nutrition plan will lead to an increase in effective demand which will need to be matched by an increase in supply. It should be noted that, by this approach, food planning is very largely a question of inducing changes in supplies to match desired patterns of consumption and planned market demand while nutrition planning is a matter of ensuring that need is translated into effective demand. Unless it is so translated there is no point in planning for supplies to meet needs. Attempts to do so are more than likely to produce 'surpluses' while aggravating the nutrition problem.

Thus, at the heart of the nutrition problem is an income distribution problem. True, there is still a challenge of finding ways of producing more food but the trick is not simply to find improved farming—and manufacturing—technologies but to apply them in ways which spread their benefits. New technologies may be irrelevant to poor farmers facing a depressed market. To regard failures to spread benefits as short-term problems to be treated by applied nutrition programmes is appropriate only when they are truly transitional features, of manageable proportions, of otherwise well-conceived development strategies. . . .

THE ROLE OF THE ECONOMIST

It seems worthwhile to review the role of the economist in food and nutrition planning.

The economist's first major role is in his contribution to the design of an effective planning process. Broadly, this means insisting on an effective, operationally relevant, diagnosis of the nutrition problem in terms of 'who is short of what and why'; insisting on the identification of relevant alternative measures in relation to the diagnosis of the nature and causes of the problem; and insisting on explicit attempts to predict the impact of alternative measures in relation to health and performance and in relation to other policy objectives. He should contribute to the formulation of programmes of data collection and analysis and to procedures for mobilising, co-ordinating and reviewing contributions from relevant departments and agencies. He should insist, too, that the problem is seen as a dynamic one and that micro and regional level analyses are incorporated into a macro and general equilibrium framework.

Secondly, he has an important contribution to make in drawing attention to and analysing the short- and long-term impact of broad development strategies upon the nature and extent of the nutrition problem. Agrarian strategies involving technical and structural change (mechanisation, irrigation, land reform, etc.); extension and credit programmes as they affect small and large farmers, landlords, tenants and labourers; marketing and transport developments; trade policies; prices, taxes and subsidies; policies for industrialisation and urbanisation; public health programmes—these and other major policies, interacting with demographic and social changes, affect the numbers of people who cannot subsist. It has been argued that the major control instruments for affecting the nutrition problem lie in these fields and it follows that the economist has a role in ensuring an understanding of the relative importance of the various determinants of malnutrition and of policy instruments through which they might be controlled.

A functional classification of the sub-sets of the nutrition problem is an indispensible planning tool which the economist should press for. He should be concerned for its operational relevance and for the necessary degree of reliability of the numbers—present and future—ascribed to the sub-sets thus defined.

Economists—and agricultural economists especially—still have much to contribute to the development of local level planning and this should place nutrition objectives and nutrition programmes in the context of local, and national, opportunity cost perspectives. Where the idea of making health and nutrition a community responsibility has an appeal, the question of local taxation for the finance of such programmes may pose problems worthy of attention.

The design and appraisal of applied nutrition programmes has in the past been inadequate and contributions by economists are needed for improvements here. Appraisal is needed *ex ante* and *ex post* and the economist has a role in guiding the adaptive control of programmes according to their performance. The economist must also insist on equi-marginal returns thinking, especially with regard to the relative roles of health and nutrition measures. All of this still implies, however, the devising of practical and relevant appraisal methods using cost-benefit logic with relevant and practical approaches to valuation problems.

For policy purposes perhaps the most important single contribution that the economist can make is to correct the current supply-oriented approach by emphasising the overwhelming importance of effective demand and the need to seek social rather than technical solutions to the problems.

But perhaps the major challenge is in theoretical and empirical analysis. We need still to be able to identify alternative policy measures for raising people to a subsistence level of income and to be able to classify these in terms of their effect on the future stream of G.N.P., suitably valued to allow for income maldistribution distortions. We urgently need to know the trade-offs between income transfers and income generating resource transfers: between malnutrition today and malnutrition tomorrow.

References

Barg, B. 1971: 'The Role of Nutrition in National Development'. *Proc. International Conf. on Nutrition and National Development,* M.I.T. 1971.

Berg, A. 1970: 'Nutrition as a National Priority. Lessons from India's Experience'. *Am. Jnl Clinical Nutrition,* Vol. 23, No. 11, Nov. 1970, pp. 1396–1408.

Berg, A. and Muscat, R. 1971: 'Nutrition and Development: The View of the Planner'. Paper prepared for the U.N. Secretary-General's Statement on the Protein Problem Confronting the Developing Countries.

Call, D. L. and Levinson, F. J. 1971: 'A Systematic Approach to Nutrition Intervention Programmes'. *Proc. International Conf. on Nutrition and National Development,* M.I.T., 1971.

Dandekar, V. M. and Rath, N. 1970: *Poverty in India,* Indian School of Political Economy, Poona, and Ford Foundation, Delhi, 1970.

Dovring, F. 1959: 'The Share of Agriculture in a Growing Population'. *Monthly Bulletin of Agricultural Economics and Statistics*, Vol. 8, Aug.–Sept. 1959. F.A.O., Rome.

Gopalan, C. 1968: in *Calorie Deficiencies and Protein Deficiencies* (ed. McCance, R. A. and Widdowson, E. M.) London.

Government of India 1966: Ministry of Food, Agriculture, Community Development and Cooperation (Dept. of Food). *Report of the Study Team of Fair Price Shops, 1966*.

Joy, J. L. 1971a: 'Economic Aspects of Food and Nutrition Planning'. *Proc. First Asian Congress of Nutrition, Jan. 1971*, Hyderabad, India. Also, published together with Payne 1971 and Sukhatme 1971 in Institute of Development Studies, Sussex, Communication Series.

Joy, J. L. 1971b: Discussion of 'A Systematic Approach to Nutrition Intervention Programmes' by Call and Levinson. *Proc. International Conf. on Nutrition and National Development*, M.I.T., Oct. 1971.

Little, I. M. D. and Mirrlees, J. A. 1969: *Manual of Industrial Project Analysis in Developing Countries, Vol II. Social Cost Benefit Analysis*. Development Centre, O.E.C.D., Paris, 1969.

Miller, D. S. and Payne, P. R. 1969: 'Assessment of Protein Requirements by Nitrogen Balance'. *Proc. Nutr. Soc.*, Vol. 28, No. 2, p. 225.

Sadre, M. and Donoso, G. 1969: 'Treatment of Malnutrition' (Letter to the Editor, *The Lancet* July 12th, 1969, p. 112).

Sukahtme, P. V. 1970a: *Brit. Jnl Nutr.*, No. 24, p. 477.

Sukhatme, P. V. 1970b: *Proc. Nutr. Soc.*, Vol 29, No. 1, p. 176.

Sukhatme, P. V. 1971: *Proc. First Asian Congress of Nutrition*, Jan.–Feb., 1971, Hyderabad, India.

Sundrum, R. M. 1972: 'Studies in Planning Techniques IV–Planning the Distribution of Income'. *Economic and Political Weekly*, Vol. VII, No. 22, 1972. Bombay, India.

Wilson, D. 1971: 'The Economic Analysis of Malnutrition'. *Proc. International Conf. on Nutrition and National Development*, M.I.T., 1971.

VIII.C. EDUCATION

VIII.C.1. Investment in Human Capital—Note

Although the objective of adding to the stock of physical capital has dominated investment discussions, it has now become evident that a high priority must also be assigned to investment in human capital.

Many studies of economic growth in advanced countries confirm the importance of nonmaterial investment. These statistical investigations indicate that output has increased at a higher rate than can be explained by an increase in only the inputs of labor and physical capital. The "residual" difference between the rate of increase in output and the rate of increase in physical capital and labor encompasses many "unidentified factors," but a prominent element is the improvement in the quality of inputs. Although some of this progress may be incorporated in physical capital, the improvements in intangible human qualities are more significant.

For purposes of measurement, capital formation is usually identified with the net increase of land, structures, durable equipment, commodity stocks, and foreign claims. But the capital stock should be interpreted more broadly to include the body of knowledge possessed by the population and the capacity and training of the population to use it effectively. Expenditures on education and training, improvement of health, and research contribute to productivity by raising the quality of the population, and these outlays yield a continuing return in the future. If these expenditures are considered as capital expenditures, then the proportion of capital formation in national income in the rich countries would be much larger than is conventionally indicated in national accounts that treat these expenditures under the flow of goods to ultimate consumers rather than under capital. But since poor countries do not make many such investments in the formation of human capital, this broad interpretation of capital would not increase significantly the proportion of their national incomes devoted to capital formation.

While investment in human beings has been a major source of growth in advanced countries, the negligible amount of human investment in underdeveloped countries has done little to extend the capacity of the people to meet the challenge of accelerated development. The characteristic of "economic backwardness" is still manifest in several particular forms:[1] low labor efficiency, factor immobility, limited specialization in occupations and in trade, a deficient supply of entrepreneurship, and customary values and traditional social institutions that minimize the incentives for economic change. The slow growth in knowledge is an especially severe restraint to progress. The economic quality of the population remains low when there is little knowledge of what natural resources are available, the alternative production techniques that are possible, the necessary skills, the existing market conditions and opportunities, and the institutions that might be created to favor economizing effort and economic rationality. An improvement in the quality of the "human factor" is then as essential as investment in physical capital. An advance in knowledge and the diffusion of new ideas and objectives are necessary to remove economic

[1] Hla Myint, "An Interpretation of Economic Backwardness," *Oxford Economic Papers*, June 1954, pp. 132–63.

519

backwardness and instill the human abilities and motivations that are more favorable to economic achievement. Although investment in material capital may indirectly achieve some lessening of the economic backwardness of the human resources, the direct and more decisive means is through investment in human beings.

Emphasizing the weight that should be given to the growth in the quality of human resources, Professor Schultz illustrates the possible implications of the quality component as follows:

Suppose there were an economy with the land and physical reproducible capital including the available techniques of production that we now possess in the United States, but which attempted to function under the following restraints: there would be no person available who had any on-the-job experience, none who had any schooling, no one who had any information about the economy except of his locality, each individual would be bound to his locality, and the average life span of people would be only forty years. Surely, production would fall catastrophically. It is certain that there would be both low output and extraordinary rigidity of economic organization until the capabilities of the people were raised markedly by investing in them. Let me now take a Bunyan-like step and suppose a set of human resources with as many but no more capabilities per man than existed as of 1900 or even as of 1929 in the United States. The adverse effects on production in either case would undoubtedly be large. To continue these speculations, suppose that by some miracle India, or some other low-income country like India, were to acquire as it were overnight a set of natural resources, equipment, and structures including techniques of production comparable per person to ours— what could they do with them, given the existing skills and knowledge of the people? Surely the imbalance between the stock of

human and non-human capital would be tremendous.[2]

Recent experience with attempts to accumulate physical capital at a rapid rate in poor countries bears out the necessity of due attention to human capital. It has become evident that the effective use of physical capital itself is dependent upon human capital. If there is underinvestment in human capital, the rate at which additional physical capital can be productively utilized will be limited since technical, professional, and administrative people are needed to make effective use of material capital. In many newly developing countries the absorptive capacity for physical capital has proved to be low because the extension of human capabilities has failed to keep pace with the accumulation of physical capital.[3]

While the case for investment in human resources is gaining wider acceptance, the means of attaining an increase in this type of investment have still received only superficial consideration compared with the intensive investigations that have been made of the problems of investment in physical goods.

It is not difficult to identify the more important categories of activities that improve human capabilities. As Professor Schultz suggests, a typical list would be:

(1) health facilities and services, broadly conceived to include all expenditures that affect the life expectancy, strength and stamina, and the vigor and vitality of a peo-

[2] T. W. Schultz, "Reflections on Investment in Man," *Journal of Political Economy*, Supplement, October 1962, pp. 2–3.

[3] For strong arguments that "the experience of planning seems to suggest that knowledge (and certainly not investment resources) is the most important scarce factor in underdeveloped countries with otherwise favorable social climate," see B. Horvat, "The Optimum Rate of Investment," *Economic Journal*, December 1958, pp. 751–3.

ple; (2) on-the-job training, including old-style apprenticeship organized by firms; (3) formally organized education at the elementary, secondary, and higher levels; (4) study programs for adults that are not organized by firms, including extension programs notably in agriculture; (5) migration of individuals and families to adjust to changing job opportunities.[4]

Underlying each of these activities, however, are a number of questions that should be studied more seriously.[5] At the outset, the problem of measurement presents several difficulties: Is it possible to separate the consumption and investment part of expenditures on these activities? Can the particular resources entering into each of these components be identified and measured? Can the rates of returns from these activities be identified and measured? And can the rate of return on investment in education be compared with the rate of return on investment in some other alternative use? As yet, no completely satisfactory empirical procedure for answering these questions has been devised. Although a few studies have recently made noteworthy steps in the direction of measuring some consequences of an increase in tangible capital,[6] no empirical study of investment in human capital is yet free from some arbitrary elements, and more statistical evidence is needed.

Another problem of particular importance to a country engaged in development programming is to determine at what phase of development the formation of intangible capital is most significant. It can be argued that a high rate of increase in the demand for improvements in the quality of inputs appears only at a fairly advanced phase of development. The early industrialization in Western Europe, for example, appears to have been accomplished without requiring as prerequisites marked improvements in skills and knowledge and health of workers.[7] And the contribution of education to American growth has been most pronounced in the more recent decades, while capital investment was more important in earlier decades.[8] Unlike the earlier historical situation, however, it may now be necessary to have a relatively high level of skill and much more knowledge to take advantage of the more complex equipment and techniques that may be obtained from advanced countries.

There are additional questions to be raised concerning what types of education should be emphasized, to what degree, and how soon. Some economists have such questions in mind when they criticize—from the viewpoint of the economic, though not social or moral, value—proposals for mass education or extensive systems of higher education in newly developing nations. They contend that these countries do not yet have an effective demand for large numbers of educated workers; it will take considerable time to raise the presently limited absorptive capacity of the economy for educated persons; and a poor country can not afford to pay for as much education as can rich countries.[9]

[4] T. W. Schultz, "Investment in Human Capital in Poor Countries," in P. D. Zook (ed.), *Foreign Trade and Human Capital*, Dallas, 1962, pp. 3–4, 11–12.

[5] The remainder of our discussion concentrates on education and training. For a consideration of human capital formation through health services, see Selma J. Mushkin, "Health as an Investment," *Journal of Political Economy*, Supplement, October 1962, pp. 129–57.

[6] For example, Mary Jean Bowman, "Human Capital: Concepts and Measures," in *Money, Growth, and Methodology*, Essays in Honor of Johan Akerman, Lund, 1961, pp. 147–68.

[7] Cf. Schultz, "Investment in Human Capital," pp. 3–4, 11–12.

[8] Edward F. Denison, "Education, Economic Growth, and Gaps in Information," *Journal of Political Economy*, October 1962, p. 127.

[9] These arguments are cogently presented by W. Arthur Lewis, "Education and Economic Development," *International Social Science Journal*, Vol. 14, No. 4, 1962, pp. 685–99; Thomas Balogh,

Since educational outlays compete for resources that have an alternative use in directly productive investment, it is essential to determine what proportion of national income should be devoted to education. And within the education system itself it is necessary to establish priorities for the various possible forms of education and training.

From the standpoint of accelerating development, the immediate requirements may call for emphasis on vocational and technical training and adult education rather than on a greatly expanded system of formal education. Considering its high cost and the problems of absorption that it raises, even the case for universal primary education is questionable. Professor Lewis expresses such skepticism in the following comments on African proposals:

The limited absorptive capacity of most West African economies today—especially owing to the backwardness of agriculture—makes frustration and dislocation inevitable if more than 50 per cent of children enter school. This, coupled with the high cost due to the high ratio of teachers' salaries to average national income, and with the time it takes to train large numbers of teachers properly, has taught some African countries to proceed with caution; to set the goal of universal schooling twenty years ahead or more, rather than the ten years ahead or less associated with the first flush of independence movements. Such a decision is regarded as highly controversial by those for whom literacy is a universal human right irrespective of cost.... On the other hand, considering that in most African territories less than 25 per cent of children aged six to fourteen are in school, a goal of 50 per cent within ten years may be held to constitute revolutionary progress.[10]

More immediately serious than the lack of universal primary education is the deficiency in secondary education. The most critical manpower requirement tends to be for people with a secondary education who can be managers, administrators, professional technicians (scientists, engineers, agronomists, doctors, economists, accountants, etc.), or subprofessional technical personnel (agricultural assistants, technical supervisors, nurses, engineering assistants, bookkeepers, etc.). Lewis characterizes the products of secondary schools as "the officers and noncommissioned officers of an economic and social system. A small percentage goes on to university education, but the numbers required from the university are so small that the average country of up to five million inhabitants could manage tolerably well without a university of its own. Absence of secondary schools, however, is an enormous handicap.... The middle and upper ranks of business consist almost entirely of secondary school products, and these products are also the backbone of public administration."[11]

Also deserving of high priority is the infusion of new skills and knowledge into the agricultural sector. In order to achieve a system of modern agriculture, the quality of labor in agriculture needs to be improved as an input in its own right and also to allow the use of better forms of nonhuman capital (equipment, seeds, insecticides, etc.). In many countries that have experienced substantial increases in agricultural production, the key factor has not been new land or land that is superior for agriculture; nor has it been mainly the addition of reproducible capital. More importantly, the agricultural transformation has been based predominantly upon new skills and useful knowledge required to develop a modern agriculture.[12] Educational facilities for agriculture may also provide a way of encouraging rural

---

"Misconceived Educational Programmes in Africa," *Universities Quarterly*, June 1962, pp. 243–9.

[10] Lewis, "Education and Economic Development," p. 689.

[11] Ibid., pp. 688–90.

[12] Cf. Schultz, "Investment in Human Capital," p. 9.

school-leavers to take up work in the rural sector rather than migrating to the towns, and the special training of young school-leavers may allow them to act as the agents for introducing new and improved agricultural techniques.

For the broader problems of educational requirements, the making of "manpower surveys" (as discussed in selection VIII.C.4) may furnish a useful basis for determining the principal skill shortages and what types of training activities should be emphasized. At least for the short term, the provision of agricultural extension services, training in mechanical and technical skills, and training in supervisory and administrative skills may contribute the most to fulfilling manpower requirements. After overcoming the immediate bottlenecks of scarce personnel in specific key occupations, the education system should then be devised to provide a balance between general education, prevocational preparation, and vocational education and training.

We may conclude that the recent attention to investment in human capital should prove salutary in cautioning against an overemphasis on physical capital to the neglect of the more intangible factors. When considered for a poor country, however, investment in human capital calls for new approaches and special emphases that differ from those in advanced economies. An extensive system of formal education is a commendable objective—but it must necessarily be a distant objective. Instead of attempting to imitate the educational system of an advanced country, newly developing countries may more suitably concentrate, at least in the early phases of their development programs, on methods of informal education and on the objectives of functional education. These efforts are less time-consuming, less costly, and more directly related to manpower requirements than is a formal educational system. As such, they are likely to prove most effective in improving the economic quality of human resources.

VIII.C.2. Educational Investment in Developing Countries*

The educational product, in the context of economic development . . . not only includes the components of education usually distinguished as consumption (i.e., enjoyment of the fuller life permitted by education) and as direct investment (with the gains accruing "internally" in the form of increased earnings to the educated person), but also education as investment in the functioning of the economic and social system at large. These

*From Richard A. Musgrave, "Notes on Educational Investment in Developing Nations," in OECD Study Group in the Economics of Education, *Financing of Education for Economic Growth*, Paris, 1966, pp. 31–9. Reprinted by permission.

latter gains accrue "externally," not only to those in whom the educational input is invested, but also to other members of the community.

The theory of investment planning may be looked at from the micro or macro level. In macro terms, the problem is to determine the alternative growth path available to the economy, assuming the best structure of capital formation to apply in each case, and then to choose the optimum path on the basis of the community's time preference. In micro terms, the problem is one of rating alternative investment projects and of deciding which one is to be included within a given level of overall capital formation.

There is no reason why investment in human resources by education should not be included in such an analysis. However, education investment has certain characteristics—quite apart from the previously noted factor of externality—which pose special problems and should be noted at the outset.

CHARACTERISTICS OF EDUCATIONAL INVESTMENT

The product of education outlays, to begin with, carries joint features of consumption and investment. For this reason, the share of resources allocated to education cannot be considered wholly an investment outlay. The consumption component has to compete with alternative forms of consumption, while the investment component must compete with alternative forms of capital formation. To the extent that the two parts are inseparable, the proper allocation of resources to education should leave the rate of return thereon (computed as ratio of the present value of additional earnings to investment cost) below that of alternative investments which do not carry joint consumption components.

This distinction between the consumption and capital formation aspects of education outlays, however, is somewhat misleading. The consumption product of education may be divided into current consumption (the delights of attending school) and future consumption (the ability to appreciate life more fully later on). Since the latter is much the major element, the consumption component is largely in the nature of a durable consumer good and hence investment. The essential distinction, thus, is not between the consumption and investment aspects of education output, but between education investment which generates imputed income (the fuller life later on) and education investment which generates increased factor earnings to the labour supplied by the educated person.

What weight is to be given to the two components in the development context, and how is this to be reflected in the pattern of the education programme? Recent writers have pointed to the extension of secondary education as being the primary goal of education policy in countries with a low level of educational capital stock, with extension of elementary education and technical training at the subsequent level of capital stock, and expansion of higher education at a more advanced stage.[1] While this priority is derived from the projected needs for various types of skill and training, it also suggests that the imputed-income component of the education mix tends to be of particularly great importance at the early stages.

Secondly, investment in education is characterized by a gestation period which is substantially longer than that of many other types of capital formation. Indeed, education seems the time-consuming, Boehm-Bawerkian type of investment *par excellence*. Periods of ten to twenty years may be involved, depending on how far the education process is carried, and even longer spans must be allowed for if teacher-training is taken into consideration. Even though certain skills may be acquired fairly rapidly, especially if a previous foundation is laid, the educational capital stock cannot be changed quickly, particularly for the more advanced type of education. This introduces a constraint in investment planning and demands a correspondingly longer planning horizon which in turn points to the need for public policy guidance seen in the context of a long-term development perspective, if not development plan.

A similar consideration relates to a further feature of investment in education, i.e., the relatively long useful life of the education asset. Consideration of returns over, say, a thirty-year period, lends great weight

[1] See Frederick Harbison and Charles A. Myers, *Education, Manpower and Economic Growth*, New York, 1964, Chapters 4—6.

to the importance of the discount factor in assessing the relative productivity of investment in education. Since the useful life for competing investments tends frequently to be shorter, the relative case for investment in education is low if the appropriate rate of discount is high. Thus, the selection of the appropriate rate of discount is of particular importance in assessing the proper share for education in total capital formation. There being no developed capital markets which provide a clear indicator of this rate, its determination becomes essentially a matter of public policy. Investments should be ranked by a present value rather than an internal rate of return criteria. Moreover, there may well be a difference between the government's and the private investor's evaluation of present, relative to future, needs. To the extent that public policy takes a longer view, it will also tend to require a larger share for education in investment outlays.

The relatively long, useful life, moreover, makes it necessary that the type of education be chosen in order to meet future demands for particular skills. This applies less to general and elementary education, which lays a more flexible basis, but becomes of great importance for specialized and technical types of training that do not permit easy conversion. As already noted, educational planning in the context of a longer-term development view is essential.

Finally, a word regarding the resource cost of education. Recent discussions of the economics of education[2] emphasize, and rightly so, that this cost not only includes teachers' salaries, buildings and equipment, but also the opportunity cost of lost income on the part of the student. Depending on the structure of the developing country, this latter component may be of varying significance. Where there is a general surplus of labour supply, the opportunity cost of forgone earnings will be small or non-existent. Under other conditions, customary use of child labour may produce the opposite situation. While the former is the more typical case, other components of education cost (school teachers' salaries in particular) tend to be relatively high in underdeveloped countries.[3] Even though the income stream from a given factor input into education will be large (educated workers are needed to take advantage of modern techniques, and education is highly complementary to other types of capital formation) the rate of return on educational investments (relative to that on other investments) is therefore not as high as suggested by the income stream alone.

EXTERNALITIES

The standard procedure for determining the value of investment in education is to estimate the future stream of incremental earnings which accrue to the student, and to discount it to obtain the present value. This present value is then related to the cost of investment in obtaining the rate of return. This procedure excludes additions to output which accrue externally and to the benefit of others rather than to the educated person alone. Such oversight may be acceptable in assessing the value of education for a developed economy, but hardly for the underdeveloped country, where external benefits constitute a substantial part of the total gain.

Perhaps the most important aspect of the external benefits of education lies in the change in the social and cultural climate, incident to the widening of horizons, which education entails. As has been pointed out many times, such a change is an essential condition of success for many developing

[2] For a survey of this literature, see Chapter I in William J. Bowen, *Economic Aspects of Education*, Princeton, 1964.

[3] See W. Arthur Lewis, "Priorities for Educational Expansion," *Policy Conference on Economic Growth and Investment in Education*, OECD, Washington, 1961, Part III, p. 37.

nations. At the same time, this benefit result is not an automatic consequence of education at large, but only of the proper type, quality and quantity of education. Supply of professional people who cannot be absorbed into appropriate positions may readily become an external dis-economy and source of instability.

As noted previously, different types of investments in the early stages of development tend to be highly complementary, and this holds *par excellence* for the proper combination of investment in education and capital equipment. Without a capable labour force modern capital equipment cannot be operated, and it is precisely the access to superior techniques that is the one hopeful factor in the development picture. Now it is true that the existence of such complementarity need not, *per se*, constitute an externality which would fail to be recorded in a perfectly functioning pricing system. If tractors can be substituted for oxen only if trained drivers are available, this will be reflected in corresponding higher wages for the driver. The trouble, however, lies in the fact that in an economy where there are as yet no tractors, the supply of drivers is unlikely to be forthcoming, and *vice versa*. The generation of growth (whether "balanced" in an overall Nurkse sense or not) requires a concerted effort to provide a chain of investments, thereby reducing the risks of individual investment and making it possible for an investment programme to succeed where individual investments would fail.

This necessity for investment planning exists even for investments which, given the necessary supply of entrepreneurial talent, would be appropriately undertaken privately. It exists *par excellence* for investment in education. Left to household decisions, neither the market knowledge, foresight or financial requirements are present which are needed to secure adequate supplies. This is especially the case in underdeveloped countries where the whole attitude towards education has to overcome conventional barriers and become reoriented to the development process. . . .

Sensible education targets, therefore, must be developed by considering the needs of the particular economy and the demands posed by its specific plans. This raises a question of the rate at which the system needs to, or can absorb additional supplies of educated manpower. Arthur Lewis stresses the fact that absorption capacity is limited by the high cost of education in developing countries. To quote:

The main limitation on the absorption of the educated in poor countries is their high price, relatively to average national output per head. . . . In consequence, all production . . . which depends on using educated people is much more expensive, in relation to national income, in poor than in rich countries. The poor countries may need the educated more than the rich, but they can even less afford to pay for or absorb large numbers. . . . In the long run, the situation adjusts itself because the premium for education diminishes as the number of educated increases. . . . As the premium for education falls, the market for the educated may widen enormously.

And he further notes that

to give eight years of primary education to every child would cost at current prices about 0.8 per cent of national income in the USA, 1.7 per cent in Jamaica, 2.8 per cent in Ghana and 4.0 per cent in Nigeria. The main reason for this difference is that, while the average salary of a primary school teacher is less than one and a half times per capita national income in the USA, a primary school teacher gets three times per capita national income in Jamaica, five times in Ghana, and seven times in Nigeria.[4]

[4] W. A. Lewis, *op. cit.*, pp. 37–38.

The fact that school teachers' wages are high relative to average wages in the under-developed country need not mean that the absorptive capacity, as we understand it, is low. The rate of return on education equals the ratio of present value of wages or earn-ings due to education, to the cost of produc-ing it. The high relative wage of the educated person may merely express the extreme scarcity of the education factor, and hence its ability to command a high return at the given cost of producing it. The high wage might be an indicator of under- rather than over-supply, as demand may prove elastic if only increased supplies could be made avail-able. At the same time, the cost of pro-ducing education may be high at early stages of development, relative to that of produc-ing other capital goods, say tractors. If so, the rate of return on education (relative to that on tractors) will not be as high as sug-gested by the high income stream (wages) accruing to the educated factor alone. The cost of producing education must be low-ered before increased investment in education is profitable. This, however, is subject to the previously noted condition that education is highly complementary to other forms of capital formation.

In addition to genuine scarcity, the high salaries demanded for work in positions re-quiring education reflect conventional fac-tors and the desire to absorb the status previ-ously held by the colonial official. As a result, there is frequently a "minimum wage structure" for high-level work which exceeds the economic return on such work, and prices educated services out of the market. Such rigidities need to be broken down to permit an effective education policy, and to the extent that they are permitted to prevail, appropriate allowance must be made in for-mulating realistic education targets. A policy which results in a supply of education that cannot be absorbed is obviously inefficient.

A further aspect of the cost problem which deserves special attention is the extent to which the educational effort involves a need for foreign exchange. Capital formation in the developing countries is frequently limited by the fact that capital goods cannot be produced at home, and that the foreign exchange available for acquiring them abroad is scarce. The question arises whether investment in education is more or less capi-tal intensive than are other, and to some extent alternative, forms of capital forma-tion. The answer depends on the level of education. While the exchange component of elementary education cost tends to be relatively low, it rises at the middle level, and for higher education it becomes ex-tremely high. At later stages, this pattern may fit the needs and resources of the coun-try but at the earlier stages, where emphasis is on middle-level education, the match tends to be an unfortunate one and points to the need for an all-out effort in domestic teacher-training.

PRIORITIES

The matter of educational priorities is obviously of vital importance. Unless the right kind of education is provided, setting overall targets has little meaning. Educated people who are unable to find suitable jobs, not only fail to add to the national product but become a source of political instability. Since the cost of various types of education (primary versus secondary versus advanced; liberal arts versus technical, and so forth) differs greatly, the very setting of overall targets has to be derived from the structural composition of the education supply.

VIII.C.3. Investment in the Social

Infrastructure*

This idea [of investment in social and human capital] has proved attractive to many people, both economists and non-economists, and there have been attempts to consider how to strike a correct balance between investment in material capital and investment in human capital, between economic development and social development. Unfortunately, however, as currently stated, this idea remains rather vague, based upon an analogy which has not been systematically drawn. Thus as a possible subject for discussion among social scientists of different disciplines, we may begin by drawing attention to some of the conceptual problems as they appear to an economist.

To begin with, it should be noted that even with respect to material capital, there is no simple mechanical relationship between the amount of resources invested and the *value* of the capital formation which results from it. Although national income statistics automatically equate the two, it can readily be seen that say an amount of one million pounds of savings invested may result in capital goods which may be worth many times more or many times less than one million pounds, depending on how and where it is invested and how far the resultant capital goods serve the future productive requirements of the country and how far people value the products which these capital goods can help to produce. In the extreme case, it has not been unknown for large sums

*From Hla Myint, "Social Flexibility, Social Discipline and Economic Growth," Paper presented to UNESCO Expert Working Group on Social Prerequisites to Economic Growth, Kyrenia, Cyprus, April 1963; mimeographed, UNESCO/SS/SP/13, Paris, December 1962, pp. 3–6. Reprinted in *International Journal of Social Science*, Vol. 16, No. 2, 1964, pp. 252–60. Reprinted by permission.

of money to be so wrongly invested as to serve no useful purpose so that the value of capital formation resulting from them is zero. The problems of trying to establish a causal quantitative relation between the expenditure on resources invested and the value of capital formation which results from it are multiplied manifold when we move from material capital to human capital. To start with the most general difficulty: in dealing with material capital the economists have a reasonably clear idea of what they mean by the productive structure and how an additional piece of material capital may contribute to it, either by changing and improving its efficiency or by fitting into an identifiable gap in it. But no such established conceptual framework exists when we move to human capital. By analogy, we must suppose that the value of a given investment in human capital will depend on its contribution to the "social infrastructure," either by improving and changing this infrastructure or by fitting into a gap in it. But what is this "social infrastructure" and in what direction do we wish to change and improve it?

At this point the economist will look askance at the social scientists from other disciplines, many of whom have been using the fashionable concept of "social and human capital" as much as some of the economists. If hard pressed to define the "social infrastructure" further, the economist can only carry the analogy one or two stages more. He would suppose that in the same way as there is an intimate connexion between the material production structure of a country and its natural resources, there would be a similar connexion between the social infrastructure and the social conditions and characteristics of a country. Material production structure represents the adaptation and improvement of natural resources through investment in material capital. Some investment would exploit the special advantages of these natural resources and other investment would make up for the deficiencies in these natural resources. He would then have to ask the other social scientists whether this analogy is meaningful when extended to cover the relationship between the social infrastructure and the social conditions of a country.

Carrying the analogy a stage further, the economist would point out that the consequences of a wrong choice of investment project may be very different between material capital and human capital. Frequently, a wrong investment in material capital and attempts to salvage it have a distorting effect on the whole production structure. For instance, a wrongly sited railway system or a "show piece" but uneconomic factory may be maintained by government subsidy, grants of exclusive monopolistic privileges or by protection against foreign competitors. But at the last resort a wrong investment in material capital can be scrapped when it proves too expensive to salvage. Wrong choice of investment in human capital will presumably have similar distorting effects on the social infrastructure, but wrong pieces of human capital cannot be scrapped; they tend to be self-perpetuating and have the habit not merely of distorting but actually of disrupting the social infrastructure. For instance, the growing problem of graduate unemployment in Asian countries, due to the production of too much of the wrong type of "human capital" is a very clear illustration of this danger.[1]

In this connexion, it may be noted that for the economist the material production structure of a country is a different thing from the economic institutions which mobilize resources and feed them into the production structure. But when we come to the concept of social infrastructure, the distinction between these two different functions is blurred. As currently used, the idea of social infrastructure seems to serve both as the social equivalent of the production structure which absorbs resources and also to have the more active function of the social and institutional framework which mobilizes and allocates resources. This makes assessment of the productivity in investment in human capital doubly difficult. For instance, increased educational opportunities, say through films, radio and other mass media, may widen the horizons of the people and stimulate the growth of new wants (through demonstration effects) and new ideas. This may possibly increase the long run productivity of the people and thus may be regarded as an improvement in the social infrastructure in the first sense. But on the other hand, the effect of these new educational opportunities may also weaken and disrupt the ability of existing social values and social hierarchies to mobilize resources and thus undermine the social infrastructure in the second sense.

We started by saying that the conflicting requirements of social flexibility and social discipline in promoting economic development at the earlier pre-take-off stages of development can be illustrated by two approaches: the first in terms of the growth of the money economy and the second in terms of increasing investment in social and human capital. It now appears that this conflict is latent even if we concentrate on the second approach only although to some extent it is hidden by the vagueness in the concept of the "social infrastructure." Certain changes which might widen the educational horizon of a people and thus increase their longer run productivity might at the same time undermine the coherence of the social and institutional framework to mobilize resources to increase capital formation both in human and material capital.

This conflict may be further illustrated by human investment in higher education for economic development where the great-

[1] See Hla Myint, "The Universities of South East Asia and Economic Development," *Pacific Affairs*, Summer 1962.

est long run increases in productivity have been frequently claimed. When people make this claim, they have two distinct ideas at the back of their minds. Firstly, they are thinking of the dynamic effects of higher education, in stimulating new discoveries and innovations and in adopting new methods of production. This implies a sort of intellectual yeast which will ferment and change the whole of the production structure and presumably the social infrastructure with it. Here the productivity of investment in human capital is conceived in terms of greater flexibility and adaptability of the social and institutional framework which will create favourable conditions both in stimulating changes and for receptiveness and adaptability to these changes. Secondly, they are also thinking of shortages of skilled people of particular types who are needed as "missing components" to be fitted into a desired pattern of economic development. Of course some flexibility has to be allowed even in the most rigid and comprehensive type of planning. But it is fair to say that the *basic* reasons for claiming high productivity as a result of investment in education are different in these two types of argument. In popular terms, the first type of argument is thinking in terms of creating square pegs to fit into round holes with the hope that the pattern of holes will be stretched and changed into more productive directions. The second type of argument is thinking in terms of trying to create round pegs to fit into round holes, as though fitting the miss-

ing pieces into a jigsaw puzzle within the framework of a given and fixed pattern of production and planning requirements.

These conflicting considerations become bewildering when we look closely at the skilled manpower problems of any newly independent countries. Firstly, there is an obvious need to fill up the gaps left in the civil service, and those left in all sectors of the economy by departing foreign personnel. The missing components have to be produced to maintain the old economic and administrative structure. But at the same time there is a great desire to change very quickly "the old colonial structure," not only politically but also economically and socially. Logically, one might perhaps expect a great upsurge of a liberal educational policy encouraging individualism, enterprise and innovations to break down the rigidities both of the traditional and of the colonial systems. But given the prevailing intellectual atmosphere that such quick change can only be forced through by economic planning, the prevailing bias is against both economic liberalism and "liberal education" in favour of detailed skilled manpower planning integrated with programmes of technical education which ideally specify the exact type of training and the exact number of trainees. Thus we get back to the problem of manufacturing the "missing components" for the jigsaw puzzle, the only trouble being that the old puzzle has been torn down and the new puzzle has not been constructed.

VIII.C.4. Approaches to Human-Resource Development*

Most modernising economies are confronted simultaneously with two persistent, yet seemingly diverse, manpower problems: *the shortage of persons with critical skills* in the modernising sector and *surplus labour* in both the modernising and traditional sectors. Thus, the strategy of human resources development is concerned with the twofold objective of building skills and providing productive employment for unutilised or underutilised manpower. The shortages and surplus of human resources, however, are not separate and distinct problems; they are very intimately related. Both have their roots in the changes which are inherent in the development process. Both are related in part to education. Both are aggravated as the tempo of modernisation is quickened. And, paradoxically, the shortage of persons with critical skills is one of the contributing causes of the surplus of people without jobs. Although the manpower problems of no two countries are exactly alike, there are some shortages and surpluses which appear to be universal in modernising societies.

The manpower shortages of modernising countries are quite easy to identify, and fall into several categories:

1. In all modernising countries there is likely to be a shortage of highly educated professional manpower such as, for example, scientists, agronomists, veterinarians, engineers, and doctors. Such persons, however, usually prefer to live in the major cities

rather than in the rural areas, where in many cases their services are most urgently needed. Thus, their shortage is magnified by their relative immobility. And, ironically, their skills are seldom used effectively. In West Africa and also in many Asian and Latin American countries, for example, graduate engineers may be found managing the routine operation of an electric power substation or doing the work of draughtsmen. Doctors may spend long hours making the most routine medical tests. The reason is obvious.

2. The shortage of technicians, nurses, agricultural assistants, technical supervisors, and other sub-professional personnel is generally even more critical than the shortage of fully qualified professionals. For this there are several explanations. First, the modernising countries usually fail to recognise that the requirements for this category of manpower exceed by many times those for senior professional personnel. Second, the few persons who are qualified to enter a technical institute may also be qualified to enter a university, and they prefer the latter because of the higher status and pay which is accorded the holder of a university degree. Finally, there are often fewer places available in institutions providing intermediate training than in the universities.

3. The shortage of top-level managerial and administrative personnel, in both the private and public sectors, is almost universal, as is the dearth of persons with entrepreneurial talents.

4. Teachers are almost always in short supply, and their turnover is high because they tend to leave the teaching profession if and when more attractive jobs become available in government, politics, or private enterprise. The scarcity is generally most serious in secondary education, and particularly

*From Frederick H. Harbison, "Human Resources Development Planning in Modernising Economies," *International Labour Review*, Vol. 85, No. 5, May 1962, pp. 2–5, 7–8, 20–23; ____, "A Systems Analysis Approach to Human-Resource Development Planning," in UNESCO, *Manpower Aspects of Educational Planning*, Paris, 1968, pp. 57–8, 59–64. Reprinted by permission.

acute in the fields of science and mathematics. This shortage of competent teachers is a "master bottleneck" which retards the entire process of human resources development.

5. In most modernising countries there are also shortages of craftsmen of all kinds as well as senior clerical personnel such as bookkeepers, secretaries, stenographers, and business machine operators.

6. Finally, there are usually in addition several other miscellaneous categories of personnel in short supply, such as, for example, radio and television specialists, airplane pilots, accountants, economists and statisticians.

I shall use the term "high-level manpower," or alternatively "human capital," as a convenient designation for the persons who fall into categories such as those mentioned above. The term "human capital formation," as used in this paper, is the process of acquiring and increasing the numbers of persons who have the skills, education, and experience which are critical for the economic and political development of a country.

The analysis of human capital formation is thus parallel and complementary to the study of the processes of savings and investment (in the material sense). In designing a strategy for development, one needs to consider the total stock of human capital required, its rates of accumulation, and its commitment to (or investment in) high-priority productive activities.

The rate of modernisation of a country is associated with both its stock and rate of accumulation of human capital. High-level manpower is needed to staff new and expanding government services, to introduce new systems of land use and new methods of agriculture, to develop new means of communication, to carry forward industrialisation, and to build the educational system. In other words, innovation, or the process of change from a static or traditional society, requires very large "doses" of strategic human capital. The countries which are making the most rapid and spectacular innovations

are invariably those which are under the greatest pressure to accumulate this kind of human capital at a fast rate. Here we may make two tentative generalisations:

First, the rate of accumulation of strategic human capital must always exceed the rate of increase in the labour force as a whole. In most countries, for example, the rate of increase in scientific and engineering personnel may need to be at least three times that of the labour force. Sub-professional personnel may have to increase even more rapidly. Clerical personnel and craftsmen may have to increase at least twice as fast as the labour force, and top managerial and administrative personnel should normally increase at a comparable rate.

Second, in most cases, the rate of increase in human capital will need to exceed the rate of economic growth. In newly developing countries which already are faced with critical shortages of highly skilled persons, the ratio of the annual increase in high-level manpower to the annual increase in national income may need to be as high as three to one, or even higher in those cases where expatriates are to be replaced by citizens of the developing countries.

The accumulation of high-level manpower to overcome skill bottlenecks is a never-ending process. Advanced industrial societies as well as underdeveloped countries are normally short of critical skills. Indeed, as long as the pace of innovation is rapid, the appetite of any growing country for high-level manpower is almost insatiable.

As indicated above, no two countries have exactly the same manpower problems. Some have unusually serious surpluses, and others have very specialised kinds of skill bottlenecks. Politicians and planners, therefore, need to make a systematic assessment of the human resources problems in their particular countries. Such assessment may be called "manpower analysis."

The objectives of manpower analysis are as follows: (1) the identification of the principal critical shortages of skilled manpower in each major sector of the economy, and an analysis of the reasons for such shortages; (2) the identification of surpluses, both of trained manpower as well as unskilled labour, and the reasons for such surpluses; and (3) the setting of forward targets for human resources development based upon reasonable expectations of growth. Such forward targets are best determined by a careful examination and comparison, sector by sector, of the utilisation of manpower in a number of countries which are somewhat more advanced politically, socially and economically.

Manpower analysis cannot always be based on an elaborate or exhaustive survey. It is seldom possible to calculate precisely the numbers of people needed in every occupation at some future time. But, whether statistics are available or not, the purpose of manpower analysis is to give a reasonably objective picture of a country's major human resources problems, the inter-relationships between these problems, and their causes, together with an informed guess as to probable future trends. Manpower analysis is both qualitative and quantitative, and it must be based upon wise judgment as well as upon available statistics. In countries where statistics are either unavailable or clearly unreliable, moreover, the initial manpower analysis may be frankly impressionistic. . . .

Once the manpower problems of a newly developing country are identified, a strategy must be developed to overcome them effectively. The essential components of such a strategy are the following: (1) the building of appropriate incentives; (2) the effective training of employed manpower, and (3) the rational development of formal education. These three elements are interdependent. Progress in one area is dependent upon progress in the other two. The country's leaders should not concentrate on only one or two of them at a time; they must plan an integrated attack on all three fronts at once.

The argument has been made that investments in formal education alone are not likely to solve either critical skill shortages or persistent labour surpluses in modernising societies. Investments in education are likely to contribute effectively to rapid growth only (1) if there are adequate incentives to encourage men and women to engage in the kinds of productive activity which are needed to accelerate the modernisation process; and (2) if appropriate measures are taken to shift a large part of the responsibility for training to the principal employing institutions. The building of incentives and the training of employed manpower, therefore, are necessary both as a means of economising on formal education and as a means of making the investment in it productive. . . .

The third component of the strategy is wise judgment and prudent investment in building the system of formal education. This calls for giving priority to investment in and development of broad secondary education. It requires that the costs of universal primary education be kept as low as possible by applying new technologies which can make effective use of relatively untrained teachers and which can multiply the contribution of a very small but strategic group of highly trained professionals. Finally, in the area of higher education, the strategy stresses the need for giving priority to investment in intermediate-level training institutions and the scientific and engineering faculties of universities. But this does not mean that the production of liberally educated persons should be neglected.

The three essential components of the strategy are interdependent, and call for a well-designed and integrated attack on all three fronts at once. And it is imperative that the strategy of building and utilising human resources be an integral part of a country's national development programme.

The major thesis of this paper is that the manpower approach should encompass much more than a tabulation of "heads and hands" in precise occupational categories. It must go far beyond the construction of purely quantitative forecasts, projections, or targets for formal education. It should be related to a broad strategy of human-resource development rather than to a narrow concept of education planning.

Without questioning the usefulness and importance of the kind of quantitative analysis which is characteristic of most manpower surveys, I suggest that it may now be appropriate to use in addition a systems analysis concept. It should be possible to look at the various constituent elements of human-resource development as a system which is somewhat analogous to a system for the generation and distribution of electric power. In using this frame of reference, one can identify skill-generating centres, such as, for example, schools, universities, training institutes, and employing organizations, which develop people on the job. The linkages between such centres are analogous to transmission lines. The manpower problems, such as skill shortages and labour surpluses, encountered by developing countries may be thought of as attributable to power failures in particular generating centres, ineffective linkages between these centres, or faulty design resulting in the failure of the total system to carry the loads expected of it. A system of human-skill generation, should be designed to carry varying loads; it must have built-in flexibility to meet such loads; it must be adequate in size; and above all its components must be properly balanced. The systems-analysis approach makes it easier to identify in operational terms major problem areas, and it compels the analyst to examine the critical inter-relationships between various manpower, education, and economic-development programmes. It provides a logical starting-point for building a strategy of human-resource development.

HUMAN-RESOURCE PROBLEMS IN DEVELOPING ECONOMIES

The major human-resource problems in developing societies are: (a) rapidly growing population; (b) mounting unemployment in the modern sectors of the economy as well as widespread underemployment in traditional agriculture; (c) shortage of persons with the critical skills and knowledge required for effective national development; (d) inadequate or underdeveloped organizations and institutions for mobilizing human effort; and (e) lack of incentives for persons to engage in particular activities which are vitally important for national development. There are obviously other major human-resource development problems such as nutrition and health, but these lie for the most part in other technical fields and are thus beyond the scope of this paper.

The manpower analyst, of course, is particularly interested in the present and future size of the labour force, its growth rates in both the traditional and modern sectors, and the factors which determine labour-force participation of various groups. Of necessity he must also be concerned with the consequences of policies to limit population growth. For example, a reduction in birthrates will not immediately lead to a reduction in the labour force, but at the same time it would probably increase a country's propensity to save and to invest in productive activities. Population control, therefore, in addition to its other obvious benefits, may contribute directly to greater labour productivity. Certainly, the human-resource development strategist should give very close attention to population problems and assume greater responsibility for proposing population-control measures.

Mounting unemployment in urban areas is probably the most serious and intractable problem facing today's newly developing countries. . . .

Although he might wish that somehow or other the problem would "go away," the human-resource development planner cannot escape responsibility for considering ways and means of absorbing surplus manpower and directing it into productive activities.

The evaluation of occupational needs and

skill-generating capacity has been a traditional concern of manpower specialists. Here, unlike the situation with unemployment, it is possible to suggest viable solutions for rather clearly defined problems. Manpower requirements can be determined; appropriate programmes of formal education and on-the-job training can be devised; and progress toward achievement of goals can be measured.

In setting targets for education and training programmes, the analyst is concerned with two related but distinct concepts—"manpower requirements" and "absorptive capacity." "Manpower requirements" may be defined as clearly evident needs for persons with particular education, training, and experience. The assumption here is that such persons are necessary, if not indispensable, for the achievement of a programme of national development. "Absorptive capacity" is a looser term which refers to a country's capacity to provide some kind of useful employment for persons with certain educational qualifications. In effect, "manpower requirements" should express *minimum* or essential needs; "absorptive capacity" should express the *maximum* number of persons who can be employed without encountering redundancy or serious under-utilization of skill. The skill-generating centres, therefore, should produce trained manpower within this range between the maximum and the minimum; otherwise the skill-generation system is distorted or unbalanced.

The "demand" for education or training must be distinguished from the allowable range between manpower requirements and absorptive capacity. Demand stems from social and political pressures for various kinds of education as well as from the willingness of people to pay fees to acquire it. Thus, for example, the demand for university education may be very high because of the status, prestige, and pay enjoyed by graduates; but, in many countries, this results in the production of graduates who cannot be effectively absorbed in the economy.[1] When demand is clearly out of step with requirements or absorptive capacity, the country's educational system is clearly distorted or out of balance with the needs for national development. In using the systems analysis approach, a major task of the human-resource planner is to detect actual and potential distortion and to consider measures for achieving a proper balance.

Another type of distortion in many countries is the underdevelopment, if not outright neglect, of appropriate measures of training persons in employment. A great deal of money is wasted in formal pre-employment craft or technical training which could be provided more efficiently and cheaply by employing establishments. Also the efficiency of skill-generating systems could be greatly improved by closer linkages between schools and universities and the employing institutions. For some reason, education planners have been inclined to think that on-the-job development lies beyond their legitimate concern, and at the same time they appear to have ignored the task of building the necessary bridges between formal education and in-service training. The systems-analysis approach helps to highlight this underdeveloped area of concern.

In the past, manpower analysis has centred on measurement of needs for various categories of high-level manpower, and in doing so it has usually overlooked the vital problem of organization and institution building. Successful development requires the building of effective government organizations, private enterprises, agricultural extension forces, research institutions, producer and consumer co-operatives, education systems, and a host of other institutions which mobilize and direct human energy

[1] In India, for example, it has been estimated that the number of unemployed educated persons in 1975–76 will about equal the total stock of educated persons in 1960–61. See Institute of Applied Manpower Research, *Working paper no.* 11, New Delhi, 1965, Part IV, p. ii.

into useful channels. Organization is a factor of production, separate from labour, high-level manpower, capital, or natural resources. The essence of organization is the co-ordinated effort of many persons toward common objectives. At the same time the structure of organization is a hierarchy of superiors and subordinates in which the higher levels exercise authority over the lower levels.

The successful leaders of organizations, or more accurately the "organization builders," are in any society a small but aggressive minority committed to progress and change. They feed the aspirations, give expression to the goals, and shape the destinies of peoples. They play the principal roles on the stage of history, and they organize the march of the masses.

A major problem in many developing countries is "organizational power failures." Often government ministries, commercial and industrial organizations, or educational institutions simply fail to "deliver the goods." Usually, the trouble may be traced to a dearth of "prime movers of innovation."

Who then are these prime movers of innovation? Certainly the entrepreneur who perceives and exploits new business ventures belongs to this group, as does the manager or top administrator in public establishments. He may not always have new ideas of his own, but his function is to organize and stimulate the efforts of others. He structures organizations, and either infuses hierarchies with energy and vision or fetters them with chains of conformity. But effective organizations also need other creative people. The agronomist who discovers better measures of cultivation, and the agricultural assistants who teach the farmers to use them, belong to the innovator class, as do public-health officers, nurses, and medical assistants. Engineers are in essence designers of change, and engineering technicians and supervisors put the changes to work. And last but not least, professors, teachers, and administrators of educational institutions in many countries

may constitute the largest group of prime movers of innovation, as they are the "seed-corn" from which new generations of manpower will grow.

Some innovators are "change-designers" who make new discoveries, suggest new methods of organization, and plan broad new strategies. Others are "change-pushers" who are able to persuade, coach and inspire people to put new ideas to work. Some innovators, of course, are at the same time change-designers and change-pushers. But whether they are designers, pushers, or a combination of the two, the prime movers of innovation must have extensive knowledge and experience. Thus, for the most part, they are drawn from the ranks of high-level manpower. But they need more than proven intelligence and thorough technical training. They should have in addition keen curiosity, a capacity for self-discipline, and an unquenchable desire for accomplishment. They should be adept at asking questions. They should have the knack of stimulating others to produce ideas and to activate the ablest minds about them; and they should be able to sell ideas to superiors, subordinates, and associates. The prime mover of innovation must be convinced that change can occur as a result of individual action, and he must have the drive within him to bring it about. This may stem from a desire to rise in social status, to build up material wealth, to acquire political influence, or to preserve an already established prestige position.

Many of the persons holding commanding positions in organizations are conformists or even obstructors of innovation. They must be systematically replaced by more creative innovators. The human-resource development planner should be able to locate the critical points of power loss in organizational structures and to suggest remedial measures.

A final problem area in human-resource development is incentives. It is one thing to estimate the needs for manpower of various qualifications but quite another to induce persons to prepare for and engage in occupations which are most vital for national growth. In most developing countries, it is incorrect to assume that relative earnings and status reflect the value of the contribution of individuals to development. Pay and status are often more related to tradition, colonial heritage, and political pressures than to productivity. Characteristically, for example, the rewards of subprofessional personnel and technicians are far from sufficient to attract the numbers needed—the pay of teachers is often inadequate; the differentials in compensation between the agricultural officer and agricultural assistant are too great; and the earnings of scientists and engineers, in comparison with administrative bureaucrats in government ministries, are too low. The preferences for urban living, the forces of tradition, and historical differentials all tend to distort the market for critical skills. It follows then that the demand for certain kinds of education, particularly at the university level, is inflated relative to the country's absorptive capacity. The human-resource development planner must therefore consider deliberate measures to influence the allocation of manpower into high-priority activities and occupations. Such measures may include major changes in the wage and salary structure, scholarship support for particular kinds of education and training, removal of barriers against upward mobility,

and in some cases outright compulsion. As many developing countries have learned to their chagrin, investments in education can be wasted unless men and women have the will to prepare for and engage in those activities which are most critically needed for national development.

These then are the problems and tasks which face the human-resource development planner—the consequences of population increases and the measures for controlling them; underemployment and unemployment in both the traditional and modern sectors; skill shortages and the processes of developing high-level manpower to overcome them; organizational weakness and the need to find prime movers of innovation for institutional development; and provision of both financial and non-financial incentives in order to direct critically needed manpower into productive channels. Some of these are subject to quantitative analysis; others are purely qualitative; and a few are subject only to intuitive judgment. But, they are all interrelated. The systems approach forces the analyst to examine them simultaneously as he searches for the weak spots—the points of power failure or the major areas of distortion—in a country's over-all effort to effectively develop and utilize its human resources.

VIII.C.5. Education and Employment*

Although the linkages between education and employment are complex and, in the past, often analyzed with simplistic notions of causality, recent research results have yielded new insights about the nature of these linkages.[1] A number of international

*From Edgar O. Edwards and Michael P. Todaro, "Education, Society and Development: Some Main Themes and Suggested Strategies for International Assistance," World Development, January 1974, pp. 27–30. Reprinted by permission.

[1] For the most recent and comprehensive analysis of the interrelationships between education

organizations, including the ILO and the Ford and Rockefeller Foundations, have been engaged in intensive analyses and have conducted numerous conferences and meetings on the employment topic over the past two years.[2] The authors have participated in a number of these activities and the follow-

and employment, see Mark Blaug, Education and the Employment Problem in Developing Countries, Geneva, 1973.

[2] Edgar O. Edwards (ed.), Employment in Developing Nations, New York, 1974; and ILO,

ing represents a condensed statement of our current thinking about the principal relationships between education and employment. In the interests of brevity, the argument is put forward as a series of major propositions and derivative strategies relating to the education-employment nexus.

SEVEN BASIC PROPOSITIONS ABOUT EDUCATION AND EMPLOYMENT

Proposition 1. *Pressures outside the educational system will force it to overproduce in terms of the real manpower needs of development, giving rise to the phenomenon of educated unemployment.*

As discussed in Section 1, an educational system in any society both reflects and adapts itself to the political and economic circumstances of that society. Economic signals or incentives and socio-political constraints operative in the society are the primary factors determining the employment aspirations of individuals and hence the level and composition of the aggregate private demand for education. This demand in turn influences the supply, composition, and academic standards of educational opportunities, both public and private. Political pressures force the public educational system to attempt to meet quantitatively the aggregate demand for school places. In the event that the number of these places is limited by public financial constraints or policy decisions, the private sector will tend to find alternative ways of meeting unmet educational demand.[3] The educational composition of the system's output also will accord with the dictates of aggregate demand with the private system once again meeting needs

Scope, *Approach and Content of Research Oriented Activities of the World Employment Programme*, Geneva, 1972.

[3] Some examples of private-sector initiatives in response to unsatisfied, aggregate demands include the Harambee school movement in Kenya and the proliferation of private colleges and universities in India and the Philippines.

unmet by the public system. Since aggregate private demand will normally exceed job opportunities and since this demand will tend to be satisfied either politically (through the public system) or privately, educational systems in LDCs are likely to overproduce in terms of the real manpower needs of the nation. Moreover, this divergence between the output of the educational system and the number of new job opportunities is likely to grow over time. Given these inexorable pressures to overproduce, major modifications in the educational system must depend primarily on changes in economic incentives and social constraints and *not* on isolated initiatives taken within the educational system itself.

Proposition 2. *Education, in conjunction with the development of a modern sector, transforms various kinds of underemployment into open unemployment, primarily through rural-urban migration.*

In traditional societies it has been customary for members to share among themselves the work which the community considered necessary to perform. Even in feudal landlord-tenant settings, the landlord often regarded it as his responsibility to share available work among all of those who accepted his patronage. In most LDCs the development of a modern sector has introduced very different working arrangements such as the discipline of a standard work-week and minimum wages. The modern sector has also been characterized by an urban, industrial bias and a need for a new set of specialized occupational skills. Educational systems responded quickly to these modern sector needs, focusing curricula on modern-sector educational requirements and strengthening urban schools more quickly than those in rural areas. These several contemporaneous events have meant that many young people previously underemployed in rural areas have flocked to the cities in search of education or jobs in numbers substantially in excess of the opportunities available. Many, indeed growing numbers, have become openly unemployed, a vivid and visible transformation of widely dispersed rural underemployment into the far more troublesome and potentially explosive problem of open urban unemployment. Recent LDC research on rural-urban migration has demonstrated that the propensity to migrate increases with increasing educational attainment and that the ranks of the urban unemployed are increasingly being swelled by the more educated.[4]

Proposition 3. *Limited job opportunities tend to be rationed by educational certification with the more educated replacing the less well educated, even though higher qualifications may not be needed to perform the task adequately.*

Given the chronic tendency of educational systems of LDCs increasingly to overproduce in terms of available employment opportunities, the problem of rationing limited modern-sector jobs assumes growing importance. Typically these jobs are allocated to those with higher levels of educational attainment regardless of whether that education is really necessary for satisfactory job performance. The educationally less fortunate are relegated to the ranks of the unemployed and underemployed on the fringes of the urban sector. This rationing device has the appealing political merit of being apparently objective, relatively untainted by obvious favor, and patently dependent for its operation on many private as well as public decisions. But its operation does not relieve unemployment or improve the allocation of resources beyond insuring that those most over-educated are indeed eventually employed. So the magnitude of the problem is left to grow and an apparently fair rationing mechanism is unlikely to provide continuing political cover for an increasingly explosive situation.[5]

[4] See, for example, M. P. Todaro, "Education, migration, and fertility", paper presented at IBRD conference on *The Economics of Education: Alternative Strategies for Investment*, Washington, D.C., October 1973 (mimeo).

[5] For a more detailed discussion of the job rationing by educational certification phenome-

Proposition 4. *Rising unemployment, distorted wage differentials, and excessive education must be taken into account if social rate-of-return and benefit/cost calculations are to play a role in educational planning.*

Although political factors are dominant in LDC government decisions with regard to the supply of educational opportunities, economic analyses of social and private rates of return to investment in various levels of education remain a tool of considerable potential importance in assessing the wisdom of educational investment decisions, both for local governments and donor agencies. This analytical tool has been much maligned, sometimes justifiably so and other times as the result of a critic's misunderstanding of the legitimate, albeit limited, role which these calculations can play.[6] For the most part, however, rate-of-return calculations have not taken account of factors such as educational displacement, rising unemployment among the more educated, and distorted wage and price signals in the economy as a whole. We believe that many manpower plans based on these calculations would be considerably modified, especially with respect to their projections of needed quantitative expansion among the highly educated, if the above factors were taken into account. In particular, the apparent discrepancy between rates of return to investment in education as compared to alternative investment in other sectors of the economy would not be nearly so wide if the factors mentioned above were given adequate treatment.

non, see E. O. Edwards and M. P. Todaro, "Educational demand and supply in the context of growing unemployment in less developed countries", *World Development*, March/April 1973.

[6] For a further exposition of the role of cost-benefit analysis in a political setting, see Edgar O. Edwards, "Investment in education in developing nations: Conflict among social, economic, and political signals", paper presented at IBRD conference on *The Economics of Education: Alternative Strategies for Investment*, Washington, D.C., October 1973 (mimeo).

Proposition 5. *Public subsidies to education, especially at the higher levels, contribute to the widening gap between "private" and "social" benefit/cost calculations and thus lead to excessive levels of aggregate private demand for higher education; these subsidies also limit financially the ability of the public sector both to supply educational opportunities and to create jobs.*

In many LDCs both the percentage and absolute amount of educational costs borne privately tend to decrease with increasing levels of educational attainment. This phenomenon, in combination with the positive relationship between educational attainment and expected income from employment, creates an explosive private demand for higher levels of education. In order to satisfy this demand, primary and secondary facilities must be expanded by some multiple of the demand for higher education to take account of the large percentage of students who will not make it to the higher levels. The irony of the situation is that the wider the gap between *perceived* "private" benefits and costs of secondary versus primary and tertiary versus secondary education and the more unprofitable a given level of education becomes as a *terminal point* (e.g., primary education), the more demand for it increases as an *intermediate stage* or precondition to the next level of education! This puts increased pressure on the government in conjunction with donor agencies to expand lower-level facilities in order to meet the demand for higher-level education.[7]

Public subsidies not only stimulate the demand for education; they also limit the ability of governments to create both educational and job opportunities. Reducing these subsidies would release government funds for job-creating investments, raising the economy's capacity to absorb educated manpower in productive employment. Such an increase in the demand for educated manpower would itself justify a more rapid growth in educational opportunities. Thus a

reduction in public subsidies should (*a*) reduce the excess demand for education, (*b*) increase employment opportunities and (*c*) provide developmental justification for a larger educational system than would otherwise be the case.

Proposition 6. *Constraints on upward mobility in the labor market force many of those discriminated against to seek social and economic advancement through the educational system, thus increasing the already heavy burden carried by it.*

Those who expect that without substantial education their employment and promotion opportunities will be limited because of caste, race, creed, tribe, or the simple lack of overvalued exit credentials from the educational system, may seek to circumvent these obstacles through further education. This implies, of course, that educational systems are on the whole characterized by fewer discriminatory practices than the labor market itself. In these circumstances, the existence of substantial social and political biases in hiring and promotion practices may contribute to the overloading of the educational system. If, on the other hand, such labor-market constraints can be reduced, some resources of the educational system will be freed for the improved performance of its other essential functions.

Proposition 7. *Employment, in addition to providing income, is also a major means for disseminating work-related knowledge.*

Employment is often regarded by those seeking it in developing countries as a reward for the successful completion of a continuous segment of the educational process. Education is regarded as a preparation for work; work is seldom seen as a learning experience in its own right or even as a useful basis for further education. Unfortunately, this view is frequently reinforced by hiring practices of employers and incentive schemes supported by policy-makers, and it reflects a rather common underevaluation of the learning which can be obtained through participation in the labor market. Moreover, the learning potential inherent in employment opportunities does not seem to be sig-

[7]See Edwards and Todaro, op. cit. and Blaug, op. cit.

nificantly realized in practice. For example, the wider sharing of available work among members of the labor force would spread the associated learning experience over a larger number of beneficiaries; social and economic policies which promoted variety in an individual's work experiences, whether with one or several employers, rather than narrow, routine specialization would enrich his life and his potential for contributing to a nation's development; and the use of information on an individual's degree of success in work settings as a means for evaluating his potential to gain from further education would add an important dimension to the criteria currently in common use in determining who progresses in the educational system.

SOME STRATEGIES FOR IMPROVING EDUCATION AND EMPLOYMENT

In the light of the above propositions, the following strategies for improving the relationship between education and employment are offered:

1. *Minimizing imbalances, incentive distortions, and socio-political constraints will improve both education and employment.*

Policies which tend to remedy major economic imbalances (e.g., those between rural and urban areas), to correct distortions in incentives (e.g., in income and wage differentials), and to alleviate social and political constraints on upward mobility, will have the multiple beneficial effect of increasing job opportunities, modifying the accelerated rate of rural-urban migration, and facilitating development-related modifications of educational systems.

2. *Where politically feasible, educational budgets should grow more slowly and be more oriented towards primary education.*

In the light of growing unemployment among the educated, educational budgets should grow more slowly than in the past to permit more funds to be used for the creation of employment opportunities. Moreover, a larger share of educational budgets

should be allocated to the development of primary, as opposed to secondary and higher, education as a basis for self-education and work-related learning experiences. If a slowdown in subsidized public higher education is off-set by expansion of the private sector, there is at least the favorable incentive effect that the beneficiaries must pay more of the cost of their education.

3. *Work-sharing arrangements should be encouraged.*

In the absence of full employment, policies should be explored which will encourage a wider sharing of available work as a means of dispersing income, spreading work-related learning experiences, and reducing the numbers openly unemployed. It is not, however, a simple task to identify appropriate incentive mechanisms which will induce the private sector to assume the additional managerial costs which might be required in order to realize the social benefits of work sharing. This need not be a constraint on public-sector employment practices where social benefit calculations can enter directly into employment decisions.[8]

4. *Job-rationing by educational certification must be modified.*

In order to break the vicious circle in which overstated job specifications make overeducation necessary for employment, policies are needed which will induce or require both public and private employers to seek realistic qualifications even though the task of job rationing may be made somewhat more difficult as a result.[9]

5. *Subsidies for upper-level education should be reduced.*

As a means of overcoming distortions in the aggregate private demand for education induced by excessive subsidies to education especially at higher levels, policies should be

[8] For some theoretical arguments in support of work-sharing arrangements, see Edgar O. Edwards, "Work effort, investable surplus, and the inferiority of competition", *Southern Economic Journal*, October 1971.

[9] The ILO Ceylon Report, op. cit., makes extensive recommendations along these lines.

promoted by which the beneficiary of education (as opposed to his family or society as a whole) would bear a larger and rising proportion of his educational costs as he proceeds through the system—either directly, through loan repayments, or by service in rural areas.[10]

6. *Inequities and discrimination in both education and employment should be minimized.*

In order to reduce the burden on the

[10] See Edwards and Todaro, op. cit., for further discussions of the distributive implications of current methods of post-primary education in the context of rising levels of unemployment among the educated.

educational system and to improve the performance of its essential functions, policies should be pursued which (1) reduce social and educational discrimination in hiring and promotion in labor markets, (2) encourage greater reliance on job-related learning experiences as a basis for occupational advancement and (3) stimulate the use of successful work experience as a criterion for advancement in the educational system.

Insofar as possible, donor agencies should ensure that their policies of support for public education reinforce strategies, such as those listed above, which tend to make education appropriate, quantitatively and qualitatively, for the employment opportunities likely to emerge in the coming decade.

VIII.C.6. Development as a Generalized

Process of Capital Accumulation*

The contemporary interest in the economics of education, and more broadly in the economics of all processes connected with the augmentation and application of knowledge, represents a confluence of interests derived from concerns with widely divergent problems. These problems include such matters as the economic value of education, the contribution of education to past economic development in advanced countries, and the role of education and expenditure on increased education in the planned development of underdeveloped countries.[1]

*From Harry G. Johnson, "Towards a Generalized Capital Accumulation Approach to Economic Development," in OECD Study Group in the Economics of Education, *The Residual Factor and Economic Growth*, Paris, 1964, pp. 219–25. Reprinted by permission.

[1] Cf. T. W. Schultz, ed., "Reflections on Investment in Man," *Journal of Political Economy, Supplement*, October 1962, pp. 1–8.

The formulation of concern with the economics of education (in a broad sense) in these particular terms, while appropriate to the current state of economic research and thinking, is for this very reason both restrictive in its implications and likely to appear before much more time has passed as a transient stage in the evolution towards a more comprehensive formulation of economic development problems in terms of a broadly conceived concept of capital accumulation. . . .

Concentration on the role of human capital has already proceeded far enough to generate the beginnings of a counter-revolution. The general outlines of the counter-revolution are indeed already apparent. On the one hand, the recent emphasis on human capital formation in growth accountancy is based on the recognition that conventional measures of labour input fail to take account of improvements in the quality of labour and aims primarily at more accurate measurement of labour inputs. Application of the same criteria to inputs of capital suggests that the contribution of capital may also have been grossly underestimated, as a result both of understatement of the flow of capital services into production by the conventional equation of service flow with the depreciated value of capital stock, and of failure to measure accurately improvements in the performance characteristics ("quality") of capital equipment.[2] On the other hand, the evidence on rates of return to educational investment in the United States does not suggest that there has been serious general underinvestment in education there, while both casual empirical observation of underdeveloped countries and some detailed research on the relative returns to investments in education and material capital in them[3] suggest that at least in some cases the proportion of resources devoted to human capital formation may be too high rather than too low.[4] A rehabilitation of investment in material capital as a potent source of economic growth may therefore be in prospect. What is more important, while the process of increasing economic knowledge proceeds in phases of exaggerated concentration on one or another aspect of a problem, both the effect and the intent are to arrive at a unified and more powerful synthesis of explanations of economic phenomena. The con-

temporary phase, in which the concepts of human capital and of investment in it figure as corrections of emphasis in a system of economic ideas dominated by material capital, is bound to merge into one in which human and nonhuman capital are treated as alternative forms of capital in general. The desirability of achieving such a synthesis is not merely a matter of scientific economy and elegance, it is also a pre-requisite for rational discussion and formulation of policy for economic growth in both advanced and underdeveloped countries. The purpose of this paper, accordingly, is to sketch the outlines of such a synthesis, in the form of a generalised capital accumulation approach to economic development, and to discuss some of its implications for social and economic policy.

The essential elements of a generalised capital accumulation approach to economic development are already present in the literature of economics, and at least some applications of the approach (for example, the explanation of wage differentials) have been familiar to economists ever since economics became established as a separate subject of study. The foundations of it were explicitly laid in Irving Fisher's classic work on capital and income, and carried forward by F. H. Knight's work on the theory of capital; and the approach is exemplified, and its potency demonstrated, in the recent research of T. W. Schultz, Gary Becker, and others on human capital.[5] The essence of it is to regard "capital" as including anything that yields a stream of income over time, and income as the product of capital. From this point of view, as Fisher pointed out, all categories of income describe yields on various forms of capital, and can be expressed as rates of interest or return on the corresponding items of capital. Alternatively, all forms of income-yielding assets can be given an equivalent capital value by capitalising the income they yield at an appropriate rate of interest. By extension, the growth of income that

[2] Cf. Zvi Griliches, "The Sources of Measured Productivity Growth: U.S. Agriculture, 1940–1960," *Journal of Political Economy*, August 1960.

[3] Cf. Arnold C. Harberger, *Investment in Man Versus Investment in Machines: The Case of India*, a paper prepared for the Conference on Education and Economic Development, University of Chicago, April 4–6, 1963. Harberger finds the rate of return on real investment in India to be substantially higher than the rate of return on investment in education.

[4] This proposition becomes almost a truism if the concept of investment in human capital formation is extended to include expenditures on improved health, whose effects on the rate of population increase constitute one of the major economic problems of underdeveloped countries.

[5] See T. W. Schultz, *op. cit.*

defines economic development is necessarily the result of the accumulation of capital, or of "investment"; but "investment" in this context must be defined to include such diverse activities as adding to material capital, increasing the health, discipline, skill and education of the human population, moving labour into more productive occupations and locations, and applying existing knowledge or discovering and applying new knowledge to increase the efficiency of productive processes. All such activities involve incurring costs, in the form of use of current resources, and investment in them is socially worth while if the rate of return over cost exceeds the general rate of interest, or the capital value of the additional income they yield exceeds the cost of obtaining it. From the somewhat different perspective of planning economic development, efficient development involves allocation of investment resources according to priorities set by the relative rates of return on alternative investments.

The conception of economic growth as a process of accumulating capital, in all the manifold forms that the broad Fisherian concept of capital allows, is a potent simplification of the analytical problem of growth, and one which facilitates the discussion of problems of growth policy by emphasising the relative returns from alternative investments of currently available resources. The Fisherian concept of capital, however, and the approach to the analysis of production and distribution problems associated with it, are not as yet characteristic of the work and philosophical approach of the majority of economists, and to some the implications of the approach for policy with respect to human beings appear to be positively repugnant. Must economists instead employ a narrower concept of capital that identifies capital with material capital goods and equipment used in the production process, and distinguishes it sharply from labour? . . .

As already mentioned, the limitations of accumulation of material capital as an explanation of a prescription for growth have prompted the contemporary interest in human capital formation, and suggest a generalisation of the concept of capital accumulation to include investment in all types of capital formation. An important obstacle to such a generalisation is that the treatment of human beings as a form of capital, even if only conceptually, seems offensive to some economists as being contrary to democratic political philosophy. This reaction, however, involves a confusion of analytical approach and normative recommendations unfortunately only too common in discussions of economic problems with policy connotations. To recognise that important areas of socio-economic policy involve decisions analytically identical with decisions about investing in machines is not at all to imply that people should be regarded as no different from machines; on the contrary, refusal to recognise the investment character of a problem because people are involved may result in people receiving worse treatment than machines. One might, indeed, hazard the generalisation that democratic free-enterprise economies tend to make wasteful use of their human resources, precisely because people are not sufficiently regarded as socially productive assets.

Conception of economic growth as a generalised process of capital accumulation provides a unifying principle for the statistical explanation of past growth and the formulation of policy for future growth or plans for economic development. It does not, however—and cannot be expected to—dispose of any real problems, though it does clarify understanding of them. Instead, it transforms these problems into problems of the special characteristics of particular types of capital, or of the specification of efficient investment programmes.

From the point of view of economically relevant differentiations, items of capital can be classified in a variety of ways. One fundamental distinction to be drawn relates to the nature of the yield or contribution to economic welfare—the distinction between consumption capital, which yields a flow of services enjoyed directly and therefore contributing to utility, and production capital, which yields a flow of goods the consumption of which yields utility. The returns from production capital are directly observable, and therefore more amenable to measurement than the returns on consumption capital.

Another fundamental distinction relates to the form in which capital is embodied—here it seems necessary not only to distinguish capital embodied in human beings from capital embodied in non-human material forms, but also to distinguish between capital embodied in both human and non-human physical forms and capital embodied in neither, the latter category comprising both the state of the arts (the intellectual production capital of society) and the state of culture (the intellectual consumption capital of society). The significance of this distinction is closely related to a third distinction—one which is particularly relevant to policy problems—between types of capital according to whether the returns to investment in capital accumulation accrue to the investor or to others. Here it seems necessary to distinguish: (a) capital goods which render specific services to production or consumption by the owner; (b) human capital, the distinguishing characteristic of which is that, both inherently and by legal tradition, control over the use of the capital is vested in the individual embodying the capital, regardless of the source of finance of the investment in it; (c) social capital or collective capital, the distinguishing characteristic of which is that for reasons of inherent necessity or administrative convenience its services to production or consumption are not charged to individual users but are paid for by taxation of the community at large; (d) intellectual capital or knowledge, the distinguishing characteristic of which is that, once created it is a free good, in the sense that use of it by one individual does not diminish its availability to others.

All forms of capital other than capital goods rendering specific services to production or consumption raise serious problems for economic analysis measurement and policy formation. The fusion of human capital with the personality of its owner raises among other things the problem of how far expenditure on the creation of human capital should be accounted as investment, and how far it should be classed as consumption; while the vesting of control over the use of capital in the individual invested in, given the imperfection of markets for personal credit, poses the problem of how far education should be provided at public expense. The divergence of private and social costs and benefits inherent in free or subsidised education raises some particularly difficult problems in conjunction with the fact that educated people are especially mobile interregionally and internationally, so that resources devoted to education in poor countries may run substantially to waste in unilateral transfers of human capital to richer countries.[6] Social capital investment involves a similar separation of costs of investment from benefits, and a similar mixture of equity and efficiency considerations. Investment in knowledge raises the thorniest of all problems, since the zero marginal cost of knowledge to additional users implies that

[6] Brinley Thomas has emphasised the economic absurdity of the contemporary migration pattern between advanced and underdeveloped countries, in which the advanced countries cream off the professional talent of the underdeveloped countries by immigration and attempt to replace it by their own experts supplied at great expense as part of development aid. See Brinley Thomas, "International Factor Movements and Unequal Rate of Growth," *The Manchester School of Economic and Social Studies,* January 1961. The ease of migration of educated people from underdeveloped countries, especially those in which English is the language of instruction, to advanced countries is a serious limitation on the potentialities of achieving economic development by educational investment and suggests the social desirability of devising means of obliging either the emigrants themselves or the countries receiving them to repay the social capital invested in them to their countries of origin.

no system of recouping the cost of investment in knowledge-creation by charging for its use can be economically efficient. . . .

The distinctions discussed above do not include a distinction between natural resources (natural capital) and man-made capital. For most economic purposes, such a distinction is unnecessary—natural resources, like capital goods, can be appropriated, transferred, and invested in. Natural resources do, however, raise two sorts of special problems. First property rights in some range of natural resources are typically vested in society or the state; this poses the problem of ensuring efficient exploitation of these resources through appropriate accounting and charging for the use of the state's natural capital, a problem particularly important at the time when resources are first brought into use. Secondly, some kinds of natural resources, which are likely to be of particular importance to developing countries, are nonrenewable, and pose the problems of efficient depletion and exhaustion— of efficient capital decumulation, rather than accumulation. The problems of achieving economic development through the exploitation of depleting natural resources become particularly acute and politically highly charged when such exploitation is dependent on the participation of foreign capital and enterprise.

Conception of economic development as a generalised process of capital accumulation, in conjunction with recognition of economically significant differences between various types of capital, has important implications for the efficient programming of investment of economic development. These implications centre on the relationships of complementarity and substitutability in both production and consumption that may exist between types of capital provided by different investment processes, and the consequent desirability of aiming at both balanced investment in the production of complementary types of capital and the selection of the most efficient combinations of types of capital in the light of the relative costs of different kinds of investment. The complementarity between modern equipment and technology, a skilled labour force, and social overhead capital in the transportation and distribution systems is by now sufficiently recognised for development planning to aim at producing integrated investment programmes comprising investment in education and vocational training (manpower programmes) as well as investment in industrial and social overhead. For such comprehensive development investment programmes to maximise the contribution of investment to economic growth, however, recognition of complementarity must be allied with recognition of substitutability and analysis of rates of return on the total investment of capital in alternative programmes involving investment in capital goods, human capital, social capital and the acquisition of new knowledge.

Much of the literature on economic development assumes far too easily that low-wage labour is necessarily cheap industrial labour, ignoring the magnitude of the investments in human and social capital that may have to be made to convert rural workers into skilled industrial labour, and the possibility that investment of the same capital in agricultural improvement might yield far higher returns. On the other hand, there is a strong possibility, exemplified by the successful development of exports of some technologically fairly advanced products from otherwise underdeveloped countries, that the greatest comparative advantage for such countries lies in skilled-labour-intensive products, for the reason that a generally low wage level makes the cost of investment in human capital low (especially forgone earnings and the cost of instruction and educational structures) by comparison with comparable costs in advanced countries. In addition, such countries may be able to catch up with the advanced countries far more rapidly in the accumulation of knowledge than in the accumulation of material capital.

Apart from its implications for planning for economic growth, a generalised capital accumulation approach to economic development points to the potential fruitfulness of research into and analysis of the efficiency of a wide range of processes and policies that involve the allocation of capital but are not usually thought of as concerned with investment. It has, for example, been amply demonstrated by empirical research that rates of return on investment in education vary widely between different levels of the education system; and there is good reason for doubting that existing educational systems are very efficient when considered as an industry producing extremely long-lived capital assets. The field of public health and medical care, viewed as an industry concerned with the repair and maintenance of human capital, also offers scope for economic analyses of rates of return on alternative investments. Institutional arrangements for supporting and rewarding fundamental and applied research, considered as an industry producing intellectual capital, provide an even greater challenge to economists. Within the traditional scope of economics, labour mobility, unemployment policy, and policy respecting the location of industry all demand the application of capital theory. Perhaps the most important area requiring rationalisation in terms of a broadened concept of capital accumulation, however, is the theory and practice of public finance. Not only do income tax systems typically make a very poor adjustment for the capital investment element in personal income, but the necessity of recouping by income and profits taxation the costs of investments in human capital customarily provided free or at a subsidised price to the people invested in creates disincentives to the efficient use and accumulation of capital of all kinds.

VIII.D. ENTREPRENEURSHIP

VIII.D.1. The Supply of

Entrepreneurship*

Our starting point is the following observation: all the theory builders, despite many sensitive insights and distinctions with regard to specific problems, end up by positing that the creative (or achievement-oriented, or rational, or innovative) entrepreneur with his special facility is either *present* or *absent*, and that business performance is uniformly lackluster and tradition-bound or it is innovative and expansive in all aspects. The writer's own experience in West Africa and a perusal of the empirical literature on this subject for other underdeveloped countries suggest that this binary conception of the entrepreneurship problem is neither fruitful nor in accord with what we observe.

Let us start by sketching the potential scope of the entrepreneurial task in an underdeveloped economy. Widening the typical three- of four-function description of the industrialist's job to a more appropriate degree of articulation, thirteen roles or specific kinds of activities that the entrepreneur himself might have to perform for the successful operation of his enterprise are given below. It will be convenient for later discussion to categorize these roles into four subgroupings: exchange relationships (1–4), political administration (5–7), management control (8–9), and technology (10–13).

1. Perception of market opportunities (novel or imitative).
2. Gaining command over scarce resources.
3. Purchasing inputs.

*From Peter Kilby (ed.), *Entrepreneurship and Economic Development*, The Free Press, New York, 1971, pp. 27–30, 35. Reprinted by permission.

4. Marketing of the product and responding to competition.
5. Dealing with the public bureaucracy (concessions, licenses, taxes).
6. Management of human relations within the firm.
7. Management of customer and supplier relations.
8. Financial management.
9. Production management (control by written records, supervision, coordinating input flows with orders, maintenance).
10. Acquiring and overseeing assembly of the factory.
11. Industrial engineering (minimizing inputs with a given production process).
12. Upgrading processes and product quality.
13. Introduction of new production techniques and products.

Under the strict assumptions of the economist's model the entrepreneur himself (or the entrepreneurial team in the case of a large corporation) will only perform activities 1 and 2; the skills for the remaining eleven functions will be purchased in the market place. In practice, the economist may attribute as many as the first four functions to the entrepreneurial unit. The extent to which the entrepreneur can *actually* parcel out activities to competent lieutenants depends upon the following four factors:—

i. The scale of production—the larger the enterprise the more scope there is for utilizing specialized executive personnel, in so far as factors 2 to 4 permit.
ii. The degree of development of the high-level manpower market.

iii. Social factors governing the amount of responsibility with which hired personnel will perform.

iv. The entrepreneur's comparative efficiency in utilizing high-cost managerial employees.

While one can observe greater delegation of entrepreneurial tasks in the more advanced and socially disciplined economies, by and large the effect of the latter three factors has been to hold to a maximum the number of activities performed by the entrepreneur, in whole or in part, up to a threshold firm size somewhere between 100 and 200 employees. Because of the greater importance of firms falling below this threshold, in conjunction with underdeveloped factor input markets, the demands placed upon the entrepreneurial unit are considerably more extensive in low-income as compared to high-income economies.

This conceptualization of entrepreneurship as the performance of services that are required but not available in the market (or not available in sufficient divisibility) can usefully be contrasted with other formulations. The entrepreneurial function is defined in terms of activities rather than in terms of attributes such as innovation or risk-taking which may or may not characterize a particular activity. No invariable set of activities, such as investment decisions or designing market strategy, is identified as constitutive of the entrepreneurial function. The entrepreneurial unit provides the variable, residual non-marketed services and receives the residual profit income as payment. But let us return now to our principal objective of empirically assessing differential role performance.

Evidence from contemporary underdeveloped economies for evaluating entrepreneurial performance in the thirteen roles we have enumerated is found in a number of descriptive studies of on-going industrial entrepreneurship and in studies of productive efficiency in factory enterprise. The former are cross-sectional surveys covering one or a number of industries in individual countries. Investigators report energetic and skillful performance in roles 1 to 7: these business men are highly responsive to economic opportunities, they are willing to risk their own capital in long-term ventures, they are adept at marketing, and (with the exceptions noted) they maintain harmonious relations with their staff, suppliers, and the public bureaucracy.[1] Moreover, making allowance for capital entry requirements, these entrepreneurs are recruited from a broad range of occupational and social strata; there is no evidence of blocked mobility which would lead to inadequate numbers of entrepreneurs.

Seeming to bear out the speculations about the critical entrepreneurial tasks in late developing countries, the domain where performance is reported to be least satisfactory is that of technology and production management. Cochran, Harris, Kilby, and Nafziger identify this area as the major bottleneck to indigenous industrial development. Papanek also views in-factory managerial efficiency as the principal problem in Pakistan but considers it to be of manageable proportions even in the near-term. In

[1] J. J. Berna, *Industrial Entrepreneurship in Madras State* (New York: 1960), Chs. 4–6; J. J. Carroll, *The Filipino Manufacturing Entrepreneur* (Ithaca: 1965), Ch. 6; T. C. Cochran, *The Puerto Rican Businessman* (Philadelphia: 1959), Ch. 4; J. R. Harris, *Industrial Entrepreneurship in Nigeria*, unpublished doctoral dissertation (Northwestern University: 1967), Ch. 8; Peter Kilby, *African Enterprise: The Nigerian Bread Industry* (Stanford: 1965), Chs. 7–8; E. W. Nafziger, *Nigerian Entrepreneurship: A Study of Indigenous Businessmen in the Footwear Industry*, unpublished doctoral dissertation (University of Illinois: 1967), Chs. 3–5; G. F. Papanek, *Pakistan's Development, Social Goals and Private Incentives* (Cambridge, Mass.: 1967), Chs. 2–3; Y. A. Sayigh, *Entrepreneurs of Lebanon* (Cambridge, Mass.: 1962), Chs. 1–4. Limited information on role performance can be gleaned from A. P. Alexander, "Industrial Entrepreneurship in Turkey: Origins and Growth," *Economic Development and Cultural Change* (July, 1960), pp. 349–365.

his fifty-two machinery-making firms, Berna ranks inadequacies in industrial engineering and technological betterment with rigid attitudes toward labor relations as the principal impediments to further industrial expansion. Sayigh and Carroll, because of the type of data they collected, do not mention any "internal" deficiencies in entrepreneurial performance.

All but two of these investigators interpret these shortcomings as transient and as being a function of the scarcity of market supplied skill inputs, lack of competitive pressures (especially in Pakistan, Turkey, and the Philippines), and inexperience. In short, these authors take the position that there is little or no problem of entrepreneurial supply, rather that the difficulties lie primarily in external market conditions. Only Thomas Cochran and the present writer see managerial and technological shortcomings as enduring impediments rooted in sociological variables on the supply side. One can isolate two factors that might have biased the majority of investigators toward their predominantly demand interpretation. First, by and large they all approached their subject with an economist-like conception of what constitutes the entrepreneurial function, i.e., a primary emphasis on roles 1 to 4.

Second, because their studies are cross-sectional rather than longitudinal and their descriptive data on entrepreneurial performance are limited to a single point in time, actual observation of persisting managerial and technological problems is precluded. In contrast, the effect of differing market circumstances in intra-sample entrepreneurial performance is clearly seen. Moreover, even when measurements of entrepreneurial performance are obtained on a time-series basis, the influence of slow-changing supply variables will be obscured unless the period is long enough to average out shifts in economic conditions. . . .

Summarizing the foregoing review of available empirical evidence from underdeveloped countries, it was found that with a few exceptions entrepreneurial performance in those roles involving exchange relationships and "political administration" is vigorous and effective. On the other hand, entrepreneurs typically do not apply themselves with equal intensity or skill to their tasks in the realms of management control and technology. Deficiencies in these latter areas represent in many instances the operational bottleneck to indigenous industrial development.

VIII.D.2. Achievement Motive and Entrepreneurship*

In the mid-twentieth century few possibilities fascinate man more than that of shaping his own destiny. Scientific knowledge holds out precisely that promise. In the struggle for peace he seems far from achieving such a goal, but in the war on want he may be

*From David C. McClelland and David G. Winter, *Motivating Economic Achievement*, The Free Press, New York, 1969, pp. 1–2, 9–11, 20–21, 23–5, 28–31, 33–7. Reprinted by permission.

faring better. More and more studies are accumulating which purport to show what factor or factors are important for economic growth. Among these is D. C. McClelland's *The Achieving Society* (1961), which summarized an interlocking series of empirical studies suggesting that a particular human motive, the need for Achievement, promotes entrepreneurship, which in turn is a key to economic growth. The book ends with the scientist's traditional hope that the knowledge so painstakingly collected will some-how be useful in helping man shape his des-tiny. At the time it was little more than a pious hope, since it was not at all clear how a development specialist or a leader of a new nation could make use of the knowledge accumulated about the achievement motive. If anything, the general import of the find-ings was discouraging to anyone attempting to accelerate economic growth: the need to Achieve (n Achievement) seemed to be a relatively stable personality characteristic rooted in experiences in middle childhood. Didn't this imply that all a developer could do was to try to change parental habits of child-rearing—known to be very resistant to change—and then hopefully wait for the chil-dren to grow up with a stronger need to Achieve? Such a reading of the findings in *The Achieving Society* may be correct, but it was certainly discouraging, not only prac-tically, but scientifically. For the scientist would like to explore further the investiga-tion of the role of n Achievement in devel-opment.

If n Achievement can be increased only through child-rearing techniques, then fur-ther scientific investigation is impracticable for a variety of reasons. It is probably too difficult to change parental attitudes consis-tently enough over time to observe any changes in n Achievement. Even if n Achievement could be changed, it would be a long wait until the children grew up and showed the expected increases in entrepre-neurial activity and economic growth. Fur-thermore, the study would have to be done on a massive scale, since many of the chil-dren would be unlikely to go into business in any case. The final results could scarcely be obtained in the lifetime of the scientist; he could not even expect enough feedback to help give his hypothesis a better test by trying different techniques of developing achievement motivation in children. And if he changed his strategy, he would again have to wait a generation to detect any results.

If a theory cannot really be tested, maybe it needs restatement. Furthermore, the

urgent problem of accelerating economic growth in poor nations persists. Is there not some way that achievement motivation can be developed in adults—particularly in those businessmen whose actions are likely to bring most immediate returns in expanded enterprise? Can it be shown that direct in-creases in n Achievement in individuals can have significant economic impact on a com-munity? . . .

THE URGE TO IMPROVE

Many scholars have stressed that eco-nomic modernization and growth require a whole new set of values and attitudes, and marked changes in social organization. In a cross-cultural study, Inkeles has identified the following attitudes accompanying mod-ernization: "a disposition to accept new ideas and try new methods; a readiness to express opinions; a time sense that makes men more interested in the present and fu-ture than in the past; a better sense of punc-tuality; a greater concern for planning, organ-ization and efficiency; a tendency to see the world as calculable; a faith in science and technology; and, finally, a belief in distribu-tive justice" (summarized by Weiner, 1966, p. 4). Smelser (1966) points out that these value changes are often associated with po-litical reorganization and changes in the edu-cational system, in religion, in family struc-ture, and in social stratification. No one doubts that man changes his thinking and actions enormously during development, but it is hard to know which of these changes, if any, is crucial and whether any of them precedes or follows development.

The need to Achieve, or to give it a less esoteric title, the urge to improve, ought to be viewed simply as one variable among the many or as an index reflecting various habits or thoughts and actions which are important for economic development. There is no rea-son to believe that the n Achievement index is unique, that these same key attitudes could not be tapped by some other measure. All one can say is that they have not been so tapped as yet, and as an index, the *n* Achievement [*n* Ach] score has certain advantages. Research data have accumulated on it for more than 20 years—in the laboratory, in the field, in history, and in many different countries. Thus when one uses such a measure, he is not talking about some vague psychological quality; rather the quality has been quantitatively measured in a variety of contexts and has been carefully interpreted in terms of a general theory of human motivation (see McClelland *et al.*, 1953; McClelland, 1961; Atkinson, 1958, 1964). . . .

What is the evidence that *n* Ach is a key factor in economic growth? It can be briefly summarized (after McClelland, 1961). The *n* Ach content of popular literature has been shown to have increased on several occasions prior to rapid economic growth in a country and to have declined prior to a slackening in the rate of growth. When *n* Ach content is coded among modern nations in children's textbooks, those countries that scored higher in *n* Ach in 1925 and again in 1950 subsequently developed at a faster rate economically than countries that scored lower. These crude measures of general concern for achievement in a nation at a particular time presumably also reflect the number of active achievement-oriented people in the country. And how do achievement-oriented people behave? Laboratory studies of individuals with high *n* Ach show that in general they behave like successful, rationalizing, business entrepreneurs. That is, they set moderately difficult goals for themselves, neither too easy nor too hard, so as to maximize the likelihood of achievement satisfaction. They are more than normally interested in concrete feedback on how well they are doing. In this respect they seem to be particularly like businessmen who, more than professionals, get concrete feedback in concrete performance terms as to their relative success or failure. They like assuming personal responsibility for solving problems, because in that way they can get a sense of achievement satisfaction from completing a task,

whereas they cannot if success depends on luck or circumstances beyond their control, or if they are working exclusively on someone else's problem. Finally, those with high *n* Ach generally show more initiative and exploratory behavior, continually researching the environment to find tasks that they can solve to their satisfaction. The similarities in these types of behavior to the actions characteristic of a successful entrepreneur were striking. So it was predicted that entrepreneurial business executives should universally score higher in *n* Achievement than professionals with similar social and educational backgrounds. This turns out to be the case in several advanced and not so advanced countries, including Poland, which is not operating under the free enterprise system (see McClelland, 1961, Ch. 7). . . .

A GENERAL MODEL OF ECONOMIC DEVELOPMENT

Let us take stock of this discussion so far. First, we have reviewed several related theories which, for the sake of convenience, we shall call the rational model of economic development. This model holds that most men—in the West, in developing countries, and in peasant societies—naturally seek to maximize their interests, given the particular situations and constraints in which they find themselves. Hence any attempt to change their economic activity should concentrate on changing the incentives and constraints of their situations. This may involve both closing off some possibilities (e.g., land reform in Pakistan) and creating other opportunities (e.g., improved agricultural techniques). The model is appealing because it is simple and close to our ordinary experience of why men act as they do. It offers clear policy recommendations; in many instances such policies have had important effects on economic development. So it is not surprising that the rational model has considerable repute in academic and policy circles.

However, there is widespread evidence that economic development does not always and everywhere proceed according to the predictions made from the rational model. . . .

It is important to turn from a general appraisal of economic development to a careful study of some particular policies. How do different kinds of people act in different situations? Here we begin to question the adequacy of the rational model as it is usually formulated. As pointed out above, only a very small proportion of the potential entrepreneurs in Pakistan took advantage of the changed situation after 1947. In Nigeria, the Ibo responded with unique vigor and success to situational conditions that they shared with several other, less active tribes. Why is it that groups respond differently to similar conditions? . . .

We have introduced the psychological concept of achievement motivation, or *n* Achievement, to account for the differences in response to similar conditions. There is impressive evidence that *n* Achievement is associated with more vigorous effort and greater success in economic activity: in highly industrialized Western countries such as the United States (McClelland, 1965; Sheppard and Belitsky, 1966) and Finland (Kock, 1965); in developing countries such as Mexico (Andrews, 1967) and Nigeria (LeVine, 1966); and even among peasants (Rogers and Nill, 1966). The laboratory research on *n* Achievement shows that different *n* Achievement (and fear of failure) levels will lead to very different responses to situations and incentives which are externally identical. Certain motive patterns actually lead to withdrawal from "improved" incentives. We are, therefore, suggesting that motivation is an important variable which has to be taken into account in policy as well as theory, if we are to understand the way in which situations and incentives can affect behavior.

Does the *n* Achievement research suggest that the rational model is of no use in understanding and predicting economic behavior? It does not. The model of Atkinson posits

motive strength (an individual disposition) as only one factor in the complex interaction of motive, expectation, and incentive that leads to behavior. How can we reconcile the *n* Achievement research with the compelling if ambiguous simplicity of the rational model? Let us review the terms of the rational model: Men act so as to *maximize* their *interest(s) or return(s)* over some *time period*, given the *perceived constraints of the situation*. Each of the emphasized terms of this statement of the rational model contains ambiguities that need to be clarified. . . .

We here suggest that for the rational model to be useful, several of its terms have to be specified. Certain patterns of terms seem to lead to economic development, and certain patterns do not. From our review of research on *n* Achievement, we concluded that it was a motive that led to vigorous economic activity. At this point we shall attempt to show how various aspects of the *n* Achievement behavior syndrome are precisely those that are necessary to make the rational model work in a way that promotes economic development. That is, we shall review the characteristics of *n* Achievement in terms of interests, strategy of maximizing, time perspective, and perception of the environment.

First, what interests or desires for return are characteristic of men with high *n* Achievement? The evidence seems clear that these men are interested in excellence for its own sake, rather than for rewards of money, prestige, or power. Men high in *n* Achievement will not work harder at a task when money is offered as a reward (Atkinson and Reitman, 1956). They evaluate roles on the basis of the opportunities for excellence rather than those for prestige (Burnstein, Moulton, and Liberty, 1963). Their achievement concern is not affected by having to work for the group rather than for only themselves (French, 1958). They pick experts rather than friends as work partners (French, 1956). Over time they tend to become successful entrepreneurs, rather than equally wealthy men in other roles (McClelland, 1961, 1965). This connection between entrepreneurial activity and *n* Achievement holds even in Poland, a social system where presumably the direct individual financial return from profits is considerably attenuated (McClelland, 1961, pp. 262–65). So it seems clear that *n* Achievement leads to an interest in entrepreneurial excellence in its most general sense, and not to interests which may be superficially associated with it or confused with it in Western industrial culture, such as wealth, prestige, or individual prominence and influence.

What strategies of maximizing will a man with high *n* Achievement follow? From Heckhausen's summary (1967, pp. 91–103) of many studies of goal setting under conditions of risk, the following propositions seem to be valid: (1) Men high in *n* Achievement are more concerned with achieving success than with avoiding failure. That is, they are not likely to select defensive strategies which minimize failure at the cost of giving up decisive individual action. (2) Compared with men low in *n* Achievement, they pay more careful attention to the realistic probabilities of success which are attached to various alternative actions in a given situation. This suggests that they are more likely to make informal calculations of the expected values of outcomes, and to select over time those alternatives which have the highest expected values. (3) They sharply distinguish situations in which they have some control from situations where results depend largely on chance. That is, they do not assume that the world is unreasonably benevolent or malevolent, but they are aware of what they can do in it. Taking these propositions together, it seems clear that *n* Achievement leads to a strategy of maximization that is most likely to achieve success in the environment of economic decision-making. This particular strategy is no doubt assumed to be a part of the framework of the rational model, although it is by no means a universal strategy.

The evidence is clear that men with high *n* Achievement have a greater future time perspective. They are more concerned with the future, especially the medium- to long-term future. They are more willing to postpone immediate rewards in favor of large future rewards (see studies summarized in Heckhausen, 1967, pp. 42–45). The relevance of this future time perspective to the rational model seems clear. First, men with high *n* Achievement will be maximizing their interests over a longer time span, so that they are less likely to slip into the trader mentality. Second, their greater concern with the future probably enables them to form more accurate estimates of the probabilities of success and failure and this enhances their maximizing strategy.

Are there any general effects of *n* Achievement on the perceptions of the environment? Here we draw together some findings assembled by Heckhausen (1967, pp. 113–14, 122–24, 134–36). First, a man with high *n* Achievement is, surprisingly, better able to recall his failures and the tasks that were not completed and therefore counted as failures. Moreover, given the opportunity, he is more likely to return to these tasks in order to succeed if there is a reasonable probability of success. Even under situational pressures, men with high *n* Achievement are more likely to apply quick perception, practical reasoning, and insight to arrive at new and creative solutions to problems. In perceiving the environment, they are likely to be more independent: They make judgments based on their own experience and standards, rather than become overwhelmed by the perceptual environment or the opinions and pressures of other people. Any integration of these findings must remain tentative; however, taken together, they do suggest that *n* Achievement leads a man to pay more careful and accurate attention to his situation. He is perhaps less likely to rationalize or ignore his failures, and is more likely to maintain independence of judgment. Obviously such a cognitive style has important effects on the extent to which a man can use cues from the environment to maximize his interests over time. So we tentatively propose that *n* Achievement aids the perception of the situation in ways that make economic activity rational.

We have suggested that the n Achievement syndrome is associated with a particular configuration of terms in the rational model. Further, we suggest that this particular configuration of terms has usually been a hidden and unacknowledged assumption in the argument that economic activity can be stimulated by improving the incentives and opportunities in the situation. Of course vigorous economic activity has been and can be successfully encouraged by a policy of changing incentives alone; but only if the "target population" (entrepreneurs, managers in public enterprises, and the like) have the appropriate interests, strategies, time perspective, and perceptions—in short if they have the appropriate structure of response to the situation. Changing the situation works only to the extent that the target population has a structure of response appropriate to the perception, evaluation, and action on these changed incentives. The many and varied experiences with development programs over the past two decades suggest that sometimes it does and sometimes it does not.

INCREASING THE URGE TO IMPROVE

How are human values to be changed? Can we rely on social and economic or technical changes in the environment to produce the human characteristics necessary to support them? Many social theorists believe that human beings in the aggregate will adjust to their environment, that certain changes in the environment are more-or-less inevitable, and therefore, that the whole process of development of necessary values and attitudes is more-or-less automatic and can be expected to occur by natural processes. Often economists invoke the "demonstration effect" as the main source of changed wants and values. Poor people everywhere are gradually exposed to modern products such as fountain pens, better seed, or eyeglasses.

They observe that the products have real utility for them. They want to purchase such articles, but in order to get enough money to do so, they have to work harder. Their achievement motivation is directly aroused by the promise of material gains. Douvan (1956) found that achievement motivation was significantly aroused in students from working-class backgrounds following failure only when they had been promised a reward in dollars if they succeeded. For the middle-class students, failure alone was sufficient to arouse achievement motivation. Sociologists such as Inkeles stress such major motivating-shaping forces as urbanization, the mass media, creation of the nation state, and the factory. "The city is itself a powerful new experience. It encourages, and indeed to some degree obliges, the individual to adopt many new ways of life" (Inkeles, 1966, p. 147). The individual is exposed to new consumer goods and new ideas. He may learn about being on time to catch a bus or how to rely almost entirely on money as a means of surviving. He will almost certainly be exposed more to the mass media. As Pool says, "Where radio goes, there modernizing attitudes come in" (1966, p. 100). As the nation state becomes stronger and better organized, the individual is exposed to political rallies, posters, radio messages, the army, the police, the tax-collector—all sorts of influences that will eventually shape him into a man with more modern attitudes. Or if he works in a factory as Inkeles points out, he should be under powerful influences to change. "There is always an intense concentration of physical and mechanical power brought to bear on the transformation of raw materials; orderly and routine procedures to govern the flow of work are essential; time is a powerful influence in guiding the work processes; power and authority generally rest on technical competence; and, as a rule, rewards are in rough proportion to performance" (1966, p. 149).

The strange part of this argument is that development ought to be fairly automatic, easy, and rapid. Yet it clearly is not. The literature is full of examples of how men have failed notably to be influenced by such factors, have failed to act in their own self-interest. Villagers can be exposed endlessly to radio messages on how to improve their farming practices, with almost no effect unless they are organized into discussion and action groups. In Inkeles's own study, it may be those who are most ready to be influenced by the factory who will expose themselves to it by working there. Thus one can argue that while the factory accelerates change, it may not be considered the primary influence initiating change. Oscar Lewis's reports on the urban poor in Mexico City (1961) show little evidence that they are developing high n Achievement from exposure to various "demonstration effects." Over and over again technical assistance has failed to evoke automatically the attitudes it should if it is to be considered a really effective source of attitude change....

Most theorists feel that education must be the answer to the problem. And in its more general sense it must be. Man must learn new habits, values, motives, attitudes. And it would certainly be more efficient if he could learn them directly through education rather than indirectly through gradual social and economic forces. But what kind of education? A case can be made for just any kind of education—that is, just the number of years of schooling of any type. Schooling and level of economic development are highly correlated around the world. For example, Harbison and Myers (1964) report that among 75 nations, GNP per capita is correlated .67 with primary school enrollment, .82 with secondary school enrollment, and .74 with third level enrollment. Becker (1964) has made a careful analysis to show that men with more education make more money over their lifetime, even when ability and background variables are equated for those who go on to school as compared with those who do not. The cross-national comparisons do not indicate which come first, that is, whether wealth made more education possible or education led to more wealth. But Becker's individual studies suggest that more education preceded and made possible the increase in individual income. McClelland (1966) has shown elsewhere on an international basis that countries which invested heavily in secondary education on the average developed more rapidly economically a number of years later, when the educated population would have reached its peak capacity in the working force. It looks as if more of every kind of education would pay off in the human resources that accelerate economic growth.

But can the type of education that is most useful be specified even further? It certainly cannot be concluded that more of any kind of education will increase n Achievement. For example, social class data show that while those with the least education have the lowest n Achievement, those with a moderate level of education in the middle classes have the highest n Achievement. Those with the most education have somewhat less n Achievement on the average than those from the middle classes (Rosen, 1959). The best guess is that education is most likely to produce the kind of people motivated to improve when it takes place in an achievement-oriented atmosphere....

But how can an education be made achievement oriented? Most of the information on this question has come from studies dealing with a very special form of education—namely, child-rearing or early socialization practices. As noted previously, this research tradition was guided by the theoretical supposition that since motives are formed early in life, one must study how parents treat their children to find out how n Achievement is produced. The studies showed that parents of boys who were high in n Achievement set moderately high standards for them and were warm and encouraging in their attitudes toward their son's efforts to achieve. The fathers furthermore were generally nondominating, leaving the sons free to try things out on their own. But this result only raises another question. How did the parents get that way? What made them achievement-oriented in the first place? Answers have so far been fairly numerous but inconclusive.

For example, Whiting *et al.* (1966) fall back on what amounts to an environmental explanation based on classical economic reasoning. They note that cross-culturally the extended family is associated with obedience training and the nuclear family with self-reliance and independence training, which in turn have been shown to be related to n Achievement. So whenever a household shifts from an extended family pattern to a nuclear family pattern, there ought to be an increase in n Achievement. . . . But if we now conclude that parental child-rearing is not so important as it once seemed to be, the question still remains: Where does an increase in achievement concern in individuals come from? Variations in national n Achievement levels do vaguely fit the "ideological reform" hypothesis. That is, countries such as Russia and China that were swept by zealous Communist ideological revolutions have shown marked increases in n Achievement level as measured in children's textbooks (see McClelland, 1961 and 1963). Communist revolutionaries certainly talked and acted like ideological reformers with strong achievement concerns. They also thought of themselves as superior in some sense to traditional bourgeois societies, just as the early Protestants felt in reforming the church. Furthermore, many new nations that have had to fight their way to freedom from colonial rule have elevated n Achievement levels in their textbooks (see McClelland, 1961).

But one can still ask: Where do the reformers come from? What sets such a dynamic "revival movement" in motion? LeVine (1966) has sought an answer in social structure. In trying to explain why the Ibo in Nigeria are much more upwardly mobile and achievement-oriented than the Hausa, he points out that the Ibo have traditionally had a social system in which a young man can gain prestige by becoming a member of certain honorary societies. Getting into one of these societies depends on achieving occupational success and wealth. Thus, every parent, or every young man for that matter, sees that he ought to strive for achievement if he is ever to be successful in Ibo society. On the other hand, in Hausa society, the way to gain success is to attach oneself to a more powerful leader in a kind of client relationship, since rewards are bestowed from the top. A young Hausa sees that he is likely to gain recognition by being part of the entourage of a powerful person whose success he must therefore work for. According to LeVine these different traditional status mobility systems promote different ideological systems, which in turn create different personality types. Certainly such social systems should reinforce and help maintain certain patterns of motivation, but one wonders how a system ever gets up that way in the first place, or more particularly, how it would be possible to change it, once it has been set up. In fact, as noted above, a social-systems analysis is not very helpful in suggesting ways in which a particular pattern can be changed. For instance, suppose someone decided that the Hausa should become more achievement oriented. How could such a change be brought about? One might try to introduce the honorary society system employed by the Ibo, but could it succeed, unless the ideology of the Hausa had somehow been prepared to accept it?

So while the n Achievement mystique may have various sources, and while it may be maintained in various ways by the social structure, it is hard to imagine a more effective way to introduce it than by some kind of direct educational technique. Other, more indirect methods may work in the long run. But a brief survey of the evidence suggests that they will work best if there is already some receptivity, some elements of an achievement orientation present among the people to be influenced. Thus, a direct attempt to increase levels of achievement motivation in people and in a community seems to be eminently worth trying. No doubt an economic rationalist would admit that an increased *n* Achievement might add something to the effectiveness of the economic opportunities and incentives he is manipulating. The personality specialist might grant that the evidence does not clearly show that one has to wait a generation until specially trained children grow up. The historian might conclude that ideological reform movements, as in the Protestant Reformation, Communist revolutions, or the nationalism of new nations all have been important sources of increases in social *n* Achievement levels. These reform movements furthermore have usually affected minority groups, which have thought of themselves as superior to the masses around them and which have often had higher achievement motivation and greater entrepreneurial success. All might then grant that it is conceivable the same type of dedication could be created among a band of entrepreneurs whose achievement motivation had been directly influenced. Such a project would obviously have great theoretical and practical importance. The ultimate test that *n* Achievement is a key ingredient in economic growth must

be an experiment aimed at altering it to see what the effects would be. One must always wonder whether all the studies—historical, experimental, theoretical—have been interpreted in the only possible way. The network of linked findings reported in *The Achieving Society* and since may seem persuasive, but it is nowhere near as persuasive as an actual demonstration that would show the effect of an increase in *n* Achievement on economic growth directly and empirically. On the practical side, if the experiment proves to be successful, planners and policy-makers everywhere who are interested in accelerating economic growth would have a new tool. And planners need new tools; there is no question about that. The normal tools may be working—more investment in everything from schools to roads to banks to steel mills—but they are working slowly and it is difficult to establish priorities among them. It would indeed be exciting if we could discover that a specific short-term educational input in a tiny segment of the population would have far-reaching economic effects. . . .

VIII. SELECT BIBLIOGRAPHY

1. A general introduction to the importance of human capital is provided by the following: Hans W. Singer, "Social Development: Key Growth Sector," *IDR*, March 1965; N. Rosenberg, "Neglected Dimensions in the Analysis of Economic Change," *Bulletin of Oxford Institute of Economics and Statistics*, February 1964; OECD, *The Residual Factor and Economic Growth*, Paris, 1964; United Nations, ECAFE, *Economic Development and Human Resources*, Bangkok, 1966; Anne O. Krueger, "Factor Endowments and Per Capita Income Differences Among Countries," *EJ*, September 1968; F. H. Harbison, *Human Resources as the Wealth of Nations*, New York, 1973.

2. A number of studies have considered the benefits and costs of population control programs: A. J. Coale and E. M. Hoover, *Population Growth and Economic Development in Low-Income Countries*, Princeton, 1958; P. M. Hauser (ed.), *The Population Dilemma*, Englewood Cliffs, 1963; Bernard Berelson (ed.), *Family Planning and Population Programs*, Chicago, 1966; Goran Ohlin, *Population Control and Economic Development*, Paris, 1967; Dudley Kirk and Dorothy Nortman, "Population Policies in Developing Countries," *EDCC*, January 1967; R. R. Nelson, "A Theory of the Low-Level Equilibrium Trap," *AER*, December 1956; J. E. Meade, "Population Explosion, The Standard of Living, and Social Conflict," *EJ*, June 1967; J. Spengler, "The Economist and the Population Question," *AER*, March 1966; R. A. Easterlin, "Effects of Population Growth on the Economic Development of Developing Countries," *The Annals*, January 1967; S. Enke, "Economic Aspects of Slowing Population Growth," *EJ*, March 1966; E. E. Hagen, "Population and Economic Growth," *AER*, June 1959; Harvey Leibenstein, "Socio-Economic Fertility Theories and their Relevance to Population Policy," *ILR*, May–June 1974; _____, "An Interpretation of the Economic Theory of Fertility: Promising Path or Blind Alley," *JEL*, June 1974; _____, "Pitfalls in Benefit-Cost Analysis of Birth Prevention," *Population Studies*, July 1969; Dudley Kirk, "A New Demographic Transition?" in National Academy of Sciences, *Rapid Population Growth—Consequences and Policy Implications*, Baltimore, 1971; Timothy King et al., *Population Policies and Economic Development*, Baltimore, 1974.

3. Problems of health and nutrition are beginning to receive increasing attention. Some general studies are: M. H. King, *Medical Care in Developing Countries*, Nairobi, 1967; IBRD sector policy paper on *Health*, Washington, D.C., March 1975; M. J. Sharpston, "Health and Development," *JDS*, April 1973; _____, "Uneven Geographical Distribution of Medical Care," *JDS*, January 1972; Burton A. Weisbrod et al., *Disease and Economic Development*, Madison, 1973; Alan Berg, *The Nutrition Factor: Its Role in Economic Development*, Washington, D.C., 1973; H. G. Birch and J. D. Gussow, *Disadvantaged Children*, New York, 1970; Marcelo Selowsky and Lance Taylor, "The Economics of Malnourished Children: An Example of Disinvestment in Human Capital," *EDCC*, October 1973; Shlomo Reutlinger and Marcelo Selowsky, *Undernutrition and Poverty*, IBRD Working Paper No. 202, Washington, D.C., 1975; Victor W. Sidel and Ruth Sidel, *Serve the People: Observations on Medicine in the People's Republic of China*, Boston, 1974.

4. For an extensive annotated bibliography on education and development, see Mark Blaug, *The Economics of Education*, London, 1966. Several writings by T. W. Schultz are

highly instructive on the role of education in development: "Capital Formation by Education," *JPE*, December 1960; "Investment in Human Capital," *AER*, March 1961; "Education and Economic Growth," in N. B. Henry (ed.), *Social Forces Influencing American Education*, Chicago, 1961; "Investment in Human Capital in Poor Countries," in P. D. Zook (ed.), *Foreign Trade and Human Capital*, Dallas, 1962. The special supplement of the *JPE*, October 1962, also contains a number of pertinent papers covering particular aspects of the problem of "Investment in Human Beings."

Especially perceptive are the country studies by A. R. Jolly, "Educational Planning in Zambia," in *World Year Book of Education, 1967*, London, 1968; David B. Abernethy, *The Political Dilemma of Popular Education: An African Case*, Stanford, 1969; Hla Myint, "The Universities of Southeast Asia and Economic Development," *Pacific Affairs*, Summer 1962; Adam Curle, *Planning for Education in Pakistan*, Cambridge, 1966; F. Harbison and C. A. Myers (eds.), *Manpower and Education*, New York, 1965; Anne O. Krueger, "Rates of Return to Turkish Higher Education," *Journal of Human Resources*, Fall 1972; J. Bhagwati, "Education, Class Structure and Income Equality," *WD*, May 1973.

Rigorous models of educational planning are presented by S. Bowles, "A Planning Model for the Efficient Allocation of Resources in Education," *QJE*, May 1967; G. Correa and J. Tinbergen, "Quantitative Adaptation of Education to Economic Growth," *Kyklos*, 1962; R. G. Davis, *Planning Human Resource Development*, Chicago, 1966; J. Tinbergen and H. C. Bos, *Econometric Models of Education*, Paris, 1965.

More general studies are: C. A. Anderson and Mary Jean Bowman (eds.), *Education and Economic Development*, second ed., Chicago, 1965; Adam Curle, *Educational Strategy for Developing Countries*, London, 1963; E. A. G. Robinson and J. E. Vaizey (eds.), *The Economics of Education*, London, 1966; J. W. Hanson and C. S. Brembeck (eds.), *Education and the Development of Nations*, New York, 1966; IBRD sector working paper on *Education*, Washington, D.C., December 1974; Mark Blaug, *Education and the Employment Problem in Developing Countries*, Geneva, 1975.

5. An extensive bibliography on accelerating economic development through psychological training is presented by D. C. McClelland and D. G. Winter, *Motivating Economic Achievement*, New York, 1969. Critiques of the influence of achievement motivation on entrepreneurship are offered by S. N. Eisenstadt, "The Need for Achievement," *EDCC*, July 1963; S. P. Schatz, "*n* Achievement and Economic Growth," *QJE*, May 1965.

Other instructive studies of entrepreneurship are F. H. Harbison, "Entrepreneurial Organization as a Factor in Economic Development," *QJE*, August 1956; E. Hagen, *On The Theory of Social Change*, Homewood, 1962; W. P. Glade, "Approaches to a Theory of Entrepreneurship Formation," *Explorations in Entrepreneurial History*, Spring/ Summer 1967; Peter Marris, "The Social Barriers to African Entrepreneurship," *JDS*, October 1968; G. F. Papanek, *Pakistan's Development*, Cambridge, 1967, Chap. 2; Peter Kilby (ed.), *Entrepreneurship and Economic Development*, New York, 1971.

An important work on sociological and psychological modernization is Alex Inkeles and D. H. Smith, *Becoming Modern*, Cambridge, 1975. For an annotated bibliography, see John Brode, *The Process of Modernization*, Cambridge, 1975.

CHAPTER IX

Agricultural Strategy

In this chapter and the next we consider the mutually reinforcing roles of agricultural and industrial development, placing particular emphasis on the employment potentials of agricultural and industrial strategies. We have repeatedly referred to the removal of the agricultural bottleneck as a strategic policy issue: the attainment of a proper balance between the establishment of industries and the expansion of agriculture is a persistently troublesome problem for developing nations. In the earlier days of development planning, deliberate and rapid industrialization was often advocated. Experience, however, has shown the limitations of overemphasizing industrialization, and it is increasingly recognized that agricultural progress must have a vital role in the development process. The earlier confrontation of industrial development *versus* agriculture has been shown to be a false issue, and the concern now is rather with the interrelationships between industry and agriculture and the contribution that each can make to the other.

Agricultural progress is essential to provide food for a growing nonagricultural labor force, raw materials for industrial production, savings and tax revenue to support development of the rest of the economy, to earn more foreign exchange (or save foreign exchange when primary products are imported), and to provide a growing market for domestic manufactures. As the theme of section IX.A emphasizes, the intersectoral relations between agriculture and industry will determine the course of structural transformation in a developing economy: if in the longer run, there is to be a diminishing share of agriculture in output, there first must be in the short run successful policies of agricultural development to facilitate this transformation.

Another theme in this chapter is the special effort that must be made to help the rural poor take advantage of the potential now provided by the Green Revolution. Section IX.B examines some of the issues raised by the new seed-fertilizer technology, especially policies that might increase yields among small-scale, low-income producers of traditional crops, and policies that might provide more employment for small farmers and landless labor. With the present concern over absolute poverty and unemployment, rural development takes on a new importance in its own right—and not simply for its instrumental value for industrial development. Agricultural development is now crucial for amelioration of absolute poverty and for labor absorption.

Even with all due allowance for the imprecision of the data, the general enormity of the problem can be sensed from the World Bank's estimates that of the 2 billion people in the developing countries, some 40 per cent are in absolute poverty, and that of these 800 million who are the absolute poor, some 80 per cent, or 640 million, are in the rural areas. Given the magnitude of the numbers in rural poverty, and the incapacity to reduce significantly these numbers by any feasible amount of rural-urban migration, the rural proportion of the total population of people in poverty is likely to remain high in many LDCs. In these countries, rural development on a massive scale will be needed for decades. The World Bank now recognizes this in the reorientation of its activities. But the progress of rural development will be crucially dependent upon the outcome of the Green Revolution, measures of land reform, land settlement at the extensive margin, new forms of rural institutions, and various special programs designed to increase the productivity and incomes of the rural poor.

While the Green Revolution provides a potential for increasing farm output by technical innovations that increase the productivity of labor and land, it is necessary—from the standpoint of labor absorption—to realize the advantages of a labor-using and yield-increasing strategy of agricultural development. In this connection, the transformation of Japanese agriculture is instructive. The "Japanese model" has three important characteristics: first, agricultural output has been increased within the unchanged organizational framework of the existing small-scale farming system. This was possible because of increases in the productivity of the existing on-farm resources of land and labor, and was associated with small demands on the scarce resources of capital and foreign exchange. Second, the bulk of the nation's farmers have been involved in increases in agricultural productivity associated with the use of improved varieties of seeds, fertilizers, and other current inputs; and technological progress of this type has continually been the source of greater agricultural productivity. Third, agricultural and industrial development moved forward together in a process of "concurrent" growth.[1]

Emphasis is therefore placed in section IX.C on the relevance of a "unimodal strategy" such as occurred historically in the Japanese pattern of a small-scale farming system and the participation of the bulk of the nation's farmers in the increase of agricultural productivity. Such a strategy, however, must also be linked to changes in the land tenure system, technological development in agriculture, and persistent concern with the effects on employment generation.

[1] Kasuzhi Ohkawa and Bruce F. Johnston, "The Transferability of the Japanese Pattern of Modernizing Traditional Agriculture," in Erik Thorbecke (ed.), *The Role of Agriculture in Economic Development*, New York, 1969, pp. 277–8.

IX.A. INSTRUMENTAL VALUE OF AGRICULTURE

IX.A.1. Agriculture's Contribution to Development—Note

Ever since at least the time of Ricardo, the "theology" of development has emphasized that agricultural progress contributes to the support of greater productivity throughout the economy. In his *Principles of Political Economy and Taxation*, Ricardo viewed the problem of diminishing returns in agriculture as crucial. He believed that a limitation on the growth of agricultural output set the upper limit to the growth of the nonagricultural sector and to capital formation for economic expansion.

It is now customary to summarize in four ways how greater agricultural productivity and output contribute to an economy's development: (1) by supplying foodstuffs and raw materials to other expanding sectors in the economy; (2) providing an "investible surplus" of savings and taxes to support investment in another expanding sector; (3) selling for cash a "marketable surplus" that will raise the demand of the rural population for products of other expanding sectors; and (4) relaxing the foreign exchange constraint by earning foreign exchange through exports or by saving foreign exchange through import substitution.

Kuznets summarizes these contributions as the "market contribution" and the "factor contribution."

A given sector makes a contribution to an economy when it provides opportunities for other sectors to emerge, or for the economy as a whole to participate in international trade and other international economic flows. We designate this contribution the market type because the given sector provides such opportunities by offering part of its product on domestic or foreign markets in exchange for goods produced by the other sectors, at home or abroad. . . .

Thus agriculture makes a market contribution to economic growth by (1) purchasing some production items from other sectors at home or abroad; (2) selling some of its product, not only to pay for the purchases listed under (1) but also to purchase consumer goods from other sectors or from abroad, or to dispose of the product in any way other than consumption within the sector. In all these ways, agriculture makes it feasible for other sectors to emerge and grow and for international flows to develop; just as these other sectors and the international flows make it feasible for the agricultural sector to operate more efficiently as a producing unit and use its product more effectively as a consuming unit.[1]

The "factor contribution" occurs "when there is a transfer or loan of resources from the given sector to others. Thus if agriculture itself grows, it makes a product contribution; if it trades with others, it renders a market contribution; if it transfers resources to other sectors, these resources being productive factors, it makes a *factor* contribution."[2]

In this traditional interpretation, the development process is viewed as one of structural transformation from an economy in which agricultural employment and output dominate to a decline in the share of the

[1] Simon Kuznets, *Economic Growth and Structure*, New York, 1965, pp. 244–5.
[2] Ibid., p. 250.

labor force in agriculture and a decrease in the share of agriculture in GNP. But this structural transformation is itself dependent on agricultural progress. Industrial development will be cut short by lack of agricultural progress—unless the economy is in the exceptional situation of being able to export manufactures for imports of foodstuffs and raw materials (compare, Hong Kong). In Lewis' dual-sector model, we saw that if food supplies to the modern sector do not keep up with the modern sector's demand for labor, the modern sector will have to consume a larger share of its output in feeding its labor force, and this will leave a smaller surplus for capital accumulation. More generally, it is widely believed that "both in concept and in practice it is possible for the agricultural sector to make large net transfers of resources to other sectors. If these transfers are used productively, the rate of economic growth can be accelerated."[3]

Agriculture's contribution of foodstuffs—the "wage good" in classical terminology—is clear. If the labor force for manufacturing or another expanding sector is drawn from agriculture, the new workers must "take their lunch" with them when they leave the rural sector. A growing urban labor force must be supported by an expanding supply of foodstuffs. A growing population must also be supported with increased food supplies. The annual rate of increase in demand for food is given by $D = p + \eta g$, where p and g are the rate of growth of population and per capita income, and η is the income elasticity of demand for agricultural products.[4] As indicated by Johnston and Mellor,[5] not only are there high rates of population growth in the LDCs, but the income elasticity of demand for food in these countries is considerably higher than in high-income countries—probably on the order of .6 or higher in the low-income countries versus .2 or .3 in Western Europe, the United States, and Canada. A given rate of increase in per capita income therefore has a considerably stronger impact on the demand for agricultural products in the lower-income countries than in the economically advanced countries.

Johnston and Mellor observe that:

The increase in farm output in Japan between the 1880's and 1911–20, which seems to have been of about the same magnitude as the growth of demand during that period, corresponded to an annual rate of increase in demand of approximately 2 per cent. With current rates of population growth and a modest rise in per capita incomes, the annual rate of increase of demand for food in a developing economy can easily exceed 3 per cent, a formidable challenge for the agriculture of an underdeveloped country. Moreover, as a result of the expansion of population in cities and in mining and industrial centers dependent upon purchased food, the growth of demand for marketed supplies is a good deal more rapid than the overall rate of increase. Thus there are additional problems in developing transportation links and marketing facilities in order to satisfy the requirements of the nonagricultural population.

If food supplies fail to expand in pace with the growth of demand the result is likely to be a substantial rise in food prices leading to political discontent and pressure on wage rates with consequent adverse effects on industrial profits, investment, and economic growth. There is scant evidence concerning the price elasticity of demand for food in underdeveloped countries. At least in the case of an increase in prices as a result

---

[3] John W. Mellor, "Accelerated Growth in Agricultural Production and the Intersectoral Transfer of Resources," *Economic Development and Cultural Change*, October 1973, p. 5.

[4] K. Ohkawa, "Economic Growth and Agriculture," *Annals Hitotsubashi Academy*, October 1956, pp. 45–60.

[5] Bruce F. Johnston and John W. Mellor, "The Role of Agriculture in Economic Development," *American Economic Review*, September 1961, pp. 571–81.

of demand outstripping supply, there is a strong presumption that the price elasticity for "all food" is extremely low, probably lower than in economically advanced countries. Cheap starchy staple foods—cereals and root crops—provide something like 60 to 85 per cent of the total calorie intake in low-income countries, so there is relatively limited scope for offsetting a rise in food prices by shifting from expensive to less costly foods; and the pressure to resist a reduction in calorie intake is strong.

The inflationary impact of a given percentage increase in food prices is much more severe in an underdeveloped country than in a high-income economy. This is a simple consequence of the dominant position of food as a wage good in lower-income countries where 50 to 60 per cent of total consumption expenditure is devoted to food consumption compared with 20 to 30 per cent in developed economies.

Owing to the severe economic and political repercussions of a substantial rise in food prices, domestic shortages are likely to be offset by expanded food imports, provided that foreign exchange or credits are available.[6]

Through the transfer of capital and labor to nonfarm activities, agriculture may also provide an investible surplus. The transfer of labor has been repeatedly discussed in the context of the Lewis model and needs no further attention here. But it should be noted that agriculture can be a source of capital formation in ways other than the simple lending of voluntary savings. There may be a compulsory transfer from agriculture for the benefit of other sectors, ordinarily through taxation in which the burden on agriculture is greater than the governmental services provided to agriculture. Kuznets remarks:

The measurement of such forced contributions of agriculture to economic growth is not easy; the incidence of some indirect taxes is difficult to ascertain and the allocation of government expenditures in terms of benefits to agriculture and to economic growth elsewhere is far from simple. But this factor contribution by agriculture was clearly quite large in the early phases of economic growth in some countries. Thus in Japan in the last two decades of the nineteenth century the land tax was over 80 percent of central government taxation, and the direct tax ratio to income produced was between 12 and 22 percent in agriculture, compared with from 2 to 3 percent in the nonagricultural sectors. Forced extraction of surplus from agriculture by taxation, confiscation, and other measures also probably financed a considerable part of industrialization in the Soviet Union. Indeed, one of the crucial problems of modern economic growth is how to extract from the product of agriculture a surplus for the financing of capital formation for industrial growth without at the same time blighting the growth of agriculture, under conditions where no easy *quid pro quo* for such surplus is available within the country. It is only the open economy, with access to the markets of the more highly developed countries, both for goods and for capital loans, that can minimize this painful task of initial capital accumulation.[7]

Another way of transferring resources from the agricultural to the nonagricultural sectors is by the government turning the terms of trade against agriculture by imposing price controls on agricultural products, taxation, or the use of multiple exchange-rates that discriminate against agriculture. If the improvement in the terms of trade in the nonagricultural sectors raises nonagricultural incomes, and the beneficiaries save at a higher marginal rate than the decreased agricultural incomes, aggregate saving rates will increase, and agriculture will have made a net contribution to total saving in an indirect manner. The next selection gives some

[6] Ibid., p. 573.

[7] Kuznets, *Economic Growth*, pp. 250–51.

indication of what has actually occurred in recent years by way of income transfers from agriculture.

A "marketable surplus" from agriculture is needed not only to provide the wage good to industry, but also to widen the home market for the industrial products. The demand for industrial products depends on growth of farm cash income, unless the country can export its growing industrial output. Barring unlimited export possibilities, and with 70 to 90 per cent of the home market in the rural sector, the nature of rural demand will affect the growth of nonfarm employment and output. Increased agricultural productivity, a growing marketable surplus, and rising real income are necessary to raise the rural sector's demand for industrial output.

Finally, agriculture may be a major source of foreign exchange. It is clear that agricultural exports dominate in a country's early phase of development. But also important in relaxing the foreign exchange constraint is the possibility in several developing countries to save foreign exchange by replacing imports of foodstuffs with home production. Export promotion and import substitution are activities not only for the industrial sector but also for agriculture.

Considering these various contributions of agriculture, development economists have insisted that if there is to be in the longer run a structural transformation in output and labor force, there must first be in the short run "successful policies of agricultural development" to facilitate this transformation. But what specifically do "successful policies of agricultural development" entail? And is the purpose of agricultural development simply to underwrite the expansion of nonagricultural sectors—even at the expense of an "agricultural squeeze"? Now, in view of the emphasis on absolute poverty and the employment problem, is it not necessary to concentrate on agricultural development for the sake of employment and a diminution in inequality? Even though the longer-term ob-

jective is structural transformation—the absorption of a larger fraction of the rural population in new income-earning opportunities—there remains the complex problem of the timing of this transformation and the intertemporal sequence of policies to accomplish it. The lessons of recent history have shown that an "urban bias" can discriminate against agriculture;[8] and that, as illustrated in the next selection, the net outflow of resources from agriculture may be excessive. Not only may there be an inefficient use of the resources transferred to the nonagricultural sectors, but the transfer may itself be at the expense of more employment and higher income in the agricultural sector. Should not the "growth-promoting interactions between agriculture and industrial development" mean more than that agricultural development should have simply instrumental value for industrial development?

In the early years of development planning, Viner wisely anticipated the answer to this question:

Let us now suppose that *real* incomes are lower in agriculture than in industry, and that by tariff protection or subsidies industry can be made to expand and to draw workers from the country into the cities. Is this sound economic policy?

The correct answer depends on why *per capita* real incomes are lower in agriculture than in manufacturing. There may be urban exploitation of agriculture, through monopolistic pricing by employers, or through labour monopolies in the factories which by forcing wages up force up also the prices which the agricultural population has to pay for urban products and services—including government services. The tariff, supported as providing better employment opportunities for the agricultural population, may itself be

[8] Michael Lipton, "Strategy for Agriculture: Urban Bias and Rural Planning," in Paul Streeten and Michael Lipton (eds.), *The Crisis of Indian Planning*, London, 1968, Chap. 4.

a major instrument whereby agricultural real incomes are depressed. Government may also operate to depress agricultural real incomes by imposing its taxes, mainly or largely, directly or indirectly, on agriculture, and directing its expenditures mainly to the benefit of the urban population. Even though the rural population may have lower *per capita* incomes than the urban, it may nevertheless be the only economically healthy part of the population, the only part which gives good value to the community in exchange for what it gets from the community. Where the situation is one—as it often is—of urban exploitation of the rural population, to propose as a remedy the further subsidization of urban industry as a means of drawing rural workers to the city is equivalent to proposing to remedy the exploitation of worker bees by the drones by transforming the worker bees also to drones. It is obvious that it can work at all only as long as there still remain worker bees in the fields to be exploited.

The refutation of bad argument does not necessarily refute the conclusions reached by such argument. It is not my position that the path to economic progress is not, for many countries and even for most countries, by way of industrialization and urbanization. I have in fact conceded that as any country or any region becomes more prosperous it will normally tend to increase the ratio of its population which is non-agricultural. My position is a different one, and I will now state it frankly and positively for the first time. The real problem in poor countries is not agriculture as such, or the absence of manufactures as such, but poverty and backwardness, poor agriculture, or poor agriculture and poor manufacturing. The remedy is to remove the basic causes of the poverty and backwardness. This is as true in principle, and probably nearly as true in practice, for industrialized countries as for predominantly agricultural countries.

Misallocation of resources as between agriculture and manufactures is probably rarely a major cause of poverty and backwardness, except where government, through tariffs, discriminatory taxation and expenditure policies, and failure to provide on a regionally non-discriminatory pattern facilities for education, health promotion, and technical training, is itself responsible for this misallocation. Where there is such government-induced misallocation, it is today more likely to consist of the diversion of agrarian-produced resources to the support of parasitic cities than of overinvestment of resources in primary industries and in workers in such industries.

Economic improvement may call for greater industrialization, but this should be a natural growth, appropriately facilitated by government but not maintained under hothouse conditions. In many countries, the most promising field for rapid economic development lies in agriculture, and the measures needed are primarily such as will promote health, general education, technical training, better transportation facilities, and cheap rural credit for productive use. There are no inherent advantages of manufacturing over agriculture, or, for that matter, of agriculture over manufacturing. It is only arbitrarily in fact that the line separating the two can be drawn. The choice between expansion of agriculture and expansion of manufactures can for the most part best be left to the free decisions of capitalists, entrepreneurs, and workers. To the extent that there is need for government decision, it should be made on rational grounds, in the light of considerations of costs and of comparative returns from alternative allocations of scarce national resources, human and material. If direction is accepted from maxims and arbitrary dogmas and prejudices, from unsubstantiated and incredible natural laws of the inherent inferiority of one type of industry over another, then it is highly probable that the result will be the squandering of resources so scanty in supply that they need to be carefully husbanded, and the sore disappointment of the wishes of the great masses of population crying to be relieved of their crushing poverty.[9]

The emphasis on agricultural development now is not only for its instrumental value in sustaining expansion elsewhere in the nonagricultural sectors, but for its own absorption of labor and its own increase of real income among the rural poverty target groups of the small farmers and the landless laborers. The widely expressed view now is that the root of the employment problems lies in the fact that modern economic activity is not being diffused to the countryside. An agricultural strategy that would improve the rural-urban balance now requires the extension of planning, infrastructure, appropriate technology, and complementary resources to the rural sector.[10] If in earlier decades of development, agricultural development had instrumental value, in future decades it must have an intrinsic value of its own.

[9] Jacob Viner, *International Trade and Economic Development*, London, 1953, pp. 51–3.

[10] See, for instance, Edgar O. Edwards (ed.), *Employment in Developing Nations*, New York, 1974, pp. 30–31.

IX.A.2. Strategies for Transferring Agricultural Surplus*

The agricultural sector is of particular interest and concern with respect to capital accumulation in the early stages of economic development. The agricultural sector is initially dominant in the economy, containing the bulk of national income, labor and capital resources. In the long run, the nonagricultural sectors must grow at a substantially more rapid rate than the agricultural sector, gradually providing a transformation of the economy from one dominated by agriculture to one dominated by other sectors. It is logical to presume that this process of economic transformation will proceed more rapidly if a net transfer of income and savings can be made from the agricultural sector to other sectors of the economy.

The recent literature on the role of agriculture in economic development has been enhanced by a number of essays on intersectoral capital flows in relation to the transformation of traditional agriculture in less developed countries. Two different viewpoints can be categorized from these papers. One is that agriculture does not require a large amount of capital for its transformation. Agriculture, therefore, is a great contributor of capital to industrialization. The other opinion is that the investment requirements for agricultural transformation are so large that capital may have net inflow from nonagriculture to agriculture. These views are based primarily on different emphases of how to modernize the traditional agriculture.

Obviously, there are many differences between countries in social-institutional arrangements with which to mobilize the resources from the agricultural sector to the nonagricultural sector. According to the ini-

*From T. H. Lee, "Strategies for Transferring Agricultural Surplus under Different Agricultural Situations in Taiwan," Conference on Agriculture and Economic Development, Japan Economic Research Center, September 6–10, 1971, pp. 1–7, 12–15, 21–5; also in Lee, *Intersectoral Capital Flows in the Economic Development of Taiwan, 1895–1960*, Cornell University Press, Ithaca, 1971, pp. 8–12, 131–4, 139–42. Reprinted by permission.

tial level of agricultural productivity and resource endowment, capital requirement for transforming traditional agriculture will be different between countries.

Infusions of the new technology into traditional agriculture are gaining dramatic results in Southeast Asia. Several countries in this area have begun shifts in production as strategic moves toward agricultural development. There is a spreading optimistic belief that the transformation is already sufficient to lift away the spectre of famine and to postpone, at least, the materialization of the Malthusian trap. These gains have been most noticeable in basic food grains (rice, corn and wheat) and have been realized mainly from new high-yield varieties with adequate supplies of fertilizer, pesticides, water and modern implements. It is expected that the new technology will quickly spread within the nations and across national boundaries. Therefore, provided that increased production is actually obtained by the presently developing countries, a new set of agricultural problems can be anticipated, for which new solutions must be discovered. How to maintain the current increase in agricultural production with more inputs and investment in agriculture, and how to effectively siphon off such gains in agricultural production for the nation's industrial development, are most important and urgent tasks in the Southeast Asian countries.

The experience of Taiwan in economic development is an example of a country with a traditional agricultural pattern successfully advancing and transforming its economy as a whole. . . .

FRAMEWORK FOR MEASUREMENT

The interrelationships between agricultural production and nonagricultural production are dealt with here by dividing the areas

[1] The letters in brackets are the symbols used for the given item in the algebraic expression of these variables and relationships presented in equations below.

participating in the economic transactions of the national economy of Taiwan into six sectors: agricultural production, agricultural household, nonagricultural production, nonagricultural household, government, and foreign trade.

In the agricultural production sector, services of primary production factors such as land and labor flow from the agricultural household sector (D_a).[1] The sector also produces agricultural output (Y_a). The agricultural production sector consumes production goods such as chemical fertilizer, feed, and other material manufactured in the nonagricultural production sector (R^a_n). Agricultural products used in agricultural production are provided from the gross agricultural output within the sector. The net agricultural output is partially consumed by the agricultural household sector (C^a_a). The remaining amount of net output is sold to the nonagricultural production sector as raw materials (R^n_a), to the nonagricultural household sector for consumption (C^n_a), and directly to foreign trade as exports (E_a). The total quantity of agricultural products sold amounts to the sum of $R^n_a + C^n_a + E_a$. In nonagricultural production, services of production factors flow from the nonagricultural household sector (D_n). The sector produces two products, consumer goods and capital goods. Consumer goods flow from the nonagricultural production sector to the nonagricultural household sector (C^n_n), to the agricultural household sector (C^a_n), to the government sector (C^g_n), and to exports (E_n). Capital goods are distributed to the agricultural production sector as intermediate goods (R^a_n), as investment goods (I_a), and for investment in its own sector (I_n). No capital goods export is assumed in this case. The government sector collects taxes (G_a) from the agricultural household sector and (G_n) from the nonagricultural household sector, and allocates the revenue for consumption of industrial goods (C^g_n), and for government savings (S_g). In the foreign trade sector, the government exports agricultural products (E_a), and industrial consumer goods (E_n), in exchange for consumer goods (M_c), and capital goods (M_i). The balance of international trade represents an additional variable (F).

Income generation is represented by flows in the opposite direction from the commodity flows between sectors. In addition to the commodity transactions between sectors, income also flows from the agricultural household sector to the nonagricultural sector in the form of payment of land rent, wages, and interest. The agricultural household sector also receives income from the nonagricultural household sector.

These commodity and income flows can be summarized in the following accounting equations:[2]

$$
\begin{array}{ll}
\textit{Inflows} & \textit{Outflows} \\
D_a + R^a{}_n & = C^a{}_a + C^n{}_a + R^n{}_a + E_a (1) \\
D_n + R^n{}_a + M_c + M_i & = C^n{}_n + C^a{}_n + C^g{}_n + R^a{}_n (2) \\
& \quad\quad + I + E_n \\
C^a{}_a + C^a{}_n + S_a + G_a = D_a & \quad\quad (3) \\
C^n{}_a + C^n{}_n + S_n + G_n = D_n & \quad\quad (4) \\
C^g{}_n + S_g \quad\quad = G_a + G_n & \quad\quad (5)
\end{array}
$$

Adding the five equations and cancelling out similar terms on both sides of the resulting equality, we have:

$$
S_a + S_n + S_g = \\
I + (E_a + E_n) - (M_c + M_i) \quad (6)
$$

or

$$
I_n = (S_a - I_a) + S_n + S_g + F \quad (7)
$$

where $I = I_a + I_n$, and $F = (E_a + E_n) - (M_c + M_i)$. The terms S_a, S_n, and S_g in the above equations denote the savings of agricultural household, nonagricultural household, and government. Equation (6) is the financing equation indicating the relationship between savings and investment for the national economy as a whole. Equation (7) indicates the sectoral interdependence. The investment in the nonagricultural sector depends upon the amount of net capital flow from agriculture,

[2] Fei and Ranis, *Development of the Labor Surplus Economy, Theory and Policy*, p. 57.

size of savings in its own and government sectors, and the export surplus. Adding equations (1) and (3) for the agricultural sector, we have:

$$
S_a = C^n{}_a + R^n{}_a + E_a - C^a{}_n - R^a{}_n - G_a (8)
$$

As government taxing on agriculture is not greatly in the form of commodities, the term (G_a) in equation (8) may be better included in the term (S_a) from equation (8) and the term $(S_a - I_a)$ in equation (7); then we can draw the following cases, indicating the balance of commodity flows between agriculture and nonagriculture.

$$
C^n{}_a + R^n{}_a + E_a - C^a{}_n - R^a{}_n \gtreqless I_a \quad (9)
$$

or

$$
C^n{}_a + R^n{}_a + E_a - C^a{}_n - R^a{}_n - I_a = B \, (9')
$$

The terms on the left side of equation $(9')$ indicate the commodity transactions between two sectors, and the term B is the balance showing the physical aspect of capital outflow from agriculture. The term B is also the balance of capital accounting between two sectors.

Generally speaking, it is more common and more useful to set up both capital and current operating (income) accounts in order to investigate the sectoral commodity and financial transactions. Capital account shows the changes in assets and liabilities. An increase in assets or decrease in liabilities indicates the outflow of capital. A decrease in assets or an increase in liabilities indicates the inflow of capital. The term B can, therefore, be expressed as follows:

$$
B = R + K \quad (10)
$$

The term R on the right side of the above equation is the balance of current financial transactions between sectors, including the net payments of land rent, wages, and interest, and government taxing and subsidies. The term K is the balance of the capital account between sectors, including the net changes in outstanding short-term and long-term loans and investment.

The above exposition of the accounting system of sectoral interdependence between agriculture and nonagriculture is based on commodity and income flows and the sectoral capital accounting. The important fact is that both of the above sectoral accounts of income and capital are related to the expense accounts of income, consumption, and savings-investment in the agricultural and the nonagricultural sector. This means that the above sectoral accounts can be derived statistically from the social income accounts including income, consumption, and savings-investment in a sector. When we construct the social income account for the agricultural sector, the sectoral accounts can be systematically derived from it.

Equations (9') and (10) are generally valued at current prices of commodities and services in the transactions. The effects of changes in price ratios or sectoral terms of trade on sectoral capital flows are not reflected in equations (9') and (10). The term B in the equations, therefore, should be adjusted for changes in the price ratios. The equation (9') in real terms thus can be expressed:

$$(C^n_a + R^n_a + E_a) / P_a - (C^a_n + R^a_n + I_a) / P_n = B' \quad (11)$$

where P_a and P_n are price indices for agricultural products and nonagricultural products bought by the agricultural sector. When capital flows out from the agricultural sector, the term B' can be expressed:

$$B' = B/P_a + (C^a_n + R^a_n + I_a) / P_n (P_n/P_a - 1) \quad (12)$$

The first term on the right side of the equation is the financial amount of capital outflow from agriculture in real terms, and the second term is the amount of capital outflow caused by the change in the sectoral terms of trade between agriculture and nonagriculture. We call the former the visible net

real capital outflow and the latter the invisible net real capital outflow. . . .

STRATEGIC MEASURES FOR AGRICULTURAL DEVELOPMENT AND CAPITAL TRANSFER

With a systematic examination of Taiwan's experience for the period 1895–1960, we set out to provide a statistical framework for empirical analysis of intersectoral capital flow between the agricultural sector and the nonagricultural sector. A statistical scale for measuring the intersectoral capital flows was developed by the social accounting system based on the definition of capital, and an effort was made to identify the determinants of the net capital outflow from the agricultural sector. Conclusions may be summarized as follows:

(a) The direction of the intersectoral net capital flow was identified as an outflow from the agricultural sector in Taiwan throughout the entire period. The amount of net capital outflow showed a slightly increasing trend in terms of real price up to 1940, but has tended to decline since 1950. Invisible net real capital outflow caused by terms of trade against agriculture was less important in the prewar period but increased in relative importance to more than 50 percent of the total net real capital outflow in the postwar period. Financially, current transfers of rent payment and taxes occupied the most important role in the financial accommodation of net agricultural surplus in the prewar period, and direct capital transfer of farmers' savings became increasingly important in the postwar period.

(b) The size of the intersectoral capital flow is dependent in part on the changes in the terms of trade, but it is also significantly dependent on the physical and financial measures by which development can be achieved. Certain measures and conditions significantly influenced the intersectoral capital outflow in Taiwan: (1) Under the Japanese administration a new system of government taxes and levies was imposed while the inherited system of agricultural squeeze was not abolished. Since institution of land-reform program in the postwar period, taxation and levies by means of both direct and hidden methods have been strengthened. (2) Despite the high-gross squeeze, agricultural productivity of land and labor in the sector was not affected. After the shift from traditional agriculture in the period 1926–1930, the increase in agricultural productivity was accelerated. Neither the initial resource endowment nor the level of agricultural productivity in Taiwan in 1895 was any more favorable than in countries presently developing. However, the successful transformation of traditional agriculture in Taiwan could be accomplished while maintaining a continuous net outflow of capital from the agricultural sector. A heavy investment in irrigation was initiated in the transformation period, yet it did not bring a net inflow of capital from the nonagricultural sector with it. This important aspect of agricultural development particularly with reference to the role of government and technological progress in agriculture is discussed below.

(c) The empirical tests showed that Taiwan's experience departed appreciably from the conventional hypotheses regarding net capital outflow from agriculture. (1) Taiwan has maintained a continuous outflow of net capital from the agricultural sector under the high growth rate of agricultural population and labor force. This fact disproves the broadly held viewpoint that decelerating the rate of population growth is a necessary condition for accelerating the growth of agricultural surplus. (2) The agricultural wage rate or per capita consumption of farmers improved through time, despite the increase of population in agriculture. However, the proportion of total agricultural income going to agricultural labor has tended to decline relatively in contrast to the nonagricultural sector where the proportion of total income to labor increased. In the context of net capital outflow from the agricultural sector, the relative decline of the share of labor income in agriculture is thus a more important concept that that of constant institutional wage rate in agriculture. (3) Heavy investment in irrigation is necessary in order to transform traditional agriculture in the paddy farming areas. Intensive innovation in the use of capital has been witnessed in the period of transformation of traditional agriculture. This departs from the conventional viewpoint of a complementary relation between capital and labor in agricultural innovation. (4) As for the amount of net capital outflow, it is clearly shown by the statistical comparison in the text that the concept of "net agricultural savings" is not appropriate. (5) Financial adjustment of the net agricultural surplus is one of the important factors determining the magnitude of the net capital outflow from the agricultural sector. The problem of intersectoral capital flow can be discussed from the viewpoint of financial adjustment and the commodity transferring process as well as from the viewpoint of increase in agricultural productivity.

(d) Finally, agricultural development is primarily concerned with the feasibility of increasing net agricultural surplus or net capital outflow form the agricultural sector. In less-developed countries like Taiwan, mobilization of internal capital must depend on agricultural development. The development of agriculture and the application of economic squeeze on agriculture are closely related to government strategies for agricultural development.

In relation to the intersectoral capital outflow from agriculture, four important government measures toward agricultural development can be derived: (a) allocation of capital to agriculture, (b) technological progress, (c) agricultural taxation, and (d) organizational improvements. . . .

IMPLICATIONS OF TAIWAN'S EXPERIENCE

In considering the implications of the above discussion, it is important to generalize the relationship between determinants of the intersectoral capital flow in order to provide a measurement of agricultural development. The resource endowment and the level of agricultural productivity determine the size of agricultural investment that can be undertaken to achieve a given rate of agricultural growth. Basically, land productivity and per capita land area or man-land ratio are the determinants of the level of agricultural productivity in terms of labor. Consequently, given the increase in population, limited land resource and heavy food requirements in a low income country, a big increase is required in irrigation and land improvements. For this reason, Ishikawa and Ruttan have concluded that the agricultural sector may require a net inflow of capital from the nonagricultural sector for the transformation of agriculture in Asia.[3] This obviously does not apply to Taiwan's experience, since a big push in irrigation and land improvement had not been undertaken in Taiwan before a surplus in the government budget and technological progress were realized. Two important factors need to be noted in this context: (a) determined government action, and (b) technological relation between the fixed capital input and biological technology. The former is related to the basic problem of capital allocation in the whole national economy. Since agriculture is generally considered the mainstay of the economy, better utilization of slack in agriculture is preferred to additional input of scarce

[3] Ishikawa, *Economic Development in Asian Perspective*, pp. 346–347; V. W. Ruttan, *Considerations in the Design of a Strategy for Increasing Rice Production in Southeast Asia*.

capital funds. The latter is concerned with the availability of new varieties of seeds, with the farmers' skill in application of chemical fertilizer, and with the method of cultivation in relation to the heavy irrigation investment. The requirement for heavy irrigation investment seems to be large in the period of transition from extensive to intensive farming in paddy farming areas. With the high pressure of population, there is a general tendency for labor intensive cultivation in agriculture. To absorb more labor input in farming, expansion of productive capacity in terms of land is naturally necessary. However, the intensity of farming is greatly dependent on the demand for crops and livestock as well as the quantitative and qualitative relationships between inputs. Landowners, as receivers of large shares of land rent from the additional increase of output, will play some role in encouraging such intensive farming. In Taiwan, promotion of new varieties of seeds, chemical fertilizers, and irrigation investment represented such an effort on the part of landlords.

Agricultural transformation which simultaneously maintains a net capital outflow calls for a variety of strategies. The more important of these are: (a) the basic agricultural investment should be accompanied by technological improvement; (b) an appropriate investment scheme with large labor input and less input of capital goods should be selected; and (c) a capital transfer mechanism should be established. According to the different conditions or stages of agricultural development, the above strategic components will change in relative importance, as the experience of Taiwan has shown. . . .

IX.A.3. Recent History of Intersectoral Resource Transfers*

This section is organized around three themes in the recent economic history of developing countries. First, it has become abundantly clear that government policies can markedly affect the terms of trade of agriculture and other relative prices; that such changes in relative prices can result in substantial transfers of income among sectors; and that entrepreneurs in all sectors of the economies of LDCs respond quite rapidly to changes in relative prices, both of inputs and factors and of output. Second, concerns about productivity growth that preoccupied economists somewhat earlier in developed country studies have begun to concern economists in LDCs. Rapid productivity growth in agriculture has in some cases substantially increased price elasticities of supply; and such growth has also exacerbated some problems of income distribution and of direct taxation of the agricultural sector. In addition, the *failure* of total factor productivity to grow rapidly in import-substituting manufacturing sectors has resulted in high and growing burdens on the sectors that must subsidize protected industry. Third, and related to the first two themes, there has been growing unemployment and related unrest in a large number of LDCs and a substantial increase in concern for the distribution, as opposed to the growth, of income.

EFFECTS OF POLICY ON RELATIVE PRICES

The impact of government policies in changing relative prices immediately raises the question: changing them from what? Existing studies have used two different definitions of the situation with which to compare the price structure at some point in time. One set of studies, emphasizing the effects of price distortions resulting from protection, has used international relative prices facing the country, or international trade opportunity costs. The other set of studies has used the structure of domestic prices in some base period and has generally been concerned primarily or exclusively with movements in the domestic terms of trade of agriculture. The data requirements for any of these studies are formidable indeed. Data availability explains why most studies comparing domestic and foreign price structures have been single-year studies, while those concerned with movements of prices over time have been largely confined to movements of relative prices domestically.

The appropriate price comparisons, when one is interested in the possible distorting effects of policies, are between domestic relative prices and the set of prices (or, where appropriate, marginal revenues) the country faces in international markets. If one is interested in agriculture's terms of trade under a given policy regime, the relevant set of prices with which to compare *actual* prices received and paid by agriculture is the set of prices agriculture would have faced had there not been particular policies with respect to foreign trade taxes, domestic taxes, and exchange rates that distorted the domestic price structure from that which would face the country in international trade. The comparison of the domestic terms of trade today with the domestic terms of trade in some

*From Stephen R. Lewis, Jr., "Agricultural Taxation and Intersectoral Resource Transfers," *Food Research Institute Studies in Agricultural Economics, Trade, and Development*, Vol. 12, No. 2, 1973, pp. 96–105. Reprinted by permission.

past period may be of interest for some purposes. But, past prices do not present an alternative set of prices which could have been paid or received by agriculture today in the same way that today's international prices present a real alternative.

Recent studies indicate that government policies in many countries have indeed had major effects on the structure of domestic (relative to world) prices, and that substantial amounts of income have been transferred both between sectors and between producers of different goods within sectors. Detailed comparative studies of a number of LDCs sponsored by the World Bank focused on the impact of indirect taxes, exchange rate policies, tariffs, and quantitative restrictions on imports in protecting or subsidizing various activities at the expense of others (1). Manufacturing industry was generally the beneficiary and agriculture the sector discriminated against, but within each sector there were a variety of subsectors subsidized and others "taxed" by the protective system. In some extreme cases, activities were found that yielded *negative* returns to domestic factors when the tradable output and the tradable inputs of the sector were evaluated at international rather than domestic prices; real national income would be higher if the activities simply ceased to exist. This result has generally come from tariff "cascading," with a lower price of foreign exchange implicit in prices of inputs than in prices of output.

The studies sponsored by the Organization for Economic Co-operation and Development (OECD) (summarized, interpreted, and extended in the volume by I. M. D. Little, Tibor Scitovsky, and M. FG. Scott [11]), focused broadly on manufacturing and trade policies, and made it clear that policies that favored manufacturing in many countries did so at the expense of agriculture. By recalculating the gross domestic product (GDP) at international instead of domestic relative prices, Little et al. found that agriculture was subsidizing manufacturing by 10 to 20 percent or more of agricultural value added as a result of trade policies. Studies in Pakistan indicated that in the 1950s perhaps as much as 10 to 15 percent of agricultural income was being transferred out due to adverse terms of trade relative to world prices (9; 10). . . . T. H. Lee's study of Taiwan, while using domestic base period prices instead of international prices as the point of comparison, indicates that the deterioration of agriculture's terms of trade in the 1950s and 1960s as compared with the 1930s involved an implicit (or, as he says, invisible) transfer from agriculture equivalent to one-half to two-thirds of the real capital outflow from agriculture in the latter two decades (7). R. P. Echevarria's study of Chile examines changes in relative prices (including changes in international prices of goods actually traded) over several subperiods and by calculating the transfer of resources involved in changes during the period from prices existing in the immediately preceding period (2). He found that agriculture as a whole gained as much as 15 percent of its value added from changes in relative prices from 1959/61 to 1962/64, which suggests a similar loss of income in the earlier period relative to the later one.

The amount of resources transferred from agriculture through the use of trade and indirect tax policies, then, have been very substantial in relation to agricultural output in a number of countries. The amounts are even larger in importance relative to the size of direct agricultural taxes, or industrial output, or government revenue and expenditures.

What have been the consequences of these large gross transfers? In the context of the well-behaved two-sector model, depressing agriculture's terms of trade and improving them for the modern sector might have improved the saving rate and rate of investment for the economy, the rate of growth in output and employment in the modern sector, and the rate of growth of output of the economy as a whole. The principal adverse effects might have been disincentives and lack of investment resources in agriculture which would eventually result in inadequate growth of agricultural output and marketed surplus and deceleration of the growth rate of the modern sector.[1]

The principal difficulty encountered by countries following the policy of turning the terms of trade against agriculture, however, is the inefficiency with which the nonagricultural sectors used the transfered resources. The nature of the trade policies followed encouraged the establishment of manufacturing industries aimed primarily at the domestic market, using imported (or exportable) raw materials, and capital goods purchased at favorable exchange rates compared to the exchange rate implicit in the prices at which they sold output. The nominal extent to which domestic prices of import substitutes exceeded their international prices (c.i.f.) substantially understated the extent of subsidy to value added in the import substituting industries. *If* the import substituting sectors' profits had increased by the full amount of their subsidy from protection, and *if* profits were heavily reinvested, *then* the mechanism for accelerating development through the use of trade restricting devices might have worked.[2] However, detailed studies of protection in most countries show that a substantial portion of the increase in gross returns made possible by protection subsidized the inefficient use of capital, labor, and intermediate inputs (*1; 11*). Thus, a continuing subsidy to the indus-

[1] To the extent that capital is mobile, disincentives to agricultural investment might result in a shift to nonagricultural investment. It might also be that lower rates of return on agricultural investment would result in higher consumption and lower saving by farmers.

[2] Even in this case, to the extent that the protection raised the private rate of return artificially above that of projects with equivalent social rates of return in agriculture, overall growth would be lower if capital moved in response to private rates of return.

tries became necessary simply to support the level of output and value added in such industries. And, therefore, the agricultural sector was being "taxed" *not* to increase overall saving in the economy, but rather to give an ongoing subsidy to industries that were unable to compete in international markets, even with a correction for the overvaluation of currencies that existed in countries following this pattern of "growth." . . .

GROWTH OF PRODUCTIVITY

Certainly the most dramatic events of the past six years in the LDCs are related to the Green Revolution and to the impact of such rapid productivity growth in some parts of agriculture on taxation and resource transfer. One of the most obvious impacts has been the effect on domestic relative prices of agricultural commodities. These changes in domestic production costs and relative prices are directly related to the problems of the last subsection with an interesting set of twists.

If governments try to maintain some historical level of relative domestic prices (especially for import-substitute products, such as foodgrains on the South Asian subcontinent) in the face of falling domestic costs, resources will be drawn out of subsectors of agriculture that are efficient producers of tradables into these sectors in which real costs are falling but prices are being prevented from doing so. Studies in Pakistan have suggested that the introduction of the new varieties may make cropping patterns even more sensitive to changes in relative prices than they had been under traditional conditions;[3] just as political pressures build

[3] See the study by C. H. Gotsch and W. P. Falcon (5). To some extent the added sensitivity comes from the lack of specificity of the new technologies (i.e., tubewell water that can be applied to supplement many crops, so cropping patterns are not tied to timing of canal irrigation or rains; or new varieties have different growing sea-

up to prevent endogenous changes in relative prices, the need to make sure that prices reflect opportunity costs becomes even more important.

Another aspect of the rapid increase in productivity in some parts of LDC agriculture has been that the long-standing problem of lack of income-elastic taxes on agriculture has been made even more acute. Those countries with land-based taxes and relatively long periods between reassessment of the base for taxation have experienced substantial increases in agricultural incomes with no way to tap them because of the structure of taxation. In addition, the political pressure to maintain the prices of the products in which productivity increases have taken place means a further drain on government resources to maintain subsidies or guaranteed price purchasing arrangements. Thus, if prices do not fall substantially, a tax-policy question becomes: how does one capture some of the productivity gains in parts of agriculture for use by society as a whole?

The possibility of rapid productivity growth in agriculture has another interesting dimension. As pointed earlier, if there is little productivity growth in the protected nonagricultural sector, the expansion of that sector will require an increasing subsidy from agriculture (and from the efficient parts of nonagriculture) simply to keep going. The rapid growth of productivity in agriculture, then, can effectively postpone the time when nonagriculture must become efficient. If the nonagricultural sector was really in the process of cutting its real cost of production, this extra breathing room before balance-of-payments and other problems closed in would be welcome indeed. But if the nonagricultural sector were increasing its need for subsidy and remaining an inefficient producer of tradables, the increase in the growth rate of agriculture

would simply enable the sector to put off the day of reckoning and would waste the productivity gains in agriculture.[4]

Growth of productivity in agriculture has another dimension relevant to both efficiency and equity. If rapid productivity growth puts downward pressure on the price of the commodity in question, it will have a depressing effect on the net barter terms of trade of agriculture. But, the income terms of trade need not deteriorate, a point often forgotten in discussions of the effect of the Green Revolution on farm welfare.[5] In addition, since a very large fraction of farms in many LDCs are net purchasers of food crops, the effects of productivity growth even with falling prices are likely to be favorable to farm welfare. Also, changes in the net barter terms of trade arising from productivity growth do not have decisive consequences for the incentive to use improved inputs or new techniques. The expected payoff for improved inputs involves both the physical productivity of the inputs (rising with improved techniques) and the price of output (falling with new techniques) relative to the costs of the input.

Finally, the new agricultural technologies often involve the need for more sophisticated (and expensive) water control systems; in general, it appears that benefits from the new technologies will be optimized only with increased use of fertilizers and pesticides, which increase the need for working capital in agriculture. Even in "labor surplus" economies, the need for more careful

sons from traditional varieties and may affect profitability of growing crops in seasons other than those in which they themselves are grown).

[4] It seems reasonably clear to me that the sudden increase in agricultural growth, combined with large inflows of foreign aid, provided the manufacturing sector in Pakistan with just such an increase in the availability of subsidy in the early 1960s and put off the need to rationalize the sector, thus maintaining the need to have a growing subsidy from the rest of the economy in order to expand. See (8) for a more detailed discussion of the intersectoral subsidy question.

[5] See Falcon (4) and Mellor (12) on the points raised in this paragraph.

preparation of fields and the increases in the sizes of harvests have led to a genuine (i.e., not caused by price distortions) need for investment in equipment of various kinds; and the increased input needs and physical output flows have created transport and storage problems which can be solved only by additional capacity in these systems. Such considerations suggest that the absolute allocation of private and public capital to agriculture will have to rise to optimize growth for the economy as a whole; but at the same time the growth of productivity stemming from the Green Revolution makes agriculture better able both to meet its own needs and to transfer capital to other sectors.[6] It would be dangerous to try to conclude anything "in principle" about net transfers from or to agriculture given this set of conflicting forces.

EMPLOYMENT AND INCOME DISTRIBUTION QUESTIONS

The shortage of domestic saving was *the* "development problem" of the 1950s. It was replaced briefly by the need for education and training in the early 1960s, but that gave way to the scarcity of foreign exchange in the mid- to late 1960s. Since the problems of employment and of equitable distribution of income appear to be the main foci of attention at the beginning of a new decade, one can only hope that as a profession we will sort out the relevant from the irrelevant, and the helpful from the harmful, sooner than we have on these other problems.

A number of papers on the Green Revolution have pointed out that, to a large extent, the initial beneficiaries of the new varieties and other new agricultural technologies have been the larger farmers (4; 13). Part of this has to do with "progressiveness," part with

---

[6] See 12. Note too, however, that the growing capital needs of agriculture come from increased higher-productivity investment opportunities, thus raising the opportunity cost of wasting-resources in lower-productivity protected sectors.

ability to take risks, part with the need for working (and perhaps fixed) capital to exploit the new technologies. In any case, the new technologies seem to have increased the incomes of larger farmers faster than farm incomes as a whole. In addition, the new technologies have had a regional bias in some countries, most dramatically perhaps in India and Pakistan, which has added political strains of a different kind (4). Thus, the technological revolution in agriculture has created a need for a system of taxing agriculture to tap the additional incomes which are exacerbating already serious problems of unequal income distribution.

An additional problem in income distribution is the rise of modern sector wages ahead of labor scarcity. The rationale of squeezing agriculture to raise rates of saving and employment growth is lost when the resources are absorbed by rising urban wage rates. While the higher wage rates improve the income position of employed modern sector workers relative to large rural landlords and managerial classes in the cities, they do so at the expense of parts of the agricultural sector that cannot boast such large incomes as the groups to which they are transferring income; and, whether from the effects of reduced levels of saving and investment or from effects of capital-labor substitution resulting from higher wage rates, the employment opportunities in the modern sector at higher wages than available in traditional agriculture are diminished from what they might have been. In addition, since higher costs would limit competitiveness with some imports and in export markets, there is a reduction in demand for output which will also reduce employment opportunities. Incomes policy for the modern sector is therefore relevant to methods and levels of taxation of agriculture.

Product price distortions in agriculture and manufacturing involve questions both of income distribution and of employment growth. The overvaluation of currencies, bolstered by protective systems that leave prices of capital goods artificially low, in conjunction with interest rates facing the modern sector in both agriculture and manufacturing that substantially understate the opportunity cost of capital, present a set of conditions prevalent in a large number of countries. It should not be surprising, then, to find such countries experiencing problems of unemployment and unequal income distribution. This is particularly so in light of the experience of Japan and Taiwan, and more recently Korea, where, while government policies encouraging industry and agriculture as well could hardly be called neutral, the peculiar problems of recurring balance-of-payments problems, unemployment, discrimination against exports, and lack of local capital goods do not seem to be present in such abundance as in other countries which have pursued the somewhat stylized set of policies outlined above.

The policies that have sharply biased the prices of capital and of capital goods downward, thus lowering the user cost of capital relative to labor have had three kinds of effects. First, and most obvious, there is an incentive for capital-labor substitution, especially where the urban wage rate has moved well above the traditional sector wage, but also in agriculture, where the wage rate may not be much above the opportunity cost of labor but the price of capital is heavily subsidized (see 3; 6). This effect reduces the amount of employment for any given industry structure and for any given technology. Second, the distorted prices of labor and capital lead to a choice of industry structure inconsistent with the resource endowment of the country, further reducing employment below what it could be with the available capital, and, in addition, putting pressure on the balance of payments from the inappropriate choice of techniques (and, where agriculture supplies most exports, placing an additional burden on agriculture as a whole). Third, the failure to price imported capital goods at their opportunity costs will discriminate against the production of capital goods domestically, which may have two effects: since capital goods

industries are relatively labor intensive (in hand-skilled labor generally) a set of industries is further discriminated against that would have provided more employment opportunities (and more real output) per unit of capital than other industries; and since the locally made capital goods would be more likely to reflect local factor availabilities (and maintenance tolerances), the discrimination against local production of capital goods will result in a capital stock embodying higher capital-labor ratios than would be the case with a larger proportion of locally produced capital goods in the total.

References

1. B. Balassa and Assoc., *The Structure of Protection in Developing Countries* (Baltimore, 1971).
2. R. P. Echevarria, "The Effect of Agricultural Price Policies on Intersectoral Income Transfers" (Cornell Univ., Dept. Agr. Econ., Occas. Paper No. 30, Ithaca, June 1970).
3. C. K. Eicher, T. Zalla, J. Kocher, F. Winch, *Employment Generation in African Agriculture* (Michigan State Univ., Inst. of Int. Agr. Res., Rep. No. 9, East Lansing, July 1970).
4. W. P. Falcon, "The Green Revolution: Generations of Problems," *Amer. J. Agr. Econ.,* Dec. 1970.
5. C. H. Gotsch and W. P. Falcon (eds.), "Agricultural Price Policy and the Development of West Pakistan," Vol. II (Organ. for Soc. and Tech. Innovation [OSTI], Cambridge, 1969 and 1970, mimeo.).
6. Hiromitsu Kaneda and F. C. Child, "Small-Scale, Agriculturally Related Industry in the Punjab" (Univ. Calif., Dept. Econ., Working Paper No. 11, Davis, Sept. 1971).
7. T. H. Lee, *Intersectoral Capital Flows in the Economic Development of Taiwan* (Ithaca, 1971).

8. S. R. Lewis, Jr., "The Effects of Protection on the Growth Rate and the Need for External Assistance" (Williams College, Res. Memo. No. 49, and Inst. Dev. Studies, Nairobi, Disc. Paper No. 140, 1972).

9. ____, "Interrelations Between Agricultural and Industrial Development: Discussion," *J. Farm Econ.*, Dec. 1967.

10. ____, *Pakistan: Industrialization and Trade Policies* (London, 1970).

11. I. M. D. Little, Tibor Scitovsky, and M. FG. Scott. *Industry and Trade in Some Developing Countries* (London, 1970).

12. J. W. Mellor, "Technological Change in Agriculture and Intersectoral Resource Flows" (Cornell Univ., Dept. Agr. Econ., Occas. Paper No. 34, Ithaca, June 1970).

13. J. W. Mellor and Uma J. Lele, "A Labor Supply Theory of Economic Development" (Cornell Univ., Dept. of Agr. Econ., Occas. Paper No. 43, Ithaca, June 1971).

IX.B. THE GREEN REVOLUTION

IX.B.1. Green Revolution in Southeast Asia*

The Green Revolution which started in Southeast Asia during the latter part of the 1960s represents a major advance in agricultural technology. It is likely to be the most important of the new economic factors affecting Southeast Asia's economy in the 1970s.

The fundamental question raised by the Green Revolution is: what are the economic policies required to turn it from a technological innovation into a genuine dynamic force for economic development? We shall devote much of this chapter to trying to answer this question because there is a danger that, without appropriate policies, the Green Revolution might be cut short before its full potential economic benefits are realized. We shall deal somewhat more briefly with the possible undesirable side effects of the Green Revolution: externally, on the traditional rice-exporting countries of Southeast Asia, particularly Thailand; and internally, by widening the gap between the bigger and smaller farmers.

The policies required to turn the Green Revolution into a dynamic force for economic development may be considered on the basis of three inter-related sets of problems.

THE TECHNICAL PROBLEMS

First, there are the technical problems. (1) The higher yields which can be obtained by the new varieties of rice introduced by the Green Revolution are very substantial.

*From Hla Myint, *Southeast Asia's Economy in the 1970s*, Asian Development Bank, Praeger Publishers, New York, 1971, pp. 5–11, 15–17. Reprinted by permission.

But they require not only large quantities of fertilizer and pesticide but also a well-developed system of irrigation capable of proper control over the water supply to the individual fields to give their full potential yield. The problem of supplying these modern inputs on an adequate scale is very considerable: perhaps the most formidable problem will arise from the provision of the irrigation facilities. The problem of water control is particularly difficult in the conditions which characterize the traditional rice-exporting countries of the mainland of Southeast Asia, where the main rice crop is grown in the wet season in the broad flooded river valleys and where it does not pay the farmer to apply fertilizer because it will simply be washed away. (2) The new rice varieties are not only high yielding but can be harvested in a shorter period. They therefore offer a real opportunity for a more intensive use of available land by growing at least two crops a year instead of the single crop which characterizes the extensive agriculture of much of Southeast Asia. But to take advantage of this opportunity requires not only a far-reaching change in cropping patterns but also a change in harvesting methods. Mechanical drying and increased storage facilities will be required for harvesting rice during the wet season. (3) Finally, it is important to dispel the illusion that the Green Revolution is a once-for-all technical break-through resulting in the 'miracle seeds'. On the contrary, in order to sustain it there would have to be continuous research, not only by the international research centers but also by individual countries. Apart from the longer-term research on plant protection and diversified breeding to reduce the risks of large-scale crop failure through disease and infestation, there are at least three fields of research of immediate economic importance. First, research is needed to adapt the new high-yielding varieties to the divergent local conditions of different Southeast Asian countries. For instance, the Green Revolution has not spread to the Central Plain of Thailand, both because of the difficulties of water control and the unsuitability of the dwarf varieties to flood conditions. Second, more research is needed to make the new varieties of rice more appealing to the consumers' tastes. Otherwise the market for them will remain limited. Third, in order to obtain the full benefits from the Green Revolution, a more intensive use of land and multiple cropping is necessary. It has been suggested that in order to recover the overhead costs of the elaborate irrigation facilities when required, four or five crops may have to be grown annually on a given piece of land. This makes it especially important to diversify the crops, since the market for rice will be saturated soon. So far, of the new high-yielding varieties only rice has made its impact on Southeast Asia. Research to widen the range of the Green Revolution to other crops is an important condition for maintaining its momentum.

THE ORGANIZATIONAL PROBLEMS

Next, there are the organizational problems. The Green Revolution requires the building up of an organizational framework which can carry out efficiently the two complementary functions: (1) of distributing the improved seeds, fertilizers, pesticides and irrigation water to millions of farmers, and (2) of collecting the output from them and storing it where necessary and transporting it until it reaches the final consumers.

At one time or another, many Asian countries have tried to use their government departments to distribute the seeds and fertilizer to the farmers. Some of them have also tried to use State Agricultural Marketing Boards to collect the product from the farmer and sell it to the export market. The experiences of using these government agencies in distribution and marketing have not been encouraging. It is fair to say that few government departments in the underdeveloped countries have been able to cope with the task of supplying the inputs in the right quantities and at the right time and place to a large number of farmers all over the country. Thus there has been an increasing tendency to rely on the private marketing network of the village shops, the retailers and wholesalers to supply the inputs to the farmers. Similarly, the State Marketing Boards have proved to be inefficient, particularly when they try to buy the rice directly from the farmer, instead of indirectly through the millers and middlemen. The organizational problem of marketing the rice through a State Marketing Board for the domestic market is more demanding than selling it to the export market. The task of supplying the domestic market will have to be left mainly to private traders if the development of a black market on a large scale is to be avoided.

The Green Revolution puts a heavy burden on the existing distribution and marketing organization and emphasizes the need for a rapid development of markets, not only for the inputs and the crops but also for agricultural credit. In many parts of Southeast Asia, the marketing facilities are geared to a situation in which the farmer sells only the surplus part of his output not required for family consumption. Given the expansion of output through the Green Revolution, the farmer will retain only a small proportion of the extra output for family consumption: the bulk of it will be sold on the market. This can strain the existing storage and transport facilities and may cause local gluts. Further, the new technology requires the farmer to substitute the traditional inputs which he can supply for himself with large quantities of modern inputs which he must buy with money. A much larger cash outlay is now needed to produce a given quantity of output. A correspondingly larger amount of agricultural credit is needed to finance the new cash-intensive form of agriculture.

The question of how far the distribution of seeds, fertilizers and credit to the farmers should be left to private enterprise and market forces and how far it should be undertaken by the government agencies and other non-market institutions, such as cooperatives, farmers' associations, etc., is a source of perennial debate. In some countries, there is an ideological objection to the market system as such on the ground that it enables the middlemen, money lenders and the landlords to exploit the peasants. Frequently this is reinforced by antagonism towards a particular section of the community prominent in trading and money lending. Purely in terms of organizational efficiency, however, the task of distributing inputs and collecting output from a large number of farmers all over the country is generally found to be more efficiently performed by the market network of traders and middlemen than by a centralized agency, whether government or private. It is costly for the central agency to open a sufficiently large number of local branches to deal directly with the farmers: the overhead costs of the local traders and money lenders are much lower. Further and more important, while the traders and middlemen trying to maximize profits coordinate their decisions flexibly and automatically through the market system, the task of coordinating the work of the central agency and its local branches must be done through administrative procedures. These generally tend to be rigid, cumbersome and unadaptable to local conditions. This is one of the reasons why the non-institutional sources of credit, such as the money lender, the village shopkeeper or the landlord, will continue to play an important part in financing the Green Revolution. Of course, the Southeast Asian countries should actively pursue policies for promoting the spread of modern banking to the rural areas and the develop-

ment of cooperative societies and farmers' associations. But, if they desire organizational efficiency, they should also allow the traders and middlemen freely to perform their functions to the full extent they are competitive with the alternative agencies.

This lesson is, if anything, strengthened by recent experiments to use the modern corporation in 'agri-business' to supply the farmers with seeds, fertilizers and pesticides in an appropriately combined package. This idea is promising, since the Green Revolution requires not only large quantities of the modern inputs but also technical advice on how to use them effectively. With the technical resources of a large modern corporation, the sales-cum-advisory staff may be able to offer the farmers a better technical service than they can obtain from the ordinary retailer or from the government agricultural extension service. So far, however, the organizational problems of dealing with a large number of farmers on a retail basis remains formidable, even if the commodity to be retailed is modern technology. It is increasingly realized that the agri-business corporation is not a short cut which can entirely by-pass the existing network of local traders. The Esso Fertilizer Company in the Philippines is said to have run into difficulties in recruiting a sufficient number of trained staff to man its local branches. The failure of the Bimas Gotong Rojong program in Indonesia, under which the foreign companies contracted with the government to supply the farmers with packaged inputs but left it to the government agency to collect the output, is even more instructive. It suggests two lessons: (1) the local trading network is likely to perform the retail distribution of inputs to the farmers more cheaply than large foreign companies, and (2) in order to be viable, the organizational network must also be capable of collecting the output from the farmers to pay for the inputs.

The second point is of considerable practical importance. When the inputs are supplied to the farmers by private traders, they make it their business to collect the payment for the inputs. On the other hand, the government agencies have been generally found to be unable or unwilling to collect the full payment for the inputs they supply to the farmer. The Green Revolution requires a large and rapid expansion in the irrigation services to be provided by the government. This raises very considerable problems of financial administration concerning the appropriate charges to be made for the water and collecting these charges. These problems deserve special attention when the ability of Southeast Asian governments to meet the deficits on the irrigation services out of general taxation is very limited.

THE CENTRAL ECONOMIC ISSUES

We now come to the central economic issues raised by the Green Revolution.

(1) First, there is the basic question: how to allocate the available resources more effectively to take advantage of the opportunities created by the Green Revolution? This applies to the resources both in the private sector and the public sector.

Typically, the Green Revolution has been launched by raising the price of rice to the farmers by government price supports or by import restrictions which raise the domestic price above the world market price. This is reinforced by the distribution of seeds, fertilizers and other inputs at subsidized prices, or sometimes free of charge. This has undoubtedly succeeded in inducing the farmers to expand their output rapidly through the private profit motive. But the question is whether the economic incentives given to the farmers are appropriate for the efficient allocation of the resources between rice production and other crops, and more generally, between the agricultural sector and the rest of the economy.

A similar question arises in the allocation of resources in the public sector. It is apparent that the Green Revolution is going to require heavy government investment, par-

ticularly in the irrigation facilities, not to speak of auxiliary investment required for improving transport and storage facilities. Thus we have to face the question how much of the available resources should be allocated to promoting the Green Revolution and how much of it should be allocated to public investment in other sectors of the economy.

(2) The Green Revolution however is not merely a matter of growing more rice by a once-for-all change in the allocation of resources. It is bound to set up a far-reaching chain of consequences which calls for policies of continuous adjustment and adaptation if its full potential benefits are to be realized. The need to grow a succession of crops, rather than a single rice crop, to meet the overhead cost of large irrigation works involves radical changes in cropping and harvesting in order to achieve an appropriately diversified pattern of agriculture, producing both food and non-food crops. Given the high productivity of the new technology, some land and labor will be released from crop production, and these will have to be reabsorbed in other uses such as livestock farming, forestry or tree crops. If these changes can be carried out successfully, the result will be an increase in output of the whole agricultural sector (a) in rice and food grains, (b) in a wide range of other foodstuffs such as vegetables, meat and dairy products, and (c) in raw materials available for export and for the domestic industry.

(3) The Green Revolution is likely to require large amounts of new investment both from the private and the public sector. Its momentum can be maintained only by policies which increase the total volume of investible resources from domestic sources to supplement the available funds from external sources. In particular, governments should resist the temptation to keep the rates of interest too low to provide cheap loans to the farmers. This type of policy has been tried in some countries in the past to promote domestic industrialization, with very unfortunate consequences. Firstly,

those who are able to obtain loans at artificially low rates of interest are tempted to employ excessively capital-intensive methods of production using too little labor. Secondly, by keeping down the rate of interest below the level which equates the demand and supply, an excess demand for credit is generated, and government agencies have to take an increasing part in rationing loans among the borrowers. By accident or design, such a mechanism tends to favor bigger enterprises, if only for the fact that the small man is unable to cope with the complexities and delays of administrative procedures. Finally, artificially low rates of interest discourage saving, especially where the real value of savings is quickly eroded by inflation. In general the domestic financing of the Green Revolution can be more effectively done by keeping interest rates up to equate demand and supply for loans, and by giving equal opportunities to banks, cooperative societies and private money lenders to compete with each other in providing the farmers with credit. . . .

THE SIDE EFFECTS OF THE GREEN REVOLUTION

Finally, we may briefly touch upon the possible undesirable side effects of the Green Revolution.

First, there are the external effects on the traditional rice-exporting countries in the region, such as Thailand. Here the best way to reduce these effects is already contained in our suggestion that free trade in rice within the region should be restored as soon as possible. In so far as import-substitution has taken place by protecting high-cost producers in the deficit countries, free trade would benefit both the rice exporters and rice-deficit countries. In so far as the Green Revolution has genuinely shifted comparative costs to the hitherto rice-deficit countries, then the rice-exporting countries will have to accept the new situation and make suitable adjustments to it. Malaysia herself has successfully adapted to the new situation

introduced by synthetic rubber. Thailand in her turn will have to adapt to the changes which are inevitably part of technological progress. It is even possible that the same forces of technological progress will hasten the spread of a bigger and better Green Revolution to the broad river valleys of mainland Southeast Asia. As yet, we cannot even begin to imagine the tremendous consequences which this might have on the rest of the region.

Second, there are the possible disequalizing effects of the Green Revolution on the bigger and the smaller farmers within the country. These disequalizing effects may arise, not because of the economies of large-scale production but because the Green Revolution increases the amount of modern inputs which the farmers have to buy, and thus sharply raises the cash outlay required for efficient farming. Many people fear that this will lead to the larger and more commercialized farmers buying out small proprietors and evicting small tenants, and thus increasing social and political tensions. They ask whether the Southeast Asian countries should not adopt policies to control the growth of the larger farmers and try to carry out the Green Revolution based on small farmers as in Japan and Taiwan. . . .

The bigger farmers may do better out of the Green Revolution for rational economic reasons such as that they are willing and able to adapt to modern methods more quickly, or that the organizational costs of distributing inputs and credit to the larger units are lower. In so far as these reasons operate, the attempt to control the growth of the larger farms will tend to slow down the agricultural revolution. On the other hand, the bigger farmers may do better for less rational reasons: they may be better placed to obtain subsidized loans or scarce foreign exchange to buy capital equipment; or they may be able to use their influence to get a lion's share of the available public services, particularly irrigation. It is difficult in practice to draw a sharp line between the rational and the irrational factors which favor the bigger farmers. Furthermore, it should be pointed out that it is not only the free market forces but also and more importantly the working of government controls (including in some cases the land reform laws themselves) which favor the bigger farmers.

One commonly observed effect of the existing imperfections in the market and the government controls is that the bigger farmers are frequently encouraged to use excessively mechanized methods of farming which waste scarce capital resources and result in too little employment. It is a moot point whether this should be prevented by breaking up the large farms or by using less drastic measures such as removing government controls which have the effect of supplying the inputs on more favorable terms to bigger farmers, and by imposing excise taxes on heavy tractors.

The strongest case for trying to preserve the pattern of smallholders arises from what may be described as the practical problems of labor relations. Given the 'revolution of rising expectations', workers in most underdeveloped countries including the Southeast Asian countries tend to demand a higher wage rate than that which is consistent with the full employment of the existing abundant labor supply. This insistence on 'fair' wages, frequently backed by government legislation, creates a situation of 'dualism' in which a small section of the labor force is employed at high wages in the modern manufacturing industry and in government enterprises, with adverse effects on the wage and employment opportunities for others who cannot get on these 'high-wage islands'. The extension of this pattern from the urban centers to the agricultural sector through the Green Revolution will tend to create serious problems of unemployment and disparities. A policy of trying to preserve the pattern of smallholdings may serve to relieve these problems. Given the intensification of commercialization of agriculture which accompanies the Green Revolution, it will be difficult to preserve the ownership of the smallholdings. Individual farmers will have to be permitted to buy and sell their land freely if they are to participate in the Green Revolution. What can be preserved is the small-scale tenancy. Theoretically, with perfect markets, it should make little difference whether a person works as a laborer for a big farmer or works as a small tenant. But in practice a tenant may be prepared to work for much lower real wages on his farm than he is willing to work for as a laborer on a large farm. This will help to increase the volume of agricultural employment. But one must add the warning that the Green Revolution on the Japan-Taiwan model is not likely to succeed unless the small farmers of Southeast Asia are prepared to work as their counterparts in those countries, growing a succession of crops throughout the year.

IX.B.2. Generations of Problems*

In the regions of Asia where the production revolution has occurred, the impact on marketed surplus has been nothing short of phenomenal. Even with a moderately high on-farm demand from increased output, marketings have risen much more than propor-

*From Walter P. Falcon, "The Green Revolution: Second-Generation Problems," *American Journal of Agricultural Economics*, December 1970, pp. 701–9. Reprinted by permission.

tionately to production. While the response of public and private sectors in a few regions has been good, the pace of change, the preoccupation with production, and the ability of policy makers to handle only a few issues simultaneously have meant that few policy actions were taken before crises erupted. Transportation bottlenecks often have been a problem, as an example from West Pakistan will illustrate. In Sind (the lower half of the hour-glass-shaped Indus Basin), rail marketings of rice in 1969 completely swamped the system. Large, uncovered piles of rice accumulated at railheads, and prices to farmers fell substantially. Millers were working equipment at capacity and were running into severe inventory and working capital constraints. (As usual, they were blamed for the decline in price.) It nearly required a French-style, pitchfork rebellion to obtain more rail cars, to change government policy to permit trucks to deliver rice to the port, etc. In the meantime, however, farmers were "hurt," at least relative to what would have been the case with a better transport system and faster-moving government policy machinery.

Similar stories on milling, grading, storage, and transport can be told for other countries as well. The problem of limited, old-style mills, unable to handle increased supplies or to produce "export-quality" rice, is well documented in reports and government documents that I have seen for at least five Asian countries. These physical problems of marketing have been exacerbated by social factors in several countries of Southeast Asia, where specific ethnic or racial groups have traditionally controlled most of the commerce. Regardless of the efficiency of the marketing system, rural problems have tended to be blamed on these groups. Justly or unjustly, middlemen are an important factor in social and political unrest in these countries. This unrest, in turn, has posed the problem of either taking over milling in the public sector or developing a set of incentives and guidelines for the private trade that will protect the public interest as seen by the policy makers. Efficiency and ideology are often in conflict on this point, and the net result in many regions has been that the developments in marketing skills have lagged.

There have also been varietal-quality questions that have posed difficulties both domestically and internationally.... However important these difficulties may have been in the short run, they are clearly transitional in nature. New varieties are already being developed and introduced that will overcome many of the most severe quality problems.

In addition to the readily identifiable milling, transport, and grading questions, there are also formidable second-generation problems concerned with pricing and markets. There are economic and political dimensions to these questions, and both aspects must be incorporated into meaningful answers.

A number of the food-deficit countries have historically had a structure of relative prices that bore little relationship to world prices. Although in allocative efficiency terms such a structure has always had drawbacks, the problem takes on even more serious proportions when countries and regions close their food import gap and become potential exporters. Adjusting domestic support prices, which at the official exchange rate are often double or more the world price, is no easier politically in these countries than in the United States.

In addition to internal pricing difficulties an even larger problem looms ahead on the international side. For those regions "lucky" enough to emerge as surplus areas the problems of breaking into international grain markets have rarely appeared so difficult. The International Wheat Agreement appears to be seriously undermined, and there has been a considerable softening in rice prices, particularly in the lower-quality grades.

Several elements of the international dimension deserve mention. What happens to "world prices" for wheat and rice is obviously dependent on what happens to the green revolution in the developing countries as well as to the agricultural policies of the developed nations. As indicated previously, there are reasons to believe that portions of Indonesia, India, and East Pakistan are likely to be net importers for some time. On the other hand, the quantity traded internationally is so small relative to production— less than four percent in the case of rice— that increases in production in key countries such as India are likely to have important international price repercussions. Perhaps even more important than what happens in the developing countries is what happens to agricultural policy in the advanced countries. Unable to adapt to rapid technological advances and structural change themselves, these countries have instituted support systems that use commodity exports to solve sectoral income distribution problems. In short, less-developed countries breaking into export markets will be faced with three kinds of problems: (a) a tenacity among developed countries in fighting for shares of the commercial market and a willingness to cut prices to retain them; (b) an increasing amount of foodgrains being supplied by developed countries at concessional terms to countries that might "normally" be trading partners of developing countries; and (c) an inability, or at least difficulty, of the less-developed world to compete in "buyers'" markets in terms of specific grades, quality, deliverability, etc. This does not mean that the developing countries cannot sell in international markets. What it does mean is that planners in these countries must be hard-headed about the quantities and especially the prices at which wheat and rice can be exported and about the concomitant internal price adjustment (or export subsidy) that will be required at these levels.

The foregoing marketing and demand problems, any one of which could be the subject of a major paper, suggest several conclusions:

First, the production gains in certain regions have shown how rapidly second-generation marketing problems can arise. It is to be hoped that in the future policy makers will heed earlier the warnings given by marketing specialists and will react before crisis situations develop. Unless these milling and transport problems are solved, farm prices will decline steeply and the quality problems of exporting will be all the more difficult. What is particularly needed in several Asian countries is a marketing strategy that resolves the basic public/private/foreign investment question on marketing facilities. Also needed is an explicit recognition of the interaction of price support policies and techniques with the behavior and efficiency of marketing firms.

Second, planners must pay increasing attention to the adjustment and pricing problems attendant on the new varieties. The narrow focus on foodgrains and relative neglect of other crops must be reevaluated in a multicrop setting. In particular, the cropping patterns of many of the irrigated areas of Asia which can best use the new varieties are quite sensitive to profitability changes. What constitutes an appropriate incentive price for foodgrains in these areas with the new varieties has changed substantially; unfortunately, the rhetoric of the later 1950's and early 1960's regarding the need for ever higher agricultural prices has not changed. Vested interests in agriculture are already a fact of life in these countries, and economists concerned with agriculture must keep in mind the overall needs of development, not just the needs of the agricultural sector. Since most agricultural goods are tradable, what is especially needed in the less-developed countries is an assessment of the domestic costs of earning or saving foreign exchange from producing various agricultural and nonagricultural commodities. The real tragedy would be for those countries to retain outmoded pricing policies which lead to great inefficiencies in resource use, stock accumulations, and/or highly subsidized agricultural exports—exports that were uneconomically grown in real terms in the first place. Unfortunately, experience in dealing with such problems in developed countries does not inspire confidence, nor do recent policies in a number of Asian countries.

Third, the advanced countries must consider more seriously the distorting effects of their dumping programs. The talk of *a* world market price for wheat or for rice is largely a fiction, and concessional pricing arrangements will be a sharp deterrent to the generation of third-country foodgrain exports.

Fourth, since there is little reason to have confidence in the developed countries' ability to deal with their sectoral income distribution problems without resort to concessional efforts, the developing countries should look increasingly to domestic markets for absorbing additional supplies. On this point there is some room for optimism. What has been seriously underestimated, I believe, is the investment and employment uses to which wheat and rice, the wage goods, can be put. The basic elements in this argument can be stated as follows: With significant increases in production, foodgrain prices in a closed economy would fall. However, given the fact that much of the increase came from cost-free technological change, prices could fall somewhat and still provide adequate incentives to farmers. In addition, with substantial supplies of grain, the government can have a much more expansionary fiscal and monetary policy. (Indeed, in India and Indonesia the lack of adequate food supplies and a fear of rising prices have been constraints on the size of the development budget.) The more expansionary monetary and fiscal policy—particularly if it is directed toward labor-intensive public projects—can shift the demand curve for grains, helping to counteract some of the decline in prices. Given the fact that the price of the wage good is a major development constraint in much of Asia, especially as seen by finance ministers, the increases in production from the green revolution can thus continue after initial import substitution has been exhausted. These increases can be converted into investible resources through fiscal and monetary expansion, and the country (perhaps even the agricultural sector, if the investments are rural) could be much better off. This should be one element of development strategy for countries moving into foodgrain surpluses; moreover, it seems especially important for countries who find themselves with seriously distorted internal prices. This approach should provide time both to solve the institutional problems of entering international trade and to make transitional changes in relative and absolute price levels without having to rely on stock accumula-

tion or "excessive" subsidies to agriculture. Such a strategy also has much in common with a sensible P.L. 480 policy which can effect shifts in the demand curve through investment policies, thereby helping to counteract much of the decline in prices that would have resulted from increased supplies.

The first-generation production problems and the second-generation marketing and demand difficulties created by the green revolution are a formidable list. Nevertheless, they are largely short-run issues on which economists have worked for years. By contrast, the third-generation problems, having to do with equity, welfare, employment, and social institutions generally are questions that have received inadequate attention even in the developed countries. . . .

These third-generation factors arise from four principal sources: (a) population growth rates in excess of 2.5 percent annually in areas already extraordinarily densely populated; (b) very low average income levels, coupled simultaneously with great regional and personal disparities in income, wealth, and political power; (c) limited opportunities for nonfarm employment, even if the manufacturing and service sectors grow very rapidly; and (d) the possibility for technological leap-frogging with agricultural inputs and techniques, which are often of a labor-displacing nature. The resulting dilemma can be baldly stated: The Asian countries need agricultural growth if ever they are to break the chains of poverty; but they need equity as well, for obvious humanitarian reasons and in order not to find themselves in a continuous cycle of violence and repression. The challenge of these forces is far greater in magnitude than the problems ever faced by the United States and most other presently developed nations. Moreover, the latter are not in a position to help. Although they are perhaps capable of exporting the growth technology, they have few institutional forms to export that can come to grips with the income distribution and employment questions that now plague Asia.

India, Pakistan, and Indonesia—three

enormously large and regionally heterogeneous countries—present stark examples of the problems outlined above.

Perhaps even more important than the direct effects, and often neglected in discussions on employment, are the side effects of increased food supplies and lower food prices on public and private savings and investment generally. As noted earlier, the food-price constraint is an important one and has a pervasiveness that extends far beyond the agricultural sector. Here, too, the green revolution helps, provided that its potential for increasing savings is realized and is transferred into real investment.

Far more disturbing, however, are two other effects of the green revolution on employment, welfare, and stability. Both of these derive basically from the unequal regional growth that seems to be a concomitant of the new technology. The process is as follows: The regions with irrigation, such as the Punjab, have the ability to respond rapidly to the new technology. A combination of the resulting production plus an agricultural price policy that reflects concerns for nongrowing districts as well as vested agricultural interests will mean that incomes in the irrigated regions will grow at phenomenal rates. That is all to the good; the difficulty is that welfare, between regions as among people, is more a relative concept than an absolute idea. In this interregional sense, therefore, the green revolution is hardly a stabilizing influence.

Within a given region, the mechanism producing greater income inequality is much the same, and the form is even more virulent. Although in theory the new seeds and fertilizer are neutral to scale, in practice they are not. Under rationed conditions, and unfortunately these often prevail for inputs in Asia, it is the larger farmers who obtain the fertilizer and receive the irrigation water. Moreover, with the prices and technology now prevailing, agricultural incomes of large farmers have risen dramatically. This too is not "bad," but the side effects may be. Land prices are rising rapidly, as farmers seek to expand size and find new outlets for their increased incomes. Even more important is the drive that these windfall gains are providing for certain types of mechanization. Although this is a broad question, deserving also of a separate study, several points deserve mention. First, there are powerful forces that are pressing for mechanization of all kinds. Large farmers, foreign and domestic industrialists, politicians, and even aid agencies have vested interests in promoting various implements, including tractors. Some forms of mechanization may be labor-displacing, others not. However, large farms in wheat areas are an example of where tractors and combines will be introduced, barring strong government action to the contrary. The net result will be to make tenants into laborers and to increase the number of people displaced from agriculture. Just as in the interregional illustration, the intraregional effects of the green revolution are likely to increase the inequality of incomes within agriculture. There will indeed be agricultural growth in these areas, but probably increasing tension among classes as well. Perhaps the growth in service and supply industries in small towns can absorb this additional displacement. But the adjustment problems, with which the United States had trouble in coping under much more favorable demographic circumstances and over a century, must be dealt with in Pakistan in 20 years. This labor-displacement process was not "easy" in the United States; in Asia the situation is distressing even to contemplate. . . .

Several recommendations and reconsiderations are suggested in the light of these third-generation questions. First, as long as the new varieties remain limited to a few regions and as long as farm incomes are primarily dependent on acreage rather than people, it is naive to believe that the new technology for agriculture is likely to be a stabilizing influence. Growth generally is destabilizing, and this form of unequal agricultural development is particularly so. Even if the first borrowings of technology are neutral to scale (which in practice probably they are not), subsequent borrowings are likely to be labor displacing unless strong policy measures are introduced. The magnitude of this phenomenon will vary by commodity and region, but the direction seems fairly clear. Second, some way must be found to close the gap between social and private benefits from certain forms of agricultural technology. It is not sufficient to appeal to the "Japanese method" of cultivation, to urge labor-intensive techniques for agriculture and industry, or to proclaim the virtues of small-scale industry. Such pronouncements must be transformed into instruments of direction and control: high taxes on tractors; a possible lowering of wheat and rice prices as a stimulant to the rest of the economy; much higher interest rates on capital and higher de facto rates for foreign exchange; progressive land taxes; and perhaps even ceilings on farm size so as to make uneconomical, from a private point of view, certain forms of technology. And in any Asian country, no one should discount the size and power of the forces that are likely to be against most of these policies.

Third, neither growth nor equity problems in Asia can be solved by the green revolution or even by the agricultural sector alone. The employment problem in particular is total-economy in character, whose solution requires increased savings, more foreign exchange, higher investment rates, altered factor- and product-pricing structures—in short, economic development. While agricultural policies should not aggravate the situation, meaningful answers to these issues must look to other sectors as well.

Fourth, given the tearing effect that unequal regional growth has on the national fabric, there is need to stress again the importance of developing new technology for the monsoon/dryland areas.

Finally, while there is need to keep social and private benefits from diverging among the large farms, the opposite side of the coin is to assist small farmers.... Given the resources available and the political interests that are involved, a broad-based welfare system does not seem to be the answer. Nor

do special loan or credit arrangements to small farmers which are used for unproductive investments. There is reason to be even more skeptical, as amply demonstrated in the United States, about price support or input subsidies as an instrument. It is the large farmer who has the marketed surplus and who uses most of the inputs. (Nearly one-third of the farmers in Indonesia, Pakistan, and India, for example, are net purchasers of grains.) It is spurious to argue for higher farm prices or increased subsidies to "help the small farmer," for it would be hard to design a more inefficient system for reaching them. (Some rough calculations for India and Pakistan indicate that of $10 transferred via a price-support system, only about $1 goes to "small" farmers.) The small-farmer argument, which is always offered by the representatives of larger farmers whenever pricing is an issue, should be viewed very skeptically.

Except for the obvious and important point of assuming a ready supply of inputs such as fertilizer, the literature of agricultural development has little to offer in the way of positive suggestions for dealing with the agricultural production alternatives for millions of small Asian farmers. Providing credit in kind (as under the BIMAS program in parts of Indonesia) has worked in some circumstances, as have a few cooperative arrangements. The program at Comilla in East Pakistan, for example, has shown the merit of cooperative credit, marketing, and pump facilities at the village level. On the other hand, most of the cooperatives of South and Southeast Asia have been run as heavy-handed government agencies with little local support except among the rural elite who have benefited from them. Similarly, loan programs especially designed for small farmers have generally had little success because of prohibitively high transaction costs for issuing and monitoring small loans. Perhaps most promising as an aid to the smaller operator is the provision of adequate supplies of irrigation water. The employment effects from this type of infrastructure are substantial, and reliable water supplies may provide the flexibility for diversifying and intensifying output. On the whole, however, the outlook is far from bright for the smaller farmer.

CONCLUDING COMMENTS

The foregoing assessment of the green revolution is hardly one of wild enthusiasm. The purpose has not been to argue that it should not have happened or to deny its great production successes in certain regions. Rather, the intent has been to indicate how limited a solution the revolution is, given the broader development problems of South and Southeast Asia.

Four central themes stand out in the analysis. First, impressive as the gains to date have been, the term "revolution" can be applied correctly only to about 10 to 15 percent of Asia. One of the greatest second-generation obstacles is that set of individuals who believe, explicitly or implicitly, that the first-generation solutions have been found. Many additional answers are needed, and any complacency on varietal research would be most unfortunate both in terms of growth and regional equity. Clearly also, a real revolution will require greatly expanded investments in irrigation and substantial improvements in systems for pest control.

Second, the sudden increases in agricultural output have already or will soon necessitate basic pricing decisions on the parts of governments. It would be a great pity if the nations of Asia, in the face of remarkable productivity changes, maintained pricing structures that did not keep in mind the needs of the entire economy. As a result of the increased production from the green revolution, there is considerable potential for expanding the development effort with

investment programs that are wage-good intensive. As regards exports, the developed countries could play a major facilitating role; however, their probable increased use of dumping programs will provide the most formidable kinds of competition for those developing nations who generate export surpluses. Hence, the internal market opportunities and the external market difficulties indicate the probable need for downward adjustments in relative grain prices in several Asian nations.

Third, the limited technological revolution in agriculture has permitted an easing of one critical development constraint. It has not, however, provided a panacea for the employment and equity problems, and indeed has probably been destabilizing in the sense that it has widened income disparities within and between regions. Lest this view be regarded as too bleak, it should also be emphasized that without the green revolution, the development situation in these countries would now be even more dire.

Finally, although it is important to recognize and understand what has happened in the past, the great challenge of the future will be to forge institutions that can deal simultaneously with the demographic explosion, rapid economic growth, and equality of income distribution. Certain obvious mistakes in policies can be avoided, such as the subsidization of tractors. However, there is little in the way of a broad, institutional blueprint in the history of the developed countries or in the general writings of agricultural economists that is now of much help on this issue. The Asian challenge of the 1970's will be to encourage growth elements in the economy—such as the green revolution—while at the same time fostering equity so as to prevent an ascending spiral of violence and repression.

IX.C. RURAL DEVELOPMENT
AND EMPLOYMENT

IX.C.1. The Case for a Unimodal Strategy*

The historical experience in a number of countries, and the recent technical breakthroughs of the Green Revolution, justify major emphasis on increases in factor productivity. It is, however, the experience of Japan and Taiwan that is especially useful in demonstrating that an *appropriate* sequence of innovations based on modern scientific knowledge and experimental methods makes possible an expansion path for the agricultural sector that is characterized by large increases in factor productivity *throughout* the agricultural sector. Such a strategy enables a widening fraction of the working population in agriculture to be associated with increasingly productive technologies, based mainly on expanded use of purchased inputs that are divisible and neutral to scale. It is because the new inputs of seed and fertilizer, that are the essence of the Green Revolution, are complementary to the large amounts of labor and land already committed to agriculture that these increases in factor productivity can have such a large impact on total farm output. At the same time, by involving an increasingly large fraction of the rural population in the process of technical change, such a strategy means that the fruits of economic progress are widely shared.

The thrust of this argument is that it is possible and desirable to devise and imple-ment agricultural strategies which are efficient in terms of a number of objectives, including but not confined to the objective of achieving desired increases in farm output at low cost. The following objectives, which are examined later in some detail, seem to be especially relevant to the design of strategies for agriculture that are efficient in this broad sense:

(1) Contributing to the overall rate of economic growth and the process of structural transformation,

(2) Achieving a satisfactory rate of increase in farm output at minimum cost by encouraging sequences of innovations which exploit the possibilities for technical change most appropriate to a country's factor endowments,

(3) Achieving a broadly based improvement in the welfare of the rural population, and

(4) Facilitating the process of social modernization (including the lowering of birthrates, the extension and improvement of rural education, and the strengthening of entrepreneurial capacities) by encouraging widespread attitudinal and behavioral changes among farm households.

I believe that it is useful to assess the "total efficiency" of alternative agricultural strategies in terms of their relative success in achieving those four objectives.

The concept of total efficiency is, quite obviously, difficult to define operationally. That is inherent in the nature of the problem. But the problem must be confronted because only when a country's agricultural strategy is efficient in this broad sense is the trade-off between the goal of increased

*From Bruce F. Johnston, "Criteria for the Design of Agricultural Development Strategies," *Food Research Institute Studies in Agricultural Economics, Trade, and Development*, Vol. 11, No. 1, 1972, pp. 35–7, 42–54. Reprinted by permission.

output and other objectives likely to be minimized. Indeed, it is my contention that with an agricultural strategy that is designed with those multiple objectives in view, the trade-off is likely to be small or nonexistent.

A country's overall strategy for agriculture is a composite of substrategies relating to research, education, water resources development, promotion of farmers' organizations, marketing and price policy, credit and the distribution of inputs, agricultural taxation, land tenure, policies affecting the nature and pace of mechanization, and other elements. The total efficiency of the strategy depends on the complementarities among those various activities and the quality of implementation as well as decisions with respect to the allocation of funds and personnel and policies for individual substrategies. . . .

THE CHOICE BETWEEN UNIMODAL AND BIMODAL AGRICULTURAL STRATEGIES

The most fundamental issue of agricultural strategy faced by the late developing countries is to choose between a bimodal strategy whereby resources are concentrated within a subsector of large, capital-intensive units or a unimodal strategy which seeks to encourage a more progressive and wider diffusion of technical innovations adapted to the factor proportions of the sector as a whole. The essential distinction between the two approaches is that the unimodal strategy emphasizes sequences of innovations that are highly divisible and largely scale-neutral. These are innovations that can be used efficiently by small-scale farmers and adopted progressively. A unimodal approach does not mean that all farmers or all agricultural regions would adopt innovations and expand output at uniform rates. Rather it means that the type of innovations emphasized are appropriate to a progressive pattern of adoption in the twofold sense that there will be progressive diffusion of innovations within particular areas and extension of the

benefits of technical change to new areas as changes in environmental conditions, notably irrigation facilities, or improved market opportunities or changes in the nature of the innovations available enable farmers in new areas to participate in the process of modernization. Although a bimodal strategy entails a much more rapid adoption of a wider range of modern technologies, this is necessarily confined to a small fraction of farm units because of the structure of economies in which commercial demand is small in relation to a farm labor force that still represents some 60 to 80 per cent of the working population.

The late developing countries face a wide choice of farm equipment embodying large investments in research and development activity in the economically advanced countries. The performance characteristics of these machines are impressive, and representatives of the major manufacturing firms in the economically advanced countries are experienced and skillful in demonstrating their equipment. And they now have added incentive to promote sales in the developing countries to more fully utilize their plant capacity which is large relative to domestic demand (mainly a replacement demand since the period of rapid expansion of tractors and tractor-drawn equipment in the developed countries has ended). The availability of credit under bilateral and international aid programs temporarily eliminates the foreign exchange constraint to acquiring such equipment; and when such loans are readily available it may even appear to be an attractive means of increasing the availability of resources—in the short run. Within developing countries there is often considerable enthusiasm for the latest in modern technologies. But little attention is given to research and development activity and support services to promote the manufacture and wide use of simple, inexpensive equipment of good design, low import content, and suited to the factor proportions prevailing in countries where labor is relatively abundant and capital scarce. . . .

Under a bimodal strategy frontier firms with their high capital to labor ratio would account for the bulk of commercial production and would have the cash income required to make extensive use of purchased inputs. Inasmuch as the schedule of aggregate commercial demand for agricultural products is inelastic and its rightward shift over time is essentially a function of the rate of structural transformation, to concentrate resources within a subsector of agriculture inevitably implies a reduction in the ability of farm households outside that subsector to adopt new purchased inputs and technologies. In addition, the high foreign exchange content of many of the capital inputs employed in the frontier sector implies a reduction in the amount of foreign exchange available for imported inputs for other farm firms (or for other sectors). It is, of course, because of these purchasing power and foreign exchange constraints that it is impossible for the agricultural sector as a whole to pursue a crash modernization strategy. It might be argued that a proper farm credit program could eliminate the purchasing power constraint, but the availability of credit (assuming that repayment takes place) merely alters the shape of the time horizon over which the constraint operates. And capital and government revenue are such scarce resources in a developing country that government subsidy programs are not feasible means of escaping from this constraint. In brief, bimodal and unimodal strategies are to a considerable extent mutually exclusive.

Under the bimodal approach the divergence between the factor intensities and the technical efficiency of "best" and average firms is likely to become progressively greater as agricultural transformation takes place. Moreover, both the initial and subsequent divergences between the technologies used in the two sectors are likely to be accentuated because the factor prices, including the price of imported capital equipment, faced by the modern sector in contemporary developing countries typically diverge from social opportunity cost. This divergence is obvious when subsidized credit is made available on a rationed basis to large farmers and when equipment can be imported with a zero or low tariff at an official exchange rate that is overvalued. In addition, the large-scale farmers depend on hired labor rather than unpaid family labor. The wages paid hired labor may be determined by minimum wage legislation, and even without a statutory minimum the price of hired labor is characteristically higher than the opportunity cost of labor to small farm units. . . .

Under the unimodal strategy with its emphasis on highly divisible and scale-neutral innovations, the best firms in the agrarian sector display essentially the same factor intensities as average firms. Interfarm differences in performance will be large, especially during transitional periods as farmers are learning how to use new inputs efficiently, but this will reflect mainly differences in output per unit of input rather than major differences in factor proportions. Inasmuch as the expansion path for the agricultural sector associated with a unimodal strategy inplies a level of capital intensity and foreign exchange requirements that are compatible with a late developing country's economic structure, more firms within the agricultural sector are able to expand their use of fertilizer and the other divisible inputs that dominate purchases under this strategy. Thus, the diffusion of innovations and associated inputs will be more broadly based, and the divergence in factor intensities between frontier firms and average firms will be moderate.

Although the foregoing has emphasized the contrast in the pattern of technical change, it is apparent that the two strategies will have significantly different impacts on many dimensions of economic and social change. Most obvious are the differences in the nature of demand for farm inputs, but the structure of rural demand for consumer goods will also be very different under a unimodal as compared to a bimodal strategy.

A major difference in income distribution is to be expected because of the likelihood that under a bimodal strategy the difficult problem of absorbing a rapidly growing labor force into productive employment would be exacerbated whereas under a unimodal strategy there is a good prospect that the rate of increase in demand for labor would be more rapid than the growth of the labor force. Underemployment and unemployment would thus be reduced as a result of wider participation of the rural population in improved income-earning opportunities. This improvement in income opportunities available to members of the rural work force would result in part from increased earnings as hired labor since rising demand for labor would tend to raise wage rates and the number of days of work available during the year for landless laborers and for very small farmers whose incomes derive to a considerable extent from work on farms that are above average size.

Most important, however, would be the increased incomes earned by farm households cultivating their own or rented land. The extent to which tenants would be able to share in the increased productivity resulting from yield-increasing innovations will be determined by forces considered later in a section discussing land reform as an aspect of broadly based improvement in the welfare of the rural population. Basically, however, it will depend upon the rate of growth of the rural population of working age seeking a livelihood in farming or in nonfarm activities relative to the rate of expansion of income-earning opportunities. The latter will be influenced strongly by the demand on the part of landowners for labor "hired" indirectly through tenancy arrangements, or hired directly as laborers on owner-operated farms.

THE MULTIPLE OBJECTIVES OF AN AGRICULTURAL STRATEGY

In the paragraphs that follow I comment briefly on some of the reasons why the design of an efficient strategy for agriculture should be guided by explicit consideration of four major objectives of an agricultural strategy and the interrelationships among them. . . .

Contributions to overall economic growth and structural transformation.—It is conventional when considering agriculture's role in economic development to catalog a number of specific "contributions." Several of these contributions imply a net transfer of factors of production out of the agricultural sector as the process of structural transformation takes place. Typically the farm sector provides foreign exchange, public and private investment resources, and labor to the more rapidly expanding sectors of the economy as well as increased supplies of food and raw materials to support a growing urban population and manufacturing sector.

These contributions are, of course, synonymous with the increased sectoral interdependence that characterizes a developing economy. Outward labor migration and increased farm purchasing power are synchronized with the growing importance of commodity flows between agriculture and other sectors: a flow of food and raw materials out of agriculture and a return flow of farm inputs and consumer goods from the manufacturing sector. Tertiary activities of government, transport, marketing and other service industries expand to meet the needs of individual sectors and to facilitate the linkages between them.

Agricultural exports have special significance here for two reasons. First, in countries that have experienced little structural transformation there are usually few alternative means of meeting the growing demands for foreign exchange that characterize a developing economy. Secondly, expanded production for export makes it possible to enlarge farm cash incomes when the domestic market for purchased food is still very small, and at the same time it provides a stimulus and the means to establish some of the physical infrastructure and institutions that are necessary for the creation of a national, market-oriented economy.

The structure of rural demand for farm inputs associated with alternative agricultural strategies exerts an important influence on the growth of local manufacturing as well as on the pattern of productivity advance within agriculture. I emphasize the composition of this demand because the capacity of the agricultural sector to purchase inputs from other sectors is powerfully constrained by the proportion of the population living outside agriculture. Pathological growth of population in urban areas only loosely related to the growth of off-farm employment opportunities is a conspicuous and distressing feature of many of the contemporary less developed countries, but basically this growth of urban population depends on the transformation of a country's occupational structure that is a concomitant of economic growth.

The nature of the linkages between agriculture and the local manufacturing sector and the seriousness of foreign exchange and investment constraints on development will be influenced significantly by the structure of rural demand for both inputs and consumer goods. Because of their differential effects on the sequence of innovations and on rural income distribution, a bimodal and a unimodal strategy will differ greatly in their aggregate capital and foreign exchange requirements.

The more capital-intensive bimodal strategy emphasizes rapid adoption of mechanical innovations such as tractors along with chemical fertilizers and other inputs essential for increasing crop yields. Even if that type of machinery is manufactured locally, the foreign exchange requirements for capital equipment and for components are high, and the production processes require a high level of technical sophistication, large plants, and capital-intensive technologies.

The unimodal strategy with its emphasis on mechanical innovatons of lower technical sophistication and foreign exchange content, such as improved bullock implements and low-lift pumps, appears to offer greater promise for the development of local manufacturing which is less demanding in its technical requirements and which is characterized by lower capital-labor ratios and lower foreign exchange content. On the basis of experience in Japan and Taiwan as well as an analysis of the nature of the supply response to the two patterns of demand, it seems clear that a unimodal strategy will have a much more favorable impact on the growth of output and especially on the growth of employment in local manufacturing and supporting service industries. The reasons cannot be pursued here except to note the wider diffusion of opportunities to develop entrepreneurial and technical skills through "learning by doing" that leads to increasing competence in manufacturing. Progress in metalworking and in the domestic manufacture of capital goods are especially significant because they are necessary to the creation of an industrial sector adapted to the factor proportions of a late developing economy.

Increasing farm productivity and output.—The differences in farm productivity between modern and traditional agriculture are, of course, to be attributed mainly to their use of widely different technologies. Those differences in turn are based on large differences in their use of fixed and working capital and associated differences in their investments in human resources that affect the level and efficiency of agricultural research and other supporting services as well as the knowledge, skills, and innovativeness of the farm population.

The importance of distinguishing between inputs and innovations that are mainly instrumental in increasing output per acre and those that make it possible for each farm worker to cultivate a larger area has already been noted. Biological and chemical innovations increase agricultural productivity mainly through increasing yields per acre. In general the effect on yield of farm mechanization *per se* is slight, although certain mechanical innovations, notably tubewells and low-lift pumps may be highly complementary to yield-increasing innovations. Indeed, for some high-yielding varieties, especially rice, an ample and reliable supply of water is a necessary precondition for realizing the genetic potential of the new varieties.

This distinction between yield-increasing and labor-saving innovations is significant because the relative emphasis given to these two types of innovations largely determines whether development of agriculture will follow a unimodal or bimodal pattern.

The thrust of a unimodal strategy is to encourage general diffusion of yield-increasing innovations and such mechanical innovations as are complementary with the new seed-fertilizer technology. The bimodal strategy emphasizes simultaneous adoption of innovations that increase substantially the amount of land which individual cultivators can efficiently work in addition to the yield-increasing innovations emphasized in the unimodal approach.

For reasons discussed above, it is not possible for developing countries to pursue the unimodal and bimodal options simultaneously. In placing emphasis on reinforcing success within a subsector of large and capital-intensive farms, a bimodal strategy may have an advantage in maximizing the rate of increase in the short run because it bypasses the problems and costs associated with involving a large fraction of the farm population in the modernization process. In a longer view, however, a unimodal strategy appears to be more efficient, especially in minimizing requirements for the scarce resources of foreign exchange and loanable funds.

Policies and programs to ensure that the seed-fertilizer revolution is exploited as widely and as fully as possible are clearly of central importance. This emphasizes the importance of adaptive research and of training and extension programs to promote further diffusion of new varieties and to narrow the gap between yields at the farm level and the potential yields obtainable. Investments in infrastructure and in land and water development required to provide environmental conditions favorable to the introduction of more productive technologies are also priority needs. . . .

The distribution of land ownership and, more particularly, the size distribution of operational units are highly important factors influencing the choice of technique and the factor proportions that characterize the expansion path of the agricultural sector. Both are influenced by policies and practices affecting land tenure which are discussed in the following section.

Achieving broadly based improvement in the welfare of the rural population.—In a longer term view substantial improvement in the welfare of the rural population depends upon the process of structural change which, inter alia, makes possible a reduction in the absolute size of the rural population, a large increase in commercial demand for farm products, and large increases in the capital-labor ratio in agriculture. There are, however, some more direct relationships between strategies for agriculture and the improvement of rural welfare that need to be considered.

Rural works programs are probably the most frequently discussed measure aimed directly at improving the welfare of the poorest segments of the farm population. There is much to be said for such programs as a means of providing supplemental employment and income to the most disadvantaged members of the rural population and at the same time building infrastructure important to agriculture and other sectors. But because of the organizational problems and particularly the severe fiscal constraints that characterize a developing country, it seems doubtful whether this approach can have a very substantial effect on underemployment and unemployment in rural areas. . . .

Other programs also merit attention because they offer the promise of substantial benefits relative to their cost, and some of them can also make a substantial contribution to the expansion of output by improving the health and productivity of the rural population. Public health programs such as malaria control are notable examples. The success of such programs is, of course, a major factor underlying the population explosion and the urgent need for policies and programs that will have both direct and indirect effects in encouraging the spread of family planning. Nutritional programs also deserve attention. The effects on well-being of increased farm productivity and incomes can be enhanced considerably if diet changes are informed by practical programs of nutrition education. Encouragement of the manufacture and distribution of products that are especially effective in meeting the needs of vulnerable categories (e.g., Vitasoy, Incaparina, and other low-cost sources of high quality protein) also offer the possibility of large returns at small cost.

Although it is foolhardy to attempt to treat the complex and controversial subject of land tenure in a few paragraphs, the positive and negative effects on rural welfare of land reform programs cannot be ignored. In Asia the land tenure situation is dominated by the fact that the area of arable land is small relative to the large and growing farm population entirely or mainly dependent on agriculture for their livelihood. One implication of this, which is distressing but beyond dispute, is that for the agricultural sector as a whole in these countries the average farm size will become even smaller—or at least that the number of agricultural workers per acre of arable land will continue to increase for several decades until a structural transformation turning point is reached.

It is sometimes argued that because of the connection between size of holding and choice of technique, redistributive land reform is a necessary condition for a unimodal strategy. Indeed it is even claimed that the success of unimodal strategies in Japan and Taiwan is attributable to their postwar land reforms, notwithstanding the fact that in both countries the basic pattern of progressive modernization of small-scale, labor-intensive, but technically progressive farm units was established long before World War II.

I am persuaded that an effectively implemented land reform program that brings about a more equal distribution of landed wealth will not only contribute to the goal of equity but will also tend to facilitate low-cost expansion of farm output based primarily on yield-increasing innovations. Although such a program would appear to be desirable, there is reason to believe that for a good many Asian countries it is not a likely outcome. It therefore seems important to emphasize that historical evidence and logic both contradict the view that in the absence of land reform the pattern of agricultural development will inevitably accentuate the problems of rural underemployment and unemployment and the inequality of income distribution.

The critical factor determining the choice of technique and factor proportions in agriculture is the size distribution of operational (management) units rather than ownership units. Past experience, for example in prewar Japan and Taiwan, demonstrates that a highly skewed pattern of land ownership is not incompatible with a unimodal size distribution of operational units. To a considerable extent the widespread condemnation of tenancy, particularly of share tenancy, seems to stem from a tendency to confuse what is really a symptom with the root cause of the miserable existence that is the plight of so many tenant households in underdeveloped countries. The fact that tenants are prepared to accept rental arrangements that leave them such a meager residual income is fundamentally a consequence of the extreme lack of alternative income-earning opportunities. The proposition, briefly stated, is that bargaining between landowners and tenants will tend to result in equilibrium arrangements with respect to the rental share, the amount of land rented to individual tenants, the cropping pattern and other farm practices, and sharing of expenses of inputs. These arrangements will tend to maximize the land owner's rental income subject to the constraint that a tenant and members of his household must obtain residual income that represents a "wage" approximately equal to his best alternative earnings or they will not enter into the agreement. To the extent that the proposition is valid, it means that improvement in the welfare of tenants must depend primarily on improving the income-earning opportunities available, including the possibility of enlarging their own holdings by redistributive land reform as well as the increase in demand for labor within and outside agriculture.

The advantages of organizing agricultural production primarily on the basis of small-scale units appropriate to the unfavorable man-land ratios that characterize the agricultural sector in late developing countries are enhanced by the new technical possibilities resulting from the seed-fertilizer revolution. Although those advantages are to a considerable extent a function of the size of operational units, there are some specific advantages of owner cultivation related to productivity considerations as well as the more obvious effects on income distribution. Although in principle, investments in land improvement that are profitable will be made by the landowner, by the tenant, or under some joint agreement, the division of responsibility in decision-making is likely to delay or prevent investments even though they would be to the advantage of both parties. Owner cultivation also avoids the difficulties that arise when landlords, responding to higher yields, raise the percentage share of output that they demand as rent. But if redistributive land reform is not a realistic possibility, widespread renting of land seems clearly preferable to the further concentration of land in large operational units and the bimodal pattern which is thereby accentuated.

Agricultural development that depends on fostering economic and technical change among the rural population, buttressed by a network of institutions and in organizing institutions and networks of communication and delivery to provide the supporting services on which a unimodal strategy depends. To the extent that developing countries have a commitment to expand education, however, such activities provide a range of opportunities for worthwhile employment of those leaving school at various educational levels. Moreover, the spread of rural education and other institutions useful in promoting the modernization of agriculture are capable of bringing many other benefits to the countryside.

Facilitating the processes of social modernization by encouraging widespread attitudinal and behavioral changes.—The spread of economic and technical change among the rural population, buttressed by a network of institutions and communication links, undoubtedly has significant effects on the process of social modernization that go beyond their effects on economic growth. It seems likely that the broad impact of a unimodal strategy would have favorable effects in three areas important to this process of social change. First, the wide diffusion of familiarity with the calculation of costs and returns and of opportunities to acquire managerial experience would appear to provide a favorable environment for the training and recruitment of entrepreneurs. The same would apply, of course, to the wider diffusion of learning experiences in manufacturing which is associated with a unimodal strategy.

Secondly, a broadly based approach to agricultural development seems likely to generate strong support for rural education as well as the institutions more directly related to promoting increased agricultural productivity. It is sometimes argued that large-scale, highly commercialized farm enterprises are easier to tax than millions of small units. Because of the power structure maintained or created by a bimodal strategy, however, the greater administrative convenience may in practice mean very little. The fact that public education, and especially rural education, in most of South America seems to lag behind progress in other developing countries where average incomes are considerably lower seems to provide some support for this generalization.

Thirdly, and most important, the reduction in birthrates in the countryside, resulting from spontaneous changes in attitudes and behavior as well as behavioral changes induced by government population programs, are likely to be more widespread and have a greater effect on the national birthrate under a unimodal than a bimodal strategy. For reasons examined earlier, the bulk of the population in the late developing countries is going to be in the agricultural sector for several decades or more. Under those circumstances rapid reduction in a country's birthrate to bring it into tolerable balance with a sharply reduced death rate cannot be achieved unless family planning spreads in the countryside as well as in towns and cities. It seems probable that reasonably rapid changes in this domain of behavior are more likely to take place if the dynamic processes of economic and technical change affect a large fraction of a rural population involved to an increasing extent in formal and informal education and communication networks (including mass media). It also seems likely that the wider spread of improved income and educational opportunities will affect motivations in ways favorable to the practice of family planning. . . .

IX.C.2. Agricultural Technology and Agrarian Structure*

One of the characteristics of the so-called "Japanese Model" is that the bulk of the nation's farmers have been involved in increases in agricultural productivity associated with the use of improved varieties, fertilizers, implements and other complementary inputs within the almost unchanged organizational framework of the existing small-scale farming system. This type of technological progress is called biological-chemical (BC for short).

The "Green Revolution" which emerged in south and southeast Asia is in essence of the same type of technological progress as it is often called a seeds-fertilizer revolution. Nevertheless, the organizational framework of the existing farming system appears to have undergone some changes. According to S. Ishikawa the pattern of response to the new high-yield varieties is not uniform to all strata of the agricultural community: the innovators have emerged from only the upper strata; capitalist-type tenant farmers have newly appeared as the innovators; the non-cultivating landlords have become cultivators, at least partly, if not fully, engaging in direct farming operations or they have been leading their tenants to adopt the new technology. It is too early to say definitely which will be the dominant pattern among these at present as the Green Revolution is still going on. It is also to be noted that there is a case where the response has emerged from almost all strata of the agricultural community. However, a question can be posed—why does the Green Revolution appear to produce such organizational changes in other Asian countries whereas in Japan the organizational framework remained virtually unchanged?

Being motivated by this question, we have been interested in a comparative survey of Japan's experience and what has been brought about by the Green Revolution. This empirical survey leads me to an analytical problem—some kind of relationship should be searched for between the type of agricultural technology and the pattern of agrarian structure. By agrarian structure I

*From Kazushi Ohkawa, *Differential Structure and Agriculture—Essays on Dualistic Growth*, Kinokuniya Bookstore Co. Ltd., Tokyo, 1972 (Economic Research Series No. 13, The Institute of Economic Research, Hitotsubashi University), pp. 277–83, 285–92. Reprinted by permission.

TABLE 1. Productivity by Size of Farm, 1964, Japan.

Unit Size	(ha)	Thousand Yen per ha Y/B	Yen per Hour Y/B	Thousand Yen per Worker K/L	Thousand Yen per ha K/B	Labor Hour per 0.1 ha L/B
(1)	Under 0.5	510	75	235	100.0	679
(2)	0.5–1.0	479	96	301	85.3	495
(3)	1.0–1.5	421	110	336	70.2	381
(4)	1.5–2.0	378	124	360	59.1	306
(5)	2.0–2.5	344	143	341	46.0	241
(6)	2.5–3.0	343	158	348	41.9	217
(7)	Over 3.0	345	200	372	34.5	163
(8)	Average	402	115	326	63.9	350

Source: *Farm-households Economy Survey*, Ministry of Agriculture and Forestry, 1964, Vol. 7, published in 1966, which classifies farm-households into several types. The source is for *Sengyo*, the farm-households excluding part-time farming. The tabulation excludes Hokkaido.

Remarks: Y = net product, B = area of cultivated land, K = fixed capital stock and L = working hour, or number of workers.

mean a combined distributive composition of the owner-tenureship of land and the size of farming operation. The problem is too big and too broad to be treated in such a small paper and here I will confine myself to the specific aspects of the problem which, I believe, are relevant to the question posed above. They are:

(1) Is it possible to identify the factors which are common to both Japan and other Asian countries with respect to the stabilized (a sort of equilibrium) relationship between the existing technology and the agrarian structure?

(2) Is it possible to understand in a systematic way the impacts of technological changes on the direction of changes in agrarian structure?

(3) What are the major factors which are responsible for the difference between Japan and other Asian countries in the response to the emergence of new technologies in agriculture?

A SIMPLE MODEL

A most simplified but useful model for approaching the aspect of the problem (1)

mentioned above is, I believe, a production function of the Cobb-Douglas type with specified behavior of producers regarding the self-evaluation of labor and land.

A number of cross-section measurements of an agricultural production function of this type give a fairly firm empirical basis, showing common features: first, the output elasticity of land is bigger than the output elasticities of labor and capital, approximating to the average relative income shares of production factors; and second, constant returns to scale is broadly revealed. The point here is that with the existing agrarian structure the pattern of agricultural production of the community as a whole can be described homogeneously by such simple relationships.

I would like to draw your attention to two major features of productivity distribution which widely prevail in agricultural production both in Japan and other countries in Asia under the operation of the functional pattern above described. First, with regard to average labor productivity, its level tends to vary with the size of farm-operation in terms of land-holding: the bigger the size the higher the level. Second, with regard to the average land productivity also we see a relationship to the farm-operation size, but the relationship is reverse. As an example, Table 1 is presented.

Regarding Y/L, average labor productivity, a remarkable difference by farm-size is seen with regular association mentioned above, whereas for Y/B, average land productivity we see a narrower range of difference. (To other terms, K/B and L/B we shall return later). The prewar data (though lacking data for K) show similar tendencies: taking the size group of 0.5–1.0 ha as 100, Y/L is 120–140, Y/B is 65–80 for the size group of over 2.0 ha for the 1922–40 period. It is to be noted that a range of Y/B difference was much wider in prewar than in postwar years.

I believe such a size-associated distribution of productivity variation is important. In order to interpret it, two inter-related assumptions are introduced: one is that the smaller the size of farms the lower the self-evaluation of labor; and the other the smaller the size of farms the higher the self-evaluation of land. These assumptions about the subjective behavior of peasants can be positively treated in terms of marginal products of labor and land. Let α, β, and γ stand for the output elasticity of labor, land and capital respectively, and suffix 1 for larger farm-size and 2 for smaller farm-size. Assuming equal output elasticities, we have

$$\frac{\partial Y_1}{\partial L_1} = \alpha \frac{Y_1}{L_1}, \frac{\partial Y_2}{\partial L_2} = \alpha \frac{Y_1}{L_1} \text{ and } \frac{\partial Y_1}{\partial L_1} > \frac{\partial Y_2}{\partial L_2} (1)$$

$$\frac{\partial Y_1}{\partial B_1} = \beta \frac{Y_1}{B_1}, \frac{\partial Y_2}{\partial B_2} = \beta \frac{Y_2}{B_2} \text{ and } \frac{\partial Y_1}{\partial B_1} < \frac{\partial Y_2}{\partial B_2} \quad (2)$$

A state of equilibrium implies (1) and (2), namely that the marginal product of labor is bigger in farm 1 than in farm 2, whereas the reverse is true for the marginal product of land. If our assumptions are all valid, this confirms that the agrarian structure contains the differentials of marginal productivities with respect to labor and land at a state of

equilibrium in the sense mentioned above. This is a kind of differential structure.

Under the operation of a single production function of the above mentioned type, we have

$$\frac{Y}{L} = A \left(\frac{B}{L}\right)^\beta \left(\frac{K}{L}\right)^\gamma \qquad (3)$$

$$\frac{Y}{B} = A \left(\frac{L}{B}\right)^\alpha \left(\frac{K}{B}\right)^\gamma . \qquad (4)$$

These present the relations between average productivities and factor intensities. By use of (3) and (4), it is intended to discuss the relation between what has been said and the role of capital. According to our assumption about the peasants' behavior, B/L must be larger in farm 1 than in farm 2 and actually an empirical endorsement is given in Table 1 in terms of L/B—the fact that a much greater labor input per unit land area prevails in farm 2. With equation (3) this can explain a lower level of average labor productivity of farm 2 even if the capital intensity, K/L, is equal between farms 1 and 2. With equation (4) likewise, the higher level of L/B of farm 2 can explain its higher level of Y/B even if the capital-land ratio, K/B, is the same as between the two farms.

In a very backward condition of agricultural production, the above simple interpretation may not be far from reality as the role of capital may be minor. As technological progress goes on its role becomes increasingly significant and productivities of both labor and land will be influenced by the inequality of both K/L and K/B as between various farm sizes. Under the assumed production function, however, the self-evaluation behavior of labor and land, with market prices of capital, will be responsible for determining K/L and K/B. If K/L is bigger in farm 1 than in farm 2, Y/L will be higher to that extent in the former. If K/B is bigger in farm 2 than in farm 1, Y/B will be higher to that extent in the former. In Table 1 we see a moderate increase of K/L as the farm-size becomes bigger whereas a sharp reverse tendency is seen with respect to K/B.

So far we have described a very simple model which can link the differential level of productivity with the structure of size distribution of farm holdings. The point is that the linked relationship is possible at a state of equilibrium, which can be identified under the operation of constant returns to scale. It seems to me that there has been some confusion in this respect. The well-known controversies with regard to possible polarization in agriculture have been mainly discussed in terms of productivity. Those in favor of polarization assert the higher labor productivity of larger farms while those against the polarization thesis assert the advantage of higher land productivity of smaller farms. It is my view that if there exist differentials of evaluating labor and land in the agricultural community (and I believe these do exist in Asian countries), the productivity differentials need not necessarily be a dynamic factor and that they can be a static phenomenon in a sort of equilibrium relationship with the existing agrarian structure. . . .

IMPACT OF TECHNOLOGICAL CHANGES

Having described a static equilibrium relationship between technology and structure, let us discuss the impact of technological changes—a dynamic process.

Since the man-land ratio is the basic factor which determines the pattern of agrarian structure, the industrialization, particularly its capacity for absorbing rural labor force cannot be ignored. Rather we can discuss industrialization as the major dynamic factor but this would need a separate treatment. In the following this will be discussed only implicitly so far as is reflected in changes in our terms used in the preceding section.

To begin with the impact on the size distribution of farm operation units, first, two types of agricultural technologies are to be distinguished: the BC type, mentioned in the Introduction and the other mechanical or engineering type (M for short). The former is neutral with respect to scale while the latter has economies of scale. These two, however, cannot function separately. Every agricultural technology is a combination of the two and accordingly it would be better to speak of the BC element and the M element. The technology which has BC elements as its core is neutral with respect to scale whereas the technology of which the core is M elements has scale economies. The nature of BC elements is clear enough but that of M elements needs clarification as their function varies. At least two different functions are to be distinguished: one is substitution for labor and the other complementary with labor. These are not necessarily always separable, but in essence the former is the case for the technology of which the core is M elements and the latter is the case for the technology of which the core is BC elements. With these qualifications, for simplicity I will use the terms BC and M technology.

The state described in the preceding section is of course characterized by BC technology and the impact of its progress should first be discussed within this framework. It goes without saying that the observable indicator of the progress is yield or output per unit area, Y/B. From the viewpoint of the characteristics of BC technology, an increase in Y/B can take place in all strata of farm-size, without discrimination. In reality, however, we cannot necessarily expect such a homogeneous case. Larger scale farmers will first be the innovators. Using notations, Y_1/B_1 increases in comparison with Y_2/B_2—as a result of an increase in K_1/B_1 as mentioned previously. Such changes can take place within the existing agrarian structure to a certain extent. The eventual impact will be found in two different cases. First, if farm 2 could follow farm 1 in implementing the new technology sooner or later, there will be no change in the agrarian structure. Second, if the increase in Y_1/B_1 could not be followed by an increase in Y_2/B_2 a change will take place in the initial framework. For example if Y_1/B_1 becomes equal to Y_2/B_2 and this relation is stabilized, the assumed properties of the original state cannot be maintained.

In the former case we can assume that the output elasticities of production factors are eventually not altered by the impact of introducing improved varieties. If we look at the process of its diffusion, it may appear to bring forth some changes in the output elasticities. But this should be understood afterall as a temporary phenomenon. What kind of changes will take place in the latter case? Answer cannot be given in general but can be illustrated by the example of the competitive relation between owner-cultivator and rentier discussed in the preceding section. If the value of the ratio of Y_2/B_2 to Y_1/B_1, the left hand side of equation (2), becomes smaller than the value of the right hand side, to be a rentier is disadvantageous to the land-owners. There will be an incentive to be owner-cultivators and the agrarian structure will change.

From the viewpoint of the production function approach, it is not possible to say definitely what kind of changes will correspond to the state illustrated above. It would be possible, however, to say that the output elasticities of production factors will eventually be altered but the production structure still retain the property of constant returns to scale. This can be conceived by assuming a situation where farm 1 and farm 2 have different output elasticities. It can be simply expressed by $\beta_1 < \beta_2$ as we should still retain the assumption that the self-evaluation of land is higher in farm 2; we have

$$\frac{\partial Y_1}{\partial B_1} < \frac{\partial Y_2}{\partial B_2} \text{ for a special case of } \frac{Y_1}{B_1} = \frac{Y_2}{B_2}.$$

Because of the lack of empirical studies, we cannot tell the actual contents of the elasticity difference by farm-size in general. I believe, however, it is meaningful to consider this case. The point is to answer the question why different technologies (defined in terms of different elasticities) can exist concur-

rently? Analytically this should be a state of equilibrium and the differentials of peasants' behavior, regarding not only self-evaluation of production factors but also elasticity of substitution etc. may be involved. In the following an answer will be given from rather an empirical point of view.

Given the pattern of agrarian structure, there are various factors which are responsible for differentials among farmers with respect to their capability of responding to new technology. These I would like to call *"differentiating factors"*. A higher level of BC technology needs an increase in complementary inputs like fertilizers, insecticides as well as for irrigation facilities etc. It goes without saying that there is great variation of financial capability to providing these supplies. Personal capabilities are also different with respect to implementing farm technology as well as commanding technological knowledge. These cannot be discussed comprehensively, but two points are particularly relevant to our discussion here.

First, the institutional aspect of the differentiating factors and second, the degree of gap between the level of new technology and the farmers' capabilities—these two inter-related aspects, characterize the patterns of impact. To begin with the former, let us take up, for example, a case where the lack of adequate credit organization is the major differentiating factor. So long as this is not reformed, the development of new technology will be limited only to the upper strata of the rural community, and no follow-up can be expected for the innovation. Such institutional *restraints* are sometimes influential and sometimes not according to the level and pattern of the initial conditions. In my view, as far as the BC technology is concerned, the major differentiating factors are restraints of this type. Japan's experience may be cited as an example of the case where such institutional restraints were not influential whereas in most of south and southeast Asia such restraints are influential. Coming back to the question posed before, my answer is that the co-existence of different technologies is possible if the institutional restraints continue to exist with the impact of new BC technology.

The degree of gap between the level of new technology and the farmers' capability involves various factors, all of which cannot be discussed here. What I would like to draw particular attention to is the thesis of borrowed technology in the context of economic backwardness. When technology is introduced from advanced countries exogenously to an economically backward country, its level is high relative to the general capabilities of the people. This is true also in agriculture. Where the pattern of agrarian structure is differential in that the level of capability has a wide range of variance, naturally the differentiating factor will operate much more strongly.

This is most relevant to the present process of Green Revolution in south and southeast Asia, whereas in Japan BC technology has been developed, so to speak "endogenously" and its new level was not far beyond the capability of the mass of peasants.[1]

[1] In the Japanese literature on the prewar agrarian structure the following arguments are often found. (1) A tendency of bi-polarization of agrarian structure in terms of operating farm size took place in Meiji Era: *tezukuri-jinushi*, landlords-*cum*-cultivators had expanded. (2) "Parasitic" landlords took the place of landlords-*cum*-cultivators towards the beginning of this century. (3) Medium-scale farmers increased while both large-scale and small-scale farmers decreased in both their absolute number and relative weights, during the twenties and thirties.

My own view is as follows. The statistical data upon which (1) depends are not reliable enough to confirm the tendency of bi-polarization although the landlords undoubtedly were innovators. (2) and (3) can be explained basically by a tendency of $Y_2/B_2 > Y_1/B_1$ due to the progress of BC technology although the changes in agrarian structure were not so remarkable as has been argued. By international comparison, therefore, we can say broadly that the organizational framework of prewar agriculture had remained almost unchanged in Japan.

Now let us proceed to the discussion of M technology. In the Philippines, Pakistan, India and perhaps other countries, large-scale farming with mechanization has recently developed with impacts of new technology of the BC type. In prewar Japan no such phenomenon took place. It goes without saying that what has been said above with regard to the differentiating factors should be applied to the case of M technology much more strongly. Distortion of factor prices by government aid policy, it is said, furthermore has been aggravating the operation of the differentiating powers. At any rate we see distinctly a co-existence of different levels of M technology in the agriculturally backward countries.

From the standpoint of strategy of agricultural development, desirability of large scale mechanization is a controversial issue. I have no intention here to join the policy debate. Two points are relevant to the present discussion. One is that mechanization in itself is the most distinct differentiating factor because of its associated economies of scale, and the other is that both in postwar Japan and in other Asian countries a leveling-up of yield or output per unit area appears to be an indispensable condition for mechanization on the part of larger scale farms.

The first point is almost self-evident. Even in the case of small-scale mechanization which took place widely in postwar Japanese agriculture, measurements of the production function give results which suggest a tendency of increasing returns to scale. I believe that large-scale mechanization in other Asian agriculture undoubtedly has scale economies, together with labor-substituting effects at least in the first instance. How about its impact on the agrarian structure? In answering this question, let us recall its initial pattern which we described in the preceding section—a state of no economies of scale. Surely the agrarian structure will change in favor of larger scale farming. The discussion of the second point, mentioned above, will reveal its features more.

The degree of difference of output per unit area between farm 1 and farm 2, to use our terminology, has been described as the crucial indicator in the case of BC technology. This is understandable as it is originally of the land-saving type. An interesting fact is that in comparing prewar and postwar Japanese agriculture, the range of difference has been narrowed to a considerable extent. This took place with the progress of mechanization. . . .

How about the eventual result of the impact of technological progress of this type? This is a most difficult question to answer at present. However, in a longer-run perspective the following two points can be stated to be most relevant to the answer.

First, the mechanization for the sake of labor-substitution, as distinguished from the complementary use of machines with labor input, will face a certain limit of its expansion sooner or later. It is true that the price of machines at present is much lower as compared with the prewar Japanese case. But on the other hand, in most of the south and southeast Asian regions wage rates will continue to be low. Therefore, the relative factor prices will discourage the labor-replacement requirement—a fact which differs from the postwar Japanese agriculture, whose mechanization has developed for the sake of replacing labor because of the higher wages caused by the rapid industrialization.

Second, the expansion or contraction of large-scale farming based on M technology will depend much on the future performance of land productivity, output per unit area of land, of small-scale farms, which, in turn, will depend heavily upon the possibility of reforms of the existing differentiating factors of institutional-organizational nature. If these reforms will succeed in leveling up of land productivity of small-scale farms by accelerating the diffusion of BC technology, as has been explained earlier, this will discourage the expansion of large-scale farming by mechanization.[2]

[2] This statement assumes that the seed-fertilizer technology and mechanization are essentially separable in a technical sense.

IX.C.3. Relation Between Land Reform and Development*

Professional economists neglect the subject of land reform, because it concerns the institutional framework of society, which economic analysis accepts as given. The study of change in economic institutions, it is assumed, can be left to the historian. Yet, as we have seen, the historical approach can tell us only about the experience of advanced

*From Doreen Warriner, *Land Reform and Economic Development*, National Bank of Egypt Fiftieth Anniversary Commemoration Lectures, Cairo, 1955, Lecture II. [Corrected version reprinted in Carl Eicher and Lawrence Witt (eds.), *Agriculture In Economic Development*, McGraw-Hill Book Co., New York, 1964, pp. 280–90.] Reprinted by permission.

countries: it does not serve as a guide for the countries that are now commonly described as underdeveloped. If we are to consider the effects of land reform on agricultural production, investment and employment, in these countries, we must attempt to use the methods of economic analysis. These methods include the theory of competition and monopoly, the theory of the firm, and the theory of investment.

The economist's approach is valuable, because it forces us to define the assumptions underlying any general argument for or against land reform. Most of the economic arguments commonly used against land reform are really political arguments in disguise. There is, for example, the argument that land reform will lead to a fall in production. In Egypt, this argument has been proved false by experience; economic analysis can show the conditions in which it does not apply even in theory. If we use the methods of economic analysis, and are careful to define our assumptions, we can perhaps show that there is a positive relation between reform and development, in the conditions of "under-developed countries." ...

To a very great extent—to the extent of 90% perhaps—under-development is coterminous with overpopulation, for Asia dominates the whole picture. However, this conceptual definition does not quite fit with the descriptive definition, which includes some regions in Africa and Latin America which are not at present overpopulated. For these countries, we require another conception, that of unbalanced or lop-sided development. We may use the two situations defined by Professor Nurkse: the vicious circle and the lop-sided economy. Both are conceptions of capital shortage. In the first, no net capital formation is occurring, in the second, net capital formation occurs principally in one branch of the economy, leaving the rest primitive and backward. (The countries of the Fertile Crescent, with their modern and highly efficient oil industry and their primitive agriculture, are an obvious example of the second situation.) ...

We have to ask what land reform can do for these villages which take up such an enormous percentage of the world's population.

We must be clear that we are generalising about the land systems of three vast continents. There is great variety in institutions, in types of farming and natural conditions, and it is dangerous to generalise too broadly.

Each country has a land system peculiar to itself, though it is not so peculiar as it is believed to be. At first sight we seem to be confronted by sheer multiplicity. In fact, there is much more uniformity than appears at first sight. If we compare the different forms of land tenure, three distinct patterns emerge, and we can say that from the standpoint of economic analysis there are really three distinct problems of reform. We can leave out some land systems altogether as irrelevant to our subject—the peasant systems, in which land ownership is more or less equally distributed, and communal tenure systems, in which the land is communally owned (mainly prevalent in Africa). These may need other types of reform—reforms of the agrarian structure—but they do not need redistribution of ownership. We can concentrate on the land systems in which the large estate is the predominant form of tenure.

We must, however, distinguish sharply between the different types of large estate. One of the great difficulties in the study of this subject is that we have no accepted vocabulary. Much confusion arises from lack of precise terminology. "Large estate" itself is an ambiguous term, referring to at least three different forms of tenure and three different types of economic organisation. The three types are:

1. The type of ownership characteristic of Asian countries, in which the land holding is only a property and not a large farm or large producing unit. The property is leased in small units to tenant cultivators, either on the basis of money rent or on a basis of share-cropping rents.

2. The large estate, characteristic of South European countries and of Latin America, which is both a large property and a large enterprise. This type of estate is managed by salaried officials and worked by labourers and people of indeterminate status, squatters or share-croppers. Estates of this kind are usually extensively cultivated, or used as cattle ranges. We may call them latifundia, since this is the term used in the countries where they prevail; they are the direct descendants of the slave-tilled ranches of the Roman Empire.

3. Plantation estates. These are also both large properties and large enterprises. They are usually owned by a company with for-

eign capital and foreign management, though estates of a plantation type may also be found in private ownership. The methods of cultivation are usually intensive.

Many countries have agrarian structures which include estates of two or even three of these types. The land system of Egypt in certain features resembles the Asian form of ownership, while in other features it is a plantation system.

These forms of ownership and enterprise have very little in common with the types of large-scale farming found in advanced countries, i.e. in countries with an industrialised economy and commercialised agriculture. The Asian system is found principally in subsistence economies, while latifundia and plantations produce mainly for export.

From the standpoint of economic analysis, the most obvious feature of all these types of ownership is the existence of an institutional monopoly. In Asian countries, where demographic pressure is high, the level of rents is determined not by the fertility of the land, but by the fertility of human beings. Land is a scarce factor of production, and would command a high price in terms of its produce, whatever the system of land tenure. The existence of institutional monopoly allows the landowner to raise rents to a still higher level. In latifundian systems and in plantation systems, the estate owner is a monopoly buyer of labour, controlling the use of land rather than its price, and he uses his monopoly power to keep wages low.

The main economic argument for land reform is the need for securing a more equal distribution of income by eliminating these monopoly elements. In the first case the aim is to reduce the price for the use of land, i.e. a reduction in rents, and in the second case, the aim is to subdivide big holdings and secure a fuller use of land, an increased demand for labour, and higher wages for the farm worker.

But, it may be objected, will not this redistribution of ownership reduce productivity by dividing up efficient large estates? If we wish to use this argument, we must consider in what sense these estates are to be regarded as efficient. The theory of the firm is always difficult to apply in agriculture, and as far as the under-developed countries are concerned, it seems to have very limited application.

The argument that the division of large agricultural enterprises will cause a decline in productivity is true on two assumptions: (1) that there is competition between the factors of production and (2) that there are economies of large scale production. These assumptions are generally valid in industrialised countries. In England, for example, a large farm has generally become large because it is a more efficient producer, i.e. it produces at lower costs; it can compete more effectively for the factors of production and combine them more efficiently, using more capital and using it more fully; it can also use more efficient management and more specialised labour. In such conditions there is a presumption that the size of farms is more or less adjusted to an optimum scale of output for certain types of farming. This optimum scale of output is difficult to define precisely, and in practice means the minimum area needed to utilise power-driven machinery. In Sweden and France, for example, agricultural economists are now much concerned with the problem of farm sizes, because farms in the smaller size groups are not large enough to use modern technical methods, and the farming structure is not so well adjusted to technical advance as it was 50 years ago. Even in advanced countries, therefore, there may be institutional factors which prevent adjustment to larger scale production. But the conception of an optimum scale of output is always valid, simply because capital equipment plays a large part in farming.

When we try to apply this argument about the scale of production to the under-developed countries, we shall find that over a very wide range of conditions it has no validity at all. In Asian land systems, large estates are not large producing units. Land reform in such systems simply means the transfer of ownership from the landowner to the cultivator of the existing small holding. The size of the farm is not affected, for there are no large farms. When the Governments of India and Pakistan speak of "uneconomic farms," they mean farms which fall below a subsistence minimum, not below a technical optimum. Nor does the argument about efficient large estates apply generally to latifundian systems. The haciendas in Mexico and many of the latifundia in Southern Italy were not efficient large estates on any standard. They wasted both land and labour.

So generally speaking, the argument about "efficient large estates" does not seem to apply to the first type or the second type of estates which we have distinguished. It does seem to apply to plantation estates which use intensive methods of cultivation and modern methods. Every plantation system is a special case. Where there is reason to believe that sub-division of the estate would lead to a decline in production, then the monopoly effect on labour must be tackled by a policy for raising wages, and taxing profits to secure reinvestment in other types of farming producing for local needs. Or the estate may be divided with safeguards for maintaining efficiency, as under the Egyptian Land Reform.

I have examined this argument at some length because it serves to illustrate the danger of using the methods of economic analysis without making explicit the assumptions on which the analysis is based. The assumptions of competition and economies of large scale production which are valid in advanced countries are generally not valid in relation to the land systems of the under-developed countries, simply because capital plays so small a part in production.

Several other arguments used against land reform are false because they are based on projections of conditions in advanced countries, and do not take these basic differences into account. One argument frequently encountered in international discussions is that because tenancy works very well in England

there can be no reason for Asian countries to abolish tenancy by redistribution of ownership: what they need is legislation to improve the security of tenure for tenants. This argument overlooks the monopoly influence in Asian countries. It is true that tenancy works well in England, because the conditions of tenancy are regulated by law, and also because land is only one of the many forms of holding wealth. If a landowner attempts to take too high a rent, the tenant will prefer to invest his capital in other ways. But in Asian conditions tenancy laws will never suffice to counteract the effects of monopoly ownership.

Another argument of this kind is that there is no need for expropriation by compulsion. This argument runs as follows: "If governments wish to encourage ownership, they can do this by giving tenants special credit facilities enabling them to buy their holdings. In Switzerland (or Denmark or Sweden) the land system has evolved itself by gradual adjustment to modern conditions, and Asian countries should therefore adjust their systems gradually, without drastic legislation to expropriate owners of land." The logical fallacy in this argument is obvious. In advanced countries, an improvement in the economic position of agriculture will enable the tenant to buy his land, and special credit facilities can encourage the acquisition of ownership. In the United States, the proportion of ownership to tenancy rises when agriculture is prosperous, and special legislation aids farm purchase. In European countries, particularly in Scandinavia, governments have helped tenants to become owners by giving them easy credit terms. But in Asian countries, the market price of land is too high in terms of what it produces to allow the tenant to purchase his land. If agriculture becomes more prosperous, either as a result of higher prices or better harvests, the share-cropping tenant will not be able to buy his holding, because the landlord benefits equally from the increased income, and the tenant's position in relation to the landlord has not improved. There is no price which the tenant can afford to pay which the landlord will be willing to accept. If the tenant is to acquire ownership, the price of land must be fixed at a level which he can pay, and this will inevitably be much lower than the market value of the land. All land reforms involve expropriation to some extent for this reason.

In economic terms, there can be no ground for paying compensation at all, since the existing prices of land are monopoly prices. The price that is actually fixed in reform legislation is determined by political bargaining power.

We can conclude therefore that the existence of institutional monopoly creates a strong argument for land reform on the ground of equalizing incomes. We can conclude that in Asian systems and in latifundian systems the redistribution of ownership will not have adverse effects on production through the division of efficient large units, though in plantation systems sub-division may have bad effects, and other ways of equalizing incomes may have to be used.

These arguments, however, tell us nothing about the positive effects of reform on development. They are negative arguments which show it will not do harm. If we are to consider the effects on economic development, this is not enough, and it is the investment aspect that must be considered.

The general economic argument for land reform as distinct from the social argument for more equality is that these systems of ownership give rise to large incomes which are not reinvested in production. They give rise also to social attitudes inimical to investment. Landowners spend conspicuously; buy more land; or invest in urban house property; or lend at extortionate rates of interest to cultivators for non-productive purposes. This argument applies with great force to Asian tenancy systems and to latifundian systems. It does not apply generally to plantation systems. These may have bad social consequences, but whatever their defects may be, failure to invest productively is not one of them, or not generally one. (There

are exceptions where plantations keep land out of cultivation, and these systems cause trouble.)

In general, the land systems of Asia and Latin America are strong deterrents to investment and aggravate the shortage of capital by draining capital from agriculture. They undervalue the future. The landowners' preference for land as a form of holding wealth can be explained simply as a result of the secure and high return on capital which results from institutional monopoly; there is no need to introduce the Keynesian liquidity preference analysis.

The crucial question is whether land reform—the change to small ownership—will give better results in the future. Can it promote more investment? . . .

All we can say as to the investment effect is that results depend mainly on what can be done to give inducements to invest, through special credit facilities and special forms of village organisation. We cannot say that reform will *cause* more investment: but we can certainly say that it is a condition, for without more income in the hands of the cultivator, no investment programme for agriculture is likely to have much effect.

Can we say anything about the production effects of reform, when there is actually sub-division of the land?

Here too we can only say that results will depend on how far the new owners can intensify farming, either by the use of more labour on the land, or by the use of more labour and more capital. . . .

It would be possible to carry the investment argument very much further. We might regard these three types of land system as the institutional framework for the typical development models set up by Professor Nurkse, the vicious circle situation and the lop-sided economy.

Asian tenancy systems, in certain conditions, though not universally, might be regarded as a determinant of the vicious circle situation. The *zamindari* system in India seems to have been such a determinant. This system was instituted by Lord Cornwallis, at the end of the eighteenth century, in an attempted imitation of the English landlord system. It conferred rights of ownership on tax collectors, the *zamindars*, and under the permanent settlements, fixed the tax on land in cash in perpetuity. As population and production increased, the zamindars could increase their demand for rent from the cultivators, but the state could not increase its demand for revenue. Monopoly ownership, low taxation and a high propensity to consume, add up to a vicious circle condition. Asian tenure system need not have this effect, if the state practices a policy of financing development from land revenues obtained through a stiff tax policy, as it did in Japan.

In Latin American countries, the latifundian system promotes lop-sided development. The great inequality of incomes prevents the expansion of the internal demand for food, while the great inequality in farm sizes prevents an expansion of supply of

food for the home market. So far as investment takes place in agriculture, it is concentrated in the branches producing for export. Many examples might be quoted of the distortions in the land use pattern reflecting this one-sided development, as for example in Venezuela where fertile land round the capital is used for cattle grazing, while food for the city is grown on remote small holdings.

If these situations are to be changed, then clearly the institutional framework of society must be changed also. Of course, institutional change will not reverse the course of development and repair the damage done in the past through the loss of capital. It can only be the first step towards breaking the circle or getting a more balanced development. But it is, in such conditions, an essential first step. We can therefore conclude that land reform, in the conditions of many under-developed countries, is certainly a condition of development.

IX.C.4. Agricultural Strategy and Rural Income Distribution*

Of the alternative agricultural policies, land redistribution is the most likely to attain increased equity along with increased production. However, due to political constraints it is frequently the least likely policy to be carried out. Nevertheless, land redistribution deserves particular attention because

*From William R. Cline, "Interrelationships Between Agricultural Strategy and Rural Income Distribution," *Food Research Institute Studies in Agricultural Economics, Trade, and Development*, Vol. 11, No. 1, 1972, pp. 143–7, 155–6. Reprinted by permission.

of its potential for joint increase in output and equity.

THEORY

Land redistribution away from large landowners toward family, cooperative, or state farms for former tenants, workers, unemployed laborers, and farmers with minuscule plots, has been cited as a policy which can increase production through the general effect of increasing incentive of the operator to use the land. The conventional emphasis is on the lack of utilization by large traditional owners holding land primarily for prestige (most frequently cited for the Latin American case), and on the incentive distortions of tenancy due to share-cropping arrangements or lack of long-term investment horizons associated with uncertain tenancy. Concerning income distribution, land redistribution should tend to equalize rural income over time since land is the principal factor of agricultural production; furthermore, the less compensation paid to expropriated landowners, the more immediate and radical is the redistribution of rural wealth.

The two principal issues that affect land reform's impact on production are whether economies of large-scale production exist, and whether land utilization does in fact decline as farm size (in area) rises. If there are increasing returns to scale, fragmenting large producing units will lower output, and even installing small units on formerly unused land will create a structure unable to attain efficient production. The primary reason to expect possible scale economies would be the argument that minimum areas are required to utilize certain farm machines (such as tractors and self-propelled combines). However, in a labor surplus context these machines are not likely to be profitable at appropriate capital, exchange rate, and product prices, and *a fortiori* are not likely to be socially profitable if labor is shadow-priced. Even if they are profitable, these machines can in principle be supplied on a custom service basis, so that their availability need not depend on farm size. In short, the agricultural economies of scale argument warrants little weight in the context of the developing countries.

In contrast, there are several reasons to expect land utilization to decline as farm size rises, in addition to the "prestige" and "incentive" factors already mentioned. First, there exists a "labor market dualism" between small family-labor farms and large hired-labor farms analogous to the dualism between the traditional and modern sectors in the established "surplus labor" theories.

The large capitalist farms pay the institutional wage, and equate labor's marginal product to it. Small family farms utilize their available stock of labor in combination with their limited amount of land to the point where the marginal utility of product equals the marginal disutility of effort. However, this small-farm equilibrium results in a marginal product of labor below the institutional wage and therefore below the marginal product of labor on large farms. This disequilibrium between the two sectoral marginal products results in part from physical friction (i.e., the infeasibility of sending wage supplement from the family to the out-hired member) and in part from the general rigidities which prevent sectoral marginal product equalization between the "traditional" sector and the "modern" sector in the economy at large (primarily, the unwillingness to work for a wage below an institutionally accepted minimum despite the fact that to do so could somewhat enlarge the total family income, so long as marginal product of the family-leaver fell short of any outside wage whatsoever).

Lower marginal product of labor on small family farms means greater utilization of land: for a given profile of Ricardian declining fertility of land, a larger percentage of land would be brought into cultivation on a unit prepared to accept a lower marginal product of labor working with that land. In sum, the labor market dualism consideration would predict poorer utilization of land by large capitalist farms than by small family farms.

A second explanation for declining land use by farm size is the tendency among larger owners to hold land as a portfolio asset rather than a production input, thereby obtaining prospective capital gains (or at least maintenance of real asset value) without incurring additional current expenses and risk by making outlays for labor and capital costs of production. This phenomenon seems to be particularly important in certain Latin American countries with prolonged inflationary experience. Further reasons to expect land use to decline with increasing farm size include imperfection in the land market, not only in the form of greater availability of credit to large buyers, but also the fact that, for constant quality of land, unit price is lower in large block transactions; the possible effect of oligopsony in a region dominated by a few large landlords who affect the regional wage by their activities and therefore attain a below-competitive production and land-use equilibrium; and the fact that small farms produce in part for their own consumption and are therefore less exposed to market risk than larger farms.

The one major counter-explanation of declining land-use intensity is the argument that larger farms tend to have lower quality land, in terms of fertility and location.

EMPIRICAL EVIDENCE

Two types of information exist for hypothesized effects of land redistribution on output and income equity: *ex ante* data on agrarian structure and *ex post* historical data for countries which have carried out redistribution. For Latin America, there is a large consensus of interpretation of the *ex ante* data, to the effect that the observed pattern of high output per total farm area on small farms, low output per total farm area on large estates, and underutilization of labor crowded onto minuscule plots or merely unemployed, suggests a substantial potential for increased production as well as increased employment through land redistribution. Data on agrarian structure in India show a similar pattern of lower production per available area on larger farms, implying potential output gains from land redistribution (4).

My own empirical tests using data for approximately 1,000 farms in Brazil indicated: (1) returns to scale for inputs used are constant: the sum of factor elasticities does not differ significantly from unity, based on production function estimates; (2) land utilization (on alternative measures) declines significantly as farm size rises even when the influence of land quality is removed by inclusion in regression models of land price as a proxy for quality; (3) if present land and other input use patterns relating to farm size, and present production functions, were to prevail after land redistribution to a family farm structure, farm output would increase a predicted 20 to 25 percent under a "total redistribution," or 5 percent under a conservative prediction exempting intermediate size farms and farms with below average land price from redistribution; both calculations understate output gains by ruling out product shifts due to a lack of information on land quality (1, pp. 78, 130–31, 165).

The historical or *ex post* empirical evidence is more cloudy. The principal problem is one of separating temporary disruption phenomena from long-run structural effects. Poor data availability, particularly with regard to total production as opposed to marketed production, further complicates analysis of *ex post* cases. For the Mexican case, Dovring has indicated that revised historical data dispute earlier data showing lower production in 1925–29 than before the 1910 revolution (3, p. 265). In any case, declining or stagnant production could have been expected given the uncertainty generated by lack of definition of the agrarian reform prior to the vigorous land redistribution activities of the Cardenas regime in the 1930s. Furthermore, the subsequent relative stagnation of the *ejido* sector and dynamism of the new private sector cannot be accepted as evidence against land reform's production effects. The new dynamism itself required the land reform's pressures for land utilization (for example, farm-size ceilings) as its precondition; most of the new resources of irrigated land and credit have been channeled to the private sector (5, p. 12); and the *ejido* sector uses labor-intensive techniques that are probably more appropriate on a shadow-price basis than the capital intensive techniques of the dynamic private sector (3, p. 273).

Doreen Warriner describes land reform experience in the Middle East in terms of the overriding importance of irrigation and the need for administrative structures to preserve its availability, attended to by large landlords prior to reform. Egypt, with very great land scarcity, was not characterized by unused land on large farms prior to reform; a good public administration did manage to maintain production after reform, although increases in productivity could not be attributed to land redistribution but to other measures. Iraq, with better production effect potential in view of land-use patterns, suffered worse results due to a long period of uncertainty, while Iran maintained productivity and reached a fourth of the rural population with a quick and decisive implementation of land reform (6).

The postwar reform in Japan turned tenants into owners, and rapid inflation virtually eliminated the real value of their repayment burden and landlords' compensation. Subsequent agricultural growth was dynamic, but it is difficult to analyze the extent to which growth through increased use of fertilizers and new varieties would have taken place even in the absence of any incentive efforts of the structural reform (2).

While it is far beyond the scope of this discussion to reach verdicts about the historical evidence on land reform's production effect, it is justifiable to conclude that the wide diversity of historical experience shows the importance of: (1) the incidence of underutilized land prior to reform, (2) the speed and degree of certainty with which reform is implemented, and (3) the degree to which credit and modern inputs are made available to the reform's beneficiaries. Therefore, the evidence suggests that with appropriate policy in the latter two dimensions, the expected output gains based on *ex ante* data can be realized.

A final caveat on the income distributional impact of land redistribution is required. To the extent that programs are implemented on a limited basis, with land made available to an elite minority of farmers or even former urban residents, the policy ceases to be a significant instrument for improving equity. . . .

The principal conclusions of this study are the following: (1) In the absence of specific policy measures to improve rural income distribution, it will tend to remain skewed or to grow more concentrated, due to labor force expansion in the face of improved seed-output gains concentrated on large farms and farm mechanization stimulated by artificially low capital prices. (2) Land redistribution is the policy most likely to bring both production gains and improved equity. Empirical studies indicate that potential output and employment increases through land redistribution are particularly large in Latin America. (3) Although varietal improvements are highly desirable, they may have a negative income distributional impact in the face of unitary or lower price elasticity of demand. (4) Farm mechanization with tractors or combines should be avoided except where it can be demonstrated that mechanization will raise output rather than merely replace labor; the available evidence suggests these instances will be rare. Estimates for rice in southern Brazil indicate negligible net effects of mechanization on yield per hectare. Even where output would be increased by mechanization by the breaking of timing bottlenecks, allowing increased cropping intensity, the extra output evaluated at social prices would have to be sufficient to exceed investment evaluated with high capital and foreign exchange shadow-prices, to justify a mechanization program. Efforts should be made to achieve improvements in implements used in bullock technology. (5) Experiments with rural family budget data for Brazil and Mexico suggest that the channeling of output gains to the low income rural families would not involve major sacrifice of potential savings.

The principal policy implications are that governments truly seeking rural equity should look to land redistribution as a principal means to this end; they should terminate current price distortions favoring mechanization; they should make farm machines available to small farmers on a custom service basis when and if mechanization is found economically desirable at social prices; they should increase levels and enforcement of land and rural income taxation; and channel credit toward the poorer farmers. The policy implications for external lending agencies are: (1) leverage should be exercised to induce income equalizing policies that would otherwise be rejected due to political structures in recipient countries; (2) past flirtations with loans for agricultural mechanization should be discontinued until strong evidence on its economic desirability is found; and (3) sample surveys examining agricultural techniques, and surveys permitting the development of reliable data on income distribution, deserve special attention for financing.

References

1. W. R. Cline, *Economic Consequences of a Land Reform in Brazil* (Amsterdam, 1970).
2. R. P. Dore, *Land Reform in Japan* (London, 1959).
3. Folke Dovring, "Land Reform and Productivity in Mexico," *Land Econ.*, Aug. 1970.
4. Morton Paglin, " 'Surplus' Agricultural Labor and Development: Facts and Theories," *Amer. Econ. Rev.*, Sept. 1965.
5. Leopoldo Solis, "Mexican Economic Policy in the Post-War Period: The Views of Mexican Economists," *Amer. Econ. Rev.*, June 1971 (supp.).
6. Doreen Warriner, "Employment and Income Aspects of Recent Agrarian Reforms in the Middle East," *Intl. Labour Rev.* (Geneva), June 1970.

IX.C.5. Technological Change in Agriculture and Employment*

Our consideration of employment has been of the factors limiting agricultural incomes and the provision of more opportunities for productive, remunerative employment in the agricultural sectors of developing countries. The question of how much involuntary unemployment there may be in traditional agriculture has been set aside, largely because when involuntary agricultural unemployment is properly defined (and defined in such a way as to be comparable with involuntary industrial unemployment) it becomes almost impossible to measure. . . .

*From Montague Yudelman et al., *Technological Change in Agriculture and Employment*, OECD Development Center, Employment Series No. 4, Paris, 1971, pp. 161–8. Reprinted by permission.

Conditions of both supply and demand can limit agricultural incomes and the provision of employment opportunities. Among the conditions of supply, the following appear to be the most important: (i) at an aggregate level, a highly inelastic supply of at least one resource which complements labour in agricultural production, along with an insignificant substitutability between labour and the scarce resources at a given level of technology; (ii) a tendency for part of the agricultural labour force to be undernourished; (iii) the seasonal nature of agricultural production; and (iv) the pattern of ownership of the scarce agricultural resources and the associated institutional structure of farming.

Technological change (or an innovation) is considered to involve the substitution of a new and relative abundant resource for a scarce conventional resource. Consequently, it can be, in principle, an appropriate means of inducing agricultural growth. A full judgement as to the appropriateness of a particular change in technology, however, must also have regard to all of the factors limiting agricultural employment and determining the distribution of income. A particular change must be considered within the context of, for example, the initial institutional structure.

If a technological change is to promote productive employment and income generation within as many as possible of households currently within agriculture, it would appear that the innovation itself and all agricultural institutions governing its diffusion must be such as to allow smallholders to adopt the innovation as readily as neighbouring large landowners. It is postulated that the adoption of an innovation by an individual entrepreneur depends on the profitability of the innovation, the entrepreneur's awareness of the way in which it would change his production, his ability to finance it, and his aversion to risk. Thus, if the postulate is valid, the size pattern of farm holdings, tenurial arrangements, credit facilities, channels of communication, and the technical divisibility of new inputs are all relevant to an examination of technological change. In view of these factors, it is clear that not all farm households are able to adopt any innovation simultaneously. There is, instead, a gradual diffusion of an innovation throughout a region.

It is an essential part of an unregulated market economy that successful technological change among those firms first to innovate encourages other firms to follow suit and forces them out of business if they do not. In most developing countries, if smallholders cannot quickly be made as well able to innovate as large landowners, a large proportion of agricultural householders are likely to be left entrapped in greater relative poverty than was their lot to begin with.

Land-augmenting technological changes are clearly appropriate, at an aggregate level, in densely populated countries. However, they may not be neutral with respect to scale of enterprise, although they are commonly highly divisible. In other words, the spread of even the land-augmenting innovations and the realisation of their benefits may be confined by institutional factors to only relatively large "commercial" landowners. A decline in output prices resulting from even the limited spread of technological change can be expected to further impoverish many smallholders or to force them to dispose of their holdings. Any such tendency as a result of land-augmenting technological change is much greater in the case of mechanization, especially large-scale mechanization. Some form of mechanization may be appropriate. The point is, though, that there are often several financial and social factors which make it privately rational for farmers to undertake large-scale mechanization that is inappropriate from an aggregate (or social) point of view. Perhaps one of the most important factors is the managerial and technical difficulty of employing a large labour force; as the scale of enterprise increases, the total non-wage cost of employing the labour force required in the absence of mechanization may increase at a greater rate.

In the absence of change in agricultural institutions, the ultimate effect of non-selective mechanization plus land-augmenting technological change is likely to be, in most developing countries, a replication of the pattern of evolution shown by Western agriculture. That would create, however, a group of entrapped or disenfranchised households numerically and proportionately much larger than has been seen anywhere in the West.

The most relevant pre-emptive institutional changes are thought to be the following: (i) land reform; and (ii) the formation of cooperatives (the details of which would vary from one society to another) to administer credit, marketing, the dissemination of technical knowledge and, in some cases, the sharing of large-scale equipment between smallholders.

There is good reason to expect that a structure of small-holdings (grouped to some extent into cooperatives) assures a greater level of welfare for the majority of agricultural households than the alternative which would be a structure that involved a relatively small group of highly mechanized but highly productive and highly-taxed farms; the obverse aspect of the structure would need to be an administrative transfer of tax revenue to a large number of unemployed. However, this alternative, at least, must be considered to be anathema to genuine development.

We have examined the *ex post* effects of the two different kinds of technological changes (land-augmenting and labour-replacing) on the demand for labour at the farm level. This examination has been based on a limited number of sample surveys. The nature of the samples, the problems inherent in an analysis of this kind and the differences in conditions in the regions concerned can make any generalization of results misleading. The surveys indicated that in the cases considered, land-augmenting technological changes *increased* labour requirements by around 30% and that large-scale mechanization tended to *reduce* labour requirements by between 17% and 27% depending on the case examined. Two case studies were examined to indicate what might happen if a particular operation were to be mechanized. In both instances it appears that selective mechanization, which is short of complete mechanization, would add to output without unduly displacing farm labour. In the same vein we have considered the possible gains from selective mechanization—compared with full mechanization—in reducing the seasonal labour shortage that is anticipated in parts of India

when and if land augmenting inputs are more widely used than at present. It appears that there are advantages in selective mechanization at least from the point of view of increasing output per man without having the labour displacing effect of complete mechanization. . . .

Technological change involves the introduction of new or improved inputs in the process of production. These new inputs can be classified into reproducible and manufactured inputs according to industrial origin. The origin of both kinds of new inputs is in research and product development. Research and development on new or improved reproducible inputs for producing basic staples tends to be a public sector activity. In contrast, research and product development of modern manufactured inputs such as agro-chemicals and tractors tends to be a private sector activity.

The great bulk of public sector research on reproducible inputs is undertaken in the developed countries; since the developed countries are in the temperate zones and public sector expenditures have to be linked to the national interest this has precluded work on products that are grown exclusively in the tropics. There is thus little product-specific technology to be transferred. Research and product development, supported by the public sector, has also been undertaken in the developed countries on staples that are grown in both temperate and tropical climates. The new inputs evolved, though, have to be adapted if their full potential is to be realizable in locations other than that in which the basic research was undertaken. The process of adaptation has to be in the agro-climatic environment of the importing country. Thus complementary research is an important factor in the transfer, from developed to developing country, of the technology embodied in reproducible inputs. This entails public sector support. However, low levels of public sector support and difficulties in research management militate against the successful transfer of this technology. Fortunately these obstacles have been overcome—in part—by the creation of international research centres.

Modern, manufactured inputs used by farmers are usually end products of research and product development undertaken by large-scale corporations. (The manufacture of items such as tractors and agro-chemicals tends to be capital intensive and subject to economies of large-scale operations.) The corporations in question are profit-conscious and so are concerned about the market potential of their new products. The largest markets for modern inputs (including divisible inputs) are in the farm areas of the developed countries. As is to be expected, the emphasis in research and product development is on products that are attractive to farmers in these areas, that is, products that can be used effectively in labour-scarce temperate zone agriculture on commercial farms. Very often these same products are the new inputs used by farmers in developing countries in which they may not be fully appropriate, given the local economic, social and climatic conditions. From the manufacturers' point of view, the costs of developing location or product specific inputs, or of adapting existing inputs, may not warrant the investment in these inputs that would be required because the size of the market for them is too small. This depends, though, on the profit perspective of the manufacturers who may have a "safe" market in developed countries.

INFERENCES FOR POLICY

This final section deals with some of the possible inferences for policies on technological change and the demand for labour at the farm level in surplus economies. We would like to emphasize, though, that these suggestions be read in the light of the following *caveats*:

a) Governments have their own preferences in regard to objectives and instruments of policy and these may relate to social and economic criteria different from those we have taken as desirable in this study.

b) Our conclusions are based on limited data and we have focused on one problem among many: policies need to be related to implications in the context of the economy as a whole.

c) Even if our focus were a great deal wider than it is, good policies would be those tailored for particular situations: almost any general policy conclusion is found to be wrong in a great many situations.

With these *caveats* in mind we suggest the following:

The adoption of land-augmenting technologies tends to increase the demand for labour at the farm level. Given the size of the employment problem facing most countries, there would appear to be a strong case for improvement and the extension of such technologies. Extensions and improvements originate in research activities. In particular it would appear desirable that research on improving reproducible inputs and techniques of production be oriented toward technical objectives that increase the demand for labour. Illustrations of such objectives might include:

a) The development of varieties that, *ceteris paribus*, would permit labour intensive, multiple cropping and reduce seasonal conflicts in the demand for labour (without necessarily resorting to mechanization). For example, a shortened growing period could allow the growing of three crops of rice in many areas where only two now grow; characteristics that permit a greater staggering of timing of planting could lead to an increase in demand for labour without simultaneously creating seasonal conflicts in labour utilization and thus a constraint on output.

b) Much of the land-augmenting technology has been confined to varieties that flourish when properly irrigated. The diffusion of this technology with its subsequent increase in the demand for labour will depend, in part, on the expansion of irrigation and more effective use of existing supplies of water. (And so the effective use of water is necessarily a subject for increased research.) However, most farmers in developing countries are engaged in non-irrigated or dry land farming. There is thus a need for greater research efforts into yield-increasing technologies in "dry land" areas if there is to be an increase in demand for farm labour in these regions. . . .

The most important manufactured inputs used by farmers are of two kinds— "mechanized" and "agro-chemical". Agro-chemicals tend to be part of the land-augmenting technology, while large scale mechanization tends to be labour-saving or displacing. Most of these inputs originate in the private sector in developed countries and are intended, primarily, for use in those countries.

To increase the demand for labour at the farm level it is likely that:

a) Machine technology appropriate to small scale farm conditions needs special promotional effort. Some experience with sophisticated small scale equipment, however, also suggests that simplicity in maintenance and operation is important. The specific task needs are for machinery which reduces seasonal bottlenecks in the demand for labour;

b) Similarly existing types of agro-chemical inputs, notably pesticides, represent a technology that is often directly transferred from developed to developing countries. They may not be as effective as would be location and product specific alternatives.

The specification of what constitutes an appropriate technology, given the circumstances prevailing in a country, is presumably a task for scientists, agronomists,

engineers and economists. There is plenty of scope here for inter-disciplinary approaches. The identification of particular needs will require field research and the widest forms of co-operation among both national and international institutions. . . .

The demand for labour at the farm level is influenced by economic policies that favour one form of technological change over another. Such policies include those that relate to factor prices and to the allocation of foreign exchange for imports (when there is a foreign exchange constraint). When economic policies effectively increase the price of a relatively abundant factor, such as labour, and effectively lower the price of a relatively scarce factor, such as capital, then profit oriented producers will be encouraged to substitute capital for labour. Capital inputs in agriculture include large-scale mechanization which substitutes for labour (and animal draft power). There is no doubt that the scope for substituting capital for labour in agriculture is extremely important so that policies in this area really do matter. Consequently:

a) policies that result in lowering costs of large-scale mechanization to producers should be discouraged. These policies include duty-free imports, special subsidies on fuel and subsidized credit to purchase equipment;

b) when it is considered desirable to encourage selective mechanization to ameliorate seasonal shortages of labour then it may be necessary to discriminate in favour of certain types of equipment. This can be done through tax exemptions and, possibly, subsidies;

c) when there is a scarcity of foreign exchange the allocation of foreign exchange for the importation of agricultural inputs may have important consequences for the demand for labour. The use of scarce foreign exchange to make available large-scale mechanization may well reduce the demand for labour at the farm level. Aid donors' policies are important here and have not always, in the past, taken sufficient account of repercussions on the labour market.

The demand for labour at the farm level is influenced by the rate of diffusion of innovations. This depends in good measure on the awareness of the possibilities of introducing technological change, profitability of innovating and the availability of inputs. The rapid diffusion of innovations that increase the demand for labour may well require:

a) price and other policies that minimize the risks of adopting the new technology. Price stability would appear to be important in this respect; in addition risks can be reduced by the availability of crop insurance and adequate market facilities, as well as by a distribution system that increases the availability of inputs when and as they are needed;

b) as a general rule the operation of agencies intended to provide goods and services to promote and facilitate appropriate technological changes tends to be biased against small-scale, low-income producers. Where such biases do exist it may be necessary to create and provide adequate staff and finance for special agencies whose function is to assist those producers who are unable to take advantage of existing services. In addition, as small-scale producers tend to have a greater aversion to risk than do larger-scale producers, it may be important to provide special incentives for this group of producers to use yield-increasing and labour-intensive inputs. These incentives might well include subsidization of inputs that are part of the yield-increasing technology.

The operation of market forces usually tend to work to the advantage of innovators who are primarily the larger, commercially-oriented farmers. With a higher rate of adoption of innovations the more "progressive" farmers would tend to absorb the less pro-

gressive. But large-scale farming based on hired labour and profit maximization may well lead to lower levels of labour utilization than if the same land were to be in individual holdings in which producers sought to maximize output. With the emergence of large-scale, capital-intensive farming there will also be a worsening of income distribution in agriculture and the increased impoverishment of large numbers of producers, associated with the displacement of labour with at best only very meagre alternative sources of employment. An appropriate system of taxation might be effective in diminishing the worsening of income distribution and the absorption of small holdings by larger land holders. Where such systems cannot be made effective, more drastic alternatives may become necessary, for example an upper limit on the size of holding per farm family. It should be emphasized that land reform, while it can provide a breathing space, is not a long term solution where land is scarce and population is increasing rapidly. But nor, in these circumstances, is any acceptable solution likely to emerge through the operation of free market forces...

In brief, the inferences for policy outlined above include considerations of the most appropriate forms of technology, the institutions that support agriculture, and land reform. Where there is conflict between increasing output or increasing labour utilization in agriculture, this may pose a difficult choice for policy makers. In addition the financial costs of increasing employment in agriculture may be higher than concentrating on increasing output without regard to numbers employed. Nevertheless given the limited alternatives for labour, it is our conviction that governments must consider the issue of labour utilization *pari passu* with increasing output in agriculture. The real costs of following policies that lead to an increase in unemployed or underemployed rural labour and an entrapped, backward subsector may be beyond economic calculation.

IX.C.6. Employment Generation in

African Agriculture*

Since there is a marked heterogeneity of natural and human resource endowments within and between African nations, the causes of, and solutions to, unemployment problems will vary widely from nation to nation and from one period to another. Also, an analysis of unemployment in agriculture must go beyond an analysis of agricultural policies and include economic and social policies and the policies of external donors. For these reasons, we have summarized in Table 1 the major policies—economic, social, and agricultural—which affect unemployment and underemployment in African agriculture and migration from agriculture to urban areas.

Two points stand out in Table 1. First a range of poor policies—economic, social, and agricultural—can contribute in a major way to unemployment and underemployment. Second, approaches to planning, such as the *ad hoc* project approach and maximum growth rate plans, often sidestep unemployment problems. A third point, not included in Table 1, is the crucial role of enlightened political leadership in aggressively supporting rural development and employment generation in agriculture. Improved agricultural policies, improved policy coordination, and improved approaches to planning will be to no avail if political leaders lay down a monolithic strategy of development through import substitution industrialization which is financed by supplier credits and surpluses from farmers.

The reader should note that Table 1 contains a list of general economic and social

*From Carl Eicher et al., "Employment Generation in African Agriculture," Michigan State University, Institute of International Agriculture, Research Report No. 9, July 1970, pp. 18–20, 37–41. Reprinted by permission.

policies. In this section we shall focus on agricultural policies which directly or indirectly exacerbate unemployment or inhibit employment generation in agriculture. We shall then demonstrate how improved agricultural policies—in combination with improved economic and social policies, improved policy coordination, and improved approaches to planning—are key steps which African nations can take to develop an efficient and consistent strategy for agricultural expansion and employment generation.

In contrast to Latin America and Asia, Africa does not have major land tenure problems which require public action and land reforms. Africa's land tenure system of smallholder production is remarkably capable of absorbing labor, provided incentives are available at the farm level.

Some of the major causes of unemployment in agriculture in African countries are linked to poor agricultural policies. These policies are summarized as follows.

1. Subsidized (big) tractor mechanization
2. Anti-export agricultural policies
3. Self-sufficient food policies which may raise consumer prices and induce higher minimum statutory wage rates
4. Overemphasis on direct government production schemes which are capital intensive—(a) state farms, (b) land settlements, (c) irrigation
5. Lack of national R and D policies and programs which are geared to the factor endowments of the nation. . .

Rising unemployment in Africa is a major social, political, and economic problem. A convergence of forces, including the population explosion, has led to rising rates of unemployment which are expected to increase in the 1970's. Only a modest percent of the increase in population will be able to

TABLE 1. Some Causes of Unemployment and Underemployment in African Agriculture and Migration from Agriculture.

Types of Policies and Approaches to Planning Pursued by African Governments				Policies of External Donors
General Economic Policies	Social Policies	Agricultural Policies	Approaches to Planning	
1. "Industrial fundamentalism" of the 1960's	1. Colonial legacy of developing capital cities	1. Subsidized tractor mechanization	1. Overemphasis on comprehensive plans under comprehensive uncertainty	1. Emphasis on projects rather than *assisting* in developing consistent economic policies for the agricultural sector
2. Minimum wage legislation and social service benefits which are extended to plantations and estates	2. Unbalanced educational expansion	2. Anti-export policies	2. Overemphasis on single target—high growth rate plans	2. Trade barriers to LDC exports
3. Capital investment allowances for adopting capital-intensive technology in processing and in farming	3. Urban bias in social services	3. Self-sufficiency food policies which may raise consumer prices and induce higher minimum statutory wage rates	3. Overemphasis on project approach and on financial rather than economic returns	3. Tied aid—e.g. tractors
4. Fiscal policies which tax agricultural exports and increase the gap between rural incomes	4. Educational curriculum oriented to modern urban industrial careers	4. Lack of attention to key role of producer incentives	4. Lack of attention to agricultural sector planning	4. Token emphasis on financing local cost components—especially labor—of projects
5. Import substitution industrialization which often raises the price of farm inputs	5. "Wait and see" attitude to family planning	5. Overemphasis on government direct production schemes which are capital intensive a) irrigation b) state farms c) land settlements	5. High level manpower requirements computed to meet the needs of urban/industrial sector	5. Token support for local research on technology appropriate to local factor endowments
6. Statutory wage rates which raise the price of manual laborer above the real cost to society of employing him	6. Political and ethnic barriers to the development of a national labor market	6. Lack of national R & D systems which are development-oriented and geared to the factor endowments of the nation		6. Emphasis on single target—high growth rates (Pearson report 6% target for 1970's)
	7. Housing subsidies in urban areas			7. Token support for development of farm management research and experimental types of farm organizations—nucleus plantations, cooperatives

find jobs in Africa's urban centers. There is now a consensus of opinion among researchers that over the next 10 to 15 years solutions to employment generation in Africa will have to be found to a large degree in the agricultural sector. However, with the exception of a few countries such as Tanzania, the Ivory Coast, and recently Nigeria, African political leaders have not made an all out commitment to employment generation in agriculture. Likewise, most African political leaders have adopted a "wait and see" attitude to checking the population growth rate through family planning as they perceive there are few short-term political gains from launching a family planning program.

The decision to reduce the size of the labor force in the late 1980's must be taken today as the size of the labor force for the next 15 years (1970–1985) is already determined by living children. For these reasons family planning policy should be considered as an integral part of a nation's long-run strategy for coping with employment problems.

A consensus has now been reached by researchers on the following common causes of unemployment in African economies.

1) population explosion
2) factor price distortions
3) rising labor productivity
4) increasing gap between rural and urban incomes
5) urban bias in the provision of social services
6) unbalanced educational expansion
7) tied aid
8) political and ethnic barriers to internal and external migration
9) ecological constraints

Approaches to planning such as high growth rate (GDP) plans and the *ad hoc* project-by-project approach often sidestep the employment problem. Project selection criteria should be expanded so as to come to grips with employment generation. Present techniques of investment analysis contain a built-in urban bias because they usually do not include as a social cost the differential complement of urban amenities involved in creating employment in urban as compared with rural areas.

We have pointed out that Africa's smallholders land tenure system is remarkably labor-absorptive provided incentives are available at the farm level. Even though there is not a clearly identified land market in many countries, there is substantial evidence of land tenure bottlenecks "yielding" when sufficient incentives are available at the farm level. For these reasons we contend that there is little need in most African countries—as contrasted with many countries in Latin America and Asia—for direct government action to modify land tenure systems in order to make them more labor-absorptive.

Unemployment in agriculture and premature rural to urban migration in many African countries has been abetted by poor and inconsistent government agricultural policies. Policies which have inhibited employment generation in African agriculture include:

a) subsidized tractor mechanization
b) anti-export agricultural policies
c) self-sufficient food policies which raise consumer prices and induce higher minimum statutory wage rates
d) overemphasis on government direct production schemes which are capital intensive. Such schemes include large-scale irrigation, state farms, and land settlements.

One of the major findings of this paper is that poor and inconsistent government policies are major barriers to employment expansion in African agriculture. A summary of these poor policies—agricultural, social, and economic—is found in Table 1.

Attempts by African governments to use direct public sector investments to expand agricultural output and employment have generally met with disaster. There is little reason to expect much improvement in the 1970's. Directly productive government investment schemes such as large-scale irrigation, land settlements, state farms, and youth brigades will likely be ineffective in efficiently generating employment. They may, in fact, have adverse effects on employment. The big government schemes may utilize mechanical technology which will replace labor.

The key to employment generation in African agriculture in the 1970's lies mainly in the selective use of *indirect* measures such as improved and better coordinated internal policies—economic, agricultural, and social—and improved and better coordinated policies of external donors.

Even though improved policies—economic, agricultural, and social—are fundamental in designing an efficient strategy for employment generation in agriculture, we find that relatively few African nations are pursuing an efficient set of policies and strategies for developing their agriculture. Most African countries do not have political leadership firmly committed to seeking significant employment generation in agriculture. An efficient strategy for agricultural development and employment generation most likely will not be forthcoming unless there is high-level political support. A drastic reorientation of the political leadership is required in many African countries to recognize that the relative emphasis in planning in the 1970's should shift from urban/industrial to rural development and from a "wait and see attitude" to family planning to expanded demographic research, pilot family planning programs and the introduction or expansion of nationwide family planning programs when it is politically and administratively feasible.

Agricultural planning in many African countries is a mechanical exercise which includes public sector projects to expand agricultural output, and the mere listing of a string of investment projects for possible funding by external donors. Only modest attention is usually paid to interrelating economic, social and agricultural policies to facilitate the expansion of smallholder production which has been the "dynamic" of African agricultural development. Implementation of agricultural projects is spotty and the manpower, recurrent and capital budgets are usually not integrated.

The above shortcomings in agricultural planning are partially a result of the difficulties in planning for agriculture under conditions which Stolper describes as "comprehensive uncertainty" and partially the result of token research on agricultural policy and micro-level problems. Only a few countries have amassed sufficient studies of payoffs on agricultural investments to begin to assemble a reasonably efficient agricultural sector strategy. Nigeria is among the few African countries which—after ten years of agricultural economics research—can proceed to develop an efficient agricultural strategy which is supported by facts. Most African countries therefore require substantial high-level assistance in agricultural policy research and micro-level rural development research during the 1970's so they can develop improved agricultural strategies as the decade progresses. Also, African nations need to step up substantially project appraisal training courses in Africa.

African countries are "locked into" the use of technology—particularly mechanical technology—from developed countries. This "technology trap" makes it virtually impossible to develop mechanical technology appropriate to the labor surplus conditions in African agriculture for the following reasons. First, almost all—95 percent—of the world's R and D expenditures originate in developed countries. Second, this technology is invariably developed to solve problems in developed countries and is inappropriate to the factor endowments in African countries. Third, although much of this technology is inappropriate it is exported to developing countries under "tied aid arrangements." Fourth, much of the mechanical technology which LDCs import under tied aid agreements is "subsidized" by African governments. The combination of the above four factors produce a "technology trap" and leads to a pessimistic outlook for African countries in developing the technology—

particularly mechanical technology—which is appropriate to its factor endowments.

If the above steps are taken to develop improved policies and if improved approaches to planning are introduced, a number of African countries can begin to develop a more efficient strategy for their agricultural development. If a more efficient strategy for agriculture is developed and implemented, we contend that substantial employment generation can take place in smallholder agriculture which will reduce the need for special government employment generation programs. However, the government has a major role to play in promoting pilot rural development schemes, expanding R and D which is relevant to local factor endowments, providing subsidies for new inputs for limited periods of time, experimenting with new types of farm organizations, and aggressively searching for new markets in Africa and overseas.

IX. SELECT BIBLIOGRAPHY

1. A major study of agricultural problems and development is Bruce F. Johnston and Peter Kilby, *Agriculture and Structural Transformation*, New York, 1975. Other general studies are: J. W. Mellor, *Economics of Agricultural Development*, revised ed., Ithaca, 1974; T. W. Schultz, *Transforming Traditional Agriculture*, New Haven, 1964; ____, *Economic Growth and Agriculture*, New York, 1968; C. K. Eicher and L. W. Witt (eds.), *Agriculture in Economic Development*, New York, 1964; H. M. Southworth and B. F. Johnston (eds.), *Agricultural Development and Economic Growth*, Ithaca, 1967; Clifton R. Wharton (ed.), *Subsistence Agriculture and Economic Development*, Chicago, 1969; Y. Hayami and V. W. Ruttan, *Agricultural Development: An International Perspective*, Baltimore, 1971; E. Boserup, *Conditions of Agricultural Growth*, Chicago, 1965; IBRD sector policy paper on *Rural Development*, Washington, D.C., February 1975; Nurul Islam (ed.), *Agricultural Policy in Developing Countries*, New York, 1974.

2. On the need for land reform in connection with the development of agriculture, see United Nations, *Land Reform: Defects in Agrarian Structure as Obstacles to Economic Development*, New York, 1951; D. Warriner, *Land Reform and Development in the Middle East*, London, 1957; ____, *Land Reform in Principle and Practice*, London, 1969; D. Felix, "Agrarian Reform and Industrial Growth," *IDR*, October 1960; K. H. Parsons (ed.), *Land Tenure*, Madison, 1951; P. M. Raup, "The Contribution of Land Reforms to Economic Development," *EDCC*, October 1963; Anthony Y. C. Koo, *The Role of Land Reform in Economic Development—A Case Study of Taiwan*, New York, 1968; Philip Raup, "Land Reform and Economic Development," in H. M. Southworth and B. F. Johnston (eds.), *Agricultural Development and Economic Growth*, Ithaca, 1967; Dale Adams, "The Economics of Land Reform: Comment," *Food Research Institute Studies*, 1973; B. S. Minhas, "Rural Poverty, Land Redistribution and Development Strategy: Facts and Policy," *Indian Economic Review*, 1970; Peter Dorner, *Land Reform and Economic Development*, London, 1972; R. Albert Berry, "Land Reform and Agricultural Income Distribution," *Pakistan Development Review*, Spring 1971.

3. Studies of the Green Revolution are T. T. Poleman and D. K. Freebairn (eds.), *Food, Population, and Employment: The Impact of the Green Revolution*, New York, 1973; Keith Griffin, *The Political Economy of Agrarian Change*, Cambridge, 1975; Clive Bell, "The Acquisition of Agricultural Technology," *JDS*, October 1972; B. F. Johnston and J. Cownie, "The Seed-Fertilizer Revolution and Labor Force Absorption," *AER*, September 1969; B. F. Johnston and Peter Kilby, *Agriculture and Structural Transformation*, New York, 1975.

4. The following consider more specialized topics relating to agricultural development: J. W. Mellor, "The Process of Agricultural Development in Low-Income Countries," *Journal of Farm Economics*, August 1962; W. H. Nicholls, "Investment in Agriculture in Underdeveloped Countries," *AER*, May 1955; ____, "Industrialization, Factor Markets, and Agricultural Development," *JPE*, August 1961; ____, "An 'Agricultural Surplus' as a Factor in Economic Development," *JPE*, February 1963; B. F. Johnston and S. T. Nielsen, "Agricultural and Structural Transformation in a Developing Economy," *EDCC*, April 1966; ____, and G. S. Tolley, "Strategy for Agriculture in Development," *Journal*

of Farm Economics, May 1965; W. Owen, "The Double Squeeze on Agriculture," *AER*, March 1966; M. June Flanders, "Agriculture versus Industry in Development Policy: The Planner's Dilemma Re-examined," *JDS*, April 1969; Michael Lipton, "The Theory of the Optimising Peasant," *JDS*, April 1968; D. L. W. Anker, "Rural Development Problems and Strategies," *ILR*, December 1973.

An excellent survey article is B. F. Johnston, "Agriculture and Structural Transformation in Developing Countries: A Survey of Research," *JEL*, June 1970.

5. Some country studies are: S. M. Makings, *Agricultural Problems of Developing Countries in Africa*, London, 1968; John C. de Wilde et al., *Experiences with Agricultural Development in Tropical Africa*, Vols. 1 and 2, Baltimore, 1967; Montague Yudelman, *Africans on the Land*, Cambridge, 1964; René Dumont, *False Start in Africa*, second ed., New York, 1969; I. G. Stewart (ed.), *African Primary Products*, Edinburgh, 1965; G. K. Helleiner, *Peasant Agriculture, Government, and Economic Growth in Nigeria*, Homewood, 1966; "Agricultural Development and Planning in the Caribbean," Special Number of *Social and Economic Studies*, September 1968; United Nations, ECLA, "Agriculture in Latin America: Problems and Prospects," *Economic Bulletin for Latin America*, October 1963; W. P. Falcon, "Agricultural and Industrial Interrelationships in West Pakistan," *Journal of Farm Economics*, December 1967; J. W. Mellor et al., *Developing Rural India*, Ithaca, 1968.

The Japanese case has been examined in great detail. Some important studies (that include extensive references to other literature on Japanese agricultural development) are: B. F. Johnston, "Agriculture and Economic Development: The Relevance of the Japanese Experience," *Food Research Institute Studies*, Vol. 6, 1966; W. W. Lockwood (ed.), *The State and Economic Enterprise in Japan*, Princeton, 1965, Chaps. 2, 6; Saburo Yamada, "Changes in Output and in Conventional and Nonconventional Inputs in Japanese Agriculture Since 1880," *Food Research Institute Studies*, Vol. 7, 1967; Lawrence Klein and Kazushi Ohkawa (eds.), *Economic Growth: The Japanese Experience Since the Meiji Era*, Homewood, 1968, Part I; K. Ohkawa and B. F. Johnston, "The Transferability of the Japanese Pattern of Modernizing Traditional Agriculture," in E. Thorbecke (ed.), *The Role of Agriculture in Economic Development*, New York, 1969; K. Ohkawa, *Differential Structure and Agriculture: Essays on Dualistic Growth*, Tokyo, 1972; M. Akino and Y. Hayami, "Agricultural Growth in Japan, 1880–1965," *QJE*, August 1974.

CHAPTER X

Industrialization Strategy

While the initial development plans of LDCs emphasized programs of deliberate industrialization, the role of industrialization is now being reappraised. Instead of industrialization via import substitution, which involved an output mix and choice of techniques that conflicted with other development objectives, there is now the advocacy of a simpler, more appropriate type of industrialization. As Streeten states,

The disenchantment with industrialization in recent writings and speeches has been based on a confusion: it is a disenchantment with the form that economic growth had taken in some developing countries and with the distribution of its benefits. . . . After a reorientation of goals, industrialization as the servant of development regains its proper place in the strategy. Industry should produce the simple producer and consumer goods required by the people, the majority of whom live in the countryside; hoes and simple power tillers and bicycles, not air conditioners and expensive cars and equipment for luxury flats. . . .

In simple mass consumption goods, often produced in a labour-intensive, capital saving way, the developing countries have a comparative advantage and could expand their trade among themselves. But all this depends upon countries opting for a style of development that gives priority to satisfying the simple needs of the large number of poor people. Industries producing clothing, food, furniture, simple household goods, electronics, buses and electric fans would thrive without the need for heavy protection in a society that had adopted this style of industrialization and development. Much of the recent criticism of inefficient, high-cost industrialization behind high walls of protection and quantitative restrictions should be directed at the types of product and of technique which cater for a highly unequal income distribution and reflect entrenched vested interests. It is in no way a criticism of industrialization for the needs of the people.[1]

The future of industrialization lies in a shift from industrialization via import substitution to a different pattern of domestic output and industrialization via export substitution. As a corollary of this shift, the old dispute about whether to give priority to industry or agriculture is not a real issue. The question instead is how to achieve concurrently both agricultural and industrial development.

Section X.A indicates that industrialization offers substantial dynamic benefits that are important for changing the traditional structure of the less developed economy, and the advocacy of industrialization may be particularly compelling for primary export countries that confront problems of a lagging export demand while having to provide employment for a rapidly increasing labor force. Systematic support is given to the industrialization argument in Rosenstein-Rodan's emphasis on the external economies to be realized through industrialization, and his advocacy of a "big push" in the form of a high minimum amount of industrial investment in order to jump over the economic obstacles to development. Although the "balanced growth" doctrine is sometimes related to the big push theory, we should note that the principle of balanced growth is not a necessary component of the big push theory, and balanced growth need not be dependent upon a large amount of public investment or dominance of the public sector.

Section X.B also summarizes the present status of the much-discussed "balanced growth" versus "unbalanced growth" approaches to investment. By emphasizing that investment decisions are mutually reinforcing and that overall supply "creates its own demand," the balanced growth doctrine has considerable appeal as a means of initiating development. Critics of the doctrine, however, argue that a poor country does not have the capacity to attain balanced investment over a wide range of industries and that, moreover, the method of balanced growth cannot bring about as high a rate of development as can unbalanced growth. Instead of striving for balanced investment, proponents of unbalanced growth advocate the creation of strategic imbalances that will set up stimuli and pressures which are needed to induce investment decisions. As expressed by Hirschman, for instance, "our aim must be to keep *alive* rather than eliminate the disequilibria of which profits and losses are symptoms in a competitive economy. If the economy is to be kept moving ahead, the task of development policy is to maintain tensions, disproportions, and disequilibria."[2]

According to this view, the central task of a development strategy is to overcome the lack of decision-taking in the economy; for this purpose, unbalanced growth is necessary to induce investment decisions and thereby economize on the less developed economy's principal scarce resource, namely, genuine decision-making.

It has now become clear that the phrases "balanced growth" and "unbalanced growth" initially caught on too readily and that each approach has been overdrawn. After much reconsideration, each approach has become so highly qualified that the controversy is now essentially barren. Instead of seeking to generalize either approach, we should more appropriately look to the conditions under which each can claim some validity. It may be concluded that while a newly developing country should aim at balance as an investment criterion, this objective will be attained only by initially following in most cases a policy

---

[1] Paul Streeten, "Industrialization in a Unified Development Strategy," *World Development*, January 1975, p. 3.

[2] Albert O. Hirschman, *The Strategy of Economic Development*, New Haven, 1958, p. 66.

of unbalanced investment. In operational terms, the crucial question has become how to determine what is the proper sequence of investment decisions in order to create the right amount of imbalance in the right activities.

Much of the industrialization effort in LDCs has been founded on a strategy of industrialization by import substitution, and the Note in X.B.1 appraises the special arguments for import-substituting industrialization. It will be of interest to consider in the next chapter what have been the actual results of the policy of industrialization by import substitution. The other selections in section X.B indicate additional lessons of recent history. Finally, section X.C traces the evolution toward current demands for industrialization via the export of manufactures.

X.A. PATHS TO INDUSTRIALIZATION

X.A.1. The Theory of the "Big Push"*

An institutional framework different from the present one is clearly necessary for the successful carrying out of industrialisation in international depressed areas. In what follows arguments are submitted tending to show why the whole of the industry to be created is to be treated and planned like one huge firm or trust.

The first task of industrialisation is to provide for training and "skilling" of labour which is to transform Eastern European peasants into full-time or part-time industrial workers. The automatism of *laissez-faire* never worked properly in that field. It broke down because it is not profitable for a private entrepreneur to invest in training labour. There are no mortgages on workers—an entrepreneur who invests in training workers may lose capital if these workers contract with another firm. Although not a good investment for a private firm, it is the best investment for the State. It is also a good investment for the bulk of industries to be created when taken as a whole, although it may represent irrecoverable costs for a smaller unit. It constitutes an important instance of the Pigovian divergence between "private and social marginal net product" where the latter is greater than the former. Training facilities (including transport and housing) of one million workers per annum would involve costs of certainly more than

£100 million per annum—a sum which may be too great to be borne by the State (or the Eastern European national economy) if taken *apart* from the costs of the 50% participation in its own "Eastern European Industrial Trust" that we shall propose. It should be counted as capital investment in the Eastern European Industrial Trust (E.E.I.T.).

That is not, however, the most important reason in favour of such a large investment unit.

Complementarity of different industries provides the most important set of arguments in favor of a large-scale planned industrialisation. In order to illustrate the issues involved, let us adopt the somewhat roundabout method of analysing two examples. Let us assume that 20,000 unemployed workers in Eastern and South-Eastern Europe are taken from the land and put into a large shoe factory. They receive wages substantially higher than their previous meagre income *in natura*. It would be impossible to put them into industry at their previous income standard, because they need more foodstuffs than they had in their agrarian semi-unemployed existence, because these foodstuffs have to be transported to towns, and because the workers have to pay for housing accommodation. If these workers spent all their wages on shoes, a market for the products of their enterprise would arise representing an expansion which does not disturb the pre-existing market, and 90% of the problem (assuming 10% profit) would be solved. The trouble is that the workers will not spend all their wages on shoes. If, instead, one million unemployed workers were taken from the land and put, not into one industry, but into a whole series of indus-

*From Paul N. Rosenstein-Rodan, "Problems of Industrialization of Eastern and South-Eastern Europe," *Economic Journal*, June–September 1943, pp. 204–7; "Notes on the Theory of the 'Big Push,'" in Howard S. Ellis (ed.), *Economic Development for Latin America*, Macmillan and Co. Ltd., London; St. Martin's Press, New York, 1961, pp. 57–8, 60–62, 65–6. Reprinted by permission.

tries which produce the bulk of the goods on which the workers would spend their wages, what was not true in the case of one shoe factory would become true in the case of a whole system of industries: it would create its own additional market, thus realising an expansion of world output with the minimum disturbance of the world markets. The industries producing the bulk of the wage goods can therefore be said to be complementary. The planned creation of such a complementary system reduces the risk of not being able to sell, and, since risk can be considered as cost, it reduces costs. It is in this sense a special case of "external economies."

It may be added that, while in the highly developed and rich countries with their more variegated needs it is difficult to assess the prospective demand of the population, it is not as difficult to foresee on what the formerly unemployed workers would spend their wages in regions where a low standard of living obtains.

Two other types of "external economies" will arise when a system of different industries is created. First, the strictly Marshallian economies external to a firm within a growing industry. The same applies, however (secondly), to economies external to one industry due to the growth of other industries. It is usually tactily assumed that the divergence between the "private and social marginal net product" is not very considerable. This assumption may be too optimistic even in the case of a crystallised mature competitive economy. It is certainly not true in the case of fundamental structural changes in the international depressed areas. External economies may there be of the same order of magnitude as profits which appear on the profit and loss account of the enterprise.

The existing institutions of international and national investment do not take advantage of external economies. There is no incentive within their framework for many investments which are profitable in terms of "social marginal net product," but do not appear profitable in terms of "private mar-

ginal net product." The main driving-force of investment is the profit expectation of an individual entrepreneur which is based on experience of the past. Experience of the past is partly irrelevant, however, where the whole economic structure of a region is to be changed. An individual entrepreneur's knowledge of the market is bound to be insufficient in this case because he cannot have all the data that would be available to the planning board of an E.E.I.T. His subjective risk estimate is bound to be considerably higher than the objective risk. If the industrialisation of international depressed areas were to rely entirely on the normal incentive of private entrepreneurs, the process would not only be very much slower, the rate of investment smaller and (consequently) the national income lower, but the whole economic structure of the region would be different. Investment would be distributed in different proportions between different industries, the final equilibrium would be below the optimum which a large E.E.I.T. could achieve. In the international capital market the existing institutions are mostly used to invest in, or to grant credit to, single enterprises. It might easily happen that any one enterprise would not be profitable enough to guarantee payment of sufficient interest or dividends out of its own profits. But the creation of such an enterprise, e.g., production of electric power, may create new investment opportunities and profits elsewhere, e.g., in an electrical equipment industry. If we create a sufficiently large investment unit by including all the new industries of the region, external economies will become internal profits out of which dividends may be paid easily.

Professor Allyn Young's celebrated example elucidates our problem. He assumed that a Tube line was to be built in a district and that an accurate estimate was made of costs and receipts. It was found that the rate of profit would be below the usual rate of yield on investments obtainable elsewhere. The project was found not profitable and was abandoned. Another enterprising company bought up the land and houses along the proposed Tube line and was then able to build the line. Although the receipts from the passenger traffic would not pay a sufficient rate of profit, the capital appreciation on the houses and land more than made up the deficiency. Thus the project was realised, the Tube line was built. The problem is: Is it desirable—*i.e.*, does it lend to an optimum allocation of resources and maximisation of national income—that this form of capital gain (external economy) be included as an item in the calculus of profitability, or is it not? Allyn Young hints that it is not desirable because the capital appreciation of houses and land along the Tube line due to an influx of people from other districts has an uncompensated counterpart in a capital depreciation of houses and land in districts out of which people moved into the Tube-line district. Agricultural land in Eastern and South-Eastern Europe will, however, not depreciate when the agrarian excess of population moves out. In this case external economies should be included in the calculus of profitability.

* * *

"There is a minimum level of resources that must be devoted to . . . a development program if it is to have any chance of success. Launching a country into self-sustaining growth is a little like getting an airplane off the ground. There is a critical ground speed which must be passed before the craft can become airborne. . . ."[1] Proceeding "bit by bit" will not add up in its effects to the sum total of the single bits. A minimum quantum of investment is a necessary, though not sufficient, condition of success. This, in a nutshell, is the contention of the theory of the big push.

This theory seems to contradict the conclusions of the traditional static equilibrium theory and to reverse its famous motto *na-*

tura non facit saltum. It does so for three reasons. First, it is based on a set of more realistic assumptions of certain indivisibilities and "nonappropriabilities" in the production functions even on the level of static equilibrium theory. These indivisibilities give rise to increasing returns and to technological external economies. Second, in dealing with problems of growth this theory examines the path towards equilibrium, not the conditions at a point of equilibrium only. At a point of static equilibrium net investment is zero. The theory of growth is very largely a theory of investment. Moreover, the allocation of investment—unlike the allocation of given stocks of consumer goods (equilibrium of consumption), or of producers' goods (equilibrium of production)—necessarily occurs in an imperfect market, that is, a market on which prices do not signal all the information required for an optimum solution.[2] Given an imperfect investment market, pecuniary external economies have the same effect in the theory of growth as technological external economies. They are a cause of a possible divergence between the private and the social marginal net product. Since pecuniary, unlike technological, external economies are all-pervading and frequent, the price mechanism does not necessarily put the economy on an optimum path. Therefore, additional signalling devices apart from market prices are required. Many economists, including the author, believe that these additional signals can be provided by programming. Third, in addition to the risk phenomena and imperfections characterizing the investment equilibrium, markets in under-developed countries are even more imperfect than in developed countries. The price mechanism in such imperfect markets does not provide the signals which guide a perfectly competitive economy towards an optimum position. . . .

---

[1] Massachusetts Institute of Technology, Center for International Studies, *The Objectives of United States Economic Assistance Programs,* Washington, D.C., 1957, p. 70.

[2] See P. N. Rosenstein-Rodan, "Programming in Theory and in Italian Practice," in Massachusetts Institute of Technology, Center for International Studies, *Investment Criteria and Economic Growth,* Cambridge, Mass., 1955.

Indivisibilities of inputs, processes, or outputs give rise to increasing returns, that is, economies of scale, and may require a high optimum size of a firm. This is not a very important obstacle to development since with some exceptions (for instance in Central America) there is usually sufficient demand, even in small, poor countries, for at least one optimum scale firm in many industries. There may be room, however, only for one or a few firms with the obvious danger of monopolistic markets.

As Allyn Young pointed out, increasing returns accrue to a firm not only with the growth of its size but also with the growth of the industry and with the growth of the industrial system as a whole. Greater specialization and better use of resources become possible when growth helps to overcome indivisibilities generating pecuniary external economies. The range of increasing returns seems to be very wide indeed.[3]

Social overhead capital is the most important instance of indivisibility and hence of external economies on the supply side. Its services are indirectly productive and become available only after long gestation periods. Its most important products are investment opportunities created in other industries. Social overhead capital comprises all those basic industries like power, transport, or communications which must precede the more quickly yielding, directly productive investments and which constitute the framework or infrastructure and the overhead costs of the economy as a whole. Its installations are characterized by a sizeable initial lump and low variable costs. Since the mini-

mum size in these basic industries is large, excess capacity will be unavoidable over the initial period in under-developed countries.[4] In addition, there is also an irreducible minimum industry mix of different public utilities, so that an under-developed country will have to invest between 30–40 per cent of its total investment in these channels. Since over-all vision is required as well as a correct appraisal of future development, programming is undoubtedly required in this lumpy field. Normal market mechanisms will not provide an optimum supply.

Social overhead capital is characterized by four indivisibilities. First, it is indivisible (irreversible) in time. It must precede other directly productive investments. Second, its equipment has high minimum durability. Lesser durability is either technically impossible or much less efficient. For this and other reasons it is very lumpy. Third, it has long gestation periods. Fourth, an irreducible minimum social overhead capital industry mix is a condition for getting off the dead-end.

Because of these indivisibilities and because services of social overhead capital cannot be imported, a high initial investment in social overhead capital must either precede or be known to be certainly available in order to pave the way for additional more quickly yielding directly productive investments. This indivisibility of social overhead capital constitutes one of the main obstacles to development of under-developed countries.

Relatively few investments are made in the small market of an under-developed country. If all investment projects were inde-

[3] The capital-output ratio in the United States has fallen over the last eighty years from around 4 : 1 to around 3 : 1, while income per head, wage-rates, and the relative importance of heavy industry were rising. This is due to technical progress (change in production functions), increasing returns on balance (increasing returns prevailing over decreasing returns), and to the rising demand for labour-intensive services characteristic of high-income economies. It is my conviction that increasing returns played a considerable part in it.

[4] We may distinguish in fact between the developmental social overhead capital which provides for a hoped for but uncertain future demand and the rehabilitation social overhead capital which caters to an unsatisfied demand of the past. The first with its excess capacity will necessarily have a big sectoral capital-output ratio (10–15 : 1); the second, through breaking bottlenecks, has a certain high indirect productivity and a much lower capital-output ratio.

pendent (which they are not) and if their number grew, the risk of each investment project would decline by simple actuarial rules. The lower marginal risk of each investment dose (or project) would lead to either higher or cheaper credit facilities and these would thus constitute internal economies. In reality, however, various investment decisions are not independent. Investment projects have high risks because of uncertainty as to whether their products will find a market.

Let us restate our old example, at first for a closed economy. If a hundred workers who were previously in disguised unemployment (so that the marginal productivity of their labour was equal to zero) in an underdeveloped country are put into a shoe factory, their wages will constitute additional income. If the newly employed workers spend all of their additional income on the shoes they produce, the shoe factory will find a market and will succeed. In fact, however, they will not spend all of their additional income on shoes. There is no easy solution of creating an additional market in this way. The risk of not finding a market reduces the incentive to invest, and the shoe factory investment project will probably be abandoned. Let us vary the example. Instead of putting a hundred previously unemployed workers in one shoe factory, let us put ten thousand workers in one hundred factories and farms which between them will produce the bulk of the wage-goods on which the newly employed workers will spend their wages. What was not true in the case of one single shoe factory will become true for the complementary system of one hundred factories and farms. The new producers will be each other's customers and will verify Say's Law by creating an additional market. The complementarity of demand will reduce the risk of not finding a market. Reducing such interdependent risks naturally increases the incentives to invest. . . .

A high minimum quantum of investment requires a high volume of savings, which is difficult to achieve in low income, underdeveloped countries. There is a way out of this vicious circle. In the first stage when income is increased due to an increase in investment which mobilizes additional latent resources, mechanisms must be provided which assure that in the second stage the marginal rate of saving is very much higher than the average rate of saving. Adam Smith's dictum that frugality is a virtue and prodigality a vice has to be adapted to a situation of growing income. Economic history does not show that the proportion saved from the increase in income was higher than the previous average rate of saving.

A zero (or very low) price elasticity of the supply of saving and a high income elasticity of saving thus constitute the third indivisibility.

These three indivisibilities and the external economies to which they give rise, plus the external economies of training labour, form the characteristic pattern of models of growth of under-developed countries.

The economic factors discussed so far give only the necessary, but not the sufficient, conditions of growth. A big push seems to be required to jump over the economic obstacles to development. There may be finally a phenomenon of indivisibility in the vigour and drive required for a successful development policy. Isolated and small efforts may not add up to a sufficient impact on growth. An atmosphere of development may only arise with a minimum speed or size of investment. Our knowledge of psychology is far too deficient to theorize about this phenomenon. This does not make it a less important factor. It may well constitute the difference between necessary and sufficient conditions for success.

X.A.2. Critique of the "Big Push"

Argument*

... [T]he theories I am considering have several characteristics which warrant their being grouped together. For one thing, these theories are generally strongly interventionist, at least so far as concerns the assumption of responsibility by the state for a greatly increased rate of saving, and—extending out from this basis according to the predilections of the individual writer—to more or less, and generally more, control (and sometimes operation) of the specific lines of investment and production. Secondly, these "big push" theorists usually consider manufacture as inherently superior to primary production as a vehicle of development. These two characteristics are so general that I shall terminate the list with these alone for greater emphasis; but it would be tempting to point to the frequency also of an inflationary bias in writings of this sort, to autarkical leanings and to a fondness for general equilibrium planning as implied by linear or nonlinear programming. But the interventionist and other features of these theories, upon which I shall want to comment later, are their overtones rather than their substance.

The substantive bases for an accelerated rate of investment through state intervention are principally three: a demographic argument, a line of reasoning involving the propensity to consume (or to save), and thirdly, conclusions reached from the technical discontinuities or "lumpiness" of investment. Let me say clearly in advance that in no case do I reject the reasoning completely; but that in all cases I attach much greater weight than do the proponents of these theories to

the limits of possible gain, to the risks and costs of the proposed line of action, and to the merits of alternative policies. . . .

The chief basis upon which the "big push" of investment has been justified, since its original enunciation by Paul Rosenstein-Rodan a decade and a half ago, has been the possibility of realizing extensive external economies, and this ground is still a favorite with nearly all writers of this persuastion. But the great offset to the possibility that domestic development programs should give rise to further external economies has been definitely set forth by Professor Viner: foreign trade makes available to the developing country the much more substantial economies realized upon world markets, independently of home investment.[1] This fact is now recognized by Professor Rosenstein. But he fails to give overt recognition to the further fact adduced by Viner that the newly developing countries nowadays are chiefly primary producers, and, as such, investment for exports and for marginal import substitutes, where external economies are presumably negligible, occupies a very large part of total investment. For this entire sector, the "big push" loses its specific justification from external economies.

We are left then with that portion of production for the domestic market which does not substitute for imports. Still, this can be a very substantial field, embracing purely local consumer goods production and most public utilities—transportation, com-

*From Howard S. Ellis, "Accelerated Investment as a Force in Economic Development," *Quarterly Journal of Economics*, November 1958, pp. 486, 491–5. Reprinted by permission.

[1] Jacob Viner, "Stability and Progress: the Poorer Countries' Problem," First Congress of the International Economic Association, Rome, September 6–11, 1956; mimeographed paper, pp. 27–31. [Reprinted in Douglas Hague (ed.), *Stability and Progress in the World Economy*, New York, 1958.]

munication, power, water and sewerage facilities, and the like. Even here, however, there are limits to potential external economies. Viner points out that certain investments—presumably in the case of fairly inelastic demand—are cost-reducing rather than output-expanding. Since external economies depend upon expansion of output in the initial industry, they become negligible for this category of investment. I should like to call attention to two further limitations of considerable significance. In the field of purely domestic goods, a large fraction will be personal services and very light industry (a good deal of food and raiment production) in which the "chunkiness" of fixed investment is unimportant because fixed investment is itself a small fraction of costs. Since external economies are simply internal economies in adjacent industries, their significance is correspondingly small in these cases. It is furthermore worth remembering that, in the case of public utilities, potential external economies do not pertain to the cost of the *equipment* of these industries if it can be more cheaply imported.

Taken together, all of these limitations need not entirely remove the possibility of external economies. But they are neither as universal as often supposed nor, when they actually exist, as substantial. Furthermore and finally, though their existence does increase the productivity of the economy for given magnitudes of investment, they do not constitute a reason for a *concentration of investment in point of time* if—as would appear probable in any but the smallest countries—the "chunkiness" of individual investments levels out to a fairly full utilization of capacities in the aggregate for all capital facilities together. This is a decidedly relevant consideration if "accelerated investment" is taken, not as simply synonymous with more investment continually, but as a "big push" followed by a lower rate.

Beyond its substantive theoretical basis in the population, savings, and external economies arguments, the doctrine of accelerated rates of investment has overtones for policy which its proponents, I am sure, would not

be content to have ignored. One of these is the predilection for manufacturing over agricultural and other primary industries. In part this predilection may simply reflect a sentimental desire to see the country "independent" of its neighbors, particularly the richer ones; but in part it may rest on rational arguments, such as the improvement in labor morale which is supposed to attend factory production, the cultural and demographic effects of large cities, which are supposed to be favorable to economic progress, and the risks of primary production from the fluctuations of world markets. On the other hand, agricultural and primary types of production have in their favor that they utilize the relatively abundant factors of land and labor and economize capital; that characteristically in the less developed countries they provide two-thirds or more of the national income; and that, by the same token, they supply the chief wherewithal for industrial imports and investment in general.

It would scarcely seem necessary at the present stage of the debate concerning economic development to say that the merits of investment in agriculture versus industry have to be settled according to the peculiarities of each country. By consequence, whatever merits may inhere in crash programs of investment may just as well be associated with agriculture—irrigation, drainage, transportation facilities, reform of fragmented landholdings, etc.,—as with building industrial plants; in particular cases, indeed, more so.

Somewhat similar reflections would be germane to the penchant of the "big push" economists for planning, state direction of investment, and extensive controls. Linear programming, for example, is essentially an information service, and the benefits of its information may just as well be made available to private as to public entrepreneurs. In and of itself, linear programming does not supply any rationale for accelerated investment. If it should appear desirable to supplement private voluntary savings by the fiscal arm of the state, the funds can be lent to private firms. The theoretical underpinning of accelerated investment programs pertains to a *rate* of investment, and not necessarily to government controlled investment. Ordinary economic motivations of the individual and the firm are a powerful engine of economic progress. It would be regrettable if the economists of the free world created an impression to the contrary.

What, in conclusion, may be said of the general merits of the "big push" philosophy of economic development? As a starting point for development some kind of impulse is, of course, necessary; a change from stagnation is not likely to come by almost imperceptible degrees. Economic historians and cultural anthropologists have pointed to various prime movers in economic change: to the roles of the foreign trader and foreign capital, to immigration and the transfer of techniques, to the process of technical innovation itself, to cultural change, and to political revolution. Among these, intensive programs of state investment, as in the Japanese and Russian cases, should certainly take their place. But they are by no means the only or even the chief channel through which development can be achieved; and the demographic advantages, the capital accumulation, and the external economies to be expected from crash programs of government investment can easily be overrated.

A statistical summary of recent economic development throughout the world by John H. Adler reaches the important conclusion, among others, that "a relatively low level of investment 'pays off' well in the form of additional output."[2] The author emphasizes this conclusion most sharply in connection with India and Pakistan; but the chief reason for this conclusion, the prevailing low capital-output ratio, is also characteristic of many other of the less developed countries of Asia and Latin America as his statistics reveal. Thus it appears that it is far from generally true that a massive injection of capital is a precondition of growth.

[2] John H. Adler, "World Economic Growth—Retrospect and Prospects," *Review of Economics and Statistics*, Aug. 1956, p. 279; cf. also p. 283.

A general weakness of the "big push" doctrine is that it frequently ignores the conditions for *evoking* the investment to which it ascribes such potency in the general picture of development, as well as neglecting the conditions under which investments, once made, can be fruitful. It is through the assumption of a *deus ex machina*, the state, which does all or most of the investing, that this theory is able to avoid the problems of securing not only the saving, but also the willingness to undergo risk, which is implied in investment. And it is only through a singular narrowness that the theory often implies that it tells the whole story of the successful operation of the economy, once the investment is made.

In point of fact, the conditions for the evoking of private investment and the conditions for the profitable use of capital are largely the same. I should place high upon this list the existence of stable and honest government, the absence of inflation, and the accessibility of the economy to the gains of foreign trade and commerce. But other factors, such as the improvement of general and technical education, the amelioration of agriculture (which bulks large in nearly all low-income countries), and progress along the family-limitation front would seem to be equally critical. Taken together, or in some cases even singly, we would seem to have identified a number of factors in economic progress which could outweigh a burst of state-engineered investment.

Some food for thought concerning programs of intensive investment would seem to be offered by certain points made recently by Simon Kuznets. His statistical and historical studies lead to the conclusion that "current international differences in *per capita* income are congealed effects of past differences in the rate of growth of *per capita* income." How far would it be necessary to go back into the history of the more advanced countries to reach levels comparable to the *per capita* incomes of the currently less developed countries? The answer is that we should have to go back about ten decades to reach the current income level of Latin

America and about fifteen decades for that of Africa and Asia.[3] Thus, even at a very

[3] Simon Kuznets, "Quantitative Aspects of the Economic Growth of Nations," in *Economic Development and Cultural Change*, Oct. 1956; see especially pp. 23–5.

early stage in the industrialization of Western Europe, per capita incomes were probably as high as in Latin America today and certainly higher than in Asia and Africa. The economic development of the most advanced countries, at least, scarcely seems to be the result of crash programs.

X.A.3. The Case for Balanced Growth*

It is no longer so certain that the less developed countries can rely on economic growth being induced from the outside through an expansion of world demand for their exports of primary commodities. In these circumstances reliance on induced expansion through international trade cannot provide a solution to the problem of economic development. It is not surprising therefore that countries should be looking for other solutions. It is important to keep these things in mind, because they form the background to the case for balanced growth which is now so much in vogue.

The circumstances indicated do not apply to all underdeveloped countries today: Kuwait and perhaps Iraq have nothing to worry about. But in so far as these circumstances do exist in reality it is clear that the poorer countries, even if they are only to keep pace with the richer, to say nothing about catching up with them, must expand production for their own domestic markets or for each others' markets. Now domestic markets are limited because of mass poverty due to low productivity. Private investment in any single industry considered by itself is discouraged by the smallness of the existing market.

*From Ragnar Nurkse, "The Conflict Between 'Balanced Growth' and International Specialization," *Lectures on Economic Development*, Faculty of Economics (Istanbul University) and Faculty of Political Sciences (Ankara University), Istanbul, 1958, pp. 170–76. Reprinted by permission.

The limits set by the small size of the local market for manufactured goods are so plainly visible to any individual businessman that we are fully justified in taking for granted conditions of imperfect competition, and not the pure atomistic competition which even in advanced economies does not exist to any significant degree, outside the economics textbooks.

The solution seems to be a balanced pattern of investment in a number of different industries, so that people working more productively, with more capital and improved techniques, become each others' customers. In the absence of vigorous upward shifts in world demand for exports of primary products, a low income country through a process of diversified growth can seek to bring about upward shifts in domestic demand schedules by means of increased productivity and therefore increased real purchasing power. In this way, a pattern of mutually supporting investments in different lines of production can enlarge the size of the market and help to fill the vacuum in the domestic economy of low income areas. This, in brief, is the notion of balanced growth.

Isolated advance is not impossible. A solitary process of investment and increased productivity in one industry alone will certainly have favorable repercussions elsewhere in the economy. There is no denying that through the normal incentives of the price mechanism other industries will be induced to advance also. But this may be a snail's pace of progress. The price mechanism works but it may work too slowly. That is one reason for the frequently observed fact that foreign direct investments in extractive export industries have created high productivity islands in low income areas and have had little impact on the level of productivity in the domestic economy.

Within the domestic economy itself, advance in one direction, say in industry A, tends to induce advance in B as well. But if it is only a passive reaction to the stimulus coming from A, the induced advance of B may be slow and uncertain. And B's slowness and passiveness will in turn slow down and discourage the initial advance in A. The application of capital to one industry alone may therefore be subject to sharply diminishing returns. As a way of escape from slowness if not from stagnation, the balanced growth principle envisages autonomous advance along a number of lines more or less simultaneously.

Viewed in this way, balanced growth is a means to accelerated growth. Some economists treat the problem of achieving balanced growth as quite separate from the problem of speeding up the rate of advance in a backward economy. I admit that this may be a convenient distinction to draw on other grounds. But in my view, balanced growth is first and foremost a means of getting out of the rut, a means of stepping up the rate of growth when the external forces of advance through trade expansion and foreign capital are sluggish or inoperative.

In the existing state of affairs in low income areas the introduction of capital-using techniques of production in any single industry is inhibited by the small size of the market. Hence the weakness of private investment incentives in such areas. The balanced growth principle points to a way out of the deadlock. New enterprises set up in different industries create increased markets for each other, so that in each of them the installation of capital equipment becomes worth while. As Marshall said, "The effi-

ciency of specialized machinery ... is but one condition of its economic use; the other is that sufficient work should be found to keep it well employed" (*Principles*, p. 264). The techniques that have been developed in production for mass markets in advanced countries are not well adapted and sometimes not adaptable at all to output on a more limited scale. It is easy to see that the relationship between the size of the market and the amount of investment required for efficient operation is of considerable importance for the theory of balanced growth.

Frequently the objection is made: But why use machinery? Why adopt capital-using methods in areas where labor is cheap and plentiful? Why not accordingly employ techniques that are labor-intensive instead of capital-intensive?

The answer is obvious. As an adaptation to existing circumstances, including the existing factor proportions, the pursuit of labor-intensive production methods with a view to economizing capital may be perfectly correct. But the study of economic development must concern itself with changing these circumstances, not accepting them as they are. What is wanted is progress, not simply adaptation to present conditions. And progress depends largely on the use of capital, which in turn depends on adequate and growing markets, which in the absence of a strongly rising world demand for the country's exports means a diversified output expansion for domestic use.

Reference has been made to the importance of autonomous advance in a number of mutually supporting lines of production. How is this achieved? Autonomous advance in different branches simultaneously may come about through the infectious influence of business psychology, through the multiplier effects of investment anywhere which can create increased money demand elsewhere, or through deliberate control and planning by public authorities. According to some writers the balanced growth argument implies that the market mechanism is eliminated and that investments must be effected according to a coordinated plan. This opinion, which is widely held, seems to me dubious. There are many important reasons for government planning, but this is not necessarily one of them. As a means of creating inducements to invest, balanced growth can be said to be relevant primarily to a private enterprise system. State investment can and often does go ahead without any market incentives. Planning authorities can apply capital, if they have any, wherever they may choose, though if they depart too much from balance as dictated by income elasticities of demand they will end by creating white elephants and intolerable disproportionalities in the structure of production. It is private investment that is attracted by markets and that needs the inducement of growing markets. It is here that the element of mutual support is so useful and, for rapid growth, indispensable.

X It is important to note that the doctrine under consideration is not itself concerned with the question of where the capital is to be found, for all the balanced investment which it envisages. I have tried to make it clear in my discussion of it that the argument is primarily relevant to the problem of the demand for capital; it takes an increased supply of capital for granted. In my presentation balanced growth is an exercise in economic development with unlimited supplies of capital, analogous to Professor Lewis's celebrated exercise in development with unlimited labor supplies.

In reality, of course, capital supplies are not unlimited. It may be that the case for state investment stems chiefly from the fact that capital is scarce and that government efforts are necessary to mobilize all possible domestic sources of saving. Measures to check the expansion of consumer demand may be necessary to make resources available for investment but may at the same time weaken the private inducement to invest. This is a famous dilemma to which Malthus first called attention in his *Principles of Political Economy*. A case for state investment may clearly arise if and when the mobilization of capital supplies discourages private investment activity and so destroys the demand for capital. But this case is entirely separate from the principle of balanced growth as such. It might only be added that the capital supply problem alone creates a strong presumption against relying on the indiscriminate use of import restriction which may reduce a country's real income and therefore make it harder to increase the flow of saving.

Elsewhere I have tried to explain how the balanced growth idea is related to the classical law of markets. Supply creates its own demand, provided that supply is properly distributed among different commodities in accordance with consumers' wants. An increase in consumable output must provide a balanced diet. Each industry must advance along an expansion path determined by the income elasticity of consumer demand for its product. This simple idea must be the starting point in any expansion of production for domestic markets in the less developed countries, in so far as external demand conditions do not favor the traditional pattern of "growth through trade." Yet, as often happens in economic discussion, critics have tended to dismiss this idea either as a dangerous fallacy or as an obvious platitude. It is hardly necessary to add that the pattern of consumable output cannot be expected to remain the same in successive stages of development. The content of a balanced diet of a man with a thousand dollars a year will differ from that of a man with a hundred dollars.

The relation between agriculture and manufacturing industry offers the clearest and simplest case of balance needed for economic growth. In a country where the peasantry is incapable of producing a surplus of food above its own subsistence needs there is little or no incentive for industry to establish itself: there is not a sufficient market for manufactured goods. Conversely, agricultural improvements may be inhibited by lack of a market for farm products if the non-farm sector of the economy is backward or undeveloped. Each of the two sectors must try to move forward. If one remains passive the other is slowed down.

It is important in this connection to make a clear distinction between two concepts that are frequently confused: the marketable surplus and investible surplus of the farm sector. The farm sector's marketable surplus of farm products determines the volume of non-farm employment in manufacturing and other activities. It reflects simply the farm sector's demand for non-agricultural commodities. This is the concept that is relevant to the balanced growth principle.

An investible surplus of farm products represents an act of saving in the farm sector. It can conceivably result from a transfer of surplus labourers from the farms to capital construction projects: a food surplus may then arise through forced or voluntary saving in the farm sector for maintaining the workers engaged on capital projects. This is the concept relevant to the problem of capital supply. It is obvious that even a large marketable surplus of food need not involve any saving by the farmers. It presents a very helpful inducement, but does not in itself create the means, for capital investment outside the agricultural sector. A fuller discussion of the interrelationship between marketable and investible surpluses would take us too far from our present subject. It seemed desirable to mention the distinction here merely for the sake of conceptual clarity. So much for the relation between agriculture and industry.

Within the manufacturing field alone the case for balanced investment implies a horizontal diversification of industrial activities all pushing ahead, though naturally at varying rates. The objection can be made that such diffusion of effort and resources over many different lines of activity must mean a loss of dynamic momentum in the economy. This is possible. The dispersal of investment over a variety of consumer-goods industries can undoubtedly be carried to excess. The balanced growth principle can be and has been interpreted far too literally. Producing a little of everything is not the key to progress. The case for balanced growth is concerned with establishing a pattern of mutually supporting investments over a range of industries wide enough to overcome the frustration of isolated advance, in order precisely to create a forward momentum of growth. The particular factors that determine the optimum pattern of diversification have to do with technology, physical conditions and other circumstances that vary from country to country. There can be no standard prescription of universal applicability. We are concerned with a point of principle and cannot deal with the precise forms of its implementation in practice. Just as it is possible for manufacturing industry as a whole to languish if farmers produce too little and are too poor to buy anything from factories, so it is possible for a single line of manufacturing to fail for lack of support from other sectors in industry as well as agriculture; that is, for lack of markets.

X.A.4. Balanced versus Unbalanced Growth*

... Before we enter upon a discussion of the merits and faults of the doctrines of balanced growth (BG) and of unbalanced growth (UG), it is necessary to clarify two questions to which the contributors to the debate have not given clear and satisfactory answers. The first question, most relevant in the present context of our discussion, concerns the role of planning; the second question [concerns] the role of supply limitations and supply inelasticities.

*From Paul Streeten, "Balanced versus Unbalanced Growth," The Economic Weekly, April 20, 1963, pp. 669–71. Reprinted by permission.

In the controversy the role of government (or for that matter private) planning has not always been brought out clearly. In particular, it is not always clear whether the question under consideration relates to planning, or whether it relates to an attempt to explain development that takes place without planning, or with only an initial impulse of planning in the form of an investment project, while things are thereafter left to take their own course with market forces responding to demand and supply.

Nurkse thought that BG is relevant primarily to a private enterprise economy. It is (he argued) private investment that needs market inducements. In his doctrine, the choice between public and private investment and between direct controls and market incentives is mainly a matter of administrative expediency. But he seems to be wrong in this. The indivisibilities assumed in BG imply the need for coordination, i.e. planning, although it would, in principle, be possible to have either private or public coordination.

UG as propounded by Hirschman is consistent with, but does not require, initial *and* continued planning. His state administrators are—or should be—subject to the same kind of pressures as private entrepreneurs. The role of the state is both to induce and to repair disequilibria. Thus state action becomes a dependent, as well as an independent, variable. But again, on closer inspection it would seem that UG, to be most effective, does require planning and preferably state planning, because no private firm may want or be able to carry the surplus capacity and the losses, and because private horizons are too narrow.

It is not surprising that both BG and UG should, to be most effective, presuppose (each a different kind of) planning, for they are both concerned with lumpy investments and complementarities. Coordination is needed in order both to get things done that otherwise would not be done, and in order to reap the rewards of complementarities. Market forces look best after adjustments that can be made in infinitesimally small steps. This is why the concept "marginal" plays such as important part in neo-classical Western economic theory. It is also one of the important differences between developed and underdeveloped countries. In the former a new profitable investment project is normally small relative to the size of existing capital equipment (however measured), relatively to new investment, and relatively to the hinterland of facilities on which it can draw. In underdeveloped countries indivisibilities are more prominent and marginal adjustments rarer for at least four reasons.

First, both the existing stock of equipment and the additions to it are small compared with those in advanced countries with comparable populations. Since plant and equipment often have to be of a minimum size for technical reasons, the addition of a plant or a piece of equipment makes a greater proportionate difference both to the stock of capital and to total investment.

Second, economic development is usually directed at moving people from agriculture to industrial enterprises. This normally implies an increase in the number of indivisible units.

Third, the necessary social overhead capital and the basic structure of industry (power, steel, transport, housing, government buildings) consist of large indivisible units.

Fourth, complementarities between enterprises and activities are likely to be more important in the meagre economies of underdeveloped countries, so that a given investment is more liable to require complementary and supplementary investments. Both BG and UG give rise to external economies. A cost incurred by A creates profit opportunities for B. If steps are taken to seize these opportunities at once and in one type of sequence (BG), the results will be different than if they are seized later and in a different type of sequence (UG). But there is no guarantee that A will be induced by market forces to incur these costs, indeed there is a presumption that he will not be so induced.

We next turn to the role of supply limitations and supply inelasticities in the controversy. Nurkse explicitly confined his discussion to the demand side. He assumed supplies to be available and asked what would investment have to be like to justify them? He wrote:

There is no suggestion here that, by taking care of the demand side alone, any country could, as it were, lift itself up by its bootstraps. We have been considering one particular facet of our subject. The more fundamental difficulties that lie on the supply side have so far been kept off-stage for the sake of orderly discussion.[1]

Nevertheless, the position of this chapter in his book and the emphasis laid on it have led to misinterpretations. If BG stresses *markets* as the main limitation on growth, UG in the Hirschman version stresses *decisions*. The implication of Hirschman's theory is that supplies will be forthcoming with relative ease if only the lack of decision-taking can be overcome. This shift of emphasis to an attitude, usually assumed either constant or automatically adjusted to precisely the required extent, should be welcomed. Hirschman has been charged with excessive preoccupation with *investment* decisions. Much of his book indeed focuses attention on them, but it is clear that he had a wider concept in mind, as is shown by his use of the terms "development decisions" and "developmental tasks."

Insofar as BG is concerned with the creation of markets through complementary investment projects and the inducement to invest by providing complementary markets for final goods, it stresses a problem which is rarely serious in the countries of the region. Final markets can often quite easily be created without recourse to BG, by import restrictions and, less easily, by export expansion.

[1] *Problems of Capital Formation in Underdeveloped Countries*, pp. 30–31.

On the other hand, although UG is correct in pointing to the scarcity of decision-taking in some countries, it should not be contrasted, but it should be combined with the provision of more supplies. The contrast drawn by UG between scarcity of physical resources and scarcity of decision-taking can be misleading. Those who stress resources say that decisions will be taken as soon as resources are available; those who stress decision-taking say that resources will flow freely as soon as adequate inducements to take decisions are provided. The former group of experts go out on missions and advocate high taxation in order to "set resources free," the latter recommend low taxation in order to "encourage enterprise."

Both views reflect misplaced aggregation and illegitimate isolation, two types of bias introduced by the careless use of Western concepts and models. No general formula will serve. The correct division often cuts across these categories. The question is what combination of resource policy, reform of attitudes (including "incentives") and of legal, social and cultural institutions, is necessary in a particular situation.

Moreover, the tendency of both BG and UG to underplay supply limitations diverts attention from the fact that planning must be directed as much at restricting supplies in certain directions as at *expanding* them in others. The policy package presupposes a choice of allocating limited supplies, i.e., supplies growing at a limited rate, and in response to certain stimuli, to the most important uses, combined with inducements to decisions of all kinds (not only investment decisions). These supply limitations are considerably less important in advanced industrial countries now and were less important in the early developing phase of many now advanced countries, like Sweden or the regions of recent settlement. These countries had almost unlimited access to capital at low interest rates, a reserve of skilled labour and plentiful natural resources. Again, certain underdeveloped regions in advanced countries (Southern Italy, the South of the USA) can draw on supplies but lack development decisions.

The models developed in the BG vs. UG controversy seem to have drawn on this kind of experience from "ceilingless economies" which is relevant to South America but not to the entirely different problems of South Asia. The two important differences between, on the one hand, advanced countries now and in their development phase, and, on the other hand, the underdeveloped countries of South Asia are:

1. that investments in advanced countries can more often be treated as marginal than in underdeveloped countries, and

2. that advanced countries are and were high supply-elasticity economies with responses and institutions already adapted to economic growth.

Both doctrines have certain faults. The trouble with advocating UG is that, for countries embarking on development, unbalance is inevitable, whether they want it or not, and governments and planners do not need the admonitions of theoreticians. All investment creates unbalances because of rigidities, indivisibilities, sluggishness of response both of supply and of demand and because of miscalculations. There will be, in any case, plenty of difficulties in meeting many urgent requirements, whether of workers, technicians, managers, machines, semi-manufactured products, raw materials or power and transport facilities and in finding markets permitting full utilisation of equipment. Market forces will be too weak or powerless to bring about the required adjustments and unless coordinated planning of much more than investment is carried out, the investment projects will turn out to be wasteful and will be abandoned.

Insofar as unbalance does create desirable attitudes, the crucial question is not whether to create unbalance, but *what* is the *optimum* degree of unbalance, *where* to unbalance and *how much*, in order to accelerate growth; which are the "growing points," where should the spearheads be thrust, on which slope would snowballs grow into avalanches? Although nobody just said "create any old unbalance," insufficient attention has been paid to its precise composition, direction and timing.

The second weakness of UG is that the theory concentrates on stimuli to *expansion*, and tends to neglect or minimise *resistances* caused by UG. UG argues that the active sectors pull the others with them, BG that the passive sectors drag the active ones back. While the former is relevant to South America, the latter is relevant to South Asia. It would, of course, be better, as Nurkse would have liked it, if *all* sectors were active, and the wish may have been father of the thought behind these models. But the problem is how to activate them. Activation measures must take the form both of positive inducements and of resistances to resistances.

The UG model in the Hirschman version has the great merit, in comparison with many other models, of including attitudes and institutions, and in particular investment incentives, normally assumed fully adjusted to requirements, and of turning them from independent variables or constants into dependent variables. In particular Hirschman's discussion of forward and backward linkages is provocative and fruitful. It brings out the previously neglected effects of one investment on investment at earlier and later stages of production. But the doctrine underplays obstacles and resistances (also in attitudes) called into being by imbalance. Shortages create vested interests; they give rise to monopoly gains; people may get their fingers burnt by malinvestments and may get frightened by the growth of competition. The attitudes and institutions evolving through development will arouse opposition and hostility. Some of these resistances may be overcome only by state compulsion, but the governments of the "soft states" are reluctant to use force and the threat of force. Once again, the absence of this type of reaction from the models is both appropriate for Western countries and is opportune to the planners in South Asia, but it introduces a systematic bias and neglects some of the most important issues.

Turning now to BG, we have seen that its main weakness is that it is concerned with the creation of complementary domestic markets as an inducement to invest, whereas markets in the countries of the region can usually be created by import restrictions, and, where possible, export expansion. This relates to final goods and principally to consumers' goods. As far as intermediate markets are concerned, Nurkse came out in favour of UG (vertical imbalance) in his second Istanbul Lecture.[2] Social overhead investment provides the conditions and inducements for consequential direct productive investment. As for horizontal balance, he believed that the case "rests on the need for a 'balanced diet.' "[3] But he later drew a distinction between BG as a method and BG as an outcome or objec-

---

[2] R. Nurkse, *Equilibrium and Growth in the World Economy*, pp. 259–78.

[3] "The difficulty caused by the small size of the market relates to individual investment incentives in any single line of production taken by itself. At least in principle, the difficulty vanishes in the case of a more or less synchronized application of capital to a wide range of different industries. Here is an escape from the deadlock; here the result is an over-all enlargement of the market. People working with more and better tools in a number of complementary projects become each others' customers. Most industries catering for mass consumption are complementary in the sense that they provide a market for, and thus support, each other. This basic complementarity stems, in the last analysis, from the diversity of human wants. The case for 'balanced growth' rests on the need for a 'balanced

tive.[4] What remains of the doctrine is the emphasis on the complementarity of markets for final goods as an ultimate objective for investment incentives. But not only is absence of markets not normally a serious obstacle to development; even where it is, it is by no means the main obstacle and, in any case, balanced growth cannot always remove it.

What is sound in BG is the stress on the investment package, on the need for coordination, on the structure of an investment complex. But investment is not the only component in this package: and there is too much stress on the complementarity of final markets. What is needed is a package of policy measures containing

a. complementary investments;
b. actions to reform attitudes and institutions, including the desire to invest, but also the ability and willingness to work, (which may involve raising *consumption*), to organise and manage and in particular to administer politically;
c. a carefully thought-out timetable showing the sequence of the various measures which would be determined by technological, political and sociological factors;
d. controls checking undesirable or less desirable investments; and
e. policies designed to weaken or eliminate obstacles and inhibitions to development, including resistances induced by measures (a) to (d).

---

diet.' " *Problems of Capital Formation in Underdeveloped Countries*, pp. 11f.
[4] Op. cit., p. 279.

X.B. LESSONS OF RECENT HISTORY

X.B.1. Industrialization via Import Substitution—Note

In many LDCs—especially in Latin America and Asia—the dominant strategy of industrialization has been the production of consumer goods in substitution for imports. Given an existing demand for imported consumer goods, it was simple to base the postwar rationale for industrialization on the home replacement of these finished goods (in most industries by importing the components and engaging in the final assembling process, in the hope of proceeding to "industrialize from the top downwards" through the ultimate production of the intermediate products and capital goods). Besides allowing the home replacement of an existing market, import substitution also had considerable appeal by virtue of the common belief that it would help meet the developing country's balance of payments problem.

Although the widespread pursuit of import substitution has in practice been based mainly on the objectives of industrialization and balance-of-payments support, the policy has been rationalized by a number of protectionist arguments. Proponents of industrial protectionism have adduced several special arguments in the context of development—arguments that should be considered more seriously than the usual simple assertions about a "natural" inferiority of agriculture or the supposed necessity of industrialization to achieve a rising level of income.

Support for import replacement comes partly from an appeal to the experience of industrialized countries. Historical studies of some countries show not only that the share of industrial output rises with development, but also that the growth of industries based on import substitution accounts for a large proportion of the total rise in industry.[1] It is also true that "much of the recent economic history of some rapidly developing underdeveloped countries can be written in terms of industrialization working its way backward from the 'final touches' stage to domestic production of intermediate, and finally to that of basic, industrial materials."[2] At first, the country may import semifinished materials and perform domestically the "final touches" of converting or assembling the almost-finished industrial imports into final products. Later on, with the growth in demand for the final product, a point may be reached at which the import demand for intermediate components and basic goods is sufficiently high to warrant investment in their production at home; the market has become sufficiently large to reach a domestic production threshold.[3]

As with any interpretation of historical development, however, it is one thing to determine what has happened to make the course of development in one country a "success story" and quite another to infer from this experience that the same result could now be induced more rapidly in another country through deliberate policy measures. The historical evidence on the contribution of import substitution to industrialization applies only to some countries; in other countries, the replacement of im-

[1] For evidence, see H. B. Chenery, "Patterns of Industrial Growth," *American Economic Review*, September 1960, pp. 639–41, 651.
[2] A. O. Hirschman, *The Strategy of Economic Development*, New Haven, 1958, p. 112.
[3] Ibid., p. 114.

ports was not significant. Moreover, we should recognize that the rise of industry through import replacement was in large part due to systematic changes in supply conditions, not simply to a change in the composition of demand with rising income.[4] The changes in factor supply—especially the growth in capital stock per worker and the increase in education and skills of all kinds— were instrumental in causing a systematic shift in comparative advantage as per capita income rose. But for a presently underdeveloped country there is no reason to expect that a tariff on industrial imports would cause the supplies of capital, human skills, and natural resources to change in a way that would favor the substitution of domestic production for imports. The changes in supply conditions that occurred in other countries cannot now be duplicated simply by a policy of industrial protection.

Nor is industrial protection justified by reference to the historical pattern of industrialization working its way backward from the "final touches" stage to domestic production of formerly imported materials. On the contrary, this pattern demonstrates that it is the growth of imports which subsequently induces domestic production; in offering proof that a market exists, the imports can fulfill the important function of demand formation and demand reconnaissance for the country's entrepreneurs, and the imports can act as a catalytic agent that will bring some of the country's underemployed resources together in order to exploit the opportunities they have revealed.[5] For the objective of eventually replacing imports with domestic production, it would thus be self-defeating to restrict imports at too early a stage and thereby forgo the awakening and inducing effects which imports have on industrialization.[6] An increase in imports—not their restriction—is the effective way to prepare the ground for the eventual creation of an import-replacing industry. Only after the domestic industry has been established can the country afford to dispense with the "creative" role played by imports, and only then would there be a case for protection of the domestic industry. Although in promoting the demand for import substitutes, restrictions on imports allow the country to bypass the difficulties of having to build up internal demand simultaneously with supply,[7] nonetheless such a protective commercial policy is designed merely to replace imports; this in itself is no guarantee of cumulative growth. Even though industrialization may be initiated through import substitution, there still remains the problem of sustaining the industrialization momentum beyond the point of import replacement.

Another special argument for industrialization via import substitution rests on the contention that a peripheral country's demand for industrial imports increases much more rapidly than does the foreign demand for its exports, so that the country must supply all those industrial products which cannot be imported in view of the relatively slow growth of its exports. If we accept the contentions that there is disparity in the income elasticities of demand for imports and exports, that the industrial imports are essential and must be either imported or produced at home, and that the country has no other means of increasing its capacity to import, then there is *prima facie* a case for industrial protection to encourage import substitutes. What is relevant for individual primary exporting countries, however, is not the overall income elasticity of demand for primary products, but the prospects for their individual exports. It is unreasonable to believe that export prospects are equally unfavorable for foodstuffs, minerals, and raw materials, or for all commodities in each of these broad categories. Moreover, though the elasticity of demand for a commodity may be low on world markets, it may be high for

[4] Chenery, "Patterns of Industrial Growth," pp. 624–5, 628–9, 644.

[5] Hirschman, *Strategy of Economic Development*, p. 123.

[6] Ibid., p. 124.

[7] Cf. Gunnar Myrdal, *An International Economy*, New York, 1956, p. 276.

the commodity from a particular source of supply. Nor can the future demand of industrial countries for imports be inferred simply from their income elasticity of demand for imports. Their import requirements will also depend on their growth rates in income (a high growth rate may offset a low income elasticity of demand), on shifts of the long-term supply elasticities within the industrial countries (domestic output of certain minerals and fuels, for example, has not kept pace with demand, so that import requirements are rising relatively to income growth), and on the degree of liberalization in the importing countries' commercial policies. Without undertaking individual commodity and country studies, it is therefore difficult to gauge how applicable is the argument for industrialization because of a weak export position.

We should also allow for the fact that a developing country's capacity to import industrial products will depend not only on its export earnings, but also on the inflow of foreign capital, changes in the terms of trade, and the capacity to replace other imports (such as foodstuffs and raw materials) with domestic production. To the extent that these other factors may raise the capacity to import industrial products, there is less need for industrial protection.

The case is also weakened if in attempting to offset the limited demand for exports, the policy of import substitution should in turn give rise to limitations on the supply side and deter exports. Such a worsening of the export situation may occur when the country's scarce financial and human resources are concentrated on industrialization, resources are diverted from the export sector, home consumption limits the available export supply, or the industrialization program is inflationary.

Another facet of the argument for replacing industrial imports with domestic production is related to the objective of expanding employment outside of agriculture. It may be contended that industrialization is necessary to provide employment opportunities

for the presently underemployed, to absorb manpower that would otherwise become redundant when agricultural productivity rises through the adoption of more advanced techniques, and to take up the increase in the size of the labor force as population grows.

The promotion of new employment opportunities is certainly a crucial component of development programming, and in this connection there is considerable point to the emphasis on industrialization. The relevant questions here, however, are whether investment should be directed toward import-replacing industries, and whether industrial protectionism is the most appropriate policy for facilitating the expansion of nonagricultural employment.

It is possible that the objectives of more employment and a more rapid rate of development are incompatible, and this conflict in social objectives must first be resolved. A policy of industrialization through import substitution must also be compared with a policy of gradually inducing industrialization through agricultural improvement, or promoting industry through the production of manufactured exports (as discussed in XI.D). There is also a tendency to exaggerate the amount of employment that could be provided by substituting home manufacture for imports; as country studies show, the direct employment which can be provided by replacing imports with domestic manufacture is generally limited for a poor country.

Further, it can be questioned whether industrialization through protection is the best remedy for underemployment. The effect of surplus labor in agriculture is low productivity, but the remedy for this is capital formation, not industrialization as such. Although the surplus labor constitutes an "investible surplus," this surplus can be applied in various investment outlets, and we cannot simply conclude that the optimum resource use is in import-competing industries. We should also recognize that other policies might be more effective in stimulating labor mobility than would protection.

When occupational mobility is restricted by institutional and cultural barriers, the supply responses to the price and income stimuli of protection are necessarily weak, and extra-economic measures are required in such forms as education and training, land tenure reforms, and policies that foster cultural change. Finally, we must distinguish between the mere availability of surplus laborers and their actual transference into productive employment as efficient and fully committed industrial workers. This raises all the complex problems of creating and disciplining an industrial labor force.[8]

A more sophisticated version of the employment argument is that industry should be protected by a tariff in order to offset the effects of an excessively high wage rate for labor in the importable manufacturing industries.[9] It is claimed that the wage differential between the agricultural and industrial sectors overvalues labor for the industrial sector in the sense that industrial wage rates exceed the social opportunity costs of employing more labor in industry. This may be due to the alleged fact that industrial wages are based on agricultural earnings, which are determined by the average product of labor in agriculture rather than by the marginal product of labor which is lower (compare the discussion of Lewis's model in III.D above); or it may be due to market imperfections that make the gap between agricultural and industrial wages greater than can be accounted for by "net advantages" as between

agricultural and industrial work. In either case, there is a distortion in the labor market which raises the private cost of labor in industry above its social opportunity cost (the marginal product of labor in agriculture). This results in an inefficient allocation of labor between agriculture and industry, and it also understates the profitability of transforming agriculture into manufactures.[10] It is therefore concluded that protection of manufacturing industry may increase real income above the free trade level by making the relative price of manufactures higher and facilitating the redistribution of labor from agriculture to import-competing industries.

This conclusion, however, can be criticized in several respects. Insofar as it is concerned with absorbing underemployed agricultural labor into import-competing industries, this aspect of the argument is subject to the same qualifications raised previously for the general argument of expanding employment through industrial protection. More pointedly, with regard to the alleged distortion in the labor market, it can be questioned whether the mere existence of a differential between industrial and agricultural wages is proof of a distortion. To the extent that the wage differential might be explained entirely by rational considerations of differences in costs and preferences as between industrial and agricultural work, there is no genuine distortion.[11] Considering

---

[8] Cf. W. Galenson (ed.), *Labor and Economic Development*, New York, 1959; W. E. Moore and A. S. Feldman (eds.), *Labor Commitment and Social Change in Developing Areas*, New York, 1960.

[9] For a detailed analysis of this argument, see E. E. Hagen, "An Economic Justification for Protection," *Quarterly Journal of Economics*, November 1958; J. Bhagwati, "The Theory of Comparative Advantage in the Context of Underdevelopment and Growth," *Pakistan Development Review*, Autumn 1962, pp. 342–5; J. Bhagwati and V. K. Ramaswami, "Domestic Distortions, Tariffs and the Theory of Optimum Subsidy," *Journal of Political Economy*, February 1963, pp. 44–50.

[10] In technical terms, the wage differential against industry causes the feasible production possibility curve to be drawn inwards within the maximum attainable production possibility curve based on a uniform wage. It also makes the commodity price ratio diverge from the domestic rate of transformation, so that the optimum conditions characterized by the equality of the foreign rate of transformation, domestic rate of transformation in production, and domestic rate of substitution in consumption are violated in the free trade case. See Bhagwati and Ramaswami, "Domestic Distortions," pp. 48–9.

[11] For a list of conditions under which wage differentials do not represent a genuine distortion, see ibid., pp. 47–8.

the other possible reason for a distortion in the labor market—that industrial wages are related to agricultural earnings, but these earnings exceed the marginal productivity of agricultural labor—we must recognize that this result is based on the assumption of surplus agricultural labor and the ability of the worker to receive the average product because the supply of labor is the family which works on its own account and not for wages. This consideration is not relevant, however, for thinly populated countries or for plantation labor. And, regarding the concept of surplus labor and any estimate of its extent, we should recall all the reservations discussed in our earlier analysis of the labor surplus economy (III.C).

Even if we assume, however, that the wage differential does represent a genuine distortion, we must still recognize that the effects of this distortion may be better offset by domestic policies rather than a tariff on industrial imports. The difficulty with protection by a tariff is that it seeks to remedy the distortion by affecting foreign trade whereas the distortion is in a domestic factor market.[12] In this case, a policy of subsidization of production of the import-competing commodity, or of taxation of agricultural production, would be superior to a tariff.[13] A policy of subsidization on the use of labor in the import-competing industry, or a tax on its use in agriculture, would be an even better solution; since it directly eliminates the wage differential, this policy yields a higher real income than

[12] A tariff could make the foreign and domestic rates of transformation equal, but it destroys the equality between the domestic rate of substitution and the foreign rate of transformation.

[13] A policy of subsidization or taxation of domestic products could equate the domestic and foreign rates of transformation and the domestic rate of substitution. But since it does not eliminate the inefficiency of labor-use induced by the excessive wage differential, it achieves this equality along the production possibility curve that is within the maximum attainable production possibility curve.

would a tariff, and an even higher real income than can be attained by a tax-cum-subsidy on domestic production.[14] A tariff on industrial imports is thus the least effective way of offsetting a distortion in the labor market.

Although we have so far been skeptical about the validity of protectionist arguments for import substitution, there remain two arguments that have more merit—the infant industry case and the attraction of foreign investment argument.[15] Temporary tariff protection of an infant industry is generally accepted as a valid policy for establishing an industry that would eventually be able to produce at lower costs and compete favorably with foreign producers. Nonetheless, to justify government intervention, it is not sufficient to anticipate solely the realization of internal economies of scale. For if the future benefits were to accrue only to the

[14] A policy of tax-cum-subsidy on the use of labor could achieve the equality of the domestic rate of transformation, foreign rate of transformation, and the domestic rate of substitution, and it can do this along the maximum attainable production possibility curve. For in this case, the wage differential against the industrial sector is directly removed, and both the inefficiency in labor allocation and the divergence of commodity prices from opportunity costs are simultaneously eliminated.

[15] We omit the more general external economies argument and the terms of trade case for protection. These arguments are analytically correct, but are not among the most relevant for import-substitution in a poor country. The external economies argument merges with the balanced growth doctrine. There is, moreover, no *a priori* reason why—among all possible alternative investment opportunities—we should expect the net external economies to be greatest in import-competing industries. And again, a policy of tax-cum-subsidy on domestic production may be shown to be superior to a tariff. Cf. Bhagwati and Ramaswami, "Domestic Distortions," pp. 45–7.

Although it is possible that a nation may succeed in improving its terms of trade by switching production from exportables to import-substitutes, this policy has little practical relevance for poor countries that cannot exercise sufficient monopoly or monopsony power in foreign trade.

firm, the investment might then still be made by a private firm without protection insofar as the firm can cover its earlier costs of growth out of its later profits. Protection should instead be based on the condition that the social rate of return exceeds the private rate of return on the investment. The social benefit is likely to exceed the private benefit in an infant industry for two special reasons that are particularly relevant for a newly developing country: the knowledge of new industrial protection techniques acquired in the protected industry may also be shared with other producers, and the training of the labor force may also redound to the benefit of other employers. When external economies are present, social benefits will exceed private benefits, and market forces would not yield the social optimum output. To gain the additional benefits, government aid may then be advocated.

It should be realized, however, that protection causes society to bear not only the losses that would be incurred by the industry during its period of infancy, but also the cost to consumption in the form of higher-priced import substitutes during this period. The ultimate saving in costs, therefore, ought to be sufficient to compensate the community for the excess costs during the "growing up" period.

Finally, when the social rate of return exceeds the private, the preferable policy, in a way analogous to the other cases of domestic distortions, would be a direct subsidy on facilities to further the "learning process" of new production methods, or provisions by the government for the training of labor. These subsidies are superior to a protective tariff, since they avoid the intermediate loss to consumption that occurs with protection.

Protection may, however, be an effective policy for fostering an import-replacing industry when its successful establishment depends on the acquisition of better technical knowledge and experience. For when the country imposes prohibitive tariffs, or other import restrictions, against foreign manufactures, the foreign manufacturer may be induced to escape the import controls against his product by establishing a branch plant or subsidiary behind the tariff wall. Although the protection would have little effect in attracting supply-oriented industries, the inducement may be significant for the creation of "tariff factories" in market-oriented industries. It may be particularly effective in encouraging the final stages of manufacture and assembly of parts within the tariff-imposing country when there is an import duty on finished goods while raw materials or intermediate goods remain untaxed. This assumes, of course, that a sufficiently high domestic demand exists for the product of the tariff factory. And in determining whether the attraction of additional private foreign capital provides a net gain, we must again recall the earlier discussion about the various costs and benefits of foreign capital.

From the foregoing appraisal of the various protection arguments, we may conclude that they must be highly qualified, the costs of protection not underestimated, and superior alternative policies not overlooked. Beyond these analytical considerations, the actual experience of many developing countries with industrial protectionist policies also confirms the conclusion that developing countries are likely to overemphasize the scope for replacement of industrial imports. A policy of import-substitution industrialization becomes increasingly difficult to follow beyond the consumer goods phase because with each successive import-substitution activity through the intermediate and capital goods phases, the capital intensity of import-substitution projects rises, resulting in a larger import content of investment. On the demand side, the projects tend to require increasingly large domestic markets for the achievement of a minimum efficient scale of production.[16]

The limitations and deleterious effects that have resulted in practice from actual

[16] David Felix, "The Dilemma of Import Substitution—Argentina," in Gustav F. Papanek (ed.), *Development Policy—Theory and Practice*, Cambridge, 1968, pp. 60–61.

import-substitution policies will be discussed in greater detail in the next chapter. We may simply note now that in many instances, the protectionist policies have resulted in higher prices, a domestic product of inferior quality, excess capacity in the import-competing industries, and a restraint on agricultural output and on the expansion of exports. A number of country studies can now document the contention that overinvestment has occurred in import-replacing industry.

In some countries the promotion of import substitutes through tariff rates that escalate with the degree of processing (low on imported intermediate goods and high on final goods) has actually resulted in negative value added. Although high protection of final goods makes production of the import substitute privately profitable in local currency, the value of inputs at world prices exceeds the value of the final product at world prices; the process of import substitution is socially inefficient.[17]

Not only has the actual process of import substitution been inefficient in resource use; it has also often intensified the foreign exchange constraint. At the same time as policies have subsidized import replacement, they have inhibited expansion of exports, but there has not been a net saving of imports since the replacement of finished import commodities has required heavy imports of fuels, industrial materials, and capital goods, as well as foodstuffs in cases where agricultural development has also suffered.

After a period of import-substitution industrialization, the problems of maldistribution in income and unemployment have also become more serious than they were in the first place. The use of subsidies, overvalued exchange rates, rationing of underpriced import licenses, high levels of effective protection, and loans at negative real interest rates have induced the production of import substitutes by capital-intensive, labor-saving methods and have resulted in industrial profits in the sheltered sector and high industrial wages for a labor elite, aggravating inequalities in income distribution. As noted repeatedly, employment creation in the urban import-replacement industrial sector has not kept pace with the rural-urban migration, and the unemployment problem has been aggravated by the transfer of the rural underemployed into open unemployment in the urban sector.

The references to country studies in the next chapter will provide some supporting evidence for the disenchantment with industrialization via import substitution, and at the same time they will reinforce our conclusion that an LDC must now focus on the possibilities of inducing a gradual process of industrialization through agricultural development, and on the potential industrialization through the export of manufactured products. Having realized the limitations of an inward-looking strategy of industrialization, many LDCs—as represented through the pronouncements of UNCTAD—have in fact recently changed their emphasis and are now seeking measures that will promote industrialization via the substitution of exports of processed primary products, semimanufactures, and manufactures instead of exports of primary commodities.

[17] See selections in section XI.C, below.

X.B.2. Industrialization, Employment, and Urban Growth*

Disappointment of the hopes that industrialization would lead to high employment has been the most important reason for the Southeast Asian countries' disenchantment with industrial growth. This failure, however, is not due to industrialization as such but to the Southeast Asian countries' concentration on import replacement for the westernized urban markets, and to the failure to promote labor-intensive exports on a substantial scale. Singapore is an exception. Its export-oriented industrialization policies have transformed unemployment levels of at least 10 per cent in 1966 and 1967 into negligible unemployment, confined largely to high-school leavers whose educational qualifications are too high for unskilled or semi-skilled factory labor but who are not qualified for skilled manufacturing labor. The manufacturing work force grew by an average of 12·7 per cent per annum from 1963 to 1967, and by 23·1 per cent from 1967 to 1968 when the impact of export promotion policies really began to be felt. Singapore is admittedly a special case. Its entrepot trade, relatively high standards of living and the concentration of the population in one urban area together with an extremely vigorous urban development program, enabled employment opportunities created by investment in manufacturing and other sectors to be fully exploited. However, many of the policies which Singapore followed apply in other countries, and the extent to which other Southeast Asian countries are able to increase manufacturing em-

*From Helen Hughes, "The Manufacturing Industry Sector," Part 3 of Asian Development Bank, *Southeast Asia's Economy in the 1970s*, Longman, London, 1971, pp. 227–33. Reprinted by permission.

ployment in future depends on the industrial strategies they follow.

The social costs and benefits of industrialization are intimately bound up with the problems of urbanization. Industrial development has taken place mainly in the capital cities for a number of reasons. Manufacturing industries are most economically situated when they are close both to their sources of raw materials and to their markets, although the latter are more important. In most Southeast Asian countries, capital cities serve as the principal collecting points for most local raw material supplies, and their ports provide access to imported raw materials. Since Southeast Asian industrialization has been highly dependent on imported raw materials, this has generally meant that capital city location has provided raw material sources and market location simultaneously. Government regulations, policies and incentives have been extremely important in the development of manufacturing, and this gives manufacturers the quickest access to government departments. Managers, technicians and owners, particularly foreign staff, prefer to live in urban communities which provide the facilities associated with modern life, and in most Southeast Asian countries such facilities are only available in capital cities, so that it is therefore extremely difficult to attract managerial and technical staff to outlying areas. The capital cities, independently of industrialization, have been the principal pools of labor in Southeast Asia. It is a fact of life, not only in Southeast Asia, that the most energetic and enterprising people, and particularly young people, want to move from the countryside and its provincial centers to the metropolis. The growth of industrialization has added to the attraction of the city with the promise of new and interesting as well as relatively highly paid jobs.

Once a small nucleus of industry is created, external economies which arise out of the agglomeration of industry make it much more economic for new industries to locate in existing industrial centers than elsewhere. Various industrial and commercial services such as metal plating, foundries, advertising, import and export agencies and banks especially accustomed to industrial lending rather than merely commercial lending, are attracted to the area. Manufacturers benefit from the movement of workers and technical and managerial staff from firm to firm. In countries where inventories of raw materials and spare parts have to be high to ensure continuous production in case of import difficulties, it is convenient for similar firms to be able to help each other out at short notice. Specialized textile weaving manufacturers, for example, borrow fixtures from each other. In Singapore, they point out that Hong Kong, with much larger groups of specialized textile manufacturers, is more fortunate in this respect. Thus although the high cost of land and difficulties in obtaining it even at high cost pushes manufacturers to the outskirts of large cities, and although industrial agglomeration leads to the crowding of transport and port facilities, the private cost of such crowding to the manufacturer is lower than the benefit he gains from being part of the agglomeration. In terms of social cost, however, unplanned industrial development in the capital cities is uneconomic. The problems of urban growth in Bangkok, Manila and Djakarta have clearly reached the point where urban planning, or alternative solutions to urban growth, are necessary if industry is not to be burdened with excessively high costs and if cities are to be fit for human habitation.

Decentralization, with the implication that industry should be distributed throughout a country, province by province, while widely supported for political reasons, is not a viable economic proposition. Provincial centers lack all those facilities which make location in capital cities attractive to industry and to individuals. Such facilities cannot be provided in provincial centers for many years to come. Proposals to offset the disadvantages of country location by incentives such as tax or freight concessions are generally unsuccessful. If firms take advantage of freight concessions, they burden transport systems with high costs, for which there are rarely any economic returns. Decentralization of this type has not only been unsuccessful in Southeast Asia but in the rest of the world as well.

An alternative to both decentralization and urban sprawl which would minimize the social costs of industrialization and bring private costs and benefits closer together to social costs and benefits, lies in vigorous urban development not only in the capital cities, but where appropriate, in a limited number of urban development poles based on provincial centers or ports which are already developing rapidly. In Thailand, a second industrial center on a deep-water port on the east coast of the Gulf of Thailand is urgently needed, and there is room for several poles in Indonesia and the Philippines. This does not mean that provincial centers need be neglected. An improvement in the efficiency of agricultural processing presupposes some increase in the scale of individual units and their concentration around provincial centers so that, albeit on a small scale, they could take advantage of the external economies of scale which the presence of half a dozen efficient managing concerns would create. Small-scale, labor-intensive industries might find opportunities for local production in competition with large-scale manufacturing units at the center. In due course, some of these provincial centers would grow sufficiently to qualify as development poles.

The principal contribution which planning for industry can make to urban development is the creation of industrial estates of various types, ranging from flatted factories and other types of mini-estates in population centers to cater to small-scale and labor-intensive industries whether for domestic markets or for exports, to mixed estates of small-, medium- and large-scale industries, with both local and foreign participation. The value of an industrial estate lies in overcoming land bottlenecks and at the same time in making the provision of adequate infrastructure services more economic than if industrialization is spread throughout an urban area. It is important that industrial estates be planned for the needs of Southeast Asian industries rather than on lines suitable for European and United States industrial development. To be successful, industrial estates have to be well situated with regard to ports and transport, and they should be able to take advantage of existing public utilities as far as possible. This means some hard decisions to make suitable land available, rather than delays and unworthy attempts to sell unsuitable land to industrial estate authorities. Estates should also be close to where workers live to avoid transportation problems, and the provision for small-scale industry on the estate itself or its outskirts in the shape of the two-storied dwelling workshops typical of small-scale industry establishments in Southeast Asia should be included. Industrial estates can form the nucleus of demonstration metal centers, standards laboratories and industrial training for skilled workers, all of which are important to the growth of local manufacturing enterprises. They can be used to establish and improve industrial relations. Where the reform of administration is difficult and therefore a long-term prospect, industrial estates can be turned into free zone areas to avoid lengthy custom procedures.

The success of industrial estate-type development also depends on the degree to which estates are integrated with the urban community. The problems of urban development have largely been shelved in Southeast Asia in the past 20 years, and with the exception of Singapore and Phnom Penh, the cities have simply sprawled as they would, with chronic shortages of housing not only for the squatters who dwell on

their outskirts, but also for the middle classes. Housing can play a vital role in creating employment, providing a market for industrial products, particularly for small-scale industries, but again only if the problem of the availability of suitable land can be overcome. Except in Singapore, housing needs are at present so great that grandiose solutions are not in order. Once land is made available at reasonable prices, middle-class housing can be constructed on a large scale. In some cases the existing mortgage facilities of government insurance schemes are available, and new savings institutions can be created and directed towards this end. A start has been made on these lines in several cities, but land is the bottleneck. The task of providing housing for workers presents much greater problems. It is clearly impossible to emulate Singapore's success in this direction, as none of the other Southeast Asian countries have the government resources which include not only the building of low-cost high-rise apartments but also the very extensive social work which turns slum dwellers and squatters into apartment dwellers. However, as is evident to the most casual passerby, most of the squatters in Southeast Asian cities clearly demonstrate their willingness and ability to build their own dwellings, in spite of the insecurity of tenure and the lack of sanitary services. The mere provision of well-situated small plots of serviced land for sale on easy terms to such families would be sufficient to begin the decent housing of thousands of people who now live in unhealthy and demoralizing squalor.

The existing cities of Southeast Asia have some urban infrastructure facilities and frequently have considerable potential for more. For example, several of the capital cities have railway lines running strategically through their center. These could be used as a trunk passenger railway system together with buses and jeepneys, providing that sensible urban transport policies, including some judgment about the use of private motor cars, were adopted. This is an area where international technical and financial assistance would be particularly useful, but it is also an area where planning and the use of local resources would have large returns.

In most Southeast Asian countries, industrialization is now at a crossroads. The further pursuit of import-substituting, inward-oriented industrialization strategies will lead to more high costs and balance of payments difficulties. In the Philippines, industrial growth had already slowed down in the 1960s, and in Malaysia and Thailand, where achievements in import replacement are also substantial, industrial growth is in danger of slowing down in the 1970s because the relatively easy import-substitution possibilities have been exhausted. An alternative, outward-looking industrialization strategy, already adopted with such remarkable success in Singapore, entails a difficult and painful adjustment of policies. In the short run such a strategy may not create as many investment opportunities or as much employment as import replacement. But whereas further import replacement without reference to costs will lead to increasing difficulties and halting development during the 1970s, an outward-looking strategy promises the possibility of competitive costs, exports of industrial products, and continuing, self-sustaining industrial growth with far greater long-term impact on employment than does an import-substitution policy.

A forward-looking industrial strategy cannot be built around specific industry targets. It is the very essence of such a strategy that it seeks rather to create a vigorous, competitive industrial sector structured appropriately for each of the Southeast Asian countries. It is true that past neglect and fiscal discrimination point to industries which at present need particular encouragement—notably primary processing, mass consumption and export-oriented industries. Improved productivity is needed in agricultural processing both for local consumption and for exports, and there are opportunities in mineral processing, particularly for exports.

Increasing productivity and efficiency in mass consumption goods could reduce costs in these industries, and hence lead to larger markets, greater capacity utilization and increasing profitability. Labor-intensive industries with assured markets such as electronic and other component assembly now present excellent export opportunities. By the mid-1970s, however, new opportunities may lie elsewhere, and this will certainly be so by the end of the decade. The aim of the strategy outlined here is to ensure that whatever opportunities arise—whether for large- or small-scale industries, whether in domestic or international markets—energetic entrepreneurs should be able to exploit them economically and profitably both for the individual enterprise and the economy.

The application of such an industrial strategy is difficult because it requires the coordinated use of a battery of economic policies centered around appropriate monetary and fiscal policies. It implies, moreover, not only legislative change, but also administrative reform. This is not to ignore the role which a well-organized investment promotion agency can play in blockbusting through existing legislative and administrative obstacles, but valuable and important though such tactics may be, they cannot make up for the absence of policies appropriate to the encouragement of a competitive manufacturing sector, or for the lack of administrative efficiency. Soundly based long-run development leading to self-sustaining growth requires an attack on basic policy and administrative short-comings, that is, on the essential problem of underdevelopment itself. The time for such changes is now opportune. The years of independence have seen a considerable maturing of government administration, and well-trained young men have been gaining experience in policy formulation and administration. A reassessment and restructuring of policies and administrative practices is not impossible. . . .

X.B.3. Industrialization and Social Objectives*

In very recent years some doubt has been cast on the validity of the role of industrialization in development. The reasons advanced have taken a form that has led to the fear of a trend of thought opposed to industry. The arguments supporting that position have appeared not only in economic writing; they are largely a culmination of the thinking in other fields that are concerned with the social objectives of society. The concern for social welfare is certainly valid, but the premise that industrialization is the cause of social ills may be debatable. If the model exemplified by the pattern of industrial development of the developed countries is under attack, industrialization as such should not be blamed, but rather the faults embodied in that system.

The present arguments against industry, although they could be answered easily, may have some validity. Most developing countries emerged after the Second World War from a long colonial era with great aspirations for economic development. They pinned their hopes on industry for an accelerated growth in income, which would lead to a surplus that in turn would further stimulate economic development. They hoped for a faster growth in output and the diversification of that output, which would lead to the structural change conducive to sustained income and economic growth. Such diversification, coupled with higher productivity and efficiency, would prompt the growth and diversification of manufactured exports, where favourable terms of trade prevailed, enhancing these countries'

*From UNIDO, *Industrial Development Survey*, Vol. 5, 1973, pp. 33–6. Reprinted by permission.

capacities to meet the increased import requirements for development. At the same time it was hoped that industrialization would bring social transformation, social equality, higher levels of employment, more equitable distribution of income and a well-balanced regional development. Industrialization, whatever the mode in which it was carried out, was thought to be synonymous with economic growth. It was to bring relief from the underdevelopment suffered by these countries for centuries.

This pattern of reasoning is not shared by all developing countries. It is claimed that, instead of solving many of these problems, industrialization has not led to the economic or social gains expected from it. The growth of income and the pace of development in many of these countries, it is argued, have not been satisfactory, unemployment has tended to increase, and social unrest has become a major problem. The argument continues that all this has taken place despite the over-concentration on industrial development in these countries at the cost of the development of other sectors. From this it is concluded that having failed to fulfil the aspirations of the developing countries, industry should receive less emphasis and other sectors should be given more attention.

Although some of the arguments referred to above are sound, at present no examination is made of the reasons why such aspirations have not been achieved. Developing countries no doubt appreciate the fact that industrialization by itself could not achieve economic growth, and that if stated objectives could not be fulfilled, industry should not be blamed. It is essential to recognize that, while the industrial sector may be the most dynamic sector in the economy, the way to industrialization and thus to the transformation of society and the fulfilment of social and economic objectives is very long indeed and involves a highly complex process. Furthermore, industry does not operate in a vacuum. If development is to entail the transformation of a present economic structure into another characterized by higher efficiency, diversification of output and social justice, the role of industry, although certainly central, is just one of the many complementary roles to be played by all sectors. This is a crucial point to remember, since industrialization has been regarded so far by many developing countries as a separate effort rather than as a complementary component of an over-all economic development strategy, conceived on the basis of the particular circumstances, comparative advantages and stated objectives of the country concerned.

The fulfilment of the goals and aspirations of countries, therefore, depends in the first place on the strategies and policies adopted by these countries, with industry playing its part but not substituting for the other sectors. An appreciation of this point is basic to dispel many of the misconceptions about industrialization and the achievement of national objectives. There is no place for a rigid dichotomy between industry and the other sectors, since their complementarity is essential for development. An arbitrary division of the sectors risks undermining industrial development and runs counter to the concept of economic development. If placed in proper perspective as part of an over-all development strategy, industry should fit into a pattern of industrial development that is suited to a particular country. A wide variety of industrial-development patterns exist from which a country may choose.

When viewed in this perspective, can industry be blamed for the failure of some countries to achieve such social objectives as the elimination of mass poverty, unemploy-

ment and underemployment; the attainment of greater social justice and self-reliance; the effective participation of individuals in the process of development and the sense of responsibility and dignity that this gives to them? Industry should be judged solely on the measure of its achievement of the quantitative objectives set for it, assuming that the other complementary factors play their parts. The realization of social objectives, which are of great importance, depends then on the co-operation of all sectors and, above all, on the will of Governments to institutionalize the necessary policies and strategies to achieve such goals. Individual sectoral strategies may be fitted into an over-all strategy. It should be made clear, however, that should the international community put too great stress on social goals, and neglect the quantitative objectives of growth that are basic to the achievement of social objectives, developing countries may doubt the sincerity of the international effort to assist in their development. It is important instead that the real causes for a slackening of development and a failure to achieve social aims be seriously investigated.

In judging the achievement of industry in terms of the objectives set by the developing countries, the constraints imposed on the industrialization of these countries by the international climate should not be overlooked. Reference has been made to the concentration of world manufacturing output and its implication for the relationship between the developing and the developed countries. It should be taken into consideration in assessing the past performance of the developing countries. Reference has also been made to the rigid pattern of manufacturing trade and the restrictions imposed on the flow of exports of commodities from the developing countries. Other sectors do not have to contend with such a discriminatory situation, and the international climate is not of such importance to their development. Further, at the root of the opposition to industry appears to be the mistaken idea that the pattern of development of the developed countries is likely to be followed by the developing countries.

Although no alternative pattern of development to that of the developed countries has appeared, the assumption that the developing countries must necessarily follow the same pattern is questionable and may indeed have contributed to the confusion. The present ills of the industrialized societies, perhaps caused by excessive industrialization and perhaps by lack of institutional arrangements and social policies, do not pertain to the developing countries, at least in the short term. It is recognized by some opponents of industrialization that it will be a long time before the ills of modern society can appear in the developing countries. Meanwhile, it is hoped that the corrections and solutions now sought by the developed countries will serve to caution the developing countries in designing the future development, not only of their industrial sector but also of the other sectors.

The need of the developing countries to industrialize, however, is not only appreciated by the opponents of excessive industrialization, but it is deemed essential, provided that the pattern of industrial development fits into an over-all strategy of development to achieve the economic and social objectives set by Governments. In this respect, industry could play its role as a major sector in achieving the objectives of such a strategy and the desired change in the style and pattern of development. Characteristics of the industrial sector are its power to inno-

vate and its forceful impact on the process of change. The capacity to innovate often gives it a dynamism that affects the other sectors and other aspects of life, including social and political aspects. Hence, industrialization is not only a way to increase output or national income; it is also a means of introducing modern technology into the economy and of changing attitudes towards development and towards a way of life. Naturally, the results are not automatic, but require changes in the structure of society and its institutions, and these depend on the will of Governments and their capacities to institute the necessary decision-making bodies and the machinery to implement such changes. There are indeed some changes that would strike at the roots of the structure of society, and some Governments may be reluctant to initiate them. Industrialization, by its very nature, either requires such changes or leads to them, and this may account for some of the opposition to industrialization.

From an economic and developmental standpoint, the case for industrialization needs no further argument. Its acknowledged capacities are: to produce more goods through higher productivity; to generate employment, directly and indirectly, through its backward and forward linkages with other sectors, which are often considered front-runners in employment generation; to improve the balance of payments; and to infuse greater efficiency into the whole economy.

X.B.4. Industrialism and Industrial Man*

The decade that has passed since our *Industrialism and industrial man* was first published[1] has been marked both by further rapid development of industrialisation around the world and by continuing commentaries upon it by many observers. Our views of this transformation of world society have undergone some modifications as we have seen the developments of the past decade and studied the views of other contemporary observers and the reactions of reviewers to our book.... This postscript will be primarily concerned with the changes in emphasis we would now make in our earlier views and additional comments we would now add.

MAJOR THEMES REAFFIRMED

Basically, however, we reaffirm the central points of our earlier analysis:

(1) That industrialisation is a central dynamic force at work around the world. It is, of course, only a part of the modernisation process, which includes political and cultural developments as well. A degree of modernisation can, and sometimes does, occur without industrialisation, but industrialisation is usually a basic aspect of modernisation. By "industrialisation" we have meant the totality of relations involving workers, employers and society as they develop to

*From Clark Kerr et al., "Postscript to 'Industrialism and Industrial Man,'" *International Labour Review*, June 1971, pp. 519–26. Reprinted by permission.

[1] *Industrialism and industrial man: the problems of labor and management in economic growth* (Cambridge, Massachusetts), Harvard University Press, 1960; British edition, London and Edinburgh, Heinemann Educational Books, 1962; revised edition, New York, Oxford University Press, 1964. Page references in the present article are to the revised edition.

make use of the new machines, processes and services that modern technology has made possible.[2] These relations are quite distinct from those in a commercial and handicraft, or an agricultural, or a hunting and fishing, society. Industrialisation embodies the new modes of conduct affecting men in the productive process as they shift from the windmill to the steammill—to borrow a phrase from Marx—and as they move towards a society characterised by a wide range of products and services.

(2) That there is a central logic to industrialisation that can be seen in every society using the new technology, regardless of its historical background or current political orientation. This is the common denominator of new and more diverse skills, larger-scale productive endeavours, more large cities and much else. Industrial societies, despite all their differences, are more like each other than they are like pre-industrial societies.

(3) That different societies have taken and still take separate paths on the way to industrialisation. To the central logic that unites all industrialising societies is added the diversity of arrangements that men fashion around this logic, the variations that men devise on the basic theme. These variations relate primarily to the approaches of the élites who organise the industrialisation process—the middle class, the dynastic leaders, the revolutionary intellectuals, the colonial administrators and the nationalist leaders. We would now give greater emphasis to the mixtures of approaches within systems and would rename one of the élites given in 1960, as will be noted below. But these remain, in our view, the five major

[2] The advanced industrial society is particularly characterised by a vast expansion of service industries of all kinds, so that white-collar employment often exceeds blue-collar employment.

variations on the theme of industrialisation.

(4) That, in addition to what is uniform to all and what is related by major approach, there are specific aspects of industrialisation in each country, and even parts of each country, which are quite distinctive. However, the forces of industrialisation have appeared in many countries to be stronger, and cultural factors somewhat less of a force, than we thought in 1960.

(5) That management moves from a paternal or political orientation to a professional one. As we emphasized, professionals are fast becoming more highly trained technically; and the "techno-structure", as Galbraith has termed it, takes over more of the managerial function.

(6) That the central problem of industrial relations around the world is not capital versus labour, but rather the structuring of the labour force—how it gets recruited, developed and maintained. This is the daily business of industrial relations everywhere. Here again, the similarities of actions belie the ideological conflicts.

(7) That workers adapt themselves to and accept industrialisation much more readily than was once thought possible, even avidly at times. We would now add that they tend to become more moderate than we once envisaged, some indeed becoming conservative members of the body politic.

(8) That systems of industrial relations, almost universally tripartite, develop with a substantial degree of compatability among the component parts. These systems originate and administer the "web of rules" that comes to govern daily operations within the system. The organisations of the workers become more a part of the system than an opponent. The system is subject more to evolutionary change than to revolutionary revision.

(9) That industrial societies that start with an atomistic approach (middle class élites) or a monolithic approach (revolutionary intellectuals) tend to move towards pluralistic arrangements lying between full dependence on either the individual or the

State; that the individual, the State and the middle-level organisation all have prominent roles to play. This convergence will never be total and may take longer than we once thought, as we note below, but it remains a major tendency of industrialisation. Also, we now give a greater emphasis to what we called, in 1960, the "new Bohemianism," somewhat redefined. But it still seems to us that the future of man's productive effort lies within the broad band of arrangements which we called "pluralistic industrialism".

As we review our work ten years later we should like to emphasise, once again, that we are engaged in analysis and not in prescription; that we are describing what we see and not what we consider to be a more nearly perfect solution. Industrialisation places many burdens on man besides bringing him greater benefits. We do believe that there are ways in which the burdens could be lightened and the benefits increased. Our analysis, however, is not concerned with our several versions of Utopia, but rather with the nature of the new society that is shaping the present and the future for so much of mankind.

A RE-EXAMINATION OF CRITICAL PROBLEMS IN EARLY STAGES OF DEVELOPMENT

For the developing countries, particularly in their earlier stages of development, the path towards industrialisation is more like an obstacle-race than a paved highway. As we stressed (pp. 78–81), it may be obstructed by conflicts of cultural patterns or retarded by organisational and economic constraints. In *Industrialism and industrial man* we identified most of these obstacles, but some appear to have been overcome without great difficulty while others have turned out in the past decade to be much more formidable than we had anticipated.

In expanding their modern-sector enclaves, for example, the developing countries have generally had less difficulty in overcoming cultural barriers than we thought likely. Constraints such as the family structure, class and race, or religious and ethical values have seldom impeded rapid development in the modern sectors. Nearly all of the less developed countries have modern office buildings, hotels, factories, airports and highways in the urban areas. Coca Cola, Bata shoes, Hilton hotels, TV and grocery supermarkets are almost as ubiquitous in Abidjan, Lagos, Addis Ababa or Bogotá as they are in Copenhagen, Berlin or Tokyo. The new culture of the cities acts like a magnet drawing ever larger numbers of migrants from the rural areas, who quickly conform to a new culture of urban life.

The commitment of a labour force to employment in modern factories has been less difficult than expected. By paying relatively high wages and providing appropriate on-the-job training, employers have been able to minimise the problems of turnover and absenteeism and to build up productive labour forces. The newcomers to modern industrial employment are quick to make a permanent attachment to it, and, with rapidly expanding education in urban areas, the supply of trainable workers has been constantly expanding.

Even the selection, development and training of supervisors and managerial personnel, although not an easy task, appear to offer no insurmountable obstacles. In most countries, the replacement of expatriates by local nationals, particularly in the public service, has proceeded much more rapidly than expected, although government bureaucracies are still not very efficient. Staff training programmes in both the public and the private sectors have proved to be more effective than anticipated for upgrading managerial personnel, and the time required to build experience on the job has in most cases been shorter than most colonial administrators would have predicted. Where local talent is not available, the developing countries can "rent" it from abroad. On the whole, the experience of the last decade

indicates clearly that the developing countries can muster, train or rent the managerial, technical and skilled personnel to operate modern industrial complexes. Indeed, it is probable that the staffing of a steel mill is for them an easier task than the organisation and training of cadres for the promotion of rural development.

Finally, formal education, particularly at the secondary and higher levels, has expanded much more quickly than even the most optimistic planners ever expected. In the modern sectors of most developing countries, quantitative targets for educational expansion have been achieved if not overfulfilled during the past decade. The average annual percentage increase per head in expenditures on public education in many developing countries has exceeded by three or four times the average increase per head in GNP. . . .

In other significant respects, however, some problems connected with industrialisation have loomed larger than we expected. Of these the most serious are: (1) rural stagnation, (2) the mushrooming growth of the urban underclass, (3) education poorly geared to development needs, (4) organisational "power failures" in government bureaucracies, and (5) excessively high rates of growth of the population and the labour force. Each will be reviewed briefly.

(1) A rural transformation is ordinarily an indispensable requirement for continuing industrial development in the absence of substantial exportable natural resources. Rapid development in the isolated modern-sector enclaves provides no easy short cut. An increase in the quantity and particularly the quality of agricultural and livestock production is the core of any rural transformation, but along with this there must be expansion of small industries, improved education and health facilities, better housing, water supplies, sanitation, roads and other public services. Rural transformation calls for the progressive modernisation of traditional rural life, and this in turn requires the

investment of resources, brainpower and human effort in programmes for raising the levels of living of rural people. During the past decade, rural development has often been neglected in favour of rapid industrialisation in the urban areas.

Industrialisation, of course, will provide much of the impetus for rural development. For example, modern science and technology are responsible for the improved seeds, fertilisers, pesticides and techniques that are the basis of possible "green revolutions" in many countries. A sizeable part of the necessary resources may be generated in the rural areas themselves, for experience has shown that rural residents are willing to devote both labour and tax moneys to projects from which they can clearly derive tangible benefits. But some of the profits generated in the modern sectors must also be siphoned off to help finance rural development. Yet, unfortunately, the problems of creating the organisations and developing the appropriate skills for the rural transformation are still largely unsolved. Here perhaps is the most underdeveloped area in the whole field of knowledge on modernisation.

(2) Unemployment and the widespread underemployment of human resources in sprawling urban areas now perhaps constitute the central and most baffling problem facing the developing countries. At best, employment in the modern sectors increases by 3 to 5 per cent a year, but characteristically urban labour forces are growing over twice as fast. Furthermore, an increasing proportion of job seekers are persons with considerable formal education whose expectations far exceed their chances of gaining access to work in government agencies or modern industrial and commercial enterprises. And behind those openly unemployed are growing armies of stall-holders, shoe-shiners, pedlars, beggars, casual labourers and petty thieves who constitute a poverty-stricken, restless and disillusioned urban underclass. In the advanced countries this underclass is usually a small minority

consisting of the undereducated, discriminated-against minority groups, ghetto dwellers, migrant farm workers and others rejected by the institutions of industrialism. But in the urban areas of the less developed countries, this underclass is in the majority even in cases where industrial growth has been most impressive.

The causes of urban unemployment in the industrialising countries are easy to identify: high wages and salaries compared with rural area earnings, which attract droves of hopeful job seekers to the cities; the rise of aspirations fuelled by education oriented to the modern sector; the increase in population growth; and the use of labour-saving technology in modern enterprises. In many respects, therefore, industrialisation concentrates the unemployed in urban areas, even as it creates new employment. The remedies, however, are difficult to implement, for they include wage restraint in the modern sector, greater investment in rural development, more emphasis on labour-intensive industries and population control.

(3) The remarkable expansion of education in the developing countries has drawbacks as well as advantages. For the most part, the underlying purpose of education is more education. In other words, the principal goal of primary schools is to prepare students for entry into secondary schools, and the purpose of secondary schools is to prepare the most promising students for the university and other establishments of higher education. This "single-axis" orientation of the educational systems of many industrialising countries overemphasises preparation for entry into the modern-sector enclaves. It tends to produce intellectuals who are often unemployable, and it creates expectations which are inconsistent with realistic opportunities provided by developing economies. The experience of the last decade has emphasised what we stressed earlier, namely that irrelevant education can waste human and financial resources which otherwise might be channeled into more productive

activities (pp. 18–20 and 99–100).[3] Now the overinvestment in the wrong kinds of formal education compared with non-formal means of acquiring skills and knowledge is becoming more generally recognised, and the importance of employing organisations in providing on-the-job training and work experience is more widely understood.

(4) Government ministries and bureaus, though relatively easy to man in numbers, are slower in developing efficiency. In many countries, the capacity of governments to plan, organise, manage and implement development programmes suffers from chronic "organisational power failure". Even the simplest tasks are poorly performed; the most urgent policy decisions remain unimplemented; rivalries and in-fighting between ministries forestall logical decision-making; and corruption and laziness sap the resources allocated to development programmes. All countries are subject to the danger of becoming mired in their bureaucracies, and many of the developing nations appear to be particularly susceptible to this disease. In particular, the achievement of independence has not enabled the new nationalist leaders to streamline government machinery and cleanse it of corruptive influences to the extent that we might have hoped.

(5) Today nations are more aware of the population menace. Most of the developing countries now have rates of population increase in excess of 2.5 per cent a year (and these rates are still increasing) in contrast with less than half such rates in the industrialised countries. The consequent high proportion of persons in the non-working age groups places almost intolerable burdens on public services, schools, health, and other programmes for improving the lot of the people. Rapidly increasing population lies at the root of mounting unemployment and underemployment. It forestalls the rapid rise

[3] See also Frederick Harbison and Charles A. Myers: *Education, manpower and economic growth. Strategies of human resource development* (New York, London, McGraw-Hill, 1964).

of income per head. It retards the rate of savings. In short, rapidly rising population growth may halt the march towards industrialisation in many countries during the next decades.

In general, it is clear that the developing countries can build industrialised enclaves more quickly than they can develop their rural sectors. For this they have access to modern technology, high-level manpower and even external financial resources. But such industrial systems produce goods and services largely for the minority of the population who are fortunate enough to be attached to the modern-sector enclaves. The result is often dual economies in which the disparities between the rich and the poor are widened. And the notion that growth in the modern-sector enclaves will in itself lead to the transformation of entire traditional societies is now open to question. Internal markets for the outputs of modern-sector enterprise are very thin, and external markets are difficult to penetrate because of ever-increasing international competition. Unless there are rising incomes for the masses in rural areas, therefore, the industrialisation process can slow down once the import-substitution industries have satisfied the economic demands of the fortunate few in the modern enclaves.

In brief, industrialisation in many countries has proceeded more rapidly than we anticipated. In particular, cultural restraints have been less confining, management has been more available, workers have adapted themselves more readily and the educational system has expanded more quickly than we expected ten years ago. However, rural sectors have remained more stagnant, urban unemployment has increased more rapidly, educational expansion has created more unrealistic expectations, government bureaucracies have remained more lethargic or corrupt and population increases have accelerated faster than we once anticipated, and these have proved to be great obstacles in many countries. In many African and Latin American countries industrialisation has increased the disparities between the rich and the poor and between urban and rural areas. It has meant a new and challenging life for a small minority but it has largely bypassed the rural masses. Particularly where there are high rates of population increase and mounting unemployment, industrialisation, by itself, without appropriate measures to reduce the degree of inequality in incomes, offers no ready solution for the problem of poverty in many less developed countries. . . .

X.C. FUTURE

INDUSTRIALIZATION

X.C.1. Goals and Patterns*

The experience of the last two decades underlines above all the need for taking a fresh look at the basic purposes of industrialization and the methods adopted to promote it. Industrialization is not an end in itself, it is only a means of achieving other more basic objectives; and, if the progress made so far has been well below expectations, part of the explanation may be that these objectives have been lost sight of and, consequently, that policies and instruments adopted have not matched the objectives. The dangers of a purely technocratic approach are greater in industrialization than in almost any other sphere of development.

The Committee emphasizes that industrialization should be viewed primarily as a means of improving the conditions of work and living standards of poverty-stricken masses the world over, and not merely as a means of producing a wider variety of products by application of modern technology. If this is not kept in mind, efforts to industrialize may leave the lives of the majority of the people untouched.

If industrialization is to have a broad impact on living conditions in the less developed countries, it has to be closely interwoven with the development of all other sectors of the economy, more particularly agriculture. In fact, without the harmonious development of agriculture and industry, neither can proceed very far. Many of the tensions that have emerged in the developing countries in recent times are

directly or indirectly a reflection of imbalances in the development of these two sectors.

It is not enough, however, for agriculture and industry to achieve high rates of growth of output; such high rates can sometimes be realized by fostering a kind of enclave development within each. It is essential that incomes generated in the process of economic growth are distributed sufficiently widely to promote perceptible improvements in living standards all round. If there is such broad-based generation of incomes, it will also tend to become reflected in the composition of the output corresponding more closely to the requirements of the masses of the people.

Another important objective of industrialization is that it should promote a greater sense of confidence and self-reliance among the developing countries which have hitherto suffered from excessive dependence on others. Yet such self-reliance does not imply autarky. One of the merits of industrialization is, in fact, that while it makes it possible for countries to satisfy their own requirements to a greater degree, it also creates through the very complexity of the processes involved a web of interrelationships which over a period of time bring the countries closer together and make them more dependent on one another. The Committee believes that this kind of balanced interdependence promoted by industrialization can be an important factor in building up the economic foundations for more stable co-operative relationships among nations.

None of these objectives can be realized, however, unless special attention is paid to

*From United Nations, Committee on Planning, Department of Economic and Social Affairs, *Industrialization for New Development Needs*, New York, 1974, pp. 8–12. Reprinted by permission.

the adequacy of the policies and instruments adopted for industrialization. As in other spheres, the broader environment within which particular programmes are undertaken and the means used often have an independent effect of their own on what is actually achieved. Failure to take this into account has been a major weakness hitherto, and the Committee would therefore like to dwell on it at greater length.

Since the industrial sector is, to begin with, a relatively small one in the developing countries, whether its importance is measured in terms of its contribution to total output or its share of the total labour force, the pattern of its further development is apt to be influenced very considerably by the pulls and pressures generated by the rest of the economy. Particularly important in this context are the distribution of wealth and income in the agricultural sector and the biases introduced by trading and financial institutions. Unless the institutional framework in this broad sense of the term is suitably oriented to the promotion of broad-based development, the process of industrialization will inevitably become lop-sided. This has happened in many countries. To that extent the remedy lies not so much in policies and programmes relating to industry as such as in creating a social and economic environment more conducive to development along the desired lines.

Still another general environmental factor affecting industrialization in the developing countries has been the policy of protection followed by the more advanced industrial countries. This has restricted the options available and forced many developing countries to follow policies which they would not have had to follow otherwise. In many instances these policies have taken the form of import restrictions which have led to oligopolistic profits and capital-intensive methods of production with undesirable impacts on exports, income distribution and the standard of living of most of the people. For many developing countries, especially those with a narrow economic base, the opportunity to participate in a more liberal and open world economy and to plan their development in harmony with that of other countries, developed and developing, is indispensable if they are to make full use of their natural and human resources for industrialization.

It is the Committee's view that, if industrialization is to achieve the goals set, there have to be stronger and more concerted efforts to come to grips with these larger issues. If this is not forthcoming, progress in the future may not be very much better than that experienced hitherto.

In order to encourage future industrialization along sound lines, it is necessary to provide an expanding market both internally and externally, and this requires a series of co-ordinated measures. The basis for industrialization must be broadened geographically by giving more attention to the expansion and modernization of agriculture and to the development of small and middle-sized urban centres in the rural areas. This would create the conditions for the development of a pattern of industrialization that would include among its objectives the processing of agricultural and other local materials. Such a pattern of industrialization would in turn help to raise incomes in rural areas and thus provide an expanding market for mass-produced industrial consumer goods. Moreover, there would be a need for increasing manufactured inputs for agriculture and other rural activities.

Such efforts to create a larger market for the products of industry need to be promoted by a lowering of costs in these industries. One means to this end is to improve labour productivity at all levels by training and technical assistance. Another is a progressive reduction of the level of protection in the already well-established industries by more trade in industrial and other products among developing countries. Many developing countries have now reached a stage in their industrial development where they could greatly benefit from more trade among themselves.

The impact of industrialization on employment will however depend mainly on the over-all rate of investment and on the allocation of investment among sectors and subsectors. A sufficiently high rate of investment, together with a harmonious allocation of investment among sectors and subsectors, can offer rapidly expanding employment opportunities. Industrialization will fulfil its key role in the development process when increased production of manufactured goods makes possible substantial increases in other sectors such as agriculture, construction, housing services and infrastructure. It is in that wider sense that industrialization is to be regarded as the main instrument for expanding levels of employment.

Industrialization entails of course not only a quantitative expansion of industrial output but also an improvement in the variety and quality of goods. New and better commodities must appear. This is necessary both for meeting a widening range of domestic demand and for gaining competitiveness in external markets. At the same time, developing countries have to avoid as far as possible excessive differentiation within products, when such differentiation leads to wasteful use of resources, including redundant advertising, and serves no purpose other than helping producers to practise monopolistic pricing.

Most developing countries are heavily dependent on the technologies for industrialization available in the industrialized countries. Research efforts in the developing countries to develop technologies more suited to their requirements need to be strengthened. A primary aim of technological innovation in these countries should be to make available at the lowest possible cost the basic necessities of life for the mass of the people, utilizing to the fullest extent the resources of manpower and materials available in them. The Committee believes that there is considerable scope for such innovative work in which the industrially advanced countries could also help. While, as to technological adaptation, the dominant need

now is for developing, by adaptation or innovation, appropriate technologies that are less capital-intensive, it should also be noted that in due course developing countries will tend to experience technological adjustments of the opposite kind: as they accumulate capital and industrial experience and broaden the range of their industrialization and scientific sophistication, their technologies can be expected to converge more and more with those of the most advanced economies.

Is is often argued that a transfer of technologies for industrialization can best be accomplished by foreign investment that combines technology, management, marketing and capital in a package form. This type of transfer, however, sometimes causes social and political friction in the host countries. Moreover, foreign investment sometimes enters into areas of low priority in terms of the national objectives of development. To avoid such undesirable effects of foreign investment, it may sometimes be desirable for the Governments of developing countries to import foreign investment selectively or to import technology separated from foreign capital and management controls.

Naturally industrialization requires not only the expansion of physical capital, but also the expansion and development of human capital. The latter is perhaps even more important than the former, since it will be the permanent basis of self-reliance. Training of skilled workers, education at all levels, a good selection and training of managerial staff, support for research—these are activities indispensable for successful industrialization.

The choice between specialization and diversification is a dilemma for some developing countries. Pushed to an extreme, neither emphasis is likely to be satisfactory. Specialization offers the chance to exploit economies of scale and to acquire an increasing routine and a growing international reputation as a producer of certain manufactured goods. At the same time, risk is involved. If an external market is lost, the troubles of a highly specialized industry may affect the whole economy. High specialization brings with it an increased dependence on the external market, sometimes on a narrow set of foreign buyers. "Defensive" diversification, on the other hand, may lead to a scattering of resources, higher costs and a less established selling position. Each country must make its own choice, not overlooking the possibility of a deliberate combination, as is the case, for example, in those countries which have chosen to diversify among industries but then to specialize—and to exchange products with trading partners—within industries. Countries are likely to make different specialization-diversification choices at different stages of development and also, of course, to relate their choices to their size and geographical position. All of these factors, together with the country's general development goals and the possibilities of integration with other developing countries, deserve to be taken into account.

Industrialization, the Committee wishes to reiterate, is for people and has to be accomplished by people. It will help them to live better if it widens and cheapens the range of goods they can consume, in the long term as well as the short. There must also be concern for the welfare of people as participants in industrial enterprises—for their job satisfaction, training, working conditions, freedom of association, protection from abuse—and likewise for their protection against the health hazards that so often accompany industrialization.

The International Development Strategy for the Second United Nations Development Decade envisions greater efforts at promoting the industrial development of the developing countries as a principal means of enabling them to produce for themselves the resources for modernization and for the solution of the problems of mass poverty, unemployment and general backwardness. The Committee believes that this is still a necessary part of an appropriate development strategy for the years ahead. For several countries the task of industrialization has of course to start from a very low base; they need to create first the appropriate environment and the institutions for the promotion of industry; and this will take time. For these countries, therefore, the case for an immediate start is all the stronger.

X.C.2. Industrialization via Export

Substitution—Note

In contrast with industrialization via import substitution, there is an increasing interest in the potentialities of an industrialization strategy that emphasizes export substitution—that is, nontraditional exports such as processed primary products, semimanufactures, and manufactured commodities in substitution for traditional primary product exports. It can be argued that the export-substitution process has some distinct advantages over the import-substitution process. In terms of relaxing a country's foreign exchange constraint, a unit of foreign exchange saved by import substitution is equivalent to a unit of foreign exchange earned by export substitution. But there are other considerations in favor of export substitution. The domestic resource cost of earning a unit of foreign exchange tends to be less than the domestic resource cost of saving a unit of foreign exchange. In other words, the resources used in import substitution could have earned a greater amount of foreign exchange through export expansion than the foreign exchange saved in import substitution that relies on high effective rates of protection. Some empirical studies of the factor requirements of industrial exports and imports indicate that if capital and foreign exchange are true constraints and labor is not, the value of exports that could be produced with a given use of scarce factors is greater than the value of imports that could be replaced.[1]

Moreover, to the extent that it rests on exogenous world demand, the process of industrialization through export substitution is not limited to the narrow domestic market of the import-substitution process. The inflow of foreign capital to support export substitution is not dependent on home market protection but is induced by considerations of efficiency on the side of resource cost.

Foreign investment for export substitution also tends to have more linkages to agriculture when it involves the processing of primary products. It also upgrades labor skills when it involves the production of labor-intensive semimanufactures or manufactures. Most importantly, export substitution contributes more than does import substitution to the objectives of greater employment and improvement in the distribution of income. Being labor-intensive in production technique, and dependent on exogenous demand, the nontraditional exports may directly absorb more labor than import replacement, and they may also reduce the cost of employment in terms of the complementary use of scarce factors of capital and imported inputs. The export-substitution process utilizes the surplus factor of labor more intensively than does the import-substitution process, and it also allows the scarce complementary factors to be more productive.

Furthermore, export substitution indirectly aids employment creation in the urban-industrial sector by avoiding an agri-

[1] John Sheahan, "Trade and Employment: Industrial Exports Compared to Import Substitution in Mexico," Williams College Research Center for Development Economics, Research Memorandum 43, 1971.

cultural bottleneck that would otherwise handicap urban-industrial employment. By exporting manufactures and semimanufactures, the developing countries are able to import agricultural goods and thereby keep the real wage low as expressed in terms of industrial goods. If on the contrary, there is a slow growth of agricultural production, and the price of agricultural goods rises relative to that of industrial goods, the real wage in terms of industrial goods would rise. This in turn would induce a substitution of capital for labor, and it would also reduce profit margins, thereby causing savings to decline and the rate of capital formation to decrease. Industrial employment would thereby be adversely affected.[2]

It is, of course, just as possible to oversubsidize in export substitution through a set of discriminatory governmental policies as it is in import-substitution industrialization. As a condition of optimal resource allocation, the marginal cost of earning foreign exchange should be equated with the marginal cost of saving foreign exchange. It is therefore just as inefficient to promote the earning of foreign exchange at all costs as it is to favor the saving of foreign exchange at all costs. To the extent that excessive subsidization of exports occurs, social inefficiency in resource allocation will appear in the same way as under policies that subsidize import substitution. There is, however, evidence that oversubsidization of the export-substitution process is less likely to occur than oversubsidization of import-substitu-

[2] For an elaboration of this point, see J. C. H. Fei and Gustav Ranis, "Development and Employment in the Open Dualistic Economy," Yale Economic Growth Center, Discussion Paper No. 110, April 1971. Fei and Ranis show that countries actually have adjusted to agricultural stagnation by expanding food imports by means of labor-intensive industrial exports. Contemporary examples are Korea and Taiwan, while historical cases include the repeal of the Corn Laws in the United Kingdom and Japanese food imports from her colonies after 1900.

tion industrialization. From a study of several developing countries, Bhagwati and Krueger conclude:

Among the more interesting results that appear to emerge from our preliminary analysis of individual countries' experience is that countries which have had export-oriented development strategies appear, by and large, to have intervened virtually as much and as "chaotically" on the side of promoting new exports as other countries have on the side of import substitution. Yet, the economic cost of incentives distorted toward export promotion appears to have been less than the cost of those distorted toward import substitution, and the growth performance of the countries oriented toward export promotion appears to have been more satisfactory than that of the import-substitution oriented countries. If that conclusion is valid, the lesson is that policy should err on the side of allowing a higher marginal cost for earning than for saving foreign exchange.

There are several theoretical reasons which would explain such an asymmetry in outcomes, and the empirical evidence does point in their direction. In theory, there are four reasons why export promotion may be the superior strategy.

(1) Generally speaking, the costs of excess export promotion are more visible to policymakers than are those of import substitution.

(2) An export-oriented development strategy generally entails relatively greater use of indirect, rather than direct, interventions. There is considerable evidence from the individual country studies that direct intervention may be considerably more costly than is generally recognized.

(3) Exporting firms, however much they may be sheltered on the domestic market, must face price and quality competition in international markets.

(4) If there are significant indivisibilities or economies of scale, an export-oriented

strategy will enable firms of adequate size to realize them. If indivisibilities and/or economies to scale are important, an export-oriented strategy will provide better incentives for expansion of capacity in existing lines. As such, an export-oriented growth strategy is better suited to achieving whatever economies of scale are present than is an import-substitution strategy where firms are generally limited in their horizons by the size of the domestic market.[3]

The evidence from the past two decades does show that the range of labor-intensive manufactures exported from LDCs has indeed widened, and the number of LDCs engaged in export substitution has increased. In conformity with hypotheses about export-based development (see XI.A.6), the evidence indicates that export growth-rates explain a significant portion of the variance in income growth-rates which cannot be explained by the growth in primary inputs; that generally the greatest increase in the GNP of various LDCs is better correlated with exports than any other variables; that the higher-income LDCs have a higher ratio of exports to GDP and a faster rate of growth; and that the higher rate of growth is correlated with a more diversified export base.[4]

Recognizing the potential for a new industrialization strategy, an increasing number of LDCs desire to promote nontraditional exports. A report prepared for the Asian Development Bank is typical in proposing that "to obtain a satisfactory basis for industrialization during the 1970's, the Southeast Asian countries should move away from import-substitution policies towards a radically different approach to industrialization. This

[3] Jagdish N. Bhagwati and Anne O. Krueger, "Exchange Control, Liberalization, and Economic Development," *American Economic Review, Papers and Proceedings*, May 1973, pp. 420–21.

[4] See C. Michaloupoulos, "Growth of Exports and Income in the Developing World," AID Discussion Paper No. 28, November 1973.

new industrialization strategy should be based on the following considerations."

1. Southeast Asian countries have small domestic markets; but they have abundant natural resources and an increasing supply of labor. Their abundant natural resources have enabled them to enjoy rapid economic development through the expansion of primary exports, and this process is likely to continue during the 1970s. Granted this, the new industrialization strategy, if it is to succeed, must be fitted into this general pattern of economic development. Thus, instead of orienting their industrial pattern towards their limited domestic markets, the Southeast Asian countries should orient it towards the export market and should also try to take advantage of their abundant endowment of natural resources. This means that they should make a determined effort to break into the market for manufactured exports during the 1970s.

2. But what type of manufactured exports? In the market for labor-intensive manufactures typified by the textiles and other light consumers' goods, they are likely to face stiff competition, from the neighboring Asian countries, from Pakistan and India on the one hand and from Taiwan and Hong Kong on the other. Singapore has already succeeded in following the path taken by the latter group of countries, but this may be more difficult for other Southeast Asian countries. In order to succeed in the export of labor-intensive manufactures, wage costs must be kept low. Wage costs depend not only on the level of wages but also on the productivity of labor. But initially, when the Southeast Asian countries are trying to break through as latecomers into the export market for labor-intensive manufactures, it may be necessary to keep their wage levels low also. Traditionally, given the sparse population on the available agricultural land, the Southeast Asian peasants tend to require a higher level of wages to induce them to work in the mines and plantations compared with the immigrant labor from the densely popu-

lated countries of India and China. If this high wage tradition is carried into manufacturing, the Southeast Asian countries are likely to find it difficult to compete with neighboring countries in terms of sheer cheapness of unskilled labor. Their best prospect lies in specializing in particular lines of manufactures where they can make the best use of the specific skills and aptitudes of their labor force.

3. A more promising line of export expansion may be found in "export-substitution", that is to say, substituting the existing exports of raw materials by the exports of processed and semi-processed materials. The Philippines and Thailand have already made a start in this direction. Given the range and volume of Southeast Asia's primary exports, there would seem to be a considerable scope for increasing the degree of processing done locally in a wide variety of mineral, timber and agricultural products. But it should be noted that nearness to the source of raw materials does not, by itself, ensure that the processing industries will be profitable. Their success will depend on a number of other factors, such as the productivity of labor in processing activities relative to the prevailing wages, the availability of transport facilities which can exploit the locational advantage, and the availability of an adequate source of power supply. In many cases, the success of the "export-substitution" policy may be held back by the lack of these facilities. But, taking it by and large, this policy still offers the Southeast Asian countries the most promising way of expanding manufactured exports.

4. Southeast Asia's attempt to expand her manufactured exports, whether in the form of labor-intensive finished products or in the form of processed and semi-processed materials, will have to contend with the trade obstacles placed against these products by the advanced countries which represent the largest potential markets. In particular, "tariff escalation", i.e. the system of raising the rate of duty imposed on the processed materials according to the stages of process-

ing they have passed through, is widely practised by the advanced countries, and this can be very damaging to a policy of export-substitution. For the moment, without minimizing the difficulties of overcoming the trade obstacles, it still seems true to say that export-substitution is likely to offer a more promising path to industrialization than import-substitution.[5]

The new industrialization strategy has not, however, gone unchallenged. Some analysts interpret the promotion of labor-intensive processes and component manufacturing as the replacement of a nineteenth-century "plantation society" with the twentieth-century creation of a "branch plant society," as involving undue bargaining power in favor of the foreign enterprise; or as resulting in an unequal international distribution of the gains from trade and investment. Thus, Helleiner cautions about the dependence effects:

Export-oriented labour-intensive industries selling to multinational firms, and totally unintegrated with the rest of the economies in which they are located, would seem to combine some of the most disagreeable features of outward orientation and foreign investment. Particularly where there are "export processing zones", the manufactured export sector constitutes an "enclave"—an "outpost of the mother country"—in as real a sense as any foreign-owned mine ever did. These disagreeable features, moreover, are combined in a manner which leaves the host country with a minimum of bargaining advantage.

Not only is the export manufacturing activity extraordinarily "foot-loose", dependent as it is on neither local resources nor local markets, but it is also likely to bind the host country both to sources of inputs and to market outlets over which it has an absolute minimum of control. Bargaining

strength is likely to be considerably less for a country manufacturing components or undertaking middle-stage processing than it is even for a raw material exporter; for copper or cocoa beans can, after all, be sold on a world market or bartered with socialist states or even used domestically. What is a country to do, however, with tuners designed to meet the particular specifications of Philco television receivers—other than sell them to Philco? Production for export within the multinational firm may indeed be a means for acquiring a share of the expanding markets in products for which world demand is income-elastic; but it may render the host country exceptionally "dependent" upon powerful foreign actors; foreign firms and/or governments may be in a strong position to influence the host countries' policies—both external and domestic—either directly or through their employees or local suppliers where they dominate so utterly particular sectors of their economies. The fundamental problem with this dependency relationship is that continuation or further development in the field of these manufactured exports is subject to the decisions of foreign firms over which the host countries can have extraordinarily little influence—decisions over plant location, new product development, choice of techniques, market allocations, etc. One might therefore sensibly hesitate before committing oneself overly in this direction.[6]

To the extent that export substitution rests on foreign investment by vertically integrated transnational firms, it has been criticized by Vaitsos as constituting only "shallow development." Vaitsos analyzes the export-substitution activities of transnational enterprises as follows:

In the case of exports of processed goods, such firms develop to be important suppliers

[5] Asian Development Bank, *Southeast Asia's Economy in the 1970s*, London, 1971, pp. 19–21.

[6] G. K. Helleiner, "Manufacturing for Export, Multinational Firms and Economic Development," *World Development*, July 1973, p. 17.

of unskilled-labor-intensive know-how. For example, the average fixed capital necessary for each unit of labor in the Taiwan export processing zone in Kaohsiung is about $1,500.

Such a structure raises further issues on the repercussions of foreign firms in developing countries since the former still control the ownership, management, the marketing and technology used. They, in turn, pursue activities related to, what has been called, "shallow development" in the host developing economies (see below for reasons). Furthermore, such firms through their transfer pricing can separate the causes concerning the *location* of production (based on comparative production cost structures) from those related to the *values* or prices registered for the goods that are traded and produced. The latter are affected by tariff levels, absolute and relative tax differentials, political considerations on profit declarations, and government pressures on balance of payments and income effects.

The basic attraction offered by developing countries to such export activities by transnational firms is obviously due to the very low wages of unskilled labor in such countries given minimum productivity rates. Table 1 presents some international comparisons on wage differentials (including supplementary compensation) for comparable job classifications.

The development of this type of international sourcing by transnational firms has important repercussions for developing countries. Their comparative advantage in this case rests in specializing in unskilled labor whose wages have to stay comparatively low while importing a package of inputs (both physical and intangibles) from abroad. Since skills and technology, capital, components and other goods are mobile internationally while unskilled labor is not (or is preferred not to be, due to the heavy social costs involved), transnational firms will be induced to intensify such international sourcing, diversifying their sources of unskilled labor among different developing

countries to assure a continuous availability of supply, or the products of that input.

The "shallowness" of such a development process is a result of the following reasons. The type of labor utilized represents generally the weakest and less organized part of the labor class, thus limiting possibilities for increasing labor returns unless a general shortage of labor takes place in the country, in which case opportunity cost considerations arise for the host economy. If wages increase foreign investors will tend to shift to other countries since their locational interests stem from the existence of low wages given some minimum productivity levels. The training necessary for local labor in such activities is generally very small, limiting spill-over effects. Of critical importance is the absence of marketing knowhow effects for the host country since the goods traded are within the captive markets of affiliates. Final product promotion is handled abroad by the foreign centers of decision making.

The concentration on low wage, unskilled-labor-intensive, export promoting activities has been compared to the older enclave structures in the extractive industry. The basic difference between them, though, is that in the former the foreign investor is not very much captive once he has committed his activities in a country since the investment is very low, the shifting of activities to other nations is easy to undertake since there is no uniqueness in the local supply of inputs and the tapping of local resources did not imply the expensive discovery of previously unknown resources (as in the extractive sector). Thus, the possibility of enhancing the bargaining power of the host government to share in a more equitable distribution of the surplus involved is minimal or non-existent.[7]

From the preceding quotations, it is clear that the issues raised by a strategy of indus-

[7] Constantine V. Vaitsos, "Employment Effects of Foreign Direct Investments," in Edgar O. Edwards (ed.), *Employment in Developing Nations*, New York, 1974, pp. 339–41.

TABLE 1. Average Hourly Earnings of Workers Processing or Assembling U.S. Materials Overseas and in the United States

	Average Hourly Earnings Abroad (Dollars)	Average Hourly U.S. Earnings (Dollars)	Ratio of U.S. Earnings to Earnings Abroad
Consumer electronic products			
Hong Kong	0.27	3.12	11.8
Mexico	0.53	2.31	4.4
Taiwan	0.14	2.56	18.2
Office machine parts			
Hong Kong	0.30	2.92	9.7
Mexico	0.48	2.97	6.2
Korea	0.28	2.78	10.1
Singapore	0.29	3.36	11.6
Taiwan	0.38	3.67	9.8
Semiconductors			
Hong Kong	0.28	2.84	10.3
Jamaica	0.30	2.23	7.4
Mexico	0.61	2.56	4.2
Netherlands Antilles	0.72	3.33	4.6
Korea	0.33	3.32	10.2
Singapore	0.29	3.36	11.6
Wearing Apparel			
British Honduras	0.28	2.11	7.5
Costa Rica	0.34	2.28	6.7
Honduras	0.45	2.27	5.0
Mexico	0.53	2.29	4.3
Trinidad	0.40	2.49	6.3

Source: United States Tariff Commission, *Economic Factors Affecting the Use of Items 807.00 and 806.30 of the Tariff Schedules of the United States* (Washington, D.C., 1970) as cited by Helleiner, "Manufactured Exports from Less Developed Countries and Multinational Firms," *Economic Journal*, March 1973, p. 45.

trialization via export substitution are controversial. They cannot be resolved in isolation. The efficacy of this industrialization strategy is dependent upon the performance of foreign investment, relations between multinational enterprises and host countries, and the trade policies of the developed importing countries. This topic should therefore be considered alongside the selections in VI.C and VI.D, above, and the next chapter.

X.C.3. A Two-Pronged Strategy*

The Philippine economy is of the labour-surplus type.[1] It is, however, also blessed with a relatively good natural resources base, which has meant and still means a strong pattern of cash crop exports—logs, sugar, copra, coconut, tobacco, pineapples and bananas. It was exploitation of these basic resources which constituted the main economic driving force in the colonial period.

The Mission's analysis indicates that the post-Second World War era saw the initiation of two profound changes in the historical pattern of Philippine development: (1) a marked acceleration of population growth, and (2) an attempt to foster rapid growth of the relatively narrow large-scale industrial sector. This meant, on the one hand, that in spite of the relatively rich endowment in natural resources, population began to press increasingly against the land frontier by the end of the 1960s and, on the other, that the rural sector—with its two components of domestically-oriented food production and export-oriented cash crops—had to be relied upon to finance much of the rapid expansion of the industrial sector.

In this situation, some import substitu-

*From Gustav Ranis, "Employment, Equity, and Growth: Lessons from the Philippine Employment Mission," *International Labour Review*, July 1974, pp. 18–24. Reprinted by permission.

[1] A labour-surplus economy is one in which the real agricultural wage is often higher than the marginal product of agricultural labour and in which the relative price of the capital-intensive good understates its opportunity cost in terms of food, i.e. the wage good. For a theoretical exposition, see J. C. H. Fei and Gustav Ranis: *Development of the labor surplus economy: theory and policy*, Homewood, 1964; also M. S. Ahluwalia: "Tax-subsidy intervention and employment", in ILO: *Fiscal measures for employment promotion in developing countries*, Geneva, 1972, and I. Little, T. Scitovsky and M. Scott: *Industry and trade in some developing countries*, London, 1970.

tion sub-phase of transition growth was probably inevitable and, in fact, desirable if the economy was to be restructured away from its pre-independence colonial pattern. Under import substitution the proceeds of the cash crop agricultural subsector, augmented by the reinvestment of industrial profits and foreign capital inflows, were typically used to build up the large-scale industrial sector. The record of the past quarter of a century in the Philippines indicates, however, that import substitution, while constituting a legitimate and desirable post-independence political package, was pursued too much and too long and that one of its major consequences was the above-mentioned conflict among the various desirable goals of national development. It resulted in the relatively vigorous continued growth of both export-oriented agriculture and large-scale domestically-oriented manufacturing but in the relative stagnation of subsistence agriculture and virtually everything else. A careful review of the past quarter of a century makes it possible not only to place the present problems in proper perspective but also to marshal the local evidence bearing on the probable consequences of major policy shifts in the future. For example, while industrialisation aiming at the substitution of consumer good imports—with all the normal paraphernalia of protection, overvalued exchange rates, low interest rates, etc.—was a major phenomenon of the 1950s and 1960s, examination of a particular sub-period, such as 1962–68, during which there was some deviation from that pattern, is bound to be particularly instructive.

A quarter of a century of accelerated industrialisation and population growth, impinging on a mainly rural economy which had not drastically changed since the colonial era, led to mounting difficulties. On the one hand, with domestic markets running out and with no encouragement of international competitiveness, the industrial sector's own growth began to run out of steam. On the other, the rural sector's ability to continue to finance this growth through the contributions of agricultural exports and/or domestic agricultural surpluses diminished with time. This was reflected in a long-term deterioration of the urban industrial sector's terms of trade, both domestic and foreign, as well as in declining rates of return—certainly social and even private—within that sector.

Meanwhile, left to one side in the course of this 25-year effort to maximise urban industrial growth through import substitution were the majority of the would-be economic actors in the society: the medium- and small-scale producers, both agricultural and non-agricultural. The sub-period 1962—68 showed some deviation from extreme import substitution policies and also gave rise to a much faster growth of medium- and small-scale industry than took place before or since. But it is essentially the non-participation of more than four-fifths of the population in productive and innovative activity which lies at the root of the problems to which the Mission was asked to address itself.

A TWO-PRONGED STRATEGY

With respect to the future, all of the Mission's suggestions fall under two strategic headings: to achieve, on the one hand, balanced rural mobilisation and, on the other, a shift towards export-oriented labour-intensive industrial growth. This basic two-pronged strategy reflects the Mission's assessment that the so-called employment problem, which is fundamentally one of low incomes, can be solved only if both the agricultural and the non-agricultural components of the rural sector are mobilised in a balanced, mutually reinforcing fashion and if the industrial sector is able to contribute to its own further growth by exporting competitively in labour-intensive industrial export markets. Only in this fashion can the narrow growth of the past be replaced by broadly based development in the future.

So far as the first aspect of the proposed two-pronged strategy is concerned, the underlying cause of the unemployment and income maldistribution problem and of the social and political unrest threatened thereby is seen by the Mission as the failure of the rural sector to hold its people in productive employment—a failure due especially to the inability of secondary crops and rural industrial activities to become important contributors and, in turn, to help generate sustained productivity increases in the traditional food crop sector. This has resulted in substantial migration to the city which, in the absence of a simultaneous increase in the wages fund to provide additional urban jobs, has caused ever-increasing urban underemployment. The temptation must be resisted to continue to rely exclusively on exports of commercialised cash crops, even under the present temporarily favourable terms of trade. To give way to that temptation would be to forgo substantial additional incomes, additional markets and the entrepreneurial and innovative involvement of the majority of the population.

The second and related aspect of the proposed strategy is concerned with the nature of future as opposed to past urban industrial development. The Philippines should now be ready to combine its relatively plentiful supply of indigenous entrepreneurs with its relatively high-quality labour force in order to penetrate international markets through major changes in output mix and technology. In other words, the path of urban industrial growth can substantially change to absorb the rural migrants arriving in the urban areas complete with their wages fund, i.e. additional food to help provide the additional urban jobs. In view of the labour shortage and substantial wage increases which other labour-intensive exporters in the region such as South Korea and Hong Kong have been experiencing in recent years, the Philippines has an opportunity of stepping into their rather profitable shoes. If the response is inadequate, there are other labour-surplus countries in the region which might well push ahead.

In short, the Mission's analysis of the past indicates that accelerated growth along the old path, that is, "more of the same", cannot work. An increasingly capital-intensive urban industrial sector which at present absorbs less than 10 per cent of the total working population cannot be expected to absorb the new migrants from the rural areas, quite aside from mopping up the existing backlog of urban underemployment. Moreover, the fuelling of import-substituting industrialisation through the generation of food surpluses and/or the export of the traditional products of the soil would become less and less adequate and more and more expensive. . . .

The Mission believes that a redirection of the economy of the Philippines from unbalanced growth to balanced development is eminently feasible. It sees the possibility of: (1) a marked change in the performance of the rural sector resulting from a substantial expansion of rural industrial activities which are at present, by international standards, much too restricted—activities which would grow, in a mutually reinforcing fashion, with primary and secondary food crops and animal husbandry; (2) a rapidly growing role for both existing and new labour-intensive industrial exports, which would be directed to the markets not only of developed but also of other developing countries; (3) an increase in the demand for the (efficient) use of labour in rural and urban industrial activities sufficient not only to absorb the increments in the labour force over the next decade but also to mop up much existing rural and urban underemployment; (4) an improvement in the distribution of income during the next decade resulting from increases in family incomes as more members of the typical working family find jobs, as each member of the family works longer hours and as hourly wages rise, even if only

moderately; (5) sustained increases in wages and major improvements in the distribution of income once underemployment has been eliminated and unskilled labour has become scarce and (6) as a consequence of this much more labour-intensive and broadened development path, the immediate achievement of much higher annual rates of savings and growth than in the past—in excess of 15 per cent and 9 per cent respectively. . . .

"RADICAL" AND "CONVENTIONAL" SOLUTIONS

Another point to be emphasised is that the distinction often drawn between so-called "radical" and "conventional" solutions to the problems of unemployment and maldistribution of income is largely artificial. The policy package that the Philippine Mission recommends contains proposals for a number of structural reforms. They include a vigorous land reform extending beyond what is currently being planned, by providing for differential compensation according to size of holding, a lowering of the existing retention limits for rice and maize and possible reforms in respect of other crops; a thoroughgoing decentralisation of public sector administrative and fiscal powers, at the *barrio* and sub-municipal government level, in order to improve the quality of decision making on issues affecting small farmers and rural industrialists; a comprehensive review of the regional dimensions of development in the Philippines, with a programme of both differential taxation and reallocation of direct expenditure designed to correct the present excessive concentration of economic activity in Manila; and, last but not least, a substantial overhaul of the machinery for promoting investment and innovative activity in a now dormant rural industrial sector oriented to the domestic market.

Much of the rest of the Mission's policy package may be regarded as "conventional".

One of the proposals is for a major reform of the system of interest rates whereby a larger share of the function of credit allocation would be shifted to the banks and away from unofficial markets; medium- and small-scale participants in both the agricultural and the non-agricultural rural sector would be provided with easier access to credit; and unearned or windfall profits would be withdrawn from the large-scale urban industrialist and landlord classes, with the incidental result that a narrowing of the spread between lending and borrowing rates would stimulate the banks to become more competitive by opening more branches in the rural areas. Another proposal is for a progressive readjustment of public sector tax and expenditure policies, including programmes designed to ensure stable prices for the major wage goods and a modest programme of poverty redressal in favour of the poorest sections of the population. There are proposals, too, for a major effort of technical assistance to rural medium- and small-scale industry focusing both on the scope for adaptive technology and on adaptive commodities serving mainly the domestic market, and for a strategy of liberalising the industrial protection and tariff system linked to an adjustment assistance programme for affected existing industries.

But the difference between the so-called "radical" and "conventional" components of the Mission's proposed package pales into insignificance on closer examination. Major changes in the equity with which various groups are treated, e.g. in access to credit before and after an interest rate reform, are just as "radical", in terms of their impact on the elimination of windfall profits, as is asset redistribution (e.g. land reform). To the extent that existing inequality is due to the accumulated effect of market imperfections, monopoly positions, the existence of protected sectors benefiting from tariff policy, credit discrimination, etc., liberalisation is a most effective way to improve the function-

ing of the system, including the distribution of income. The policies suggested by the Mission with a view to promoting institutional change and improving markets are intended not to discourage profits *per se* but to discourage unearned profits and ensure that more profits accrue to the small competitive enterprise rather than to the large protected oligopoly, to small owner-operated farms and rural industries rather than to absentee landlords and metropolitan firms.

The really critical issue is not, however, one of differentiating between the "radical" and the "conventional" portions of the Mission's proposed policy package: both portions have the same purpose of releasing the energies of large numbers of persons who are at present economically disenfranchised. The real issue is, rather, to make sure that the various parties to the social contract understand that there is a need for a change in the nature of the growth path and that a changed path can be expected to yield a better distribution of income, a solution to the employment problem and higher growth rates to boot.

A major lesson to be drawn by other labour-surplus developing economies is that the basis for a simultaneous solution to the employment, income distribution and growth problems lies in the encouragement of a much more sustained demand for unskilled labour. The Mission has suggested policies having significant direct and indirect income redistribution effects, as, for example, through a redistribution of assets, through a decentralisation of public infrastructure, especially in the rural sector, through improvements in the functioning of the credit market, through public sector tax and expenditure readjustments, but mainly through an increase in the demand for labour due to the changes in technology and output mix resulting from balanced rural mobilisation and a new industrial export orientation. . . .

X. SELECT BIBLIOGRAPHY

1. The balanced growth versus unbalanced growth controversy can be examined more intensively in the following references. The list includes readings on the various concepts of external economies which underlie advocacy of balanced growth. Some references also subject the balanced growth doctrine to historical analysis, and others relate the doctrine to foreign trade: H. W. Arndt, "External Economies in Economic Growth," *Economic Record*, November 1955; H. B. Chenery, "The Interdependence of Investment Decisions," in Moses Abramovitz et al. (eds.), *The Allocation of Economic Resources*, Stanford, 1959; M. Fleming, "External Economies and the Doctrine of Balanced Growth," *EJ*, June 1955; J. R. T. Hughes, "Foreign Trade and Balanced Growth: The Historical Framework," *AER*, May 1959; M. Lipton, "Balanced and Unbalanced Growth in Underdeveloped Countries," *EJ*, September 1962; H. B. Malmgren, "Balance, Imbalance, and External Economies," *OEP*, March 1963; J. M. Montias, "Balanced Growth and International Specialization: A Diagrammatic Analysis," *OEP*, June 1961; H. Myint, "The Demand Approach to Economic Development," *Review of Economic Studies*, Vol. 27, No. 2; S. K. Nath, "The Theory of Balanced Growth," *OEP*, June 1962; Goran Ohlin, "Balanced Economic Growth in History," *AER*, May 1959; Tibor Scitovsky, "Growth-Balanced or Unbalanced?" in Moses Abramovitz et al. (eds.), *The Allocation of Economic Resources*, Stanford, 1959; Ragnar Nurkse, *Problems of Capital Formation in Underdeveloped Countries*, London, 1960; Harvey Leibenstein, *Economic Backwardness and Economic Growth*, New York, 1957; A. O. Hirschman, *Strategy of Economic Development*, New Haven, Chaps. 5, 11; Dalip S. Swamy, "Statistical Evidence of Balanced and Unbalanced Growth," *RES*, August 1967.

2. Specialized aspects of the development of secondary industry are considered in the following: H. G. Aubrey, "Small Industry in Economic Development," *Social Research*, September 1951; G. B. Baldwin, *Industrial Growth in South India: Case Studies in Economic Development*, Glencoe, 1959; H. Belshaw, "Observations on Industrialization for Higher Income," *EJ*, September 1947; H. B. Chenery, "The Role of Industrialization in Development Programs," *AER*, May 1955; B. F. Hoselitz, "Small Industry in Underdeveloped Countries," *Journal of Economic History*, December 1959; E. A. J. Johnson, "Problems of 'Forced-Draft' Industrialization," *First International Conference of Economic History*, Stockholm, 1960; W. A. Lewis, "Industrial Development in Puerto Rico," *Caribbean Economic Review*, December 1949; ____, "Industrialization of the British West Indies," *Caribbean Economic Review*, May 1950; ____, *Aspects of Industrialization*, Cairo, 1953; H. W. Singer, "Problems of Industrialization of Underdeveloped Countries," in L. Dupriez (ed.), *Economic Progress*, Louvain, 1955; OECD, *Methods of Industrial Development*, Paris 1962; United Nations, *Management of Industrial Enterprises in Underdeveloped Countries*, New York, 1958; ____, *Processes and Problems of Industrialization in Underdeveloped Countries*, New York, 1955; ____, *Industrial Development in Asia and The Far East*, Manila, 1965; UNIDO, *Report of the International Symposium on Industrial Development*, TD/B/21, February 2, 1968 (includes list of documents prepared for the Symposium); A. B. Mountjoy, *Industrialization and Underdeveloped Countries*, Chicago, 1967; A. F. Ewing, *Industry in Africa*, London, 1968; W. Baer and M. Herve, "Employment and Industrialization in Developing Countries," *QJE*, February 1966; OECD Development Center, *Manual of Industrial Project Analysis in Developing Countries*, Paris, 1969; R. B. Helfgott and S. Schiavo-Campo, "An Introduction to

Industrial Planning," *Industrialization and Productivity*, No. 16, 1970; I. Sachs and K. Laski, "Industrial Development Strategy," *Industrialization and Productivity*, No. 16, 1970, pp. 35–48; K. Griffin and J. Enos, *Planning Development*, London, 1971, Chap. 9.

3. The following consider in general some theoretical aspects of industrialization via import substitution or export substitution. (Empirical aspects are considered in the next chapter.) M. Bruno, "The Optimal Selection of Export Promoting and Import Substituting Projects," in United Nations, *Planning the External Sector*, New York, 1967; ____, "Optimal Patterns of Trade and Development," *RES*, 1967; A. O. Hirschman, "The Political Economy of Import Substituting Industrialization," *QJE*, February 1968; K. H. Raj and A. K. Sen, "Alternative Patterns of Growth under Conditions of Stagnant Export Earnings," *OEP*, February 1961; H. Bruton, "The Import Substitution Strategy of Economic Development," *Pakistan Development Review*, Summer 1970; I. M. D. Little, T. Scitovsky, and M. Scott, *Industry and Trade in Some Developing Countries*, London, 1970, Chaps. 2–3; Hollis Chenery; "Comparative Advantage and Development Policy," *AER*, March 1961; Joel Bergsman, "Commercial Policy, Allocative Efficiency and 'X-Efficiency,' " *QJE*, August 1974.

CHAPTER XI

Trade
Strategy

This chapter concentrates on the problems connected with the transmission of development through trade. It is especially concerned with whether there is a conflict between market-determined comparative advantage and the acceleration of development—whether in pursuing the gains from trade, a country might limit its attainment of the gains from growth.

Materials in the first section present opposing views on this question. Some economists argue that the accrual of the gains from trade is biased in favor of the advanced industrial countries, that foreign trade has inhibited industrial development in the poorer nations, and that—contrary to what would be expected from classical trade doctrine—free trade has in reality accentuated international inequalities. In contrast, others maintain the traditional position that foreign trade can contribute substantially to the development of primary exporting countries and that the gains from international specialization merge with the gains from growth. A more eclectic approach attempts to identify the various conditions that favor—or inhibit—a process of export-led development.

Phenomena associated with a changing international division of labor may also exert strong influence on the rate and structural pattern of a country's development. The concern over the role of the LDCs in a new international economic order is connected with problems of facilitating a new international division of labor: To what extent can primary producing countries exercise "resource bargaining power"? What is the scope for import substitution? What are the potentials for export of nontraditional products?

In demanding the reform of international trading arrangements, the LDCs in UNCTAD are seeking not merely more trade, but more trade at higher export prices. In essence the trade proposals of UNCTAD attempt to internationalize protection or invert protection in the sense of having it practiced by developed importing countries in favor of the less developed exporting countries.[1] Both international commodity agreements for primary products and preferences for manufactured exports have the objective of improving the LDCs' terms of trade by raising export prices, thereby effecting a transfer of real resources from consumers in developed countries to producers in LDCs. If balance-of-payments and budgetary considerations make it unlikely that more resources can be transferred through taxpayers in the developed countries in the form of "open aid," then the transfer may have to come more covertly through implicit taxation of consumers in the developed importing countries. The selections in section XI.B discuss how the character of trade in primary products might be changed through the use of "producer power" and international commodity agreements.

The trade policy of a developing country is closely related to the problems raised by the foreign exchange constraint on the country's development. A number of theoretically sophisticated arguments support a protectionist trade policy for a developing country. In actual practice, however, protectionist policies have rarely been adopted out of a reasoned consideration of how protectionism might improve the terms of trade, raise the savings ratio, take account of external economies, or overcome distortions in the labor market. On the contrary, it has been the persistent shortage of foreign exchange that has dominated considerations of trade policy, and protectionist policies have been much more in the nature of ad hoc responses to recurrent balance-of-payments crises.

These policies have, however, been disappointing in most countries. The policies have not succeeded in reducing the foreign exchange constraint; indeed, in some cases, it can be claimed that import-substitution policies have actually intensified the shortage. Nor have the policies of import replacement succeeded in achieving any widespread degree of industrialization beyond the immediate replacement of the final imported consumer goods; nor has there been the expected progression from import-replacement to production for export markets (as in the earlier Japanese case); nor has industrial protection been an effective means of ameliorating the labor absorption problem. Nonetheless, import-substituting policies have become self-justifying in LDCs as their trade gap has widened, and the countries have resorted to yet another round of import restrictions to meet the balance-of-payments problem. These disappointing results of import substitution in practice are reviewed in section XI.C.

There is now a notable shift of emphasis away from import-replacing policies to the outward-looking policies of export promotion, particularly of semimanufactured and manufactured exports. This requires consideration of a variety of policies—not only the granting of tariff preferences for exports from the LDCs, but even more importantly a reduction of the effective rates of protection, and a removal of nontariff barriers. If their nontraditional exports are to be promoted, the LDCs will also have to pursue policies to take advantage of the new opportunities provided by the underlying real forces of a changing international division of labor.

Proposals for regional integration, as a means of lessening the dependence on primary exports and accelerating development, have also gained increasing favor. The Note in section XI.E appraises the contributions that a customs union or free trade area might make to the development of its member nations.

The issues raised in this chapter tend to cut across the objectives of international efficiency in resource allocation, international stabilization of primary export revenue,

---

[1] H. G. Johnson, *Economic Policies Toward Less Developed Countries*, Washington, D.C., 1967, *passim*.

and international redistribution of income. In the more orthodox view of trade theory, these objectives are kept quite separate, and different policy instruments are advocated as being "first-best" policy for each objective. In international policy discussions, however, the problems become only too easily intermixed. And just as there is a political controversy over whether the international monetary system should be linked to development finance, so too there is political disagreement over "aid through trade policy," over the sacrifice of efficiency in international resource allocation for the sake of an international transfer of resources, and over the burden-sharing of adjustments to a changing international division of labor.

XI.A. INTERNATIONAL TRADE AND INTERNATIONAL INEQUALITY

XI.A.1. Trade as a Mechanism of International Inequality*

Our inherited economic theory would . . . lead us to expect that international inequalities should not be so large as they are and not be growing. In any case this theory does not furnish us with an explanation in causal terms of these inequalities and their tendency to increase.

"The fact that many under-developed countries do not derive the advantages from modern transportation and commerce that theory seems to demand is one of the most pertinent facts in the present international situation and cannot be easily dismissed"—I am quoting from a recent paper by a Swedish economist, Mr. Folke Hilgert.[1] . . .

Hilgert points out that huge movements of labour and capital from Europe have transformed the plains in the temperate belts into "white man's land" with high, rapid and sustained economic development and rising levels of living. "Yet the gradual filling of the 'empty spaces' has not reduced the pressure of population in, for instance, Asia's over-populated regions where labour is most abundant."

Let us remember, however, that according to the classical doctrine movements of labour and capital between countries would not be necessary for bringing about a devel-

opment towards equilisation of factor prices and, consequently, earnings and incomes; in fact, the theory of international trade was largely developed on the abstract assumption of international immobility of all factors of production. That trade itself initiated a tendency towards a gradual equalisation of factor prices was implicit already in the expositions by the classical authors, though their method of stating the law of comparative costs in terms of only a single factor, labour—which, however, could have different "qualities" or degrees of "effectiveness"—turned the emphasis in other directions.

After Eli F. Heckscher's paper on the equalising influence of trade on factor prices and Bertil Ohlin's restatement of the classical theory of international trade in terms of a general equilibrium theory of the Lausanne school type,[2] trade appeared more clearly as a substitute, or an alternative, to factor movements in permitting an adjustment of industrial activity to adapt itself to the localisation of natural and population resources with the result that the relative scarcity of labour and capital became less different. Upon this foundation there has in recent years been a lively discussion between

---

*From Gunnar Myrdal, *Development and Underdevelopment*, National Bank of Egypt Fiftieth Anniversary Commemoration Lectures, Cairo, 1956, pp. 9–10, 47–51. Reprinted by permission.

[1] "Uses and Limitations of International Trade in Overcoming Inequalities in World Distribution of Population and Resources," *World Population Conference*, Rome, 1954.

[2] Eli F. Heckscher, "The Effect of Foreign Trade on the Distribution of Income," *Readings in the Theory of International Trade*, selected by a committee of the American Economic Association, Allen & Unwin, London, 1950 (translation from the Swedish original 1919); Bertil Ohlin, *Interregional and International Trade*, Harvard University Press, Cambridge, Mass., 1933.

688

the econometricians elaborating, under specific, abstract and static, conditions, the relative effectiveness of this tendency to equalisation of factor prices as a result of international trade.[3]

The inadequacy of such theories for explaining reality cannot be accounted for by pointing to the relative breakdown of the multilateral trading system as it functioned prior to the First World War, a change which is related as both effect and cause to the increase of national trade and payments restrictions. For, as Hilgert observes, a similar confrontation of the facts of international inequality with the theory of international trade for the period before 1914 reveals the same discord. And I would add that it is not self-evident but, indeed, very much up to doubt whether today a freer trade would necessarily lead to less of international inequality or whether in general trade between developed and (densely populated) under-developed countries has ever had that effect. . . .

Contrary to what the equilibrium theory of international trade would seem to suggest, the play of the market forces does not work towards equality in the remunerations to factors of production and, consequently, in incomes. If left to take its own course, economic development is a process of circular and cumulative causation which tends to award its favours to those who are already well endowed and even to thwart the efforts of those who happen to live in regions that are lagging behind. The backsetting effects of economic expansion in other regions dominate the more powerfully, the poorer a country is.

Within the national boundaries of the richer countries an integration process has

taken place: on a higher level of economic development expansionary momentum tends to spread more effectively to other localities and regions than those where starts happen to have been made and successfully sustained; and inequality has there also been mitigated through interferences in the play of the market forces by organised society. In a few highly advanced countries—comprising only about one-sixth of the population in the non-Soviet world—this national integration process is now being carried forward towards a very high level of equality of opportunity to all, wherever, and in whatever circumstances they happen to be born. These countries are approaching a national harmony of interest which, because of the role played by state policies, has to be characterized as a "created harmony"; and this has increasingly sustained also their further economic development.

Outside this small group of highly developed and progressive countries, all other countries are in various degrees poorer and mostly also less progressive economically. In a rather close correlation to their poverty they are ridden by internal economic inequalities, which also tend to weaken the effectiveness of their democratic systems of government in the cases where they are not under one form or another of oligarchic or forthright dictatorial rule.

The relations between relative lack of national economic integration and relative economic backwardness run, according to my hypothesis of circular cumulative causation, both ways. With a low level of economic development follow low levels of social mobility, communications, popular education and national sharing in beliefs and valuations, which imply greater impediments to the spread effects of expansionary momentum; at the same time the poorer states have for much the same reasons and because of the very fact of existing internal inequalities often been less democratic and, in any case, they have, because they are poorer, been up against narrower financial and, at bottom, psychological limitations on policies

[3] The recent discussion of the problem of factor price equalisation as a result of international trade was initiated by Professor Paul A. Samuelson in two articles in the *Economic Journal*, 1948 and 1949; for fuller reference see Svend Laursen, "Production Functions and the Theory of International Trade," *The American Economic Review*, 1955, pp. 540 ff.

seeking to equalise opportunities. Inequality of opportunities has, on the other hand, contributed to preserving a low "quality" of their factors of production and a low "effectiveness" in their production efforts, to use the classical terms, and this has hampered their economic development.

On the international as on the national level trade does not by itself necessarily work for equality. A widening of markets strengthens often on the first hand the progressive countries whose manufacturing industries have the lead and are already fortified in surroundings of external economies, while the under-developed countries are in continuous danger of seeing even what they have of industry and, in particular, their small scale industry and handicrafts outcompeted by cheap imports from the industrial countries, if they do not protect them.

It is easy to observe how in most under-developed countries the trading contacts with the outside world have actually impoverished them culturally. Skills in many crafts inherited from centuries back have been lost. A city like Baghdad, with whose name such glorious associations are connected, today does not harbour any of the old crafts, except some silver smithies, and they have adopted patterns from abroad requiring less craftsmanship; similarly it is only with the greatest difficulties that one can buy a book of Arabic literature, while cheap magazines in English or Arabic are in abundance.

If international trade did not stimulate manufacturing industry in the under-developed countries but instead robbed them of what they had of old-established crafts, it did promote the production of primary products, and such production, employing mostly unskilled labour, came to constitute the basis for the bulk of their exports. In these lines, however, they often meet inelastic demands in the export market, often also a demand trend which is not rising very rapidly, and excessive price fluctuations. When, furthermore, population is rapidly rising while the larger part of it lives at, or near, the subsistence level—which means that there is no scarcity of common labour—any technological improvement in their export production tends to confer the advantages from the cheapening of production to the importing countries. Because of inelastic demands the result will often not even be a very great enlargement of the markets and of production and employment. In any case the wages and the export returns per unit of product will tend to remain low as the supply of unskilled labour is almost unlimited.

The advice—and assistance—which the poor countries receive from the rich is even nowadays often directed towards increasing their production of primary goods for export. The advice is certainly given in good faith and it may even be rational from the short term point of view of each under-developed country seen in isolation. Under a broader perspective and from a long term point of view, what would be rational is above all to increase productivity, incomes and living standards in the larger agricultural subsistence sectors, so as to raise the supply price of labour, and in manufacturing industry. This would engender economic development and raise incomes *per capita*. But trade by itself does not lead to such a development; it rather tends to have backsetting effects and to strengthen the forces maintaining stagnation or regression. Economic development has to be brought about by policy interferences which, however, are not under our purview at this stage of the argument when we are analysing only the effects of the play of the market forces.

Neither can the capital movements be relied upon to counteract international inequalities between the countries which are here in question. Under the circumstances described, capital will, on the whole, shun the under-developed countries, particularly as the advanced countries themselves are rapidly developing further and can offer their owners of capital both good profits and security.

There has, in fact, never been much of a capital movement to the countries which today we call under-developed, even in earlier times—except tiny streams to the economic enclaves, mainly devoted to export production of primary products which, however, usually were so profitable to their owners that they rapidly became self-supporting so far as investment capital was concerned and, in addition, the considerably larger but still relatively small investments in railways and other public utilities which had their security in the political controls held by colonial governments. The bulk of European overseas capital exports went to the settlements in the free spaces in the temperate zones which were becoming populated by emigration from Europe. After the collapse of the international capital market in the early 'thirties, which has not been remedied, and later the breakdown of the colonial system, which had given security to the foreign investor, it would be almost against nature if capital in large quantities were voluntarily to seek its way to under-developed countries in order to play a role in their economic development.

True, capital in these countries is scarce. But the need for it does not represent an effective demand in the capital market. Rather, if there were no exchange controls and if, at the same time, there were no elements in their national development policies securing high profits for capital—i.e. if the forces in the capital market were given unhampered play—capitalists in under-developed countries would be exporting their capital. Even with such controls and policies in existence, there is actually a steady capital flight going on from under-developed countries, which in a realistic analysis should be counted against what there is of capital inflow to these countries.

Labour migration, finally, can safely be counted out as a factor of importance for international economic adjustment as between under-developed and developed countries. The population pressure in most under-developed countries implies, of course, that they do not need immigration and the consequent low wages that immigrants are not tempted to come. Emigration from these

countries would instead be the natural thing. For various reasons emigration could, however, not be much of a real aid to economic development, even if it were possible.

And the whole world is since the First World War gradually settling down to a situation where immigrants are not welcomed almost anywhere from wherever they come; people have pretty well to stay in the country where they are born, except for touristing by those who can afford it. And so far as the larger part of the under-developed world is concerned, where people are "coloured" according to the definition in the advanced countries, emigration is usually stopped altogether by the colour bar as defined by the legislation, or in the administration, of the countries which are white-dominated and at the same time better off economically.

If left unregulated, international trade and capital movements would thus often be the media through which the economic progress in the advanced countries would have backsetting effects in the under-developed world, and their mode of operation would be very much the same as it is in the circular cumulation of causes in the development process within a single country.... Internationally, these effects will, however, dominate the outcome much more, as the countervailing spread effects of expansionary momentum are so very much weaker. Differences in legislation, administration and *mores* generally, in language, in basic valuations and beliefs, in levels of living, production capacities and facilities, etcetera make the national boundaries effective barriers to the spread to a degree which no demarcation lines within one country approach.

Even more important as impediments to the spread effects of expansionary momentum from abroad than the boundaries and everything they stand for is, however, the very fact of great poverty and weak spread effects within the under-developed countries themselves. Where, for instance, international trade and shipping actually does transform the immediate surroundings of a port to a centre of economic expansion, which happens almost everywhere in the world, the expansionary momentum usually does not spread out to other regions of the country, which tend to remain backward if the forces in the markets are left free to take their course. Basically, the weak spread effects as between countries are thus for the larger part only a reflection of the weak spread effects within the under-developed countries themselves.

Under these circumstances the forces in the markets will in a cumulative way tend to cause ever greater international inequalities between countries as to their level of economic development and average national income *per capita.*

XI.A.2. Transnational Capitalism and National Disintegration*

The approach proposed here takes the characteristics of underdevelopment as a set of normal features inherent in the functioning of a given system. In other words, the structure of the system defines the manner in which it functions, and, therefore, the results which it produces. These results are well known in the case of underdeveloped countries: low income and slow growth, regional disequilibria, instability, inequality, unemployment, dependence on foreign countries, specialization in the production of raw materials and primary crops, economic, social, political and cultural marginality, etc. The conventional student takes those symptoms of underdevelopment as deviations from the ideal, or the teething troubles of an infant economy which would be overcome with economic growth and modernization. He does not perceive that at the root of these characteristics there exists a system which normally produces and continues to produce those results as long as development policy continues to attack the symptoms of underdevelopment without dealing with the basic structural elements which give rise to underdevelopment.

Historical insight is essential for the identification of such structural elements, explanation of the functioning of a system with a given structure, and analysis of structural change itself. This seems to be the more decisive aspect of development analysis, because if the results of the process are seen as a function of the structure of the system, these results will change only if the structure of the system undergoes change.

If one were to apply this orientation to Latin American countries, it becomes quite clear that external links and relationships have exercised a fundamental influence on the shaping of the structure of our systems, and, therefore, on their functioning and outcome, as well as on the process of structural transformation. Nevertheless, the importance attached to these external links should not lead us to underestimate the existence of structures of underdevelopment internal to the system. Although external influences probably tend to prevail as main factors in the long term process of transformation, structural transformation is the product of the interaction between external and internal variables. . . .

In sum, an adequate analytical framework for the study of underdevelopment and development must rest on the notions of process, structure and system. According to an approach of this kind, it is not possible to admit that underdevelopment is a moment in the evolution of a society which is economically, politically and culturally autonomous and isolated. On the contrary, it is postulated that underdevelopment is part and parcel of the historical process of global development of the international system,

*From Osvaldo Sunkel, "Transnational Capitalism and National Disintegration in Latin America," *Social and Economic Studies,* Special Number, Vol. 22, No. 1, March 1973, pp. 135–40, 145–9, 154, 163–70. Reprinted by permission.

and therefore, that underdevelopment and development are simply the two faces of one single universal process. Furthermore, underdevelopment and development have been, historically, simultaneous processes which have been linked in a functional way, that is, which have interacted and conditioned themselves mutually.

The evolution of this global system of underdevelopment-development has, over a period of time, given rise to two great polarizations which have found their main expression in geographical terms. First, a polarization of the world between countries: with the developed, industrialized, advanced, "central northern" ones on one side, and the underdeveloped, poor, dependent, and "peripheral southern" ones on the other. Second, a polarization within countries, between advanced and modern groups, regions and activities and backward, primitive, marginal and dependent groups, regions and activities.

Development and underdevelopment should therefore be understood as partial but interdependent structures, which form part of a single whole. The main difference between the two structures is that the developed one, due basically to its endogenous growth capacity, is the dominant structure, while the underdeveloped structure, due largely to the induced character of its dynamism, is a dependent one. This applies both to whole countries and to regions, social groups and activities within a single country.

This approach focuses attention on two types of polarization processes, one at the level of international relations, the other at the domestic level. We shall now examine some of the more relevant aspects of both processes from the dominant viewpoint of this paper, viz., the interaction between the international and domestic levels of the dual process of polarization.

INTERNATIONAL POLARIZATION

The theories which relate the national development process to the system of international economic relations, and which underline the interpretation of past and present trends, may be classified in three main groups: the neoclassical theory of international trade, the Marxist theory of capitalistic-imperialist exploitation and the theories of the "backwash effect" of international trade.

The liberal *laissez faire* approach is a rather inappropriate basis for analysis and recommendations, because of the highly unrealistic and restrictive assumptions upon which it is based, of which one is particularly damaging. I refer to the identification of the concepts of "economy" and "country" which means that countries are conceived as selfcontained economic units which exchange products in the international market place, these then being their "international economic relations". Quite apart from the very partial aspect of international economic relations implicit in this approach, such an approach fails to grasp one of the essential characteristics of the international economy, viz., that it is basically made up of transnational conglomerates, firms which operate simultaneously in various *national* markets, thus constituting an international economic system which penetrates and overlaps with the national economic system.

The Marxist theory of imperialism is based precisely on the recognition of this fact, since it suggests that international monopolies penetrate national economies in search of raw materials and market outlets in order to use and add to their increasing economic surplus. Nevertheless, until relatively recently, the Marxist approach had restricted itself mainly to the role of *international monopoly capitalism*, neglecting to some extent an element which seems most essential from our point of view: the "spread" and "back-wash" effects of the international extensions of some national economic systems into other national economic systems.

This analysis, which was associated originally with the names of Myrdal, Singer, Prebisch and others, and which has been a central concern in important Marxist and non-Marxist contributions in recent years, suggests that in the interaction of industrial economies with primary producing economies, the former tend to benefit relatively more than the latter, and that this gives rise to cumulatively divergent trends in the development of the two groups of countries. Although there are many different arguments advanced in favour of this hypothesis, they essentially boil down to the following: a) the nature of foreign owned or controlled primary production for export, which tends to be an "enclave" with little relation to or influence over the local economy but with substantial promotional effects over the home economy where most procurement, financing, storing, processing, research, marketing and reinvestment take place; b) the characteristics of the local economy, which lacks trained manpower, entrepreneurial talent, capital and physical as well as institutional infrastructure, and is therefore unable to respond positively to the potential opportunities of an expanding export activity; c) the relative behaviour of the prices of raw material exports and manufactured imports—the worsening of the terms of trade of primary producers—as well as the instability of primary product prices; d) the generally monopolistic nature of the primary export activity which, when the firm is foreign owned, implies an outflow of excess profits.

This approach introduces a most important perspective since it focusses attention on the interaction between the external agents and the domestic economic, social and political structures. Nevertheless, it is still somewhat partial and requires further generalization and systematization.

Apart from other considerations, it is partial because it has concentrated its analysis of the differential effects of the interaction between developed and underdeveloped countries exclusively on the primary producing export activities of the latter. One of the results of this bias in the analysis was the conclusion that these countries had to industrialize because industrialization would re-sult in a cumulative process of self-enforcing "spread" effects—Rostow's "take-off into self-sustained growth". To a large extent this seems to have been the consequence of applying the European model of the Industrial Revolution to the Latin American cases.

But the model of import substituting industrialization that has characterized Latin America seems to be something quite different. It is in fact very difficult to understand if, apart from the internal peculiarities of each country, reference is not made to the framework of external links conditioning factors and pressures that have influenced industrial development so decisively in our countries. In fact, its dynamics, its structure and the nature of the productive processes adopted, especially with reference to technology, have been induced to a large extent by external conditions.

When Latin American countries embarked on a deliberate policy of industrialization, they were confronted with the need for substantially expanding specialized manpower, skilled human resources, entrepreneurs, machinery and equipment, raw materials and inputs, financial resources, sales, marketing, credit and publicity organizations, as well as the technology and know-how necessary for all these tasks. When industrial development outgrows its initial stages, the scarcity and urgency of all these elements become more and more critical, particularly when industry enters the more complex fields of basic manufactures and consumer durables.

Under such conditions, the forces of industrialization have had to rely heavily and increasingly on external support, for know-how, technology, administrative capacity, equipment, financing, etc. These various international contributions to domestic industrial development, clearly indispensable in view of the precarious base from which such development started, have taken place in various forms manifesting different modalities. External financial contributions, for instance, have come as public or private loans, portfolio investments, immigration of foreign capitalists, foreign subsidiaries wholly or partially foreign-owned. Skilled human resources have also come in different ways: immigration of qualified people, hiring of foreign experts, training of personnel both at home and abroad. Technological transfers also conform to different modalities—through foreign subsidiaries which bring their own technology by means of licences, patents, trade marks, technical assistance contracts, etc., and by adapting or developing technology locally.

All these various ways of incorporating foreign inputs for industrial development have resulted in different costs and effects. Until about the middle of the 50s, the nature of external contributions to industrial development was such that it contributed to the development of a *national* manufacturing sector in our economies. Since then, however, a period of denationalization and of "subsidiarization" of industrial development has ensued, coinciding with the end of the decades of crisis and coldwar, (the accelerated expansion of the transnational conglomerate and a more advanced phase in the import substitution process in Latin America).

The change that has taken place in the ways in which foreign resources have been attracted and incorporated into domestic industrial development has probably been one of the most important factors determining the nature of the results of industrialization, contribution to the growth of the economy, the level of employment, the distribution of income, institutional characteristics (concentration of property, vertical and horizontal integration, conglomeration, etc.,) structure of production, exports and imports, external financial flows, transfer of technology, etc.

It is therefore clear that the process of industrialization via import substitution, although stimulated and induced by the crisis in international relations and international crises in general and balance of payments problems in particular, and also by a deliberate policy of protection, has not taken place in isolation, as a spontaneous process.

On the contrary, it has meant new and very important, though different, links with the international economy, and particularly with the United States. Industrialization did not reduce foreign dependence; a primary-exporting economy is fatally condemned, by its very structure, to depend almost entirely on its basic exports, unless and until industrialization changes that situation, which import-substituting industrialization has not been able to do.

In other words, at a higher level of abstraction, the phase of import-substituting industrialization, just as the period of primary export expansion that preceded it, constitutes, in the final analysis, a new way of integration of the underdeveloped economy, at a different level of evolution and through different means, into a new type of international capitalist system. Although this new system is again organized in terms of developed and dominant economies on the one side, and underdeveloped and dependent economies on the other—ever more closely interrelated—it is necessary to take into account that this new model of international economic relations is based operationally on the transnational conglomerate, a new kind of business organization that has experienced an enormous growth during the last decades. This is particularly the case in the United States, mainly as a consequence of the enormous expansion of government expenditure—especially in armaments and space exploration—and of the resulting spectacular technological progress.

In the factories, laboratories, design and publicity departments and in the centres of decision, planning and finance which constitute its super-structure and which is always situated in a developed country, the transnational corporation develops: a) new products, b) new ways of manufacturing these products, c) the machines and tools necessary for manufacturing them, d) the synthetic and natural raw materials and inputs needed for their production, and e) the publicity needed for the creation and dynamization of the market for these goods.

On the other hand, the final stages of assembly and production of these goods take place in the underdeveloped economy through an industrialization process that proceeds by means of the importation of new equipment and inputs and the use of the corresponding marks, patents and licences, both by public and private national firms, as well as by the wholly or partially owned foreign subsidiaries of the transnational conglomerate. This process is of course supported by public and private international finance as well as by international technical assistance, which constitute efficient aid for the expansion of the international markets of the American, European and Japanese transnational conglomerates.

In a world of protected markets but helpless consumers, a new international division of labour appears with its new agent: the international manufacturing oligopoly. As in earlier stages, there is also a new international specialization in the generation of scientific and technological knowledge in the metropolitan countries, and of its routine "consumption" in the peripheral countries. If the above line of argument is valid, then we are now again in a period of organization of a centre-periphery model of a new kind, despite our prior belief that import-substituting industrialization was leading us away from it.

We should not be surprised by the consequences of such a process, with which we are only too familiar: a) a persistence and even worsening of the primary exporting character of the economy; b) exogenous source of the economy's dynamism; c) exogenous character of most of the fundamental centres of decision in finance, economic policy, science and technology, access to foreign markets, etc.; d) acute and persistent tendency to foreign indebtedness, denationalization and subsidiarization; e) a great danger of Latin American integration efforts ending up in favour of transnational conglomerates: a definitive liquidation of the remaining local enterprise; f) a growing income gap between developed and underdeveloped countries, etc.

THE INTERNAL POLARIZATION

Let us now return to the central theme of this essay—the hypothesis that we are in the midst of a simultaneous process of dual polarization, international and national. We have just described the first, we shall now turn to the second.

The internal process of polarization can be seen as a growing division between modern dominant and advanced economic activities, social groups and regions on the one hand, and backward, marginal and dependent activities, groups and regions on the other. In fact, the geographic, economic, social, political and cultural centres of modernity and development are closely associated with the rise and fall of the activities linked more closely—directly or indirectly—to the developed countries. This is the case of regions, cities or ports which are subject to the direct influence of the investments and expansion of the traditional export activities, and also of those other cities or regions which, either because they are administrative centres or areas producing inputs for the export sector are able to capture part of the income generated in the export sector and redistribute it to other regions and social groups.

In the import-substituting industrialization phase, the activities which concentrate a large part of the investments and which expand fastest are of course manufacturing, i.e., the activities which produce their inputs and the infrastructures most necessary for industrial development. As this industrialization is basically oriented toward consumer goods, it tends to concentrate around the larger population centres, thereby reinforcing the tendency of urban concentration so characteristic of Latin America. This tendency is frequently further accentuated by the stagnation and/or modernization of the traditional export sector and of domestic agriculture, a phenomenon which is usually accompanied by a growing concentration of ownership of the means of production in these activities. All three elements—stagnation, modernization, and concentration—accelerate the exodus of the population directly or indirectly related to export and agricultural activities.

When this polarization of population corresponds to the decline of economic activity in traditional export and/or agricultural activity, it leads to acute and growing spatial imbalances. . . .

THE RELATIONSHIPS BETWEEN THE PROCESSES OF INTERNATIONAL AND NATIONAL POLARIZATION

The examination of the internal and international processes of polarization clearly suggests a further step in the analysis. If we look at countries as composed of developed and underdeveloped functions, groups and regions, and remember the basic characteristics of the international economy—the penetration of the underdeveloped economies by the economies of the developed countries through the extractive, manufacturing, commercial and financial transnational conglomerates—it becomes apparent that there must be a close correlation and connection between the extension of the developed economies into the underdeveloped countries, and the developed, modern and advanced activities, social groups and regions of these countries.

From such a perspective of the global system, apart from the distinction between developed and underdeveloped countries, components of importance can be observed:

a) a complex of activities, social groups and regions in different countries which conform to the developed part of the global system and which are closely linked transnationally through many concrete interests as well as by similar styles, ways and levels of living and cultural affinities;

b) a national complement of activities, social groups and regions partially or totally excluded from the national developed part of the global system and without any links with similar activities, groups and regions of other countries.

In this conception of the phenomena associated with the development-underdevelopment continuum which implicitly claims to incorporate the aspects of domination-dependence and marginality which form an inherent part of it, the so-called developed countries would be those where the developed structure—economic, social and spatial—prevails, while the backward and marginal activities, social groups and regions would appear as exceptional, limited and secondary situations.

Conversely, the so-called underdeveloped countries would be those in which the phenomenon of marginality affects a significant proportion of the population, activities and areas, and therefore would appear as an urgent and acute problem, not only in relative terms but also for the reason that large segments of population are affected by it at extremely low absolute levels of living. The modern activities, social groups and areas would, on the other hand, constitute more or less restricted portions of these countries. . . .

The interpretation so far advanced suggests that the international capitalist system contains an internationalized nucleus of activities, regions and social groups of varying degrees of importance in each country. These sectors share a common culture and "way of life", which expresses itself through the same books, texts, films, television programmes, similar fashions, similar groups of organization of family and social life, similar style of decoration of homes, similar orientations to housing, building, furniture, and urban design. Despite linguistic barriers, these sectors have a far greater capacity for communication among themselves than is possible between integrated and marginal persons of the same country who speak the same language. An advertisement in *Time* magazine expresses this idea with the perfection to be expected from publicity aimed precisely at the international market constituted by the nucleus of internationalized population:

Time's 24 million readers are apt to have more in common with each other than with many of their own countrymen. High incomes. Good Education. Responsible positions in business, government and the professions. *Time* readers constitute an international community of the affluent and influential, responsive to new ideas, new products and new ways of doing things.

For this international community, inhabiting different countries—developed and underdeveloped—to have similar patterns of consumption, it must also have similar patterns of income. However, it is well known that the average levels of income *per capita* of developed nations are greater by a factor of considerable magnitude than that of underdeveloped countries. But these averages are highly questionable, particularly if the national universe which they claim to represent is highly heterogeneous, as is particularly the case in underdeveloped economies, where income distribution is very unequal. In fact, depending upon whether greater or lesser weight is attached to the modernized, integrated or internationalized segment of each underdeveloped economy, more or less significant proportions of the population in these economies will accumulate substantial shares of total income, thereby obtaining *per capita* incomes similar to those prevailing in the developed countries. In the case of Chile, for example, with an average *per capita* income of about U.S.$600, the privileged 10 per cent of the population which receives about 40 per cent of the total income has a *per capita* income of U.S.$2,400, a figure

significantly higher than the average for any European economy. . . .

One basic element of the approach developed in this essay is the hypothesis of the central role played by the external links in the structural formation and transformation of our economies. To understand the nature and consequences of those external links, it is essential to have a clear conception of the characteristics of the international economic system. To begin with, it is important to recognize that the international economic system, as any other social system, is simultaneously a system of power and a system of domination-dependence, that has systematically been biassed in favour of the developed countries and against the underdeveloped countries. This system has evolved through various historical periods—mercantilism, liberalism, neo-mercantilism—with the type of hegemonic power and the instruments of domination which each has used. . . .

TRANSNATIONAL INTEGRATION AND NATIONAL DISINTEGRATION

In the previous sections, an effort has been made to interpret the five concepts, problems and processes that engage us in this essay—development, underdevelopment, dependence, marginality and spatial imbalances—in such a way as to render their interrelationships apparent. We believe that we have suggested that they are not only interrelated, but that in fact they are different manifestations of a single global process, which is simultaneously a process of transnational integration and national disintegration.

The main actor in this process is the transnational conglomerate, in the sense that this is the basic economic institution of the post-war capitalist world, an institution of tremendous dynamism, which is bringing about a fundamental transformation of the structure and financing of that system, not only in the central countries but in the whole world, creating in the final analysis a new model of civilization represented by the superconsumption society exemplified by the U.S.

For our present purpose it is necessary to stress only two aspects viz.,: a) The TRANCOS do in fact constitute a new economic system—both national and international; and b) This new system favours the development of local segments integrated into the internationalized nucleus of the capitalist system, in particular, those segments which are more directly connected with the TRANCOS, while at the same time tending to disrupt the rest of the economy and society, segregating and marginalizing significant sections of the population....

The nucleus of the TRANCO is its headquarters, which is located in the metropolis, and which is the central planning bureau of the corporation. The headquarters is something quite distinct from its productive activites, which can be classified in three main types—extractive, industrial and marketing—and which are located also in the metropolitan country, but with subsidiaries, branches or affiliates in the peripheral countries. The headquarters consists essentially of a group of people who plan and decide what will be produced and sold, how, where, how much and over what period of time. In order to perform the decision-making process rationally, it has developed a highly efficient system of communications through which the necessary information, personnel, scientific and technological knowledge, finance and decisions flow.

Between the productive activities of the TRANCO there develops a flow of goods and services within an institutional framework of vertically and horizontally highly integrated oligopolistic enterprises—both nationally and internationally. In this manner, the TRANCO replaces to a large extent the market—again both national and international—since it takes over the sources of supply of its inputs and the outlets of its production. Moreover, it is able to influence significantly the demand for its goods and

services through the pressure it is able to exercise over the individual consumer as well as over governments. As can be seen, the new industrial system also entails the disappearance of the classical entrepreneur, the suppliers of capital and capital markets, and their replacement by the top planners and managers who constitute the corporate techno-structure. These same technocrats ... are in fact replacing the national entrepreneurial class in the underdeveloped countries, as we shall see presently.

For the reasons indicated above, and since the expenditures in research, design and technology have become a major item in the TRANCO fixed cost structure, it has every interest in spreading these costs over an ever increasing total output, including the output sold in the metropolitan markets and overseas markets. Therefore, the capturing of more and more consumers at home and abroad is absolutely central to the long term profitability of the TRANCO....

Nearly every country in the world has in the past made efforts to attract foreign private capital for every country experienced the acute need for the contributions that foreign capital was supposed to make (capital, technology, markets, entrepreneurship etc.). But the nature of traditional enterprise based on foreign capital was different from the new international industrial system built around the TRANCO. It is now becoming increasingly clear that the claims traditionally made regarding the contributions of foreign private capital are not necessarily valid.

In fact, the contributions of new additional capital are rather small, as the subsidiaries finance themselves in large measure with local resources. Remittances abroad of profits, interest, royalties, payments for technical assistance, foreign inputs, etc., are normally several times larger than the net inflow of capital, with the consequence of a substantial net outflow of resources (this amount is generally underestimated because of the possibility of overpricing in the case of each of the items of payments abroad, facilitated by the transnational integration of the firms).

Technological transfer also manifests some very special peculiarities. As it occurs within the framework of the TRANCO, it is not to be expected that any substantial effort will be made to adapt techniques to local conditions or to stimulate local scientific and technological activity; therefore, we learn to "consume" new techniques through this kind of transfer, but not to adapt or generate science and technology. Something similar occurs with the national entrepreneur—he is converted into an international technocrat or bureaucrat, or becomes marginalized. Finally, with respect to the opening of new foreign markets, experience, at least in the case of manufacturing, has been entirely negative.

On the other hand, multinational business through the proliferation of subsidiaries, has grown so large and influential that nationstates, through which its influence extends itself challenging national decision-making processes, are becoming increasingly restless. . . .

It is possible to identify a number of problems which keep recurring:

i) the multinational corporation is a medium for the intrusion of the laws, politics, foreign policy and culture of one country into another. This relationship is asymmetrical for the flow tends to be from the parent country to the subsidiary country rather than vice versa. The issue of extra-territoriality with regard to such things as anti-trust and trading with the enemy is one of the main focuses of debate and concern.

ii) Multinational corporations reduce the ability of the government to control the economy. Multinational corporations, because of their size and international connections, have a certain flexibility for escaping regulations imposed in one country. The nature and effectiveness of traditional policy instruments—monetary policy, anti-trust, taxation—change when important segments of the economy are foreign-owned.

iii) The multinational corporation tends to centralize research and entrepreneurial decision-making in the home country. Unless countermeasures are taken, the "backwash" effects may outweigh the "spread" effects, and the technology gap may be perpetuated rather than alleviated. Over-reliance on multinational corporations may cause the country to remain a margin rather than become a centre.

iv) Multinational corporations often occupy a dominant position in their industry. Countries are concerned that they will not get a fair share of production and exports. Decisions depend on the horizons and outlook of the head office management, which can be limited and biased. Each country is aware that other countries, including the United States, put pressures on the multinational corporation to produce, export, import or invest in a particular way. A country without the ability to make its presence effective in the decision-making process may end up with a smaller share than otherwise.

v) Natural resource industries are sometimes highly oligopolistic, and have only a relatively small number of firms. The price a country obtains for its raw materials is not set objectively in a free market, but is determined by bargaining and negotiation with the dominant corporations. Unless a country has the requisite knowledge and effectiveness, it may get a smaller than possible share of the benefits.

Some of the effects of the process of transnational conglomeration on the underdeveloped countries are the following:

a) The increasing capacity of the TRANCO to take the fullest possible advantages of size and diversification—economies of scale, large accumulations of capital, long range planning, market power, scientific and technological research, predominantly internal sources of finance, reduction of uncertainty and risk, choice of best opportunities over a very wide economic horizon, etc., accrues mainly to the country where the basic functions of the TRANCO are located, constituting a kind of external economy which integrates, increases the degree of complexity and specialization, and dynamizes the rest of the economy of the metropolis. The subsidiaries and affiliates of the TRANCO located in the peripheral country—not only in the primary producing sectors but in all activities of the underdeveloped economy—do not create a similarly integrated industrial complex with the rest of the local economy, but on the contrary, remain integrated with the TRANCO. Moreover, they even have some disintegrating effects, among other factors, in view of the parallelism of productive activities which they tend to produce. This is due to the fact that TRANCOS never leave the market to competitors (which means excess capacity in small markets), and also to the massive introduction of highly capital-intensive technologies displacing local activities, including their entrepreneurs, workers, etc. Since the subsidiaries remain as closely tied to the TRANCO as possible in terms of inputs, technology, personnel, property, administration, product and process innovation, etc., the effects of the spread over the local economy tend to be less important than the backwash effects or the spread effects over the economy of the metropolitan country.

b) Since, for various reasons, the TRANCO needs permanently to expand its markets, underdeveloped countries are subject to a massive offensive of the consumerism characteristic of developed societies. There is of course a ready market for these goods among the small segment of higher income groups which are integrated into the developed part of the global system, but the demonstration effect also trickles down to the lower income groups. This introduces serious distortions and irrationalities into the structure of demand and in the allocation of private and public investment resources, while at the same time it reduces savings.

c) The activities in which TRANCOS operate are frequently of a highly oligopolistic nature. A few primary exporters may buy from a large number of small agricultural or mining firms, while a few producers of consumer durables may sell to a large number of independent consumers. Under these conditions, the TRANCOS could well underpay local producers and overcharge local consumers, obtaining excess profits on both accounts and either sending them back to the headquarters or reinvesting them locally, initiating a process of cumulative accentuation.

The above analysis leads us to the following tentative conclusion: the capitalist system of world economy is in the process of being reorganized into a new international industrial system whose main institutional agents are the TRANCOS, increasingly backed by the governments of the developed countries; this is a new structure of domination sharing a large number of characteristics of the mercantilist system, which concentrates the planning of the deployment of natural, human and capital resources and the development of science and technology in the "brain" of the new industrial system (i.e. the technocrats of TRANCOS, international organizations and governments of developed countries), and which tends to reinforce the process of economic, social, political and cultural underdevelopment of the Third World, deepening foreign dependence and exacerbating internal disintegration. . . .

The classification of integrated and segregated groups now overlaps with a class structure, so that integrated and non-integrated groups appear among entrepreneurs, middle class and workers, as well as in a segment of "absolutely" marginalized population. It should be emphasized that the classification used here and the relative importance of the seven segments into which society has been divided are mainly of an illustrative nature. This compartmentalization of society will assume different forms, depending upon the actual situation prevailing in different countries.

The hypothesis that has been elaborated in this essay suggests that this social structure derives an important part of its dynamism from the influence that the internationalized or integrated sector receives from the central countries. At the level of the productive structure, this influence makes itself felt through the massive and extraordinarily dynamic penetration of the transnational conglomerate and its subsidiaries and affiliates; at the technological level, by the large scale introduction of highly capital intensive techniques; at the cultural and ideological level, by the overwhelming and systematic promotion and publicity of the super-consumption civilization, and at the concrete level of development policies and strategies, by the pressure of national and international public and private interests in favour of the production of higher income consumption goods and services and the process of transnational integration.

As was indicated in the section on the international process of polarization, modernization implies the gradual replacement of the traditional productive structure by another of much higher capital intensiveness. In the conditions that were specified then, this process appears to produce two opposed tendencies. On the one hand, the process of modernization incorporates into the new structures the individuals and groups that are apt to fit into the kind of rationality that prevails there; on the other hand, it expels the individuals and groups that have no place in the new productive structure or who lack the capacity to become adapted to it. It is important to emphasize that this process does not only prevent or limit the formation of a national entrepreneurial class, as indicated by Furtado, but also of national middle classes (including national intellectuals, scientists, technologists, etc.) and even a national working class. The advancement of modernization introduces, so to speak, a wedge along the area dividing the integrated from the segregated segments. . . .

XI.A.3. Dynamic Benefits of Trade*

I shall now positively and systematically state what I think the contribution of international trade to economic development was in the past and what it can be in the future. My overall conclusion is that international trade has made a tremendous contribution to the development of less developed countries in the 19th and 20th centuries and can be expected to make an equally big contribution in the future, if it is allowed to proceed freely. It does not necessarily follow that a 100% free trade policy is always most conducive to most rapid development. Marginal interferences with the free flow of trade, if properly selected, may speed up

*From Gottfried Haberler, *International Trade and Economic Development*, National Bank of Egypt Fiftieth Anniversary Commemoration Lectures, Cairo, 1959, pp. 5–7, 9–14. Reprinted by permission.

development. But I do not want to leave any doubt that my conclusion is that substantially free trade with marginal, insubstantial corrections and deviations, is the best policy from the point of view of economic development. Drastic deviations from free trade can be justified, on development grounds,—and this is very nearly the same thing as to say on economic grounds—only if and when they are needed to compensate for the adverse influence of other policies inimical to economic development, for example, the consequences of persistent inflation or of certain tax and domestic price support policies. Let me guard against a possible misunderstanding. If I say that drastic interferences with the market mechanism are not needed for rapid development, I refer to trade policy and I do not deny that drastic measures in other areas, let me say, land reform, education, forced investment (if the projects are well chosen) etc. may not speed up growth. . . .

International division of labor and international trade, which enable every country to specialize and to export those things that it can produce cheaper in exchange for what others can provide at a lower cost, have been and still are one of the basic factors promoting economic well-being and increasing national income of every participating country. Moreover, what is good for the national income and the standard of living is, at least potentially, also good for economic development; for the greater the volume of output the greater can be the rate of growth—provided the people individually or collectively have the urge to save and to invest and economically to develop. The higher the level of output, the easier it is to escape the "vicious circle of poverty" and to "take off into self-sustained growth" to use the jargon of modern development theory. Hence, if trade raises the level of income, it also promotes economic development. . . .

In most underdeveloped countries international trade plays quantitatively an especially important role, that is, a larger percentage of their income is spent on imports, and a larger percentage of their output is being exported, than in the case of developed countries of comparable economic size. (Other things being equal, it is natural that the "larger," economically speaking, a country, the smaller its trade percentages.) Many underdeveloped countries are highly specialized also in the sense that a very large percentage of their exports consists of one or two staple commodities. . . .

This high concentration of exports is not without danger. One would normally not want to put so many of one's eggs into one basket. But the price of diversification is in most cases extremely high. I shall touch on that topic once more. At this point, let me simply say that a high level of concentrated trade will, in most cases, be much better than a low level of diversified trade. How much poorer would Brazil be without cof-fee, Venezuela, Iran and Iraq without oil, Bolivia without tin, Malaya without rubber and tin, Ghana without cocoa, and, I dare say, Egypt without cotton. The really great danger of concentration arises in case of deep and protracted slumps in the industrial countries—slumps of the order of magnitude of the Great Depression in the 1930's. In my opinion, and here I am sure the overwhelming majority of economists in the Western world agrees, the chance that this will happen again is practically nil.

The tremendous importance of trade for the underdeveloped countries (as well as for most developed ones, with the exception of the US and USSR, which could, if need be, give it up without suffering a catastrophic reduction in their living standard) follows from the classical theory of comparative cost in conjunction with the fact that the comparative differences in cost of production of industrial products and food and raw materials between developed countries are obviously very great, in many cases, in fact, infinite in the sense that countries of either group just could not produce what they buy from the other.[1] . . .

For our purposes I will distinguish among the changes which constitute economic development two types—those that take place independently of international trade and those that are induced by trade or trade policy.

As far as the first group—let me call them autonomous changes—is concerned, I can see no difficulty resulting from them for the applicability of the classical theory of comparative cost. Such changes are the gradual improvement in skill, education and training of workers, farmers, engineers, entrepreneurs; improvements resulting from inven-

---

[1] In many cases very expensive and poor substitutes can be produced. There is not much sense in contemplating extreme situations. But if I were pressed to guess, I would say that the developed countries as a group, and a few of them individually, could get along without trade a little easier (although still at a terrific loss) than the underdeveloped countries.

tions and discoveries and from the accumulation of capital—changes which in the Western world stem for the most part from the initiative of individuals and private associations, but possibly also from conscious government policies.[2]

These changes come gradually or in waves and result in gradually increasing output of commodities that had been produced before or in the setting up of the production of goods that had not been produced earlier. Analytically, such development has to be pictured as an outward movement of the production possibility curve (often called substitution or transformation curve). Depending on the concrete turn that autonomous development (including improvements in transportation technology) takes, the comparative cost situation and hence volume and composition of trade will be more or less profoundly affected. But since these changes only come slowly and gradually and usually cannot be foreseen (either by private business or government planners) in sufficient detail to make anticipatory action possible, there is no presumption that the allocative mechanism as described in the theory of comparative cost will not automatically and efficiently bring about the changes and adjustment in the volume and structure of trade called for by autonomous development.

I turn now to the second type of changes in the productive capabilities of a country which are more important for the purposes of my lectures, namely, those induced by trade and changes in trade including changes in trade brought about by trade policy. Favorable as well as unfavorable trade-induced changes are possible and have to be considered. Alleged unfavorable trade-induced changes have received so much attention from protectionist writers from List to Myrdal (which has induced free trade economists, too, to discuss them at great

length), that there is danger that the tremendously important favorable influences be unduly neglected. Let me, therefore, discuss the latter first.

If we were to estimate the contribution of international trade to economic development, especially of the underdeveloped countries, solely by the static gains from trade in any given year on the usual assumption of given[3] production capabilities (analytically under the assumption of given production functions or given or autonomously shifting production possibility curves) we would indeed grossly underrate the importance of trade. For over and above the direct static gains dwelt upon by the traditional theory of comparative cost, trade bestows very important indirect benefits, which also can be described as dynamic benefits, upon the participating countries. Let me emphasize once more that the older classical writers did stress these "indirect benefits" (Mill's own words).[4] Analytically we have to describe these "indirect," "dynamic" benefits from trade as an outward shift (in the northeast direction) of the production possibility curve brought about by a trade-induced movement along the curve.

First, trade provides material means (capital goods, machinery and raw and semi-finished material) indispensable for economic development. Secondly, even more important, trade is the means and vehicle for the dissemination of technological knowledge, the transmission of ideas, for the importation of know-how, skills, managerial talents and entrepreneurship. Thirdly, trade is also the vehicle for the international movement of capital especially from the developed to the underdeveloped countries. Fourthly, free international trade is the best antimonopoly policy and the best guarantee for the maintenance of a healthy degree of free competition.

[2] I am not speaking here of policies concerning international trade such as the imposition of import restrictions. Changes resulting from trade policy measures are trade-induced and not autonomous changes.

[3] This includes autonomously shifting.
[4] In the neo-classical theory they have been somewhat neglected. The reason is perhaps that these factors do not lend themselves well to precise mathematical treatment.

Let me now make a few explanatory remarks on each of these four points before I try to show how they fit into, and complement, the static theory of comparative advantage.

The first point is so obvious that it does not require much elaboration. Let us recall and remember, however, the tremendous benefits which the underdeveloped countries draw from technological progress in the developed countries through the importation of machinery, transport equipment, vehicles, power generation equipment, road building machinery, medicines, chemicals, and so on. The advantage is, of course, not all on one side. I stress the advantage derived by underdeveloped countries (rather than the equally important benefits for the developed countries), because I am concerned in these lectures primarily with the development of the less developed countries.

The composition of the export trade of the developed industrial countries has been changing, as we all know, in the direction of the types of capital goods which I have mentioned away from textiles and other light consumer goods. This shift has been going on for a long time; it is not a recent phenomenon. But it has proceeded rapidly in recent years, and there is no reason to doubt that it will continue.

Secondly, probably even more important than the importation of material goods is the importation of technical know-how, skills, managerial talents, entrepreneurship. This is, of course, especially important for the underdeveloped countries. But the developed countries too benefit greatly from cross-fertilization aided by trade among themselves and the less advanced industrial countries can profit from the superior technical and managerial know-how, etc. of the more advanced ones.

The late-comers and successors in the process of development and industrialization have always had the great advantage that they could learn from the experiences, from the successes as well as from the failures and mistakes of the pioneers and forerunners. In the 19th century the continental European countries and the U.S. profited greatly from the technological innovation and achievements of the industrial revolution in Great Britain. Later the Japanese proved to be very adept learners and Soviet Russia has shown herself capable of speeding up her own development by "borrowing" (interest free) immense amounts of technological know-how from the West, developing it further and adopting it for her own purposes. This "trade" has been entirely onesided. I know of not a single industrial idea or invention which the West has obtained from the East. Today the underdeveloped countries have a tremendous, constantly growing, store of technological know-how to draw from. True, simple adoption of methods developed for the conditions of the developed countries is often not possible. But adaptation is surely much easier than first creation.

Trade is the most important vehicle for the transmission of technological know-how. True, it is not the only one. In fact this function of trade is probably somewhat less important now than it was a hundred years ago, because ideas, skills, know-how, travel easier and quicker and cheaper today than in the 19th century. The market where engineering and management experts can be hired is much better-organized than formerly. There is much more competition in this field as well as in the area of material capital equipment. In the 19th century Great Britain was the only center from which industrial equipment and know-how could be obtained, and there were all sorts of restrictions on the exportation of both. Today there are a dozen industrial centers in Europe, the US, Canada, and Japan, and even Russia and Czechoslovakia all ready to sell machinery as well as engineering advice and know-how.

However, trade is still the most important transmission belt. What J. S. Mill said 100 years ago is still substantially true: "It is hardly possible to overrate the value in the present low state of human improvement, of placing human beings in contact with persons dissimilar to themselves, and with modes of thought and action unlike those with which they are familiar. . . . Such communication has always been, peculiarly in the present age one of the primary sources of progress."[5]

The third indirect benefit of trade which I mentioned was that it also serves as a transmission belt for capital. It is true that the amount of capital that an underdeveloped country can obtain from abroad depends in the first place on the ability and willingness of developed countries to lend, which is of course decisively influenced by the internal policies in the borrowing countries. But it stands to reason—and this is the only point I wanted to make at this juncture—that, other things being equal, the larger the volume of trade, the greater will be the volume of foreign capital that can be expected to become available under realistic assumptions. The reason is that with a large volume of trade the transfer of interest and repayments on principal is more easily effected than with a small volume of trade; and it would be clearly unrealistic to expect large capital movements if the chance for transfer of interest and repayments is not good. There is, furthermore, the related fact that it is much easier to get foreign capital for export industries with their built-in solution of the retransfer problem than for other types of investments which do not directly and automatically improve the balance of payments. This preference of foreign capital for export industries is regrettable because other types of investment (such as investment in public utilities, railroads, manufacturing industries) may often (not always) be more productive and may make a greater indirect contribution, dollar per dollar, to economic development by providing training to native personnel and in various other ways than export industries which sometimes (by no means always) constitute foreign enclaves in native soil. If the direct and indirect contribution of non-export industries to national income and economic development are in fact greater than those of the

[5] *Principles of Political Economy.*

export industry, they should be preferred, because their indirect contribution to the balance of payments position will then also be such as to guarantee the possibility of smooth retransfer of principal and interest— *provided* inflationary monetary policies do not upset equilibrium entailing exchange control that then gets in the way of transfer. But with inflationary monetary policies and exchange control practices as they are in most underdeveloped countries, the preference of foreign capital for export industries is readily understandable and must be reckoned with and foreign capital in export is better than no foreign capital at all.

The fourth way in which trade benefits a country indirectly is by fostering healthy competition and keeping in check inefficient monopolies. The reason why the American economy is more competitive—and more efficient—than most others is probably to be sought more in the great internal free trade area which the US enjoys rather than in the antimonopoly policy which was always much more popular in the US than in Europe or anywhere else. . . .

Increased competition is important also for underdeveloped countries, especially inasmuch as the size of their market is usually small (even if the geographic area is large). A reservation has nevertheless to be made. The first introduction of new industries on infant industry grounds may justify the creation of monopolistic positions, depending on the size of the country and the type of industry. But the problem will always remain how to prevent the permanent establishment of inefficient exploitative monopolies even after an industry has taken root and has become able to hold its ground without the crutches of imports restriction.

The general conclusion, then, is that international trade, in addition to the static gains resulting from the division of labor with given (or autonomously changing) production functions powerfully contributes, in the four ways indicated, to the development of the productive capabilities of the less developed countries. Analytically we have to express that, in the framework of modern trade theory, by saying that trade gradually transforms existing production functions; in other words, that a movement along the production possibility curves in accordance with the preexisting comparative cost situation, will tend to push up and out the production possibility curve.

XI.A.4. Patterns of Trade and Development*

[It is] instructive to take a look at past experience and see how economic growth in certain areas was induced through international trade in the nineteenth century. The areas involved in this process of growth through trade were chiefly the so-called regions of recent settlement in the temperate latitudes outside Europe. These areas, in which the United States may be included, received a large inflow of labour as well as capital from Europe, but a basic inducement that caused them to develop was the tremendous expansion of Western Europe's, and especially Great Britain's, demand for the foodstuffs and raw materials which they were well suited to produce. Growth at the periphery was induced, through trade, by growth in the rising industrial centre.

Alfred Marshall referred to "the splendid markets which the old world has offered to the products of the new."[1] He forgot to mention the crucial point that these were growing markets, but this he probably assumed as a matter of course. The penultimate chapter of his *Principles* is entitled "General Influences of Economic Progress"

and begins as follows: "The field of employment which any place offers for labour and capital depends, firstly, on its natural resources; secondly, on ... knowledge and ... organization; and thirdly, on ... markets in which it has a superfluity. The importance of this last condition is often underrated; but it stands out prominently when we look at the history of new countries."[2]

It was under the impression of this experience that Marshall made the following pronouncement: "The causes which determine the economic progress of nations belong to the study of international trade."[3] In the second half of the twentieth century this may seem to us a curious statement. It can be understood only in the light of certain historical conditions, and it embodies the particular experience of Britain's economic relations with the new countries overseas. Economic growth in these areas was due not to international specialization alone but more particularly to the fact that the character of trade was such that the rapid growth which was taking place in the centre was transmitted to the outlying new countries through a vigorous increase in the demand for primary products.

Trade in the nineteenth century was not simply a device for the optimum allocation

*From Ragnar Nurkse, "Trade Theory and Development Policy," in H. S. Ellis (ed.), *Economic Development for Latin America*, Macmillan and Co. Ltd., London; St. Martin's Press, New York, 1961, pp. 236–45. Reprinted by permission.
[1] Alfred Marshall, *Principles of Economics*, 8th ed., London, 1920, pp. 668–9.

[2] Ibid., p. 668.
[3] Ibid., p. 270.

of a given stock of resources. It was that too, but it was more than that. It was above all "an engine of growth." This profoundly important observation is one which we owe to Sir Dennis Robertson.[4]

It helps us to see things in perspective, but in doing so it serves also to limit the significance of classical trade theory to its proper sphere. The conventional tendency has been to credit international specialization as such with the spectacular growth of the new countries in the nineteenth century. In the light of Robertson's remark it may perhaps be suggested that classical specialization theory, which in the nature of the case is a static analysis, has derived more prestige from nineteenth-century experience than it has deserved. The dynamic nature of trade as a transmitter of growth was overlooked during an era in which progress was taken for granted, like the air we breathe.

There is no doubt that international trade was peculiarly important in the conditions of the nineteenth century. In real volume it increased tenfold between 1850 and 1913, twice as fast as world production. Imperialism had very little to do with the expansion of trade. As was shown by J. A. Hobson himself,[5] the tropical colonies took a minor share in the growth of British trade. Continental Europe and the new countries outside as well as within the British Empire took the major share. The regions of recent settlement were high-income countries from the start, effective markets as well as efficient producers. Their development was part of the growth of international trade itself.

So much for the new countries. Elsewhere, in the truly backward areas, economic growth induced through international trade in some cases carried with it certain features that were, and still are, regarded as undesirable. It sometimes led to a lopsided pattern of growth in which production of

primary products for export was carried on with the aid of substantial investment of foreign capital, while the domestic economy remained far less developed, if not altogether primitive. This picture applies especially to tropical areas. It is the familiar picture of the dual economy resulting from trade and from foreign business investment induced by trade. Areas of outpost investment producing for foreign markets often showed a lack of social as well as economic integration internally. Moreover, their export activities were subject to the familiar hazards of cyclical instability.

Nevertheless, even unsteady growth through foreign trade is surely better than no growth at all. Mr. Bauer has given impressive examples of progress resulting from peasant production for export in some parts of West Africa during the early half of the twentieth century.[6] Elsewhere foreign capital working for export has usually led to an additional demand for local labour, increased wage incomes, expenditures on local materials, new sources of taxation, and, in the case of mineral concessions, lucrative profit-sharing arrangements. All these benefits have helped to promote expansion in the domestic economy.

The traditional pattern of development through production for expanding export markets is not to be despised and ought not to be discouraged. Indeed, I should like to assume that all opportunities in this direction are fully exploited. The trouble is that in the mid-twentieth century, with a few notable exceptions, conditions for this type of growth do not, by and large, appear to be as promising as they were a hundred years ago.

Since 1913 the quantum of world trade has increased less than world production. To be sure, in the last five or six years we find the volume of trade in the non-communist world increasing at just about the same pace as production. But when we look at it more

---

[4] D. H. Robertson, *Essays in Monetary Theory*, London, 1940, p. 214.

[5] J. A. Hobson, *Imperialism*, 3rd ed., London, 1938, ch. 2.

[6] P. T. Bauer, *West African Trade*, Cambridge, 1955.

closely we find that it is chiefly among the advanced industrial countries that international trade has been expanding in the recent past. These countries, including above all the United States, are themselves efficient primary producers, especially for food. Their demand for exotic raw materials like crude rubber, silk, nitrates, jute, vegetable oils, hides, and skins has been, and will probably continue to be, affected by the growth of the chemical industry in the twentieth century. . . . Professor D. D. Humphrey in his voluminous study, *American Imports*,[7] attaches great importance to the technological factor. He estimates that, in its effect on total United States imports, the displacement of imported raw materials by synthetic products has more than offset the 75 per cent reduction in the American tariff which has taken place in the last twenty years partly through duty reductions and partly through the effect of price inflation on the burden of specific duties. While tariff changes have mainly affected imports of manufactured goods from other industrial countries, technological displacement has particularly affected United States imports from the less developed countries.

Only for minerals are conditions generally favorable, although even here it should be noted that, first, the demand for metals is affected by the increasing efficiency of scrap collection and recovery in the industrial countries. Second, mineral deposits are gifts of nature, and if a country does not happen to have any, it can do nothing in response to the rise in world demand. Some countries that have deposits fail to exploit them. Nevertheless, the point remains that while Guatemala, for example, can at least try to grow chicle, she cannot try to grow nickel. Third, the export of minerals involves in an obvious sense an element of living on capital.

The growth of synthetic materials is undoubtedly one explanation of the findings which Professor Kindleberger reaches in his

book on *The Terms of Trade: A European Case Study*. This study lends some support to the view that the poorer countries' terms of trade have shown a tendency to deteriorate. Kindleberger has calculated industrial Europe's terms of trade separately for various parts of the world, including in particular two groups of countries overseas, the areas of recent settlement, not including the United States, and the poorer countries (the rest of the world in his grouping). Difficulties due to quality changes and transport costs apply to both groups. Both the new countries and the poor countries are exporters of primary products and importers of manufactured goods. From 1913 to 1952, according to these estimates, Europe's terms of trade with the areas of recent settlement showed a 20 per cent improvement, while in trade with the poorer countries Europe's terms seem to have improved by as much as 55 per cent.[8]

Other recent studies have provided evidence that world demand for the poorer countries' export products has tended to rise much less than in proportion to the production and incomes of the advanced countries.[9] It is therefore not surprising that, according to the report of the Contracting Parties to the General Agreement on Tariffs and Trade, we find the following distribution of international trade in the non-

---

[7] D. D. Humphrey, *American Imports*, New York, 1955.

[8] C. P. Kindleberger, *The Terms of Trade: A European Case Study*, New York, 1956, p. 234.

[9] For the post-war period this conclusion is documented in United Nations, *World Economic Survey*, 1956, and also in the annual report of the Contracting Parties to the General Agreement on Tariffs and Trade, *International Trade*, 1955, Geneva, 1956.

For a longer period, Professor Cairncross has made a careful statistical study of world exports of manufactured goods since 1900 showing that the manufactured goods which the industrial countries export to each other have constituted a steadily increasing proportion of their total exports of manufactured articles; A. K. Cairncross, "World Trade in Manufactures since 1900," *Economia Internazionale*, November 1955.

communist world in 1955. The exports of twenty advanced industrial countries (United States, Canada, Japan, and Western Europe) to each other constitute as much as 40 per cent of total exports. Exports from these twenty countries to all less developed countries outside the communist orbit amount to 25 per cent of the total. Exports from the less developed to the advanced countries represent another 25 per cent. Only 10 per cent of the total are exports of the less developed countries to each other, even though the more than hundred countries in this group contain two-thirds of the total population of the non-communist world.[10] Why is it that so little of the coffee, tea, rubber, and tin produced in these countries goes to other countries in the same group? Obviously the main explanation is the low purchasing power of people in these countries, which in turn is a reflection of their low productivity.

The fact that the economically advanced countries are each others' best customers is now more than ever a central feature of world trade. It is chiefly within this small circle of countries that international trade is now expanding. With the leading exception of petroleum and a few other minerals, it can hardly be said that primary producing countries are enjoying a dynamic expansion in world demand for their exports. . . .

Professor T. W. Schultz in his paper on "Economic Prospect of Primary Products" shows that the demand for all raw materials, whether imported or domestically produced, has lagged far behind the increase in output in the United States. What we are considering therefore is merely the international aspect of a fairly general tendency. In a country amply supplied with capital and technical know-how, it seems a perfectly natural tendency for investment in research and development to displace crude materials

[10] *International Trade*, 1955. The figures given in this report exclude trade within the communist orbit. For the sake of comparability I have adjusted them so as to exclude trade between communist and non-communist countries as well.

with synthetic products made from a few basic elements of mostly local origin. These trends are not confined to the United States. They are affecting the trade of other advanced areas as well.[11]

If this is the situation of the mid-twentieth century, the mental habits which economists have inherited from the mid-nineteenth may no longer be altogether adequate. It will be recalled that Professor Hicks's analysis of the long-run dollar problem was based on what he described as "a change in economic atmosphere between the nineteenth and twentieth centuries."[12] His analysis in regard to the dollar problem was open to criticism, yet I believe that in emphasizing the varying incidence of productivity changes on international trade he made an important point, a point that had been noted some years earlier by Professor Haberler.[13] While Britain's ratio of imports to national income showed a rising tendency during most of the nineteenth century, the United States import ratio has been practically halved in the last five decades.[14] This has happened in spite of the fact that in short period comparisons the United States typically shows a rather high income elasticity of imports. There seems to have been a long-run downward shift in the United States import function, resulting from changes in economic structure. It is not certain that tariff policy provides the major

[11] A. K. Cairncross and J. Faaland, "Long-Term Trends in Europe's Trade," *Economic Journal*, March 1952, pp. 26–7.

[12] J. R. Hicks, "An Inaugural Lecture," *Oxford Economic Papers*, June 1953, p. 130.

[13] G. Haberler, "Dollar Shortage?" in S. E. Harris (ed.), *Foreign Economic Policy for the United States*, Cambridge, Massachusetts, 1948, pp. 438–9.

[14] United States exports as a percentage of gross national product fell from 5.7 per cent in the period 1896–1914 to 2.97 per cent in 1955. See W. Lederer, "Major Developments Affecting the United States Balance of International Payments," *Review of Economics and Statistics*, May 1956, p. 184.

part of the explanation. It seems very likely that the incidence of technological advance has had a good deal to do with it.

The slight increase which has occurred in the last few years in the United States import ratio has been due to increased imports of finished and semi-finished manufactures. This has meant increased trade with other industrial countries, Canada, Western Europe, Japan. Imports of crude materials, largely from under-developed areas, have not regained their pre-war position in relation to United States gross national product. All this does not mean that the absolute volume of United States imports has failed to expand. It increased by 44 per cent from 1929 to 1955.[15] But notice two things. This increase is much less than proportional to the growth of United States output. Moreover, it is much less than the rate of growth of British imports in the nineteenth century, which during any comparable period showed a two to threefold increase in volume.

It is useful to keep in mind these elementary facts about American imports because the United States is now the dominant economy not only in world production but also in world trade. Some economists are more inclined to stress the future prospect of expansion in United States imports, but that is a debatable matter. It is never quite safe, and for present purposes really unnecessary, to engage in predictions. The facts for the recent past are sufficient to indicate a change in the economic atmosphere of international trade

---

[15] The quantum of crude material imports, as already stated, increased by only 23 per cent. The other commodity groups showed the following percentage increases from 1929 to 1955: crude foodstuffs, 33 per cent; manufactured foodstuffs, 55 per cent; semi-manufactures, 76 per cent; finished manufactures, 52 per cent. Is it not possible, however, that the relatively small rise in imports of crude commodities may be due, not to a low rate of growth of United States demand, but rather to a deficiency on the supply side? The answer is in Professor Schultz's paper, where the strategic role of demand is clearly demonstrated.

between the nineteenth and twentieth centuries.

It will be remembered that in Hicks's analysis of the dollar shortage, the balance of payments problem resolves itself into a terms of trade problem. This seems a plausible simplification. Any country in foreign exchange difficulties can normally restore its balance of payments by accepting a worsening in its terms of trade. In Hicks's model external balance is maintained by changes in terms of trade.

But can we not go a step further? There has been a tendency, in Britain and elsewhere, to exaggerate both the actual extent and the economic significance of changes in the terms of trade. We are sometimes apt to think of these changes as if the resources of each country were for ever committed to the existing export industries. This view may be all right for the short run, but in the longer run labour and capital within each country can usually move to other occupations, and do in fact move. If the relationship of export prices to import prices undergoes a marked increase or decline, it is entirely natural that factors of production should tend to move from export industries to import-competing industries or vice versa. This may involve simply changes in the allocation of *increases* in factor supplies rather than movements of existing factors. In any event, the point is that a change in the terms of trade tends to induce shifts in production and in the distribution of resources, which will tend to reverse or counteract the change in the terms of trade. What remains is growth and change in the volume of productive activity induced through international trade. On this view, changes in the terms as well as in the balance of trade are a transient and relatively insignificant element in the mechanism by which processes of economic growth (or decline) may be transmitted from one country to others.

This does not imply that shifts in external demand do not matter. Fortunate indeed is the country with an expanding export market for the commodity in whose production it has a comparative advantage; for it can then draw increasing supplies in limitless variety from the outside world. The suggestion is merely that, because of the possibility of internal factor shifts in response to varying price relationships, long-term trends in external demand conditions need not be reflected fully, if at all, in changes in the terms of trade.

In considering the international mechanism of development it is necessary at any rate to admit the possibility of variation in the conditions of growth transmission through trade. Just as the limited extent to which the United States economy transmits its own growth rate to primary producing countries is fully understandable in the light of its own abundant natural resources combined with its ample capital supplies and technical know-how, so the nineteenth century experience was conditioned by the fact that the industrial revolution happened to originate on a small island with a limited range of resources, at a time when the chemical industry was yet unborn.

As a result, the rate of growth in the import demand of the dominant economy of the twentieth century seems different from that of the nineteenth. If this is so, it is not certain that the less developed countries can rely on economic growth being induced from the outside through an expansion of world demand for their exports of crude materials.[16] In these circumstances reliance on induced expansion through international trade may not be able to provide the main solution to the problem of development. It is not surprising, therefore, that countries should be looking for other types of solution. It will be useful to keep these things in mind, because they form the background to the case for balanced growth which is now so greatly in vogue.

[16] To ask the less developed countries to increase their export quantities of primary products in the face of a price-inelastic and not an upward-shifting demand schedule would be to ask, in effect, for an income transfer from poor to rich countries through a change in the terms of trade in favour of the latter. If one of several countries exporting the same primary commodity were to cut its export costs and prices, its export proceeds could indeed increase, but only at the expense of a fall in the other countries' export proceeds. The balance of payments adjustment process alone (whether through exchange rate variations or domestic price changes) would lead the latter to cut their export prices too, and all will be worse off at the end than they were at the start.

XI.A.5. Contribution of Trade to

Development*

Let me begin . . . by emphasizing the importance—indeed, the uniqueness—of the contribution that foreign trade can make to economic development. There is nothing necessarily regrettable about dependence on foreign trade. It is true that in engaging in trade a country puts itself at the mercy of external events: this is the price that any international division of labour exacts. But a country that seeks development must invite foreign influences if it is to succeed. It needs foreign equipment, foreign capital and foreign ideas. How can it pay for this equipment without earning foreign currency by exporting? Or arrange a transfer of capital, in or out, without those other transactions in goods and services that give effect to the transfer? Or allow the economy to be permeated with the ideas that are the seed of true development without the kind of contacts

*From A. K. Cairncross, *Factors in Economic Development*, George Allen & Unwin, London, 1962, pp. 214–20, 223–8. Reprinted by permission.

with foreigners that trade automatically produces? Trade is no mere exchange of goods, least of all when it takes place between economies at different stages of development. As often as not, it is trade that gives birth to the urge to develop, the knowledge and experience that make development possible, and the means to accomplish it.

The importance of foreign trade is particularly great in countries that lack an engineering industry and are obliged to import almost all their machinery. In such countries exports may easily become the limiting factor on productive investment and on the successful development of the economy. The common experience in under-developed countries is not that exports are already a dangerously large element but that they are not large enough to give adequate elbow room in the financing of new investment. A high level of exports enlarges the volume of imports of equipment that can be financed without endangering the balance of payments, and this greater degree of freedom makes it easier to take a long view and plan domestic investment without the constant interruption that destroys half its value.

There is nothing particularly surprising when external demand bears on a narrow sector of the economy. This presumably reflects the much higher productivity of resources, especially land, in some specialized use, such as the growing of coffee, than in any less specialized alternative use. Foreign trade opens up large possibilities of immediate gain by concentrating on a product that foreigners will buy and for which they will pay a relatively attractive price. It helps to transform subsistence into monetary economies by providing a market for cash crops, and raises the standard of living of monetary economies by bringing a higher return for the same effort. But it does not and cannot by itself do more than this. It does not, for example, result in an automatic modernization of agricultural methods; nor does it guarantee that the domestic market which it creates or widens will nurse local industry to factory-scale volume. The attitudes, prac-

tices and tenures of peasant cultivators may be little altered and they may buy their manufactures not from the towns but from abroad. Development may be blocked by a social structure that keeps the response to economic forces within narrow channels and itself withstands transformation by those forces. An expanding foreign demand will not be translated into a self-sustaining process of development in every sector of the economy unless many other conditions are fulfilled simultaneously. But the chances are that if these conditions are not fulfilled the same obstacles will stultify development so long as the forces of change are purely economic.

I confess to some scepticism about the supposed ineffectiveness of foreign trade in producing innovation and development. It does not strike me as entirely plausible to speak as if foreign trade could be contained within an enclave without transmitting its dynamic influences to the rest of the economy. How can one contain the so-called demonstration effects? By what magic is a steel mill supposed to revolutionize an economy while a railway or a copper smelter leaves it essentially unchanged? Every new departure is initially an enclave and it takes time for all innovations to work through and be absorbed. The influence of foreign trade may also make itself felt slowly. Sometimes the influence is bound to be indirect; there is not much in an oil refinery that will transform the agriculture of an Arab country. But indirect influences are not to be discounted: they may embrace half the profits of the oil companies and a good deal of free technical education for the local staff. As Professor Swerling has pointed out, "the tax machinery can remove much economic remoteness even from mineral enclaves."

Most of the countries that we now think of as advanced have been at one time or another dependent on just as narrow a range of exports. Japan in the early stages of industrialization was heavily dependent on exports of silk, the United States and Canada on exports of grain, Britain on exports of wool, or, at a later stage, on textile manufactures which once supplied over 70 per cent of her export earnings. If you want to make a start you must use what you have, not lament that the other fellow who is ahead of you is less highly specialized. The more foreign exchange is felt to be a bottleneck, the more important it is to foster in every possible way the limited range of activities from which foreign exchange can be derived.

Yet the risks of specializing on a narrow front are very real. In the long run there is the danger of a substitute produced at lower cost by factory methods; in the short run there is the danger of wide fluctuations in price. Of these two the long-run danger is the more alarming even if, so far, it has been rare for a natural product to be superseded by a synthetic one. The world's consumption of cotton, rubber, jute, butter and other products threatened by substitutes is higher than ever before in spite of the rise of synthetics. The function of the synthetic product has generally been to supplement an inelastic natural supply and meet rapidly expanding industrial requirements rather than to displace the natural products altogether.

Far too much emphasis is put in current literature on the forces operating to limit or diminish the demand for primary produce and far too little on the constant opening up of new requirements throughout the world as the standard of living rises. It is a useful exercise to list the major raw materials in use today and consider how many of them were available, even a hundred years ago. Steel and petroleum are barely a hundred years old. In 1860 aluminum was a precious metal used like platinum in royal gifts. Rubber, newsprint, synthetic fibers are for all practical purposes twentieth century creations. Nor is it only the advanced countries that benefit when new materials emerge. The less advanced countries, with luck, can shift from one crop to another or find within their borders the mineral products that technological change brings to the front. If there are losers through the obsolescence of materials, there are gainers as well. . . .

This brings me to what seems to be the central issue. Is the market for the exports of the under-developed countries so inelastic that it no longer provides a satisfactory engine of growth? Is their development being cramped by stagnation of world demand for their traditional exports?

That the nineteenth century process of growth-transmission works rather differently nowadays is not in dispute. The under-developed countries are no longer the frontiers of an expanding world economy and the division of labour between them and the individual countries of North America and Western Europe does not involve those vast territorial shifts in primary production that lie behind the rapid growth of world trade in the nineteenth century. In the middle of the nineteenth century that growth averaged about 13 per cent annually, the total volume trebling within thirty years largely as a result of the inflow into Europe of primary produce from countries overseas.[1] Since the scope for similar displacements is now far more limited and the industrial countries are less willing to see their agriculture contract further, it is unlikely that trade will ever grow so fast again over so long a period. To the extent that the under-developed countries have to rely on exports of tropical produce, there can be very little displacement of production and the rate of expansion is bound to be limited by the growth of world demand. For other products, however, notably base metals and petroleum, this limitation does not apply. . . .

Every under-developed country is unique and is affected by the market conditions and prices for its own products and not by the movement of index numbers. To aggregate or average the experience of the group of countries that we think of as under-developed is to presume common elements that may have no real existence.

Nevertheless, it may help to give some concreteness to my argument if I turn at this

[1] A. H. Imlah, *Economic Elements in the Pax Britannica*, pp. 96–7, 190.

point to consider just what the under-developed countries as a group do export and what part trade plays in their economy. For simplicity I shall divide the world into the three poorest and the three richest continents, the first group being made up of Africa, Asia and Latin America and the second of Europe, North America and Oceania. This means that one or two advanced countries such as South Africa and Japan will be included in the poor countries but their exclusion would make little difference to the results. At times I have been obliged to use a grouping prepared by GATT which adds Australasia to the three poorer continents and labels the mixture "non-industrial areas." The Communist bloc of countries is excluded throughout, unless otherwise indicated.

The so-called non-industrial areas, on examination, turn out to be very far from non-industrial. According to GATT they import only about one-third of their consumption of manufactures, and this proportion is falling.[2] The remaining two-thirds of their consumption of manufactures is produced at home. Many of them already have a flourishing textile industry and some of them are net exporters of textiles. Of the manufactured goods which they import, a high proportion consists of capital goods, base metals, and so on, while manufactured consumption goods are relatively small, constituting not much more than 10 per cent of total imports. Nor are they by any means entirely dependent on foreign markets for the sale of their primary produce. This is particularly true of food and feeding stuffs; nine-tenths of the output is consumed at home while only the remaining tenth is exported. Many of the foodstuffs that form their staple diet are quite unimportant in foreign trade. Exports of fuel and raw materials (including materials of agricultural origin) take a higher proportion of total production—on the average, about two-fifths,[3]

and sometimes, as in the oil countries, nearly 100 per cent.

Just as it is a mistake to think that under-developed countries have no industries, so it is a mistake to think of them as the major sources of primary produce. Every country is a primary producer, and the more advanced it is, the larger, broadly speaking, is its output of primary produce. There can be few countries that fail to grow at least half their food supply or to produce a wide range of raw materials. It is true that some advanced countries employ very little of their manpower in agriculture and that their raw materials are often manufactured rather than mined or grown. But the fact remains that the advanced countries produce more food and more raw materials than the less advanced countries. What they import from the less advanced countries meets only one-tenth of their requirements of food and one-quarter of their requirements of raw materials.[4] Nor are they all net importers. Some of them are large exporters, and the three richer continents account for roughly half of world exports of primary produce. They are in fact larger exporters, just as they are larger producers, of primary products than the so-called primary-producing countries.[5]

The less advanced countries, in the same way, are importers as well as exporters of primary produce: indeed, their imports are half as large as their exports. Thus it is quite wrong to think of the world as if it could be divided into two sets of countries, the advanced and the less advanced, with primary produce flowing exclusively in one direction. On the contrary, international trade brings the primary producers of every country into competition with one another, and the margin of advantage does not necessarily shift steadily in one direction.

Seven items or groups make up nearly three-quarters of the total exports of pri-

---

[2] International Trade 1959, GATT, 1960, p. 14.
[3] Ibid., p. 13.

[4] Ibid., p. 14.
[5] This is true only if we exclude Australasia from the primary-producing countries. See my "International Trade and Economic Development," Kyklos, Vol. XIII (1960), p. 549.

mary produce from the under-developed countries. Listed in order of size they are: petroleum, beverages, textile fibers, base metals, sugar, oilseeds and fats, and rubber. The same group of items make up less than 40 per cent of the exports of primary produce from the developed countries. But what is perhaps of more significance is the change that has taken place over the past century. For the seven items selected the share of the under-developed countries in world trade has risen from 43 per cent to 64 per cent. For all other items, representing nearly half the total volume of world trade in primary products, the share of the under-developed countries has remained a little below 30 per cent. It has been where their share was already high that it expanded most. . . .

From this analysis of the trade of the under-developed countries I draw four conclusions.

First of all they are highly dependent on a very narrow range of exports. A large proportion of these exports consists of gifts of nature: petroleum, mineral ores, crude fertilizers. How much a country can earn from exports of this kind is largely a matter of luck and willingness to make use of foreign capital. Other exports suffer from great variability in supply and low elasticity of supply. The source of these exports tends to be either foreign-owned plantations or peasants who may lack the means, the knowledge or the incentives to adopt modern methods of production. On top of all this nearly all capital equipment has to be imported, and a shortage of foreign exchange frequently sets a sharp limit to the scale and firmness of any forward planning of investment. These facts point strongly to the desirability of widening the range of exports wherever possible and developing domestic sources of the simpler types of imported manufactures.

Secondly, it would seem that exports from the under-developed countries are governed less closely by the level of world demand than is usually supposed. Where they are in direct competition with the more ad-

vanced countries, their share of the market depends also on the terms on which they are able to compete: on the movement of their costs and in the alternatives which they can choose. If their exports have lagged behind the exports of the more advanced countries, this is partly because they have been running a large external deficit . . . and this necessarily implies some downward drag on their exports compared with the exports of the countries from which they buy. Other, but not unrelated, factors tending to hold back their exports have been inflation, relatively high prices, and the encouragement of other sectors of their economies.

Thirdly, since agriculture is by far the most important activity and is usually directed more towards domestic than export markets, there is everything to be gained by trying to expand agricultural production. Without a general improvement in agricultural production and incomes, the mass of the population will remain hungry and poor and domestic industry will be industry will be stifled for lack of markets. Such an improvement is not dependent on some precise rate of growth of exports. An expanding foreign market can, however, contribute, both by putting more cash in the hands of the cultivators and by introducing a competitive element that may make technical change in agriculture more acceptable.

But what, fourthly, if agriculture proves unresponsive and the government has to think of industrialization without any expansion in foodstuffs? The fact that under-developed countries produce about two-thirds of the manufactured goods which they consume shows that some progress towards industrialization has already been made. Industrial development *is* occurring, assisted by higher export earnings and foreign investment and loans. But the industries that have grown up are not, as a rule, very efficient. It is curious, for example, that Latin American countries meet nearly all their own textile requirements but have a negligible share in each other's markets or, indeed, in any foreign market.

One of the principal obstacles to more rapid industrialization is the limited scale of operations in a manufacturing plant supplying only the domestic market of an underdeveloped country. It is precisely this limitation which international trade can remove. If, therefore, we are anxious to encourage development in the poorer countries and doubt whether agricultural expansion will clear the way for industry, might we not turn to a new model of the traditional engine of development and see what could be done through freer trade in manufactured goods?

XI.A.6. Conditions of Export-Led Development—Note

The foregoing materials raise a central question: Under what conditions can a process of export-induced development follow upon an expansion of the export sector? How can export expansion also act as an engine of domestic development? Notwithstanding the possibility of lagging exports in more recent decades, most of the underdeveloped countries have experienced long periods of export growth. In most cases, after a country was exposed to the world economy, its exports grew markedly in volume and in variety. Yet, despite their secular rise, exports in many countries have not acted as a key propulsive sector, propelling the rest of the economy forward. Although the classical belief that development can be transmitted through trade has been confirmed by the experience of some countries that are now among the richest in the world, trade has not had a similar stimulating effect for countries that have remained underdeveloped. Why has not the growth in exports in these countries carried over to other sectors and led to more widespread development in the domestic economy?

As noted above, some critics of the classical position contend that the very forces of international trade have been responsible for inhibiting development. They argue that the development of the export sector by foreign capital has created a "dual economy" in which production has been export-biased, and the resultant pattern of resource utiliza-tion has deterred development. This argument, however, tends to contrast the pattern of resource utilization that actually occurred with some other ideal pattern. More relevant is a comparison between the actual pattern and the allocation that would have occurred in the absence of the capital inflow. There is little foundation to the assertion that if there had been no foreign investment, a poor country would have generated more domestic investment; or that, in the absence of foreign entrepreneurs, the supply of domestic entrepreneurs would have been larger. Contrary to what is often implied by the critics of foreign investment, the real choice was not between employing the resources in the export sector or in domestic production, but rather between giving employment to the surplus resources in export production or leaving them idle.[1] It is difficult to substantiate the argument that foreign investment was competitive with home investment, or that the utilization of resources in the export sector was at the expense of home production.

Another contention is that trade has impeded development by the "demonstration

---

[1] Cf. Hla Myint, "The Gains from International Trade and the Backward Countries," *Review of Economic Studies*, Vol. 22, No. 58, 1954–55; "The 'Classical Theory' of International Trade and the Underdeveloped Countries," *Economic Journal*, June 1958, pp. 317–37.

effect": the international demonstration of higher consumption standards in more developed countries has allegedly raised the propensity to consume in the less developed countries and reduced attainable saving rates. By stimulating the desire to consume, however, the international demonstration effect may also have operated on incentives and been instrumental in increasing the supply of effort and productive services—especially as between the subsistence sector and the exchange economy.[2] This positive effect on the side of factor supply may have more than offset any negative effect on saving.

More serious is the argument that international market forces have transferred income from the poor to rich nations through a deterioration in the terms of trade of the less developed countries. The significance of this argument is also overdrawn, and it can be questioned on both theoretical and empirical grounds. The alleged trend is based not on the measurement of prices within the poor countries, but rather on inferences from the United Kingdom's commodity terms of trade or the terms of trade between primary products and manufactured products.[3] This does not provide a sufficiently strong statistical foundation for any adequate generalization about the terms of trade of poor countries.[4] The import-price index conceals the heterogeneous price movements within and among the broad categories of foodstuffs, raw materials, and minerals; no allowance is made for changes in the quality of exports and imports; there is inadequate consideration of new commodities; and the recorded terms of trade are not corrected for the substantial decline in transportation costs. The introduction of new products and qualitative improvements have been greater in manufactured than in primary products, and a large proportion of the fall in British prices of primary products can be attributed to the great decline in inward freight rates. The simple use of the "inverse" of the United Kingdom's terms of trade to indicate the terms of trade of primary producing countries involves therefore a systematic bias which makes changes appear more unfavorable to the primary exporting countries than they actually were.

Even if it were true that the less developed countries experienced a secular deterioration in their commodity terms of trade, the question would still remain whether this constituted a significant obstacle to their development. The answer depends on what caused the deterioration and whether the country's factoral terms of trade and income terms also deteriorated. If the deterioration in the commodity terms is due to increased productivity in the export sector, the single-factoral terms of trade (commodity terms corrected for changes in productivity in producing exports) can improve at the same time. As long as productivity in its export industries is increasing more rapidly than

---

[2] For an instructive analysis of the general process by which the money economy has developed through expansion of export production induced by the growth of new wants for imported consumers' goods, see Hla Myint, *The Economics of Developing Countries*, London, 1964, Chaps. 1–5.

[3] United Nations, Department of Economic Affairs, *Relative Prices of Exports and Imports of Under-Developed Countries*, New York, 1949, pp. 7, 13–24; W. A. Lewis, "World Production, Prices, and Trade, 1870–1960," *Manchester School*, May 1952, p. 118.

[4] For detailed criticisms, see R. E. Baldwin, "Secular Movements in the Terms of Trade," *American Economic Review, Papers and Proceedings*, May 1955, pp. 267ff.; P. T. Ellsworth, "The Terms of Trade Between Primary Producing and Industrial Countries," *Inter-American Economic Affairs*, Summer 1956, pp. 47–65; T. Morgan, "The Long-Run Terms of Trade Between Agriculture and Manufacturing," *Economic Development and Cultural Change*, October 1959, pp. 6–17; Gottfried Haberler, "Terms of Trade and Economic Development," in H. S. Ellis (ed.), *Economic Development for Latin America*, New York, 1961, pp. 275–97; Jagdish Bhagwati, "A Skeptical Note on the Adverse Secular Trend in the Terms of Trade of Underdeveloped Countries," *Pakistan Economic Journal*, December 1960; G. M. Meier, *International Economics of Development*, New York, 1968, Chap. 3.

export prices are falling, the country's real income can rise despite the deterioration in the commodity terms of trade: when its factoral terms improve, the country benefits from the ability to obtain a greater quantity of imports per unit of factors embodied in its exports. Also possible is an improvement in the country's income terms of trade (commodity terms multiplied by quantity of exports) at the same time as its commodity terms deteriorate. The country's capacity to import is then greater, and this will ease development efforts. When due weight is given to the increase in productivity in export production and the rise in export volume, it would appear that the single-factoral terms and income terms of trade actually improved for many poor countries, notwithstanding any possible deterioration in their commodity terms of trade.

Having rejected the view that international trade operated as a mechanism of international inequality, we must look to other factors for an understanding of why trade has not had a more stimulating effect in underdeveloped countries. If the export sector is to be a propelling force in development, it is essential that the export sector not remain an enclave, separate from the rest of the economy; instead, an integrated process should be established, diffusing stimuli from the export sector and creating responses elsewhere in the economy. A more convincing explanation of why export-led development has occurred in some countries, but not in others, would therefore distinguish the differential effects of the integrative process by focusing on the varying strength of the stimuli in different countries from their exports and on the different response mechanisms within the exporting countries.[5]

Different export commodities will provide different stimuli, according to the tech-

nological characteristics of their production. The nature of the export good's production function has an influence on the extent of other secondary changes elsewhere in the economy, beyond the primary increase in export output.[6] With the use of different input coefficients to produce different types of export commodities, there will be different rates of learning and different linkage effects. The degree to which the various exports are processed is highly significant in the determination of external economies associated with the learning process; the processing of primary-product exports of modern methods is likely to benefit other activities through the spread of technical knowledge, training of labor, demonstration of new production techniques that might be adapted elsewhere in the economy, and the acquisition of organizational and supervisory skills.

In contrast, growth of the export sector will have a negligible carry-over if its techniques of production are the same as those already in use in other sectors, or if its expansion occurs by a simple widening of production without any change in production functions. If the introduction or expan-

---

[5] The following paragraphs draw upon G. M. Meier, "External Trade and International Development," in Louis Gann and Peter Duignan (eds.), *Colonialism in Africa*, New York, 1975, Chapter 11.

[6] Although more empirical research is needed, some illustrative cases are suggested by D. C. North, "Location Theory and Regional Economic Growth," *Journal of Political Economy*, June 1955, pp. 249–51; Dudley Seers, "An Approach to the Short-Period Analysis of Primary-Producing Economies," *Oxford Economic Papers*, February 1959, pp. 6–9; R. E. Caves and R. H. Holton, *The Canadian Economy*, Cambridge, 1959, pp. 41–7; J. V. Levin, *The Export Economies*, Cambridge, 1960; R. E. Baldwin, "Export Technology and Development from a Subsistence Level," *Economic Journal*, March 1963, pp. 80–92; M. H. Watkins, "A Staple Theory of Economic Growth," *Canadian Journal of Economics and Political Science*, May 1963, pp. 141–58; V. D. Wickizer, "The Plantation System in the Development of Tropical Economics," *Journal of Farm Economics*, February 1958, pp. 63–77; Dudley Seers, "The Mechanism of an Open Petroleum Economy," *Social and Economic Studies*, June 1964, pp. 233–42; M. J. Herskovitz and M. Horwitz, *Economic Transition in Africa*, Evanston, 1964, pp. 312–18.

sion of export crops involves simple methods of production that do not differ markedly from the traditional techniques already used in subsistence agriculture, the stimulus to development will clearly be less than if the growth in exports entailed the introduction of new skills and more productive recombinations of factors of production. More favorable linkages may stem from exports that require skilled labor than from those using unskilled labor. The influence of skill requirements may operate in various ways: greater incentives for capital formation may be provided through education; on-the-job training in the export sector may be disseminated at little real cost through the movement of workers into other sectors or occupations; skilled workers may be a source of entrepreneurship; skilled workers may save more of their wage incomes than unskilled workers.[7] The level of entrepreneurial skill induced by the development of an export is also highly significant. The level will be expanded if the development of the export commodity offers significant challenge and instills abilities usable in other sectors, but is not so high as to require the importing of a transient class of skilled managerial labor.

Although the processing of a primary product provides forward linkages in the sense that the output of one sector becomes an input for another sector, it is also important to have backward linkages. When some exports grow, they provide a strong stimulus for expansion in the input-supplying industries elsewhere in the economy. These backward linkages may be in agriculture or in other industries supplying inputs to the expanding export sector, or in social overhead capital. The importance of linkages has been stressed by Hirschman.[8]

The notion is emphasized also by Perroux, who refers to a developing enterprise as a "motor unit" when it increases its demands on its suppliers for raw materials or communicates new techniques to another enterprise. The "induction effect" that the motor unit exerts upon another unit may be considered in two components that frequently occur in combination: (1) a dimension effect that is the augmentation of demand by one enterprise to another by increasing its supply; and (2) an innovation effect that introduces an innovation which for a given quantity of factors of production yields the same quantity of production at a lower price and/or a better quality. When a motor unit is interlinked with its surrounding environment, Perroux refers to a growth pole or a development pole.[9] The emphasis on generating new skills, innovations in the export sector or other sectors linked to exports, and technical change are important in determining the learning rate of the economy.

Beyond this, the nature of the production function of the exports commodity will also determine the distribution of income, and, in turn, the pattern of local demand and impact on local employment. The use of different factor combinations affects the distribution of income in the sense that the relative shares of profits, wages, interest, and rent will vary according to the labor intensity or capital intensity of the export production and the nature of its organization—whether it is mining, plantation agriculture, or peasant farming. If the internal distribution of the export income favors groups with a higher propensity to consume domestic goods than to import, the resultant distribution of income will be more effective in raising the demand for home-produced products; and to the extent that these home-produced products are labor-intensive, there will be more of an impact on employment. In

[7] Richard E. Caves, "Export-led growth and the new economic history," in *Trade, Balance of Payments and Growth*, J. N. Bhagwati et al. (eds.), Amsterdam, 1971, pp. 403–42.

[8] Albert O. Hirschman, *The Strategy of Economic Development*, New Haven, 1958, Chap. 9.

[9] Francois Perroux, "Multinational Investment and the Analysis of Development and Integration Poles," in *Multinational Investment in the Economic Development and Integration of Latin America*, Bogotá, Inter-American Development Bank, April 1968, pp. 99–103.

contrast, if income is distributed to those who have a higher propensity to import, the leakage through consumption of imported goods will be greater. If income increments go to those who are likely to save large portions, the export sector may also make a greater contribution to the financing of growth in other sectors.

If the export commodity is subject to substantial economies of scale in its production, this will tend to imply large capital requirements for the establishment of enterprises, and hence extra-regional or foreign borrowing. This may then lead to an outward flow of profits instead of providing profit income for local reinvestment. But this is only part of the impact of the foreign investment. For a full appraisal, it would be necessary to consider all the benefits and costs of the foreign investment. And these too will vary according to the nature of the export sector in which the foreign investment occurs.

Finally, the repercussions from exports will also differ according to the degree of fluctuation in export proceeds. Disruptions in the flow of foreign exchange receipts make the development process discontinuous; the greater the degree of instability, the more difficult it is to maintain steady employment, because there will be disturbing effects on real income, government revenue, capital formation, resource allocation, and the capacity to import according to the degree of amplitude of fluctuation in foreign exchange receipts. To the extent that different exports vary in their degree of fluctuation, and in revenue earned and retained at home, their repercussions on the domestic economy will also differ. Depending on the various characteristics of the country's export, we may thus infer how the strength of the integrative process, in terms of the stimulus from exports, will differ among countries.

In summary, we would normally expect the stimulating forces of the integrative process to be stronger under the following conditions: the higher the growth-rate of the export sector, the greater the direct impact of the export sector on employment and personal income, the more the expansion of exports has a "learning effect" in terms of increasing productivity and instilling new skills, the more the export sector is supplied through domestic inputs instead of imports, the more the distribution of export income favors those with a marginal propensity to consume domestic goods instead of imports, the more productive is the investment resulting from any saving of export income, the more extensive are the externalities and linkages connected with the export sector, and the more stable are the export receipts that are retained at home. Some exports fulfill these conditions more readily than others, and countries specializing on these exports will enjoy greater opportunities for development.

Even with a strong stimulus from exports, however, the transmission of growth from the export-base to the rest of the economy will still be contingent upon other conditions in the economy. The weak penetrative power of exports in underdeveloped countries can be explained not only by a possibly weak stimulus from a particular type of export, but also by the host of domestic impediments that limit the transmission of the gains from exports to other sectors even when the stimulus may be strong.

After analyzing the character of a country's export base for an indication of the strength of the stimulus to development provided by its export commodities, we must go on to examine the strength of the response or diffusion mechanism within the domestic economy for evidence of how receptive the domestic economy is to the stimulus from exports. The strength of the integrative process, in terms of the response mechanism to the export stimulus, will depend on the extent of market imperfections in the domestic economy and also on noneconomic barriers in the general environment. The integrative forces are stronger under the following conditions: the more developed the infrastructure of the economy, the more market institutions are developed; the more extensive the development of human resources, the less are the price distortions that affect resource allocations, and the greater is the capacity to bear risks. Our view of the carry-over should stress not only the mechanical linkages but also a more evolutionary (and hence biological rather than mechanical) analogy that recognizes societal responses. What matters is not simply the creation of modern enterprise or modern sectors but modernization as a process. This involves not simply physical production or mechanical linkages but a change in socioeconomic traits throughout the society, and an intangible atmosphere that relates to changes in values, in character, in attitudes, in the learning of new behavior patterns, and in institutions.

In sum, the effects of a strong integrative process will be the following: (1) an acceleration in the learning rate of the economy; (2) an enrichment of the economic and social infrastructure (transportation, public services, health, education); (3) an expansion of the supply of entrepreneurship (and a managerial and administrative class); and (4) a mobilization of a larger surplus above consumption in the form of taxation and saving. These effects constitute the country's development foundations. Once these foundations are laid, the country's economy can be more readily transformed through diversification in primary production and the service industries, new commodity exports, and industrialization via import substitution and export substitution.

It follows that if a more extensive carry-over from exports is to be achieved, it is necessary to remove the domestic impediments that cut short the stimulus from exports. Many of the policy recommendations in this book refer to the need for reducing the fragmentation and compartmentalization of the economy by overcoming the narrow and isolated markets, ignorance of technological possibilities, limited infrastructure, and slow rate of human-resource development. To accomplish this, alternative forms of economic and social organization are re-

quired, and policy measures must aim at diminishing the prevalence of semimonopolistic and monopolistic practices, removing restraints on land tenure and land use, widening and expanding financial markets, promoting market facilities and increasing investment in economic and social infrastructure, and in promoting human-resource development.

It also follows that the stimulus from the export-base should be as strong as possible. While domestic limitations and impediments may have accounted for the weak carry-over of exports in the past when export markets were expanding, it may be contended (as Nurkse does, XI.A.4) that exports no longer enjoy a strongly rising world demand and do not now provide a sufficient stimulus for development in the first instance. If exports are confined to a slow rate of growth, then there can be little scope for development through trade even if the domestic obstacles are removed. To counter this "export pessimism," it is all the more necessary for underdeveloped countries to raise productivity in agriculture in order to ensure that their primary exports are competitive on world markets, and to prevent home consumption from causing a limitation of their export supplies. Further, it is important that the less developed countries pursue policies that will ensure that they specialize as much as they can in exports with the highest growth prospects. To do this, a country must have the capacity to reallocate resources—to shift, for instance, from exporting a foodstuff which may have only a slowly growing demand, to the export of an industrial raw material or a mineral for which the demand may be rising more rapidly. Of special significance is the country's potential for taking advantage of new export opportunities in manufactured goods. The exportation of manufactured commodities may play a strategic role in transmitting development to some poor countries that have a favorable factor endowment and can gain a comparative advantage by utilizing labor-intensive methods. In section XI.D, we shall consider more fully the issue of export stimulation, giving particular attention to the opportunity for exporting manufactures. Efforts at regional integration may also promote trade in manufactures among the developing nations themselves, as will be discussed in section XI.E, below.

Export prospects may also be improved by a more liberal importation policy on the part of advanced countries. A removal of trade restrictions is beneficial not only for the more traditional primary exports, but also for encouraging new manufactured exports. The export market for primary products might also be expanded if industrialized nations avoided artificial supports for the substitution of primary products by synthetic materials. And along with the liberalization of trade, it is vitally important that the LDCs should be able to look forward to the maintenance of high rates of growth in the advanced countries to which they export.

Finally, advanced countries can contribute by supporting policies to stabilize export proceeds. High and stable levels of employment in industrial nations will help reduce the short-term fluctuations in export proceeds; but in addition, national and international measures might be advocated to achieve greater short-run stability in international commodity markets. Various possible remedies for the short-term fall in export earnings are examined in the next section.

XI.B. TRADE IN PRIMARY PRODUCTS

XI.B.1. International Resource Bargaining—Note

The control of the price of oil by the Organization of Petroleum Exporting Countries (OPEC) has posed in dramatic form the question of whether the exercise of "producer power" in commodities can be generalized to other primary producers. Can there be additional producer monopoly agreements that effectively control future supplies or prices of minerals, food, and other primary products so as to create artificial scarcities and raise export prices above competitive market levels? Is oil a special situation, or can effective producer power be exercised also for bauxite, copper, tin, phosphates, coffee, tea, rubber, and other primary products?

The answers to these questions rest in the outcome of a complex process of international resource bargaining. But we might identify various conditions in this process that will determine the relative bargaining strengths of different producing and consuming countries. First, primary production in the LDCs must be disaggregated—at the least, into such categories as oil, non-fuel minerals, tropical agricultural products, cereals. Secondly, it should be recognized that market intervention can assume various forms: a cartel of exporters that takes collusive action to set production and export quotas or to raise export prices, or one producer acting as a price leader with others following, or by export controls over the flow of exports through imposition of quantitative limitations or export taxes. Whether a particular form of market intervention will be successful in raising the export price and revenue for a particular primary product will depend essentially on the existence of three conditions: (1) a dominant position by a producer country in export markets or the capacity for effective collusion by a group of producer nations; (2) an inelastic demand for the product in consumer countries; (3) a low elasticity of supply of alternative materials for consumer countries.

The economic prospects for successful market intervention must ultimately be determined by detailed econometric studies on an individual commodity basis.[1] Opposing conclusions of a general nature, however, may be summarized here.

The "threat from the Third World" has been emphasized by Bergsten, who states:

Four countries control more than 80 percent of the exportable supply of world copper, have already organized, and have already begun to use their oligopoly power. Two countries account for more than 70 percent of world tin exports, and four countries raise the total close to 95 percent. Four countries combine for more than 50 percent of the world supply of natural rubber. Four countries possess over one-half the world supply of bauxite, and the inclusion of Australia (which might well join the "Third World" for such purposes) brings the total above 90 percent. In coffee, the four major suppliers have begun to collude (even within the framework of the International Coffee

---

[1] Political prospects are as crucial as economic prospects, but they are not amenable to such systematic empirical study. That is why the problem of international resource bargaining might be characterized more aptly as a problem of international resource *diplomacy*.

Agreement, which includes the main consuming countries) to boost prices. A few countries are coming to dominate each of the regional markets for timber, the closest present approximation to a truly vanishing resource. The percentages are less, but still quite impressive, for several other key raw materials and agricultural products. And the United States already meets an overwhelming share of its needs for most of these commodities from imports, or will soon be doing so.

A wide range of Third World countries thus have sizeable potential for strategic market power. They could use that power against all buyers, or in a discriminatory way through differential pricing or supply conditions—for example, to avoid higher costs to other LDC's or against the United States alone to favor Europe or Japan.

Supplying countries could exercise maximum leverage through withholding supplies altogether, at least from a single customer such as the United States. Withholding is a feasible policy when there are no substitute products available on short notice, and when the foreign exchange reserves of the suppliers become sizeable enough that they have no need for current earnings.

The suppliers would be even more likely to use their monopoly power to charge higher prices for their raw materials, directly or through such techniques as insisting that they process the materials themselves.[2]

Considering whether oil and OPEC represent a unique case which cannot be duplicated, Bergsten states that

it is very doubtful that oil is different in any qualitative sense. Indeed, many other OPECs look much *easier* to organize and maintain. OPEC had to pool twelve countries to control 80 percent of world oil exports, but fewer countries are usually involved in production of other primary products. Most

OPEC countries are heavily dependent on oil, and cartelization was especially risky for them. Other commodity producers are more diversified. OPEC could politicize oil and threaten the world economy; its successors will have an easier task because their products are less important. And economic and political differences among OPEC countries seem much sharper than those among other potential cartelizers. So new OPECs seem at least as likely as OPEC itself.[3]

In contrast with Bergsten's view, a prominent report by 15 economists from Japan, the European Community, and North America states that

the frequent portrayal of a future world of primary commodities divided up into cartels of developing country producers, as in the Organization of Petroleum Exporting Countries (OPEC), dictating prices and turning the supply on and off to achieve political or other ends, is vastly overdrawn. Primary products are produced by many countries, imports are not everywhere a major proportion of total consumption, and industrial rather than developing countries are the leading suppliers of many internationally traded commodities. Furthermore, many primary commodities can be substituted for each other, depending on price and availability. New collusive attempts by exporters to exploit markets are entirely possible—the more so because governments now intervene more actively in setting the conditions for production and sale, because the issues have become heavily politicized, and because the prospects for short-term gains are sometimes attractive. Also, following the example of OPEC is tempting. The crucial point, however, is that the number of commodities on which collusion would be feasible or effective is small, the economic impact is likely to be limited and isolated rather than pervasive

[2] C. Fred Bergsten, "The Threat from the Third World," *Foreign Policy*, Summer 1973, pp. 107–8.

[3] C. Fred Bergsten, "The New Era in World Commodity Markets," *Challenge*, September–October 1974, p. 40.

as with oil, and the prospects for sustained success over the medium term, to say nothing for the long term, are dim.[4]

On the particular prospects for market manipulation in the markets for tropical agricultural products, the report recalls that

past attempts by exporting countries to maintain prices of coffee and cocoa above competitive levels have met with only limited and temporary success, as individual exporting countries either would not observe or could not enforce export quotas without the cooperation of importing countries. . . . Cane sugar does not lend itself to producer cartelization because of the large number of suppliers and the competition from beet sugar and substitute sweeteners. For other tropical products, such as natural rubber and fibers, attempts to rig prices would be self-defeating because of competition from synthetics. . . .

In the case of cereals, experience with the International Grains Arrangement suggests how difficult it is for exporters, even when their number is limited, to maintain world prices above competitive levels for any significant length of time. Pressure is building up for greater price stability, however, and a renewed international effort to reduce the range of price fluctuations for grains and possibly for oil seeds as well seems bound to be given consideration. But if such a negotiation does take place, it must have as participants both exporters and importers. The end result of a successful negotiation would be a joint commodity agreement rather than a producers' cartel.[5]

It is also questioned whether cartels in mineral industries can be effective.

First, rarely do the major producers and exporters of a mineral adhere to the same

political and economic objectives. . . . Second, many of the producing nations depend heavily on mineral exports for their foreign exchange earnings, so the costs to them of withholding supplies are high. . . . Third, mineral production involves high fixed costs which continue whether production takes place or not. Thus, pressure mounts to cut prices during downswings in the business cycle to keep capacity utilization from falling drastically.

All this strongly suggests that attempts by producing countries to form cartels in the mineral industries are unlikely to succeed for any extended period. In time members will find the demand for their exports falling as producers outside the cartel boost their supplies and consumers switch to substitute materials. Eventually, they will have to abandon artificially high prices to avoid losing their markets entirely.[6]

Another study reaches similar conclusions:

Even the strongest political urge, or the most adroit management, cannot alter certain basic factors that, in our judgment, severely limit the possible accomplishments of producers' alliances in non-fuel minerals.

The key economic fact is that, while demand for most non-fuel minerals is price-inelastic in the short run . . . , this is not necessarily true over the long run, certainly not to the extent that holds for oil. Calculations based on historic experience for tin, aluminum and copper, for example, suggest strongly that in the long run the drop in demand more than offsets any price increase, so that the total return to the producers eventually becomes less than before the price change. Although the econometric measurement of price elasticities is a tricky process leading to differing estimates of individual cases, there is little disagreement on the broad point about short-term and long-term price elasticity.

[4] *Trade in Primary Commodities: Conflict or Cooperation?*, A Tripartite Report, The Brookings Institution, Washington, D.C., 1974, pp. 1–2.

[5] Ibid., p. 32.

[6] Ibid., pp. 30–31.

The reasons are threefold—stockpiles, recycling possibilities, and the use of substitutes—none of which, of course, applies to oil in anything like the same way as yet.[7]

The foregoing clearly represent different views on the prospect of OPEC-like cartels being effective in various primary commodity markets. The major purpose of the cartel might be interpreted as the improvement in the producing country's terms of trade—more precisely, not simply the commodity terms of trade $\frac{P_x}{P_m}$, but rather the income terms of trade $\frac{P_x Q_x}{P_m}$, where P_x is an export price index, Q_x is an export volume index, and P_m is an import price index. This is an attempt to raise the primary country's share in the gains from trade and to increase its "capacity to import" (Q_m) derived from a given Q_x (as distinguished from the capacity to import based on a capital inflow). Thus, issues of international distributional equity and the size of a country's development program (as determined by the foreign exchange constraint), become intertwined with the process of international resource bargaining.

But to the extent that cartels and other measures to control export prices succeed, they impose real costs on the international community by inducing the production of costlier sources of supply, aggravating inflationary pressures, slowing down the rate of growth in consuming countries, and inviting retaliatory measures.

The deleterious effects on the "Fourth World" countries that are in the "resource-poor" category—that is, agricultural countries without mineral resources—should be of special concern to the international commu-

nity. The problem of acquiring minerals (and the derivatives of fertilizer and foodstuffs) at a price they can afford became in the 1970s a major handicap to the realization of development plans in resource-poor developing countries. Special arrangements that will provide these countries with the means of financing these imports or that will provide them with additional export revenue may impose additional costs on the world economy.

From the standpoint of world economic welfare, the policies of trade liberalization, additional aid, and foreign investment (with a benefit-cost ratio greater than unity) are first-best policies in comparison with cartels and related price fixing undertakings that have costly side-effects and are hence second-best as policies for increasing the gains from trade and raising the capacity to import.

The discussion of the control of trade in primary products has raised other issues that deserve attention. The use of export controls that impede access to supplies imposes costs on the world economy that are similar to those of import controls. But GATT has been concerned only with the latter. Bergsten has therefore proposed new rules to govern export controls:

Like those existing GATT rules which seek to govern the use of import controls, a set of rules on export controls would have four immediate goals:

1. To deter producing countries from erecting export controls except in clearly defined and justified circumstances.

2. To reinforce that deterrent by providing a basis for concerted response by the world trading community.

3. To limit the scope and duration of those controls which are actually applied.

4. To provide an international framework into which disputes triggered by export controls can be channeled when they are actually applied, to reduce the likelihood of unilateral reactions and emulation/retaliation cycles. . . .

[7] Bension Varon and Kenji Takeuchi, "Developing Countries and Non-Fuel Minerals," *Foreign Affairs*, April 1974, pp. 505–6. For similar views, see also Raymond F. Mikesell, "More Third World Cartels Ahead?" *Challenge*, December 1974, pp. 26–7.

The proposed set of rules would permit the use of export controls for national security purposes and "infant industry" protection, and to avoid serious injury (or the threat thereof) to national economies. But they would otherwise be proscribed.

The proscription would be backed by the requirement that any country adopting an unjustified export control had to provide adequate compensation or, more likely, accept any of a number of types of economic retaliation. Nonsignatories of the agreement could be subjected to such retaliation, broadening the scope of the deterrent, although every effort would be made to maximize membership in the new regime. Retaliation would also be authorized against "reverse dumping" and against import subsidies, in the form of import duties and "countervailing export controls," respectively.

When controls were justified, their application would be subject to agreed time limits and, for longer-term controls, the presentation of an acceptable domestic adjustment program. And they would require advance notification and consultation, undergo multilateral surveillance both at their initiation and throughout their subsequent application, have to be administered through export taxes rather than quotas whenever possible, and apply on a most-favored-nation basis. Such a regime would seem to provide a reasonable chance that export controls could be relatively depoliticized, and avoid unilateral reactions and emulation/retaliation cycles.

Any comprehensive arrangements to "assure access to supplies" must probably encompass commodity agreements as well as rules limiting the use of trade controls. Buffer stocks, agreed production levels and perhaps other arrangements to preserve agreed volumes of trade and price ranges would be needed. The nature of the decision-making machinery on all these issues would be a central concern to all negotiating parties.

Thus, from an intellectual standpoint, commodity agreements and new trade rules must be viewed together in dealing with the problem of access to supplies. But they must also be viewed in tandem from a negotiating standpoint, because together they might provide the basis for a package which served the interests of the several different groups of countries.[8]

International commodity agreements are also frequently proposed to reduce price fluctuations and stabilize foreign exchange earnings. This is discussed in the next selection.

Finally, the problem of international resource bargaining relates to two other issues discussed in previous chapters. Another objective of the exercise of "commodity power" is to increase the domestic value added from the primary commodity by inducing domestic processing of the commodity (bauxite into alumina, crude oil into refined petroleum products, etc.). This relates to the process of industrialization via export substitution, as discussed in selection X.C.2, above. An additional objective is to exercise more national control over foreign investment in primary products and to capture more of the rents from that investment. This relates to the problem of private foreign investment, as discussed in section VI.C, above.

Thus, the exercise of "producer power" raises not just one issue—that of improvement in the terms of trade—but also other related issues: (1) the stability of export prices and foreign exchange receipts in order to increase the developing country's capacity to import; (2) domestic processing of primary commodities; and (3) an increase in the benefit-cost ratio of foreign investment. For the longer-run period that is relevant to the outcome of development programs, the resolution of these other issues may well be more crucial than the shorter-run use of "producer power" to improve the terms of trade.

[8] C. Fred Bergsten, *Completing the GATT: Toward New International Rules to Govern Export Controls*, British-North American Committee, Washington, D.C., 1974, pp. 23, 51–2.

XI.B.2. An Integrated Program for

Commodities*

... The following proposals are made on the key issues that would form the core of an international approach to commodity problems:

(a) Establishment of international stocks of commodities, on a scale sufficient to provide assurance of disposal of production undertaken on the basis of a realistic assessment of consumption, as well as assurance of adequate supplies at all times for importing countries, and also large enough to ensure that excessive movements in prices—either upward or downward—can be prevented by market intervention;

(b) The creation of a common fund for the financing of international stocks, on terms and conditions that would attract to the fund investment of international capital, including the support of international financial institutions, while also reflecting in its composition the responsibility of governments of trading countries for the management of international commodity policies;

(c) The building up of systems of multilateral commitments on individual commodities, whereby governments, on the basis of a multilateral appraisal of trade requirements, enter into purchase and supply commitments as a means of improving the predictability of trade requirements and encouraging rational levels of investment of resources in commodity production. The functioning of the system, and the capacity of governments to undertake commitments on behalf of their export and import sectors, would be facilitated by arrangements for linking the commitments to the operation of interna-

*From United Nations Conference on Trade and Development, *An Integrated Programme for Commodities, Report by the Secretary-General of UNCTAD*, TD/B/C.1/166, December 9, 1974, pp. 1–4, 6–12, 14–16.

tional stocking mechanisms, and to compensatory schemes;

(d) Improved compensatory arrangements in situations of fluctuation in commodity prices and earnings for which international stocking or other arrangements could not secure suitable price and production incentives;

(e) The implementation of measures removing discrimination in trade against processed products, encouraging the transfer of technology and supporting a more intensive research effort, in order to secure rapid development in the processing of raw materials in producing countries as a basis for the expansion and diversification of export earnings. . . .

The proposal for an over-all integrated programme for commodities endeavours to launch international commodity policy onto a new course which, it is hoped, may have a greater chance of success than the approaches hitherto adopted. The proposed new approach is an attempt to move urgently from the field of consultation to the field of negotiation. To facilitate this shift, it is proposed that arrangements for a comprehensive range of commodities should be negotiated in the form of a package, so that the special interest of countries in some commodities could be an incentive to them to reach agreement on others. Although this implies a departure from the traditional piecemeal, commodity-by-commodity, approach to negotiations, it does not alter the fact that specific arrangements would have to be devised for individual commodities. It does mean, however, that the drawing up of arrangements for a substantial number of commodities would have to be agreed upon at the same time and undertaken simultaneously, or as simultaneously as possible, this being an important dynamic feature of the new approach.

Fundamental to the proposed new approach is the setting of wider objectives for international commodity arrangements, including the improvement of marketing systems, diversification (horizontal and vertical), expanded access to markets, and measures to counter inflation, in addition to the traditional objectives of stable and remunerative prices. Acceptance of these additional objectives is essential if more viable and more durable commodity arrangements are to be established. Without some kind of provision for relating prices of exports to prices of imports, for example, commodity arrangements operating in conditions of rapid international inflation would tend to break down. In the case of some commodities, provision for improved access to markets would also be essential, since the expansion of world supply in line with demand cannot be assured if efficient producing countries fear that any attempt to expand their exports will be frustrated by import restrictions, as has been notably the case with sugar and livestock products. . .

INTERNATIONAL STOCKING POLICIES

The most urgent need is for action on commodity stocks, and it is suggested that this be given priority consideration. The urgency is dictated by the recent and possible future developments in the world economy. . . .

It is proposed that international stocks should be established for a wide range of commodities by purchasing them when their prices are at an agreed floor level. Table 1 lists 18 major commodities which appear suitable for international stocking. The list is provisional. Some of these commodities, for example, wheat and wool, are exported predominantly by the developed countries, but are important to developing countries as both exporters and importers. Some others, for example, tropical beverages and natural rubber, are produced exclusively in the developing countries. The 18 commodities listed account for 55–60 per cent of the total primary product exports of developing countries other than petroleum, and their stabilization at an adequate level would have far-reaching effects on these countries.

The accumulated stocks would serve as an international reserve of foodstuffs and industrial raw materials which would help to assure an uninterrupted flow of world consumption and world industrial production. They would be released to the market or to the participating countries when prices moved above an agreed ceiling. Such international reserves should be created, since the national stocks of some key products, very large until several years ago, have now been depleted. By the end of 1973, the aggregate of existing stocks of cereals and most non-ferrous metals had fallen to under 10 per cent of world annual consumption, and of several other major foodstuffs and agricultural raw materials to under 25 per cent. Most of these stocks do not leave any reserve margin above working ("pipeline") stock requirements. Stocks will have to be rebuilt, although not necessarily to earlier levels. Since it is unlikely that any one single country will attempt in the future to hold stocks for the world economy, the question is whether there will be attempts by a number of countries to carry stocks individually, or whether there will be an international system of stock accumulation, holding, and disposal.

The present proposal is not limited to meeting the current emergency situation. The machinery of international stocks, once created, should remain in existence and would then be able to exercise a continuing stabilizing effect on world commodity markets, in the interest of both the exporters and the importers. In the absence of price support by an international stock, the exporting countries, particularly low-income ones, are frequently compelled, in periods of excess supply or weak demand marked by falling prices, to sell on a declining market, thus depressing prices and earnings even fur-

TABLE 1.   Major Stockable Commodities: Trade Values, 1972 (Millions of United States Dollars)

	Exports f.o.b.				Imports c.i.f.			
	World	Developed Market-Economy Countries	Socialist Countries	Developing Countries	World	Developed Market-Economy Countries	Socialist Countries	Developing Countries
Wheat	4,366	3,818	388	160	4,609	1,540	1,291	1,778
Maize	2,298	1.914	53	331	2,444	1,905	324	215
Rice	1,120	537	143	440	1,232	175	82	974
Sugar	3,334	921	178	2,235	3,379	2,304	460	614
Coffee (raw)	3,049	–	–	3,049	3,368	3,101	126	141
Cocoa beans	723	–	–	723	729	572	131	26
Tea	745	79	57	609	784	470	72	242
Cotton	2,828	587	484	1,757	3,055	1,714	792	549
Jute and manufactures	762	71	21	670	840	520	120	200
Wool	1,346	1,143	42	161	1,722	1,361	257	105
Hard fibers	87	3	–	84	106	92	7	7
Rubber	904	–	–	904	1,095	689	305	101
Copper	4,113	1,364	354	2,395	4,226	2,635	377	214
Lead	418	257	45	116	470	379	60	31
Zinc	862	558	110	194	938	736	77	125
Tin	730	70	28	632	758	613	53	92
Bauxite	305	82	5	218	363	325	36	2
Alumina	609	265	46	298	685	532	91	62
Iron ore	2,608	1,213	403	992	3,484	3,039	425	21
Total	31,207	12,882	2,357	15,968	34,287	23,702	5,086	5,499

Source: FAO, *Trade Yearbook 1972*, and national statistics.

ther, because they do not have enough financial resources to hold back supplies. While the support provided by an international stock may not be sufficient for them to achieve an adequate price level and other measures may be needed, such support is likely to be a necessary condition in most cases. For the importing countries, international stocks would bring security of supplies and reasonably stable prices; also, by providing producers with certainty concerning prices and markets, such stocks would help assure adequacy of supplies for the importing countries over the long run, especially if supported by investment on the part of international development agencies designed to expand output of scarce materials. A wide geographic distribution of physical location of stocks would be an additional guarantee of equal access to primary products. . . .

The cost of acquisition of the necessary volume of the 18 commodities listed in table I has been provisionally estimated at $US

10.7 billion, assuming the commodities were bought at average prices prevailing in the five-year period 1970–1974. Of this amount, $4.7 billion is accounted for by grains (wheat, rice and coarse grains). The next largest amounts are for sugar, coffee and copper, aggregating $3.2 billion. If the commodities were bought at average prices of the three-year period 1972–1974, the aggregate cost would be one-fourth higher, and at 1970–1972 prices probably one-fourth lower. . . .

International stocking mechanisms exist at present for only two of the 18 commodities, tin and cocoa. The operating experience and financial results of the tin stock, covering the last 20 years, have been favourable. The mechanism of the cocoa stock has just been established. The limited use of stocking arrangements in international commodity policy is inconsistent with the present and prospective needs of the world economy. . . .

THE FINANCING OF STOCKS

The integrated programme will need to adopt a broad solution to the financing of stocks as a key element in the programme. The illustrative example given in the study on the role of international commodity stocks suggests that the comprehensive programme envisaged might involve capital resources of the order of $11 billion (nearly half of which might be for grains alone), though the amount in use at any time might not approach this size, and would in part represent re-allocation of public expenditures already committed to stocking. International co-operation in investment of this magnitude cannot therefore be considered in a similar manner to the amounts of less than $200 million committed to the two existing international stocks.

Present stock operations suffer from financial constraints in government budgets and industry, and from the instability of interest rates. Credit shortages and "double-

digit" interest rates currently make it virtually impossible to break even on stocking operations unless price swings are wide. Financing stocking operations with an uncertain quantity and an unstable price of money cannot be expected to achieve stable prices, costs and returns for commodities. Consequently, governments supporting stocking schemes recognize that assured sources of funds at reasonable charges should be provided. Financing probably remains a major factor impeding the establishment of stocking schemes.

Although, under present arrangements, the IMF buffer-stock financing facility is a potentially large source of funds, it has not been used extensively during its five years of operation, and has not so far acted as a catalyst, as hoped, for the negotiation of new buffer-stock arrangements. The facility is intended to assist mainly developing country exporters with contributions to individual international schemes, but a serious difficulty in the use of the facility even by such countries has been the reluctance of importers generally to make their contribution directly to such schemes.

In view of the foregoing, it is proposed that stock financing should be undertaken through a common fund, constituted for the specific purpose of directly financing stocks of a number of commodities. The fund should be supported by both exporting and importing countries, so that an appropriate commitment to the financial arrangements would be shown by countries participating in the management of stocking arrangements. The financial burden for these countries would be eased if the international financial institutions extended assistance more widely and effectively to all countries among their members. Furthermore, the fund should be open to investment from other sources, as a major or supplementary source of financing. To do so, the stocking operations and the rules of the fund should provide security of investment and reasonable returns. The fund should be able to raise its finances on terms and conditions comparable to those for other official international investment. The balance of commitments accepted by governments and the international financial institutions would exercise a key influence on the objectives of international policy in the commodity field. . . .

MULTILATERAL COMMITMENTS IN COMMODITY TRADE

The objective of more stable conditions in commodity supply and demand in general, and the role and viability of international stocking operations, would be strengthened if governments encouraged sustained levels of trade by undertaking multilateral supply and purchase commitments to which stocking policies would be related. These commitments could be agreements between governments on the approximate amounts of a commodity that each government expected the economy to supply or demand, to or from all participating countries, based on forecasts of trade, including state trade, private and official bilateral contracts and open market trading. Though the agreement would carry an obligation it would not have the full character of a contract obliging governments as such to acquire or supply amounts that were not purchased or sold under the ordinary trading system of the country during the period of the commitment.

Assurance of supply is the second outstanding area of concern emerging from the chaotic commodity developments of the 1970s. Set alongside the chronic concern of primary producing countries with sustained market capacity, there is a unique opportunity for a marriage of interests in realizing more predictable and more stable movement of commodities in international trade. Governments now seem more ready to recognize that reciprocal trade volume commitments could facilitate forward planning of resource use in their domestic economic policies and in solutions for balance-of-payments difficulties. These commitments could best be achieved multilaterally, and with as wide a coverage of trade flows for particular commodities as possible. . . .

COMPENSATORY FINANCING OF COMMODITY TRADE

The foregoing measures would still leave certain countries vulnerable to export instability and to depressed trends that reflected a weak bargaining position for key exports. These would probably be countries with a significant dependence on commodities for which stocking arrangements or multilateral commitments are not feasible, or where participation in a multilateral commitment still left serious fluctuation in their prices or returns. Such commodities are less likely to have a significant influence on the trade or payments situation of importing countries, so that arrangements for compensation could be more suitably directed to the assistance of exporting countries.

The justification for such assistance is already concretely acknowledged in the international community through the IMF facility for the compensatory financing of export fluctuations, and by a major group of importing countries in the EEC proposals for a commodity compensation scheme available to associated and associable countries. Medium-term loans by the IMF are intended to smooth out fluctuations in the total export trade of primary producing members and thus compensate for fluctuations in specific commodity exports when these are reflected in downturns in over-all export receipts. The IMF scheme is self-financing, with full repayment of loans. It does not lay down conditions with regard to the domestic arrangements the financial authorities of borrowers make on producer prices or incomes. About SDR 1 billion of assistance was provided to 32 countries in 1963–1973. The EEC scheme would be applicable to a selected group of commodities, and while based on returns to those commodity sectors individually, is intended to have an income-stabilizing influence for the individual producer in recipient countries. It has provisions that would cause non-repayable expenditures, though partly self-financing. . . .

Within an integrated approach to commodity problems, it would seem best to give priority attention with regard to compensation aspects to the possibility of building on the present IMF facility, with attention being given at a later stage to any additional compensatory measures that might be required in consideration of the scope of the expanded facility.

The aspects of the facility in mind in this respect are (i) the need for more flexible conditions as regards the balance-of-payments criterion for assistance; (ii) relaxation of the limits on the amounts available as determined by IMF quotas to take account of the size of shortfalls; (iii) easier requirements on the completion of detailed export statistics within a relatively short period of the shortfall in exports; (iv) extension of the repayment period beyond the present obligation to make complete repayment within five years, including a closer link with the recovery of exports; and (v) account to be taken of changes in the import purchasing power of a country's exports.

If, however, action on these lines did not appear feasible, the problem for the exporters of the perishable commodities for which demand and prices are highly unstable would remain large enough to warrant consideration of commodity compensation schemes. The most critical point of policy in a commodity compensation scheme is that the scheme should be considered as a residual measure, to be applied when other more direct approaches are inappropriate or inadequate to meet the ultimate objective of stabilizing and maintaining the real export income of exporting developing countries.

Consequently, the scheme should be designed to provide automatic compensation payments in the form of loans to developing countries experiencing shortfalls in their export income from the commodities considered (i.e. those not covered by other arrangements). Such loans would be repaid out of part of any excess of exports over the agreed "normal" levels (from which the shortfalls were calculated). Repayment procedures might also include provision for conversion of unpaid balances into grants.

EXPANSION OF PROCESSING AND DIVERSIFICATION

The contribution of commodity production and trade to the economic development of the developing world will only be realized rapidly and efficiently if shifts in resources within the primary sectors of the developing countries and within their economies in general can occur. The measures above would create more favourable conditions for appropriate diversification and for freeing resources in a more broadly based economic structure. But in addition, separate and more constructive attention will be required in the international community to develop means of expanding the processing of primary products, removing trade discrimination in this respect, and to encourage the transfer of technology and research with this objective.

For the generality of primary commodities exported by developing countries, there is need for greater diversification into the more manufactured forms of the basic products. Expansion of trade in semi-processed and processed products is inhibited by various factors, among which are tariff and non-tariff barriers in developed countries. This situation needs to be improved through extension of GSP coverage to more products of primary origin, the removal of ceilings and quotas under the GSP, and the removal or relaxation of other non-tariff barriers.

XI.C. IMPORT SUBSTITUTION IN PRACTICE

XI.C.1. Limitations of Import Substitution*

[B]eyond the first stage in an import substitution strategy—the expansion, behind protection, of finished consumption goods production to the limits of the domestic markets—lies the necessity of developing production of intermediate goods, capital goods, and raw materials; or expanding exports; or both. It is a simple matter to formulate and implement a policy of protection for the first stage. Often this happens almost inadvertently, as was suggested above. But the crude policies of protection that may serve adequately in the first stage, and the economic structure that they encourage, are likely, in my opinion, to become barriers to growth in subsequent stages.[1] Why this is so, and what might be done to prevent it or correct it, is the subject of this paper.

Section 1 comprises a discussion of the emergence of barriers to growth under three headings: economic inefficiency (misallocation of resources); technical inefficiency (failure to minimize costs); and the saving gap (failure to achieve an adequate rise in domestic saving). While the distinctions may not always seem clearcut, this scheme of

*From John H. Power, "Import Substitution as an Industrialization Strategy," *The Philippine Economic Journal*, Vol. 5, No. 2, 1966, pp. 169–74, 191–9. Reprinted by permission.
[1] Because of a rising import bill of materials, parts and equipment to sustain production in the protected industries, and because of a resistance on the part of unprotected sectors and income groups (e.g. agriculture and labor) to any deterioration of their terms of trade, barriers to growth taking the form of balance of payments difficulties and inflation may arise long before the first stage is completed.

presentation does serve to emphasize that a naive import substitution strategy can impede growth via an adverse influence on the marginal saving rate, as well as on the social product; and that its influence on the latter over time depends as much on inducements to efficiency and innovation as on resource allocation.

ECONOMIC INEFFICIENCY

An import substitution bias means a balance of payments policy that favors import control or restriction (often via exchange control) over export encouragement. This, in turn, implies a lower value for foreign exchange than that appropriate to a policy of equal encouragement to exports and import substitution. If market prices were given and could be taken to represent unit costs and utilities at the margin, the resulting resource allocation would require a greater value of resources to save an additional unit of foreign exchange through import substitution than to earn an additional unit of foreign exchange through export expansion.

Since this kind of welfare loss is generally well understood, the persistence of this direction of bias in balance of payments policies suggests either that considerations other than economic efficiency are held to be more important, or that the assumptions underlying this kind of welfare judgment are considered to be invalid. About all an economist can do with regard to the former is to point to the cost and, since this emerges anyway in a discussion of economic efficiency, I will focus on the latter.

Before turning to the validity of the assumptions on which welfare judgments against interference with free market results are based, however, we should note another kind of misallocation that appears to be both very likely and very substantial in the context of an import substitution strategy. That is the bias against production of intermediate goods, capital goods and raw materials. The reason is, of course, that these are inputs in the industries which develop in the first stage and, as such, are usually more liberally imported than are the finished consumption goods that compete with the emerging domestic industries. This means not only a bias against vertical balance in import substitution—i.e., backward linkage is discouraged—but also an inflated and irrationally differentiated structure of protection at the finishing stages of production.

This is so because the total rate of protection depends not only on the particular rate of protection that applies to the product of that industry, but also on the particular rates that apply at the preceding stage in the production process. The former acts as a subsidy while the latter act as taxes on value added in a particular industry. It may be useful to put these relationships more formally at this point.[2]

Let Y_i represent the output of any industry and $\sum_j a_{ji} Y_i$ its intermediate inputs, both valued at given world prices—i.e., the prices that would prevail with free trade. Then

$$V_i = Y_i - \sum_j a_{ji} Y_i \qquad (1)$$

is value added at free trade prices, and

$$V_i (1 + T_i) = \\ Y_i (1 + t_i) - \sum_j a_{ji} (1 + t_j) Y_i \qquad (2)$$

is actual value added under the system of protection. The t's represent the proportions by which the system of protection permits

the actual domestic prices of the outputs of various industries to exceed their free trade prices, while T_i is the total rate of protection of the ith industry—the proportion by which its value added can exceed what would be its free trade value. This can be written also as

$$V_i (1 + T_i) = \\ Y_i + t_i Y_i - \sum_j a_{ji} Y_i - \sum_j a_{ji} t_j Y_i$$

and by substituting (1) in the right-hand side

$$V_i (1 + T_i) = V_i + t_i Y_i - \sum_j a_{ji} t_j Y_i$$

We can solve this for the total rate of protection

$$T_i = \frac{V_i + t_i Y_i - \sum_j a_{ji} t_j Y_i}{V_i} - 1$$

or

$$T_i = \frac{t_i - \sum_j a_{ji} t_j}{V_i / Y_i} \qquad (3)$$

From (3) we can see that the total rate of protection of an industry will be greater the greater is its own particular rate of protection, the smaller are the particular rates of protection of its supplying industries, and the smaller is the proportion of its value added to the total value of its output. Now consider the distorted pattern of protection that can result from a policy of restricting most severely the import of consumption goods, while permitting inputs into these industries to be more liberally imported.

First, as was noted above, exports are penalized by the lower value of foreign exchange that is consistent with the bias toward import restriction. But the extent of the bias can be much greater than the particular degrees of protection would suggest. Suppose, for example, that the protective device employed were a 50 per cent duty on consumption goods while intermediate inputs could be imported at free trade prices. Then if value added in manufacturing (at free trade prices) were 25 per cent of total (free trade) value, equation (3) tells us that the total degree of protection would be 200 per cent! If the protection is effective, the economy is paying marginal resources adding value in import-substituting industries 200 per cent more, for each unit of foreign exchange saved, than it is paying marginal resources earning a unit of foreign exchange in export industries. This could mean either higher rewards per unit or resources, or more resources—i.e., less efficiency, or both.[3]

A similar magnification of the distortion in degrees of protection occurs, of course, between industries producing consumption goods and those producing materials, parts and equipment when the latter are more liberally imported. Thus, the bias against backward-linkage import substitution is more pronounced than a simple comparison of particular rates of protection would suggest. Moreover, the resulting relative lack of domestic sources of supply for these inputs, together with the fact that the total degree of protection is inversely related to the (proportional) value added contribution of the industry, means that such a system of protection particularly encourages heavy users of foreign exchange. Finally, we should note that in protecting the balance of payments via import restriction, it is a very common practice to restrict most severely the least essential imports. This tends to bias import substitution, albeit perhaps inadvertently, in favor of less essential industries.

The conclusion is that an import substitution bias in development strategy, when accompanied—as is, I think, typical—by relatively liberal import policies with respect to "essential" imports (both in the form of inputs for domestic industries and special categories of consumption goods), can create a rather extreme distortion of incentives away from the pattern that would result from free markets. Moreover, the direction of distortion appears to be unfortunate in that it particularly discourages export expan-

[3] This assumes no terms of trade effect.

sion and backward-linkage import substitution, one or both of which is crucial to sustained industrial growth, as noted above; while it gives the greatest encouragement to industries most heavily requiring foreign exchange to produce less essential products. . . .

TECHNICAL INEFFICIENCY

A relatively high total rate of protection for an industry may, of course, imply high factor incomes or relative inefficiency, or both. I have no evidence to present on this point, but it seems to me that for several reasons we might expect relative inefficiency to be widespread among those industries with the highest total rates of protection. First, a system of protection of the kind under discussion will inevitably include under its umbrella all kinds of comparatively disadvantageous industries. Second, for others (including "infant industries"), the protection against foreign competition permits monopolistic or oligopolistic market positions that take the edge off the drive for efficiency and technical progress. Third, the dispersion of resources in horizontally-balanced industrial growth sacrifices potential gains from economies of scale and the stimulus to innovations and learning from faster concentrated growth.

It is possible, on the other hand, that some of these highly protected industries have a real comparative advantage and are reasonably efficient, so that the protection permits high factor incomes. The factor-price disequilibrium case fits here. The protection may permit the industry to pay the required excess above labor's opportunity cost that the market dictates. We have seen above, however, that this is no more than a third-best sort of argument for protection.

Finally, however, the high degree of protection may mean high profits, and high profits suggest the possibility of a saving-reinvestment growth mechanism. This brings us, then, to the effects on saving of an import-substitution bias in development strategy.

THE SAVING GAP[4]

I have argued above that to carry an import substitution strategy successfully beyond the first stage requires either breaking into the export market or extending production backward to materials, intermediate goods, and equipment. Continuing expansion of finished consumption goods for the domestic market, while perfectly compatible with a non-accumulation economy (wherein the growth of income occurs exogenously), can permit growth in capital accumulation (other than accumulation of stocks) only so long as it reduces consumption goods imports.[5] When the first stage is completed, of course, this is no longer possible. But even during the first stage there is a very real possibility that a bias toward the production of consumption goods balanced in relation to the domestic demand will tend to erode the constraints on consumption that are needed to permit accelerating growth.

To see how this might be so, consider first the identity

$$C_d + I_d + E_d = C_m + C_d + S \qquad (4)$$

where C_d, I_d, and E_d are value added in domestic production for consumption, investment, and exports. S is domestic saving

[4] The following discussion owes much to analyses of the Pakistan and Indian experiences. See A. R. Khan, "Import Substitution, Consumption Liberalization and Export Expansion," and my "Industrialization in Pakistan: A Case of Frustrated Take-Off?," both in *Pakistan Development Review* (Summer 1963). For India, an unpublished paper by V. V. Desai of the University of Bombay, entitled "Import Substitution, Growth of Consumer Goods Industries and Economic Development" was particularly useful.

[5] Of course rising capital imports could permit growing capital accumulation without any rise in domestic saving. I am assuming here, however, that some rise in domestic saving is essential.

and C_m is the imported component of consumption. The left-hand represents the national product and the right-hand side, the disposal of national income.

A rise in any component of the left-hand side implies an equal rise in saving (and investment—domestic or foreign) if consumption does not rise. Thus a case of pure import substitution (the rise in C_d being matched precisely by a fall in C_m) increases saving exactly as does a rise in the production of capital goods or exports when consumption is constant. The analysis can be extended to the more general case in which consumption rises by some proportion of the rise in national product, and the conclusion is the same. The change in saving associated with a rise in output depends on the change in consumption regardless of the kind of goods the output increase embodies.

The key question is, then, how the marginal consumption rate might be affected by alternative patterns of investment leading to different mixes of output increase. This is usually analyzed in terms of the associated sectoral income increases and saving propensities, but I propose to look at it briefly from the other side—to consider how the supply mix itself can affect consumption and saving.

Consider the following simple model of a closed economy.

$$\Delta Y = kI \qquad \text{(i)}$$
$$\Delta S = s\Delta Y \qquad \text{(ii)}$$
$$\Delta I = kaI \qquad \text{(iii)}$$
$$\Delta S = \Delta I \qquad \text{(iv)}$$

Y is national product, I is investment, S is saving, s is the marginal propensity to save, k is the incremental output-capital ratio (identical for all sectors of the economy), and a is the proportion of investment allocated to the investment goods sector.

Given ΔY (the growth target) and the investment coefficient, k, these four equations determine I, ΔS, ΔI and either s or a if the other is given. If both are given the system is overdetermined. That is, consistency is required between the marginal saving rate and the proportion of investment allocated to the investment goods sector. This leaves open the question of how consistency is achieved, however. If saving propensities govern, a must adjust to s—the allocation of investment must respond to the pattern of final demand. Alternatively, however, marginal saving could be constrained by the output mix of consumption and investment goods as determined by the investment allocation—i.e., by a. It is this latter possibility that I want to explore in the context of an import substitution strategy.

To do this we must introduce international trade into the model. This can be done most simply by assuming that any increase in exports or substitution of domestic production for imports going into consumption will result automatically in investment via import of equipment with the foreign exchange earned or saved. Allocation of investment to sectors producing for export or import substitution will then raise the rate of capital accumulation exactly as will investment in the capital goods sectors, and a can refer to the proportion of investment going to these sectors taken together.

Marginal saving depends, then, on a—the allocation of investment to capital goods production, to production of exports, and to import substitution. But the import substitution strategy described above is strongly biased via the system of protection against both exports and the production of capital goods. And within the category of import substitution it is biased against investment in the production of materials and parts. A high a must depend mainly then on (1) the rapid expansion of capacity to add value at the finishing stages of consumption goods production, and (2) the use of this capacity to reduce the import bill rather than to supply an expanding home consumption.

At first these conditions may easily be met, as import restriction serves not only as a balance of payments control, but also as a principal constraint on consumption. As domestic capacity expands rapidly in re-sponse to high rates of protection, however, two things happen. First, a kind of automatic decontrol of consumption takes place as the proportion of consumption constrained by import controls declines. This is partly due to the increased availability of goods and disappearance of scarcity premiums, and partly due to the shift in income distribution from government (customs duties) and profits of importers to income recipients in the new industries.

At the same time the expansion of consumption goods industries creates a rapidly growing demand for import of materials, parts, and equipment. These two developments shift the focus of control over consumption to taxes and imports of inputs for the new industries. If control over the latter is tightened there arises the phenomenon of excess capacity due to scarcity of imported supplies. While this should be attributed to the misallocation of investment resulting from biases in the system of protection—too much capacity installed to produce consumption goods and too little to produce materials, parts, and equipment, the pressures are inevitably on the side of permitting the necessary imports. For the availability of excess capacity always promises a cheap way to get an increase in production. Since the increased production will be consumption goods, however, this also precludes the imposition of new taxes to offset the steady erosion of control over consumption. The result is what Khan has called "consumption liberalization."[6]

Consumption liberalization occurs, in a static context, when the rise in domestic output of consumption goods is not fully matched by a decline in imports—i.e., in equation (4) (above), when the rise in C_d exceeds the fall in C_m, with a corresponding diminished effect on saving. In a dynamic context we must expect consumption to grow with growing output and the question of whether an increase in production serves

[6] Khan, op. cit., 209.

to replace imports or liberalize consumption is a more complex one.

Khan's solution[7] was to calculate a "normal" increase in consumption of a good based on population growth, per capita income increase, the planned marginal saving rate, and an expenditure elasticity of demand. Any increase in supply from production plus imports that was not exported or absorbed by normal consumption was defined as consumption liberalization. He then attempted to measure this over the period of 1951/52 to 1959/60 for four of Pakistan's important import substitution industries: cotton cloth, sugar, cigarettes, and paper. In each case he found that a very high proportion of the output increase resulted in consumption liberalization—from almost 50 per cent in cotton cloth to over 100 per cent in paper. . . .

These results are at least consistent with the hypothesis that a part of the explanation for the low saving rates in India and Pakistan during this period (despite rapid industrialization) was the bias toward consumption goods production for the home market.[8] On the other hand, because of shifts in income distribution and in the proportions of rural and urban populations, because of the existence of controls and other abnormal influences affecting consumption, and finally because of the general complexity of the relation between the consumption of particular goods and aggregate consumption, one cannot be sure how important this was.

Nevertheless, on theoretical grounds a strong case can be made against an import substitution bias in development strategy because of its likely effect on saving. First, the

[7] Ibid., pp. 208–212.

[8] A case could be made for liberalizing the consumption of certain goods (via price or other inducements) to take advantage of economies of scale or other advantages of concentration. This "consumption distortion" has merit particularly if the favored goods are essential mass consumption goods. To avoid a general consumption rise, however, taxes would have to be raised elsewhere.

various aspects of economic and technical inefficiency discussed above mean lower incomes, and especially lower profits, with obvious implications for saving. Second, the bias toward producing goods that can be consumed and against goods that cannot (e.g., capital goods and some exports) is likely to make political control of consumption more difficult.[9] Finally, at some points there is an absolute necessity to move into exports or to the earlier stages of production, or both; and the longer it is postponed and the more biased against it is the system of protection, the more likely is the economy to find itself in the kind of trap that leads to consumption liberalization.

The conclusion I reach from this critique of an industrialization strategy biased toward import substitution is that it does not promise an easy path around the difficulties facing less developed countries. This is not a happy conclusion for the difficulties are very great and the alternatives to an import substitution strategy are not very promising either.

In any case, for what they are worth the policy implications, as they pertain to a single country, have more or less emerged in the course of the critique itself. They are, in general, to avoid the kind of excessive and distorted protection that biases growth toward a horizontal balance of consumption goods production for the domestic market, penalizing both exports and backward-linkage import substitution. The costs of such a policy go beyond simple resource misallocation to adverse effects on technical efficiency, innovations and saving. More emphasis on vertical balance would seem to be essential to success in industrial growth beyond the first stage of import substitution.

This does not mean that policies should be biased against import substitution. What

[9] This has now become officially recognized in Pakistan. See the Preface to the Pakistan Third Five-Year Plan (Karachi, Government of Pakistan, March 1965), p. viii.

is needed rather are rational choices, both between import substitution and export expansion and among various potential import substitution industries. Especially important in helping the economy (public or private) to make rational choices in this area is to find some means of correcting the undervaluation of foreign exchange. . . .

Beyond difficulties of implementing exchange rate policy, however, lie more fundamental issues around which doubts will certainly arise. For what the above critique may appear to do is to reverse the classic argument of Nurkse in his lectures on "Patterns of Trade and Development."[10] There it was the difficulties faced by both traditional and new exports that dictated the option for balanced growth in relation to domestic demand. If the latter has all of the disadvantages catalogued above, however, the last escape route from economic stagnation would seem to have been closed off.

It is only fair to remind ourselves that Nurkse's view of an import-substitution strategy bore little resemblance to that pictured above. He emphasized especially the prime importance of rising agricultural productivity in balanced growth and considered the inherent difficulties in carrying through an agricultural revolution to be the reason that "industrialization for domestic markets appears as a much more formidable task."[11]

In addition he argued that: "When industrialization for the home market has taken root, it becomes easier to increase exports of manufactured goods to the more advanced economies."[12] It follows, I think, that he would have opposed measures that unnecessarily penalize such exports.

[10] Ragnar Nurkse, *Equilibrium and Growth in the World Economy*, Haberler and Stern (eds.), Harvard, 1961, pp. 282–324.

[11] Ibid., p. 315.
[12] Ibid., p. 320.

XI.C.2. Critics of Latin American Import Substitution*

Let us now turn to the various critiques which have been made of Latin American ISI [Import-Substitution Industrialization]. The critics can be divided into two groups which I shall designate as the "market critics" and the "structural critics." Although some arguments are common to both sets of critics, there is a certain philosophic-analytical similarity of the views within each

*From Werner Baer, "Import Substitution and Industrialization in Latin America: Experiences and Interpretations," *Latin American Research Review*, Spring 1972, pp. 101–8. Reprinted by permission.

camp which seem to justify the division I have made.

THE MARKET CRITICS

Many economists in this category view Latin America's ISI as an inefficient way of using resources to develop the region's countries. The more conservative economists believe that since world production can best be maximized by having each country (or area of the world) specialize in the sectors where it has the greatest comparative advantage, Latin America should have continued to specialize in the production of primary products. This specialization would have maximized world output and made possible a higher income level in all parts of the world.

Because of the declining share of food and primary products in world trade, more moderate critics recognize the need for some ISI. But they criticize the indiscriminate way in which ISI was carried on, that is, by across-the-board promotion of industries without regard even to potential comparative advantage. The Latin American ISI strategies are seen as drives towards national self-sufficiency in total disregard of the advantages of an international division of labor along newer lines. This emphasis on autarky is seen as prejudicial to rapid economic growth for a number of reasons.

Given small markets, limited capital, and a dearth of skilled manpower, autarkic industrial growth leads to the development of inefficient and high-cost industries. The situation becomes especially pronounced in industries having high fixed costs. These industries require large-scale output in order to bring costs down to levels prevailing in more advanced industrial countries. Outstanding examples are the steel and automobile industries which have been established in most of the larger Latin American countries. In the case of automobiles, the situation was worsened because a large number of these countries permitted the establishment of many firms, thus completely eliminating the possibilities of economies of large scale production. In the late Sixties, the annual output of cars and trucks in eight Latin American countries was 600,000, which was produced by ninety firms (an average of 6,700 per firm). The situation is well summarized by Scitovsky: "Protection usually confines the protected manufacturer to the domestic market and so inhibits the exploitation of

TABLE 1.

a) *Real Rate of Growth (annual) by Sectors for Latin America and Selected Countries*

	1955–60	1960–65	1955–60	1960–65	1955–60	1960–65
	Latin America		Argentina		Brazil	
Agriculture	2.7	4.8	−0.4	2.1	3.7	6.9
Manufacturing	6.6	5.6	3.8	4.1	10.3	4.9
Construction	4.2	5.9	4.3	2.0	7.2	2.8
	Chile		Mexico		Colombia	
Agriculture	2.3	3.1	3.0	3.9	3.5	3.0
Manufacturing	3.2	6.7	8.1	8.0	6.1	5.9
Construction	1.4	4.6	8.1	5.9	−0.2	1.9

Source: Naciones Unidas, *Estudio económico de América Latina, 1965.*

b) *Latin America: Growth Rates of the Total Gross Domestic Product and of Industrial Product (Annual Cumulative Rates)*

	Total Product	Industrial Product
1940–50	5.0	6.8
1950–60	4.7	6.3
1960–68	4.5	5.4

Source: United Nations, *Economic Bulletin for Latin America*, Second Half of 1969.

TABLE 2.

a) *Growth of Urban Population and Industrial Employment*
(Average Annual Rates of Growth: 1950–60)

	Urban Population	Industrial Employment
Argentina	3.0	1.7
Brazil	6.5	2.6
Mexico	5.6	4.8

b) *Growth of Industrial Product and Industrial Employment*
(Annual Growth Rates: 1950–68)

	Industrial Product	Industrial Employment
Argentina	4.5	2.2
Brazil	7.3	2.2
Colombia	6.2	2.4
Chile	4.6	2.2
Peru	7.8	3.4
Mexico	6.7	4.7
Latin America	6.0	2.8

Source: Table in Little, Scitovsky, and Scott, *Industry and Trade*, p. 84.
Source: Raúl Prebisch, *Transformatión y desarrollo: la gran tarea de América Latina,*
Washington, D.C., 1970, p. 45.

economies of scale, especially in small countries and in industries where scale economies are important and call for very large-scale operations. Moreover, governments anxious to secure the benefits of competition often encourage many firms to enter industry in order to create domestic competition where protectionist policies have suspended foreign competition." The result, however, is contrary to what is aimed for, since such government policy "... restricts the scope for economies of scale yet further and often leads to the emergence of too many firms, each with too small an output capacity, and frequently with too small a market to utilize fully even that capacity."[1]

In the last few years the concept of "effective protection" has been used by numerous economists to analyze distortions which have arisen during the ISI process. ... In a number of Latin American countries the effective tariff on consumer goods was found to be much higher than for intermediate or capital goods. Such high levels of effective protection eliminate incentives to increase production efficiency and make it difficult to bring the cost of production to international levels.

The stress on autarky—on maximizing internal vertical integration (promoting not only final goods production, but also intermediate and capital goods)—impedes growth because resources are not used in sectors where they will produce the highest possible output. Had Latin American countries specialized in only a few products with the greatest potential comparative advantage, and exported a large surplus while importing other goods, total output available would have been higher and these nations would have grown more rapidly than they actually

[1] Tibor Scitovsky, "Prospects for Latin American Industrialization within the Framework of Economic Integration," in *The Process of Industrialization in Latin America*, Washington, D.C., 1969, p. 42.

TABLE 3.

a) *Latin America's Participation in World Trade* (Latin America's Exports as a Per Cent of World Exports)

1948–10.9%
1950–10.6%
1957– 7.8%

1960–7.0%
1964–6.4%
1968–5.0%

Source: *Regional Integration and the Trade of Latin America*, Committee for Economic Development, Jan. 1968; and *International Trade, 1968*, GATT.

b) *Changes in Latin America's Import Coefficients* (Value of Imports of Goods and Services as a Per Cent of GDP)

	1928	1938	1948–9	1957–8	1962	1960*	1967*
Argentina	17.8	12.1	11.2	5.8	7.1	8.0	6.6
Brazil	11.3	6.2	6.6	5.8	4.5	7.8	5.6
Chile	31.2	14.9	11.5	9.5	11.3	15.7	15.7
Colombia	18.0	11.0	10.6	8.2	8.8	12.2	8.8
Mexico	14.2	7.0	8.5	7.8	6.8	7.8	7.8
Peru			9.6	16.1	13.6	19.0	28.1
Latin America			10.2	9.9	8.7	10.0	9.9

Source: Joseph Grunwald and Philip Musgrove, *Natural Resources in Latin American Development*, Baltimore, 1970, p. 20.
    *CEPAL, 1968.

c) *Imports as a Percentage of Total Supplies by Categories*

	Consumers' Goods	Intermediate Goods	Capital Goods
Brazil			
1949	9.0	25.9	63.7
1955	2.9	17.9	43.2
1959	1.9	11.7	32.9
1964	1.3	6.6	9.8
Mexico			
1950	2.4	13.2	66.5
1955	2.3	n.a.	63.4
1960	1.3	10.4	54.9
1965	n.a.	9.9	59.8

Source: Little, Scitovsky, and Scott, *Industry and Trade*, p. 60.

did. As it happened, autarky was practiced in each country, and no attempt was made until the late Sixties to at least promote ISI on a regional basis; in other words, to promote a complementary industrial structure within Latin America. . . .

Some economists have been concerned about the domestic resource cost involved in the type of ISI which has been promoted in Latin America. They have stressed the need to calculate for various industries the value of domestic resources required to save a unit of foreign exchange. The rate of transformation between domestic and foreign resources thus obtained should be compared to the appropriate exchange rate. The higher the former is over the latter, the greater presumably is the "waste" of resources; that is, if domestic resources had been used for export purposes, the foreign exchange earned would have fetched more goods than the goods produced by using the resources domestically.

Policies employed to stimulate industries have often been prejudicial to the functioning of the more traditional agricultural sector. The allocation of investment resources (credit) to new industries has often meant that few resources were available to increase agricultural efficiency. Overvalued exchange rates, which favored industries by providing cheap imported inputs, hurt agriculture by making its goods less competitive on the international market and/or by making it less profitable to export agricultural products. Finally, the combination of higher industrial prices caused by protection and by price control of agricultural goods, turned the internal terms of trade against agriculture. All these factors hurt agricultural production and exports. Argentina is probably the outstanding example of ISI occurring to the detriment of agriculture and agricultural exports.

Critics have also pointed to the detrimental results of neglecting exports during the heyday of ISI. Some stress the negative effects of ISI policies on the production and exportation of traditional goods, while others emphasize the failure to diversify the export structure in accordance with the changing internal economic structure which ISI brought about. While, as was mentioned earlier, the contribution of industry to GDP became dominant in the years after World War II, the commodity composition of Latin America's exports remained almost unchanged. For example, in the late Sixties, over 90 per cent of Argentina and Brazil's exports still consisted of traditional primary and food products, while about three-quarters of Mexico's exports consisted of such products. Until the Sixties, little efforts were made by Latin American countries to stimulate non-traditional exports. And while in the early Sixties the develop-

ment of the Latin American Common Market, the Central American Common Market, the introduction of drawbacks and rebates on domestic taxes for export efforts in some countries (Argentina, Mexico, Colombia) represented attempts to stimulate non-traditional exports, the net effects by the late Sixties were still slight.

The neglect of exports during the ISI period in Latin America, that is, the failure to stimulate traditional exports and to diversify the export structure, could have serious consequences. The original advocates of ISI had hoped that their policy would lead Latin American countries to greater self-sufficiency and would make their economies more independent of the vicissitudes of international trade. It appears, however, that there is a lower limit to the import coefficient (import/GDP ratio) for most economies, as becomes clear by examining Table 3 (b). While ISI was taking place, not only was the import coefficient reduced, but the commodity composition of imports changed. An increasingly larger proportion of imports consisted of raw materials, semi-finished products, and capital goods. These represented the inputs of the ISI industries which were not available domestically, and were thus the principal reason for the increasing downward stickiness of the import coefficient.

It is thus ironic that the net result of ISI has been to place Latin American countries in a new and more dangerous dependency relationship with the more advanced countries than ever before. In former times, a decline in export receipts acted as a stimulus to ISI. Under the circumstances, a decline in export receipts not counterbalanced by capital inflows can result in forced import curtailments which, in turn, could cause an industrial recession. Such results have been experienced by Argentina and Colombia, and other countries face the same danger.

To guard against such a situation, Latin American countries would have to make increasing efforts to diversify exports. Such actions, however, assume that they are able to compete in the international market. Considering the high cost structure of many Latin American ISI industries, the many bureaucratic obstacles exporters have faced, and the lack of an adequate credit mechanism to export manufactured goods, export diversification is not an easy task.

STRUCTURAL CRITICS

Since World War II, most Latin American countries have experienced a population explosion. Annual population growth for the entire region increased from 1.9 per cent to over 2.8 per cent in the late Fifties and Sixties. During the same period, migration from the countryside to the cities increased dramatically.... The urban population growth rate in the post-World War II period was over three times as large as the rural growth rate. The rate of labor absorption in industry was substantially smaller than the rate of growth of urban population. It is clear that after two decades of industrialization, the proportion of the labor force employed in manufacturing industry in Latin America as a whole actually declined somewhat, and that almost half of these workers were still engaged in artisan workshops. In some of the individual countries shown, the proportion rose a few points, but very modestly compared to the changes in the contribution of industry to GDP. The failure of ISI to create direct employment opportunities has worried both "structural" and "market" critics.

The latter blame the low labor absorption rate on price distortions. Most countries used certain types of subsidies to capital in order to stimulate industrialization. In a number of countries, domestic and foreign firms were given special exchange rate privileges to import capital equipment. Development banks gave cheap credit (often at negative real rates of interest) to help finance investment in favored industries. At the same time, wages in industry were relatively high because of labor legislation which had been introduced in the Thirties and Forties

in such countries as Argentina, Brazil, and Chile. Thus, there were no incentives to adopt labor-intensive techniques of production. On the contrary, the relative price structure of capital and labor was such as to actually stimulate the search for and adoption of capital-intensive techniques.

The structural critics of ISI worry about low labor absorption rates not only because of the social services problems of urban unemployment or underemployment which result, but also because of their implication for income distribution. With an unequal distribution of income, a fiscal system which does not redistribute income, and a leading growth sector (industry) whose incremental capital/labor ratio is high (usually substantially higher than the economy's average capital/labor ratio), the tendency will be for income to become even more concentrated than before. The evidence available for Latin American countries tends to confirm this trend.

Because of the concentration of income, the growth of demand for industrial products may not be sufficient to maintain the initial ISI momentum. What makes the situation worse is the lumpiness of many ISI industries. Because of indivisibilities, many industries were forced to build substantially ahead of demand. Thus, the existence of excess capacity which is not being rapidly filled by growing demand dampens the incentive to invest.

This situation could, of course, be avoided by various types of redistributive policies of governments—redistribution by income groups, by sectors of the economy, and by regions. Progressive tax measures and/or appropriate wage policies could be used to redistribute income among social groups; government credit and fiscal policies could redirect resources to neglected sectors (such as agriculture, housing, road building) and geographical regions.

Potential domestic demand for industrial products exists in most Latin American countries because the ISI process occurred in an unbalanced fashion. We have already mentioned the trends towards the concentration of income which could be reversed by appropriate policies and thus result in considerable demand expansion. However, there were other imbalances. As ISI proceeded, such sectors as agriculture, low income housing, transportation, and other infrastructure facilities were often neglected, threatening countries with severe bottlenecks. In the larger countries, ISI resulted in a strong regional concentration of industry and income, especially in Brazil, Mexico, and Argentina. Although such regional concentration made sense when taking into account external economies to firms settling close to suppliers, to decent infrastructure facilities, and to skilled labor supplies, etc., it was of a self-reinforcing nature. Increasing regional concentration of wealth presented many countries with the political need to redistribute income on a regional basis. All these forces make it possible to generate new demand through government policies.

Georgescu-Roegen, however, called attention to a problem which might arise from post-ISI redistribution efforts. The profile of the productive structure which resulted from the ISI process reflects the demand profile which existed at the time when the process was started. This demand profile was based on a distribution of income which, in most cases, was quite unequal. Efforts to change the distribution of income in the post-ISI era in order to achieve greater social justice, increase aggregate demand, diminish inter-

sectoral and/or inter-regional imbalances, will change the demand profile. Such changes could result in a substantial amount of imbalance or lack of synchronization between the country's productive and demand profiles. The degree of such imbalance depends, of course, on the flexibility of various productive sectors. For example, to what extent can the productive facilities of the consumer goods and capital goods industries be converted from producing luxury goods to producing mass consumption goods?

The greater the inflexibility of the country's productive structure, the greater the "structural-lock" dilemma of the country. Thus, the full use of the existing productive capacity would imply the necessity for the type of income distribution which would produce the requisite demand profile, i.e., a very unequal distribution of income. The alternative, a more egalitarian distribution of income, might imply considerable capacity in a number of industries.

This "structural lock" dilemma should be set off, however, against the import constraint problem. It has been claimed that high income inequality encourages a more import-intensive demand profile. That is, higher income groups consume technically more sophisticated goods which have relatively high direct and indirect import requirements. Thus, although a greater degree of income concentration could avoid a "structural lock" problem, it could lead to stagnation caused by import constraints.

XI.C.3. Import-Substitution Strategy*

The most pervasive impact of IS policies has been that it distorts the economy, and these distortions do not, except in rare instances, correct themselves. Indeed, economies be-

*From Henry J. Bruton, "The Import-Substitution Strategy of Economic Development: A Survey," *Pakistan Development Review*, Summer 1970, pp. 137–43. Reprinted by permission.

come increasingly distorted as the IS process continues. Three assumptions seem to underlie much of the analysis that leads to the policies that in turn produce the distortion. One has to do with the assumptions about the responsiveness of the various sectors of the system to relative price changes, the second to the existence and impact of external and internal economies that accompany the establishment of new activities, and the third to the role of capital formation in development. If one assumes that relative prices have no effect on anything then they can be safely ignored, and distortion loses much of its meaning. Consequently, the policy-maker can ignore the impact of misleading price signals on his economy. Similarly, if expected external (or internal) economies are assumed great enough, then *any* activity can be justified, and there appears great, and unsupported, optimism implied by many policies as to the existence of such economies in the newly established activities. And, an assumption seems to prevail that amounts essentially to the assertion that a high rate of physical capital formation can overcome any obstacle. Evidence from several studies strongly suggests that none of these assumptions can support the weight that it is asked to bear.

The most specific evidence on the role prices can play has to do with foreign trade. In [6], for example, John Sheahan presents regressions that leave little doubt that maintaining reasonably correct exchange rates does have a significant effect on export earnings from Colombia's exports other than coffee and oil. In [2], Paul Clark's equations explaining Brazilian imports show price elasticities ranging from $-.35$ for capital equipment to -1.62 for the construction material industry. While elasticities with respect to investment (the stand-in for GNP) were higher than the price elasticities for four of the six groups for which both investment and price elasticities were available, this evidence indicates again that sufficient substitutability between domestic and imported goods exists in Brazil, that to ignore it will induce distortion. The extent to which the Colombian and Brazilian equations represent demand or supply parameters can not be told from either set of equations. Doubtless to some extent both are effective so that the computed coefficients are probably not estimates of a structural parameter. Nevertheless, these results do indicate that a price effect does exist and which in turn indicates

substitutability and responsiveness in the economies of significant magnitude.

There is evidence on this issue on a more general level. In a study of Mexico [4], Clark Reynolds suggests that postwar policies were somewhat different from those of many other countries. Nominal tariff rates have been much lower than in most other developing countries, and have risen only moderately, if at all, since the 1930's. Also the more established firms have to supply products of reasonable quality and at a reasonable price within a few years of their initiation or their protection is reduced. The findings on Mexico also indicate that considerable substitution exists between domestic skilled labour imputs and imported intermediate goods. Finally, Mexico's IS activities appeared more heavily concentrated in labour-intensive industries than has been the case elsewhere. (Though this latter is not necessarily a desirable condition, it appears to be so in this case.) Evidently, Mexico's relatively strong showing since 1950 is explained by a great number of factors and cannot be attributed exclusively to the points just enumerated. It is, however, appropriate to emphasize that these attributes of Mexican policy did prevent the marked distortions from appearing that would impede the other advantages of Mexico from having their full effect.

A last example has to do with Pakistan. In Chapter VII of [3], S. R. Lewis' discussion of the effect of economic policy on the growth rate and composition of output shows that policies that tended to correct the distortions in the system did produce changes that resulted in a more efficient use of both domestic and aid-provided resources. Both the Export Bonus Scheme and the import-liberalization policies seemed to affect allocations in a manner that facilitated a more rational use of her resources. Other policies examined by Lewis to some extent offset these effects, but the point remains relevant.

On the question of external effects, the evidence is less clear and, what there is, is of a more negative kind than that just mentioned. It is surely clear that structural change itself does not automatically contribute significant external economies. There is virtually no empirical evidence that the often referred to, seldom specifically identified, "external" effects of new activities—labour training, technological improvement, economies of scale, etc.—occur with the establishment of import-replacing activities. Indeed the same distortions that result in activities in the developing economies being less productive than in the advanced countries also have negative effects on the realization of possible externalities. More positively, one may say that these matters must be considered explicitly with respect to individual activities, and general assumptions as to their sources are not acceptable. This is not to suggest that structural change as an end in itself may not be important. It often is, and rightly so. The point here is to emphasize that our studies do not show that such changes do, in themselves, bring about major external economies.

The third implicit assumption underlying much of IS philosophy has to do with the role of capital formation in development. This is a broad question which our studies do not directly consider. The evidence is now overwhelming that merely more investment does not mean a higher growth rate. This does not mean of course that capital formation is not important in producing growth. It does mean that merely generating a high rate of investment is not sufficient to assure growth. More specifically it means that a higher rate of investment will not in itself solve—or prevent from arising—other, growth-defeating, issues. A still more important conclusion, noted in several studies, is that concentrating attention on capital formation irrespective of other matters creates growth-defeating developments.

These arguments have two broad categories of implications. In the first place they mean that distortions are very real and must be taken into account in devising and appraising policies. For example, if there were no substitutability between labour and capital (and among products), then the relative cost of labour and capital would not be relevant to the distortion issue. Efforts to affect the distribution of income via wage policies (minimum wage rates, high severance pay, etc.) will have no effect on choice of technique or product selected. Where there is such substitutability, however, these policies do introduce distortions. Similarly, if the exchange rate's role as an allocation device is negligible, then to undervalue foreign exchange to encourage investment is acceptable policy. If, as now seems clear, the exchange rate does perform an allocative function, then to keep it below its equilibrium level does impose distortions, the damage of which cannot be overcome by the mere fact of a high rate of capital formation. In general then, we can say that the degree of flexibility and adaptability suggested by recent studies shows that many policies aimed at specific targets do impose distortions on the system that make it difficult or impossible to achieve the specified target.

The second implication is even broader than the first and follows from it. The results suggest that the misallocations produced by conventional IS policies not only reduce total output below the level that it might have otherwise reached, but it also reduces the growth rate, principally through its effect on productivity growth and the flexibility of the economy. This means simply that the distortion issue is a most strategic concept, strategic to the point that to ignore it is to court failure. This we believe to be a vital point, and more will be said on its specific policy implications later.

IS-CREATED ALIENNESS

We have emphasized that IS seems to create activities that are broadly alien to the economic and social environment of the community. Alien here applies not only to the factor endowment as such, but refers also to the whole range of characteristics and attributes of a society that affect its capacity to produce goods and services and to respond to unpredicted opportunities (and setbacks). Alienness is not independent of, but also not simply a component of, the distortion issue just discussed.

The clearest case of the point appears in [1] where evidence is presented that Latin American countries exploited the opportunities offered them during World War II in a more effective way than in later years. During the War there was no inflow of physical or financial capital. The countries were forced to use what they had, to build with what they had, and to rely exclusively on their own saving. They did all this in such a manner that productivity rose at a much higher rate than in the postwar period when foreign capital was relied on to a much greater extent. Also domestic resources were much more fully utilized in the War period than after, despite the fact that the rate of capital accumulation was much less. In being forced to use what they had, the economic structure created was much more consistent, much less alien than in later years when IS policies became so paramount.

In Lewis' discussion of changing relative prices and the manner in which costs of new activities in Pakistan decreased, there is a similar picture [3]. In activities where the inputs fit well with what Pakistan could offer and could do, relative prices—hence presumably costs—declined. Other sectors, less suitable, were also less successful. Natural resources played some role in this, but certainly the whole story is not simply one of natural resources.

Sheahan's model of the Colombia economy shows how that economy became more rigid, more dependent on imports as the alienness of its economic structure evolved [5]. This may be contrasted somewhat with Mexico, the structure of which evolved in a manner much more consistent with her social and cultural heritage, entrepreneurial ability, organizing capacity, and management skills.

These matters are difficult to separate from the distortion issue already emphasized. The key point seems to be this: that if a country's economy evolves in a manner consistent with its resource endowment, then that endowment can be near fully exploited.

PRODUCTIVITY-GROWTH DAMPENING EFFECTS OF IS

The argument above indicated that the conventional approach to IS creates conditions that dampen productivity growth, and rapid productivity growth is essential to a successful IS. So an important positive notion emerging from our studies is that countries *must* pursue policies that lead to a high productivity growth or IS *must* fail. The question of course is what are such policies? The first point to emphasise is simply that productivity growth does not just happen. It is not a time trend to be appended. It is rather a phenomenon to be explained, and despite the absence of data and argument it seems clear that it (productivity growth) is and can be affected by economic policies. In many studies where this issue is treated most explicitly, evidence seems to indicate that productivity growth is more likely to reach acceptable rates in economies where distortions and alienness are at a minimum. Certainly it is correct to say that there is nothing incompatible between distortion free economies and the achievement of an acceptable growth of productivity.

Stronger positive statements are more difficult. In general it does seem clear that most developing countries are not paying sufficient attention to the possibilities of adapting and modifying imported physical capital in such a way that it more nearly fits their domestic economies. To do this probably means the allocation of more resources explicitly to this task. It certainly means a conscious recognition of the necessity of this sort of activity by both government and the private sector. General considerations indicate that this can best be done at the firm or plant level. Hence, policies that put pressure on firms or that provide an incentive to them to seek ways to increase the productivity of their resources are an essential ingredient of development policy.

With respect to the effect of education on the productivity of labour, two general points emerge from the literature on education. In the first place, the shortage of the kind of skills learned in the classroom does not appear to be a specific bottleneck. The educational establishment does not turn out individuals who are immediately employed to break a bottleneck. Rather, the productivity effect of education is to equip a person to adapt and to respond to opportunities as they appear. Perhaps most directly they equip a person to profit from on-the-job training. The second point has to do with the quality of education. In economies where productivity is generally low, it is unlikely that it is high in the difficult tasks of educating. This means that many countries that are spending large sums on education may be doing it on rather low productivity activities. The not-very-startling idea emerges then that the developing countries may not need more education of the kind currently being provided, but rather improved productivity of the educational activities.

Productivity growth probably is not completely explained by allocation, by technological improvements, and by raising the quality of labour. These, however, are surely a significant part of the key to its understanding. The evidence that productivity growth is a strategic element in the picture of a successful IS policy means, therefore, that these matters are equally a significant part of the key to the devising of effective development policy.

In the preceding sections we have discussed the general content of the usual approach to IS, have tried to identify the specific aspects of that approach that seem to account for the difficulties that so many countries following IS policies find themselves in, and finally we sought to outline in

very broad terms what appeared as the more positive findings of our studies. In this final section we seek to consider these positive issues in terms of more specific types of policies and strategies that have emerged.

Few studies suggest a simple *laissez-faire*, free-trade approach. Similarly, few deny the advantages of industrialization in particular, or, more generally, the importance of changes in the structure of the developing economies and in the composition of their output. More importantly, the idea of a strategy, as defined earlier in this paper, has great merit. There is much evidence that many governments attack the development problem on too many fronts. The consequence of this is not only that demands are placed on the administrative machinery which cannot be met, but also that policies often counter each other and *full* consequences of all aspects of the attack are not understood. Therefore, the notion that the attack on the development objective should consist of a small number of strategic policy areas has great merit. The question of which areas the government should direct its attention depends of course on the assumptions that are made as to how the specific economy functions and as to the nature of the growth mechanism. As emphasized above, the IS strategy as conventionally practised rests on assumptions which recent studies have seriously questioned.

What then can we say about strategic variables and mechanisms of growth on the basis of the preceding discussion of our findings? And what kind of policies exploit these variables and these mechanisms at the same time that they induce industrialization and structural changes that are recognized as necessary for development?

Our analysis suggests that three items, distortion, alienness, and productivity growth, are more demanding of attention, *i.e.*, more strategic, than those variables which have occupied attention in the conventional IS model. Since governments cannot do everything, they should then concentrate on these issues. Specific policies would then be appraised as to the extent to which they *i*) distort or undistort the system, *ii*) encourage projects consistent with the other characteristics of the economy, and *iii*) encourage productivity growth. If policies are successful in these areas, then other conditions necessary for continued growth (*e.g.,* capital formation) may be expected to be induced or to be achievable without major policy measures. To repeat our well-worn theme, it is attacks on these other, these "nonstrategic," growth-producing variables that violate our strategic variables and cause the difficulties which we have found to inhere in the IS strategy.

References

1. Bruton, H. J., "Productivity Growth in Latin America," *American Economic Review*, December 1967.

2. Clark, P. G., and R. Weisskoff, *Import Demands and Import Policies in Brazil.* Research Memorandum No. 8, Williamstown, Mass.: Williams College, 1967.

3. Lewis, S. R., Jr., *Economic Policy and Industrial Growth in Pakistan.* London, 1969.

4. Reynolds, C. W., *Changing Trade Patterns and Trade Policy in Mexico.* Research Memorandum No. 17, Williamstown, Mass.: Williams College, 1967.

5. Sheahan, J. B., "Imports, Investment and Growth: Colombia Experience Since 1950," in *Development Policy—Theory and Practice*, edited by Gustav F. Papanek, Cambridge, 1968.

6. Sheahan J., and S. Clark, *The Response of Colombia Exports to Variations in Effective Exchange Rates.* Research Memorandum No. 11, Williamstown, Mass.: Williams College, June 1967.

XI.D. POSSIBILITIES OF EXPORT EXPANSION

XI.D.1. The Optimal Correspondence Between Industries and Countries*

The question "how much of what to produce where" has been posed by Tinbergen.[1] To answer this question, he developed what might be termed correspondence models in which the conditions for satisfying the age-old dictum of "the right man in the right place" are rigorously formulated. The correspondence models are not specifically tied to a single purpose, and can be used for a range of problems. Attention is concentrated, in this review, on the "Hungarian model".[2]

The essence of the correspondence model for the optimal international division of labour lies in the idea that both the tasks to be performed and the producers to perform them can be arrayed in two distributions which show, respectively, for every value of capital required or available, the amount of goods demanded and the productive capacity available for their supply. This approach involves a departure from traditional economics and the latter's emphasis on either demand or supply limitations.

The correspondence between the two distributions—that is their reconciliation—is made in such a way as to minimise costs. The optimality that is sought is analysed in terms of the solution's contribution to improvements in income distribution and the utilisation of factors. The discrepancies be-

*Reprinted from Bohuslav Herman, *The Optimal International Division of Labour*, International Labour Office, Geneva, 1975, pp. 18–20, 45–8, 131–4. Reprinted by permission.

[1] J. Tinbergen, "The Optimal International Division of Labour," *Acta Oeconomica Academiae Scientiarum Hungaricae*, 1968.

[2] Ibid.

tween what is available and what is required yield policy prescriptions concerning factor formation processes (capital accumulation, training programmes or re-schooling, etc.) as much as factor transfers: that is, there are two means of minimising those discrepancies, or in other words of ensuring that the present structure approximates more closely to the ideal that would prevail if the correspondence between industries and countries were optimal. The optimal correspondence between industries and countries that satisfies the conditions and objectives stated above would prescribe an optimal international division of labour based on comparative advantages. Each country would produce a commodity whose factor requirements would correspond most closely to the country's factor endowments.

What makes Tinbergen's contribution the most useful one, and therefore the one to be adopted when attempting solutions to the problem under consideration, is the explicit introduction of the demand for commodities. The vector of world demand, specifying the amounts of each commodity that should be produced, plays the pivotal role of unifying the whole system through the total (as opposed to unit) factor requirements that need to be mobilised, since no industry can work at zero output. This feature has three major implications.

First, the identification of industrial activities for large groups of countries is no longer a simple procedure based on their (known) factor endowments, but a more selective allocation process characterised by a harmonious combination of the industrialisation plans of each area that is distinguished.

It could be that countries with certain (unit) capital endowments offer too much (or too little) capacity; or there might not be enough demand for some commodities the production of which calls for a certain degree of capital intensity. In such situations the allocation of activities to countries that mechanically equalise factor endowments with requirements might not be conducive either to the production of all commodities or to the employment of all factors. Tinbergen's model offers a solution whereby the national targets (full employment of factors through optimal specialisation) are harmoniously combined in such a way that the international economy is better off, since the burden on each nation is minimised.

The second point is that a measure of welfare is disaggregatedly achieved in real terms through the demand pattern. What is needed is produced. This has a major political implication: well endowed countries may artificially stimulate demand for unrequired capital-intensive goods or depress demand for required labour-intensive goods, so ensuring employment to the factors of production. Only by specifying a demand pattern is the appropriate counterpart to the distribution of endowments ensured—a distribution of requirements that accords with the production of commodities in actual demand.

The third point is a consequence of the condition that all commodities must be produced, taken in conjunction with the fact of a larger dispersion in the distribution of endowments than in the range of requirements. These two elements in Samuelson's now classical theorem are incompatible since he assumed (admittedly unrealistically) that capital is immobile. Tinbergen assumes that capital enjoys a limited international mobility, so that his optimum admits transfers of one factor and, as a matter of empirical fact, is characterised by such transfers. . . .

To specify the optimal task of each nation within the context of a worldwide international division of labour, a method is required that systematically allocates such tasks, is flexible enough to reveal different possibilities and enables the optimality of any particular solution to be evaluated.

As already stated, in this analysis there will be less emphasis on trade flows than on production structures. Because the main aim is to determine how a country should specialise in industrial terms, trade flows eventually emerge accessorily. . . .

Much of the economic writing on this subject has been centred on two poles, namely the views of economists who consider that demand provides the limitations and of those who consider that supply provides them. The authors in the first group, who are essentially concerned with marketing, advise concentration on the products that are more easy to sell. In the supply-oriented class are writers who concentrate on production techniques and would prescribe, for instance, which individuals should receive what kind of training, taking account only of the qualities of the individual and not of the skills required by the economy.

History illustrates the influence of the two conceptions, each of which is correct as far as it goes. In periods of deflation, economists tend to be demand-oriented (the best-known example being Keynes), whereas during inflation supply-centred studies flourish. However, for a pair of scissors to work, both blades need to operate.

Accordingly a conceptual framework that can be described as consisting of "correspondence models" is used here. These are intrinsically equilibrium models in which two sets are mapped upon each other. The result of the mapping is a function called a "transformation equation", in which there is a one-to-one correspondence between elements of both universes over the whole range. The matching satisfies certain constraints while indicating the optimal progress that can be made towards certain targets. Such a framework is general enough to embrace a large variety of problems; here it is used for sector planning at the world level. The pattern to be determined corresponds to an ideal development path, which means that full capacity utilisation is assumed for labour and capital.

The method consists in matching the elements of two arrays in such a way that income and employment objectives are attained in an optimal way, while satisfying resource, demand and technological constraints. In the present case, where there are space and commodity variables, the former are arrayed on the basis of factor endowments per worker and the latter on the basis of factor requirements per worker.

THE UNIVERSE OF SPACES

Consider the notion of standardised "nations", each comprising a single worker, whose resource endowments are known. A cumulative frequency distribution of such nations can then be constructed on a scale of capital intensity running from zero to infinity. The total manpower requiring employment (or world productive capacity) would be equal to the available workers in all countries from the poorest to the richest. The productive capacity of all real countries endowed with up to a certain amount of capital per worker would be represented by the stock of workers available to those countries; similarly the capital endowment of countries below a prescribed amount of capital per worker could be computed by definite integration of the cumulative distribution, and integration over the whole range of countries would yield total world capital as the area under the distribution curve.

By specifying typical values of capital per worker, one can group countries into as many classes as it is wished to distinguish, though the number of such groups must be the smallest that reflects relevant differences in endowments per head between groups and minimum differences within each group. The productive capacity of every group, as well as its capital endowment, can then be computed in the manner shown above.

Relating the income generated to the

quantity of factors utilised (perhaps in conjunction with the efficiency with which they are used) yields factor productivities as a function of capital intensity (either directly, or indirectly through the effect of capital intensity on efficiency); and when factor prices are equalised to marginal factor productivities, a set of factor shadow prices is established for each group of countries.

THE UNIVERSE OF COMMODITIES

In the preceding section there was no need to define the size of nations (number of employable workers as computed for the frequency distribution) which affects the function of distribution of capital available, since the size of nations is given. The size of sectors, on the other hand, is not given but will depend on the demand assumed for goods produced in those sectors.

Before the pattern of demand and the inter-relations between demand and total factor requirements are described, it is helpful to describe the universe of commodities in a manner similar to that used for the universe of spaces, on the assumption that the size of sectors is already known. The second part of this section explains how those sizes are determined.

Imagine standardised "sectors" in each of which one worker is employed each with typical resource requirements. If the frequency of these standardised sectors is known (through the demand pattern), a frequency distribution can be constructed. The demand for goods that require up to a certain value of capital intensity would then be represented by the number of workers needed for production of those goods, and the total number of jobs available (or world demand for all goods) would be equal to all manpower required to produce the whole range of commodities (capital intensity ranging from zero to infinity).

Similarly the capital requirements of any sub-set of commodities contained between two given values of capital intensity could be computed by definite integration of the distribution function over the relevant range of goods, and integration over the whole range of commodities yields world capital requirements.

If the number of workers available in each group of countries is known, characteristic capital intensity values can be chosen to cluster sectors in such a way that the number of workers required in each cluster approximates as closely as possible to the number of workers available in each group; for by bringing into a certain cluster a neighbouring industry in the array, the average factor intensity of the cluster is raised, since commodities were arrayed according to increasing capital intensity. This would result in an inferior adaptation of requirements and availabilities.

By establishing a relationship between the income generated in a sector and the factors engaged in that sector, it is possible to choose, by parametric variations, the factor mix that optimises income subject to different values of prevailing wages.

Finally, the basket of goods demanded accords with the distribution specified in the demand vector, which contains as many elements as there are commodities distinguished. Its general element reflects the income spent on a commodity as the share of income spent on all commodities, and this vector is the pivot of the correspondence that is sought: for each million dollars of product, it tells how much will be food, how much clothing and so on. Thus the problem is not merely to determine maximum activity levels subject to given factor endowments and technological constraints, but also to take account of demand constraints. The demand vector determines how the total feasible product is to be subdivided into each of the goods required to satisfy needs.

The procedure is as follows. First, the technologically specified labour-output and capital-labour coefficients are applied to the demand vector to elicit the capital require-

ments of the basket of goods, at unit output level. Factor endowments then determine how many unit baskets can be produced. At this stage a problem appears. The available factor mix will coincide with the required factor mix only by chance. Most probably one factor will not be redundant, and the endowment of this non-redundant factor (presumably capital, but it could be oxygen, copper, oil or any other ecological factor) may turn out to be the limiting factor. Once the level of feasible supply of output is known, the demand pattern determines the level at which demand for each commodity can be met, and the size of the producing sector when demand is converted from output into labour terms. . . .

The simple but important proposition that the market is a world market is overlooked in most development studies and policies. Even in sophisticated multi-sector planning models used to design national industrial structures to serve domestic markets, it is implicitly accepted as something like a divine law that international trade must be derived as a residual. Yet it is by now quite evident that inward-looking policies do not help to foster economic development, mainly because of the large element of inefficiency that they allow. If applied at national level, multi-sector planning, however complex, should be viewed with suspicion, to say the least, since it takes as given just the entity—the country's industrial structure—that should be designed by an appropriate choice of the most efficient industries. To deal with this problem by means of multi-sector models is to beg the very question that calls for an answer.

Many suggestions have been made for dealing with this problem. The adoption of capital-intensive industrialisation has been defended on various grounds. Bhagwati, among others, was suspicious of Galenson and Leibenstein's recommendation of capital-intensive (even if inefficient) industrialisation as a means of increasing savings; he argued in favour of a direct path to efficient production which would increase savings through higher incomes. Following Bhagwati's line of thought, one may aim directly at efficiency in production, and view with suspicion all recommendations that involve inefficient production, whatever the promised benefits.

Efficiency in production is essential if regard is paid to the world market, where competitiveness is the most important factor. Adoption of this efficiency principle might seem like an unconditional act of faith in the market mechanism. To show that this is not so, it should be stated at the outset that no true development can be achieved if the harsh realities of the market mechanism are ignored. However, as Chenery made clear, if it is agreed to allow the forces generated by the market to guide development, the operation of the market should be controlled in some respects through planning in order to arrive at the optimum. This is essentially the balanced growth strategy.

Among all the theoretical solutions hitherto proposed, Tinbergen's, subsuming supply and demand in one model, is the most adequate because it embraces all the variables that must be taken into account to answer the question of how much of what to produce where. His correspondence model provides an appropriate framework for dealing with the problem of the optimal allocation of resources, besides incorporating a rigorous quantitative formulation of the Heckscher-Ohlin theorem of comparative advantages.

Analyses of relevant past experience, such as those of Balassa, confirm that the few examples of successful development which are to be found in recent times are provided by countries that have exploited their comparative advantages. Analyses of changes in trade flows over time confirm that the theory of comparative advantage is supported by empirical facts. What is of immediate importance in the present context is that a strategy based on this principle would not only accelerate the growth of income but would simultaneously have the salutary effect of creating employment in countries where the reduction of unemployment should be the prime objective.

The optimal international division of labour was approached in this study as a strategy for the optimal allocation of all resources. Since labour is the resource in respect of which there is most idle capacity, it has been taken as the core element and allocated by using the choice of industry as the instrumental variable. It was found unnecessary to consider the choice of technique within individual sectors since the range of choice was very limited, but there are many more possibilities if the choice of technique is made between sectors.

This study was grounded in the belief that the reader would appreciate an alternative to the studies of concepts and causes of underemployment of manpower, which usually do not provide guidance for positive action. What matters is the soundness of the economic principles used and not the elegance of the economic techniques employed.

To achieve the optimal international division of labour, policy makers should widen their horizons, regarding the whole world as their market and submitting to the efficiency criterion. However, certain complementary action is required.

First, a change in the direction of scientific and technological research is needed, in order that more attention may be paid to factors affecting welfare. More research into labour-intensive technology is also very important; the equation of capital intensity with progress is conducive to an indiscriminate imitation of rich countries. An efficient technology is one that economises in the use of the scarce factor, and for developing countries progressive and efficient technologies will therefore be those that economise on capital. The responsibility for research lies primarily with rich countries. However it is not merely incumbent on them to undertake it for purely humanitarian reasons; it is also in their own interest, since developing countries will become better customers if they also become increasingly important suppliers of goods.

The second line of action directly suggested by this study is the reform of trade. Comparative advantages can only generate their benefits if they operate through a market mechanism in which competition is not vitiated by tariffs. Balassa has already warned against the self-perpetuating character of protectionist measures, whatever statement of intentions may be made about their temporary character. It must be made clear, moreover, that recommending a particular industry to a particular country does not imply that special privileges should be granted to producers in that industry in that country; the optimal allocation has itself taken account of the optimal circumstances those producers already enjoy.

The third most important kind of complementary action to be taken in conjunction with an endeavour to achieve the optimal international division of labour is the retraining of manpower in order to reduce the human difficulties that can arise in the transition from the existing labour market to that which accords with optimal employment opportunities. The retraining scheme must be carefully planned, since a switch from one sector into another does not necessarily require retraining: it may well be that workers with the same skills and aptitudes are required in both the old and the new sector of employment. It is, moreover, high time that trade unions stopped supporting marginal entrepreneurs in their pleas for protection and subsidies, hopeless remedies which in the long term cannot prevent the closure of factories. It is more positive, and effective, for workers to press for retraining facilities, in order to take advantage of the increasing employment oppportunities in efficient industries which will need to expand as a result of greater specialisation.

Another point which arises in the context of the allocation of labour concerns its immobility. Sectoral re-allocation of the labour force within a country may imply internal migrations. These are practicable, since not only are they an accepted fact of life but they do not give rise to problems of socio-cultural adjustment as serious as those that arise in the case of migrations across national boundaries. In contrast, international labour migrations have not been considered as a long-term solution, since quite apart from any human suffering involved they are not conducive to appropriate development in the labour-exporting country.

Most nations have grown by exporting their resources in the shape of goods manufactured by their own members. History provides no example of a country that has grown by exporting its labour, which is hardly to be wondered at since a nation deprived of its prime mover would find it virtually impossible to accumulate other resources. . . .

Finally, at the risk of sounding repetitive, it is reiterated that the object of this study is to emphasise the need for a world-wide approach to problems of employment and industrialisation. An attempt has been made to demonstrate the advantages of world harmonisation. Attention was drawn to the chaos attributable to national-centred policies that neglect harmonisation, even if those policies are outward-looking and flawless in all other respects. Harmonisation requires consensus. It can confidently be expected that action to optimise the international division of labour will, since it is in the interest of all, itself be conducive to the emergence of a consensus reflecting the solidarity of a world corresponding to human aspirations.

XI.D.2. The Issue of Trade Preferences*

The case against preferences has not always been well presented, and some excuse is given for the tendency among LDCs to feel that vital help to their growth is being sacrificed by the DCs because of actual or feared internal political pressure from manufacturing interests—and especially from those, such as textiles and handicrafts, that are comparatively inefficient and so have the least economic claim to favoured treatment.

Gardner Patterson has published[1] a clear exposition of the anti-preference case and the best public statement of the old American position. The following summarizes his argument, and supplements it along frequently reasoned lines:

1. If a poorer country is to be able to export to a richer country where previously it could not, the delivered price of the LDC producer must be lower than the price quotation of producers in the DC, and lower also than the price of producers in other DCs plus any tariff they must still pay. But the formation of the European Common Market and Free Trade Association have been lowering tariffs within the groups toward zero. Soon the most efficient producer in any of the associated countries will hold the market. The effect is sharply to increase the competition any LDC producer outside must meet and conquer.

In addition, present tariff levels in DCs average only about 15% *ad valorem*, and with the agreements of the recent Kennedy

Round of negotiations they will drop to the neighbourhood of 9–12%. There will be great resistance among DCs to granting preferences of zero tariff duties: if the often proposed "half of the most-favoured-nation rate" should win out, then preferential duties would be around 5%. The argument continues that there are very few LDC exports that would gain decisive advantage over domestic DC producers and other free-trade-area producers from a 5% price cut, and over external DC producers from a 5% margin (since the latter must still pay a post-Kennedy Round near 10% average duty). The maximum possible price advantage is modest.

2. Setting up a system of tariff preferences would entail special costs. First, political frictions have arisen and would arise between African states that want to continue their existing preferences in the Common Market, and the other LDCs that want preferences extended uniformly. United States' granting of preferences to Latin America only, as has been urged, would be vigorously resented by the Philippines, India, Hong Kong, Malaysia, Israel, and all other LDCs outside of Latin America. Differences have arisen in the DCs among those that want no preferences, those that want selectively negotiated preferences, and those that want across-the-board ones. Second, administrative costs can be high of trying to make preferences "fair," adjusting them for different states of development, deciding the cutoff point between LDCs and DCs, and adjusting for different quota and special arrangements. Third, DC preferences will not be granted unless the United States goes along. But once Congress has opened up the Pandora's box of tariff issues, surprising and unwelcome votes may ensue: other abrogations of most-favoured-nation treatment, and special safeguards against foreign com-

*From Theodore Morgan, "Preferences Revisited," *Malayan Economic Review*, Vol. 12, No. 2, October 1967, pp. 18–24. Reprinted by permission.
[1] Gardner Patterson, "Would Tariff Preferences Help Economic Development?" *Lloyd's Bank Review*, April 1965, pp. 18–30. Harry Johnson presented a rebuttal to the Patterson article in the same *Review* a year later.

petition written in for many a domestic producer.

3. The main gain from preferences would go to only a few countries, namely, the present major exporters of manufactures— India, Hong Kong, Israel, and Mexico.

4. Non-tariff barriers, such as quota restrictions on imports of textiles, are often of major importance.

Counter-arguments. Do these points hold water? Consider them in reverse order: (4) If non-barriers are major handicaps to LDC growth, then the plausible moral is that they should be lowered or dropped, if that is politically possible. Tariff preferences offer a possible further gain, to be considered on their own merits. The case for them may be stronger, if one is pessimistic about the chance of significantly cutting non-tariff barriers. (3) Preferences do give advantage to those countries that are near-competitive already, and offer future advantage in proportion as LDC exporters are able to get their costs down. Such a reward for efficiency and energy is desirable: late-comers can be considered later, when the present advanced LDCs are themselves DCs and no longer need special help.

In the meantime, a drop in the average level of world restrictionism is a contribution to greater world productivity. And preferences to LDCs might best be considered not something temporary, to be reversed later, but a step toward freer trade generally. Their exception to the most-favoured-nation principle, which is a good principle, is to be countered, not by refusing to extend preferences or by revoking them once extended, but by lowering other world trade barriers toward the low or zero preference level.

Point (2) on administrative and political costs of having preferences is a diffuse one, depending on one's judgment of political pressures and of the kinds of administrative arrangements one envisages. A view sympathetic to preferences would seek to diminish the costs, prehaps along the lines of the recent LDC formula. Uniform preferences to all the LDC world, rather than to a group,

would minimize both political issues and administrative complications. And the disposition of the American Congress to think solicitously of local interests should be least in a time of high prosperity.

Point (1) is the sticking point. If it is true that protection is now, or will be soon, so low that future reduction of tariffs can give little added advantage, then certainly the laborious and uncertain routine of negotiation should not be undertaken; and delegations might sensibly say, as one has, "Discussion of preferences successfully avoided." To this point—the issue of what gains and losses preferences would bring—we now turn.

Variants. The problem is not only the magnitude of gains and losses to low-income countries from preferences, but also to the United States and other high-income countries.

The countries involved are a variable: the United States only, or some, or all high-income countries might extend preferences; all low income countries might receive them, or only a group. All LDC exports, or manufactures only, or some other class of products might be covered. How much preference is also a variable: tariffs and/or non-tariff barriers might be lowered partially, or lowered to zero. The criterion of gain can be economic, or political, or both; and the time horizon can be very short run, or for a moderate period of some 2 to 5 years, or still longer,

Should there be side-conditions tied to any preference-extension? For example, if a rapid rise of imports into the United States is feared, can that cost be softened while hoped-for gains to LDCs are still retained? If softening of most-favoured-nation policy is objected to, can counter-extensions of most-favoured-nation treatment be built into a preference scheme.

Finally, the gains and losses of preferences ought to be measured side by side with those of other measures for stimulating the growth of low income countries; such as aid, most-favoured-nation treatment, price-maintenance schemes for their exports, and compensation-for-decline in value of exports schemes.

Middle-of-the-road plausible assumptions are explored below: that the United States and the other main high-income countries grant preferences, as seems likely in the present climate of opinion; that both tariff and non-tariff import barriers be lowered substantially, as a limiting case to zero, for manufactures from all LDC regions; and that effects be thought of within some moderate period of 2 to 5 years—long enough so that crucial effects on resources supplies and productivity efficiency are not dropped from consideration, short enough so that effects are not lost in the murk of possible but unrelated changes in world productive efficiency and trade patterns.

Central Effects of Preferences. What are the economic results in LDCs? There are significant effects even if preferences have no influence on the supply of resources and on productive efficiency in low-income areas. One *beneficial effect* lies in "trade creation": low-cost producers in the LDCs expand, in accord with their marginal costs, as net prices received from sales in the DCs extending preferences rise. The windfall price gain will be less than the amount of any tariff remission, since price in the DCs falls with a rise in imports. A critical question is, how much will the LDC producers expand output? A second *beneficial effect* is implied: more sales will be made by the LDCs abroad at the higher net prices obtainable, depending on elasticities of DC demand and LDC supply. Increased foreign earnings for LDCs will soon be transformed into increased imports. Employment effects in LDCs are also positive, as export industries expand. A third *beneficial effect* is now being pressed in LDC arguments: that manufacturers in high-income countries will be encouraged by the chance of tariff-free importing to invest capital and know-how in LDC industries (as the British invested in India, the French in Africa, the Japanese in Korea).

On the other hand, there will be *injurious* "trade diversion" outside the preferred area. Exports to the DCs will shrink from outside the favoured group—from countries defined as not "under-developed," and from countries outside any special LDC preferred area, such as Latin America. The non-favoured group will view this shrinkage as a disadvantage. The effect also injures world efficiency of production, since previous low-cost producers are forced out of the market through administrative favour granted to the preferred group.

Conversely, in the developed countries there will be some adverse balance-of-payments and employment effects, softened to the extent that there is flexible shift of resources into relatively more efficient production for home use and for export. There will be some injury also from the rise in cost of some imports to the United States as preferences shift sources of supply away from cheaper (non-preferred) suppliers. There will be advantage from checking monopolistic practices and, in a full-employment world, from discouraging price rises.

The effects above are all "static": no account is taken of changes in resource supplies and productive efficiency. But such dynamic effects are the mainly-important potentialities from a preference system. Export markets will expand for the products of the preferred low-income countries. Domestic markets for their products are small, often very small. As the size of the market and the volume of production expand, average costs in many industries can fall sharply through a considerable range: handicraft and small-scale production are outcompeted by mechanization, use of power equipment, specialization in sub-processes, and assembly line fabrication. Expansion of the market develops other economies, feedback effects in their broadest sense: skills and entrepreneuring abilities in one industry that are useful also in others; better communications (a road or railroad developed for one business can be used by others); simplifications and standardization encouraged through producing for a large market; emergence of new industries out of the specialization encouraged by producing for a large market and from more contacts; and finally, growth of a sense of momentum and confidence in economic possibilities. Industries differ in their extent of feedbacks. It is sensible, in a preference scheme, to stimulate those that have the most.

Aside from economic effects of preferences, there is the general political effect. The drive for preferences at UNCTAD and other meetings comes not from a reasoned case, marshalling up the pros and cons, but from a profound sense of unjust treatment. Lower trade restrictions in international trade generally is not what the LDCs want. What they want is *preference*.

The United States' past opposition to preferences has been at some political cost in LDC official opinion. Supporting preferences therefore should bring some political gain. Within such a high-income country as the United States, there would be mixed political results, such as the normal opposition from American producers of products competing with plausible imports, and support from exporter and consumer interests and from groups sensitive to LDC welfare.

Would competing producers in the United States seek to raise non-tariff barriers against imports that threaten to rise rapidly? No doubt they would, and they would also find their task of persuading legislators eased by the conscious departure of policy from the anchor of most-favoured-nation treatment. The importance of this risk is a matter of political judgment. The risk does imply that a tariff preference law, or negotiations, to be meaningful, should include pledges or checks against raising such barriers. The opposition and threat could be softened by a rule limiting the rate of rise of imports; for example, that imports of a particular good from one LDC may not be imported in a quantity more than 10% above the level of any previous year without paying a penalty duty, which means that imports from all LDCs of

that commodity would usually rise by less than 10%.

Another concern is that the effect of granting preferences might be, within the United States or other grantor, a weakening of political support for further most-favoured-nation lowering of tariff and non-tariff barriers generally. The LDCs would care less for further most-favoured-nation lowering of barriers, since the effect would be to diminish their margin of preference.

Nevertheless, a preference system can be fitted into a general world context of lowered protection along most-favoured-nation lines: the high-income grantor nation could demand, as a condition for granting preferences to any one LDC, that it should schedule lowering its own tariff and non-tariff barriers to import from other LDCs, and bargain in good faith in future trade negotiations. Such a demand would then push the LDC world toward this amount of most-favoured-nation practice. As the years go by, a hoped-for general lowering of trade barriers through repeated trade negotiations would diminish the margin of preference to LDCs.

Lowered trade barriers have a special advantage to low-income countries for a reason not often highlighted. LDC economies are typically thin, subject to sporadic scarcities and surpluses of particular products due to crop failure or abundance, to industrial difficulties or successes where suppliers are few, and to failures of central planning. There is, therefore, especially large gain to their economic life from opening up freer trade channels for supplies and markets; and for this reason they ought to be devout supporters of free trade. But on the other hand, most low-income countries are heavily dependent for government revenues on customs receipts; they find it easier, politically and administratively, to obtain the bulk of their revenues from customs duties rather than from any internal source, and they are therefore forced to go slow in lowering customs levies.

XI.D.3. The Prospects for Export of

Manufactures—Note

We have frequently remarked upon the LDCs' desire to use trade policy as a means of promoting their industrialization. If the development of home production to replace imports of manufactured goods was the earlier attempted strategy of industrialization, there is now a new hope that industrialization might be based on the processing of the LDCs' primary materials for export and on the export of other manufactures and semi-manufactures in which LDCs might become competitive. Arguments in favor of an export substitution strategy of industrialization were presented in selection X.C.2, above. But what are the prospects for making such a strategy actually effective?

UNCTAD's proposal that the industrially advanced countries should grant preferential reductions in their import duties in favor of imports of manufactures and semimanufactures from the LDCs has been the LDCs' major policy recommendation for stimulating their exports.

If preferences allow exporters of the LDC to charge the consumers in the importing country a higher price than the world market price, then there is a transfer of resources. Suppose, for example, that a developed country, A, initially imposes a 50 per cent ad valorem duty on imports from both another developed country, B, and an LDC, and the export price from developed country B is 100 and from the LDC the price is 120. The import price plus duty in A will then be 150 for imports from B and 180 from the LDC. The country will therefore import from the other developed country. If, however, A now retains the 50 per cent ad valorem duty on imports from B while levying no duty on imports from the LDC (a 100 per cent preferential margin), then the LDC can export at a price up to 150 (the

import price plus duty for imports from B). Previously, A paid customs receipts of 50 (import price of 100 from B plus duty of 50) to itself; but after preferences are granted, the preference-granting country transfers to the LDC real resources equal to the value of the foregone customs receipts.[1]

The government of an LDC might reconsider its policies with respect to private foreign investment and attempt to channel such investment in the direction of manufactures for export. The prospects for the export of manufactures from developing countries may indeed be vastly improved if managerial and technological knowledge are transferred to a low-wage developing country in order to manufacture exports to a preference-granting country. The role of multinational enterprises and host-country policies relative to this changing pattern of investment, production, and trade relationships have been discussed in Chapter VI.

Besides preferences, there are other policy measures that both the developed countries and LDCs might take to encourage more exports of manufactures from LDCs. The potential impact of some of these measures may well be greater than that of tariff preferences. Moreover, some of these measures are necessary if preferences are to be effective at all. This Note therefore examines the policies—other than preferential trading arrangements—that might be adopted to improve the prospects for exports of manufactures from the developing countries.

A few basic statistical points should first be noted:

[1] See Gardner Patterson, *Discrimination in International Trade, The Policy Issues 1945–1965*, Princeton, 1966, pp. 350–51; also, John Pincus, *Trade, Aid and Development*, New York, 1967, pp. 202–4, 225–30.

In promoting the export of manufactures, the LDCs are attempting to gain a greater share of the most dynamic sector of world trade. World trade in manufactures increased at an average annual rate of 12.3 per cent in the period 1962–70, while the growth rate for primary products was only 7.6 per cent. Although the percentage of primary products in world trade declined steadily from almost 50 per cent in 1955 to less than 40 per cent in 1970, the share of manufactured and semimanufactured products improved from approximately 49 per cent in 1955 to 61 per cent in 1970.

The share of the developing countries in world trade in manufactures and semimanufactures was, however, very low throughout the period 1966–71, as may be seen in Table 1. In 1971 the share was still under 6 per cent. At the same time, the developing countries' own demand for manufactures has been met predominantly through imports from the developed countries. Of total world exports of manufactures directed to developing countries worth $40 billion in 1970, exports from other developing countries accounted for not more than $2.9 billion, or only 7 per cent.

The number of LDCs exporting manufactures is still limited, although the number of exporting countries has grown. Only the following LDCs exported more than $500 mil-

lion worth of manufactures and semimanufactures to the developed market economy countries in 1971: Hong Kong ($1,961 million), Venezuela ($772 million), Yugoslavia ($718 million), Republic of Korea ($681 million), Mexico ($642 million), Chile ($590 million), Zambia ($531 million), India ($529 million).

The range of manufactured and semimanufactured products imported by the developed market economy countries from the developing countries was narrow. But it is significant that the range of manufactures exported has been widening, as indicated in Table 2.

Finally, the pattern in trade in manufactures from developing countries is highly concentrated, as can be seen in Table 3. Of total imports of manufactures by developed countries from LDCs in 1972, the United States accounted for approximately 50 per cent, the United Kingdom for almost 11 per cent, West Germany for approximately 10 per cent, and Japan for almost 8 per cent. Together these four countries took 80 per cent of the total.

At present, the LDCs supply only about 7 per cent of the total imports of manufactures into developed countries, and only about 1 per cent of their total consumption of manufactures. But the growth rate is high and has been rising.

TABLE 1.   Share of World Exports in Manufactures and Semimanufactures (SITC sections 5–8)

		$ Million			Percentage of World Total		
Year	World	Developed Market Economy Countries	Developing Countries	Socialist Countries	Developed Market Economy Countries	Developing Countries	Socialist Countries
1966	122,460	102,132	6,980	13,348	83.4	5.7	10.9
1967	131,190	109,150	7,740	14,300	83.2	5.9	10.9
1968	150,680	125,516	9,051	16,123	83.3	6.0	10.7
1969	176,320	147,051	11,108	18,161	83.4	6.3	10.3
1970	202,090	169,351	12,732	20,007	83.8	6.3	9.9
1971	226,670	190,620	12,400	23,640	84.1	5.5	10.4

Source: United Nations, *Monthly Bulletin of Statistics.*

TABLE 2. Values of Imports from Developing Countries into Developed Market Economy Countries, 1971

	($ US Million)	Annual % Change 1962–70
1. Petroleum products	2693.3	5.3
2. Unworked non-ferrous metals	2402.4	12.7
3. Clothing	1453.4	12.7
4. Textiles	1174.2	7.8
5. Other engineering and metal products	1010.6	31.0
6. Food products	850.3	8.4
7. Miscellaneous light manufactures	755.2	26.5
8. Wood products and furnitures	664.6	11.8
9. Chemicals	510.3	9.4
10. Leather and footwear	396.8	15.7
11. Iron and steel	277.7	24.9
12. Worked non-ferrous metals	140.5	24.2
13. Drink and tobacco products	101.0	−4.5
14. Non-metallic mineral products	72.0	12.6
15. Pulp, paper, board	44.5	12.9
16. Road motor vehicles	42.7	12.0
17. Rubber products	27.8	21.5

Source: UNCTAD, *Trade in Manufactures of Developing Countries and Territories*, 1972 Review, TD/B/C.2/124/Rev. 1, p. 8.

The important question now is what is the potential for the future growth in exports of manufactures from the LDCs. In the present century, only two major countries—Japan and the United States—have succeeded in transforming their economies from being mainly commodity exporters to being exporters of finished manufactures. If a developing country is now to follow suit, it will have to overcome a number of formidable obstacles.

The technical conditions of production are likely to be unfavorable and costs of production excessive. Costs will tend to be especially high if production of a manufactured commodity requires the importation of weight-losing raw materials, heavy fuel components, special design of products, special labour skills, or a high ratio of capital to labor. And although money wages in the LDC may be low, wage costs per unit of output may actually be high if the efficiency of labor is low. Moreover, if the local market is small, it may be difficult to achieve sufficient economies of scale to become competitive on world markets. In fact, it may be contended that the range of exportable manufactured products is determined by internal demand: thus, Linder has argued that "it is a necessary, but not a sufficient, condition that a product be consumed (or invested) in the home country for this product to be a potential export product."[2] But while this "size effect" may be important for export of finished manufactures, it does not apply to the export of intermediate goods and the

[2] Staffan B. Linder, *An Essay on Trade and Transformation*, Upssala, 1961, p. 87. But see Bela Balassa, "Country Size and Trade Patterns: Comment," *American Economic Review*, March 1969, pp. 203–4.

TABLE 3. Imports of Manufactures, Excluding Non-ferrous Metals (SITC 5 to 8 (Excluding 68)) into Selected Developed Countries, 1962 and 1972 (Million Dollars c.i.f. and Per cent)

| | Value in Million Dollars c.i.f. | | | | | | |
| | Total | | From Developing Countries | | Imports from Developing Countries in Per Cent of Total Imports | | Annual Growth Rate of Imports from Developing Countries |
Importing Countries	1962	1972	1962	1972	1962	1972	1962 to 1972
United Kingdom	3683	14137	483	1196	13.1	8.5	9.5
United States[a]	6445	35816	657	5399	10.2	15.1	23.5
Norway	1108	3203	45	103	4.1	3.2	8.6
Australia[a]	1574	3514[b]	58	122[b]	3.7	3.5[b]	8.6[c]
Japan	1360	5867	59	774	4.3	13.2	29.4
Germany, Fed. Rep.	4695	22269	132	982	2.8	4.4	22.2
France	3101	16074	87	423	2.8	2.6	17.1
Switzerland	1990	6316	31	136	1.6	2.2	15.9
Belgium-Luxemburg Union	2399	9882	32	190	1.3	1.9	19.5
Denmark	1313	3509	16	70	1.2	2.0	15.9
Canada[a]	4030	15028	54	390	1.3	2.6	21.9
Sweden	1948	5717	23	154	1.2	2.7	20.9
Italy	2616	8734	26	244	1.0	2.8	25.1
Netherlands	3123	10716	31	218	1.0	2.0	21.5
Portugal	322	1425	3	106	0.9	7.4	42.8
Austria	965	3864	7	42	0.7	1.1	19.6
Spain	721	3597	5	80	0.7	2.2	32.0
TOTAL	41393	169668	1749	10629	4.2	6.3	19.8

[a]Imports f.o.b.
[b]1971
[c]1962–1971
Sources: United Nations, *Commodity Trade Statistics;* OECD, *Trade by Commodities,* Series B.

interaffiliate trade that may characterize investment by vertically integrated multinational enterprises.

In addition to the high manufacturing costs, the export of manufactures is likely to be handicapped by a failure to perceive market opportunities and an inability to over-come marketing problems. Unlike the exportation of primary products in highly organized world markets or the replacement of imports in a sheltered home market, the export of manufactures calls for a range of marketing skills that have not yet been developed within the LDCs: obtaining and evaluating market information, design, standardization, quality control, penetrating the foreign market, establishing channels of distribution and a foreign sales organization, providing credit arrangements, etc.

Manufacturers in the LDCs clearly confront more uncertainty when they try to enter export markets; accordingly, they are likely to have a high risk aversion to attempts to enter markets for manufactured exports where specialized risks exist in the sale of differentiated products.[3] A large part of the exports of manufactures from LDCs is also likely to consist of components and intermediate products rather than finished products; trade in such products requires special contacts and collaboration among producers in different countries.[4]

For these reasons it is unreasonable to expect LDCs to be able to export capital goods or products of heavy industry or even consumer goods that require high quality standards, advanced styling, or sophisticated marketing skills. There can, however, be considerable potential for exports of light processed primary products, light consumer goods, and intermediate products—commodities that are labor-intensive or resource-based and require only simple technology and cheap or little fuel.

Study of the manufactures and semi-manufactures in which the LDCs have already achieved an export position confirms that exports have been largely limited to these two types of products: products directly based on local raw materials and labor-intensive products requiring little capital equipment or technical skill.[5]

Although the absolute value of exports of manufactures from the LDCs is still low, and the exports are concentrated in a few product groups and to a few countries, nonetheless it is noteworthy that this trade has been growing very rapidly and is becoming more widely spread by both exporting and importing countries and more varied in composition. The average annual rate of increase in exports of labor-intensive manufactures from LDCs from 1962 to 1970 was 15 per cent. Exports are now growing rapidly not only from Hong Kong but also from various other sources, especially South Korea, Taiwan, Singapore, Brazil, and Mexico. And while textiles and clothing remain the largest single product group, the share of a variety of other manufactured exports is increasing—particularly various food specialties, leather goods, glassware and pottery, cutlery, jewelry, toys and sporting goods, electronic components, metal manufacturing, and plywood and other wood products.

From a study of exports of manufactures from LDCs in the 1960s, Chenery and Hughes conclude that

the experience of the 1960s suggests that semi-industrialized countries have a significant comparative advantage in a wide range of products in which they can combine relatively low labor costs, that is relatively low wages but high skills, with modern technology, management and commercial practice. Existing tariff levels cannot keep out textiles, clothing, footware, electrical products and steel; a wide variety of new products, ranging from optical instruments to hydroelectric generators, are now coming into the same category. Developed countries, working on the assumption that developing

---

[3] Raymond Vernon, "Problems and Prospects in the Export of Manufactured Goods from the Less Developed Countries," *Proceedings of UNCTAD*, Vol. 4, Trade in Manufactures, pp. 203–4.

[4] I. G. Patel, "Exports by Countries in Process of Industrialization," in *New Directions for World Trade*, a Chatham House Report, London, 1964, pp. 98–9. But standardized semimanufactures will not generally require the availability of a home market, and to this extent the problem of exporting is eased; see Balassa, "Country Size and Trade Patterns," p. 203.

[5] See UNCTAD secretariat, *The International Division of Labour and Developing Countries*, TD/40, January 19, 1968, pp. 4–5.

country exports are going to continue to be simple, labor-intensive consumer goods are likely to find themselves—indeed, are already finding themselves—totally unprepared for such new directions in international trade in manufactures.[6]

Beyond the capacity to acquire a comparative advantage in resource-based or labor-intensive commodities, there are other forces tending to widen the basis of exports of manufactures from the LDCs. Some of the effects of technological change, for example, may go in this direction. Technological change is usually interpreted as promoting more trade in new manufactured commodities which embody a high degree of research and development or are intensive in highly skilled labor.[7] Although it is true that much of the trade in manufactures is composed of products embodying advanced scientific and technical knowledge and that the LDCs lack the necessary basis for producing and exporting these products, nonetheless it must be recognized that technological advantage is not permanent, but is more or less transitory. This is because technological information is eventually diffused and a breakthrough achieved in one country stimulates emulation in other countries. More significantly, with the lapse of time, a new product will pass through a "product cycle" in the course of which the technology becomes

more standardized and thus more readily transferable to an LDC.[8]

As a product passes through its "new" and "growth" phases into its "mature" phase, its production process tends to become more standardized, requiring less of skilled management and scientific and engineering know-how and making more use of relatively unskilled labor and standardized machinery that is easily obtainable and maintainable. The production process of a mature product may thus be more easily adopted by a newly developing country (hence the early introduction of the textile industry into industrializing countries).[9] Insofar as the mature products are standardized manufactures, their export marketing is also relatively easier because specifications and prices for these nondifferentiated products are easily available and their markets are highly price sensitive.[10]

It may be expected that eventually a given technological advantage will be dissipated and will give way to conventional factor-cost advantages, so that the new line or production may become more accessible to developing countries. Indicative of this has been the rapid advance in recent years of exports from some LDCs of what were formerly considered to be fairly sophisticated products: photographic and cinematographic supplies, watches and clocks, medical and

[6] H. B. Chenery and H. Hughes, "The International Division of Labor: The Case of Industry," in *Towards a New World Economy*, 5th European Conference of the Society for International Development, Rotterdam, 1972, p. 96.

[7] See Donald Keesing, "The Impact of Research and Development on United States Trade," *Journal of Political Economy*, February 1967, pp. 38–48; Raymond Vernon, "International Investment and International Trade in the Product Cycle," *Quarterly Journal of Economics*, May 1966, pp. 190–207; G. C. Hufbauer, *Synthetic Materials and the Theory of International Trade*, London, 1966; Richard R. Nelson, "A 'Diffusion' Model of International Productivity Differences in Manufacturing Industry," *American Economic Review*, December 1968, pp. 1219–48.

[8] UNCTAD secretariat, *The International Division of Labour and Developing Countries*, pp. 6–7.

[9] Seev Hirsch, *Location of Industry and International Competitiveness*, Oxford, 1967, pp. 24–9, 114–20. To the extent that mature products may have a comparatively high capital content, they will have an undesirable attribute. But the adverse effects of the higher capital charges may be offset by the fact that the employment of other scarce inputs can be minimized: the limited need of mature industries for scientists and engineers, their relative independence of external economies, and their adaptability to imported technologies allow the LDC to economize on resources which may be even scarcer than capital (p. 114).

[10] Ibid., pp. 49–50, 120.

pharmaceutical products, plastic materials, and telecommunication apparatus.[11]

If, however, exports of manufactures are to grow more rapidly and include a wider range of products, there will have to be changes in the trade policies of the developed importing countries and also changes in policies by LDCs.

Greater access to the markets of the developed countries requires policies of trade liberalization. Although the "average" nominal tariff rate on manufactured goods in the major industrial countries has been reduced considerably through successive rounds of trade negotiations, there is still a wide dispersion of tariffs over the range of manufactures and semimanufactures of potential interest to the LDCs, and in some cases even the nominal tariff rates are very high. There is still a strong degree of protectionism in the tariff structures of the major industrial nations: nominal tariff rates still tend to rise with the degree of labor-intensiveness; effective rates of protection tend to be much higher than nominal tariff rates; and effective tariffs on the products of special interest to developing countries are generally higher than those on other products, so that the tariff structure in the major developed countries remains strongly protective against imports of labor-intensive manufactured goods from the LDCs.

Even more restrictive are the nontariff barriers—especially quotas—placed on imports from LDCs. Textiles are, for example, the most important manufactured commodities now exported by the LDCs, but textiles confront severe quota limitations. The original negotiation of the Arrangement regarding International Trade in Cotton Textiles was based on the concept of "market disruption." Members of GATT may place "restraints" on particular categories of cotton textile imports if increased imports constitute "market disruption," defined as: (1) a sharp and substantial increase in imports of a

particular item; (2) import prices substantially below domestic prices in the importing country; and (3) serious damage to domestic producers or threat thereof. Not only does the invocation of "market disruption" allow severe restrictionist measures on textiles (the major export of more developing countries than any other class of manufactured goods), but it also sets an undesirable precedent for other manufactures that might receive similar treatment. No policies promoting manufactured exports will be effective if the concept of "market disruption" is invoked to restrict the entry of manufactures into advanced markets. This possibility is most contradictory to what might be expected from the granting of preferences to LDCs. If a preference system is qualified by the imposition of tariff quotas,[12] as in the EEC's scheme, and the U.S. Trade Act of 1974,[13] then the efficacy of preferences is clearly diminished. If developed countries are to be receptive to imports from LDCs, they must provide for adjustment assistance measures to move resources out of displaced industries in which the developed countries' comparative advantage has been lost into new, more efficient, higher technology product lines.[14] Market access on a broader front through trade liberalization can be more significant for LDC exports than preferences subject to safeguards.

After prolonged but unsuccessful attempts to secure really effective preferential treatment, the LDCs may be better advised to emphasize market access across the most

---

[11] UNCTAD secretariat, *The International Division of Labour and Developing Countries*, p. 7.

[12] Under a system of tariff quotas, the importing country specifies the quantity of imports of a product it is prepared to import at the preferential duty rate, with all imports greater than this amount being subject to the full most-favored-nation rate.

[13] See G. M. Meier, *Problems of Cooperation for Development*, New York, 1975, pp. 228–45.

[14] On trade adjustment assistance, see Charles R. Frank, Jr., *Adjustment Assistance: American Jobs and Trade with Developing Countries*, Overseas Development Council Paper No. 13, Washington, D.C., January 1973.

favored nation tariffs. The implementation of a general preference system has been only partial. While the United States accounts for the largest percentage of imports of manufactures from developing countries, its Trade Act of 1974 allows for preferences only if the imports from the preference-receiving country are less than 50 per cent of the total imports of the commodity or less than $25 million. A large percentage of dutiable imports from developing countries have also been excluded completely from preferential treatment in the schemes that have been adopted. Almost nine-tenths of imports now benefiting from a general system of preferences are imported under schemes which limit preferential entry by tariff quotas and ceilings. It follows that trade liberalization which would allow greater access to developed markets under the most-favored-nation tariffs can be more effective in stimulating the export of manufactures. This requires, however, some liberal safeguard system and adjustment assistance to raise the import-absorption capacity of the developed importing countries. The basic problem is that of reducing the adjustment costs entailed by a changing international division of labor in order that the real sources of comparative advantage might operate to change the structure of trade.

To achieve the same positive stimulating effects on exports from LDCs while avoiding these difficulties that could neutralize the effects of preferences, some alternatives to preferences have been proposed.[15] One proposal is that the developed countries establish targets for imports of manufactures from the LDCs, and that these targets should be raised every year. It could also be stipulated that if the import target were not fulfilled, the developed country would then offer more explicit aid instead. Another proposal is that, taking off from the Cotton

[15] See Harry G. Johnson, "United States Economic Policy Toward the Developing Countries," *Economic Development and Cultural Change*, April 1968, p. 372.

Textiles Arrangements but proceeding in the other direction toward more trade, the importing countries assure "market hospitality" to exports from the LDCs by offering the LDCs discriminatory global tariff quotas that would rise at a certain percentage per annum. It would be desirable that the quotas become sufficiently high as to be inoperative.

At the same time that the developed countries would be removing their trade restrictions, the LDCs would have to pursue policies to take advantage of the wider opportunities. As we have seen previously, import-substitution policies, together with inflation and an overvalued exchange rate, adversely affect the LDC's export sector. If new exports are to be supported, these unfavorable domestic policies must be corrected. It is necessary to reduce money costs relative to world prices, to control domestic inflation, and to correct the overvaluation of the exchange-rate. Taxation and public expenditure policies must also be conducive for switching resources from the domestic manufacturing sector into the export sector.

More positively, a number of export promotion measures can be undertaken by the developing country's government. The range of export incentives available to governments include systems whereby a company's imports are related to its export performance; devices to penalize firms failing to meet a given export target; rebates on export prices or other forms of subsidy on inputs used in industrial exports; and an exchange-rate that is more favorable to exports. It is especially important that these various policies be considered as a set so that they are as consistent and effective as possible: the positive effects derived from tax and other incentives, for instance, should not be offset by the negative effects of an overvalued exchange-rate. Some caution must be expressed, however, lest the export of manufactures be oversubsidized. As indicated in the previous chapter, it is necessary to avoid in the strategy of export-substitution industrialization the very weaknesses of the earlier strategy of import substitution (X.B.1).

Beyond removing the price distortions which discourage exports, and providing the positive export incentives which improve the profitability of exports, the governments of LDCs have a special function to play at the microlevel in furnishing services that the ordinary manufacturing firm cannot provide for itself in export markets. Thus, the undertaking of marketing activities may require government assistance. This may even involve subsidization of new exports, based on an "infant marketing" argument for assisting inexperienced firms to enter unfamiliar foreign markets during their periods of "export infancy." The provision of export credit for manufactures may also require the government to mobilize financial resources for export finance and to develop new instruments and methods for financing the longer-term credit arrangements required for the financing of manufactured exports. Further, as an integral part of export credit, risk insurance may require government or joint government-private action in initiating insurance agencies that can cover the commercial and transfer risks involved in breaking into new export markets. The government might also undertake research and promote technological changes to improve the quality of production and reduce the manufacturing costs of exports.

The largest markets for the export of manufactures are, of course, in the more developed countries, but there is still considerable scope for trade among the LDCs. Indeed, the range and quality of manufactures from an LDC may initially be most suitable for export to another LDC rather than to an advanced industrial nation. If LDCs were to move toward a product mix that emphasized technologically simpler and more labor-intensive products, the scope for trade would increase among the LDCs themselves. Given the presently low volume of trade in manufactures among the LDCs as a group, there should be considerable potential for an expansion of such trade provided the LDCs remove their own trade barriers against each other's manufactured exports. Moreover, the case for regional preferential trading arrangements among a group of LDCs is stronger on economic efficiency grounds than it is for a general preferential system. If we begin with the actual situation of LDCs attempting to industrialize via import substitution, then the tariff cuts among the LDCs would in fact be permitting trade creation among the LDCs, as compared with the situation in which they would have industrialized behind national tariff walls.[16] Preferential trading arrangements among LDCs should therefore be encouraged as a significant means of stimulating manufactured exports from some of the developing countries.

[16] Jagdish Bhagwati, "Trade Liberalization Among LDCs, Trade Theory and GATT Rules," in J. N. Wolfe (ed.), *Value, Capital, and Growth*, Edinburgh, 1968, p. 35.

XI.E. REGIONAL INTEGRATION
AND DEVELOPMENT—NOTE

Some of the questions raised above—how to increase the gains from trade, stimulate exports, stabilize export proceeds—are now receiving increasing attention in the context of regional economic integration. Various degrees of integration are possible, but most interest centers on the potential role of customs unions and free trade areas. While both a customs union and free trade area provide for free trade among the member countries, a customs union also adopts a common external tariff.

At a level less general than a customs union or free trade association, regional integration might be directed simply toward "sectoral integration"—that is, the removal of trade restrictions on only a selected list of commodities, or the treatment of the problems of some one industry as a whole on a regional basis.

Beyond free trade in goods, a more comprehensive economic union might allow for the free movement of factors of production, a common monetary system, and the coordination of economic policies among the member countries. This is still unrealistic to expect for developing countries, and we shall therefore be concerned here with only the implications of free trade in goods.

Even though practical results are as yet only modest, there have been several efforts to secure regional integration among developing countries—notably the Latin American Free Trade Area (LAFTA), Central American Common Market, East-African Common Market, the Andean Group, and the Caribbean Free Trade Area Association (CARIFTA).

As a basis for appraising specific proposals, we consider in this Note the benefits that might be derived from economic groupings among developing countries and the difficulties that are likely to be encountered in their formation.

Advocates of an economic union believe that its formation will accelerate the development of the member countries by (a) stimulating the establishment and expansion of manufacturing industries on a more rational basis, (b) increasing the gains from trade, and (c) providing benefits from intensified competition.

In many developing countries import requirements are growing rapidly, but the export-based capacity to import is insufficient to allow an unrestricted demand for imports. To meet the need for imports of essential materials and capital goods in face of a deficiency in foreign exchange, many countries have adopted a policy of deliberate import substitution in consumer goods. When each country restricted its imports, however, and attempted to substitute home production, industrialization became unduly compartmentalized, and the uneconomic multiplication of import-competing industries was wasteful. In contrast, if manufacturing industry can be encouraged in the context of a customs union or free trade area, it may attain a higher level of productivity than resulted from industrial protection in each country. Greater specialization within the region can increase the share of exports and imports in manufacturing and reduce the excessive number of products manufactured in an excessive number of protected firms.

To reach an efficient scale of output, a modern manufacturing plant may have to produce a larger output than the low level of home demand in a single underdeveloped country can absorb. By pooling markets through the removal of internal trade barriers, a free trade union might thus provide a sufficiently wide export market to make economies of scale realizable. Within a union, secondary industry can become more efficient as specialization occurs in the member country that acquires a comparative advantage. At the same time, the other constituent countries may now replace their imported manufactures from outside the union and thereby be able to spend a higher proportion of their foreign exchange on outside imports that are essential but cannot be produced efficiently within the union. A more rational pattern of production and trade within the region may therefore be an important result of integration.

The extension of the market, together with the inducement to get behind the external tariff wall, may also be particularly effective in attracting direct private foreign investment in manufacturing. And over time, there is the further possibility that new industries can become increasingly competitive on world markets and eventually be able to export manufactured goods to nonmember countries. But this depends first on establishing a sufficiently wide market within the union to allow operation of a manufacturing industry on a large enough scale.

An expansion of trade among the member countries is also expected to result from the removal of trade barriers. If this takes the form of replacing high-cost producers within the region by lower-cost producers, the effect is one of "trade creation."[1] The gains from trade are then increased, since the international division of labor is improved as resources shift into more efficient production. On the other hand, some of the intra-union trade may merely replace trade that formerly occurred between members and nonmembers. When the formation of an economic union has this "trade-diverting" effect, the international division of labor will be worsened if the outside source of supply is actually a low-cost source, and its product now becomes higher priced within the union because of the external tariff. In this case,

there is an uneconomic diversion of output from the low-cost outside source to the high-cost supplier within the union, and the gains from trade are diminished.

In considering whether trade creation or trade diversion is likely to dominate in a particular union, we have to take into account the preunion level of tariff rates among the members, the level of the post-union external tariff compared with the pre-union tariff levels of each member country, the elasticities of demand for the imports on which duties are reduced, and the elasticities of supply of exports from the members and foreign sources. Conditions are more propitious for trade creation when each member's preunion duties are high on the others' products, the members are initially similar in the products they produce but different in the pattern of relative prices at which they produce them, the external tariff of the union is low compared with the preunion tariff levels of the members, and the production within the union of commodities that are substitutes for outside imports can be undertaken at a lower cost.

The formation of a free trade union might also result in an improvement—or at least the forestalling of a deterioration—in the region's commodity terms of trade. This is possible if there is a reduction in the supply of exports from the union, or the demand by members of the union is reduced for imports from outside, or the bargaining power of the members in trade negotiations is strengthened. But unless the members of the union are the chief suppliers on the world market or constitute a large part of the world market for their imports, they are unlikely to be able to exercise sufficient monopolistic or monopsonistic power to influence their terms of trade by raising duties on their trade with the outside world or by inducing outsiders to supply their goods more cheaply. Moreover, when free trade is confined only to the region, there is the risk of retaliation through the formation of other economic blocs. A union may thereby inhibit the realization of the more extensive

[1] Jacob Viner, *The Customs Union Issue*, New York, 1950, pp. 48–52.

gains from the "universal" approach to free trade.

Finally, regional integration might be beneficial in encouraging competition among the member countries. Technical efficiency in existing industries might then be improved as marginal firms are forced to reduce their costs, resources are reallocated from less efficient to more efficient firms, and monopolies that had previously been established behind tariff walls are no longer in a sheltered position. Further, the stimulation of competition within each country may yield not only a better utilization of given resources, but may also raise the rate of growth of productive resources. This may result from stronger incentives to adopt new methods of production, to replace obsolete equipment more rapidly, and to innovate more rapidly with more and better investment.[2]

In practice, however, a number of objections have been raised against proposals for regional integration, and actual negotiations have encountered serious difficulties. As is true for a union among even advanced countries, political problems take precedence, nations will guard against a sacrifice of their sovereignty, and the administration of the union may be extremely complex. For underdeveloped countries, these problems tend to be especially acute since many have only recently gained political independence, newly established national governments may be excessively concerned with their own national interests and needs, and the administrative requirements may be beyond their present capacity. Aside from the political and administrative difficulties, there are also several economic objections to a union.

To begin with, it may be argued that the case for an economic union is in reality weak when the constituent countries have not yet established many industries. Limitations on the supply side may be more of a deterrent to the creation of an industry than is the narrow market on the side of demand. If production conditions do not also improve, the mere extension of the consumer market will not be sufficient to create industries. Moreover, when manufacturing industry is only at a rudimentary stage in the member countries, there is not much scope for eliminating high-cost manufacturers within the region. Nor is there much scope for realizing the benefits of increased competition when there are not yet similar ranges of rival products, produced under different cost conditions, in the several member nations. A union will not cause substantial improvement in the utilization of resources unless industries have already been established but need wider markets than the national economy can provide for the realization of economies of scale, and the member countries have been protecting the same kinds of industry, but have markedly different ratios of factor-efficiency in these industries to factor-efficiency in nonprotected branches of production.

It has been pointed out that the case for a union is strongest among countries that have little foreign trade in proportion to their domestic production, but conduct a high proportion of their foreign trade with one another.[3] When these conditions prevail, there is less possibility for introducing, within each member country, a distortion of the price relation between goods from other member countries and goods from outside the union, and more of a possibility for eliminating any distortion by tariffs of the price-relations between domestic goods and imports from other member countries. There is therefore greater likelihood that the union will improve the use of resources and raise real income.

A union among underdeveloped countries, however, is unlikely to conform to these conditions. The ratio of foreign trade to domestic production is generally high for

[2] See Paul Streeten, *Economic Integration,* second ed., Leyden, 1964, pp. 26–7.

[3] R. G. Lipsey, "The Theory of Customs Unions: A General Survey," *Economic Journal,* September 1960, pp. 507–9. This conclusion rests, however, on the assumption that there are no productive economies of large scale.

these countries, and the actual volume of intraregional trade is normally only a small proportion of the region's total foreign trade. The gain from regional integration would therefore be small. The basic difficulty is that, with existing trade patterns, the formation of a union is likely to cause a considerable amount of wasteful "trade diversion." Over the longer run, comparative costs and trade patterns may change, and economies of scale may give rise to competitive advantages as development proceeds, so that the scope for "trade creation" will become greater within the union. But the immediate gain is small, and the longer-run prospects for the creation of new trade are not likely to influence current decisions to join a union.

The case for regional preferential trading arrangements is stronger than that for a general preference scheme if the regional arrangement allows the avoidance of trade diversion. GATT (Article 24) insists that tariffs among members of a customs union or free trade area be reduced to zero; it can be demonstrated, however, that in some cases, less trade diversion will result if the members reduce their internal tariffs below the external tariff but not necessarily to zero.[4] In this respect, a partial preferential arrangement has merit.

Besides the possibility of "trade diversion," other undesirable consequences may result from a union. The member countries are unlikely to benefit equally, and some members may feel that others are gaining at their expense. A country may have a strong comparative advantage in only primary products and will sell to other members only goods that it could as readily export to outside countries. At the same time, the location of manufacturing industry and ancillary activities may become localized within one member country, and "polarization" results. Other members may then contend that if they too had been able to adopt tariff pro-

tection against their partners, they would have also been able to attract industry. A nonindustrialized member country may further complain that in buying from an industrialized partner, instead of importing from the outside, it is losing revenue equal to the duty on outside manufactures. And, with a common external tariff, member countries no longer have the discretionary power to use variations in the tariff for the purpose of adjusting their national revenues to their own requirements. The internal strains that arise from uneven development among the member countries may thus make it extremely difficult to preserve a regional grouping. As one study states,

Of the many difficulties which stand in the way of the formation and effective operation of economic integration arrangements among less developed countries, perhaps the most difficult and contentious centres upon the equitable distribution of their costs and benefits. Whatever may be the situation in groupings of advanced countries, among less developed countries an equitable distribution of costs and benefits is not something which can generally be relied upon to emerge spontaneously, in the course of the integration of national markets. But if equity is not assured, the operation of existing groupings may easily be rendered ineffective or in extreme cases, they may collapse. The experience of the last few years demonstrates that this is not a remote possibility. . . . The operation of the forces making for polarization between countries may in practice be limited if there are factors at work which produce growth centres in each participating country. These include such influences as the existence of several concentrations of fixed natural resources which may each serve as a basis for industrial complexes; distribution costs; and finally the influence of public policy operating through expenditure on infrastructure, etc. Apart from these influences, the dissemination of the benefits of integration in a common market will depend on the so-called spread or trickle-down effects. The most important of

[4] Ibid., pp. 506–7; W. M. Corden, *Recent Developments in the Theory of International Trade*, Princeton, 1965, p. 54.

these is the increase of the developing country's purchases from the others which may be expected to take place if the economies are complementary.

Such influences may, in favourable circumstances, be sufficiently powerful to bring about an acceptable distribution of the costs and benefits within a common market. So far as concerns the process of economic development within national boundaries however, the evidence seems to suggest that, in less developed countries, the process of economic growth generates increasingly large inter-regional differentials and that it is only in advanced countries that the disequilibrating tendencies are sufficiently reduced in their operation to produce a tendency to convergence.[5]

It may be possible for the union to correct some of the inequalities through a system of public finance transfers among members,[6] a regional development bank, encouragement of free factor movements, regional policies for the location of industry, the pooling of overhead costs of public services, or coordination of development policies. But unless the union is strong enough to adopt these other measures and distribute the gains more evenly, its stability may be threatened.[7]

As stated in an UNCTAD study of economic integration among developing countries,

it would appear that the problem of ensuring an equitable distribution of the benefits of integration is more difficult to solve as between developing than as between developed

countries. No doubt, the principle that countries in unequal situations should not be treated equally is as valid in relations between developing countries as it should be in those between developing and developed countries. But for objective and subjective reasons, developing countries would seem to have even more difficulties in acting upon this principle in their mutual relations. Not only are the differences between developing countries within one region often more pronounced than those between developed countries in the same region; in addition, inasmuch as the specific guarantees which the weaker partner understandably wants before agreeing to integration imply a transfer of resources or other apparent sacrifices by the more advanced partner countries, the latter have at their disposal comparatively smaller resources for such measures than are available to developed countries in a similar process. Above all, these more advanced developing countries often have, within their own borders, large backward areas whose level of development is as low as that of their less advanced partners, and hence it is politically difficult for them to mobilize the resources for dealing with what appears to be another country's problem; in those cases, national integration might appear to deserve priority, and any regional scheme would have to be conceived in such a manner as not to jeopardize action in the national framework. Therefore, for a scheme to be politically negotiable, both the less advanced and the more advanced partner countries must have the feeling that each would gain concrete benefits from it.[8]

We may conclude that while there are potential benefits to be derived from an economic union, especially over the longer run, the immediate gains should not be overestimated and due attention must be given to the possible undesirable consequences. The most important lesson to be learned from

[5] United Nations, *Current Problems of Economic Integration, Fiscal Compensation and the Distribution of Benefits in Economic Groupings of Developing Countries*, New York, 1971 (Report prepared by Peter Robson), pp. 1 and 4.

[6] For various measures of fiscal compensation, see Ibid., Chap. 5.

[7] For a perceptive analysis of an actual case, see W. T. Newlyn, "Gains and Losses in the East-African Common Market," *Yorkshire Bulletin of Economic and Social Research*, November 1965, pp. 132–8.

[8] UNCTAD secretariat, *Trade Expansion and Economic Integration Among Developing Countries*, New York, 1967, p. 21.

efforts at regional integration is that if the potential benefits of integration are to be fully realized, the regional association must be a strong one and must be capable of coordinating trade policies, including exchange-rate policy, among the member countries, and must provide some means for an equitable distribution of the costs and benefits among members. Most proposals for regional integration do not yet show promise of sufficient cohesion and policy coordination.

Although a comprehensive form of free trade area or full customs union may not yet be practicable for most of the developing countries, there are still substantial advantages that can be derived from more ad hoc functional types of regional cooperation short of comprehensive integration. Measures of "partial integration" may help to avoid the costs of "micro-states" and national development along compartmentalized lines. In particular, the complementary development of specific industries through a regional investment policy has considerable potential. The realization of markets of sufficient size, avoidance of duplication, and better location of projects might result. There are a few outstanding examples of multinational investment projects, and there should be scope for many more.

It is, however, difficult to formulate project evaluation criteria for a region, and more analysis of this problem is required before there can be policy implementation. Rosenstein-Rodan states the problem succinctly:

Modern economic theory can formulate project evaluation criteria in terms of national welfare which include not only the desirable rate of growth but also other social objectives like income distribution. What can be formulated for a nation is more difficult for a conglomeration of nations for two reasons; (a) because social welfare functions of different nations may be different. One country may prefer to have a 5 per cent rate of growth instead of a possible 6 per cent for the sake of better income redistribution and fuller employment in the next one or two five-year periods. Another country may prefer to have a 6 per cent rate of growth even at the expense of less social progress and less employment in the immediate future for the sake of having more employment at a higher level of income in the second decade. (b) Are we to maximize welfare for the Latin American community as a whole, which might imply considerable emigration and a lower standard of living in some countries or do we assume that each nation should maximize its own welfare? In the first case, incidentally, international corporations and Latin American multinational corporations might be efficient instruments for the maximization of output of Latin America as a whole but would create conflicts with the welfare objectives of some countries. The Latin American social welfare function is not based on the maximization of output for Latin America as a whole. Measures agreed upon in favor of less developed areas . . . imply an agreement that the maximization for the Latin American community as a whole is to be sacrificed for the sake of a better (how much?) income distribution between nations, but without quantifying the how much we are not able to build up an operational Latin American social welfare function.

The application of different criteria to multinational and integration projects is not easy. Multinational and integration projects are two different concepts which need not coincide. It is difficult moreover to give a logically neat definition of integration projects even if we confined ourselves to the narrower concept of "project" and not to the wider integration policy which will influence the constellation, selection and location of many projects.[9]

It is also possible for more to be accomplished by way of partial liberalization of regional trade for certain products or sec-

[9] See Paul N. Rosenstein-Rodan, "Multinational Investment in the Framework of Latin American Integration," in *Multinational Investment, Public and Private, in the Economic Development and Integration of Latin America*, Round-Table, Inter-American Bank, Bogotá, April 1968, pp. 33–40.

tors. Countries might identify specific sectors or individual products for which they could commit themselves not to erect trade barriers with each other. Products that are not yet fabricated in a particular group—that is, new products for the region—might be singled out as a particularly suitable object of such a commitment, especially if supplemented by some commitments regarding a regional investment policy. The Andean Group, for instance, established in 1972 its first sectoral program for the development of metalworking products by providing shared production assignments among the members (Bolivia, Chile, Colombia, Ecuador, Peru, Venezuela), free access to the member markets, a common external tariff, and common credit, fiscal, and administrative policies.

A regional agreement might also be effective in bargaining over the entry of foreign investment and the import of technology into the region. Instead of individual countries having to engage in their own bargaining with the foreign investor or foreign supplier of technology, a regional bargaining unit may have more power and may be able to harmonize conditions of entry to greater advantage for the recipient members. Thus again, for example, the Commission of the Cartagena Agreement for the Andean Group is directed to "establish an information and control system with respect to the prices of intermediate products furnished by the suppliers of technology or foreign capital; [and to] authorize licensing agreements for the use of imported technology and the exploitation of trademarks and patents."[10] By the

Andean Foreign Investment Code, member countries are prohibited from concluding agreements to the transfer of foreign technology or to patents if the agreements oblige the recipient country to purchase capital goods, intermediate products, or forms of technology from an exclusive source; or to fix the selling or resale price of the products manufactured on the basis of the technology in question; or to subscribe to other practices that restrict the volume of production, the use of competing technologies, or the freedom to export products manufactured on the basis of the technology in question. Restrictive clauses are also prohibited for licensing agreements.

Finally, an important area of regional cooperation—and one that could be used to support other areas—is that of channeling aid through regional integration banks or development corporations. The more this is done, the more influential might the regional institutions be in promoting the regional investment policies and regional trade liberalization policies that are necessary to avoid uncoordinated duplicative national development policies.

Until the risks of joining a free trade union are diminished, this less ambitious approach involving efforts to secure sectoral integration may be the most feasible alternative. Even though a customs union may be the ultimate objective, it will still be a sizeable accomplishment in the immediate future to secure the mutually supporting measures of regional investment policies, regional trade liberalization, and regional aid institutions.

---

[10] Decision No. 24 of the Commission of the Cartagena Agreement, creating a Common Regulation for Foreign Investment and Transfer of Technology.

XI. SELECT BIBLIOGRAPHY

1. General analytical and policy-oriented studies of the trade problems of LDCs are: H. G. Johnson, *Economic Policies Toward Less Developed Countries*, Washington, D.C., 1967; G. M. Meier, *The International Economics of Development*, New York, 1968 (with specialized bibliography); R. F. Harrod and D. Hague (eds.), *International Trade Theory in a Developing World*, New York, 1963; J. D. Theberge (ed.), *Economics of Trade and Development*, New York, 1968; G. K. Helleiner, *International Trade and Economic Development*, London, 1972; Ragnar Nurkse, *Patterns of Trade and Development*, Stockholm, 1959; S. B. Linder, *Trade and Trade Policy for Development*, New York, 1967.

2. The following readings offer various interpretations of the potentials and limitations of development-through-trade: R. E. Baldwin, "Patterns of Development in Newly Settled Regions," *Manchester School*, May 1956; ____, "Export Technology and Development from a Subsistence Level," *EJ*, March 1963; P. A. Baran, "On the Political Economy of Backwardness," *Manchester School*, January 1952; K. Berrill, "International Trade and the Rate of Economic Growth," *Economic History Review*, April 1960; J. Bhagwati, "Immiserizing Growth: A Geometrical Note," *Review of Economic Studies*, June 1958; ____, "Growth, Terms of Trade, and Comparative Advantage," *Economia Internazionale*, August 1959; ____, "Economic Development and International Trade," *Pakistan Economic Journal*, December 1959; H. B. Chenery, "Comparative Advantage and Development Policy," *AER*, March 1961; G. Haberler, *International Trade and Economic Development*, Cairo, 1959; J. R. Hicks, *Essays in World Economics*, Oxford, 1959, Chap. 8; H. G. Johnson, *International Trade and Economic Growth*, Cambridge, 1958, Chap. 3; ____, "Economic Development and International Trade," *Pakistan Economic Journal*, December 1959; C. P. Kindleberger, "Foreign Trade and Economic Growth: Lessons from Britain and France, 1850 to 1931," *Economic History Review*, December 1961; J. V. Levin, *The Export Economies*, Cambridge, 1960; A. N. McLeod, "Trade and Investment in Underdeveloped Areas: A Comment," *AER*, June 1951; Hla Myint, "The Gains from International Trade and the Backward Countries," *Review of Economic Studies*, Vol. 22, No. 58, 1954–55; ____, "The 'Classical Theory' of International Trade and the Underdeveloped Countries," *EJ*, June 1958; ____, *Economics of the Developing Countries*, London, 1964, Chaps. 2–5; ____, "Inward and Outward-Looking Countries of Southeast Asia," *Malayan Economic Review*, April 1967; G. Myrdal, *Rich Lands and Poor*, New York, 1957; R. Nurkse, "Some International Aspects of the Problem of Economic Development," *AER*, May 1952; ____, *Patterns of Trade and Development*, Stockholm, 1956; ____, "International Trade Theory and Development Policy," in H. S. Ellis (ed.), *Economic Development for Latin America*, New York, 1961; H. W. Singer, "The Distribution of Gains Between Investing and Borrowing Countries," *AER*, May 1950; Eric Clayton, "A Note on the Alien Enclave and Development," *East African Economics Review*, June 1963; Margaret G. De Vries, "Trade and Exchange Policy and Economic Development," *OEP*, March 1966 (with extensive bibliography); W. A. Lewis, *Aspects of Tropical Trade 1883–1965*, Stockholm, 1969; T. B. Birnberg and S. A. Resnick, *Colonial Development: An Econometric Study*, New Haven, 1975; I. Kravis, "Trade as a Handmaiden of Growth," *EJ*, December 1970.

Studies that emphasize features of imperialism or "exploitation" are: R. Rhodes (ed.), *Imperialism and Underdevelopment*, New York, 1970; H. Magdoff, *The Age of Imperialism*, New York, 1969; K. Boulding and T. Mukerjee (eds.), *Economic Imperialism*, Ann Arbor, 1972; P. A. Baran, *The Political Economy of Growth*, New York, 1962, Chaps. 6–8; M. Dobb, *Political Economy and Capitalism*, London, 1940, Chap. 7; E. Mandel, *Marxist Economic Theory*, Vol. 2, New York, 1968, Chap. 13; K. T. Fann and D. C. Hodges (eds.), *Readings in U.S. Imperialism*, Boston, 1971; Walter Rodney, *How Europe Underdeveloped Africa*, London, 1972; D. S. Landes, "Some Thoughts on the Nature of Economic Imperialism," *Journal of Economic History*, December 1961; A. Emmanuel, *Unequal Exchange*, New York, 1972; S. Hymer and S. Resnick, "International Trade and Uneven Development," in J. Bhagwati (ed.), *Trade, Balance of Payments, and Growth*, Amsterdam, 1971; B. J. Cohen, *The Question of Imperialism*, New York, 1973.

The literature on dependency, as listed in Chapter II above, is also relevant. See also, issue on "Dependency and Foreign Domination in the Third World," *Review of Radical Political Economics*, Spring 1972; R. Rhodes, "Bibliography on Studying Imperialism," ibid., Spring 1971.

3. Three major projects investigate problems of import-substitution: the OECD series of country studies, with summary volume by I. M. D. Little, T. Scitovsky, and M. Scott, *Industry and Trade in Some Developing Countries*, London, 1970; Bela Balassa and associates, *The Structure of Protection in Developing Countries*, Baltimore, 1971; J. Bhagwati and A. O. Krueger, "Exchange Control Liberalization and Economic Development," *AER*, May 1973, an introduction to the National Bureau of Economic Research Conference Series on Foreign Trade Regimes and Economic Development (10 proposed country volumes).

4. The changing international division of labor and potentials for export substitution are examined in: Donald Keesing, "Outward-Looking Policies and Economic Development," *EJ*, June 1967; H. B. Lary, *Imports of Manufactures from Less Developed Countries*, New York, 1968; H. G. Johnson, "The Theory of Effective Protection and Preferences," *Economica*, May 1969; Alfred Maizels, *Exports and Economic Growth of Developing Countries*, Cambridge, 1968; Bela Balassa, "Growth Strategies in Semi-Industrial Countries," *QJE*, February 1970; _____, "Reforming the System of Incentives in Developing Countries," *WD*, June 1975; B. I. Cohen and D. G. Sisler, "Exports of Developing Countries in the 1960s," *RES*, November 1971; Helen Hughes (ed.), *Propsects for Partnership: Industrialization and Trade Policies in 1960s*, Baltimore, 1973; A. H. M. Mahfuzur Rahman, *Exports of Manufactures from Developing Countries*, Rotterdam, 1973; R. C. Porter and C. P. Staelin, "The Rediscovery of Exports by the Third World," *Foreign Trade Review*, January 1972; T. Murray, "How Helpful is the Generalized System of Preferences to Developing Countries?" *EJ*, June 1973; H. Giersch (ed.), *The Changing International Division of Labour, Problems and Perspectives*, Kiel, 1974; R. Codoni, *The International Division of Labor in View of the Second Development Decade*, Zurich, 1974.

5. The following may be consulted for a more intensive consideration of regional economic integration as a means of accelerating development: B. Balassa, *The Theory of Economic Integration*, Homewood, 1961; F. Andic and D. Dosser, *Theory of Economic Integration for Developing Countries*, London, 1971; J. B. Nugent, *Economic Integration in Central America*, Baltimore, 1974; S. Dell, "Economic Integration and the American

Example," *EJ*, March 1959; _____ *Trade Blocs and Common Markets*, New York, 1963, Chaps. 5, 6; _____ *A Latin American Common Market?*, New York, 1966; R. F. Harrod, "Economic Development and Asian Regional Cooperation," *Pakistan Development Review*, Spring 1962; H. G. Johnson, "The Economic Theory of Customs Union," *Pakistan Economic Journal*, March 1960; T. Scitovsky, "International Trade and Economic Integration as a Means of Overcoming the Disadvantages of a Small Nation," in E. A. G. Robinson (ed.), *Economic Consequences of the Size of Nations*, New York, 1960; M. S. Wionczek (ed.), *Latin American Economic Integration*, New York, 1966; A. Hazlewood (ed.), *African Integration and Disintegration*, London, 1967; R. H. Green and Ann Seidman, *Unity or Poverty? The Economics of Pan-Africanism*, London, 1968; D. C. Mead, "The Distribution of Gains in Customs Unions Between Developing Countries," *Kyklos*, Vol. 21, No. 4, 1968; W. T. Newlyn, "Gains and Losses in the East African Common Market," *Yorkshire Bulletin of Economic and Social Research*, November 1965; David Morawetz, *The Andean Group*, Cambridge, 1974.

CHAPTER XII

Development Planning and Policymaking

All the preceding chapters have had some relevance for development planning, and we have already related specific aspects of development planning to several substantive problems. But we now want to examine the nature and scope of development planning in a more integrated fashion. By appraising the effectiveness of development planning in light of the development record and the analyses and policy proposals that have emerged in preceding chapters, this final chapter may also serve as a summary evaluation of the leading issues in development economics.

Just beneath the surface of practically all the preceding analyses has been the issue of planning versus the price system. We now focus directly on this, with some of the materials in this chapter arguing against the effectiveness of the price system for attaining the objectives of development. The market mechanism is criticized as being either ineffective, unreliable, or irrelevant for the problems now encountered by developing nations. It is contended that the price system exists in only a rudimentary form in many of the LDCs and that market forces are too weak to accomplish the changes needed for accelerated development. Even a fairly well-defined price system may be considered unreliable, it is claimed, when market prices of goods and factors are not a true reflection of the opportunity costs to society. Above all, it is contended that the price system must be superseded insofar as the determination of the amount and composition of investment are too important to be left to a multitude of individual investment decisions, and the tasks of the economy entail large structural changes over a long period ahead instead of simply marginal adjustments in the present period.

On the other hand, it can be argued that the objections to the market system are relatively unimportant compared with the essential functions of the market and that the disadvantages of detailed planning by a central authority are far more serious than the deficiencies of the market system. The market is extremely valuable in the context of development as an administrative instrument that is relatively cheap to operate (XII.A.2). For this reason and others outlined in XII.A, development policy might be better devoted to improving and strengthening the market system than to supplanting the market with detailed administrative controls.

To the extent, however, that there has been a large measure of government direction over the rate and pattern of development, we should appraise the techniques and applicability of development planning. Taken together, the materials in sections XII.B and XII.C indicate the nature of the available programming techniques, some operational problems, and the significance of their effects in practice. Although section XII.B considers general principles of model building and provides some introduction to the theory of development planning, it does not pretend to offer a detailed exposition of modeling techniques. Development programming has become a specialized subject in its own right, requiring more familiarity with mathematical and econometric techniques than can be provided here. We also slight the administrative aspects of development planning, leaving for more specialized courses in public administration or development management the consideration of the organizational problems of policy implementation.

We are, however, most interested in proceeding beyond the theory of development to a review of planning practice in order to distinguish between the techniques discussed in development literature and those that have actually been used in various countries. Although planning models have been useful in improving the formulation of development plans, their application is still beset with practical difficulties, and it is essential to recognize their possible abuse in development planning.

The Note in section XII.D submits some general conclusions on the present state of development planning and the modifications necessary to improve its future effectiveness. This Note and other selections in this chapter may appear critical of specific plans, but it should be realized that there can be considerable value to the planning process itself. The active process of planning may indeed be of more benefit than the actual plan, for it can demonstrate the need for the collection and use of more empirical information, promote the dissemination of knowledge, clarify objectives and choices, and indicate the political and administrative preconditions necessary for implementing policies.

What ultimately matters is the benefit that can come from a dialogue between the modelbuilder and policymaker. While a model cannot provide a final answer, it can illuminate choices and indicate to the policymaker the consequences of alternative decisions. The implementation of mathematical planning is, however, dependent on the degree of maturity of nonmathematical planning. It is only clear what aims are worth striving for when there has already been established an organized institutional, nonmathematical form of planning.

In a single model only a few hundred relationships and constraints can be considered. But people working in the central planning agencies and lower-level institutions and enterprises "sense" hundreds of thousands of further constraints and relations, and they can give expression to these in their own estimates. Mathematical planning will develop successfully only when it develops as one element of well-prepared and well-oriented institutional planning, connected by many threads with real economic life in developing countries.[1]

[1] Janos Kornai, "Models and Policy: The Dialogue between Model Builder and Planner," in C. R. Blitzer et al., *Economy-Wide Models and Development Planning*, New York, 1975, Chap. 2.

XII.A. PLANNING AND THE MARKET

XII.A.1. The Flaw in the Mechanism of Market Forces*

The free and unimpeded mechanism of market forces would lead to a maximum national income according to the liberal classical doctrine. Disregarding an ethical value-judgment about personal income distribution and special cases of increasing returns to scale the maximum would also be an optimum national income. Any conscious deliberate active economic policy designed to influence the amount and the composition of investment could not, according to this school, raise national income in the long run. It is the contention of this paper that the opposite is true, that an economic policy designed to influence the amount and composition of investment can raise the rate of economic growth and increase national income.

Maximization of national income would be reached, according to the "liberal" school, by the working of the mechanism of supply and demand on assumption of competitive conditions and of small changes per unit of time, in four stages or "equilibria": (1) allocation of given stock of consumers' goods, (2) allocation of production on assumption of given stock of equipment, land, and labor, (3) allocation of investment on assumption of given stock of labor, land and capital. A fourth equilibrium condition is provided by Say's law.

*From Paul N. Rosenstein-Rodan, "Programming in Theory and in Italian Practice," in Massachusetts Institute of Technology, Center for International Studies, *Investment Criteria and Economic Growth*, Cambridge, 1955; Asia Publishing House, Bombay, 1961, pp. 19–22. Reprinted by permission.

It is true that the price mechanism works perfectly under those assumptions in the first stage, i.e., in allocation of given stocks of consumers' goods. It works less perfectly, but tolerably well, in the second stage, when we replace the assumption of given stocks of consumers' goods by flows of supply of these goods from given stocks of equipment, raw materials, and labor.

The price mechanism does not work in this sense, however, in the third equilibrium when we drop the assumption of given fixed capital and assume that the amount and composition of investment is to be determined by a multitude of individual investment decisions.

The individual investment decision may lead to nonoptimum allocation of resources for the following reasons:

a. The investor maximizes the private, not the social net marginal product. External economies are not sufficiently exploited. Complementarity of industries is so great that simultaneous inducement rather than hope for autonomous coincidence of investment is called for.

b. The lifetime of equipment is long (say ten years) so that the investor's foresight is likely to be more imperfect than that of the buyer and seller or of the producer. The individual investor's risk may be higher than that confronting an over-all investment program. The costs of an erroneous investment decision are high; punishment in the form of loss of capital afflicts not only the investor but also the national economy.

c. Because of the indivisibility (lumpiness) of capital, large rather than small changes are involved. Yet the price-mechanism works perfectly only under the assumption of small changes.

d. Capital markets though often well organized are notoriously imperfect markets, governed not only by prices but also by institutional or traditional rationing quotas.

The investment theory is indeed the weakest link in the "liberal" theory.

It is finally recognized even by the strongest advocates of a free economy that an equilibrium between aggregate demand and aggregate supply (i.e., the dynamic monetary equilibrium) cannot itself be ensured by trusting to the automatic responses of a free economy. This task can only be discharged by a deliberate policy. Without an equilibrium of aggregate demand and aggregate supply, however, prices cease to be reliable parameters of choice and the price mechanism breaks down.

The automatic responses of the market economy do not ensure an optimum allocation in two out of four markets. They allocate efficiently stocks of consumers' goods, and supplies of these goods flowing from stocks of equipment, but they do not function efficiently in the fields of investment and monetary equilibrium.

Programming is just another word for rational, deliberate, consistent, and coordinated economic policy. It is only spelling out explicitly what was always attempted implicitly in any monetary (fiscal and commercial) policy. Like Mr. Jourdain who talked prose all his life, programming at least in the field of monetary policy was always practiced, though it used shorthand rules of thumb or the "practical man's flairs, hunches, instincts and insights" rather than fully spelled out "White Papers" on output and employment. Neutral Government is as unrealistic an assumption as Neutral Money.

Monetary (fiscal and commercial) policy is a form of programming using indirect means for the achievement of its aims and targets. In its first pre-Wicksellian stage its only aim was equilibrium between aggregate demand and aggregate supply without distin-

guishing too clearly between investment and consumption. It became more purposeful in its second post-Wicksellian stage differentiating between and choosing its impact effects on various sectors of national income. In its third post-Keynesian stage it aims not only at *a* monetary equilibrium but at one which assures full employment and more and more also one (not necessarily the same) which assures the optimum rate of growth. In this third stage programming concerns not only the amount but also the composition of investment.

The *aim* of programming is to assure the maximum national income through time. For this purpose it tries to maximize the amount and to optimize the composition of investment. The *means* employed may be either indirect (monetary, fiscal and commercial policy as well as providing information on economic trends besides other incentives and disincentives) or direct (public investment). Even if no direct means were to be employed programming would be necessary in order to inform investors of short- and long-run trends, notably of intersectoral demands resulting from complementarity of industries (revealed by a periodically revised input-output table) and of indirect effects of investment on future demand of domestic, imported, or so far exported goods. Such information might guide and favorably influence the composition of investment.

The need for an active economic policy, even if it were to employ only indirect means, can hardly be denied. Agreement on this point may conceal, however, two different conceptions. The "liberal" considers State intervention as an occasionally necessary medicine. "Nobody denies that clean living is the best way to good health, but this is really not a sufficient reason to deny that it is sometimes necessary to take medicine." This view is based on the assumption that private investment decisions normally lead to an optimum position. The other view considers that a continuous active economic policy, beyond measures to assure an equilibrium between aggregate demand and aggregate supply, is necessary, since the multitude of dispersed individual uninfluenced decisions will not lead to the maximization of national income. The real question is how far programming should extend, what it should cover, what degrees of "freedom" it should leave between and within the various economic sectors. . . .

XII.A.2. The Market Mechanism as an Instrument of Development*

In recent times, there has been a retreat both in economic theory and in economic policy from the nineteenth-century ideal of the unfettered market as a principle of economic organization. But the economic pros and cons of this retreat have been fully debated, and the economist consequently has a great deal to say about the relative merits of the market as contrasted with other methods of economic organization, and the circumstances appropriate to each.

The subject of planning and the market in economic development is, therefore, one which falls definitely within the field of the economist. Before I go on to discuss it, I must define more precisely what I mean by it. "Planning and the market" may be interpreted in two different ways. First, it may refer to the contrast between direction of the economy by Government and the policy of *laissez-faire*. This is not my subject, though in a wider philosophical and historical context it offers much to discuss. For example, though *laissez-faire* and direction are often regarded as opposites, if one looks to the history of economic development one finds (as Professor Easterbrook has shown[1])

*From Harry G. Johnson, *Money, Trade and Economic Growth*, George Allen & Unwin Ltd., London, 1962, pp. 152–3, 156–9, 160–63. Reprinted by permission.

[1] Professor Easterbrook's analysis was presented in the Marshall Lectures at Cambridge University in the spring of 1956. Unfortunately these lectures have not been published, but some of the ideas are

that economic development is almost invariably a process in which planning and direction on the one hand and freedom of enterprise on the other play their part, and are mixed. There is almost no case in which economic development has been entirely planned or entirely unplanned. The usual pattern is one of some framework of control by Government, within which the entrepreneur provides his services—a mixture of bureaucracy and enterprise, in which bureaucracy takes care of the major risks of development and enterprise faces and overcomes the minor ones. Another relevant point that Easterbrook makes is that an economy which succeeds in finding a formula for growth tends to repeat that pattern after it has become inappropriate. For example, Britain has gone on trying to work the internationally-oriented pattern of her nineteenth-century development; Russia has been very successful in developing heavy industry but has not yet solved the problem of agriculture.

The alternative interpretation takes planning, in the sense of a general direction of the economy, as an established principle, and considers the market as an alternative to other and more direct means of detailed control. Given the general framework of economic planning, there is still a choice be-

available in W. T. Easterbrook, "Long Period Comparative Study: Some Historical Cases," *Journal of Economic History*, XVII, No. 4, December 1957, 571–95.

tween two alternative methods of looking after the details. One is by direct detailed planning by a central authority, the other is by leaving the working out of details as far as possible to the operation of the market. (There is a third alternative, in which the Government is itself the entrepreneur and investor, which I shall consider later.)

This alternative interpretation is the one I shall be using: I shall discuss the question of the market mechanism as against detailed planning as an instrument of economic development. I should like to make it clear from the start that I am going to make a strong case for the market, as the preferable instrument of economic development, on two main grounds. The first is that the achievement of the desired results by control methods is likely to be especially difficult and inefficient in an underdeveloped economy; at this point I should like to remind you that a large part of Adam Smith's argument for *laissez-faire* was the inefficiency and corruption he saw in the Governments of his time. The second is that the remedies for the main fault which can be found with the use of the market mechanism, its undesirable social effects, are luxuries which underdeveloped countries cannot afford to indulge in if they are really serious about attaining a high rate of development. In particular, there is likely to be a conflict between rapid growth and an equitable distribution of income; and a poor country anxious to develop would probably be well advised not to worry too much about the distribution of income.

I am going to make a fairly strong case for the market, because the market figures relatively little in the literature of economic development, and the theoretical analysis which economics has developed in relation to markets is often overlooked or disregarded....

I now want to recapitulate briefly the various economic functions of the market and the price system as a method of economic organization. I shall be brief, as the argument is a familiar one.

In the first place, the market rations supplies of consumer goods among consumers; this rationing is governed by the willingness of consumers to pay, and provided the distribution of income is acceptable it is a socially efficient process. Secondly, the market directs the allocation of production between commodities, according to the criterion of maximum profit, which, on the same assumption, corresponds to social usefulness. Thirdly, the market allocates the different factors of production among their various uses, according to the criterion of maximizing their incomes. Fourthly, it governs the relative quantities of specific types of labour and capital equipment made available. Fifthly, it distributes income between the factors of production and therefore between individuals. Thus it solves all the economic problems of allocation of scarce means between alternative ends.

These are static functions; but the market also serves in various ways to provide incentives to economic growth. Thus the availability of goods through the market stimulates the consumer to seek to increase his income; and access to the market provides an opportunity for inventors of new goods and technical improvements to profit from their exploitation. Moreover, the market serves particularly to provide an incentive to the accumulation of capital of all kinds: first to the accumulation of personal capital in the form of trained skill, since such skill earns a higher reward; and second to the accumulation of material capital, since such capital earns an income.

The argument, then, is that a properly functioning market system would tend to stimulate both economic efficiency and economic growth. And it is important to note that the market does this automatically, while it requires no big administrative apparatus, no central decision-making, and very little policing other than the provision of a legal system for the enforcement of contracts.

All this sounds very impressive; but it is clearly not the whole of the story. What, then, are the objections to the market, how serious are they, and what should be done about them in the context of economic development? I shall discuss these questions in some detail. But first I shall state briefly the central theme of my discussion. It is that in many cases the objections to the market can be overcome by reforming specific markets, so as to bring them closer to the ideal type of market; and that to overcome other objections to the market may be very expensive and may not prove to be worthwhile—in other words, the defects of the market mechanism may on balance be more tolerable than they look at first sight.

Now, what are the objections to the market? They can, I think, be classified into two main types. One type of objection is that the market does not perform its functions properly. The other type of objection is that the results produced by the functioning of the market are undesirable in themselves.

I begin with the first type of objection, that the market does not perform its function properly. Here it is useful to draw a distinction between two quite different sorts of cases—those in which the market operates imperfectly, and those in which a perfectly functioning market would not produce the best results.

Imperfect operation of the market in an underdeveloped country may be attributable to ignorance, in the sense of lack of familiarity with market mechanisms and of awareness of relevant information, or to the prevalence of other modes of behaviour than the rational maximization of returns from effort. In the first case, the appropriate Governmental policy would seem to me to be, not to assume from the market the responsibility for allocative decisions, but to disseminate the knowledge and information required to make the market work efficiently and provide the education required to use it. The second case implies a more fundamental obstacle, not only to the use of the market but also to economic development itself, and suggests that successful economic development requires a basic change in social psy-chology. To my mind, it raises a serious question of fact. Is it really true that people in underdeveloped countries are strangers to the idea of maximizing gains? The idea that they are is very common in the literature and policy-making of economic development; one of its manifestations is the implicit assumption that both supplies and demands are completely price-inelastic. I am very sceptical about this, partly because of Bauer's work and partly because at least some of the actions of Governments in underdeveloped areas presuppose that even the poorest producers are susceptible to price incentives. I personally do not think one is justified in assuming as a general proposition that ignorance and illiteracy necessarily imply that men are not interested in making money. If it is true, there will be serious difficulties in the way of economic development; but again, the appropriate Governmental policy would seem to be to educate the people in the practice of rational economic behavior.

Even if the market functions perfectly, it will not produce the best possible results by its own criteria if there is a difference between social and private benefit or cost. This type of case may be particularly relevant to economic development; it includes the case of increasing returns to scale, and can be extended to include the possibility that technical progress or capital accumulation tend to proceed more rapidly in industry than in agriculture. But it raises an immediate question of fact—whether divergences between social and private benefit or cost are numerous and important or not. This is an important question, but one on which we do not know very much for certain. The theory of increasing returns is logically intriguing, but the influence of increasing returns still has to be disentangled from that of technical progress in historical growth. Again, it is a fact that few advanced countries are not industrial; but this by itself does not establish the wisdom of a policy of forced industrialization in an underdeveloped country. Aside from the question of fact, the existence of divergences between social and private returns does not necessarily indicate a need for the government to replace the market mechanism; instead, the operation of the market can be perfected by the use of appropriate taxes and subsidies to offset any divergences between social and private returns.

I now turn to the second type of objection to the market, the point of which is not that the market does not work in the way it should, but that the results produced are undesirable in themselves. Here, I think, there are two major objections to the market. The first is that the income distribution produced by the market is unjust and socially undesirable. The distribution of income through the market depends on the wealth and talents of different individuals, and on their individual skill in seeing a profitable opportunity of employing their money or labour. If they make a wise or lucky choice, they may obtain a much higher income. The objection is that this method of determining the distribution of income is not just. But if you attempt to intervene in the distribution of income, you immediately encounter the problem that such intervention interferes with the efficiency of the market system. If people are not allowed to enjoy the income they could obtain by their decisions, their decisions in turn will be affected, and the efficiency of the system will be impaired. There is, therefore, a conflict between economic efficiency and social justice. The extent and importance of this conflict is likely to vary according to the state of economic development. The more advanced a country is, the more likely are its citizens to have consciences about the distribution of income, and to accept the high taxation necessary to correct it without disastrously altering their behaviour; and on the other hand, the higher the level of income reached, the less serious will be any slowing down of the rate of growth brought about by redistribution policies. An advanced country can afford to sacrifice some growth for the sake of social justice. But the cost of greater equality may be great to any

economy at a low level of economic development that wishes to grow rapidly, particularly as it is evident that historically the great bursts of economic growth have been associated with the prospect and the result of big windfall gains; it would therefore seem unwise for a country anxious to enjoy rapid growth to insist too strongly on policies aimed at ensuring economic equality and a just income distribution. I should add that the problem may not be in fact as serious as I have made it out to be, since in the course of time rapid growth tends in various ways to promote a more equal distribution of wealth. . . .

I have been discussing the objection to the results of the market system on the grounds that it produces an undesirable distribution of income. A second objection of the same sort is that the free market will not produce as high a rate of growth as is desirable. I think there is a strong case for this objection, because people's actions in regard to saving and investment depend very much on their guesses about the future. Now people are likely to know their own current requirements better than the Government. But the requirements of the future have to be looked at not from the individual or family point of view or that of the nation as a collection of individuals, but from the point of view of the ongoing society. The needs of society in the future, many economists agree, tend to be underprovided for by the free market.

Even if the conclusion that state action is desirable to raise the rate of growth is accepted, this conclusion nevertheless does not carry with it a number of corollaries which are often attached to it. In particular, it does not necessarily imply that the state ought to undertake development saving and investment itself. Private enterprise may be more efficient than the Government in constructing and operating enterprises, so that the best policy may be to stimulate private enterprise by tax concessions, subsidies, and the provision of cheap credit. Similarly, it may be preferable to stimulate private saving by offering high interest rates, rather than by forcing savings into the hands of the state by taxation or inflation. One argument against a policy of low interest rates and forced saving is that it may in the long run contribute to the inequality of income distribution. The reason is that the poor or small savers are mainly confined to low-yielding fixed-interest investments, directly or indirectly in Government debt, because these are safe and easily available, whereas the larger savers can invest their money in higher-yielding stocks and shares or directly in profitable enterprises. There is, therefore, an opportunity here for Government both to stimulate saving for development and to improve the distribution of income.

There is another reason for being wary of the proposition that the state should undertake development investment itself—the danger that if the Government undertakes investment itself, especially if its administrators are not too clear on their objectives, the result will be the creation of vested industrial interests inimical to further development, and resistant to technical change.

To summarize the foregoing argument from the point of view of development policy, it seems to me that much of development planning could usefully be devoted to the improvement and strengthening of the market system. This does not imply the acceptance of all the results of *laissez-faire*, especially with respect to the rate of growth; but there are reasons for thinking that too much emphasis on a fair or ethical distribution of income can be an obstacle to rapid growth.

The argument I have presented has been concerned mainly with one side of the case for the market. The other side concerns the costs and difficulties of controls, in terms of the manpower costs of the administration they require, and their effects in creating profit opportunities which bring windfall gains to some members of the community and create incentives to evasion which in turn require policing of the controls. I have touched on that side of the argument sufficiently frequently to make it unnecessary to elaborate on it further.

Instead, I shall comment briefly on international markets in relation to economic development, since so far I have been implicitly concerned with internal markets. Economic development planning inevitably has a strong autarkic bias, by reason both of its motivation and of the limitation of the scope of control to the national economy. Nevertheless, international trade can play an important part in stimulating and facilitating the development process. Access to foreign markets for exports can permit an economy with a limited domestic market to exploit economies of scale, and the potentiality of such exports can serve as a powerful attraction for foreign capital and enterprise. Similarly, the capacity to import provided by exports can give a developing economy immediate access to the products of advanced technology, without obliging it to go through the long and perhaps costly process of developing domestic production facilities. Economic nationalism and excessive fear of the risks of international trade, by fostering aversion to exploiting the advantages of the international market, can therefore retard economic development unnecessarily.

One further comment on the international aspects of the market and economic development seems to me worth making. Discussion of the international side of development has been mostly concerned with commodity trade and commercial policy. But in fact one of the most important ways in which the world market system is imperfect is with respect to the international mobility of capital and labour. The problem of international capital movements has received a fair amount of attention, labour mobility and immobility much less. Now, the process of economic development in the past, especially in the nineteenth century, was characterized by vast movements, not only of capital, but also of labour, about the world. The mass movement of labour between countries has now been more or less shut off by the growth of nationalism. I believe it is important to recognize this restriction on international competition, and its implications for programmes of economic development. It means—looking at the world economy as a whole—that the solution to the problem of maximizing world output cannot be approached directly, by bringing labour, capital technology, and natural resources together at the most efficient location; instead, the other productive factors have to be brought to the labour. To a large extent, "the economic development of underdeveloped countries" is a second-best policy,[2] in which gifts of capital and technical training by advanced to underdeveloped countries are a compensation for the unwillingness of the former to consider the alternative way of

improving the labour to resources ratio, movement of the labour to the resources. The fact that development is a second-best policy in this respect may impose severe limitations on its efficiency and rapidity.

To conclude, I have been concerned with the role of the market in economic development; and I have aimed at stressing the economic functions of the market, in automatically taking decisions about various kinds of allocations of economic resources, and the place in economic development programmes of improvements in market organization and methods. I have been advocating, not a policy of *laissez-faire*, but recognition of the market as an administrative instrument that is relatively cheap to operate and may therefore be efficient in spite of objectionable features of its operations. The general assumption on which I have been arguing is that economic development is a process of co-operation between the state and private enterprise, and that the problem is to devise the best possible mixture.

[2] See J. E. Meade, *The Theory of International Economic Policy, Volume II: Trade and Welfare* (London: Oxford University Press, 1955), and R. G. Lipsey and Kelvin Lancaster, "The General Theory of Second Best," *Review of Economic Studies*, XXIV (1), No. 63, 1956–57, 11–33.

XII.A.3. The Fragmented Economy*

While economists can usefully divide their labor as monetary theorists, tax experts, foreign trade specialists, project evaluators, and so on, a unified view of the development process is a great analytical convenience. Why is public intervention so pervasive and generally so unsuccessful? Intervention is usually prompted by the perception—sometimes correct—that a particular market is functioning badly, so that authorities feel pressed to "do something." An infant textile firm is helped by a tariff; or the price of an agricultural product may be raised to permit

*From Ronald I. McKinnon, *Money and Capital in Economic Development*, Brookings Institution, Washington, D.C., 1973, pp. 5–8. Reprinted by permission.

farmers to use a new fertilizer-intensive technology; or a tax exemption may be granted to a foreign firm for automobile assembly. This pressure for public intervention is the result of severe fragmentation in the underdeveloped economy.

THE FRAGMENTED ECONOMY

The economy is "fragmented" in the sense that firms and households are so isolated that they face different effective prices for land, labor, capital, and produced commodities and do not have access to the same technologies. Authorities then cannot presume that socially profitable investment opportunities will be taken up by the private sector, because prevailing prices need not reflect true economic scarcity—at least not for large segments of the population. There is historical justification for this view in the nineteenth and early twentieth centuries. In Asia, Latin America, and Africa, primary commodity export enclaves were controlled by foreigners, and much of the general population remained outside of the market economy. Indigenous entrepreneurs had limited access to capital, no means of acquiring advanced technologies, and little skilled labor.

Thus in the determination of where in the vast new areas of the overseas world the raw material export industries were to be established, the pre-existing domestic supply of labor, capital, and entrepreneurship played a minimal role. Where they did exist in areas of potential export production, these factors were highly immobile and could not be counted upon to engage in export industry operation.[1]

Newly independent governments quite properly felt compelled to act as agents of change to offset economic and political colonialism. In the past twenty or thirty years, poor countries have succeeded in introducing some new industrial activities—particularly the manufacture of goods previously imported—and in mobilizing some domestic factors of production. Their governments chose to do so, however, by manipulating commodity prices in a variety of ways and by intervening directly to help some individuals or sectors of the economy at the expense of others.

Consider the extraordinary lengths to which import tariffs have been used in Latin

[1] Jonathan V. Levin, *The Export Economies: Their Pattern of Development in Historical Perspective*, Cambridge, 1960, p. 169. For a good description of how small farmers, who are strongly motivated toward economic efficiency, can nonetheless be locked into a backward agricultural technology, see Theodore W. Schultz, *Transforming Traditional Agriculture*, New Haven, 1964, pp. 36–48.

America, with rates of several hundred percent on some goods and absolute prohibitions on the import of others, while still others enter freely. The situation on the Indian subcontinent is no different. Price and quantity controls on foreign trade and domestic commerce make licensing and rationing commonplace. Byzantine patterns of industrial taxes and subsidies complicate government budgetmaking. Consequently, the market mechanism has become no better, and perhaps even worse, as an indicator of social advantage.

Modern fragmentation, therefore, has been largely the result of government policy and goes beyond the old distinction between the export enclave and the traditional subsistence sector. One manifestation is the often-noted existence of small household enterprises and large corporate firms—all producing similar products with different factor proportions and very different levels of technological efficiency. Continuing mechanization on farms and in factories in the presence of heavy rural and urban unemployment is another. Excess plant and equipment with underutilized capacity are commonly found in economies that are reputed to be short of capital and that do suffer from specific bottlenecks. In rural areas, tiny landholdings may be split up into small noncontiguous parcels, with inadequate incentives for agricultural land improvements.

While tangible land and capital are badly used, fragmentation in the growth and use of human capital can be more serious and no less visible. Learning-by-doing and on-the-job training in the "organized" economy are confined to narrow enclaves—export-oriented in the past but now increasingly inward-oriented toward "modern" manufacturing—whose employment growth may be less than the growth in general population. Unemployment among the highly educated coexists with severe shortages in some labor skills.

Indigenous entrepreneurship is narrowly based and is supported by heavy government subsidy. Tariff protection, import licenses, tax concessions, and low-cost bank finance commonly go to small urban elites and create great income inequality between the wealthy few and the poverty-stricken many. This income inequality has failed to induce high rates of saving in the classical manner, but governments remain reluctant to reduce the disposable income of well-to-do investors whose unique access to investment opportunities is guaranteed by the web of official controls and by the endemic fragmentation.

LIBERALIZATION AND THE CAPITAL MARKET

How does one begin to loosen the Gordian knot? The incredibly complex distortions in commodity prices now prevailing are the unplanned macroeconomic outcome of specific microeconomic interventions. But substantial fragmentation in the markets for land, labor, and capital provided the initial motivation for public authorities to "do something" and continues to pressure governments to intervene. Thus an explicit policy for improving the operation of factor markets is necessary to persuade authorities to cease intervening in commodity markets. Carefully considered liberalization in all sectors can then move forward—not merely as a reaction to the more obvious mistakes of the immediate past, but in ways that allay legitimate fears of pure laissez-faire.

However, the knot needs to be loosened further. To say that there are "imperfections in factor markets" is distressingly vague and often signals the end of formal economic analysis. But further systematic inquiry can proceed if the neoclassical approach of treating labor, land, and capital symmetrically as primary factors is dropped. It is hypothesized here that fragmentation in the capital market—endemic in the underdeveloped environment without carefully considered public policy—causes the misuse of labor and land, suppresses entrepreneurial development, and condemns important sectors of the economy to inferior technologies. Thus appropriate policy in the domestic capital market is the key to general liberalization, and particularly to the withdrawal of unwise public intervention from commodity markets....

XII.B. POLICY MODELS

XII.B.1. Relevance of Development
Models to Planning*

Planning models have been increasing in number and complexity in the developing countries in recent years. Strictly speaking, a model is a hypothesis involving a relationship between variables which intends to explain and predict events, past and future, or prescribe policy. For policy purposes, a model distinguishes between target variables which constitute the objectives of economic policy and controlled variables which are instruments affected by policies and which, through the variations occurring in their levels, affect the levels or magnitudes of the target variables. A broader classification of variables is between exogenous and endogenous variables. The model specifies relationships, technological, institutional and behavioural, between variables. In its reduced form, a model can always be expressed in terms of number of exogenous variables, some of which are predetermined for the purpose in hand, whereas others are policy or instrument variables; the values of the endogenous variables are then solved or determined by the interactions postulated in the equation system of the model.

Models can be sector-oriented or can encompass the entire economy. A restrictive model can be designed to explain or forecast the developments or prescribe policy in a particular sector, such as agriculture. It can be directed towards illuminating narrowly defined problems such as the optimum cropping pattern, given the prices of alternative crops and the prices of inputs and given a set

*From Nural Islam, "The Relevance of Development Models to Economic Planning in Developing Countries," *Economic Bulletin for Asia and the Far East*, June–September 1970, pp. 56–61, 64–5. Reprinted by permission.

of technical-production relations between inputs and outputs in agriculture. The first attempt in a planning exercise starts from an assessment of prospects in the individual sectors of an economy. Information on individual projects is often more readily available, especially in the early stages of a country's progress in economic planning. However, the sectoral approach has the drawback that it often results in assorted projects which are not part of an integrated total. If planning ends with project analysis only, it is not possible to evaluate the projects on a consistent basis or to check the total inputs against the over-all availability of resources. Models can also encompass the entire economy; here one can mention the highly aggregative Harrod-Domar type of model, where the operations of an entire economy are conceived in terms of aggregate saving, investment and income relationships, which can further be extended to include the effects of external economic relationships in terms of interactions between income and imports or exports. The two-gap model which seeks to investigate the gap between savings and investment, on the one hand, and that between exports and imports (i.e. the demand for and supply of foreign exchange) on the other, is an obvious example. While the original Harrod-Domar model treats capital as the only relevant scarce factor of production, the elaboration of the two gap model introduces an additional scarce factor, foreign exchange, which is crucial in many developing countries.

There is a variety of planning models which, while global in character in so far as they encompass the operations of the entire economy, are highly disaggregative in the sense that they postulate quantifiable relationships between the various sectors of the economy. A simple taxonomy of the planning models of this type is: (1) input-output models, (2) simultaneous equation models of a behaviourial nature and (3) models which combine features of input-output models and of behaviourial models. The planning exercise involves the need to discover a consistent set of economic aggregates over the plan period, which are economically feasible and politically acceptable; it is necessary to connect these macro-economic aggregates with the sectors and projects which constitute the operational content of the development effort. As a general rule, input-output models provide the sectoral details and consistency checks among sectoral targets in terms of output and investment targets in the various sectors. An open input-output model seeks to provide a consistency check between the over-all import requirements and export possibilities arising out of or associated with various sectoral outputs. The input-output models provide estimates of sectoral outputs and import levels which are consistent with each other and with the estimates of final demand. They aid in the allocation of investment to achieve the projected sectoral outputs and provide a more accurate test of the adequacy of the available investment resources. The requirements for skilled labourers, if a set of skill coefficients for individual sectors is available, and for imports can be estimated; and the possibilities of import substitution can be analysed. The indirect requirements for scarce inputs such as skill, capital and imports can also be estimated. Regional input-output models help in the regional allocation of investment. The main difficulty in the use of input-output models in developing countries concerns the treatment of structural changes such as substitution of domestic production for imports, changes in technology and other shifts in the structure of intermediate demand.

An input-output model usually does not handle questions of price formulation, except indirectly by postulating an equality between costs and prices in each sector; it does not deal with questions of fiscal and monetary policies, which are among the principal instruments of economic policymaking. The standard input-output model deals with questions of fiscal policy and monetary policies as a subsequent or subsidiary exercise, once it has established the inter-sectoral flows. There is a class of macro-economic aggregative model which does not directly incorporate input-output relations among the various sectors of the economy. Such models deal with behaviourial relationships such as consumption and investment functions and institutional relationships such as those relating to tax yields, money supply, price formulation for broad classes of commodities such as agricultural and industrial commodities. They are usually expressed at high levels of aggregation. The basic elements of a traditional input-output model are the exogenously determined final demand, consisting of consumption and investment demand and the technical coefficients which quantify the inter-sectoral flows. The behavioural models concentrate on explaining behavioural relationships which are estimated from time series or cross-sectional data. They incorporate both linear and non-linear relationships among variables whereas the input-output models are linear models and postulate a relationship of proportionality between inputs and outputs. These two types of model can be and are often combined, though they run into the problems of compatibility when the behaviourial relationships are non-linear.

Over the years, the input-output model has been extended in various directions, especially in the direction of explaining the determinants of final demand by means of behaviourial and technological equations purporting to explain consumption and investment behaviour. The input-output model concentrates on consistency among sectoral outputs and inputs as well as between the former and the components of demand. In some formulations of the model, a capital-output matrix is added so that investment by sector is related to the outputs of investment goods. The input-output models do not provide solutions for the best combinations of sectoral outputs or optimal combinations of techniques of production in each of the sectors. The important problems in economic planning are the allocation of scarce resources among competing sectors and, within each sector, among alternative techniques of production. Furthermore, in each sector, there is a choice between providing the required output either by domestic production or by imports and it is necessary to find the optimum pattern of import substitution. The linear programming models provide the necessary extension of the consistency models of the input-output variety to optimization criteria. Given the objective of economic policy, which could be maximization of income or employment or any other quantifiable economic objective, the linear programming models provide optimal solutions for combinations among sectors or techniques, including optimal combinations of domestic production and imports in each sector. Optimization is subject to the restraints inherent in technological production possibilities and limited resources, which can be distinguished in terms of foreign exchange, domestic savings and skills or any other scarce resource as indicated by the policy makers.

The use of models to illuminate discussions on economic policy making and economic planning has been facilitated in recent years by an increasing sophistication on the part of policy makers in handling economic tools. In the initial years, the discussion between model builders and policy makers in the planning agencies often threatened to become sterile since there was a difficulty of communication between them. As the number of model builders proliferated, the number of planners who were given training in quantitative economics increased correspondingly. As the planners and economists began to be taken seriously by the governments and faced the incredible complexity of the economies they were asked to under-

stand, they began to look for ways to judge the possible consequences of alternative policies or actions. It was increasingly realized that models do not provide solutions but only assist in finding them. The models were as good or as bad as the assumptions on which they were based; real life complexities could hardly be all encompassed in models. They included the critical variables and key assumptions and provided the range of choice or alternatives within which the forces of political bargaining and judgement of the policy makers could function. The effectiveness of models depends in this context upon whether they are over-loaded or pushed beyond their capacity.

Furthermore, model building and model using became increasingly a part of a dialogue between the model builders and those engaged in planning and policy making. Modifications are wrought as new knowledge accumulates; new decisions or analysis designed to understand the economic process or economic behaviour or effects of policy on human economic actions are derived from quantitative work outside the model. In the planning process, model builders have to be in constant touch with conventional economists, technicians and administrators. They have to check their assumptions and postulate relationships among variables by a constant dialogue with the specialists in the field.

The relevance of models in development planning may best be discussed in connexion with the use of planning models in the actual planning process and with the discussions of development problems in the South Asian countries. The experiment with econometric models in the context of actual experience in development planning has thrown up issues and problems which have illuminated both the usefulness and the limitations of models in development planning. The following discussion of the subject is inevitably influenced by the experience in Pakistan.

In the use of models in development planning in a concrete context, several steps can be distinguished. These steps are not necessarily planned in any strict time sequence; there is always a feed-back between one step or stage and the next step and stage. However, a comprehensive linear programming model, which adequately disaggregates the economic sectors and which in addition contains dynamic elements, seeks to compress several steps into one grand exercise. In the absence of an all-embracing model used right from the beginning of the planning process, several steps can be distinguished as follows: At the first stage of plan formulation, the model can assist in producing the macro-economic framework. At this stage, interest centres mainly on broad magnitudes and their interrelationships in order to determine the tentative size of the plan or its broad orders of magnitude and to explore the relationships among growth targets, savings and the balance of payments.

At the second stage, the macro-economic framework can be further elaborated to illuminate a few critical issues such as the inter-relations between agricultural growth and over-all growth, the implications of alternative rates of savings or exports, the implications of import propensities for the balance of payments and the effects of alternative levels of foreign assistance. At the third stage, by the elaboration of an input-output model in a macro-economic framework, the implications of sectoral balance (the relationships among sectoral targets), and savings and the balance of payments can be explored. Even a relatively aggregative input-output model can help in clearing up inter-sectoral relations, the balance of payments implications of alternative growth patterns and final demand structures.

In Pakistan, for example, the first and second five-year plans were not based on any detailed input-output model. However, a macro-economic framework of the Harrod-Domar type was used in discussions relating to the broad size of the plan as well as its saving and investment implications. No model was ever formally presented, but various calculations regarding the size of the planned investment requirements were conceived in

terms of such a framework which the planners had, so to speak, at the back of their minds. The elements of such a Harrod-Domar type of model can be found not in the form of a set of equations but in the form of analysis of investment requirements and role of savings, etc. as indicated by a careful reading of the plan documents. One can say that something like the following model was implicit in the discussions relating to the plan formulation.

$$I_t = K_1 (y_t - y_{t-1}) \dots\dots\dots\dots\dots (1)$$
$$D_t = D_{t-1} + K_2 I_t \dots\dots\dots\dots (2)$$
$$GDP_t = y_t + D_t \dots\dots\dots\dots\dots (3)$$
$$GI_t = I_t + D_t \dots\dots\dots\dots\dots (4)$$
$$\overline{S}_t = GI_t - A_t \dots\dots\dots\dots\dots (5)$$
$$S_t = K_3 (y_t - y_{t-1}) + S_{t-1} \dots\dots\dots (6)$$
$$C_t = GDP_t - \overline{S}_t - G_t \dots\dots\dots\dots (7)$$
$$M_t = K_4 GDP_t \dots\dots\dots\dots\dots (8)$$
$$\overline{E}_t = M_t - A_t \dots\dots\dots\dots\dots (9)$$

Symbols:
t indicates the end, and t-1 the beginning of the plan period
I = net investment
K_1 = net capital/output ratio
y = national income
D = depreciation, and D_{t-1} is depreciation on the old stock of capital
$\overline{E}$ = required exports
A = foreign aid
K_2 = the share of investment required to account for the depreciation on the increase of the capital stock during the plan period
GDP = gross domestic product
GI = gross investment
$\overline{S}$ = required savings
S = savings
M = total imports
C = consumption
G = defence expenditure
K_3 = marginal savings rate
K_4 = import coefficient

The logic of the model is as follows. The planner sets a target in national income (y_t); on the basis of the capital/output ratio, this yields required investment (I_t) which, to-gether with depreciation requirements, yields required gross investment and the re-sultant gross domestic product. Given for-eign aid, required savings to match required investment is derived. Given initial savings, additional expected savings are thus deter-mined. If required savings are not equal to expected savings, the marginal savings rate (K_3) needs to be adjusted; K_3 is a policy variable. Consumption is a residual. Given import requirements, which with varying K_4 (that is, the degree of import substitution) and foreign aid, required exports would be derived. The balance between required ex-ports and imports can be adjusted by either import substitution or export promotion.

Such an aggregative framework is not of any relevance in the matter of choice be-tween alternative sectors, projects or tech-niques. Nor does it encompass the considera-tion of the alternative objectives of eco-nomic planning such as growth of income, expansion of employment, more equitable distribution of income, or a more equitable balance in regional development. . . .

The over-all analytical framework dis-cussed above provided the planners with a guide to the broad orders of magnitude of the investment programmes and the relation-ships with savings, growth of income and balance of payments. These orders of magni-tude provided the first tentative step in the actual formulation of the plan, which con-sisted of sector programmes and of individual projects in each sector.

At the next stage, lists of projects by sector were drawn-up, on the basis of techni-cal feasibility studies and market demand. These were related to all public sector proj-ects and to the big projects in the private sector. The small projects in the private sec-tor escaped scrutiny. The total claims on domestic resources and foreign exchange ex-ceeded the availabilities of these two scarce resources, as estimated from or as assumed in the aggregative framework. Priorities were allocated to various sectors and to projects in each sector in order to arrive at a feasible

programme. The criteria were the contribu-tion of the project to national income and the balance of payments. In the case of conflict between the two criteria, the latter received greater weight. Further adjustments were required to make the outputs of differ-ent sectors consistent with one another and to avoid bottlenecks in the production of power, cement and other critical materials. This called for an analysis of demand and supply of these key commodities and for the establishment of physical balance sheets.

The investment and foreign exchange re-quirements emerging from the analysis of sector programmes and individual projects are not necessarily consistent with the aggre-gative projections of savings, investment and balance of payments. Any such consistency has to be matter of trial and error in a process of feed-back between the two sets of exercises. The assumptions made at the start of the aggregative model have to be re-examined. The various methods of assessing priorities require the estimation of future value to the economy—as determined by ag-gregate demand and total availability of labour and foreign exchange—and the pro-spective demand for individual commodities. These magnitudes can best be derived from an inter-sectoral general equilibrium model, but approximation can be attempted on the basis of partial analysis.

Thus in Pakistan in the matter of sectoral allocation of investment and choice of proj-ects in the broad sectors, it was sought to apply some forms of cost-benefit analysis. In an ideal situation, the planning model is ex-pected to generate the shadow prices for the relevant scarce factors of production, which should then provide a guide for the solution of projects, the aggregation of which will eventually produce the sectoral allocation of investment. The derivation of scarcity prices for scarce factors by considering the supply and demand for them, without direct rela-tion to a detailed intersectoral model, is at least a partial equilibrium approach. After all, in a general equilibrium framework, the factor prices and commodity prices are to be simultaneously determined, given the supply of scarce resources, and given the structure of demand and of consumption or investment expenditures which are the functions of the over-all development programme, including its sectoral composition. Some crude estimates were made of the scarcity price of foreign exchange on the basis of a judgement regarding the possible overvaluation of the exchange rate. This kind of experiment with a simple, aggregative planning model seems to have been common to many developing countries. In India, it was the extension of the Harrod-Domar model in terms of the consumption and investment goods sectors, with different capital output ratios, which played a crucial role in the choice of investment decisions during the second five-year plan. The model was first formulated in an Indian context by P. C. Mahalanobis.

It was during the formulation of the third five-year plan in Pakistan that an attempt was made to formulate a formal planning model based on: (a) an input-output model consisting of the current flows, (b) a highly aggregated seven-sector capital-output matrix and (c) a set of expenditure functions. The seven sectors as distinguished in the model represented an aggregation of a much larger input-output model for Pakistan's economy. However, since the objective of the model was to illuminate the implication of choices in terms of some key exogenous variable such as the rate of growth of GNP, the agricultural growth rate, the savings rate, and non-agricultural exports, the more detailed input-output matrix was not used in the formal model. The sectors were: agriculture (including forestry and fisheries) manufactured consumer goods, intermediate goods, investment goods, construction, transportation and communication and other services. In the final demand sector, a distribution was made in terms of consumption, fixed investment, inventory investment, exports and import substitution. The model consists of a set of input-output relations, consumption functions, investment functions (relating the flow of in-

vestment goods by sectors of origin and destination), inventory adjustment functions, indirect tax functions and import functions. The reduced form equations of the model express agricultural exports, imports, fixed investment, balance of payments surplus and deficit, import substitution, consumption, inventory investment and seven sectoral outputs as functions of GNP, agricultural output, savings, and four different non-agricultural exports.

In the reduced form of the system of equations, the sectoral outputs, investment (fixed and inventory), agricultural exports, imports, import substitution, consumption, and the current account of the balance of payments are endogenously determined; the exogenous variables are income, agricultural output, savings and non-agricultural exports. The model, therefore, permits an examination of the implications of the changes in the exogenous variables for the rest of the economic system. . . .

The model helps planners to examine the implications of alternative values of exogenous or predetermined variables. Since the model generates a unique solution for any set of values of parameters and exogenous variables, the changes brought about by alternative parameters or exogenous variables can be deduced. Given the rate of growth of GNP, the implications of different rates of growth of agriculture on the rest of the economy, that is, on the GNP, different industrial sectors as well as on the savings-investment gap or the foreign exchange gap, can be readily estimated. A slower rate of growth of agriculture reduces the agricultural export surplus, increases the balance of payments deficit, and necessitates a larger import substitution in the non-agricultural sector, which increases investment requirements, in view of the higher capital requirements. The model makes it possible to arrive at feasible targets of over-all GNP growth and of agricultural growth and non-agricultural exports which are consistent with the maximum or feasible degree of import substitution or foreign assistance. In other words, the model can answer the following question. Given feasible levels of deficit in balance of payments, of exports, and given the ability to achieve import substitution, what growth rate of GNP can Pakistan achieve and what marginal savings rate does this growth require?

The answer—or more correctly, the best guess at the answer—to any such single question can probably be fairly quickly provided by a planning commission economist without such an elaborate and time-consuming model; but for the answers to dozens of such questions, the model is an extremely efficient device. Beyond that, moreover, is the fact that time and skilled manpower in a planning commission are so scarce that, without such a model, most of the interesting alternatives would never be explored; if they were, the research would be done at different times by different people, who would almost inevitably apply different assumptions, procedures, and degrees of optimism and therefore produce incomparable results.

There are two sorts of policy variables (or policy parameters) in the model, namely direct and indirect. The direct are those which are *fixed* by government policy, for example, the income tax rate or the size of government expenditures; the indirect are those which can only be *influenced* by government policies, such as the marginal savings ratio or the level of GNP in some future year. In the model discussed above the policy variables (or parameters) are entirely indirect with the result that the precise implications of alternative policies cannot be calculated without further work with information from outside the model. Nevertheless, a great deal of insight into direct policy problems can be gained from the model. Indeed it is often analytically convenient to break up a policy analysis into two stages, and the model may provide the answers at one stage of the work: for example, when faced with the question of the influence of a change in a direct policy variable on gross savings (which probably requires that its effect on

corporate, household, and government savings be discovered) and the effect of a changed volume of savings on the economy has to be examined. The model will not help at the first stage, though that stage may require a fairly straight-forward supplementary analysis, but it will be of much assistance at the more complex second stage of the analysis.

The policy changes about which the model offers insight are those which operate through either the exogenous variables or the parameters of the technological behavioural relations. It is clear that many aspects of government policies operate through their impact on the exogenous variables of the model (GNP, savings, agricultural output, and exports). For example, the level of savings (or alternatively the marginal savings ratio) may be influenced by excise, income, and corporate tax policies, income distribution and social welfare policies, interest rates and other monetary policies, regional growth policies, and the like. Similarly, many of the parameters of the behavioural relations are influenced by various government policies. For example, one of the relations of the model gives the consumption of each sector's product as a linear function of the aggregate consumption; but this propensity to consume from a particular sector can be altered by government price policies or excise taxes, the availability of imported substitutes (or complements), the redistribution of income, and so forth. There are very few parameters in the model which cannot be reached through government policy. Manipulation of the model will give information as to the size and direction of the impact of any changes in a parameter—and may thereby help to decide about policies which affect that parameter.

Furthermore a model of this kind permits a wide variety of sensitivity tests, tracing out the effects of changes in exogenous variables on the endogenous variables. The sensitivity tests free the model builder from the constraint of using a single value for any variable and permit him to try out a range.

But it is important to remember that the range within which various values of exogenous variables are tried is largely a matter of judgement on the part of the model user. He cannot be entirely freed from the need for exercising judgement. In determining the plausible range of values with which to experiment, history and analogy are standard guides to a policy. But both history and analogy are less reliable guides in a developing country than in a developed country. As R. Vernon puts it, "typically, the history of development in the underdeveloped areas is brief; typically, it is grossly and imperfectly recorded. Even if recorded with great accuracy, however, one would expect to find highly unstable and swiftly changing patterns at even modest levels of aggregation."[1] Therefore, judgement plays a vital role. Moreover, a wider range of alternative values has to be tried out in the particular situation.

What combination of ranges of different exogenous variables can be tested together? The variables which formally appear exogenous and independent in a model may not and are not in many cases independent. A sensitivity test for one variable at a time may not be appropriate. Sensitivity tests on the basis of alternative sets of values of exogenous variables generate a wider range of choice than the sensitivity tests of one variable at a time. It is desirable that the results of sensitivity tests should not cover a very wide range, because in that case the policy maker's scope for judgement is not appropriately reduced. The purpose of a policy model is to expand the role of quantitative analysis and to reduce as far as possible the role of intuitive judgement. . . .

CONCLUSION

In most of the developing countries, consistency models consisting of input-output

[1] R. Vernon, "Comprehensive Model Building in the Planning Process: The Case of the Less Developed Economies," *Economic Journal*, March 1966, p. 64.

tables have been most widely used. Their use has been supplemented by material balances for key commodities. Formal linear programming models have been less extensively used because of the data requirements. Moreover quantification of the multiple objectives of economic policy has been far from satisfactory. The most important problem in many developing countries has been the determination of the weights to be assigned to growth of income on the one hand and to creation of employment and attainment of a more equitable distribution of income on the other. Even when supplementary objectives such as employment creation and income distribution can be treated as constraints to a linear programming model, while the maximization of income is treated as the objective function, the problem of weighting is not to be avoided. The levels at which the constraints regarding employment and the distribution of income have to be put depend basically upon social value judgements and hence on the relative weights which are to be accorded to conflicting objectives. Most of the optimizing models have concentrated on scarce inputs of capital and foreign exchange and have assumed labour as a free input in view of the disguised and open unemployment in many countries in the ECAFE region. The most important problem in these countries is, however, the provision of employment. This has implications for the other sectors in terms of supply of wage goods, even if the objective is to put labour to work in construction projects in the rural areas. In the formal models, one could incorporate the rural public works programme as an activity and consider as its major input the supply of wage goods and a limited amount of capital goods.

Again, many models are basically one-period or terminal-year models, in which the increase in income is considered for the plan period as a whole. The models are usually conceived in terms of maximization of terminal-year income or consumption or terminal stock of capital or increase in income or capital stock. The distribution of year-by-year growth of income to be achieved during the plan period necessitates a dynamic programming model which, in terms both of data requirements and of mathematical properties or ease of computational manipulation, is not entirely satisfactory. In the actual planning process, the annual phasing of the investment programme is of crucial significance; it has implications for the generation of savings and hence for the requirements for foreign aid. The rate at which investment can be accelerated over the plan period is closely related to the absorptive capacity of an economy, conceived broadly in terms of technical and managerial ability to generate, prepare and execute development projects. This is partly an institutional problem and partly a problem of a package of appropriate policies, including the training of manpower in the various aspects of development activity. Any dynamic model has to incorporate some assumption regarding the rate at which investment can be accelerated from one year to the next during the plan period. The annual rate of acceleration which is feasible requires analysis of institutions and policies outside the formal structure of a model. In addition to postulating a feasible rate of acceleration of investment and income, such a model has also to incorporate the time lag between investment and income. The generation of income in any plan period is partly the consequence of investment which has taken place in the last planning period and partly of what is invested during the plan period itself. Again, a part of the investment in the present plan period will come to fruition and yield income in the next plan period. While the capital output relations may be satisfactory for a relatively general discussion of long-term perspectives, detailed knowledge of the projects under implementation, their completion times, the requirements for their future operations, and capacities which might become critical in the immediate future will play an important role in a five-year plan period.

It is remarkable that, in most of the developing countries, the use of models for short period planning has been very limited. The concept of annual planning except in the sense of an annual government budget, elaborating government tax and expenditure policy, has only very recently been introduced in the planning process in a few developing countries. Even though an annual plan is the instrument through which five-year plans can be implemented, little effort has gone into the elaboration of models for planning for a year. The technical and behavioural relations which may hold for a five-year period can seldom be used for annual plans. An annual plan has to be in much greater detail in terms of projects and programmes as well as in terms of fiscal, monetary and commercial policy which need be integrated with the investment and income targets. Import and export projections have to be made every year to be realistic and worthwhile, and so do the savings and investment projections. So far, input-output models have been fruitfully used in forecasting annual import requirements. The stability of import coefficients is much greater in the short run than in the medium or long run.

The optimizing models which consider only the choice between domestic production and imports for each sector implicitly assume that the currently or historically prevailing technical coefficients of production are the optimum ones, given the prices of factors and outputs. In view of the known imperfections in the factor and commodity markets, the prevailing technology is far from optimum. Unless comprehensive linear programming models, which specify alternative techniques in each sector and which encompass the problem of choice between sectors and techniques simultaneously as an integral part of the solution are used, it will be necessary to undertake supplementary analysis for the choice of the appropriate techniques in each sector in the light of the assumed opportunity cost of the scarce resources. In the absence of a formal model incorporating the choice of techniques, there is need for a process of trial and error, since the selection of techniques for each sector on the basis of the assumed scarcity prices, and the subsequent derivation of the output and investment figures, may not be consistent with the given quantity of scarce factors, which will necessitate a revision of the original prices. In a few steps of iteration a reasonably consistent solution may be found. The important supplementary analysis at the sector or project level is therefore the analysis of alternative techniques and a sensitivity analysis of how the optimal choice of techniques varies in response to change in scarcity prices.

XII.B.2. Planning Economic Development*

In the socialist countries and in the countries following a national revolutionary pattern we plan economic development, because economic development would not, under historic conditions existent, take place by itself automatically. Consequently it must be planned.

What is the essential of planning economic development? I would say that the essential consists in assuring an amount of productive investment which is sufficient to provide for a rise of national income substantially in excess of the rise in population, so that *per capita* national income increases. The strategic factor is investment, or more precisely productive investment. Consequently the problem of development planning is one of assuring that there be sufficient productive investment, and then of directing that productive investment into such channels as will provide for the most rapid growth of the productive power of national economy.

These are the essential tasks of development planning. The problems which planning faces can be divided into two categories. One is the mobilisation of resources for purposes of productive investment, the

*From Oskar Lange, *Economic Development, Planning and International Cooperation*, Central Bank of Egypt, Cairo, 1961, pp. 10–13, 15–17. Reprinted by permission.

other is the direction of the investment into proper channels. These are the essential problems implied in planning.

The first problem is that of mobilising resources for investment. Taking the experience of the socialist countries and of the countries following a national revolutionary pattern, a certain picture of methods employed for that mobilisation of resources can be drawn. These methods consist in the following: one is, and that is the method which was paramountly applied in the socialist countries, nationalisation of industries, finance, trade and the use of the profits thus derived for purposes of investment. The other method, which particularly plays a role in the countries following the national revolutionary pattern, is nationalisation of foreign owned natural resources and the use of the profits from these resources for investment purposes.

A further method is the contribution of the peasants in countries where agrarian reforms are carried out. The peasants are required, in turn, to make some contribution to the state finances, which are used for purposes of investment. This frequently does not suffice and an appeal is made to resources derived from general taxation, public loans and, in certain cases, also to deficit financing.

These methods of raising resources for investment are applied both in socialist and national revolutionary countries in various proportions. There is, also, a method which plays a particularly important role in the national revolutionary countries, and which in certain socialist countries during a transition period plays a role too. This is the inducement of private savers to undertake productive investment. This implies inducing private industrialists, traders, landowners, and financial groups, to invest a considerable part of their income in the direction which is conducive to assuring the country's rapid economic development, that means essentially investment in production. This can be achieved by various ways such as, for instance, taxation of unproductive uses of wealth, compulsory saving, restrictions of distributions of profits and of such uses of profits as do not consist of productive investment, compulsory loans and all kinds of other measures. Finally, import of foreign capital may be also a source of financing productive investments. . . .

Thus there is a whole catalogue of means applied in various proportions in different countries which provide the resources necessary for substantial productive investment. By substantial productive investment I mean investment which is large enough to achieve a break-through, or as some economists call it—to produce the "take-off," the passage from stagnation to intensive development. This obviously cannot be done by small amounts of investment which are likely to peter out in a great number of minor projects. Sufficient investment is required to produce a real, a qualitative change in the structure of national economy. This is one problem of developmental planning, namely to secure these resources for productive investment.

The second problem is the direction of investment and here I shall distinguish three sub-problems. The first is how to allocate investment so as to assure the most rapid growth of production; the second is how to secure balanced development of the economy, balance between the different branches of national economy; the third is how to assure efficiency of the use of resources in economic development, how to avoid waste and resources. These are three sub-problems of the general problem of directing investment so as to assure economic development.

The first sub-problem is the most important one. It is concerned with choosing such types of investment as will most rapidly increase the productive power of the economy. This implies a concentration of investment in fields which increase the capacity of further production; that means building up the industries which produce means of production. It is only through development of the industries which produce means of production that the production capacity of the economy can be raised.

This can be done, however, either directly or indirectly. It is done directly through investing in the construction of, say, power plants, steel plants, machine industries, raw material production and so on. It is done indirectly through foreign trade: instead of investing directly in the production, say, of certain machines it may be possible to get these machines from abroad by investing in the production of such commodities which can be sold abroad in order to import the machines required. Thus the productive power of the economy can be increased either directly through investing in the production of means of production, or indirectly through developing export industries which make it possible to import in the future the needed means of production. Which of these two methods is used depends on all kinds of circumstances, of existing facilities for developing either directly the output of means of production, or for producing commodities for export. However, if investment in exportable commodities is undertaken then obviously it must be associated with importation in exchange for these exports of machinery, steel and other means of production to increase the country's productive power.

However, investment in the production of means of production is not the only type of investment needed. There are two complementary types of investment which are necessary. One is investment in agriculture to increase food production. The experience of economic planning, particularly in the socialist countries, has shown that with the growth of industrialisation, with an increasing part of the population being employed in industries or transport services and so on, a considerable surplus of agricultural products is needed to feed the non-agricultural population. Consequently complementary to the investment in the development of the output of means of production must be investment in agriculture to increase agricultural output. Also a certain amount of investment in industries producing consumers' goods for the population is required, for the standard of living rises with the expansion of industrial employment and output. These are then the chief directions of developmental investments. The first one is the strategic one, the one which brings about economic development, and the other two are of a complementary nature necessary in order that economic development can proceed smoothly.

Finally, there is one important field of developmental investment, namely investment in the general economic infra-structure of the country, such as transport facilities, roads and also social services. These, too, are complementary investments needed to assure smooth economic development. However, they by themselves are not a factor bringing about development. One of the problems in many, if not most, underdeveloped countries was—and this was a part of the colonial or imperialist system—that there took place a large construction of this economic infra-structure purely for the needs of colonial exploitation, and not for development of the productive power of the country. . . .

There are two kinds of balances which must be secured: one is the physical balance and the other is financial or monetary balance. The physical balance consists in a proper evaluation of the relations between investment and output. In the countries which have already experience in economic planning investment coefficients are computed. These coefficients indicate the amount of investment in terms of various kinds of goods needed in order to obtain an increase of output of a product by a given amount. For example, how much iron, how much coal, how much electric power is needed in order to produce an additional ton of steel. On this basis the planned increase in output of various products is balanced with the amounts and types of investment. It is also necessary to balance the outputs of the various sections of the economy because, as we know, the output of one branch of the economy serves as input for producing the output of another branch. For instance, the output of iron ore serves as an input in the steel industry. In the last mentioned field a special technique, that of input-output analysis has been developed.

The physical balancing mentioned is necessary in order that the output of the different branches of the economy proceed smoothly. This is a condition of the internal consistency of the plan. If this condition is not observed bottlenecks appear. The plan cannot be carried out because of the physical obstacles, such as lack of raw materials, of manpower, etc.

The second kind of balancing is monetary balancing, assuring monetary equilibrium in the economy. This consists in establishing an equilibrium between the incomes of the population—wages, incomes of peasants and others—and the amount of consumers' goods which will be available to the population. If the amount of incomes, or more precisely that part of the incomes which is spent for purposes of consumption, should turn out greater than the amount of available consumers' goods, inflationary processes develop. Thus the financial or monetary balance must establish an equilibrium between the part of incomes devoted to consumption and the output of consumers' goods. Further it must establish equilibrium between the part of incomes of the population which will be used for private investment and the amount of investment goods made available to private investors. Finally, in the public sector a balance must be established between the financial funds made available for investment purposes and the amount of investment goods which will be produced or imported. In addition to these balances it is necessary to establish the balance of foreign payments and receipts. The financial balances are an important part of planning. Just like the lack of physical balance leads to physical obstacles to the smooth process of production, so the lack of financial balance leads to disturbances in the supply and demand for physical commodities, and finally also to physical disturbances in the process of production.

Looking backwards upon the experience of the countries which applied planning as a tool of economic development, I must say that it usually turned out to be difficult to maintain the proper financial balance. Few of these countries escaped inflationary processes during certain periods. These processes were due to the wage bill rising more rapidly than the output of consumers' goods. However, in theory and with the experience which has been gained in earlier years it is today quite possible to plan the financial equilibrium of economic development in a way which avoids inflationary processes.

A last point—to be only mentioned briefly—is that of securing efficiency in the use of resources in the process of economic development. This is connected with the use of the price system. The function of the price system in economic planning is two-fold. Prices serve as a means of accounting, namely as a means of evaluating cost of production, value of output, and comparing the two. For this purpose it is necessary to have a proper price system which reflects the social cost (and in the short run—the scarcity) of the various means of production and the social importance of the various prod-

ucts. Without such a price system, cost accounting would not have any objective economic significance. This is one role of the price system; the other role is that of an incentive.

The plan of economic development has two aspects: in the public sector it is a directive to various public agencies and enterprises to do certain things, e.g. to invest that much in such a way at such a cost. With regard to the private sector, the plan has not the power of a directive, but is a desire expressed which must be followed by creating such incentives as will induce private producers to do exactly the things which are required from them in the plan. It is quite clear and does not require further explanation that with regard to the private sector the price system, including interest rates, is an important incentive serving to induce the private sector to do things required from it in the plan. But also in the public sector the need for incentive exists. It is not sufficient just to address administrative directives to public agencies and public enterprises. In addition to that it is necessary to create such economic incentives that the public agencies, enterprises, etc. find it in the interest of their management and their employees to do the things which are required from them in the plan. This again requires a proper price system.

Thus the price system plays in planning a role both as a basis of accounting and as an incentive inducing the people to do the things required from them in the plan. A certain general observation may be made here. It seems rather general historical experience that in the first phase of economic development, particularly industrialisation, the problem of a proper price system is not the most important one. In both the socialist and the national revolutionary type of economic development we find that in the first period the main problem is not that of the details of accounting or incentives. The main problem is assuring rapid growth of productive capacity. The question of rapidity of growth overshadows the more subtle questions of high grade efficiency. It is more important, for instance, to develop at all the machine industry than to do it in the most efficient manner. Too much preoccupation with the subtleties of economic accounting may hold up action and slow down progress. It is only on a higher stage of economic development, when the national economy has become more complex and diversified, that the problem of efficiency and incentives become increasingly important. It is then that the subtleties of assuring the highest efficiency of economy through proper cost accounting, through properly established incentives, etc. come into play.

Thus—not wanting to minimise the importance of the problem—I do believe that it is not the most important problem in the first stage of economic development. In this first stage, the take-off stage, the real issue is to mobilise the necessary resources for productive investment, to allocate them to the branches of the economy which most rapidly increase the productive potential of the country, and to do so by the most productive technological methods. At a later stage more subtle aspects of planning come into play. Thus a certain crudeness of planning in the early stages of economic development is, I believe, quite justified.

XII.B.3. Policy Instruments and

Development Alternatives*

There has been little systematic analysis of the relative merits and defects of the policy instruments available to underdeveloped countries. Since control of international trade is administratively simpler than many other types of policy, there has been a tendency to rely heavily on it as a way of influencing the pattern of domestic production, without recognizing the drawbacks to exclusive reliance on this set of instruments. Colonial areas have been forced to devise other measures, since protection was denied to them, but they have rarely pursued overall development policies. The need for a greater variety of measures to promote development has now been widely recognized,

but there is still inadequate consideration of the range of alternatives available.

In its need to change the pattern of resource use over a relatively short period of time, the promotion of development resembles (in lesser degree) the problem of mobilization for war. The suitability of various instruments for the latter purpose has been widely discussed, and the experience of the United States and other countries has been analysed in some detail. A similar study of the actual effects of development policies is needed before very firm recommendations can be made to the under-developed countries, but some general comments may be in order.

CHARACTERISTICS OF INSTRUMENTS

Policy instruments may be classified in various ways: by the sectors of the economy on which they operate, by their use of prices or quantities as variables to be manipulated, by the extent to which they can be effectively controlled by the government, by the

*From Hollis B. Chenery, "Development Policies and Programmes," *Economic Bulletin for Latin America*, Vol. 3, No. 1, March 1958, pp. 55–60; "A Model of Development Alternatives," Vol. 8, United States Papers Prepared for the United Nations Conference on the Application of Science and Technology for the Benefit of the Less Developed Countries, Washington, D.C., 1962, pp. 82–6. Reprinted by permission.

effect that they have on private incentives and freedom of choice, etc. In Table 1 representative instruments are classified according to the extent of their application (general versus specific) and their mode of operation (through prices or quantities). The general instruments act on broad aspects of the economy—the money supply, the government budget, investment, consumption—and are widely used in developed and underdeveloped countries alike. The specific instruments are applied differentially to individual sectors of the economy, as illustrated by subsidies, tariffs, or Government investment.

To achieve a given effect on production, or use of any commodity, there is a choice between controlling a price and controlling a quantity. In this respect, tariffs are an alternative to quotas, differential interest rates are an alternative to capital rationing, and subsidies to private producers are an alternative to production by the government. These measures differ in their effects on prices and consumer choices, in administrative convenience, in the predictability of their results, and in other respects. A choice between quantity and price variables as instruments must therefore be made by balancing the advantages and disadvantages in each case.

Some of the main issues of economic policy are concerned with the choice between general and specific instruments and between using prices and quantities as control variables. There is a strong case to be made for using general instruments rather than specific ones. The rates of interest, taxation, and exchange are the orthodox means of exerting Government influence in a *laissez-faire* economy. Their immediate objectives are stability in prices and the balance of payments and the prevention of unemployment. Growth is left to free market forces. The manipulation of interest rates and exchange rates allows market forces in each sector to determine where expansion or contraction of production and consumption will take place. These instruments therefore interfere less with the choices of producers and consumers than do measures which discriminate by sector. They also require a less detailed analysis for their use and do not substitute Government judgment of what is desirable for the action of market forces.

The need for specific instruments to supplement general measures derives from the deficiencies in the price mechanism which apply primarily to specific sectors of the economy. When these factors prevent the achievement of a satisfactory rate of growth, the problem is to devise policy measures which will improve on the working of the competitive economy without losing the advantages of private initiative and the automatic adjustment of the price system.

In designing policies for specific sectors, there is an argument for using price rather than quantity instruments which is based on reasoning similar to the case for general over specific instruments. Taxes and subsidies distort the choices open to producers and users of a commodity less than do allocation systems or other quantitative restrictions and hence are conductive to greater flexibility and over-all economic efficiency. Furthermore, the administrative requirements for price intervention of this type are generally less than for quantitative controls.

Despite the general case in favour of using the price system, there are several situations in which quantitative measures may be needed:

i. When it is necessary to limit consumption of an essential commodity in short supply (e.g., imported goods), the tax needed to bring about a given reduction in use might result in such high prices that the burden of the reduction would fall on lower income groups. In this case, price controls and rationing may be preferable on welfare grounds.

ii. Where a minimum increase in production is essential to production in other sectors—as in the case of power, transport and various auxiliary facilities—the price needed to ensure adequate private investment may be too high or the response of private investors too uncertain. In this case, quantitative

TABLE 1. Classification of Policy Instruments

Area of Policy	Price Variables		Quantity Variables	
	Instrument	Variables Affected*	Instrument	Variables Affected
Monetary	interest rate	(1) level of investment (2) cost of production	open market operations	(1) money supply (2) prices
Fiscal	personal income tax	(1) consumption and saving	Government expenditure	(1) national income (2) price level
	corporate income tax	(1) profits (2) investment		
Foreign Trade	exchange rate general tariff level	(1) cost of imports (2) price of exports (3) balance of payments	exchange auctions	exchange rates
Foreign Investment	taxes on foreign profits	level of foreign investment	foreign loans and grants	(1) investment resources (2) exchange supply
Consumption	general sales tax	consumption	social insurance, relief, other transfers	(1) consumption (2) income distribution
Labour	wage rates	(1) labour cost (2) profits and investment (3) labour income	emigration and immigration	labour supply

General

810

Production	taxes and subsidies price control	Government production Government research and technical assistance	(1) profits and production (2) investment	level of production cost of production
Investment	interest rates tax exemptions	Government investment capital rationing restrictions on entry	(1) profits (2) investment by sector	level of investment (1) prices and profits (2) level of investment
Consumption	specific sales taxes	Government services (health, education)	consumption by commodity	(1) consumption (2) income distribution
Trade	export subsidies tariffs	import quotas and prohibitions exchange controls	(1) price to consumer (2) profits on domestic production (1) profits and investment	(1) level of imports (2) domestic prices
Labour	wage subsidy	labour training	(1) labour cost and use (2) profits and investment	supply of skilled labour
Natural Resources	taxes and subsidies	surveys, auxiliary investment, etc.	(1) cost of production (2) rate of exploitation	rate of development

*All taxes affect Government revenue and saving in addition to the variables cited.

measures, such as Government investment, may be more efficient because the cost to the society is less or the outcome more predictable.

iii. In general, where controls are needed for only a short period, as in the case of temporary shortages, it may be desirable to allocate supplies to more essential uses rather than upset the general price structure and distort investment decisions by allowing prices to rise. Quantitative measures are also likely to have more predictable effects in this case.

In these examples, it is the dynamic elements in the situation and the deviation from a desirable income distribution which provide the principal arguments for using quantitative measures of control.

SPECIFIC MEASURES FOR INVESTMENT ALLOCATION

Although the specific measures listed in Table 1 affect both current production and the allocation of investment resources, it is the latter aspect that is crucial for the future course of development. The various instruments affect investment decisions through the availability and cost of primary inputs (labour, natural resources, imported commodities); through the supply of inputs from other sectors (raw materials, overhead facilities); through the demand for output (sales taxes, export subsidies); through profits (taxes, subsidies); and through measures directly related to the process of investment (interest rates, capital rationing, restrictions on entry, direct Government investment). There is therefore a considerable variety of choice between quantity and price instruments and among measures more or less directly related to a particular investment.

The *a priori* arguments concerning some of the principal measures for influencing investment decisions run somewhat as follows:

i. *Measures of Protection.* As indicated earlier, protective devices are perhaps the most common instruments for influencing the pattern of investment. For this purpose, tariffs are generally preferable to quantitative restrictions—quotas, prohibitions, exchange controls, etc.—for reasons already indicated. Quantitative restrictions prevent competition with domestic producers regardless of price, raise prices to users and limit demand, and require an elaborate administrative mechanism and detailed economic analysis to be effective. Quotas also involve a loss of revenue to the Government, as compared with the use of tariffs, unless the profits of importers can be recovered through taxes.

The cases where quantitative measures may nevertheless be needed derive from the principles given in the previous section. In cases of extreme shortage of foreign exchange, tariffs (or devaluation) may be too uncertain in their results and quotas or exchange restrictions may be adopted as emergency measures.

The effect of quantitative restrictions on investment in domestic substitutes for imports or in sectors using imported commodities is generally less certain than that of tariffs. Allocations are subject to variation according to the amount of exchange available, and the profitability of domestic production is harder to determine than in the case of a tariff.

As instruments for inducing investment in new types of production, subsidies may be preferable to either quantitative restrictions or tariffs because the price is not raised above the level of world prices. Total demand is therefore greater and using sectors are not penalized in export markets. The cost of this technique in Government expenditure must be weighed against its benefits, however.

Protection from foreign competitors is only one factor in the expansion of domestic production. Also required are entrepreneurs, capital, skilled labour, raw materials, etc. When some of these are lacking, the restriction only serves to reduce imports and raise prices to consumers. Trade restrictions are therefore a rather uncertain method of directing investment unless combined with other measures affecting factor supply, and they frequently have undesirable secondary effects.

ii. *Government Investment versus Incentives to Private Investment.* Although the arguments concerning trade restrictions are based mainly on economic considerations, the choice between Government investment and incentives to private investors involves social and political factors to a large extent. In countries that do not have strong ideological preferences for either private or Government enterprise, the usual approach is to rely on private investment except in cases where it cannot be expected to work in the public interest (e.g., monopoly) or in which its performance has been demonstrably deficient. Since the reaction of investors to various incentives (tax reduction, guaranteed markets, low interest rates, etc.) is subject to considerable uncertainty, such incentives are more likely to be adequate when a general objective is to be achieved—e.g., import substitution, increase of industrial employment—than when increases in output in specific sectors are required. Because of this uncertainty, the extent to which reliance on private investment is desirable can be determined only by an actual trial of specific measures.

Another alternative for securing investment in given sectors when tax incentives are thought to be inadequate or too costly to the treasury is the intervention of a Government agency as entrepreneur but not as a long-term producer. This may be done through development corporations, which sell their investments to private enterprises as they become profitable, or through mixed corporations, in which the role of the Government declines as the enterprise becomes established.

The assumption underlying all these measures is that it is bad for the Government to continue permanently as a producer in most fields. There is a widespread view (shared by the present writer) that the lack of incentives to efficiency in Government operations makes private operation preferable even where conditions are not favourable to the initial undertaking of the investment by private enterprise. In the absence of more objective evaluations of the experience with Government and private enterprise in various countries, it is impossible to support this conclusion empirically, and it is by no means universally held among democratic Governments. In countries such as India, for example, an attempt is made to ascertain the relative merits of public and private investment in specific fields rather than starting from this premise. Even in these cases, however, the sectors that are chosen for Government investment are limited in number and characterized by specific structural features (economies of large scale production, importance of the product, tendency to monopoly, etc.)

The possibility of attracting foreign investment adds a further element to the problem. To the argument against Government investment must be added the loss of additional investment resources, while the argument against private foreign investment must include the removal of profits from the economy and the future burden on the balance of payments. A purely economic evaluation would probably weigh the value of the additional investment resources and managerial talents more heavily than the cost of obtaining them (particularly where there are unemployed labour and natural resources because of lack of these factors), but the decision is infrequently made on purely economic grounds.

QUANTITATIVE ANALYSIS AND CHOICE OF INSTRUMENTS

The preceding discussion has been entirely in qualitative terms, which at best leads to the establishment of certain cases to which particular policies apply. The identification of an actual situation with the relevant case often depends on the results of quantitative analysis. Such factors as the extent of the excess demand for imports, the future amount of unemployed labour, the magnitude of the shift in resources needed in particular sectors, and the importance to the rest of the economy of a given investment, can only be determined from such an analysis. The initial study of development possibilities should be designed to permit a choice of policy instruments in different fields. Once this has been done, the long-term programme can be formulated in more specific terms which take account of the instruments chosen.

The importance of a quantitative analysis for the choice of policy instruments will be determined in part by the presence or absence of the following factors:

i. Economies of scale in production;
ii. The possibility of imports and exports;
iii. The use of the product in other sectors of production;
iv. The predictability of demand.

In the production of consumer goods, the main objective of the development programme is likely to be a certain degree of substitution of domestic production for imports, but the choice of sector can be left to market forces. Quantitative analysis may be needed to determine the amount of employment and exchange saving which should be aimed at in the consumer goods industries, but not to determine the choice of sector.[1]

At the other extreme, the amount and distribution of investment in overhead facilities must be determined entirely from a quantitative analysis of future production because the alternative of imports is not available and output is needed to permit investment and production in other sectors. In some cases the choice between public and

private investment will also depend on the amount of output required.

Choices among policy measures in the intermediate goods sectors are more affected by the outcome of the quantitative analysis than are those in consumer goods because demands derive from the planned outputs of the using sectors. Economies of scale are also more prevalent, and there is thus more interdependence among investment plans in earlier and later stages. While imports provide alternative sources of supply for many intermediate goods, some investments will not be undertaken unless there is a domestic supply of materials available. To ensure the carrying out of several interconnected projects, Government intervention in some form is likely to be necessary because the risk to private investors would be too great. Investments centering on steel production—ore, transport, power, iron and steel, fabricating—provide a good example. Once the initial investments have been made, however, most of them will prove suitable for private ownership and operation.

The advantage to the economy—in terms of the social productivity of the total investment—of inter-related projects of this type cannot be accurately determined from a partial analysis of each investment taken separately because the profitability of one may understate its contribution to the total. This dynamic type of external economy (as opposed to the technological external economies of static analysis) can only be taken account of adequately in the framework of an overall analysis.

TYPES OF DEVELOPMENT PROGRAMMES

A development programme is an analysis which provides a basis for designing and carrying out development policy. There is, however, no sharp distinction between programming and policy making, since each influences the other. The main function of a programme is to make different policies consistent with each other. Ideally, it should go further and help to select the best policies

---

[1] This statement is not true where economies of scale are important as in the case of automobile production, because then the profitability of investment depends on an estimate of the quantity that would be demanded at the expected level of income.

and the best means of carrying them out. The decision to make a development programme does not constitute an endorsement of increased Government intervention, or of any other particular set of policy instruments, therefore.

The nature of the analysis contained in a development programme is determined in part by the information available and in part by the instruments which are being considered. For simplicity, three general types can be distinguished, which I will call aggregate programmes, sector programmes, and over-all programmes.

Aggregate programmes consist mainly of national accounts analyses and projections of other magnitudes such as industrial production, labour force, average productivity, etc. These projections are often combined with a more detailed analysis of certain aspects of the economy, such as the balance of payments, the sources of Government revenue, etc. . . .

Aggregate programmes provide a fairly adequate basis for the use of general policy instruments, but they do not furnish a check on the consistency of the results in specific sectors nor on the balance of payments. They are more likely to be adequate when the composition of production and consumption does not change too much as income increases, and when the market mechanism works well in directing investment and production decisions. . . .

Sector programmes are analyses of the demands and investment prospects in individual branches of production. Their main function is to determine the relative priority of investments within the sector. Investment programmes for the whole economy (or for all resources controlled by the Government) are sometimes constructed by merely adding up the high priority projects in each sector.

The sector approach is generally recognized to be inadequate as a basis for development policy because it does not provide a test of the consistency of the decisions made in each sector, nor a way of comparing high priority projects in one sector with those in

another. It has nevertheless been the principal basis for development policy in Latin America and in most under-developed countries until quite recently. The defects in the sector approach are less serious in primary-producing economies than in those which have reached a high degree of industrialization and hence have a greater amount of inter-dependence among the various sectors.

Over-all programmes combine the elements of aggregate programmes and sector programmes in varying degrees. The analysis may start from over-all projections or from sector analyses, but in the final result they must be reconciled. It is only by some check of this kind that the consistency of the simpler models used in the two partial approaches can be tested. . . .

The need for over-all development programmes is most acute when large structural changes are required to establish or restore a process of balanced growth. Large balance of payments deficits, unemployment, bottlenecks in over-all facilities, and lack of growth may each be evidence of such conditions. These conditions may of course be merely symptoms of an excess or deficiency of total demand, and the diagnosis of structural disequilibrium must try to identify the problems which would exist if inflationary (or, less often, deflationary) forces were offset. The design of policy in such circumstances is likely to call for an over-all analysis, however, whether the policy measures selected are general or specific in nature.

ELEMENTS OF POLICY ANALYSIS

General Scope. A policy model is designed to determine whether proposed economic policies are mutually consistent and to facilitate the choice among them. To fulfill these functions the model must: (a) incorporate the principal limits to achieving social objectives and (b) contain variables that indicate the nature of the policies implied by a given solution. To avoid becoming unwieldy, the model may omit variables which do not significantly affect the type of problem being considered or which can be handled in a separate analysis.

These considerations suggest that models designed to analyze long-run policy in the less developed countries should be significantly different from the models now used for the analysis of primary short-run policies in the advanced countries. Certain features will be emphasized, for example:

a. Long-term supply limitations, both in the aggregate and by sector, should be specified.

b. Since the less-developed country is typically quite dependent on foreign trade, exports and imports must be explicitly included.

c. The model should allow for the inflow of foreign capital as a significant element of development policy.

Objectives. The objectives of economic development are not adequately described as the maximization of any single measure of welfare, such as per capita output or consumption. All societies recognize the need to take account of a number of other social objectives, such as reduced unemployment, greater equality of income, and reduced economic instability. Some of these objectives can properly be taken as limitations on the economic system by assigning a given value or target to the appropriate variable. In most cases, however, it will be desirable to consider a range of alternative values in order to discover the opportunity cost or "trade off" between this and other objectives.

Variables. In his pioneering work on policy models, Tinbergen divides all variables into four categories.

a. *Objectives,* which reflect the aims of policy;

b. *Instruments,* which measure the direct effects of policy;

c. *Exogenous variables (data),* which are taken as given;

d. *Other endogenous* (irrelevant) *variables,* which do not directly affect either the choice of policy or the social welfare.

The first two types of variables—objectives and instruments—are the main concern of policy analysis, and I shall call them *policy variables.* Formally, the analyst's task is to maximize some (unknown) function of the objective variables. As Theil has emphasized, the social welfare is also affected by the values assumed by some of the instrument variables, such as taxes or income distribution, which thus take on some of the welfare characteristics of the objectives. Although a few policy variables, such as the exchange rate, are "pure" instruments which have no welfare implications *per se*, it will be convenient to assume that the desirability of a given type of policy is determined by the values of all the policy variables. A set of values for the policy variables may be called a *program.*

The Choice of Programs. In order to arrive at a political decision on the nature of the development policies to be followed, it is useful to focus attention on a few strategic variables having wide economic and social implications. These variables are primarily those which apply to large segments of the economy and occur in aggregate models, although a few sector decisions may be of the same degree of importance.

The formal model contributes to the choice of policy by determining *alternative feasible programs*—i.e., combinations of the strategic policy variables that are consistent with the social and economic structure of the economy. A feasible program is determined primarily by a solution to an aggregate model, supplemented by whatever elements of sector or inter-industry analysis may be necessary.

The range of programs to be considered should cover values of the policy variables that are politically as well as technically attainable. The solutions produced by the planners should indicate the possibility of achieving the several social objectives in varying degrees. In the absence of prior knowledge of the relative valuation of these objectives, the economist cannot determine an *optimum program.* At best, he can present the alternatives in such a way as to focus political attention on the problem of determining a social choice among a limited number of relevant alternatives. This is likely to be much easier than solving the larger problem of describing social preferences in general terms.

STRUCTURE OF THE MODEL

A policy model should specify the various factors limiting growth and the ways in which they can be modified by the instruments of government policy. The limits to be included depend on the present structure of the economy, the extent of the possible changes in the structure, and the data available for estimating economic relationships.

Since the economic structure may change rapidly in an underdeveloped economy, even a general planning model must pay some attention to the sector composition of demand and supply, which will affect both trade patterns and capital requirements. Once sector analyses have been made, however, their results can be incorporated into an aggregate model, which can then be used to study variations from the initial solution. This procedure will be followed here.

In designing econometric models for less developed countries, it is useful to start from the experience in advanced countries, making allowance for the differences noted above. An examination of aggregate models by Chenery and Goldberger concluded that the long-term model developed for the Netherlands by the Central Planning Bureau, came closest to fitting the needs of the less developed economies. Features of this model that are particularly relevant to the choice of development policy are:

a. The inclusion of a number of policy instruments: the savings rate, import substitution, the relation of domestic to foreign prices, migration.
b. Explicit analysis of foreign trade.
c. Incorporation of the results of inter-

industry analysis into the aggregate model by an iterative procedure.

These elements are utilized in the policy model designed by Goldberger to analyze existing data available for Argentina. The model was further developed by Chenery and Bruno to determine development alternatives in Israel. These models explicitly recognize four limits to growth:

a. The supply of capital
b. The supply of labor
c. The supply of foreign exchange
d. The composition of internal and external demand.

The first three limits are reflected in the basic equations of the aggregate model. The composition of demand at different income levels, together with the possibilities for imports and exports, determines the capital requirements and import demands. . . .

A policy model is characterized by having more variables than equations. . . . This excess of variables constitutes the number of degrees of freedom of the model. . . . To solve the model, the values of a number of variables equal to the number of degrees of freedom must be fixed in advance. In general, the planner can assign consistent values to any combination of policy variables—objectives or instruments—equal to the number of degrees of freedom and then solve for the values of the remaining variables.

The process of solution is facilitated by first eliminating some or all of the irrelevant endogenous variables—i.e., those that are not selected to represent policy objectives. In the Israel case, for example, it was found convenient to reduce the model to four equations in eight variables, of which five are instruments and three are objectives.

These two models both allow for the anticipated composition of demand in estimating import requirements. The coefficients μ_c, μ_g, μ_i, μ_e, represent the total import requirements per unit increase in the four components of final demand: private consumption, government consumption, investment, and exports. The differences in the coefficients show the importance of allowing for changes in the composition of final demand. . . .

In designing the model, the analyst has a considerable choice of variables to represent government policy. It is sometimes feasible to use a variable that directly reflects the effects of government actions, such as the exchange rate. More often there will be several intermediate links between the actual policy measures, which may affect individual sectors of the economy, and the summary measure that it is convenient to use in the general model.

The range of choice is illustrated by the alternatives proposed for the analysis of savings in Argentina. On theoretical grounds, the following set of equations was suggested:

(a) *Net Domestic Saving*
$$S = \alpha_1 W + \alpha_2 R + T - G$$
(b) *Taxation*
$$T = tY$$
(c) *Income distribution*
$$W = w (R + W)$$
Where W = Disposable wage income
R = Disposable non-wage income
T = Taxes
G = Government current expenditure
t = Tax rate
w = Share of wages in disposable income

This formulation shows the several effects of government policy on savings by using three instruments: government expenditure (G), the tax rate (t), and the share of wages (w). Since information was not available to estimate the parameters in the savings and tax functions, the formulation was first simplified to:

(d) $S = \alpha^* Y - G$
and finally to:
(e) $S = \alpha Y$

In the last form, α reflects all the government policies that influence the rate of savings. A similar range of alternatives could be shown for other instrument variables which are less directly connected to the actions of the government.

THE DETERMINATION OF ALTERNATIVE POLICIES

Procedures. The greatest value of a formal model is its ability to determine consistent sets of alternative policies. The weakness of the model approach is its oversimplification of many of the individual features of the economy in order to bring out their interrelations. This drawback can be minimized by starting from a trial program in which additional elements of detailed analysis and judgment have been introduced. The model structure should be adjusted to be consistent with these added elements.

Given a realistic starting point, the model can then be used to explore a range of solutions in which the policy variables vary within predetermined limits. This range, which I shall call the *feasible area of choice*, should cover all the consistent programs that might be of interest to policy makers.

The specified limits for each policy variable must be determined from outside sources. For example, the limits to increased saving may be set by feasible improvements in the tax structure and administration and the probable distribution of income. An optimistic estimate of these factors would set an upper limit to the savings rate that it is worth considering.

This approach demands less precision and detail in the model than would a mechanical application of a formal optimizing procedure. Additional information is used both in establishing the starting point for the analysis and in setting the range over which the equations in the model must hold. The use of linear approximations to non-linear functions can be quite accurate for a limited range when it would not be acceptable for the whole range of values.

Having specified the starting point and the allowable range for each policy variable, the analyst's next step is to fix values for a number of policy variables equal to the number of degrees of freedom in the model. If it is desired to determine the limits to the feasible area of choice, this can be done by setting the instrument variables and the objective variables alternately at their minima or maxima. A set of solutions will determine the range of values that is consistent with all the restrictions. . . .

The last step in the analytical procedure is to narrow the range of choice and finally to present a few of the leading alternative programs to the political authorities for decision. . . .

XII.B.4. Problems of Development Planning*

The basic problem of development planning is the organization of resources for growth. In this, the problem does not differ essentially from what it is in the so-called developed countries, except that in developed economies there exists a market and numerous institutions which can be used for the carrying out of planning ideas. The problem which development planners face in underdeveloped countries is fourfold. Firstly, they frequently lack the signalling system which a well-functioning market provides; secondly, they also lack the institutions by means of which ideas which might crystallize can be put into practice; thirdly, in under-developed countries there does not exist a sufficient number of people who can take the place even of a crudely working price system; and fourthly, basic information of a technical sort, particularly with respect to agriculture, is frequently enough not there, or is available only in a form in which it is not usable. Experience in many countries indicates that it would be fatal to ignore the price mechanism; this is true even in such centrally planned economies as the Soviet

Union or East Germany. And it is not a realistic alternative to say that a government can take the place of a supposedly non-existent entrepreneur class.

Any comprehensive development planning must, in my opinion, make use of all the resources which the country has: there should be no ideological blocks to the employment of both as much state activity and as much private activity as can be possibly executed. . . .

The lack of data and the shortage of trained personnel dictate, in my opinion, the following approach to comprehensive planning.

First, no man can know the future. This is especially true in open economies dependent to an unusual degree on the prices for their export products. . . .

It follows that any long-range plan must be flexible. The view is all too common that a Five-Year Programme—or whatever happens to be the mystic number chosen—is a blueprint for the future which should be altered as little as possible. It is, in fact, the view of the plan as a five-year capital and recurrent budget. On the other extreme is the cynical view of the plan as a series of telephone numbers that can be changed at will. But any realistic plan should provide primarily a sense of direction and consistency. It must, as far as Government expenditure is concerned, still be translated every year into the details of a budget. It must,

*From Wolfgang F. Stolper, "Comprehensive Development Planning," Paper prepared for the Economic Commission for Africa Working Party in Addis Ababa, January 1962, mimeographed, pp. 1, 3–6, 8–13. Reprinted in *East African Economics Review*, I, New Series, December 1964. Reprinted by permission.

therefore, be specified every year in the light of the then available information and the then available resources. Now, obviously, some projects have larger horizons than others: tree crops take longer planning than field crops; oil drilling or a steel mill more than textile mills, bottling plants or even cement plants. But the tempo of road building, of electricity expansion, of sewerage and water expansion and in fact of most programmes can be adjusted quite easily. Hence, while the long-run plan should give direction and over-all priorities, the details remain to be ironed out annually or even more frequently. It is realized that this will lay planning open to continuous political interference which in dictatorships is even more frequent and irrational than in countries that have the check of open debate. But the alternative is the carrying out of programmes even after changing events have shown them to be undesirable. . . .

The central direction, and the sense of where the economy is going, must come from an over-all view of the economy. But because any knowledge of local conditions, if it exists at all, can be found only on the spot the execution of the plan and the detailed planning itself must be decentralized. Moreover, any plan which does not envisage a vigorous growth of a private sector both in agriculture and in industry is doomed to have slower growth rates than could be otherwise achieved. . . .

I envisage a comprehensive plan to consist essentially of three parts: a capital budget for government; recurrent expenditure budgets for government; and policies towards the private sector. In addition, both recurrent expenditures and the policies require frequently the building of institutions, and everything requires the best possible use of the market mechanism, even if it exists in only an imperfect form.

The basic task of comprehensive planning is to ensure consistency and feasibility and to permit a rational determination of priorities. Any generally trained economist who is familiar with general equilibrium theory,

particularly in its modern form of inter-industry economics, knows that the characteristic of an economy is the high degree of inter-relationships among its various parts. To some extent, it is a characteristic of an under-developed economy that its major links are through exports and imports with the outside world while the internal flows are relatively small. I have frequently wondered to what extent this is due to our ignorance of the true facts, and to what extent it truly reflects reality that there are relatively minor internal flows. We take it, for example, much too much for granted that food crops are primarily grown for subsistence when in fact a casual visit to any market indicates that almost any produce—millet, guinea corn, maize, kila nuts, rice, pepper, groundnuts, and what have you—is domestically traded. . . .

No individual project can be evaluated in isolation. Whether it should or should not be executed will depend on the alternative uses which can be made of the capital requested and the manpower available. To ensure consistency, some over-all view has to be gained. The easiest and best developed method of doing so is through the development of national income statistics. . . .

The uses to which such a national income account . . . can be put [are] as follows. First, the politically determined targets in growth terms can be worked out. The projections of gross product at, say, x per cent, can be shown to be feasible by showing the implications which this growth would have. Thus, if in the past y per cent of income had to be invested to achieve x per cent of growth and if the composition of past investment among major sectors is known, it is a fair assumption that the same investment will carry the same rate of growth, unless its composition is drastically changed.

The aggregate model can, secondly, be used to determine—in admittedly rough terms—the order of magnitude of the foreign exchange gap that will develop. This permits the planner some view of whether his investment targets are realistic. It also gives him some clue how he may have to change the composition of investments to reduce the foreign exchange gap. Moreover, it is quite easy to vary such growth models and to build into them various price changes. It may be found that any inflationary trend very quickly tends to spill over into imports and tends to make it increasingly difficult to meet the required import finance.

The same model can also be used to determine the real limits of the investment programme in yet another manner. It is my firm conviction that the real limit to any governmental development programme is the ability to carry recurrent cost. It is virtually impossible to get foreign aid for recurrent cost, with the major exceptions of education and possibly health. Any development programme will raise recurrent costs. These recurrent costs can be translated with relatively minor effort into government absorption of goods and services in the national income sense. If the recurrent costs involved in the programme together with the normal administrative cost become too big and too large a percentage of GDP [Gross Domestic Product] is to be allocated, therefore, to government consumption, this will reduce the available resources in other directions and require either a further lowering of consumption or an increase in the imports to be financed. If it is politically decided that no further sacrifices can be put upon consumers and if it is not feasible to finance a larger import gap, the over-all programme must be reduced.

Finally, the aggregative model is necessary to catch all the indirect repercussions which the investment programmes, whether by government or private persons, will have; particularly on import goods. No amount of adding of additional projects will give the total effect on imports because of these indirect repercussions. The development planner in particular who is aware of the foreign exchange content of many projects should be aware of the probability that he may run into balance of payments trouble even if he got foreign aid for all the foreign exchange

content of each project. The aggregative model allows some assumption of the additional gap created by indirect repercussions and therefore of the additional percentage required either through the country's own resources or through general balance of payments support.

Any aggregative model can therefore be used to provide a planning framework into which projects and programmes are integrated. . . .

The heart of any development programme is an action programme consisting of well thought through projects. What distinguishes the comprehensive approach from a mere list of projects is, first, that an attempt is made to relate the various projects towards each other; secondly, that an attempt is made to take indirect effects into account; thirdly, that an attempt is made to relate policies for both the public and the private sector to the projects; and finally that an attempt is made to make the various projects feed into each other in timing, manpower planning, size and so forth.

It should be repeatedly stressed that many basic facts of the African economies are not known and that, therefore, it will not always be possible to get the necessary facts. Nevertheless, it is surprising how much can be learned if the right sort of questions are asked. It should also repeatedly be stressed that projects must be profitable within a reasonable time. It is not an argument that can be defended economically or politically to say that a loss industry is justifiable because it gives employment; alternative better uses of the capital would have given more employment, as profits can be reinvested while losses require constant subsidies, prevent investment elsewhere, and therefore hamper development.

The intellectual framework of detailed planning is inter-industry economics. The techniques developed by Tinbergen, Chenery, Chakravarty and others must, of course, be imginatively adopted to circumstances. No one in his right mind proposes to set up a system of equations, calculate the matrix and solve it to get the answers. It is questionable whether this would be worthwhile even if the data were available. In any case, we would not have sufficient facts to feed a high-powered modern calculating brain.

The basic problem of development is the allocation of resources in such a manner as to increase the availability of resources. Once the problem of how much consumption increase is to be permitted politically is settled, the major problem becomes one of resource allocation. The major scarcities in most African economies are skilled manpower and capital. Skilled manpower must, therefore, be allocated to raise production and not only capital. With African economies being open, foreign exchange allocation and earnings as well as saving become of paramount importance. . . .

The indirect costs and benefits must be as far as possible evaluated. This, it seems to me, is the heart of comprehensive development planning: that one keeps constantly the interrelation with other parts of the economy in mind. The factual questions must be asked in such a manner that the answers when they are received can be fed into other programmes, into budgets, manpower estimates, foreign exchange budgets, and even that they can be used by an existing development corporation anxious to invest capital or attract a foreigner with lures of a prospective profitable market and capital participation. I am not preaching perfection but only the beginning of an attempt to look at a plan *in toto* and to evaluate projects within a context. The reason is, to state the point *ad nauseum*, that all our decisions in economics are of a "more-or-less" nature and not of an "either-or" nature; that we rarely will condemn a project outright but will mainly question its size and timing and that we will make the manner of its execution and indeed whether and when it is to be executed dependent upon other decisions taken simultaneously. There is, to repeat another point already made, some notion around that if only enough unprofitable enterprises are started somehow the economy will grow. Some vague and misunderstood concept of external economies and balanced growth will usually be mentioned. . . . Moreover, there is never any virtue in investing money at a loss, even if the money is available and not at the time usable for other projects. Opportunity cost for funds is measured in interest rates which are quite high throughout the world. And losses mean that you come out with less resources than you started with, which is not development. . . .

It is, of course, impossible to do more than one thing at a time. What distinguishes comprehensive planning from a mere list of projects is not that there is no such list of projects but that the final list has been arrived at in the process of making the various individual programmes consistent with each other. They all must be added up, must be matched against each other and against the available resources. Only in this manner can some less profitable projects be shown to be undesirable. Because only then can it be conclusively shown that the execution of a less desirable project will interfere with a more desirable one. Only then can it be shown that the true choices are between a programme with a "more" and a programme with a "less" growth inducing distribution of investments. It goes without saying that the final decision must be made by the Ministers on a political level, and that is as it should be because a rapid economic development is only one of several possible and possibly conflicting political aims. I should not worry widely about the possible conflict. It is the characteristic of an optimal situation that no further improvement in one direction can be made without a deterioration in another. After all, how do you know that you are on top of a mountain and not in a saddle? All you have to do is to take steps in different directions. If the only way is down, you know you are as high as you can go. The technician must, however, have made a clear case in which the choices to be made are plain to the politician:

more projects mean more taxes and/or internal borrowing and/or foreign aid;

expansion in one direction must be balanced by contraction in another if tax increases, etc., are to be avoided;

execution of lower payoff projects will stimulate growth less than that of higher payoff projects; it will therefore reduce potential government revenues and potential domestic savings; it will therefore lead to a less fast growth in consumption, investment, employment and growth than possible in the circumstances.

All this can never be shown by treating individual projects in isolation. Nor can a sensible answer to what is a desirable project be found without tracing through as many of the repercussions as it is feasible to do in the admittedly rough circumstances with which the planner is faced.

XII.C. PLANNING EXPERIENCE

XII.C.1. On Assessing a
Development Plan*

In assessing a development plan we have to consider three matters: first, its contribution to policy-making, secondly its size, and thirdly its priorities.

POLICY-MAKING

I put policy-making first because I am convinced that sound economic policies are more important to economic development than mere expenditure of money by the Government. In private enterprise systems the amount the Government has to invest is always less than half of the total capital formation required in the country. It is therefore important to adopt policies which encourage private investment to come forward in the right magnitude in the right places. Resistance to this has been strongest among those who do not know how large are the total sums required if an even moderate rate of development is to be achieved. In my experience, resistance crumbles as soon as the figures are demonstrated.

Resistance has crumbled remarkably in all under-developed countries in the past ten years in relation to investment in manufacturing industry and in mining. Everywhere these countries are now competing in trying to create a framework which will encourage private investment. They do industrial research, set up propaganda bureaus, offer tax concessions, pass legislation to secure titles to land and to minerals, and spend lavishly on entertaining, persuading and helping business men. That this pays off is amply illus-

*From W. Arthur Lewis, "On Assessing a Development Plan," *Economic Bulletin of the Economic Society of Ghana*, May–June 1959, pp. 2–16. Reprinted by permission.

trated by the parts of the world where it is done on a substantial scale.

Attitudes have not been changed so radically in relation to agriculture. There is greater reluctance to grant concessions for agricultural enterprises than for mining or for manufacturing. More important, little progress is being made anywhere in Africa or in Asia (other than India) in creating an appropriate framework for small farming—in tackling the fragmentation of farms, in providing adequate agricultural credit, in organising adequate agricultural extension services, in building subsidiary roads, dams and irrigation facilities, or in controlling agricultural debt. Agriculture is still the Cinderella of development programmes.

In the field of housing there is even less understanding of the need to create an encouraging framework for private investment, in view of how little money the Government has, in relation to housing needs. Nearly always one finds that the planners of housing policy are discussing mainly how many houses the Government is going to build. A little arithmetic shows that the number of houses the Government can afford to build is, even at the most generous estimate, only a small fraction of the houses needed. The major problem is to encourage private building, and in countries where only a few people live in rented accommodations, the main problem is to help people build better houses for themselves. Self-help building schemes are now making their appearance. It is also coming to be understood that the Government must not fix rents at un-economic levels unless it has the money and can afford to build all the houses which private building is thereby discouraged from providing. In effect, the main objective of housing policy, in poor countries, should be to use such money as is available to stimulate building by others, rather than for the Government to build houses itself.

I think that Ghana's experience under the First Development Plan proves my proposition that policy is more important than expenditure. Very large sums of money were spent by the Government, but since the industrial, agricultural, mining, and housing policies were inappropriate, very little increased productive capacity resulted from these large expenditures. There was a remarkable increase in public facilities, such as roads, schools, electric power, water supplies, and so on, but remarkably little increase in the output of commodities. Considering also how much was wasted by overloading the building industry, one can say without hesitation that the country would have made more progress if it had spent less and had had better economic policies. So I deduce that the most important question to ask, when assessing a development plan, is whether the policies are adequate to stimulate private investment in the production of commodities. I do not think that this is fully realised in Ghana, where some people seem to be hypnotised by the magic of large numbers. However, the Second Development Plan, as drafted, laid great emphasis on creating an appropriate framework, through reasonable policies and institutions.

SIZE

This brings me to expenditure. What is the right size for a development programme? There is no scientific answer to this question. One must use one's judgment.

The normal way of making a development programme is to begin with an assessment of what the country needs. Every Minister or Department is asked to list projects and expenditures which it would consider to be beneficial. This approach provides no answer to the question how large a develop-

ment programme should be. The needs of under-developed countries are virtually unlimited. Anybody could make a development plan for Ghana, for instance, which provided for spending £G1,000 million over the next five years, and which was thought reasonable in relation to the country's need for water supplies, better roads, hospitals, schools, factories, agricultural equipment, irrigation works, and so on. Yet, any individual who based his personal expenditure programme upon his needs without regard to his resources, would soon be written off by his fellow men as irresponsible. In determining size, the basis of a development plan is not needs, but resources.

For most countries, the principal limitation on the size of the programme is now money. There are some fortunate countries where the limitation is not money, but physical resources. This was the case with Ghana under the First Development Plan. The Government tried hard to complete the Plan in five years, and at all times had more than enough money to do so, but was unable to do so. At the beginning the physical limitation was the capacity of the building industry. Construction is normally about two-thirds of capital formation, and so a sudden attempt to increase capital formation is always frustrated by lack of trained construction workers, insufficiency of building firms, and difficulties of supervision. The result, as in Ghana, is that projects cost twice as much as they should, contractors make enormous profits, works are badly designed or badly built, and everything takes much longer to achieve than was expected. This limitation is temporary, since the construction industry can expand and in time does expand to whatever extent is required. Thus, whereas the capacity of the construction industry was a bottleneck in most countries in the early nineteen-fifties, this is no longer the case. . . .

A more serious limitation in under-developed countries now is political and administrative capacity. To carry out a programme, decisions must be made at the right time, preliminary researches must be made, blueprints ordered at the right time, contracts placed at the right time, and so on. Not enough importance is attached to the absence of preliminary researches, which are a bottleneck to absorptive capacity. You cannot decide suddenly to invest in mines, without first having the geological surveys made, and this takes time. You cannot build hundreds of factories in five years, if each factory is to be properly studied, carefully designed and located, and fitted into appropriate commercial arrangements for its materials, labour management, and the marketing of its products. The political aspect of administrative competence is also important. If reasonable decisions are to be made, the people who have to make decisions must be appointed on merit, and not merely for political or racial reasons. Contracts must be awarded to people who are capable of carrying them out, and not merely to political friends. We hear much about corruption in under-developed countries, but the harm done by bribery or by theft seldom exceeds hundreds of thousands of pounds a year, and though morally deplorable, is quite small when compared with the harm which is done by appointing people to big jobs which they are not competent to do properly. Most under-developed countries are in this sense incapable of executing large development programmes. The larger the programme, the less preparation is given to each project, and the greater is the number of incompetent people appointed to public service. Programmes fall into arrears, are overcostly, and are badly executed. . . .

In most of the under-developed countries today the main limitation on the size of the programme is lack of money. Leaving aside the possibilities of credit creation, which are not relevant in West Africa, most countries either do not raise enough in taxes, or cannot borrow enough money to carry out the programmes which they could conveniently administer. . . .

One important element in deciding how large a development programme should be is to look at the effects of the programme on the ordinary budget. Capital expenditure carries with it recurring commitments, so one way of discovering how much capital to spend (assuming that you can raise the capital) is to assess how much recurrent expenditure the country can afford to bear. There is no point in building schools or hospitals, if you cannot find the money to pay teachers or nurses. And there is no sense in borrowing, if you will not be able to meet the debt charges.

It follows that one of the ways of assessing a plan is to look carefully at what that plan says about the future of the recurrent budget. If it says nothing, or very little, one can deduce either that the planners have forgotten that capital expenditure carries recurrent commitments, or else that the recurrent commitments are so large that they prefer to hide the fact that they are biting off more than they can chew.

PRIORITIES

Under this heading I deal with a number of topics which do not normally receive sufficient consideration.

First, basic surveys are usually starved of funds. I refer here to geological surveys, soil surveys, mapping, marine biology, the measurement of river flows, and fundamental agricultural research. Moreover the officials responsible for these surveys have become so used to not having the money they need, that they no longer even ask for it. The economist planner has to knock at their doors and plead with them to ask for more money. Frequently they reply that they could not get the bodies even if the money were available, because salaries are inadequate.

Next, one should look at basic training. In these days, the favourite sons in West Africa are elementary education and University education. Elementary education is being pushed so rapidly that nobody knows what to do with the half illiterates who are now forsaking the countryside and crowding the towns. At the other end money is being poured out on University education to produce, at £2,000 to £3,000 per pupil per year (because there are not enough students) what the students could get elsewhere at a cost to the Government of only £600 per pupil per year. Meanwhile, the real bottleneck in Africa, which is secondary education, is hopelessly neglected. . . . Everywhere people are concerned about technical training, for nurses, secretaries, foremen, agricultural assistants, medical assistants, and other intermediate grades. The basis for this is secondary education, and one can judge any African plan by the extent to which this is realized. I say African plan, because this is an African problem. In most of Asia, 10 per cent of the children receive secondary education, whereas in most of Africa the figure is less than 1 per cent.

The third element to look for, in a development plan, is the basis on which the demand for the services of public utilities has been estimated. This is usually quite haphazard. Perhaps somebody is bitten with the bug of electricity, and puts in twice as much as is needed; or as in Ghana, in the first Five-Year Plan, the estimator is conservative and puts in only half as much as is needed. Similarly with roads, water supplies, port services, railroads and telephones. This is the point where economists pride themselves that their techniques have something to offer. They make mathematical exercises, estimating the growth of demand. They speak of the need for consistency between public and private intentions, and they even use input-output tables to demonstrate appropriate relationships. Actually, this is the area where precise estimation matters least, because mistakes find themselves out rapidly. If the planner neglects to provide adequate services, a bottleneck develops, people fuss, and the mistake can be corrected quickly. Fortunately too, if the planner provides too much service, he is not in error for long, since rapidly growing populations and productivities soon produce enough extra de-

mand to catch up with over-capacity. The difficulty arises not in matching public supply to the needs of private commerce, but in deciding how much service to provide for domestic consumers. How high a priority should one accord to water supplies in the village, to rural electrification, to providing good road surfaces even where road traffic is small, to hospital and medical services, to broadcast rediffusion, to decent prisons, and to such other consumer facilities? These are matters for political decision. I can only answer for myself that I put these high above the prestige expenditures which clutter up so many programmes.

The next thing to look for in a development plan is the balance between what is being done for the countryside, and what is being done for the towns. It is easy to test a development programme for this by splitting up its proposed expenditures on an area basis, and calculating how much will be spent in the capital, and how much in the rest of the country. There is always a curious disparity between what the Ministers want, and what back-benchers in Parliament want. The back-benchers mostly come from the countryside, and they press the demands for water supplies, roads, hospitals, and the like. The Ministers, however, live in the capital. I have never known a Cabinet which was not persuaded that the most important thing to do with public money was to beautify the capital, leaving only scraps for rural development. Thus the capital becomes an imposing facade which impresses the tourists until they go into the countryside and see how little has been done for the great majority of the people living in the villages. The capital does not stay beautiful for long. The concentration of development there attracts people to flood into it from the countryside, and the slums multiply even faster than the magnificent structures.

The remedy for this lies in the machinery for making the development plan. One can take it as axiomatic that any programme which is made by a planning office in the capital, using data from the central ministries, will be a bad plan from this point of view. A plan should be prepared at the grass-roots, by a large number of provincial committees. One cannot escape the fact that it will fall to the centre to determine the distribution of funds between the provinces, but if the provinces are well organized, and have made good plans for themselves, their needs cannot be disregarded as easily as happens when there are no provincial committees.

One should look next at the flow from the countryside to the towns, i.e., at the rate of urbanization. In most under-developed countries urbanization is occurring too rapidly. People are coming into the towns faster than the towns can provide jobs, houses, busses, water, electricity, and other amenities. Measures are required at both ends, to diminish the flow from the countryside, and also to improve the facilities in towns.

It is not easy to diminish the flow from the countryside. The impact of primary education is only one reason for this flow, which would occur even if the school curricula were better designed to fit rural children for rural life. Towns have substantial advantages over the countryside in terms of amenities, and will always attract people. . . .

Lastly, I come to the question of prestige expenditures. In every country of the world, rich or poor, politicians believe that the greatness of their country is demonstrated by one or another kind of large useless expenditure. The United States strains to put more and more planets into orbit around the sun. The United Kingdom was unhappy without hydrogen bombs. France has an irrepressible taste for colonial wars. In the more ridiculous of the under-developed countries the leaders go in for flashy uniforms, palaces, toy armies, television, innumerable embassies, military parades and other symbols of splendour. In the more sensible of the under-developed countries the weakness for prestige shows itself not so much in the objects of expenditure which are desirable in themselves, but in doing on a lavish and magnificent scale what could be done much more cheaply, and especially in lavish expen-

diture on airports, model towns, and imposing public buildings. Since these manifestations are universal and inevitable, there is not much point in grumbling about them. There may even be something to be said for some expenditure of this kind. Most of us derive some satisfaction from wasting our own money on prestige objects and the nation as a whole is the same. Everybody takes some pride in seeing fine structures going up in one's country, and only a few realise that the cost is less money spent on giving the villages water, schools, or sanitation. Those of us who know the cost can only hope that prestige expenditure will be kept to reasonable proportions. I would give high marks to a development programme in which only 10 per cent of the expenditures was in nonsense of this kind, whereas a programme in which the figure reached 30 per cent would seem to be well below par.

One way of keeping down such expenditures, is to have a development programme made openly. The programme should be made not by the Cabinet, but by a Committee of public persons especially charged to make it, such as the Planning Commission in India, or the Planning Commission in Senegal, or Tunisia, and elsewhere. The procedure is to appoint a representative Committee consisting of some officials and some private persons, including business men, trade unionists, and members of Parliament. They consider material submitted by the Regional Committees and the proposals made by ministries and government departments, and publish what in their opinion would be the best plan. In this way one keeps to a minimum prestige objects, expenditures on political roads, excessive glorification of the capital, and similar defects. The Government is not, of course, obliged to accept what such a Committee recommends any more than it is obliged to accept the report of any other commission of inquiry. Bur if it wishes to add or exclude projects, it must give its reasons; and so it is less likely to make indefensible decisions than is the case where the whole plan is made in secret under the control of the Cabinet, without the public having the benefit of an impartial nonpolitical report with which to compare what the Government proposes.

Of course, all the foregoing presupposes that the published Plan is a serious document, in the sense that the Government means to do what it contains, and means not to do what is excluded. This is not always the case. A development programme can be used as a means of window-dressing, and is often so used. The Government omits from the plan things which it intends to do but prefers not to talk about, such as some prestige expenditures; and it puts into the plan things which will impress some readers, but which it does not intend to do. When the programme is obviously grossly excessive, because the Government has not had the courage to eliminate the lesser priorities, one cannot take it seriously at all, since it is clear that the Government cannot fulfill its promises, and it is also more than likely that what gets done will be determined rather by political pressures than by objective urgency. For this there is no remedy other than a strong public opinion, which does not exist in most under-developed countries. But this means that what must be assessed eventually is not what the Government says it will do, but what it actually does.

XII.C.2. Planned Development in India*

The structure of our economic policies in the last two decades of planned development was founded on six major premises:

(1) The only sensible long-term way of eradicating poverty must be to create more jobs by investing and growing faster; hence, redistributive measures which would tend to use up investible resources in current consumption were undesirable.

(2) In consequence, the Government must direct its major effort at raising the domestic savings rate and securing external aid to supplement domestic savings until such time as the domestic savings rate had been raised to levels adequate to do away with foreign aid altogether and achieve rapid growth with self-reliance.

(3) The industrial sector, which would grow with investment and income, had to be planned and controlled *in depth*: towards

*From Jagdish N. Bhagwati, *India in the International Economy*, Lal Bahadur Shastri Memorial Lectures, Institute of Public Enterprise, Hyderabad, 1973, pp. 3–12. Reprinted by permission.

this end, very detailed targeting and regulatory licensing of industrial establishments was considered necessary and resulted in the Industries (Development and Regulation) Act of 1951.

(4) The external accounts, *i.e.*, the balance of payments, had also to be regulated, not *via* exchange rate adjustments and the use of protective tariffs, but by resort to comprehensive exchange control so that the use of imported raw materials, capital goods and other supplies was to be regulated by an elaborate administrative mechanism.

(5) Alongside these four basic premises of economic policy was the objective of an increasing role for the public sector in the ownership of the country's resources. As the succeeding Industrial Policy Resolutions and the pronouncements of our Prime Ministers underlined, this was a political objective but also one which reflected certain economic axioms. Thus, we thought that the public sector would invest where the private sector would not invest (*e.g.,* steel in the Second Plan); and, in particular, the public sector

would generate surpluses for investment, obviating the need to raise savings exclusively *via* the politically-difficult budgetary process of taxation. These dual economic objectives in expanding the public sector went alongside with the envisaged role of the expanding public sector in conjunction with the industrial licensing policy in controlling the concentration of private economic power. There was also the additional political objective of securing public control over the so-called "commanding heights" of the economy, the "basic" or "key" sectors.

(6) Finally, while these policy instruments embraced directly the non-agricultural sector of our economy, though in turn influencing no doubt the agricultural sector, the Plan programmes repeatedly urged land reforms to transform the institutional structure in the rural economy and urged rural works programmes so that expanding production would go hand in hand with better income distribution.

Experience has now shown that these premises of our policies have been either misguided or inadequate or unrealistic in our political framework. In short, a serious restructuring of our policies is called for. Indeed, many of the more dramatic measures of recent years, especially the nationalization of banking and wholesale wheat trade, are evidence that a restructuring is either being intentionally designed or being forced by the complex of political and economic circumstances on the government. Hence a realistic appraisal of where our policy premises fell short is necessary to examine the optimal policy mix for our economy and to judge, in perspective thereof, the present and prospective governmental actions and programmes. To this task, I shall now turn.

(1) The estimates of increasing poverty in India have underlined the lesson that growing incomes do not necessarily trickle down to the bottom deciles. Even if they did, the process would be so slow that it would be intolerable in the time it would take: it is morally difficult and politically impossible to ask those in poverty to wait until perhaps the next millennium for significantly improved incomes. The early faith in the ability of growing incomes and investments to take care of the poor within the foreseeable future, in any significant fashion, is no longer with us.

(2) The failure of the income-generation mechanism to make an impact on poverty, in turn, must be traced to the inappropriateness of the other policy premises I listed earlier. The policy premise that domestic savings should be stepped up steadily and the level of external aid should be tapered off as the domestic savings took its place has been only partially fulfilled: ironically, aid has substantially fallen for exogenous reasons since the mid-60's but domestic savings which increased steadily through the first three Five-Year Plans, have stagnated since then! (It is tempting to argue, as some radical economists have recently argued elsewhere, that over the long haul the presence of foreign aid in fact may have reduced our domestic savings effort; but systematic economic analysis does not support such a charge). The Indo-Pakistan War, the refugee relief burden and the outflow of significant net resources to Bangladesh have undoubtedly contributed their share to this continuing failure to resume the rate of increment in the domestic savings rate. Nonetheless, since the mid-60's even our traditional strategy of increasing the rates of saving, investment and job-plus-income-creation has not been pursued with any degree of success.

(3) But the efficacy of this developmental strategy has been undoubtedly impaired also by the inefficiency which has resulted from our framework of industrial and foreign trade policies. Even while we heroically raised our domestic rate of saving through successive budgets, our policies which defined the *use* of these savings and accumulated capital stock have left us with intolerable inefficiencies and diminished returns to our efforts.

There are so many inefficiencies inherent in these policies that one could write volumes cataloguing them, as indeed I have! But let me highlight a few of the most obvious ones, focusing first on the industrial policy framework and next on the foreign trade regime, though the conjunction of both has disproportionately accentuated some of the unfortunate consequences of either taken by itself.

The detailed industrial targeting cannot possibly take into account costs and benefits at a micro-level. Industrial licensing has either buttressed this targeting or made the non-targeted industrial development none-the-less go through a series of substantially meaningless bureaucratic scrutinies for which no rational economic criteria have ever been defined or at least discovered. Import licensing, in combination with the principle of indigenous availability, has conferred "automatic protection" to domestic industry regardless of costs. The pro-rata-to-capacity allocations of imported (and other) materials to licensed units have, in combination with automatic protection and licensing restrictions on domestic entry, eliminated virtually all effective foreign and domestic competition, and in consequence also the incentive to efficiency and cost-reduction. The practically-assured markets for licensed units (in view of the elimination of foreign and domestic competition) and the guaranteed share in the available inputs as soon as capacity is licensed have also meant that, even when there was excess capacity in an industry or a product, there could still be adequate incentive to add to capacity: there is little doubt that, while we have been eager to blame aid-tying to project imports for much of our phenomenal underutilisation of capacity, it is very much a result of our own licensing and allocation policies which make the additional of yet more capacity to underutilized-capacity industries ever so profitable.

This pattern of "bureaucratic capitalism" is reminiscent of the "bureaucratic socialism" from which the Soviet Union is busy disengaging itself in its Liebermannist reforms; but we have stuck to it, with occa-sional Ministerial and Prime Ministerial exhortations to improve it—exhortations which are no longer amusing—never facing up to the stark and compelling fact that it is one of the supreme examples of counterproductive and ill-conceived economic policy-making. Adam Smith discovered the Invisible Hand; and economists have correctly argued, in Joan Robinson's colourful phrasing, that the Invisible Hand may often work by strangulation. But the maze of meaningless controls that we continue to work with, so that the Invisible Hand is nowhere to be seen, represents a regression, a *reductio ad absurdum* that does our intelligence little credit and our economy much harm.

Indeed, one must ask why this policy framework continues and answer that it is not merely a product of misguided thinking on the part of our intellectual Left—for several of us who are on the Left have already rejected this travesty of radicalism. It surely has to be explained, in the ultimate political analysis, as the most obvious and ideal instrument for creating an elaborate facade to delude the masses into the belief that Socialism is being practised while, in reality, the policy merely serves to create political power and patronage, essentially leading to shared economic power in the urban areas between the private sector and the politicians, and to spawn ever more, in Shakespeare's phrase, "caterpillars of the Commonwealth": the economic agents whose function is to seek out the "rents", the monopoly profits which the system itself creates through the endless generation of licensed allocations, and the bureaucratic agents, with whom they have a symbiotic relationship, whose function is to allocate these rent-earning privileges among the competing claimants.

(4) Let me turn now to the foreign trade and exchange rate policies which, as I have already indicated, have critically reinforced this inefficient policy framework.

The automatic protection mindless of the cost of import substitution and the elimination of virtually any competitive spur to efficiency, which I have already noted, were the product of the comprehensive exchange control that we settled down to as a long-term way of managing our balance of payments.

The overvalued exchange rate has also implied a continuing discrimination against exports: a phenomenon that has become so obvious that the government has repeatedly sought to offset it by special subsidies to exportation. But the several export subsidy programmes have been generally chaotic in their selectivity and have reproduced on the export front the irrationalities and inefficiencies that have afflicted the import substitution mechanism. The multiplicity of effective exchange rates for exports, necessitated by the adherence to overvalued exchange rates, is a serious source of waste and must inevitably reduce the returns to our economic sacrifices.

Compounding these inefficiencies has been our peculiar attachment, only slightly diminished through the years, to making all import allocations generally non-transferable. The resulting bottle-necks and inflexibility are a totally gratuitous source of additional, and significant, waste in the system; they must also seriously impede exports where the ability to grasp sudden opportunities and to produce with predictable and rapid access to materials without red tape is surely criticial.[1]

And let us not forget the simple but critical fact that the attempts to offset the ill-effects of over-valuation of the exchange rate on export performance through greater reliance on export incentives are also an additional source of the corruption which has now become almost endemic to our scene—and again, this is totally unnecessary as the most effective and efficient incentive to export is provided by eliminating the over-valuation of the exchange rate as some developing, and many developed, countries have now come to understand and practice.

Let me stress again that the objection to the energetic use of flexibility in setting the exchange rate has little justification in a radicalism that is concerned with socialist objectives as distinct from so-called socialist instruments of economic policy. In fact, not merely in India, but in many other developing countries which went through a phase of comprehensive exchange control in the three decades since the War, the exchange control regime has made a mockery of income distributional objectives by creating profits and privilege. And it is only the unthinking segment of intellectual opinion, which is mechanically wedded to obsolete and defunct notions, which would want to stick to overvalued exchange rates as a matter of *principle*. . . .

Finally, I must reject the widespread notion that somehow, in Indian conditions, exchange rate flexibility would be unworkable. In this regard, the experience of the June 1966 devaluation has been widely misunderstood. The 1966 devaluation turned out to have been badly planned and timed, from a political and psychological standpoint: the extreme pressure exerted by the Aid India Consortium in favour of the devaluation produced a perfectly natural nationalist reaction which put the devaluation into a politically unacceptable strait-jacket; and the second major agricultural drought that followed it led to major price increases and export supply difficulties which swamped the effects of the devaluation. Careful analysis, which is necessary to separate out the effects of the drought from the effects of the devaluation, and which Prof. T. N. Srinivasan and I have just concluded, strongly indicates that the latter were favourable; and that, in the absence of the devaluation, the economy would have been in yet worse shape thanks to the drought.[2]

(5) Turning next to the economic objectives to which the public sector was sup-

---

[1] These and other consequences of our trade and exchange rate policies were extensively discussed in J. Bhagawati and Padma Desai, *India: Planning for Industrialization*, London, 1970.

[2] Cf. J. Bhagwati and T. N. Srinivasan, *Foreign Trade Regimes and Economic Development: India*, National Bureau of Economic Research, Amsterdam, 1974.

posed to contribute, I am afraid that the outcome, while not as unfortunate as in the case of our trade and industrial policy framework, has been less than satisfactory. For one reason or another, the contribution made by the public sector enterprises to public saving has fallen considerably short of our early optimism. Brilliant economists, of whom we now have a growing number, can readily construct rational reasons why a public investment may be run at a private loss and yet contribute to social gain. But these reasons have as little to do with the actual occurrence of inadequate profits, and resulting savings, in the public sector as do the sophisticated reasons for selective taxing and subsidising of foreign trade with the situation actually obtaining and described by me earlier in this Lecture.

As for the role of the expanding public sector investments, in conjunction with industrial licensing, in restraining the growth of the concentration of economic power, the growth of the Large Industrial Houses has amply shown that we were not fully successful. At the same time, the stagnation in the rate of industrial investment, under the later policy of confining the Large Industrial Houses to the so-called "core" industries, suggests strongly that neither the public sector nor the small-scale sector has been able to fill the vacuum: so that we have run into the additional problem that a policy which seeks to confine the growth of the Large Houses to only the supposedly socially necessary "core" industries is also contributing, given the failure on the part of the public and the limited capacity of the small-scale sectors, to stagnation in industrial investments. At the same time, one cannot suppress the thought that there is little that is more than symbolic in a policy framework which leaves the Large Industrial Houses at their greatly-augmented capital stock and accompanying politico-economic power and seeks to convince the masses that somehow the prevention of a purely marginal addition to this capital stock is tantamount to ushering in socialism.

Indeed, it is somewhat ironic that we have now shifted from viewing the "core", the "basic", the "key" sectors as essentially the preserve of the public sector, in its exclusive or dominating domain, to viewing the "core" industries as the particularly choice investment field for what appear to be unsympathetic and uninvesting Large Industrial Houses. It is almost as if the attainment of the "commanding heights of the economy", that colourful phrase we learnt to use in progressive circles, had produced, not bliss but, vertigo!

(6) And let me turn finally to the sixth and last policy premise: that agricultural growth would be accompanied by improved income distribution *via* land reform and expanding rural works programmes. It is only an urban intelligentsia which needs to be reminded that, in a country such as ours, with the bulk of its population and its poor on land, socialist programmes cannot be formulated meaningfully except in so far as they involve the agricultural sector. The utmost importance attaches therefore to our agricultural land reforms. And yet, our progress on this front has been slow despite volumes of legislation on the subject. The readiness and ease with which the modern, non-agricultural sector has been subjected to the extensive pseudo-socialist regulation and control I have just discussed contrasts starkly with the lack of genuine socialist transformation in our agricultural economy, so that we have to-day an economy which is like an iceberg whose tip has the glossy look of socialism but whose bulk underneath has diverse capitalist and quasi-capitalist elements.

Nor have our rural works programmes ever become substantial or effective enough to make for a real impact on the agricultural economy. We have repeatedly built them into our Plans and talked of the numerous tasks that the "surplus" rural labour could be mobilized to perform. But, in the absence of organizational input and financial resources, we have had few results that would match our self-exhortations. Again, China has succeeded admirably here by being able to use its abundant labour in the communes, thus automatically providing the organizational framework and obviating the need to make budgetary allocations to compensate the "hired" labour.

We thus find ourselves in a situation where few of our original policy premises can be regarded as acceptable if we are to get the economy moving in the direction of rapid growth, self-reliance and social justice.

The present trade and industrial policies have reduced the returns to our investments. There are no mitigating "beneficial" effects such as increased savings in the economy or increased inducement to invest or enhanced R and D which can plausibly be cited, with supporting evidence. In our study of India's foreign trade regime,[3] Professor T. N. Srinivasan and I have examined these aspects at length, only to conclude that there is no escape from the unpleasant evidence of the harmful effect of our policies on industrial efficiency and thence on the overall performance and growth of our economy.

These policies have also increased our external dependence—a paradox only if you believe that comprehensive exchange controls and licensed allocations must necessarily eliminate such dependence. By adversely affecting our export performance, and by reducing the value added and hence

[3] Bhagwati and Srinivasan, Ibid.

increasing the consequent demand for external resources, *ceteris paribus*, corresponding to any investment in import substitution, we have compounded our dependence on foreign aid beyond what our early planners envisaged as the period during which we could take "aid to end aid". . . .

And finally let me stress the unpleasant but incontrovertible fact that our policies have been inadequate to the task of bringing social justice to our society. By reducing efficiency and the rate of growth, our trade and industrial policies have in fact cut into even the small but probable improvement in the incomes of the poor that we had hoped for. And as for their direct impact on income distribution, they have essentially redistributed income from the rich to the *nouveau riche*: the poor have indeed no way of asserting themselves in the marketplace but, in our policy framework, they equally cannot afford to wait in queues for licences nor do they have the position, privilege and resources to push past the line. Nor has our targeting and industrial licensing diminished the continuing and increasing use of resources to satisfy the needs of the rich, and the not-so-rich. And, as I noted earlier, our rural programmes and halting land reforms have left us with only increasing numbers below the poverty line in the last two decades.

A restructuring of our policy framework is, therefore, called for.

XII.C.3. Role of the State in the Least

Developed Countries*

Nine major elements in the implementation of development can be sketched out from the experience and aspirations of the least developed countries. As will become evident when they are examined, they all imply a central role for the State. This is hardly surprising—it is a historical fact that, with quite minor exceptions, the later a political-economic unit has embarked on a serious development effort and the greater the disparities between its own levels of institutional and productive forces and those of highly developed political-economic units, the greater has been the role of the State. Regardless of their attitudes towards private enterprise, income distribution or socialism, States starting development late and at a comparative disadvantage have found massive social and economic intervention essential.

The first element in development is increasing national self-reliance. National self-reliance, it should be underlined, no more means autarky than personal self-reliance means being a hermit. The key element here is ideological: self-reliance must be seen as both desirable and possible (indeed necessary) before much progress can be made towards attaining it. Too often in the least developed countries it is believed that nothing can be done without foreign funds, personnel and decisions. This pattern is, of course, self-perpetuating. The danger does not lie in using external finance, expatriate personnel and the world's stores of knowledge and ideas. It flows from substituting

*From Reginald H. Green, "The Role of the State as an Agent of Economic and Social Development in the Least Developed Countries," *Journal of Development Planning*, No. 6, United Nations, New York, 1974, pp. 15–26, 37–8. Reprinted by permission.

them for national efforts and national resources, instead of using them as subordinate complements to such efforts and resources. In a majority of the least developed countries, the patterns of education, the life style and the attitudes of the dominant élite give rise to attempts to deal with national realities in Western terms (no matter how strong the verbal reaction against Western domination), to take an even more negative and unrealistic view of the human and productive potential of the majority of the people than do expatriates, and to foster a series of illusions including that of greater powerlessness and inability to achieve development on their own terms and by their own efforts than is actually the case.

Three key areas for action once a dynamic belief in national self-reliance has been implanted are finance, high-level manpower for managerial and technical posts, and the over-all concept of development. No State dependent on foreign funds for almost all capital spending (and often a good deal of recurrent spending as well), with its Government "guided", its modern productive and service sectors dominated by expatriate cadres and its concept of development imported, can be self-reliant or pursue nationally relevant development very far, regardless of the motives of the providers of funds, personnel and ideas. Power is not and cannot be neutral, nor can total powerlessness be creative. The means for augmenting government revenues and domestic investible surpluses are rather widespread in many of the least developed countries. Tax reforms and increases (especially in middle and upper income groups and business units) are possible—if not popular. The United Republic of Tanzania, for example, has raised taxes and similar charges to 30 per cent of monetary

GDP and thus quadrupled recurrent revenue in one decade, while also reducing purchasing power inequalities through its selection of direct and graduated indirect taxes. . . .

The creation of national manpower capacity and a national concept of development are interrelated. Once surveys of existing and medium-term requirements are made—even approximately—a 20-year plan for local institutions and (inevitably, particularly in the early years and for highly specialized subjects) for overseas training can be worked out and given priority in funding. Once this programme begins to build up a significant body of national managerial and technical (as well as administrational) competence, the task of turning social and political aims and insights into an operational national development strategy becomes manageable.

Manpower development, the second element, is the most widely emphasized, but less frequently is this done in the context of a national manpower development strategy, served by a related national education programme and backed by manpower allocation to ensure that the right individuals in fact go to the critical jobs (or groups of jobs) in some order of priority. All too often in reality the administrative and primary-secondary educational cadres are in the hands of nationals, with government technical, productive sector technical and higher managerial cadres remaining *de facto* expatriate preserves. Even among countries which are by no means least developed the Ivory Coast and Senegal present examples of this. That pattern creates an illusion of citizen control, not a reality; it may be a first step but it is a relatively easy and short one.

Manpower planning and development takes time. The greatest difficulties arise in determining relevant approaches and curricula—especially in the adult, primary, agricultural-rural, and semi-skilled vocational areas where imported patterns and institutions are least appropriate—and in ensuring that all unnecessary expenditure is cut to allow a more rapid generalization of what is essential.

Manpower allocation is harder, especially because it must be backed by incomes policies which in the absence of a widely shared national sense of purpose and progress will lead to a massive exodus of high-level national manpower, either to other countries or to foreign controlled units at home. Manpower allocation must not be run by units—an establishments office or a ministry of education, for example—with a bias towards particular job needs; otherwise managerial technical and productive sector posts in general will be left empty.

If a large proportion of the productive sector is foreign or controlled by a resident foreign minority, firm pressure and sustained monitoring of progress will be needed to achieve a transfer of jobs to nationals. Smaller foreign and minority community firms often resist any such transfer on a significant scale, larger ones increasingly welcome it at middle levels but not in key decision-making posts.

The third element is a rural development strategy broader than the implantation of selected export crops (or, more rarely of internal urban market crops, such as sugar and tobacco). The vast majority of the population of the least developed countries now and for the next four decades (or longer) will be living in rural areas and most of them will be engaged in agriculture, herding, fishing and, in some cases, forestry. No strategy and no programme or plan which does not place central attention on broadly based gains in output and expansion of services for the rural population has any claim to be called national.

Tools to achieve such emphasis are varied; no single approach will solve all problems anywhere and no single tool is applicable everywhere in a single country, let alone in all 25 of the least developed. A few examples include supervised rural credit backed by extension advice; encouragement to create new villages as nuclei to which basic services (education facilities, health services, water, feeder roads, agricultural services, advice on nutrition and home economics) can be provided as they cannot be to scattered homesteads; the creation of locally controlled development committees served by local, technical officials and provided with central funds to be used (within broad guidelines) for projects of their own choice in conjunction with locally provided labour and materials; the adjustment of price and tax policies to encourage rural output (and especially cash output) by improving the internal terms of the agricultural sector and enhancing its viability. To make the division of gains and costs acceptable, such programmes must show a significant contribution to the over-all national output and to the improvement of the foreign balance and must be combined with measures reducing rural costs, increasing rural incomes or shifting other taxes (a protected industry, to all practical intents and purposes, levies a tax on its customers) away from the low-income farmers at least. Even more important, general attention must be paid to the terms of trade of the rural economy with the urban sector.

The difficulties in the creation of a rural development strategy include identifying genuine problems in the existing context; actually following out intentions on a long-term, case-by-case basis (the least developed countries are littered with the evidence of sound rural initiatives gone wrong because the interest in the initial concepts was not followed up with the more critical, but more tedious, day-to-day work of application and generalization); decentralizing individual operating decisions to a level at which they can be taken promptly and efficiently, while over-all coherence is maintained and the evaluation of results continued; fending off the claims of expensive, large and technically advanced projects which may be desirable in themselves but are not really essential to national growth of output or to rural development.

Altering economic structures to attain a more dynamic natural growth rate and greater productive capacity per person constitutes a fourth element of the implementation of development. The difficulty—especially for the least developed countries—is in

working out, holding to and implementing practicable and cost-efficient programmes to this end. Random industrialization is clearly not a viable approach, nor is massive unselective assistance to all comers. A number of least developed country programmes, such as those of Mali and Somalia during the period 1961–1969, have seemed quite divorced from reality; factories were indeed built, but with rather minimal regard to input supply, plausible domestic or export demand, or cost—so much so that in the event many came to represent consumption rather than investment.

What structural alterations to processing, manufacturing and the provision of key services (such as transportation and power) are possible, what combination to devise of general and specific incentives to private investors with direct public-sector initiatives, and which group of units to stress first (for example, mass consumer goods, agricultural inputs, or a vertical cluster from—say—raw timber to furniture, to construction materials, to plastics, to paper) are all questions which can be answered specifically only in the context of a particular political-economic unit and after the compilation and analysis of rather more empirical data than most of the least developed countries now possess. Random import substitution may be a start, but unless supported by a more sophisticated strategy, it will lead to a dead end even in countries with higher *per capita* incomes and more favourable geographical conditions than the least developed, as was the case in Chile, the Congo and Senegal. The same is almost certainly true of random export manufacturing operations based on local cheap labour and imported components; the experience of the Caribbean countries in this field is instructive if largely dispiriting.

One evident problem in achieving structural change is that the results tend to be achieved only over a relatively long period and the direct recipients are for the most part urban dwellers, while the costs are high in the short run and often largely borne by rural or other non-benefiting consumers. It really does not help the farmer to provide him with locally produced hoes and fertilizer, if the prices are raised by 50 per cent nor to process agricultural products before export, if the producer price has to be reduced to ensure processing unit viability.

The maximum rate of structural change that is socially and politically possible may well be determined by constraints on taxation and the extraction of investible surpluses from the rural economy and by the impact of such policies on patterns of income distribution. Whatever the merits of extracting surpluses from relatively wealthy landlords, as was done at Meiji, Japan, or from peasants living significantly above the subsistence level as in the early USSR, especially when such groups have access to growing markets, to do so from peasants living near the subsistence level has economic, technical, social and political limits. If both rapid growth and lessened inequality are sought in a least developed country, output growth and mass rural living standards (including access to public services) must speedily be raised. Only in this way will it be possible to expand the potential investible surplus and to tap it, without either increasing inequality by taxing the rural poor to the benefit of the urban rich or not-so-poor (either directly or by means of price shifts) and/or choking off rural growth by making it economically pointless for the farmer to increase officially marketed output.

Control over economic activity, the fifth element, arises partly from a general desire to assert the reality of independence and partly from a growing realization of how hard it is to exert significant national leverage over the direction and rate of change in an externally open, "free" market economy (more realistically, one where the market is free to decision-making by oligopolies), dominated by foreign firms. Some measures are fairly obvious—though far from universally adopted: the creation of an independent central bank as an apex institution with leverage over the policies of other financial institutions (requiring *inter alia*, local incor-

poration of all commercial banks, including branches of foreign ones); trade and industrial licensing; a selective protective tariff policy; and the regulation of foreign exchange transactions and imports.

Unfortunately, there is a tendency to multiply control systems over a period of time, partly to cover loopholes, partly because new controls are added without reference to the possible removal or simplification of the old. The result is cumbersome, contradictory, self-defeating, corruption-inviting mazes riddled with loopholes. Economic development cannot be regulated, much less induced, primarily by the application of complicated bureaucratic rules, especially when the civil servants applying the rules are too few and too inexperienced, have an insufficient grounding in political or technical economics, are possessed of too few instruments to direct and impose sanctions for evasion or avoidance of the rules, and are too badly paid (and often too weakly motivated) to be even reasonably immune from either overt or covert bribery by those they are supposed to control. At worst the control systems create corruption and stagnation with destructive effects on civil service effectiveness, morale and morals and bring the Government into contempt in the eyes of the business community and the majority of the population.

Evidently some controls are needed and some must be administered on a case-by-case basis. However, the standard temptation—once controls are used to any significant extent—is to use them too readily. Further it is an illusion that control without substantial ownership is an effective way for a small and weak State to influence positively a broad range of decisions made by units of foreign-controlled firms.

The sixth element, public-sector participation in directly productive activity, flows partly from a perception of the limitations of controls; partly from a realization that private enterprise has not led and—to say the least—does not seem likely to lead to rapid development on a broad front in the least developed countries; partly from a commitment to state ownership which may or may not take the form of a transition to socialism; and partly from the realization that in the absence of substantial citizen capital and entrepreneurship a basically private, large-scale productive sector will inevitably be a basically foreign one.

Initially, and sometimes for extended periods, public ownership takes the form of an *ad hoc* provision of public utilities and/or remedying deficiencies, while the over-all strategy remains one of encouraging private enterprise. Unfortunately, this approach seems to result in a very poor general record of performance for state enterprises both individually and collectively. This is not to say that States with a broad range of directly productive units and a commitment to expanding the publicly-owned share of modern, large-scale sector output have a uniformly good record, but that those concentrating on remedying deficiencies, making random acquisitions and nationalizing "sinking sands" (that is, critically important, but badly managed and unprofitable industries) along the lines adopted in the United Kingdom have a uniformly bad one.

Loan and minority equity investment really is a form of incentive to the private sector, not of state ownership. It is likely to be critically valuable only in building up reasonably strong, experienced domestic-owned units that lack capital and is best done by some type of quasi-autonomous development bank (it may be hoped, together with some contribution of soft foreign capital and managerial-technical expertise).

The ownership of existing units—however acquired—is a means of increasing the influence of the public sector in economic decision making both directly and by setting up a framework. For example, a petroleum refinery or wholesale distribution company can control pump prices while filling station ownership cannot be expected to give much leverage in the other direction. The ownership of existing units is also a means of speeding up the transfer of jobs to nationals;

of building up local management and planning capacity; of directing expansion in a desired direction; and of gaining a net flow of investible funds to the State. Formal ownership, however, is rather like formal sovereignty. It is a necessary condition for genuine economic decision-making power as sovereignty is for social and political decision making; but, like sovereignty, it is not a sufficient condition. Serious national and productive unit planning, analysis, implementation and review are necessary, although in their absence appropriate taxes will yield more revenue and selective incentives more effective expansion of output. To dabble in over-all public ownership can be highly expensive to a political economic unit.

The promotion of new units is harder than the management or expansion of existing ones, partly because the problems and losses of the initial period are easy to underestimate and hard to handle without past institutional experience. However, in the least developed countries, to nationalize existing units even on a basis that makes the initial capital compensation about equal to or less than the profits derived (such conditions appear to have been more than fulfilled in the United Republic of Tanzania, if one takes the instances of nationalization and the negotiated takeovers as a group) will not achieve much. For practical reasons related to general personnel, knowledge and finance needs, across-the-board non-compensated acquisition also has its limitations. Whatever the ethics of the matter, its effective use requires an ability on the part of the State to run the units independently and to make do with low levels of non-socialist capital and personnel inflows. For most of the least developed countries this is simply impossible (Cuba, China and the Democratic Republic of Viet-Nam are neither typical nor directly comparable cases). Development requires new initiatives. For these, at the outset foreign management and technical personnel, access to data and experience, and funds (preferably soft loans, not normally equity, and certainly not supplier credit) are often, albiet not always, of critical importance. Minority private, or foreign public, ownership should be judged case by case in terms of its probable contribution to development and its cost and should be balanced against other possible management, technical, sales and supply contract arrangements.

The capacity for economic, business and legal analysis that would be of assistance in making successful choices and negotiating contracts is notoriously lacking in the least developed countries and is all too often viewed as a boring and unattractive accomplishment by the most competent citizens. Yet it can have a very high payoff. . . .

Income distribution and national mobilization, the seventh and eighth elements, are closely linked. The price of a serious attempt to gain a measure of economic independence and rapid development is almost always the need for austerity. Indeed, it is probably true to say that it always is so in the case of the least developed countries. In practice, this means slightly greater initial austerity (and, it may be hoped, rather less in the medium term) for the poor and genuine austerity for those with an income of over $2,000 plus severe restriction of spending in the government and State-owned productive sector. In the short run a *laissez-faire* policy, foreign investment, aid and deficits may allow an easier life, especially to the most politically effective groups, including organized labour, but they rapidly lead to *de facto* insolvency, stagnation and almost insuperable difficulties for the creation of a new foundation on which to build further. . . .

The acceptance of the need to marshal resources, to enhance the efficiency of the labour force and expand the output (especially monetized output) of small-scale farmers and the parallel necessity of maintaining reasonably broad support for, and very broad acceptance of, the political system mean that, when it is not possible to provide rapidly rising levels of personal consumption, national mobilization and commitment

by education, example and demonstration are essential. To preach austerity and efficiency and to impose it on the broad masses of the population, while allowing ostentation, corruption and inefficiency among the *élite* and in the State-owned public sector is to arouse massive dissatisfaction leading, at the least, to disastrous effects on morale, productivity and output and, at the worst, to political upheaval. The Congo, Ghana, Nigeria, the Sudan and Uganda have at one point or another illustrated this. . . .

Income distribution can be controlled by a combination of tax policies (including differential indirect taxes that particularly affect the prices of amenity and luxury goods); agricultural pricing; selective price controls (to prevent profiteering and warn consumers with regard to "bargained" prices); incomes policies that are harder on salaries than on wages and that limit total *per capita* increases to 5 per cent or to the possible percentage increase in agricultural incomes, whichever is higher; controls on fringe benefits in the public sector; limits on price increasing incentives (for example, protective tariffs) to producers; and special assistance to the poorest regions and sectors. These policies are not simple, and their effect is very hard to judge with much precision, given the weakness of data on income distribution. Experience in the United Republic of Tanzania suggests, however, that they certainly can at least reduce disparities in purchasing power among wage and salary earners, halt the normal broadening of the gap between urban and rural dwellers and achieve a significant dispersion of new economic activity to areas other than the central metropolis (albeit not to the very poorest towns or areas). Again the matter is one which is rarely pursued consistently or in detail at the planning level or in any coherent fashion during data collection, individual policy formulation or evaluation.

A general verbal commitment to a more equitable income distribution that is not seriously supported by policy probably soon becomes worse than nothing; the "automatic" forces tend to inequality and the gap between rhetoric and reality leads to the charge of hypocrisy. If a Government believes that increasingly unequal private income distribution partly counter-balanced by expanded public services is crucial to economic, and compatible with social, development, it is probably politically as well as morally more desirable to say so openly as, for example, do Singapore and, to a lesser degree, Kenya.

Mobilization and less unequal income distribution are desirable on purely economic as well as on social and political grounds. To reduce imports requires more monetized food and industrial input production and this will not come without greater material incentives being given to the farmer and without his having a greater belief in his own participation in national development. Amenity and luxury goods (including unnecessarily elaborate buildings, plant and equipment quite as much as radiograms, air conditioners and high quality watches) have an import content of nearly 100 per cent. Goods with a broader market, such as beer, cigarettes, textiles, sugar, simple construction materials, wooden furniture and cement can have a local content of well over 50 per cent. Similarly in the least developed countries, the savings of the upper income group are usually relatively low, often licitly or illicitly exported, and when invested usually put into personally profitable but nationally low priority commodities such as luxury housing for the foreign and local *élite*. Taxation seems a more effective way to extract national savings, which can, if desired, be utilized to help in the financing of local private, as well as public investment, than do incentives to non-controlled private savings by means of low tax rates.

Austerity can be carried to extremes. The end purpose of develpoment is human welfare not burgeoning statistical indices. The provision of a more varied and nutritious diet, the improvement of construction and furnishing standards and the supply of bicycles, low-cost radios and gramophones with locally produced records, ice chests, air coolers (not air conditioners), improved hot plates (not complete electric or gas stoves) and similar intermediate level consumer goods can be carried on with relatively low capital and import intensity, a relatively high impact on employment and more widespread effects reaching smaller towns and smaller firms (including component manufacturers). Such activity will also provide significant incentives for farmers and wage-earners who today have to settle for either a small range of low-quality goods plus a few improved ones or a quite unattainable range of expensive high-quality items of use only to the local and foreign *élite*.

The limitations imposed by unequal size and the concentration of economic relations with a few industrial economies lead to the final element in the implementation of development, namely, the diversification of external economic links, with emphasis on regional economic co-operation. The greater the number of export markets, import suppliers, sources of capital and expert personnel an economy has to draw upon, the less dependent it is on its relations with any foreign economy or interest group. As a result, the greater is its potential ability to secure co-operation on terms acceptable to it over a broad range of activities selected according to its own political and economic priorities rather than those of foreign partners. Such a policy of diversification has been pursued to some degree by all but the smallest and most dependent economies. . . .

The only short-term means to increasing the economic mass and, therefore, the bargaining basis of the least developed countries is to pool economic sovereignty. It may well be the only possible, and certainly appears to be the most efficient, route to the long-term creation of fully viable, integrated economies, given the present economic scale, population and resources of those countries. Co-operation can range from the co-ordination of policies on specific issues of common concern (as, for example, within the International Coffee Agreement), through the preparation of joint strategy positions for international forums ... to full-scale economic unions such as the Customs and Economic Union of Central Africa (UDEAC) and the East African Community. The co-ordination of policy affords an opportunity for maximizing the influence of the regional groups by making national initiatives complementary, instead of competitive, and by reducing the room for outside interests to manoeuvre least developed States into positions detrimental to their own concerns. Economic unions are a much more basic strategic component designed to broaden the economic opportunities (and the range of resources for taking advantage of them) open to each partner State and to the economic region as a whole. . . .

To include too many elements in a policy package is to lose one's sense of direction, one's ability to evaluate results and one's power to control. To include too few is just as deadly; the essential is the ability to identify what are the key pressure points and instruments of inducing change and to create a co-ordinated programme concentrating on them.

A short list of a few of the priorities in state action for development in the least developed countries may have instructive implications for those prone to pay too much attention to theory, strategy and initial decision making:

(a) Rural education (including extension courses) that is relevant and effective;

(b) Agricultural research, *inter alia*, on questions of economic viability and farm management, that is applicable and actually applied;

(c) Small-scale rural works programmes maximizing local effort, satisfaction and decision making within a coherent framework of techniques and goals;

(d) Decentralized, small-scale industries directed towards local markets and able to provide reasonably priced goods, while improving the standard of living and the skills of their workers;

(e) Work towards economic integration with other least developed (and with other developing) States that—through specialization and the division of labour in co-ordinated production and infrastructural planning and provision—will really constitute effective co-operation against poverty and for development;

(f) Bargaining capacity based on economic, social and legal competence to ensure that the Governments of the least developed countries and their public corporations are, at least, less inequitably treated in negotiations and contracts than in the past.

In each of these areas a central goal needs to be identified, a strategy worked out and new ideas and initiatives canvassed. That is happening increasingly often in a number of the least developed countries. What is not so generally accepted is that 90–99 per cent of the work remains to be done even when the strategy is outlined, programmes derived from it and implementation ordered. It is equally true that most of the implementation, data collection, negotiation and revision will be hard work with little glamour and offering no sense of vast accomplishment in the detail of its execution.

To devise a programme budget for one of the least developed countries and to identify its potential uses is intellectually compelling; to work out a framework for its inauguration is less so; to collect, check, correct, organize and reproduce the hundreds of thousands of figures necessary to work it, is not at all glamorous or exciting. Yet it is the last not the first task which finally determines whether the new tool is of any value. In several of the least developed countries workable procedures for project evaluation, loans, tax concessions and the like, data formats and decision-taking bodies exist, but are seriously (sometimes fatally) weakened by the fact that the data are not collected, checked and presented in a coherent way. Thus a great deal of time is wasted and, in the end, *ad hoc* decisions are taken on desperate guesses and in desperate haste.

Infinite care over detail may or may not constitute genius and can certainly be carried too far. However, as a precondition for a significantly greater contribution to economic and social development than has been achieved by them in the past, most of the least developed States should take far greater pains with the implementation of their planning, by using what data and procedures are available and by making continuous reporting and evaluation automatically a part of the work of implementation and subsequent decision making.

It is not enough to set goals and pass on to setting further goals. One must also work out appropriate and feasible means for their achievement, given the resources that are or may be made available. For example, to set farmers the goal of marketing produce is quite useless without working out means for storing, transporting and marketing the produce; the second task is all too often ignored. Until effective methods are chosen and implemented, further talk about goals is useless.

Solving the problem of method includes putting the solution into practice. Without a coherent strategy frame, it is impossible to work out consistent decisions, but without individual decisions and action to implement them, the strategy will remain empty of content. In the context of a long-term development strategy, each decision, each implementation is both an arrival and a point of departure for future decisions and each is a step towards or away from the achievement of the broad strategic aims.

XII.C.4. Plan Implementation*

The type of plans with whose implementation we are here concerned are those that are sufficiently detailed and specific so that they are both broadly capable of implementation and so that progress in their implementation can be tested. Let us turn to an examination of some of the necessary characteristics of a feasible and implementable plan.

In the first place, major targets must be fully specified, sector by sector, with a sufficient breakdown so that those lying within the responsibilities of major decision-making units are separately identifiable. Since feasibility must be tested in both financial and physical terms, the targets must be stated so far as possible both ways.

*From Max F. Millikan, "Comments on Methods for Reporting and Evaluting Progress Under Plan Implementation," in United Nations, Department of Economic and Social Affairs, *Planning and Plan Implementation,* New York, 1967 (67.II.B.14), pp. 178–81. Reprinted by permission.

Second, the targets must be stated in both capital and current terms. That means they must specify both stocks of resources for production presumed to have been created by the end of the planning period and the current flows of output which it is hoped to achieve in time. Questions will frequently arise as to whether shortfalls are a result of delays in the installation of facilities or equipment, or to the impossibility of employing such facilities to capacity. Separate accounting for capital and current items in both physical and financial terms is essential to answer such questions. In this connexion it is worth noting that some activities conventionally classified as belonging in the current account are designed to produce changes in the resource base or fundamental structure of the economy and should be classified differently from current consumption. A case in point is educational expenditures designed to improve the capability of the labour force. Some countries employ a category of developmental expenditures not included in the capital budget but distinguished from current consumption to deal with this problem. The significance of this distinction for reporting purposes is that associated with these expenditures there should be procedures for reporting progress in the developmental changes they are designed to accomplish.

A third requirement is that there must be a full specification of all project and programme activities designed to lead to the achievement of the specified targets. The first important distinction here is between activities to be carried out in the public sector and those for which it is presumed the private sector will take principal responsibility. Techniques of implementation and control and, more important, techniques of reporting and evaluation will be radically different in these two cases. For public sector activities, programme and performance budgeting, which includes both financial and physical measures of performance, is an essential tool. For the private sector which is not under the direct financial control of the Government, special reporting procedures are required which we discuss further later. It is important for subsequent follow-up purposes that the plan itself group the principal activities which it contemplates under the main organizational units, either public or private, which will have the responsibility for carrying them out.

A fourth requirement, seldom if ever met in actual planning practice, is that all the major activities just described must have their time dimensions fully specified. For capital projects with substantial gestation periods, the periods of time assumed to be required for the phases of planning and design, placing of orders, delivery of equipment and components, construction, and operation must all be clearly indicated. In certain cases some operations must be completed before others can be begun, such as the building of a road or a dam site before dam construction can start, or the comple-

tion of a power grid before an electric pumping operation can be put in motion. Many a development programme has been severely delayed because in the planning and design phases the temporal interdependencies of its various parts were not adequately specified. Unless these sequential operations are fully spelled out in the planning process itself, many of the reasons for delays will not become apparent until it is too late to take remedial action, and potential bottle-necks cannot be adequately foreseen in advance. This is important both at the project and at the overall programme level. . . .

A fifth requirement for an implementable plan, which is obvious but all too seldom met, is a full specification of the initial conditions in the economy which it is presumed will prevail at the beginning of the planning period. This includes not just the usual aggregate indices of prices, national output and its composition, rates of investment, levels of employment and the like, but estimates of physical capacity and physical output in major sectors, various forms of working capital on hand, levels of support available from the social overhead industries such as power, transport and communications and stocks of housing. Especially important and usually missing is a specification of capital projects in process, that is of projects initiated before the beginning of the planning period but expected to be completed some time thereafter.

A time-phased schedule both of anticipated expenditures and of required flows of physical inputs for the completion of these projects during the planning period is critical. New projects or programme activities specified in the plan may very well be held up with serious consequences because of delays in completing the implementation of projects carried over from earlier plans or from a pre-plan period. Similarly, of course, the plan must include time-specific provision for the early phases of projects to be begun during the planning period but not completed until after the end of the current plan.

A sixth requirement is that the plan must

be thoroughly tested for what we can call, in short, input-output consistency. This means that the interdependencies among the various projects in the plan and among the various sectors of the economy and decision-making units having responsibility for its implementation must be fully specified to reveal possible bottle-necks in the output or supply of intermediate goods and services like materials, power, transport, agricultural raw materials, and the like which are essential inputs to other activities. The usual static input-output test for the terminal year of a plan is wholly inadequate here since the time-phasing of requirements for many kinds of resources will be critical and cannot be presumed to be smooth or uniform. Unless time-phased interdependencies of this kind have been spelled out in advance of the planning process, it will be impossible to predict in advance, and difficult to determine afterwards, precisely where bottle-necks have occurred. Since the statistical resources of the developing countries are limited it will be difficult for them to keep continually abreast of all supply-demand balances for all intermediate goods in the economy. A careful advance testing of the time-phased input-output relations of a plan can focus attention on likely trouble spots and provide guidance for priorities in current reporting.

A seventh requirement, which is an elaboration of one aspect of the preceding one, is that the plan should include a time-phased indication of the proposed allocation of those financial, physical, and human resources, other than produced intermediate goods, that are likely to constitute important bottle-necks to development activities. On the financial side, these include funds for investment required in both the public and private sectors, total foreign exchange resources and their sectoral allocation. With respect to human resources, in most developing countries specific skills and talents are much more likely to be in short supply than unskilled labour, and the manpower sections of the plan should be broken down in some

detail by skill categories. Social overhead requirements in power, transport, and communications have been mentioned above but are worth further attention both because lead times for expansion of capacity here tend to be long and because the effects of shortages are likely to be pervasive throughout the economy. In new locations, housing and community facilities such as water, sewage, medical and educational facilities, and the like may be critical. Most plans include aggregate requirements for these resources for the plan as a whole, but what is needed for effective monitoring is the kind of time-phased requirements that can only emerge from detailed time schedules of activities within each sector.

A final requirement is that for major commodity groups the levels of demand likely to be generated in each period by the incomes flowing from the planned levels of productive activity should be reasonably consistent with the levels of supply implicit in the physical productive targets. If, for example, the targets for food production plus food imports are substantially smaller than the levels of demand for food likely to result from the planned level and distribution of national income, there may well result either serious inflationary pressures or unanticipated requirements for foreign exchange for food purchases, or both, which may interfere in important ways with the achievement of other targets. Or, on the other hand, an excess production of food in one period over and above what can be exported and marketed domestically at current income levels may, by depressing prices and generating unsaleable surpluses, create negative incentives which will prevent the achievement of production targets in foodstuffs in subsequent periods. Precise forecasting of these demand-supply balances is neither possible nor necessary. One function of a good price system is to stimulate and guide all the minor adjustments in the allocation of resources to particular commodities which changes in supply-demand balances dictate. On the other hand, for economies undertaking, as are most of the developing countries, major planned structural change, some testing of the gross supply-demand consistency of the plan in major sectors is an important element in appraising its implementability and in designing reporting procedures for monitoring its progress.

We may summarize these required characteristics of an implementable plan and their implications for reporting procedures by reviewing a brief classification of the major reasons for shortfalls in implementation.

The first of these is that major decisions required for the implementation of the plan either do not get made at all or do not get made in time for the plan's targets to be achieved. If, as in some plans, the necessary decision points have not even been identified, it is of course not possible to report these decision-making failures. If in general the organizational responsibilities, public and private, for making the major decisions implied in the plan have been clearly stipulated, but no time-table for these interrelated and sequential decisions has been specified, it will be very difficult in a post audit to find where the trouble lies. If a clear time-table on the other hand is specified, with built-in procedures for reporting on the times at which major decisions are in fact taken, discrepancies between plan and performance will show up very quickly. In general there will be some decisions whose timing is very much more critical to the progress of the plan as a whole than others. These decisions, lying on what has been called the critical path of the decision network of a project or programme, deserve an especially high priority in designing reporting procedures. . . . Since the phases of project planning and design lie on the critical path of virtually all projects and sectors, and since they customarily take longer than anticipated to accomplish, the reporting of progress in the planning and design phases is, if

anything, more important than the reporting of progress in physical execution.

A second reason for shortfalls is that, even though decision points are identified and critical decisions are made on schedule, implementation may be inhibited by the unavailability of critical supply items which are bottle-necks. These may be physical items like raw materials, equipment, or trained manpower, or they may be financial items such as credit or foreign exchange. They may be items required for the completion of capital facilities or, on the other hand, current inputs necessary for the utilization of available capacity. If the plan has identified potential bottle-neck resources and indicated both the time-phasing of their presumed availability and their allocation period by period, then current reporting on the availability and allocation of these bottle-neck items should reveal where the trouble lies.

Third, even when decisions are made on time and inputs are available as required, failure of implementation may be due to delays in the carrying out of certain activities called for by the plan. . . . [C]ompletion times of some activities will be very much more critical to plan implementation than those of others. It is these activities on the critical path which should be given priority in detailed and timely reporting on progress under plans and programmes.

Finally, there may be distortions in supply-demand relationships compared to those postulated in the plan, not because supply diverges from plan levels but because demand does so. If anticipated levels of effective demand, period by period and sector by sector, have been specified in the plan, and if there is effective current reporting on actual levels of demand through an appropriate national income accounting system, failures of implementation resulting from this source should be identifiable.

XII.C.5. The Cost of Inaction*

In our report we have made a number of far-reaching suggestions. Far-reaching changes in many sectors of the economy seemed to us to be urgently required if the aims that formed the subject of our brief—the creation of a Kenya where there would be much more widespread chances of earning a reasonable living—were to be rapidly achieved. Sometimes we wondered whether it was proper for an international mission to presume to make such recommendations, but we were encouraged by the expressed wish of the Government that we should not shrink from bold and radical approaches. Moreover, we believe that our recommendations remain within the framework of the essential principles governing Kenya's society and economy, a mixed economy conforming to the pragmatic guidelines of Sessional Paper No. 10 of 1965.[1] Finally, we did not hesitate to make our recommendations because we realise that in any case it will be for the Government and Parliament of Kenya to decide whether our recommendations are found acceptable or not. This applies both to the broad sweep of re-orientation intrinsic to our recommendations as a whole and to each one taken individually.

In considering our proposals, it is important not to lose sight of this broad sweep of re-orientation. The details of the policies can be varied—and in some cases there are major alternatives within the policies themselves. But in one way or another, certain new directions must be established if the prob-lems identified earlier in the report are to be solved.

These new directions, outlined in the preceding chapters, can be summarised as follows:

(1) Kenya's population policy, a pioneering policy in its time, must, over the coming years, be implemented much more effectively and on an increasing scale.

(2) Technological policy must be approached in a multitude of ways, being concerned with what is produced as well as how it is produced, and covering the more selective importation of technology as well as stimulating, wherever appropriate, the development of indigenous technology.

(3) There must be a major shift in agricultural policy in favour of the small farmer, through a whole range of extension, research, credit, input, pricing and marketing policies, as well as through land and land-tax policies designed to encourage further subdivision of large holdings.

(4) Integrated rural development should be stimulated through a wide range of rural works and activities which would improve rural incomes, amenities and living standards and reduce the risks of periodic famine and loss. Local planning, which is already being initiated, will need much greater resources and support in order to implement the minimum income approach and make integrated rural development a reality.

(5) Industrialization should press ahead, but with a more selective approach to foreign investment and large-scale production and more support for small-scale, regionally dispersed local industry, and of industries exporting processed agricultural products.

(6) A radical change in local and central government policy towards the informal sector is required, with legal restrictions being replaced by a positive approach in which the

---

*From *Employment, Incomes and Equality, A Strategy for Increasing Productive Employment in Kenya*, Report of an Inter-Agency team financed by the United Nations Development Program and organized by the International Labor Office, Geneva, 1972, pp. 325–9.

[1] *African Socialism and its application to planning in Kenya.*

initiative and dynamism of the informal sector is encouraged to develop freely.

(7) Fundamental reform of the educational system must be set in motion, breaking the negative backwash effects of the existing examination system and moving towards a system in which repetition and differential enrolment between districts are replaced by a period of universal basic education for all children, followed by opportunities for relevant training which avoid sharp divisions between school and training and training and work.

(8) Major inequalities in access to land, education and employment—which underly a great deal of today's frustration among school-leavers and job-seekers—must be sharply reduced, in part by the provisional use of quotas to ensure fairer treatment between men and women, between persons of different tribal and ethnic backgrounds, and between different districts.

(9) An incomes policy covering wages and other incomes along the lines specified in the Development Plan, but effectively implemented, is essential.

(10) A major re-structuring of government revenue and expenditures is required in favour of the rural areas, the more backward districts and the lower income groups.

(11) Kenya's international policies towards aid, trade and foreign investment need to be more selective, to reduce dependence and ensure greater alignment of activities in each of these areas with Kenya's national interests.

We realise that in many cases action along these lines may be difficult—politically, administratively, financially and psychologically. It may represent a break with familiar traditions and offend or hurt sectional interests. But when the cost of action is weighed we plead that the cost of inaction be also considered. The problem that the Government of Kenya considered serious enough for our advice to be sought on it is the result of past history, and of past conditions and policies. If they are not changed there must be a presumption that the problem will remain, that it will in fact continue to grow. There are transitional problems, especially in developing countries, which can be expected to right themselves in due course; but problems of lack of employment and maldistribution of income-earning opportunities are not among them. Moreover, the cost of dealing with problems may be much higher once they pass the threshold of what is considered tolerable, since the opportunities of dealing with them by rational and consistent methods and by national consensus may be greatly lessened.

When we try to assess the consequences of inaction in more concrete terms, there is a danger of apocalyptic exaggerations. We have been asked to deal with one of the deficiencies in Kenya's economic growth and development. There is a danger that a group of people who concentrate on the problem of that particular deficiency may forget about growth and development. In our report, we had to concentrate on the aspects of Kenya's structure in respect of which we believe changes to be necessary. This is the place to remind ourselves that our view is partial. Kenya has an enviable record in terms of over-all growth, as in a number of other respects. Signs of progress abound. Indeed, many of our suggestions would be unthinkable had we not considered that Kenya's past achievements provided the basis and the means for achieving them. We do believe, however, that without such action as we suggest the particular problems with which we have been dealing will not disappear. And nobody can say that these problems are merely like the mild toothache of an otherwise healthy person: they are more like the broken leg of an otherwise vigorous person, which prevents him from exercising his strength until the matter is put right.

In the past, Kenya has been assisted by a number of factors which have given impetus to its progress and provided a breathing space for dealing with problems or temporary solutions which made it safe to defer more fundamental policies. The achievement of independence was the major event from which much of this impetus and many opportunities have flowed. The settlement of the Scheduled Areas, the abolition of many restrictions on the African small-holder and producer, Kenyanisation, which opened many new avenues in the higher ranges of economic opportunities, the East African Community, the emergence of Nairobi as the metropolis of East Africa, the strong and harmonious international relations of Kenya, the flood of tourists attracted by the great beauty of the country, the vigorous self-help movement, the burning desire for education and training, the inflow of foreign investment and aid . . . again and again these have released forces which provided new outlets and opportunities—enough to keep the troubling problem of imbalance and insufficiency of productive employment within manageable proportions.

No doubt the future will bring to light new sources of strength of this kind, although some of those enumerated above cannot be relied upon for the future. There are still chances of settlement, and indeed some of our proposals are based on this; there are the existing although uncertain prospects of pushing the land frontier out into the vast expanse of drier land still available; there is still scope for Kenyanisation; the East African Community may be revitalised or expanded and new methods of African and world co-operation may develop; mineral resources may be found; new technologies may emerge (even without action of the kind we suggest), the balance of payments may again turn in Kenya's favour, and so forth. These things may, and some of them no doubt will, happen and provide new opportunities and even partial relief of unemployment and poverty. Above all, as long as underlying economic growth continues, the scope for dealing with some aspects of the unemployment problem by the financing of relief or by redistribution of incomes after they are earned will constantly improve and widen.

But when all this is said, we can and must nevertheless state, without distorting the over-all perspective, that the danger of inaction is great. The population increases relentlessly, and if there are no results from the family planning policy which we have recommended, Kenya may have to support a population of 30 or 40 million people by the year 2000, on what may still be a small area of high-potential land concentrated along a narrow axis in a small part of the country. The balance of payments may set serious limits to continued economic growth in the present framework, and increase international dependence at a time when the forces of international co-operation may be even weaker, or at any rate no stronger, than now. It would be better to create a less dependent economy now (our recommendation would move the country in that direction) than to have to take ad hoc or crisis measures in the future. The frustration of younger people in search of opportunities— frustration instilled by their present preparation for life—may lead to alienation and intolerable tensions. In this, as in many other fields in which we make recommendations, it is necessary to take the first steps towards a new structure now, in order to be able to cope with problems that may be 10 or 20 years distant. If Kenyanisation is to be a full reality in industry in 10 or 20 years, the restructuring of industry and technology as well as training and selection must start today. Once a structure of demand and production has been created which is incompatible with fuller employment, it becomes progressively more difficult and expensive to reverse it later; it is far better to take early action to create a different structure. An ossified structure may create a situation in which any interference will only aggravate unemployment in the short run (and possibly beyond the limits of what is tolerable) while the structure itself prevents the implementation of the policies required for full and widespread employment. Thus the problem may become insoluble in future, whereas it can still be avoided by timely action.

XII.D. THE FUTURE OF DEVELOPMENT PLANNING—NOTE

After all the discussion of the preceding chapters, we are left with the ultimate question of why the success stories of development planning have been so few and the disappointments so many. In this final Note, it may be most appropriate to concentrate on the limits of development planning, instead of its accomplishments, because concerted attention in the immediate future must be given to those countries with a dismal development record even after experiencing two or more decades of planning. To this end, it is necessary first to isolate the reasons why development planning has not succeeded in coping more effectively with the strategic policy issues discussed in this book. We may then consider ways to improve the practice of development planning.

Many economists would suggest that the reasons for past failures are to be found mainly in an inability or unwillingness to implement development plans. Planning agencies in the developing countries are now capable of approximating the elements of a well-formulated plan in a creditable fashion. And yet we are left with the disconcerting question: has the ability to implement a development plan improved *pari passu* with the ability to formulate a plan? It can be maintained that the record of development planning reveals that problems of implementation now need more attention than problems of formulation.

In this vein, Sir Arthur Lewis prefaces his book *Development Planning* with the observation that "The economics of development is not very complicated; the secret of successful planning lies more in sensible politics and good public administration."[1] The implication of this statement is that the major problems of development planning center upon implementation—that the secret of successful planning lies essentially in political stability and political leadership and in competent and effective public administration of the policy instruments by which the goals of development can be reached. But this has additional implications—namely, that economists know why poor countries have remained poor and that they also know what policy measures would accelerate their development.

Before placing so much emphasis on implementation, we should raise, however, the logically prior question of whether economists really do know what is wrong and how to put it right. In answering this question, we might reasonably argue that a major difficulty with development planning has been the economists' inadequate understanding of the development process, and that the secret of successful planning is not only—nor even mainly—a matter of implementation.

From the foregoing chapters we can identify three areas about which we need fundamental understanding before there can be a more intelligent basis for development planning. One area is that of the "unexplained residual factor." To the extent that our knowledge of the sources of economic development remains inadequate, we must also remain ignorant of relevant policy variables. This constitutes a severe limitation on the efficacy of development planning. Even if we were to succeed in disaggregating the residual into recognizable elements (such as advances in technical, managerial, and organizational knowledge), it would still be difficult to specify exactly how these elements are to yield to planning. Planning may operate effectively on the supply of inputs, but it

[1] W. Arthur Lewis, *Development Planning*, London, 1966, Preface.

is quite a different matter to bring the techniques of planning to bear on the income-raising forces constituting the residual.

Similarly, it is uncertain by what means a development plan can have an impact on population growth. And yet in many countries, a major challenge to development planning is the control of the income-depressing forces associated with heavy population pressures. The record of development planning in this area has so far been disappointing, but many development practitioners would now contend that it is of prime importance to acquire new meaningful sociological and scientific knowledge of the determinants of the birth rate and to institute as an essential element of development planning a set of policies aimed at birth control.

This brings us to the third set of factors with which it is difficult for development planning to cope—namely, the sociocultural and other noneconomic factors that have an effect on the process of development. If we are to improve our understanding of the two problem areas already discussed—the residual factor and population growth—we must also be able to evaluate more thoroughly the noneconomic factors in the development process. It is now stating the obvious to say that economic, social, and political change are all interrelated. Nonetheless, we do not yet know under what conditions and by what mechanisms it is possible to have the types of sociocultural and political changes that will be most favorable for development. Without such knowledge, we cannot expect development planning to be very successful. Exactly how is planning to bring about cultural change? Are attitudes, motivations, and institutions amenable to change by planning? Or is planning actually counterproductive, inhibiting the emergence of the favorable sociocultural factors? If policymakers cannot identify the functional relationships among economic and noneconomic factors, and their quantitative significance, how can they determine whether to operate on economic incentives, or attitudes, or organizational structure, or social rela-

tions, or any of the many other factors that connect economic and noneconomic change? Despite the countless assertions that the interaction between economic and noneconomic variables is of utmost importance, the past emphasis has been on *economic* planning. The planning of social or political change has been negligible. But the future success of economic planning may depend upon an understanding of how to plan social and political transformations. And to achieve this, more than "sensible policies and good administration" are required.

At the same time as (and possibly because) policymakers have remained ignorant about these fundamental aspects of the development process, a number of biases have been revealed within the actual planning process.[2] What has been unfortunate about these biases is that some of them have actually intensified the constraints on development and others have kept the actual rate below the attainable rate of development.

If we may refer to a characteristic style of development planning, three types of bias have been prominent: a bias toward macromodels in plan formulation to the relative neglect of the microeconomic aspects of planning (such as project analysis); a bias toward the quantitative aspects of planning to the relative neglect of other development forces that are not quantifiable but are of crucial importance (for instance, many aspects of human-resource development and sociocultural and political changes for which no data exist); a bias toward concentration on the formulation of a development plan without due regard for its implementation (even though formulation and implementation should be inseparable).

As for their substantive content, many development plans have until recently emphasized inward-looking policies to the relative neglect of outward-looking policies; the

[2] These are biases in the sense of both statistical skewness and unwarranted valuations. Cf. Gunnar Myrdal, *Asian Drama*, New York, 1968, Appendix 4.

development of the urban industrial sector with much less concentration on rural development; and the simple imitation of the advanced countries' institutions at the expense of innovation and adaptation.

The quantitative bias in the theory of development planning tends to reinforce the other biases in development planning. Intersectoral programming models and other planning models are generally national planning models because the locus of industrial policy and the sources of data are usually national.[3]

Data accessibility also reinforces the macro bias, an emphasis on physical rather than human capital, and a focus on a few large projects rather than many small projects. Plans for industrial development also tend to dominate insofar as the outputs of industry are more easily measured and industrial inputs are more readily specified than in agriculture.[4]

In our previous discussions of the need to mobilize domestic and external resources, promote agricultural development, encourage foreign trade, and invest in human capital, we have repeatedly encountered arguments in support of those very policies that have actually been ignored by many of the past development plans. Recognizing the past biases in development planning, many development economists now maintain that the time has come to rethink the nature and scope of development planning. It has been increasingly recognized that the comprehensive "heavy-type" of central planning is still premature for most of the LDCs.

The plea is not, however, for a reversal to laissez-faire—but a plea for *competent* plan-

ment must devote more research to determining. To achieve this, students of developmining the appropriate range and forms of planning for a developing country (for instance, indicative versus controlling, or formal versus informal planning). The problem is to identify and institutionalize the most appropriate way of planning for the particular country at a particular period. An evolution of the planning approach itself would therefore be expected as the country develops.

More immediately, some major revisions of development planning can be suggested to remove the biases and secure more benefits from planning in the future. These revisions amount, on the one side, to making greater use of the market mechanism as an instrument of development policy within the domestic economy, while encouraging, on the other side, an extension of multinational planning in the international economy.

Many economists have come to believe that in order to overcome past deficiencies in planning and undertake policies that conform more closely to their present needs and capabilities, the majority of LDCs should retrench to a lighter type of planning. This would rely more on decentralized decisions operating through the market mechanism, and greater attention would be given to devising policies that might make private action more effective.

The advocacy of greater use of the market mechanism should not be interpreted as a call for a diminished role for the government, but rather a different role. Governmental policies are needed to strengthen the market system, and a stronger market system is in turn needed to allow public policy to operate more effectively through the market. Thus, in a sense, more planning is actually required to overcome the results of inadequate planning in the past: improved planning is now necessary to remove the distortions caused by arbitrary direct administrative controls that have produced a disequilibrium system and a set of trade, fiscal,

[3] See Don Humphrey, "Some Implications of Planning for Trade and Capital," in Max F. Millikan (ed.), *National Economic Planning*, New York, 1967.

[4] Cf. Michael Lipton, "Urban Bias and Agricultural Planning," in Paul Streeten and Michael Lipton (eds.), *The Crisis of Indian Planning*, London, 1968.

financial, industrial, and wage policies that are often contradictory and self-defeating.

The case for a high degree of planning, with a large amount of public investment and deliberate industrialization constituting the core of the plan, may remain strong for countries that suffer seriously from the pressure of population on the land but have the potential for large domestic markets (such as India or China). For other countries, however, in which there are underutilized natural resources but only small internal markets, it can be persuasively argued that the basic problem is one of creating a favorable social and economic environment which will lead to expansion of private activity, more effective use of the underutilized resources, and capitalization on the existing opportunities for international trade (as is being done in the Philippines, Thailand, Malaya, and some Latin American countries).[5]

If the private sector is to be enlarged, how is this now to be accomplished? Instead of allowing any economic resources to be left unemployed, governmental policies must try to mobilize through positive economic incentives and inducements the latent skills and capital in the private sector. Fundamentally, the stimulation of multiple centers of initiative depends on the establishment of markets and encouragement of market institutions. Economic and social overhead capital can help to establish the physical conditions for a market to exist and can support the interdependence of markets. The government also has a crucial role in building institutions such as a banking system, a money and capital market, agricultural cooperatives, labor organizations, rural credit institutions, training institutes. It must also be recognized that many policy measures that can affect individual action by altering the economic environment are not of the usual monetary or fiscal type of policy, but rather of a kind that involve the legal

[5] See Hla Myint, "Inward and Outward Looking Countries of Southeast Asia," *Malayan Economic Review*, April 1967.

and institutional framework, such as land tenure legislation, commercial law, property rights.

Once market imperfections are reduced and the structure of markets improved, the market mechanism can itself be used as an instrument of development—promoting governmental policies as well as more effective private activity. Instead of relying on comprehensive and detailed administrative controls, the government can alter prices to execute policy and can provide price and income stimuli for an expansion in private output, an increase in exports, and a widening of domestic markets. These price changes may extend to foreign exchange rates, interest rates, tariffs, taxes, and subsidies. Subsidy and tax schemes can be especially relevant in inducing firms to value inputs according to their social opportunity costs, to exploit external economies, or to introduce new techniques of production.

Of most importance is the need to remove the distortions in internal price relations which have resulted from the use of numerous specific controls. We have repeatedly noted criticisms that interest rates are artificially low in the urban sector, exchange rates are overvalued, unskilled wages are too high in labor surplus economies, subsidization of import-substitutes has become suboptimal, exports and agriculture are being discriminated against. Accordingly, there are now more proponents advocating the adoption of flexible exchange-rates to avoid currency overvaluation, the removal of price controls on foodstuffs, and the liberalization of foreign trade controls with the substitution of domestic subsidy and tax schemes. It is argued that a more realistic price structure would remove the need for detailed investment planning and would induce additional private activity. If the price mechanism is no longer distorted, there is likely to be both greater total investment and the undertaking of private projects that previously appeared unprofitable. With an overvalued exchange rate, this is especially relevant for export projects. Most significant is the possibility that corrections of the price structure would promote a reallocation of resources away from the subsidized manufacturing, import-substitution, and consumption sectors, and would also encourage as well the more efficient use of resources in all sectors.

If the market mechanism should have a larger role within the LDC's domestic economy, there is at the same time a need for more multinational planning for development within the international economy. One objective of this planning should be to realize the potential for more coordination of policies among the LDCs themselves. This is necessary to avoid competition among the LDCs in such policies as the attraction of private foreign investment, or the promotion of import-replacement industries. The more positive case for regional integration in trade policy has been presented in XI.E. Further, the regional coordination of national development plans would also improve the allocation of foreign aid and make feasible projects on a multinational basis that would otherwise be impossible on a national basis.

Beyond regional planning, it would also be desirable to have more international planning of trade and aid policies. Preferential trading arrangements, trade liberalization in the developed countries, more multilateral aid programs, harmonization of aid terms, compensatory financing measures, international stabilization policies, supplementary financial measures—all these policies depend upon cooperative international action.

Perhaps the most general limitation to the efficacy of development policymaking can be expressed in terms of the absence of an international public sector. In the domestic economy, the public sector is charged with the correction of market failure, redistribution of income, and maintenance of full employment. But where is the responsibility for the performance of analogous functions in the international economy? Can surplus labor be absorbed without some form of international deficit financing and interna-

tional full employment policy? Can there be an international redistribution of income without some more effective mechanism for transferring resources from rich countries to poor? Can the cases of international market failure—whether expressed as "backwash effects," or price distortions, or inappropriate transfers—be corrected without some international authority that can transcend the limits of national jurisdication? Can national development programs be effective without the existence of an international public sector?

In lieu of the existence of an international public sector, alternative arrangements must be sought. In Tinbergen's words,

Only a world policy, or, as a second best, a stronger international policy can prevent us from sliding into a complete failure of development policy and all the political consequences of such a failure.... At the moment, the development policies of the various national governments are much less coordinated than is desirable from the point of view of all concerned: both poor and rich countries. The process of development must be speeded up. New industries should be chosen in order to meet the increased demand for the various types of products to be expected from increased incomes and to equip each country with the industries that fit its special capabilities. Education and training, financial and commercial policies, and many specific measures should all be geared to this process. For this whole complex of activities to run smoothly a fair degree of world and continental planning will be needed. Some useful beginnings have been made, but more can be done, keeping in mind the appropriate division of tasks between all agencies involved. Such an intensified action may make a sizable contribution to the gradual establishment of a world order, at least in matters of economic policy.[6]

[6] Jan Tinbergen, "International Economic Planning," in Stanley Hoffman (ed.), *Conditions of World Order*, Boston, 1968, pp. 260, 284–5.

To realize the potentialities for more extensive international planning, some international economic institutions may have to be reformed, and the specialized international agencies will have to coordinate their programs more fully. Improvements in development policy are likely to come ultimately from more cooperation among the international specialized agencies, regional agencies, and national governments of rich and poor countries alike. If instead of supporting an international order for development policy, each LDC simply pursues narrow national policies, we shall have to expect a continued deterioration in developmental performance.

As we began in the Preface to this book, so we must end: "A development economist might be defined as one who has accepted the inevitability of a number of departures from the basic premises of neo-classical economics and is thus forced to operate in the ill-defined world of the theory of 'second-best.' "[7] In such a world there are no simple *a priori* rules for establishing a second-best optimum, and the policymaker cannot operate with textbook precision. But, if the underdeveloped economy is a fragmented economy, so too has there been fragmentation in policymaking. This *ad hoc* piecemeal approach to policy has left a distorted policy framework which is third—or fourth—or n[th] best. It is to be hoped that at least the basic economic principles emphasized here, together with the lessons of recent economic history, might provide a basis for future progress toward more effective development policymaking. Even if the perfect set of policies cannot be formulated and implemented, better policymaking can do much to mitigate absolute poverty, improve the distribution of income, and provide more employment.

[7] Hollis B. Chenery, Review of Paul Streeten, *The Frontiers of Development Studies*, in *Journal of Economic Literature*, March 1975, p. 66.

XII. SELECT BIBLIOGRAPHY

1. The literature on the general topic of planning and the price system is extensive, but the following references may be cited for the particular problem of assessing the relative merits of the market mechanism and planning in the context of development: Hugh C. J. Aitken (ed.), *The State and Economic Growth*, New York, 1959; P. T. Bauer, *Dissent on Development*, London, 1972, Chap. 2; A. K. Cairncross, *Factors in Economic Development*, London, 1962, Chap. 19; Amlan Datta, *Socialism, Democracy and Industrialization*, London, 1962; Elliot J. Berg, "Socialism and Economic Development in Tropical Africa," *QJE*, November 1968; Maurice Dobb, *An Essay on Economic Growth and Planning*, London, 1960, Chap. 1; A. H. Hanson, *Public Enterprise and Economic Development*, London, 1959; A. O. Hirschman, "Economic Policy in Underdeveloped Countries," *EDCC*, July 1957; E. S. Mason, *Economic Planning in Underdeveloped Areas*, New York, 1958; R. M. Solow, "Some Problems of the Theory and Practice of Economic Planning," *EDCC*, January 1962; A. M. Watson and Joel B. Dirlam, "The Impact of Underdevelopment on Economic Planning," *QJE*, May 1965; Raymond Vernon, "Comprehensive Model-Building in the Planning Process: The Case of the Less Developed Countries," *EJ*, March 1966; Gustav Ranis, "Planning for Resources and Planning for Strategy Change," *Weltwirtschaftliches Archiv*, Summer 1965; H. B. Chenery, "The Structuralist Approach to Development Policy," *AER*, May 1975.

2. Outstanding general introductions to development planning are provided by W. Arthur Lewis, *Development Planning*, London, 1966; Jan Tinbergen, *Development Planning*, New York, 1967; K. Griffin and J. Enos, *Planning Development*, London, 1971; M. P. Todaro, *Development Planning*, Nairobi, 1971; Mike Faber and Dudley Seers (eds.), *The Crisis in Planning*, London, 1972; G. Ranis (ed.), *Government and Economic Development*, New Haven, 1971.

An excellent survey article on development policymaking and planning is D. T. Healy, "Development Policy; New Thinking about an Interpretation," *JEL*, September 1972.

3. Planning models of development include macroeconomic, multisectoral, equilibrium simulation, and optimizing models. For studies of the design and use of econometric models and planning models, see H. B. Chenery (ed.), *Studies in Development Planning*, Cambridge, 1971; C. R. Blitzer et al., *Economy-Wide Models and Development Planning*, New York, 1975. An excellent survey article is A. S. Manne, "Multi-Sector Models for Development Planning," *JDE*, Vol. 1, No. 1, 1974. Other useful references are: S. Chakravarty, *Capital and Development Planning*, Cambridge, 1969, Chaps. 1–5; E. Malinvaud and M. D. L. Bacharach (eds.), *Activity Analysis in the Theory of Growth and Planning*, London, 1967, Chap. 7; H. B. Chenery, "The Use of Interindustry Analysis in Development Programming," in T. Barna (ed.), *Structural Interdependence and Economic Development*, New York, 1956; ____, and K. S. Kretschmer, "Resources Allocation for Economic Development," *Econometrica*, October 1956; ____, and P. Clark, *Interindustry Economics*, New York, 1959, Chaps. 1–3; L. Johansen, *A Multi-Sectoral Study of Economic Growth*, Amsterdam, 1960; Roy Radner, *Notes on the Theory of Economic Planning*, Athens, 1963; J. K. Sengupta and G. Tintner, "On Some Economic Models of Development Planning," *Economia Internazionale*, February 1963; J. Tinbergen and H. C. Bos, *Mathematical Models of Economic Growth*, New York, 1962; S. Chakravarty and

L. Lefeber, "An Optimizing Planning Model," *Economic Weekly*, February 1965; I. Adelman and E. Thorbecke (eds.), *The Theory and Design of Economic Development*, Baltimore, 1965; M. Bruno, "Experiments with a Multi-Sector Programming Model," *RES*, November 1967; Russell Ackoff, "Operations Research and National Planning," *Operations Research*, August 1957; Charles Hitch, "A Dissent," *Operations Research*, October 1957; M. Bronfenbrenner, "A Simplified Mahalanobis Development Model," *EDCC*, October 1960; Amartya Sen, "Interrelation Between Project, Sectoral and Aggregate Planning," *Economic Bulletin for Asia and the Far East*, June/September 1970.

4. A large number of case studies are now available for an appraisal of development planning in practice. A selected list of readings follows: I. G. Patel, "Strategy of Indian Planning," in P. Chaudhuri (ed.), *Aspects of Indian Economic Development*, London, 1971; J. N. Bhagwati and S. Chakravarty, "Contributions to Indian Economic Analysis: A Survey," *AER*, September 1969 (supplement), Part 2; R. S. Eckaus and K. Parikh, *Planning for Growth*, Cambridge, 1967; ____, "Planning in India," in M. F. Millikan (ed.), *National Economic Planning*, New York; B. S. Minhas, *Planning and the Poor*, New Delhi, 1974; Pranab K. Bardhan, "India," in Hollis Chenery et al., *Redistribution with Growth*, London, 1974, pp. 255–62; J. H. Power, "Industrialization in Pakistan: A Case of Frustrated Take-off," *Pakistan Development Review*, Summer 1963; F. C. Shorter, "Planning Procedures in Pakistan," *Pakistan Development Review*, Autumn 1961; Mahbub ul Haq, *The Strategy of Economic Planning: A Case Study of Pakistan*, New York, 1964; Gustav F. Papanek, *Pakistan's Development*, Cambridge, 1967; W. P. Falcon and G. F. Papanek (eds.), *Development Policy: The Pakistan Experience*, Cambridge, 1971; A. MacEwan, *Development Alternatives in Pakistan*, Cambridge, 1971; I. Adelman (ed.), *Practical Approaches to Development Planning: Korea's Second Five-Year Plan*, Baltimore, 1969; G. T. Brown, *Korean Pricing Policies and Economic Development in 1960s*, Baltimore, 1973; D. C. Cole and P. N. Lyman, *Korean Development: The Interplay of Politics and Economics*, Cambridge, 1971; Raymond Vernon, *The Dilemma of Mexico's Development*, Cambridge, 1963; Wolfgang Stolper, *Planning Without Facts*, Cambridge, 1966; Andrew Kamarck, *Economics of African Development*, revised edition, New York, 1971; Paul G. Clark, *Development Planning in East-Africa*, East African Publishing House, 1965; R. H. Green, "Four African Development Plans," *Journal of Modern African Studies*, Vol. 3, No. 2, 1966; George B. Baldwin, *Planning and Development in Iran*, Baltimore, 1967; Bertram M. Gross (ed.), *Action Under Planning: The Guidance of Economic Development*, New York, 1967; Albert Waterston, *Development Planning: Lessons of Experience*, Baltimore, 1969.

INDEX

Abramovitz, M., 2
Absorptive capacity, 253, 335–6, 360–61, 522–3
Accounting prices, 433, 456–7. *See also* Price
   distortions; Project appraisal; Shadow prices
Achievement motivation, 483, 550–58
Adelman, Irma, 27ff.
Aggregation: problems of, 64–5, 83–5
Agrarian economics, 58–61
Agrarian reform, *see* Green Revolution; Land
   reform; Rural development
Agriculture, 6, 86–8, 90, 95, 160; as bottleneck,
   44; in China, 102–3; and development, 563–8;
   and employment, 622–6; factor contribution,
   563–4; Green Revolution, 586–92; and income
   distribution, 578–9, 612–16; land reform,
   607–12; market contribution, 563; productivity
   of, 576–8; resource transfer, 568–79; in Southeast Asia, 581–6; strategy objectives, 596–9; in
   Taiwan, 568–73; and taxation, 281–4; and
   technology, 601–7, 616–21; unimodal strategy,
   592–601; underemployment in, *see* Disguised
   unemployment, Dualistic development. *See also*
   Rural development
Ahluwalia, M.S., 18ff.
Aid-tying, 358–60

Backwardness: degrees of, 90–93
Baer, W., 741 ff.
Balance of payments, 375, 432
"Balanced growth": vs. "unbalanced growth,"
   630–31, 643–7. *See also* Industrialization
   strategy
Baldwin, R.E., 392, 718
Baran, P.A., 292, 294
Barber, W., 162
Bargaining, 393–4, 412ff.
Bauer, P.T., 66ff., 353ff., 708
Beckerman, W., 13, 16
Berg, A., 503ff.
Bergsten, C. Fred, 724–5
Bhagwati, J.N., 673, 756, 828ff.
"Big Push," 632–40
Bird, R.M., 284ff.
Boeke, J.H., 128, 130ff.
Bruton, H.J., 747ff.
Buffer stocks, *see* Commodities

Cairncross, A.K., 74, 84, 261ff., 712ff.
Campos, Roberto de Oliveira, 316ff.

Capital accumulation, 44, 93, 105, 253–5, 261–70,
   421–8, 542–7; cost of, 256–8; and taxation,
   271–4. *See also* Investment; Savings
Capital-output ratio, 83, 253, 258–61; net ratio,
   273. *See also* Investment criteria
Capital requirements, 333–6
Capital stretching, 409–12
Capital transfer, 33–7, 44–5
Capital turnover criterion, 429–30, 442–3
"Carry-over" problem, *see* Export-led development
Cartels, in primary products, 724–8
Caves, R.E., 391
Chelliah, R.J., 275ff.
Chenery, H.B., 10, 26ff., 33ff., 335–6, 341, 422ff.,
   430, 432–3, 808ff., 817, 821, 855
China, 100–108
Choice of techniques, 433–47
Cline, W.R., 612ff.
Colombia: unemployment in, 193–200
Commodities: integrated program, 729–34;
   resource bargaining, 724–8
Complementarities, 632–40, 643–7
Constraints on development, 43–4. *See also*
   Agriculture; Foreign exchange; Human resources;
   Savings
Corden, W.M., 775
Cost-benefit analysis, *see* Project appraisal; Social
   cost-benefit analysis
Critical minimum effort, *see* "Big push"
Cuba, 108–13
Currie, Lauchlin, 425
Customs union, 772–8

Debt servicing capacity, 351–3
Demographic change: and social change, 488–95
Demonstration effect, 71, 717–18
Dependency, 5, 52. *See also* Polarization;
   Transnational capitalism
Development decades, 4, 10–11
De Vries, Bernard A., 351ff.
Dobb, Maurice, 422ff.
Dualistic development, 31–2, 125–67; and
   intersectoral relationships, 157–63; technological
   dualism, 139–41, 153; and wage differentials,
   151–6

Eckstein, O., 422ff., 431
Economic development: defined, 6–7
Education, 10, 64, 542–7; and employment,

859